FAMILY LAW

ASPEN CASEBOOK SERIES

FAMILY LAW
THEORETICAL, COMPARATIVE, AND SOCIAL SCIENCE PERSPECTIVES

James Dwyer

Arthur B. Hanson Professor of Law
William and Mary Law School

Wolters Kluwer
Law & Business

Published by Wolters Kluwer Law & Business in New York.

Wolters Kluwer Law & Business serves customers worldwide with CCH, Aspen Publishers, and Kluwer Law International products. (www.wolterskluwerlb.com)

To contact Customer Service, e-mail customer.service@wolterskluwer.com, call 1-800-234-1660, fax 1-800-901-9075, or mail correspondence to:

Wolters Kluwer Law & Business
Attn: Order Department
PO Box 990
Frederick, MD 21705

Printed in the United States of America.

1 2 3 4 5 6 7 8 9 0

ISBN 978-1-4548-1366-8

Library of Congress Cataloging-in-Publication Data

Dwyer, James.
Family law : theoretical, comparative, and social science perspectives / James Dwyer.
p. cm.—(Aspen casebook series)
Includes index.
ISBN 978-1-4548-1366-8
1. Parent and child (Law)—United States—States. 2. Domestic relations—United States—States. 3. Parent and child (Law)—United States—States—Cases. 4. Domestic relations—United States—States—Cases. 5. Parent and child (Law) 6. Domestic relations. I. Title.
KF540.D89 2011
346.7301'5—dc23

2012017366

SUSTAINABLE FORESTRY INITIATIVE
Certified Sourcing
www.sfiprogram.org
SFI-01234
SFI label applies to the text stock

About Wolters Kluwer Law & Business

Wolters Kluwer Law & Business is a leading global provider of intelligent information and digital solutions for legal and business professionals in key specialty areas, and respected educational resources for professors and law students. Wolters Kluwer Law & Business connects legal and business professionals as well as those in the education market with timely, specialized authoritative content and information-enabled solutions to support success through productivity, accuracy and mobility.

Serving customers worldwide, Wolters Kluwer Law & Business products include those under the Aspen Publishers, CCH, Kluwer Law International, Loislaw, Best Case, ftwilliam.com and MediRegs family of products.

CCH products have been a trusted resource since 1913, and are highly regarded resources for legal, securities, antitrust and trade regulation, government contracting, banking, pension, payroll, employment and labor, and healthcare reimbursement and compliance professionals.

Aspen Publishers products provide essential information to attorneys, business professionals and law students. Written by preeminent authorities, the product line offers analytical and practical information in a range of specialty practice areas from securities law and intellectual property to mergers and acquisitions and pension/benefits. Aspen's trusted legal education resources provide professors and students with high-quality, up-to-date and effective resources for successful instruction and study in all areas of the law.

Kluwer Law International products provide the global business community with reliable international legal information in English. Legal practitioners, corporate counsel and business executives around the world rely on Kluwer Law journals, looseleafs, books, and electronic products for comprehensive information in many areas of international legal practice.

Loislaw is a comprehensive online legal research product providing legal content to law firm practitioners of various specializations. Loislaw provides attorneys with the ability to quickly and efficiently find the necessary legal information they need, when and where they need it, by facilitating access to primary law as well as state-specific law, records, forms and treatises.

Best Case Solutions is the leading bankruptcy software product to the bankruptcy industry. It provides software and workflow tools to flawlessly streamline petition preparation and the electronic filing process, while timely incorporating ever-changing court requirements.

ftwilliam.com offers employee benefits professionals the highest quality plan documents (retirement, welfare and non-qualified) and government forms (5500/PBGC, 1099 and IRS) software at highly competitive prices.

MediRegs products provide integrated health care compliance content and software solutions for professionals in healthcare, higher education and life sciences, including professionals in accounting, law and consulting.

Wolters Kluwer Law & Business, a division of Wolters Kluwer, is headquartered in New York. Wolters Kluwer is a market-leading global information services company focused on professionals.

To my family law colleagues everywhere,
from whom I have learned so much.

SUMMARY OF CONTENTS

CONTENTS

PREFACE

Family law is inherently interesting to students, regardless of whether they intend to practice in the field, and many come to the subject with strong beliefs about how the law ought to be. A family law course therefore presents an excellent opportunity to develop certain skills that are important to any area of practice but that are typically under-emphasized in the law school curriculum. This text exploits that opportunity.

Statutory interpretation skills are vital to law practice today, and excellent lawyers can rigorously dissect and present competing and novel interpretations of code language. Statutes are rarely unambiguous, and lawyers who rely on courts or other lawyers to tell them what statutes mean cannot effectively represent or counsel clients. But reading statutes closely, especially in an educational rather than practice setting, is usually painful for most people. However, because students come to family law with heightened interest in its content, often having had relevant personal experiences, they are more receptive to, and even enjoy, examining and playing around analytically with family law statutes. This text therefore includes substantial statutory material and interpretive questions, to help students develop this essential skill.

Increasingly, lawyers are expected to use and analyze scientific studies in their practice, in counseling clients and in litigating. Students need to become comfortable with reading social science literature in particular, and there is an abundance of it relating to family relationships. Lawyers should view it as part of their ongoing professional experience to digest the empirical work relevant to their field. For example, any attorney who does not understand the attachment process for infants will be less effective at representing a client with infant children in a paternity or divorce custody dispute. Divorce attorneys are more effective in advising and litigating as to property distribution and support if they are well-versed in relevant economics literature. Lawyers must also develop the skill of critiquing scientific studies, which are often poorly designed by the researchers and misused by legal actors. This text weaves social science writings into each major topic and poses critical questions to help students become adept at finding weaknesses in study design and flaws in the reasoning based on the data.

A much overlooked lawyering skill is the ability to do normative analysis and argument. Law is a normative enterprise, and most legal rules rest on assumptions about social policy and morality. Lawyers cannot fully understand and explain to clients the rules they work with unless they appreciate the normative underpinnings. They cannot effectively advocate for clients unless they develop the capacity to argue on the basis of public policies and moral beliefs. It is no longer sufficient for you to say simply that you do not like someone else's opinions. You need to be able to participate in normative debate with others if you want to be a competent attorney, because judges, legislators, agency officials, and other lawyers all have personal opinions that you need to deal with. In fact, the law often explicitly calls for normative judgments—for example, what is an "illicit relationship" to which adults should not expose children or what constitutes "cruelty" toward a spouse. As will be apparent from the cases in this text, and indeed from the cases in most law textbooks, even when legal rules do not clearly call for normative judgments, legal actors are inevitably influenced in their decision making by their beliefs about what is best for society and about what is right and wrong. Getting good results for your clients will often require changing others' beliefs or convincing them that their beliefs support a different conclusion than they had supposed. Simply dismissing their beliefs as benighted or repulsive will not do; as a lawyer, you must engage.

Effective counselors and litigators therefore need to be familiar with the policies and moral attitudes that typically inform the thinking of legislators, judges, administrators, and people more generally in relation to their area of practice, and they need to be able to deconstruct others' normative reasoning and construct their own competing theories. Great lawyers are really good at this. Yet students generally receive little guidance or practice in normative analysis and argument in law school, so many feel reluctant to jump into a debate in order to sharpen their abilities. Family law, because of students' strong antecedent interest in and beliefs about family life, is a topic that ordinarily reticent students might be more willing to discuss in a classroom setting. Other students are quite comfortable voicing their views to anyone who will listen, especially their views about family life, but they are not used to having their views intensely scrutinized. It is possible, though, to think in a disciplined and rigorous way about family life, and this text aims to help students do that. It encourages and guides normative debate throughout, by posing questions that challenge students to justify the convictions they hold and by presenting sustained scholarly criticisms of fundamental premises at the base of several topical areas. The critical theory should foster the inclination and capacity to look at a legal rule or social practice and rethink it, to look at it upside down and sideways to see if there is a new and creative way to approach it. Great lawyers do that as well.

Also supporting the aim of improved critical and creative thinking is the comparative law feature of this text. On many of the course's topics, the text includes laws and descriptions of practices in other countries that differ significantly from those in the U.S. It asks whether the differences are explicable in terms of divergent cultures, history, or contemporary circumstances and whether family life in the U.S. might be improved by importing something from a foreign legal system. A broader geographical scope gives us a better idea of what is possible, offers examples we can cite in advocating for particular changes in the law, and improves understanding of our own norms. In addition, the very structure of the book, which organizes the subject of family law in a novel way, is designed to inspire critical reexamination of the rules at the core of family formation, regulation, and dissolution. As to each of these three sites of state involvement in family life, the text pairs a chapter on the parent-child relationship with a chapter on intimate partnerships between adults. The comparison generates insight into the normative assumptions at the core of the state's treatment of the two relationships, and the text challenges students to explain or justify any differences in that treatment. It is a comparison we are not accustomed to making, but the unfamiliar analogy is a powerful tool in creative lawyering.

Students who embrace the novel aspects of this text, and who welcome a new kind of law school classroom experience, should at the end of the semester feel they have expanded their lawyering tool set. I hope that they will also have enjoyed the intellectual experience, and that this will encourage them to make intellectual reflection and exploration a regular part of their lives as lawyers. Law school tends to have an unfortunate deadening effect on the natural curiosity of smart people, and that is part of the explanation for the high rate of alienation and unhappiness among young attorneys. Use this course to revive and fortify that important aspect of your personality. Lawyering is like parenting in this respect: the more you enjoy it and the more parts of yourself that it satisfies, the better at it you will be.

James Dwyer

June 2012

ACKNOWLEDGMENTS

The author would like to thank the copyright holders of the following publications for permission to reproduce exerpts herein:

Scott Altman, *A Theory of Child Support,* 17 INT'L J.L. POL'Y & FAM. 173 (2003). Reprinted with permission of the Oxford University Press and Scott Altman.

Katharine K. Baker, *Bargaining or Biology? The History and Future of Paternity Law and Parental Status,* 14 CORNELL J.L. & PUB. POL'Y 1 (2004). Reprinted with Permission of the Cornell Journal of Law and Public Policy and Katharine K. Baker.

Laura Bradford, *The Counterrevolution: A Critique of Recent Proposals to Reform No-Fault Divorce Laws,* 49 STAN L. REV. 607 (1997). Reprinted with permission of the Stanford Law Review and Laura Bradford.

Alicia Brokars Kelly, *Money Matters in Marriage: Unmasking Interdependence in On-going Spousal Economic Relations,* 47 U. LOUISVILLE L. REV. 113 (2008). Reprinted with permission of the University of Louisville Law Review and Alicia Brokars Kelly.

K. Alison Clarke-Stewart and Cornelia Brentano, *Divorce: Causes and Consequences* (Yale University Press, 2006). Reprinted with permission of the Yale University Press, K. Alison Clarke-Stewart and Cornelia Brentano.

James G. Dwyer, *A Constitutional Birthright: The State, Parentage, and the Rights of Newborn Persons,* 56 UCLA L. Rev. 755 (2009). Reprinted with permission of the University of California Law Review and James G. Dwyer.

James G. Dwyer, "Children's Rights" in A COMPANION TO THE PHILOSOPHY OF EDUCATION (Blackwell Publishers, 2003). Reprinted with permission of the Blackwell Publishers and James G. Dwyer.

Ann Laquer Estin, *Unofficial Family Law,* 94 IOWA L. REV. 449 (2009). Reprinted with permission of the Iowa Law Review and Ann Laquer Estin.

Elizabeth T. Gershoff and Susan H. Bitensky, *The Case Against Corporal Punishment of Children,* 13 PSYCHOL. PUB. POL'Y & L. 231. Reprinted with permission of the American Psychology Association, Elizabeth T. Gershoff, and Susan H. Bitensky. Copyright 2008 by the American Psychology Association.

Leigh Goodmark, *Autonomy Feminism: An Anti-Essentialist Critique of Mandatory Interventions in Domestic Violence Cases,* 37 Fla. St. U. L. Rev. 1 (2009). Reprinted with permission of the Florida State University Law Review and Leigh Goodmark. Florida State University Law Review is the original publisher and copyright holder of the reproduced material.

Alan J. Hawkins, *Will Legislation to Encourage Premarital Education Strengthen Marriage and Reduce Divorce?,* 9 J.L. & Fam. Stud. 79 (2007). Reprinted with permission of the Journal of Law and Family Studies and Alan J. Hawkins. Originally published in the Journal of Law and Family Studies, 9 J.L. & Fam. Stud. 79 (2007).

Linda Kelly Hill, *Disabusing the Definition of Domestic Abuse: How Women Batter Men and the Role of the Feminist State,* 30 Fla. St. U. L. Rev. 791 (2003). Reprinted with permission of the Florida State University Law Review and Linda Kelly Hill. Florida State University Law Review is the original publisher and copyright holder of the reproduced material.

Miriam Jordan, *Abuse Case Sparks a Clash over Limits of Tough Parenting,* The Wall Street Journal, January 22, 2011. Reprinted with permission of The Wall Street Journal and Miriam Jordan.

Twila L. Perry, *Alimony: Race, Privilege, and Dependency in the Search for Theory,* 82 Geo. L.J. 2481 (1994). Reprinted with permission of the Georgetown University Law Center and Twila L. Perry. Copyright 1994 by the Georgetown Law Journal.

Laura A. Rosenbury, *Two Ways to End a Marriage: Divorce or Death,* 2005 Utah L. Rev. 1227. Reprinted with permission of the Utah Law Review and Laura A. Rosenbury. Originally published in the Utah Law Review, 2005 Utah L. Rev. 1227.

Jeannie Suk, *Criminal Law Comes Home,* 116 Yale L.J. 2 (2006). Reprinted with permission of the Yale Law Journal and Jeannie Suk.

Julie C. Suk, *Are Gender Sterotypes Bad for Women? Rethinking Antidiscrimination Law and Work-Family Conflict,* 110 Colum. L. Rev. 1 (2010). Reprinted with permission of the Columbia Law Review and Julie C. Suk.

Claudia Zahir, *When a Woman's Marital Status Determined Her Legal Status: A Research Guide on the Common Law Doctrine of Converture,* 94 L. LIBRA. J. 459 (2002). Reprinted with permission. Claudia Zahir, copyright holder.

FAMILY LAW

INTRODUCTION

> "**Family**"—from the Latin *famulus* (servant or slave), origin in Late Middle English, meaning "the servants of a house or establishment"
>
> —OXFORD ENGLISH DICTIONARY

Janet Halley, What Is Family Law?: A Genealogy Part I

23 YALE J.L. & HUMAN. 1, 2-7, 82-83 (2011)

. . . In the early nineteenth century, there was no family law. The law of husband and wife and the law of parent and child were separate, parallel, and closely related legal topics, but they were equally proximate to the law of guardian and ward and . . . the law of master and servant. This pattern corresponded with a social order in which cohabitation, legitimate sexual relations, reproduction, and productive labor were assumed to belong in one place: the household. A single figure was assumed to serve as husband, father, and master. He was not one but three legal persons. The wife, the child, and the servant were not just subordinate; they were similarly subordinate.

By mid-century . . . pressure to divide marriage from the law of an emerging capitalist market order began to build. . . . [S]eparation of the law of familial intimacy from the law of productive labor . . . coincided with the emancipation of the servant from indenture and slavery and with the emergence of the laborer and employee selling his work for a wage. Socially, it coincided with the emergence of a market for labor, an ideology of laissez faire for the market, and an ideology of domestic intimacy that could be articulated as the opposite of the market. . . . Contract, quasi-contract, and tort became the law of everyone—the faceless individual of liberalism—while the law of marriage became the law of special persons, incapacitated to varying degrees from contract: the wife and the child across the board or nearly so. . . . In the corresponding ideology, the husband, wife, and child constituted "the family" and lived in an affective, sentimental, altruistic, ascriptive, and morally saturated legal and social space. . . . The term chosen to describe those relations was "domestic": the law of "Domestic Relations" was born. . . .

Family Law . . . in law schools today . . . houses the entry rules of marriage, divorce, and . . . marriage alternatives (cohabitation and civil union). It includes the law of parentage (who is a parent?), including adoption. Constitutionally-driven rights in reproduction and parenthood take up a big segment of the course. But the course is mostly about the formation of the core relationships, which are paradigmatically marital and parental, and about the dissolution of marriage and its consequences for adults and children. . . .

[W]hat has remained constant is the division of intellectual labor between the law of the market and the law of the family. . . . This . . . distinction is not ideologically innocent. It carries with it the idea . . . that the market is free, while the family is entrenched in moral or natural command; it carries the idea that the market is the site of progress, while the family is or should be slow to change. . . . [In fact,] the family and family law are hidden but crucial mechanisms for the distribution of social goods of an immense variety of kinds: material resources like money, jobs, nutrition; symbolic resources like prestige and degradation; psychic resources like affectional ties, erotic attraction and repulsion, the very conditions of access to human personality. . . . [I]t serves as a legally regulated private welfare system, as a site of legally regulated productive labor, as a crucial unit of production and consumption. Many of the "culture wars" fights that now occupy the field obscure these distributional consequences and make it impossible to have descriptively adequate discussions of the stakes of various policy choices. . . .

The concept of family has changed substantially from the classical era, when citizens were men and "family" referred to a man's household servants, including his women, his children, and his slaves. The concept now comprises persons of equal moral standing who are related to each other by blood, marriage, and/or close affective ties. Men and women are equal in moral and political status, and adult unions are assumed to endure because of emotional bonds rather than power and dependency. Even children are deemed persons and right-holders today, and "family" connotes care of children rather than service by children. Family in its ideal form exudes mutual respect and caring.

Family *law* today is largely a response to departures from this ideal—that is, to lack of respect and caring in close personal relationships. Its operation is most evident when the state steps in to force people to shoulder costs they create by their behavior in relationships (as in paternity, child support, and alimony actions), to block efforts by some to oppress others within the home (as in domestic violence and child abuse proceedings), or to compel sharing of goods generated jointly in a shared household (as in property distribution at divorce). If people always approached sexual relations, household sharing, and dissolution of relationships with full respect and concern for one another, the state would not need to do these things and most of family law would not exist.

But there are also aspects of family law today that suggest a lack of *government* respect for persons, and some that serve to facilitate rather than prevent private domination. The law of parentage, other than adoption law, arguably treats newborn children as property of their biological parents rather than as persons whose interests should matter equally in state decisions about family formation. The law of domestic violence substitutes for and preempts application of the general law of violence, which is less tolerant and forgiving of physical domination and harm. The legal doctrine of parental child-rearing rights sometimes empowers parents to deny children basic things such as education and medical care, and one might plausibly view this as simply privileging parental desires over children's welfare, implicitly treating children as lesser persons or non-persons.

A recurrent question in this course is whether modern family law rules serve to eliminate or to perpetuate the master/servant structure of the classical household. You will be asked to imagine what rules and practices would prevail if family members all received equal respect, and accordingly to assess whether existing rules and practices are adequately respectful of all affected persons. The basic structure of this text is designed in part to facilitate that sort of inquiry. At successive stages of state involvement in family relationships (i.e., their creation, their regulation, and their dissolution), the text invites a comparison of the two "core relationships" of family—that is, adult partnerships and parent-child relationships. Careful examination of what is similar and what is different as between these two relationships can be very illuminating and can challenge our ingrained assumptions about what the law should be.

This comparison of the two relationships on which family law focuses is not meant to suggest that any adults are entirely like children or that children are functionally just like adults, nor that the two types of relationships do or should operate similarly or involve similar emotional experiences. Obvious differences between the two relationships are that one involves only autonomous persons whereas the other involves a non-autonomous person, and that one is today assumed to be horizontal and operationally egalitarian whereas the other remains—and, it would seem, appropriately so—vertical and operationally hierarchical. But there are also characteristics that the two relationships share and that distinguish them from other types of relationship, and this makes the comparison appropriate. Both relationships are assumed to be intimate, carried on in a physical space deemed "private," able to satisfy needs deemed fundamental, connecting individuals of equal moral worth, and based on love and altruistic caring. Comparing the two relationships serves at least two purposes: 1) to illuminate how those particular characteristics of a relationship make particular types of legal rules and processes fitting, and 2) to facilitate critical examination of legal rules pertaining to each, by demanding explanation of any differences in the rules as between these two relationships, given their important similarities.

Another recurrent question in this course is what interests society as a whole has at stake in the way family life goes on and whether any such interests are a proper basis for legal rules aimed at encouraging people to behave in particular ways in their home lives. For example, there is a collective interest in minimizing the costs of operating a court system, but can that interest be a proper basis for legal rules that coerce people into remaining in a marital relationship rather than divorcing? Society as a whole might have an interest in cultural pluralism, but is that a legitimate reason to empower some parents to insulate their children from mainstream culture? Family-shaping social policies drive not only the rules making up what we now view as "family law," but also some rules typically studied only in other courses, such as employment law or tax law, and some effort is made in this text to reveal the connections between these other legal subjects and family life.

The structure of the course is simple. This text has three substantive Parts, one each for formation, regulation, and dissolution of family relationships. Within each Part there is first a chapter about one of the two core family relationships (marital or parental) and then a chapter about the other. At the end of the text is a fourth Part containing several problems that serve as review exercises and as vehicles for learning some non-substantive rules and common practices, such as special ethical rules for family law practice, alternative dispute resolution of divorce disputes, and jurisdictional rules.

This text goes beyond imparting substantive knowledge and inviting critical analysis, however. It aims to promote certain lawyering skills that many law schools' curricula under-emphasize. One is policy-based and morality-based argument. The most successful lawyers in every area of practice go beyond legal analysis and argument in attempting to explain the law to clients or to convince a judge or legislator to adopt a particular interpretation or new rule. The text will frequently ask you to mount policy or moral arguments in favor of a position. Importantly, this is quite different from stating your personal opinions; you should offer reasons why others should take a position, and your having a particular position will not itself constitute a reason for them to do so. In fact, you should become adept at arguing for positions independently of whether you personally agree with them. Family law is especially well suited to developing this capacity. To present moral arguments, you must begin with moral premises that others hold or could be persuaded to hold (based on other moral premises which they already hold), and demonstrate that those premises lead to a certain conclusion. To present policy reasons, you must identify societal interests that the outcome you advocate would serve.

Another skill, crucial to successful practice in family law and many other fields, is statutory interpretation. On almost any question you would encounter in family law practice, the place to start your research is a governing statute. Statutes can be beautiful things, elegantly crafted but economical and clear condensations of directives for multifarious factual circumstances. More often, they are comically convoluted contraptions full of ambiguities. In either case, it can be great fun dissecting them and discovering how you can interpret them in different, competing ways. If you master that, you will have a powerful lawyering tool at your disposal. There are well-established and fairly uniform rules, or "canons," of statutory interpretation (as well as some that are quite contested). Read the summary of canons below and refer back to it when you come to a statutory interpretation exercise in the text.

Canons of Statutory Interpretation

1) The overriding aim is to give effect to what the legislature intended in passing the statute.
2) Begin with the text of the statute. If its meaning is plain (i.e., clear and unambiguous), given the statute's own definitions of its terms or, if none, dictionary definitions of its words, then apply that meaning unless it would produce an absurd result. An absurd result suggests the legislature erred in drafting.
3) If and only if the text is ambiguous or would produce an absurd result, apply the aids to construction below (a partial list, not exhaustive), relying first on methods that look within the state's code and, only if they are indeterminate, look to external sources.

<u>Intrinsic Sources of Interpretation</u>

In pari materia: Look to other statutes on the same subject matter for context and for use of the same terms, applying an assumption that the legislature intended a consistent usage of any given term throughout an act or code chapter.

Noscitur a sociis: Interpret an ambiguous word in light of the other words with which it is grouped. For example, the meaning of "bay" would be one thing if the sentence it appears in refers to putting a boat on it, another if the sentence refers to putting a saddle on it.

Ejusdem generis: Where a statute lists specific classes of persons or things and then refers to them in general, the general statements only apply to the same kind of persons or things specifically listed. For example, if a law refers to "automobiles, trucks, tractors, motorcycles and other motor-powered vehicles," "vehicles" would not include airplanes, because the list was of land-based transportation.

Generalia specialibus non derogant: If two statutes conflict, the specific trumps the general. If neither is more specific, the later enacted trumps the earlier enacted.

Avoid surplusage: Avoid interpretations that would make a provision or words in it superfluous; assume that every word and provision has independent meaning.

Interpret consistent with explicit legislative purpose: Some acts contain a preamble or initial section stating the legislature's intent in passing a law, the public policies it is aiming to serve, the perceived problem it is addressing. Judges frequently cite these in choosing an interpretation of an ambiguous statute. Less important but in some states potentially relevant—if written by the legislature (as opposed to the publisher of acts and statutes)—are the long and short titles of acts, code title names, and chapter or section headings.

Expressio unius est exclusio alterius: Inclusion of one thing implies exclusion of others. [Note: Some states have rejected this canon.]

<u>Extrinsic Sources of Interpretation</u>

Avoid conflict with the constitution: If a statute is reasonably susceptible to more than one interpretation, prefer one that is less likely to render the statute unconstitutional.

Rule of lenity: Statutes that punish people with fines or imprisonment should be construed strictly; any ambiguity remaining after intrinsic sources of interpretation are consulted should be resolved against the state.

Interpret consistently with public policies and moral principles: Many state legislatures have explicitly directed courts to interpret statutes in such a way as to serve the state's public policies or general moral principles. See, e.g., Texas Government Code §312.006 ("The Revised Statutes . . . shall be liberally construed to achieve their purpose and to promote justice.") Judges in family law cases are remarkably comfortable appealing to their own understanding of what is good and just, and of what is immoral and indecent.

Look to legislative history for meaning and intent: If the state publishes legislative history (some do not), start with conference committee reports, then committee reports, and then earlier versions of the bill and rejected amendments. In some jurisdictions, courts might also look to drafters' commentary, floor statements for and against the bill, or bills on the same subject that the same legislature considered and rejected.

Harmonize interpretation of uniform acts: When a state adopts a uniform act, interpretive decisions of courts in other states that have also adopted that act are persuasive authority.

For fuller explanation of the canons of statutory interpretation, see, e.g., LINDA D. JELLUM, MASTERING STATUTORY INTERPRETATION (2008), and Jacob Scott, *Codified Canons and the Common Law of Interpretation*, 98 GEO. L.J. 341 (2010).

Part I

STATE CREATION OF FAMILY RELATIONSHIPS

Humans form social relationships of many sorts, by many means. We are concerned here with the role of the state in formation of relationships intimate and enduring enough to be characterized as family relationships. The state's role is most apparent in connection with formation and regulation of relationships between an adult caregiver and a child and relationships between two adults in intimate partnerships. Those two relationships are therefore the principal focus of this course. Some other types of family relationships, such as that between siblings or that between grandparents and grandchildren, arise only incidentally from creation of parent-child relationships and intimate partnerships, though the state does sometimes act directly to protect those other relationships after they have formed.

In analyzing the state's involvement in formation of parent-child relationships and adult partnerships, keep in mind the distinction between a social relationship—that is, interpersonal interactions and emotional bonds between people—and a legal relationship—that is, a status the law confers on people, entailing legal ramifications. One interesting aspect of family law is the manner in which social relationship and legal status interact; sometimes the former gives rise to the latter, and sometimes the opposite occurs.

In Part I of this text, you will study the laws that create legal parent-child relationships and legal marital relationships. Creation of legal marriages today has no necessary effect on social relationships between spouses. The law does not require spouses to spend time with each other nor give one spouse control over where the other lives; a spouse is legally free to dissociate herself completely from the other. Nor is legal marriage necessary today in order for two people to cohabit or otherwise interact in particular ways. Creation of legal parent-child relationships also does not necessarily produce a social relationship, because the law does not force legal parents to spend time with their children. However, legal parenthood does generally entail a right to possess or at least spend time with a child, and the legal system does generally force children to live with or at least spend time with their legal parents if the parents want to do so. And without legal parent status, one might be precluded from cohabiting or even interacting at all with a child. Thus, in most cases, the state's creation of the legal parent-child relationship might be said also to create the social relationship, or to determine with whom a newborn child will form social family relationships, because of the rights, powers, immunities, and liabilities that the state attaches to the legal relationship.

In addition to compelling or fostering relationships, the state can also act to prevent formation of certain social relationships, by creating disincentives, by refusing legal recognition, or by outright prohibiting them. One of your tasks in Part I is to determine whether and to what extent the state ever obstructs formation of social relationships, and what legitimate justifications there might be for its doing so. For example, does the state make it more difficult for two adults to carry on an intimate relationship if it does not confer legal marital status on the relationship? If so, what could justify the state's picking and choosing which relationships it will facilitate or discourage? Does the state inhibit development of bonds between children and men who are not their biological fathers but who are raising them with the children's mothers, if it confers legal father status on biological fathers regardless of their relationship with the mothers?

Where should one begin in studying family formation? There are several possible organizing principles. Temporal priority is one, but whether adult partnerships or parent-child relationships came first is, almost literally, a chicken versus egg sort of question, at least from an historical perspective. Within any individual's life, though, the parent-child relationship comes first—that is, we are children with legal parents first, and we enter into a legal intimate partnership only much later, if ever. That temporal priority might be some reason to begin with the parent-child relationship. Prevalence in society is another possible criterion, and on that measure, too, the parent-child relationship would come first, as nearly everyone in the world is in one as a child, whereas a large number of people never enter into any adult intimate partnership (because of early death, disinclination, or lack of opportunity) and a large number who do form adult partnerships never involve the state in their relationship. Professor Kessler notes: "Unmarried parents now make up one-third of households with children less than eighteen years old, and unmarried parenthood is the predominant family form in the African-American community." Laura T. Kessler, *Transgressive Caregiving*, 33 Fla. St. U. L. Rev. 1, 3 (2005). Likewise, prevalence in legal practice cuts in favor of parentage; paternity and adoption constitute a substantial portion of the family court docket, whereas formation or formalization of adult partnerships involves lawyers much less often (typically only when the parties execute a pre-nuptial agreement) and courts rarely. For the most part, state involvement in the process of getting married is limited to clerks' issuing licenses and certificates, and couples generally need no attorney to assist them in dealing with those clerks.

Social or personal importance would also seem to favor parent-child relationships. How one is raised impacts one's development and welfare more fundamentally than does partner intimacy as an adult, and the need for state involvement in creating and regulating relationships is much clearer with respect to parent-child relationships than with respect to adult partnerships. Though no one seriously maintains that we could get along without parentage laws, many scholars have argued for the abolition of legal marriage. Professor Fineman, for example, contends that "for all relevant and appropriate societal purposes we do not need marriage, per se, at all. . . . The pressing problems today do not revolve around the marriage connection, but the caretaker-dependent relationship. . . . Rather than marriage, we should view the parent-child relationship as the quintessential or core family connection, and focus on how policy can strengthen this tie." Martha Fineman, *Why Marriage?*, 9 Va. J. Soc. Pol'y & L. 239, 245 (2001). The ease with which marriages can dissolve, relative to the onerous process for terminating parental rights, likewise suggests that the parent-child relationship is more important to individuals' lives, to society, and to the state. Professor Carbone observes: "Across the academy, the courts, classrooms, and election campaigns, the code of family responsibility is being rewritten in terms of the only ties left—the ones to children." JUNE CARBONE, FROM PARTNERS TO PARENTS: THE SECOND REVOLUTION IN FAMILY LAW, at xiii-xiv (2000).

Despite these several reasons for giving priority to the parent-child relationship, other family law textbooks give priority of place to adult partnerships and typically arrive at consideration of the parent-child relationship only midway through the semester. Why do you suppose that is the case? The best explanation might be that historically in modern Western society, marriage was considered the essential core of a family. Parenthood without marriage was viewed as deviant and condemnable. As recently as 2009, the Supreme Court of Ireland proclaimed that people sharing a life and home could be protected as a "family" within the meaning of Article 41 of the Irish Constitution, which "guarantees to protect the family in its constitution and authority, as the necessary basis of society and indispensible to the welfare of the Nation and the State," only if the cohabitation and shared life are "founded on the institution of marriage." McD v. L [2009] IESC 81, ¶61. The U.S. Supreme Court has repeatedly referred to marriage as the foundation of the family. See, e.g., Maynard v. Hill, 125 U.S. 190, 211 (1888) ("[Marriage] is an institution, in the maintenance of which in its purity the public is deeply interested, for it is the foundation of the family and of society, without which there would be neither civilization nor progress.").

Throughout most of the West, however, courts in recent decades have abandoned this view. The European Court of Human Rights, the U.S. Supreme Court, and numerous other courts have applied constitution-like provisions and doctrines relating to family life also to non-marital children and their parents. See, e.g., Kroon and others v. The Netherlands, App. No. 18535/91 paras. 10, 28 (Eur. Ct. H.R. Oct. 27, 1994) (holding that an unwed father who had cared for his child enjoyed the Human Rights Convention protection of "family life" and stating that the "notion of 'family life' . . . is not confined . . . to marriage-based relationships and may encompass other de facto 'family ties' where parties are living together . . ."); Stanley v. Illinois, 405 U.S. 645 (1972) (first in a series of U.S. Supreme Court decisions recognizing a substantive Fourteenth Amendment right of unwed fathers to legal parenthood). U.S. Supreme Court decisions have denounced discrimination against and stigmatization of non-marital births. See Solangel Maldonado, *Illegitimate Harm: Law, Stigma, and Discrimination Against Nonmarital Children*, 63 FLA. L. REV. 345 (2011) (discussing doctrine and urging elimination of remaining discriminatory laws). Marriage still has a special status among adult relationships, but it is no longer deemed essential to the existence of a family.

A rationale for prioritizing marriage that is more in keeping with modern attitudes toward family might be that marriage is a paradigm of relationship formation. Two autonomous persons come together, get to know each other, and then freely choose to commit to sharing a life and a home together, after determining that doing so is the best available option for both of them. The high rate of marriage failure, however, suggests that this process does not work especially well, so it seems suspect to treat it as paradigmatic.

Thus, neither the position that marriage is the essential foundation of family life nor the view that marriage as we know it is an exemplar of human relationship formation provides a compelling reason for privileging marriage in the study of family formation. This text will instead begin with the study of state formation of the parent-child relationship, principally for the reasons stated above, and especially because of the relative importance of parent-child relationships. The idea of beginning with a good model, though, does suggest a more specific jumping off point within the realm of parent-child relationships. What if we were to begin by studying the area of family law in which state actors are most heavily involved in creating family relationships and in which the state arguably has the highest rate of success, if success is measured in terms of whether family relationships are enduring and healthy? What area would that be?

The law governing "new family" adoption (as opposed to step-parent adoption) ostensibly requires extensive agency review, careful matching of adults and children, lengthy effort and deliberation by potential parents, and an individualized court determination that the relationship is in the best interests of the child. Arguably this is a model of relationship formation superior to marriage. Adoption resembles marriage insofar as it involves mutual choice (by proxy, for the child) and a determination on the part of both parties that forming the relationship is best for both of them. However, new-family adoption arguably is superior to marriage and to biology-based parentage insofar as it entails a rational assessment of proposed relationships by an objective observer and exclusion of people with characteristics or histories that make them unsuitable for the relationship. Many adults become spouses or biological parents with little thought, and neither marriage nor biology-based parentage requires a background check or any demonstration of suitability for the relationship. People can legally marry regardless of any history of marriage failure or violence toward partners. And under existing parentage rules, adults who have committed the most heinous abuse of other children nevertheless automatically become legal parents to any additional offspring they produce.

Perhaps because of the relatively objective best-interest assessment that precedes them, parent-child relationships that arise from new-family adoption are statistically more successful than either biology-based parent-child relationships or marriages. The rates of maltreatment and dissolution are lower for parent-child relationships arising from new-family infant adoption than they are for biology-based parent-child relationships or for marriages. A great number of biological/legal parents choose not to participate in a social relationship with their offspring, or do so initially and then drift away, and the rate of abuse and neglect is higher among biological parents than among adoptive parents. Abuse is also more common between intimate adult partners than it is in parent-child relationships by adoption, and marriages are on average far less enduring than either sort of parent-child relationship. Perhaps, then, adoption presents the best model for relationship formation. Perhaps all parent-child relationships should develop from a process that approximates the adoption process, and perhaps the state should do more to promote rational and informed decision making in adult partnerships. The overarching question Part I raises is this: What is the optimal state role in formation of family relationships?

1

STATE CREATION OF PARENT-CHILD RELATIONSHIPS

Family law impacted you at the very outset of your life, when state parentage laws dictated who your first legal parents would be and state custody statutes conferred custodial rights on those parents. We are generally unmindful of the state's role in creating parent-child relationships. This is in part because legal parent status usually arises without any individualized agency review or court approval, but rather by ministerial application of statutes conferring that status on people presumed to be a child's biological parents. Pregnant women and their husbands or boyfriends simply fill out paperwork at the birthing facility and then receive a birth certificate with their names on it in the mail soon after returning home. It is also in part because we take for granted that newborn babies will go home from the hospital with their birth parents, which seems a fact of nature rather than state action. But the truth is that it is only because state laws conferred legal parenthood and custodial legal rights on your birth parents that they had legal permission and the practical ability to do what might otherwise be kidnapping—that is, to take another person (you) to their home and confine that person there without that person's consent. A nurse or doctor present at your birth might have wanted to take you home themselves, but the state prohibited them from doing that and empowered your biological parents to do so instead, with police prepared to enforce that state decision if necessary.

In contrast, we are quite cognizant of the state's role in creating a parent-child relationship between a child and an adult who is not the child's biological parent, through adoption. State institutions and employees, or private professionals and agencies licensed and empowered by the state, devote substantial effort in order for the relationship to come into existence. Yet the legal status created, that of parenthood, is exactly the same as that held by persons who become legal parents under parentage laws by virtue of biological parenthood, with all the same legal rights and duties. And in the case of newborn adoption, the family experience is virtually the same; those who adopt children placed with them very soon after birth will really be the children's first social parents and likely the children's only social parents.

A. ADOPTION

Roughly 134,000 adoptions occurred in the United States in the most recent year for which figures were reported. This is nearly double the number of adoptions that occurred in 1951, but over 40,000 less than occurred in 1970. In addition to domestic adoptions, Americans currently adopt around 20,000 children from other countries each year. Among domestic adoptions today, 43 percent are adoptions by an existing family member—that is, a step-parent or a biological relative. Of the 57 percent that are "unrelated domestic adoptions," 56 percent are through state agencies, which generally means adoption of children whom the state removed from unfit parents or whose parents voluntarily relinquished them to the state because they felt unable to care for the children. Twenty-six percent of all unrelated domestic adoptions are through private adoption agencies, which could involve children transferred from the state child protection/foster care system or relinquished by parents directly to the private agency. Seventeen percent of unrelated domestic adoptions are "private placement" adoptions, which means birth parents voluntarily relinquished their children to specific individuals. In 1951, private placement adoptions were half of all unrelated domestic adoptions; this phenomenon has dropped dramatically because of *Roe v. Wade* and reduction of the stigma of out-of-wedlock pregnancy. See National Council for Adoption, Adoption Fact Book V 11-27 (2011). Regardless of the type of adoption, lawyers are likely to be involved—lawyers for state agencies, for private agencies, for birth parents, and/or for the adopting parents.

People become adoptive parents as the result of a court order. The basic rule the court applies, after finding that birth parents have forfeited their status as legal parents, is simply that the adoption is good for the child. See, e.g., Cal. Fam. Code §8612(c) ("If satisfied that the interest of the child will be promoted by the adoption, the court may make and enter an order of adoption of the child by the prospective adoptive parent or parents."); 750 Ill. Comp. Stat. 50/14(e) (court must find "that the adoption is for the welfare of the child and that there is a valid consent [by birth parents], or that no consent is required."). When someone petitions to adopt an older child, the child's consent is also required. See, e.g., Cal. Fam. Code §8602 (children over age 12 must give consent).

To determine whether an adoption is good for a child, the state ostensibly requires a thorough investigation of adoption applicants. This is often waived for step-parent adoptions, see, e.g., Va. Code Ann. §63.2-1242, but for new-family adoptions it is typically quite invasive. In addition to filling out a lengthy application, unrelated applicants must undergo a background check in criminal and child maltreatment registries and a home study. The home study entails visits by an employee of a state or private adoption agency to the applicants' home, assessment of the quality of the home and neighborhood environment, and interviews of the applicants, other family members, and references. The law also typically requires that adoptive parents successfully complete a probationary period—for example, six months after initially receiving the child into their home, with additional visits by adoption agency workers during that period—before the court can finally vest parental status in them. Here is a trimmed-down version of the regulations governing agency approval of adoptive parents in Georgia:

Georgia Administrative Code
Title 290. Rules of Department of Human Resources
Subtitle 290-9. Office of Regulatory Services
Chapter 290-9-2. Child-Placing Agencies

290-9-2.06. ADOPTION SERVICES. . . .

(3) **Home Study of Prospective Adoptive Family**. The Agency shall make a written evaluation, or study, of each prospective adoptive family prior to the placement of a child in the home. . . .

(a) This home study . . . shall include at least three visits on separate days. At least one visit shall be in the home and the applicant and all other family members shall be seen and interviewed. . . .

(d) The study shall include at least the following information . . . :

. . . 2. Motivation to adopt and the family members' attitude(s) toward childlessness;

3. Description of each family member, to include:

(i) Date and place of birth;

(ii) Physical description;

(iii) Family background and history;

(iv) Current relationships with immediate and extended family members;

(v) Education;

(vi) Social involvements; and

(vii) Personal characteristics, such as personality, and interests and hobbies;

4. Evaluation of marriages and family life: . . .

(ii) History and assessment of marital relationship;

(iii) Family patterns; and

(iv) Previous marriages (verification of divorces, if applicable);

5. Evaluation of parenting practices:

(i) Description of parenting knowledge, attitudes, and skills;

(ii) Behavior management practices;

(iii) Child rearing practices; and

(iv) Experience with children;

6. Evaluation of physical and mental health needs . . . :

(i) Summary of health history and condition of each family member;

(ii) Documentation of a physical examination of the . . . applicants . . . ;

(iii) A statement from a licensed physician, physician's assistant, or public health department regarding the general health status of other members of the prospective adoptive family . . . ; and

(iv) An informal assessment of the emotional and mental health of each member of the prospective adoptive family;

7. Evaluation of the understanding of and adjustment to adoptive parenting:

(i) The understanding of adoption and how adoption will be handled with the child;

(ii) Attitude toward birth parent(s);

(iii) Understanding of how adoptive parenting is different from biological parenting;

(iv) Attitude toward rearing a child biologically not their own;

(v) Understanding of the possibility of inherited traits and the influence of genetics vs. environment;

(vi) Expectations of the adopted child, including intellectual and physical achievement;

(vii) Understanding of loss in adoption;

(viii) Attitudes of other children residing in the home and extended family members toward adoption; and

(ix) The support network in place for the prospective adoptive family, including support systems for single parent families, if applicable;

8. Evaluation of the prospective adoptive parent(s)' finances and occupation:

(i) Employment history of family members;

(ii) Combined annual income . . . ; and

(iv) Projected financial impact of the addition of an adopted child to the home;

9. A description of the home and community:

(i) Description of the neighborhood;

(ii) Physical standards of the home, including space, and water supply and sewage disposal systems which, if other than public systems, have been approved by appropriate authorities;

(iii) A statement to verify that any domestic pets owned or residing with the family have been inoculated against rabies as required by law;

(iv) A statement verifying that all firearms owned and in the home are locked away from children;

(v) A statement verifying that if a swimming pool is present at the home, it is fenced with a locked gate to prevent unsupervised access and that it meets all applicable community ordinances;

(vi) A statement that smoke alarms are present and functioning on each level in the home;

(vii) Verification that gas heaters are vented to avoid fire and health hazards, with any unvented fuel-fired heaters equipped with oxygen depletion safety shut-off systems;

(viii) Assessment of community resources, including accessibility of schools, religious institutions, recreation, and medical facilities;

10. A statement regarding the results of a criminal records check . . . for each prospective adoptive parent. . . .

11. A minimum of three character references. . . .

(7) **Services Following an Adoption Placement.**

(a) The Agency caseworker shall make at least two home visits after the placement of the child and prior to the filing of the petition for adoption. . . .

(b) Home visits shall be made with the prospective adoptive family at least once a month prior to the filing of a petition for adoption to verify that the prospective parent(s) are delivering care in a safe and healthy environment to the children. . . .

(e) Documentation of home visits should include but not be limited to a summary of the entire family's adjustment to the prospective adoptive placement, any problem or issue that has arisen, and the resolution of the problem or issue. . . .

(10) **Behavior Management and Emergency Safety Interventions.**

. . . (c) 1. The agency shall make available to prospective adoptive parent(s) information on the kinds of behavioral problems of the children that might arise and appropriate techniques of behavior management for dealing with such behaviors.

2. The following forms of behavior management shall not be used by prospective adoptive parent(s) receiving services through the licensed agency;

(i) Assignment of excessive or unreasonable work tasks;

(ii) Denial of meals and hydration;

(iii) Denial of sleep;

(iv) Denial of shelter, clothing, or essential personal needs;

(v) Denial of essential services;

(vi) Verbal abuse, ridicule, or humiliation;

(vii) Restraint, manual holds, and seclusion used as a means of coercion, discipline, convenience, or retaliation;

(viii) Corporal punishment;

(ix) Seclusion or confinement of a child in a room or area which may reasonably be expected to cause physical or emotional damage to the child; or

(x) Seclusion or confinement of a child to a room or area for periods longer than those appropriate to the child's age, intelligence, emotional makeup and previous experience, or confinement to a room or area without the supervision or monitoring necessary to ensure the child's safety and well-being. . . .

When deciding whether to marry someone. Does one usually have more or less information about that person than what the home study aims to uncover as to adoption applicants? Does one ordinarily have higher or lower expectations for a spouse than these regulations suggest the state has for adoptive parents? Are there some things on the list you believe to be inappropriate considerations or requirements? Is there anything you would add? What justification, if any, is there for imposing on adoption applicants during the probationary period greater restrictions on disciplinary techniques than the law generally imposes on parents (e.g., prohibiting corporal punishment)?

In addition to establishing the suitability of applicants as parents—in general and for a particular child—the application process also aims to help the applicants make an informed and rational decision whether to go forward. The process and the generally high cost of adopting make it unlikely that anyone enters into a parent-child relationship through adoption without careful and lengthy deliberation. Both the process and the cost are much less burdensome in the case of step-parent adoption, which constitutes roughly half of all adoptions in the United States, but they are still significant and likely to make an adopting step-parent deliberate more rationally than people on average do before reproducing or marrying.

Significantly, some characteristics reasonably assumed to make one unprepared to parent adequately, such as being too young, operate in the adoption context categorically to exclude persons from legal parent status. In the United States, one generally must be an adult—that is, at least 18, to adopt, though in some states married couples under 18 might be permitted to do so. See, e.g., Fla. Stat. §63.042. In a few states, the minimum age is higher—for example, 25 in Georgia. Ga. Code Ann. §19-8-3. Some states also, or instead, require that the prospective adoptive parent be at least ten years older than the person to be adopted. E.g., Cal. Fam. Code §8601(a). France takes duration of marriage into account also, requiring that applicants for adoption other than step-parents be 28 years old unless they have been married for more than two years. Other characteristics that suggest danger of child maltreatment, such as drug abuse or a history of child maltreatment, would of course make it very unlikely that an applicant would receive agency or court approval.

Thus, with the basic rules for new-family adoption, we have what might seem the best approach to establishing a relationship between two people. In this context, you have one or two adults on one side of family formation, and those adults have freely chosen, typically after long deliberation and rigorous examination by a third party, to enter into the relationship. On the other side, you have a child, usually too young to choose but represented by an agency with expertise in making proxy decisions for children as to with whom they should enter into a family relationship. On both sides there must be a decision that entering into the relationship is in the parties' best interests, in light of available alternatives. And there is a testing period to make sure the relationship gets off to a good start, before it is made permanent. Would it be possible and desirable to reform parentage or marriage law and practice so that they more closely resemble this model?

That said, there are several ways in which adoption law and practice arguably fall short of such an ideal. First, the home study and approval process might in many cases be much less rigorous than the laws and regulations suggest—principally, those cases in which wealthy parents can shop around for a private agency more interested in their money than in fulfilling the aims of the law, those involving step-parent applicants, and those involving adoption of children from foreign countries. See ELIZABETH BARTHOLET, FAMILY BONDS: ADOPTION, INFERTILITY, AND THE NEW WORLD OF CHILD PRODUCTION 73-74 (1999).

The more relaxed procedures for step-parent adoptions likely reflects in part an assumption that an existing parent would not choose as a second parent for his or her child (or as a spouse) someone who would not make at least a minimally adequate parent. It might also reflect recognition that, absent a report that the spouse has abused the child, the child will live in the household with that spouse anyway. The adoption simply confers legal status on a social relationship that already exists and is likely to continue regardless. But it might nevertheless be detrimental to a child to have a step-parent become a legal parent, if the step-parent has a troubling history, perhaps a criminal or child maltreatment history of which the child's birth parent is unaware. Following adoption, that person would have all the same rights of custody and control over the child as any other legal parent. There is therefore still much value for the child in conducting the background check and home study.

Adoption by Persons Who Are Homosexual or by Same-Sex Couples

A second way in which adoption law and practice arguably fall short of the ideal is that certain sub-rules in adoption law have excluded some persons from adoption who arguably should not be excluded, or have made adoption by such persons unreasonably difficult. For example, the law in some U.S. states and in many other countries precludes same-sex couples from adopting jointly, either explicitly or, in jurisdictions where same-sex couples may not marry, incidentally by allowing only married persons to petition jointly. See, e.g., Miss. Code Ann. §93-17-3(5) ("Adoption by couples of the same gender is prohibited."); Utah Code Ann. §78B-6-117(3) ("A child may not be adopted by a person who is cohabiting in a relationship that is not a legally valid and binding marriage under the laws of this state.") One member of the couple might be able to adopt alone, but then there is no legal recognition of the child's relationship with the other caregiver. As a result, some children might not be adopted by anyone, and some might be adopted by only one of two co-parents, leaving their social parent-child relationship with the other co-parent vulnerable to arbitrary severance. Chapter 4 addresses the possibility of petitioning for visitation or shared custody as a non-parent in such cases.

Relatedly, prevailing step-parent adoption rules, designed for adoption by "spouses" of birth parents, do not allow for a same-sex partner of a biological parent to become the child's legal parent, absent liberal interpretation by a court, in states that do not recognize same-sex marriages. In re Adoption of K.S.P., 804 N.E.2d 1253 (Ind. Ct. App. 2004) (construing statute liberally to allow for step-parent adoption by same-sex partner); In Interest of Angel Lace M., 516 N.W.2d 678 (Wis. 1994) (refusing to apply step-parent adoption provision to same-sex partner); see also, e.g., Adoption of M.A., 930 A.2d 1088 (Me. 2007) (construing statute liberally to allow joint adoption petitions by members of a same-sex couple). Professor Polikoff critiques this aspect of adoption law, and she urges reform modeled after parentage laws in other countries that contemplate initial legal parent status for both members of lesbian couples who conceive using artificial insemination. See Nancy D. Polikoff, *A Mother Should Not Have to Adopt Her Own Child: Parentage Laws for Children of Lesbian Couples in the Twenty-First Century*, 5 STAN. J. C.R. & C.L. 201 (2009) (citing examples in Quebec, other Canadian provinces, Australia, and several European countries).

Regardless of whether a same-sex couple is able to achieve legal parent status for both of them, if the relationship dissolves and one member of the couple relocates to another state, there could be special problems faced in trying to enforce an adoption or parentage order or to secure continued contact with the child, if one state refuses to recognize rulings of courts in another. See Courtney G. Joslin, *Interstate Recognition of Parentage in a Time of Disharmony: Same-Sex Parent Families and Beyond*, 70 OHIO ST. L.J. 563 (2009). A highly publicized, long-running duel between socially conservative Virginia and more liberal Vermont finally ended with Virginia courts deferring to the civil union dissolution orders of Vermont courts, which granted child visitation rights to the former lesbian partner of a biological mother. See Miller v. Jenkins, 2010 WL 605737 (Va. Ct. App.).

In some places, historically, homosexuals have not been permitted to adopt at all, singly or as members of a committed couple. Thus, even if, on the facts of particular cases, children would benefit from having such persons adopt them, the child could not enter into a legal parent-child relationship with those persons. For the most part, this is true today only where laws limit adoption to married couples, so the exclusion is incidental and perhaps unintentional. Florida adoption law, however, contains a provision stating: "No person eligible to adopt under this statute may adopt if that person is a homosexual." Fla. Stat. Ann. §63.042. A gay man who had been a successful foster parent to several children challenged this statutory obstacle to his adopting one of his foster children, and a Florida intermediate appellate court held in 2010 that it violates the state constitutional rights of homosexuals and of children who have bonded with homosexual foster parents. See Florida Dep't of Children and Families v. Adoption of X.X.G. and N.R.G., 45 So. 3d 79 (Fla. Dist. Ct. App. 3d Dist. 2010). France had a practice of limiting adoption to heterosexuals until the European Court of Human Rights held, in *E.B. v. France* (2008), that this was a violation of both the equal protection and the family life articles of the European Convention on Human Rights. Prior to this ruling, the U.K. Parliament had explicitly banned discrimination against homosexuals in adoption. Equality Act (Sexual Orientation) Regulations 2007 (United Kingdom).

Should it even be a factor in an adoption that an applicant is homosexual or that joint applicants are a same-sex couple? In other words, all else being equal, should an adoption agency favor a heterosexual couple or individual over a homosexual couple or individual? What rule would you want in place if you were going to be a newborn child again and would be placed by your birth parents for adoption? For contrasting views on the child welfare effects of having gay parents, see Courtney G. Joslin, *Searching for Harm: Same-Sex Marriage and the Well-being of Children,* 46 HARV. C.R.-C.L. L. REV. 81 (2011), and Lynn D. Wardle, *The "Inner Lives" of Children in Lesbigay Adoption: Narratives and Other Concerns,* 18 ST. THOMAS L. REV 511 (2005).

Trans-Racial Adoption

Other substantive considerations in adoption placement do not categorically exclude or disadvantage particular groups of people with respect to adoption but rather exclude or disadvantage particular applicants in placement of particular children. One such consideration that has been the subject of long-standing controversy is race. Some U.S. states once had statutes explicitly precluding trans-racial adoption. See, e.g., Tex. Rev. Civ. Stat. Ann. art. 46a, §8 (Vernon 1969) ("No white child can be adopted by a negro person, nor can a negro child be adopted by a white person.") (repealed 1974).

Federal law in the United States now proscribes categorical race-matching policies, but some observers believe that many public and private adoption agencies today nevertheless follow an unofficial policy of categorical race-matching—that is, applying a very strong, perhaps irrebuttable, presumption against trans-racial placement, because beliefs about community ownership of children or about the unnaturalness of mixed-race family relationships are deeply entrenched. Historically, there has also been an aversion in many societies to inter-racial marriage. How do you suppose opposition to mixed-race relationships differs as between the parent-child relationship and the martial relationship, in terms of who is opposed and why?

Ralph Richard Banks, The Multiethnic Placement Act and the Troubling Persistence of Race Matching

38 Cap. U. L. Rev. 271 (2009)

Prior to the passage of the Multiethnic Placement Act (MEPA) in 1994, . . . [s]ocial work policy and practice was animated by the sense that children belonged with parents from their own racial group. Some jurisdictions created a formal presumption in favor of same race placement. Others simply accorded social workers the discretion to take account of race, which many did. The emphasis on racial commonality was one expression of the more general assumption that children should be placed in a family as similar as possible to the biological family into which the child was born.

MEPA was Congress' response to criticism that the widespread preference for placing black children with black parents—a practice known as race matching—had exacerbated the disproportionate representation of black children among those awaiting adoption from foster care. . . . In some cases, white foster parents with whom a black child had lived were denied the opportunity to adopt the child. As originally enacted, MEPA prohibited officials from delaying or denying the placement of a child "solely on the basis of race." This language permitted child placement decisions in which race was one factor among many, ironically making MEPA the first federal statute to condone race matching. After a public outcry, Congress amended MEPA in 1996, deleting the "solely" language. . . . Some commentators . . . think the law has not been pushed far enough, and that more vigorous enforcement is needed to ferret out covert forms of race matching. . . .

The Preference Policy

In South Carolina, state adoption agency officials typically asked prospective adoptive parents about their preferences with respect to the child they hoped to adopt. Among the many preferences elicited by state adoption agencies were preferences related to race. . . . South Carolina agency officials could reasonably argue that by deferring to parental preferences, they were not delaying or denying placement of children on the basis of race; they were attempting to expedite the placement of children. . . . Not only did the policy help to give parents what they wanted, but also it aimed to give children what they needed. . . . [I]t "may not be in the child's best interest to remain with or be placed with a family that has stated their preference is another race." . . .

There are at least two problems with the procedures in South Carolina. First, there is reason to conclude the state social workers . . . accorded racial preferences deference precisely because they knew that doing so would result in monoracial families, which the social workers wanted to create. Additionally, . . . according weight to racial preferences dramatically limited the pool of parents available to black children in particular. . . .

The second problem with the South Carolina approach is that even if state officials were not intentionally attempting to race match, their treatment of parental preferences unquestionably reflected the view that the desire for a child of one's own race is natural and normal, whereas a desire for a child of a different race is suspect. The assumption that parents' racial preferences are always more deeply held and less malleable than other preferences is almost certainly incorrect. . . . Some prospective parents might have expressed a preference for a same race child because they suspected, correctly, that the adoption process would become a lot more cumbersome had they expressed an openness to a transracial placement. Others may have answered that they would prefer to adopt a child of their own race because that seemed to be the "right" answer, what friends, family, and the social worker would expect one to say. . . .

Social workers would regularly query parents who wanted a healthy young child, for example, whether they would agree to adopt a child with some physical health issues or who was slightly older. . . . Yet, many social workers would not dare ask anyone to reconsider their racial preference. . . . Social workers could have assumed race is no more important than, for example, eye or hair color, and left it to the parents to determine if it was. . . . The state could also have actively encouraged potential parents to be more open about the race of their potential adoptive child and to consider a transracial adoption if the parents' other preferences were met. . . .

The Cultural Competency Policy

Confronted with a potential transracial placement, officials in Ohio typically investigated prospective adoptive parents' racial views, whether the parents lived in a racially-diverse neighborhood, how they felt about various issues in black history, and what they would do to raise the child with an awareness of his or her cultural heritage. . . . State adoption officials assume that black parents are culturally competent to raise black children. . . . These practices led the Office of Civil Rights to determine that prospective parents were subject to "different treatment and standards based upon their race and the race of the children in which they expresse[d] an interest in adopting." . . .

Maintaining a child's cultural heritage, developing a healthy racial identity, and acquiring the tools to deal with discrimination—these aspects of cultural competency are means of promoting the child's best interests. . . . But . . . social workers in Ohio seemed to reflect the same judgment that animated the matching process in South Carolina: that race should be accorded primacy. . . . [For example, they] regard the child's "racial needs" as more important than any needs arising from the child's medical condition. . . . The same logic that would have caused the adoption officials to prefer a racially integrated setting would have made an African American family seem better still. . . .

Ohio officials "urged parents interested in transracial placements to consider moving to integrated neighborhoods, to attend integrated churches, to obtain African American artwork, and to become familiar with what workers perceived as African American culture." One could scarcely imagine black adoptive parents being given similar directives. And if they were, most people would recoil from that degree of state interference with personal tastes and lifestyle preferences. . . . African American potential parents willing to adopt African American children waited an average of 89.8 days to be matched with a child, while white parents who were open to adopting African American or biracial children waited an average of 201.5 days—more than twice as long. Children, too, may have waited longer for families to adopt them due to officials' desire to find a family with appropriate cultural competency. . . .

In 1972, the National Association of Black Social Workers released a statement in which they strongly opposed transracial adoption as a form of cultural genocide . . . :

> Only a black family can transmit the emotional and sensitive subtleties of perception and reaction essential for a black child's survival in a racist society. . . . We stand firmly, though, on conviction that a white home is not a suitable placement for black children and contend it is totally unnecessary.

. . . [E]ven some ostensible opponents of race matching probably do not believe that there is no reason to favor same race placements. . . .

[S]hould race matching be illegal even if there were more than enough black families to adopt all the available black children? . . . Suppose that black children placed in white families tend to believe that "people are people, and that race doesn't really matter," and that black children adopted into black families are more likely to think "race should be a crucial component of one's identity." Is there any reason to prefer one form of identity over another? Is it better to understand race as a fundamental part of one's self or as a trivial part of one's self? . . . Given the impossibility of any non-ideological way of resolving this issue, social workers should refrain from preferring one racial identity to another in their adoptive placements. For them to promote any particular sort of racial identity constitutes the sort of governmental imposition of values against which our Constitution guards. . . .

There are consistent findings that "transracial adoptees do as well as other children on standard measures of self-esteem, educational achievement, behavioral difficulties, and relations to peers and other family members." Moreover, there is no reason to expect that black parents would be better able to teach black children how to succeed in American society. Certainly, black parents would have experienced racism and discrimination. But why would one conclude that they have been ennobled rather than damaged by such experiences? And why would white parents not have benefited from all their years spent on the white side of the racial divide? Who better than a white parent to explain to a black child how white people are likely to view and respond to him? . . .

Professor Bartholet responds that a broader range of state-created forces promote single-race families:

> "Banks's article focuses on . . . private preferences in adoption only, and only as facilitated by the state. Private preferences, however, are conditioned by public policy in the entire family-decisionmaking arena, not simply in adoption. Public policy encourages the creation of same-race families by a multitude of laws and practices. For example, states "facilitate" private race preference when they license marriage partners without inquiry into the role race played in partner selection. Our society encourages racially matched parenting through employment and health insurance policies that subsidize procreation, through constitutional doctrines that protect the 'right' to procreate, through free market policies that allow the purchase and sale of sperm, eggs, embryos, and surrogacy services, and through social conditioning that puts a high value on parenting genetically related children. At the same time, our society discourages adoption through restrictive regulation, making adoption expensive while failing to provide the financial subsidies that we accord procreation, and stigmatizing adoption as a second-class form of parenting. And in discouraging adoption, we discourage transracial families, because the children in need of adoptive homes here and abroad are, overwhelmingly, non-Caucasian, and the adults seeking to become adoptive parents are, overwhelmingly, Caucasian."

Elizabeth Bartholet, *Private Race Preference in Family Formation*, 107 YALE L.J. 2351, 2352 (1998).

Professor Bartholet also doubts that the amended MEPA is having the effect Congress intended, stating that "there is enormous resistance to this law, and it appears so far to have had little impact. State social service agencies tend to be committed from top to bottom to their race-matching ways." Id. at 2354. See also RANDALL KENNEDY, INTERRACIAL INTIMACIES: SEX, MARRIAGE, IDENTITY, AND ADOPTION (2004). For skeptical views on trans-racial adoption, see, e.g., Twila L. Perry, *Transractial Adoption and Gentrification: An Essay on Race, Power, Family and Community*, 26 B.C. THIRD WORLD L.J. 25 (2006).

A phenomenon similar to race-matching is federal legislation that confers on Native American tribes, in many family matters, jurisdiction over children who have some connection to a tribe, and that requires state child welfare agencies, when placing a child with such a connection in foster care or adoption, to give preference to members of Native American tribes. Application of the Indian Child Welfare Act of 1978 has caused the disruption or delay of many adoptions, when tribes have received notice only after a child has been placed with adopting parents that the child has some tribal connection. Transfer of the child's case to a tribal court typically results in a denial of the adoption petition, even in the many cases when the birth mother supports completion of the adoption.

Barbara Atwood, The Voice of the Indian Child: Strengthening the Indian Child Welfare Act Through Children's Participation

50 Ariz. L. Rev. 127, 128-130 (2008)

The Indian Child Welfare Act, a response to the wide-scale separation of American Indian children from their families and tribes, has now been on the books for thirty years. The positive results of the Act are many, including greater respect for tribal authority over the placement of Indian children and an expansion of tribal family preservation programs. Moreover, while Indian children are still removed from their homes in disproportionately higher numbers than non-Indian children, the rate of removal has decreased as has the rate of placement with non-Indian caregivers. Nevertheless, the policies underlying the Act remain deeply controversial.

One of the key criticisms of the Act is that it objectifies Indian children as tribal "resources" and mandates certain jurisdictional and placement outcomes that benefit tribes without regard to children's interests. Critics argue that Congress ignored the socioeconomic ills that continue to ravage American Indian communities and instead fashioned a cheap fix by increasing tribal power over child welfare matters and providing placement criteria for the adoption and foster care of Indian children that serve tribal goals. Similarly, the view that the Act requires wooden preferences for tribal placements that disregard children's unique circumstances seems to drive state court resistance. As a result, some courts have relied on ill-founded doctrines that permit them to avoid the Act altogether or to refuse transfers of ICWA proceedings to tribal courts by prematurely assessing children's interests.

I agree that the federal government needs to devote significantly more resources to reservations and tribal communities, both for family preservation services and tribal child welfare programs. A shortage of Indian foster homes is the result, in part, of inadequate or non-existent federal funding. . . . At the same time, I disagree with those who condemn ICWA as a misguided use of children to serve tribal ends. When an Indian tribe achieves vitality and respect as a sovereign, the tribe's members, including children, stand to benefit. The Act is an essential piece of the overall federal policy of tribal self-determination, and growth in de facto tribal sovereignty correlates strongly with a tribe's economic well-being. Moreover, . . . the Act's procedural and substantive provisions should be read to permit state courts to bring "a multidimensional, situated interpretation to the goal of advancing the interests of individual Indian children."

Suppose a tribe is today far from achieving "vitality." Is it plausible to say that a child born today "stand[s] to benefit" from an ICWA-driven decision that prevents her from being adopted by persons outside the tribe who live in an already-vital community and that results in her growing up in a non-vital social environment with people who are not her parents? If the positive effects for the tribe that Professor Atwood posits would occur only gradually over several decades, is it not treating the child instrumentally as a tribe resource to maintain that such a child should be kept in the tribal environment in order to support this progress? If it is, would that be wrong? Do not all societies expect individual members to sacrifice their own interests to some degree for the good of the community? Do not many people, even in mainstream America, view children as a resource and think that education and other aspects of child rearing should be designed to produce good citizens and workers, for the benefit of the community or the nation?

For competing views on the animating idea and implementation of ICWA, see, e.g., Cheyañna L. Jaffke, *The "Existing Indian Family" Exception to the Indian Child Welfare Act: The States' Attempt to Slaughter Tribal Interests in Indian Children,* 66 LA. L. REV. 733 (2006); Christine Metteer, *Hard Cases Making Bad Law: The Need for Revision of the Indian Child Welfare Act,* 38 SANTA CLARA L. REV. 419 (1998). Christine D. Bakeis, *The Indian Child Welfare Act of 1978: Violating Personal Rights for the Sake of the Tribe,* 10 NOTRE DAME J.L. ETHICS & PUB. POL'Y 543, 546-547 (1996). For a recent state court decision applying ICWA to a jurisdictional dispute, see People ex rel. South Dakota Dep't of Soc. Servs., 795 N.W.2d 39 (S.D. 2011) (holding that DSS demonstrated good cause for deviating from ICWA's preferences for an adoption placement).

International Adoption

Americans began to adopt across national borders in substantial numbers after World War II, and the practice grew steadily in the ensuing decades, though there has been a drop off in recent years. International adoption poses additional costs and administrative hurdles for would-be adopters. They generally must pay many thousands of dollars to an agency that specializes in international adoption, satisfy the legal requirements for adoption in the child's country as well as their own, and in most instances travel to the child's country and negotiate a legal process conducted in a language they likely do not speak. After managing the foreign component, traditionally they have also had to go through the normal process for an adoption in their home state. There has been movement in recent years at the federal level and in some states toward eliminating this additional step at home, but the law in many states still requires persons who adopt abroad to file a petition in a court in their home state after receiving custody of the child. See, e.g., 750 Ill. Comp. Stat. 50/5(A) ("In the case of a child born outside the United States or a territory thereof, if the prospective adoptive parents of such child have been appointed guardians of such child by a court of competent jurisdiction in a country other than the United States or a territory thereof, such parents shall file a petition as provided in this Section within 30 days after entry of the child into the United States."). They generally must also undergo the same home study to which parents in domestic adoptions are subjected. See, e.g., 750 Ill. Comp. Stat. 50/6(B).

The primary motivation for adopters to endure the added expense and hassle of a foreign adoption seems to be the vastly greater pool of available children in the global adoption arena. The number of newborns available for adoption in the United States has plummeted in the past several decades, as abortion became legal, contraception became widely available, and the stigma of non-marital pregnancy largely disappeared. Rather than adopt a child who has been in the foster care system, many Americans prefer to look abroad for a child whom they can raise almost from birth. Professor Maldanado suggests that racial preference also plays a role, noting that children available for adoption in the United States are predominantly black, whereas by adopting abroad Americans can more readily find an available child who is white or Asian. She proposes that adoption laws in the United States be amended to require that Americans seeking to adopt abroad present non-race-based reasons for doing so. See Solangel Maldonado, *Discouraging Racial Preferences in Adoptions*, 39 U.C. Davis L. Rev. 1415 (2006).

Debates about trans-racial adoption and about ICWA raise the question of whether children "belong to" a group. International adoption raises this same question. A primary cause of the drop off in the number of inter-country adoptions in recent years is that many nations that have served as source countries for American and western European adopters have recently imposed greater restrictions on adoption of "their" children, or stopped it altogether. For example, the Ukraine now limits inter-country adoptions, absent special circumstances, to children age five or older, even if children are placed in orphanages at birth. Guatemala stopped accepting new adoption applications in 2008. South Korea has announced an intention to end foreign adoptions. Many countries restrict who may adopt, precluding single people or homosexuals or persons above or below a certain age from adopting, again regardless of how many children languish in their orphanages. For a description of current policies across the globe, see Bureau of Consular Affairs, Intercountry Adoption, http://adoption.state.gov/index.php.

Such policies have the effect of preventing some orphaned children from forming a family with adults who want to raise them, even though, apart from considerations of cultural belonging, doing so would appear to be clearly the best thing for them. Scholars debating the propriety of trans-national adoption, like those debating trans-racial adoption, focus on the significance of native culture for a baby. They also express concerns about the symbolic implications of Westerners using their wealth to take babies away from less developed countries and about the threat of baby-selling or trafficking of children. Compare David M. Smolin, *Child Laundering and the Hague Convention on Intercountry Adoption: The Future and Past of Intercountry Adoption*, 48 U. Louisville L. Rev. (2010) (voicing concerns about child trafficking), and Shani King, *Challenging Monohumanism: An Argument for Changing the Way We Think About Intercountry Adoption*, 30 Mich. J. Int'l L. 413 (2009), with Elizabeth Bartholet, *International Adoption: The Human Rights Position*, 1 Global Pol'y 91 (2010), and Sara Dillon, *Making Legal Regimes for Intercountry Adoption Reflect Human Rights Principles: Transforming the United Nations Convention on the Rights of the Child with the Hague Convention on Intercountry Adoption*, 21 B.U. Int'l L.J. 179 (2003) (presenting children's rights arguments for removing barriers to international adoption). For discussion of inter-country adoption by same-sex couples, see Lynn D. Wardle, *The Hague Convention on Intercountry Adoption and American Implementing Law: Implications for International Adoptions by Gay and Lesbian Couples or Partners*, 18 Ind. Int'l & Comp. L. Rev. 113 (2008).

In light of these various limits on who may adopt and who may be adopted, adoption law on the whole arguably does not match the posited ideal of rational, mutually optimal decision making based on extensive information and open consideration of all available alternatives. But in the most common case of married heterosexual couples adopting children viewed as of the same race, the governing rules for the most part are designed to ensure such decisions. Arguably aspects of adoption law that detract from this model should be eliminated. But we see a much greater departure from this model in the case of biology-based parentage, and a much stronger popular conviction that children "belong to" certain people regardless of whether that is best for them. We turn now to this important area of domestic relations practice.

B. ASSIGNMENT OF CHILDREN TO THEIR FIRST LEGAL PARENTS

Except in rare cases of abandonment, the state will identify at least one person as a baby's legal parent immediately after birth. A person's initial legal parents remain his or her legal parents for life unless the state terminates their rights through a child protective or adoption proceeding. In the United States, state creation of first-parent legal status is in almost all cases based on proof or presumption of biological parentage. Because this is such a simple rule to apply, the state generally expends little or no effort in creating initial parent-child relationships. Even in cases of contested paternity, there is typically little need for court proceedings, except to secure an order for genetic testing, in order for the state to create the legal parent-child relationship. (Custody, visitation, and support matters, *after* the parent-child relationship is established, do frequently give rise to substantial litigation.) The main question for you to ponder as you read the materials to follow is whether the state should be more circumspect with first-parent assignments, perhaps at a minimum making an effort to exclude the most unfit biological parents from becoming legal parents.

An important subsidiary question is what is the significance of the biological relationship, as an empirical and moral matter. Is it so important to children's well being that exceptionless biology-based parentage amounts to always doing what is best for newborn children, and therefore is just as protective of children's interests as is the qualification process for adoption? Many other legal systems place less emphasis on biological connection, at least with respect to fathers. Some make a woman's husband the father of any children she bears regardless of who the actual biological father is. And in the case of births to unmarried women, some never confer parental status on the biological father or do so only if this is shown to be in the best interests of the child. See, e.g., McD v. L [2009] IESC 81 (decision of the Supreme Court of Ireland holding that biological father of child born to unmarried woman had no constitutional right to legal parent status or custody but rather just a statutory right to apply for guardian status, with decision on such application to be based principally on the welfare interests of the child).

1. Maternity

Perhaps the closest thing to a globally uniform rule in family law is that the woman who gives birth to a child is the child's first legal mother, with a presumptive right to custody. California's maternity rule is typical, and in fact derives from the 1973 Uniform Parentage Act, which 19 states adopted:

California Family Code
Division 12. Parent and Child Relationship
Part 3. Uniform Parentage Act
Chapter 2. Establishing Parent and Child Relationship

§7610. METHOD OF ESTABLISHMENT

The parent and child relationship may be established as follows:

(a) Between a child and the natural mother, it may be established by proof of her having given birth to the child, or under this part.

§7650. ACTION TO DETERMINE EXISTENCE OR NONEXISTENCE OF MOTHER AND CHILD RELATIONSHIP

(a) . . . Insofar as practicable, the provisions of this part applicable to the father and child relationship apply.

The "or under this part" language in §7610 connects that section to §7650, which in turn allows for extension to maternity of provisions governing establishment of paternity, in the rare cases when it is uncertain who gave birth to a child—for example, if a birth mother initially abandoned a baby. In nearly all cases, though, women give birth in birthing facilities, the facilities report the name of child and birth mother to a state agency, which then issues a birth certificate naming the birth mother as the child's legal mother, and that is all that is necessary to establish the legal parent-child relationship.

A recent medical phenomenon, likely not contemplated by the California legislature when it adopted the Uniform Parentage Act, is the possibility of two women in an intimate relationship having a child together, by having one of them artificially inseminated or by implantation of the fertilized egg of one in the uterus of the other. In such cases, the women typically want, at least initially, for both of them to be legal parents. Whether legislatures and courts choose to confer legal maternity on both partners in these cases will likely determine how widespread the practice becomes. As it has been in many areas of family law, California has been on the forefront of liberalizing parentage rules.

Elisa B. v. Superior Court

117 P.3d 660 (Cal. 2005)

Moreno, J.

. . . On June 7, 2001, the El Dorado County District Attorney filed a complaint in superior court to establish that Elisa B. is a parent of two-year-old twins Kaia B. and Ry B., who were born to Emily B., and to order Elisa to pay child support. Elisa filed an answer in which she denied being the children's parent. . . .

Elisa testified that she entered into a lesbian relationship with Emily in 1993. . . . They introduced each other to friends as their "partner," exchanged rings, opened a joint bank account, and believed they were in a committed relationship. Elisa and Emily discussed having children and decided that they both wished to give birth. Because Elisa earned more than twice as much money as Emily, they decided that Emily "would be the stay-at-home mother" and Elisa "would be the primary breadwinner for the family." At a sperm bank, they chose a donor they both would use so the children would "be biological brothers and sisters."

After several unsuccessful attempts, Elisa became pregnant in February, 1997. Emily was present when Elisa was inseminated. Emily began the insemination process in June of 1997 and became pregnant in August, 1997. Elisa was present when Emily was inseminated and, the next day, Elisa picked up additional sperm at the sperm bank and again inseminated Emily at their home to "make sure she got pregnant." They went to each other's medical appointments during pregnancy and attended childbirth classes together so that each could act as a "coach" for the other during birth, including cutting the children's umbilical cords.

Elisa gave birth to Chance in November, 1997, and Emily gave birth to Ry and Kaia prematurely in March, 1998. Ry had medical problems; he suffered from Down's Syndrome, and required heart surgery. They jointly selected the children's names, joining their surnames with a hyphen to form the children's surname. They each breast-fed all of the children. Elisa claimed all three children as her dependents on her tax returns and obtained a life insurance policy on herself naming Emily as the beneficiary so that if "anything happened" to her, all three children would be "cared for." Elisa believed the children would be considered both of their children.

Elisa's parents referred to the twins as their grandchildren, and her sister referred to the twins as part of their family and referred to Elisa as the twins' mother. Elisa treated all of the children as hers and told a prospective employer that she had triplets. Elisa and

Emily identified themselves as co-parents of Ry at an organization arranging care for his Down's Syndrome. Elisa supported the household financially. Emily was not working. Emily testified that she would not have become pregnant if Elisa had not promised to support her financially, but Elisa denied that any financial arrangements were discussed before the birth of the children. Elisa later acknowledged in her testimony, however, that Emily "was going to be an at-home mom for maybe a couple of years and then the kids were going to go into day care and she was going to return to work." They consulted an attorney regarding adopting "each other's child," but never did so. Nor did they register as domestic partners or execute a written agreement concerning the children. Elisa stated she later reconsidered adoption because she had misgivings about Emily adopting Chance.

Elisa and Emily separated in November, 1999. Elisa promised to support Emily and the twins "as much as I possibly could" and initially paid the mortgage payments of approximately $1,500 per month on the house in which Emily and the twins continued to live, as well as other expenses. Emily applied for aid. When they sold the house and Emily and the twins moved into an apartment in November, 2000, Elisa paid Emily $1,000 a month. In early 2001, Elisa stated she lost her position as a full-time employee and told Emily she no longer could support her and the twins. At the time of trial, Elisa was earning $95,000 a year. . . .

The UPA . . . expressly provides that in determining the existence of a mother and child relationship, "[i]nsofar as practicable, the provisions of this part applicable to the father and child relationship apply." (§7650.) . . . The issue before us in *Johnson* was whether a wife whose ovum was fertilized in vitro by her husband's sperm and implanted in a surrogate mother was the mother of the child so produced, rather than the surrogate. (Johnson v. Calvert, 851 P.2d 776 (1993). . . . No provision of the UPA expressly addresses the parental rights of a woman who, like the wife in *Johnson v. Calvert*, has not given birth to a child, but has a genetic relationship because she supplied the ovum used to impregnate the birth mother. But . . . we looked to the provisions regarding presumptions of paternity and concluded that "genetic consanguinity" could be the basis for a finding of maternity just as it is for paternity. We concluded, therefore, that both women—the surrogate who gave birth to the child and the wife who supplied the ovum—had "adduced evidence of a mother and child relationship as contemplated by the Act."

Anticipating this result, the American Civil Liberties Union appearing as amicus curiae urged this court to rule that the child, therefore, had two mothers. Because it was undisputed that the husband, who had supplied the semen used to impregnate the surrogate, was the child's father, this would have left the child with three parents. We declined the invitation, stating: "Even though rising divorce rates have made multiple parent arrangements common in our society, we see no compelling reason to recognize such a situation here. The Calverts are the genetic and intending parents of their son and have provided him, by all accounts, with a stable, intact, and nurturing home. To recognize parental rights in a third party with whom the Calvert family has had little contact since shortly after the child's birth would diminish [the wife]'s role as mother." We held instead that "for any child California law recognizes only one natural mother," and proceeded to conclude that the wife, rather than the surrogate, was the child's mother: "We conclude that although the Act recognizes both genetic consanguinity and giving birth as means of establishing a mother and child relationship, when the two means do not coincide in one woman, she who intended to procreate the child—that is, she who intended to bring about the birth of a child that she intended to raise as her own—is the natural mother under California law." . . .

[W]hat we considered and rejected in *Johnson* was the argument that a child could have three parents: a father and two mothers.[4] We did not address the question presented in this case of whether a child could have two parents, both of whom are women.

We perceive no reason why both parents of a child cannot be women. That result now is possible under the current version of the domestic partnership statutes, which took effect this year. (§297 et seq.) Two women "who have chosen to share one another's lives in an intimate and committed relationship of mutual caring" and have a common residence (§297) can file with the Secretary of State a "Declaration of Domestic Partnership" (§298). Section 297.5(d) provides . . . : "The rights and obligations of registered domestic partners with respect to a child of either of them shall be the same as those of spouses."

Prior to the effective date of the current domestic partnership statutes, we recognized in an adoption case that a child can have two parents, both of whom are women. In *Sharon S. v. Superior Court* (2003), we upheld a "second parent" adoption in which the mother of a child that had been conceived by means of artificial insemination consented to adoption of the child by the mother's lesbian partner. If both parents of an adopted child can be women, we see no reason why the twins in the present case cannot have two parents, both of whom are women. . . .

Subdivision (d) of section 7611 states that a man is presumed to be the natural father of a child if "[h]e receives the child into his home and openly holds out the child as his natural child." The Court of Appeal in *In re Karen C.* (2002) held that [this] "should apply equally to women." . . . There is no doubt that Elisa satisfied the first part of this test; it is undisputed that Elisa received the twins into her home. . . . The circumstance that Elisa has no genetic connection to the twins does not necessarily mean that she did not hold out the twins as her "natural" children under section 7611.

We held in *In re Nicholas H.* (2002) that the presumption . . . that a man who receives a child into his home and openly holds the child out as his natural child is not necessarily rebutted when he admits he is not the child's biological father. The presumed father in *Nicholas H.*, Thomas, met the child's mother, Kimberly, when she was pregnant with Nicholas. Nevertheless, Thomas was named as the child's father on his birth certificate and provided a home for the child and his mother for several years. . . . The Court of Appeal . . . observ[ed] that "the Legislature has used the term 'natural' to mean 'biological'" and . . . is rebutted under section 7612, subdivision (a) by clear and convincing evidence "that the man is not the child's natural, biological father." We noted, however, that the UPA does not state that the presumption under section 7611, subdivision (d), *is* rebutted by evidence that the presumed father is not the child's biological father, but rather that it *may* be rebutted *in an appropriate action* by such evidence. We held that *Nicholas H.* was not an appropriate action in which to rebut the presumption because no one had raised a conflicting claim to being the child's father. Applying the presumption, therefore, would produce the "harsh result" of leaving the child fatherless. We quoted . . . "[a] man who has lived with a child, treating it as his son or daughter, has developed a relationship with the child that should not be lightly dissolved. . . . This social relationship is much more important, to the child at least, than a biological relationship of actual paternity. . . ."

The Court of Appeal in *In re Karen C.* applied the principles discussed in *Nicholas H.* regarding presumed fathers and concluded that a woman with no biological connection

4. We have not decided "whether there exists an overriding legislative policy limiting a child to two parents." . . .

to a child could be a presumed mother. . . . Twelve-year-old Karen C. petitioned for an order determining the existence of a mother and child relationship between her and Leticia C., who had raised her from birth. Leticia admitted she was not Karen's biological mother, explaining that Karen's birth mother had tried unsuccessfully to abort her pregnancy and then agreed to give the child to Leticia. The birth mother falsely told the hospital staff that her name was Leticia C. so that Leticia's name would appear on the child's birth certificate. The birth mother gave Karen to Leticia promptly after the child was born. . . . The Court of Appeal . . . determin[ed] that Leticia was the child's presumed mother under section 7611 because she had taken Karen into her home and raised her as her child. . . .

Similarly, the Court of Appeal in *In re Salvador M.* held that a woman who had raised her half brother as her son could be the child's presumed mother. . . . In that case, the child's mother died when he was three years old and he was raised by his 18-year-old half sister, who had a four-year-old daughter of her own and later gave birth again. The child believed that his half sister was his mother and that her offspring were his siblings. His half sister revealed her true relation to the child "'in official matters, such as school registration,'" but maintained that "'to the rest of the world [the child] is my son.'" The Court of Appeal . . . stat[ed]: "The paternity presumptions are driven, not by biological paternity, but by the state's interest in the welfare of the child and the integrity of the family. The court concluded that the half sister had openly held out the child as her own, despite admitting to various officials that she was the child's half sister, noting that "the most compelling evidence" that she held out the child as her own was that the eight-year-old child "*believed* appellant was his mother" which supported the conclusion that she held the child "out to the community as her son." . . . [T]he court concluded that this was "clearly *not* an appropriate case" to find the presumption was rebutted by the fact that she was not the child's birth mother, "because there was no competing maternal interest and to sever this deeply rooted mother/child bond would contravene the state's interest in maintaining the family relationship."

We conclude that the present case . . . is not "an appropriate action" in which to rebut the presumption of presumed parenthood with proof that Elisa is not the twins' biological parent. . . . It is undisputed that Elisa actively consented to, and participated in, the artificial insemination of her partner with the understanding that the resulting child or children would be raised by Emily and her as coparents, and they did act as coparents for a substantial period of time. Elisa received the twins into her home and held them out to the world as her natural children. . . . She breast-fed all three children, claimed all three children as her dependents on her tax returns, and told a prospective employer that she had triplets. Even at the hearing before the superior court, Elisa candidly testified that she considered herself to be the twins' mother.

Declaring that Elisa cannot be the twins' parent and, thus, has no obligation to support them because she is not biologically related to them would produce a result similar to the situation we sought to avoid in *Nicholas H.* of leaving the child fatherless. The twins in the present case have no father because they were conceived by means of artificial insemination using an anonymous semen donor. Rebutting the presumption that Elisa is the twin's parent would leave them with only one parent and would deprive them of the support of their second parent. Because Emily is financially unable to support the twins, the financial burden of supporting the twins would be borne by the county, rather than Elisa. . . . "There is a compelling state interest in establishing paternity for all children. Establishing paternity is the first step toward a child support award, which, in turn, provides children with equal rights and access to benefits, including, but not limited to, social security, health insurance, survivors' benefits, military benefits, and inheritance rights. . . ." By recognizing the value of determining paternity, the Legislature implicitly recognized the value of having two parents, rather than one, as a source of both emotional and financial support, especially when the obligation to support the child would otherwise fall to the public. . . .

Although Elisa presently is unwilling to accept the obligations of parenthood, this was not always so. . . . Elisa actively assisted Emily in becoming pregnant, with the understanding that they would raise the resulting children together. Having helped cause the children to be born, and having raised them as her own, Elisa should not be permitted to later abandon the twins simply because her relationship with Emily dissolved. As we noted in the context of a husband who consented to the artificial insemination of his wife using an anonymous sperm donor, but later denied responsibility for the resulting child: "One who consents to the production of a child cannot create a temporary relation to be assumed and disclaimed at will, but the arrangement must be of such character as to impose an obligation of supporting those for whose existence he is directly responsible." . . .

We were careful in *Nicholas H.*, therefore, not to suggest that every man who begins living with a woman when she is pregnant and continues to do so after the child is born necessarily becomes a presumed father of the child, even against his wishes. The Legislature surely did not intend to punish a man like the one in *Nicholas H.* who voluntarily provides support for a child who was conceived before he met the mother, by transforming that act of kindness into a legal obligation. But our observation in *Nicholas H.* loses its force in a case like the one at bar in which the presumed mother . . . acted together with the birth mother to cause the child to be conceived. . . .

Can you critique the court's statutory analysis using the canons of interpretation? What about its assumption as to what is best for the child? Is there no downside for a child to a ruling like this? We will ask the same question with respect to contested paternity. But is there no practical difference between the situation in this case and one in which the birth mother is disputing the paternity of a man, as the court appears to assume? When you study the paternity rules below, think about what other provisions California courts might someday be asked to extend to claims of maternity.

Does dual maternity become easier when same-sex marriage is legalized? In 2009, the Iowa Supreme Court ordered that legal marriage be opened to same-sex couples, and in 2012, an Iowa court applied the marital presumption of that state's paternity laws to a woman who was the wife of the birth mother. It ordered the Department of Public Health to place the wife's name on the birth certificate of a child created by artificial insemination using donated sperm. See Gartner v. Iowa Dep't of Public Health, 2012 WL 28078, (Iowa Dist. Ct.).

In the same year as its *Elisa B.* decision, the California Supreme Court addressed the somewhat different scenario of one woman's fertilized egg being implanted in a female partner's uterus. Couples who do this must contend with state laws governing gamete donation, which were written to help infertile married couples reproduce with the help of a third party, and which typically dictate that the donor shall have no rights as to any resulting child. In K.M. v. E.G., 117 P.3d 673, 679 (Cal. 2005), the court held that there was no "true egg donation" because "K.M. did not intend to simply donate her ova to E.G., but rather provided her ova to her lesbian partner with whom she was living so that E.G.

could give birth to a child that would be raised in their joint home." Id. at 679. In 2011, an intermediate Florida appellate court followed *K.M.* and conferred maternal status on two women formerly in an intimate partnership. T.M.H. v. D.M.T., 2011 WL 6437247 (Fla. Dist. Ct. App. 5th Dist.). The Florida statute was written to cover sperm and egg donation and likewise used the term "donor." Fla. Stat. §742.14 ("The donor of any egg, sperm, or preembryo . . . shall relinquish all maternal or paternal rights and obligations. . . ."). The court relied more explicitly than did the California Supreme Court on a supposition that "donor" has a meaning distinct from "provide" or "transfer." It also reasoned that interpreting "donor" to mean any transfer of an egg from one woman to another "eliminates Appellant's right to procreate and parent a child of her own" and "eliminates that right for all lesbian couples," and to do this "violates Appellant's constitutional rights to equal protection and privacy."

De Facto Motherhood

In addition to sometimes treating two women as parents of a child based on joint intent and effort to create the child, the legal system is increasingly conferring parental status based on participation in raising a child. The concept of de facto parent was first applied to men who were not biological fathers but who had co-parented a child with the child's mother, a topic covered in the next subsection. But in recent years, many women, after ending an intimate relationship with another woman who was a birth mother to one or more children, have sought to protect the relationship they formed with the children by claiming de facto parent status. Some courts have used their equitable power to establish a common-law rule predicating parenthood on having occupied a parental role in a child's life. See, e.g., In re Parentage of L.B., 122 P.3d 161 (Wash. 2005); E.N.O. v. L.M.M., 711 N.E.2d 886 (Mass. 1999); Rubano v. DiCenzo, 759 A.2d 959, 975-976 (R.I. 2000). In addition, some states' legislatures have amended their maternity statutes to authorize courts to recognize such claims.

Delaware Code
Title 13. Domestic Relations, Chapter 8. Uniform Parentage Act
Subchapter II. Parent-Child Relationship

§8-201. ESTABLISHMENT OF PARENT-CHILD RELATIONSHIP

(a) The mother-child relationship is established between a woman and a child by:

(1) The woman's having given birth to the child;

(2) An adjudication of the woman's maternity;

(3) Adoption of the child by the woman; or

(4) A determination by the court that the woman is a de facto parent of the child. . . .

(c) De facto parent status is established if the Family Court determines that the de facto parent:

(1) Has had the support and consent of the child's parent or parents who fostered the formation and establishment of a parent-like relationship between the child and the de facto parent;

(2) Has exercised parental responsibility for the child . . . ; and

(3) Has acted in a parental role for a length of time sufficient to have established a bonded and dependent relationship with the child that is parental in nature.

See also Mont. Code Ann. §40-4-228(2) ("A court may award a parental interest to a person other than a natural parent when it is shown by clear and convincing evidence that: (a) the natural parent has engaged in conduct that is contrary to the child-parent relationship; and (b) the nonparent has established with the child a child-parent relationship . . . and it is in the best interests of the child to continue that relationship.") Courts have upheld such statutory provisions against constitutional challenge by birth mothers who claimed the provisions violated their parental rights. See, e.g., Smith v. Guest, 16 A.3d 920 (Del. Super. Ct. 2011); Kulstad v. Maniaci, 220 P.3d 595 (Mont. 2009).

Should satisfying the requirements in paragraph (c) of the Delaware statute be sufficient to establish parental status? Conversely, is it proper for Montana to require that the "natural parent" have engaged in some sort of misconduct, in order to recognize the relationship that the child has with the natural parent's former partner?

Surrogacy

Surrogacy is an arrangement by which a couple unable to reproduce on their own arranges with a woman to have her gestate a baby for them. Typically the baby is conceived with the sperm of a male member of the couple. Most often today, the egg comes from a woman in the couple ("gestational surrogacy") and physicians implant the fertilized egg in the surrogate's womb. But it is also common to conceive the child by using a contracting male's sperm to fertilize an egg of the surrogate herself ("traditional surrogacy"). There is no reliable data collection to establish the prevalence of surrogacy, but one source estimates that in the United States "the number of infants born to gestational surrogates almost doubled from 2004 to 2008, from 738 babies born to nearly 1,400." See Magdalina Gugucheva, Surrogacy in America, Council for Responsible Genetics (2010), http://www.councilforresponsiblegenetics.org/pageDocuments/KAEVEJ0A1M.pdf.

Because maternity laws like the California statute above generally predicate legal motherhood on giving birth, in the absence of a special statute relating to surrogacy, a contract between a surrogate and "intending parents" is essentially a pre-commitment by the surrogate to relinquish her legal parent status following the birth, so that the intending parents can adopt the child. The legal system has been mostly hostile to such agreements. In the widely publicized case of *Baby M,* the New Jersey Supreme Court viewed such a deal as baby-selling and therefore contrary to public policy. In re Baby M, 537 A.2d 1227 (N.J. 1988). See also In re Parentage of a Child by T.J.S. and A.L.S., 16 A.3d 386 (N.J. Super. Ct. App. Div. 2011) (holding that only way for infertile wife to become legal parent of child born as result of gestational surrogacy using husband's sperm and donor ova was by step-parent adoption in which surrogate voluntarily relinquished parental rights). Courts asked to enforce such contracts in other states without statutory authorization have also mostly refused. But see J.F. v. D.B., 879 N.E.2d 740 (Ohio 2007) (holding that gestational surrogacy contract was not contrary to public policy and was enforceable). Even where such contracts have not been enforceable, though, people have continued to enter into surrogacy arrangements, with "intended parents" compensating a surrogate to carry a baby for them and hoping that the surrogate will follow through with the plan for her voluntarily to relinquish to the intended mother the legal parent status that state law confers on birth mothers. As with adoption, Americans increasingly have looked abroad to become parents by surrogacy, contracting with women in other countries. See, e.g., Liz Zemba, *Debate Swirls Around Overseas Surrogacy*, PITTSBURGH TRIB.-REV., Feb. 6, 2011.

Recognizing that people have continued to make surrogacy agreements even where unenforceable, or out of concern for the parenting aspirations of infertile couples, legislators in some states have in recent years passed legislation authorizing the practice and conferring legal parent status on the "intended parents." Over a dozen states now enforce surrogacy contracts, at least in some circumstances. In some, only a married couple can contract for surrogacy. See, e.g., N.H. Rev. Stat. Ann. §168-B:1(VII); Nev. Rev. Stat. §126.045(1); Tex. Fam. Code Ann. §160.754(b). At the same time, in some states it is a crime to enter into such an agreement. States are thus quite polarized on the appropriateness of this approach to parenthood. For a recent summary of the law, see Darra L. Hofman, *Mama's Baby, Daddy's Maybe: A State-by-State Survey of Surrogacy Laws and Their Disparate Gender Impact*, 35 WM. MITCHELL L. REV. 449 (2009). Roughly half of U.S. states still have no legislation or judicial doctrine on surrogacy, leaving parties to such contracts uncertain as to their bindingness. See, e.g., A.L.S. v. E.A.G., 2010 WL 4181449 (Minn. Ct. App.) (applying parentage law straightforwardly to confer legal motherhood on the traditional surrogate and legal fatherhood only on the member of the same-sex contracting couple who was the biological father, noting the absence of any Minnesota statute authorizing an overriding of the parentage law by contract).

Professor Roberts writes: "The literature on reproductive technologies designed to create genetic ties . . . divides mainly into liberal defenses that promote the individual's right to procreate without government interference on the one hand (citations) and feminist critiques that view these technologies as a means of gender oppression on the other hand (citations). "Dorothy E. Roberts, *The Genetic Tie*, 62 U. CHI. L. REV. 209, 248-249 (1995). This rich literature includes Elizabeth S. Scott, *Surrogacy and the Politics of Commodification*, 72 LAW & CONTEMP. PROBS. 109 (2009); Carol Sanger, *Developing Markets in Baby-Making: In the Matter of Baby M*, 30 HARV. J.L. & GENDER 67 (2007); Marsha Garrison, *Law Making for Baby Making: An Interpretive Approach to the Determination of Legal Parentage*, 113 HARV. L. REV. 835 (2000); Margaret Friedlander Brinig, *A Maternalistic Approach to Surrogacy: Comment on Richard Epstein's* Surrogacy: The Case for Full Contractual Enforcement, 81 VA. L. REV. 2377, 2388 (1995); Mary Becker, *Four Feminist Theoretical Approaches and the Double Bind of Surrogacy*, 69 CHI.-KENT L. REV. 303, 309 (1993). For an argument that surrogacy disputes should be resolved on the basis of what is in the child's best interests, see Browne C. Lewis, *Three Lies and a Truth: Adjudicating Maternity in Surrogacy Disputes*, 49 U. LOUISVILLE L. REV. 371 (2011).

CONCEPTUAL ANALYSIS

The normal process of "having children" might be divided into several components: 1) having sex, 2) conceiving a child, 3) giving birth to a child, and 4) raising a child once it is born. Do we have a basic moral right to do all of these things? Would the argument for asserting that we do need to be different for each component? What might justify state infringement of such a right as to each component? What would be the nature of the right or rights that underlie an argument against state interference with, or refusal to enforce, surrogacy contracts? Cf. S.H. v. Austria, App. No. 57813/00, paras. 9-10, 12 (Eur. Ct. H.R. Apr. 1, 2010) (decision of the European Court of Human Rights holding that Austria's prohibition of reproduction by *in vitro fertilization* using third-party sperm or ova violated the right to family life guaranteed by Article 8 of the European Convention on Human Rights).

CROSS-CULTURAL PERSPECTIVE

In the Kashmir region of India, it is not uncommon for a fertile couple to procreate for the purpose of supplying a child to a family member who is unable to procreate with his or her spouse. See JAIN MAIR & ESIN ORUCU, THE PLACE OF RELIGION IN FAMILY LAW: A COMPARATIVE SEARCH 30 (2011). Should legislators in the United States consider facilitating and even encouraging this practice, as an alternative to contracts with strangers? If so, how might they do so?

CLIENT COUNSELING EXERCISE

Two couples, one lesbian and one gay, all good friends with each other, call your office to arrange a consultation with you. Each of the four individuals wants to become a legal parent, and they thought they could save money by consulting with you as a group. Make a list of all the options for each couple, then draw a conclusion about which option is easiest/least costly for each and about which couple has the easiest options available. For classroom discussion purposes, you might also consider whether there is any policy or constitutional reason for the state to be concerned about any dramatic difference in difficulty as between male and female couples. In doing so, take into account that states devote significant effort and resources to helping infertile heterosexual couples adopt.

Declining Motherhood?

Note that the California statutory rule for maternity does not permit a birth mother to decline legal motherhood; if the state is aware of who gave birth to a child, it will impose legal parenthood regardless of her wishes. In contrast, several European countries give women the option of declining legal parenthood. France has for over a century authorized anonymous births in birthing facilities, allowing a woman to give birth and leave the facility without the child and without disclosing her name. Some women from neighboring countries travel to France to give birth anonymously. Anywhere in the United States, though, birthing facilities must elicit identifying information from women who arrive to give birth and must transmit that information to the state's department of health or vital records.

In the United States, a birth mother could try to avoid legal motherhood by giving birth in secret and then abandoning the child, or she might informally relinquish legal motherhood immediately after its conferral by abandoning the child. If she abandons the child in a way that endangers the child, it could subject her to criminal prosecution. Today, though, every state has a "Safe Haven" law, immunizing from maltreatment charges parents who anonymously drop off their newborn children at a designated facility, such as a hospital or firehouse. The principal aim of such laws is to prevent grievous harm to children before or after birth, as the opportunity for an anonymous transfer of a baby is assumed to make it less likely that a mother would have an abortion, commit infanticide, or abandon a baby in an unsafe manner. These laws resemble long-standing practice in Europe, first begun by the Catholic Church in the eighteenth century and now carried out by some local governments. Several localities in Germany, for example, have Babyklappe, or "baby boxes," on the exterior of designated public buildings, in which mothers can place a child, ring a bell, and walk off. Babies abandoned in such a way would then be available for adoption, and in Western nations the demand for adoption of newborn babies is high.

POLICY QUESTION

What are the pros and cons of allowing women to give birth anonymously or to abandon their babies anonymously? Should a woman be able to change her mind and go back to reclaim the baby? What justification is there for forcing legal parenthood on any birth mother if she does not want it? Consider these questions from the perspectives of all interested parties. For discussion of concerns raised by Safe Haven laws, see Carol Sanger, *Infant Safe Haven Laws: Legislating in the Culture of Life,* 106 COLUM. L. REV. 753 (2006) (discussing implications for women's reproductive freedom), and Jeffrey A. Parness, *Lost Paternity in the Culture of Motherhood: A Different View of Safe Haven Laws,* 42 VAL. U. L. REV. 81 (2007) (highlighting biological fathers' interest in raising their offspring).

Excluding Unfit Mothers?

Maternity rules also do not allow for excluding any birth mother from initial legal parenthood on the grounds that she is unfit to be a parent. The vast majority of birth mothers are capable of caring for their children, but a significant percentage are not capable at the time of birth and are very unlikely to become capable within a reasonable period of time, yet they receive legal parent status as readily as fit birth mothers. A woman might have her rights as to one child terminated today, because of severe maltreatment and a failure to respond to rehabilitative efforts, but then automatically become the legal parent to another child to whom she gives birth tomorrow. Women who give birth in prison are made legal parents to their offspring regardless of how long they will remain in prison after the birth.

In at least one non-Western nation, Japan, the law does allow for denial of legal parenthood to birth mothers in some cases, in order to serve the welfare of children. The rules for parental status and rights dictate that they may not be conferred upon a "minor, incompetent, or quasi-incompetent" unless a court finds that this would be in the best interests of the child. Satoshi Minamikata et al., *Japan, in* INTERNATIONAL ENCYCLOPEDIA OF LAWS, VOLUME II: OF FAMILY AND SUCCESSION LAW 133 (W. Pintens ed., 1999). In other non-Western nations, the law might deny women legal status with respect to their children on patriarchal grounds—that is, in order to afford men exclusive dominion over their offspring. See BLAIR ET AL., FAMILY LAW IN THE WORLD COMMUNITY 397 (2009) ("The concept that a child belongs to the father's family is common to many of the patrilineal societies in sub-Saharan Africa"). There might be a child welfare justification for this, where a child's material well-being depends on being in the care of the father, who can provide support and an inheritance in a very poor society where men generally own what little wealth there is. Id. at 398. But that, of course, does not make mothers unfit.

There is some sentiment in the United States in favor of denying parenthood to some biological mothers. In 2004, a family court judge in Rochester, New York, made national headlines by ordering a woman who was homeless, addicted to drugs, and regularly engaged in prostitution to stop having children, as a condition for return of four children she had borne who were in foster care, all of whom had been subjected to cocaine ingestion during pregnancy. Noting that she had "seen as many as nine children from one family surrendered to foster care," the judge lamented:

> All babies deserve more than to be born to parents who have proven they cannot possibly raise or parent a child. This neglected existence is an immense burden to place on a child and on society. The cycle of neglect often created by such births needs to stop. Our society has reached the breaking point with respect to raising neglected children, often born with extraordinary needs. One need only look at our schools, our jails, our Division of Human and Health Services budgets, and our Family Courts to see that a serious change of direction is necessary in the interests of children, the taxpayers, and the community as a whole.

In re Bobbijean P., 784 N.Y.S.2d 919, 2004 N.Y. Slip Op. 50286U, at *5 (Monroe Cty. Fam. Ct. 2004). See also Janice G. Inman, *How Will It Play in New York?*, 5 N.Y. Fam. L. Monthly, June 1, 2004 (describing similar court orders in other states).

The woman was still consistently using cocaine and had shown no interest in the removed children. Yet when, despite the judge's order, the mother became pregnant again soon after this ruling, the law of New York State made her the legal parent of the newborn baby as well, with the result that this baby, too, would be placed in foster care, rather than beginning life in a family with capable, permanent parents. Later in this chapter we will consider arguments for and against modifying maternity (and paternity) rules to exclude manifestly unfit birth parents.

As this New York case suggests, there are situations in which a legal mother will not have *custody* of a child after birth. When a local child protection agency is aware that a baby has been born to birth parents with serious maltreatment histories, substance abuse problems, or mental illness, it might take custody of the baby and place the baby in foster care and then attempt to help the mother become fit. In addition, a birth mother who does not wish to raise a child can execute a relinquishment of her parental rights. The state might accept the relinquishment, though, only if there are other adults who wish to adopt the child and if the birth father also consents, and state laws generally allow mothers to change their mind for some period of time.

2. *Paternity*

Paternity is a substantial area of domestic relations practice today, reflecting the greater uncertainty, relative to maternity, of biological fatherhood, and also reflecting cultural acceptance today of unwed fathers as potential legal parents. The latter produced, and in turn was accelerated by, U.S. Supreme Court decisions establishing constitutional protection in some circumstances for unwed fathers' desire to be involved in child rearing. We will first study state statutory law governing paternity today, the rules attorneys work with on a daily basis in family court, to give you a sense of the history and competing policy and moral concerns underlying paternity law. Then we will look at the constitutional doctrine, which attorneys also often invoke in practice, with that history and those concerns in mind, and you can then judge whether the statutory rules are more protective of unwed fathers than the Court's doctrine suggests they need to be.

a. Statutory Rules

Statutory rules for paternity are more complicated, more contested, and more variable across jurisdictions than are maternity rules, reflecting the greater difficulty of identifying the biological father of a child, the absence of a presumption that biological fathers expend pre-birth child-care labor or are as predisposed as biological mothers to be nurturing, and a traditional assumption that the mother-child relationship is the core relationship for a child. As a general matter, though, paternity rules in the United States today also predicate legal parenthood, and a set of rights entailed in that status, on biological parenthood. Legal paternity is generally evidenced by a child's birth certificate, so the question is how a man's name comes to be on a child's birth certificate.

With a majority of births, the mothers are married and their husbands are present at the birthing facility when a child is born. Absent objection by mother or husband, the birthing facility will report the husband's name as the father to the state department of health or vital records, which in turn will issue a birth certificate naming the husband as the child's legal father. Thereafter, whenever the husband needs to demonstrate that he is the child's legal father, he will present a copy of the birth certificate. The mother or husband might object if she or he has reason to believe the husband is not in fact the biological father. In addition, another man believing himself to be the biological father might object to having the husband treated as the legal father. When any party objects, one must look to state statutes to see whether and when the marital presumption of paternity can be overcome. Examples of different state law approaches appear below.

With roughly 40 percent of births, the mother is unmarried. In such cases, a man present at the birth will be listed on the birth certificate if he and the mother execute an "acknowledgment of paternity." Federal law, motivated by a state interest in imposing a child support obligation on more men, now requires birthing facilities to present acknowledgment forms to birth mothers and to men present at a birth. This New York code provision sets forth the content of such an acknowledgment.

New York Public Health Law
Chapter 45, Article 41. Vital Statistics
Title III. Registration of Births

§4135-B. Voluntary Acknowledgments of Paternity; Child Born out of Wedlock

1. (a) Immediately preceding or following the in-hospital birth of a child to an unmarried woman, the person in charge of such hospital or his or her designated representative shall provide to the child's mother and putative father, if such father is readily identifiable and available, the documents and written instructions necessary for such mother and putative father to complete an acknowledgment of paternity witnessed by two persons not related to the signatory. . . . The acknowledgment shall . . . provide in plain language (i) a statement by the mother consenting to the acknowledgment of paternity and a statement that the putative father is the only possible father, (ii) a statement by the putative father that he is the biological father of the child, and (iii) a statement that the signing of the

acknowledgment of paternity by both parties shall have the same force and effect as an order of filiation entered . . . by a court . . . , including an obligation to provide support for the child. . . .

Alternatively, a "putative father" (i.e., someone believed to be the biological father) can petition a court for a paternity order, or the mother or a state child support agency can ask a court to impose such an order on a putative father. The court order would then be the basis for putting the man's name on the birth certificate. In most cases, the basis for a court order of paternity is genetic tests, which are highly accurate today, though sometimes men (unwisely) concede their paternity without undergoing testing, perhaps to solidify their relationship with a birth mother. In some states, a man can request legal paternity for himself, regardless of what genetic tests might show, on the basis of his having acted as if he were the child's father for a significant period, as reflected in the Texas statute below.

Below are two statutory models for establishing paternity. The first, from New York, represents a majority approach. The second, from Texas, was derived from the Uniform Parentage Act (UPA), which a large minority of states adopted. The two are distinguished principally by the UPA's greater reliance on explicit presumptions.

New York Family Court Act
Article 5. Paternity Proceedings

§516-A. Acknowledgment of Paternity

(a) An acknowledgment of paternity . . . shall establish the paternity of and liability for the support of a child . . . No further judicial or administrative proceedings are required to ratify an unchallenged acknowledgment of paternity.

(b) (i) An acknowledgment of paternity . . . may be rescinded by either signator's filing of a petition with the court to vacate the acknowledgment within the earlier of 60 days of the date of signing the acknowledgment or the date of an administrative or a judicial proceeding (including a proceeding to establish a support order) relating to the child in which either signator is a party. . . . The court shall order genetic marker tests or DNA tests for the determination of the child's paternity. No such test shall be ordered, however, upon a written finding by the court that it is not in the best interests of the child on the basis of res judicata, equitable estoppel, or the presumption of legitimacy of a child born to a married woman. If the court determines, following the test, . . . that the person who signed the acknowledgment is not the father of the child, the acknowledgment shall be vacated.

(ii) After the expiration of 60 days of the execution of the acknowledgment, either signator may challenge the acknowledgment of paternity in court by alleging and proving fraud, duress, or material mistake of fact. . . . If the petitioner proves to the court that the acknowledgment of paternity was signed under fraud, duress, or due to a material mistake of fact, the court shall order genetic marker tests or DNA tests for the determination of the child's paternity. No such test shall be ordered, however, upon a written finding by the court that it is not in the best interests of the child on the basis of res judicata, equitable estoppel, or the presumption of legitimacy of a child born to a married woman. If the court determines, following the test, . . . that the person who signed the acknowledgment is not the father of the child, the acknowledgment shall be vacated.

§517. Time for Instituting Proceedings

Proceedings to establish the paternity of a child may be instituted during the pregnancy of the mother or after the birth of the child, but shall not be brought after the child reaches the age of twenty-one years, unless paternity has been acknowledged by the father in writing or by furnishing support.

§522. Persons Who May Originate Proceedings

Proceedings to establish the paternity of the child and to compel support under this article may be commenced by the mother . . . , by a person alleging to be the father . . . , by the child or child's guardian or . . . by a public welfare official. . . .

New York's paternity statutes make no reference to the marital status of birth mothers, though the health code provision above regarding acknowledgments refers to "an unmarried woman." Yet there is a marital presumption in New York. Courts there typically cite a common-law rule when announcing the marital presumption, and pursuant to judicial doctrine that presumption is rebuttable by genetic tests. See, e.g., Ghaznavi v. Gordon, 558 N.Y.S.2d 46 (N.Y. App. Div. 1990) ("One of the strongest and most persuasive presumptions in law is that a child born to a married woman is presumed to have been fathered by her then husband. The result of a properly administered blood test which excludes the husband's paternity is sufficient to rebut the presumption."). There is a reference to marital status of parents in the Code article relating to marriage, though it seems to presuppose that the spouses are the biological and legal parents and to concern itself just with the status of the child as "legitimate":

McKinney's Consolidated Laws of New York
Domestic Relations Law
Chapter 14, Article 3. Solemnization, Proof and Effect of Marriage

§24. Effect of Marriage on Legitimacy of Children

1. A child . . . born of parents who prior or subsequent to the birth of such child shall have entered into a civil or religious marriage . . . is the legitimate child of both natural parents. . . .

STATUTORY INTERPRETATION EXERCISE

Suppose a woman in New York who is legally married is intimate with a man other than her husband and becomes pregnant. If the baby is born and then mother and non-husband sign an acknowledgment, is it valid and effective? Does it matter whether the woman was still with her husband at the time of conception or instead was separated from him? Does it matter whether she is still married at the time of the birth? If the acknowledgment is valid, could the husband challenge it and get a court order for genetic testing?

Vernon's Texas Statutes and Codes—Family Code
Title 5, Subtitle B, Chapter 160. Uniform Parentage Act
Subchapter C. Parent-Child Relationship

§160.204. Presumption of Paternity

(a) A man is presumed to be the father of a child if:

(1) he is married to the mother of the child and the child is born during the marriage;

(2) he is married to the mother of the child and the child is born before the 301st day after the date the marriage is terminated by death, annulment, declaration of invalidity, or divorce; . . .

(4) he married the mother of the child after the birth of the child . . . , he voluntarily asserted his paternity of the child, and:

(A) the assertion is in a record filed with the bureau of vital statistics;

(B) he is voluntarily named as the child's father on the child's birth certificate; or

(C) he promised in a record to support the child as his own; or

(5) during the first two years of the child's life, he continuously resided in the household in which the child resided and he represented to others that the child was his own.

(b) A presumption of paternity established under this section may be rebutted only by:

(1) an adjudication under Subchapter G [below]; or

(2) the filing of a valid denial of paternity by a presumed father in conjunction with the filing by another person of a valid acknowledgment of paternity. . . .

Subchapter D. Voluntary Acknowledgment of Paternity

§160.301. Acknowledgment of Paternity

The mother of a child and a man claiming to be the biological father of the child may sign an acknowledgment of paternity with the intent to establish the man's paternity.

[Other sections of this subchapter set out, just as the New York statute does, a 60-day time limit for rescission and a requirement that after 60 days a signatory must prove fraud, duress, or material mistake of fact in order to nullify the acknowledgment. Texas imposes a four-year limitation on such challenges. A non-signatory can also challenge within that four-year period.]

Subchapter G. Proceeding to Adjudicate Parentage

§160.631. Rules for Adjudication of Paternity

(b) The paternity of a child having a presumed, acknowledged, or adjudicated father may be disproved only by admissible results of genetic testing excluding that man as the father of the child or identifying another man as the father of the child. . . .

§160.602. STANDING TO MAINTAIN PROCEEDING

(a) [A] proceeding to adjudicate parentage may be maintained by:
(1) the child;
(2) the mother of the child;
(3) a man whose paternity of the child is to be adjudicated;
(4) the support enforcement agency or another government agency authorized by other law;
(5) an authorized adoption agency or licensed child-placing agency; . . .
(8) a person who is an intended parent.

§160.606. CHILD HAVING NO PRESUMED, ACKNOWLEDGED, OR ADJUDICATED FATHER

A proceeding to adjudicate the parentage of a child having no presumed, acknowledged, or adjudicated father may be commenced at any time. . . .

§160.607. TIME LIMITATION: CHILD HAVING PRESUMED FATHER

(a) . . . [A] proceeding brought by a presumed father, the mother, or another individual to adjudicate the parentage of a child having a presumed father shall be commenced not later than the fourth anniversary of the date of the birth of the child.
(b) A proceeding seeking to disprove the father-child relationship between a child and the child's presumed father may be maintained at any time if the court determines that:
(1) the presumed father and the mother of the child did not live together or engage in sexual intercourse with each other during the probable time of conception; and
(2) the presumed father never represented to others that the child was his own.

§160.608. AUTHORITY TO DENY MOTION FOR GENETIC TESTING

(a) . . . [A] court may deny a motion for an order for the genetic testing of the mother, the child, and the presumed father if the court determines that:
(1) the conduct of the mother or the presumed father estops that party from denying parentage; and
(2) it would be inequitable to disprove the father-child relationship between the child and the presumed father.
(b) In determining whether to deny a motion for an order for genetic testing under this section, the court shall consider the best interest of the child, including the following factors:
(1) the length of time between the date of the proceeding to adjudicate parentage and the date presumed father was placed on notice that he might not be the genetic father;
(2) the length of time during which the presumed father has assumed the role of father;
(3) the facts surrounding the presumed father's discovery of his possible nonpaternity;
(4) the nature of the relationship between the child and the presumed father;
(5) the age of the child;
(6) any harm that may result to the child if presumed paternity is successfully disproved;

(7) the nature of the relationship between the child and the alleged father;

(8) the extent to which the passage of time reduces the chances of establishing the paternity of another man and a child support obligation in favor of the child; and

(9) other factors that may affect the equities arising from disruption of the father-child relationship between the child and the presumed father or the chance of other harm to the child. . . .

(e) If the court denies a motion for an order for genetic testing, the court shall issue an order adjudicating the presumed father to be the father of the child.

POLICY QUESTIONS

1) What are the advantages and disadvantages of using presumptions to establish legal fatherhood rather than simply relying on genetic tests? Before answering this question, try to figure out when exactly any of the presumptions would be invoked or have practical effect.

2) §160.204(a)(2) presumes that a man is the father of a child if the man divorces the mother during her pregnancy. Does that make sense?

3) §160.204(a)(4) imputes fatherhood to men who marry single mothers and claim parenthood of any of her children. What are the policy pros and cons of doing so?

4) §160.602(a)(4) gives local child support enforcement standing to initiate a paternity suit. Is that wise? Who benefits from state efforts to impose paternity on an absent or unwilling biological father? Who might be harmed?

Regarding question 4), consider this typical statute requiring mothers on welfare to assist state agencies seeking to impose a support obligation on biological fathers:

Code of Virginia
Title 63.2. Welfare (Social Services), Subtitle II. Public Assistance
Chapter 6. Temporary Assistance for Needy Families Program

§63.2-602. ELIGIBILITY FOR TEMPORARY ASSISTANCE FOR NEEDY FAMILIES (TANF)

. . . B. An applicant for TANF shall:

. . . 2. Assign the Commonwealth any rights to support from any other person such applicant may have on his own behalf or on behalf of any other family member for whom the applicant is applying for or receiving aid . . . ;

3. Identify the parents of the child for whom aid is claimed, subject to the "good cause" provisions or exceptions in federal law. . . . However, this requirement shall not apply if the child . . . was conceived as the result of incest or rape; and

4. Cooperate in (i) locating the parent of the child with respect to whom TANF is claimed, (ii) establishing the paternity of a child born out of wedlock with respect to whom TANF is claimed, (iii) obtaining support payments for such applicant or recipient and for a child with respect to whom TANF is claimed, and (iv) obtaining any other payments or property due such applicant or recipient for such child.

Any applicant or recipient who intentionally misidentifies another person as a parent shall be guilty of a Class 5 felony.

C. . . . If paternity is not established after 6 months . . . due to the caretaker relative's non-cooperation, the local department may suspend the entire grant or the adult portion. . . .

NOTES AND QUESTIONS

Most states apply the good cause exception description contained in federal regulations issued pursuant to the Aid to Families with Dependent Children legislation, which preceded TANF. It excused parents from assisting with child support enforcement against the other parent if they could demonstrate that doing so would be likely to result in emotional or physical harm to the child or themselves, that the child resulted from rape or incest, or that the child was being put up for adoption. Does that exception address all the concerns raised by the cooperation requirement? Might it go too far in some cases? For an argument that welfare agency efforts to locate and extract money from unwed fathers harms children in several ways, including alienating fathers from their children, see Daniel L. Hatcher, *Child Support Harming Children: Subordinating the Best Interests of Children to the Fiscal Interests of the State,* 42 Wake Forest L. Rev. 1029 (2007), and Solangel Maldonado, *Deadbeat or Deadbroke: Redefining Child Support for Poor Fathers,* 39 U.C. Davis. L. Rev. 991 (2006).

Sperm donors

Paternity laws generally allow a biological father to challenge the paternity of a mother's husband, and thus in some instances to intrude into intact families. Most jurisdictions have a special provision, however, for sperm donors, in order to facilitate assisted reproduction for married couples who are unable to procreate because of a husband's infertility. For example, N.Y. Domestic Relations Law §73 provides: "Any child born to a married woman by means of artificial insemination performed by persons duly authorized to practice medicine and with the consent in writing of the woman and her husband, shall be deemed the legitimate, natural child of the husband and his wife for all purposes." See also Ala. Code §26-17-21(a) ("If, under the supervision of a licensed physician and with the consent of her husband, a wife is inseminated artificially with semen donated by a man not her husband, the husband is treated in law as if he were the natural father of a child thereby conceived."); Cal. Fam. Code §7613(a) (same); Colo. Rev. Stat. §19-4-106(1) (same); Ill. Comp. Stat. ch. 750 40/3(a) (same); Minn. Stat. §257.56 Subd. 1; Mo. Rev. Stat. §210.824(1) (2000) (same); N.J. Stat. Ann. §9:17-44(a) (same); Ohio Rev. Code Ann. §3111.95(A) (similar); Wis. Stat. §891.40(1) (same). Some add explicitly what is implicit in the New York statute, that the sperm donor will not be a legal parent. See, e.g., Cal. Fam. Code §7613(b) ("The donor of semen provided to a licensed physician and surgeon for use in artificial insemination of a woman other than the donor's wife is treated in law as if he were not the natural father of a child thereby conceived."); Ala. Code §26-17-21(b) (1992) (same); Minn. Stat. §257.56 Subd. 2 (same); Mo. Rev. Stat. §210.824(2) (same).

Several states now authorize unmarried women to use the artificial insemination route to pregnancy, and they generally establish a default rule that the sperm donor will not become a legal parent, thus creating a situation in which a newborn child will have only one initial parent. See, e.g., Cal. Fam. Code §7613; Kan. Stat. Ann. §38-1114; Ark. Code Ann. §9-10-201; Ohio Rev. Code Ann. §3111.93, 95; Ill. Comp. Stat. ch. 750 40/3(b); Wis. Stat. §891.40(2); Colo. Rev. Stat. §19-4-106(2); Conn. Gen. Stat. §45a-775; Idaho Code Ann. §39-5405; Va. Code Ann. §20-158(A)(3). Is that wise? Why should a state facilitate such a practice? Should it make a difference whether the woman is in a committed non-marital relationship, or whether any such relationship is with a man or with a woman? Cf. Act (2006:351) on Genetic Integrity, Ch. 6, Sec. 1 (Sweden) (permitting women to be artificially inseminated only if they are married or cohabiting, and only if the spouse or partner consents). Could you make an argument that it is constitutionally required for states to create a means for single women to become mothers without having sex and without having a co-parent? For competing views on the child welfare significance of parents' marital status, compare Courtney G. Joslin, *Protecting Children(?): Marriage, Gender, and Assisted Reproductive Technology*, 83 S. CAL. L. REV. 1177 (2010), and Vivian E. Hamilton, *Family Structure, Children, and Law*, 24 WASH. U. J.L. & POL'Y 9, 21 (2007), with W. Bradford Wilcox & Robin Fretwell Wilson, *Bringing up Baby: Adoption, Marriage, and the Best Interests of the Child*, 14 WM. & MARY BILL RTS. J. 883 (2006).

Importantly, these statutory provisions, creating legal exceptions to paternity laws for sperm donors, typically require that the sperm donation occur through a licensed medical professional. There have been many instances in which women who wanted to become pregnant asked a man they knew to give his sperm in a more informal way, with the understanding between them that he would not become a legal parent if and when a child is born and would not have a duty to support the child. After all, why should a woman have to pay thousands of dollars to a sperm bank for injection of some stranger's sperm, when a simpler and more comfortable approach is available? Such an understanding is of no legal effect in that situation, however, so if either of them later changes his or her mind and seeks to establish paternity, the original intention will not preclude a determination of legal paternity. See, e.g., Ferguson v. McKeirnan, 940 A.2d 1236 (Pa. 2007) (holding agreement unenforceable even when conception occurred in a clinical setting using in vitro fertilization); Jhordan C. v. Mary K., 179 Cal. App. 3d 386, 224 Cal. Rptr. 530 (Cal. Ct. App. 1986) (conferring legal parent status on a man who supplied sperm to one member of a lesbian couple, despite his initial agreement with the couple that he would waive paternity, because they had not used a doctor for the insemination). But cf. McIntyre v. Crouch 780 P.2d 239 (Or. 1989) (holding that Oregon's artificial insemination statute does not require that the insemination occur through a sperm bank in order for the provision excluding the sperm donor from parenthood to apply). What are the policy pros and cons of requiring involvement of a licensed physician in order to make a non-paternity agreement with the sperm donor legally effective?

In some instances, unmarried women who seek artificial insemination agree with a donor that he *will* have parent status and be involved in raising the child. Several of the states that adopted statutes authorizing unmarried women to receive artificial insemination also sanctioned such agreements, providing that the donor can become a legal parent. See Kan. Stat. Ann. §38-1114(f), Ark. Code Ann. §9-10-201; Fla. Stat. §742.14; N.H. Rev. Stat. Ann. §168-B:3(I)(e); N.J. Stat. Ann. §9:17-44(b); N.M. Stat Ann. §40-11-6(B).

In contrast with the increasingly liberal legal authorization of artificial insemination in most of the western world, Italy bans the practice of sperm (and egg) donation altogether, reflecting the Catholic Church's condemnation of artificial insemination, on the grounds that it entails masturbation and, in the case of married women, conception through involvement of an outsider to the marital union.

Are there other concerns raised by artificial insemination? What interest do the children have with respect to their biological fathers? Several European countries ban anonymous sperm donations, concerned for children's desire to know who their biological fathers are. See, e.g., Human Fertilisation and Embryology Authority (Disclosure of Donor Information) Regulations 2004, No. 1511 (requiring that British donors' identities be available to donor-conceived children when they turn 18, if the children so request); Netherlands Embryos Bill, Article 3 Dutch Ministry of Health, Welfare, and Sport (2004) (establishing right of such children to information about their biological fathers at age 16); Act (2006:351) on Genetic Integrity, Ch. 6, Sec. 5 (Sweden). Is such a rule truly protective of children's interests if it might deter some men from donating sperm? See Angus Roxburgh, *Dutch Sperm Laws Threaten Donations*, BBC News Online, Aug. 14, 2004, http://news.bbc.co.uk/2/hi/europe/3555202.stm.

Artificial insemination laws in the United States do not limit the number of children that can be conceived from a given donor. The laws in many other countries do impose limits—anywhere from 5 to 25. Can you guess why? However, there is a global market for sperm, so any given man could be the biological father of a limitless number of children despite such numerical restrictions, by having his sperm exported. Danish sperm is the most sought after, and it is exported from Denmark to over 50 countries.

Fatherhood by Surrogacy

Though the practice of surrogacy initially developed to provide married couples in which the wife was infertile a means by which to become parents, many male same-sex couples have also contracted with a woman to bear a child for them. Sir Elton John and his partner David Furnish might be the most famous such couple to have done so, having gone that route in 2010 after Ukrainian authorities refused to let them adopt a Ukrainian child. Male couples can use the sperm of one or both to impregnate the surrogate by artificial insemination, or they can use their sperm to fertilize a donated ovum *in vitro* and have it implanted in the surrogate's uterus. Courts have even been asked in recent years to give effect to surrogacy agreements initiated by just one man who wants to become a lone parent to a child. See, e.g., In re Roberto d.B., 923 A.2d 115 (Md. 2007) (holding that gestational surrogate could be excluded from legal parent status, leaving child with biological father as only parent); J.F. v. D.B., 879 N.E.2d 740 (Ohio 2007) (enforcing gestational surrogacy contract in favor of single man and against surrogate and her husband). Ricky Martin might be the most famous such man, having twins by a surrogate in 2008.

Disestablishing Paternity

From the paternity rules set forth above, one can glean various ways in which legal fatherhood can arise without genetic testing—namely, based on a man's being married to the mother at some point, based on a man and the mother signing an acknowledgment, based on a man's living with a child and holding the child out as his own, or based on a man's admitting to paternity in court. In a significant percentage of cases in which legal fatherhood arises in one of these ways, the men are actually not the biological father. Usually they did not know this when the legal relationship first arose; the birth mother might have deceived them or it might be that both the birth mother and the man were mistaken. Sometimes, though, men are aware the biological father is someone else but nevertheless agree to raise the child with the mother. As a result, there has been a great deal of litigation over whether and when the legal relationship can later be severed because of the lack of biological connection.

Sometimes it is the actual biological father who seeks to disestablish paternity, potentially disrupting an intact family. With limited exceptions, state laws today enable so-called "putative fathers" to do this. Below you will read U.S. Supreme Court decisions regarding the constitutional rights of men to claim legal parent status based on biological paternity. In other cases, it is the presumed father or the mother who wishes to disestablish the relationship, typically when their relationship ends. In fact, often it is a man's discovery that he has been mistaken or defrauded (and, accordingly, that his wife or girlfriend had relations with another man) that precipitates dissolution of the relationship. Mothers might at that point ask a court to disestablish the man's paternity so that he will not have a right to visitation with the child. Such efforts by mothers usually fail when the man wishes to continue an established relationship with the child, unless the biological father wishes to occupy the paternal role.

R.W.E. v. A.B.K. and M.K.

961 A.2d 161 (Pa. Super. Ct. 2008)

Opinion by DONOHUE, J.:

. . . Mother and Robert were involved in an on-again, off-again relationship between approximately February 2002 and November 2003, during which they periodically resided together. In November 2003, Mother and Robert separated for several months before reconciling in mid-February 2004, at which time Robert moved back in with Mother. During this separation between November 2003 and February 2004, Mother became sexually involved with another man, later identified as Father.

In mid-March 2004, Mother told Robert that she was pregnant. She also informed him that she had been sexually intimate with another man and that there was a possibility that this other man was the father of her unborn child. Because of the time frame of her relationships with Father and Robert, Mother believed there was a "50-50" chance that either man could be the father of her child. Mother and Robert agreed to proceed with the pregnancy, that Robert would parent the child, and that neither of them would undergo genetic testing to establish paternity. Mother and Robert resided together during the pregnancy, and Robert was present at the birth of Child on November 12, 2004. Father, who was deployed to Kuwait by the National Guard shortly after his relationship with Mother ended, was not informed of Mother's pregnancy or of Child's birth.

Days after Child's birth, Mother and Robert signed an acknowledgment of paternity form at the hospital provided by the Pennsylvania Department of Public Welfare pursuant to 23 Pa. C.S.A. §5103. Robert was also identified as Child's father on Child's birth certificate. Mother and Robert continued to live together until sometime in 2005, when Robert moved out of the home occupied by Mother and Child.[2] Robert alleged that Mother initially allowed him to see Child after their separation but then abruptly terminated his visits. . . .

2. The record reflects a discrepancy in the date of Robert's departure, with Mother claiming that Robert moved out between August and October of 2005, and Robert claiming that he did not move out until November 2005.

Robert filed a custody complaint and a petition for emergency relief on December 8, 2005. . . . The results of genetic testing revealed a zero percent probability that Robert was the biological father of Child. In January 2006, Father was advised for the first time that he might be the biological father of Child. . . .[3]

Mother identified Father as the biological father of Child, and the trial court granted the oral motion of Mother's counsel to join Father as an additional defendant. The trial court resolved the cross motions by ordering additional genetic testing on Father, Mother and Child. . . . The genetic testing confirmed . . . a 99.99 percent probability that Father was the biological father of Child. [Father filed a] petition to set aside the acknowledgment. . . .

Robert argues that section 5103 does not provide a third party with standing to challenge an acknowledgment of paternity, and that the statute specifically limits those who can challenge the acknowledgment to signatories to the acknowledgment. . . . A court must construe the words of a statute according to their plain meaning. Section 5103 provides that the "signatories" of an acknowledgment of paternity may rescind such acknowledgment within sixty days. In the provision permitting challenges to acknowledgment based on fraud, duress, or material mistake of fact, however, our Legislature opted for different language. 23 Pa. C.S.A. §5103(g)(2) provides:

> After the expiration of the 60 days, an acknowledgment of paternity may be challenged in court only on the basis of fraud, duress or material mistake of fact, which must be established by the *challenger* through clear and convincing evidence. . . .

There is nothing in section 5103(g)(2) that limits the identity of potential challengers to signatories to the acknowledgment of paternity. If our Legislature had intended such an application, we conclude they would have used the term "signatories" in section 5103(g)(2) to express that limitation. By choosing the broader term "challenger," the Legislature intended to grant non-signatories the power to challenge the acknowledgment under the limited circumstances delineated in subsection (g)(2).[5] . . .

Next, Robert argues that the trial court improperly rescinded the acknowledgment of paternity he signed at Child's birth when no evidence of fraud existed. . . . The governing statute, 23 Pa. C.S.A. §5103, states that:

> (a) Acknowledgment of paternity.—The father of a child born to an unmarried woman may file with the Department of Public Welfare, on forms prescribed by the department, an acknowledgment of paternity of the child which shall include consent of the mother of the child, supported by her witnessed statement. . . . In such case, the father shall have all the rights and duties as to the child which he would have had if he had been married to the mother at the time of the birth of the child, and the child shall have all the rights and duties as to the father which the child would have had if the father had been married to the mother at the time of birth.

3. The trial court also entered an interim order awarding Mother primary physical and legal custody of Child, and Robert, partial custody every Sunday from 9:00 A.M. to 8:00 P.M.

5. Robert also argues that Father lacks standing to challenge the acknowledgment of paternity signed in this case, relying on Moyer v. Gresh, 904 A.2d 958 (Pa. Super. 2006). In *Moyer*, a custody dispute, the trial court applied the doctrine of paternity by estoppel and dismissed a biological father from the action, finding that he had voluntarily waived standing by playing a limited role in his son's life. . . . An important distinction between *Moyer* and this case, however, is that in *Moyer*, the biological father was made aware that he was the father at the time of the child's birth and thereafter voluntarily allowed another man to hold himself out as the father of the child for nine years. . . .

In *B.O. v. C.O.* (1991), this Court stated that "when an allegation of fraud is injected in [an acknowledgment of paternity] case, the whole tone and tenor of the matter changes. It opens the door to overturning settled issues and policies of the law." This Court went on to create a narrow fraud exception for challenging paternity, which is otherwise a settled issue based on the signed acknowledgment. We adopted the traditional elements of fraud established in Pennsylvania jurisprudence:

> (1) a misrepresentation, (2) a fraudulent utterance thereof, (3) an intention by the maker that the recipient will thereby be induced to act, (4) justifiable reliance by the recipient upon the misrepresentation, and (5) damage to the recipient as the proximate result.

Recent cases have moved away from this rigid five-prong test which this Court acknowledged in *B.O.* as problematic and somewhat circular. Our recent decision of *Glover v. Severino* (Pa. Super. 2008) provides additional guidance as to the elements of fraud in the context of challenges to acknowledgments of paternity:

> A misrepresentation need not be an actual statement; it can be manifest in the form of silence or failure to disclose relevant information when good faith requires disclosure. Fraud is practiced when deception of another to his damage is brought about by a misrepresentation of fact or by silence when good faith required expression. Fraud comprises anything calculated to deceive, whether by single act or combination, or by suppression of truth, or suggestion of what is false, whether by direct falsehood or innuendo, by speech or silence, word of mouth, or look or gesture.

In *Glover*, a mother had a brief sexual relationship with a putative father and became pregnant. . . . [T]he putative father signed an acknowledgment of paternity and paid child support, though his involvement in the child's life was minimal and sporadic. Mother insisted that putative father was the father of the child, despite the results of later testing that revealed he was not. This Court held that despite the mother's strong belief as to the identity of the biological father, her silence on the issue of other possible fathers and her failure to be forthcoming about the true probabilities of paternity constituted fraud by omission. Though the facts of this case are different from those in *Glover*—most notably, because the defrauded party is the biological father and not Robert, the putative father—the guiding principles regarding fraud are the same. . . . We find the exception particularly applicable to this agreement intended to defraud a biological father of his paternity rights. . . .

Paternity by estoppel has been defined as:

> [T]he legal determination that because of a person's conduct (e.g. holding out the child as his own, or supporting the child) that person, regardless of his true biological status, will not be permitted to deny parentage, nor will the child's mother who has participated in this conduct be permitted to sue a third party for support, claiming that the third party is the true father. As the Superior Court has observed, the doctrine of estoppel in paternity actions is aimed at "achieving fairness as between the parents by holding them, both mother and father, to their prior conduct regarding paternity of the child."

The doctrine of paternity by estoppel has been applied by courts to prevent putative fathers who hold themselves out as the fathers of their children from subsequently denying their parentage. Our appellate courts have not expanded this doctrine to allow putative fathers to use the doctrine offensively, in order to assert their paternity rights by and through their prior conduct. We decline to do so here, particularly at the expense of a biological father who did not earlier claim paternity only because of Mother's and Robert's decision to deprive him of the opportunity to do so. . . .

A "best interests" analysis is applicable to, and the paramount concern in, any child custody case. Accordingly, we decline to address the issue of whether Child's best interests would be served by having Robert play a continuing role in his life, which would be better addressed as part of the subsequent custody phase of this case, if there is one. In its written opinion, the trial court stated that it was "deciding paternity only," and "not whether [Robert] has established *in loco parentis* for purposes of standing to request custodial rights." As Robert's third-party custody rights are not presently at issue in this appeal, the issue of Child's "best interests" is outside of our jurisdiction and we decline to address it. . . .

The court's definition of fraud makes crucial reference to "good faith." Did good faith in fact require Mother to disclose anything to Father at an earlier time? How should a court answer that question? By reference to moral theories? To the writings of legal scholars? To surveys of popular attitudes? To what the judges think they would do in the same circumstances? To what is within a range of reasonable decision making for a pregnant woman in that situation? Would all of these bases for assessing good faith lead to the same conclusion?

Assuming that Robert moved out when the child was a year old and spent every Sunday with her during the subsequent years of litigation, how should the trial court rule on a petition by Robert for continued visitation, following this final determination that he will not be a legal parent of the child? What further facts might you want to have in order to make a best-interests determination? Should the child's best interests control if Father wants to assume a full parental role and opposes continued contact with Robert? You will study the law governing non-parent requests for custody or visitation in Chapter 4.

More difficult for courts to resolve have been the many cases in which a man who has acted as father to a child for a substantial period, under the belief that he is the biological father, wishes to be relieved of parental responsibilities sometime after he learns that he is not. The New York and Texas statutes above and the Pennsylvania Superior Court decision in *R.W.E.* suggest that someone seeking to disestablish paternity can be estopped on equitable grounds from challenging the presumed paternity, and many other states have adopted this rule as well. What are the equities on each side in such a case? The following two cases address them in two contexts, one in which a husband knew all along that he was not the biological father and one in which a husband did not know until the time of divorce.

Weidman v. Weidman

808 A.2d 576 (Pa. Super. Ct. 2002)

CAVANAUGH, J.:

. . . Robert and Melissa Weidman were married on March 20, 1992. A son, Jordan, was born on November 13, 1992. A daughter, Miranda, was born on September 26, 1994. After the births of these two children, appellee underwent a vasectomy on January 20, 1995. Thereafter, appellant conceived Xavier, who was born on September 28, 1998. The parties separated in January, 2000. Appellee sued for divorce in February, 2001, and the decree in divorce was entered on September 28, 2001. There is no dispute that appellee is not the biological father of Xavier.

At the evidentiary hearing conducted pursuant to appellant's petition for support of Xavier, . . . Robert testified as to his relationship with Xavier. He stated that he knew as soon as Melissa was pregnant that he could not be the father. Xavier's Birth Certificate and Birth Record from the Good Samaritan Hospital lists Robert as the father. When questioned about this, Robert admitted that he agreed to put his name on these documents because he did not want the other children to ask questions. Robert testified that in the two and a half years that the parties remained married after Xavier was born, he never told anyone that Xavier was his son. He did not correct Xavier when he called him daddy, again, because he did not want the other children to know the difference. Robert did have all three children's names tattooed on his chest. At the Hearing, he testified that he recently had the tattoo of Xavier's name altered.

Robert testified that he did take care of Xavier when he and Melissa were married. He bought him food, clothes and diapers. He fed him, bathed him and changed his diapers. He also testified that he would care for Xavier during the night because Melissa would not get up and do so and that Melissa would go out at night until two or three a.m. and he would watch all three children. Furthermore, he testified that he lost three or four jobs because Melissa would call him while he was at work, and he would have to leave work to take care of the children. As Robert put it, he did not want Xavier to die or be dirty. Since Robert and Melissa separated, Robert has not visited Xavier nor has Xavier come to Robert's home. Although Jordan and Miranda are covered by Robert's medical insurance, Xavier is not. . . .

A (former) husband may be estopped from denying paternity of a child born during a marriage if either he or his wife holds the child out to be the child of the marriage. The doctrine of estoppel will not apply when evidence establishes that the father failed to accept the child as his own by holding it out and/or supporting the child. In finding that the doctrine of estoppel applied, the supreme court in *Fish* considered the following facts as indicia of holding out the child as one's own and/or providing support:

1. Mother assured her husband that he was the child's father;
2. Mother named husband as the father on the child's birth certificate;
3. Child bears husband's last name;
4. Child listed as a dependent on the couple's income tax returns;
5. Child was otherwise treated as a child of the marriage which remained intact until three years after the birth of the child when mother informed husband that he was not the father;
6. Child continues to believe that husband is his father;
7. Father-son relationship formed during first three years of child's life;
8. Following separation, for at least two years, husband continued to treat all three children equally;
9. Mother and husband continued to hold child out to the community as the child of their marriage.

In *McConnell*, this court determined that the doctrine of estoppel applied against a putative unwed father (appellee) based upon the following:

1. Mother never told appellee that he was the biological father of child;
2. Appellee accompanied mother to hospital for child's birth;

3. Appellee signed acknowledgment of paternity on child's birth certificate;
4. Appellee insisted that child should bear his surname and requested that child be named after him;
5. Appellee resided with mother and child for four months after birth;
6. After separation, appellee continued to visit mother and child and brought child presents;
7. Appellee voluntarily signed a stipulated support agreement for the child;
8. Child continued to call appellee "Daddy."

Holding that a step-mother was estopped from denying the paternity of her former husband, this court in *Tregoning*, found the following facts probative of the issue:

1. Child bore father's last name;
2. Former husband was named as father on birth certificate;
3. Couple lived as family unit with child for two years;
4. Former wife named former husband as father in two support petitions;
5. Child was listed as daughter on father's passport.

Looking to the facts of the instant case, we find that the lower court erred in failing to find that appellee was estopped from denying paternity of Xavier. There is no issue of fraud by the mother. . . . Appellee treated Xavier from birth until the age of two years as he did his other two children. Appellee is named as father on Xavier's birth certificate, and Xavier was claimed as a dependent on the jointly filed tax returns while the parties remained married. Appellee provided support and care for Xavier. . . . Xavier's name had been tattooed on appellee's chest, along with the names of Jordan and Miranda. . . .

The [lower] court found that appellee had attempted to do the "right thing" by accepting Xavier while trying to maintain the family unit. However, . . . mother never attempted to mislead appellee into believing he was the father of Xavier, [and] appellee never believed himself to be the father. He voluntarily accepted Xavier into his family and provided support for him. That appellee never represented to anyone that Xavier was his biological son is not determinative of the issue of estoppel, since even absent a "holding out", the provision of support may warrant application of the estoppel doctrine. As in *McConnell*, appellee only contested paternal status when he decided that he did not wish to provide financial support for the child.

We recognize that there exists a split of authority among other jurisdictions regarding application of the doctrine of estoppel in situations where a husband provides support for an infant child that he knows not to be his issue. The argument against application of estoppel is that it is inequitable to impose upon a man who is not the biological father of a child the permanent and substantial financial burden of support for the child. *See J.C. v. G.C.* (Conn. Super. 1998), wherein the court observed:

> The issue in this case really goes to the "desirability of encouraging husbands in this situation . . . to assume voluntarily support of children without the fear that doing so may obligate them permanently." *K.B. v. D.B.*, (Mass. App. Ct. 1994). This Court believes that such conduct should be encouraged and concludes that a finding of estoppel would discourage, rather than encourage, individuals such as the Plaintiff from getting involved.

The court then quoted from cases from Wisconsin and Maryland which did not apply estoppel, so as to encourage the voluntary support of nonmarital children.

We conclude that the law in Pennsylvania is not in accord with these cases, since Pennsylvania places the greatest emphasis on the prior conduct of the husband and the effect such conduct has upon the child. The guiding principle in these cases was stated in *Brinkley* [*v. King*, 549 Pa. 241, 701 A.2d 176 (1997)] as the following:

> If a certain person has acted as the parent and bonded with the child, the child should not be required to suffer the potentially damaging trauma that may come from being told that the father he has known all his life is not in fact his father.

Based upon the evidence, we conclude that appellee did act as a parent to Xavier and did bond with the child. Therefore, the lower court erred in not finding that appellee was estopped from denying paternity of Xavier.

The Connecticut and Pennsylvania court decisions discussed here both allude to moral principles for their opposite conclusions. The *J.C.* holding might be said to rest on the principle of "Don't punish good deeds." The *Brinkley* holding might be said to rest on the principle of "Innocent children should not suffer for the choices adults make." Does the *Weidman* court offer any reason for giving one of these principles more weight than the other, besides the fact that *Brinkley* was also decided in Pennsylvania? Is it possible to rank them?

Parker v. Parker

916 So. 2d 926 (Fla. Dist. Ct. App. 4th Dist. 2005)

TAYLOR, J.

. . . The petition filed by appellant alleged that the parties were married on June 26, 1996. A minor child was born of the marriage on June 10, 1998. The former wife represented to the former husband that he was the biological father, and the former husband had no reason to suspect otherwise.

On December 5, 2001, when the child was three and a half years old, the parties entered into a marital settlement agreement which obligated the former husband to pay $1,200 monthly in child support. . . . The marital settlement agreement was incorporated into the final judgment of dissolution dated December 7, 2001. During the dissolution of marriage proceeding, the former wife represented to the court and the former husband that the former husband was the child's biological father.

On or about March 28, 2003, the former wife filed a motion for contempt and enforcement, alleging that the former husband owed her certain monies for child support and the child's medical expenses. One week later, the former husband subjected the child to DNA paternity testing. The testing excluded the former husband as the child's biological father.

Immediately after the child's fifth birthday, the former husband filed this independent action, alleging that at all material times, the former wife knew that the former husband was not the child's biological father due to sexual relations she had with another man. He claims that she purposefully concealed the fact that he was not the child's biological father to collect child support from him.

PROCEDURAL SETTING

. . . Because we are faced here with an attempt to upset the marital presumption of legitimacy in favor of a conclusion of illegitimacy and adultery, we are in territory "fraught with difficult social issues." One report states that as many as ten percent of all children born to married women during the 1940's were the product of adultery. There is little reason to suspect that this number has declined. The advancing technology has made the temptation to DNA test a child even greater:

> While testing at one time involved a blood draw, many laboratories now offer testing with sample collection by mail . . . using cheek swabs. Testing hair and other materials easily collected without the knowledge or cooperation of the subject is increasingly available.

Thus, the instant case presents a question which can be expected to recur with increasing frequency.

FLORIDA PATERNITY LAW

In *Daniel v. Daniel* (Fla. 1997), the trial court had required the former husband to pay child support as part of the marital dissolution decree, despite the fact that the child born during the marriage was not his biological child. The Second District Court of Appeal reversed. The Florida Supreme Court approved that decision, declaring it:

> . . . the well-settled rule of law in this state that "a person has no legal duty to provide support for a minor child who is neither his natural nor his adopted child and for whose care and support he has not contracted."

Thus, had the former husband in this case presented the DNA test results at the time of dissolution, *Daniel* would have controlled and he would have no child support obligation. However, because he did not present these test results until more than a year after the dissolution decree, he runs headlong into principles of res judicata. . . . In *D.F. v. Department of Revenue* (Fla. 2002), the Florida Supreme Court stated bluntly:

> We hold that a final judgment of dissolution of marriage which establishes a child support obligation for a former husband is a final determination of paternity. Any subsequent challenge of paternity must be brought under the provisions of Florida Rule of Civil Procedure 1.540.

RELIEF FROM JUDGMENTS IN FLORIDA

. . . The former husband argues, and we agree, that his action is essentially an attempt to set aside the dissolution decree's paternity and child support obligations for fraud on the court, i.e., extrinsic fraud. . . . "Extrinsic fraud, which constitutes fraud on the court, involves conduct which is collateral to the issues tried in a case.". . . [E]xtrinsic fraud occurs "where a defendant has somehow been prevented from participating in a cause." It defined intrinsic fraud as "fraudulent conduct that arises within a proceeding and pertains to the issues in the case that have been tried or could have been tried." . . .

> When an issue is before a court for resolution, and the complaining party could have addressed the issue in the proceeding, such as attacking the false testimony or

> misrepresentation through cross-examination and other evidence, then the improper conduct, even though it may be perjury, is intrinsic fraud and an attack on a final judgment based on such fraud must be made within one year of the entry of the judgment.

. . . We believe that the basic misrepresentation alleged in this case concerned an issue that could have been raised in the dissolution proceedings, rather than an issue collateral to those proceedings. . . .

THE LAW IN OTHER JURISDICTIONS

Our research discloses numerous cases wherein courts in other jurisdictions have considered this extrinsic fraud question. The prevailing view appears to be that the nondisclosure of true paternity presents a question of intrinsic fraud.

Texas appellate courts have the highest number of reported cases on this issue. They have consistently ruled that concealment or misrepresentation of paternity during divorce proceedings involves intrinsic fraud. . . . The most recent decision in *Temple* is typical. There the former wife was alleged to have represented to the former husband that he was the father. After the divorce it became apparent to him that his daughter did not look like him. Paternity testing then excluded him as the father. The court stated:

> Paternity, although not contested, was an issue agreed to by the parties and addressed and resolved by the trial court. . . . The decree establishes the parent-child relationship. Temple did not allege any act on the part of Archambo that prevented him from contesting the issue of paternity. . . . He did not allege that he could not contest paternity at the final divorce hearing or that he was denied that defense as a matter of law. We conclude that Temple alleged only intrinsic fraud because his "meritorious defense" could have been fully presented at the original proceeding.

Although not as developed, Arkansas law is similar.

The Vermont Supreme Court's decision in *Godin v. Godin* (1998), took a slightly different tack in reaching the same result. That court held that the mother's representation in the original divorce proceeding that the child was "born of the marriage" merely signified that the child was born while the parties were legally married, so that it was not a materially false statement. It went on to hold that the mere non-disclosure to an adverse party of facts pertinent to a controversy does not constitute fraud on the court for purposes of vacating the judgment. . . .

[The court then cites similar decisions in Oklahoma, South Carolina, and Alabama.]

We note that Nevada has held that a wife's misrepresentations of paternity are extrinsic fraud which will permit reopening the divorce decree. However, we disagree with this apparent minority view.

POLICY CONSIDERATIONS

Because the effect of our conclusion is to create a one-year window after the divorce to perform any DNA testing or be forever barred, we now discuss whether a time-based limitation is supportable as a matter of policy. There is ample authority that post-dissolution challenges to paternity should not be permitted beyond a "relatively brief passage of time." We consider it significant that many states have legislatively adopted a "statute of limitations" approach based on the age of the child. The original Uniform Parentage Act (UPA), which has been adopted by 19 states (in whole or in part) mandated a five-year limitations period, so that any petition to disestablish would have to be brought by the child's fifth birthday or be forever barred. Several other states (including California and Oklahoma) and the 2000 version of the UPA (adopted by four states), now provide for a two-year limitations period from the child's birth. Had the minor child in this case lived in any of these states, his legitimacy would be safe from disruption, as he was five years old at the time this petition was filed.

In her dissenting opinion in *Mr. G,* Judge Hearn pointed out a potential policy ramification of refusing a post-dissolution disestablishment suit:

> The holding that the allegations of fraud contained in Mr. G's complaint cannot serve as the basis for attacking a judgment may be interpreted by the Family Court bar to require every male litigant in a domestic proceeding to request and secure a blood test.

While this view appears a bit extreme, there may be some merit in telling divorcing fathers who are in doubt to "test now, or forever hold your peace."

Many courts state that there is an overriding special concern for the finality of judgments in this area. In *Ince,* 58 S.W.3d at 191, the Texas appeals court said of the parental relationship established by the divorce decree:

> The relationship was . . . recognized, confirmed and became final under all the rules and with the formalities and solemnities accorded the creation and recognition of other legal relationships. The judgment at issue in this case should not be set aside because one of the individuals involved has become unhappy with the continued existence of it.

The Vermont Supreme Court agreed that finality is important, taking the view that the public interest primarily derives from the interests of the child:

> Thus, the State retains a strong and direct interest in ensuring that children born of a marriage do not suffer financially or psychologically merely because of a parent's belated and self-serving concern over a child's biological origins. These themes underlie the conclusion, reached by numerous courts, that the public interest in finality of paternity determinations is compelling, and that the doctrine of res judicata therefore bars subsequent attempts to disprove paternity.

Godin.

The fundamental choice in these cases is between the interests of the legal father on the one hand and the child on the other. The Vermont Supreme Court stated:

> Although we understand plaintiff's interest in ascertaining the true genetic makeup of the child, we agree with the many jurisdictions holding that the financial and emotional welfare of the child, and the preservation of an established parent-child relationship, must remain paramount. Where the presumptive father has held himself out as the child's parent, and engaged in an ongoing parent-child relationship for a period of years, he may not disavow that relationship and destroy a child's long-held assumptions, solely for his own self-interest. *Id.*; *see also In re Marriage of Wendy M.* (Wash. App. 1998) (stating that while former husband had an interest in avoiding erroneous child support, he could not sacrifice the child's interest to protect his own); *Hackley v. Hackley* (Mich. 1986) (holding that best interests

of child must prevail over unfairness to former husband challenging paternity nine years after his divorce).

The main issue affecting the child in a disestablishment suit is the psychological devastation that the child will undoubtedly experience from losing the only father he or she has ever known. As Theresa Glennon pointed out, these children are hit with a "double-whammy." First, they must endure the trauma of divorce, then experience the pain of their parentage in dispute.

We realize that as judges, we cannot order a man to love a child. In *Paternity of Cheryl* (Mass. 2001), the Massachusetts Supreme Court stated that it harbored no illusions about its ability to protect the child fully from the consequences of the former husband's decisions. Still, it felt that relieving the former husband of his financial obligations might itself "unravel the parental ties, as the payment of child support 'is a strand tightly interwoven with other forms of connection between father and child,' and often forms a critical bond between them." Or, as the Iowa Supreme Court more bluntly put it, "We hope that David's heart will follow his money." *Dye v. Geiger* (Iowa 1996).

Other courts have been less kind. The Vermont Supreme Court in *Godin*, said:

> The fact that plaintiff chose for self-serving purposes to jeopardize his relationship with Christina is beyond our control. We need not, however, award plaintiff a financial windfall for his conduct, or deprive Christina of not only a father's affection, but also the legal rights and financial benefits of the parental relationship.

By refusing to set aside paternity decrees based on belated requests, courts "will help deter other parents who might otherwise seek, for financial or other self-serving reasons, to dissolve their parental bonds." Stability and continuity of support, both emotional and financial, are essential to a child's welfare. Indeed, one of the factors most important to a child's post-divorce adjustment is the degree of economic hardship.

We recognize that the former husband in this case may feel victimized. However, Theresa Glennon argues cogently that:

> [w]hile some individuals are innocent victims of deceptive partners, adults are aware of the high incidence of infidelity and only they, not the children, are able to act to ensure that the biological ties they may deem essential are present. . . . The law should discourage adults from treating children they have parented as expendable when their adult relationships fall apart. It is the adults who can and should absorb the pain of betrayal rather than inflict additional betrayal on the involved children.

Theresa Glennon, *Expendable Children: Defining Belonging in a Broken World*, 8 DUKE J. GENDER L. & POLICY 269 (2001).

CONCLUSION

In sum, we conclude, along with the majority of states, that the issue of paternity misrepresentation in marital dissolution proceedings is a matter of intrinsic fraud. It is not extrinsic fraud, or a fraud upon the court, that can form the basis for relief from judgment more than a year later. Any relevant policy considerations that would compel a different result are best addressed by the legislature.

NOTES AND QUESTIONS

The Pennsylvania Supreme Court denied an appeal of the *Wiedman* decision. The Florida Supreme Court upheld the *Parker* decision, adopting its reasoning wholesale, and added by way of explanation this remarkable statement: "The presumption of legitimacy is a constitutional right afforded to every child born into a marriage granting the child the right to remain legitimate, both legally and factually, if doing so is in the child's best interest." Parker v. Parker, 950 So. 2d 388 (Fla. 2007). What basis could there be for such a constitutional right?

Is the policy reasoning in *Weidman* or *Parker* adequate? What rule would produce the best consequences for children over the course of their minority, in terms of what behavior it induces in husbands and boyfriends? Some family law scholars have called for mandatory paternity testing at the birth of every child, to prevent cases like *Parker* and cases in which boyfriends execute acknowledgments of paternity based on the mistaken assumption that they are the father of their girlfriend's baby. See, e.g., June Carbone & Naomi Cahn, *Which Ties Bind? Redefining the Parent-Child Relationship in an Age of Genetic Certainty*, 11 WM. & MARY BILL RTS. J. 1011 (2003). Would that be socially desirable? Is the policy analysis different as between cases in which the mother is married and cases in which she is not? How would you advise a man in either case? Some evolutionary psychologists have suggested that women are actually better off in a situation of paternity uncertainty, because this results in "both material and genetic benefits, and protection of self and young from future mistreatment by males as a result of having distributed some possibility of paternity." Margo Wilson & Martin Daly, *Lethal and Nonlethal Violence Against Wives and Evotionary Psychology of Male Sexual Proprietariness, in* RETHINKING VIOLENCE AGAINST WOMEN 211 (Russell B. Dobash ed., 1998).

b. Constitutional Rights of Unwed Fathers

Because non-marital births are so common today, and because most such births involve biological parents who are not in a stable relationship with each other, the situation of the unwed father merits special attention. Paternity cases make up a major component of any juvenile court's docket. In nearly all cases of non-marital births, if the mother is fit she will assume primary custody of the baby after the birth. Biological fathers, once established as legal parents, commonly seek and receive orders of visitation and are put under an obligation of financial support.

The status of unwed fathers in the United States is dramatically different today relative to half a century ago. Before the 1960s, non-marital pregnancy was a cause of great shame and stigma, and the main options for the woman were abortion, carrying the child to term as secretly as possible and then relinquishing the child for adoption, or marrying the biological father if he was agreeable. Few unwed mothers undertook to raise non-marital children. The biological father had little control over the situation; his choices were to propose marriage or not. If he proposed and was rejected or if he did not agree to marry (despite any shotguns pointed at him . . .), he would be treated as irrelevant to the situation. He could not compel or prohibit an abortion, and he could not block an adoption. If the child was born, he was not treated as a legal parent. He had neither rights nor responsibilities.

The cultural and sexual revolution of the '60s led to many more non-marital children being born and kept by their mothers, rather than being relinquished for adoption, which in turn swelled welfare rolls, which in turn made states want to go after biological fathers for child support, which in turn led them to amend their parentage laws to give legal parent status to unwed fathers. States could have imposed a financial obligation on biological fathers without making them legal parents and without conferring full parental rights. In Denmark, biological fatherhood is a sufficient basis for imposing a support obligation on a man, but unwed fathers do not acquire any parental rights unless the mother agrees to it. See Susanne Storm et al., *Denmark, in* INTERNATIONAL ENCYCLOPEDIA OF LAWS, VOLUME I: OF FAMILY AND SUCCESSION LAW 94 (W. Pintens ed., 2002). In Germany, an unwed father has only a limited right to visitation and cannot seek custody unless the mother consents to it or is unable to have custody herself, but is subject to a support obligation in any case. See Hamilton & Perry, FAMILY LAW IN EUROPE 317-318; Nekvedavicius v. Germany, (2004) 38 EHRR CD1.

However, in a series of decisions starting with *Stanley v. Illinois* in 1972, the U.S. Supreme Court created a substantive right to legal parent status for some unwed fathers, under the Due Process Clause of the Fourteenth Amendment. The Court also rendered several decisions holding that states may not discriminate against non-marital children in their laws and benefit programs, which incidentally further diminished the stigma attached to non-marital pregnancy. In response to welfare exigencies and constitutional doctrine, states all came to adopt paternity laws conferring legal parent status on unwed biological fathers, even in some cases when they do not want it.

As you read the Supreme Court decisions below, think about whether states have gone farther than they are constitutionally required to in conferring legal parent status on unwed fathers. Certainly states could constitutionally exclude those who do not want to be legal parents, absent a (highly unlikely) judicial determination that some other party (e.g., the child) has a constitutional right to imposition of paternity on such men. But it is somewhat unclear when states must give that status to biological fathers who want it, because the precise content of unwed fathers' constitutional rights remains uncertain, despite five Supreme Court decisions addressing the matter. Most legal scholars interpreted the Court's first four unwed father decisions, culminating in *Lehr v. Robertson* below, as establishing a two-part test for an unwed father having a constitutional right to become a legal parent—namely, biological connection plus having demonstrated commitment to assuming the responsibilities of parenthood. Yet the parentage laws set out above do not make demonstrated commitment a prerequisite to paternity. (On the other hand, adoption laws in many states make an unwed father's having financially supported and/or visited a child determinative of whether he can block an adoption.) As you read *Lehr*, see if there is in fact an implicit third requirement—namely, that a putative father must be fit to serve as a parent.

Lehr addressed principally a procedural due process claim, but the Court summarized its prior holdings as to substantive due process and as to the permissibility under the Equal Protection Clause of treating fathers differently from mothers. The *Michael H.* decision that follows *Lehr* below focused on substantive due process, and the plurality reinterpreted the prior cases as establishing a quite different test.

Lehr v. Robertson

463 U.S. 248 (1983)

STEVENS, Justice.

. . . Jessica M. was born out of wedlock on November 9, 1976. Her mother, Lorraine Robertson, married Richard Robertson eight months after Jessica's birth. On December

21, 1978, when Jessica was over two years old, the Robertsons filed an adoption petition. . . . On March 7, 1979, the court entered an order of adoption. In this proceeding, appellant contends that the adoption order is invalid because he, Jessica's putative father, was not given advance notice of the adoption proceeding.

The State of New York maintains a "putative father registry." A man who files with that registry demonstrates his intent to claim paternity of a child born out of wedlock and is therefore entitled to receive notice of any proceeding to adopt that child. Before entering Jessica's adoption order, the Ulster County Family Court had the putative father registry examined. Although appellant claims to be Jessica's natural father, he had not entered his name in the registry.

In addition to the persons whose names are listed on the putative father registry, New York law requires that notice of an adoption proceeding be given to several other classes of possible fathers of children born out of wedlock—those who have been adjudicated to be the father, those who have been identified as the father on the child's birth certificate, those who live openly with the child and the child's mother and who hold themselves out to be the father, those who have been identified as the father by the mother in a sworn written statement, and those who were married to the child's mother before the child was six months old.

Appellant admittedly was not a member of any of those classes. He had lived with appellee prior to Jessica's birth and visited her in the hospital when Jessica was born, but his name does not appear on Jessica's birth certificate. He did not live with appellee or Jessica after Jessica's birth, he has never provided them with any financial support, and he has never offered to marry appellee. Nevertheless, he contends that the following special circumstances gave him a constitutional right to notice and a hearing before Jessica was adopted.

On January 30, 1979, one month after the adoption proceeding was commenced in Ulster County, appellant filed a "visitation and paternity petition" in the Westchester County Family Court. In that petition, he asked for a determination of paternity, an order of support, and reasonable visitation privileges with Jessica. Notice of that proceeding was served on appellee on February 22, 1979. Four days later appellee's attorney informed the Ulster County Court that appellant had commenced a paternity proceeding in Westchester County; the Ulster County judge then entered an order staying appellant's paternity proceeding until he could rule on a motion to change the venue of that proceeding to Ulster County. On March 3, 1979, appellant received notice of the change of venue motion and, for the first time, learned that an adoption proceeding was pending in Ulster County.

On March 7, 1979, appellant's attorney telephoned the Ulster County judge to inform him that he planned to seek a stay of the adoption proceeding pending the determination of the paternity petition. In that telephone conversation, the judge advised the lawyer that he had already signed the adoption order earlier that day. According to appellant's attorney, the judge stated that he was aware of the pending paternity petition but did not believe he was required to give notice to appellant prior to the entry of the order of adoption. Thereafter, the Family Court in Westchester County granted appellee's motion to dismiss the paternity petition, holding that the putative father's right to seek paternity ". . . must be deemed severed so long as an order of adoption exists." . . .

The Due Process Claim

The Fourteenth Amendment provides that no State shall deprive any person of life, liberty, or property without due process of law. When that Clause is invoked in a novel context, it is our practice to begin the inquiry with a determination of the precise nature of the private interest that is threatened by the State. Only after that interest has been identified, can we properly evaluate the adequacy of the State's process. . . .

I

The intangible fibers that connect parent and child have infinite variety. They are woven throughout the fabric of our society, providing it with strength, beauty, and flexibility. It is self-evident that they are sufficiently vital to merit constitutional protection in appropriate cases. In deciding whether this is such a case, however, we must consider the broad framework that has traditionally been used to resolve the legal problems arising from the parent-child relationship.

In the vast majority of cases, state law determines the final outcome. Rules governing the inheritance of property, adoption, and child custody are generally specified in statutory enactments that vary from State to State. Moreover, equally varied state laws governing marriage and divorce affect a multitude of parent-child relationships. The institution of marriage has played a critical role both in defining the legal entitlements of family members and in developing the decentralized structure of our democratic society. In recognition of that role, and as part of their general overarching concern for serving the best interests of children, state laws almost universally express an appropriate preference for the formal family.

In some cases, however, this Court has held that the Federal Constitution supersedes state law and provides even greater protection for certain formal family relationships. In those cases, as in the state cases, the Court has emphasized the paramount interest in the welfare of children and has noted that the rights of the parents are a counterpart of the responsibilities they have assumed. Thus, the "liberty" of parents to control the education of their children that was vindicated in *Meyer v. Nebraska* (1923) and *Pierce v. Society of Sisters* (1925) was described as a "right, coupled with the high duty, to recognize and prepare [the child] for additional obligations." The linkage between parental duty and parental right was stressed again in *Prince v. Massachusetts* (1944), when the Court declared it a cardinal principal "that the custody, care and nurture of the child reside first in the parents, whose primary function and freedom include preparation for obligations the state can neither supply nor hinder." In these cases the Court has found that the relationship of love and duty in a recognized family unit is an interest in liberty entitled to constitutional protection.

. . . This Court has examined the extent to which a natural father's biological relationship with his illegitimate child receives protection under the Due Process Clause in precisely three cases: *Stanley v. Illinois* (1972), *Quilloin v. Walcott* (1978), and *Caban v. Mohammed* (1979). *Stanley* involved the constitutionality of an Illinois statute that conclusively presumed every father of a child born out of wedlock to be an unfit person to have custody of his children. The father in that case had lived with his children all their lives and had lived with their mother for eighteen years. There was nothing in the record to indicate that Stanley had been a neglectful father who had not cared for his children. Under the statute, however, the nature of the actual relationship between parent and child was completely irrelevant. Once the mother died, the children were automatically made wards of the state. Relying in part on a Michigan case recognizing that the preservation of "a subsisting relationship with the child's father" may better serve the child's best interest than "uprooting him from the family which he knew from birth," the Court held that the Due Process Clause was violated by the automatic destruction of the custodial relationship without giving the father any opportunity to present evidence regarding his fitness as a parent.

Quilloin involved the constitutionality of a Georgia statute that authorized the adoption of a child born out of wedlock over the objection of the natural father. The father in that case had never legitimated the child. It was only after the mother had remarried and her new husband had filed an adoption petition that the natural father sought visitation rights and filed a petition for legitimation. The trial court found adoption by the new husband to be in the child's best interests, and we unanimously held that action to be consistent with the Due Process Clause.

Caban involved the conflicting claims of two natural parents who had maintained joint custody of their children from the time of their birth until they were respectively two and four years old. The father challenged the validity of an order authorizing the mother's new husband to adopt the children; he relied on both the Equal Protection Clause and the Due Process Clause. Because this Court upheld his equal protection claim, the majority did not address his due process challenge. The comments on the latter claim by the four dissenting Justices are nevertheless instructive, because they identify the clear distinction between a mere biological relationship and an actual relationship of parental responsibility.

Justice Stewart correctly observed:

> "Even if it be assumed that each married parent after divorce has some substantive due process right to maintain his or her parental relationship, it by no means follows that each unwed parent has any such right. *Parental rights do not spring full-blown from the biological connection between parent and child. They require relationships more enduring.*"[16]

In a similar vein, the other three dissenters in *Caban* were prepared to "assume that, *if and when one develops*, the relationship between a father and his natural child is entitled to protection against arbitrary state action as a matter of due process."

The difference between the developed parent-child relationship that was implicated in *Stanley* and *Caban*, and the potential relationship involved in *Quilloin* and this case, is both clear and significant. When an unwed father demonstrates a full commitment to the responsibilities of parenthood by "com[ing] forward to participate in the rearing of his child," his interest in personal contact with his child acquires substantial protection under the due process clause. At that point it may be said that he "act[s] as a father toward his children." But the mere existence of a biological link does not merit equivalent constitutional protection. The actions of judges neither create nor sever genetic bonds. "[T]he importance of the familial relationship, to the individuals involved and to the society, stems from the emotional attachments that derive from the intimacy of daily association, and from the role it plays in 'promot[ing] a way of life' through the instruction of children as well as from the fact of blood relationship."[17]

16. In the balance of that paragraph Justice Stewart noted that the relation between a father and his natural child may acquire constitutional protection if the father enters into a traditional marriage with the mother or if "the actual relationship between father and child" is sufficient. "The mother carries and bears the child, and in this sense her parental relationship is clear. The validity of the father's parental claims must be gauged by other measures. By tradition, the primary measure has been the legitimate familial relationship he creates with the child by marriage with the mother. By definition, the question before us can arise only when no such marriage has taken place. In some circumstances the actual relationship between father and child may suffice to create in the unwed father parental interests comparable to those of the married father. But here we are concerned with the rights the unwed father may have when his wishes and those of the mother are in conflict, and the child's best interests are served by a resolution in favor of the mother. It seems to me that the absence of a legal tie with the mother may in such circumstances appropriately place a limit on whatever substantive constitutional claims might otherwise exist by virtue of the father's actual relationship with the children."

17. Commentators have emphasized the constitutional importance of the distinction between an inchoate and a fully developed relationship. See Comment, 46 Brooklyn L. Rev. 95 (1979) ("the unwed father's interest springs not from his biological tie with his illegitimate child, but rather, from the relationship he has established with and the responsibility he has shouldered for his child"); Note, 58 Neb. L. Rev. 610 (1979) ("a putative

The significance of the biological connection is that it offers the natural father an opportunity that no other male possesses to develop a relationship with his offspring. If he grasps that opportunity and accepts some measure of responsibility for the child's future, he may enjoy the blessings of the parent-child relationship and make uniquely valuable contributions to the child's development.[18] If he fails to do so, the Federal Constitution will not automatically compel a state to listen to his opinion of where the child's best interests lie.

In this case, we are not assessing the constitutional adequacy of New York's procedures for terminating a developed relationship. Appellant has never had any significant custodial, personal, or financial relationship with Jessica, and he did not seek to establish a legal tie until after she was two years old.[19] We are concerned only with whether New York has adequately protected his opportunity to form such a relationship.

II

The most effective protection of the putative father's opportunity to develop a relationship with his child is provided by the laws that authorize formal marriage and govern its consequences. But the availability of that protection is, of course, dependent on the will of both parents of the child. Thus, New York has adopted a special statutory scheme to protect the unmarried father's interest in assuming a responsible role in the future of his child.

After . . . *Stanley*, the New York Legislature appointed a special commission to recommend legislation that would accommodate both the interests of biological fathers in their children and the children's interest in prompt and certain adoption procedures. The commission recommended, and the legislature enacted, a statutory adoption scheme that automatically provides notice to seven categories of putative fathers who are likely to have assumed some responsibility for the care of their natural children. If this scheme were

---

father's failure to show a substantial interest in his child's welfare and to employ methods provided by state law for solidifying his parental rights . . . will remove from him the full constitutional protection afforded the parental rights of other classes of parents"); Note, 29 Emory L.J. 845 (1980) ("an unwed father's rights in his child do not spring solely from the biological fact of his parentage, but rather from his willingness to admit his paternity and express some tangible interest in the child"). See also Poulin, Illegitimacy and Family Privacy: A Note on Maternal Cooperation in Paternity Suits, 70 Nw. U. L. Rev. 910 (1976); Developments in the Law, 93 Harv. L. Rev. 1156 (1980); Note, 18 Duquesne L. Rev. 375 (1980); Note, 19 J. Family L. 440 (1980); Note, 57 Denver L.J. 671 (1980); Note, 1979 Wash. U. L.Q. 1029; Note, 12 U.C. D. L. Rev. 412 (1979). [Note the Court's heavy reliance on law student Notes for this crucial empirical/legal assumption. Yet below the Court dismisses the opinions of "family psychologists" as irrelevant.—Ed.]

18. Of course, we need not take sides in the ongoing debate among family psychologists over the relative weight to be accorded biological ties and psychological ties, in order to recognize that a natural father who has played a substantial role in rearing his child has a greater claim to constitutional protection than a mere biological parent. New York's statutory scheme reflects these differences, guaranteeing notice to any putative father who is living openly with the child, and providing putative fathers who have never developed a relationship with the child the opportunity to receive notice simply by mailing a postcard to the putative father registry.

19. This case happens to involve an adoption by the husband of the natural mother, but we do not believe the natural father has any greater right to object to such an adoption than to an adoption by two total strangers. If anything, the balance of equities tips the opposite way in a case such as this. In denying the putative father relief in *Quilloin*, we made an observation equally applicable here:

> "Nor is this a case in which the proposed adoption would place the child with a new set of parents with whom the child had never before lived. Rather, the result of the adoption in this case is to give full recognition to a family unit already in existence, a result desired by all concerned, except appellant. Whatever might be required in other situations, we cannot say that the State was required in this situation to find anything more than that the adoption, and denial of legitimation, were in the 'best interests of the child.'"

likely to omit many responsible fathers, and if qualification for notice were beyond the control of an interested putative father, it might be thought procedurally inadequate. Yet, as all of the New York courts that reviewed this matter observed, the right to receive notice was completely within appellant's control. By mailing a postcard to the putative father registry, he could have guaranteed that he would receive notice of any proceedings to adopt Jessica. The possibility that he may have failed to do so because of his ignorance of the law cannot be a sufficient reason for criticizing the law itself. The New York legislature concluded that a more open-ended notice requirement would merely complicate the adoption process, threaten the privacy interests of unwed mothers, create the risk of unnecessary controversy, and impair the desired finality of adoption decrees. Regardless of whether we would have done likewise if we were legislators instead of judges, we surely cannot characterize the state's conclusion as arbitrary.

Appellant argues, however, that even if the putative father's opportunity to establish a relationship with an illegitimate child is adequately protected by the New York statutory scheme in the normal case, he was nevertheless entitled to special notice because the court and the mother knew that he had filed an affiliation proceeding in another court. . . . The Constitution does not require either a trial judge or a litigant to give special notice to nonparties who are presumptively capable of asserting and protecting their own rights. . . .

THE EQUAL PROTECTION CLAIM. . . .

The legislation at issue in this case . . . is intended to establish procedures for adoptions. Those procedures are designed to promote the best interests of the child, protect the rights of interested third parties, and ensure promptness and finality.[25] To serve those ends, the legislation guarantees to certain people the right to veto an adoption and the right to prior notice of any adoption proceeding. The mother of an illegitimate child is always within that favored class, but only certain putative fathers are included. Appellant contends that the gender-based distinction is invidious.

As we noted above, the existence or nonexistence of a substantial relationship between parent and child is a relevant criterion in evaluating both the rights of the parent and the best interests of the child. In *Quilloin v. Walcott,* [we] therefore found that a Georgia statute that always required a mother's consent to the adoption of a child born out of wedlock, but required the father's consent only if he had legitimated the child, did not violate the Equal Protection Clause. Because, like the father in *Quilloin,* appellant has never established a substantial relationship with his daughter, the New York statutes at issue in this case did not operate to deny appellant equal protection.

We have held that these statutes may not constitutionally be applied in that class of cases where the mother and father are in fact similarly situated with regard to their relationship with the child. In *Caban v. Mohammed* (1979), the Court held that it violated the Equal Protection Clause to grant the mother a veto over the adoption of a four-year-old girl and a six-year-old boy, but not to grant a veto to their father, who had admitted paternity and had participated in the rearing of the children. . . .

Jessica's parents are not like the parents in *Caban.* Whereas appellee had a continuous custodial responsibility for Jessica, appellant never established any custodial, personal, or financial relationship with her. If one parent has an established custodial relationship with the child and the other parent has either abandoned or never established a

25. Appellant does not contest the vital importance of those ends to the people of New York. It has long been accepted that illegitimate children whose parents never marry are "at risk" economically, medically, emotionally, and educationally.

relationship, the Equal Protection Clause does not prevent a state from according the two parents different legal rights.

Justice WHITE, with Justices MARSHALL and BLACKMUN, dissenting.

. . . As Jessica's biological father, Lehr either had an interest protected by the Constitution or he did not. If the entry of the adoption order in this case deprived Lehr of a constitutionally protected interest, he is entitled to notice and an opportunity to be heard before the order can be accorded finality.

According to Lehr, . . . Lorraine told Lehr that she had reported to the New York State Department of Social Services that he was the father. Lehr visited Lorraine and Jessica in the hospital every day during Lorraine's confinement. According to Lehr, from the time Lorraine was discharged from the hospital until August, 1978, she concealed her whereabouts from him. During this time Lehr never ceased his efforts to locate Lorraine and Jessica and achieved sporadic success until August, 1977, after which time he was unable to locate them at all. On those occasions when he did determine Lorraine's location, he visited with her and her children to the extent she was willing to permit it. When Lehr, with the aid of a detective agency, located Lorraine and Jessica in August, 1978, Lorraine was already married to Mr. Robertson. Lehr asserts that at this time he offered to provide financial assistance and to set up a trust fund for Jessica, but that Lorraine refused. Lorraine threatened Lehr with arrest unless he stayed away and refused to permit him to see Jessica. Thereafter Lehr retained counsel who wrote to Lorraine in early December, 1978, requesting that she permit Lehr to visit Jessica and threatening legal action on Lehr's behalf. On December 21, 1978, perhaps as a response to Lehr's threatened legal action, appellees commenced the adoption action at issue here.

The "nature of the interest" at stake here is the interest that a natural parent has in his or her child, one that has long been recognized and accorded constitutional protection. We have frequently "stressed the importance of familial bonds, whether or not legitimized by marriage, and accorded them constitutional protection." If "both the child and the [putative father] in a paternity action have a compelling interest" in the accurate outcome of such a case, it cannot be disputed that both the child and the putative father have a compelling interest in the outcome of a proceeding that may result in the termination of the father-child relationship. "A parent's interest in the accuracy and justice of the decision to terminate his or her parental status is . . . a commanding one." *Lassiter v. Department of Social Services* (1981). It is beyond dispute that a formal order of adoption, no less than a formal termination proceeding, operates to permanently terminate parental rights. . . .

A "mere biological relationship" is not as unimportant in determining the nature of liberty interests as the majority suggests. "[T]he usual understanding of 'family' implies biological relationships, and most decisions treating the relation between parent and child have stressed this element." *Smith v. Organization of Foster Families*. The "biological connection" is itself a relationship that creates a protected interest. Thus the "nature" of the interest is the parent-child relationship; how well-developed that relationship has become goes to its "weight," not its "nature." Whether Lehr's interest is entitled to constitutional protection does not entail a searching inquiry into the quality of the relationship but a simple determination of the *fact* that the relationship exists—a fact that even the majority agrees must be assumed to be established. . . .

Any analysis of the adequacy of the notice in this case must be conducted on the assumption that the interest involved here is as strong as that of *any* putative father. That is not to say that due process requires actual notice to every putative father or that adoptive parents or the State must conduct an exhaustive search of records or an intensive investigation before a final adoption order may be entered. The procedures adopted by the State, however, must at least represent a reasonable effort to determine the identity of the putative father and to give him adequate notice.

In this case, of course, there was no question about either the identity or the location of the putative father. The mother knew exactly who he was and both she and the court entering the order of adoption knew precisely where he was and how to give him actual notice that his parental rights were about to be terminated by an adoption order. . . . The State is quite willing to give notice and a hearing to putative fathers who have made themselves known by resorting to the putative fathers' register. It makes little sense to me to deny notice and hearing to a father who has not placed his name in the register but who has unmistakably identified himself by filing suit to establish his paternity and has notified the adoption court of his action and his interest. . . .

NOTES AND QUESTIONS

The *Lehr* majority affirmed the principle established in the Court's three prior unwed father cases: "When an unwed father demonstrates a full commitment to the responsibilities of parenthood by 'com[ing] forward to participate in the rearing of his child,' his interest in personal contact with his child acquires substantial protection under the due process clause." Did the Court apply that principle poorly in this case, at least if the dissenters' account of the facts is correct? As clear as that principle might seem from *Lehr* and its predecessors, the plurality in *Michael H.*, six years later, set out below, denied that the Court's prior decisions stood for such a principle.

The *Lehr* Court was less clear about whether just the fact of being a biological parent gives rise to some substantive or procedural constitutional rights and, if so, what exactly those rights are. Can you articulate a rule established by the Court in *Lehr* as to rights arising from biology alone? In reading the *Michael H.* opinions below, try to determine what a majority of the Justices would have concluded about whether biology alone gives rise to some constitutional protection.

States *could* conclude from *Lehr* at least that having a putative father registry and requiring adoption courts to give notice to biological fathers on it would satisfy unwed fathers' procedural due process rights. After *Lehr* many states created registries, and increasingly states are making failure to register itself a basis for obviating a biological father's consent to adoption by another man. Unwed fathers in such states therefore stand to lose a great deal simply by not contacting the state's putative father registry office when their offspring are born. Have you ever heard of such a registry in any state where you have lived? Would you know what government agency to call if you or a friend might have fathered a child outside of marriage, in order to preserve paternal rights?

Michael H. v. Gerald D.

491 U.S. 110 (1989)

Justice Scalia announced the judgment of the Court and delivered an opinion, in which The Chief Justice joins, and in all but footnote 6 of which Justices O'Connor and Kennedy join.

... The facts of this case are, we must hope, extraordinary. On May 9, 1976, in Las Vegas, Nevada, Carole D., an international model, and Gerald D., a top executive in a French oil company, were married. The couple established a home in Playa del Rey, California, in which they resided as husband and wife when one or the other was not out of the country on business. In the summer of 1978, Carole became involved in an adulterous affair with a neighbor, Michael H. In September 1980, she conceived a child, Victoria D., who was born on May 11, 1981. Gerald was listed as father on the birth certificate and has always held Victoria out to the world as his daughter. Soon after delivery of the child, however, Carole informed Michael that she believed he might be the father.

In the first three years of her life, Victoria remained always with Carole, but found herself within a variety of quasi-family units. In October 1981, Gerald moved to New York City to pursue his business interests, but Carole chose to remain in California. At the end of that month, Carole and Michael had blood tests of themselves and Victoria, which showed a 98.07% probability that Michael was Victoria's father. In January 1982, Carole visited Michael in St. Thomas, where his primary business interests were based. There Michael held Victoria out as his child. In March, however, Carole left Michael and returned to California, where she took up residence with yet another man, Scott K. Later that spring, and again in the summer, Carole and Victoria spent time with Gerald in New York City, as well as on vacation in Europe. In the fall, they returned to Scott in California.

In November 1982, rebuffed in his attempts to visit Victoria, Michael filed a filiation action in California Superior Court to establish his paternity and right to visitation. [F]rom March through July 1983, Carole was again living with Gerald in New York. In August, however, she returned to California, became involved once again with Michael ... [and the filiation action was dropped].

For the ensuing eight months, when Michael was not in St. Thomas he lived with Carole and Victoria in Carole's apartment in Los Angeles and held Victoria out as his daughter. In April 1984, Carole and Michael signed a stipulation that Michael was Victoria's natural father. Carole left Michael the next month, however, and instructed her attorneys not to file the stipulation. In June 1984, Carole reconciled with Gerald and joined him in New York, where they now live with Victoria and two other children since born into the marriage.

In May 1984, Michael and Victoria, through her guardian ad litem, sought visitation rights for Michael *pendente lite.* To assist in determining whether visitation would be in Victoria's best interests, the Superior Court appointed a psychologist to evaluate Victoria, Gerald, Michael, and Carole. The psychologist recommended that Carole retain sole custody, but that Michael be allowed continued contact with Victoria pursuant to a restricted visitation schedule. The court concurred and ordered that Michael be provided with limited visitation privileges *pendente lite.*

On October 19, 1984, Gerald, who intervened in the action, moved for summary judgment on the ground that under Cal. Evid. Code §621 there were no triable issues of fact as to Victoria's paternity. This law provides that "the issue of a wife cohabiting with her husband, who is not impotent or sterile, is conclusively presumed to be a child of the marriage." The presumption may be rebutted by blood tests, but only if a motion for such tests is made ... by the husband or ... by the wife. ... [T]he Superior Court granted Gerald's motion for summary judgment. ...

On appeal, Michael asserted, *inter alia,* that the Superior Court's application of §621 had violated his procedural and substantive due process rights. Victoria also raised a due process challenge to the statute, seeking to preserve her *de facto* relationship with Michael as well as with Gerald. She contended, in addition, that as §621 allows the husband and, at least to a limited extent, the mother, but not the child, to rebut the presumption of legitimacy, it violates the child's right to equal protection. . . .

III

. . . California law, like nature itself, makes no provision for dual fatherhood. Michael sought to be declared *the* father of Victoria. The immediate benefit he sought to obtain from that status was visitation rights. But if he were successful in being declared the father, other rights would follow-most importantly, the right to be considered as the parent who should have custody, a status that "embrace[s] the sum of parental rights with respect to the rearing of a child, including the child's care; the right to the child's services and earnings; the right to direct the child's activities; the right to make decisions regarding the control, education, and health of the child; and the right, as well as the duty, to prepare the child for additional obligations, which includes the teaching of moral standards, religious beliefs, and elements of good citizenship." All parental rights, including visitation, were automatically denied by denying Michael status as the father. . . .

Michael contends as a matter of substantive due process that, because he has established a parental relationship with Victoria, protection of Gerald's and Carole's marital union is an insufficient state interest to support termination of that relationship. This argument is, of course, predicated on the assertion that Michael has a constitutionally protected liberty interest in his relationship with Victoria.

It is an established part of our constitutional jurisprudence that the term "liberty" in the Due Process Clause extends beyond freedom from physical restraint. . . . In an attempt to limit and guide interpretation of the Clause, we have insisted not merely that the interest denominated as a "liberty" be "fundamental" (a concept that, in isolation, is hard to objectify), but also that it be an interest traditionally protected by our society.[2] As we have put it, the Due Process Clause affords only those protections "so rooted in the traditions and conscience of our people as to be ranked as fundamental." Our cases reflect "continual insistence upon respect for the teachings of history [and] solid recognition of the basic values that underlie our society. . . ."

This insistence that the asserted liberty interest be rooted in history and tradition is evident, as elsewhere, in our cases according constitutional protection to certain parental rights. Michael reads the landmark case of *Stanley v. Illinois* and the subsequent cases of *Quilloin v. Walcott, Caban v. Mohammed,* and *Lehr v. Robertson,* as establishing that a liberty interest is created by biological fatherhood plus an established parental relationship—factors that exist in the present case as well. We think that distorts the rationale of those cases. As we view them, they rest not upon such isolated factors but upon the historic respect—indeed, sanctity would not be too strong a term—traditionally accorded to the relationships that develop within the unitary family.[3] In *Stanley*, for example, we forbade

2. We do not understand what Justice Brennan has in mind by an interest "that society traditionally has thought important . . . without protecting it." The protection need not take the form of an explicit constitutional provision or statutory guarantee, but it must at least exclude (all that is necessary to decide the present case) a societal tradition of enacting laws *denying* the interest. Nor do we understand why our practice of limiting the Due Process Clause to traditionally protected interests turns the Clause "into a redundancy," *post*, at 2351. Its purpose is to prevent future generations from lightly casting aside important traditional values—not to enable this Court to invent new ones.

3. Justice Brennan asserts that only a "pinched conception of 'the family' " would exclude Michael, Carole, and Victoria from protection. We disagree. The family unit accorded traditional respect in our society, which we have referred to as the "unitary family," is typified, of course, by the marital family, but also includes the household of unmarried parents and their children. Perhaps the concept can be expanded even beyond this, but it will bear no resemblance to traditionally respected relationships—and will thus cease to have any

the destruction of such a family when, upon the death of the mother, the State had sought to remove children from the custody of a father who had lived with and supported them and their mother for 18 years. As Justice Powell stated for the plurality in *Moore v. East Cleveland*: "Our decisions establish that the Constitution protects the sanctity of the family precisely because the institution of the family is deeply rooted in this Nation's history and tradition."

Thus, the legal issue in the present case reduces to whether the relationship between persons in the situation of Michael and Victoria has been treated as a protected family unit under the historic practices of our society, or whether on any other basis it has been accorded special protection. We think it impossible to find that it has. In fact, quite to the contrary, our traditions have protected the marital family (Gerald, Carole, and the child they acknowledge to be theirs) against the sort of claim Michael asserts.[4]

The presumption of legitimacy was a fundamental principle of the common law. Traditionally, that presumption could be rebutted only by proof that a husband was incapable of procreation or had had no access to his wife during the relevant period. As explained by Blackstone, nonaccess could only be proved "if the husband be out of the kingdom of England (or, as the law somewhat loosely phrases it, *extra quatuor maria* [beyond the four seas]) for above nine months. . . ." And, under the common law both in England and here, "neither husband nor wife [could] be a witness to prove access or nonaccess." The primary policy rationale underlying the common law's severe restrictions on rebuttal of the presumption appears to have been an aversion to declaring children illegitimate, thereby depriving them of rights of inheritance and succession, and likely making them wards of the state. A secondary policy concern was the interest in promoting the "peace and tranquillity of states and families," a goal that is obviously impaired by facilitating suits against husband and wife asserting that their children are illegitimate. Even though, as bastardy laws became less harsh, "[j]udges in both [England and the United States] gradually widened the acceptable range of evidence that could be offered by spouses, and placed restraints on the 'four seas rule' . . . [,] the law retained a strong bias against ruling the children of married women illegitimate."

We have found nothing in the older sources, nor in the older cases, addressing specifically the power of the natural father to assert parental rights over a child born into a woman's existing marriage with another man. Since it is Michael's burden to establish that such a power (at least where the natural father has established a relationship with the child) is so deeply embedded within our traditions as to be a fundamental right, the lack of evidence alone might defeat his case. But the evidence shows that even in modern times-when, as we have noted, the rigid protection of the marital family has in other respects been relaxed-the ability of a person in Michael's position to claim paternity has not been generally acknowledged. For example, a 1957 annotation on the subject: "Who may dispute presumption of legitimacy of child conceived or born during

constitutional significance—if it is stretched so far as to include the relationship established between a married woman, her lover, and their child, during a 3-month sojourn in St. Thomas, or during a subsequent 8-month period when, if he happened to be in Los Angeles, he stayed with her and the child.

4. Justice Brennan insists that in determining whether a liberty interest exists we must look at Michael's relationship with Victoria in isolation, without reference to the circumstance that Victoria's mother was married to someone else when the child was conceived, and that that woman and her husband wish to raise the child as their own. We cannot imagine what compels this strange procedure of looking at the act which is assertedly the subject of a liberty interest in isolation from its effect upon other people-rather like inquiring whether there is a liberty interest in firing a gun where the case at hand happens to involve its discharge into another person's body. The logic of Justice Brennan's position leads to the conclusion that if Michael had begotten Victoria by rape, that fact would in no way affect his possession of a liberty interest in his relationship with her.

wedlock," 53 A.L.R.2d 572, shows three States (including California) with statutes limiting standing to the husband or wife and their descendants, one State (Louisiana) with a statute limiting it to the husband, two states (Florida and Texas) with judicial decisions limiting standing to the husband, and two states (Illinois and New York) with judicial decisions denying standing even to the mother. Not a single decision is set forth specifically according standing to the natural father, and "express indications of the nonexistence of any . . . limitation" upon standing were found only "in a few jurisdictions."

Moreover, even if it were clear that one in Michael's position generally possesses, and has generally always possessed, standing to challenge the marital child's legitimacy, that would still not establish Michael's case. What is at issue here is not entitlement to a state pronouncement that Victoria was begotten by Michael. It is no conceivable denial of constitutional right for a State to decline to declare facts unless some legal consequence hinges upon the requested declaration. What Michael asserts here is a right to have himself declared the natural father *and thereby to obtain parental prerogatives*. What he must establish, therefore, is not that our society has traditionally allowed a natural father in his circumstances to establish paternity, but that it has traditionally accorded such a father parental rights, or at least has not traditionally denied them. Even if the law in all states had always been that the entire world could challenge the marital presumption and obtain a declaration as to who was the natural father, that would not advance Michael's claim. Thus, it is ultimately irrelevant, even for purposes of determining *current* social attitudes towards the alleged substantive right Michael asserts, that the present law in a number of states appears to allow the natural father-including the natural father who has not established a relationship with the child-the theoretical power to rebut the marital presumption. What counts is whether the states in fact award substantive parental rights to the natural father of a child conceived within, and born into, an extant marital union that wishes to embrace the child. We are not aware of a single case, old or new, that has done so. This is not the stuff of which fundamental rights qualifying as liberty interests are made.[6]

In *Lehr v. Robertson*, a case involving a natural father's attempt to block his child's adoption by the unwed mother's new husband, we observed that "[t]he significance of the biological connection is that it offers the natural father an opportunity that no other male possesses to develop a relationship with his offspring," and we assumed that the Constitution might require some protection of that opportunity. Where, however, the child is born into an extant marital family, the natural father's unique opportunity conflicts with the similarly unique opportunity of the husband of the marriage; and it is not unconstitutional for the State to give categorical preference to the latter. . . . In accord with our traditions, a limit is also imposed by the circumstance that the mother is, at the time of the child's conception and birth, married to, and cohabitating with, another man,

6. We do not understand why, having rejected our focus upon the societal tradition regarding the natural father's rights vis-à-vis a child whose mother is married to another man, Justice Brennan would choose to focus instead upon "parenthood." Why should the relevant category not be even more general-perhaps "family relationships"; or "personal relationships"; or even "emotional attachments in general"? Though the dissent has no basis for the level of generality it would select, we do: We refer to the most specific level at which a relevant tradition protecting, or denying protection to, the asserted right can be identified. . . . The need, if arbitrary decisionmaking is to be avoided, to adopt the most specific tradition as the point of reference-or at least to announce, as Justice Brennan declines to do, some other criterion for selecting among the innumerable relevant traditions that could be consulted-is well enough exemplified by the fact that in the present case Justice Brennan's opinion and Justice O'Connor's opinion, which disapproves this footnote, *both* appeal to tradition, but on the basis of the tradition they select reach opposite results. . . .

both of whom wish to raise the child as the offspring of their union.[7] It is a question of legislative policy and not constitutional law whether California will allow the presumed parenthood of a couple desiring to retain a child conceived within and born into their marriage to be rebutted.

We do not accept Justice Brennan's criticism that this result "squashes" the liberty that consists of "the freedom not to conform." It seems to us that reflects the erroneous view that there is only one side to this controversy—that one disposition can expand a "liberty" of sorts without contracting an equivalent "liberty" on the other side. Such a happy choice is rarely available. Here, to *provide* protection to an adulterous natural father is to *deny* protection to a marital father, and vice versa. If Michael has a "freedom not to conform" (whatever that means), Gerald must equivalently have a "freedom to conform." One of them will pay a price for asserting that "freedom"—Michael by being unable to act as father of the child he has adulterously begotten, or Gerald by being unable to preserve the integrity of the traditional family unit he and Victoria have established. Our disposition does not choose between these two "freedoms," but leaves that to the people of California. Justice Brennan's approach chooses one of them as the constitutional imperative, on no apparent basis except that the unconventional is to be preferred.

IV

We have never had occasion to decide whether a child has a liberty interest, symmetrical with that of her parent, in maintaining her filial relationship. We need not do so here because, even assuming that such a right exists, Victoria's claim must fail. Victoria's due process challenge is, if anything, weaker than Michael's. Her basic claim is not that California has erred in preventing her from establishing that Michael, not Gerald, should stand as her legal father. Rather, she claims a due process right to maintain filial relationships with both Michael and Gerald. This assertion merits little discussion, for, whatever the merits of the guardian ad litem's belief that such an arrangement can be of great psychological benefit to a child, the claim that a State must recognize multiple fatherhood has no support in the history or traditions of this country. Moreover, even if we were to construe Victoria's argument as forwarding the lesser proposition that, whatever her status vis-à-vis Gerald, she has a liberty interest in maintaining a filial relationship with her natural father, Michael, we find that, at best, her claim is the obverse of Michael's and fails for the same reasons.

Victoria claims in addition that her equal protection rights have been violated because, unlike her mother and presumed father, she had no opportunity to rebut the presumption of her legitimacy. We find this argument wholly without merit. . . . The primary rationale underlying §621's limitation on those who may rebut the presumption of legitimacy is a concern that allowing persons other than the husband or wife to do so may undermine the integrity of the marital union. When the husband or wife contests the legitimacy of their child, the stability of the marriage has already been shaken. In contrast, allowing a claim of illegitimacy to be pressed by the child—or, more accurately, by a court-appointed guardian ad litem—may well disrupt an otherwise peaceful union. Since it

7. Justice Brennan chides us for thus limiting our holding to situations in which, as here, the husband and wife wish to raise her child jointly. . . . We limit our pronouncement to the relevant facts of this case because it is at least possible that our traditions lead to a different conclusion with regard to adulterous fathering of a child whom the marital parents do not wish to raise as their own. It seems unfair for those who disagree with our holding to include among their criticisms that we have not extended the holding more broadly.

pursues a legitimate end by rational means, California's decision to treat Victoria differently from her parents is not a denial of equal protection.

Justice Brennan, with Justices Marshall and Blackmun, dissenting.

. . . Five Members of the Court refuse to foreclose "the possibility that a natural father might ever have a constitutionally protected interest in his relationship with a child whose mother was married to, and cohabiting with, another man at the time of the child's conception and birth." . . . Four Members of the Court agree that Michael H. has a liberty interest in his relationship with Victoria, and one assumes for purposes of this case that he does, see *ante* (Stevens, J., concurring in judgment). . . . If we had looked to tradition with such specificity in past cases, many a decision would have reached a different result. Surely the use of contraceptives by unmarried couples, *Eisenstadt v. Baird* (1972), or even by married couples, *Griswold v. Connecticut* (1965) . . . and even the right to raise one's natural but illegitimate children, *Stanley*, were not "interest[s] traditionally protected by our society" at the time of their consideration by this Court. . . .

In the plurality's constitutional universe, we may not take notice of the fact that the original reasons for the conclusive presumption of paternity are out of place in a world in which blood tests can prove virtually beyond a shadow of a doubt who sired a particular child and in which the fact of illegitimacy no longer plays the burdensome and stigmatizing role it once did. Nor, in the plurality's world, may we deny "tradition" its full scope by pointing out that the rationale for the conventional rule has changed over the years . . . ;[1] instead, our task is simply to identify a rule denying the asserted interest and not to ask whether the basis for that rule-which is the true reflection of the values undergirding it-has changed too often or too recently to call the rule embodying that rationale a "tradition." . . .

. . . The better approach—indeed, the one commanded by our prior cases and by common sense—is to ask whether the specific parent-child relationship under consideration is close enough to the interests that we already have protected to be deemed an aspect of "liberty" as well. . . . [Our prior decisions] produced a unifying theme: although an unwed father's biological link to his child does not, in and of itself, guarantee him a constitutional stake in his relationship with that child, such a link combined with a substantial parent-child relationship will do so.[2] "When an unwed father demonstrates a full commitment to the responsibilities of parenthood by 'com[ing] forward to participate in the rearing of his child,' . . . his interest in personal contact with his child acquires substantial protection under the Due Process Clause. At that point it may be said that he 'act[s] as a father toward his children.'" . . . Michael H. is almost certainly Victoria D.'s natural father, has lived with her as her father, has contributed to her support, and has from the beginning sought to strengthen and maintain his relationship with her.

Yet they are not, in the plurality's view, a "unitary family," whereas Gerald, Carole, and Victoria do compose such a family. The only difference between these two sets of relationships, however, is the fact of marriage. . . . However, the very premise of *Stanley* and the cases following it is that marriage is not decisive in answering the question whether the

1. See In re Marriage of Sharyne and Stephen B., 124 Cal. App. 3d 524 (1981) (noting that California courts initially justified conclusive presumption of paternity on the ground that biological paternity was impossible to prove, but that the preservation of family integrity became the rule's paramount justification when paternity tests became reliable).

2. The plurality's claim that "[t]he logic of [my] position leads to the conclusion that if Michael had begotten Victoria by rape, that fact would in no way affect his possession of a liberty interest in his relationship with her," ignores my observation that a mere biological connection is insufficient to establish a liberty interest on the part of an unwed father. . . .

Constitution protects the parental relationship under consideration. These cases are, after all, important precisely because they involve the rights of *unwed* fathers. It is important to remember, moreover, that in *Quilloin, Caban,* and *Lehr,* the putative father's demands would have disrupted a "unitary family" as the plurality defines it; in each case, the husband of the child's mother sought to adopt the child over the objections of the natural father. Significantly, our decisions in those cases in no way relied on the need to protect the marital family. . . . [The plurality's] pinched conception of "the family" . . . is jarring in light of our many cases preventing the states from denying important interests or statuses to those whose situations do not fit the government's narrow view of the family. From *Loving v. Virginia* (1967), to *Levy v. Louisiana* (1968), and *Glona v. American Guarantee & Liability Ins. Co.* (1968), and from *Gomez v. Perez* (1973), to *Moore v. East Cleveland* (1977), we have declined to respect a State's notion, as manifested in its allocation of privileges and burdens, of what the family should be. Today's rhapsody on the "unitary family" is out of tune with such decisions.

The plurality's focus on the "unitary family" is misdirected for another reason. It conflates the question whether a liberty interest exists with the question what procedures may be used to terminate or curtail it. It is no coincidence that we never before have looked at the relationship that the unwed father seeks to disrupt, rather than the one he seeks to preserve, in determining whether he has a liberty interest in his relationship with his child. To do otherwise is to allow the State's interest in terminating the relationship to play a role in defining the "liberty" that is protected by the Constitution. According to our established framework under the Due Process Clause, however, we first ask whether the person claiming constitutional protection has an interest that the Constitution recognizes; if we find that he or she does, we next consider the State's interest in limiting the extent of the procedures that will attend the deprivation of that interest. By stressing the need to preserve the "unitary family" and by focusing not just on the relationship between Michael and Victoria but on their "situation" as well, today's plurality opinion takes both of these steps at once.

The plurality's . . . careful limitation of its holding . . . suggests that if Carole or Gerald alone wished to raise Victoria, or if both were dead and the State wished to raise her, Michael and Victoria might be found to have a liberty interest in their relationship with each other. But that would be to say that whether Michael and Victoria have a liberty interest varies with the State's interest in recognizing that interest, for it is the State's interest in protecting the marital family—and not Michael and Victoria's interest in their relationship with each other—that varies with the status of Carole and Gerald's relationship.

The atmosphere surrounding today's decision is one of make-believe. Beginning with the suggestion that the situation confronting us here does not repeat itself every day in every corner of the country, moving on to the claim that it is tradition alone that supplies the details of the liberty that the Constitution protects, and passing finally to the notion that the Court always has recognized a cramped vision of "the family," today's decision lets stand California's pronouncement that Michael—whom blood tests show to a 98 percent probability to be Victoria's father—is not Victoria's father. When and if the Court awakes to reality, it will find a world very different from the one it expects.

Generally speaking, a plurality decision rejecting a constitutional challenge to a state law establishes little except that a law like the one challenged is constitutional, at least as applied to persons similarly situated to the losing plaintiffs. In all U.S. states today, however, state statutes or common law make the marital presumption rebuttable by a putative father. But cf. E.W. v. T.S., 916 A.2d 1197 (Pa. Super. Ct. 2007) (refusing to order husband to undergo genetic test so that putative father could disprove husband's marital presumption of paternity, even though paternity statute clearly contemplated putative father's contesting marital presumption based on genetic tests). California law at that time was unusual in making the marital presumption "conclusive," and the state legislature later amended the law to make the presumption rebuttable. See Cal. Fam. Code §7541. Moreover, the plurality indicated that they might come out differently even as to a conclusive marital presumption in circumstances where mother and husband were not together. The European Court of Human Rights reached such a decision in Kroon v. Netherlands, ECHR 18535/91 (1994), holding that in such circumstances application of Netherlands' conclusive marital presumption of paternity to a biological father who had established a relationship with his child violated the man's "right to respect for his private and family life" under Article 8 of the European Convention on Human Rights.

Does it make sense to say that whether a biological father has a constitutional right to legal parent status depends on whether the mother is married to and living with another man? Or should such a fact instead be a consideration in assessing whether the state has sufficient justification for infringing such a right? The dissenters maintain that Michael does have a protected liberty interest, but do they suggest how they would balance that interest against the state's interest in protecting the unitary family Carole and Gerald had formed with Victoria? What is really best for a child in such a situation?

Though *Michael H.* was a plurality decision, it might nevertheless have significance beyond its specific conclusion, because the plurality's approach to consecrating substantive due process rights has become the dominant approach, and because the several opinions as a whole reflect a devaluing of an adult's biological connection to a child. It is implicit in the plurality opinion that biology alone does not trigger any constitutional protection, and Justice Brennan's dissent says this more explicitly. Lower courts have generally held that biology alone does not give rise to constitutional protection for unwed fathers. See, e.g., Randy A.J. v. Norma I.J, 677 N.W.2d 630 (Wis. 2004); Dawn D. v. Superior Court, 952 P.2d 1139, 1144-1145 (Cal. 1998).

What interest does a man have as a result of being the biological father of a child per se? It seems that knowledge of this fact generates a certain longing in him to have a connection with the child, but how important is an interest in having that longing satisfied? Is it more important than having satisfied a longing for a relationship with a particular woman? That interest receives no constitutional protection absent a reciprocal longing on her part. What is different about the longing for a parent-child relationship, and why should any such difference have constitutional significance?

Is it plausible to maintain that children have a constitutional right presumptively to be raised by their biological parents? How important is the biological connection, as an empirical matter, for the flourishing of parent-child relationships and for the welfare of children, relative to other considerations? Might it be different for the mother-child relationship than it is for the father-child relationship?

William Marsiglio, Procreative Man

33-34 (N.Y.U. Press 1997)

Regardless of what types of social structures our early ancestors were accustomed to, it is safe to assume that for a considerable period of time prehistoric humans did not recognize that men played a role in reproducing children. Men had intercourse with women because it was instinctive and physiologically pleasurable. . . . [T]hese males probably witnessed, or were at least aware, that the females with whom they had had sex were also undergoing physiological changes during gestation and eventually bearing children in many cases. However, for a long time they did not have a clue as to why these females were experiencing these changes.

Ira Reiss, a sociologist, has speculated that the physiologically gratifying experience of copulation, not knowledge of their paternity, first lead some males to bond with female partners and to develop feelings toward their partners' offspring. . . . In discussing the probable living patterns of the protohominids who lived some eight million years ago, Helen Fisher posits that a selection process took place where females with physiological attributes that enabled them to be more sexually active were able to gain advantages for themselves and their children. She argues that this process leads to what she refers to as the "sexual contract":

> As generations passed, selection gradually produced more and more female protohominids who copulated for a longer period of their monthly cycle; who made love during pregnancy; who had sex sooner after parturition. Protohominid females were beginning to lose their period of heat. . . . With the stimulus of constantly available sex, protohominids had begun the most fundamental exchange the human race would ever make. Males and females were learning to divide their labors, to exchange meat and vegetables, to share their daily catch. Constant sex had begun to tie them to one another and economic dependence was tightening the knot.

Fisher goes on to suggest that some females were supposedly more capable than others of deriving intense physical pleasures from their sexual episodes. Consequently, she argues that a selection process enhanced the chances for survival for highly sexualized females. In her words:

> These components of an extremely high sex drive are not necessary for procreation today, and they weren't necessary millions of years ago either. But they were essential to survival—because the males liked them. They were sex attractants and those who had them clinched economic ties with males. These females lived. They reproduced. Their children lived with the economic prosperity induced by male attention, and the phenomenally high sex drive of the female protohominid was passed along to the females of today.

If we accept this theory of human evolution, then it is likely that men had occasion to extend their protective child care services and affection to children born to their favorite sexual partner(s). This may have occurred even though, unbeknownst to them, the children had actually been sired by other men. Thus, being involved with and taking care of children was coincidental for men in that they were available to partake in some of these activities primarily because they were interested in having sex with the children's mother. Their commitment to "their" children was therefore not based on their concern for biological relatedness, rather interpersonal ties fueled their familial commitment. . . .

Elizabeth Bartholet, Guiding Principles for Picking Parents

27 Harv. Women's L.J. 323 (2004)

. . . [B]iology has never been all-determinative in defining parentage, whether in nature or under law. In nature some animals are raised by both biological parents, but in most species "fathers" exist only in the sense that they create life. Further, like humans, animals sometimes "adopt" others' offspring.

For as long as law has governed various family matters among humans, it has looked at biology as only one among a number of factors to be used in deciding how to allocate parental rights and responsibilities. . . . The dominant trend in law today is in the direction of reducing the importance of biology as a factor in defining parentage. Increasing emphasis is being placed on established and intended parenting relationships, . . . in part to deal with the new complexity of family life, as the nuclear family has broken up and children are more often dependent on nurturing relationships with people other than their genetic parents. Both courts and legislatures have helped develop the functional parent doctrine, giving those who have developed actual parenting relationships with children the right to come into court and compete for some piece of the total parenting rights package with those who became parents through biology. . . .

Sociobiology, or evolutionary psychology, is enjoying something of a revival today, providing new energy for claims that genetics should play a yet more important role than it has traditionally in defining parentage. Some of its adherents claim that, because of "biological favoritism," child rearing by nonrelatives is "inherently problematic." They say that human beings, like the rest of the animal kingdom, are genetically programmed to produce and to favor their own progeny over others': "It is not that unrelated individuals are unable to do the job of parenting, it is just that they are not as likely to do the job well." Richard Dawkins, who has done much to popularize evolutionary psychology, describes adoption as a "mistake," a "misfiring of a built-in rule." He claims that "the generous female is doing her own genes no good by caring for the orphan. She is wasting time and energy that she could be investing in the lives of her own kin, particularly future children of her own." Martin Daly and Margo Wilson, leading proponents of evolutionary psychology, write in their well-known *Homicide* book:

> Perhaps the most obvious prediction from a Darwinian view of parental motives is this: Substitute parents will generally tend to care less profoundly for children than natural parents, with the result that children reared by people other than their natural parents will be more often exploited and otherwise at risk. Parental investment is a precious resource, and selection must favor those parental psyches that do not squander it on nonrelatives. Sexual strategies theory promotes a related claim—that men are genetically programmed to choose women who will faithfully raise their progeny. Thus, when DNA evidence shows that a child a man thought was his biological child is not his, revealing that the woman has betrayed him, he reacts with anger toward both the woman and the child.

. . . Daly and Wilson's well-known study of step-parenting . . . purports to provide empirical grounding for the biological favoritism claim, by demonstrating higher rates of abuse, both physical and sexual, in stepparent households and by stepparents as compared to genetically related parents within households. However, some highly respected research questions the generally accepted conclusion that stepparents are in fact disproportionately responsible for abuse. Even assuming the higher abuse rates claimed, Daly and Wilson's arguments . . . fail entirely to address the many obvious factors other than genetics that could explain disproportionate abuse in stepparent households. . . .

The stepparent evidence is in any event countered by powerful evidence that looks in the opposite direction. . . . Adoption studies show adoptive parent-child relationships working essentially as well as biological parent-child relationships. . . . Carbone and Cahn's analysis of studies of fathers who move from one adult relationship to another show that these men appear to care more for the non-related children with whom they are living than the related children they left behind. Apparently, any "biological favoritism" that may exist is outweighed by the adult relationship factor. Carbone and Cahn show that biological favoritism theorists typically fail to take into account the complexity of human beings and their institutional lives:

> Humans act not just through direct provisions for their children and indifference (or even hostility) toward others but through the creation of complex customs and institutions that instill values and habits including altruism and selfishness. The trick in using sociobiology to make sense of parental behavior therefore lies in identifying the competing tendencies and the possible tradeoffs among them.

. . . Biology may matter. Human beings may be genetically programmed to prefer their genetic offspring over other children. But factors other than biology also matter in shaping parenting desires and capacities. Social conditioning has a huge impact. Moreover, it seems likely that we would maximize human happiness if we were to shape our culture in ways that reduced rather than reinforced any natural tendency to prefer our genetic relatives over others. . . . [A] weak version of the biological favoritism thesis seems plausible and fits with a broadly shared sense that it is "natural" to want to create and raise genetic progeny. It should be possible to cater to this desire while simultaneously encouraging love for unrelated others.

Children also have at least some significant interest in knowing their biological heritage. Certainly this is true in a society that places the high value ours does on that heritage. . . . So in cases where it does not make sense for the genetic parent to be the legal parent, we should consider giving children at least an informational link with the genetic parent. This is complicated, because in a society that over-values genetics, as I believe ours does, creating that informational link risks exacerbating this problem, adding to the sense that genetics are overwhelmingly important. It may also create pressure to define the biological parent as the legal parent. However, we need to move forward to a stage where we can put biology in its place and keep it there. We need to recognize that in some situations the genetic contributor is a relevant person, but a nonparent, and the social parent is a fully real legal parent. . . .

NOTES AND QUESTIONS

How strong are children's interests in being raised by biological parents in a "normal" family? Is it much less today than it was decades ago when adoption was rare? What should be made of the search many adopted children undertake to find their biological parents? Certainly not all adopted children undertake such a search, and the situation of children who are adopted (who usually know that they were adopted) might be quite different from the situation of children, like Victoria in *Michael H.*, whose legal father is such by virtue of a marital presumption. But those who in any context advocate placing great weight on biological parenthood in creating and maintaining legal parent-child relationships often point to this phenomenon of searching for birth parents as demonstrating that the state should do everything it can to make sure children grow up in the custody of their biological parents. Does it in fact demonstrate that? Is wanting information about one's biological parents, or wanting to meet one's biological parents, equivalent to concluding that one would have been better off if raised by one's biological parents (with whatever dysfunctions they might have had) rather than by one's adoptive parents?

Many adopted children also report feeling a sense of loss for most of their lives. Again, though, one must be careful not to make an illogical inference from the assumption that persons have a certain interest (here, in avoiding a permanent sense of loss) to the conclusion that serving that interest is more important than any other consideration or even to the conclusion that such an interest is very weighty. It might be that all or most people go through life with some significant misgivings about lost opportunities of one sort or another—for example, a career or relationship they failed to pursue. In addition, there might be more than one way to serve a given interest. With respect to adoptions, Professor Bartholet alludes to an alternative way of serving children's interest in knowing their biological parents and heritage—open adoption, which has been the subject of much scholarly and political discussion. Should it satisfy an unwed father to be told after his offspring is adopted without his consent, or if he were excluded from paternity because not in a relationship with the mother, that the child would be told about him and perhaps meet him someday? Should the state care about satisfying him, or should its focus just be on what is best for the child or on what the child's birth mother wants?

Unwed Fathers Disrupting Adoptions

The Supreme Court's unwed father decisions are currently having their greatest impact in the realm of adoptions. Generally, state laws in the United States require the consent of biological parents to an adoption, unless the biological parents' legal status has previously been terminated in a child protection proceeding. This is in most states an ironclad requirement with respect to birth mothers, but states have in various ways increasingly weakened the requirement as to unwed fathers. In some states, an unwed father's consent is not required if he has not had custody of the child or taken steps to legally establish his paternity prior to the filing of a divorce petition. See, e.g., Alaska Stat. §25.23.040; Ark. Code Ann. §9-9-206. Many states' laws provide for overriding an unwed father's objection to an adoption where he has failed to communicate with the child for a lengthy period or failed to support the mother during pregnancy. See, e.g., Ark. Code Ann. §9-9-207(a); Fla. Stat. §63.064; Ohio Rev. Code Ann. §3107.07; Wash. Rev. Code §26.33.120. A few authorize adoption over the biological father's objection simply on the basis of a finding that his objection is contrary to the child's best interests. See, e.g., Alaska Stat. §25.23.180(c); Cal. Fam. Code §7664; Iowa Code §600.7; Mass. Gen. L. 210 §3. In the United Kingdom, by way of comparison, the consent of the birth mother *and* the biological father can be waived based just on a finding that "the welfare of the child requires the consent to be dispensed with." Adoption and Children Act of 2002, §52(1).

Whenever state law allows for adoption of a child without the biological father's consent, that invites a constitutional challenge by such men, based on the Supreme Court decisions. Even where state adoption law is very protective of biological fathers, such men who object to adoption of their offspring might need to invoke the Supreme Court doctrine, if an adoption goes forward despite state law because the biological father is not notified of the proceedings until after the child is placed with adopting parents. Once the child is placed, adopting parents might assert an associational right of the child or themselves against operation of state statutes, or they might live in a different state, one that is less protective of biological fathers. Following public outrage at a few "disrupted adoption" cases in the 1990s, when after several years of litigation children four or five years of age were taken away from adoptive parents and handed over to biological fathers, several states passed laws to protect children's interests in those situations. See Diane S. Kaplan, *The Baby Richard Amendments and the Law of Unintended Consequences*, 22 CHILD. LEGAL RTS. J. (Winter 2002-2003). These laws dictate that, if an adoption must be undone because of a violation of a biological father's statutory rights, a court should hold a best-interests hearing to determine what should be done next, and can order that adoptive parents retain custody, as guardians. Biological fathers are likely to challenge these laws as unconstitutional.

For accounts of recent disrupted adoption cases, see Mary McCarty, *"Baby Vanessa" Improperly Taken from Ohio, Biological Father Argues*, DAYTON DAILY NEWS, Mar. 8, 2011; Lou Grieco, *Baby Vanessa's Father Sentenced to Prison*, DAYTON DAILY NEWS, June 14, 2011; Matt Thacker, *Ohio Supreme Court Will Not Reconsider Vaughn Adoption Decision*, NewsAndTribune.com, Oct. 7, 2010; Larua Oren, *Thwarted Fathers or Pop-Up Pops?: How to Determine When Putative Fathers Can Block the Adoption of Their Newborn Children*, 40 FAM. L.Q. 153 (2006).

One moral and policy question such cases raise is to what extent a mother should be able to decide the future care of her child, as against the wishes of the biological father.

Katharine K. Baker, Bargaining or Biology? The History and Future of Paternity Law and Parental Status

14 Cornell J.L. & Pub. Pol'y 1 (2004)

. . . [T]he law should abandon its interest in determining biological paternity. The legal rights and duties of fatherhood should emanate from commitment and contract, not from sex or genes. . . . [This article] suggests and defends two ideas that are likely to be controversial. First, a gestational mother holds all initial rights and obligations to a child. With some built-in limitations, the mother has parental rights and obligations to contract away as she chooses. Second, the obligation to support a child can be limited temporally, so that the paternal obligation reflects what was bargained for in the agreement between mother and father, not a static notion of fatherhood. . . . Alternatively, as is the case in many other countries, biological fathers could be held accountable for their reproductive activity without necessarily becoming legal fathers. . . . This kind of partial responsibility could deter irresponsible sexual behavior without making fathers out of people who never intended to be or acted as parents. . . .

III. THE CONTRACT

. . . De facto, if not de jure, it is the gestational mother who controls whether a biological father or any other person is able to establish a relationship with the child and thereby secure parental rights. As a preliminary matter, it is the pregnant woman and only the pregnant woman who decides whether to remain pregnant. Once that decision is made, the pregnant woman can, with remarkable ease, prevent a biological father from ever knowing about a child's existence. For biological parents who are not living together, it is the woman who decides whether the biological father knows about the pregnancy, how participatory the biological father (or any other potential "father") can be during the pregnancy, and, at least when the child is young, how much contact the father can have. She can thereby all but ensure that his parental rights will never be exercised. She can also take measures to make it very likely that parental status will be vested in someone else. She can do that by marrying someone else, letting someone else adopt the child, or simply sharing her life with someone else. As numerous researchers have found, women have always determined the extent of paternal involvement with children. From conception on, de facto parental status is something that the woman has and can, at her discretion, mete out to someone else.

Although courts have never put it in these terms, the above suggests that the gestational mother gains parental status through her gestational investment, not through her genetic contribution. A father gains parental status through his relationship with the mother. If the gestational mother has not contracted her labor out (in a gestational surrogacy contract) or previously agreed (through marriage or another form of contract) to share parental rights, then she has exclusive control. Once she agrees, either explicitly or implicitly, to share that control, she has a co-parent.

To some, this paradigm may seem highly unfair. The woman, by virtue of labor that a man cannot give, has more access to parenthood than a man. Yet the very same factors that make it unfair to hold an unwilling man liable for a child that he never wanted make it appropriate to vest the gestational mother with sole parental status. It is her decision to undergo the huge and very costly burdens of pregnancy. Up until birth, the mother has, of necessity, invested far more of herself than has the biological father. Conscientious men may try to invest time and money in the pregnancy, but the decision as to whether to accept that effort is the mother's. At a very basic level, there is simply no comparison between what a mother necessarily gives during pregnancy and what a man can give. Thus, by virtue of her sole responsibility and labor, the mother obtains sole parental rights. It follows, then, that she should shoulder the entire obligation. . . .

To a certain extent, the degree to which a mother shares the rights and responsibilities that she acquires by virtue of gestation is up to her, but the number of people she can contract with and the extent to which she can completely alienate her parental status must be limited. Scholars disagree about the relative harms and benefits of multiple parental figures in a child's life, but most can probably agree that there should be some limit on the number of legal "parents" a child should have. The more adults who have standing to assert visitation rights and challenge the parenting decisions of others, the greater the likelihood of litigation. . . . The extraordinary pecuniary and emotional toll this can take on a child suggests that, for the child's sake, the law should limit the number of contracts a mother can make with regard to any one child.

On the other hand, if a father abandons a mother and child, the mother should be able to contract with someone else. . . . If she contracts with someone else, that new person becomes the father with his own parental rights and obligations. The first father stays obligated until the mother contracts with someone else. Once she does, the first father loses rights and obligations. This is what currently happens in the adoption context. . . .

Unfortunately, parenting studies suggest that abandonment by fathers is common. Nearly 40% of children do not live with their fathers. Only one in six children in fatherless households see their father at least once a week. 40% of children who live in fatherless households have not seen their fathers at all in the past year. The chances of a child not having seen his or her father increase with time. One study found that ten years after divorce, nearly two-thirds of the children of those divorces had not seen their father at all in the past year. Abandonment by mothers is not unheard of, but noncustodial mothers are much more likely than noncustodial fathers to visit their children. . . .

The prevalence of abandonment by fathers suggests that a legal label of father does not keep men sufficiently connected to their children to ensure that child support gets paid or that contact is maintained. Thus, it is not clear we would have any fewer involved and paying fathers if the law acknowledged such abandonment and deprived abandoning fathers of their legal status as parents. . . . If, because they could avoid child support, most men would avoid having children in their lives, it tells us something remarkably disturbing about the likelihood that men will be responsible parents. If we cannot count on men to be responsible parents, it is not clear why we should be concerned about granting them parental rights at all. . . .

The financial and emotional burdens of single parenthood, though not insurmountable, are significant. By finding someone with whom to share those burdens, a mother helps ensure that a child has both the emotional and financial support that he or she needs. Currently, the law often assigns a second parent on the basis of biology. Empirical research and common sense suggest that biology alone is a significantly inferior proxy of willingness to support than is an agreement with the mother. . . . Far more deliberation and concern is likely to go into a decision as to whether to share one's life with a woman and her child than is likely to go into a decision as to whether to have sex.

In sum, the entitlement at issue in parenting contracts is the entitlement to parental rights and responsibilities. As an initial matter, unless she has already agreed to share part of that entitlement, the mother has an exclusive right to that entitlement. If she has agreed to share it, the person with whom she has so agreed is the other parent. . . . If a former contracting partner has abandoned, a new person may assume the previous partner's status by contracting with the mother. Some examples may help bring the various strands of this proposal together.

1. THE EASY CASES

Frank . . . slept with a woman named Pamela, who told him she was using birth control when she knew that she was not. Pamela got pregnant and sued Frank for child support. In 1983, New York's highest court found Frank liable for child support in an amount proportional to what he earned. Under the proposed regime, Frank would not be liable for child support, nor would he have any rights as a father. The rights and responsibilities for any child born of the sexual liaison would be vested in Pamela alone unless and until she found someone else willing to assume the role of father.

Tamara Budnick and Frederick Silverman signed an agreement in which they agreed that Frederick would not assume any responsibility for a child born of their sexual liaison. In 2002, a Florida court found Silverman responsible for child support notwithstanding the contract. Under the proposed regime, he would not be responsible because the contract clearly indicates his intent not to parent.

Ann and Dudley Nygard met in July of 1982. In October of 1982, Ann discovered that she was 5 months pregnant. Dudley asked Ann to stay with him, notwithstanding both of their knowledge that the pregnancy could not have resulted from their sexual activity. He also agreed "to raise the child as his own." . . . A Michigan court ordered Dudley to pay child support, finding either that the oral contract was enforceable, or, if the statute of frauds barred enforcement of the contract, that Dudley was bound under doctrines of equitable or promissory estoppel. Under the proposed regime, the case would come out precisely the same way. . . .

2. THE HARDER CASES

Amy and Tom dated fairly regularly but were not married. Amy got pregnant. Tom supported her emotionally and with some financial assistance throughout the pregnancy. He was present at the birth of the child (Lisa) and stayed as a regular presence in Amy and

Lisa's life until Lisa was three years old. He contributed to Amy's household, paying for food, clothes, and other expenses for Lisa. By the time Lisa was three, Tom began to drift away. He was around much less and contributed almost nothing. By the time Lisa was four, Amy no longer knew where he was.

At this point, Amy could sue for paternity. The suit would be based on an implicit promise to support and not based on Tom's blood relationship to Lisa. The facts of this paternity case would look remarkably similar to the average facts alleged in paternity suits now. . . . What would likely be different is the extent of Tom's obligation. Tom would be liable for an amount of support that reflected Ann's reasonable reliance on his contributions. For instance, he could be liable for three years of subsequent support. During those three years he would have full parental rights. If he paid for those three years—and at any time prior to the end of those three years—he would have the right to opt into permanent parental status. If he did so, the amount of his obligation would be determined by standard child support guidelines.

If Amy did not sue Tom for paternity, it is very likely that another man (call him Bill) would enter Amy and Lisa's life and assume a parent-like role. As Bill provided continuing emotional and financial support to Amy and Lisa's household, he would make himself potentially responsible and potentially protected as a father. Whether Bill became legally responsible would depend on whether Tom had drifted away. If Tom was an obvious presence in Lisa's life, then there could be no reasonable reliance on Bill as father. However, if Tom ceased acting as father, he would be deemed to have abandoned his paternal relationship, and Bill could assume that role either explicitly or implicitly. Again, the facts of this situation are common. If Amy and Bill explicitly agreed that Bill should assume parental status, the situation would be functionally identical to the hundreds of stepparent adoptions that currently happen every year in this country. . . . Under the proposed model, a court should be free to infer such an agreement in the absence of explicit words or contract. Once that agreement can be inferred from the parties' behavior, Bill can sue Amy to maintain contact with Lisa if Amy tries to bar him from such, and Ann can sue Bill for support if Bill drifts away like Tom. . . .

IV. Advantages and Disadvantages

. . . At this point, readers concerned about sex equality are probably bristling at the labels of mother and father. . . . [T]his article uses the term mother in its biological and social sense, but not necessarily in the sense that it means "female parent." Comparably, it uses the term father to mean "partner of mother" and not necessarily "male parent." . . . What need not be salient is the sex of the person parenting. If a man is mothering a child because the female parent has abandoned the child, or for any other reason, then the law should treat that man as a mother. If a woman is fathering a child by supporting the family structure economically while someone else is doing more of the caretaking, then the law should treat that woman as a father. If both parents are doing identical jobs, then the labels are irrelevant anyway. . . .

Of course, the one place where sex is salient is at birth. Men cannot mother a child in utero. . . . Rewarding that investment with superior rights simply reflects a principle basic to the common law and to more recent trends in family law rewarding investment with rights. Refusing to honor what is unquestionably a greater contribution smacks more of oppression than equality. . . .

The distinction between mothers and fathers proposed here builds on Martha Fineman's suggestion to restructure the family relationship around the caretaking-based parent-child dyad instead of the sexually-based husband-wife dyad. . . . Fineman . . . has made us all realize how much dependencies beget dependencies. By taking care of dependents, caretakers become dependent because the person in need of care demands the time, resources, and energy that the caretaker would otherwise use to take care of herself. The proposed model recognizes that women often try to meet these dependencies by entering into relationships with others. It recognizes that in meeting those dependencies men must not be viewed simply as generous philanthropists, but as individuals willingly undertaking obligations in return for benefits. It forces men to take their family obligations seriously because it holds them responsible only for those obligations that they have willfully accepted.

Where this proposal differs from Fineman's is in its ability to incorporate fathers and reward them when they deserve it. . . . [A] world in which women have all the parental power and all the parental responsibility is not necessarily a feminist ideal. . . . Women want someone with whom to share the physical, financial, and emotional burdens and they want someone with whom to share the joy. . . . To make it worthwhile for men to share in the hardships and the fun, the law must be prepared to honor the sacrifices they make in parenting and the desires they demonstrate to parent.

By honoring those sacrifices and desires, the proposed model draws men into the family unit, but in a much more rational and just fashion than does contemporary paternity law. Instead of relying on confused and inconsistent invocations of punishment and deterrence, the proposed model links parental status to a willful acceptance of parental responsibility. Instead of assuming that genetic contribution gives rise to moral responsibility, the proposed model assumes that parental participation gives rise to moral responsibility. . . . [T]he proposed model links the child's entitlement to what the child and his or her primary caretaker have bargained for and come to rely on. It also links parental obligation to parental rights in a way that can explain why someone must continue to pay support even if he is not acting as a parent. He must continue to pay because he agreed to pay. . . .

Even if the proposed system did require greater governmental expenditure on children, budgeting for those resources would do nothing more than bring the United states up to par with the rest of the industrialized world. The current scheme in this country, which assumes bilateral obligation stemming from blood and assumes that two parents acting alone should be able to meet all of the needs of children, is followed virtually nowhere else in the world. . . . [W]ith the exceptions of China and the United States, every industrialized country has a family allowance program that provides regular cash payments to families with children regardless of need. . . . In other words, most of the industrialized world does not consider the dependency of youth a matter of private concern. If the United States could sever its allegiance to privatizing the dependency of youth, the proposed contractual framework would appear both less radical and less costly. . . . Collective responsibility for children should follow from the fact that children, like the elderly, are needy, and not from the fact that they are fatherless.

Moreover, . . . if we are deeply concerned about the moral obligation or deterrent functions that a biologically-based paternity system may serve, a tax on biological fathers could serve those functions just as well while providing additional income for children. Again looking at the United States' peer countries, most biological fathers pay something towards support of their children, but what they pay is a fraction of the subsidy that caretakers receive. The government assumes the primary responsibility for providing a minimum standard of support. Moreover, these biological fathers usually have limited, if any, parental rights. What this means is that men have less of a need to avoid detection (because they will not be responsible for that much support) and mothers have less need to hide the biological father's identity (because he cannot meaningfully interfere with her parental rights). These differences may well account for the vastly different rates of paternity establishment in the United States and its peer countries. In most of the United States' peer countries, the paternity establishment rate for children of unmarried mothers hovers around 90%. In the United States, it is 30%. Thus, perhaps ironically, making biological fatherhood significantly less important legally may make it easier to find and secure money from biological fathers.

Professor Baker's proposal, in relation to non-marital births, resembles the law of a half century ago, which largely treated unwed fathers as non-parents unless and until they entered into a marriage with the mother. Under that regime, unwed fathers might have access to a child only if the mother voluntarily allowed it, which she might do only in exchange for support. What effect might it have on men's attitudes toward parenting to return to that regime? Would it reverse progress that has been made in encouraging more involved fathering? Conversely, might it foster a salutary perception of parenthood as an earned privilege rather than a right based on nothing more than having had sex?

Is Professor Baker persuasive in justifying a post-dissolution support obligation for partners who are not a child's biological father? She states that "the proposed model links the child's entitlement to what the child and his or her primary caretaker have bargained for and come to rely on." What is the consideration that the child and primary caretaker give to a father figure in this bargain? What benefits did Robert Weidman, for example, receive in exchange for accepting Xavier into his life despite knowing that Xavier was the product of the mother's adultery? What reliance is reasonable when a mother brings a new partner into a child's life, given common knowledge about the impermanence of adult relationships? How would you identify the terms of any implicit bargain or undertaking in such a situation? What basis is there for concluding that the commitment by a partner is anything other than "I'll help out with your child as long as we are together or as long as I want to have a relationship with the child"? Do many single mothers have the bargaining power to insist on a commitment to three years of support in the event of dissolution as a prerequisite to entering into an intimate relationship?

C. STEP-PARENTS

Marrying a legal parent also gives rise to a legal status with respect to any child of that person. The 2010 Census found that 16 percent of American children live with a step-parent. (Note: If a step-parent adopts a spouse's child, as many do, then the status is no longer one of step-parent but rather becomes one of a legal parent in the full sense.) In many states, step-parents have a financial responsibility for the child's well being. See, e.g., Va. Code Ann. §63.2-510 ("A person shall be responsible for the support and maintenance of any child or children living in the same home in which he and the natural or adoptive parent of such child or children cohabit as man and wife. . . ."). In most of those states, though, it is a fall-back responsibility, kicking in only if the legal parents are unable or unwilling to provide the necessary support, and courts are rarely asked to enforce this responsibility. See Margaret M. Mahoney, *Stepparents as Third Parties in Relation to Their Stepchildren*, 40 Fam. L.Q. 81, 101-102 (2006); Haw. Rev. Stat. §577-4; Mo. Rev. State. §453.400. In some states, children are entitled to state-provided survivor benefits when a step-parent dies. See, e.g., Va. Code Ann. §65.2-515 (workers' compensation for family of deceased employee).

A step-parent might also have the power to authorize medical treatment for a step-child in an emergency situation or if the child's legal parent is unavailable for some other reason, see, e.g., Mo. Rev. Stat. §431.061, but more commonly only if a legal parent is not available, e.g., Ariz. Rev. Stat. §44-133. Medical insurance providers generally allow step-children to be covered as dependents. In addition, a step-parent might have authority to participate in school administrative proceedings relating to a child's education. See, e.g., Va. Code Ann. §22.1-213.1(4) (treating as a parent for purposes of the special education planning process "an individual acting in the place of a biological or adoptive parent (including grandparent, stepparent, or other relative) with whom the child lives"). Step-children are not, however, treated as children for inheritance purposes when a step-parent dies intestate or includes a bequest to "my children" in a will. Mahoney, supra, 40 Fam. L.Q. at 99-100.

If a step-parent's relationship with the legal parent ends by death or divorce, the step-parent will in some states have specially recognized standing among non-parents to petition for visitation with, or even custody of, a child. See id. at 103-105; Del. Code Ann. tit. 13, §733 ("Notwithstanding that there is a surviving natural parent, upon the death or disability of the custodial or primary placement parent, the Court, at the request of the stepparent shall continue the placement of the child or children with the stepparent pending a hearing on the merits, provided the child has or children have resided with the stepparent immediately prior to the death or disability of the custodial or primary placement parent. . . . [T]he Court . . . may grant permanent custody or primary physical placement to the stepparent . . . [if this is in the child's best interests, and] the stepparent shall have all of the rights and obligations of a parent. . . ."); Va. Code Ann. §20-124.1 (specifying that step-parents are "persons with a legitimate interest" who have standing to petition for custody of or visitation with a child at any time).

Court conferral of post-dissolution contact rights on former step-parents is, however, also fairly rare. See Cynthia Grant Bowman, *The Legal Relationship Between Cohabitants and Their Partners' Children*, 13 Theoretical Inquiries L. 127, 137 (2012) (explaining as to custody that "a stepparent must first establish standing based either on a state statute concerning third-party custody or by showing that he or she is a psychological or *de facto* parent to the child, or stands *in loco parentis*, all of which require the stepparent's intentional assumption of an active parental role in the child's life and the existence of a parent-child relationship between them. After establishing standing, the stepparent must still defeat the parental presumption, which can be difficult to do in the absence of a finding of parental unfitness."), id. at 144 (noting that a former step-parent is more likely to succeed in seeking visitation, provided he or she shared a household with the child for a substantial period). In a few cases, courts have ordered former step-parents to pay child support after divorcing from the child's parent. Id. at 145-146. But absent court-ordered continued contact, any financial responsibility for a child that a person had while married to the child's legal parent will terminate when the marriage ends.

Professor Bowman argues that the law should give greater protection to the relationships between children and the partners of their parents, and not just to step-parents but also to non-marital cohabitants of parents, if they have acted as de facto parents and formed a bond with the child. She would also impose a financial child support obligation on former cohabitants who receive such legal protection of their relationship with a child. Professor Mahoney advocates a voluntary registration system for step-parents who want rights and responsibilities with respect to a step-child and who have their spouse's consent. Mahoney, supra, 40 FAM. L.Q. at 105-107.

POLICY QUESTIONS

Should the status, rights, and responsibilities of step-parents, during marriage to a parent or after dissolution of that relationship, depend on the role played by and the preferences of the child's other legal parent (i.e., the legal parent, if there is one, who has not been the step-parent's spouse)? Or should they depend solely on the role that the step-parent has played in the child's life? Should the law treat the same persons who have married a legal parent and persons who have non-maritally cohabited with a legal parent? What facts might you want to have to answer these questions definitively?

For discussion of empirical research findings on step-parenting, see Judith Wallerstein & Julia M. Lewis, *Sibling Outcomes and Disparate Parenting and Stepparenting After Divorce: Report from a 10-Year Longitudinal Study*, 24 PSYCHOANALYTIC PSYCHOL. 445-458 (2007).

D. RELATIONSHIPS INCIDENTAL TO THE PARENT-CHILD RELATIONSHIP

A topic that does not neatly fit into any of this text's chapters is that of legally recognized relationships other than parent-child and intimate partnership. Those other relationships are generally incidental to one of the two core types of relationship on which family law focuses. From the parent-child relationship flow several incidental, legally recognized relationships. The step-child relationship with a spouse of the parent, if the spouse is not also a legal parent to the child, was the topic of the preceding section. In addition, when the state places a child into a legal parent-child relationship with an adult, that child then becomes a legal grandchild of the adult's legal parents, a legal sibling or half-sibling of any other legal children of that adult, and legally connected for inheritance purposes—in reciprocal fashion—with collateral legal relatives of the parent, including the parent's siblings, aunts, uncles, and cousins.

Legal ancestor and sibling relationships might generate a presumptive right to court-ordered visitation or co-residence following a divorce, death of a parent, or termination of parental rights. See, e.g., Cal. Welf. & Inst. Code §366.26(c)(1)(B)(v) (creating exception to rules for post-termination adoption for situations when this would harm a child by disrupting a sibling relationship). The extent to which legal parents are empowered to control any social dimension of these incidental relationships is a topic covered in Chapter 4. These relationships might also entail financial entitlements, such as inheritance and or compensation for wrongful death or loss of consortium. See, e.g., Dubaniewicz v. Houman, 910 A.2d 897 (Vt. 2006) (holding that brother of shooting victim could bring action against killers for damages based on wrongful death). On the other hand, a sibling relationship can make one vulnerable to involuntary harvesting of one's body parts for donation; the legal system generally empowers parents to authorize removal of tissues, bone marrow, and organs from one offspring to implant in another offspring.

See Doriane Lambelet Coleman, *The Legal Ethics of Pediatric Research*, 57 Duke L.J. 517, 555 n.156 (2007).

E. RETHINKING PARENTAGE LAW

Maternity and paternity laws take no account of birth parents' fitness. Yet we know some adults have characteristics or are in circumstances that can make them wholly unsuited to raise a child—in particular drug addiction, mental illness, history of severe child maltreatment, and long-term incarceration. Is it proper for the state to confer legal parenthood on them anyway? Certainly the state would not approve *adoption* of a child by such persons and make them the legal parents of a child who is not their biological offspring. Why, then, does the law make such persons parents of a child who is their biological offspring? Is it just what Professor Bartholet terms "blood bias"?

What the state does do to protect such children, after assigning them to legal relationships with unfit birth parents, is to step in after a local child protection agency learns of their being abused, neglected, or endangered. There is today the legal possibility of terminating birth parents' parental rights immediately after conferring them (i.e., soon after birth) in a limited set of situations, but for various reasons this almost never happens. Generally, child protection agencies are not even aware when a child is born to parents who have terrible child maltreatment histories; they become aware of the birth only after the parents have damaged the new child. And the prevailing practice is to place maltreated or endangered children in foster care for a substantial period while CPS attempts to "rehabilitate" the parents, even if CPS has made failed efforts to reform the parents previously, because of maltreatment of another child.

Some philosophers have proposed that anyone who wishes to raise a child, like anyone who wishes to drive a car, should have to qualify for a license, through a process that would, at a minimum, screen out those who are grossly unfit. Most well known is Professor Hugh LaFollette's *Licensing Parents*, 9 Phil. & Pub. Aff. 182 (1980). See also Jack C. Westman, Licensing Parents: Can We Prevent Child Abuse and Neglect? (1994). Professor Dwyer advances the more modest proposal that states engraft onto their maternity and paternity laws an unfitness exception. Under his proposal, birth parent information that hospitals currently report to a state health department would be cross-checked against child abuse registries and criminal conviction records, as is now done with applicants for foster care, adoption, and employment in schools and other child care facilities, to flag new births to parents who have previously seriously harmed a child. Birth parents identified in this way, along with birth parents who are in prison at the time of birth or who are reported to CPS because their babies are born with illegal drugs in their system, would have to request a fitness hearing and demonstrate to a court their preparedness to parent, *before* legal parenthood would be conferred on them. The idea is to deny legal parenthood in the first instance to adults who, under current law, are very likely to have their parental rights ultimately terminated anyway. As a result, children would achieve permanency with adequate caregivers earlier and would avoid foster care. See James G. Dwyer, The Relationship Rights of Children (2006). Their legal parents would then not be "adoptive parents" in the conventional sense, but rather the first and only parents the child ever has, which could have positive psychological and emotional consequences for the parents and the child. See James G. Dwyer, *First Parents: Reconceptualizing Newborn Adoption*, 37 Cap. U. L. Rev. 293 (2008).

Professor Dwyer argues in fact that newborn babies have a constitutional right to such an unfitness exclusion from parentage. Existing constitutional doctrine relating to parentage addresses almost exclusively rights of biological fathers. Can it be the case that children themselves have no constitutional rights that constrain the state when it selects the adults who will be their legal parents? Do men need or deserve greater protection for their relationship interests than do newborn babies?

Before considering the constitutional argument, it is important to have some understanding of newborns' developmental needs, and to appreciate the urgency for infants of being in the care of competent, nurturing adults who will be their permanent caregivers.

James G. Dwyer, The Child Protection Pretense: States' Continued Consignment of Newborn Babies to Unfit Parents

93 Minn. L. Rev. 407 (2008)

... Abundant research demonstrates that the state's creation of a legal parent-child relationship has an enormous impact on a child's brain development, basic psychological health and emotional make up, capacity for self-regulation, and physical health and growth. Parents largely determine an infant's experience of the world, and that experience has a tremendous effect on every aspect of the child's development. Of crucial importance to each child's healthy development are early satisfaction of physical needs, freedom from trauma, and ... "a secure attachment to a sensitive, responsive, and reliable caregiver." Infancy is "a period of extreme vulnerability in which specific child welfare experiences have the potential to have devastating, long-term consequences." ...

The neurobiological literature reveals that, during infancy of a normal child, most brain development is complete and the basis for cognitive and perceptual processes is in place. Healthy development of various parts of the brain depends on avoiding or receiving certain experiential inputs. Deleterious to neurological development are not only physical maltreatment—that is, physical trauma and malnutrition—but also social deprivation and stress during infancy. ... Studies of children with attachment disorders caused by parental neglect ... show an adverse impact on brain development. Impairment of brain development caused by social deprivation in turn hinders intellectual, linguistic, emotional, and social development.

Social science literature amply documents the crucial developmental importance of a secure attachment, which is a child's psychological identification with and emotional connection to a caregiver. A secure attachment to a caregiver is the basis of a child's understanding of and feeling about the world and about himself and therefore plays an "essential formative role[] in later social and emotional functioning. Infant-parent attachments promote a sense of security, the beginnings of self-confidence, and the development of trust in other human beings." A secure attachment initially entails a desire to stay close to a strong, protective, and nurturing figure, and ultimately, "its effective operation brings with it a strong feeling of security and contentment." That security enables a child eventually to explore the world without great anxiety and therefore to master tasks and develop a sense of competence and self-worth. It also "creates a positive expectation from the child's view that relationships can be fulfilling, helpful, and provide sufficient protection in a world that may at times be overwhelming," an expectation that will later make possible positive peer and family relationships and healthy intimacy. As a result, securely attached children become "more independent, socially competent, inquisitive, and cooperative and empathic with peers; have higher self-esteem; and demonstrate more persistence and flexibility on problem-solving tasks." They possess a "greater capacity for self-regulation, effective social interactions, positive self-representations, self-reliance, and adaptive coping skills." Conversely, if a child fails to attach to any caregiver or forms only an insecure attachment, many negative consequences for many aspects of development are likely, as discussed below.

Whether a child forms an attachment at all and whether any attachment formed is secure depends on the child's interactions with caregivers during the attachment phase of infancy, between seven months and two years of age. In this period especially, babies need "sensitive and responsive care from familiar adults in the course of feeding, holding, talking, playing, soothing, and general proximity." . . . Accordingly, it is not sufficient for a child's healthy development that a parent simply not physically endanger the child. Even if a parent is consistently present and not dangerous, a child might fail to form a secure attachment as a result of poor parenting, including "disturbed family interactions, parental rejection, inattentive or disorganized parenting, [and] neglect." . . . Any of these might result from a parent's substance abuse, mental illness, or dysfunctional relationship with another adult; "[p]reoccupation with personal stressors diminishes the parent's ability to respond in this way." . . . And of course, children likely will fail to form even an insecure attachment with parents if parents are absent for long periods, as when parents abandon or neglect a child or go to prison, or if a child's interactions with parents are often painful rather than nurturing, as when parents physically abuse a child. . . .

In addition, children are harmed by disruption of an established attachment relationship. It is very difficult to reestablish an attachment once it is disrupted and also very difficult for a child later to form an attachment to a new caregiver. Thus, children's development is adversely affected by removal from a parent after an attachment with the parent has formed, even though the removal might be necessary for the child's safety or because the parent goes to prison. Importantly, children are also adversely affected by being removed from foster parents if they have begun to attach to the foster parents, whether the removal is for the purpose of placing the child with a "rehabilitated" birth parent or for the purpose of changing foster care placements (as traditionally was done when foster parents appeared to be getting "too close" to the child). . . .

In turn, attachment disorders cause lifelong difficulties. Numerous studies of maternal deprivation have concluded that failure of attachment caused by inadequate nurturance in infancy results in "a variety of serious medical problems, physical and brain growth deficiencies, cognitive problems, speech and language delays, sensory integration difficulties and stereotypes, and . . . social and behavioral abnormalities." Attachment failure retards socio-emotional development and produces emotional withdrawal, indiscriminate socializing, lack of impulse control, failure to internalize moral norms, and psychiatric disorders such as depression, anxiety, hyperactivity, and disruptive behavior. . . .

A much larger body of social science research demonstrates a clear link between proven child maltreatment . . . and cognitive impairment, delayed language development, poor school performance, poor physical health and development, mental health problems, lack of self-control and behavioral disorders, failure to internalize moral norms, peer socialization problems, violence and other forms of delinquency, running away from home, youth suicide, substance abuse, prostitution, teen pregnancy, unemployment, criminality in adulthood, partner violence as an adult, and maltreatment of the next generation of children. . . .

Turning to predictive parental characteristics, child maltreatment strongly correlates with parental substance abuse, mental illness, and prior maltreatment of another child. Birth parents with substance abuse problems are (a) at a pronounced higher risk of child maltreatment, (b) extremely unlikely to overcome an addiction prior to the time when their baby needs to form a secure attachment to a consistent, nurturing caregiver, regardless of what assistance they receive, (c) very likely to have child protective services (CPS) remove their children from their custody at some point anyway, and (d) extremely unlikely to reunify successfully following removal. The prospects are similarly bleak for birth parents suffering from serious mental illnesses. . . .

In sum, scientific research shows that two things can seriously adversely affect an infant's physiological and psycho-emotional development—initial placement in the custody of parents who are incapable of providing consistent nurturing and, alternatively, disruption of a healthy initial attachment with good caregivers. The best child welfare policy is therefore one that aims to get parentage right at the outset and then supports whatever choice of initial parentage is made. [Yet] the state routinely confers legal parenthood and custody on birth parents even when the state is aware that the birth parents have serious maltreatment histories with other children, have intractable substance abuse or mental health problems, and/or are incarcerated. And when the state does take custody of children, temporary foster care is still the norm for placements after removal of all children, including infants, and the number of placement transitions for children in the foster care system is shockingly high—nationally, six placements per child on average.

More generally, child-protection law fails to differentiate among children by age, instead taking a "one rule fits all ages" approach. . . . Yet several things clearly differentiate newborn children from older children who come to CPS attention. First, as discussed above, the first year of life is the most important developmentally. Second, children are readily adoptable immediately after birth, but their chances for adoption diminish steadily from that point on, especially if they incur maltreatment or spend a substantial period of time in foster care. Third, newborn children have no established relationship with birth parents to maintain.

. . . [T]he prevailing practice of placing children in foster care and attempting to rehabilitate their parents is simply ineffective in a large percentage of cases. . . . [E]ven the best, most resource-intensive parent-rehabilitation programs, with all the facilities and services and encouragement experts typically recommend, have very little success with dysfunctional parents. For example, a five-year demonstration project in Cook County, Illinois that provided 1500 randomly selected parents with a comprehensive needs assessment, entry into treatment programs within twenty-four hours of assessment, and a "Recovery Coach" to coordinate their services, monitor their progress, advocate on their behalf, and give them encouragement succeeded in securing the recommended services very quickly for the vast majority of parents in the program, but raised the rate at which social workers thought it "safe" to return a child to parent custody only from 11.6% to 15.5%. Most parents whose children need to be taken into state custody have dysfunctions so deep, stemming from damage they themselves incurred as children, that they are not going to overcome them even in a couple of years, and newborns cannot wait more than six months or so for a permanent and nurturing caregiver. . . .

Moreover, reunification does not mean that a child will then have even a decent upbringing; a substantial percentage of children whom the state transfers from foster care to birth-parent custody end up in the child protective system again, after another maltreatment report, meaning that the child has multiple damaging disruptions during the crucial first years of life. Further, many of those who do remain in the parents' home thereafter will have only a marginal existence, suffering maltreatment that goes undetected or receiving parental care that is just above the local CPS agency's threshold for intervention.

Placing babies born to criminals in a holding pattern while birth parents serve jail terms is also very detrimental to the children, because of the impact on attachment and on a child's sense of identity. Even after release, incarcerated parents are generally not able for some time to establish a home for and take care of a child, so the child's wait for permanency is likely to extend well beyond the expected release date, which is itself likely to be years down the developmental road if the parents have committed felonies. In addition, most incarcerated mothers suffer from a host of personal problems—in particular, drug addiction, alcoholism, mental illness, and lack of education—that will continue to plague them after release, and accordingly they are quite likely to return to prison after being "reunited" with the babies to whom they gave birth while in prison. . . .

In short, for a substantial percentage of newborn children whose parents have previously manifested unfitness or who are currently incapacitated by reason of serious and chronic substance abuse, severe mental illness, or incarceration, there is very little chance of their having a decent life with their birth parents, and the only sensible surrogate decision in their behalf by the state would be to move for TPR and adoption immediately after birth. . . .

James G. Dwyer, A Constitutional Birthright: The State, Parentage, and the Rights of Newborn Persons

56 UCLA L. Rev. 755 (2009)

. . . [C]urrent state parentage statutes dictating the family lives of babies born to manifestly unfit birth parents predictably and substantially endanger babies' wellbeing and severely undermine their chances for a happy and fulfilling life. States do this to babies even though they could avoid doing so without great difficulty and could in addition save taxpayers a lot of money by leaving such children free for family formation with different, fit parents at the outset. Might it be unconstitutional for the state to do this to babies? . . .

II. General Principles for State Control over Personal Relationships

. . . Like a parent, the guardian of an incompetent adult is charged with primary responsibility for the welfare of the ward and receives substantial powers to direct the life of the ward. . . . In appointing a guardian for an incompetent adult, the state respects that individual's personhood by insisting that the relationship arise exclusively on the basis of a finding that the ward chose it before becoming incompetent, in an advance directive of some kind, or that the ward would now choose it if able. In other words, the law makes the state decisionmaker a surrogate for the incompetent adult, directing the appointing court effectively to give proxy consent to a legal relationship on behalf of the nonautonomous person.

When an incompetent adult has not given an advance directive as to who should be the guardian, or has named someone who now declines appointment or appears unsuitable, that proxy consent amounts to a "best interests" determination—that is, an assessment of which competent adult, among those willing to serve, would be the best caregiver for the incompetent adult. . . . Importantly, satisfying an applicant's desire for the position, no matter how intense, is not a permissible aim in selecting a guardian. Moreover, a judge aware of something rendering particular applicants unfit to serve as guardian would not appoint them. A judge . . . would certainly refuse to appoint an applicant who had previously served in a guardian role for an incompetent adult and had been removed from that role because he or she abused the ward. . . .

Thus, in the case of a relationship between adults that is structurally similar to the parent-child relationship, with one person of greater capacity in a caregiving role vis-à-vis the other, the law aims to mirror the paradigmatic case of a mutually consensual relationship between two private parties, simply substituting proxy consent for actual consent in the case of a person unable to give actual consent. . . . [C]onstitutional decisionmaking concerning incompetent adults in other contexts has established as a general principle that they possess constitutional rights equal or equivalent to those of competent adults and that state decisionmaking about fundamental aspects of their lives should aim first and foremost at exercising those rights on behalf of the incompetent adults, under the parens patriae authority of the state. . . .

B. STATE CONTROL OF PRIVATE ASSOCIATION

When the state places a newborn into a legal parent-child relationship with particular adults and confers custodial rights on those adults, it effectively compels the child to associate closely with those adults. . . . As a general matter, individuals have a constitutionally-protected right to freedom of association, which entails both the freedom to associate and the freedom not to associate with others as one chooses. There is thus a constitutional presumption against the state compelling any private person to associate with another, and the presumption is especially strong with respect to intimate association. . . .

No doubt if a state today tried to force a wife to live with her husband, a court would find that this violates the wife's right to liberty under the Due Process Clause, especially if the husband's known history or characteristics indicated the wife would be in danger. Today the only persons compelled to associate with other members of their legal family are children. The law does not require any competent adults to associate with other adults with whom they stand in some form of legal family relationships, and the law never compels any adults to associate with any children. . . .

In the . . . context of placing children in the custody of foster parents, . . . children do receive constitutional protection. Courts have established that the state . . . when it places a child in a foster care relationship . . . , while not precluded from placing children into such unchosen associations, is constitutionally required to do so with some care. Some courts apply a "professional judgment" standard, whereas others impose liability on an agency that acts with "deliberate indifference" to dangers the placement might pose for the child. Thus, were a state to select foster parents with the same disregard for child maltreatment history, drug addiction, or severe mental illness that it shows when making birth parents legal parents (for example, by choosing the first person to respond to a newspaper ad), courts would conclude that it violated a constitutional right of any children harmed as a result. Accordingly, state statutes require child protection agencies to investigate any applicants for foster parent positions and require that courts find foster parents fit and qualified prior to placing a child with them. . . .

Significantly, adults who have committed sexual or violent offenses against a child will commonly be prohibited from associating at all with any children—other than their own [later-born] offspring. Ironically, this is true even if the prior victim was their own offspring! A sex offender must register with local police and in many jurisdictions may not live near a school or other place where children regularly congregate. An adult identified with a child maltreatment history typically will not be permitted to work in a school in any capacity or even to serve as a coach for a youth sports team. Yet the state generally allows sexual predators and adults with horrible child maltreatment histories to associate in the most private and unsupervised of settings with any later offspring they have. . . .

III. Children's Due Process Right Against Bad Parentage Decisions

. . . The Supreme Court has made clear that children are persons who have rights under the federal Constitution. Thus, were a state's laws to declare, for example, . . . that the first legal parent for any newborn left at a safe haven depository shall be an unmarried male sex-offender just released from prison, we would charge the state with an atrocious abuse of state power and a violation of the abandoned babies' rights against the state. It would not matter that legislators were motivated in passing such laws by compassion for such men, who were likely abused as children themselves and who might otherwise never have an opportunity to raise a child, given that they are relatively unattractive to women as potential partners. The Constitution simply does not permit legislatures to use babies in that way to ease the suffering of adults. . . . That the state inevitably must intrude into babies' intimate lives to the extent of choosing legal and custodial parents for them does not mean that it is constitutionally unconstrained in how it does so.

The most fitting articulation of a constitutional right of newborns against the state in relation to parentage statutes would be in terms of the Fourteenth Amendment Due Process Clause. . . . The Supreme Court has stated that the Due Process Clause . . . serves the broader purpose "'to secure the individual from the arbitrary exercise of the powers of government.'" . . . [C]ourts have construed the protection of liberty to require not just that the state stay out of certain private realms altogether, but also that when the state must enter into a private realm, because an individual is incapable of self-determining choices and actions, it not do so arbitrarily or in a manner that disrespects the personhood of that individual. . . .

A. The State Action Question

. . . In *DeShaney*, the Court held that a county child protection agency did not violate the constitutional rights of a boy whose father beat him to the point of causing severe brain damage, by failing to remove the boy from his father's custody even though the agency had reason to believe the boy was in danger. The basis for the Court's rejection of the §1983 claim was that there was no state action, but rather only a failure to act.

The *DeShaney* Court . . . failed to acknowledge the state's role in creating the situation in which Joshua Deshaney was harmed—that is, by the child protection agency repeatedly removing Joshua from a safe foster home and depositing him in his abusive father's home, and by the legislature conferring legal parent status on Randy DeShaney in the first place. . . . [T]he *DeShaney* decision is also readily distinguishable. The attorney retained by Joshua DeShaney's mother directed the complaint only against the child protection agency, alleged only a failure to act, and mistakenly conceded that the State played no part in creating the danger to the boy. . . . A challenge to parentage laws, in contrast, would focus directly on affirmative conduct by the state—namely, the legislature's passage of state statutes determining every child's first legal relationships and bestowing custodial rights on the adult parties to that relationship, state agencies' implementation of those statutes, and courts' application of those statutes in individual cases. The initial creation of a legal and custodial parent-child relationship is as much state action as is creating a guardian-ward relationship, whether it occurs by operation of a statute over a large number of cases or by judicial decision in an individual case. . . .

Further, state creation of legal and custodial parent-child relationships is a state action that, in the case of unfit parents, creates a danger for the child that would not otherwise exist, because those adults would not otherwise be legally free to take the child into their household and assume control over the child's life. And, because of the exclusivity and plenary power that the state injects into legal parenthood, such state action entails cutting off potential private sources of protection, including assumption of custody by other adults who are prepared to provide a very nurturing upbringing. . . .

Few people would have difficulty seeing how creation of a legal parent-child relationship constitutes potentially wrongful state action in the case of adoption—that is, if a social services agency and court were to grant adoption of a newborn to persons the state knew to be grossly unfit to parent. Imagine an adult, reported in the newspapers today for throwing a crying baby against a brick wall, going tomorrow to a local social services agency and applying to adopt any available baby. Were the agency and a court to approve such an adoption, we would readily discern state action and would ascribe responsibility to the state if that adult then threw the adopted baby against the same brick wall. Creating a legal parent-child relationship between a newborn and birth parents who are grossly unfit is no less state action. It is certainly more clearly state action than is a state agency declining to create a legal relationship desired by private parties, such as a legal marriage between persons of the same sex, yet courts have unhesitatingly treated such refusal to create a legal relationship as state action.

B. ESTABLISHING THE SUBSTANTIVE RIGHT

. . . There are at least two reasons . . . why in this context the Court might be less reluctant to recognize a new right or to apply an old right in a new way. First, . . . the legislative process does not naturally respect and reflect the equal personhood of babies born to unfit parents and is especially likely to produce outcomes that are unjustifiable from the standpoint of those children. Only rigorous judicial review, forcing legislatures to provide convincing reasons for their decisions as to the fate of vulnerable newborns, can effectuate the most basic political right of those children to treatment as equal citizens. . . .

The second reason . . . is that the kind of state decision the right would constrain—namely, choosing family members for a person—is one the state presumptively should never be making in the first place. Such a decision is an extreme incursion into a citizen's private life. The state makes it solely because the newborn's incompetence and vulnerability necessitate some entity making decisions for them about their family relationships. Incapacity and vulnerability do not necessitate and do not justify the state using their lives to serve the common good or to gratify the wishes of other private parties (namely, unfit birth parents). Just as the self-determining choices we adults make about our intimate relationships, in the pursuit of our own happiness, receive constitutional protection from majoritarian preferences and prejudices, choices made on behalf of newborns to advance their welfare and enhance their prospects for a happy life should receive such protection as well. No doubt, if some state changed its guardianship rules to eliminate the best interests standard for guardian appointment and began appointing personal guardians without regard to fitness, courts would recognize a fundamental substantive due process right of adults against the state placing them in the custody of persons grossly unfit as caretakers—for example, persons known to have severely abused another incompetent adult. . . .

1. Grounding a Newborn's Right in History and Tradition

. . . [O]ne can find substantial historical evidence of states reacting to what they viewed as parental unfitness, in many cases by denying legal parent status in the first instance to birth parents deemed unfit. . . . [F]or most of American history the state deemed unwed fathers per se unfit and accordingly denied them legal parent status. . . . There were also interventions to prevent "cruelty," and colonists did believe children were entitled to be free from excessive abuse or neglect. Local officials were quite intrusive in family matters by today's standards, and their authority to intervene to prevent abuse of children was widely accepted. . . .

Certainly there is no evidence of society explicitly rejecting this right of children, as there is with society rejecting the right to engage in homosexual sodomy and with society rejecting the right to abortion. There have never been laws proscribing interference with unfit birth parents' relationships with their offspring, and consigning babies to unfit parents has never been a matter of moral principle, the way prohibition of sodomy has been. At worst, there has been state indifference to the plight of some children. . . .

In any event, . . . babies' interest in the state not forcing them into a harmful parent-child relationship is one instance of a more general interest every person has in not being forced to enter into intimate relationships harmful to them. . . . Babies have an interest at least as strong as that of adult women in not being compelled to live with someone who is likely to cause them bodily harm or be indifferent to their well-being. Certainly a fundamental right against the state forcing one to be in a legal relationship and intimate association likely to be quite harmful is a right deeply rooted in our history. . . .

2. Grounding a Newborn's Right in Reasoned Judgment

. . . [I]t would be difficult to find many better candidates for a fundamental right than the right of a baby not to be placed into a legal relationship and compelled intimate association with unfit parents. Apart from executions, there might be nothing more damaging that the state does to people. . . . This is so whether the state is placing children with biological parents through parentage laws or with nonbiological parents through adoption laws.

The Court has often . . . indicated that the primary reason family relationships receive constitutional protection is that they typically provide positive emotional attachments, which are the basis of identity, self-worth, and happiness. . . . The Court has also been more inclined to recognize substantive due process rights against state action that threatens substantially to undermine a person's life prospects. For example, the Court has rested the right to an abortion in large part on the connection between women's ability to control their reproductive lives and their "ability to realize their full potential." . . .

C. STATE JUSTIFICATIONS FOR INFRINGING THE RIGHT

. . . [A]voiding additional administrative costs would not be sufficient justification. Even if it were, the reality is that there would be little additional administrative burden from identifying presumptively unfit parents at the time of birth rather than after they have damaged a child. To identify birth parents presumptively unfit by virtue of past conduct, state-level child protection agencies need simply install a computer program that cross-checks databases the state already possesses—namely, birth records and records of past child maltreatment or violent felonies. To identify birth parents presumptively unfit by virtue of current substance abuse, states need only mandate testing of all newborns for drug or alcohol exposure, which some hospitals already routinely do. States already require birthing facilities that do test newborns to report positive drug toxicology results to the local child protective agency and could easily expand that mandate to include alcohol as well. Any court proceeding triggered by such identification, aimed at preventing assignment of children at birth to unfit parents (or, when likely to be effective quickly, providing services to rehabilitate the parents), would likely substitute for and obviate the need for the several court proceedings that ordinarily ensue after unfit parents maltreat children. . . .

1. Birth Parents' Constitutional Right to Be Legal Parents

Many people speak as if there is a well-recognized constitutional right of biological parents per se to become legal parents. In reality, the U.S. Constitution contains not a word about parenthood, and the Supreme Court has never held that there is such a right. . . .

The most relevant Supreme Court precedents concern unwed biological fathers' substantive due process right to be legal parents. . . . Importantly, as with the parental control cases, in none of these unwed fathers' rights cases was there an allegation that the adult asserting rights was unfit to be a parent, and the Court implied that unfitness would be a proper basis for denying the right. . . . In *Stanley v. Illinois,* the Court in fact suggested that the state could constitutionally require a hearing on an unwed father's fitness prior to conferring on him legal parental status, and indeed could put the onus on the biological father to initiate the proceeding. . . . Lower courts relying on the early fathers' rights cases have consistently indicated that unfitness obviates a biological parent's claim to a constitutional right to a relationship. . . . Courts might come to a different conclusion with respect to mothers, but . . . there is no reason to suppose that the Court would hold that fitness is irrelevant with respect to mothers. . . . A claim to a constitutional right to be a parent despite unfitness would have little plausibility. While all humans might have a strong interest in being in family relationships that generate emotional, psychological, and physical goods, they do not have a strong interest in being in dysfunctional and destructive relationships that are likely to be disrupted. Additionally, it is not part of human flourishing to be in a parental role but fail miserably at it and damage one's child. . . .

[E]ven if the Court did conclude that some constitutional right exists for biological parents per se with respect to legal parentage, its statement in numerous contexts that protecting the welfare of children is a compelling state interest suggests that it would find no violation of such a right in a state excluding from legal parenthood birth parents whom the state has good reason to suppose will seriously damage a child. Significantly, lower courts have uniformly rejected constitutional challenges to state laws that authorize TPR on the basis of a parent's prior TPR as to another child. . . .

b. The Moral Basis for State Creation of Families

. . . [I]f the only justification for the state presuming to step into the lives of private parties and make choices about their intimate relationships is that the private parties are incapable of self-determination and need decisions to be made for them, the state's authority to make such decisions should extend no further than doing for the private parties what they would do for themselves if able. . . . The state certainly could not invoke its police power to . . . compel one adult to marry another, on the grounds that, by refusing to marry, the former is making the latter intensely unhappy, or on the grounds that the latter has a fundamental right to marry, or on the grounds that compelling them into marriage would serve some broad societal purpose. Likewise, the state cannot legitimately invoke its police power to decide who a child's parents will be and thereby base its decisions on a balancing of the child's welfare against the desires or interests of the birth parents or against the interests of the rest of society. The *parens patriae* power, not the police power, is the sole appropriate basis for the state making such a decision about a person's life. . . .

[W]hen the state acts merely as proxy or agent for a private party, making a decision ordinarily within the realm of private life, its decisionmaking should replicate that of an autonomous private party making a similar decision. Assuming that autonomous persons ordinarily act, or at least are entitled to act, solely to further their own well being, the state's proxy decisionmaking should not entail sacrificing the interests of the nonautonomous person in order to serve the interests or desires of other parties. It should not entail even considering other's interests, and no rights should be attributed to other persons. No one has a legal or moral right to be chosen as a spouse, and likewise no one should be deemed to have a right to be chosen as a parent. Other adults have a right to decline a relationship with us, but no right to force us into one with them, regardless of how strongly they desire it, regardless of what connection they might feel to us, and regardless of what disparate societal impact our decision might have. Likewise, no one . . . should be viewed as having a right to be in a parent-child relationship with a newborn child that constrains the state's surrogate decisionmaking on behalf of the child. . . .

Biological parents . . . might have an equal protection-type right against a state that entirely and arbitrarily excludes them from consideration as potential legal parents, just as any adult would have a right against a state arbitrarily and categorically precluding them from ever becoming anyone's spouse. And if it is best for a newborn to be in a parent-child relationship with her biological parents . . . , such that the state's surrogate choice of parents on behalf of the newborn should be in favor of the biological parents, then both the biological parents and the baby might be said to have a constitutional right against the state preventing them from forming a relationship. But courts should conclude that biological parents have no constitutional right to use state power to force their association on a child or to be in a relationship with a child even in the absence of a reciprocal, proxy choice, just as adults have no moral or legal right to state assistance in forcing their association on another adult against the latter's actual or surrogate choice.

c. Natural Law

. . . A natural law proponent ought to say that it violates natural law for parents to abuse or neglect their offspring and, if it is the state's place to enforce natural law, that the state should therefore act to keep offspring out of relationships with and custody of such birth parents. Further, observation of human behavior might reveal that there is something natural about biologically unrelated persons caring about and for vulnerable persons who do not have an adequate caregiver, and something quite unnatural about knowingly thrusting vulnerable persons into dangerous or grossly unhealthy situations, as we collectively do now through our parentage laws. . . .

5. Adverse Maternal Reactions

The most persuasive objection to excluding some birth parents from legal parenthood relates to child welfare—a concern that it could make children on the whole worse off. Specifically, some might conjecture that fear of having their babies taken away from them could cause some pregnant women to act in ways they otherwise would not. One of those ways might be entirely salutary: some might take greater steps to prevent further pregnancy after having rights terminated as to a child or if they are substance abusers. Other possible reactions, though, would be undesirable from anyone's perspective. Women who do become pregnant and who fear being deemed unfit when they give birth might for that reason (a) have an abortion, (b) fail to get prenatal care because they fear medical facilities will report them to child protective services, or (c) give birth secretly in conditions unsafe for them and the baby. . . .

If it is proper in this context to base a legislative choice on fear of such reactions, then the constitutionality of current parentage laws might well depend on what level of scrutiny courts apply. . . . Under rational basis review, courts would give legislatures the freedom to balance the competing considerations of babies' well being before and at birth with babies' well being after birth, without second guessing a legislature's evidentiary support, wisdom, or carefulness. Under strict or rigorous scrutiny, however, courts should insist that states provide evidentiary support for the assumption that women will react in the feared ways, and demonstrate that they could not feasibly deter such reactions by means that do not entail infringing constitutional rights of babies after birth. . . . I will offer reasons for believing that states could not meet this burden.

First, the concern as stated draws no connection between harm to fetuses and denying legal parenthood to biological fathers. . . . It is not plausible to suggest that men concerned about being denied parental status would coerce expectant mothers to have an abortion, avoid prenatal care, or give birth in secret. . . .

Second, concern that the possibility of being denied legal motherhood will alter pregnant women's behavior is mere speculation. . . . [U]nder current law, states sometimes do something with respect to newborns that, from the parents' perspective, is not much different from denial of parentage. Each year thousands of babies in the U.S. are taken into custody immediately after birth and placed in foster care, usually because of maternal drug addiction. Though this is only a small fraction of the children who are at high risk of maltreatment, it is common enough that women at risk of losing custody are likely to be aware of the possibility. Most such newborns are never placed in birth parents' custody, and many who are placed in a birth parent's custody are later removed. . . . Yet there is no reported evidence of women having abortions, avoiding prenatal care providers, or giving birth in secret because of this CPS practice. . . .

Third, [an] alternative way of addressing all three concerns would be to make rehabilitation services available to pregnant women even if they do not currently have a child in the child protective system and to make the availability of those services known, by requiring abortion clinics to provide information to their patients about such services and by having CPS agencies publicize their availability. The availability of those services would signal to pregnant women that the social services agency stands ready to help them achieve parental fitness before giving birth, which would give them greater hope of avoiding or succeeding in a fitness hearing.

In addition, states could alter pregnant women's incentive structures by including in civil and/or criminal definitions of child neglect failure to secure prenatal care and giving birth to a child in unsafe conditions. Such a failure could also be a factor weighing against a parent in a fitness hearing at the time of birth, so that if dysfunctional pregnant women were in fact as aware of the law and as strategic as some suppose, this might counteract any effect from fearing detection. A few states now treat prenatal drug exposure as civil or criminal child abuse or neglect, so it would not be unprecedented to attach legal consequences to prebirth maternal behavior.

Discussion of altering the incentives for pregnant women raises concern about an additional adult right—namely, pregnant women's personal freedom. However, the proposal I advance would not burden a woman's choice to have an abortion; indeed, the concern is that it would induce abortions, and the remedy I propose for that is simply to make services available to women contemplating abortion. . . . The abortion rights cases are nevertheless relevant, because they establish that the state is permitted to limit pregnant women's freedom to some degree in order to further the state's legitimate interest in the health and safety of babies before their birth. Indeed, if the state may force women to remain pregnant once they enter the third trimester, then surely it may require them to visit a clinic a few times during a pregnancy and to give birth in a licensed facility. Doing so does not directly interfere with the procreative choice itself and is not a substantial burden on freedom; it is certainly much less of a burden than the responsibilities the law imposes on parents after a child is born. . . .

IV. Implementing the Right: A Constitutional Scheme of Parentage

. . . First, the guardian ad litem appointed to represent a child in a serious maltreatment case, or some other person or entity acting on behalf of a child who has been abused or neglected, could bring a claim for damages under 42 U.S.C. §1983, not against the child protection agency for failing to protect them (the sort of claim that failed in *DeShaney*), but against the state for enacting and implementing statutes that consigned the child to a life with birth parents known at the time of the child's birth to be unfit and likely to abuse the child. . . .

An alternative . . . would be for a representative of a baby just born or about to be born to petition for injunctive relief against application of the state's parentage statute to that baby. Social service agency workers are sometimes aware when an adult who previously had parental rights terminated as to another child is pregnant again, and some such persons might be motivated to ask the juvenile court to order guardian ad litem representation of the baby before (if state statutes allow for appointment to represent an unborn child) or immediately upon birth. Alternatively, one parent could seek to represent the child and advance the claim against the other parent, or any other relative or a child advocacy organization that is aware of the pending birth could seek "next friend" representative status and file suit. . . .

QUESTIONS

Which of the analogies relied on in the argument—e.g., adoption, guardianship for incompetent adults, adults' self-determining choices about relationships—is most persuasive? Which least persuasive?

Does anything in the opinions in *Lehr* or *Michael H.* suggest that unwed mothers might have stronger constitutional rights with respect to becoming and remaining legal parents than do unwed fathers? Cf. Katharine T. Bartlett, *Re-Expressing Parenthood*, 98 Yale L.J. 293, 333 (1988) ("Within custody law, there is a strong ideology that through pregnancy and childbirth an enduring bond develops between mother and child which cannot easily be broken.").

Are there any other legitimate and compelling state interests that need to be considered? For example, should it change the constitutional analysis that the birth parents who would be denied legal parenthood would be disproportionately poor and of minority race? Compare Dorothy Roberts, Shattered Bonds: The Color of Child Welfare (2002); Shani King, *The Family Law Canon in a (Post?) Racial Era,* 72 Ohio St. L.J. 575 602-616 (2011); Twila L. Perry, *Race Matters: Change, Choice, and Family Law at the Millennium,* 33 Fam. L.Q. 461 (1999); and Dorothy E. Roberts, *Punishing Drug Addicts Who Have Babies: Women of Color, Equality, and the Right to Privacy,* 104 Harv. L. Rev. 1419 (1991), with Elizabeth Bartholet, *The Racial Disproportionality Movement in Child Welfare: False Facts and Dangerous Directions,* 51 Ariz. L. Rev. 871 (2009).

Can you think of any way other than assertion of constitutional rights to garner greater protection for newborns whose birth parents are unfit? Consider that the Adoption and Safe Families Act, which in part aimed at inducing states to take a more preventive rather than reactive approach to child maltreatment, came only after a very difficult political struggle and ultimately had so many gaps in it that the "no reasonable efforts" component (requiring states to authorize termination of parental rights in some cases without first undertaking rehabilitative efforts with parents) has had nearly no effect in practice, largely because social workers and judges are highly resistant to "giving up" on parents.

Some would argue that what the state should do to protect children is just devote more resources to eliminating poverty and to helping parents overcome dysfunctions. Is that an adequate response? Should child welfare law and policy be based on the way things now are (perhaps thereby reinforcing the status quo) or on the way things would be in (what some people would view as) a more just society?

PROBLEMS

1. Denise recently gave birth to a son, Ethan. The law in her state requires toxicology testing of all newborns and stipulates that birth mothers of babies who manifest *in utero* exposure to certain levels of certain illegal drugs must petition for legal parenthood and demonstrate their fitness. Ethan tested positive for a high level of methamphetamine. Denise had been using meth for several years and engaging in prostitution to obtain money to buy it. Her use intensified when her boyfriend, who was not Ethan's father, became abusive during the pregnancy. The hospital reported the test results to the local CPS agency, and a social worker visited Denise in the hospital. The social worker informed Denise that her name would not be put on the birth certificate and she would not be Ethan's legal mother unless and until she requested a fitness hearing and convinced a judge that she could become capable of caring for Ethan within six months. Denise filled out the form the social worker gave her to request a fitness hearing, and she agreed to leave her boyfriend and go straight from the hospital to a residential drug rehabilitation program. Pursuant to state statute, the fitness hearing was scheduled for 30 days later. At that time, Denise is still at the treatment program and has not used any drugs since before Ethan's birth. The biological father is undiscoverable, and Denise has no family with whom she can live or who can adopt Ethan. There is a waiting list of qualified couples wishing to adopt a newborn, many of whom are willing and qualified to parent a special needs child. What arguments would you present if you were Denise's court-appointed attorney? If you were guardian *ad litem* for Ethan? What further information might you want to obtain if you were the judge?

2. Suppose you proposed legislation in your state along the lines Professor Dwyer suggests, and suppose you were told to make your case to the "Citizens Commission for Child Welfare," a legislatively created group containing representatives of various

agencies and interests. Among the following, whom would you expect to support or oppose the measure and why: a) the head of the state-level child protection agency, b) the statewide director of poverty law services, c) a juvenile court judge, d) a lawyer who represents local CPS agencies in child protection matters, e) a representative of the state ACLU chapter, f) a representative from Focus on the Family, a conservative, national family policy organization, g) the statewide head of Catholic Family Services, and h) a CPS social worker. Bear in mind that they are likely to have personal values, ambitions, and psychological needs that influence their position, as well as any concern they might have for interests and rights of persons whom the legislation would affect. What might you say to any of those from whom you expect resistance, in order to win them over?

2

STATE CREATION OF LEGAL PARTNER RELATIONSHIPS

Human adults satisfy certain desires by forming personal relationships and having intimate interactions with other adults. Relationships can take many forms, and a relationship with any given person can take on different forms over time. Physical intimacy can range from flirting to sex. Suppose you are a newly elected state legislator and you want to develop your policy on state involvement in citizens' private lives. You might begin by identifying the types of relationships or intimate interactions that you think the state has sufficient interest in to warrant laws regulating the relationships or interactions. What would that include? Friendships? Any two people living together? Any sexual conduct? Any social gathering where people might hook up? Or are private interactions and relationships none of the state's business, in your view, absent coercion or harm to third parties? In that case, would you work to repeal all laws pertaining to marriage, thereby making marriage a purely private matter?

To answer these questions, you might first wish to identify what legitimate interests the state has that might be affected by personal relationships and interactions. Then you might try to figure out how important and how greatly affected such interests must be in order to justify state involvement in this private activity. Reflect on what your general starting assumptions might be.

The current state of the law in most of the United States is such that the state involves itself in formation of personal relationships among adults only when heterosexual intimate partners ask the state to treat them as "married" and to confer on them the material benefits that the state offers to those who get legally married. The state today generally does not take any special interest in people's initiation of friendships, non-marital cohabitation, or mutually voluntary casual sex. You will find some exceptions in the materials the follow, but after *Lawrence v. Texas* they are mostly confined to situations in which such interactions adversely affect third parties, such as a spouse (e.g., in the case of adultery) or child (e.g., when the state thinks children should not be exposed to certain people or interactions). In and of themselves, adults' formation of non-marital personal relationships does not trigger any state involvement in most jurisdictions. Readings in this chapter raise the questions of why the state has drawn the line where it has, between marriage and everything else, and whether this is the best place to draw it.

At the same time, although the state takes special interest in marriage, it requires little of two people in order to confer this legal status on them. It will not confer legal marital status on certain types of pairings—for example, a brother/sister pair, a pair of ten-year-olds, or, at present in most jurisdictions, two people of the same sex. But if two people constitute the right sort of pair—paradigmatically, a biologically unrelated man/woman pair, they need only go to a local government office once or twice and declare their desire to be legally married, and the state will grant their request. The state does not require that they cohabit or be physically intimate before or after it confers the legal status. It does not require any proof of competence to be in, nor any preparation for, a marital relationship. Nor does it generally insist, in contrast to the adoption process, that each person disclose to the other information that could influence the other's decision to marry, such as any criminal background or a severe health problem. Thus, if you and a classmate thought it materially advantageous for you to be legally married to each other, even though you are merely acquaintances, perhaps to save on your taxes or so that one of you can get on the other's health insurance plan, you could accomplish this with astonishing ease. If your local court or city hall is still open, you might get yourself married before today is done.

Roughly 85 percent of Americans get married at least once. As with the parent-child relationship, we can distinguish social and legal aspects of the marital relationship. As suggested above, one can be legally married without having anything resembling a marriage in a social sense. Conversely, one can live the life of a married person, perhaps even have a wedding ceremony with family and friends, yet never have legal marital status, if one never asks the state to confer that status or asks and is refused (e.g., because one's quasi-spouse is of the same sex). But in nearly every instance when a heterosexual couple has a wedding ceremony, they elect to become legally married as well, obtaining a state license to marry and then a state-issued marriage certificate. The 85 percent figure therefore refers to those who both have a wedding ceremony of some sort and obtain a state-issued certificate of legal marriage. The great majority of people do it.

Legal marriage arises in the Western world only by the voluntary choice of both parties to the relationship. See, e.g., N.M. Stat. Ann. §40-1-1 ("Marriage is contemplated by the law as a civil contract, for which the consent of the contracting parties, capable in law of contracting, is essential."). "Should I get married?" and "should we get married to each other?" are therefore questions nearly all competent adults face at some point. To answer the first of those two questions, one would take into account any practical differences that it makes to be legally married rather than not. To answer the second, one might want to know what characteristics make a particular other person a good prospect as a spouse. We will consider both of those things in this chapter, as well as what the law requires and what it authorizes in connection with getting legally married.

As noted, getting "legally married" is entirely distinct from getting married for private, social, or religious purposes. In the vast majority of states, there is no law imposing constraints on private marriage *per se*; if some church or other organization decided to recognize and perform ceremonies for marriages between brothers and sisters, parents and their children, or people and horses, state officials have no legal authority to stop them from doing so. A few states make it a crime for those persons whom the state has authorized to perform marriage ceremonies to do so without the couple's presenting a marriage license, but such laws are almost never enforced, do not apply to persons who are not authorized by the state to perform marriages, and beg the interpretive question of whether "performing a marriage ceremony" means performing a ceremony that purports to be of a legal marriage. See, e.g., N.Y. Dom. Rel. Law §17 (making it a crime for a "clergyman or other person authorized by the laws of this state to perform marriage ceremonies" or to "solemnize or presume to solemnize any marriage" when the couple does not have a state-issued marriage license); Cal. Penal Code §360 (similar) (no cases in annotations); N.M. Stat. Ann. §40-1-19 (similar) (no cases in annotation); and People v. Greenleaf, 780 N.Y.S.2d 899 (N.Y. Just. Ct. 2004) (dismissing prosecution for performance of a same-sex marriage). Such purely private marriages would, however, have no legal effect. They would not excuse the married parties from any general legal prohibitions as to conduct (e.g., as to incest, child abuse, or bestiality), and they would not make the parties eligible for benefits that attach to legal marriage, including the protections of divorce law. See, e.g., Pinkhasov v. Petocz, 331 S.W.3d 285 (Ky. App. 2011) (holding that couple who deliberately chose not to secure marriage license prior to, or marriage certificate after, Jewish wedding ceremony, were not legally spouses, and therefore dismissing woman's suit for divorce).

A. WHY MARRIAGE?

This is a question both lawmakers and private persons should ask. What reasons does the state have for creating a special legal status called marriage? What reasons does any couple have for wanting that status?

Imagine yourself a legislator in a society with no marriage laws. You know that nearly all adults enter into intimate relationships (your society does have laws proscribing sexual activity with and among minors) and cohabit, and that most couples at some point have a private ceremony at which they declare a permanent commitment and celebrate their union with family and friends. What do you think would be better about your society if you created a legal status of "married" and passed various laws governing that particular status? Would people be happier or more satisfied as a result simply of the state's acknowledging that they have formed such a union? If so, that might also be true of friendships; perhaps as a legislator you should also propose codifying the legal status of BFF? Cf. Laura A. Rosenbury, *Friends with Benefits?*, 106 Mich. L. Rev. 189 (2007) (arguing for legal cognizance of the role that friendships play in people's lives). Proponents of same-sex marriage have at times emphasized the symbolic importance of legal marriage, or have spoken of the state honoring their relationship. But is the symbolism that concerns them really about equality rather than about the inherent value of the state calling people married? Do heterosexual married couples derive additional enjoyment from their relationship as a result of *the state* taking notice of it?

If the point of creating marriage laws would instead be to create some material or practical benefits, what are they, and why would you as a legislator choose to establish such benefits just for people who have a ceremony that they call a wedding? Is the point to encourage more people to have such a ceremony? If so, why? Would not enough people do it in a regime of no marriage laws? If that is a real concern, what do we know about the people who need state encouragement in order to have such a ceremony? Does having the ceremony generate positive changes in their relationship, or make it more healthy and enduring? If so, why?

Or would the point of creating legal marriage status and special laws for the marital relationship be simply to create a set of default contract rules that couples who wish to can sign on to as a matter of convenience? If so, would there be any reason for any couples both to enter into an individualized contract (i.e., a pre-nuptial agreement) and to enter into legal marriage? If the point is instead to create some unwaivable protections for one or both parties to a marital contract (e.g., to financial support during or after marriage if one party has no means of self-support), why does any adult in today's society need the state to do that? And does the state's intrusion have any downside?

Now, what about the motivation of private parties in the real world today? There is still a societal expectation that all heterosexuals will marry; those who never do are considered odd. But the percentage of those in the United States who never marry has risen substantially in the past half century, and increasingly people are doing it as a deliberate choice and matter of principle. See SASHA CAGEN, QUIRKYALONE (2006). The percentage of never-married men in their early 40s increased from roughly 5 percent in 1970 to roughly 20 percent in 2010. The increase for women in their early 40s over that time was from roughly 6 percent to roughly 14 percent. And it is rare for people to have a first marriage after age 45. In 1950, 78 percent of all households in the United States included a married couple, whereas the 2010 census showed that the rate is now less than 50 percent. The traditional family consisting of a married couple with their children now represents only one-fifth of all households. What is the explanation for the declining marriage rate? Here are some possible explanations:

1. Marriage used to be the only way to have sex, now it is a sexual straightjacket.
2. Divorce used to be rare and disgraceful, now it is common and accepted. The most desirable mates are therefore available for multiple, albeit only serial, marriages. "In modern times, women would rather become the second trophy wife of an older alpha male or never marry at all, than settle for an omega male." Half Sigma, Percentage of Whites Who Never Married, by Sex, Apr. 05, 2008, http://www.half-sigma.com/2008/04/percentage-of-w.html. This hypothesis is consistent with the greater increase in the never-married rate for men relative to women.
3. People today put off marrying until a later age, giving them a shorter window of time in which to find a mate before the child bearing period passes (for women) and before they become so accustomed to living alone that marriage is less attractive to them. People put off marrying because expectations for education have risen, and because higher expectations for personal fulfillment in marriage have made people pickier about whom they marry. See A.J. Cherlin, *The Deinstitutionalization of American Marriage*, 66 J. MARRIAGE & FAM. 848-862 (2004).
4. Society today is more tolerant of non-marital cohabitation and of diverse moral outlooks, so some people choose simply to live together and not involve the state in their private life by getting a marriage license, especially if they are not going to have children, which is also something more people are choosing today.
5. Women have less reason to marry today, because they now have less need than in the past for the financial support that having a husband might provide and because they now can enjoy single motherhood without the scorn that used to attend it.

For fuller explanation of declining marriage rates, see Linda McClain, *Love, Marriage, and the Baby Carriage: Revisiting the Channelling Function of Family Law*, 28 CARDOZO L. REV. 2133, 2138-2147 (2007), and *Social Indicators of Marital Health & Well-Being, in* THE STATE OF OUR UNIONS: MARRIAGE IN 2011, 60-67 (W. Bradford Wilcox ed., 2011).

The first hypothesis above reflects the fact that historically there were prohibitions on what unmarried people could legally do to or with each other that did not apply to married people, including having sex. This was once also true of violence; as discussed further in Chapter 3, it has always been criminal in the United States for a man to rape or beat a (non-slave) woman who was not his spouse, but until a half century ago many jurisdictions recognized a legal right of husbands to apply corporal punishment to a wife and to force sex on her. It seems unlikely that a desire to commit violence against women was ever a motive for men to get married, but a desire to have sex might well have been a motive for many. Non-marital sex has been criminal for most of American history, and many states today still have anti-"fornication" laws in their criminal codes, though none systematically enforce such laws. In contrast, it has, of course, always been legal to have consensual sex with one's spouse. We will consider first why marriage has historically been a necessary condition for legally having sex, and then whether states constitutionally could enforce anti-fornication laws today if they wished to do so.

The historical explanation for criminalizing sex outside of marriage is that the state has wished to channel all procreation into marriage. Especially in earlier times when birth control was not widespread or especially effective, this meant channeling all sex into marriage. See Linda McClain, *supra*, for extensive discussion of this channeling function of marriage. Such channeling is still official policy, and the availability of effective birth control has not eliminated the risk of non-marital births, so the state still has some reason to punish people for non-marital sex. But this raises the question of why there has been a policy of channeling procreation into marriage—that is, into permanently bound heterosexual pairs.

In modern times, one expressed justification for this channeling has been that a marital family, with two parents living together and cooperating in child rearing, is the best environment for child rearing. See, e.g., Hernandez v. Robles, 855 N.E.2d 1, 7 (N.Y. 2006) (discussing state justifications for limiting marriage to different-sex couples). There is empirical evidence to support that view. See Robin Fretwell Wilson, *Evaluating Marriage: Does Marriage Matter to the Nurturing of Children?*, 42 San Diego L. Rev. 847, 876-879 (2005). Another expressed justification has been that married parents internalize the costs of child rearing to a greater degree than single parents do, because they tend to be wealthier; single mothers are more likely to seek welfare payments for their children. See Linda J. Waite & Evelyn L. Lehrer, *The Benefits from Marriage and Religion in the United States: A Comparative Analysis*, 29 Population & Dev. Rev. 255, 259 (2003).

Historical *explanations* for the emergence of marriage as a custom and legal institution, however, are quite different from these expressed justifications. Some historians maintain, for example, that the Church promoted the practice of marriage and the norm of confining sex to the marriage relationships in the Middle Ages simply in order to minimize the number of babies born. At one time the Church stood to collect the estates of childless decedents, so reducing births was financially beneficial for the Church. See Kevin MacDonald, *The Establishment and Maintenance of Socially Imposed Monogamy in Western Europe*, 14 Pol. & Life Sci. 3, 10 (1995) (citing historical work). Going back much further in time, some evolutionary theorists offer this theory of pair bonding:

William Marsiglio, Procreative Man

35-36 (N.Y.U. Press 1997)

At some point in time, . . . men (and women) developed a cursory understanding that they and/or others had contributed to the birth of infants through sexual acts. . . . [T]hese early men experienced a dilemma because while they had a crude sense that babies were created through sexual intercourse, they were physiologically detached from the gestation and labor process. This, in turn, made the establishment of paternity problematic. These men had no way of being absolutely certain that a child was, in fact, their child. Documenting one's paternity was consequently an act of personal faith reinforced by community cooperation. Men's tacit acceptance of other men's paternity claims provided the collusion necessary to perpetuate patriarchal social systems. In short, others in the tribe, clan, or community had to accept men's paternity claims for this sytem to work. . . . [M]en's efforts to develop an ideology of continuity that linked fathers to their offspring, solidifying the patriarchal system, necessitated that they develop social and legal institutions such as marriage in order for them to lay legal claim to their children. This practice connected the biological paternity of children and social fatherhood with men's marital relationships. Men were, in effect, indirectly appropriating their children by asserting their paternal rights vis-à-vis their legal relationship with, and ownership of, their children's mother. . . .

This account does not make clear why men, upon discovering their role in the reproductive process, were motivated to lay claim to the children produced with their involvement. If ownership of children per se was of value, why would it matter who was involved in producing them? What is the thought process connecting "this baby was born because I had sex with that woman" to "I want to possess that baby"? If having played a role in production did not matter to men, and instead men simply wished to own any children, why would not marriage have developed before humans became aware of how reproduction worked, as an indirect means for men to possess some children? If, on the other hand, possessing children per se was not something early males desired, why would they want to possess children resulting from their sexual acts, after they became aware of that causal reality? Perhaps possessiveness about one's genetic offspring, entailing an inclination to exert dominion over the mother of those offspring, is itself simply another trait that natural selection favored, rather than a conscious choice men made when they discovered that children resulted from sex? Is it plausible to suppose that a random genetic variation inclined some men to care specifically about children they helped to produce, thereby giving those children (who would inherit that genetic variation) a greater chance of survival? Would the evolutionary explanation for maternal care be pretty much the same?

In more recent times, the desire of men to control women has been manifest in legal rules disempowering women upon marriage. Before the mid-nineteenth century, "coverture" law in the United States essentially made women non-persons, precluding them from owning property or bringing legal actions in their own name. Today wives and husbands in the United States have equal legal rights, but coverture regimes remain in place in some developing countries. Chapter 3 addresses this topic.

A contrary hypothesis is that marriage developed in order to constrain men, whose naturally best reproductive strategy is to impregnate as many women as possible, and so to leave any sexual partner immediately after conception in order to go find another. One family policy organization asserts:

> Marriage emerged in virtually every known society to wrestle with the problematic of fatherhood, the biologically based sexual asymmetry in which men and women jointly have sex, but women alone bear children. The process of gestation and birth ensures that at a minimum, the mother is around when the baby is born. But no identical biological imperative connects that father to his child, or to the mother of his children. Marriage emerges out of the child's need for a father and the mother's need for a mate.

Institute for American Values and Institute for Marriage & Public Policy, Marriage and the Law: A Statement of Principles 15 (2006).

Professor Murray explains that before the middle of the twentieth century, criminal seduction laws effectively forced into marriage any man who induced a single woman to have sex with him by promising to marry her; men faced years in jail if prosecuted for seduction, but could avoid this by marrying the "victim." Professor Murray maintains that still today marriage is a "disciplinary institution," entailing imposition of legal obligations and societal norms and "deprivation of certain liberties and freedoms," with the aim of channeling sex into marriage. Melissa Murray, *Marriage as Punishment,* 112 Colum. L. Rev. 1 (2011). Viewed from another perspective, the law of marital privileges and responsibilities reflects a normative ideal of intimate life, and the criminal law reinforces the ideal by criminalizing certain behavior outside of marriage and failure to fulfill prescribed responsibilities. See Melissa Murray, *Strange Bedfellows: Criminal Law, Family Law, and the Legal Construction of Intimate Life,* 94 Iowa L. Rev. 1253 (2009).

Is it more plausible to believe marriage arose as a means of serving men's desire to control women or to believe that it arose as a means to constrain men's behavior for the sake of women and children? Could both hypotheses be correct?

Still another explanation for the emergence of permanent pair bonding as a custom links it to the need for tribal alliances and an efficient means of wealth transmission.

Kerry Abrams & Peter Brooks, Marriage as a Message: Same-Sex Couples and the Rhetoric of Accidental Procreation

21 Yale J.L. & Human. 1, 7-13 (2009)

Lévi-Strauss argued that marriage had nothing to do with the regulation of sexuality or procreation but rather with the creation of alliances among different kinship groups. . . . [U]nless small kinship groups attempted to reach out to other groups, creating tribes (and ultimately nations), they were vulnerable to attack and extinction. . . . [M]arriage . . . creates alliances between families that in turn create communities, governments, and organizations of membership and belonging. For Lévi-Strauss, this need for exogamy is the reason behind the incest taboos that seem to exist in almost all cultures. Sex and procreation with members of one's own family prevents a person from using sex and procreation as tools of alliance building—prevents the development of culture, law, the state. . . .

In the English legal tradition, the exchange of women through marriage served not only the function of creating alliances for purposes of survival but also for maintaining control over private property. Marriage can be seen as an efficient method of determining which children would become heirs, and would therefore be legally entitled to inherit property. Children born outside marriage—bastards—were not able to inherit. . . . Marriage provided . . . a way for men to determine how to transmit wealth independent of accidental procreation. Men could procreate, whether intentionally or accidentally, and widely, but it was only those children born within marriage or those children a man chose to legitimate who could become heirs. Marriage thus functioned not as a check on the wildness of male heterosexuality but as a way for men to maintain sexual freedom without adverse financial consequences to themselves or their (official) families. . . .

Historians have observed a marked difference in the cultural purpose of marriage in the past two centuries: the rise of companionate marriage, in which spouses are expected to satisfy each others' emotional needs. This is a highly personal, individualistic view of marriage where the couple's personal desires take precedence over the needs of the individuals' fathers to control their property, their extended families to create alliances, or the community's need to discipline sexuality. These historians describe the twentieth century family as an "encounter group," or a private sphere where couples can "express creativity . . . individuality . . . shared identity, and . . . changing commitments . . . love." This most recent version of family life puts particular pressure on marriage to be fulfilling. As John Demos puts it, "[m]onogamous marriage is liable to become boring and stultifying; in other things, after all, variety is 'the spice of life' . . . 'spice' and 'space': these are, in fact, the qualities for which we yearn most especially. And the family severely limits our access to either one." Lawrence Friedman is careful to insist that this emphasis on the individual does not mean that the family has declined, fallen, or dissolved. Rather, it has "changed and broadened . . . become more elastic." Certainly it has become less tethered to procreation and more bound up in fulfillment. . . .

Three developments in particular have had a major impact on why we are now able to think about marriage as an individual act of personal fulfillment: effective contraception, legal abortion, and child support statutes. Despite the myriad problems with enforcement of child support statutes, they still provide a method of regulating male reproductive sexuality much more broadly than marriage ever could. Whereas marriage put men in the driver's seat, allowing them to determine which children they fathered would be legal children, the presumption behind child support statutes is that any child fathered by a particular man has a financial claim for support from that man, regardless of the father's intention at the time of conception. Access to abortion and contraception have further decreased the need for a disciplining institution, at least for those people who are willing to use them; it is no longer self-evident that the only result of heterosexual intercourse will be procreation.

Is it plausible to think that marriage still serves the function of creating alliances that hold communities and even nations together? That it still has implications for wealth transmission that are important to families—if not consciously so for newlyweds, perhaps for their parents?

In terms of its positive functions today (we will soon consider possible negative consequences as well), marriage is believed to benefit society in additional ways. Sharing a household generates efficiencies, and people who undertake a long-term commitment to care for each other spare the state from having to pay for the needs of anyone who is not financially self-sufficient. Cf. Angela Onwuachi-Willig, *The Return of the Ring: Welfare Reform's Marriage Cure as the Revival of Post-Bellum Control*, 93 Cal. L. Rev. 1647 (2005) (critiquing pro-marriage aspects of welfare reform legislation and arguing that the state should better enable single persons to be economically self-sufficient). Related to the modern, individualistic view of marriage as a vehicle of personal fulfillment, some assert that a well-functioning marriage makes spouses psychologically healthier and more stable than they would be if single, which in turn makes them more productive, independent, and law-abiding. In addition, marriage is said to strengthen communities, in ways other than by creating procreative alliances: "Because of the social roles attached to marriage, . . . marriage embeds individuals in more social networks. To be precise, marriage leads men (but not women) to join voluntary associations, and it reduces withdrawals by both men and women from voluntary associations. . . . Greater participation in voluntary associations in the United States improves the performance of state governments, and in both the United States and Europe, greater participation in voluntary associations increases the trust that individuals have in other people. A rise in the level of trust in a society promotes the quality of government and fosters not only adequate physical infrastructure in a country but adequate educational facilities as well. An increase in trust in a country also lowers the overall homicide rate." Larry D. Barnett & Pietro Saitta, *Societal Properties and Law on Same-Sex Non-Marital Partnerships and Same-Sex Marriage in European Union Nation,* 25 J. Civ. Rts. & Econ. Dev. 625, 636-637 (2011). Cf. Jennifer Wriggins, *Marriage Law and Family Law: Autonomy, Interdependence, and Couples of the Same Gender,* 41 B.C. L. Rev. 265 (2000) (maintaining that exclusion of same-sex couples from marriage undermines community by treating members of such couples as atomistic individuals).

Whatever the correct historical explanation for the social practice of marriage, as a matter of modern legal history it is clear that marriage until recently effected a transition from a position of not being legally permitted to have sex at all, with anyone, to the position of being permitted to have sex with precisely one person. It still means this for minors who are able to marry. See, e.g., State v. Pryes, 771 N.W.2d 930 (Wis. App. June 10, 2009) (upholding statutory exemption for inter-spousal intercourse from statutory rape law, against equal protection challenge by man who had sex with a minor who was not his wife). But for adults today marriage instead means going from being able legally to have sex with any other consenting, unmarried, unrelated adult in the world to an expectation (legally enforceable in some ways in some states) that one will have sex with only one person, for as long as the marriage lasts. This makes single life more attractive for many people than it used to be. Fornication prohibitions remain in the criminal codes of about ten states, but the Supreme Court's 2003 decision in *Lawrence v. Texas,* holding that states may not criminalize homosexual sexual activity, implies that anti-fornication laws are unconstitutional. Legal tests are not likely to come from prosecutions for fornication, because states simply do not enforce anti-fornication laws. Instead they will arise, if at all, indirectly, as in this Virginia case:

Martin v. Ziherl

607 S.E.2d 367 (Va. 2005)

Opinion by Justice Elizabeth B. Lacy.

Martin and Ziherl were unmarried adults in a sexually active relationship from approximately October 31, 2001 through November 3, 2003. Martin experienced a vaginal outbreak in June 2003, which her physician diagnosed as herpes. Martin filed a motion for judgment against Ziherl alleging that he knew he was infected with the sexually transmitted herpes virus when he and Martin were engaged in unprotected sexual conduct, knew that the virus was contagious, and failed to inform Martin of his condition. . . . Martin asserted claims of negligence, intentional battery and intentional infliction of emotional distress and sought compensatory and punitive damages.

Ziherl filed a demurrer asserting that Martin's injuries were caused by her participation in an illegal act and therefore [she] did not state a claim upon which relief could be granted. . . .

Martin asserts that the reasoning of the Supreme Court of the United States in *Lawrence v. Texas* renders Virginia's statute criminalizing the sexual intercourse between two unmarried persons, Code §18.2-344, unconstitutional. The issue in *Lawrence* . . . was "whether the petitioners were free as adults to engage in the private conduct in the exercise of their liberty under the Due Process Clause of the Fourteenth Amendment to the Constitution." Lawrence had been convicted of violating a Texas statute that made it a crime for two persons of the same sex to engage in certain intimate sexual conduct described as the act of sodomy. . . . The Court explained that the liberty interest at issue was not a fundamental right to engage in certain conduct but was the right to enter and maintain a personal relationship without governmental interference. The Court determined that the statutes proscribing certain acts between persons of the same sex sought to control a personal relationship that is "within the liberty of persons to choose without being punished as criminals." The Court explained that the constitution protects the liberty interests of persons to maintain a personal relationship "in the confines of their homes and their own private lives" and that an element of that relationship is its "overt expression in intimate conduct."

In overruling *Bowers*, the Court also stated that the analysis of Justice Stevens in his dissenting opinion in *Bowers* . . . "should control" in *Lawrence*. That analysis is:

> Our prior cases make two propositions abundantly clear. First, the fact that the governing majority in a State has traditionally viewed a particular practice as immoral is not a sufficient reason for upholding a law prohibiting the practice; neither history nor tradition could save a law prohibiting miscegenation from constitutional attack. Second, individual decisions by married persons, concerning the intimacies of their physical relationship, even when not intended to produce offspring, are a form of "liberty" protected by the Due Process Clause of the Fourteenth Amendment. Moreover, this protection extends to intimate choices by unmarried as well as married persons.

Applying Justice Stevens' analysis, the Court stated, "The State cannot demean their existence or control their destiny by making their private sexual conduct a crime. Their right to liberty under the Due Process Clause gives them the full right to engage in their conduct without intervention of the government."

We find no relevant distinction between the circumstances in *Lawrence* and the circumstances in the present case.* . . . We find no principled way to conclude that the specific act of intercourse is not an element of a personal relationship between two unmarried persons or that the Virginia statute criminalizing intercourse between unmarried persons does not improperly abridge a personal relationship that is within the liberty interest of persons to choose. Because Code §18.2-334 . . . is an attempt by the state to control the liberty interest which is exercised in making these personal decisions, it violates the Due Process Clause of the Fourteenth Amendment.

. . . [T]he trial court held, that Code §18.2-344 withstands constitutional scrutiny because "[v]alid public reasons for the law exist," including protection of public health and "encouraging that children be born into a family consisting of a married couple." Regardless of the merit of the policies referred to by the trial court, the Supreme Court in *Lawrence* indicated that such policies are insufficient to sustain the statute's constitutionality.

*Indeed, but for the nature of the sexual act, the provisions of Code §18.2-344 are identical to those of the Texas statute which *Lawrence* determined to be unconstitutional.

The Supreme Court did not consider the liberty right vindicated in *Lawrence* as a fundamental constitutional right which could be infringed only if the statute in question satisfied the strict scrutiny test. Rather, the Court applied a rational basis test, but held that "[t]he Texas statute furthers no legitimate state interest which can justify its intrusion into the personal and private life of the individual." This statement is not limited to state interests offered by the state of Texas in support of its statute, but sweeps within it all manner of states' interests and finds them insufficient when measured against the intrusion upon a person's liberty interest when that interest is exercised in the form of private, consensual sexual conduct between adults. As we have said, this same liberty interest is invoked in this case when two unmarried adults make the choice to engage in the intimate sexual conduct proscribed by Code §18.2-344. Thus, as in *Lawrence*, the Commonwealth's interests do not warrant such encroachment on personal liberty. . . .

It is important to note that this case does not involve minors, non-consensual activity, prostitution, or public activity. The *Lawrence* court indicated that state regulation of that type of activity might support a different result. . . . Our holding does not affect the Commonwealth's police power regarding regulation of public fornication, prostitution, or other such crimes.

The rule applied in *Zysk* was that "a party who consents to and participates in an immoral and illegal act cannot recover damages from other participants for the consequence of that act." We adhere to that rule. However, in light of our determination regarding the constitutionality of Code §18.2-344, the sexual activity between Martin and Ziherl was not illegal and "the fact that the governing majority in a State has traditionally viewed a particular practice as immoral is not a sufficient reason for upholding a law prohibiting the practice." Therefore, *Zysk* is no longer controlling precedent to the extent that its holding applies to private, consensual sexual intercourse.

For the reasons stated above, we will reverse the judgment of the trial court and remand the case for further proceedings consistent with this opinion.

Is a court really applying a rational basis test if it begins with an assumption that "all manner of states' interests" are insufficient to justify interference with "private, consensual sexual conduct between adults"? Would the *Lawrence* Court, addressing the constitutionality of applying to gay men a statute criminalizing sodomy, have had reason to consider the state's policy of "encouraging that children be born into a family consisting of a married couple"? Is not the possibility of unintended pregnancy a real and important difference between heterosexual intimacy and homosexual intimacy, one that gives the state a stronger basis for criminalizing heterosexual fornication than it has for criminalizing homosexual sodomy? Putting aside the constitutional issue, should Martin have been able to sue Ziherl for her injury?

Martin is the sole decision of a high state court ruling on the constitutionality of a fornication law post-*Lawrence*. A county level court in North Carolina reached the same conclusion as *Martin* in Hobbs v. Smith, 2006 WL 3193998 (N.C. Super. Ct. Sept. 12, 2006), when a woman challenged that state's law after being forced out of her government job because she was living with her boyfriend. It is difficult to imagine any state court coming out differently on the question of an anti-fornication law's constitutionality. If unmarried individuals have a constitutional right to sexual intimacy with someone of the same sex, it would be impolitic, if not illogical, to deny unmarried individuals a constitutional right to have sex with someone of the opposite sex. The factual difference between the two cases—that is, the potential for conception in the latter case—is not likely to suffice for any court as a justification for different treatment. Do you think moral conservatives would still want anti-fornication laws upheld, given that same-sex intimacy is now constitutionally protected?

Nearly half of U.S. states make adultery a crime. What would the implications of the *Martin* holding be for such laws? Are they unconstitutional as well? How about laws of the sort we will see in later chapters that attach financial consequences to adultery in divorce proceedings? Should a "rational basis" be sufficient to uphold any law that punishes consensual sexual behavior between adults? Adultery prosecutions are exceedingly rare, though some do occur. See, e.g., Jonathan Turley, *Of Lust and the Law*, WASH. POST, Sept. 8, 2004, at p. B01 (reporting guilty plea of former town attorney prosecuted for adultery). Where adultery remains a crime, former spouses can use that fact to sway a child custody decision against an ex who commits it. Adulterers can also use it to their advantage in a divorce or custody trial, however, by asserting a Fifth Amendment privilege against self-incrimination in response to any hostile questioning about intimate relationships with third parties.

Sex/Wealth Exchanges

The *Martin* court emphasized that its ruling would have no effect on Virginia's law criminalizing prostitution. Such a law is an enduring instance of state regulation of intimacy outside of marriage. Thus, in Virginia today, providing or purchasing "escort services" is criminal, but the following interactions are entirely legal: 1) two people meet at a party, have mutually consensual sex that night simply for the sake of having physical pleasure, or so that they can boast to friends, and never interact with each other again; 2) a person with little wealth dates and then has sex on a regular basis with another person who is quite wealthy, simply because the first person wants to get some of the other person's wealth, in the form of gifts, dinners out, a nice place to stay, etc.; 3) a law student has sex with a professor solely in the hope that this will result in a better grade; 4) an employee has sex with a supervisor solely in the hope that this will result in a raise or promotion; 5) a woman agrees to have sex with her boyfriend only after he gives her an engagement ring; 6) women in a particular minority cultural group will marry only after receiving a bride price, and will only have sex when married; 7) an 18-year-old marries a 90-year-old billionaire, after they sign a pre-nuptial agreement in which he commits to executing a will leaving her half his estate. Has Virginia drawn the line of state regulation of intimacy in the correct place? Or should it move the line in one direction or the other, either legalizing explicit exchanges of sex and money or making some forms of implicit or indirect sex/wealth exchange illegal? Cf. Jill Hasday, *Intimacy and Economic Exchange*, 119 HARV. L. REV. 491 (2005) (arguing that "legal efforts to denote the sanctity of intimate relationships by regulating and restricting the exchange of economic resources within them appear to systematically perpetuate and exacerbate distributive inequality for women and poorer people").

In light of the inefficacy of fornication laws and the virtual disappearance of the social norm of celibacy till marriage, permission to have sex is no longer a reason to get married for many people. Why do it then? Why when you fall in love with someone, and decide that you want to live together and create a family life together, do you go tell the state about it and get its approval? Why don't you just do it and limit your public declarations of ecstasy to your family and friends? Increasingly, couples in the United States are choosing to do that, to keep their intimate lives private. Scandinavian countries are ahead of (or behind, depending on your outlook) us in this regard; there couples who seek state recognition of their relationship are only a slim majority of all cohabiting couples.

The same-sex marriage debate in the United States, though it has been about symbolism as well, has focused to a great extent on the material benefits that marriage affords. No longer applying the stick of criminal prosecution for fornication in order to drive people into marriage, the state now dangles the carrots of financial incentives and practical advantages in order to draw them into marriage. In holding that the state must, as a matter of equal protection, afford same-sex couples some legal status equivalent to marriage, the Vermont Supreme Court itemized many of the practical benefits at stake:

> [T]he benefits and protections incident to a marriage license under Vermont law have never been greater. They include, for example, the right to receive a portion of the estate of a spouse who dies intestate and protection against disinheritance through elective share provisions; preference in being appointed as the personal representative of a spouse who dies intestate; the right to bring a lawsuit for the wrongful death of a spouse; the right to bring an action for loss of consortium; the right to workers' compensation survivor benefits; the right to spousal benefits statutorily guaranteed to public employees, including health, life, disability, and accident insurance; the opportunity to be covered as a spouse under group life insurance policies issued to an employee; the opportunity to be covered as the insured's spouse under an individual health insurance policy; the right to claim an evidentiary privilege for marital communications; homestead rights and protections; the presumption of joint ownership of property and the concomitant right of survivorship; hospital visitation and other rights incident to the medical treatment of a family member; and the right to receive, and the obligation to provide, spousal support, maintenance, and property division in the event of separation or divorce.

Baker v. State, 744 A.2d 864 (Vt. 1999).

In addition to this list, there is an income tax benefit for high income earners who marry someone with little or no income. See generally Martha T. McCluskey, *Taxing the Family Work: Aid for Affluent Husband Care*, 21 COLUM. J. GENDER & L. 109 (2011). Professor McCluskey observes that "the affluent breadwinner-homemaker family form often held out as the model of self-sufficiency instead relies on special government tax support amounting to over thirty billion dollars a year." Id. at 114.

Which of those benefits would matter most to you in thinking about whether to marry? Which can you enjoy without marriage, by private contracting or by executing other documents, such as a will, power of attorney, or health care proxy? Could state bestowal of special benefits on married people ever be so coercive as to violate individuals' constitutional right to freedom of choice with respect to marriage?

Some of these benefits of marriage entail state subsidization of marriage, and therefore amount to wealth transfers from single people to married people. Is that transfer fair to unmarried taxpayers? Recall the discussion above of the supposed positive externalities of marriage—that is, optimal child-rearing environment, greater productivity, stability, community cohesion. But see Laura A. Rosenbury, *Friends with Benefits?*, 106 MICH. L. REV. 189 (2007) (arguing that the law unjustifiably overlooks the ways in which persons in non-"family" personal relationships also provide each other with care, support, and companionship), and McCloskey, supra (noting that many unmarried persons support a lower-income partner and/or pay for—without tax deduction—many services that a homemaker spouse typically provides to a breadwinner spouse). See also Dorothy A. Brown, *The Marriage Penalty/Bonus Debate: Legislative Issues in Black and White,* 16 N.Y.L. Sch. J. Hum. Rts. 287, 295-296 (1999) (showing that at every level of income, a smaller percentage of married African Americans than married white couples receive marriage bonuses).

Holning Lau & Charles Q. Strohm, The Effects of Legally Recognizing Same-Sex Unions on Health and Well-Being

27 Law & Inequality 107 (2011)

. . . Social scientists have studied the effects of marriage on different-sex couples by comparing individuals who are married, cohabiting (but unmarried), and single. This body of research finds that married couples, on average, enjoy better mental and physical health, exercise better health behaviors, and report greater life satisfaction than their unmarried counterparts. Although some studies find that men benefit from marriage more than women do, most recent studies find that the positive effects of marriage accrue to both men and women. . . . Although several studies suggest that self-selection is a factor [i.e., "individuals who are healthier and happier may be more likely to enter and remain in marriages"], other research suggests that self-selection only provides a partial explanation. . . .

Why might marriage have this transformative effect on couples? The most prominent explanations developed by scholars can be organized into three main parts. First, the legal rights and responsibilities of marriage can promote care between spouses, thereby contributing to their health and well-being. For example, spouses have rights to medical leave to attend to each other's needs. The legal responsibility of spousal support also enforces caregiving. Some rights associated with marriage may improve health and well-being even if they do not foster caregiving. For example, the federal government offers health care benefits to spouses of federal employees, which may improve their health regardless of the nature of their marriages. Second, the social meaning of marriage promotes commitment between the couple, which in turn fosters care. For example, the widely-held understanding of marriage as a long-term relationship of mutual dependence motivates partners to encourage each other's healthy behaviors and provide sanctions for unhealthy behaviors. Third, marriage can legitimize a relationship in the eyes of third parties such as family, friends, and other private actors. As a result, family and friends may offer greater social support to married couples than to unmarried partners, and such social support can enhance health and well-being. Similarly, private employers might limit their support, in the form of health care coverage, to legally recognized partners of employees. . . .

Others hypothesize that marriage lowers risk-taking behaviors in males, and therefore also their injuries to self, others, and property, because much such behavior is an unconscious strategy for attracting a mate. If you are single, do such accounts of marriage's salutary effects persuade you that the state should take some of your income and give it to married people? Does this forced single-to-married wealth transfer make you more inclined to get married yourself?

Marriage can also reduce state-provided financial benefits, however. Two-earner couples are likely to pay more in taxes collectively than their combined tax liability prior to marriage, and having a spouse might reduce or eliminate one's welfare or disability payments. See Robert E. Rains, *Disability and Family Relationships: Marriage Penalties and Support Anomalies,* 22 GA. ST. U. L. REV. 561 (2006).

Securing Material Benefits of Marriage Without Marrying

One argument sometimes advanced against same-sex marriage is that many of the benefits or protections of marriage that the Vermont court identified in *Baker v. State* are available to unmarried couples by contract or other private arrangement. As is true of any other two people, intimate non-marital partners can create for each other the same rights of inheritance and decision making in the event of incapacity that state law creates for spouses, by executing wills, powers of attorney, health care proxies, and the like. In addition, although intimate partners cannot secure by contract the special welfare and tax benefits that states confer on spouses, they can contract to impose on each other obligations of the sort that state laws governing marriage and divorce now impose on couples as a matter of default rule, such as property or support rights in the event of relationship dissolution. Though averse to enforcing contracts between unmarried partners in an earlier era, today courts are generally willing to do so. As the opinions in the following case reflect, however, there is great variety among the states as to what is required in order for an enforceable contract to exist, and as to what relief is available to a former domestic partner in the absence of a valid contract. States generally reject claims for ongoing post-dissolution support in the absence of a contract, but some are receptive to equitable claims for property or restitution awards.

Devaney v. L'Esperance

949 A.2d 743 (N.J. 2008)

Justice WALLACE, Jr., delivered the opinion of the Court.

. . . In 1983, plaintiff, Helen Devaney, then 23 years old, began working for defendant, Francis L'Esperance, Jr., as a receptionist for his ophthalmology medical practice. At that time, defendant was 51 years old and had been married to his current wife for approximately twenty years. Plaintiff and defendant embarked on a romantic relationship. . . .

In the beginning of their relationship, plaintiff lived in a variety of places, all of which were rented in her own name and mostly self-financed. At some point, defendant began paying plaintiff's telephone bill and gave her money for various other things. . . . She continued working for defendant in various capacities, at first full-time, and then part-time. For about ten years, plaintiff and defendant saw each other regularly and would spend vacations together. However, when the parties were not traveling, they rarely stayed overnight together. Defendant frequently had dinner at plaintiff's house, but he invariably returned home to his wife.

Plaintiff testified that defendant repeatedly told her that he would divorce his wife and marry her. In 1993, plaintiff terminated her employment with defendant and pursued educational opportunities. . . . A year later, she moved to Seattle, Washington, where she remained for approximately three years. Plaintiff testified that her decision to move was based primarily on defendant's unfulfilled promise to divorce his wife. During her stay in Seattle, plaintiff frequently spoke by telephone with defendant and requested money from him. Defendant would send her approximately four hundred dollars a month to cover her incidental expenses. During the time that plaintiff lived in Seattle, defendant visited her six or seven times.

In 1997, defendant asked plaintiff to return to the East Coast. Plaintiff testified that defendant promised that he would "make things right" by divorcing his wife, marrying plaintiff, and having a baby with her. She testified that she agreed to move back after defendant showed her a separation agreement that was signed by both defendant and his wife. Plaintiff also testified that defendant promised to buy her a home.

Plaintiff returned to New Jersey in 1997, and moved into a North Bergen condominium that defendant leased for her. In 1999, defendant purchased the condominium unit and plaintiff continued to reside there. Defendant also purchased a car that plaintiff used; gave her money for various expenses; and paid for her undergraduate and graduate education. Plaintiff ultimately received a Master's degree. Despite the increased support that defendant provided to plaintiff, the parties saw each other no more than two or three evenings at the condominium for dinner each week and sometimes one day on the weekend. During the seven years that plaintiff lived in the condominium, defendant spent only six or seven nights there.

In 2003, the parties considered having a child together. However, at some point, plaintiff learned that she would have difficulty conceiving a child. Defendant also changed his mind about wanting to have another child in August 2003 and conveyed that to plaintiff. Finally, defendant told plaintiff that he wanted to discontinue the relationship. Plaintiff continued to live in the North Bergen condominium, and in December 2003, she began a relationship with another man. In February 2004, defendant attempted to visit the condominium when plaintiff's new boyfriend was present, but defendant was denied entrance by plaintiff.

Shortly thereafter, defendant sought to remove plaintiff from the condominium and filed an action for ejectment. Eventually, the trial court granted defendant possession of the condominium and the judgment was affirmed on appeal. Plaintiff filed a complaint for palimony in October 2004. . . . The [trial] judge found that defendant had made "general promises" to plaintiff that he would take care of her and that "things would work out," [but] never promised to provide plaintiff with lifetime financial support. . . .

[A] cause of action for palimony . . . is a claim for support between unmarried persons. We first recognized such a cause of action in *Kozlowski v. Kozlowski* (1979). Prior to that decision, our courts would not enforce support agreements between unmarried individuals or married persons who lived together with someone other than their spouses because they were considered meretricious.

In *Kozlowski*, both the defendant and the plaintiff were married to other persons when the defendant induced the plaintiff to leave her husband and come live with him. The parties lived as a normal family unit for approximately six years. During that time, three of the four children of the two families came to live with the couple in their new home. Although a serious disagreement caused them to separate for a week, the defendant wanted to resume the relationship and promised to take care of and provide for the plaintiff for the rest of her life if she would return. The plaintiff agreed and the parties resumed their relationship for about nine more years before the defendant broke it off for another woman. The plaintiff filed suit against the defendant, seeking, among other things, future support for life. The trial court found that the defendant expressly agreed to support the plaintiff for the rest of her life and that such a promise was enforceable. . . .

[T]his Court . . . acknowledged the changing mores that resulted in many unmarried persons living together . . . :

> "[T]he prevalence of nonmarital relationships in modern society and the social acceptance of them, marks this as a time when our courts should by no means apply the doctrine of the unlawfulness of the so-called meretricious relationship to the instant case . . . [which] rested upon the fact that such conduct, as the word suggests, pertained to and encompassed prostitution. To equate the nonmarital relationship of today to such a subject matter is to do violence to an accepted and wholly different practice.
>
> We are aware that many young couples live together without the solemnization of marriage, in order to make sure that they can successfully later undertake marriage. This trial period, preliminary to marriage, serves as some assurance that the marriage will not subsequently end in dissolution to the harm of both parties. We . . . cannot impose a standard based on alleged moral considerations that have apparently been so widely abandoned by so many. . . . [E]xpress agreements will be enforced unless they rest on an unlawful meretricious consideration."

[Id. (quoting Marvin v. Marvin, 134 Cal. Rptr. 815 (1976)).]

The Court recognized that such an agreement may be expressed or implied because the "[p]arties entering this type of relationship usually do not record their understanding in specific legalese." The Court concluded that "an agreement between adult parties living together is enforceable to the extent it is not based on a relationship proscribed by law, or on a promise to marry." . . .

[T]he question we have not previously addressed is whether the parties may have a marital-type relationship, which is the underpinning of the consideration needed to support a claim for palimony, when they have not cohabited. . . . We . . . opt for a more flexible approach that seeks to achieve substantial justice in light of the realities of the relationship. It is the promise to support, expressed or implied, coupled with a marital-type relationship, that are the indispensable elements to support a valid claim for palimony. Indeed, whether the parties cohabited is a relevant factor in the analysis of whether a marital-type relationship exists, and in most successful palimony cases, cohabitation will be present. . . . [H]owever, . . . [t]here may be circumstances where a couple may hold themselves out to others as if they were married and yet not cohabit (i.e., couples who are separated due to employment, military, or educational opportunities and who do not cohabit). . . .

The trial judge in the present case . . . found that the parties did not live together; they did not spend significant periods of time together; they did not commingle their property or share living expenses; and they did not hold themselves out to the public as husband and wife. The trial judge correctly considered . . . the fact that defendant continued to live with his wife. Consequently, . . . "the parties' relationship was best characterized as a dating relationship." . . .

Justice Long, concurring.

I write separately to express my view that although the Court's opinion is an entirely correct paradigm in an implied contract case like the one before us, it should not be read in the future as applicable to an express contract. The right to support in a palimony action "does not derive from the relationship itself but rather is a right created by contract." To be enforceable, a contract must be supported by valuable consideration which involves a detriment incurred by a promisee or a benefit received by a promisor, at the promisor's request. The nature and sufficiency of the consideration is not a factor so long as it has been bargained for. Even where those requirements are satisfied, however, today, as at common law, certain contracts cannot be enforced, for example, contracts that are illegal or violative of public policy.

At common law, that bar applied where promises were based in whole or in part on sexual intercourse outside of the marriage relationship. Indeed, in a broad sweep, courts tended to view any contract arising from such a relationship as "meretricious" and unenforceable even if the relationship was not an express part of the bargain. . . . *Marvin* established the limited principle that cohabitation in itself is not meretricious. . . . Cohabitation only played a part in [*Marvin* and *Kozlowski*] because it was advanced as an *impediment* to an otherwise maintainable contract action. In turn, a marital-type relationship was only considered in *Marvin* and *Kozlowski* because it raised the spectre of cohabitation. Indeed, all that *Marvin* and *Kozlowski* established was that living together in a marital-type relationship is *not* a meretricious disqualifier, not that those circumstances are the only route to a contract claim.

That is not to suggest that the existence of a marital-type relationship is irrelevant. . . . Indeed, in an implied contract case such as the one before us, where courts look beyond what was said to the parties' acts, it is hard to imagine that any scenario other than a marriage-type relationship would sustain the conclusion that an implied promise of lifetime support was made. It is for that reason that I concur in the result reached here. I note as well that a party's actual willingness to live in a marital-type relationship is relevant to a consideration analysis. . . . My concern is that the Court's broad requirement of a marital-type relationship, which is entirely appropriate in an implied contract case such as this, will be carried over and bar enforcement of an express contract for lifetime support based on some other type of consideration. . . .

Justice RIVERA-SOTO, concurring in the result.

. . . The majority does not mention, much less discuss, the objective fact that the overwhelming weight of authority nationwide rejects a claim for palimony—a post-nonmarital relationship support or alimony obligation—and instead limits recovery to what a cohabitant has contributed to the relationship.

As a threshold matter, Alabama, Idaho, Oklahoma, South Carolina and Utah recognize common law marriages, and, for that reason, do not allow palimony claims. The vast majority of states that do not acknowledge common law marriages also have rejected a cause of action for palimony, although most have allowed parties to recoup either assets brought into the relationship or the value of the services they have provided to the relationship. Thus, even though Alaska does not explicitly recognize a *Marvin* palimony cause of action, it does allow for the division of property acquired during cohabitation, noting that "to the extent it is ascertainable, intent of the parties should control the distribution of property accumulated during the course of cohabitation." *Tolan v. Kimball* (Alaska 2001). Arkansas too does not recognize a palimony claim. . . . *Brissett v. Sykes* (Ark. 1993). Connecticut expressly states that "no right to palimony exists under Connecticut law." *Vibert v. Atchley* (Conn. Super. Ct. 1996). However, Connecticut "[c]ourts will enforce a contract, express or implied, between non marital partners, and may employ equitable remedies to enforce those agreements where necessary." *Hrostek v. Massey* (Conn. Super. Ct. 2007). Delaware likewise rejects palimony claims, particularly when one of the parties is already married. *Wells v. Boardley* (Del. Ch. 1981).

Georgia explicitly rejects any palimony claims. *Long v. Marino* (1994). Illinois jettisons palimony claims as surrogates for outlawed common law marriages. *Hewitt v. Hewitt* (1979). Although it does not recognize palimony claims, Iowa allows unmarried cohabitants to enforce property claims based on "a recognized legal theory outside marriage to support the claim." *In re Marriage of Martin* (Iowa 2004). Kansas disallows a palimony claim, but provides for "equitable division of the property accumulated by the parties during the period they were living together[,]" *Eaton v. Johnston* (Kan. 1984), a view also shared by Mississippi, Montana, New Hampshire, South Dakota and West Virginia. *Davis v. Davis* (Miss. 1994); *In re Kynett* (Mont. Dist. Ct. 1994); *Tapley v. Tapley* (N.H. 1982) (refusing to "recognize a contract which is implied from the rendition and acceptance of 'housewifely services[,]'" but acknowledging that "upon the dissolution of a non-marital living arrangement, either party may seek a judicial determination of the equitable rights of the parties in particular property"); *Bracken v. Bracken* (S.D. 1927) ("[i]f a woman should assume the duties of a housewife and care for a home, while the man assumed the duties of a husband and ran the farm, although both parties knew there was no marriage, such assumed relation might have a great bearing in determining the right to wages of one against the other, or upon the interest of each in the property acquired in the joint enterprise"); *Thomas v. LaRosa* (W. Va. 1990).

Kentucky rejects palimony claims for a straightforward and logical reason: "[w]ere it otherwise, the courts, in effect, would be reinstituting by judicial fiat common law marriage which by expressed public policy is not recognized." *Murphy v. Bowen* (Ky. Ct. App. 1988). Louisiana too rejects palimony claims. *Schwegmann v. Schwegmann* (La. Ct. App. 1983). Holding that "[i]t is not right to treat unmarried people as if they were married[,]" Maine does not recognize a palimony claim, but does allow recovery for "business[-]related services" and for "domestic services performed solely to allow the defendant to devote more time to his business[.]" *Ring v. Thompson* (Me. Super. Ct. Aug. 29, 1996). Maryland bars a palimony cause of action based on a continued sexual relationship, *Donovan v. Scuderi* (Md. 1982), or a promise to marry "whether attired in the full raiment of the prohibited action or disguised as another type of action." *Miller v. Ratner* (Md. App. 1997). Michigan explicitly rejects, as a matter of public policy, the palimony cause of action set forth in *Marvin*. *Carnes v. Sheldon* (Mich. App. 1981).

New York does not enforce contracts implied from the relationship of unmarried cohabitants, but does enforce express contracts for the distribution of earnings and assets acquired during the cohabitation. *Morone v. Morone* (N.Y. 1980). Ohio "decline[s] to follow [*Marvin*, supra, and like decisions] insofar as they recognize a new legal status for persons living together without benefit of marriage[,]" holding that "[t]here is no precedent in Ohio for dividing assets or property based on mere cohabitation without marriage[.]" *Lauper v. Harold* (Ohio App. 1985). Tennessee and Vermont do not allow palimony claims, but do enforce claims for property acquired during the relationship on a partnership theory. *Bass v. Bass* (Tenn. 1991) (explaining that "[t]he fact that the parties cohabited . . . has absolutely no bearing whatsoever [as a] partnership can be implied in this case while completely ignoring the parties' social relationship"); *Harman v. Rogers* (Vt. 1986).

Several states—Arizona, Colorado, Hawaii, Indiana, Massachusetts, Missouri, Nebraska, Nevada, New Mexico, North Carolina, Oregon, Pennsylvania, Rhode Island, Washington and Wyoming—do not explicitly address whether a palimony claim for support is cognizable, focusing instead on whether assets acquired during the non-marital cohabitation relationship are divisible. *See, e.g., Cook v. Cook* (Ariz. 1984) (stating that although "[t]he law will not give to non-marital cohabiting parties the benefit of community property rights, since these rights derive solely from the marital relationship[,]" nevertheless "'the fact that the parties engaged in a meretricious relationship does not bar either from asserting against the other such claims as would be otherwise enforceable[,]'"); *Salzman v. Bachrach* (Colo. 2000); *Maria v. Freitas* (Haw. 1992) (recognizing that "marriage holds 'positive and negative legal consequences for each party [and that a] person who is not legally married does not qualify for the positive legal consequences of marriage.'"); *Bright v. Kuehl* (Ind. Ct. App. 1995) (holding that in context of claim for compensatory damages arising out of cohabitation, "a party who cohabitates with another without subsequent marriage is entitled to relief upon a showing of an express contract or a viable equitable theory such as an implied contract or unjust enrichment"); *Davis v. Misiano* (Mass. 1977) (holding that unmarried partners have no right to support or alimony); *Wilcox v. Trautz* (Mass. 1998) (explaining that Massachusetts "do[es] not recognize common law marriage, do[es] not extend to unmarried couples the rights possessed by married couples who divorce, and reject[s] equitable remedies that might have the effect of dividing property between unmarried parties"); *Hudson v. DeLonjay* (Mo. Ct. App. 1987) (stating that "[t]he relevant inquiry is whether there was an agreement, either express or implied in fact, between the parties which was supported by valid consideration . . . even though the parties' contemplation of cohabitation may have been the reason for their entering into such an agreement at the outset"); *Taylor v. Frost* (Neb. 1979) (adopting rule that "'[a] bargain in whole or in part for or in consideration of illicit sexual intercourse or of a promise thereof is illegal; but subject to this exception such intercourse between parties to a bargain previously or subsequently formed does not invalidate it'"); *Western States Constr., Inc. v. Michoff* (Nev. 1992) (holding that "[u]nmarried couples who cohabit have the same rights to lawfully contract with each other regarding their property as do other unmarried individuals" (Nev. 1984); *Dominguez v. Cruz* (N.M. App. 1980) (holding that "if an agreement such as an oral contract can exist between business associates, one can exist between two cohabiting adults who are not married if the essential elements of the contractual relationship are present"); *Suggs v. Norris* (N.C. App. 1988) (allowing "recovery by a plaintiff partner to an unmarried but cohabiting or meretricious relationship, from the other partner's estate, for services rendered to or benefits conferred upon the other partner through the plaintiff's work in the operation of a joint business when the business proceeds were utilized to enrich the estate of the deceased partner"); *Shuraleff v. Donnelly* (Or. App. 1991) (reaffirming that "'courts, when dealing with the property disputes of a man and a woman who have been living together in a nonmarital domestic relationship, should distribute the property based upon the express or implied intent of those parties'"); *Knauer v. Knauer* (Pa. 1983) (finding "no public policy in Pennsylvania against entertaining suits between non-married cohabitors in property disputes"); *Doe v. Burkland* (R.I. 2002) (holding that assisting cohabitant in career and providing homemaking, business, consulting and counseling services is not illegal consideration "irrespective of the fact that the parties may have been living together when they entered into the contract"); *Connell v. Francisco* (Wash. 1995); *Watts v. Watts* (Wis. 1987) (explaining that "statute providing guidelines for property division upon dissolution of marriage, legal separation, etc., could also be applied to divide property acquired by unmarried cohabitants in what was 'tantamount to a marital family except for a legal marriage'"); *Shaw v. Smith* (Wyo. 1998) noting that "a cohabiting couple can enter into binding contracts as long as the agreement complies with Wyoming's law of contracts" and that it "will not . . . reject a claim based on well-established principles of contract or equity solely because the parties have cohabited").

Two states, by statute, have required that palimony claims must satisfy the statute of frauds in order to be enforceable. Minnesota provides that

> [i]f sexual relations between the parties are contemplated, a contract between a man and a woman who are living together in this state out of wedlock, or who are about to commence living together in this state out of wedlock, is enforceable as to terms concerning the property and financial relations of the parties only if: (1) the contract is written and signed by the parties, and (2) enforcement is sought after termination of the relationship.

[Minn. Stat. §513.075 (2007).]

Texas likewise provides that a

> promise or agreement [made on consideration of marriage or on consideration of nonmarital conjugal cohabitation] is not enforceable unless the promise or agreement, or a memorandum of it, is (1) in writing; and (2) signed by the person to be charged with the promise or agreement or by someone lawfully authorized to sign for him.

[Tex. Bus. & Com. Code Ann. §26.01 (2007).]

Finally, as a matter of decisional law, Florida and North Dakota also do not acknowledge a palimony claim in the absence of a writing confirming the agreement of support. *Posik v. Layton* (Fla. Dist. Ct. App. 1997); *Kohler v. Flynn* (N.D. 1992) (barring both palimony claims and equitable division claims by unmarried cohabitants, explaining that "[i]f live-in companions intend to share property, they should express that intention in writing").

The lesson to be gleaned is clear: nowhere—save for those limited instances where a claim for palimony is based on a writing confirming an agreement of support—can a palimony claim be sustained absent proof of cohabitation. The rationale undergirding that obvious rule is equally self-evident: because they are easy to allege yet inherently contrary to fundamental legal concepts that have governed our jurisprudence for centuries, palimony claims must be viewed with great skepticism and must be subjected to harsh and unremitting scrutiny. . . .[3]

Even California—the birthplace of the *Marvin* palimony cause of action—requires cohabitation as a prerequisite to recovery on a palimony claim. *Taylor v. Fields* (Cal. Ct. App. 1986). California explains that "[c]ohabitation is necessary not in and of itself, but rather, because from cohabitation flows the rendition of domestic services, which services amount to lawful consideration for a contract between the parties." *Bergen v. Wood* (Cal. Ct. App. 1993). More to the point, California makes the critical "observation that if cohabitation were not a prerequisite to recovery, every dating relationship would have the potential for giving rise to such claims, a result no one favors[,]" *ibid.*, because "a

3. Cohabitation is defined as "[t]o live together as spouses" or "[t]o live together in a sexual relationship when not legally married." *Webster's II New College Dictionary* 218 (1995). This Court has defined the term as follows:

> Cohabitation is not defined or measured solely or even essentially by "sex" or even by gender. . . . The ordinary understanding of cohabitation is based on those factors that make the relationship close and enduring and requires more than a common residence, although that is an important factor. Cohabitation involves an intimate relationship in which the couple has undertaken duties and privileges that are commonly associated with marriage. These can include, but are not limited to, living together, intertwined finances such as joint bank accounts, sharing living expenses and household chores, and recognition of the relationship in the couple's social and family circle.

[*Konzelman v. Konzelman* (N.J. 1999).]

recovery under *Marvin* 'requires a showing of a stable and significant relationship arising out of cohabitation.'" *Cochran v. Cochran* (Cal. Ct. App. 2001). . . . Without such a bright-line requirement, the concept of "marital-type" relationship is unacceptably vulnerable to duplicitous manipulation.

> Requiring cohabitation as an element of a palimony action also provides a measure of advance notice and warning, to both parties to a relationship, and to their respective family members, that legal and financial consequences may result from that relationship. . . . Thus, in contrast to an extramarital affair, even a long-term one, cohabitation announces to the ones most affected by the existence of the relationship, the innocent spouse and dependent children, that defendant has entered into a relationship that may result in significant and long-term impairment of family assets.

[*Levine*, supra, 383 N.J. Super. at 10-11, 890 A.2d 354.]

. . . As stated in *Roccamonte*,

> . . . A marital-type relationship is . . . the undertaking of a way of life in which two people commit to each other, foregoing other liaisons and opportunities, doing for each other whatever each is capable of doing, providing companionship, and fulfilling each other's needs, financial, emotional, physical, and social, as best as they are able. . . . Whatever other consideration may be involved, the entry into such a relationship and then conducting oneself in accordance with its unique character is consideration in full measure. . . .

[A] distinct cohabitation requirement stands as a formidable bulwark against emotion-based yet meritless claims. . . . [P]laintiff has failed to prove the element of cohabitation. . . .

Helen Devaney's strongest moral argument for continued financial support might be one based on reliance. Francis told her that he would take care of her and that he would marry her. Was she less justified in relying on such representations than is someone who relies on marital vows today, when divorce is so common? Might there also be a policy argument in her favor, based on a state interest in deterring people like Francis from behaving and making promises the way Francis did to keep Helen available to him and to induce her to move across the country to be near him? If so, are any of the policy rationales cited by the New Jersey Supreme Court Justices weightier than these reliance or deterrence bases for giving Helen relief? From another perspective, why should cohabitation strengthen a claim for financial redress? Devaney's opportunity cost would be the same whether she lived with Francis or not, yet the benefits she received in return for accepting that cost were presumably less than they would have been if she had lived with Francis. Should not the courts say to a dependent person who cohabitated that she benefitted substantially during the cohabitation (e.g., free rent, food, companionship, etc.) and now has no basis for complaint simply because the free ride ended?

Common-Law Marriage

If a former intimate partner cannot succeed in a contract or equitable claim for financial protection following dissolution of the relationship, he or she might try to establish that a marriage existed even though the couple never had a formal ceremony and state license. The laws of 11 states today allow for "common-law marriage"—Alabama, Colorado, Idaho, Iowa, Kansas, Montana, Pennsylvania, Rhode Island, South Carolina, Texas, and Utah. They will treat a couple as married, despite the absence of formalization, when a couple has agreed to be, and has acted as if they are, married. Many other jurisdictions in the world also have common-law marriage, in some places called "customary marriage."

A common-law marriage, when established, is a marriage for all purposes, just like a formal or ceremonial marriage. To end it, formal divorce proceedings are necessary; a couple cannot simply cease cohabitation and thereby become unmarried. See, e.g., Pirri v. Pirri, 631 S.E.2d 279 (S.C. App. 2006) (resolving dispute over property distribution and alimony in dissolution of common-law marriage).The same impediments to formal marriage exist also for common-law marriage—for example, that one or both persons is too young, that the couple are brother and sister, or that one or both persons is already married to someone else. Conversely, being already in a common-law marriage precludes entering into a formal or informal marriage with someone else. Cf., Nguyen v. Nguyen, 2011 WL 1496746 (Tex. App.—Hous. (1 Dist.) 2011) (rejecting husband's argument that divorce petition by wife should be dismissed because their marriage was invalid, where husband could not demonstrate that at time of wedding ceremony he was in a common-law marriage with another woman).

Dispute over whether a common-law marriage arose can occur in any kind of legal proceeding in which the existence of a marriage is a relevant fact. This would include any legal action in which one person lays claim to property of another by virtue of having been that person's spouse, including divorce and distribution of a decedent's estate. See, e.g., In re Estate of Collier, 2011 WL 2420989 (Tex. App.—Beaumont 2011) (addressing claims by two women, both claiming to have had a common-law marriage with an intestate decedent and therefore an entitlement to inherit from him); In re Estate of Duffy, 707 S.E.2d 447 (S.C. App. 2011) (rejecting cohabitant's claim for spousal elective share of decedent's estate). There are also many cases in which people claim benefits from third parties based on common-law marital status. See, e.g., In re Hyde, 255 P.3d 411 (Okla. 2011) (addressing woman's claim for spouse death benefits from male cohabitant's employer); Fravala v. City of Cranston, 996 A.2d 696 (R.I. 2010) (holding that woman established common-law marriage to deceased firefighter and was therefore entitled to his pension benefits); Anguiano v. Larry's Elec. Contracting, 241 P.3d 175 (Kan. App. 2010) (rejecting claim for death benefits from state worker's compensation agency).

In another category of cases, one person alleges that another has entered into a common-law marriage with a third person, in order to terminate a financial obligation. For example, in Cont'l Cas. Ins. Co. v. Lavender, 2011 WL 2306832 (Tex. App.—Fort Worth 2011), an insurance company that had been paying worker's compensation surviving spouse death benefits to a woman sought to cease making payments to her, because the benefits were to be paid only while she remained unmarried. The woman had been living with a man, but they had not had any wedding ceremony, so the company attempted, unsuccessfully, to demonstrate that her behavior satisfied the elements under Texas law for establishing a common-law marriage. See also PPL v. Workers' Comp. Appeal Bd., 5 A.3d 839 (Pa. Commw. 2010) (same). More common are cases in which alimony payors allege that their ex-spouses have formed a common-law marriage with someone else, because a payee's remarriage typically terminates a former spouse's alimony obligation.

A century ago, most U.S. states had common-law marriage. It was needed especially in less populated states, because preachers were few and far between. Many states eliminated it as population growth lessened the need for it, preferring that people take simpler and clearer steps to becoming married in the eyes of the law. Utah, however, bucked the trend by authorizing non-ceremonial marriage for the first time in the late 1980s, by statute. Why do you suppose the Utah legislature chose to do this? The statutory rule resembles the traditional common-law test:

Utah Code
Title 30. Husband and Wife
Chapter 1. Marriage

§30-1-4.5. Validity of Marriage Not Solemnized

(1) A marriage which is not solemnized according to this chapter shall be legal and valid if a court or administrative order establishes that it arises out of a contract between a man and a woman who:

(a) are of legal age and capable of giving consent;

(b) are legally capable of entering a solemnized marriage under the provisions of this chapter;

(c) have cohabited;

(d) mutually assume marital rights, duties, and obligations; and

(e) who hold themselves out as and have acquired a uniform and general reputation as husband and wife.

The statute's reference to a "contract" prior to the list of specific requirements is crucial. The ultimate question under common-law doctrine on informal marriage has been whether the parties *agreed* to be legally married. Common-law marriage was not something to be foisted on people who never intended to marry. In theory, then, a marriage should arise in the absence of prescribed formalities only when both members of a couple are aware that it is possible under the law of their state to become married without a license or ceremony and they decide together that they want to do that. Determining whether there was such an agreement usually requires courts to sift through complex facts about how two people lived, interacted, and spoke of themselves to others. Such fact-specific assessments are very subjective and therefore highly susceptible to bias yet very difficult to appeal. Are your intuitions about the following two cases consistent with the court's conclusion?

Jilverto Martinez v. Martha Lopez

2011 WL 2112806 (Tex. App.—Hous. (1 Dist.))

Evelyn V. Keyes, Justice.

. . . Martinez and Lopez began dating in 2000 while Lopez was pregnant with A.L., a child from a previous relationship, and while Martinez was separated from his wife, Maria Martinez. Martinez's divorce from Maria was finalized in June 2001. Before the divorce was finalized, Lopez became pregnant with Martinez's son, G.M., who was born in July 2001. Martinez and Lopez, along with A.L., began living together upon G.M.'s birth.

Martinez and Lopez's second child, J.M., was born in 2002. Martinez and Lopez continued to live together until March 2008. G.M. and J.M. both lived with Lopez until

May 2008, when G.M. moved in with Martinez. Martinez filed a Suit Affecting the Parent-Child Relationship requesting custody and visitation with J.M. Lopez answered and counter-petitioned for divorce, alleging that she and Martinez had a common-law marriage. Martinez denied that they had such a marriage.

At trial, Martinez testified that he and Lopez began living together when G.M. was born because he wanted to care for his son. Lopez testified that although Martinez never told her that they were married, she used to introduce Martinez as her husband and he represented to his friends and family that she was his wife. Lopez also testified that they shopped for property and a trailer together, but she admitted that her name was not on the title to that property. Lopez also acknowledged that Martinez bought a truck while they were together and that her name was not on the title of the truck, stating, "He never named me on anything of his." Lopez also testified that she did not work outside the home while she was living with Martinez. Instead, she prepared all of the meals and provided all of the child care. Regarding Martinez's and Lopez's own views of the status of their relationship, Lopez testified:

> *[Counsel]:* And why do you think it is that he never put you on the taxes.
> *[Lopez]:* Well, because he always looked at me like I was just anything, like I had no value to him.
> *[Counsel]:* Not as a wife?
> *[Lopez]:* To him, no. He didn't see me like that.
> *[Counsel]:* You're basically just the mother of his children?
> *[Lopez]:* Yes.
> *[Counsel]:* And he would treat you as such?
> *[Lopez]:* Yes.
> *[Counsel]:* Did you ever feel like you were his wife?
> *[Lopez]:* Well, yes.
> *[Counsel]:* Even though he pretty much told you that he wasn't?
> *[Lopez]:* Yeah, either way. For me, my life with him was [sic] his wife.
> *[Counsel]:* But, of course, he didn't see it that way?
> *[Lopez]:* No.
> *[Counsel]:* And you knew that?
> *[Lopez]:* He will make me feel that way.
> *[Counsel]:* So the question—I'm sorry. I'm just asking it, so you knew that, though?
> *[Lopez]:* Yes.

Martinez's counsel also questioned Lopez about her statement that she shopped for the property and trailer with Martinez but did not insist on having her name on the title:

> *[Counsel]:* And whenever you bought the property, you never insisted on your name being put on there?
> *[Lopez]:* Yes.
> *[Counsel]:* And it was not added though?
> *[Lopez]:* No, because he comes from a marriage where he lost everything, so he is afraid that the same thing will happen with me.
> *[Counsel]:* So he is basically very careful not to pass as your husband?
> *[Lopez]:* Of course.
> *[Counsel]:* And the same thing happened with the truck?
> *[Lopez]:* Yes.

[Counsel]: So in the end, he made sure to let you know and basically informed you that he was not your husband?

[Lopez]: Well, yes.

. . . Martinez's 2007 federal income tax return [showed] A.L., G.M., and J.M. as dependents, and . . . that Martinez was filing as the head of household. . . .

A valid informal, or common-law, marriage consists of three elements: (1) agreement of the parties to be married; (2) after the agreement, their living together in Texas as husband and wife; and (3) their representing to others in Texas that they are married. Tex. Fam. Code §2.401(a)(2) (Vernon 2006). The . . . party seeking to establish existence of the marriage bears the burden of proving the three elements by a preponderance of the evidence. . . . It is uncontested that the parties cohabitated throughout their relationship. . . .

1. Agreement to Marry

To establish an agreement to be married, "the evidence must show the parties intended to have a present, immediate, and permanent marital relationship and that they did in fact agree to be husband and wife." A proponent may prove an agreement to be married by direct or circumstantial evidence. The testimony of one of the parties to the marriage constitutes some direct evidence that the parties agreed to be married. Conduct of the parties, cohabitation, and representations to others may constitute circumstantial evidence of an agreement to be married. However, "[a] finding that there is legally and/or factually sufficient evidence of cohabitation and public representation will not necessarily constitute legally and/or factually sufficient evidence of an agreement to be married." "[T]he circumstances of each case must be determined based upon its own facts." *Id.* . . .

Martinez himself never testified regarding whether he and Lopez agreed to be married, but he characterizes Lopez's testimony as "direct evidence" that he never agreed to marry her, and thus, "any possible circumstantial evidence . . . cannot outweigh an outright repudiation of an agreement." . . . This testimony is insufficient to support a conclusion as a matter of law that Lopez made an "outright repudiation of an agreement" to be married or that Lopez's testimony was "direct evidence" that Martinez never agreed to marry her. Furthermore, Lopez also testified that Martinez had been her sole source of support from the birth of G.M. until the end of their relationship in March 2008. She testified that she lived with Martinez as his wife during that time, taking care of his home and children, and shopping for property and a trailer with him. Lopez also testified that she and Martinez identified each other as husband and wife to friends and family, that she believed she was his wife, and that they raised their children together as the mother and father of the children. . . . Lopez's testimony provides legally sufficient evidence that she and Martinez "intended to have a present, immediate, and permanent marital relationship and that they did in fact agree to be husband and wife." *See City of Keller* (holding that we examine evidence in light most favorable to trial court's finding when reviewing legal sufficiency). . . .

Martinez did not contest that he provided the sole financial support for Lopez and their children, that Lopez provided all of the domestic and child care for himself and their children, that they shopped for the property and trailer together, or that he and Lopez lived together exclusively and raised the children as their father and mother. Nor did Martinez contest Lopez's testimony that Martinez himself referred to them as being married to his friends and family. . . .

2. Representations to Others of Marriage

. . . "The statutory requirement of 'represented to others' is synonymous with the judicial requirement of 'holding out to the public.'" Spoken words are not necessary to establish representation as husband and wife—it may be proven by the conduct and actions of the parties. Occasional introductions as husband and wife are not sufficient to establish the element of holding out. Thus, whether the evidence is sufficient to establish that a couple held themselves out as husband and wife turns on whether the couple had a reputation in the community for being married. . . .

[T]he fact that Lopez is not mentioned in the financial documents is not direct proof that the couple did not represent themselves as husband and wife. Furthermore, Lopez unequivocally testified that she introduced Martinez as her husband and that he represented that she was his wife to all of their friends and family. Lopez also testified that she lived with Martinez as his wife, beginning when G.M. was born, that Martinez was her sole source of support during the time they lived together, that she took care of the home they shopped for together, and that they raised their children together. Viewed in the light most favorable to the trial court's finding, Lopez's testimony provides legally sufficient evidence that she and Martinez represented to others that they were married and supports an inference that they had a reputation in the community for being married. . . . Martinez did not offer any testimony on this element himself or provide any evidence contradicting Lopez's testimony. . . . We affirm the judgment of the trial court.

If you were representing either party, you would attempt to make the evidence cohere into a plausible account supportive of your position. Can you think of any reason why a man would tell his family he is married if he never actually decided to be married? Conversely, what explanation could there be for the supposed wife having the impression that he did not view her as his wife, if he did in fact consider himself married?

Does it make sense to consider as evidence of marital reputation anything that is commonly done by non-marital cohabitants (e.g., living together) or even by mere friends (e.g., shopping together)? What today is distinctive of the marital relationship, and therefore arguably more pertinent? Just saying that one is married? Do you suppose the judges hearing this case were pre-disposed to find a marriage? If so, why?

As indicated in the opinion above, Texas codified its informal marriage doctrine. In other states, it remains just a common-law rule.

John Lewis Reese v. Kathleen T. Holston

67 So. 3d 109 (Ala. Civ. App. 2011)

Thomas, Judge.

. . . On January 29, 2008, Holston filed a complaint for a divorce in the trial court, alleging that she and Reese had entered into a common-law marriage on December 23, 1999. Among other things, Holston requested that the trial court award her a house that she alleged had been the parties' marital residence ("the property"). In response, Reese filed an answer denying that he and Holston had a common-law marriage. . . .

"'Courts of this state closely scrutinize claims of common law marriage and require clear and convincing proof thereof.'" "In Alabama, recognition of a common-law marriage requires proof of the following elements: (1) capacity; (2) present, mutual agreement to permanently enter the marriage relationship to the exclusion of all other relationships; and (3) public recognition of the relationship as a marriage and public assumption of marital duties and cohabitation. . . .

According to Holston, in late December 1999, Reese asked her to marry him and she accepted his proposal. . . . Reese gave her an engagement ring. . . . [S]he "said [a] prayer for us to be bound together as husband and wife until the day when he had set up for a wedding, for May 2, 2002. And we was in agreement for that." Holston stated that they never had the planned wedding ceremony but that they lived together as husband and wife from December 23, 1999, forward. Delmonica Holston Wise, Holston's daughter, testified that she and her husband were at her grandmother's house on December 24, 1999, and that, on that date, Holston and Reese arrived at the house and announced that they had married. Wise also stated that Holston was wearing a wedding ring. She further testified that the parties had held themselves out to Holston's family as husband and wife. Ethleen Jones, Holston's sister, testified that on December 24, 1999, she had a telephone conversation with Holston, in which Holston told Jones that Holston and Reese had just married.

Reese denied that he had given Holston an engagement ring or a wedding ring. He also denied ever asking Holston to marry him. Reese further testified that he had been dating three other women in December 1999.

Both parties testified that they did not have any joint bank accounts, credit cards, loans, or other financial instruments. Additionally, the parties did not purchase any jointly held property-real or personal. Holston testified that she and Reese filed a joint tax return in 2000 but that she had told Reese to stop filing joint returns because she had outstanding student loans and the loan providers had attempted to reach the parties' tax refund. Holston did not enter the alleged joint tax return into evidence. Holston testified that she and Reese filed separate tax returns from 2001 to the present. Holston further testified that she continued to use Holston as her last name rather than Reese to protect Reese being liable for her debts. According to Holston, she did obtain a credit card under the name of Kathleen Reese . . . after she had filed her complaint for a divorce.

Reese purchased the property from Holston in February 1999; the property was in foreclosure at the time. After Reese purchased the property, Holston continued to live on the property and agreed to pay Reese $250 per month in rent. According to Holston, the payments were pursuant to an agreement between Holston and Reese for her to pay Reese back for his purchase of the property. Holston testified that she had paid Reese every month until she moved off of the property in 2007. Holston also testified that in 2004 she started helping to pay the electricity bill and the water bill associated with the property. Reese testified that Holston did not pay the agreed-upon rent for any month that she had lived on the property.

According to Holston, in December 1999, the parties started living together as husband and wife in Reese's home in Waverly. Holston stated that the parties moved from Reese's home in Waverly in 2001 and began living on the property. Wise testified that she lived on the property in 2000 and paid Holston $250 per month in rent; she stated that Holston was living with Reese in Waverly at that time.

In contrast, Reese testified that the parties never lived together in Waverly. He testified that Holston would sometimes spend the night with him in Waverly but that she did not leave any of her belongings in his home. Reese did admit that the parties had lived together on the property; however, he described the relationship as more of a landlord/ tenant relationship. According to Reese, he and Holston had separate bedrooms, although he did state that they sometimes had sexual relations. Reese testified that he sent Holston two eviction notices by certified mail in February 2004. Reese introduced the notices into evidence. . . .

Holston testified that everyone at her church believed that she and Reese had been ceremonially married. Holston stated that the people in her church believed that she and Reese were married because she had told them so and because her family had told them so. Holston did not state that Reese had represented to anyone at her church that the parties were married. In fact, Holston testified that Reese refused to attend her church. According to Holston, she sometimes attended Reese's church; however, she stated that the only people at his church who believed that they were married were Reese's family. Holston introduced into evidence, over Reese's objection, two funeral programs that listed her as Kathleen Reese. The first funeral program was for Holston's mother, who had died in 2001. . . . The second funeral program was for Reese's first cousin, who died in 2008. . . .

We conclude that the evidence presented by Holston is insufficient to show by clear and convincing evidence that the parties' relationship was publicly recognized as a marriage and that the parties publicly assumed marital duties. "It is indispensable that the parties must comport themselves in such a manner as to achieve public recognition of their status as common-law man and wife." We have stated:

> "'[T]he marriage relationship may be shown in any way that can be known by others, such as living together as man and wife, referring to each other in the presence of others as being in that relation, declaring the relation in various types of documents and transactions, sharing household duties and expenses, and generally engaging in "all of the numerous aspects of day-to-day mutual existence of married persons."'"

The fact that the parties may have lived together or cohabited, standing alone, is insufficient. . . . "[T]he man and woman, following their mutual consent to live as man and wife, must so live as to gain the recognition of the public that they are living as man and wife rather than in a state of concubinage."

Although Holston testified that she had told people at her church that she and Reese were married, it is also apparent from the record that Reese did not attend that church with her. Instead, Reese attended a separate church, where, according to Holston, only Reese's family members believed that he and Holston were married. Holston did not present any testimony from members of her church or other members of the public regarding the existence of a common-law marriage. Similarly, the statements by Wise and Jones only prove that members of Holston's family believed that Holston and Reese were married. The only other proof of public recognition of the parties' alleged common-law marriage were the two funeral programs offered by Holston. These two isolated documents, created by family members, are insufficient to "meet the required standard of a persuasive pattern of unambivalent conduct, but rather are too few and isolated." . . . Consequently, . . . we hold that the parties were not married. . . .

Could the judges in this case have had any reason to be pre-disposed *against* finding the existence of a marriage? Does a ruling like this invite devious behavior, by men trying to convince a woman to have sex with him or live with him?

Why is recognition by the public outside the family so important as to make it a separate element? In some other common-law marriage jurisdictions, it would be simply a factor to consider in determining whether there was an agreement to be married. Consider also that a ceremonial marriage can be done in great privacy, in some states even without witnesses, and need not be publicized.

States that do not have common-law marriage themselves usually will recognize as valid a common-law marriage arising in another jurisdiction that does have it. See, e.g., Christiansen v. Christiansen, 253 P.3d 153 (Wyo. 2011) (noting example of situation in which Wyoming courts will do so); Clark Sand Co., Inc. v. Kelly, 60 So. 3d 149 (Miss. 2011) (recognizing common-law marriage that arose in Alabama); Segal v. Lynch, 11 A.3d 407 (N.J. Super. A.D. 2011) (adjudicating custody issue in dissolution of common-law marriage that arose in Canada under Canadian law). If a common-law marriage arises in one state and one or both parties moves to another, the marriage remains valid and effective despite the move. In addition, if a couple created a common-law marriage prior to abolition of the doctrine in a given state, that marriage remains valid and might be asserted in a legal dispute today. Thus, a domestic relations attorney in any state could end up handling a dissolution of a common-law marriage, with all the same matters of grounds for divorce, property distribution, support, and custody at issue, or handing any other kind of legal dispute in which a client's common-law marriage is relevant.

Importantly, when couples move together from one state to another, any evidence either would offer as proof of a common-law marriage should be of conduct, statements, and events in the state where the marriage is alleged to have arisen. What transpires before moving to a common-law marriage state or what transpires after leaving a common-law marriage state should be irrelevant. See, e.g., Callen v. Callen, 620 S.E.2d 59 (S.C. 2005) ("Even assuming . . . that the parties lived together in Florida, New York, Massachusetts, and Ireland, and further assuming that they moved together from Florida to South Carolina in August 2000, no common-law marriage could have been formed, if at all, until after the move. . . . It must be presumed that Sean and Page's relationship remained non-marital after the move. . . . Consequently, Page has the burden of proving that the parties entered into a marital agreement after moving to South Carolina.").

Also irrelevant are conduct, statements, and events that occurred while an impediment to the marriage existed, such as being too young or married to someone else. There should be a decision and agreement to be married at a time when the couple lives in a common-law marriage state and is under no impediment to marry. Further, both persons must know that their decisions and actions have the legal effect of making them married. See id. ("A party need not understand every nuance of marriage or divorce law, but . . . [i]f a party does not comprehend that his 'intentions and actions' will bind him in a 'legally binding marital relationship,' then he lacks intent to be married. . . . South Carolina does not impose marriage upon a couple merely because they intend to be together forever.").

Reese v. Holston illustrates the need for in-depth factual inquiry to determine whether a common-law marriage has arisen. This gives states at least one reason to abolish common-law marriage—namely, to conserve judicial resources. The cases above suggest that many couples would also be well served by having greater clarity about the legal status of their relationship. Why, then, would any state today retain this mechanism for treating as married people who cannot be bothered to obtain a marriage license and go through at least a cursory ceremony? Formal marriage can be exceedingly easy. In Alabama, for example, there is no waiting period after issuance of a license and no witnesses are required. There are typically public wedding officiants at the same location as the office that issues marriage licenses. A couple might therefore be able to get married by making one half-hour visit to a municipal office building. The cost for a license is $43.50. Many officiants do not charge a fee for the ceremony. Why not make this process mandatory?

CROSS-CULTURAL PERSPECTIVE

Non-marital cohabitation is quite uncommon in some European countries, particularly in the south. In Spain, for example, instead of living with a boyfriend or girlfriend, young adults typically live with their parents into their late 20s and even 30s. This is not because of a moral taboo; pre-marital sex is pretty well accepted there. Rather, it is largely because the unemployment rate and housing costs are both high; young people cannot afford to live independently, even if they share a household. It is also less common in Spain to have in-town visitors come to one's house, let alone sleep over, so people who are dating generally do not have much opportunity for pre-marital sex. One consequence of this is the extraordinary amount of making-out and groping one sees in public parks. Additional, perhaps more desirable, consequences are that the non-marital birth rate is much lower than that in the United States and that squabbles over financial matters at the termination of a non-marital cohabitation arise much less frequently. See Constanza Tobio, *Marriage, Cohabitation, and the Residential Independence of Young People in Spain*, 15 INT'L J.L. POL'Y & FAM. 68 (2001). Does this picture of young adult life suggest any lessons for public policy in the United States?

In contrast to the extremely low rates of non-marital cohabitation in southern European countries, Scandinavian countries have quite high rates. Roughly half of Swedes in their 30s are living in a non-marital cohabitation, and only 60 percent of Swedes marry at some point. Common explanations for the relative unpopularity of marriage in Scandinavia include: Scandinavians are not very religious, and Scandinavian governments have created a separate legal status for non-marital cohabitants that is practically similar to marriage, so many people choose this purely civil status. Sweden has a very generous welfare state, and government benefits are not tied to marital status, so there is not the financial inducement to marry that exists in the United States. If you believe a high rate of marriage is essential or at least conducive to a well-ordered society, what do you make of the fact that Sweden, despite its low marriage rate, consistently ranks at or near the top globally in health and happiness?

A number of European countries, and some autonomous regions in Spain, such as Catalunya (Barcelona region), have statutes creating a set of default rules for non-marital cohabitants ("stable couples") that differs significantly from those for marriage. These rules govern any couple, straight or gay, that voluntarily chooses to be governed by them and any couple that has had unbroken cohabitation for two years. The rules provide some financial protection, but not as great as those which the law of marriage does; after dissolution, one can receive support from the other in limited circumstances, and one can demand compensation for any labor supplied to improve the residence or to help the other with her or his work. Some jurisdictions in the United States now have civil unions, but these are really marriages in all but name. Should U.S. states have a more varied menu of legal relationship statuses and, correspondingly, of default rule packages, for all couples? For an argument in favor, see Jennifer A. Drobac & Antony Page, *A Uniform Domestic Partnership Act: Marrying Business Partnership and Family Law*, 41 GA. L. REV. 349 (2007).

New Zealand by statute foists a legal relationship on cohabiting unmarried couples. Under the New Property (Relationships) Act, following amendment in 2001, if a couple has lived in a "de facto relationship" for at least three years, upon dissolution of the relationship a court will order equal division of property acquired during the relationship, unless the parties have entered into a contract to the contrary. This is a step beyond the equitable remedy of *Marvin v. Marvin*, insofar as the rule is codified, applies automatically without regard to either party's representations or reliance, and stipulates an equal sharing. It looks somewhat like forced marriage or marriage by default. What are the likely consequences of such a statute?

B. WHOM TO MARRY?

Having answered the question of why one might want to marry, there is the question of with whom one may or ideally should marry. If one were to approach this systematically, one might first narrow the field by determining with whom the state will not permit one to form a legal marriage, and then one might look for particular characteristics among those who are available within the remaining pool. Again, recall the social/legal distinction: Everyone is free to have a private wedding ceremony with anyone or anything they wish, but for the state to treat one as married, one must choose a spouse that the state considers appropriate.

The state has limited the spouse options for people in many ways over the centuries. The most basic and universal limitation was that one's spouse must be human. Perhaps the second most basic and universal requirement historically was that prospective spouses be presumptively capable of reproducing with each other, which in part meant that they must be of the opposite sex. The requirement—"assumption" might be the better term—that a spouse should be of the opposite sex was even more universal and bedrock than the requirement of autonomous consent; in many cultures historically, including much of Western society until the Middle Ages, arranged marriages, even involving young children, have been common, and in some it remains so today. Yet today, states in the Western world are steadily abandoning the opposite-sex limitation, for reasons we will examine.

Clearly, autonomous consent by both parties to a marriage is required today, in most of the world, and so a further limitation is that a prospective spouse must be capable of giving free and independent consent and actually do so. This explains minimum age requirements in state marriage laws. In recent centuries, the state has also ruled out marriage to immediate family members, and this remains a widespread limitation. Another enduring limitation is that one may have only one spouse at a time, though the state today imposes no numerical limitation on the number of spouses one may have seriatum. The polygamy context, though, is one in which the line between legal and social marriage blurs, because the state is especially concerned about people skirting the aims of anti-polygamy laws by having multiple social marriages without seeking legal marriage status. We will study how successful the state has been at doing this.

Other limitations on choice of legal spouse have disappeared, in the United States primarily as a result of courts' holding that the limitations violated liberty- or equality-based constitutional rights of individuals. We will examine the history of this constitutional doctrine, leading up to the current wave of challenges to opposite-sex-only marriage laws, and then consider whether this doctrine might in the future support challenges to other common limitations on marriage. Finally, we will go beyond legal limitations to look at empirical evidence one might rely on to choose the best possible spouse from among those legally and practically available.

1. *Constitutional Challenges to Marriage Restrictions*

In chronological order, the U.S. Supreme Court has adjudicated constitutional challenges to state laws prohibiting polygamy, inter-racial marriage, marriage by or to a child support delinquent, and marriage by or to a prisoner. It has yet to accept for review a constitutional challenge to states' limiting of marriage to opposite-sex couples, but it will likely do so in the next decade. The European Court of Human Rights decided in 2010 that there is no right to same-sex marriage under the European Convention on Human Rights. Schalk and Kopf v. Austria, Application no. 30141/04, Council of Europe: European Court of Human Rights, 24 June 2010, available at http://www.unhcr.org/refworld/docid/4c29fa712.html (accessed 25 June 2011). There has been plenty of lower court litigation in the United States over same-sex marriage, and we will look at that. There have also been lower court challenges to some other marriage restrictions.

As you follow the doctrine, pay careful attention to the nature of the constitutional right the Court articulates. Does the doctrine establish a basic *liberty* right to state-conferred *legal* marital status? Or is any basic liberty right really to engage in social family formation, with a right to legal marriage merely incident to that more basic right? The Court's last marriage decision was in 1987, a year after its *Bowers v. Hardwick* decision upholding an anti-sodomy law, so all of the Court's marriage decisions have been rendered at a time when state laws criminalizing non-marital sex were common and generally viewed as constitutional, even if rarely enforced. Legal marriage was necessary then in order legally to live what might be termed a "social marriage"—that is, living together, being intimate, and conceiving children. As we saw above, the Court's 2003 decision in *Lawrence v. Texas*, and subsequent lower court decisions like *Martin v. Ziherl*, appears to have changed the situation completely, to have decoupled social and legal marriage. Is the Court today therefore likely to say that, as a matter of constitutional entitlement, there is only a basic *liberty* right to engage in *social* marriage? With respect to *legal* marriage, is there now at best only an *equality* right, protecting groups of people against unjustifiable discrimination in distribution of this state-conferred status and its attendant benefits?

If there is only an equality right as to legal marriage today, must an excluded group show that it is especially deserving of judicial protection from adverse outcomes of the political process (i.e., that it is a "suspect class"), in order to mount a successful constitutional challenge? Given the decoupling of social and legal marriage, is it no longer plausible to allege regarding legal marriage that an extremely important basic interest is at stake that should itself trigger rigorous judicial scrutiny? Professors Widiss and Tebbe highlight the distinction among these different arguments for heightened scrutiny in federal constitutional jurisprudence—that is, fundamental liberty, suspect-class-based equal protection, and important-interest-based equal protection. They maintain that the last of these—that is, an equal protection claim asserting that heightened scrutiny is warranted because an important interest is at stake—is the most promising for proponents of same-sex legal marriage. See Deborah A. Widiss & Nelson Tebbe, *Equal Access and the Right to Marry*, 158 U. Pa. L. Rev. 1375 (2010). But how important is the interest at stake with access to legal marriage, in an era when legal marriage is no longer a prerequisite to social marriage? Has *Lawrence*, ironically, weakened the case for same-sex marriage, by guaranteeing same-sex couples the freedom to live their private lives as they wish without state interference? And how important are any interests left unsatisfied by a civil union law, in states where such exists?

In some of the decisions below, courts are considering whether a particular person (e.g., a child support delinquent, a prison inmate, a minor) has a right to marry anyone. In other cases, the question is whether two individuals, each of whom definitely has a right to marry someone, have a right to marry each other (e.g., despite racial difference). The section headings below reflect the perspective of individuals wondering who is legally available to them for marriage, even though what is at issue is both that and whether certain other persons are able to marry anyone. For example, *Zablocki* addresses both your freedom to marry someone who is delinquent in child support and the right of someone who is delinquent in child support to marry at all. The headings are intended to suggest a way of looking at the cases additional to the customary way.

a. Right to Marry Someone Who Is Already Married to Someone Else

The HBO series *Six Feet Under* arguably was a bellwether and partial cause of societal acceptance of homosexual relationships. The more recent HBO hit *Big Love* might well be the same for polygamous families. A second television series featuring polygamy, *Sister Wives*, was launched in 2010, suggesting significant public interest in the practice. Unlike same-sex marriage, however, polygamous marriage has already been addressed by the Supreme Court, and unfavorably. But that was 125 years ago, long before the Court developed a substantial jurisprudence of individual liberty and equal protection under the Fourteenth Amendment. The Court in *Reynolds* addressed only a First Amendment Free Exercise Clause objection to a criminal prosecution for bigamy.

Reynolds v. United States

98 U.S. 145 (1878)

Error to the Supreme Court of the Territory of Utah.

This is an indictment . . . charging George Reynolds with bigamy, in violation of sect. 5352 of the [federal] Revised Statutes . . . :

> Every person having a husband or wife living, who marries another, whether married or single, in a Territory, or other place over which the United States have exclusive jurisdiction, is guilty of bigamy, and shall be punished by a fine of not more than $500, and by imprisonment for a term of not more than five years.

Mr. Chief Justice WAITE delivered the opinion of the court.

. . . On the trial, the plaintiff in error, the accused, proved that at the time of his alleged second marriage he was, and for many years before had been, a member of the Church of Jesus Christ of Latter-Day Saints, commonly called the Mormon Church, and a believer in its doctrines; that it was an accepted doctrine of that church "that it was the duty of male members of said church, circumstances permitting, to practise polygamy; . . . that this duty was enjoined by different books which the members of said church believed to be of divine origin, and among others the Holy Bible, and also that the members of the church believed that the practice of polygamy was directly enjoined upon the male members thereof by the Almighty God, in a revelation to Joseph Smith, the founder and prophet of said church; that the failing or refusing to practise polygamy by such male members of said church, when circumstances would admit, would be punished, and that the penalty for such failure and refusal would be damnation in the life to come." He also proved "that he had received permission from the recognized authorities in said church to enter into polygamous marriage; . . . that Daniel H. Wells, one having authority in said church to perform the marriage ceremony, married the said defendant on or about the time the crime is alleged to have been committed, to some woman by the name of Schofield, and that such marriage ceremony was performed under and pursuant to the doctrines of said church." . . .

Congress cannot pass a law for the government of the Territories which shall prohibit the free exercise of religion. The first amendment to the Constitution expressly forbids such legislation. . . . Congress was deprived of all legislative power over mere opinion, but was left free to reach actions which were in violation of social duties or subversive of good order.

Polygamy has always been odious among the northern and western nations of Europe, and, until the establishment of the Mormon Church, was almost exclusively a feature of the life of Asiatic and of African people. At common law, the second marriage was always void (2 Kent, Com. 79), and from the earliest history of England polygamy has been treated as an offence against society. After the establishment of the ecclesiastical courts, and until the time of James I., it was punished through the instrumentality of those tribunals. . . . By the statute of 1 James I. (c. 11), the offence, if committed in England or Wales, was made punishable in the civil courts, and the penalty was death. As this statute was limited in its operation to England and Wales, it was at a very early period re-enacted, generally with some modifications, in all the colonies. In connection with the case we are now considering, it is a significant fact that on the 8th of December, 1788, after the passage of the act establishing religious freedom, and after the convention of Virginia had recommended as an amendment to the Constitution of the United States the declaration in a bill of rights that "all men have an equal, natural, and unalienable right to the free exercise of religion, according to the dictates of conscience," the legislature of that State substantially enacted the statute of James I., death penalty included, because, as recited in the preamble, "it hath been doubted whether bigamy or poligamy be punishable by the laws of this Commonwealth." 12 Hening's Stat. 691. From that day to this we think it may safely be said there never has been a time in any State of the Union when polygamy has not been an offence against society, cognizable by the civil courts and punishable with more or less severity.

In the face of all this evidence, it is impossible to believe that the constitutional guaranty of religious freedom was intended to prohibit legislation in respect to this most important feature of social life. Marriage, while from its very nature a sacred obligation, is nevertheless, in most civilized nations, a civil contract, and usually regulated by law. Upon it society may be said to be built, and out of its fruits spring social relations and social obligations and duties, with which government is necessarily required to deal. In fact, according as monogamous or polygamous marriages are allowed, do we find the principles on which the government of the people, to a greater or less extent, rests. Professor Lieber says, polygamy leads to the patriarchal principle, and which, when applied to large communities, fetters the people in stationary despotism, while that principle cannot long exist in connection with monogamy. Chancellor Kent observes that this remark is equally striking and profound. 2 Kent, Com. 81, note (*e*). An exceptional colony of polygamists under an exceptional leadership may sometimes exist for a time without appearing to disturb the social condition of the people who surround it; but there cannot be a doubt that, unless restricted by some form of constitution, it is within the legitimate scope of the power of every civil government to determine whether polygamy or monogamy shall be the law of social life under its dominion. . . .

This being so, the only question which remains is, whether those who make polygamy a part of their religion are excepted from the operation of the statute. If they are, then those who do not make polygamy a part of their religious belief may be found guilty and punished, while those who do, must be acquitted and go free. This would be introducing a new element into criminal law. Laws are made for the government of actions, and while they cannot interfere with mere religious belief and opinions, they may with practices. Suppose one believed that human sacrifices were a necessary part of religious worship, would it be seriously contended that the civil government under which he lived could not interfere to prevent a sacrifice? Or if a wife religiously believed it was her duty to burn herself upon the funeral pile of her dead husband, would it be beyond the power of the civil government to prevent her carrying her belief into practice? . . . To permit this would be to make the professed doctrines of religious belief superior to the law of the land, and in effect to permit every citizen to become a law unto himself. Government could exist only in name under such circumstances. . . .

Can an argument against the right to engage in polygamy be persuasive if it must rely on comparison with human sacrifice and self-immolation? Cf. Nathan B. Oman, *Natural Law and the Rhetoric of Empire:* Reynolds v. United States, *Polygamy, and Imperialism*, 88 WASH. U. L. REV. 661, 689 (2011) ("In comparing 'suttee' to polygamy and the Mormons to Indians, the Court cast the federal government as an agent of civilization against barbarism, akin to the civilizing British imperialism under Macaulay in India. . . . This racially charged rhetoric was typical of an age where 'Progress' had replaced 'Reason' as an ideological talisman and where imperialism was in full swing. . . . Mormons were cast—along with 'Asiatic and African' peoples—as a benighted race in need of civilizing imperial masters."). Does the Court identify any justification for the ban on polygamy, any aspect of the practice that makes it barbaric, other than a concern about "the patriarchal principle"? Did that concern really distinguish polygamy from monogamy and mainstream American society in 1878? Cf. Bradwell v. State, 83 U.S. 130 (1872) (upholding Illinois law barring women from practicing law).

Under current Free Exercise Clause doctrine, the Court would likely come out the same way on a First Amendment claim, unless it were shown that anti-polygamy laws specifically target Mormons. Similarly, an equal protection challenge would seem unpromising. It remains to be seen, however, how the Court would respond to a Fourteenth Amendment claim that polygamy prohibitions unjustifiably infringe basic liberty rights. The outcome might depend on whether a particular state merely refuses to confer legal recognition on a multiple-marriage family or goes further and prosecutes people for engaging in the social practice of multiple marriage. Courts are more likely to uphold the former against constitutional challenge. Litigation involving a claim of the latter sort is now developing, as the *Sister Wives* family has brought suit in federal court to challenge Utah's anti-polygamy law. We will return to this topic below, after completing examination of the constitutional doctrine.

b. Right to Marry a White Person

Very few nations have prohibited interracial marriage. On this issue, the United States is in the company of apartheid South Africa and Nazi Germany. For most of our nation's history, it has been illegal in most of the United States for non-white people to be intimate with a white person, and a crime for a non-white person to attempt to effect a marriage with a white person. In 1883, in *Pace v. Alabama,* the U.S. Supreme Court upheld the felony conviction of an Alabama couple for interracial sex, rejecting a claim that this violated the Fourteenth Amendment. The Court took the position that the criminal prohibition was not discriminatory, because whites and non-whites were punished in equal measure for the crime. States generally did not proscribe marriages across other racial lines; the main concern was with the purity and separateness of the white race. For a fascinating account of societal attitudes toward interracial intimacy in the early twentieth century, see Angela Onwuachi-Willig, *A Beautiful Lie: Exploring* Rhinelander v. Rhinelander *as a Formative Lesson on Race, Identity, Marriage, and Family,* 95 CAL. L. REV. 2393 (2007).

In the early morning hours of July 11, 1958, Richard and Mildred Loving, married five weeks before in Washington, D.C., were in bed in their home in Virginia, when "the county sheriff and two deputies, acting on an anonymous tip, burst into their bedroom and shined flashlights in their eyes. A threatening voice demanded, 'Who is this woman you're sleeping with?' Mrs. Loving answered, 'I'm his wife.' Mr. Loving pointed to the couple's marriage certificate hung on the bedroom wall. The sheriff responded, 'That's no good here.' . . . After Mr. Loving spent a night in jail and his wife several more, the couple pleaded guilty to violating the Virginia law, the Racial Integrity Act . . . [, which] had been on the books since 1662." See Douglas Martin, *Mildred Loving, Who Battled Ban on Mixed-Race Marriage, Dies at 68,* N.Y. TIMES, May 6, 2008. In *Loving v. Virginia,* the U.S. Supreme Court ordered Virginia, and the other 15 states that had one at that time, to remove their anti-miscegenation (race-mixing) provisions. Equal Protection Clause challenges to laws excluding same-sex couples from legal marriage typically cite *Loving,* so in reading *Loving* consider to what extent the Court's reasoning about interracial marriage carries over to same-sex marriage.

Loving v. Virginia

388 U.S. 1 (1967)

Mr. Chief Justice WARREN delivered the opinion of the Court.

. . . In June 1958, two residents of Virginia, Mildred Jeter, a Negro woman, and Richard Loving, a white man, were married in the District of Columbia pursuant to its laws. Shortly after their marriage, the Lovings returned to Virginia and established their marital abode in Caroline County. . . . [A] grand jury issued an indictment charging the Lovings with violating Virginia's ban on interracial marriages. On January 6, 1959, the Lovings pleaded guilty to the charge and were sentenced to one year in jail; however, the trial judge suspended the sentence for a period of 25 years on the condition that the Lovings leave the State and not return to Virginia together for 25 years. He stated in an opinion that:

> Almighty God created the races white, black, yellow, malay and red, and he placed them on separate continents. And but for the interference with his arrangement there would be no

> cause for such marriages. The fact that he separated the races shows that he did not intend for the races to mix.

After their convictions, the Lovings took up residence in the District of Columbia. On November 6, 1963, they filed a motion in the state trial court to vacate the judgment and set aside the sentence on the ground that the statutes which they had violated were repugnant to the Fourteenth Amendment. . . . The Supreme Court of Appeals [of Virginia] upheld the constitutionality of the antimiscegenation statutes. . . .

The Lovings were convicted of violating §20-58 of the Virginia Code:

> Leaving State to evade law.—If any white person and colored person shall go out of this State, for the purpose of being married, and with the intention of returning, and be married out of it, and afterwards return to and reside in it, cohabiting as man and wife, they shall be punished as provided in §20-59, and the marriage shall be governed by the same law as if it had been solemnized in this State. The fact of their cohabitation here as man and wife shall be evidence of their marriage.

Section 20-59, which defines the penalty for miscegenation, provides:

> Punishment for marriage.—If any white person intermarry with a colored person, or any colored person intermarry with a white person, he shall be guilty of a felony and shall be punished by confinement in the penitentiary for not less than one nor more than five years. . . .[4]

Virginia is now one of 16 States which prohibit and punish marriages on the basis of racial classifications.[5] Penalties for miscegenation arose as an incident to slavery and have

4. Section 20-54 of the Virginia Code provides:

> . . . For the purpose of this chapter, the term 'white person' shall apply only to such person as has no trace whatever of any blood other than Caucasian; but persons who have 1/16 or less of the blood of the American Indian and have no other non-Caucasic blood shall be deemed to be white persons.

The exception for persons with less than one-sixteenth 'of the blood of the American Indian' is apparently accounted for, in the words of a tract issued by the Registrar of the State Bureau of Vital Statistics, by 'the desire of all to recognize as an integral and honored part of the white race the descendants of John Rolfe and Pocahontas.'

> . . .
>
> Section 1-14 of the Virginia Code provides:
>
> Colored persons and Indians defined.—Every person in whom there is ascertainable any Negro blood shall be deemed and taken to be a colored person, and every person not a colored person having one fourth or more of American Indian blood shall be deemed an American Indian; except that members of Indian tribes existing in this Commonwealth having one fourth or more of Indian blood and less than one sixteenth of Negro blood shall be deemed tribal Indians. Va. Code Ann. §1-14 (1960 Repl. Vol.).

5. After the initiation of this litigation, Maryland repealed its prohibitions against interracial marriage, Md. Laws 1967, c. 6, leaving Virginia and 15 other States with statutes outlawing interracial marriage: Alabama, Ala. Const., Art. 4, §102, Ala. Code, Tit. 14, §360 (1958); Arkansas, Ark. Stat. Ann. §55-104 (1947); Delaware, Del. Code Ann., Tit. 13, §101 (1953); Florida, Fla. Const., Art. 16, §24, F.S.A., Fla. Stat. §741.11 (1965) F.S.A.; Georgia, Ga. Code Ann. §53-106 (1961); Kentucky, Ky. Rev. Stat. Ann. §402.020 (Supp. 1966); Louisiana, La. Rev. Stat. §14:79 (1950); Mississippi, Miss. Const., Art. 14, §263, Miss. Code Ann. §459 (1956); Missouri, Mo. Rev. Stat. §451.020 (Supp. 1966), V.A.M.S.; North Carolina, N.C. Const., Art. XIV, §8, N.C. Gen. Stat. §14-181 (1953); Oklahoma, Okla. Stat., Tit. 43, §12 (Supp. 1965); South Carolina, S.C. Const., Art. 3, §33, S.C. Code Ann. §20-7 (1962); Tennessee, Tenn. Const., Art. 11, §14, Tenn. Code Ann. §36-402 (1955); Vernon's Ann. Texas, Tex. Pen. Code, Art. 492 (1952); West Virginia, W. Va. Code Ann. §4697 (1961). Over the past 15 years, 14 States have repealed laws outlawing interracial marriages: Arizona, California, Colorado, Idaho, Indiana, Maryland, Montana, Nebraska, Nevada, North Dakota, Oregon, South Dakota, Utah, and Wyoming.

been common in Virginia since the colonial period. The present statutory scheme dates from the adoption of the Racial Integrity Act of 1924, passed during the period of extreme nativism which followed the end of the First World War. The central features of this Act, and current Virginia law, are the absolute prohibition of a "white person" marrying other than another "white person," a prohibition against issuing marriage licenses until the issuing official is satisfied that the applicants' statements as to their race are correct, certificates of "racial composition" to be kept by both local and state registrars, and the carrying forward of earlier prohibitions against racial intermarriage.

I

. . . [T]he Supreme Court of Appeals of Virginia [in] its 1955 decision in *Naim v. Naim* . . . [stated] the reasons supporting the validity of these laws . . . : "to preserve the racial integrity of its citizens," and to prevent "the corruption of blood," "a mongrel breed of citizens," and "the obliteration of racial pride," obviously an endorsement of the doctrine of White Supremacy. . . .

[T]he State contends that, because its miscegenation statutes punish equally both the white and the Negro participants in an interracial marriage, these statutes, despite their reliance on racial classifications do not constitute an invidious discrimination based upon race. . . . [I]n *Pace v. State of Alabama* (1883) . . . , the Court upheld a conviction under an Alabama statute forbidding adultery or fornication between a white person and a Negro which imposed a greater penalty than that of a statute proscribing similar conduct by members of the same race. The Court reasoned that the statute could not be said to discriminate against Negroes because the punishment for each participant in the offense was the same. However, as recently as the 1964 Term, . . . we stated "*Pace* represents a limited view of the Equal Protection Clause which has not withstood analysis in the subsequent decisions of this Court." *McLaughlin v. Florida*. . . . [T]he Equal Protection Clause requires the consideration of whether the classifications drawn by any statute constitute an arbitrary and invidious discrimination. The clear and central purpose of the Fourteenth Amendment was to eliminate all official state sources of invidious racial discrimination in the States.

There can be no question but that Virginia's miscegenation statutes rest solely upon distinctions drawn according to race. The statutes proscribe generally accepted conduct if engaged in by members of different races. Over the years, this Court has consistently repudiated "(d)istinctions between citizens solely because of their ancestry" as being "odious to a free people whose institutions are founded upon the doctrine of equality." At the very least, the Equal Protection Clause demands that racial classifications, especially suspect in criminal statutes, be subjected to the "most rigid scrutiny," and, if they are ever to be upheld, they must be shown to be necessary to the accomplishment of some permissible state objective, independent of the racial discrimination which it was the object of the Fourteenth Amendment to eliminate. . . .

There is patently no legitimate overriding purpose independent of invidious racial discrimination which justifies this classification. The fact that Virginia prohibits only interracial marriages involving white persons demonstrates that the racial classifications must stand on their own justification, as measures designed to maintain White Supremacy.[11] We have consistently denied the constitutionality of measures which restrict the

11. . . . We . . . find the racial classifications in these statutes repugnant to the Fourteenth Amendment, even assuming an even-handed state purpose to protect the "integrity" of all races.

rights of citizens on account of race. There can be no doubt that restricting the freedom to marry solely because of racial classifications violates the central meaning of the Equal Protection Clause.

II

These statutes also deprive the Lovings of liberty without due process of law in violation of the Due Process Clause of the Fourteenth Amendment. The freedom to marry has long been recognized as one of the vital personal rights essential to the orderly pursuit of happiness by free men. Marriage is one of the "basic civil rights of man," fundamental to our very existence and survival. To deny this fundamental freedom on so unsupportable a basis as the racial classifications embodied in these statutes, classifications so directly subversive of the principle of equality at the heart of the Fourteenth Amendment, is surely to deprive all the State's citizens of liberty without due process of law. . . . These convictions must be reversed. It is so ordered.

Try to articulate the nature of the discrimination inherent in the Virginia statute. What did the state give to one racial group and that it did not give to another? Is that thing something of fundamental importance? Does it make sense to think about the Virginia statute in that way, or is the basic problem that the statute aimed to perpetuate racial segregation and subordination? Is the reasoning of *Loving* translatable to a case involving discrimination on any basis other than race or "ancestry"? If one were to ask, why may a state not aim to keep races distinct, would one find in *Loving* any response other than the positive law (and perhaps circular) answer that the Fourteenth Amendment does not permit it?

States have advanced the "equal application" theory in same-sex marriage litigation also, arguing that they evenhandedly afford the right to marry someone of the opposite sex to everyone and the right to marry someone of the same sex to no one. Is that argument more plausible in one context than the other (i.e., race or sex)? Is a racial restriction on marital partner more or less burdensome than a sex restriction?

The "fundamental freedom" argument at the end of the opinion made sense in an era when a couple could not legally cohabit and enjoy intimacy without being legally married. Does the argument make any sense today, when becoming legally married does not remove any restrictions on a couple's conduct? If all that legal marriage practically offers today is some protection of one's investment (financial and physical) in an intimate relationship (e.g., by ensuring a share of property in the event of divorce) and some state-conferred financial benefits, can it be said that legal marriage is an aspect of persons' fundamental freedom? Might some people feel unfree to get married in a social sense absent the legal protections and state benefits that legal marriage still provides today?

Despite the *Loving* decision, several states stubbornly refused to remove anti-miscegenation laws from their state codes, even though they could no longer enforce the laws. Alabama was the last to relent, in 2000.

The 2010 Census found 4.5 million interracial marriages, or 8 percent of all marriages, in the United States. Although *Loving* was very much about perpetuation of the subordination of African Americans, blacks actually have the lowest rate of intermarriage among all racial groups. Intermarriage is typically between a white person and a non-white person (there is relatively little marriage between people of two different minority races), but most common are marriages of whites to Asian Americans, and next to Hispanic persons. Forty percent of U.S.-born Asian Americans and 38 percent of U.S.-born Hispanics who married had white spouses. When there are intermarriages between white and black persons, it is almost three times as likely to be with a black man as it is to be with a black woman: 14.4 percent of black men and 6.5 percent of black women are currently in mixed-race marriages.

Professor Banks hypothesizes that

> . . . black women became subject to greater cultural and political pressure not to intermarry. . . . The pressures faced by black women stemmed from the increased centrality of the black family in racial equality discourse during the 1960s and 1970s. . . . Conservatives who wanted to cast African-Americans in an unsympathetic light could strenuously argue that, in a post–Jim Crow era, continued inequality reflected the deficiencies of the African-American community and the failings of the black family. . . . Although, in theory, claims of a deficient family or culture might implicate black men and women equally, in practice such claims put into question the responsibilities of women. Just as men are associated with the market, women are associated with the family. And so the problems of the black family would be seen as the responsibility of black women. . . . It was the woman's responsibility to uphold the sanctity of the black family, and that task could not be accomplished through marriage to a white man. Indeed, such marriages might be taken as evidence of the fragility of the black family. . . . As Professor Renee Romano has stated, "black women might feel a greater sense of responsibility to maintain the future of the community by building strong black families and raising black children." . . . If black women became more committed to the black family as a cultural signifier, the myriad expressions of that commitment might have caused white men to be less inclined to enter relationships with black women.

R. Richard Banks, *The Aftermath of Loving v. Virginia: Sex Asymmetry in African American Intermarriage*, 2007 Wis. L. Rev. 533. See also Ralph Richard Banks, Is Marriage for White People? (2011).

Professor Robinson cautions

> . . . against uncritical celebrations of increasing interracial intimacy as a sign of reduced prejudice and social progress. Our celebrations should be tempered by the awareness that race structures even our most intimate relationships. Although two people have crossed racial lines and may have even committed to spending their lives together, we cannot easily conclude that they have transcended race. Because race and gender intersect to determine an individual's value in the romantic marketplace, the two partners are unlikely to be similarly situated in terms of their options for leaving the relationship should it become unhappy. For instance, black heterosexual men enjoy greater options for interracial coupling than do black heterosexual women. Further, people of color who are in interracial relationships may have to suffer racialized microaggressions in order to maintain the relationship. Yet these subtle insults may escape the awareness of the white partner in the relationship, who might not intend to cause any harm or see the comments as racially offensive. One source of such racialized harms is likely to arise from racial disagreements in perceiving discrimination. Because black people and white people tend to view allegations of discrimination through fundamentally different lenses, they are likely to disagree as to the existence of discrimination, even when they are in an intimate relationship.

Russell Robinson, *Structural Dimensions of Romantic Preferences*, 76 Fordham L. Rev. 2787, 2787-2788 (2008).

Sociologists have found that interracial marriages are on average less happy and more likely to end in divorce than same-race marriages, and suggest that the primary explanations are things external to the relationships—namely, stress arising from familial disapproval and stress from dealing with the more complex relationship histories that members of such unions tend to have, including children conceived with previous partners. They find that white-Hispanic marriages are the happiest and most enduring among interracial marriages, and speculate that this is because there is less "social distance" between whites and Hispanics. See Bryndl E. Hohmann-Marriott & Paul Amato, *Relationship Quality in Interethnic Marriages and Cohabitations*, 87 Soc. Forces 825 (2008). Professors Onwuachi-Willig and Willig-Onwuachi identify a special form of discrimination against interracial couples in certain markets. See Angela Onwuachi-Willig & Jacob Willig-Onwuachi, *A House Divided: The Invisibility of the Multiracial Family*, 44 Harv. C.R.-C.L. L. Rev. 231 (2009) (explaining that "housing discrimination statutes assume that plaintiffs will be monoracial, heterosexual couples, and fail to fully address the harms to interracial, heterosexual couples who are subjected to discrimination in housing and rental searches because of their interraciality (e.g., because they have engaged in race-mixing)" and arguing for amendment to discrimination laws to address discrimination based on a couple's being of mixed race). See also Onwuachi-Willig, *A Beautiful Lie*, supra, 95 Cal. L. Rev. 2393 (describing social condemnation of persons who appear to violate expectations for their race, including by marrying someone of a different race).

Richard Loving died in 1975 in an automobile accident. Mildred died of pneumonia in 2008, in Virginia. The year before her death, Mrs. Loving issued a public statement prepared for the fortieth anniversary of the Supreme Court's decision. It included these words:

> Surrounded as I am now by wonderful children and grandchildren, not a day goes by that I don't think of Richard and our love, our right to marry, and how much it meant to me to have that freedom to marry the person precious to me, even if others thought he was the "wrong kind of person" for me to marry. I believe all Americans, no matter their race, no matter their sex, no matter their sexual orientation, should have that same freedom to marry. Government has no business imposing some people's religious beliefs over others. Especially if it denies people's civil rights. I am still not a political person, but I am proud that Richard's and my name is on a court case that can help reinforce the love, the commitment, the fairness, and the family that so many people, black or white, young or old, gay or straight seek in life. I support the freedom to marry for all. That's what Loving, and loving, are all about.

c. Right to Marry a Child Support Delinquent

Zablocki v. Redhail

434 U.S. 374 (1978)

Mr. Justice Marshall delivered the opinion of the Court.

At issue in this case is the constitutionality of a Wisconsin statute, which provides that members of a certain class of Wisconsin residents may not marry, within the State or elsewhere, without first obtaining a court order granting permission to marry. The class is defined by the statute to include any "Wisconsin resident having minor issue not in his custody and which he is under obligation to support by any court order or judgment." The statute specifies that court permission cannot be granted unless the marriage applicant submits proof of compliance with the support obligation and, in addition, demonstrates that the children covered by the support order "are not then and are not likely thereafter to become public charges." . . .

I

In January 1972, when appellee was a minor and a high school student, a paternity action was instituted against him in Milwaukee County Court, alleging that he was the father of a baby girl born out of wedlock on July 5, 1971. After he appeared and admitted that he was the child's father, the court entered an order . . . adjudging appellee the father and ordering him to pay $109 per month as support for the child until she reached 18 years of age. From May 1972 until August 1974, appellee was unemployed and indigent, and consequently was unable to make any support payments.

On September 27, 1974, appellee filed an application for a marriage license with appellant Zablocki, the County Clerk of Milwaukee County, and a few days later the application was denied on the sole ground that appellee had not obtained a court order granting him permission to marry. . . . [H]e would not have been able to satisfy either of the statutory prerequisites for an order granting permission to marry. First, he had not satisfied his support obligations to his illegitimate child, and as of December 1974 there was an arrearage in excess of $3,700. Second, the child had been a public charge since her birth, receiving benefits under the Aid to Families with Dependent Children program. . . . [S]he would have been a public charge even if appellee had been current in his support payments. . . .

II

In evaluating [the statute] under the Equal Protection Clause, "we must first determine what burden of justification the classification created thereby must meet, by looking to the nature of the classification and the individual interests affected." Since our past decisions make clear that the right to marry is of fundamental importance, and since the classification at issue here significantly interferes with the exercise of that right, we believe that "critical examination" of the state interests advanced in support of the classification is required.

The leading decision of this Court on the right to marry is *Loving v. Virginia*. . . . The Court's opinion could have rested solely on the ground that the statutes discriminated on the basis of race in violation of the Equal Protection Clause. But the Court went on to hold that the laws arbitrarily deprived the couple of a fundamental liberty protected by the Due Process Clause, the freedom to marry. . . . Long ago, in *Maynard v. Hill* (1888), the Court characterized marriage as "the most important relation in life," and as "the foundation of the family and of society, without which there would be neither civilization nor progress." In *Meyer v. Nebraska* (1923), the Court recognized that the right "to marry, establish a home and bring up children" is a central part of the liberty protected by the Due Process Clause, and in *Skinner v. Oklahoma* (1942), marriage was described as "fundamental to the very existence and survival of the race."

More recent decisions have established that the right to marry is part of the fundamental "right of privacy" implicit in the Fourteenth Amendment's Due Process Clause. In *Griswold v. Connecticut* (1965), the Court observed:

> . . . Marriage is a coming together for better or for worse, hopefully enduring, and intimate to the degree of being sacred. It is an association that promotes a way of life, not causes; a

> harmony in living, not political faiths; a bilateral loyalty, not commercial or social projects. Yet it is an association for as noble a purpose as any involved in our prior decisions.

. . . [I]n *Carey v. Population Services International* (1977), we declared:

> . . . [I]t is clear that among the decisions that an individual may make without unjustified government interference are personal decisions "relating to marriage, procreation, contraception, family relationships, and child rearing and education."

. . . As the facts of this case illustrate, it would make little sense to recognize a right of privacy with respect to other matters of family life and not with respect to the decision to enter the relationship that is the foundation of the family in our society. The woman whom appellee desired to marry had a fundamental right to seek an abortion of their expected child, or to bring the child into life to suffer the myriad social, if not economic, disabilities that the status of illegitimacy brings. Surely, a decision to marry and raise the child in a traditional family setting must receive equivalent protection. And, if appellee's right to procreate means anything at all, it must imply some right to enter the only relationship in which the State of Wisconsin allows sexual relations legally to take place.[11]

By reaffirming the fundamental character of the right to marry, we do not mean to suggest that every state regulation which relates in any way to the incidents of or prerequisites for marriage must be subjected to rigorous scrutiny. To the contrary, reasonable regulations that do not significantly interfere with decisions to enter into the marital relationship may legitimately be imposed. The statutory classification at issue here, however, clearly does interfere directly and substantially with the right to marry. . . . Some of those in the affected class, like appellee, will never be able to obtain the necessary court order, because they either lack the financial means to meet their support obligations or cannot prove that their children will not become public charges. These persons are absolutely prevented from getting married. Many others, able in theory to satisfy the statute's requirements, will be sufficiently burdened by having to do so that they will in effect be coerced into forgoing their right to marry. And even those who can be persuaded to meet the statute's requirements suffer a serious intrusion into their freedom of choice in an area in which we have held such freedom to be fundamental.[12]

III

When a statutory classification significantly interferes with the exercise of a fundamental right, it cannot be upheld unless it is supported by sufficiently important state interests and is closely tailored to effectuate only those interests. . . . There is evidence that the challenged statute . . . was intended merely to establish a mechanism whereby persons with support obligations to children from prior marriages could be

11. Wisconsin punishes fornication as a criminal offense:

> "Whoever has sexual intercourse with a person not his spouse may be fined not more than $200 or imprisoned not more than 6 months or both." Wis. Stat. §944.15 (1973).

12. The directness and substantiality of the interference with the freedom to marry distinguish the instant case from *Califano v. Jobst*. In *Jobst*, we upheld sections of the Social Security Act providing, *inter alia*, for termination of a dependent child's benefits upon marriage to an individual not entitled to benefits under the Act. . . . The Social Security provisions placed no direct legal obstacle in the path of persons desiring to get married, and . . . there was no evidence that the laws significantly discouraged, let alone made "practically impossible," any marriages. . . .

counseled before they entered into new marital relationships and incurred further support obligations. . . . The statute actually enacted, however, does not expressly require or provide for any counseling whatsoever, nor for any automatic granting of permission to marry by the court. . . . Even assuming that counseling does take place . . . this interest obviously cannot support the withholding of court permission to marry once counseling is completed.

[A]ppellant's counsel suggested that . . . the statute provides incentive for the applicant to make support payments to his children. This "collection device" rationale cannot justify the statute's broad infringement on the right to marry. First, with respect to individuals who are unable to meet the statutory requirements, the statute merely prevents the applicant from getting married, without delivering any money at all into the hands of the applicant's prior children. More importantly, . . . the State already has numerous other means for exacting compliance with support obligations, means that are at least as effective as the instant statute's and yet do not impinge upon the right to marry. Under Wisconsin law, whether the children are from a prior marriage or were born out of wedlock, court-determined support obligations may be enforced directly via wage assignments, civil contempt proceedings, and criminal penalties. And, if the State believes that parents of children out of their custody should be responsible for ensuring that those children do not become public charges, this interest can be achieved by adjusting the criteria used for determining the amounts to be paid under their support orders.

There is also some suggestion that §245.10 protects the ability of marriage applicants to meet support obligations to prior children by preventing the applicants from incurring new support obligations. But the challenged provisions of §245.10 are grossly underinclusive with respect to this purpose, since they do not limit in any way new financial commitments by the applicant other than those arising out of the contemplated marriage. The statutory classification is substantially overinclusive as well: Given the possibility that the new spouse will actually better the applicant's financial situation, by contributing income from a job or otherwise, the statute in many cases may prevent affected individuals from improving their ability to satisfy their prior support obligations. And, although it is true that the applicant will incur support obligations to any children born during the contemplated marriage, preventing the marriage may only result in the children being born out of wedlock, as in fact occurred in appellee's case. Since the support obligation is the same whether the child is born in or out of wedlock, the net result of preventing the marriage is simply more illegitimate children.

The statutory classification . . . thus cannot be justified by the interests advanced in support of it. . . .

Mr. Justice Stewart, concurring in the judgment.

. . . Like almost any law, the Wisconsin statute now before us affects some people and does not affect others. But to say that it thereby creates "classifications" in the equal protection sense strikes me as little short of fantasy. The problem in this case is not one of discriminatory classifications, but of unwarranted encroachment upon a . . . liberty protected by the Due Process Clause of the Fourteenth Amendment.

I do not agree with the Court that there is a "right to marry" in the constitutional sense. That right, or more accurately that privilege, is under our federal system peculiarly one to be defined and limited by state law. A State may not only "significantly interfere with decisions to enter into marital relationship," but may in many circumstances absolutely prohibit it. Surely, for example, a State may legitimately say that no one can marry his or her sibling, that no one can marry who is not at least 14 years old, that no one can marry without first passing an examination for venereal disease, or that no one can marry who has a living husband or wife. But, just as surely, in regulating the intimate human relationship of marriage, there is a limit beyond which a State may not constitutionally go. . . . If Wisconsin had said that no one could marry who had not paid all of the fines assessed against him for traffic violations, I suppose the constitutional invalidity of the law would be apparent. For while the state interest would certainly be legitimate, that interest would be both disproportionate and unrelated to the restriction of liberty imposed by the State. But the invalidity of the law before us is hardly so clear, because its restriction of liberty seems largely to be imposed only on those who have abused the same liberty in the past. . . . [The law] reflects a legislative judgment that a person should not be permitted to incur new family financial obligations until he has fulfilled those he already has. . . .

On several occasions this Court has held that a person's inability to pay money demanded by the State does not justify the total deprivation of a constitutionally protected liberty. . . . The Wisconsin law makes no allowance for the truly indigent. . . . To deny these people permission to marry penalizes them for failing to do that which they cannot do. . . . [T]he law is substantially more rational if viewed as a means of assuring the financial viability of future marriages. . . . But the State's legitimate concern with the financial soundness of prospective marriages must stop short of telling people they may not marry because they are too poor or because they might persist in their financial irresponsibility. The invasion of constitutionally protected liberty and the chance of erroneous prediction are simply too great. . . .

Mr. Justice Powell, concurring in the judgment.

. . . The Court apparently would subject all state regulation which "directly and substantially" interferes with the decision to marry in a traditional family setting to "critical examination" or "compelling state interest" analysis. Presumably, "reasonable regulations that do not significantly interfere with decisions to enter into the marital relationship may legitimately be imposed." The Court does not present, however, any principled means for distinguishing between the two types of regulations. Since state regulation in this area typically takes the form of a prerequisite or barrier to marriage or divorce, the degree of "direct" interference with the decision to marry or to divorce is unlikely to provide either guidance for state legislatures or a basis for judicial oversight. . . .

In my view, analysis must start from the recognition of domestic relations as "an area that has long been regarded as a virtually exclusive province of the States." The marriage relation traditionally has been subject to regulation, initially by the ecclesiastical authorities, and later by the secular state. . . . [A] State "has absolute right to prescribe the conditions upon which the marriage relation between its own citizens shall be created, and the causes for which it may be dissolved." The State, representing the collective expression of moral aspirations, has an undeniable interest in ensuring that its rules of domestic relations reflect the widely held values of its people. . . . A "compelling state purpose" inquiry would cast doubt on the network of restrictions that the States have fashioned to govern marriage and divorce. . . .

The opinion of the Court amply demonstrates that the asserted counseling objective bears no relation to this statute. . . . The so-called "collection device" rationale . . . [fails because of its] failure to make provision for those without the means to comply with child-support obligations. . . . The third justification, only obliquely advanced by appellant, is that the statute preserves the ability of marriage applicants to support their prior issue by preventing them from incurring new obligations. The challenged provisions of §245.10

are so grossly underinclusive with respect to this objective, given the many ways that additional financial obligations may be incurred by the applicant quite apart from a contemplated marriage, that the classification "does not bear a fair and substantial relation to the object of the legislation." . . . Because the State has not established a justification for this unprecedented foreclosure of marriage to many of its citizens solely because of their indigency, I concur in the judgment of the Court. . . .

Mr. Justice STEVENS, concurring in the judgment.

. . . Under this statute, . . . within the class of parents who have fulfilled their court-ordered obligations, the rich may marry and the poor may not. This type of statutory discrimination is . . . inconsistent with our tradition of administering justice equally to the rich and to the poor. . . . The statute prevents impoverished parents from marrying even though their intended spouses are economically independent. Presumably, the Wisconsin Legislature assumed (a) that only fathers would be affected by the legislation, and (b) that they would never marry employed women. . . . To the extent that the statute denies a hard-pressed parent any opportunity to prove that an intended marriage will ease rather than aggravate his financial straits, it not only rests on unreliable premises, but also defeats its own objectives. . . . The prohibition on marriage applies to the noncustodial parent but allows the parent who has custody to marry without the State's leave. Yet the danger that new children will further strain an inadequate budget is equally great for custodial and non-custodial parents, unless one assumes (a) that only mothers will ever have custody and (b) that they will never marry unemployed men. Characteristically, this law fails to regulate the marriages of those parents who are least likely to be able to afford another family, for it applies only to parents under a court order to support their children. The very poorest parents are unlikely to be the objects of support orders.[9] . . .

. . . Even assuming that the right to marry may sometimes be denied on economic grounds, this clumsy and deliberate legislative discrimination between the rich and the poor is irrational in so many ways that it cannot withstand scrutiny under the Equal Protection Clause of the Fourteenth Amendment.

Mr. Justice REHNQUIST, dissenting.

. . . I think that under the Equal Protection Clause the statute need pass only the "rational basis test," and that under the Due Process Clause it need only be shown that it bears a rational relation to a constitutionally permissible objective. . . . Earlier this Term the traditional standard of review was applied in *Califano v. Jobst*, despite the claim that the statute there in question burdened the exercise of the right to marry. The extreme situation considered there involved a permanently disabled appellee whose benefits under the Social Security Act had been terminated because of his marriage to an equally disabled woman who was not, however, a beneficiary under the Act. . . . The Court concluded that, upon a beneficiary's marriage, Congress could terminate his benefits, because "there can be no question about the validity of the assumption that a married person is less likely to be dependent on his parents for support than one who is unmarried." Although that assumption had been proved false as applied in that individual case, the statute was nevertheless rational. "The broad legislative classification must be judged by reference to characteristics typical of the affected classes rather than by focusing on selected, atypical examples." . . .

9. . . . A parent who is so disabled that he will never earn enough to pay child support is unlikely to be sued, and a court order is unlikely to be granted.

Here, too, the Wisconsin Legislature has "adopted this rule in the course of constructing a complex social welfare system that necessarily deals with the intimacies of family life." Because of the limited amount of funds available for the support of needy children, the State has an exceptionally strong interest in securing as much support as their parents are able to pay. Nor does the extent of the burden imposed by this statute so differentiate it from that considered in *Jobst* as to warrant a different result. In the case of some applicants, this statute makes the proposed marriage legally impossible for financial reasons; in a similar number of extreme cases, the Social Security Act makes the proposed marriage practically impossible for the same reasons. . . .

The Court's decision rested entirely on equal protection grounds, and application of heightened scrutiny depended entirely on the supposition that refusal of legal marriage thwarted a fundamental interest. The decision therefore clearly invites the question, again, whether the outcome should be the same in a post-*Lawrence* environment when legal marriage is unnecessary to social marriage. Do people have a fundamental interest in legal marital status *per se*? If not, it would seem that heightened scrutiny of any exclusions from legal marriage cannot be predicated on the nature of the interest at stake. Would conditioning marriage on support of prior children fail rational basis review anyway? Can the state not use the incentive of legal marriage to induce people to remedy their failure to fulfill any legal responsibilities? Why can't a state require someone to pay up on their parking tickets before receiving a marriage license? The restriction in *Zablocki* was actually related to marriage; Wisconsin believed that people are better prepared for marriage if they are on top of existing family financial obligations. In light of the Court's reasons for rejecting that rationale, how do you suppose a state would fare if it required, as a condition for receiving a marriage license, that a person who is an alcoholic demonstrate a year of sobriety? Or that a person who has been convicted in the past of domestic violence prove completion of counseling and classes designed to avoid further acts of violence? If states may not constitutionally do any of these things, why was Justice Stewart so blithe about the constitutionality of denying marriage to people under 14, to siblings, to people who refuse to take a venereal disease test, and to polygamists? What is different about these other restrictions?

The concurring Justices placed great emphasis on the disparate impact on the poor. If it is unconstitutional to deny people the opportunity to marry because they are poor, is it also unconstitutional to deny people the opportunity to adopt a child because they are poor? As we saw in Chapter 1, the law does not categorically exclude the poor from adoption, but it is quite unlikely that an agency would approve non-relative applicants for a new-family adoption if they had little or no income. If discrimination in adoption based on wealth is constitutionally permissible, how would you distinguish those two relationship opportunities? Isn't exclusion from a new-family adoption (i.e., not a step-parent adoption) a more severe deprivation, given that it typically means people will have no social relationship whatsoever with the child they would otherwise adopt?

Justice Powell noted that domestic relations has "long been regarded as a virtually exclusive province of the States." That is hardly an accurate description of domestic relations law today. In addition to the decisions relating to marriage in this section, the Supreme Court has imposed constitutional limits on state discretion with respect to paternity, child rearing, and termination of the parent-child relationship, and

Congress has passed important legislation pertaining to adoption, domestic violence, child protection, and child support. What justifications are there for federal involvement in family law and family life?

d. Right to Marry a Prisoner

Turner v. Safley

482 U.S. 78 (1987)

Justice O'Connor delivered the opinion of the Court.

. . . The Renz prison population includes both male and female prisoners of varying security levels. Most of the female prisoners at Renz are classified as medium or maximum security inmates, while most of the male prisoners are classified as minimum security offenders. . . . The challenged marriage regulation . . . permits an inmate to marry only with the permission of the superintendent of the prison, and provides that such approval should be given only "when there are compelling reasons to do so." The term "compelling" is not defined, but prison officials testified at trial that generally only a pregnancy or the birth of an illegitimate child would be considered a compelling reason. . . .

[W]hen a prison regulation impinges on inmates' constitutional rights, the regulation is valid if it is reasonably related to legitimate penological interests. . . . Thus, a regulation cannot be sustained where the logical connection between the regulation and the asserted goal is so remote as to render the policy arbitrary or irrational. . . . Where "other avenues" remain available for the exercise of the asserted right, courts should be particularly conscious of the "measure of judicial deference owed to corrections officials . . . in gauging the validity of the regulation." A third consideration is the impact accommodation of the asserted constitutional right will have on guards and other inmates, and on the allocation of prison resources generally. . . . Finally, the absence of ready alternatives is evidence of the reasonableness of a prison regulation. . . .

It is settled that a prison inmate "retains those [constitutional] rights that are not inconsistent with his status as a prisoner or with the legitimate penological objectives of the corrections system." The right to marry, like many other rights, is subject to substantial restrictions as a result of incarceration. Many important attributes of marriage remain, however, after taking into account the limitations imposed by prison life.

First, inmate marriages, like others, are expressions of emotional support and public commitment. These elements are an important and significant aspect of the marital relationship. In addition, many religions recognize marriage as having spiritual significance; for some inmates and their spouses, therefore, the commitment of marriage may be an exercise of religious faith as well as an expression of personal dedication. Third, most inmates eventually will be released by parole or commutation, and therefore most inmate marriages are formed in the expectation that they ultimately will be fully consummated. Finally, marital status often is a precondition to the receipt of government benefits (*e.g.*, Social Security benefits), property rights (*e.g.*, tenancy by the entirety, inheritance rights), and other, less tangible benefits (*e.g.*, legitimation of children born out of wedlock). These incidents of marriage, like the religious and personal aspects of the marriage commitment, are unaffected by the fact of confinement or the pursuit of legitimate corrections goals. Taken together, we conclude that these remaining elements are sufficient to form a constitutionally protected marital relationship in the prison context. Our decision in *Butler v. Wilson* (1974), summarily affirming *Johnson v. Rockefeller* (SDNY 1973), is not to the contrary. That case involved a prohibition on marriage only for inmates sentenced to life imprisonment; and, importantly, denial of the right was part of the punishment for crime. . . .

The security concern emphasized by petitioners is that "love triangles" might lead to violent confrontations between inmates. With respect to rehabilitation, prison officials testified that female prisoners often were subject to abuse at home or were overly dependent on male figures, and that this dependence or abuse was connected to the crimes they had committed. The superintendent at Renz, petitioner William Turner, testified that in his view, these women prisoners needed to concentrate on developing skills of self-reliance, and that the prohibition on marriage furthered this rehabilitative goal. Petitioners emphasize that the prohibition on marriage should be understood in light of Superintendent Turner's experience with several ill-advised marriage requests from female inmates. . . .

There are obvious, easy alternatives to the Missouri regulation that accommodate the right to marry while imposing a *de minimis* burden on the pursuit of security objectives. See, *e.g.*, 28 CFR §551.10 (1986) (marriage by inmates in federal prison generally permitted, but not if warden finds that it presents a threat to security or order of institution, or to public safety). . . . Common sense likewise suggests that there is no logical connection between the marriage restriction and the formation of love triangles: surely in prisons housing both male and female prisoners, inmate rivalries are as likely to develop without a formal marriage ceremony as with one. Finally, . . . where the inmate wishes to marry a civilian, the decision to marry (apart from the logistics of the wedding ceremony) is a completely private one.

Nor, on this record, is the marriage restriction reasonably related to the articulated rehabilitation goal. . . . Missouri prison officials testified that generally they had experienced no problem with the marriage of male inmates, and . . . that generally they had no objection to inmate-civilian marriages . . . The rehabilitation concern appears from the record to have been centered almost exclusively on female inmates marrying other inmates or ex-felons; it does not account for the ban on inmate-civilian marriages. . . . Of the several female inmates whose marriage requests were discussed by prison officials at trial, only one was refused on the basis of fostering excessive dependency. . . . We conclude, therefore, that the Missouri marriage regulation is facially invalid. . . .

Courts generally treat prison regulations, like military regulations, as sui generis, in a way that results in greater deference to the regulators. It is striking, therefore, that the Court in *Turner* unanimously ruled in favor of the inmates with respect to the exclusion from legal marriage, especially given that prisoners are generally practically incapable of doing the one thing for which legal marriage has historically been a legal precondition—namely, physical intimacy with an opposite-sex partner. In prior decisions, the Court spoke in a single phrase of marriage and procreation, tying the importance of marriage to its connection with sex and child bearing. The only mention of this connection in *Turner* is to the possibility of "consummation" when both parties to the marriage are out of prison, but the prison regulation in no way inhibited convicted criminals from marrying after getting out of prison.

The supposed bases for concluding that prisoners' interest in marriage was great enough to warrant constitutional protection were therefore just 1) that "inmate marriages, like others, are expressions of emotional support and public commitment"; 2) that "for some inmates and their spouses . . . the commitment of marriage may be an exercise of religious faith"; and 3) that "marital status often is a precondition to the receipt of government benefits (*e.g.*, Social Security benefits), property rights (*e.g.*, tenancy by the entirety, inheritance rights), and other, less tangible benefits (*e.g.*, legitimation of children born out of wedlock)." The first two of these interests can be satisfied with a private, non-legal marriage. Therefore, if there are any interests that prisoners actually have while in prison that can only be satisfied by legal marriage, they appear to be just interests in receiving special government benefits, in being able to title jointly owned real estate in a particular way, and in having their offspring be "legitimate." The Court had never spoken of government benefits or titling of real estate in prior decisions about the family. Are these interests really sufficient to attribute a constitutional right—that is, the power to have a court overrule a policy decision by the elected branches of government?

Does the Court adequately distinguish its earlier decision in Butler v. Wilson? Could it not also be said of any criminal sentence involving incarceration in Missouri that denial of the right to marry "was part of the punishment for crime"? Is not the Court in *Turner* really holding that states may not make exclusion from marriage an element of criminal punishment? Would the Court's reasoning also apply to denial of the constitutional right to become a parent, the right at issue in Lehr v. Robertson in Chapter 1? For example, if a state modified its parentage laws to say legal parent status will not vest in any biological parent incarcerated at the time of a child's birth, how would you, after reading *Turner*, expect the Court to analyze such a statute?

e. Right to Marry a Person of the Same Sex

This issue was mostly a curiosity in family law courses until 2006. There were early (i.e., ~1990), surprising decisions in a couple of states (Alaska and Hawaii) holding that exclusion of same-sex couples from legal marriage violated state equal protection constitutional provisions. In both states, however, public uproar over the court decisions quickly resulted in amendment to the state constitutions. Then a couple of states went for civil unions—in Vermont because the state's supreme court said the state constitution required more equal treatment, and in Connecticut by legislative choice. Other states responded with legislation and constitutional amendments prohibiting their courts from recognizing civil unions or anything like them created in such jurisdictions (i.e., in seeming opposition to the federal Full Faith and Credit Clause). Still, it seemed like a fringe issue, one likely to arise in practice only rarely. Not anymore.

In 2006, the Massachusetts Supreme Court held that the state must recognize same-sex unions as "marriages." In 2008, the Massachusetts legislature decided that non-residents could marry in Massachusetts, the new governor of New York announced that state agencies must recognize same-sex marriages created in other jurisdictions, and the highest courts of Connecticut and California held that those states, too, must confer legal marriage per se on same-sex couples. California voters later overturned the court decision by a referendum known as "Proposition 8," returning same-sex couples to the position of being able to register domestic partnerships with the state but not receive the appellation of "marriage." Same-sex couples then challenged Prop 8 itself, and discussion of that ongoing litigation appears below. Then in 2009, the Supreme Court of Iowa held that same-sex couples have a right under that state's constitution to marry. That decision, the most recent of the state supreme court decisions addressing state constitutional challenges, also appears below.

Rather than relying on judicial action, legislatures in several states have taken it upon themselves to introduce statutory measures to legalize same-sex marriage. In September 2009, same-sex marriages became legal in Vermont, and New Hampshire and the District of Columbia followed in 2010. The New York State Legislature did the same in 2011:

2011 New York Assembly Bill No. 8354

§3. The Domestic Relations Law Is Amended by Adding . . . :

§10-a. Parties to a marriage. 1. A marriage that is otherwise valid shall be valid regardless of whether the parties to the marriage are of the same or different sex.

2. No government treatment or legal status, effect, right, benefit, privilege, protection or responsibility relating to marriage, whether deriving from statute, administrative or court rule, public policy, common law or any other source of law, shall differ based on the parties to the marriage being or having been of the same sex rather than a different sex. . . .

§10-b. . . . [A] corporation incorporated under the benevolent orders law . . . or a religious corporation . . . shall be deemed to be in its nature distinctly private and therefore, shall not be required to provide accommodations, advantages, facilities or privileges related to the solemnization or celebration of a marriage. . . .

3. [N]othing in this article shall be deemed or construed to prohibit any religious or denominational institution or organization . . . from limiting employment or sales or rental of housing accommodations or admission to or giving preference to persons of the same religion or denomination or from taking such action as is calculated by such organization to promote the religious principles for which it is established or maintained.

Washington State followed suit in 2012. Other state legislatures continued debating same-sex marriage bills, with public support steadily increasing. In addition to states that have legalized same-sex marriage, Rhode Island, Maryland, and Illinois recognize same-sex marriages performed in other states.

As an alternative to same-sex marriage, many states now have "domestic partner" or "reciprocal beneficiary" or "civil union" statutes that to varying degrees approximate legal marital status, including California, Colorado, Delaware, Hawaii, Illinois, Maine, Maryland, Nevada, New Jersey, Oregon, Rhode Island, Wisconsin, and Washington. Europe has experienced the same gradual transformation, with much of the same turmoil. Beginning with the Netherlands in 2001, a half dozen or so European states have legalized same-sex marriage, and several more are now considering it, while another dozen have some sort of domestic partner registry. France's civil union status is available to gay or straight couples, and remarkably the overwhelming majority of couples opting for that status (95% in 2009) are heterosexual. In fact, 40 percent of straight couples in France choose to enter into a *pacte civil de solidarité* rather than a "marriage," and so the marriage rate has dropped considerably. See Scott Sayare & Maia de la Baume, *In France,*

Civil Unions Gain Favor over Marriage, N.Y. TIMES, Dec. 15, 2010. Our neighbor Canada now has same-sex marriage as well, and like Massachusetts it allows non-residents to come in for a wedding vacation. Outside America and Europe, legal marriage is available to same-sex couples in Argentina and South Africa, and some form of civil union status is available in Australia, Brazil, Israel, New Zealand, and Uruguay.

Thus, same-sex marriage has great momentum now. Soon there will be hundreds of thousands of same-sex married couples living in this country. The battle has shifted to some extent to the federal courts, so there might soon be a U.S. Supreme Court ruling on the issue, potentially mandating same-sex marriage nationwide. When children born today become adults, will they take same-sex legal marriage for granted, just as we now do the legality of interracial marriage?

Varnum v. Brien

763 N.W.2d 862 (Iowa 2009)

CADY, Justice.

. . . The Iowa legislature amended the marriage statute in 1998 to define marriage as a union between only a man and a woman. . . . Except for [this] statutory restriction . . . the twelve plaintiffs met the legal requirements to marry in Iowa. . . .[5]

B. LEGAL TESTS TO GAUGE EQUAL PROTECTION

The foundational principle of equal protection is expressed in article I, section 6 of the Iowa Constitution, which provides: "All laws of a general nature shall have a uniform operation; the general assembly shall not grant to any citizen or class of citizens, privileges or immunities, which, upon the same terms shall not equally belong to all citizens." Like the Federal Equal Protection Clause found in the Fourteenth Amendment to the United States Constitution, Iowa's constitutional promise of equal protection "'is essentially a direction that all persons similarly situated should be treated alike.'"[6] . . .

D. SIMILARLY SITUATED PEOPLE

. . . The County . . . asserts the plaintiffs are not similarly situated to opposite-sex couples . . . because the plaintiffs cannot "procreate naturally." . . . In considering whether two classes are similarly situated, a court cannot simply look at the trait used by the legislature to define a classification under a statute and conclude a person without that trait is not similarly situated to persons with the trait. . . . In the same way, the similarly situated requirement cannot possibly be interpreted to require plaintiffs to be identical in every way to people treated more favorably by the law. No two people or groups of people are the same in every way, and nearly every equal protection claim could be run aground onto the shoals of a threshold analysis if the two groups needed to be a mirror image of one another. . . . In other words, to truly ensure equality before

5. One commentator has found that, since the same-sex marriage debate started, 27 states have passed constitutional amendments prohibiting same-sex marriage, and 17 of those state amendments also ban other official forms of same-sex relationships, such as civil unions. . . .

6. . . . Generally, we view the federal and state equal protection clauses as "identical in scope, import, and purpose." At the same time, we have jealously guarded our right to "employ a different analytical framework" under the state equal protection clause as well as to independently apply the federally formulated principles. Here again, we find federal precedent instructive in interpreting the Iowa Constitution, but we refuse to follow it blindly.

the law, the equal protection guarantee requires that laws treat all those who are similarly situated *with respect to the purposes of the law* alike. . . . For these reasons, the trait asserted by the County is insufficient to support its threshold argument.

Nevertheless, we have said our marriage laws "are rooted in the necessity of providing an institutional basis for defining the fundamental relational rights and responsibilities of persons in organized society." These laws also serve to recognize the status of the parties' committed relationship. Therefore, with respect to the subject and purposes of Iowa's marriage laws, we find that the plaintiffs are similarly situated compared to heterosexual persons. Plaintiffs are in committed and loving relationships, many raising families, just like heterosexual couples. Moreover, official recognition of their status provides an institutional basis for defining their fundamental relational rights and responsibilities, just as it does for heterosexual couples. Society benefits, for example, from providing same-sex couples a stable framework within which to raise their children and the power to make health care and end-of-life decisions for loved ones, just as it does when that framework is provided for opposite-sex couples. . . .

E. CLASSIFICATION UNDERTAKEN IN IOWA CODE SECTION 595.2.

. . . It is true the marriage statute does not expressly prohibit gay and lesbian persons from marrying; it does, however, require that if they marry, it must be to someone of the opposite sex. Viewed in the complete context of marriage, including intimacy, civil marriage with a person of the opposite sex is as unappealing to a gay or lesbian person as civil marriage with a person of the same sex is to a heterosexual. Thus, the right of a gay or lesbian person under the marriage statute to enter into a civil marriage only with a person of the opposite sex is no right at all. Under such a law, gay or lesbian individuals cannot simultaneously fulfill their deeply felt need for a committed personal relationship, as influenced by their sexual orientation, and gain the civil status and attendant benefits granted by the statute. Instead, a gay or lesbian person can only gain the same rights under the statute as a heterosexual person by negating the very trait that defines gay and lesbian people as a class-their sexual orientation. The benefit denied by the marriage statute—the status of civil marriage for same-sex couples—is so "closely correlated with being homosexual" as to make it apparent the law is targeted at gay and lesbian people as a class. . . . Thus, we proceed to analyze the constitutionality of the statute based on sexual orientation discrimination.

F. FRAMEWORK FOR DETERMINING APPROPRIATE LEVEL OF JUDICIAL SCRUTINY.

. . . [T]he political power of gays and lesbians, while responsible for greater acceptance and decreased discrimination, has done little to remove barriers to civil marriage. Although a small number of state legislatures have approved civil *unions* for gay and lesbian people without judicial intervention, no legislature has secured the right to civil *marriage* for gay and lesbian people without court order. The myriad statutes and regulatory protections against discrimination based on sexual orientation in such areas as employment, housing, public accommodations, and education have not only been absent in the area of marriage, but legislative bodies have taken affirmative steps to shore up the concept of traditional marriage by specifically excluding gays and lesbians. Like Iowa, over forty other states have passed statutes or constitutional amendments to ban same-sex marriages. . . . We are convinced gay and lesbian people are not so politically powerful as to overcome the unfair and severe prejudice that history suggests produces discrimination based on sexual orientation. . . .

In summarizing the rationale supporting heightened scrutiny of legislation classifying on the basis of sexual orientation, it would be difficult to improve upon the words of the Supreme Court of Connecticut:

> Gay persons have been subjected to and stigmatized by a long history of purposeful and invidious discrimination that continues to manifest itself in society. The characteristic that defines the members of this group—attraction to persons of the same sex—bears no logical relationship to their ability to perform in society, either in familial relations or otherwise as productive citizens. Because sexual orientation is such an essential component of personhood, even if there is some possibility that a person's sexual preference can be altered, it would be wholly unacceptable for the state to require anyone to do so. Gay persons also represent a distinct minority of the population. It is true, of course, that gay persons recently have made significant advances in obtaining equal treatment under the law. Nonetheless, we conclude that, as a minority group that continues to suffer the enduring effects of centuries of legally sanctioned discrimination, laws singling them out for disparate treatment are subject to heightened judicial scrutiny to ensure that those laws are not the product of such historical prejudice and stereotyping. . . .

Because we conclude Iowa's same-sex marriage statute cannot withstand intermediate scrutiny, we need not decide whether classifications based on sexual orientation are subject to a higher level of scrutiny. "To withstand intermediate scrutiny, a statutory classification must be substantially related to an important governmental objective." . . .

3. Governmental Objectives

The County has proffered a number of objectives supporting the marriage statute. These objectives include support for the "traditional" institution of marriage, the optimal procreation and rearing of children, and financial considerations. . . .

a. Maintaining Traditional Marriage

. . . The governmental objective identified by the County—to maintain the traditional understanding of marriage—is simply another way of saying the governmental objective is to limit civil marriage to opposite-sex couples. Opposite-sex marriage, however, is the classification made under the statute, and this classification must comply with our principles of equal protection. Thus, the use of traditional marriage as both the governmental objective and the classification of the statute transforms the equal protection analysis into the question of whether restricting marriage to opposite-sex couples accomplishes the governmental objective of maintaining opposite-sex marriage. This approach is, of course, an empty analysis. It permits a classification to be maintained "'for its own sake.'" . . . If a simple showing that discrimination is traditional satisfies equal protection, previous successful equal protection challenges of invidious racial and gender classifications would have failed. Consequently, equal protection demands that "'the classification ([that is], the exclusion of gay [persons] from civil marriage) must advance a state interest that is separate from the classification itself.'"

"[W]hen tradition is offered to justify preserving a statutory scheme that has been challenged on equal protection grounds, we must determine whether the *reasons underlying that tradition* are sufficient to satisfy constitutional requirements."[25] . . . Because the County offers no particular *governmental* reason underlying the tradition of limiting civil

25. The preservation of traditional marriage could only be a legitimate reason for the classification if expanding marriage to include others in its definition would undermine the traditional institution. The County has simply failed to explain how the traditional institution of *civil* marriage would suffer if same-sex civil marriage were allowed. There is no legitimate notion that a more inclusive definition of marriage will transform civil marriage into something less than it presently is for heterosexuals.

marriage to heterosexual couples, we press forward to consider other plausible reasons for the legislative classification.

b. Promotion of Optimal Environment to Raise Children

. . . The "best interests of children" is, undeniably, an important governmental objective. . . . Plaintiffs presented an abundance of evidence and research, confirmed by our independent research, supporting the proposition that the interests of children are served equally by same-sex parents and opposite-sex parents. On the other hand, we acknowledge the existence of reasoned opinions that dual-gender parenting is the optimal environment for children. These opinions, while thoughtful and sincere, were largely unsupported by reliable scientific studies.[26]

Under intermediate scrutiny, the relationship between the government's goal and the classification employed to further that goal must be "substantial." In order to evaluate that relationship, it is helpful to consider whether the legislation is over-inclusive or under-inclusive. . . . The civil marriage statute is under-inclusive because it does not exclude from marriage other groups of parents—such as child abusers, sexual predators, parents neglecting to provide child support, and violent felons—that are undeniably less than optimal parents. . . . The ban on same-sex marriage is substantially over-inclusive because not all same-sex couples choose to raise children. Yet, the marriage statute denies civil marriage to all gay and lesbian people in order to discourage the limited number of same-sex couples who desire to raise children.

At the same time, the exclusion of gay and lesbian people from marriage is under-inclusive, even in relation to the narrower goal of improving child rearing by limiting same-sex parenting. Quite obviously, the statute does not prohibit same-sex couples from raising children. Same-sex couples currently raise children in Iowa, even while being excluded from civil marriage, and such couples will undoubtedly continue to do so. Recognition of this under-inclusion puts in perspective just how minimally the same-sex marriage ban actually advances the purported legislative goal. A law so simultaneously over-inclusive and under-inclusive is not substantially related to the government's objective. . . . Likewise, exclusion of gays and lesbians from marriage does not benefit the interests of those children of heterosexual parents, who are able to enjoy the environment supported by marriage with or without the inclusion of same-sex couples. . . .[27]

c. Promotion of Procreation

The County . . . points out that procreation is important to the continuation of the human race, and opposite-sex couples accomplish this objective because procreation occurs naturally within this group. . . . [T]he County fails to address . . . whether *exclusion* of gay and lesbian individuals from the institution of civil marriage will result in *more* procreation. . . . [T]he sole conceivable avenue by which exclusion of gay and lesbian people from civil marriage could promote more procreation is if the unavailability of civil marriage for same-sex partners caused homosexual individuals to "become" heterosexual

26. The research appears to strongly support the conclusion that same-sex couples foster the same wholesome environment as opposite-sex couples and suggests that the traditional notion that children need a mother and a father to be raised into healthy, well-adjusted adults is based more on stereotype. . . .

27. The County does not specifically contend the goal of Iowa's marriage statute is to deter gay and lesbian couples from having children. Such a claim would raise serious due process concerns. *See Eisenstadt v. Baird*, 405 U.S. 438 (1972) (noting due process concern with governmental interference with decision to conceive children).

in order to procreate within the present traditional institution of civil marriage. The briefs, the record, our research, and common sense do not suggest such an outcome. . . .

d. Promoting Stability in Opposite-Sex Relationships

. . . While the institution of civil marriage likely encourages stability in opposite-sex relationships, we must evaluate whether excluding gay and lesbian people from civil marriage encourages stability in opposite-sex relationships. The County offers no reasons that it does, and we can find none. . . .

e. Conservation of Resources

. . . Iowa's marriage statute causes numerous government benefits . . . to be withheld from plaintiffs.[28] . . . Excluding any group from civil marriage—African-Americans, illegitimates, aliens, even red-haired individuals—would conserve state resources in an equally "rational" way. Yet, such classifications so obviously offend society's collective sense of equality that courts have not hesitated to provide added protections against such inequalities.

. . . 4. Conclusion

. . . While the objectives asserted may be important . . . , none are furthered in a substantial way by the exclusion of same-sex couples from civil marriage. . . .

RELIGIOUS OPPOSITION TO SAME-SEX MARRIAGE

Now that we have addressed and rejected each specific interest advanced by the County to justify the classification drawn under the statute, we consider the reason for the exclusion of gay and lesbian couples from civil marriage left unspoken by the County: religious opposition to same-sex marriage. . . . While unexpressed, religious sentiment most likely motivates many, if not most, opponents of same-sex civil marriage and perhaps even shapes the views of those people who may accept gay and lesbian unions but find the notion of same-sex marriage unsettling.[29]

28. Plaintiffs identify over two hundred Iowa statutes affected by civil-marriage status. *See, e.g.*, Iowa Code §85.31 (dependent surviving spouse receives benefits when spouse death caused by work injury); *id.* §135J.1(4) (hospice patient's family includes spouse); *id.* §142C.4 (spouse has power to make decision concerning anatomical gifts); *id.* §144A.7 (patient's spouse determines application of life-sustaining procedures in absence of declaration); *id.* §144C.5 (surviving spouse controls disposition of decedent's remains in absence of declaration); *id.* §252A.3(1) (spouse liable for support of other spouse); *id.* §252A.3(4) (children of married parents legitimate); *id.* §422.7 (spouses may file joint tax return); *id.* §422.9(1) (optional standard deduction for married taxpayers); *id.* §422.12(1)(*b*) (spouses eligible for personal exemption credit); *id.* §450.3 (inheritance rights of surviving spouses); *id.* §450.9 (surviving spouse exempt from inheritance tax on property passed from decedent spouse); *id.* §450.10(6) (spousal allowance for surviving spouse); *id.* §523I.309 (surviving spouse must consent to decedent spouse's interment); *id.* §613.15 (spouse may recover value of services and support of decedent spouse for wrongful death or negligent injury); *id.* §622.9 (restriction of testimony of communication between husband and wife); *id.* §633.211(1) (surviving spouse receives decedent spouse's entire estate in intestacy); *id.* §633.236 (surviving spouse has right to elective share); *id.* §633.272 (surviving spouse takes under partial intestacy if elective share not exercised); *id.* §633.336 (damages for wrongful death). The Government Accounting Office, as of 2005, had identified more than 1000 federal legal rights and responsibilities derived from marriage.

29. A survey in the *Des Moines Register* in 2008 found 28.1% of individuals surveyed supported same-sex marriage, 30.2% opposed same-sex marriage but supported civil unions, and thirty-two percent of respondents opposed both same-sex marriage and civil unions. The *Register* survey is consistent with a national survey by the PEW Research Center in 2003. This PEW survey found that fifty-nine percent of Americans oppose same-sex marriage, and thirty-two percent favor same-sex marriage. However, opposition to same-sex marriage jumped to eighty percent for people "with a high level of religious commitment," with only twelve percent of such people in favor of same-sex marriage. *Id.*

. . . Yet, such views are not the only religious views of marriage. As demonstrated by amicus groups, other equally sincere groups and people in Iowa and around the nation have strong religious views that yield the opposite conclusion.[31]

. . . Our constitution does not permit any branch of government to resolve these types of religious debates and entrusts to courts the task of ensuring government *avoids* them. The statute at issue in this case does not prescribe a definition of marriage for religious institutions. Instead, the statute declares, "Marriage is a civil contract" and then regulates that civil contract. . . . State government can have no religious views, either directly or indirectly, expressed through its legislation. This proposition is the essence of the separation of church and state. . . . Religious doctrine and views contrary to this principle of law are unaffected, and people can continue to associate with the religion that best reflects their views. A religious denomination can still define marriage as a union between a man and a woman, and a marriage ceremony performed by a minister, priest, rabbi, or other person ordained or designated as a leader of the person's religious faith does not lose its meaning as a sacrament or other religious institution.

V. Remedy. . . .

. . . The high courts of other jurisdictions have remedied constitutionally invalid bans on same-sex marriage in two ways. Some courts have ordered gay and lesbian people to be allowed to access the institution of civil marriage. *See* [decisions in California, Connecticut, and Massachusetts]. Other courts have allowed their state legislatures to create parallel civil institutions for same-sex couples. *See* [decisions in New Jersey and Vermont]. . . . A new distinction based on sexual orientation would be equally suspect and difficult to square with the fundamental principles of equal protection embodied in our constitution. Consequently, the language in Iowa Code section 595.2 limiting civil marriage to a man and a woman must be stricken from the statute, and the remaining statutory language must be interpreted and applied in a manner allowing gay and lesbian people full access to the institution of civil marriage.

This was a surprising and not especially popular decision in heartlands Iowa. In November 2010 retention elections, voters dismissed three of the judges who were in the *Varnum* majority. Republicans launched a campaign to amend the state constitution to eviscerate the decision, but at this time have not yet succeeded.

In reasoning about the appropriate level of scrutiny, the court noted that "the political power of gays and lesbians . . . has done little to remove barriers to civil marriage." This is a core consideration in equal protection level of scrutiny analysis. The court noted that no state legislature had enacted a same-sex marriage law without being ordered by a court to do so. But since *Varnum*, several legislatures have passed without judicial compulsion bills authorizing same-sex marriage. Does this undermine the case for heightened scrutiny? Is there some tension between the legislative agenda and the judicial agenda of same-sex marriage proponents?

31. Many religions recognize same-sex marriage, such as Buddhists, Quakers, Unitarians, and Reform and Reconstructionist Jews. Amicus curiae Iowa and National Faith Leaders, Communities, and Scholars point out the United Church of Christ encourages, but does not require, its local congregations to adopt wedding policies that do not discriminate between heterosexual, gay, and lesbian couples, while the Episcopal Church permits priests to perform liturgies and blessings at same-sex weddings as a matter of pastoral care. Additionally, many groups and clergy within various religions are working to achieve inclusion of same-sex marriage.

Much academic literature addresses the question of what is the strongest doctrinal argument for same-sex legal marriage. The prevailing view seems to be that equal protection is more promising than substantive due process. The most common argument in state court litigation has been an equal protection claim asserting discrimination based on sexual orientation, as in *Varnum.* However, federal constitutional doctrine to date offers less support for heightened scrutiny of laws discriminating on that basis, so litigation in federal court might need to take another tack. Professor Case contends there is strong federal doctrinal support for a claim based on sex discrimination, on the theory that denying marriage to same-sex couples conflicts with the Supreme Court's prior condemnation of laws enforcing "'fixed notions concerning the roles and abilities of males and females.'" Mary Anne Case, *What Feminists Have to Lose in Same-Sex Marriage Litigation,* 57 UCLA L. Rev. 1199, 1227 (2010). As Professor Case acknowledges, state courts have not been very accepting of the notion that exclusion of same-sex couples from marriage discriminates on the basis of sex, rather than on the basis of sexual orientation, id. at 1218-1220, but she is optimistic about acceptance of this view in federal court. As noted above, Professors Widiss and Tebbe take the position that the strongest constitutional argument is an equal protection claim asserting that heightened scrutiny is warranted because an important interest is at stake, rather than because of the nature of the class discriminated against. Cf. Angela Onwuachi-Willig, *Undercover Other,* 94 Cal. L. Rev. 873, 873-874, 885-886 (2006) (analyzing the analogy between prohibition of same-sex marriage and prohibition of interracial marriage).

Regardless of what level of scrutiny applies, in defense of the different-sex requirement for marriage states uniformly assert a connection between marriage and child rearing. How close is that connection? If it is very close, would you support restricting marriage to couples who already have a child? Would a state violate constitutional rights if it excluded from legal marriage persons who are sterile or impotent? Is the connection stronger or weaker than it was at the founding of the country? Is the court right to suggest that availability of legal marriage has no effect on whether same-sex couples choose to have and raise children? Does it matter to you whether you are married if and when you have children?

The *Varnum* court concluded from its research that being raised by a gay couple is equally as good for a child as being raised by a heterosexual couple. What criteria do you think the researchers used? Should it matter whether this is true? Is there any reason to think gay couples might be *better* parents on average? Comparison with adoptive parents might be informative. The court cited a number of reasons other than child rearing why people get married. Should a government care about any of those reasons?

Now let us look at the developing federal court doctrine.

Perry v. Brown

671 F.3d 1052 (9th Cir. 2012)

Before Reinhardt, Hawkins, and N.R. Smith, Circuit Judges.

Opinion by Reinhardt, Circuit Judge:

I

. . . Marriage in California was understood . . . well into the twentieth century, to be limited to relationships between a man and a woman. In 1977, that much was made explicit by the California Legislature, which amended the marriage statute to read,

"Marriage is a personal relation arising out of a civil contract between a man and a woman, to which the consent of the parties capable of making that contract is necessary." The 1977 provision remains codified in California statute. Following the enactment of the Defense of Marriage Act of 1996 (codified in relevant part at 1 U.S.C. §7), which expressly limited the federal definition of marriage to relationships between one man and one woman, dozens of states enacted similar provisions into state law. California did so in 2000 by adopting Proposition 22, an initiative statute, which provided, "Only marriage between a man and a woman is valid or recognized in California." The proposition ensured that same-sex marriages performed in any state that might permit such marriages in the future would not be recognized in California, and it guaranteed that any legislative repeal of the 1977 statute would not allow same-sex couples to marry within the State, because the Legislature may not amend or repeal an initiative statute enacted by the People.

Meanwhile, however, California had created the designation "domestic partnership" for "two adults who have chosen to share one another's lives in an intimate and committed relationship of mutual caring." At first, California gave registered domestic partners only limited rights, such as hospital visitation privileges, and health benefits for the domestic partners of certain state employees. Over the next several years, however, the State substantially expanded the rights of domestic partners. . . . The 2003 Domestic Partner Act provided broadly: "Registered domestic partners shall have the same rights, protections, and benefits, and shall be subject to the same responsibilities, obligations, and duties under law, whether they derive from statutes, administrative regulations, court rules, government policies, common law, or any other provisions or sources of law, as are granted to and imposed upon spouses." It withheld only the official designation of marriage and thus the officially conferred and societally recognized status that accompanies that designation.

In 2004, same-sex couples and the City and County of San Francisco filed actions in California state courts alleging that the State's marriage statutes violated the California Constitution. . . . [T]he California Supreme Court . . . held the statutes to be unconstitutional. . . . In re Marriage Cases, 183 P.3d 384 (Cal. 2008). . . . The court remedied these constitutional violations by striking the language from the marriage statutes "limiting the designation of marriage to a union 'between a man and a woman,'" invalidating Proposition 22, and ordering that the designation of "marriage" be made available to both opposite-sex and same-sex couples. Following the court's decision, California counties issued more than 18,000 marriage licenses to same-sex couples.

Five California residents . . . collected voter signatures and filed petitions with the state government to place an initiative on the November 4, 2008, ballot. Unlike Proposition 22, this was an initiative constitutional amendment, which would be equal in effect to any other provision of the California Constitution, rather than subordinate to it. The Proponents' measure, designated Proposition 8, proposed to add a new provision to the California Constitution's Declaration of Rights, immediately following the Constitution's due process and equal protection clauses. The provision states, "Only marriage between a man and a woman is valid or recognized in California." According to the official voter information guide, Proposition 8 "[c]hanges the California Constitution to eliminate the right of same-sex couples to marry in California." Following a contentious campaign, a slim majority of California voters (52.3 percent) approved Proposition 8. Pursuant to the state constitution, Proposition 8 took effect the next day, as article I, section 7.5 of the California Constitution.

II

Two same-sex couples—plaintiffs Kristin Perry and Sandra Stier, and Paul Katami and Jeffrey Zarrillo—filed this action under 42 U.S.C. §1983 in May 2009, after being denied marriage licenses by the County Clerks of Alameda County and Los Angeles County, respectively. . . . The district court held a twelve-day bench trial, during which it heard testimony from nineteen witnesses and . . . built an extensive evidentiary record. In a thorough opinion in August 2010, the court made eighty findings of fact[4] and . . . held Proposition 8 unconstitutional. . . .

Proponents appealed immediately . . . [when Governor Schwarzenegger and other government defendants declined to do so]. . . . California law confers on "initiative sponsors" the authority "to defend, in lieu of public officials, the constitutionality of initiatives made law of the State." . . .

V

The district court held Proposition 8 unconstitutional for two reasons: first, it deprives same-sex couples of the fundamental right to marry, which is guaranteed by the Due Process Clause, and second, it excludes same-sex couples from state-sponsored marriage while allowing opposite-sex couples access to that honored status, in violation of the Equal Protection Clause. . . . Plaintiffs and Plaintiff-Intervenor San Francisco also offer a third argument: Proposition 8 singles out same-sex couples for unequal treatment by *taking away* from them alone the right to marry, and this action amounts to a distinct constitutional violation because the Equal Protection Clause protects minority groups from being targeted for the deprivation of an existing right without a legitimate reason. Romer v. Evans, 517 U.S. 620 (1996). Because this third argument applies to the specific history of same-sex marriage in California, it is the narrowest ground for adjudicating the constitutional questions before us, while the first two theories, if correct, would apply on a broader basis. Because courts generally decide constitutional questions on the narrowest ground available, we consider the third argument first.

Proposition 8 worked a singular and limited change to the California Constitution: it stripped same-sex couples of the right to have their committed relationships recognized by the State with the designation of "marriage," which the state constitution had previously guaranteed them, while leaving in place all of their other rights and responsibilities as partners—rights and responsibilities that are identical to those of married spouses and form an integral part of the marriage relationship. . . . Now as before, same-sex partners may:

- Raise children together, and have the same rights and obligations as to their children as spouses have, *see* Cal. Fam. Code §297.5(d);

4. The court found, among other things, that (1) marriage benefits society by organizing individuals into cohesive family units, developing a realm of liberty for intimacy and free decision making, creating stable households, legitimating children, assigning individuals to care for one another, and facilitating property ownership; (2) marriage benefits spouses and their children physically, psychologically, and economically, whether the spouses are of the same or opposite sexes; (3) domestic partnerships lack the social meaning associated with marriage; (4) permitting same-sex couples to marry would not affect the number or stability of opposite-sex marriages; (5) the children of same-sex couples benefit when their parents marry, and they fare just as well as children raised by opposite-sex parents; (6) Proposition 8 stigmatizes same-sex couples as having relationships inferior to those of opposite-sex couples; (7) Proposition 8 eliminated same-sex couples' right to marry but did not affect any other substantive right they enjoyed; and (8) the campaign in favor of Proposition 8 relied upon stereotypes and unfounded fears about gays and lesbians.

- Enjoy the presumption of parentage as to a child born to either partner, *see Elisa B. v. Super. Ct.* (Cal. 2005) or adopted by one partner and raised jointly by both, *S.Y. v. S.B.* (Cal. App. 2011);
- Adopt each other's children, *see* Cal. Fam. Code §9000(g);
- Become foster parents, *see* Cal. Welf. & Inst. Code §16013(a);
- Share community property, *see* Cal. Fam. Code §297.5(k);
- File state taxes jointly, *see* Cal. Rev. & Tax. Code §18521(d);
- Participate in a partner's group health insurance policy on the same terms as a spouse, *see* Cal. Ins. Code §10121.7;
- Enjoy hospital visitation privileges, *see* Cal. Health & Safety Code §1261;
- Make medical decisions on behalf of an incapacitated partner, *see* Cal. Prob. Code §4716;
- Be treated in a manner equal to that of a widow or widower with respect to a deceased partner, *see* Cal. Fam. Code §297.5(c);
- Serve as the conservator of a partner's estate, *see* Cal. Prob. Code §§ 1811-1813.1; and
- Sue for the wrongful death of a partner, *see* Cal. Civ. Proc. Code §377.60 . . .

Proposition 8 . . . simply took the designation of 'marriage' away from lifelong same-sex partnerships, and with it the State's authorization of that official status and the societal approval that comes with it. . . .

By emphasizing Proposition 8's limited effect, . . . we emphasize the extraordinary significance of the official designation of "marriage." That designation is important because "marriage" is the name that society gives to the relationship that matters most between two adults. A rose by any other name may smell as sweet, but to the couple desiring to enter into a committed lifelong relationship, a marriage by the name of 'registered domestic partnership' does not. The word "marriage" is singular in connoting "a harmony in living," "a bilateral loyalty," and "a coming together for better or for worse, hopefully enduring, and intimate to the degree of being sacred." As Proponents have admitted, "the word 'marriage' has a unique meaning," and "there is a significant symbolic disparity between domestic partnership and marriage." It is the designation of 'marriage' itself that expresses validation, by the state and the community, and that serves as a symbol, like a wedding ceremony or a wedding ring, of something profoundly important.

We need consider only the many ways in which we encounter the word 'marriage' in our daily lives and understand it, consciously or not, to convey a sense of significance. We are regularly given forms to complete that ask us whether we are "single" or "married." Newspapers run announcements of births, deaths, and marriages. We are excited to see someone ask, "Will you marry me?," whether on bended knee in a restaurant or in text splashed across a stadium Jumbotron. Certainly it would not have the same effect to see "Will you enter into a registered domestic partnership with me?" Groucho Marx's one-liner, "Marriage is a wonderful institution . . . but who wants to live in an institution?" would lack its punch if the word 'marriage' were replaced with the alternative phrase. So too with Shakespeare's "A young man married is a man that's marr'd," Lincoln's "Marriage is neither heaven nor hell, it is simply purgatory," and Sinatra's "A man doesn't know what happiness is until he's married. By then it's too late." We see tropes like "marrying for love" versus "marrying for money" played out again and again in our films and literature because of the recognized importance and permanence of the marriage relationship. Had Marilyn Monroe's film been called *How to Register a Domestic Partnership with a Millionaire*, it would not have conveyed the same meaning as did her famous movie, even though the underlying drama for same-sex couples is no different. The *name* "marriage" signifies the unique recognition that society gives to harmonious, loyal, enduring, and intimate relationships. . . . We do not celebrate when two people merge their bank accounts; we celebrate when a couple marries. The designation of "marriage" is the . . . principal manner in which the State attaches respect and dignity to the highest form of a committed relationship and to the individuals who have entered into it. . . . Before Proposition 8, California guaranteed gays and lesbians both the incidents and the status and dignity of marriage. Proposition 8 left the incidents but took away the status and the dignity. . . .

Withdrawing from a disfavored group the right to obtain a designation with significant societal consequences is different from declining to extend that designation in the first place, regardless of whether the right was withdrawn after a week, a year, or a decade. . . . This is not the first time the voters of a state have enacted an initiative constitutional amendment that reduces the rights of gays and lesbians under state law. In 1992, Colorado adopted Amendment 2 to its state constitution, which prohibited the state and its political subdivisions from providing any protection against discrimination on the basis of sexual orientation. Amendment 2 was proposed in response to a number of local ordinances that had banned sexual-orientation discrimination in such areas as housing, employment, education, public accommodations, and health and welfare services. The effect of Amendment 2 was "to repeal" those local laws and "to prohibit any governmental entity from adopting similar, or more protective statutes, regulations, ordinances, or policies in the future." . . . The Supreme Court held that Amendment 2 violated the Equal Protection Clause because "[i]t is not within our constitutional tradition to enact laws of this sort"—laws that "singl[e] out a certain class of citizens for disfavored legal status," which "raise the inevitable inference that the disadvantage imposed is born of animosity toward the class of persons affected." The Court . . . concluded that the law "classifie[d] homosexuals not to further a proper legislative end but to make them unequal to everyone else."[13]

Proposition 8 is remarkably similar to Amendment 2. Like Amendment 2, Proposition 8 "single[s] out a certain class of citizens for disfavored legal status. . . ." Like Amendment 2, Proposition 8 has the "peculiar property" of "withdraw[ing] from homosexuals, but no others," an existing legal right—here, access to the official designation of 'marriage'—that had been broadly available, notwithstanding the fact that the Constitution did not compel the state to confer it in the first place. Like Amendment 2, Proposition 8 . . . "carves out" an "exception" to California's equal protection clause, by removing equal access to marriage, which gays and lesbians had previously enjoyed, from the scope of that constitutional guarantee. Like Amendment 2, Proposition 8 "by state decree . . . put[s] [homosexuals] in a solitary class with respect to" an important aspect of human relations, and accordingly "imposes a special disability upon [homosexuals] alone." And like Amendment 2, Proposition 8 constitutionalizes that disability, meaning that gays and lesbians may overcome it "only by enlisting the citizenry of [the state] to amend the State Constitution" for a second time. . . . Proposition 8 is no less problematic than Amendment 2 merely because its effect is narrower; to the contrary, the surgical precision with which it excises a right belonging to gay and lesbian couples makes it even more suspect. A law that has no practical effect except to strip one group of the right to use a

13. *Romer* did not apply heightened scrutiny . . . Instead, *Romer* found that Amendment 2 "fail[ed], indeed defie[d], even [the] conventional inquiry" for non-suspect classes, concerning whether a "legislative classification . . . bears a rational relation to some legitimate end." Amendment 2 amounted to "a classification of persons undertaken for its own sake, something the Equal Protection Clause does not permit." . . .

state-authorized and socially meaningful designation is all the more "unprecedented" and "unusual" than a law that imposes broader changes, and raises an even stronger "inference that the disadvantage imposed is born of animosity toward the class of persons affected." . . . There is no necessity in either case that the privilege, benefit, or protection at issue be a constitutional right. We therefore need not and do not consider whether same-sex couples have a fundamental right to marry, or whether states that fail to afford the right to marry to gays and lesbians must do so. Further, we express no view on those questions.

D

Ordinarily, "if a law neither burdens a fundamental right nor targets a suspect class, we will uphold the legislative classification so long as it bears a rational relation to some legitimate end." . . . We first consider four possible reasons offered by Proponents or amici . . .

1

The primary rationale Proponents offer for Proposition 8 is that it advances California's interest in responsible procreation and childrearing. . . . Proposition 8 had absolutely no effect on the ability of same-sex couples to become parents or the manner in which children are raised . . . Proposition 8 in no way modified the state's laws governing parentage, which are distinct from its laws governing marriage. . . . *See* Cal. Fam. Code §297.5(d) ("The rights and obligations of registered domestic partners with respect to a child of either of them shall be the same as those of spouses."). Similarly, Proposition 8 did not alter the California adoption or presumed-parentage laws, which continue to apply equally to same-sex couples. . . . California's "current policies and conduct . . . recognize that gay individuals are fully capable of . . . responsibly caring for and raising children." And California law actually prefers a non-biological parent who has a parental relationship with a child to a biological parent who does not; in California, the parentage statutes place a premium on the "social relationship," not the "biological relationship," between a parent and a child. . . .

Proponents' second argument is that there is no need to hold out the designation of "marriage" as an encouragement for same-sex couples to engage in responsible procreation, because unlike opposite-sex couples, same-sex couples pose no risk of procreating accidentally. . . . *See* Johnson v. Robison, 415 U.S. 361, 383 (1974) ("When . . . the inclusion of one group promotes a legitimate governmental purpose, and the addition of other groups would not, we cannot say that the statute's classification of beneficiaries and nonbeneficiaries is invidiously discriminatory."). But . . . *Johnson* concerns decisions not to *add* to a legislative scheme a group that is unnecessary to the purposes of that scheme, but Proposition 8 *subtracted* a disfavored group from a scheme of which it already was a part.[21]

Under *Romer*, it is no justification for taking something away to say that there was no need to provide it in the first place; instead, there must be some legitimate reason for the act of taking it away, a reason that overcomes the "inevitable inference that the disadvantage imposed is born of animosity toward the class of persons affected." In order to explain how *rescinding* access to the designation of "marriage" is rationally related to the State's interest in responsible procreation, Proponents would have had

21. Moreover, *Johnson* did not involve a dignitary benefit that was withdrawn from one group . . . ; it concerned only a specific form of government assistance.

to argue that opposite-sex couples were more likely to procreate accidentally or irresponsibly when same-sex couples were allowed access to the designation of "marriage." We are aware of no basis on which this argument would be even conceivably plausible. . . . The same analysis applies to the arguments of some amici curiae that Proposition 8 not only promotes responsible procreation and childrearing as a general matter but promotes the single best family structure for such activities. *See, e.g.*, . . . Br. Amicus Curiae of Am. Coll. of Pediatricians 15 ("[T]he State has a legitimate interest in promoting the family structure that has proven most likely to foster an optimal environment for the rearing of children."). . . . Proposition 8 . . . makes no change with respect to the laws regarding family structure. . . .

We in no way mean to suggest that Proposition 8 would be constitutional if only it had gone further—for example, by also repealing same-sex couples' equal parental rights or their rights to share community property or enjoy hospital visitation privileges. Only if Proposition 8 had actually had any effect on childrearing or "responsible procreation" would it be necessary or appropriate for us to *consider* the legitimacy of Proponents' primary rationale for the measure. . . .

To the extent that it has been argued that withdrawing from same-sex couples access to the designation of "marriage"—without in any way altering the substantive laws concerning their rights regarding childrearing or family formation—will encourage heterosexual couples to enter into matrimony, or will strengthen their matrimonial bonds, we believe that the People of California "could not reasonably" have "conceived" such an argument "to be true." It is implausible to think that denying two men or two women the right to call themselves married could somehow bolster the stability of families headed by one man and one woman. . . .

3

We briefly consider two other potential rationales . . . First is . . . the religious-liberty interest that Proposition 8 supposedly promoted . . . to decrease the likelihood that religious organizations would be penalized, under California's antidiscrimination laws and other government policies concerning sexual orientation, for refusing to provide services to families headed by same-sex spouses. But Proposition 8 did nothing to affect those laws. . . . Second is the argument . . . that it would "protect[ ] our children from being taught in public schools that 'same-sex marriage' is the same as traditional marriage." Yet . . . before and after Proposition 8, schools have not been required to teach anything about same-sex marriage. . . . And both before and after Proposition 8, schools and individual teachers have been prohibited from giving any instruction that discriminates on the basis of sexual orientation; now as before, students could not be taught the superiority or inferiority of either same- or opposite-sex marriage or other "committed relationships." . . . Schools teach about the world as it is; when the world changes, lessons change. . . .

Simply taking away the designation of "marriage" . . . did not do any of the things its Proponents now suggest were its purposes. . . . We therefore need not, and do not, decide whether any of these purported rationales for the law would be "legitimate," or would suffice to justify Proposition 8 if the amendment actually served to further them.

E

We are left to consider why else the People of California might have enacted a constitutional amendment that takes away from gays and lesbians the right to use the designation of "marriage." One explanation is the desire to . . . "restore the traditional definition of marriage. . . ." But tradition alone is not a justification for *taking away* a right that had already been granted, even though that grant was in derogation of tradition. . . . Laws may be repealed and new rights taken away if they have had unintended consequences or if there is some conceivable affirmative good that revocation would produce, but new rights may not be stripped away solely *because* they are new. . . .

Absent any legitimate purpose for Proposition 8, we are left with "the inevitable inference that the disadvantage imposed is born of animosity toward," or . . . mere disapproval of, "the class of persons affected." . . . Disapproval may . . . be the product of longstanding, sincerely held private beliefs. Still, while "[p]rivate biases may be outside the reach of the law, . . . the law cannot, directly or indirectly, give them effect." . . . Just as the criminalization of "homosexual conduct . . . is an invitation to subject homosexual persons to discrimination both in the public and in the private spheres," *Lawrence*, so too does the elimination of the right to use the official designation of 'marriage' for the relationships of committed same-sex couples send a message that gays and lesbians are of lesser worth as a class—that they enjoy a lesser societal status. . . . Proposition 8 enacts nothing more or less than a judgment about the worth and dignity of gays and lesbians as a class. Just as a "desire to harm . . . cannot constitute a *legitimate* governmental interest," neither can a more basic disapproval of a class of people. . . . Society does sometimes draw classifications that likely are rooted partially in disapproval, such as a law that grants educational benefits to veterans but denies them to conscientious objectors who engaged in alternative civilian service. Those classifications will not be invalidated so long as they can be justified by reference to some *independent* purpose they serve; in *Johnson*, they could provide an incentive for military service and direct assistance to those who needed the most help in readjusting to post-war life. . . . Proposition 8 is a classification of gays and lesbians undertaken for its own sake. . . .

VII

By using their initiative power to target a minority group and withdraw a right that it possessed, without a legitimate reason for doing so, the People of California violated the Equal Protection Clause. We hold Proposition 8 to be unconstitutional on this ground. . . .

Given the court's analysis, would a straightforward claim to same-sex marriage as a fundamental due process right or equal protection right, in the absence of any history of once having had the right under state law, have lost? In other words, is the "withdraw vs. extend" distinction crucial to the outcome here? If so, is the distinction really as meaningful as the court suggests, or is it an artificial one?

Is the court correct that Prop 8 is a greater offense to LGBT persons than Colorado's Proposition 2 was? Is there something wrong with this reasoning: "Proposition 8 is no less problematic than Amendment 2 merely because its effect is narrower; to the contrary, the surgical precision with which it excises a right belonging to gay and lesbian couples makes it even more suspect . . . and raises an even stronger 'inference that the disadvantage imposed is born of animosity toward the class of persons affected.'"

Relatedly, to what extent is the decision dependent on the fact that California has a registered domestic partnership law that confers all the practical rights that state law can? Would the analysis yield the same conclusion as to a state that did not have that alternative—that is, where the law went from no recognition to marriage and back to no recognition?

As noted above, most states have reacted to litigation over same-sex marriage with legislation or constitutional amendments to prevent local infection—that is, to prevent recognition within their borders of such marriages effected elsewhere. Roughly 40 states now have a Defense of Marriage Act (DOMA), and their uncertain scope and constitutionality also provide grounds for litigation. Here is one example, adopted by referendum in 2004:

Constitution of Michigan

§25 MARRIAGE

To secure and preserve the benefits of marriage for our society and for future generations of children, the union of one man and one woman in marriage shall be the only agreement recognized as a marriage or similar union for any purpose.

The same sentiment earlier produced federal legislation, signed in 1996 by President Clinton, attempting to avoid application of the Full Faith and Credit Clause.

United States Public Laws
104th Congress—Second Session
PL 104-199 (HR 3396), September 21, 1996
Defense of Marriage Act

SEC. 2.(a) Chapter 115 of title 28, U.S. Code, is amended by adding:

"§1738C. Certain acts, records, and proceedings and the effect thereof

"No State, territory, or possession of the United States, or Indian tribe, shall be required to give effect to any public act, record, or judicial proceeding of any other State, territory, possession, or tribe respecting a relationship between persons of the same sex that is treated as a marriage under the laws of such other State, territory, possession, or tribe, or a right or claim arising from such relationship."

SEC. 3. Chapter 1 of title 1, United States Code, is amended by adding at the end the following:

"§7. Definition of 'marriage' and 'spouse'

"In determining the meaning of any Act of Congress, or of any ruling, regulation, or interpretation of the various administrative bureaus and agencies of the United States, the word 'marriage' means only a legal union between one man and one woman as husband and wife, and the word 'spouse' refers only to a person of the opposite sex who is a husband or a wife."

Section 3 of the Act prevents same-sex marriage proponents from experiencing complete victory in states where courts or legislatures have sided with them; they still feel the sting of the federal government's refusal to treat them as married. In February 2011, the Obama administration concluded that §3 of the Act is unconstitutional and announced that it would not defend that provision against legal challenge in courts. However, the administration also said that unless and until Congress repeals the law or the Supreme Court invalidates the law, it will continue to enforce §3. Thus, for the present the federal government continues to refuse to recognize same-sex couples as married for purposes such as income and estate tax and social security benefits, even if they have effectuated a legal marriage in a state that allows it. There are several constitutional challenges to §3 percolating in the federal court system now. Thus far, those efforts have been mostly successful. See In re Balas, 449 B.R. 567 (Bankr. C.D. Cal. 2011) (holding that refusal based on §3 of the federal DOMA to allow same-sex couple legally married in California from filing joint Chapter 13 bankruptcy petition violated equal protection guarantee of federal constitution); Gill v. Office of Pers. Mgmt., 699 F. Supp. 2d 374 (D. Mass. 2010) (holding that DOMA-based denial of federal spousal health and social security survivor benefits to same-sex couples legally married in Massachusetts violated the U.S. Constitution). See also Massachusetts v. U.S. Dep't of Health & Hum. Servs., 698 F. Supp. 2d 234 (D. Mass. 2010) (successful federalism-based challenge to §3 by Massachusetts). These cases do not address whether states must confer legal marriage status on same-sex couples, however, but only whether the federal government must recognize same-sex marriages when states do choose to confer it.

State DOMAs also continue to be enforced across most of the country, thereby inhibiting the mobility of same-sex couples who marry. These state versions have had the effect not just of preventing new rights for same-sex couples within a state, but in some jurisdictions also of eliminating rights previously granted and benefit programs already in place. For example, in May 2008, the Supreme Court of Michigan ruled in National Pride at Work, Inc. v. Governor of Michigan that the constitutional provision above prohibits public employers from continuing to provide health-insurance benefits to their employees' same-sex domestic partners, as state agencies had been doing. So the backlash made same-sex couples worse off than they had been in important respects. State DOMAs also create a great obstacle to divorce for same-sex couples who marry and then move to another state. As Professor Oppenheimer explains, the new state will not grant a divorce, because its DOMA precludes courts from recognizing that a marriage exists, and the state of marriage will not entertain a divorce petition because states generally have a residency requirement for divorce proceedings. See Elisabeth Oppenheimer, *No Exit: The Problem of Same-Sex Divorce,* 90 N.C. L. Rev. 73 (2011). Even in a state without a DOMA, courts might not know what to do with a same-sex couple, legally married in another state or country, that petitions for a divorce. See, e.g., Christiansen v. Christiansen, 253 P.3d 153 (Wyo. 2011) (overturning a trial court decision that it lacked subject matter jurisdiction over a divorce petition filed by a same-sex couple who had married in Canada, holding that Wyoming courts can in fact apply Wyoming's divorce law to such couples).

The effects of DOMAs can extend to parent-child relationships as well. As illustrated by the *Miller-Jenkins* case mentioned in Chapter 1, when a same-sex marriage or civil union dissolves and a court in the state that conferred the legal status issues a decree splitting custody between the parties, the biological parent to the child might try to exclude his or her former partner from the child's life by moving with the child to a state with a strong DOMA, hoping that that state will refuse to respect the custody order.

Passage of state and federal DOMAs, along with other elements of political backlash and resistance to same-sex marriage, reflect large-scale popular opposition to same-sex marriage. Less evident is any robust scholarly opposition, given that the family law academy is in general politically liberal. But there is some:

Lynn D. Wardle, The "Constitution" of Marriage, and the "Constitutions" of Nations

45 U.S.F. L. Rev. 437, 450-451, 464-466 (2010)

The Founders considered certain domestic habits or virtues (or, as de Tocqueville later called them, "habits of the heart") as necessary "preconditions" for maintaining the constitutional Republic. These domestic habits included and were nurtured by marriage and the marital family. The Founders believed that marriages and families were the first schoolrooms of democracy, the institutions in which essential civic virtue is inculcated. . . .

Legalizing same-sex marriage will change the meaning and morality of the social institution of marriage through "the transformative power of inclusion." . . . When same-sex marriage is legalized, the moral qualities of homosexual relations and lifestyles will become part of, and will have an altering effect upon, the qualities and characteristics of the institution of marriage. . . . The moral and relational expectations of gays and lesbians differ drastically from married men and women. For example, promiscuity, infidelity, multiple sexual partners, dangerous sexual practices, and instability are the behavioral norms among gay couples (and also, to a clear but lesser extent, among lesbian couples), rather than monogamy and sexual self-control which are the norms fostered by and nurtured in heterosexual marriages. A study by Dutch AIDS researchers, published in 2003 in the journal AIDS, reported on the number of partners among Amsterdam's homosexual population. They found . . .

- Gay men with steady partners had eight other sex partners ("casual partners") per year, on average.
- The average duration of committed relationships among gay steady partners was 1.5 years.

Likewise, a study of 2,583 older sexually active gay men reported that "the modal range for number of sexual partners ever was 101-500," while 10.2 percent to 15.7 percent had between 501 and 1,000 partners, and another 10.2 percent to 15.7 percent reported having had more than one thousand sexual partners in their lifetime. Other researchers theorize that "the cheating ratio of 'married' gay males, given enough time, approaches 100%."

Thus, redefining marriage to include gay and lesbian relationships will have a profound impact upon fidelity, promiscuity, sexual morality, and public health in the institution of marriage. Moral standards and behavioral expectations in marriage will change as homosexual relations are deemed marital relations. . . . Defining marriage to include homosexual couples will alter the meaning and moral message of our most basic social institution.

Supporters of same-sex marriage and courts striking down marriage laws excluding same-sex couples typically dismiss out of hand suggestions that heterosexual married couples might be affected in some adverse way by inclusion of same-sex couples in the institution of legal marriage. But is it not extremely common for people who want to justify some morally questionable behavior to point to a group of people among whom the behavior is accepted? It used to be that almost any casual conversation about adultery led to comparison with supposed acceptance of mistresses among the French. It is, in fact, one aim of comparative legal and cultural studies to get people to rethink the normative assumptions that prevail in their own culture and legal system, by pointing out that other cultures live by different norms. So why should it be implausible to conjecture, as Professor Wardle does, that opening marriage to same-sex couples could change heterosexual couples' beliefs about acceptable behavior for married people, in the direction of greater toleration for extra-marital sexual relations and a quicker trigger for divorce, if that is how heterosexuals view same-sex relationships? And that such a change in beliefs could make heterosexual marriages even less stable than they already are? And that less stable marriages would translate to a deterioration of important virtues and social skills? If such conjectures are plausible, might the posited adverse societal consequences be great enough to override the equality right of persons in same-sex relationships?

Relatedly, the *Perry* court rejected out of hand, as have other courts, the suggestion that extending marriage to same-sex couples could lessen heterosexual couples' estimation of the importance or specialness of marriage, and thereby make them less desirous of entering or less averse to exiting marriage. But imagine that a state eliminated all restrictions on marriage, including any relating to age, mental capacity, biological relatedness, sex of partner, and existing marriage. If any two humans could become legally married to each other, would that not be likely to affect how everyone views marriage, in a way that makes it seem less special and important, less worthy of entering into or being committed to? If so, why could not elimination of just one restriction, that pertaining to sex of partner, not have such an effect, perhaps just more modestly? A court would still have to ask whether any such effect justifies retaining the restriction, but are courts right to reject this alleged state concern as factually fanciful?

Another potential effect on heterosexuals is a reduction in financial incentives to become and remain married. Marriage is subsidized by the state in various ways now, and the state does not have infinite resources, so if the number of married couples swells significantly with the addition of same-sex couples, governments might well choose to reduce the per-couple amount of state financial support rather than increase the size of the overall marriage subsidy pie. Married couples would then be worse off materially, and that would marginally diminish the attractiveness of being married relative to being single. Is that a price heterosexual couples and society as a whole simply must pay?

2. *Unchallenged Statutory Limitations*

There are several other common restrictions on whom one may marry that have not been subject to constitutional challenge, at least not to a significant degree.

a. Right to Marry a Child

The requirement that people reach a particular age, something approaching adulthood, in order to marry legally aims to prevent young people from getting married when they want to and to prevent parents or other adults from forcing young people into marriage. In either case, we might ask, what is the big deal? Is it just that marriage makes sex legal for the couple, and society does not want to facilitate sex between children? Is it the assumption that married people live together and by themselves, and we do not think children are able to do that? Or is there something bad about being married per se when one is very young? What harm would it have done if you got married in sixth or seventh grade, if your life otherwise remained the same?

In the United States, people generally must be at least 18 years old to get a marriage license without parental approval. There is some variation among states as to when people under 18 can get married with parental consent. Here are three variations, ranging from a firm 16 years of age minimum in Michigan to no minimum in New Jersey:

Michigan Compiled Laws
Chapter 551. Marriage
Marriage License

551.103. Persons Capable of Contracting Marriage; Proof of Age; Consent to Marriage of Persons Less Than 18 Years of Age

Sec. 3. (1) A person who is 18 years of age or older may contract marriage. A person who is 16 years of age but is less than 18 years of age may contract marriage with the written consent of 1 of the parents of the person or the person's legal guardian. . . . The consent shall be given personally in the presence of the county clerk or be acknowledged before a notary public or other officer authorized to administer oaths.

551.51. Prohibition of Marriage by Persons Under 16 Years of Age

Sec. 1. A marriage in this state shall not be contracted by a person who is under 16 years of age, and the marriage, if entered into, shall be void. . . .

New Jersey Statutes
Title 37. Marriages and Married Persons
Chapter 1., Article 2. Marriage Licenses

37:1-6. Consent of Parents or Guardian of Minor; When Required

A marriage or civil union license shall not be issued to a minor under the age of 18 years, unless the parents or guardian of the minor, if there be any, first certify under their hands and seals, in the presence of two reputable witnesses, their consent thereto, which consent shall be delivered to the licensing officer issuing the license. . . . When a minor is under the age of 16 years, the consent required by this section must be approved in writing by any judge of the Superior Court, Chancery Division, Family Part. . . .

The New Jersey statute does not set forth any standard for judicial approval of parental consent, so it would seem that if the parents of a six-year-old wish to have her married, to a male of any age, the Superior Court Judge must accept it. In between the Michigan and New Jersey models are code provisions establishing an exception in cases of pregnancy:

Code of Virginia
Title 20. Domestic Relations

§20-48. Minimum Age of Marriage with Consent of Parents

The minimum age at which persons may marry, with consent of the parent or guardian, shall be sixteen. In case of pregnancy when either party is under sixteen, the clerk authorized to issue marriage licenses in the county or city wherein the female resides shall issue a proper marriage license with the consent of the parent or guardian of the person or persons under the age of sixteen only upon presentation of a doctor's certificate showing he has examined the female and that she is pregnant, or has been pregnant within the nine months previous to such examination. . . .

What are the good and bad consequences, for the teen involved and for the broader society, of conditioning permission to marry for a 14-year-old on her being pregnant? Would it be preferable to eliminate the pregnancy rule and either lower the age of marriage with parental consent to the age of menstruation or to require that a teen mom wait to marry until she reaches the normal age of consent? Note that the divorce rate in the United States is highest for those who marry in their teens or early 20s. See June Carbone, *Age Matters: Class, Family Formation, and Inequality*, 48 Santa Clara L. Rev. 901, 930 (2008).

STATUTORY INTERPRETATION QUESTIONS

Can a 15-year-old girl who has a one-year-old baby marry the baby's father in Virginia if she has parental permission?

Can a 14-year-old girl in Virginia who just had an abortion marry a 30-year-old man who was not the aborted child's biological father, if one of her parents consents?

Most provisions authorizing marriage of minors with parental consent require the consent of only one parent, which can result in conflict between a child's parents.

Kirkpatrick v. District Court

64 P.3d 1056 (Nev. 2003)

Shearing, J.

SierraDawn Kirkpatrick Crow is the daughter of Karen Karay and petitioner Bruce Kirkpatrick. In 1990, Karay and Kirkpatrick were divorced in California. As part of the divorce decree, Karay and Kirkpatrick were awarded joint legal and physical custody of SierraDawn. In 1992, Karay and SierraDawn moved from California to New Mexico. In December 2000, when SierraDawn was fifteen years old, she informed her mother that she desired to marry her guitar teacher, 48-year-old Sauren Crow. SierraDawn's mother approved of the marriage.

However, under New Mexico law, SierraDawn was not permitted to marry. Therefore, SierraDawn, her mother, and Crow traveled to Las Vegas where SierraDawn and Crow could marry, if granted permission by the court. Karay filed a petition with the Clark County district court to obtain judicial authorization for SierraDawn's marriage. With the petition, Karay filed an affidavit consenting to the marriage, in which she stated that she has "seen no other couple so right for each other," that they "have very real life plans at home, in the town in which we all reside," and that "[t]heir partnership and their talents will be most effectively utilized by this marriage." The district court found that good cause existed under Nevada law for the marriage, and ordered that a marriage license be issued to SierraDawn and Crow. January 3, 2001, SierraDawn and Crow were married in Las Vegas. . . .[3]

Kirkpatrick filed this petition seeking a writ of mandamus to compel the district court to vacate its order authorizing SierraDawn's marriage and to annul the marriage. . . .

It is well settled that states have the right and power to establish reasonable limitations on the right to marry. This power is justified as an exercise of the police power, which confers upon the states the ability to enact laws in order to protect the safety, health, morals, and general welfare of society. Pursuant to this power, the Nevada Legislature enacted NRS 122.025, which states:

> 1. A person less than 16 years of age may marry only if he has the consent of either parent . . . and such person also obtains authorization from a district court as provided in subsection 2.
> 2. In extraordinary circumstances, a district court may authorize marriage of a person less than 16 if the court finds that: (a) The marriage will serve the best interests of such person. . . .

Kirkpatrick argues that this statute violates his constitutional interest in the care, custody, and management of his daughter since it neither requires his consent nor gives him an opportunity to be heard on the issue of his daughter's marriage. The United States Supreme Court has held that parents have a fundamental liberty interest in the care, custody, and management of their children. However, the United States Supreme Court has also held that, although these rights are fundamental, they are not absolute. The state also has an interest in the welfare of children and may limit parental authority. The Supreme Court has even held, where justified, that parents can be totally deprived of their children forever. If the state can completely eliminate all parental rights, it can certainly limit some parental rights when the competing rights of the child are implicated.

The United States Supreme Court has held that the right to marry is a fundamental right. . . . Minors, as well as adults, are protected by the Constitution and possess constitutional rights." However, the Court has also recognized that states have the power to make adjustments in the constitutional rights of minors.[21]

As marriage comprises the most sacred of relationships, the decision of whom and when to marry is highly personal, often involving reasons that are complex and vary from individual to individual. The decision to marry should rest primarily in the hands of the individual, with little government interference. As a society, we recognize that

3. At common law, marriage is generally sufficient to constitute emancipation. Although NRS 129.080 provides that a child "who is at least 16 years of age, married or living apart from his parents . . . may petition the . . . court . . . for a [judicial] decree of emancipation," this statutory provision does not expressly abrogate the common law effect of marriage as emancipating a minor. It does not appear that judicial action is required for emancipation to occur. A judicial decree, however, provides an emancipated minor with tangible evidence of his or her emancipated status.

21. *Ginsberg v. New York* (U.S. 1968) (children's access to pornography).

reasonable constraints on the right to marry are appropriate, especially when the marriage involves a minor.[25]

There is no one set of criteria that can be set forth as a litmus test to determine if a marriage will be successful. Neither is there a litmus test to determine whether a person is mature enough to enter a marriage. Age alone is an arbitrary factor. The Nevada Legislature recognized that although most fifteen-year-olds would not be mature enough to enter into a marriage, there are exceptions. Nevada provided for the exceptional case by allowing a fifteen-year-old to marry if one parent consents and the court approves. The statute provides a safeguard against an erroneous marriage decision by the minor and the consenting parent, by giving the district court the discretion to withhold authorization if it finds that there are no extraordinary circumstances and/or the proposed marriage is not in the minor's best interest, regardless of parental consent. The statute strikes a balance between an arbitrary rule of age for marriage and accommodation of individual differences and circumstances.

Consent of both parents is by no means a constitutional requirement for even the most important of decisions regarding minors, as Kirkpatrick alleges. In *Hodgson v. Minnesota*, in declaring a two-parent notification requirement for an abortion unconstitutional, the United States Supreme Court stated:

> It is equally clear that the requirement that *both* parents be notified, whether or not both wish to be notified or have assumed responsibility for the upbringing of the child, does not reasonably further any legitimate state interest. . . . In the ideal family setting, of course, notice to either parent would normally constitute notice to both. . . . In many families, however, the parent notified by the child would not notify the other parent. In those cases the State has no legitimate interest in questioning one parent's judgment that notice to the other parent would not assist the minor or in presuming that the parent who has assumed parental duties is incompetent to make decisions regarding the health and welfare of the child. . . .

Contrary to what is apparently Kirkpatrick's view, the parental relationship does not end with the emancipation of a child. The only right that he has lost by his daughter's emancipation is his right to exercise legal control over his daughter during her minority. He still has all the other legal and social attributes of parenthood. Kirkpatrick retains the legal rights of inheritance, as well as all the bonds of love, care, companionship, and influence that any parents have after emancipation of their children. How he chooses to foster those bonds is up to him. . . .

In this case, we have the interest of the daughter in marriage and the interest of the mother in her daughter's welfare and happiness balanced against the father's interest in the legal control of his daughter for the remainder of her minority. NRS 122.025 strikes an appropriate balance between the various interests. . . . Nevada has an interest in promoting stable marriages, while not treating minors arbitrarily by denying them a right based solely on a few months' difference in age. In fact, at common law, although minors could not enter other contracts, they were allowed to contract for marriage at age twelve for a girl and age fourteen for a boy. Other state legislatures are free to set a different public policy for their states, but that does not invalidate Nevada's public policy. . . .

AGOSTI, C.J., with whom LEAVITT and BECKER, JJ., agree, dissenting.

. . . Marriage is a civil contract between parties with the capacity to contract. A child under the age of eighteen has no capacity to contract absent some limited statutory

25. The United States Supreme Court has made clear that states can regulate marriage with respect to bigamy, incest, or underage marriages. *See Zablocki*, (Stewart, J., concurring); *id.* at 399 (Powell, J., concurring); *id.* at 404 (Stevens, J., concurring). [NB: 3 concurring opinions = "the Court"?—ED.]

authority. The majority acknowledges that states can place limitations on a minor's ability to marry, yet in the same breath suggests that a minor has a fundamental liberty interest in marriage. But the Supreme Court has never declared or suggested that a minor has a fundamental right to marry. And Nevada's statute, even if deemed constitutional, recognizes that a minor has no independent constitutional right to marry—the minor must obtain parental and court consent or have no right at all.

This limited statutory right cannot be equated with an adult's fundamental marriage right. Even if a child could be deemed to have some constitutionally recognized interest in marriage, the United States Supreme Court has pointed to the following three reasons why children's constitutional rights are not equivalent to those of adults: "the peculiar vulnerability of children; their inability to make critical decisions in an informed, mature manner; and the importance of the parental role in child rearing." Our legal system recognizes time and time again that children are not capable of making all the decisions necessary to lead an adult life and are not vested with the same spectrum of constitutional rights afforded adults.

The majority misses the mark with its citation to an abortion case, *Hodgson v. Minnesota*. . . . A minor's abortion decision concerns recognized privacy interests and must be made in a very limited period of time. . . . A minor's desire to marry implicates contracts, parental control and the adult responsibilities that arise in a marital relationship. If marriage is delayed, the minor may marry later, if she and her intended spouse continue to want such a relationship. . . .

The only way to balance the interests at issue here and ensure that the district court makes an informed decision is to require the district court to give interested and involved parents like Kirkpatrick notice and an opportunity to participate before making its decision. . . . Although the majority concludes that Kirkpatrick has suffered no real injury, he has lost his daughter. He no longer has the right to see her, to care for her, to have her live with him, or to participate in any of her important life decisions. How his interest in his daughter's growth and development, and his concomitant loss of her companionship, can be characterized as "minimal" is bewildering. . . .

If the state's policy is to foster *appropriate* marriages, then requiring proper notice and a meaningful hearing in cases such as this would assist the state in determining whether the marriage *is* appropriate. . . . Suggesting that the court would be financially or administratively burdened by fully performing its task is ridiculous. . . .

The majority opinion is necessarily devoid of any discussion concerning the district court's finding of extraordinary circumstances or that the proposed marriage was in SierraDawn's best interests, since no such circumstances existed. The district court did not even engage in this analysis. Thus, I do not see how the statute provided SierraDawn any protection.

Moreover, pregnancy alone does not establish that the minor's best interests will be served by marriage, nor is pregnancy required by the court as a condition necessary for its marriage authorization. . . . If pregnancy, in and of itself, does not demonstrate that the minor's best interests rest in marriage, then "extraordinary circumstances" and "best interests" must mean that the circumstances justifying the marriage are extreme and unusual. . . . The district court apparently relied exclusively on Karay's observations that SierraDawn and Crow had "very real life plans," and that Karay has "seen no other couple so right for each other." Surely these cursory observations neither establish extraordinary circumstances, nor serve to demonstrate how the marriage is in SierraDawn's best interests. Since Karay was not personally present before the district court when it granted the petition to marry, the court did not have an opportunity to investigate her credibility or motives. And, although there is an approximate 30-year disparity between SierraDawn and Crow, and SierraDawn was only 15 years old at the time, the district court failed to ask Karay more specifically why it was in SierraDawn's best interests to marry Crow. . . . The court did not interview the parties or conduct any meaningful hearing. . . .

As the majority would have it, under Nevada's marital consent statute, a father could permit his thirteen-year-old son to marry the son's forty-two-year-old soccer coach, and the boy's mother would have nothing to say about it. The mother, according to the majority, would have lost nothing but a desire to "control" her son. Now, one parent, without the other parent's knowledge, can turn what would otherwise be a crime worthy of headline news into state sanctioned, constitutionally protected conduct. I would point out that the Utah Court of Appeals recently upheld the conviction of a thirteen-year-old girl's father, after concluding that the evidence supported a finding that the father knew and intended that the daughter have sexual intercourse with his forty-eight-year-old friend, the daughter's alleged "husband."[31] There, the father conducted a ceremony to marry his young daughter to his friend. The father instructed the daughter that as a wife, she was expected to engage in sexual relations with her husband. Eventually, the daughter left the relationship and informed a law enforcement officer of the marriage and her sexual relations with the "husband." The father was arrested and convicted, after a jury trial, of three counts of child rape as an accomplice. The "husband" was charged with child rape and fled the jurisdiction. The father would have been completely protected from serious criminal liability, while at the same time achieving his objective of a consummated marriage for his daughter, had he simply brought her to Nevada and executed an affidavit, as Karay did, along with a petition to permit his daughter to marry.

The majority also fails to address the fact that Nevada's marriage consent statute includes no minimum age for marriage. Under the statute, an eight-year-old child could marry a forty-year-old adult, with one parent's consent and the district court's authorization. . . . [U]nder the majority's view, absolutely no one would be in a position to challenge it. . . .

Interestingly, the legislative history reveals that the actual impetus for passing the statute was money. In 1977, when the Nevada Legislature amended the marriage consent statute to allow a minor under the age of sixteen to marry with the consent of only one parent, the legislature made clear that the decision was driven by the Nevada Wedding Association's successful lobbying efforts. Apparently, during the late 1970s, because Nevada required both parents to consent to the marriage of a minor under sixteen, a small percentage of non-residents who came to Nevada to get married were turned away because they traveled with only one parent, or presented the signature of only one parent.[39]

---

31. State v. Chaney, 989 P.2d 1091 (Utah Ct. App. 1999).

39. Other states have enacted statutes that are in keeping with due process requirements. Some require both parents to consent to a minor child's marriage, if both parents are available. *See, e.g.*, Ga. Code Ann. §19-3-37(b) (1999); Iowa Code §595.2(4)(a) (2001); La. Child. Code Ann. art. 1545(A) (1995); *see also* N.J. Stat. Ann. §37:1-6 (West 2002) (requiring that both parents consent unless one of them is "of unsound mind"). Another state requires that the court appoint an attorney guardian ad litem for the minor and consider the opinion of both parents when determining whether marriage is in the child's best interests. *See, e.g.*, N.C. Gen. Stat. §51-2.1(a)(1) (2002). Indiana requires that both parents receive notice of the hearing regarding marriage authorization, if both parents are involved with the child and are competent to testify. Ind. Code §31-11-1-6(2) (1997).

How do you suppose the U.S. Supreme Court would respond to the suggestion that SierraDawn possessed some constitutional right with respect to marriage? Recall that the Supreme Court decisions establishing a constitutional right to marry predicated that right on the fundamental interest in procreation and parenting. To attribute this constitutional right to marry to minors would therefore seem to presuppose that they have a constitutionally protected fundamental interest in procreating and parenting while they are minors. And in that case, it would seem that laws prohibiting sex before age 18 presumptively are unconstitutional.

If you remember what you were like at 15, or if you have a younger sibling about that age, what would you suppose is the mindset of a girl who chooses to marry a 48-year-old man? If your younger sister were preparing to do that, what would you do? What should the state do? Is the best rule never to allow, always to allow, or sometimes to allow? Can a 15-year-old be *harmed* by getting married? How? On the other hand, on what basis could a court ever conclude that it is in her best interests to marry now (rather than a few years later, if she still wishes to do so)? If you were the Nevada judge asked to approve Sierra-Dawn's request for a marriage license, what questions would you ask? Should the law take into account not only whether each prospective spouse is over a certain age but also how far apart in age the two are? Would you be less concerned about SierraDawn if she wanted to marry a 20-year-old guitar teacher? Is a three-decade age difference troubling even in the case of two adults—for example, if a 25-year-old law student accepted a marriage proposal from a 55-year-old professor?

There have been several other, highly publicized cases in recent years involving parents consenting to marriage of sexually active minors. In 2005, Nebraska prosecutors charged with statutory rape a 22-year-old man, Matthew Koso, who had recently wed in Kansas his 14-year-old girlfriend. The developmentally delayed Mr. Koso had been intimate with the girl since she was 12. Popular opinion was overwhelmingly hostile to the prosecution. See Jodi Wilgoren, *Rape Charge Follows Marriage to a 14-Year-Old*, N.Y. TIMES, Aug. 30, 2005. Koso served 15 months in prison, then rejoined his wife and child, and they had several more children together. He is now a convicted felon, must register as a sex offender, and is not permitted to visit his children at school. See Colleen Kenney, *Epilogue: Koso Couple Still in Love*, LINCOLN J. STAR, Feb. 8, 2010.

If very young people are precluded from marrying, because of their presumed incapacity rationally to consent to the consequences of marriage, should there also be a minimum IQ standard for marriage?

CROSS-CULTURAL PERSPECTIVE

Looking back in time to Colonial America or across the globe today, one can find norms setting both lower and higher ages for marriage than the prevailing U.S. rule. There is also variation in the extent to which marital choices are left to the prospective bride and groom or instead made or influenced by parents or community leaders. Do the different rules across time and nations reflect differences in maturity, in expectations for adult life, in value placed on individual happiness versus community well being, or something else? Is there anything inherent in the phenomenon of marriage that suggests absolute limits on how young someone can be to marry, or does it depend entirely on social circumstances?

It is commonly thought that in the days before industrialization and near-universal college attendance, people commonly married in their teens. In fact, Americans generally married later in the colonial period than they did in the mid-twentieth century, in large part because many were indentured at age 21 and not free to marry until their late 20s. See DALE TAYLOR, EVERYDAY LIFE IN COLONIAL AMERICA. Likewise, in seventeenth-century England, the average age of marriage for women was 26. See NAOMI CAHN & JUNE CARBONE, RED FAMILIES V. BLUE FAMILIES: LEGAL POLARIZATION AND THE CREATION OF CULTURE 33 (2010). The median age of first marriage in the United States has crept back up to 26 for women and 28 for men in recent years, from an all-time low of 20 and 23 in the mid-twentieth century, with college education rather than indentured servitude being the primary reason for later marriage today.

Marriage in Colonial America was also much controlled by parents, at least among families of significant wealth, because marriage was viewed in large part as a financial transaction. Parents used their control over inheritance to enforce the expectation of parental control over mate selection. See TAYLOR, supra.

Some other countries today have laws requiring or encouraging marriage at an age later than U.S. laws generally allow and/or giving parents a greater role in mate selection than is typical in the United States. Is there any reason to think the following model would not be appropriate in the United States?

The Family Code of the Philippines

ART. 14.

In case either or both of the contracting parties . . . are between the ages of 18 and 21, they shall, in addition to the requirements of the preceding articles, exhibit to the local civil registrar, the consent to their marriage of their father, mother, surviving parent or guardian, or persons having legal charge of them, in the order mentioned. . . .

ART. 15.

Any contracting party between the age of 21 and 25 shall be obliged to ask their parents or guardian for advice upon the intended marriage. If they do not obtain such advice, or if it be unfavorable, the marriage license shall not be issued till after three months following the completion of the publication of the application therefor.

ART. 16.

In the cases where parental consent or parental advice is needed, the party or parties concerned shall, in addition, attach a certificate issued by a priest, imam or minister authorized to solemnize marriage or a marriage counselor to the effect that the contracting parties have undergone marriage counseling. Failure to attach said certificates of marriage counseling shall suspend the issuance of the marriage license for a period of three months from the completion of the publication of the application. . . .

What is the likely rationale for the Philippines' parental consent requirement for 20-year-olds and parental consultation requirement for 24-year-olds? Is it just to protect the welfare of young people or is there also an intent to protect the interests of parents? Suppose your parents own substantial wealth and want to leave it all to you, to benefit you, their grandchildren, etc. Do they not have an interest in whom you marry? Might it be better to have a legal rule and cultural norm of obtaining parental approval rather than forcing parents who object to a marriage to threaten their offspring with disinheritance?

Another factor leading to later marriage in some other countries is mandatory military service. Chinese marry at a later age because of legal restrictions on procreation. China's marriage law also exemplifies the historically common norm of specifying a lower minimum age for females than for males.

Marriage Law of the People's Republic of China
Chapter II. Marriage Contract

ARTICLE 6

No marriage may be contracted before the man has reached 22 years of age and the woman 20 years of age. Late marriage and late childbirth shall be encouraged.

The converse of parents prohibiting or delaying marriage is parents arranging a marriage or forcing a child into a marriage. This was once common in Western society, and condoned by the Christian Church until the Middle Ages. See John Witte, *More Than a Mere Contract: Marriage as Contract and Covenant in Law and Theology*, 5 U. ST. THOMAS L.J. 595 (2008). Marriage of children under ten remains fairly common in parts of Asia and Africa. See, e.g., UNICEF, Early Marriage Thwarts Girls' Potential in Ethiopia, www.unicef.org/infobycountry/ethiopia_early_marriage.html. What would drive any parent today to do this?

In 2008, two girls in Yemen, nine and ten years old respectively, made international news, when one fled to a hospital to seek treatment for rapes and beatings by her 36-year-old husband and the other went to a courthouse and told a judge she wanted a divorce from her abusive 30-year-old husband. See Robert F. Worth, Tiny Voices Defy Child Marriage in Yemen, N.Y. Times (June 29, 2008). The world was shocked to learn that the average age of marriage in some parts of Yemen is 12 or 13. But the local community was shocked that the girls dared to make their unhappiness public. Conservative Islamic leaders in Yemen confidently defended the practice, citing Muhammad's marriage to a nine year old, and local tradition supports the practice as conducive to early training of females for dutiful behavior as wives. The father of 10-year-old, four-foot-tall Nujood told a reporter he consented to the marriage because two of the girl's older sisters had been kidnapped and forcibly married. He thought it better to give the younger girl a proper marriage, rather than risk a similar horror for her. With sixteen children altogether and no job, the father also had a financial motivation for accepting the offered bride price. Id.

Do you find adequate the father's explanation for arranging Nujood's marriage? If not, would it change your mind if the father had done so only after he explained to his daughter the alternatives facing her and then getting her consent? Suppose an eight- or ten-year-old girl in such a culture decided that she wanted to marry a certain 30-year-old, preferring that to the risk of kidnapping and rape. Should the law respect her wish and authorize her to marry?

It is not inconceivable that a man from Yemen or one of the many other countries where child brides are common could come to the United States, achieve permanent resident status, and then petition to have his ten-year-old bride join him in the United States. Or a U.S. citizen might go abroad and arrange to marry an eight-year-old girl, and then petition for a spouse visa for her. As with polygamous marriages, U.S. agencies and courts would have to figure out how to balance competing considerations that include respect for foreign law and custom, our strong public policy against forced marriage and sex with children, and the possibility that it would make the girl even worse off to refuse to recognize the marriage. The United Kingdom attempted to address the issue of forced marriages by adding to its immigration rules a minimum age of 22 for entry of foreign spouses, but the England and Wales Court of Appeal invalidated the provision as over-inclusive. See Quila & Others v. Sec'y of State for the Home Dep't, [2010] EWCA Civ. 1482.

Forced child marriage is not confined to less developed countries. Despite legal age restrictions, children in some insular communities in the United States also find themselves informally married at a very young age.

In re Texas Department of Family & Protective Services

255 S.W.3d 613 (Tex. 2008)

Per Curiam.

The Yearning for Zion Ranch is a 1,700-acre complex near Eldorado, Texas, that is home to a large community associated with the Fundamentalist Church of Jesus Christ of Latter Day Saints. On March 29, 2008, the Texas Department of Family Protective Services received a telephone call reporting that a sixteen-year-old girl named Sarah was being physically and sexually abused at the Ranch. On April 3, about 9:00 p.m., Department investigators and law enforcement officials entered the Ranch, and throughout the night they interviewed adults and children and searched for documents. Concerned that the community had a culture of polygamy and of directing girls younger than eighteen to enter spiritual unions with older men and have children, the Department took possession of all 468 children at the Ranch without a court order. The Department calls this "the largest child protection case documented in the history of the United States." It never located the girl Sarah who was the subject of the March 29 call. . . .

[T]he district court issued temporary orders continuing the Department's custody of the children and allowing for visitation by the parents only with the Department's agreement. Thirty-eight mothers petitioned the court of appeals for review by mandamus, seeking return of their 126 children. The record reflects that at least 117 of the children are under 13 and that two boys are 13 and 17. . . .

On the record before us, removal of the children was not warranted. The . . . Family Code gives the district court broad authority to protect children short of separating them from their parents and placing them in foster care. The court may make and modify temporary orders . . . "restraining a party from removing the child beyond a geographical area identified by the court." The court may also order the removal of an alleged perpetrator from the child's home. . . . The Code prohibits interference with an investigation, and a person who relocates a residence or conceals a child with the intent to interfere with an investigation commits an offense. While the district court must vacate the current temporary custody orders . . . , it need not do so without granting other appropriate relief to protect the children, as the mothers involved in this proceeding concede in response to the Department's motion for emergency relief. . . .

Justices O'Neill, Johnson Willett, concurring in part, dissenting in part.

. . . On April 3rd, the Department entered the Ranch along with law-enforcement personnel and conducted nineteen interviews of girls aged seventeen or under, as well as fifteen to twenty interviews of adults. In the course of these interviews, the Department learned there were many polygamist families living on the Ranch; a number of girls under the age of eighteen living on the Ranch were pregnant or had given birth; both interviewed girls and adults considered no age too young for a girl to be "spiritually" married; and the Ranch's religious leader, "Uncle Merrill," had the unilateral power to decide when and to whom they would be married. Additionally, in the trial court, the Department presented "Bishop's Records"—documents seized from the Ranch—indicating the presence of several extremely young mothers or pregnant "wives"[1] on the Ranch: a sixteen-year-old "wife" with a child, a sixteen-year-old pregnant "wife," two pregnant fifteen-year-old "wives," and a thirteen-year-old who had conceived a child. The testimony of Dr. William John Walsh, the families' expert witness, confirmed that the Fundamentalist Church of Jesus Christ of Latter Day Saints accepts the age of "physical development" (that is, first menstruation) as the age of eligibility for "marriage." Finally, child psychologist Dr. Bruce Duncan Perry testified that the pregnancy of the underage children on the Ranch was the result of sexual abuse because children of the age of fourteen, fifteen, or sixteen are not sufficiently emotionally mature to enter a healthy consensual sexual relationship or a "marriage."

Evidence presented thus indicated a pattern or practice of sexual abuse of pubescent girls, and the condoning of such sexual abuse, on the Ranch—evidence sufficient to satisfy a "person of ordinary prudence and caution" that other such girls were at risk of sexual abuse as well. This evidence supports the trial court's finding that "there was a danger to the physical health or safety" of pubescent girls on the Ranch. . . .

[T]he Family Code requires only that the Department make "reasonable efforts, consistent with the circumstances" to avoid taking custody of endangered children. Evidence presented in the trial court indicated that the actions of the children and mothers precluded the Department from pursuing other legal options. When the Department arrived at the YFZ Ranch, it was treated cordially and allowed access to children, but those children repeatedly pled "the Fifth" in response to questions about their identity, would not identify their birth-dates or parentage, refused to answer questions about who lived in their homes, and lied about their names—sometimes several times. Answers from parents were similarly inconsistent: one mother first claimed that four children were hers, and then later avowed that they were not. Furthermore, the Department arrived to discover that a shredder had been used to destroy documents just before its arrival.

1. Although referred to as "wives" in the Bishop's Records, these underage girls are not legally married; rather, the girls are "spiritually" married to their husbands, typically in polygamous households with multiple other "spiritual" wives. Subject to limited defenses, a person who "engages in sexual contact" with a child younger than seventeen who is not his *legal* spouse is guilty of a sexual offense under the Texas Penal Code. Those who promote or assist such sexual contact, or cause the child to engage in sexual contact, may also be criminally liable.

Thwarted by the resistant behavior of both children and parents on the Ranch, the Department had limited options. Without knowing the identities of family members or of particular alleged perpetrators, the Department could not have sought restraining orders under section 262.1015 as it did not know whom to restrain. Likewise, it could not have barred any family member from access to a child without filing a verified pleading or affidavit, which must identify clearly the parent and the child to be separated.

Furthermore, . . . the mothers themselves believed that the practice of underage "marriage" and procreation was not harmful for young girls . . . This is some evidence that the Department could not have reasonably sought to maintain custody with the mothers. Thus, evidence presented to the trial court demonstrated that the Department took reasonable efforts, consistent with extraordinarily difficult circumstances, to protect the children without taking them into custody. . . . I would hold that the trial court did not abuse its discretion as to the demonstrably endangered population of pubescent girls . . .

Do the New Jersey or Virginia statutes relating to age at marriage prohibit spiritual marriage of children to old men, at the direction of a non-parent but with parental acquiescence? Earlier in Western history, and still today in some non-Western cultures, "the age of 'physical development' (that is, first menstruation)" has been definitive of marriage preparedness. Don't communities within the United States that want to live by such norms have a right to do so, as a matter of cultural tolerance and First Amendment freedom of religious practice? Correspondingly, should we judge what is acceptable for children by reference to the culture where their parents live, whether it be Yemen or the YFZ Ranch, rather than on the basis of mainstream norms? That is essentially what the U.S. Supreme Court said with respect to Amish parents' desire to to deny their children schooling after the eighth grade, in the *Wisconsin v. Yoder* decision you will study in Chapter 4. Is parents' denying their children secondary (and thus, effectively, post-secondary) education, and requiring them to commence prescribed occupations at an early age, less worrisome than parents' arranging marriages for their adolescent offspring, in a community where that is normal? Both practices severely limit life options, by forcing on minors behaviors and lifestyles that are put off until adulthood for most in mainstream society but that were undertaken at much earlier ages in centuries past. Recall that some states today have no minimum age for marriage with parental consent, and bear in mind that marriage to a minor in any state makes statutory rape laws inoperative, so that having sex with the minor becomes legal.

b. Right to Marry a Family Member

Based in part on concern about consanguineous intercourse producing children with birth defects, states throughout the United States have forbidden marriage between close family members. Vermont's law is relatively minimalist:

Vermont Statutes
Title 15. Domestic Relations
Chapter 1. Civil Marriage

§1A. PERSON FORBIDDEN TO MARRY A RELATIVE

No person shall marry his or her parent, grandparent, child, grandchild, sibling, sibling's child, or parent's sibling.

No reported decisions clarify whether the list refers to biological relatives or legal relatives. Other states make clear that even a non-consanguineous relationship between some close legal family members—that is, where the relationship results from a marriage or adoption—is ineligible for legal marriage. What is the rationale for prohibiting marriage by people with no biological connection, such as siblings by adoption?

Code of Alabama
Title 13A. Criminal Code
Chapter 13. Offenses Against the Family

§13A-13-3. INCEST

(a) A person commits incest if he marries or engages in sexual intercourse with a person he knows to be, either legitimately or illegitimately:

(1) His ancestor or descendant by blood or adoption; or
(2) His brother or sister of the whole or half-blood or by adoption; or
(3) His stepchild or stepparent, while the marriage creating the relationship exists; or
(4) His aunt, uncle, nephew or niece of the whole or half-blood.

You probably do not want to think about this too much, but can you posit reasons other than concern about birth defects why you are not permitted to marry your aunt or uncle?

The Vermont and Alabama statutes, along with those of 17 other states, the District of Columbia, and pretty much the rest of the world, allow for marriage between first cousins. In many non-Western societies, cousin marriages are actually preferred, and in some places marriages between close biological relatives account for 20 to 60 percent of all marriages. Though the risk of birth defects is assumed to be very high when siblings procreate, modern genetic studies indicate that procreating with a first cousin elevates the risk of a birth defect just from 3-4 percent to 4-6 percent.

Yet roughly half of U.S. states prohibit first cousins from marrying. They will, however, respect marriage certificates issued to first cousins in other jurisdictions.

Ghassemi v. Ghassemi

998 So. 2d 731 (La. Ct. App. 1st Cir. 2008)

KUHN, J.

. . . Tahereh Ghassemi filed suit in the East Baton Rouge Parish Family Court seeking a divorce, spousal support, and a partition of community property. In her petition, she alleged that she and the defendant, Hamid Ghassemi, were married in Bam, Iran in 1976, at which time both parties were citizens of Iran. She further alleged that a son, Hamed, was born of their union in 1977. Ms. Ghassemi contends that in that same year, Mr. Ghassemi entered the United States (U.S.) on a student visa. Ms. Ghassemi avers that when Mr. Ghassemi left Iran in 1977, it was with the understanding that he would return to Iran after he completed his studies or that he would arrange for her and Hamed to join him and establish a residence in the U.S.

Unbeknownst to Ms. Ghassemi, after entering the U.S., Mr. Ghassemi contracted a "marriage" with an American woman, allegedly to enhance his legal status in this country. However, this purported "marriage" ultimately ended in "divorce." . . . Mr. Ghassemi made the necessary applications that allowed Hamed to enter the U.S. as his "son." However, no efforts were made on behalf of Ms. Ghassemi for her to enter the U.S. Subsequently, in 2002, Mr. Ghassemi "married" yet another woman in Baton Rouge, Louisiana, where he had become domiciled. In 2005, through the efforts of her son, Hamed, Ms. Ghassemi finally entered the U.S. as a permanent resident and also settled in Baton Rouge. On May 22, 2006, she filed the present suit. Mr. Ghassemi responded . . . that the purported marriage to Ms. Ghassemi was invalid [because] he and Ms. Ghassemi are first cousins. . . .

LSA-C.C. art. 3520 . . . provides:

> A. A marriage that is valid in the state where contracted, or in the state where the parties were first domiciled as husband and wife, shall be treated as a valid marriage unless to do so would violate a strong public policy of the state whose law is applicable to the particular issue under Article 3519.
>
> B. A purported marriage between persons of the same sex violates a strong public policy of the state of Louisiana and such a marriage contracted in another state shall not be recognized in this state for any purpose, including the assertion of any right or claim as a result of the purported marriage.

. . . Thus, it is the public policy of Louisiana that every effort be made to uphold the validity of marriages. Moreover, if a foreign marriage is valid in the state where it was contracted, the marriage is accorded a presumption of validity. . . . Because a marriage between first cousins is valid in Iran, it is accorded the presumption of validity. To rebut that presumption . . . , Mr. Ghassemi must prove that the recognition of a foreign marriage between first cousins would violate "a strong public policy" of this state. . . .

Louisiana Civil Code article 90 . . . provides as follows:

> A. The following persons may not contract marriage with each other:
>
> (1) Ascendants and descendants.
> (2) Collaterals within the fourth degree, whether of the whole or of the half blood.
>
> B. The impediment exists whether the persons are related by consanguinity or by adoption. Nevertheless, persons related by adoption, though not by blood, in the collateral line within the fourth degree may marry each other if they obtain judicial authorization in writing to do so.

The phrase "collaterals within the fourth degree" includes aunt and nephew, uncle and niece, siblings, and first cousins. Pursuant to LSA-C.C. art. 94, a marriage is absolutely null when contracted in this state . . . in violation of an impediment. However, the mere fact that a marriage is absolutely null when contracted in Louisiana does not mean that such a marriage validly performed elsewhere is automatically invalid as violative of a strong public policy. . . . Indeed, the jurisprudence is replete with decisions recognizing that if a common-law marriage is contracted in a state whose law sanctions such a marriage, the marriage will be recognized as a valid marriage in Louisiana, even though a common-law marriage cannot be contracted in this state. Similarly, this state has recognized a foreign marriage contracted by procuration, even though such a marriage would be absolutely null if contracted here.[25, 26] . . .

[M]arriage between first cousins has not always been prohibited in Louisiana. . . . [P]rior to 1902, there was absolutely no bar to marriages between first cousins in this state. . . . [In addition], the Louisiana Legislature thereafter repeatedly ratified marriages between collaterals in the fourth degree that had been contracted in violation of the prohibition. . . . In light of all of the foregoing, and for reasons more fully explained below, we are compelled to conclude that Louisiana does not have a strong public policy against recognizing a marriage between first cousins performed in a state or country where such marriages are valid.[31]

However, we emphasize that . . . we make a clear distinction between the marriage of first cousins and marriages contracted between more closely-related collaterals. While the former is commonly accepted, the latter is greatly condemned. . . . A marriage between first cousins neither violates natural law[32] nor is it included in the wider list of prohibited relationships set forth in Chapter 18 of the Bible's Book of Leviticus, the font of Western incest laws.

Thus, while "incestuous" marriages have traditionally constituted an exception to the general rule that a marriage valid where contracted is valid everywhere, that historical exception excludes marriages contracted between first cousins. *See* Mark Strasser, *Unity, Sovereignty, and the Interstate Recognition of Marriage,* 102 W. Va. L. Rev. 393, 405 (1999). Our recognition of this distinction is further buttressed by the fact that relations between first cousins are not encompassed by our criminal incest statute, LSA-R.S. 14:78, which provides, in pertinent part:

> A. Incest is the marriage to, or sexual intercourse with, any ascendant or descendant, brother or sister, uncle or niece, aunt or nephew, with knowledge of their relationship.

. . . [F]irst cousins may legally cohabitate, have intimate relations, and even produce children; however, they are merely prohibited from regularizing their union by marriage. . . .

25. A marriage by procuration occurs when one party is not present but, instead, is represented by another person.

26. Obviously, given its prohibition, Louisiana does have a policy against such marriages. However, the prerequisites to a valid marriage in Louisiana vary in their significance. Some are more serious, while others are less so.

31. In so concluding, we note that the Louisiana Legislature has not expressly outlawed marriages between first cousins regardless of where they are contracted, as it has emphatically done in the case of purported same-sex marriages. *See* La. Const. Art. XII §15; LSA-C.C. art. 3520(B). . . .

32. Only marriages between those in the direct lineal line of consanguinity or those contracted between brothers and sisters are thought to violate natural law. *See* P.H. Vartanian, Annotation, *Recognition of Foreign Marriage as Affected by Policy in Respect of Incestuous Marriages,* 117 A.L.R. 186, 190(1938).

Furthermore, we note that marriages between first cousins are widely permitted within the western world. "Such marriages were not forbidden at common law." Additionally, no European country prohibits marriages between first cousins. *See* Ann Laquer Estin, *Embracing Tradition: Pluralism in American Family Law*, 63 Md. L. Rev. 540, 564 (2004). Marriages between first cousins are also legal in Mexico and Canada, in addition to many other countries.

Actually, the U.S. is unique among western countries in restricting first cousin marriages. Even so, such marriages may be legally contracted in Alabama, Alaska, California, Colorado, Connecticut, Florida, Georgia, Hawaii, Maryland, Massachusetts, New Jersey, New Mexico, New York, North Carolina, Rhode Island, South Carolina, Tennessee, Vermont, Virginia, and the District of Columbia.[34] An additional six states, Arizona, Illinois, Indiana, Maine, Utah, and Wisconsin, also allow first cousin marriages subject to certain restrictions.

Accordingly, Louisiana is one of only 25 U.S. states that flatly prohibits such marriages. However, even other states that prohibit marriages between first cousins, have nonetheless found that such marriages do not violate public policy and thus recognize such marriages as valid, if they are valid in the state or country where they were contracted. Like the foregoing courts, we too find that although Louisiana law expressly prohibits the marriages of first cousins, such marriages are not so "odious" as to violate a strong public policy of this state. Accordingly, a marriage between first cousins, if valid in the state or country where it was contracted, will be recognized as valid pursuant to LSA-C.C. art. 3520. . . .

If 20 U.S. jurisdictions permit first cousin marriage and the rest do not have a strong public policy against it, could exclusion of first cousin pairs from legal marriage survive constitutional challenge? As with child support delinquents and some other categories of people that states have at times excluded from marriage, the question arises with first cousins what sense it makes to exclude a couple from marriage if they are free to have a non-marital relationship that produces children. Is it not better policy to channel any such couples into legal marriage? Or does conferring legal marriage status encourage more people to enter into that kind of relationship, which might be tolerated but not preferred?

The court notes that a handful of states permit first cousin marriage only under certain conditions. The principal condition is that the couple must show it is presumptively or demonstrably incapable of conceiving children, because of age, natural sterility, or surgery. Does that amount in some cases to conditioning legal marriage on a willingness to undergo a vasectomy or hysterectomy?

c. Polygamy Reconsidered

Polygamy is likely to be an increasingly prominent issue in America, in part because there is significant demand for it domestically, in part because the same-sex marriage movement is producing a more general liberalizing of attitudes toward marriage, and in part because it is legal in much of the world and already polygamously married

34. . . . As of September 1, 2005, Texas no longer allows first-cousin marriages. Tex. Fam. Code Ann. §2.004(6).

immigrants are continually coming to the United States in significant numbers and sometimes seeking legal recognition. Polygamy might be the next frontier in marriage reform.

David P. Schmitt, Fundamentals of Human Mating Strategies

in The Handbook of Evolutionary Psychology 258-291 (David M. Buss ed., 2005)

Monogamy may be *perennial*, when two members of the opposite sex form a lifelong mating bond, or *serial*, when members of the opposite sex are faithful to one another while they are paired, but the pairing does not last a lifetime. . . . Among mammals, both forms of monogamy are quite rare, emerging in perhaps 3% of all species. This may be due to large sex differences in the obligatory parental investments of mammals. . . . In humans, . . . only 16% of the world's preindustrial cultures have monogamous marriage systems. The official or preferred marriage system in most cultures (over 80%) is polygyny. . . . When given a chance, most men prefer to have status and the multiple wives that status affords. . . .

Female-defense or *harem* polygyny occurs when a single male mates with and defends numerous females against influences of invading males. *Resource-defense* polygyny occurs when a male is able to command and defend food supplies, territories, or other resources with regularity. Females preferentially desire and seek mateships with this high-resource male, even though he already is mated. According to the polygyny threshold model, when the costs of mating polygynously with a given male (e.g., sharing his resources and having a rivalry with other females and their children) are outweighed by the benefits (e.g., acquiring a male with ample resources and high-quality genes), females tend to mate polygynously. This often occurs in species where males vary significantly in their genetic quality and in the resources they can accrue and monopolize. . . . [M]any women preferentially choose to mate with high-status men with ample resources rather than low-status men who would be unable to support a family. . . .

In modern cultures, men with high status and ample resources are often legally prohibited from obtaining additional wives. However, some evidence suggests modern men with high status still have a greater potential for fertility by copulating more often, having sex with more partners, engaging in more extrapair copulations or affairs, and practicing legalized de facto polygyny by divorcing and remarrying a series of highly fertile women over time. These same high-fertility tendencies appear to hold true for men with other traits that women especially desire, including intelligence, dominance, athleticism, above-average height, and maturity.

Today polygamy is legal in over 60 nations and is commonly practiced in many other nations despite laws denying recognition to or prohibiting polygamous unions. Obviously, polygamy can work and arguably is as "natural" for humans, if not more so, than monogamy. Arguably it works better than the serial multiple matings common today among males in Western countries that prohibit polygamy, and better than mating with two or more women at the same time but concealing this from the women, which also occurs with some frequency.

Why, then, does the law in the United States label as criminals men who engage in multiple mating in a relatively responsible and dignified way, by forming stable families and homes based on the informed consent of all adult parties, and dedicating themselves to supporting and being involved in the lives of all the children they produce? Is this just a reflection of the fact that in democracies weaker, poorer males have more relative power than they do in a more primitive or non-democratic society? Might not society benefit if more reproduction were done by wealthier males and less by poorer males? Would not women in general benefit from having more men to choose from? Is it fair to women to limit their coupling options to males that no one else has taken yet? Are weaker, poorer males the only people who would suffer under legalized polygamy? But see James Gorman, *Baboon Study Shows Benefits for Nice Guys, Who Finish 2nd,* N.Y. TIMES, July 14, 2011 (reporting results of study of five troops of wild baboons in Kenya, finding that "alpha males showed very high stress levels, . . . probably because of the demands of fighting off challengers and guarding access to fertile females. Beta males, who fought less and had considerably less mate guarding to do, had much lower stress levels. They had fewer mating opportunities than the alphas, but they did get some mating in. . . .").

In recent decades, polygamy has become a significant social phenomenon in U.S. and European cities with large numbers of immigrants coming from countries where polygamy is common. For example, some estimate that there are several thousand African polygamists in New York City and over 120,000 in France. See Nina Bernstein, *Polygamy Practiced in Secrecy, Follows Africans to New York City,* N.Y. TIMES, Mar. 23, 2007. Polygamy is also still practiced in some Native American tribes in the United States. States must therefore decide whether to recognize such plural marriages; not doing so could harm some women. U.K. courts do recognize polygamous marriages legally entered into in other countries, for purposes such as ensuring support and property rights to dependent polygamous spouses. See JANE MAIR & ESIN ORUCU, THE PLACE OF RELIGION IN FAMILY LAW: A COMPARATIVE SEARCH 38-41 (2011). Significantly, many U.S. states have in recent years considered legislation that would prohibit their courts from considering Shariah law in any legal proceedings. See, e.g., Awad v. Ziriax, 2012 WL 50636 (C.A.10 (Okla.)) (invalidating on Establishment Clause grounds Oklahoma's proposed "Save Our State Amendment" to its state constitution, which would have ordered that state courts "when exercising their judicial authority, . . . shall not consider international law or Sharia Law").

But Americans associate polygamy principally with the Mormon religion. At one time, mainstream Mormons believed their faith compelled them to practice polygamy. Today, fundamentalist Mormons continue to hold to this belief and they maintain that their constitutional right to free exercise of religion should protect them from state interference in their polygamist lifestyle.

Irwin Altman, Polygamous Family Life: The Case of Contemporary Mormon Fundamentalists

1996 Utah L. Rev. 367

The Mormon religion, officially known as the Church of Jesus Christ of Latter-day Saints ("LDS church" or "Mormon church"), is a uniquely American version of Christianity. . . . Joseph Smith is believed to have received and translated, with divine intervention, golden plates containing the history of an American people and religion. This scripture, the Book of Mormon, describes an ancient people and their ancestors who migrated to the American continent and established a religion. . . .

Early Mormonism was one of several conservative counter-reactions to emerging liberal values of the late eighteenth and early nineteenth centuries. Several conservative religious movements of the times opposed greater freedom of choice of marital partners, women's rights, easier divorces, abortions, and a general rise in individual rights. These groups called for reestablishment of strong families, patriarchal leadership, adherence to stable and orderly community and religious structures, and restoration of gender roles, with women assuming traditional domestic and child-rearing responsibilities.

In the 1830s and 1840s, Joseph Smith and his followers migrated to Ohio, Missouri, and Illinois, and were eventually driven out because of their religious beliefs and political and economic activities. In 1847, following Joseph Smith's assassination, the new leader, Brigham Young, led the people to Utah, where they eventually became a dominant religious, economic, and political force in the Rocky Mountain region. There are currently more than nine million members of the Mormon church worldwide, and it is a religion that is growing rapidly by virtue of a worldwide missionary proselytizing program and because of a high birth rate among its members.

Joseph Smith secretly practiced polygyny early in his leadership, but it did not become official church doctrine until 1852. Polygyny was openly practiced by members of the church until 1890. There were several religious bases for polygyny, including the teachings of biblical patriarchs in the Old Testament, a belief in a polygynous hereafter in heaven, the importance of righteous men procreating in large numbers, and a male patriarchal value system. A key principle involved patriarchy, or the idea that a stable and orderly family life depends, in part, on a husband/father functioning as a religious and social leader. . . . This notion was linked to the biblical patriarchs, who were empowered with religious priesthood roles and presided over polygynous families with multiple wives and many children.

Nineteenth-century religious doctrine developed by Joseph Smith also promulgated the principle of polygyny as a religious value regarding marriage and life in the hereafter. According to doctrine, a religiously "righteous" man and his wife or wives can live as a "king" and "queen(s)" in the hereafter in their own heavenly universe, surrounded by their progeny, if married for "time and eternity." Original Mormon doctrine postulated that marriages in the civil system were for "time" only, i.e., for earthly life, while marriages conducted by religious leaders were for "time and eternity," extending into the hereafter forever. Because religiously righteous men are in a minority in the world, women were encouraged to marry such men, even in a polygynous mode, to achieve the promise of a heavenly existence in the afterlife. Through this doctrine it became possible for polygynous marriages to be conducted within the church, thereby bypassing the civil system and avoiding direct confrontation between secular and religious principles. Mormon fundamentalists continue to hold these beliefs today. . . .

As polygyny began to be practiced openly in the nineteenth century and as the Mormons began to claim greater independence from the U.S., successive U.S. Congresses enacted legislation to control plural marriages and restrict the rights of church members. Eventually the Mormon church succumbed to governmental pressures and first rejected the practice of polygyny in 1890. Although some members and leaders continued to consummate polygynous marriages, the practice declined until the 1930s and 1940s. At that time, groups of fundamentalists began to publicly and more actively advocate and engage in polygyny. Since then the number of people in fundamentalist groups who condone plural marriage has increased; some estimates are that 20,000 to 40,000 or more people presently belong to fundamentalist Mormon groups in the western U.S. . . . [T]he main LDS Church vigorously and unequivocally rejects the practice of polygyny, does not recognize fundamentalists as Mormons, excommunicates any of its members who are affiliated with fundamentalist groups, and has historically assisted and condoned the actions of civil authorities against fundamentalists who practice plural marriage. . . .

[T]he social landscape is now populated by a great diversity of close relationships and family types. . . . If we can penetrate the superficial and often inaccurate stereotypes about others who live differently from us, then we may be able to achieve a greater degree of social unity, peace, and good will amidst the diversity and plurality that will be with us for decades to come. . . .

Professor Altman goes on to describe common aspects of life within polygamous households and communities, showing that complex norms strike a balance among adult household members between dyadic relationships (i.e., between the husband and each wife) and communal living. Such norms differ in some respects from one community to another; some communities are more hierarchical and patriarchal, with a "prophet" exerting substantial control over family formation and regulation, while others are more democratic and egalitarian. The norms govern the justifications for and the process of adding a new wife, living arrangements (e.g., one family in an ordinary neighborhood versus a polygamous "compound," separate houses for each wife versus all living under one roof with separate bedrooms), how much time the husband spends alone with each wife, family celebrations, financial management, and household decision making. All of these things are well illustrated in HBO's *Big Love* series. If you have no other exposure to polygamy, you should watch the show and think of the different models of polygamous life portrayed in it when assessing policy and constitutional arguments for and against legalization of polygamy. That show and the more recent TLC series *Sister Wives* attest to popular interest in polygamy.

As Professor Altman notes, law and society now accept a great variety of family forms, and public support is available for many more kinds of households than just the ever-disappearing traditional family. Should this give rise to a presumption in favor of accepting, and even supporting, polygamous families? If so, what should be shown in order to overcome the presumption? Is there something inherently harmful about polygamy? Or is it just the case that abuse is possible within such arrangements, as it is in traditional families? Is abuse inherently more likely, so much so that the state should refuse to recognize, and even criminalize, such family arrangements, rather than just targeting any abuse? Why is it that polygamy gets associated with child marriages? Are men drawn to it more likely than other men to be pedophiles? Or is it that, in a social and legal environment where monogamy is the norm and polygamy is criminal, few adult women would freely choose to be someone's second or third wife, so polygamists "grab 'em early" when they are still susceptible to adult control? Assuming there are some men disposed to polygamy who are not pedophiles, and some fully autonomous adult women who would choose it, are there sufficient state policies to stop them from having it, policies that cannot be served by other means?

In the United States, several states have constitutional provisions explicitly prohibiting plural marriage, typically as a qualification to a general statement of religious freedom. For example:

> **Utah Const. Art. 3:** Perfect toleration of religious sentiment is guaranteed. No inhabitant of this State shall ever be molested in person or property on account of his or her mode of religious worship; but polygamous or plural marriages are forever prohibited.

Utah was required to prohibit polygamy as a condition for being admitted to the union in 1895. Federal legislation at that time even denied the vote to polygamists. More common are statutory provisions declaring a bigamous marriage void and threatening criminal prosecution of people who attempt it.

Code of Virginia
Title 20. Domestic Relations
Chapter 3. Unlawful Marriages Generally

§20-38.1 Certain Marriages Prohibited

(a) The following marriages are prohibited:

(1) A marriage entered into prior to the dissolution of an earlier marriage of one of the parties;

§20-40. Punishment for Violation

If any person marry in violation of §20-38.1 he shall be confined in jail not exceeding six months, or fined not exceeding $500, in the discretion of the jury. . . .

§20-43. Bigamous Marriages Void Without Decree

All marriages prohibited by law on account of either party having a former wife or husband then living shall be absolutely void, without any decree of divorce, or other legal process.

Code of Virginia
Title 18.2. Crimes and Offenses Generally
Chapter 8. Crimes Involving Morals and Decency
Article 4. Family Offenses; Crimes Against Children, Etc.

§18.2-362. Person Marrying When Husband or Wife Is Living

If any person, being married, shall, during the life of the husband or wife, marry another person in this Commonwealth, or if the marriage with such other person take place out of the Commonwealth, shall thereafter cohabit with such other person in this Commonwealth, he or she shall be guilty of a Class 4 felony. . . .

STATUTORY INTERPRETATION EXERCISE:

1. Is it illegal in Virginia for a man to have a legal marriage with one woman and then simply live also with two additional women, being intimate and living communally with all three women?

2. Could a Virginia prosecutor charge a man under §18.2-362 if he has a private marriage ceremony with a new bride while legally married to another woman, if the man does not seek a marriage license or ask for state recognition of his second, bigamous marriage?

It turns out to be rather difficult to draft a statute making the practice of polygamy unlawful. It is easy to draft a law dictating that a request for a marriage license will be denied and result in criminal prosecution if one of the parties is already legally married, or to criminalize efforts to obtain government or private benefits by claiming to be legally married to more than one person at the same time. But polygamists typically do not seek legal recognition from anyone of a second or third marriage; they seek simply to be left alone while they carry on multiple social marriages at the same time.

State v. Holm

137 P.3d 726 (Utah 2006), cert. denied, 549 U.S. 1252 (2007)

DURRANT, Justice:

¶1 In this case, we are asked to determine whether Rodney Hans Holm was appropriately convicted for bigamy and unlawful sexual conduct with a minor. . . .

¶2 Holm was legally married to Suzie Stubbs in 1986. Subsequent to this marriage, Holm, a member of the Fundamentalist Church of Jesus Christ of Latter-day Saints (the "FLDS Church"), participated in a religious marriage ceremony with Wendy Holm. Then, when Rodney Holm was thirty-two, he participated in another religious marriage ceremony with then-sixteen-year-old Ruth Stubbs, Suzie Stubbs's sister. After the ceremony, Ruth moved into Holm's house, where her sister Suzie Stubbs, Wendy Holm, and their children also resided. By the time Ruth turned eighteen, she had conceived two children with Holm, the second of which was born approximately three months after her eighteenth birthday.

¶3 Holm was subsequently arrested in Utah and charged with three counts of unlawful sexual conduct with a sixteen- or seventeen-year-old[3] . . . and one count of bigamy[4] . . . — all third degree felonies.

3. Utah Code section 76-5-401.2 provides, in pertinent part, as follows:

> A person commits unlawful sexual conduct with a minor if, under circumstances not amounting to [other, more serious sexual offenses], the actor who is ten or more years older than the minor at the time of the sexual conduct . . . has sexual intercourse with a minor. . . .

4. Utah Code section 76-7-101 provides, in pertinent part, as follows:

> A person is guilty of bigamy when, knowing he has a husband or wife or knowing the other person has a husband or wife, the person purports to marry another person or cohabits with another person.

¶4 At trial, Ruth Stubbs testified that although she knew that the marriage was not a legal civil marriage under the law, she believed that she was married. . . . Stubbs testified that, at the ceremony, she had answered "I do" to the following question:

> Do you, Sister [Stubbs], take Brother [Holm] by the right hand, and give yourself to him to be his lawful and wedded wife for time and all eternity, with a covenant and promise on your part, that you will fulfil all the laws, rites and ordinances pertaining to this holy bond of matrimony in the new and everlasting covenant, doing this in the presence of God, angels, and these witnesses, of your own free will and choice?

Stubbs testified that she had worn a white dress, which she considered a wedding dress; that she and Holm exchanged vows; that Warren Jeffs, a religious leader in the FLDS religion, conducted the ceremony; that other church members and members of Holm's family attended the ceremony; and that photographs were taken of Holm, Stubbs, and their guests who attended the ceremony.

¶5 Stubbs also testified about her relationship with Holm after the ceremony. She testified that she had moved in with Holm; that Holm had provided, at least in part, for Stubbs and their children; and that she and Holm had "regularly" engaged in sexual intercourse at the house in Hildale, Utah. Evidence was also introduced at trial that Holm and Stubbs "regarded each other as husband and wife." . . .

¶7 During the course of the trial, the court denied Holm's request to present rebuttal evidence . . . about the deeply held religious belief among FLDS adherents that this type of marriage is "necessary to their personal salvation," the history of polygamy, and the social health of polygamous communities.

¶8 The jury returned a guilty verdict. . . . The trial court sentenced Holm to up to five years in state prison on each conviction, to be served concurrently, and imposed a $3,000 fine. Both the prison time and the fine were suspended in exchange for three years on probation, one year in the county jail with work release, and two hundred hours of community service.

Holm appealed his conviction on all charges. . . . Holm argues that he did not "purport to marry" Ruth Stubbs, as that phrase is used in the bigamy statute, because the word "marry" in subsection 76-7-101(1) refers only to legal marriage and neither Holm nor Stubbs contemplated that the religious ceremony solemnizing their relationship would entitle them to any of the legal benefits attendant to state-sanctioned matrimony. . . .

[W]e must interpret that provision within its context in the Utah Code. "[O]ur primary goal in interpreting statutes is to give effect to the legislative intent, as evidenced by the plain language, in light of the purpose the statute was meant to achieve." "We presume that the legislature used each word advisedly and give effect to each term according to its ordinary and accepted meaning." Furthermore, "[w]e read the plain language of the statute as a whole, and interpret its provisions in harmony with other statutes in the same chapter and related chapters." Only when we find that a statute is ambiguous do we look to other interpretive tools such as legislative history. . . . Both parties to this appeal agree that "purport" means "[t]o profess or claim falsely; to seem to be." *Black's Law Dictionary* 1250 (7th ed. 1999). The definition of "marry," however, is disputed. . . .

¶19 First, the common usage of "marriage" supports a broader definition of that term than that asserted by Holm. The dictionary defines "marry" as "to join in marriage according to law *or* custom," or "to unite in close and [usually] permanent relation." Holm argues that such a definition of "marriage" is unsupportable and asks us to read the term "legally" into the bigamy statute. To support his argument that "marry" should be construed narrowly in this fashion, Holm relies on *Black's Law Dictionary,* which defines "marriage" as "[t]he legal union of a man and woman as husband and wife." While *Black's* does offer this as one definition of marriage, a review of the dictionary's various entries and editions makes clear that the dictionary itself does not confine its use of the term "marriage" to legally recognized unions. . . . For example, "plural marriage" is defined as "[a] *marriage* in which one spouse is already married to someone else; a bigamous or polygamous union,"; "bigamy" is defined as "[t]he act of *marrying* one person while legally married to another,"; and "polygamy" is "[t]he state of being simultaneously *married* to more than one spouse; multiple marriages." If we were to adopt Holm's construction of "marry," these definitions would be nonsensical, as one could not "marry" another while legally married.

¶20 Furthermore, *Black's Law Dictionary* contains several definitions of different types of marriage that are, by definition, not legally recognized. For example, "putative marriage" is "*marriage* in which husband and wife believe in good faith that they are married, but for some technical reason are not formally married (as when the ceremonial official was not authorized to perform a marriage)"; "clandestine marriage" is "*marriage* that rests merely on the agreement of the parties" or "*marriage* entered into in a secret way, as one solemnized by an unauthorized person or without all required formalities"; and "void marriage" is "*marriage* that is invalid from its inception, that cannot be made valid, and that can be terminated by either party without obtaining a divorce or annulment."

¶21 Moreover, the *Black's Law Dictionary* definition of the term "marriage," unadorned by modifiers, states that "[a]lthough the common law regarded marriage as a civil contract, it is more properly the civil status or relationship existing between a man and a woman who agree to and do live together as spouses." Thus, the plain meaning of the term "marry," as it is used in the bigamy statute, supports our conclusion that it encompasses both marriages that are legally recognized and those that are not.

¶22 Second, when we look, as we must, at the term "marry" in the context of the bigamy statute, as well as statutes in the same chapter and related chapters of the Utah Code, it is clear that the Legislature intended "marry" to be construed to include marriages that are not state-sanctioned. Most significantly, . . . the bigamy statute does not require a party to enter into a second marriage (however defined) to run afoul of the statute; cohabitation alone would constitute bigamy pursuant to the statute's terms.[6]

¶23 Also, looking at related statutes in the Utah Code, it is clear that the Legislature did not intend to limit "marriage," as it is used throughout the Utah Code, to legally recognized marriages. By expressly recognizing unsolemnized marriages and allowing for a judicial determination to establish a legal marriage at some point prior to the request for a judicial decree, the Legislature has acknowledged that the attainment of a marriage license from the State is not determinative of whether a marriage exists. In other words, the Utah Code contemplates that there will be "marital relationships" or "marriages" that are not legally recognized from inception, but which the State has the ability to legally recognize, even if the parties to that relationship do not desire such recognition. The Utah Code also recognizes that a marriage may be solemnized even though the marriage is illegal. Utah Code Ann. §30-1-15 (1998) (penalizing anyone who "knowingly . . . solemnizes a *marriage* . . . prohibited by law").

6. . . . Beyond dictionary definitions, it is evident that when the Territory of Utah enacted a law criminalizing polygamy, the term "marry" was not confined to legally recognized marriage. *See* 1892 Utah Laws, ch. VII, §1, at 5-6 ("Every person who has a husband or wife living, who, hereafter *marries* another . . . is guilty of polygamy."). As with the definition of bigamy found in *Black's Law Dictionary,* the territorial law criminalizing polygamy would be nonsensical if the term "marry" is considered limited to legally recognized marriage.

¶24 Holm contends that the term "marry" should be given the same breadth of meaning wherever it appears in the Utah Code. Accordingly, Holm argues that the term "marry" must be limited to legally recognized marriages because, if a broader definition is applied here, we would have to construe "marry" to encompass informal solemnizations in other sections of the bigamy statute specifically and the Utah Code generally. . . . [S]ubsection three of the bigamy statute . . . provides that "[i]t shall be a defense to bigamy that the accused reasonably believed he and the other person were legally eligible to remarry." Utah Code Ann. §76-7-101(3). Holm argues that the term "remarry" in subsection three clearly refers to a legal marriage and that the term "marry" in subsection one should carry the same meaning. *See Spring* Canyon Coal Co. v. Indus. Comm'n of Utah, 74 Utah 103, 277 P. 206, 206-11 (1929) ("The same meaning will be given to a word or phrase used in different parts of a statute.").

¶25 We are not persuaded that the term "remarry," as used in subsection three, is so clearly limited to legally recognized marriage. Consequently, we are not convinced that a broader interpretation of "marry" as used in subsection one is inconsistent with other uses of that term in the bigamy statute. Rather, in the absence of language limiting the definition of the term, it is appropriate to give the term chosen by the Legislature its full force, applying it to marriages recognized both by law and by custom. Conceived in this fashion, the defense offered by subsection three merely excuses bigamous marriages commenced with a *reasonable* belief that initiating the marital relationship would not run afoul of this State's bigamy law.

¶26 Third, although we need not look at other interpretive tools when the meaning of the statute is plain, our construction of "marry" is supported by the legislative history and purpose of the bigamy statute. [T]he . . . bigamy statute was intended to criminalize both attempts to gain legal recognition of duplicative marital relationships and attempts to form duplicative marital relationships that are not legally recognized. This court has previously recognized that the legislative purpose of the bigamy statute was to prevent "all the indicia of marriage repeated more than once." *State v. Green (2004).* In *Green,* we allowed an unsolemnized marriage to serve as a predicate marriage for purposes of a bigamy prosecution. If an unlicensed, unsolemnized union can serve as the predicate marriage for a bigamy prosecution, we are constrained to conclude that an unlicensed, solemnized marriage can serve as a subsequent marriage that violates the bigamy statute.

¶27 The dissent nevertheless adopts Holm's position that "purports to marry" means "purports to legally marry," "claims to enter a legally recognized marriage," or "claims benefits from the State based upon married status." In addition to the reasons proffered by Holm, the dissent seeks to support its reading of the statute by referring to our case law, which at times has used the term "purported marriage" to refer to a marriage that is presented as legally valid and recognized, when in reality the marriage enjoys no legal recognition. These cases do not, however, delineate the scope of the term "purports to marry" as the term is used in the bigamy statute, but instead involve situations in which the proper resolutions of various claims are dependent in some fashion on the existence, or absence, of a legally recognized marriage. It is true that, in assessing such claims, we have referred to the claim that a valid, legally recognized marriage exists as a claim of a "purported marriage." It does not, however, necessarily follow that the phrase "purports to marry," as used in the bigamy statute, is similarly confined to claims that a legally valid and recognized marriage has been performed. Simply because one may also purport to enter into a legally recognized marriage does not foreclose the possibility that one may purport to marry without claiming any legal recognition of the marital relationship.

¶28 In sum, we are not convinced that the plain language of the statute, which fails to adorn the term "marry" with any limiting modifiers, justifies the inference drawn by the dissent, and we decline to import such a substantive term into the language of the statute. *See* Arredondo v. Avis Rent A Car Sys., Inc., 2001 UT 29 (stating that this court will not "infer substantive terms into the [statutory] text that are not already there"). Accordingly, we read the plain language of our bigamy statute as prohibiting an individual from claiming to marry a person when already married to another. Further, we conclude that the term "marry" is not confined to legally recognized marriages. In other words, one need not purport that a second marriage is entitled to legal recognition to run afoul of the "purports to marry" prong of the bigamy statute. . . . [T]he ceremony in which Holm and Stubbs participated appeared, in every material respect, indistinguishable from a marriage ceremony to which this State grants legal recognition on a daily basis. . . . [T]he relationship formed by Holm and Stubbs was a marriage, as that term is used in the bigamy statute. . . .

¶32 [T]he dissent assigns central importance, in fact almost exclusive importance, to the lack of a marriage license recognizing the marital commitments made by Holm and Stubbs. But while a marriage license represents a contract between the State and the individuals entering into matrimony, the license itself is typically of secondary importance to the participants in a wedding ceremony. The crux of marriage in our society, perhaps especially a religious marriage, is not so much the license as the solemnization, viewed in its broadest terms as the steps, whether ritualistic or not, by which two individuals commit themselves to undertake a marital relationship. . . . The fact that the State of Utah was not invited to register or record that commitment does not change the reality that Holm and Stubbs formed a marital bond and commenced a marital relationship. . . .

1. The Bigamy Statute Does Not Impermissibly Infringe Holm's Federal Free Exercise Right

. . . Holm argues that *Reynolds* is "nothing more than a hollow relic of bygone days of fear, prejudice, and Victorian morality," and that modern free exercise jurisprudence dictates that no criminal penalty can be imposed for engaging in religiously motivated polygamy. . . . *Reynolds,* despite its age, has never been overruled by the United States Supreme Court and, in fact, has been cited by the Court with approval in several modern free exercise cases, signaling its continuing vitality. . . . Moreover, . . . the United States Supreme Court held in *Employment Division, Department of Human Resources v. Smith* (1990), that a state may, even without furthering a compelling state interest, burden an individual's right to free exercise so long as the burden is imposed by a neutral law of general applicability. The Court has since clarified that a law is not neutral if the intent of that law "is to infringe upon or restrict practices because of their religious motivation." . . . Utah's bigamy statute is a neutral law of general applicability and any infringement upon the free exercise of religion occasioned by that law's application is constitutionally permissible. . . .

2. Holm's Conviction Does Not Offend the Due Process Clause of the Fourteenth Amendment

¶53 Holm argues that the State of Utah is foreclosed from criminalizing polygamous behavior because the freedom to engage in such behavior is a fundamental liberty interest that can be infringed only for compelling reasons and that the State has failed to identify a sufficiently compelling justification for its criminalization of polygamy. . . . Holm relies primarily on the United States Supreme Court's decision in *Lawrence v. Texas* (2003). . . .

¶55 Despite its use of seemingly sweeping language, the holding in *Lawrence* is actually quite narrow. Specifically, the Court takes pains to limit the opinion's reach to decriminalizing private and intimate acts engaged in by consenting adult gays and lesbians. In fact, the Court went out of its way to exclude from protection conduct that causes "injury to a person or abuse of an institution the law protects." Further, after announcing its holding, the Court noted the following: "The present case does not involve minors. It does not involve persons who might be injured or coerced or who are situated in relationships where consent might not easily be refused. It does not involve public conduct. . . ."

¶56 In marked contrast to the situation presented to the Court in *Lawrence*, this case implicates the public institution of marriage, an institution the law protects, and also involves a minor. In other words, this case presents the exact conduct identified by the Supreme Court in *Lawrence* as outside the scope of its holding.

¶57 First, the behavior at issue in this case is not confined to personal decisions made about sexual activity, but rather raises important questions about the State's ability to regulate marital relationships and prevent the formation and propagation of marital forms that the citizens of the State deem harmful.

> Sexual intercourse . . . is the most intimate behavior in which the citizenry engages. [*Lawrence*] spoke to this discreet, personal activity. Marriage, on the other hand, includes both public and private conduct. Within the privacy of the home, marriage means essentially whatever the married individuals wish it to mean. Nonetheless, marriage extends beyond the confines of the home to our society.

¶58 The very "concept of marriage possesses 'undisputed social value.'" Utah's own constitution enshrines a commitment to prevent polygamous behavior. That commitment has undergirded this State's establishment of "a vast and convoluted network of . . . laws . . . based exclusively upon the practice of monogamy as opposed to plural marriage." Our State's commitment to monogamous unions is a recognition that decisions made by individuals as to how to structure even the most personal of relationships are capable of dramatically affecting public life.

¶59 The dissent states quite categorically that the State of Utah has no interest in the commencement of an intimate personal relationship so long as the participants do not present their relationship as being state-sanctioned. On the contrary, the formation of relationships that are marital in nature is of great interest to this State, no matter what the participants in or the observers of that relationship venture to name the union. We agree with the dissent's statement that any two people may make private pledges to each other and that these relationships do not receive legal recognition unless a legal adjudication of marriage is sought. That does not, however, prevent the legislature from having a substantial interest in criminalizing such behavior when there is an existing marriage.

¶60 As the dissent recognizes, a marriage license significantly alters the bond between two people because the State becomes a third party to the marital contract. It is precisely that third-party contractual relationship that gives the State a substantial interest in prohibiting unlicensed marriages when there is an existing marriage. Without this contractual relationship, the State would be unable to enforce important marital rights and obligations. In situations where there is no existing marriage, the Legislature has developed a mechanism for legally determining that a marriage did in fact exist, even where the couple did not seek legal recognition of that marriage, so that the State may enforce marital obligations such as spousal support or prevent welfare abuse. There is no such mechanism for protecting the State's interest in situations where there is an existing marriage because, under any interpretation of the bigamy statute, a party cannot seek a legal adjudication of a second marriage. Thus, the State has a substantial interest in criminalizing such an unlicensed second marriage.

¶61 Moreover, marital relationships serve as the building blocks of our society. The State must be able to assert some level of control over those relationships to ensure the smooth operation of laws and further the proliferation of social unions our society deems beneficial while discouraging those deemed harmful. The people of this State have declared monogamy a beneficial marital form and have also declared polygamous relationships harmful. As the Tenth Circuit stated in *Potter*, Utah "is justified, by a compelling interest, in upholding and enforcing its ban on plural marriage to protect the monogamous marriage relationship."

¶62 Further, this case features another critical distinction from *Lawrence*; namely, the involvement of a minor. Stubbs was 16 at the time of her betrothal, and evidence adduced at trial indicated that she and Holm regularly engaged in sexual activity. Further, it is not unreasonable to conclude that this case involves behavior that warrants inquiry into the possible existence of injury and the validity of consent. *See, e.g.*, *Green*, 2004 UT 76 ("[P]olygamy . . . often coincides with crimes targeting women and children. Crimes not unusually attendant to the practice of polygamy include incest, sexual assault, statutory rape, and failure to pay child support.").

¶63 Given the above, we conclude that *Lawrence* does not prevent our Legislature from prohibiting polygamous behavior. The distinction between private, intimate sexual conduct between consenting adults and the public nature of polygamists' attempts to extralegally redefine the acceptable parameters of a fundamental social institution like marriage is plain. . . .

II. We Affirm Holm's Conviction for Sexual Conduct with a Minor

. . . Sec. 76-5-407 exempts a married individual from operation of the unlawful sexual conduct statute where the individual engages in the proscribed conduct with his or her spouse. . . . Holm argues that the State has no rational justification for endorsing consensual sexual conduct between a sixteen- or seventeen-year-old girl and a man ten years her elder where the two have entered a legal marriage with the consent of one of the girl's parents, while criminalizing such conduct where the two are not legally married. He points out that if the distinction is based solely on the minor's inability to give valid consent, such a concern would not apply in this case because Stubbs's father consented to her religious union with Holm. Contrary to Holm's suggestion, we agree with the State that its interest in the distinction goes beyond any concern with obtaining parental consent. The state-determined framework within which the legal status of marriage exists provides a minor with certain protections under the law that are absent where the union is not a legal marriage and thus falls outside this framework.

¶102 The protections afforded persons who are married in the eyes of the law include rights, vis-à-vis their spouses, to support and maintenance, to the fulfillment of certain procedural requirements before the union can be dissolved, to a fair distribution of property and debt obligations in the event such a dissolution occurs, and to inherit all or a portion of the spouses' estates in the event of their death. . . . Having provided such a framework of support, the State may rationally distinguish between minors who are within its protection and those who are not.

¶104 We conclude that Holm was properly convicted of both bigamy and unlawful sexual conduct with a minor. . . .

The court's statutory interpretation is filled with flawed reasoning. If you can explain why, you are well on your way to being an effective attorney. To discover just one instance, imagine reading the cited *Black's Law Dictionary* entries in the context of one of the 60-plus nations in the world where legal polygamy exists. Would Holm's interpretation of "marry" then render the Black's definitions of plural marriage, bigamy, and polygamy nonsensical? The court unjustifiably read into those definitions an assumption that legal plural marriage was impossible. See how many other logical missteps you can find.

A concurring opinion in essence suggested the court should jettison the canons of interpretation and just do what the legislature obviously wanted courts to do—namely, to criminalize what people like Holm were doing. Would you support that approach? As a drafting exercise, try to write a statutory provision with language that more clearly conveys an intention to prohibit the private practice of polygamy, with a precise definition of the targeted conduct. Oddly, the court ignored the phrase in the polygamy statute referring to "cohabiting," which might be more straightforward. Can you imagine any difficulty with establishing that Holm cohabited with Ruth Stubbs?

What outcome would you expect under the statute if Holm had not become legally married to anyone, but rather had only a social marriage with even his first "wife"? Would it be difficult for the court to interpret "wife" as anything other than a legal spouse? If so, would FLDS members be better off not having any legal marriages? Why might Holm have secured a legal marriage with his first wife, Suzie, if he anticipated having more wives?

As an alternative to prosecuting for bigamy, could Utah simply enforce its law criminalizing adultery? Or would that lead to other problems (e.g., an equal protection or free exercise violation if only FDLS members are targeted)? If Utah is not worried about sex with multiple partners so much as people "purporting" to be in non-legal marriages with more than one wife, why is that? Is that more troubling than a man who has a wife at home and a mistress or two living under a separate roof? Do not adulterers and non-marital cohabitants also "attempt[] to extralegally redefine the acceptable parameters of a fundamental social institution like marriage," perhaps in less admirable ways? Note: In most states, adultery is not unlawful, and the divorce laws of many states preclude a private remedy for it even at the time of divorce. So what is the real, inherent problem with private polygamy? What is the harm to which the majority repeatedly alluded? And how can a state rationally justify prosecuting a married man who has another intimate relationship openly and with his legal wife's consent while not prosecuting married men who have other intimate relationships clandestinely and without their wives' consent?

Is the court too quick to dismiss the implications of *Lawrence* for polygamy? Consider whether, following *Lawrence*, a state could constitutionally criminalize any of the following: 1) a man is dating two women at the same time and having sex with each; 2) a male law student is sharing a house with two female classmates, not married in any sense to either and not committed to or supporting either, but having sex with each on occasion; 3) a man is cohabiting with two women and the three have expressed a commitment to stay together and support each other for life, without using the term "marriage." If the central principle of *Lawrence* extends to protect these arrangements, then how could it be constitutionally permissible for a state to treat the man in any of these scenarios as a *criminal* if instead he accepts the legal responsibilities of marriage as to one of the women with whom he is having sex, and if that woman accepts his intimacy with the other woman? If the state's answer would be that legal marriage is a benefit the state offers to people who accept the state's terms, and that one important term is monogamy, then why isn't the state's response to polygamy simply to remove legal marriage status as to the first wife, leaving all the parties involved free to do what they want but without state sanction? How can a criminal law response be warranted? Cf. Ann E. Tweedy, *Polyamory as a Sexual Orientation*, 79 U. Cin. L. Rev. 1461 (2011) (arguing that "a preference for having multiple romantic relationships simultaneously—should be defined as a type of sexual orientation for purposes of anti-discrimination law").

Holm filed a petition for certiorari to the U.S. Supreme Court. The Court asked for briefs, signaling some openness to accepting a polygamy case, but ultimately declined review. In July 2011, TLC polygamist family Koby Brown and his four wives filed suit in Utah challenging Utah's criminalization of polygamy. The Utah attorney general predicted the case will go to the Supreme Court. The Browns present a better case than Holm for challenging the Utah criminal statute, because state investigators have found no evidence of abuse or underage relations in the Brown situation.

In addition to *Lawrence*, a claim for legal recognition of polygamous marriage (as opposed to simply not criminalizing a polygamous lifestyle) would rest on the doctrine you studied establishing a Fourteenth Amendment right to marry. Does the doctrine support multiple legal marriage? If you think not, would you say the same about a right to remarry—that is, a right to marry if one has already been married once and gotten divorced? What if a state amended its marriage law to exclude people who were married once already and divorced because of their own adultery or abuse? Would the new restriction survive constitutional challenge?

Which do you think is the stronger case for legal acceptance: A man who is already married asserts a right to marry a second time while remaining married to the first wife versus a woman who has never been married asserting a right to marry a man who already has one wife? Try to construct the constitutional argument for each. Which minority cultural group would you expect to fare better in asserting a constitutional right against prosecution for polygamy: A Native American tribe in the United States in which polygamy has always been a cultural practice versus a recent immigrant polygamous family from Sudan, where polygamy is legal and encouraged by the government?

As in the case of drugs and prostitution, some scholars argue that the state's best stance toward polygamy is legalization and regulation, because criminalization drives the practice underground and thereby exacerbates and inhibits protection against abuse of vulnerable people. See, e.g., Emily J. Duncan, *The Positive Effects of Legalizing Polygamy: "Love is a Many Splendored Thing,"* 15 Duke J. Gender L. & Pol'y 315 (2008); Shayna M. Sigman, *Everything Lawyers Know About Polygamy Is Wrong*, 16 Cornell J.L. & Pub. Pol'y 101 (2006) ("Children and women in polygynous families may be at greater risk to suffer abuse precisely because of the premium placed on silence and privacy. These are the greatest weapons an abuser has."). It stands to reason that when the state criminalizes a practice, the persons who nevertheless choose to do it will be on average those with less to lose from prosecution—that is, those who have little wealth or social standing, those on the margins of society. And so we see that those who practice polygamy today are generally not very wealthy or reputable, and they must secure wives by means (i.e., coercion) other than attracting autonomous women away from less desirable males. In a realm of legalized polygamy, we might well see it become practiced instead more by reputable, wealthy men and uncoerced women. Is there anything you find attractive about a polygamous lifestyle? Can you imagine someone like you choosing to do it and it not entailing the problems of subordination and child abuse that much of the public associates with polygamy?

Perhaps the most surprising sources of support for polygamy are far left groups:

Adrienne D. Davis, Regulating Polygamy: Intimacy, Default Rules, and Bargaining for Equality

110 Colum. L. Rev. 1955, 1970-1974 (2010)

Some groups in the United States have urged polygamy as a way of preserving the black family, viewed by many as the bedrock of the black community. Made in its weaker form, the argument is a pragmatic one: Distorted gender ratios, lack of economic options, and sexual norms have reduced black marriage to a statistical oddity. The result: 67.1% of black children are born outside of marriage and 34.5% grow up in poverty. In this view, what might be thought of as "crisis" polygamy, or "pragmatic" or "charitable" polygamy, represents a practical way of providing black women with (black) husbands, and black children with more present and committed fathers. In its stronger form, the black nationalist argument embraces polygamy as a way to rescue black masculinity and restore patriarchy to the black community. . . . In this view, polygamy offers not only pragmatic multiplicity, but also reinforces conventional gender roles as well. . . . Black nationalists and conventional conservatives may both view marriage as the best antidote to poverty and sexual immorality, far preferable to government entitlements or restructuring the family. Yet, while mainstream conservatives additionally support black marriage as an assimilationist strategy, black nationalists advocate plural marriage as a way to further separate the black community culturally, morally, and, ultimately, politically and economically from mainstream American culture.

Meanwhile, some radical feminists urge polygamy as a potential weapon in dyadic marriage's ongoing battle of the sexes. . . . [M]any women continue to complain that conventional marriage leaves them craving deeper emotional intimacy and more equitable divisions of household labor. Thus far, frustrated wives have had three options: surrender and consign themselves to gender inequity and personal exhaustion; remain locked in battle with their husbands; or divorce. . . . For some women, increasing the ratio of women to men in a household might be more effective than pressuring husbands to "change" and conform to women's expectations. Done properly—that is, among women committed to feminist principles—polygamy can provide a "sisterhood" within marriage, generate more adults committed to balancing work/family obligations, and allow more leisure time for each wife. As Luci Malin, vice chairman of Utah's National Organization for Women, once remarked, "[Polygamy] seems like a pretty good idea for professional women, who can proceed with their careers and have someone at home they can trust to watch their children." . . . Contra polygyny as identitarian bonding among women, others laud polygamy as destabilizing the conventional gender roles assigned by dyadic marriage's "yin and yang." In this view, polygamy arguably has the potential to "queer" marriage.

Feminist endorsements of polygyny might seem to have little in common with black nationalist ones: The latter sees polygamy as patriarchy's savior, the former as its death knell. Still, what they share is attention to the material realities that shape intimacy and the ways marriage can foster such things as "gender" or "racial" community. . . .

A final defense of polygamy that does not fall neatly into either of the above categories rests on a sort of gendered pragmatic moralism rooted in an essential distinction between male and female nature. The logic runs as follows. Men are, by nature, sexually unfaithful. Women, who are less interested in sex, are not. To the contrary, women prefer monogamy. Part of the virtue, then, of polygamy is its transparency: It permits men's basic (base?) instincts while using the marital structure to domesticate and discipline them. Following this logic, men may serve their biological impulses for multiplicity, but may not be deceitful or disrespectful. They may have multiple sexual partners, but they may not turn women into "prostitutes." In sum, . . . plural marriage is defended as preferable to the alternative of men's inevitable adultery and infidelity.

Davis herself recommends decriminalization so that the state can better monitor and regulate the practice, and she explains how commercial partnership law presents a useful model for such regulation. Other support for polygamy comes from the LGBT community, based on a general principle of not discriminating against people based on their particular form of intimate life. See, e.g., Elizabeth M. Glazer, *Sodomy and Polygamy*, 111 COLUM. L. REV. SIDEBAR 66 (2011). And from those who criticize monogamy as promoting possessiveness and jealousy and as leading to boredom and cheating. See, e.g., Elizabeth Brake, *Minimal Marriage: What Political Liberalism Implies for Marriage Law*, 120 ETHICS 302, 321 (2010) (summarizing arguments of "polyamorists").

Other scholars maintain that the practice of polygamy is inherently problematic in many ways and so the state should do more to detect and prosecute polygamists:

Maura Strassberg, The Crime of Polygamy

12 Temp. Pol. & Civ. Rts. L. Rev. 353, 357-358 (2003)

. . . [M]odern Mormon fundamentalist polygyny consistently harms the liberty interests of teenage plural wives and should continue to be criminalized as long as it involves such teenage girls. The analysis of women who enter into polygyny as adults is more complicated. For some adult plural wives, polygyny furthers their liberty interests, while, for others, it becomes a systematic deprivation of their civil rights. I find it difficult to justify the criminalization of polygyny to protect adult women who choose to enter into such marriages for religious reasons.

However, modern Mormon fundamentalist polygyny is also instrumental in the development of small theocratically governed communities that largely evade both regulation by the secular government and economic contribution to that government. The evasion allows modern Mormon fundamentalist communities to shield illegal conduct from governmental observation and prosecution while at the same time making it possible to divert mainstream resources for the exclusive support and growth of local theocratic institutions. This role of polygyny in the creation and maintenance of these Mormon fundamentalist communities raises two concerns that are relevant to the question of criminalizing polygyny.

My first concern is for the loss of individual civil rights that members of these communities suffer as a result of the inability of traditional government institutions to observe, investigate or regulate almost any facet of life occurring in these communities. Given the crucial importance of teenage plural brides to the Mormon fundamentalist practice of polygyny and the extreme difficulty of regulating polygyny in any way in the isolated, theocratically governed communities that practice such polygyny, it would be impossible to protect teenage girls and very young women from the identified evils of polygynous marriage for them while allowing polygynous marriage in general. This in itself provides some justification for banning all polygynous marriages, even those involving mature adult women, on the grounds that the practice viewed more widely will inevitably and significantly target and victimize teenagers as plural wives. Furthermore, while most attention is traditionally given to the effects of polygyny on women, the indirect effects of unregulated polygynous communities on the civil rights of children and men, particularly those who dissent or oppose those in power, has yet to be documented.

My second concern is for the impact of such communities on the larger society in which they exist. To the extent that polygyny plays a crucial role in the creation of unregulated communities whose social and economic activities unfairly draw resources from regulated social and economic institutions with little or no return, polygyny must be understood as a practice that is socially problematic, even if not as broadly threatening to society as it was in the nineteenth century. If only the burdens of polygynous communities are exported, while the economic benefits of a modern democracy are siphoned off and used to strengthen an alternative political structure that is inconsistent with our own political values, this may also serve as justification for criminalizing the marriage practice, which is both the foundation and pillar of such communities. . . .

There are numerous books written by women who escaped from or males who were forced out of authoritarian and abusive polygamous communities. They include Brent W. Jeffs, Lost Boy: The True Story of One Man's Exile from a Polygamist Cult and His Brave Journey to Reclaim His Life (2010); Flora Jessop, Church of Lies (2010); Susan Ray Schmidt, Favorite Wife: Escape from Polygamy (2009); Elissa Wall, Stolen Innocence: My Story of Growing Up in a Polygamous Sect, Becoming a Teenage Bride, and Breaking Free of Warren Jeffs (2008); and Carolyn Jessop, Escape (2007).

Strassberg's main argument against legalizing polygamy is that "it would be impossible to protect teenage girls and very young women from the identified evils of polygynous marriage for them while allowing polygynous marriage in general." Could the same not also be said of sex, and really of any activity that is legal for adults but not for minors? If adult members of relatively reclusive groups are determined to have minors engaging in those activities, it will be difficult to stop them. One might think the concern less pronounced with marriage, which is relatively public, than with activities like sex, drinking alcohol, or smoking marijuana that are not inherently public.

What change, if any, might you expect in the norms and practices of polygamist communities if states struck this bargain with them: "We will henceforth legalize polygamy and even confer marriage certificates and marriage benefits for multiple marriages, but in return you will accept an absolute minimum age of eighteen for marriage, closer monitoring to guard against child abuse and violations of that minimum age, mainstream schooling of children to ensure their exposure to mainstream culture and development of autonomy, so that they can decide freely for themselves, and very aggressive prosecution and punishment of violators." Do you think such communities would accept this bargain?

d. Other Restrictions on Marriage

Should U.S. states consider adopting any of the following restrictions on who may marry?

Civil Code of Spain
Chapter II. Of the Requirements for Contracting Marriage

ART. 47

The following are also forbidden from contracting marriage: . . .

3. Those found guilty, as perpetrators or accomplices, of the malicious killing of the spouse of either of them.

Marriage Law of the People's Republic of China

ARTICLE 7

No marriage may be contracted under any of the following circumstances: . . .

(2) if the man or the woman is suffering from any disease, which is regarded by medical science as rendering a person unfit for marriage.

Civil Code 2002, Turkey

ARTICLE 132

If the marriage has ended, the woman cannot marry for three hundred days starting from the end of the marriage.

3. Who Is a Good Bet for Marriage?

Once you have figured out what pool of potential spouses is available to you as a legal matter, you might do some research in order to develop a profile of a spouse with whom you are more likely to have a happy, healthy, and permanent marriage.

Unsurprisingly, some of the traits that are attractive to people when they begin dating are also traits that make success in marriage more likely—for example, maturity, higher education, higher income, egalitarian attitudes, a clean slate, and a positive disposition. Studies consistently show marital discord and divorce are substantially more likely for people who marry when they are less than 25 years old relative to people who marry in their late 20s or 30s. PAUL R. AMATO ET AL., ALONE TOGETHER: HOW MARRIAGE IN AMERICA IS CHANGING 77-79 (2007). Relatedly, higher-income people marry later but have more enduring marriages with lower levels of conflict and violence, consistent with the common perception that financial struggle is a primary cause of marital discord. Burgess et al., *The Role of Income in Marriage and Divorce Transitions Among Young Americans,* 16 J. POPULAR ECON. 455 (2003). Decision-making equality is associated with greater marital satisfaction for both husbands and wives, so women or men with controlling or dominating tendencies are less promising as spouses. See Amato et al., *Continuity and Change in Marital Quality Between 1980 and 2000,* 65 J. MARRIAGE & FAM. 1 (2003). Having previously cohabited with another partner, having been married before, and having a child from another relationship are all significant risk factors. Amato & Hohmann-Marriott, *A Comparison of High- and Low-Distress Marriages That End in Divorce,* 69 J. MARRIAGE & FAM. 621 (2007). Naturally, the cause of a partner's prior divorce is relevant—for example, whether it resulted from your partner's infidelity or violence rather than simply from an incompatibility that is not replicated in your current relationship. And research suggests that you should ask a potential partner to bring some childhood photos with them on your first date. An Indiana study found that people with the brightest smiles as children were three times more likely to have a strong marriage than chronic frowners. See Clara Moskowitz, *Smile! It Could Predict Success of Your Marriage,* MSNBC.com, Apr. 16, 2009.

Some traits that one might not deem significant in dating are actually quite significant to odds of divorce. Intergenerational transmission of divorce has received much attention, and studies consistently show significantly higher divorce rates for couples in which one spouse has divorced parents and dramatically higher rates for couples in which both spouses have divorced parents. Amato & Hohmann-Marriott, supra. Research also shows lower marital happiness and longevity in marriages that are inter-faith or interracial, seemingly attributable to "complex relationship histories . . . , fewer shared values and less support from parents." See Bryndl E. Hohmann-Marriott & Paul Amato, *Relationship Quality in Interethnic Marriages and Cohabitations,* 87 SOC. FORCES 825-856 (2008). Persons who have liberal or individualistic family-related values—in particular, believing that people should be free to do what makes them happy and greater acceptance of divorce—are more likely to divorce.

There is also great variation in divorce rates across occupations, which could suggest that certain professions place great stress on a marriage, that some traits that incline people to certain professions also make them more or less likely to divorce, or something else. Clergy and legislators are among those least likely to divorce, as are farmers and dentists. Lawyers who do not become legislators do not do quite so well, but they are significantly better than average at marital success. Contrary to popular belief, military personnel also have a below-average divorce rate. Police officers have an average rate of divorce, but corrections officers are significantly above the average. The rate for bartenders is about twice the average, second highest among professions. You might think a massage therapist would make for a great spouse, but they have the third highest rate of divorce. Who has the highest rate? Dancers. See Shawn P. McCoy & Michael G. Aamodt, *A Comparison of Law Enforcement Divorce Rates with Those of Other Occupations,* 25 J. POLICE & CRIM. PSYCHOL. 1, 5-16 (2010) (listing divorce rates for 449 occupations).

Whether the amount of time that a potential spouse spends working affects marital happiness appears to depend on whether high work demands correspond with high income. Above normal work demands per se create stress and instability, especially when it is a wife who is working, but substantially higher family income increases marital happiness. Thus, marrying a workaholic might be okay if her or his devotion to work produces a very high income, but marrying someone who devotes a great amount of time to low-pay or volunteer work might be a bad idea, at least if that work reduces spousal interaction time or participation in household tasks.

Reports on correlations between divorce and some other traits are less consistent. Many studies have found greater marital satisfaction and a substantially lower divorce rate among persons who participate regularly in religious activities. See, e.g., Andrew J. Weaver et al., *A Systematic Review of Research on Religion in Six Primary Marriage and Family Journals:*

1995-1999, 30 AM. J. FAM. THERAPY 293, 302 (2002). But sociologist Brad Wilcox's research showed that male conservative Protestants who do not regularly participate in religious activities are more likely than average to be abusive husbands and to divorce. W. BRADFORD WILCOX, SOFT PATRIARCHS, NEW MEN: HOW CHRISTIANITY SHAPES FATHERS AND HUSBANDS 15-16, 181-182 (2004). Another study found that Jews have a divorce rate roughly three times that of Muslims. With respect to race, some studies show significantly higher divorce rates for blacks than for whites. See, e.g., Megan M. Sweeney & Julie A. Phillips, *Understanding Racial Differences in Marital Disruption: Recent Trends and Explanations*, 66 J. MARRIAGE & FAM. 639, 643 (2004). But the U.S. Census Bureau American Community Survey 2005-2009 found similar rates for whites and blacks, and also a somewhat lower rate than either for Hispanics and a very low rate for Asian Americans.

Nearly all the foregoing traits are readily discernible through dating. Other information one presumably would want to have, however, could be easy to conceal. In contrast to formation of parent-child relationships through adoption, the state does not require investigation of potential spouses before issuing a marriage license. One kind of information one might not discover from dating, because one's partner either is not aware of it or is not forthcoming, is whether one's partner has a disease or genetic condition that is transmittable or that could predispose him or her to an early death or disability. Another bit of information many people would deem very important that is very unlikely to be discovered in the courting process is whether the other person is capable of reproducing. At one time, most states required applicants for a marriage license to first get tested for sexually transmittable diseases and/or fertility and to disclose the results to their partner. Today only Connecticut, Indiana, Mississippi, and Montana require blood tests. Why have most states eliminated this requirement? Would testing for STDs and fertility not serve any good purpose today? What would your reaction be if you and your partner were required to undergo such testing before marrying?

Any history of criminal or violent behavior or child maltreatment would presumably also be relevant to a marriage decision. How likely is it that anyone you were dating who had such a history would disclose it to you? How likely that you would detect a propensity to such behavior while dating? Applicants for adoption must undergo a background check that includes review of government databases for criminal behavior and child maltreatment. Yet while some states have made discovery of undisclosed felonies a basis for annulment, none have required a pre-marriage records check as a condition for receiving a marriage license. Given the Supreme Court's decision in *Turner*, states presumably could not constitutionally deny a license to someone on the basis of a criminal record or child maltreatment record, but they could perhaps require disclosure to the other party of anything the background check reveals. Would you favor such a condition for obtaining a marriage license?

The idea of a background check in connection with adult partnership formation is not entirely unfamiliar to the U.S. legal system. In recent years, an explosion in the number of trans-national marriages, with the Internet providing innumerable sites for American men to find "e-mail order brides" from poor countries, has triggered federal legislation requiring background checks on those men. International marriages can pose special challenges for couples: cultural and linguistic differences, arranging to spend time together, the immigration process, etc. In addition, the women who enter into such marriages, so that they can move to the United States and pursue a better life than is available in their native countries, are in a highly vulnerable position. They typically have less than a normal amount of information about their fiancé before marrying, and they must remain married for at least two years in order to remain in the United States. There is evidence that some husbands take advantage of this high cost of exiting marriage for their foreign bride, trapping her in an abusive relationship. Indeed, some men might use the international bride agencies very cognizant of the fact that they will have tremendous power over any woman they can induce to come live with them in the United States. A foreign bride is also less likely to discover that a man is already married, even at the time of procuring a marriage license (there are generally no checks for existing marriages, and certainly no checks across state lines) and so might unwittingly become a man's non-legal second or third wife, her marriage a nullity as a matter of law. Or he might conceal the existence of offspring until after the wedding. At the extreme, operators of prostitution rings might try to lure foreign women to the United States under pretense of a marriage proposal and then force the women into prostitution.

In an effort to lessen the number of women who end up in abusive or unexpected situations, Congress passed the International Marriage Broker Regulation Act of 2005, which makes some effort at ensuring foreign brides are aware of any history of domestic violence an American man might have.

United States Code Annotated
Title 8. Aliens and Nationality
Chapter 12., Subchapter II. Immigration

§1375A. Domestic Violence Information and Resources for Immigrants and Regulation of International Marriage Brokers

. . . (d) Regulation of international marriage brokers

(1) Prohibition on marketing children

An international marriage broker shall not provide any individual or entity with the personal contact information, photograph, or general information about the background or interests of any individual under the age of 18.

(2) . . . [M]andatory collection of background information

(A) (i) Each international marriage broker shall search the National Sex Offender Public Registry or State sex offender public registry. . . .

(ii) Each international marriage broker shall also collect the background information listed in subparagraph (B) about the United States client to whom the personal contact information of a foreign national client would be provided.

(B) The international marriage broker shall collect a certification signed (in written, electronic, or other form) by the United States client accompanied by documentation or an attestation of the following background information about the United States client:

(i) Any temporary or permanent civil protection order or restraining order issued against the United States client.

(ii) Any Federal, State, or local arrest or conviction of the United States client for homicide, murder, manslaughter, assault, battery, domestic violence, rape, sexual assault, abusive sexual contact, sexual exploitation, incest, child abuse or neglect, torture, trafficking, peonage, holding hostage, involuntary servitude, slave trade, kidnapping, abduction, unlawful criminal restraint, false imprisonment, or stalking.

(iii) Any Federal, State, or local arrest or conviction of the United States client for—

(I) solely, principally, or incidentally engaging in prostitution;

(II) a direct or indirect attempt to procure prostitutes or persons for the purpose of prostitution; or

(III) receiving, in whole or in part, of the proceeds of prostitution.

(iv) Any Federal, State, or local arrest or conviction of the United States client for offenses related to controlled substances or alcohol.

(v) Marital history of the United States client, including whether the client is currently married, whether the client has previously been married and how many times, how previous marriages of the client were terminated and the date of termination, and whether the client has previously sponsored an alien to whom the client was engaged or married.

(vi) The ages of any of the United States client's children under the age of 18.

(vii) All States and countries in which the United States client has resided since the client was 18 years of age.

(3) Obligation of international marriage brokers with respect to informed consent

(A) An international marriage broker shall not provide any United States client or representative with the personal contact information of any foreign national client unless and until the international marriage broker has—

(i) performed a search of the National Sex Offender Public Registry, or of the relevant State sex offender public registry for any State . . . in which the United States client has resided during the previous 20 years, for information regarding the United States client;

(ii) collected background information about the United States client required under paragraph (2);

(iii) provided to the foreign national client—

(I) . . . a copy of any records retrieved from the search required under paragraph (2)(A)(i) or documentation confirming that such search retrieved no records;

(II) . . . a copy of the background information collected . . . ; and

(III) . . . the pamphlet developed under subsection (a)(1) of this section; . . .

(5) Penalties

An international marriage broker that violates (or attempts to violate) paragraph (1), (2), (3), or (4) is subject to a civil penalty of not less than $5,000 and not more than $25,000 for each such violation . . . [and] shall be fined in accordance with Title 18, or imprisoned for not more than 5 years, or both. . . .

(6) International marriage broker

(A) The term "international marriage broker" means a corporation, partnership, business, individual, or other legal entity . . . that charges fees for providing dating, matrimonial, matchmaking services, or social referrals between United States citizens or nationals . . . and foreign national clients by providing personal contact information or otherwise facilitating communication between individuals.

(B) Exceptions. Such term does not include—

(i) a traditional matchmaking organization of a cultural or religious nature that operates on a nonprofit basis . . . ; or

(ii) an entity that provides dating services if its principal business is not to provide international dating services between United States citizens or United

States residents and foreign nationals and it charges comparable rates and offers comparable services to all individuals it serves regardless of the individual's gender or country of citizenship.

The pamphlet referred to in 3(A)(iii)(III) is to provide information on the "illegality of domestic violence, sexual assault, and child abuse in the United States and the dynamics of domestic violence"; on "[d]omestic violence and sexual assault services in the United States, including the National Domestic Violence Hotline and the National Sexual Assault Hotline"; on the "legal rights of immigrant victims of abuse and other crimes in immigration, criminal justice, family law, and other matters, including access to protection orders"; on the "obligations of parents to provide child support for children"; and about "[m]arriage fraud under US immigration laws and the penalties for committing"; as well as a "warning concerning the potential use of K nonimmigrant visas by US citizens who have a history of committing domestic violence, sexual assault, child abuse, or other crimes." The federal law requires the State Department to mail a copy of the pamphlet "to each applicant for a K nonimmigrant visa at the same time that the instruction packet regarding the visa application process is mailed to such applicant," which is typically while the foreign bride is still in her home country.

In addition, the law requires that when an American files a petition for a foreign person to receive a non-immigrant fiancée visa to come to the United States, the Department of Homeland Security must do a criminal background check on the U.S. petitioner and transmit any interesting results to the State Department. The State Department conducts an interview with the foreign fiancée at a foreign embassy, prior to deciding whether to issue the visa, and in the interview process is supposed to disclose any results of the background check. It would thus seem unlikely today that a foreign bride could come to the United States on a fiancée visa without knowing of the man's criminal history.

IMBRA might be a good model for a background check component of U.S. marriage license law; Americans with a history of family abuse are likely to try to conceal this also from any American partner, and it might not be that much more difficult to succeed in doing so. In practice, though, the IMBRA appears to be not very effective; men with problematic histories can evade detection fairly easily.

First, most of the international dating agencies' obligations are written as conditions on their providing contact information, but many agencies simply allow their foreign clients to provide the contact information themselves, during conversations that the agencies facilitate on their websites, just as domestic dating sites like Match.com do. Second, the government conducts background checks and discloses results only in connection with non-immigrant fiancée visas, but there are at least two other ways by which an American can get his foreign bride to the United States. He can marry her abroad, prior to applying for any kind of visa for her, and then petition for a spouse immigrant visa instead. Or he can encourage his foreign fiancée to apply for a tourist visa, which is usually obtainable much more quickly than a fiancée visa, quickly marry her after her arrival in the United States, and then petition for her to receive immigrant status as a spouse. This second route constitutes immigration fraud, but it is difficult for INS to prove that the foreign bride applied for the tourist visa with the intent of getting married upon arrival in the United States (the law requires that anyone with such an intent should apply for a fiancée visa). Many couples choose to do one of these things even in the absence of a desire to conceal background information, because the fiancée visa route is typically longer and more expensive. Lastly, many thousands of foreign women come to the United States on temporary employment visas each year, and while they are here some meet an American man and decide to marry hastily before their visa expires. Neither a marriage broker nor the government would collect any information about the American husband prior to the marriage in that case.

Those weaknesses in IMBRA would not arise with a marriage law under which any local government office issuing marriage licenses was required to do a background check on any applicants. Such a law would address the problem of foreign brides marrying while here on a tourist or employment visa. Would you support such a law? Do Americans need this protection as well? Is there an equal protection problem with giving less protection to Americans than to foreigners?

Feminism in Peril?

Professor Abrams explains that immigration policy changed in the late '60s from a system of quotas for different nations to one based predominantly on preferences for particular types of people, most importantly people related by birth or marriage to U.S. citizens and residents. As a result, U.S. citizens have the extraordinary power to create citizenship for foreign nationals by marrying them. Moreover, immigration rules currently place no aggregate numerical limits on visas for fiancées and spouses of U.S. citizens, even though there are countless people around the world who would like to marry an American in order to move here. And as a result of the Internet, it is very easy for a U.S. citizen to meet many very eager potential spouses online. See Kerry Abrams, *Immigration Law and the Regulation of Marriage*, 91 MINN. L. REV. 1625 (2007). Between 1992, when the Internet was barely hatched, and 2005, the number of fiancée visas increased from 8,651 to 53,968. Professor Abrams reports that immigrant visas for spouses numbered nearly 300,000 in 2005.

Yet those who deliberately search abroad for a partner are almost all men, and the vast majority of fiancée visas are for women. A Google search for "foreign husband" turns up no websites with profiles of Ukrainian or Chinese or Guatemalan men available to American women, because American women are not interested. A Google search for "foreign bride," on the other hand, turns up hundreds of websites each with numerous, even thousands, of profiles of available women, mostly from Eastern Europe, Asia, and Latin America. The reality therefore seems to be that the pool of men for American women remains domestic, whereas the pool of women for American men has become global. Some observers of the foreign bride industry allege that American men look abroad for women who are subservient, because they are unhappy with the norm of gender equality toward which America has developed in recent decades. It would be very difficult to prove such an allegation, but suppose for the sake of argument that it is true, and that men can readily find abroad and bring to the United States women content to be subservient housewives, and that they are doing so in large and ever-increasing numbers.

Do immigration policies therefore have the potential to cause a setback to American feminism, both by facilitating the entrance annually of a huge number of women who adopt traditional feminine roles and by creating competitive pressure on American women? Is this concern great enough to impose new restrictions on marriage-based immigration? Or for the state to create other obstacles to international courting?

The discussion above of traits predictive of successful marriage was largely gender neutral and mostly presupposed that everyone wants a happy, permanent marriage. It is a truism in anthropology and evolutionary theory, however, that women and men are differently disposed with respect to mating. Because of sex dimorphism (difference in size between females and males) and females' much greater reproductive investment (pregnancy + lactation period versus males' momentary copulation), women evolved to prefer mates who would stick around after sex to protect and provide for them and their offspring, whereas for men the best reproduction strategy would be to have as many sex partners as possible, which means devoting as little time to each as possible. Men's strategy was altered to some extent by females' ability to reject some mates and accept others, which caused a natural selection of genes for males who display greater commitment to each female with whom they copulate (but not necessarily exclusive commitment). Of course, in modern Western culture, where physical size is of relatively little importance, women are equally capable of securing resources, and law and social norms more or less impose monogamy on men, a rational calculus today would be different. But genetic dispositions do not disappear in the blink of an evolutionary eye. Robust cross-cultural studies show that men and women still differ in some ways in their long- and short-term mate preferences.

David M. Buss, The Psychology of Human Mate Selection: Exploring the Complexity of the Strategic Repertoire

in Handbook of Evolutionary Psychology: Ideas, Issues, and Applications 413-414
(Charles B. Crawford & Dennis L. Krebs eds., 1998)

Both sexes desire mates who are kind, understanding, intelligent, dependable, healthy, and creative. Neither sex likes long-term mates who are cruel, stupid, undependable, riddled with diseases, or boring. Furthermore, both sexes place a premium on love and mutual attraction in a long-term mate . . . because these signal the depth of a person's commitment. Specifically, . . . love signals the commitment of a host of reproductively valuable resources: economic (e.g., gifts, food), physical (e.g., protection), sexual, psychological (e.g., helping mate when he or she is down), and reproductive (e.g., such as having children together). . . .

The study of 37 cultures revealed two clusters of universal or near-universal sex differences. . . . [W]omen universally desire men with good financial prospects . . . and place a greater premium on a man's income than men do on a woman's income. Women also tend to desire characteristics in men that lead to resources over time. Thus, women in most cultures place a premium on a man's social status, his ambition and industriousness, and his older age—qualities known to be linked with resource acquisition. The study . . . found only two qualities that men universally desired more than women: youth and physical attractiveness. Not a single culture showed a reversal of this trend. . . . Youth is a known correlate of reproductive value. . . . Furthermore, . . . men's standards of beauty are highly uniform across cultures; linked with cues such as smooth skin, clear skin, and a youthful appearance; linked with a low waist-to-hips ratio, which signals fertility; and linked with symmetrical features, which signals health and youth.

Many studies show that men's standards generally plummet in short-term mating as contrasted with long-term mating. Men are willing to accept lower levels on a host of mate characteristics, such as intelligence, kindness, dependability, and emotional stability. . . . Men value physical attractiveness more in a short-term mate than in in a long-term mate . . . [and] place a greater premium on sex appeal and sexual experience in the short-term mating context. Women who are sexually experienced may be more easily accessible than women who lack sexual experience. . . . [M]en are not at all turned off by promiscuity in a short-term mate, whereas they find promiscuity highly repugnant in a long-term mate. . . . Men dislike in a short-term mate, more than in a long-term mate, women who want a commitment, have a low sex drive, are prudish, lack sexual experience, and are physically unattractive. . . .

[W]omen maintain high standards in the short-term mating context . . . [and] place a greater premium on physical attractiveness in a short-term mate compared with a long-term mate. . . . [W]omen may be seeking good genes from a short-term mate. Women also elevate the importance they attach to immediate resources in short-term mating contexts. They desire men who spend a lot of money on them early on, who give them gifts early on, and who have an extravagant lifestyle. Women also dislike men who are stingy early on. These findings are consistent with the hypothesis that women seek immediate resources in the short-term mating context. . . .

[C]ultures differ substantially in the value they place on attractiveness. . . . [T]he prevalence of parasite degrades physical appearance . . . [and] too many parasites can be extremely dangerous to health and longevity. . . . [W]e were able to account for an astonishing 50% of the cultural variation in the premium placed on appearance by ecological variation in parasite prevalence. Another cultural variation in mating is the prevalence of short-term versus long-term mating. . . . According to the sex ratio hypothesis, cultures in which there is a surplus of women should be characterized by a shift to short-term mating. . . . In contexts where there are not enough men to go around, . . . some women have to shift to a short-term mating strategy or forego mating altogether. The presence of women willing to engage in short-term mating causes men to be more reluctant to commit to long-term mating; whey they do, there are more frequent opportunities for affairs. Furthermore, should they tire of their mate, there are plenty of women to take their place, and so one source of impediment to divorce is lacking when there is a surplus of women. In contexts characterized by a surplus of men, in contrast, both sexes are predicted to shift to a long-term mating strategy. . . . Evidence from other cultures, and from our own culture over time, supports the sex ratio hypothesis.

This account suggests that one might want to move to an hospitable demographic environment before looking for an individual with particular desirable traits. There are numerous websites providing male-female ratios for cities across the United States.

On the other hand, would anyone so consciously strategic about mate choice as to choose a place to live based on sex ratios and to carry around a list of pro-marriage personal traits probably not be romantic enough to make for a good spouse themselves? See Miss Alpha, *The Pitfalls of Dating with a Checklist* ("Each person wants to be wanted for their uniqueness and loved in spite of their flaws. They want to feel like the last piece in a challenging jigsaw puzzle, not like a universal adapter."), http://askmissalpha.com/2010/05/pitfalls-dating-checklist/. Some have observed that mating appears inevitably, perhaps inherently, a highly irrational activity among humans.

> Thou blind fool, Love, what dost thou to mine eyes,
> That they behold, and see not what they see?

> They know what beauty is, see where it lies,
> Yet what the best is take the worst to be.
> WILLIAM SHAKESEPEARE, *from Sonnet 137*

C. PREPARING TO MARRY

The vast majority of people who marry have a ceremonial wedding, and for most it is the most elaborately planned event of their entire lives, at least the first time around. Preparing for the event is typically an intense experience for first-time engaged couples and their families. Despite, or perhaps because of, the great excitement about the wedding, few such couples devote much time or energy to confirming the wisdom of their decision or to rationally preparing for married life. Caught up in the excitement of buying rings and dresses, selecting invitations and china, and being at the center of attention, they are unlikely to seek an objective assessment of their long-term compatibility, to contemplate the reality of decades of family life, or to think about the possibility of divorce.

Contrast this with the process of adopting a child. Becoming an adoptive parent is also typically an intense emotional experience, but the process usually entails an objective assessment of compatibility, substantial education about the nature and demands of the relationship, and discussion of the possibility of failure. In this section, we will first look at the steps couples can take to inject some rationality and realism into their union and consider whether the state should encourage or require more couples to take these steps. Then we will examine the fun parts of getting married—rings, parties, and ceremony.

1. Education

The legal system has been inconsistent or ambivalent about whether to require pre-marital education.

Alan J. Hawkins, Will Legislation to Encourage Premarital Education Strengthen Marriage and Reduce Divorce?

J.L. & Fam. Stud. (2007)

. . . Five states—Florida, Maryland, Minnesota, Oklahoma, and Tennessee—have passed legislation encouraging couples to participate in formal premarital education: education or counseling to help couples explore relationship strengths and weaknesses and learn what it takes to have a successful marriage. Other states . . . have considered this legislation but not acted upon or rejected it. . . . Minnesota's statute requires twelve hours of education or counseling and specifies a minimum set of topics to cover. Other statutes generally require fewer hours of instruction or counseling; some are not as detailed about the content. All statutes allow for clergy members as well as secular educators or counselors to offer premarital education training. And couples who participate in marriage preparation in these five states can receive a discount on their marriage license fee. . . . [T]he reduction in the cost of a marriage license (generally between $20 and $50 off) may not seem like much of an incentive. Nevertheless, legislators reason that this incentive will support cultural change that encourages greater personal investment in marriage preparation activities, and that greater preparation before marriage will reduce the number of divorces and their accompanying public costs. . . .

Certainly, many divorces are necessary to preserve the physical or psychological safety of an individual or to reinforce the moral boundaries of the institution of marriage. However, recent research suggests that most divorces are initiated because of "softer" personal or relationship problems, such as falling out of love, changing personal needs, lack of satisfaction, feelings of greater entitlement, and so forth. And this is especially true for more educated and well-off individuals. . . . [T]wo-thirds of divorces come from marriages with low amounts of conflict. . . . [R]esearch suggests that many divorces occur for reasons that can at least be addressed with effective premarital education. . . .

Typically, premarital education involves a couples-group format and includes instruction and discussions about expectations for marriage, effective communication and problem-solving skills, managing finances, and other important topics. In addition, it is common for premarital education programs to have couples complete a relationship inventory that provides them an in-depth profile of their personal and relationship strengths and possible weaknesses. These inventories are based on factors that research has shown to be related to marital success. . . . A majority of formal premarital education in the United States takes place under the auspices of a religious organization in conjunction with religious-based wedding plans. Thus, . . . many premarital education programs also include religious instruction about the sanctity of marriage and religious principles related to forming and sustaining healthy marriages. . . . Some premarital education is done in private, one-on-one settings with a professional counselor or religious minister. . . .

Many high schools include elective classes focused on helping adolescents understand how to build healthy relationships, but this is different from formal premarital education that is targeted at engaged or seriously dating couples. Florida is the only state to mandate education for high school students on building healthy relationships and marriages. All Utah high school students have the option to take a year-long course with content on financial literacy and building healthy relationships. However, there is little data yet on whether this kind of early education will translate into future healthy marriages and reduced divorce rates. . . .

Not all premarital education is formal, of course. Many individuals and couples approaching their weddings seek out self-help books or consult privately with friends and family members. However, there has been no research evaluating informal marriage preparation. . . .

According to the NFI marriage study, about 37% of ever-married adults in the United States have participated in formal marriage preparation. . . . [M]ost Americans think formal preparation for marriage is a good idea, regardless of their involvement in it. . . . In the NFI marriage study, respondents were asked if they would attend premarital education classes if they were made available at no cost; 73% said yes. . . . 86% of American adults agreed that "all couples considering marriage should be encouraged to get premarital counseling." . . .

[A] few generations ago, marriage involved more prescribed roles and responsibilities, lower expectations for personal fulfillment, stronger support systems, stronger beliefs in permanence, and higher barriers to ending a relationship. In these circumstances, perhaps a "learn-as-you-go" approach to marriage was more feasible. . . . Today, however, marital roles for most are as negotiated as they are prescribed, marriage carries high expectations for personal fulfillment, marriage is a more private institution with fewer social and cultural supports, the belief in marital permanence has eroded, and barriers to ending a marriage are much lower than in the past due to unilateral, no-fault divorce laws and women's greater economic independence. Accordingly, compared to the past, there is an increasing need for greater knowledge and relationship skills for contemporary marriages to succeed. And because the highest risk for divorce occurs during the first five years of marriage, early education seems to make sense.

In addition, there is a modern version of the "learn-as-you-go" approach to marriage. About five million individuals are cohabiting in the United States, and most young people today (66% of boys and 61% of girls) believe that living together before marriage is a good way to increase the chances of a successful marriage. . . . However, scientific evidence shows that cohabitation is a substantial risk factor for later divorce unless one cohabits with only one partner and eventually marries that partner, which is not the norm. Moreover, research suggests that those who cohabit before marrying have poorer marital quality than those who do not cohabit, even controlling for various selection effects. No research to date suggests that cohabitation is an effective means for enhancing marital success. . . . Cohabiting couples should benefit from premarital education, as well. . . .

A synthesis of studies (meta-analysis) evaluating the outcomes of formal marriage preparation found evidence supporting the effectiveness of these programs. Of the thirteen most rigorous studies, twelve found that couples who participated in premarital education programs had significantly higher relationship skills and marital quality after the program compared to couples who did not participate. [S]ix months to three years after the end of these premarital programs, program participants generally maintained the relationship skills they were taught, including effective conflict negotiation, positive communication, empathy, and self-disclosure. . . . In another recent study, researchers . . . found that couples who sought out premarital education had a substantially lower rate of separation and divorce in the early years of marriage, even controlling for a host of other factors that could influence the likelihood of divorce. . . .

In addition, data from state surveys provide some support for the notion that premarital education can make a positive difference in marital quality. Of Utahns who said they participated in formal premarital education, 84% reported that they were "very happy" in their marriages compared to 71% who did not participate in formal premarital education. Those who participated in formal premarital education also reported higher scores on talking to each other as friends, lower negative interaction scores, and lower divorce proneness scores. Similar results were found in surveys of representative samples of adults in other states. . . .

Scott Stanley has suggested three ways that premarital education works to promote healthy marriages and reduce divorce. First, Stanley argues that formal premarital education fosters greater deliberation by slowing couples down in their starry-eyed flight to the altar. . . . Research demonstrates that couples with short engagement periods have significantly higher divorce rates. . . . 10% to 15% of couples involved in premarital education decide not to marry . . . This greater deliberateness may be especially important for couples who marry much younger than average and come from sub-cultures that idealize marriage.

A second way . . . is that it reinforces the idea that marriage is worthy of commitment and depends primarily on knowledge and skills rather than romance and luck. . . . A third way . . . is that couples who participate in premarital education may be more likely to seek marital therapy for relationship problems down the road, and seek help earlier, if they already have had experience with interventions to strengthen marriages. They also may be more likely to seek out marital enrichment education or activities to keep their relationship strong, especially if they had a positive experience with premarital education. . . . Oklahoma and Utah marriage surveys . . . found that nearly 90% of adults who had some formal premarital education said they would be interested in further relationship enrichment classes compared to 68% of those who did not participate. . . .

[T]here are at least two additional reasons. First, public policy to encourage premarital education is, in itself, a strong message that a healthy, stable marriage matters not only to individuals but also to the broader communities that depend on those marriages to sustain a strong society. . . . Finally, when legislatures encourage premarital education, marriage practitioners in those states may be energized to reach out more effectively to offer premarital services. . . .

[I]t is not the only legislative option being discussed and tried. . . . One legislative option passed by three states (Arizona, Arkansas, Louisiana), and considered by more than twenty others, goes beyond encouraging premarital education to promoting a fuller package of requirements designed to promote healthy marriages and reduce divorces. . . . Covenant Marriage is an alternate set of rules couples may choose to govern their entrance into and any exit from marriage. . . . Couples who choose to marry under Covenant Marriage rules must participate in premarital education before marrying. Also, they must affirm that they have disclosed anything that could reasonably affect their partner's decision to marry (e.g., financial debt, children of previous relationships). They also legally bind themselves before they marry to seek marital counseling, either secular or religious, if they encounter problems that threaten the marriage. Finally, they legally limit their grounds for divorce to the "hard" reasons (e.g., abuse, infidelity, addiction, imprisonment, abandonment) or a longer waiting period for divorce (generally eighteen to twenty-four months). . . . [B]ecause only a small proportion—less than two percent—of couples are selecting it, and because those who choose it have a lower-risk profile for divorce, Covenant Marriage is unlikely at this time to reduce divorce rates. . . .

See also Stanley et al., *Premarital Education, Marital Quality, and Marital Stability: Findings From a Large, Random Household Survey*, 20 J. FAM. PSYCHOL. 117, 122-123 (2006) (concluding from four-state study that, for people of all races, income levels, and education levels, "participation in premarital education is associated with higher levels of marital satisfaction, lower levels of destructive conflicts, and higher levels of interpersonal commitment to spouses," and for the survey population as a whole "with a 31% decrease in the odds of divorce"). In addition to the laws mentioned in the article, a few additional states today have laws concerning pre-marital education. South Carolina provides a $50 state tax credit to couples who complete at least six hours of pre-marital counseling. S.C. Code Ann. §20-1-230. Texas and Wisconsin chose simply to exhort marrying couples. Tex. Fam. Code Ann. §2.013(a) ("Each person applying for a marriage license is encouraged to attend a premarital education course of at least eight hours during the year preceding the date of the application for the license."); Wis. Stat. §765.001(2) ("The seriousness of marriage makes adequate premarital counseling and education for family living highly desirable and courses thereon are urged upon all persons contemplating marriage."). A few states require pre-marital counseling for minors. E.g., Cal. Fam. Code §304; Utah Code Ann. §30-1-9.

There has been little opposition to legislation that simply creates a small financial incentive (waiver of license fee) to obtaining pre-marital education or counseling.

Who would oppose legislation *mandating* pre-marital education? Are those people likely to be of a substantial number? If not, why have so many legislative proposals to that end failed? As an intermediate alternative, states could increase the financial incentive, perhaps even pay couples for attending marriage preparation classes, in addition to waiving or reimbursing their marriage license fee. Would that be cost-effective for the state?

Opposition to legislative proposals for Covenant Marriage has been much greater, even though such laws simply give marrying couples an option to make a stronger commitment. When they apply for a marriage license, they are offered a choice: Covenant Marriage or regular old marriage. Is it coercive to present that choice to couples? The fact that only a tiny percentage of people in states that have Covenant Marriage choose it suggests that it is not coercive. What choice would you make?

2. *Pre-Nuptial Agreements*

Another antidote to runaway hormones and romance is to get lawyers involved in the wedding preparations. The history of the law's treatment of pre-marital agreements in the Anglo-American tradition reflects changes over time in the nature of marriage more broadly, which according to the standard account was from an origin as a contract between families to a church- or state-imposed status and in modern times back to contract. Originally, of course, there was neither contract nor marriage status; in the pre-civilized world, people simply coupled to have sex and make babies, without ceremony or official recognition. At some point in every civilization, though, when people began to accumulate wealth that could be passed on to descendants, wealthier families began to take a more formal and deliberate approach to the mating of the young. Parents would arrange, or at least approve, a marriage and negotiate an agreement over how much wealth each would pass on to the couple and what would happen to the couple's wealth in case of death, infertility, etc. In much of the world, especially in Muslim societies, such marriages grounded in a negotiated contract between sets of parents have been the norm ever since. See Nathan B. Oman, *How to Judge Shari'a Contracts: A Guide to Islamic Marriage Agreements in American Courts,* 2011 Utah L. Rev. 287, 307.

But the history of marriage followed a different path in the West.

Joseph A. Pull, Questioning the Fundamental Right to Marry

90 Marq. L. Rev. 21, 68-74 (2006)

. . . In Roman times, the state established a few marital eligibility rules (citizens needed permission to marry a foreigner and "could not marry slaves or prostitutes") but other than that "did not get involved in ratifying marriage or divorce." . . . As the Catholic Church gained ascendance in Europe, both as belief system and as agent exercising social control, it sought ways to enforce its teachings on sexuality and marriage. . . . Marriage, which alone legitimated sexual activity, was considered a sacrament, and divorce was prohibited. Eventually, the canon law was considered "the one universal law of the West," and the Church enforced it upon all persons.

Such a regime required clear rules about entry into marriage. Church doctrine declared mutual consent between a man and a woman sufficient to create a marriage.

This, however, created problems. Individuals could, and did, marry clandestinely. These secret marriages could be disclaimed by one spouse against the wishes of the other; conversely, an individual could falsely claim he or she had secretly married another, thus potentially marrying that person against his or her will. Once marriage was established in the eyes of the Church, it was permanent—and carried heavy consequences for almost every aspect of one's life. These consequences included strictly differentiated domestic sex roles; the man was required to be the husband/provider/legal representative of the marriage unit, while the woman was required to be a wife/dependant/domestic worker without separate legal personality. Additionally, the two members of the couple were considered to merge into a single legal person, represented in the person of the husband. The wife lost all legal identity.

Evidentiary problems in evaluating claims of marriage, the loss of control over the descent of property caused by children marrying without their parent's knowledge, and the desire to prevent individuals from secretly marrying and divorcing pushed the Church to find a way of controlling marriage. It began formally licensing marriages and requiring public marriage ceremonies as an attempt to cut down on secret marriages. Thus, when popular-marriage did not conform marital and sexual behavior to Church expectations (the Church's natural-law-marriage), the Church created legal-marriage to regulate personal-marriage behavior.

As secular governments became increasingly powerful, they began to compete with the Church for control over marriage. The Protestant Reformation allowed governments in Protestant areas to take charge of marriage licensing because, unlike Catholic teaching, Protestant theology did not consider marriage a sacrament, and thus did not consider direct church control of legal-marriage necessary or desirable. Though regulation of marriage began shifting from church to state, religious doctrine still shaped the substantive content of marriage regulation. Protestant political units sought to "tame" sexuality and prevent people from marrying merely out of sexual desire. . . .

This is the context in which marriage regulation was initially exported to the English colonies in North America: the government exercised marital controls based on a Christian view of marriage and morality. However, by the time of American independence, the Christian moral-behavior justification for legal-marriage began to be supplemented in the United States with another view of the purpose of legal-marriage: creating virtuous republican citizens through virtuous republican families centered on virtuous republican marriages. As the new nation launched into the 1800s, the republic-shaping view of marriage was in turn challenged by Enlightenment-inspired individualism and the growing belief in free contract principles, both of which argued against expansive state regulation of marriage. This individualist enthusiasm caused a contraction in public regulation of marriage on all levels (family, community, and state) during the first half of the nineteenth century, with private contracting and dispute resolution in courts filling the void left by the retreating state. As a result, informal marriages flourished. The courts responded by developing the doctrine of common-law marriage.

During this period, as the republic-shaping view and then the private-contract view of marriage held ascendance, legal-marriage (and popular-marriage) began to slowly, almost imperceptibly, separate from their theoretical foundation on Christian natural-law-marriage. The republic-shaping view of marriage had social-instrumental underpinnings, and the private-contract view was based on notions of individual consent alone. However, inertia kept the substantive content of the marriage regulation mostly static, even when a sense of family crisis prompted re-regulation of marriage following the Civil War.

The return of state legislatures to marriage in the last half of the nineteenth century forced courts to decide cases which pitted old common-law marriage rules against new statutes. The new statutes required that personal-marriages be solemnized by certain formalities in order for them to qualify as legal-marriages, but these formalities were often ignored by couples. Upon the death of a property-holder, disputes could arise over the estate, with one side claiming the existence of a valid legal-marriage and the other saying the formalities had not been observed so the marriage could not be given legal effect in probate. The responses of judges to such controversies illustrated the uncertainty surrounding the nature of legal-marriage, for they often ignored the unambiguous command of the statutes in favor of the common law.

Ebb and flow of the extent of marriage regulation aside, the now-entrenched non-religious theories behind legal-marriage (the social-instrumental view and the private consent view) made it possible for states to begin changing the boundaries of legal-marriage in ways contrary to religious teachings, most notably in easing access to divorce. While marriage rhetoric remained Christian (public figures spoke of marriage as a self-existent, traditional institution), underneath its rhetorical surface legal-marriage was abandoning the boundaries of religious natural-law-marriage for boundaries defined by popular preferences.

As the 1900s began, the abandonment of the traditional natural-law-marriage template was reinforced and speeded by industrialization and new ideals about the status of women, who entered the workforce on a large scale and sought treatment as coequals with men. The increasing independence of women brought the former political citizenship nature of marriage into question, for now all persons had a direct relationship with the state regardless of marital status. . . . The gradual (theoretical) general rejection of laws intended solely to enforce moral values changed legal-marriage by rendering its original justification—moral coercion—illegitimate. By the 1920s, Christian sexual mores were also slowly being discarded, and the legal-marriage monopoly on socially acceptable sexual activity was broken. . . .

The process of dismantling state regulation of sexuality was slow, however. Court decisions continued to reaffirm state power to regulate sexual activity for decades after common practice had embraced extramarital sexuality. And the growth of the administrative state during the Depression and following World War II saw marriage revived as a convenient tool for government economic treatment of the family. In the 1960s, though, the effects of the social change began to be felt in law. The "Enlightenment contractarian model" of marriage was "implemented legally." The Supreme Court began to strike down government attempts to regulate individual sexual and marital behavior, proclaiming individual liberty to live a life of one's own choosing.

With its skeleton of sex roles rejected, its monopoly on sexuality broken, and its religious justification discarded, marriage was loudly questioned in the 1970s. Still, out of habit (and, for some, a lingering belief in natural-law-marriage) people continued to enter into legal-marriage. The marriage shell began to be filled by a new popular-marriage, which redefined legal-marriage in solely personal terms—privacy, personal fulfillment, and autonomy[—an] institution whose shape and meaning is determined by each individual in terms of his or her personal preferences. . . .

Important additional parts of the story are charity and divorce. The Church was once the principle source of aid to persons unable to support themselves, but in the modern era that role has been taken over by the state. The Church did not allow divorce, but the secular post-Enlightenment state did, at first in a very limited way and more recently in a very liberal way. Because many people could be left destitute after divorce, the state had an interest in minimizing the likelihood of divorce and in imposing rules for marriage dissolution, especially regarding ownership of property and ongoing support, so as to minimize the financial burden on the state. Greater appreciation for women's contribution to acquisition of family wealth added a fairness rationale for legal imposition of special rules for marriage, deviations from the norms of title-based ownership, and of non-obligation for the needs of unrelated persons. Marriage as "status" is a role in society with such state-imposed rules for behavior and property management during marriage and for property ownership and ongoing support after divorce.

Because of the public policies motivating the state to control marriage and exit from it, the law in most U.S. states up through the mid-twentieth century was hostile to pre-nuptial agreements. Public officials believed a practice of negotiating such agreements prior to marriage would encourage people to enter this status thinking about divorce. They also thought people should not be able to thwart the policies underlying the default rules for property distribution and spousal support by contracting for different rules. But the dramatic liberalizing of private life in the '60s and '70s, and the increasingly individualistic and hedonic outlook of Americans, ultimately led to judicial acceptance of and willingness to enforce pre-marital agreements.

Today state codes across the country authorize pre-nuptial agreements and courts are quite deferential to them, at least as to those aspects of them dealing with financial matters upon divorce. Most apply general rules of contract enforcement. For policy reasons, courts are less deferential toward, and in some states will simply ignore, any provisions dealing with conduct during the marriage (e.g., "the parties agree to have sex at least once a week" or "wife agrees to keep herself in good physical shape") and any provisions dealing with custody or support of children following divorce (because the state does not want to support children and because children are now viewed as separate persons entitled to some protection of their welfare).

Even with respect to financial aspects of an agreement, though, courts in some states will scrutinize the circumstances of contracting and even the content of agreements somewhat more rigorously than they would with a commercial contract, out of concern for exploitation of a weaker party entering the marriage and for post-divorce dependency. Is such paternalism defensible? England and Ireland still take the position that pre-nuptial agreements are not enforceable per se, though the U.K. Supreme Court ruled in 2010 that courts may, in "appropriate cases" and when it would not "operate unfairly," give such agreements "compelling weight" in deciding upon a fair distribution of marital property upon divorce. Katrin Radmacher v. Nicolas Granatino, [2010] UKSC 42.

Brian Bix, Bargaining in the Shadow of Love: The Enforcement of Premarital Agreements and How We Think About Marriage

40 Wm. & Mary L. Rev. 145 (1998)

. . . One commentator has stated that "[t]he purpose and effect of most premarital agreements is to protect the wealth and earnings of an economically superior spouse from being shared with an economically inferior spouse." . . . Other possible purposes of such agreements include: (1) ensuring that children from a prior marriage retain certain family wealth, despite possible claims by the new spouse; (2) assuring the economically weaker spouse-to-be that he or she will have adequate economic protection after divorce; (3) attempting to make any eventual divorce simpler and less contentious; and (4) assuring that certain family heirlooms or family wealth stay within a family upon divorce. . . .

[T]he most recent restatement of contract law continues to declare: "A promise that tends unreasonably to encourage divorce or separation is unenforceable on grounds of public policy." . . . Current applications of the Restatement rule seem to emphasize the "unreasonably" part rather than the "encourage . . . separation" part, with most courts concluding, if they reach the question at all, that premarital agreements do not encourage separation "unreasonably." Agreements in reported cases that one might characterize as "unreasonably encouraging divorce" still appear, but they are few and far between. One such agreement in California contained unusually generous terms; it promised the previously destitute spouse a house and at least half a million dollars upon divorce. Perhaps not surprisingly, the marriage ended after only seven months. The wife sued for divorce, but the California Court of Appeals refused to enforce the agreement. The court stated that the wife had been "encouraged by the very terms of the agreement to seek a dissolution, and with all deliberate speed, lest the husband suffer an untimely demise, nullifying the contract and the wife's right to the money and property." . . . [C]ourts historically treated death-focused premarital agreements somewhat differently. These . . . did not give either party an incentive to divorce. . . .

In . . . the 1970s and early 1980s, the public policy argument began to lose its persuasiveness. . . .[28] Some might argue that the "normal," deferential enforcement of premarital contracts [today] reflects the "current reality" of marriage in some parts of America-that marriage is less a commitment for life, and more a kind of serial monogamy. . . . The image of marriage . . . is one of an institution subject to substantial private ordering, and one which people enter realizing that it may very well not be "until death." . . . Some people . . . deny that marriage is, or should be, about anything other than love or the desire to raise a family. Other people have a tendency to deny that marriage is about anything other than maximizing utility, or the like. The prosaic facts likely are: (1) that most marriages have . . . elements of each (e.g., that a partner can offer security may be part of his or her "romantic" allure); and (2) that the mixture of the romantic and the practical/economical likely will vary not only from generation to generation, but also at any given time from one marriage to the next, and even within a single marriage as the partners' perceptions, needs, and values evolve. . . .

Most people, though, want the law to stop short of purely private ordering in all matters all of the time, whether because they think "market failure" is pervasive, or because they believe that there are social interests or interests in justice and fairness that occasionally or frequently trump autonomy and individual gain. . . . One hypothetical situation that tests the contractual/libertarian approach involves a couple in which one person, for some reason, refuses to get married without a premarital agreement. . . . [A]ssume that the person insists upon an unreasonable one-sided agreement. The other party, though

28. Some might argue that the push toward writing and enforcing premarital agreements also came from another direction: the willingness of courts to award large sums to partners in long-term cohabitation relationships, under theories of express contract, implied contract, unjust enrichment, and the like. Such awards meant that the rich could not assume that they could avoid having to give large portions of their property to their current domestic partners simply by not getting married. Marriage, but with a premarital agreement, became one obvious alternative.

unhappy about the agreement, would rather be married with the agreement than not married without the agreement. Does society tell this couple that it will not give them the option of being married with an enforceable agreement, even though that would be their preference? . . .

One also can ask the question from the other side: What is the interest couples have in being married if they are able to shape their relationship as they wish when they remain unmarried? . . . Many individuals . . . clearly seem to want marriage for its own sake, beyond whatever monetary or "practical" benefits may come from that status and beyond simple questions of family or community approval. Part of the value of marriage is the public commitment involved and the community support that mobilizes to support the marriage relationship. Even beyond that, marriage has a positive social meaning and an attractiveness as an institution. . . .

[P]remarital agreements might seem less problematic if there were a "sunset provision" that ended the effectiveness of some or all of the agreement's provisions once the marriage lasted a certain number of years or once children were born. Legislation could implement such a provision, though of course the parties themselves would be free to insert such terms within an agreement. Sunset provisions offer a compromise between the interest in private ordering and concerns about rationality—concerns which grow the longer a couple is married and the more their lives change—and between the interest in private ordering and the state interest that parties not be left destitute at the end of a long marriage. Like escalator clauses within premarital agreements, [i.e., clauses providing that post-separation alimony will be greater the longer the marriage lasted] sunset provisions might create unfortunate incentives for parties otherwise uncertain about their marital future to act decisively for divorce before the rights under the contract expire or change. It is possible, however, that courts could mitigate this problem by using a "good faith" requirement and not giving full contractual effect to terminations timed for such reasons.

. . . There are particular situations and circumstances in which parties are particularly unlikely to act in a rational way, and the law—especially contract law—should respond to that reality. . . . [E]ven those who are well educated in such matters, e.g., law students in a family law course, carry an unduly optimistic view about the chances that their marriage will last. More general studies in psychology have confirmed that people tend to evaluate causal theories in a self-serving manner; though people may know that 50% of marriages end in divorce, they convince themselves—with little grounding for their conclusions—that they have characteristics that will put them in the portion that will endure. People who assume that they will not divorce will not work hard to establish a fair deal contingent on divorce occurring, just as parties do not bargain hard for reasonable terms on the failure of installment payments, as they do not expect to ever fail in their payments. Additionally, parties may have some sense of the consequences of failure one year from now, but it may be harder to foresee . . . consequences of failure 15 years from now—after one or both partners have made sacrifices in their careers and perhaps after children have been born.

Robert Nozick argued that one criterion of being in love is the belief that it—both the feeling and the relationship underlying it—will go on forever. If one thinks that it will end in a few weeks—or even a few years—then one is not in love. . . . [P]eople know divorce is not rare, but keeping a pragmatic eye on things—here, on the likelihood of failure—seems just the type of attitude that may make failure more likely. The other problem . . . is that the issue is whether the parties have consented to a change in the standard rules that apply to parties during marriage or upon divorce, and it is far from clear that most people entering a marriage ever knew of those rules from the beginning. . . . "In terms of nondisclosure of its legal effects, marriage may be the ultimate consumer fraud on unsuspecting innocents acting in an emotional fog." . . .

Requiring each party to consult with an independent lawyer for premarital agreements to be enforceable may partly solve [the rationality] problem. . . . [Another] option is to force couples about to marry to choose from a menu of options. This likely would have the similar effect of forcing parties to think through matters they otherwise might have been less willing or less able to address. It also would remove the "signaling" problem—the situation in which a party decides not to present a premarital agreement, even though the agreement is reasonable given the couple's circumstances—because the act of presenting an agreement may make the presenter appear to be saying that he or she does not think the marriage will last. . . . [Another] possibility is to treat premarital agreements as some courts treat restrictive covenants in employment agreements. . . . In some jurisdictions, when a court finds a restrictive covenant unreasonable—e.g., limiting employment for too long a period of time, or over too broad a geographical area—the court will not void the provision entirely, but will "blue pencil" it. This method enforces the provision to the extent reasonable—that is, to the extent necessary to protect the legitimate interests of the employer, taking into account the interests of the employee and the public. . . .

[T]he court in *Simeone* argued that the standard of the fairness approach, allowing enforcement of premarital agreements only if substantive and procedural fairness were proven, reflected a paternalistic attitude toward women that had lost justification. . . . As one commentator summarized . . . : "Is it possible to protect women from the oppressive consequences of harmful, constrained choices . . . without divesting women of agency?" . . . [But] one should consider the argument by Robin West that women, by nature, may be more likely to accede to authority or to enter masochistic situations. Also, some have argued that women are disadvantaged in general by bargaining, whether in negotiating contracts or in mediation processes, as they are by nature or socialization less selfish and less self-centered.

A more common . . . proposition [is] that courts should continue or strengthen the requirements of substantive and procedural fairness because the actual effect of neutral, nonintrusive rules would be to impoverish women, who tend to be the poorer parties being asked to waive their rights in such agreements. . . . Anecdotally or stereotypically, it is the woman who more often wants the commitment of marriage while the man resists—and thus, . . . it would be the woman more often than the man who would be willing to waive rights to enter into marriage . . . Additionally, one must consider the now-standard argument that rules or standards meant to protect weaker parties by allowing them to avoid contractual obligations . . . makes it harder for them to enter agreements they want to enter because other parties will refuse to enter agreements with members of the group when they know that the members of the group can avoid enforcement. . . .

How might a pre-marital agreement encourage divorce? Is it possible to draft a pre-marital agreement that would *lessen* likelihood of divorce? Could any provision discourage *both* parties from divorcing at any given time, or does what discourages one party inevitably encourage the other? Professor Bix notes a concern that a sunset provision will cause a spouse to pull the divorce trigger sooner than he or she would otherwise, but for a spouse who will be in a better position after the sunset, the provision has the opposite effect; it creates an incentive to stay in at least that long and thus possibly delaying such a decision.

Remember that, absent an agreement, default rules apply. When you study those rules, you should think about whether and how they encourage or discourage divorce. If the default divorce rules would make one spouse better off financially than he or she is in the marriage, presumably that creates an incentive to divorce.

Bix suggests a reform that could largely obviate pre-nups: Offer marrying couples a varied menu of default rules for financial aspects of marriage and divorce, as Alaska and several European governments do. The Catalan Family Code, for example, offers six different property regimes from which marrying couples should choose. One choice resembles the old common-law property system that once prevailed in the United States, under which whoever held title to an asset would keep it after divorce. Another is like the modern common-law property system, with equitable division at divorce of assets acquired during marriage by effort, regardless of title. And another is like the community property regime that operates in nine U.S. states, with joint ownership arising during marriage for assets acquired by effort of either spouse. We will study those systems in Chapters 3 and 6. The other three choices in Catalonia present variations on joint versus separate ownership and on management of property during the marriage and at the time of divorce. What advantages might a menu approach have? Is there any downside?

In most jurisdictions that have such a menu, it is combined with a rule permitting couples to draft an entirely individualized pre-marital agreement; the menu is a convenience, simply making available more than one package of rules that couples can adopt instead of incurring the costs of individualized negotiations. Switzerland represents an intermediate position between that approach and a regime in which there is only one set of rules and parties may not contract around them. Swiss law offers couples three marital regimes and treats any individualized agreements as non-binding. Is that the best balance of choice, on the one hand, and judicial economy and fairness on the other?

Bix notes that over half of U.S. states have adopted the Uniform Premarital Agreement Act (UPAA), though many have tweaked the model to suit their own policy choices. Provisions as to which matters may be included in an agreement are largely the same for all UPAA states, but many states have modified the UPAA's enforceability test to match their own judgment about whether and when procedural or substantive fairness should matter. Connecticut is at one end of the enforceability spectrum, creating several independent grounds for setting aside an agreement:

Connecticut General Statutes
Title 46B. Family Law
Chapter 815E. Marriage

§46B-36C. Form of Premarital Agreement

A premarital agreement shall be in writing and signed by both parties. It shall be enforceable without consideration.

§46B-36D. Content of Premarital Agreement

(a) Parties to a premarital agreement may contract with respect to:

(1) The rights and obligations of each of the parties in any of the property of either or both of them whenever and wherever acquired or located;

(2) The right to buy, sell, use, transfer, exchange, abandon, lease, consume, expend, assign, create a security interest in, mortgage, encumber, dispose of, or otherwise manage and control property;

(3) The disposition of property upon separation, marital dissolution, death, or the occurrence or nonoccurrence of any other event;

(4) The modification or elimination of spousal support;

(5) The making of a will, trust or other arrangement . . . ;

(6) The ownership rights in and disposition of the death benefit from a life insurance policy;

(7) The right of either party as a participant or participant's spouse under a retirement plan;

(8) The choice of law governing the construction of the agreement; and

(9) Any other matter, including their personal rights and obligations.

(b) No provision made under subdivisions (1) to (9), inclusive, of subsection (a) of this section may be in violation of public policy or of a statute imposing a criminal penalty.

(c) The right of a child to support may not be adversely affected by a premarital agreement. Any provision relating to the care, custody and visitation or other provisions affecting a child shall be subject to judicial review and modification.

§46B-36G. Enforcement of Premarital Agreement

(a) A premarital agreement or amendment shall not be enforceable if the party against whom enforcement is sought proves that:

(1) Such party did not execute the agreement voluntarily; or

(2) The agreement was unconscionable when it was executed or when enforcement is sought; or

(3) Before execution of the agreement, such party was not provided a fair and reasonable disclosure of the amount, character and value of property, financial obligations and income of the other party; or

(4) Such party was not afforded a reasonable opportunity to consult with independent counsel.

(b) If a provision of a premarital agreement modifies or eliminates spousal support and such modification or elimination causes one party to the agreement to be eligible for support under a program of public assistance at the time of separation or marital dissolution, a court, notwithstanding the terms of the agreement, may require the other party to provide support to the extent necessary to avoid such eligibility.

(c) An issue of unconscionability of a premarital agreement shall be decided by the court as a matter of law.

Similarly, Massachusetts law requires that an agreement be "fair and reasonable," both at the time of execution, in light of circumstances then, and at the time of divorce, in light of circumstances at that time, though the Massachusetts Supreme Court has interpreted "fair and reasonable" to mean simply that a dependent spouse is not "essentially stripped of substantially all marital interests" or left unable "to support herself." See Austin v. Austin, 839 N.E.2d 837 (2005).

The California law that controlled when San Francisco Giants baseball star Barry Bonds divorced, on the other hand, was highly protective of pre-marital agreements, and emphasized the voluntariness of signing rather than substantive fairness.

In re Marriage of Susann Margreth Bonds & Barry Lamar Bonds

99 Cal. Rptr. 2d 252 (Cal. 2000)

George, C.J.

In this case we consider whether appellant Susann (known as Sun) Margreth Bonds voluntarily entered into a premarital agreement with respondent Barry Lamar Bonds. . . .

Sun and Barry met in Montreal in the summer of 1987 and maintained a relationship during ensuing months through telephone contacts. In October 1987, at Barry's invitation, Sun visited him for 10 days at his home in Phoenix, Arizona. In November 1987, Sun moved to Phoenix to take up residence with Barry and, one week later, the two became engaged to be married. In January 1988, they decided to marry before the commencement of professional baseball's spring training. On February 5, 1988, in Phoenix, the parties entered into a written premarital agreement in which each party waived any interest in the earnings and acquisitions of the other party during marriage.[1] That same day, they flew to Las Vegas, and were married the following day.

Each of the parties then was 23 years of age. Barry, who had attended college for three years and who had begun his career in professional baseball in 1985, had a contract to play for the Pittsburgh Pirates. His annual salary at the time of the marriage ceremony was approximately $106,000. Sun had emigrated to Canada from Sweden in 1985, had worked as a waitress and bartender, and had undertaken some training as a cosmetologist, having expressed an interest in embarking upon a career as a makeup artist for celebrity clients. Although her native language was Swedish, she had used both French and English in her employment, education, and personal relationships when she lived in Canada. She was unemployed at the time she entered into the premarital agreement.

Barry petitioned for legal separation on May 27, 1994. . . . Sun requested custody of the parties' two children, then three and four years of age. In addition, she sought child and spousal support, attorney fees, and a determination of property rights. . . . Child support was awarded in the amount of $10,000 per month per child. Spousal support was awarded in the amount of $10,000 per month, to terminate December 30, 1998. . . .

Barry testified that he was aware of teammates and other persons who had undergone bitter marital dissolution proceedings involving the division of property, and recalled that from the beginning of his relationship with Sun he told her that he believed his earnings and acquisitions during marriage should be his own. He informed her he would not marry without a premarital agreement, and she had no objection. He also recalled that from the beginning of the relationship, Sun agreed that their earnings and acquisitions should be separate, saying "what's mine is mine, what's yours is yours." Indeed, she informed him that this was the practice with respect to marital property in Sweden. She stated that she

1. Primarily at issue is paragraph 10 of the agreement, which provided, in pertinent part, as follows: "Control and Earnings of Both Husband and Wife During Marriage. We agree that all the earnings and accumulations resulting from the other's personal services, skill, efforts and work, together with all property acquired with funds and income derived therefrom, shall be the separate property of that spouse. [¶] The earnings from husband and wife during marriage shall be: [¶] separate property of that spouse." The agreement also contained provisions concerning support obligations and the disposition of property upon dissolution of the marriage, including a proviso that "Each of us shall receive free and clear of all claim of the other spouse that property which was the separate property of each spouse prior to marriage . . . and as may be later acquired as separate property."

planned to pursue a career and wished to be financially independent. Sun knew that Barry did not anticipate that she would shoulder her living expenses while she was not employed. She was not, in fact, employed during the marriage. Barry testified that he and Sun had no difficulty communicating. . . .

Sun . . . testified that her English language skills in 1987 and 1988 were limited. Out of pride, she did not disclose to Barry that she often did not understand him. She testified that she and Barry never discussed money or property during the relationship that preceded their marriage. She agreed that she had expressed interest in a career as a cosmetologist and had said she wished to be financially independent. She had very few assets when she took up residence with Barry, and he paid for all their needs. Their wedding arrangements were very informal, with no written invitations or caterer, and only Barry's parents and a couple of friends, including Barry's godfather Willie Mays, were invited to attend. No marriage license or venue had been arranged in advance of their arrival in Las Vegas. . . .

Sun testified that on the evening before the premarital agreement was signed, Barry first informed her that they needed to go the following day to the offices of his lawyers, Leonard Brown and his associate Sabinus Megwa. She was uncertain, however, whether Barry made any reference to a premarital agreement. She testified that only at the parking lot of the law office where the agreement was to be entered into did she learn, from Barry's financial adviser, Mel Wilcox, that Barry would not marry her unless she signed a premarital agreement. She was not upset. She was surprised, however. . . . She did not question Barry or anyone else on this point. She was under the impression that Barry wished to retain separate ownership of property he owned before the marriage, and that this was the sole object of the premarital agreement. She was unaware the agreement would affect her future and was not concerned about the matter, because she was nervous and excited about getting married and trusted Barry. Wilcox's statement had little effect on her, because she had no question but that she and Barry were to be married the following day.

Sun recalled having to hurry to arrive at the lawyers' office in time both to accomplish their business there and make the scheduled departure of the airplane to Las Vegas so that she and Barry could marry the next day. Sun recalled that once they arrived at the lawyers' office on February 5, 1988, she, her friend Margareta Forsberg, Barry, and Barry's financial adviser Mel Wilcox were present in a conference room. She did not recall asking questions or her friend asking questions, nor did she recall that any changes were made to the agreement. She declared that her English language skills were limited at the time and she did not understand the agreement, but she did not ask questions of anyone other than Margareta Forsberg or ask for more time, because she did not want to miss her flight and she was focused on the forthcoming marriage ceremony. She did not believe that Barry understood the agreement either. Forsberg was unable to assist her. Sun did not recall the lawyers telling her that she should retain her own lawyer, that they were representing Barry and not her, that the applicable community property law provided that a spouse has an interest in the earnings and in acquisitions of the other spouse during marriage, or that she would be waiving this right if she signed the agreement. The lawyers may have mentioned the possibility of her being represented by her own lawyer, but she did not believe she needed one. She did not inform anyone at the meeting that she was concerned about the agreement; the meeting and discussion were not cut short, and no one forced her to sign the agreement.

Forsberg, a native of Sweden and 51 years of age at the time the agreement was signed, confirmed that . . . she had been unable to answer Sun's questions or explain to Sun the terminology used in the agreement. She confirmed that Sun's English was limited, that the lawyers had explained the agreement, and that Sun never stated that she was considering not signing the agreement, that she did not understand it, or that she was not signing of her own free will. Sun never said that Barry threatened her or forced her to sign, that she wanted to consult independent counsel concerning the agreement, or that she felt pressured. Forsberg understood that Brown and Megwa were Barry's attorneys, not Sun's. She testified that when the attorneys explained the agreement, she did not recall any discussion of Sun's community property rights. . . .

Barry and his attorney, Brown, recalled that approximately two weeks before the parties signed the formal agreement, they discussed with Sun the drafting of an agreement to keep earnings and acquisitions separate. Brown testified that he told Sun at this meeting that he represented Barry and that it might be in her best interest to obtain independent counsel. Barry, Brown, and Megwa testified that Wilcox was not present at the February 5, 1988, meeting, which lasted between one and two hours, and that at the meeting the attorneys informed Sun of her right to independent counsel. All three recalled that Sun stated she did not want her own counsel, and Megwa recalled explaining that he and Brown did not represent her. Additionally, all three recalled that the attorneys read the agreement to her paragraph by paragraph and explained it as they went through it, also informing her of a spouse's basic community property rights in earnings and acquisitions and that Sun would be waiving these rights. Megwa recalled it was clearly explained that Barry's income and acquisitions during the marriage would remain Barry's separate property, and he recalled that Sun stated that such arrangements were the practice in Sweden.

Furthermore, Barry and the two attorneys each confirmed that Sun and Forsberg asked questions during the meeting and were left alone on several occasions to discuss its terms, that Sun did not exhibit any confusion, and that Sun indicated she understood the agreement. They also testified that changes were made to the agreement at Sun's behest. Brown and Megwa experienced no difficulty in communicating with Sun, found her confident and happy, and had no indication that she was nervous or confused, intimidated, or pressured. No threat was uttered that unless she signed the agreement, the wedding would be cancelled, nor did they hear her express any reservations about signing the agreement. Additionally, legal secretary Illa Washington recalled that Wilcox waited in another room while the agreement was discussed, that Sun asked questions and that changes were made to the agreement at her behest, that Sun was informed she could secure independent counsel, that Sun said she understood the contract and did not want to consult another attorney, and that she appeared to understand the discussions and to feel comfortable and confident.

The trial court observed that the case turned upon the credibility of the witnesses. In support of its determination that Sun entered into the agreement voluntarily, "free from the taint of fraud, coercion and undue influence . . . with full knowledge of the property involved and her rights therein," the trial court made the following findings of fact: ". . . Respondent was not forced to execute the document, nor did anyone threaten Respondent in any way. . . . Respondent's refusal to sign the Agreement would have caused little embarrassment to her. The wedding was a small impromptu affair that could have been easily postponed. . . . Petitioner fully disclosed the nature, approximate value and extent of all of his assets to Petitioner, both prior to and on the day of the execution of the agreement. Respondent had sufficient knowledge and understanding of her rights regarding the property affected by the Agreement, and how the Agreement adversely affected those rights. Respondent had the opportunity to read the Agreement prior to executing it. . . . Respondent also had an adequate and reasonable opportunity to obtain independent counsel prior to execution of the Agreement. . . ."

II

From the inception of its statehood, California has retained the community property law that predated its admission to the Union and consistently has provided as a general rule that property acquired by spouses during marriage, including earnings, is community property. At the same time, applicable statutes recognized the power of parties contemplating a marriage to reach an agreement containing terms at variance with community property law. . . . In California, a premarital agreement generally has been considered to be enforceable as a contract, although when there is proof of fraud, constructive fraud, duress, or undue influence, the contract is not enforceable.

At one time, a premarital agreement that was not made in contemplation that the parties would remain married until death was considered to be against public policy in California and other jurisdictions, but this court concluded in 1976 that the validity of a premarital agreement "does not turn on whether the parties contemplated a lifelong marriage." . . . In order to encourage enforcement of such agreements on a more certain and uniform basis, . . . the Uniform Premarital Agreement Act was promulgated in 1983. . . . The only provisions of the Uniform Act omitted by the California Legislature were those permitting the parties to waive the right to spousal support and limiting the right to waive spousal support where such a waiver would result in a spouse's becoming a public charge. . . .

Section 1615 of the Family Code, like section 6 of the Uniform Act, regulates the enforceability of such agreements. It provides in pertinent part:

> (a) A premarital agreement is not enforceable if the party against whom enforcement is sought proves either of the following:
>
> (1) That party did not execute the agreement voluntarily.
>
> (2) The agreement was unconscionable when it was executed and, before execution of the agreement, all of the following applied to that party:
>
> (A) That party was not provided a fair and reasonable disclosure of the property or financial obligations of the other party.
>
> (B) That party did not voluntarily and expressly waive, in writing, any right to disclosure of the property or financial obligations of the other party beyond the disclosure provided.
>
> (C) That party did not have, or reasonably could not have had, an adequate knowledge of the property or financial obligations of the other party.

. . . In the present case, the trial court found no lack of knowledge regarding the nature of the parties' assets, a necessary predicate to considering the issue of unconscionability . . . We do not reconsider this factual determination, and thus the question of unconscionability is not before us. . . .

Neither the article of the Family Code in which section 1615 is located, nor the Uniform Act, defines the term "voluntarily." . . . *Black's Law Dictionary* defines "voluntarily" as "Done by design. . . . Intentionally and without coercion." The same source defines "voluntary" as "Proceeding from the free and unrestrained will of the person. Produced in or by an act of choice. Resulting from free choice, without compulsion or solicitation. The word, especially in statutes, often implies knowledge of essential facts." The *Oxford English Dictionary* defines "voluntarily" as "[o]f one's own free will or accord; without compulsion, constraint, or undue influence by others; freely, willingly." . . .

The debate that preceded the adoption of the Uniform Act indicated a basic disagreement between those commissioners at the National Conference of Commissioners on Uniform State Laws who placed the highest value on certainty in enforcement of premarital agreements and the vocal minority of commissioners who urged that such contracts routinely should be evaluated for substantive fairness at the time of enforcement. . . . [E]ventually it was settled that the party against whom enforcement of a premarital agreement was sought only could raise the issue of unconscionability, that is, the substantive unfairness of an agreement, if he or she also could demonstrate lack of disclosure of assets, lack of waiver of disclosure, *and* lack of imputed knowledge of assets. The language adopted was intended to *enhance* the enforceability of premarital agreements and to convey the sense that an agreement voluntarily entered into would be enforced without regard to the apparent unfairness of its terms, as long as the objecting party knew or should have known of the other party's assets, or voluntarily had waived disclosure. The commissioners, however, did not supply a definition of the term "voluntarily," nor was there much discussion of the term.

We find an indication of the commissioners' understanding of the term in their official comment to the enforcement provision of the Uniform Act, stating that the conditions to enforcement "are comparable to concepts which are expressed in the statutory and decisional law of many jurisdictions." In support of this statement, the comment cites cases from various jurisdictions examining the voluntariness of premarital agreements. . . . In the majority of these cases, . . . the question is viewed as one involving such ordinary contract defenses as fraud, undue influence, or duress, along with some examination of the parties' knowledge of the rights being waived, or at least knowledge of the intent of the agreement. . . . [The decisions] . . . direct consideration of the impact upon the parties of such factors as the coercion that may arise from the proximity of execution of the agreement to the wedding, or from surprise in the presentation of the agreement; the presence or absence of independent counsel or of an opportunity to consult independent counsel; inequality of bargaining power—in some cases indicated by the relative age and sophistication of the parties; whether there was full disclosure of assets; and the parties' understanding of the rights being waived under the agreement or at least their awareness of the intent of the agreement.

The . . . commissioners considered that the voluntariness of a premarital agreement may turn in part upon whether the agreement was entered into knowingly, in the sense that the parties understood the terms or basic effect of the agreement. A premarital agreement often contains at least some hallmarks of a waiver, in that it may bind a person to forgo important rights secured by community property law-rights that in the absence of an agreement would vest automatically upon marriage. . . . [M]ost frequently it is required that a waiver be entered into with knowledge of the effect of the agreement. Similarly, . . . the parties' general understanding of the effect of the agreement constitutes a factor for the court to consider. . . .

In sum, it is clear . . . that the commissioners intended that the party seeking to avoid a premarital agreement may prevail by establishing that the agreement was involuntary, and that evidence of lack of capacity, duress, fraud, and undue influence, as demonstrated by a number of factors uniquely probative of coercion in the premarital context, would be relevant in establishing the involuntariness of the agreement. . . . [T]he same intention safely may be attributed to the California Legislature, because an examination of the history of the enactment of Family Code section 1615 in California indicates that the Legislature adopted the views of the commissioners in all respects. . . .

Decisions interpreting the enforcement provision of the Uniform Act in other jurisdictions also refer to such factors as inequality of bargaining power, coercion arising from circumstances peculiar to an imminent wedding, the absence of independent counsel for one party, and the parties' knowledge of the purpose of the agreement. The factors we have identified also are in most respects consistent with recent non-Uniform Act cases in other jurisdictions that examine what often is termed the procedural fairness of premarital agreements.[10] These factors also are consistent with the circumstances previously considered in this state, prior to California's adoption of the Uniform Act, in connection with the issue of the voluntariness of a premarital agreement. In *In re Marriage of Dawley*, for example, we rejected the wife's claim that a premarital agreement waiving community property rights had been obtained through undue influence, pointing out that in the particular case the pressure to marry created by an unplanned pregnancy fell equally on both the parties, that both parties were educated and employed, and that the party challenging the agreement did not rely upon the other party's advice, but consulted her own attorney.

We . . . do not believe that the terms or history of section 1615 of the Family Code support the conclusion . . . that a premarital agreement should be subjected to strict scrutiny for voluntariness in the absence of independent counsel for the less sophisticated party or of an assertedly effective and knowing waiver of counsel comparable to that occurring in the criminal law setting (and potentially also requiring an offer by the represented party to pay for independent counsel for the other party). In the official comment to the Uniform Act, the commissioners stated: "Nothing in [the enforcement section] makes the absence of assistance of independent legal counsel a condition for the unenforceability of a premarital agreement. However, lack of that assistance may well be a factor in determining whether the conditions stated in [the section] may have existed." . . . [They added] . . . the comment that "the legislatures of the states ought [not] to be making the rights of people dependent upon whether or not they have lawyers," and the observation that such a rule would not reduce litigation but instead would transfer the litigation to malpractice actions. . . . [N]o state has made the presence of independent counsel a prerequisite to enforceability.

. . . Moreover, the overall purpose of the Uniform Act was to *enhance* the enforceability of premarital agreements. . . . When we also consider the circumstance that in a majority of dissolution cases in California at least one of the two parties apparently is not represented by counsel, it seems unlikely that our Legislature intended that the voluntariness of a premarital agreement should be subjected to strict scrutiny unless each party were represented by independent counsel or an unrepresented party had entered into a formal

10. See, for example, *In re Marriage of Spiegel, supra* (voluntariness depends in part upon an intentional relinquishment of a known right; the proximity of the wedding, a threat not to wed without an agreement, and embarrassment over the potential cancellation of the wedding do not constitute duress or undue influence, particularly because the party attacking the agreement was intelligent and educated and had the advice of independent counsel); *Lebeck v. Lebeck* (N.M. 1994) (shortness of time between agreement and wedding and desire of woman to marry to legitimize a child are not alone enough to establish involuntariness; wife failed to carry burden of proof of involuntariness in that she was 34 years of age, worked as a professional, had independent counsel, and understood the agreement, and the "threat" not to marry without the agreement does not constitute duress but is a legitimate objective); *Fick v. Fick* (Nev. 1993) (voluntariness depends upon the opportunity to consult independent counsel, the absence of coercion, the business acumen of the parties, the parties' awareness of each other's assets, and the parties' understanding regarding the rights being forfeited); *Lee v. Lee* (Ark. App. 1991) (although the wedding was soon to occur, there was no pressure to sign the agreement; husband's desire to maintain separate property had been discussed in advance; assets were disclosed, and the failure of the party challenging the agreement to read it before signing was no excuse); *Tiryakian v. Tiryakian* (N.C. App. 1988) (premarital agreement was involuntary because of proximity of wedding and because there was no disclosure of assets, no knowledge of the effect of the agreement, and no independent counsel).

knowing waiver of counsel comparable to that required in the criminal law setting. . . . Finally, [b]ecause the commissioners and our Legislature placed the burden of proof of involuntariness upon the party *challenging* a premarital agreement, it seems obvious that the party seeking enforcement should not be required to prove that the *absence* of any factor tending to establish voluntariness did *not* render the agreement involuntary. . . .

C

Although we agree with Barry that the lack of independent counsel for each party cannot alter the burden of proof that, by operation of statute, rests upon the party challenging the validity of the premarital agreement, we also agree with the Court of Appeal majority that considerations applicable in commercial contexts do not necessarily govern the determination whether a premarital agreement was entered into voluntarily. . . . Even apart from the circumstance that there is no statutory requirement that commercial contracts be entered into voluntarily as that term is used in Family Code section 1615, we observe some significant distinctions between the two types of contracts. A commercial contract most frequently constitutes a private regulatory agreement intended to ensure the successful outcome of the business between the contracting parties—in essence, to guide their relationship so that the object of the contract may be achieved. Normally, the execution of the contract ushers in the applicability of the regulatory scheme contemplated by the contract and the endeavor that is the object of the contract. As for a premarital agreement (or clause of such an agreement) providing solely for the division of property upon marital dissolution, the parties generally enter into the agreement anticipating that it never will be invoked, and the agreement, far from regulating the relationship of the contracting parties and providing the method for attaining their joint objectives, exists to provide for eventualities that will arise only if the relationship founders, possibly in the distant future under greatly changed and unforeseeable circumstances.

Furthermore, marriage itself is a highly regulated institution of undisputed social value, and there are many limitations on the ability of persons to contract with respect to it, or to vary its statutory terms, that have nothing to do with maximizing the satisfaction of the parties or carrying out their intent. Such limitations are inconsistent with the freedom-of-contract analysis espoused, for example, by the Pennsylvania Supreme Court. We refer to rules establishing a duty of mutual financial support during the marriage and prohibiting agreements in derogation of the duty to support a child of the marriage; the circumstance that a party may abandon the marriage unilaterally under this state's no-fault laws; and the pervasive state involvement in the dissolution of marital status, the marriage contract, and the arrangements to be made for the children of the marriage—even without consideration of the circumstance that marriage normally lacks a predominantly commercial object. We also observe that a premarital agreement to raise children in a particular religion is not enforceable. We note, too, that there is authority . . . to the effect that a contract to pay a spouse for personal services such as nursing cannot be enforced, despite the undoubted economic value of the services (see Silbaugh, *Marriage Contracts and the Family Economy* (1998) 93 N.W. U. L. Rev. 65, 123 [most jurisdictions will not enforce agreements with respect to personal services rendered during marriage]). These limitations demonstrate further that freedom of contract with respect to marital arrangements is tempered with statutory requirements and case law expressing social policy with respect to marriage.

There also are obvious differences between the remedies that realistically may be awarded with respect to commercial contracts and premarital agreements. Although a party seeking rescission of a commercial contract, for example, may be required to restore the status quo ante by restoring the consideration received, and a party in breach may be required to pay damages, the status quo ante for spouses cannot be restored to either party, nor are damages contemplated for breach of the marital contract. In any event, the suggestion that commercial contracts are strictly enforced without regard to the fairness or oppressiveness of the terms or the inequality of the bargaining power of the parties is anachronistic and inaccurate, in that claims such as duress, unconscionability, and undue influence turn upon the specific context in which the contract is formed. (See Bix, *Bargaining in the Shadow of Love: The Enforcement of Premarital Agreements and How We Think About Marriage* (1998) 40 Wm. & Mary L. Rev. 145)

We also have explained generally that we believe the reference to voluntariness in the Uniform Act was intended to convey an element of knowing waiver that is not a consistent feature of commercial contract enforcement. Further, . . . subtle coercion that would not be considered in challenges to ordinary commercial contracts may be considered in the context of the premarital agreement. (See, e.g., *Lutgert v. Lutgert,* [agreement presented too close to the wedding, with passage booked on an expensive cruise].) . . . The question of voluntariness must be examined in the unique context of the marital relationship.

On the other hand, we do not agree with Sun and the Court of Appeal majority that a *premarital* agreement should be interpreted and enforced under the same standards applicable to *marital* settlement agreements. First, although persons, once they are married, are in a fiduciary relationship to one another, so that whenever the parties enter into an agreement in which one party gains an advantage, the advantaged party bears the burden of demonstrating that the agreement was not obtained through undue influence, a different burden applies under the Uniform Act in the premarital setting. Even when the premarital agreement clearly advantages one of the parties, the party challenging the agreement bears the burden of demonstrating that the agreement was not entered into voluntarily. Further, under the Uniform Act, even when there has been a failure of disclosure, the statute still places the burden upon the party challenging the agreement to prove that the terms of the agreement were unconscionable when executed, rather than placing the burden on the advantaged party to demonstrate that the agreement was not unconscionable. . . .

California law also recognizes a lesser degree of confidential relationship that *may* arise, for example, between family members and between friends. In such cases "mere *lack of independent advice* is not sufficient to raise a presumption of undue influence or of constructive fraud, even when the consideration appears inadequate. But when to these factors is added some other such as great age, weakness of mind, sickness or other incapacity, the presumption arises, and the burden is on the other party to show that no oppression took place."[11]

. . . Although we certainly agree that persons contemplating marriage morally owe each other a duty of fair dealing and obviously are not embarking upon a purely commercial contract, we do not believe that these circumstances permit us to interpret our statute as

11. Under California law, even in the absence of a confidential or fiduciary relationship, a contract may be void if the person seeking relief proves undue influence. In such circumstances, the plaintiff must prove that the defendant took unfair advantage of the plaintiff's weakness of mind or "grossly oppressive and unfair advantage of another's necessities or distress." The court hearing such a claim will consider matters such as the substantial weakness of the person influenced or the excessive strength of the other party, taking into account factors such as the transaction having occurred at an unusual or inappropriate time or place, an insistent demand that the business be concluded immediately without recourse to independent advisers and an extreme emphasis on the negative consequences of delay, the concurrence of several persons in influencing the weaker party, and the absence of an independent adviser for that person.

imposing a *presumption* of undue influence or as requiring the kind of strict scrutiny that is conducted when a lawyer or other fiduciary engages in self-dealing. On the contrary, it is evident that the Uniform Act was intended to *enhance* the enforceability of premarital agreements, a goal that would be undermined by presuming the existence of a confidential or fiduciary relationship. . . .

Although community property law expresses a strong state interest in the equal division of property obtained during a marriage, so that any agreement in derogation of equal distribution should be subject to searching scrutiny for fairness, the substantive fairness of a premarital agreement is not open to examination unless the party objecting to enforcement meets the demands of Family Code section 1615, subdivision (a)(2). As explained above, with respect to division of property during marriage and upon dissolution of marriage, the Family Code provides that the parties stand in a confidential, fiduciary relationship to one another, but such a proviso does not appear in the California Uniform Act regulating premarital agreements. Marital settlement agreements must be preceded by rather elaborate disclosure of assets and liabilities, as well as income and expenses, and strict rules govern the waiver of disclosure. Such detailed requirements do not apply to premarital agreements. We are not persuaded that the policy of equal division of assets at the time of dissolution is intended to apply to premarital agreements. . . .

D

We do not believe that the case before us presents an appropriate occasion to delineate the duties that must guide an attorney in drafting a premarital agreement. . . . We do observe, however, that it is consistent with an attorney's duty to further the interest of his or her client for the attorney to take steps to ensure that the premarital agreement will be enforceable. After discussing the matter with his or her client, an attorney may convey such information to the other party as will assist in having the agreement upheld, as long as he or she does not violate the duty of loyalty to the client or undertake to represent both parties without an appropriate waiver of the conflict of interest. . . .

III

Finally, we conclude that the trial court's determination that Sun voluntarily entered into the premarital agreement in the present case is supported by substantial evidence. . . . Several witnesses, including Sun herself, stated that she was not threatened. The witnesses were unanimous in observing that Sun expressed no reluctance to sign the agreement, and they observed in addition that she appeared calm, happy, and confident as she participated in discussions of the agreement. Attorney Brown testified that Sun had indicated a desire at their first meeting to enter into the agreement, and that during the discussion preceding execution of the document, she stated that she understood the agreement. . . . [A]lthough the wedding between Sun and Barry was planned for the day following the signing of the agreement, the wedding was impromptu—the parties had not secured a license or a place to be married, and the few family members and close friends who were invited could have changed their plans without difficulty. (For example, guests were not arriving from Sweden.) In view of these circumstances, the evidence supported the inference, drawn by the trial court, that the coercive force of the normal desire to avoid social embarrassment or humiliation was diminished or absent.

Finally, Barry's testimony that the parties early in their relationship had discussed their desire to keep separate their property and earnings, in addition to the testimony of Barry and Brown that they had met with Sun at least one week before the document was signed to discuss the need for an agreement, and the evidence establishing that Sun understood and concurred in the agreement, constituted substantial evidence to support the trial court's conclusion that Sun was not subjected to the type of coercion that may arise from the surprise and confusion caused by a last-minute presentation of a new plan to keep earnings and property separate during marriage. . . .

[A]lthough Sun lacked legal counsel, . . . she . . . had sufficient awareness and understanding of her right to, and need for, independent counsel [and] an adequate and reasonable opportunity to obtain independent counsel prior to execution of the Agreement. . . . Additionally, there was evidence supporting the inference that she declined counsel because she understood and agreed with the terms of the agreement, and not because she had insufficient funds to employ counsel. . . . There is ample evidence to support the trial court's determination regarding Sun's English-language skills, in view of the circumstances that for two years prior to marriage she had undertaken employment and education in a trade that required such skills, and before meeting Barry had maintained close personal relationships with persons speaking only English. . . . In addition, the basic purport of the agreement—that the parties would hold their earnings and accumulations during marriage as separate property, thereby giving up the protection of marital property law—was a relatively simple concept that did not require great legal sophistication to comprehend and that was, as the trial court found, understood by Sun.

Finally, we observe that the evidence supports the inference that Sun was intrepid rather than a person whose will is easily overborne. She emigrated from her homeland at a young age, found employment and friends in a new country using two languages other than her native tongue, and in two years moved to yet another country, expressing the desire to take up a career and declaring to Barry that she "didn't want his money." . . . With respect to full disclosure of the property involved, the trial court found that Sun was aware of what separate property was held by Barry prior to the marriage, and . . . she failed to identify any property of which she later became aware that was not on the list of property referred to by the parties when they executed the contract. . . .

As the opinion suggests, states have struggled with the question whether there should be a fairness test for upholding pre-marital agreements. Some states' courts will invalidate an agreement they subjectively judge to be substantively "unconscionable," in the sense of departing dramatically from what the default rules would provide a spouse, even in the absence of any procedural deficiencies in the execution. Most states, like California, adopt a more procedural approach, focusing just on whether each spouse had a genuine opportunity knowingly to reject the deal. What arguments can you make for or against placing limits on how lousy an outcome is permitted to be for a spouse?

Is it true that Sun had "no lack of knowledge regarding the nature of the parties' assets" if Bonds was only making $106,000 a year when they married? Could a clever lawyer dispute that? By way of analogy, what if Bonds owned a family heirloom piece of jewelry that he and Sun at the time of marriage assumed was worth just a few thousand dollars, but sometime after marrying they had it appraised and learned it was worth millions? Could she claim to have lacked knowledge of the nature of that asset?

How would the Bonds pre-nup fare under Connecticut's version of the UPAA? Would differences between the Connecticut version and the California version lead you to take a different approach to client counseling and agreement execution if you were practicing in one state rather than the other? Which state's laws make pre-nups more attractive for marrying couples? Or is this another instance where a given rule might encourage one party and discourage the other, depending on their personal circumstances?

Many of the cases concerning voluntariness turn in part on the timing of the agreement. Agreements signed on the eve or morning of the wedding are surprisingly common, or at least those are the ones most likely to result in litigation and reported court decisions. Would you guess that in such cases the marriage is doomed from the outset? Is the simple fix for state legislatures simply to amend pre-nup statutes to say they will not be enforceable unless executed some period of time prior to the wedding, such as two weeks or a month? Would there be any downside to such a rule? In response to the *Bonds* decision and to another case the same year upholding a waiver of spousal support, the California Legislature added this paragraph to §1615 of the pre-nup statute in 2002:

> (c) For the purposes of subdivision (a), it shall be deemed that a premarital agreement was not executed voluntarily unless the court finds . . . all of the following:
>
> (1) The party against whom enforcement is sought was represented by independent legal counsel at the time of signing the agreement or, after being advised to seek independent legal counsel, expressly waived, in a separate writing, representation by independent legal counsel.
>
> (2) The party against whom enforcement is sought had not less than 7 calendar days between the time that party was first presented with the agreement and advised to seek independent legal counsel and the time the agreement was signed.
>
> (3) The party against whom enforcement is sought, if unrepresented by legal counsel, was fully informed of the terms and basic effect of the agreement as well as the rights and obligations he or she was giving up by signing the agreement, and was proficient in the language in which the explanation of the party's rights was conducted and in which the agreement was written. The explanation of the rights and obligations relinquished shall be memorialized in writing and delivered to the party prior to signing the agreement. The unrepresented party shall, on or before the signing of the premarital agreement, execute a document declaring that he or she received the information required by this paragraph and indicating who provided that information.
>
> (4) The agreement and the writings executed pursuant to paragraphs (1) and (3) were not executed under duress, fraud, or undue influence, and the parties did not lack capacity to enter into the agreement.
>
> (5) Any other factors the court deems relevant.

Does the change make execution of a pre-nup too onerous? Is it overly paternalistic?

The court in *Bonds* noted that a different, even more paternalistic, rule applied to marital (i.e., post-wedding) agreements. What is the reason for that? Does spouses' relative bargaining power change once they are married? Do other policy considerations change? In some other states, the same rules apply to pre-marital, marital, and divorce agreements.

The validity of one particular marital agreement has been big news in California recently—namely, that between Frank McCourt, owner of the Los Angeles Dodgers, and his wife Jamie. In 2004, when the couple had been married about 25 years, Frank purchased a controlling interest in the Dodgers, after a failed bid to buy the Red Sox. The McCourts executed an agreement at that time, in order to give Frank sole ownership of the team. In 2009, Jamie filed for divorce, and in 2010 a Los Angeles Superior Court judge ruled that the agreement was invalid. The couple's attorney in 2004 had prepared six copies of the agreement. At the last minute, he substituted a new version of one page of the agreement in three of the copies. The new version said the team would be owned solely by Frank. The old version in the three other copies said the team was to be owned by both Frank and Jamie. The judge concluded there was insufficient evidence to show which set of copies reflected the true intentions of the parties. See Amanda Bronstad, *Ruling in McCourt Divorce May Put Bingham at Risk of Malpractice Suit,* Nat'l L.J., (Dec. 13, 2010). Under the default, community property rules in California, the team therefore belonged to both spouses. This created financial havoc for the team, causing players and other employees to worry about getting paid, and McCourt put the team into bankruptcy. In late 2011, Frank and Jamie reached a divorce settlement in which she surrendered her claim to the team and received around $130 million. McCourt then agreed in bankruptcy court to sell the team. See Bill Shaikin, *Frank and Jamie McCourt Reach Settlement Involving Dodgers,* L.A. TIMES, Oct. 17, 2011. Jamie McCourt is the second person to exit pockets-full from a marriage with a Dodgers owner; Anna Murdoch was divorced from McCourt's predecessor, Rupert Murdoch, in 1999, and received a $1.2 billion settlement.

Is it a bad sign when someone getting married wants a pre-nup? Or could it be a bad sign when a couple has never discussed signing a pre-nup? Would you feel comfortable advising a friend or offspring to get a pre-nup before marrying? Apart from the awkwardness of the transaction, some might choose not to pursue a pre-nup simply because the default rules are fine for them. There is little reason to get lawyers involved before the marriage unless the default rules for divorce and death give one less financial protection than one wants and expects. As we will see, one circumstance in which it might be advisable for someone to get a pre-nup is when they are going to marry someone who is in or about to start law school.

What about a fiancé who purchases divorce insurance? Is that a bad sign? See Jennifer Saranow Schultz, *Divorce Insurance (Yes, Divorce Insurance),* N.Y. TIMES (Aug. 6, 2010), http://bucks.blogs.nytimes.com/2010/08/06/divorce-insurance-yes-divorce-insurance/ (reporting on first insurance company to offer a policy that would pay out after a divorce). That company's website, www.WedlockInsurance.com, offers a "Divorce Probability Calculator" promising to predict with only a 13 percent margin of error whether you will get divorced. If that Calculator is reliable, should local governments install touch-screen versions of it at the window of the clerk issuing marriage licenses?

Why do you suppose courts generally will not enforce pre-nup provisions relating to conduct during marriage, to child rearing during marriage or after divorce (e.g., with respect to the religious training or schooling of the child), or to custody and child support following divorce?

THOUGHT EXPERIMENT

Suppose the parent-child relationship also experienced a movement of sorts from status to contract. Suppose, for example, that adoption agencies began a practice of negotiating "pre-parental agreements" with adoption applicants and that states adapted their laws to ensure enforceability of these agreements. The supply/demand ratio with respect to children and parents would determine what bargaining power each side had, and the balance of power would determine the terms of the agreement. Thus, if there were a hundred applicants for each available child, the agency, as proxy for a given child, could demand much from applicants, as a condition for approving an adoption, and might even have them bid against each other. We might in that situation see applicants agree to such things as putting some portion of their wealth into trust for the child, accepting a support obligation longer than state law typically requires (e.g., to age 25 instead of 18), committing to elite private school tuition, and, if married, locking in to Covenant-Marriage–type restrictions on divorce. If, on the other hand, there were a hundred children for every qualified applicant, applicants might negotiate for such things as large signing bonuses, absolution from any support obligation in the event they end up without custody (because of divorce or because they decide they do not want the child any more), and exemption from some parental responsibilities. (*Note*: States arguably already do something like this with respect to hard-to-place children, recruiting adopters with promises of adoption subsidies, special education services, respite care, etc.).

What, if anything, is troubling about this prospect of pre-parental, negotiated contracts? The same things that are troubling about pre-marital agreements, or different things? One thing that might be troubling is that it seems to commercialize an intimate relationship, and to commodify children (in the first scenario) or parenting (in the second scenario). Is that true also of pre-nups, that they commercialize an intimate relationship and effectively commodify one party or the other? If so, is it more troubling with respect to one type of relationship than it is with the other? Another thing that might be troubling is that the children in the first scenario would likely be healthy white babies, and the children in the second scenario would likely be of minority race, disabled, and/or damaged by abuse and foster care. Is it not also true, though, that many adults who are able to demand good terms in a pre-nup can do so because of morally arbitrary personal characteristics like beauty or because the other person is highly needy, and so the pre-nup phenomenon tends to mark some people as more or less valuable than others? Is such implicit valuation more objectionable in the adoption context than in the marriage context? In the next section, we will study another and more common form of implicit spouse pricing—that is, the engagement ring.

3. Wedding Preparations

Most aspects of preparing for a wedding are potentially fun. But a lot of money is invested, and if an engagement is broken off, people get upset about that lost investment. It is not uncommon for domestic relations lawyers to get a call from a guy asking whether he can get the ring back, or from a would-be bride's parents asking whether they can recoup deposits and payments for the wedding reception and other expenses. Long ago, a bride could sue in tort for damages to her reputation and future marriageability when a man broke off an engagement. Today the only claims that succeed, if any, are for recovery of money spent in anticipation of a wedding. None of this financial element of weddings is legally required in order to get legally married; it is a self-inflicted cost incurred for social and psychological reasons. But the legal system intervenes when things go wrong and parties feel aggrieved.

Anthropological and contemporary cross-cultural study shows that several financial exchanges have been common throughout the world in connection with pair bonding. Bride price and dower are payments from a groom or his family to the bride or her family. In many cultures, the bride's family pays a "dowry" to the groom or his family and/or pays for the wedding celebration.

GEOFFREY F. MILLER, HOW MATE CHOICE SHAPED HUMAN NATURE: A REVIEW OF SEXUAL SELECTION AND HUMAN EVOLUTION, IN HANDBOOK OF EVOLUTIONARY PSYCHOLOGY: IDEAS, ISSUES, AND APPLICATIONS 99-100 (C. CRAWFORD & D. KREBS EDS., 1998): "Females can gain nongenetic benefits from mate choice by favoring males that offer material gifts. The main examples of such provisioning come from male insects giving nuptial gifts such as spermatophores or caught prey, male birds provisioning offspring and building nests in socially monogamous bird species, and sex-for-meat exchanges (e.g., prostitution and marriage). Male provisioning is useful to females because it eases the nutritional and energetic burden of producing eggs, and gestating and feeding the young. However, male provisioning of females during courtship is not common across species, and male provisioning of offspring after birth is quite rare, except in monogamous birds. Often, male provisioning may represent mating effort more than paternal effort, if females prefer males that have provisioned previous offspring."

RUTH MACE, THE EVOLUTIONARY ECOLOGY OF HUMAN FAMILY SIZE, IN OXFORD HANDBOOK OF EVOLUTIONARY PSYCHOLOGY 387 (DUNBAR & BARRETT EDS., 2007): "Intergenerational transfers of resources, such as territory, skills or wealth, are key to reproductive success in many social species, including humans. In wealth-inheriting societies, parents may have to show the colour of their money, in the form of the bride price or dowry, in order to marry off their children. Bride price is a payment from the groom or his family to the parents of the bride, and is typically associated with polygynous societies, where males use resources to monopolize several females, if they can afford to. Poorer males will lose out in such societies, unable to attract mates. Dowry (where money is paid from the family of the bride either to the newlyweds or their family) is associated with the opposite scenario, when it is females that are in competition with each other for mates. This female-female competition is most likely to arise in societies with socially imposed monogamy, frequently when societies are stratified. Whereas the benefits of wealth are likely to be diluted among many wives in polygynous societies, in monogamous societies a woman who marries a wealthy man has sole access to his wealth for the benefit of her offspring alone, and hence female-female competition for wealthy men becomes intense."

As this excerpt suggests, which practices predominate in particular cultures is influenced by the male-female ratio and by customary marriage practices, which determine to what extent marriageable women or men are more difficult to obtain. A change in cultural practice in Bangladesh illustrates this:

Farah Deeba Chowdhury, Dowry, Women, and Law in Bangladesh

24 Int'l J.L. Pol'y & Fam. 198, 198-207 (2010)

Dowry has now become more significant than dower in Bangladesh. Dower is religiously sanctioned but dowry is not supported by state or personal laws. *Dower* is an essential part of Muslim marriage in Bangladesh. . . . Dower is paid by the husband to his wife out of honour and respect and to show that he seriously desires to marry her with a sense of responsibility and obligation. *Dowry,* in contrast, refers to "the transmission of large sums of money, jewellery, cash, and other goods from the bride's family to the groom's family."

The dowry system increases the vulnerability of women in Bangladesh, turning them into liabilities for their family. . . . [T]he Dowry Prohibition Act of 1980 . . . makes giving and taking or demanding dowry a punishable offence. . . . Despite this legislation, dowry-related violence has been increasing in Bangladesh. According to *Odhikar*, a human rights organisation in Bangladesh, from 2002 to 2006, 1,683 women were the victims of dowry-related violence, 1,088 had been killed, and another 440 suffered severe physical torture. . . .

Amin and Cain (1997) argue that the emergence of the dowry system in Bangladesh was caused by a surplus of women relative to men of marriageable age, which began in 1960. They note that ". . . in 1950 there was an excess of girls of only 10 per cent, rising to 22 per cent in 1965 and 43 percent in 1975. . . ." They point out that bride price existed until 1964 and after that the dowry system emerged. . . . Rozario (1998) also argues that recent practice regarding dowry is related to a new surplus of unmarried women in Bangladesh. She writes, ". . . the shift from bridewealth to dowry in the Bangladeshi context is a consequence of women's devalorization. . . ."

The burden of marriage expenses had shifted from the groom's family to the bride's family. . . . Lindenbaum noted that by the 1950s and 1960s grooms started to demand objects that were not of Bengali origin or manufacture. Rural grooms started to demand fountain pens, watches, and sometimes transistor radios. The city grooms demanded tape recorders, record players, and television sets that were manufactured in Japan or the USA. Some demanded bicycles that were made in Britain and Germany and suits of clothing mostly from Britain. . . . "From these origins, the demand system has reached a stage where it is not a question of nabbing a 'highly desirable' groom any more but of getting a more or less 'ordinary' groom for one's daughter at quite a cost." . . .

The amount of dowry is an indication of the groom's worth. . . . "The family of the bride will often disclose to their friends, neighbors, and marriage brokers the amount of dowry they are willing to pay for a suitable groom, particularly if the proposed amount of dowry is relatively high. Both parties to the marriage contract often haggle about the price, and a marriage broker will mediate between them, often going back and forth several times with offers and counter offers. . . . A portion of the dowry may be given before the marriage ceremony takes place to help defray expenses the groom will incur at the marriage. The remaining transaction usually occurs at the marriage ceremony. Among poorer families and for marriages taking place during non-harvest periods, the parties may agree in advance that a portion of the dowry will be paid later (e.g., after the harvest)."

The strongest motivation behind paying demand is the daughter's security. . . . Geirbo and Imam (2006: 28) point out as follows:

> A common notion is that fathers give demand to ensure a happy married life for the daughter. If a daughter brings a large demand, her parents hope that she will be well treated in her in-laws house. They hope she will get her needs provided for, be loved and respected. The demand is expected to have this effect only if it is paid in full. If it is not paid in accordance with the schedule negotiated, the daughter is in danger of being abused.

. . . Geirbo and Imam (2006: 14) explain as follows:

> . . . the quality of the bride can also be a significant factor. If she is perceived as being of high quality compared to the groom, he might be willing to reduce his *demand* to marry her. If she is perceived as being of low quality compared to him, he might be willing to marry her in

> exchange for a higher *demand.* A female college teacher told that in her family they usually pay two or three lakh taka in demand. However, for one of her relatives, they had paid ten lakh because she is dark skinned and the groom has a good government job.

. . . Child marriages occur because the dowry is usually smaller when the bride is very young. The demand is much higher when the girl is not beautiful. Less attractive girls tend to face discrimination in their parents' family, and even educated girls who are less attractive have difficulty finding grooms. . . . Hossain (2008) writes as follows:

> Girls are starting to become sexual objects from a very early age, and being 'sexy' has become something very important, empowering, and a precondition of women's success. . . . In Bangladesh, women today are more conscious about how they look, what they wear, what they eat, and how much they weigh, than they were even ten years back. Women have been fed this message very, very clearly over the past decade that, however successful or educated one might be, one's looks and sex appeal comes first. No woman in today's world is allowed to carry body fat and appear unattractive, she has to be pretty and sexy in order to win the race.

In the villages, literacy is considered desirable in a bride, but . . . the groom should have a higher educational qualification than the bride. . . . It is very difficult to marry off well-educated girls because educated grooms are very expensive and demands are higher. Geirbo and Imam (2006: 15) report one mother as saying . . . "If I give more education to my daughter, I have to give more demand at her marriage, as in that case I have to find a groom with a salaried job." . . . Arends-Kuenning and Amin find that "[s]ome parents intend to limit their daughters' education before they complete secondary school because they are concerned that they will not be able to pay dowry for an educated groom". . . .

Upper-class families do not demand dowry. They know that they will benefit economically and socially from connections between their families. In these marriages, the families of grooms and brides spend large sums on wedding parties. Grooms' families buy wedding dresses for brides and brides' families buy wedding outfits for grooms. Both exchange gifts for their family members. But it is also assumed that women are inferior, and brides' families therefore feel they need to give expensive gifts to keep favour with the grooms' families. In this way, they also hope that their wealth and power will prevent their daughters being neglected in the in-laws' home. In these marriages, the brides' families provide expensive household items for the couple and after the marriage they give expensive gifts to the grooms' families. . . . Grooms' families also demand large wedding parties. They determine the numbers of guests, and the brides' families must agree to feed them. The number of people depends on the class. The grooms also determine the items of the marriage feast. One newspaper reported as follows:

> There were many items in a marriage feast. There were pulao (rice cooked with ghee), beef, goat meat, chicken, shrimp, vegetables and salad. Only there was no egg. For this reason the bride takers became angry. The bride's father wanted to make them understand that he did not get 700 eggs together in the market for the marriage feast. But the bride takers strongly insisted that it was agreed by the bride's family that there would be eggs in the marriage feast. So, they need eggs. Finally with the help of some senior men the egg problem was solved. The bride takers took the bride to the groom's house. After arriving at home the groom's family started humiliating and swearing at the bride. The groom was extremely mad. At one point, he cracked 19 eggs on the bride's head and she got hospitalized.

Obviously, wealth exchange at marriage is a highly sensitive matter in this culture. Because it signals one family's estimation of the other, the potential for insult is great. Is this also true in the United States?

Bride price is much more common than dowry, historically and across the globe today. It is mentioned in the Code of Hammurabi, the Hebrew Bible, the Talmud, and the Old Testament. Anthropologists explain the practice as principally compensation to the bride's family for loss of her labor and alienation of her reproductive capacity. Today the value of labor might depend on education, in cultures where women can work in the business world. Beauty is a proxy for the relative value of a particular woman's reproductive capacity, so the parents of women deemed beautiful can command a higher bride price. The "market" value of a woman's reproductive capacity plummets, however, after intercourse with any man, so historically the compensation was owed even if sex occurred without an intention to marry, and the man might be forced to marry. See, e.g., *Deuteronomy* 22:28-29:

> If a man find a damsel that is a virgin, which is not betrothed, and lay hold on her, and lie with her, and they be found; then the man that lay with her shall give unto the damsel's father fifty shekels of silver, and she shall be his wife; because he hath humbled her, he may not put her away all his days.

See also *Exodus* 22:16-17. Today many Asian and African cultures retain a norm of grooms paying a bride price to the bride's family. The practice has evolved so that in many cultures the negotiations are lengthy and the bestowal highly ritualized. Human rights activists today object that the practice commodifies women and, in cultures where there is an expectation that any woman who is unfaithful or seeks a divorce must repay the bride price, traps women in marriages that might be abusive. See, e.g., Jamil Ddamulira Mujuzi, *Bride Wealth (Price) and Women's Marriage-Related Rights in Uganda: A Historial Constitutional Perspective and Current Developments*, 24 INT'L J.L. POL'Y & FAM. 414 (2010).

In the United States, women and men of marriageable age are pretty much equal in number, legal monogamy is the prevailing rule, and there is formal gender equality in education and employment. Thus, women and men on the whole should have equal value and bargaining power in partnering. In addition, are we not the most enlightened society ever? We should therefore expect to see in the United States today that any practices resembling purchase of a spouse have disappeared. Is that the case?

Meghan O'Rourke, Diamonds Are a Girl's Worst Friend: The Trouble with Engagement Rings

Slate.com, June 11, 2007

. . . Most Americans can say no to the "celebrity garter belt" on offer for a mere $18.95 from Weddings With Class. But more than 80% of American brides receive a diamond engagement ring. . . . Few stop to think about what, beyond the misty promise of endless love, the ring might actually signify. . . . But there's a powerful case to be made that in an age of equitable marriage the engagement ring is an outmoded commodity—starting with the obvious fact that only the woman gets one. . . .

[T]he "tradition" of the diamond engagement ring is newer than you might think. Betrothal rings, a custom inherited from the Romans, became an increasingly common part of the Christian tradition in the 13th century. The first known diamond engagement ring was commissioned for Mary of Burgundy by the Archduke Maximilian of Austria in 1477. The Victorians exchanged "regards" rings set with birthstones. But it wasn't until the late 19th century, after the discovery of mines in South Africa drove the price of diamonds down, that Americans regularly began to give (or receive) diamond engagement rings. (Before that, some betrothed women got thimbles instead of rings.) . . . In 1919, De Beers experienced a drop in diamond sales that lasted for two decades. So in the 1930s it turned to the firm N.W. Ayer to devise a national advertising campaign—still relatively rare at the time—to promote its diamonds. Ayer convinced Hollywood actresses to wear diamond rings in public, and . . . encouraged fashion designers to discuss the new "trend" toward diamond rings. Between 1938 and 1941, diamond sales went up 55 percent. . . . By 1965, 80 percent of American women had diamond engagement rings. The ring had become a requisite element of betrothal—as well as a very visible demonstration of status. . . .

And as it happens there was another factor in the surge of engagement ring sales—one that makes the ring's role as collateral in the premarital economy more evident. Until the 1930s, a woman jilted by her fiancé could sue for financial compensation for "damage" to her reputation under what was known as the "Breach of Promise to Marry" action. As courts began to abolish such actions, diamond ring sales rose in response to a need for a symbol of financial commitment from the groom, argues the legal scholar Margaret Brinig—noting, crucially, that ring sales began to rise a few years before the De Beers campaign. To be marriageable at the time you needed to be a virgin, but, Brinig points out, a large percentage of women lost their virginity while engaged. So some structure of commitment was necessary to assure betrothed women that men weren't just trying to get them into bed. The "Breach of Promise" action had helped prevent what society feared would be rampant seduce-and-abandon scenarios; in its lieu, the pricey engagement ring would do the same. (Implicitly, it would seem, a woman's virginity was worth the price of a ring, and varied according to the status of her groom-to-be.) . . . [I]ts presence on a woman's finger suggests that she needs to trap a man into "commitment" or be damaged if he leaves. . . . Nor is it exactly "equitable" to demand that a partner shell out a sixth of a year's salary, demonstrating that he can "provide" for you and a future family, before you agree to marry him.

For those who aren't bothered by the finer points of gender equity, an engagement ring clearly makes a claim about the status of a woman's sexual currency. It's a big, shiny NO TRESPASSING sign, stating that the woman wearing it has been bought and paid for, while her beau is out there sign-free and all too easily trespassable, until the wedding. . . .

It may seem curious that feminism has made inroads on many retrograde customs—name-changing, for example—but not on the practice of giving engagement rings. . . . Women still measure their worth in relationship to marriage in ways that men don't. And many *are* looking for men who will bear the burden of providing for them, while demanding equality in other ways. . . . Women are collectively attached to the status a ring bestows on them. . . .

An engagement ring is certainly optional as a matter of law, but how many men or women feel that it is optional within their relationship? How many men would feel comfortable even broaching with a girlfriend the idea of skipping the engagement ring step to marriage? How many women would be open to that idea, or even suggest it themselves? If it is important to women to receive an engagement ring, is that just because it's a nice custom, or are they looking for a material indication of their value in the groom's eyes? How many women who are in a serious relationship with a man, knowing he could afford a nice big diamond, would be just as happy receiving a relatively inexpensive ring for their engagement, say a $300 blue topaz stone on a silver band? Cf. Lee Cronk & Bria Dunham, *Amounts Spent on Engagement Rings Reflect Aspects of Male and Female Mate Quality*, 18 HUM. NATURE 329 (2007). Is there not, in fact, an expectation from the first date that men should demonstrate their seriousness and estimation of the woman's value by bestowing gifts? What are the prospects for a relationship that begins with separate checks?

O'Rourke suggests the engagement ring functions, like a bride price, as a signal of ability to support a woman and offspring, and it also serves as a signal of possession by a man, a marker of sexual unavailability, as do wedding rings. Such marking occurs in many species. It makes mating more efficient for males; they can know at a glance that they are likely to be wasting resources by attempting to woo a female who has already bonded with another male. See David M. Buss, *The Psychology of Human Mate Selection: Exploring the Complexity of the Strategic Repertoire, in* HANDBOOK OF EVOLUTIONARY PSYCHOLOGY: IDEAS, ISSUES, AND APPLICATIONS 413-414 (Charles B. Crawford & Dennis L. Krebs eds., 1998). It might also benefit females who wish to be spared from mating overtures by other males. But is it demeaning to women to tag them as taken? In Iran, progressive couples have begun a practice of exchanging spiritually important but inexpensive items such as a volume of the Qur'an, instead of following the bride-price tradition. See http://family.jrank.org/pages/951/Iran-Marriage.html. Should progressive Americans, and feminists in particular, advocate for a new engagement custom, one that involves a mutual exchange and no implication of bride-purchasing? And for a strict rule throughout social life and dating of not accepting offers of drinks, dinners, etc.?

UMMNI KHAN, RUNNING IN(TO) THE FAMILY: 8 SHORT STORIES ABOUT SEX WORKERS, CLIENTS, HUSBANDS, AND WIVES, 9 AM. U. J. GENDER SOC. POL'Y & L. 495, 498-499 (2009): A prospective husband offers a diamond ring to his beloved for her hand in marriage. The hand of course is a metaphor, but more accurately, it is a synecdoche. It is a figure of speech where a part is used to stand in for the whole, the hand being part of the whole body. As for the ring, this adornment is explicitly tied to cold hard cash. Since the 1940s, the diamond company De Beers has infiltrated the rituals of marital courtship in order to impose a monetary imperative. To paraphrase an ad campaign for engagement rings I heard a few years ago: "Is two months' salary too much to spend for something that will last a lifetime?" But it is not just corporations telling men to fork out the cash. In her hit song "Single Ladies," Beyoncé admonishes her ex for not coming through with the ring after three years of dating: "If you liked it then you should have put a ring on it." Note that there is nothing in the lyrics to indicate that her ex mistreated her while they were together. He just didn't buy her a ring. And part of the bargain is that if he liked "it," then he is obliged to put a ring on "it." It is not completely clear what the first "it" is referring to, but the lyrics suggest that "it" stands for her body, her dance moves, and/or her looks. Thus, on some level, the song suggests that in a romantic dyad, in order for a man to respect a woman's value, he must present her with a ring (at least after three years of being together). Seen in this light, the exchange of a ring for "it" or for "her hand" seems akin, if not completely identical, to prostitution. And we all know this.

The practice of bringing an engagement ring to the marriage proposal gives rise to legal disputes when the engagement falls through, as a significant percentage do. Different people have very different intuitions about what should happen with the ring in that case, and often strong emotions attach to any difference of opinion. Divergent legal rules across the states reflect the disparate intuitions.

Fowler v. Perry

830 N.E.2d 97 (Ind. Ct. App. 2005)

Bailey, J.

From June of 1999 to October of 2000, Fowler and Perry lived together in a house in Missouri. During that time, Fowler and Perry had a son. On October 21, 1999, Fowler purchased an engagement ring for Perry for $5,499.00. . . .

In late October of 2000, Perry and her son moved to Indiana, while Fowler remained in Missouri to finish his education. Once Fowler graduated from college, he planned to move to Indiana to be with Perry and their son. From November of 2000 to April of 2001, Fowler gave Perry control of his income. According to Fowler, he did so with the expressed agreement that Perry would pay all of his bills with the money and, further, that "whatever money was leftover was to be saved so that when [he] graduated school, got a job in Indiana and [the two] got married, [they] could buy a house." . . .

In April of 2001, Perry informed Fowler that they should stop "seeing each other for a while." Subsequently, Perry attempted to pawn her "engagement ring" because Fowler had not requested it back and she no longer had a use for it. However, at some point during the time that Perry had taken the ring from "jewelry shop to jewelry shop" to pawn it, the ring was stolen from her car. As a result of the theft, Perry received insurance proceeds in the amount of $5,000.00.

On October 25, 2002, Fowler filed a complaint against Perry, seeking, in part, . . . the value of the stolen engagement ring. . . .

First, we examine whether the ring at issue constitutes a gift in contemplation of marriage. In so doing, we note that, at trial, both parties referred to the ring as an engagement ring. An "engagement ring" is defined as "a ring given in token of betrothal." Webster's Third New International Dictionary 751 (2002). The term "betrothal" refers to "a mutual promise or contract for a future marriage." . . .

Having determined that the engagement ring was given to Perry in contemplation of marriage, . . . we must determine whether the ring was intended as an absolute, or a conditional, gift. In addition to the competency of the donor, a valid inter vivos gift—i.e., an absolute gift—occurs when: (1) the donor intends to make a gift; (2) the gift is completed with nothing left undone; (3) the property is delivered by the donor and accepted by the donee; and (4) the gift is immediate and absolute. Thus, once delivery and acceptance of a gift inter vivos occurs, the gift is irrevocable and a present title vests in the donee. By contrast, a gift is conditional if it is conditioned upon the performance of some act by the donee or the occurrence of an event in the future. . . .

In our society, an engagement ring—i.e., a gift incidental to an engagement—is the symbol and token of a couple's agreement to marry. As such, marriage is an implied condition of the transfer of title to the ring and, thus, the gift does not become absolute until the marriage occurs. Put another way, marriage is a condition precedent before ownership of an engagement ring vests in the donee. Therefore, in the absence of a contrary expression of intent, an engagement ring is a conditional gift given in contemplation of marriage, and not an inter vivos transfer of personal property.[3]

The majority of jurisdictions that have considered the ownership of an engagement ring after the engagement was terminated has adopted a "fault-based" approach, wherein the donor is entitled to the return of an engagement ring only if the engagement was broken by mutual agreement or unjustifiably by the donee. The rationale behind the "fault-based" approach is, in large part, as follows:

> On principle, an engagement ring is given, not alone as a symbol of the status of the two persons as engaged, the one to the other, but as a symbol or token of their pledge and agreement to marry. As such pledge or gift, the condition is implied that if both parties abandon the projected marriage, the sole cause of the gift, it should be returned. Similarly, if the woman, who has received the ring in token of her promise, unjustifiably breaks her promise, it should be returned. When the converse situation occurs, and the giver of the ring, betokening his promise, violates his word, it would seem that a similar result should follow, i.e., he should lose, not gain, rights to the ring. In addition, had he not broken his promise, the marriage would follow and the ring would become the wife's absolutely. The man could not then recover the ring.

44 A.L.R.5th 1 (citing Sloin v. Lavine, 11 N.J. Misc. 899 (1933)). Accordingly, under this rationale, the courts should not aid a donor, who has broken his promise of marriage, to regain possession of something that he could not have regained if he had kept his promise.

A minority of jurisdictions has adopted a "no-fault" approach, i.e., the modern trend, holding that once an engagement is broken, the engagement ring should be returned to the donor, regardless of fault. Pursuant to this approach, fault is irrelevant, if ascertainable at all, because ownership of the engagement ring was conditional and the condition of marriage was never fulfilled. *Id.* (citing *Aronow v. Silver* (N.J. Super. 1987)). Some of these "no-fault" jurisdictions, for example, highlight the fact that the primary purpose behind the engagement period is to allow the couple to test the permanency of their feelings for one another, and with that purpose in mind, it would be irrational to penalize the donor for taking steps to prevent a possibly unhappy marriage. *See Fierro v. Hoel* (Iowa Ct. App. 1990). We find this latter approach to be more persuasive.

Indeed, the "no fault" approach is consistent with our "no-fault" system of divorce. . . . We do not want to require our judiciary to tackle the seemingly insurmountable task of determining which party was at fault for the termination of an engagement for marriage, as such may force trial courts to sort through volumes of self-serving testimony regarding who-did-what during the engagement. . . .

Here, Fowler's gift to Perry of the engagement ring that he purchased for $5,499.00 was conditioned upon their ensuing marriage. When the promise of marriage was not kept, regardless of fault, the condition was not fulfilled and the ring must be returned to him. Because the ring at issue was stolen, Fowler is entitled to the purchase price of the ring, i.e., $5,499.00.

---

3. We observe that other types of property may be shown to be conditional gifts given in contemplation of marriage, but such a classification would require specific evidence of such intent, as opposed to a mere showing that the ring was an engagement ring.

More recent state court decisions adopting the no-fault rule include Carroll v. Curry, 912 N.E.2d 272, 279 (Ill. App. 2d Dist. 2009) (holding in favor of man whose infidelity led to end of engagement, noting that "fault-based inquiries in the context of replevin actions raise troubling policy questions. For example, courts would be asked to consider whether and to what extent a person's sudden weight gain, change in financial status, or adoption of different ideologies constituted fault sufficient to justify breaking an engagement and to justify retaining possession of the property in question"), and Crippen v. Campbell, 2007 WL 2768076 (Tenn. Ct. App. Sept. 24, 2007).

Clippard v. Pfefferkorn

168 S.W.3d 616 (Mo. Ct. App. 2005)

MARY K. HOFF, Judge.

Plaintiff and Defendant dated for approximately four or five months in late 2002. . . . Plaintiff proposed marriage to Defendant and presented Defendant with a 2.02 carat diamond engagement ring (ring) valued at approximately $13,500. Defendant accepted Plaintiff's proposal and the engagement ring. A few days later, Defendant gave Plaintiff some Christmas gifts, including a full-length dress coat and a workout suit. In return, Plaintiff gave Defendant compact discs containing music and treated her to a dinner.

During the weeks following Christmas 2002, the couple experienced difficulties in their relationship. On or about February 8, 2003, approximately six weeks after the couple were engaged, Plaintiff terminated the engagement. . . .

Plaintiff testified that, although Plaintiff proposed marriage to Defendant only two days prior to Christmas in 2002, the ring was not a Christmas gift but a symbol of the couple's engagement. Plaintiff further testified that during the parties' engagement, there were periods in which the engagement was "off" and Defendant returned the ring to Plaintiff, but, when the parties renewed their engagement, he gave the ring back to Defendant. Plaintiff testified that when the couple finally broke up, he demanded that Defendant return the ring, but she refused. On cross-examination, Plaintiff admitted that he terminated the engagement with Defendant because he "knew [he] didn't want to marry her" and his thoughts on the matter were influenced by his family. Plaintiff also testified that he had an extensive conversation with Defendant about his reasons for terminating the engagement at the time he ended their relationship. However, on redirect examination, Plaintiff testified that the breakup was a mutual decision.

Defendant testified that the ring was a Christmas gift and an engagement ring from Plaintiff. Defendant also testified that she loved Plaintiff and intended to marry him at the time Plaintiff called off their engagement. Defendant further testified that, when Plaintiff terminated their engagement, Plaintiff explained that he could not go through with the marriage because of "pressure" from his family. . . .

Under Missouri law, the essential elements of an inter vivos gift are: 1) the donor's present intent to make a gift; 2) the donor's delivery of the property to the donee; and 3) the donee's acceptance of the gift, whose ownership takes effect immediately and absolutely. The party claiming an inter vivos gift was made must prove all the elements by clear, cogent, and convincing evidence. . . .

A completed inter vivos gift cannot be revoked by the donor once the gift is delivered and accepted by the donee. On the other hand, it is well settled that, if the donor makes a gift subject to a condition, the donee's failure or refusal to perform the condition or violation of the condition constitutes grounds for revocation of the gift by the donor. In other words, the donor retains the right to revoke the gift unless or until the condition is satisfied. Missouri courts have held that a gift given in contemplation of marriage is made upon the implied condition that the gift will become absolute when the marriage takes place. Thus, a gift given in contemplation of marriage, though absolute in form, is a conditional gift and may be revoked by the donor if the marriage engagement is breached by the donee. . . . Missouri courts have utilized a fault-based approach when applying the conditional gift rule to determine which party is entitled to the property.

For example, in *Lumsden*, an action in replevin, the plaintiff-donor sought the return of a piano he had given to his former fiancée. The plaintiff-donor there, like Plaintiff here, alleged that he had made the gift in contemplation of marriage, and, therefore, the gift was not absolute but conditioned upon the marriage taking place. The plaintiff-donor further alleged that he was entitled to the piano because his former fiancée broke the engagement. The fiancée, however, like Defendant here, claimed that the piano was a Christmas gift and was not conditioned on a pending marriage. In . . . ordering the return of the piano to him, the court of appeals applied the . . . fault-based approach:

> If the piano was given to defendant by plaintiff in contemplation of marriage, and she broke the engagement for no fault of plaintiff, then he can recover. . . . If an intended husband make[s] a present, after the treaty of marriage has been negotiated, to his intended wife, and the inducement for the gift is the fact of her promise to marry him, if she break[s] off the marriage, he may recover from her the value of such a present.

. . . Clearly, the evidence in the record established that the ring was a conditional gift made in contemplation of the parties' marriage and not merely a Christmas gift. However, under Missouri's fault-based approach to determining a party's rights to gifts made in contemplation of marriage . . . Plaintiff would have been entitled to the return of the ring if the engagement had been terminated by Defendant for no fault of Plaintiff. Logically, the reverse also applies: . . . Defendant was entitled to retain the ring because the engagement was terminated by Plaintiff for no fault of Defendant. . . . Plaintiff testified he no longer wished to marry Defendant because he thought she was not the "right" person. Both Plaintiff and Defendant testified that Plaintiff terminated the relationship due to the influence of Plaintiff's family. Although Plaintiff also testified that the parties' breakup was mutual, we defer to the trial court's superior position to determine the sincerity and credibility of the witnesses.

We also note that Defendant was entitled to retain the ring because, by terminating the engagement, Plaintiff breached his promise to marry Defendant. Plaintiff's proposal of marriage and giving of the ring and Defendant's acceptance of the ring and proposal was symbolic of their agreement to an exclusive relationship and intention to marry. If Plaintiff had not breached his promise to marry Defendant and the marriage had taken place, there is no question that Defendant would have been entitled to retain the ring as her own non-marital property. Accordingly, . . . Defendant is entitled to retain the ring. . . .

What policies counsel for or against the fault-based and the no-fault approaches? Should any gifts given during an engagement other than an engagement ring be considered conditional upon the marriage taking place? If so, should all, or can you propose some criteria for determining which gifts should be returned when an engagement ends?

Is it desirable for there to be a financial "penalty" for a broken engagement looming over an engaged couple? Is it possible to craft a rule that does not create such a penalty for one person or the other? One might also wonder whether the gift should always become irrevocable on the wedding day. What if there is an annulment or divorce very soon after, and what if it is because of something bad the bride has done?

Investment in a wedding is hardly a one-way street. In a traditional courtship, the prospective groom buys the rings and that's it; the bride's parents pay for everything else. If an engagement ends close to the date of the planned wedding, the parents may have spent a lot of money they cannot get back from the vendors, on invitations, dresses, down payments on catering and facilities, etc. Needless to say, they can be quite peeved when the couple calls off the wedding, especially if it is the prospective groom who breaks the engagement, and they might call a lawyer to see if they can sock the groom with the cost. The prospective bride might also have rearranged her life in expectation of marriage, and inevitably will have incurred some opportunity cost during the period of the engagement. And, of course, there is an emotional investment that is frustrated.

Kelsey M. May, Bachelors Beware: The Current Validity and Future Feasibility of a Cause of Action for Breach of Promise to Marry

45 Tulsa L. Rev. 331 (2009)

On July 23, 2008, Rosemary Shell finally felt vindicated. After receiving a $150,000 jury verdict against her former fiancé, she was satisfied that the legal system was just. Almost twelve months earlier in Georgia, Shell sued Wayne Gibbs, a man to whom she was previously engaged, after he ended their engagement by leaving her a note in the bathroom. Believing he owed her for the emotional hardship and expenses she incurred as a result of their broken engagement, she asked for pecuniary damages, including damages for humiliation and mental anguish. She took him to court and withstood a three-day jury trial, offering testimony and evidence supporting her position that Gibbs breached a binding contract. And she won.

Under the common law claim of "breach of promise to marry," an individual may recover damages due to an unfulfilled future promise of marriage. The claim itself is based on contract principles, but the available remedies resemble those of a tort claim. . . . Twenty-eight states and the District of Columbia have formally abolished the breach of marriage promise action, but the claim is evidently still valid in twenty-two states through adoption and recognition of the common law: Arizona, Arkansas, Georgia, Hawaii, Idaho, Illinois, Iowa, Kansas, Louisiana, Mississippi, Missouri, Nebraska, New Mexico, North Carolina, Oklahoma, Oregon, Rhode Island, South Carolina, South Dakota, Tennessee, Texas, and Washington. . . .

Differing somewhat from the nature of commercial contracts, available remedies are not limited to pecuniary damages, but, because of the special nature of this specific contractual relationship, a plaintiff may be awarded all of the damages that naturally flow from the defendant's breach. . . . A plaintiff may seek a multitude of damages, including "out-of-pocket expenses, personal injuries such as mental and emotional suffering and illness, damage to reputation, humiliation, embarrassment, 'loss of worldly advantage' (expectation of sharing defendant's wealth, social position, home, and other marital incidents), and punitive damages."

Traditional defenses to a breach of marriage contract resemble those of any other contractual breach, but there are additional defenses peculiar to this cause of action.

These defenses include: an unchaste character of the plaintiff that was unknown to the defendant at the time of the proposal (sometimes classified as a "misrepresentation"), an inability to marry because the defendant was already married (and this was made known to the plaintiff), certain hereditary conditions and diseases, and, in some cases, evidence of cohabitation before marriage. . . .

Although the actions can be abolished by judicial common law, they are most often barred through legislation that has come to be known as "anti-heart balm" statutes. The first "anti-heart balm" statute was introduced in 1935 by Roberta West Nicholson, the only female member of Indiana's legislature. Her apparent motivation in introducing the statute was to curb the bad reputation such actions had due to the fear that they were only used for blackmail purposes. . . .

Gilbert v. Barkes

987 S.W.2d 772 (Ky. 1999)

Stephens, Justice.

. . . Ms. Suzanne Barkes . . . and Dr. Alvin Gilbert . . . entered into a relationship beginning in January of 1989 which continued until June of 1994. Ms. Barkes claims that in September of 1990, Dr. Gilbert proposed marriage to her and that in December of 1990, she accepted. Ms. Barkes submits that she received an engagement ring from Dr. Gilbert. In reliance upon her impending marriage and at Dr. Gilbert's insistence, Ms. Barkes claims that she took early retirement in 1992. Subsequently, Ms. Barkes sold her home in January of 1993 and moved into Dr. Gilbert's home. Sometime in 1994, the parties' relationship began to deteriorate and Ms. Barkes left Dr. Gilbert's home. In June of 1994 Ms. Barkes filed an action for Breach of Promise to Marry (BPM). . . .

I. History of Action for Breach of Promise to Marry

The right of an individual to sue for Breach of Promise to Marry is a common law hybrid of tort and contract. Its origin, however, goes back to canon law, which only enforced such a breach through specific performance of the promise. Through time such harsh measures were no longer enforced. The common law has since adopted the action.

In the fifteenth century, English courts embraced the action, primarily because the basis of marriage was largely viewed as a property transaction. However, in those early times, the aggrieved party was only able to recover monies expended on a deceitful promise to marry. In the seventeenth century, the need to prove deceit was eliminated from the cause of action.

Following the lead of England, the American colonies adopted the action. The action found a receptive audience in this country eventually becoming more popular in America than in England. However, by the end of the last century commentators became highly critical of the BPM action and favored restricting or eliminating it. Today, the concept of marriage is generally no longer perceived as an economic transaction. Rather is regarded as a union of two persons borne out of love and affection, rather than a device by which property is exchanged.

The elements of the BPM action are predicated upon contract principles with the exception of damages, which has its roots in tort. . . . First, there must be mutual promises to marry one another. Furthermore, an offer and acceptance of the promise must be proven for an action to lie. The offer, however, need not be formal. "Any expression . . . of readiness to be married is sufficient." In addition, the contract to marry must be free from fraud based on the presumptions of innocence and purity of each promising party when entering into the agreement.

When the contract to marry has been breached, the injured party must suffer some form of damages. Because the issue of damages stems from tort principles, the amount is not limited to what is recoverable in the typical contract action for a breach of promise. Three general classes of damages have emerged from this action: compensatory damages relating to the loss of the marriage, aggravated damages for seduction under promise of marriage, and punitive damages for malicious conduct. In Kentucky, this Court laid down an exhaustive list of factors to consider when estimating damages:

> [I]t is proper to consider anxiety of mind produced by the breach; loss of time and expenses incurred in preparation for the marriage; advantages which might have accrued to plaintiff from the marriage; the loss of a permanent home and advantageous establishment; plaintiff's loss of employment in consequence of the engagement or loss of health in consequence of the breach; the length of the engagement; the depth of plaintiff's devotion to defendant; defendant's conduct and treatment of plaintiff in his whole intercourse with her; injury to plaintiff's reputation or future prospects of marriage; plaintiff's loss of other opportunities of marriage by reason of her engagement to defendant; plaintiff's lack of independent means; her altered social condition in relation to her home and family, due to defendant's conduct; and the fact that she was living unhappily at the time of the alleged promise.

The last case in which this Court issued a ruling on the breach of promise to marry action was in the 1937 *Scharringhaus* case.

II. Should the Cause of Action for Breach of Promise to Marry Be Abolished from Kentucky Common Law?

. . . The primary argument in favor of abolition of the BPM action is that society's view of marriage and women have changed dramatically since this cause of action was adopted. While technically either a man or a woman could bring the cause of action in question, this Court is unaware of a man ever asserting such claim before the courts of the Commonwealth. The cases which interpret this cause of action make clear the party who is sought to be protected:

> A promise to marry is not infrequently one of the base and wicked tricks of the wily seducer to accomplish his purposes by overcoming that resistance which female virtue makes to his unholy designs.

This language reflects the sexism and paternalism that pervade this cause of action. While one could certainly debate whether equality has been achieved between women and men in our society, it is certainly beyond issue that women today possess far more economic, legal and political rights than did their predecessors. Accordingly, we must examine the utility of the BPM action in the context of the present day, not in the era in which it was created.

Our review of the actions taken by other jurisdictions indicates that 28 states have legislatively or judicially abolished the Breach of Promise to Marry action. The work of various commentators on this issue demonstrates criticism starting late in the last century and continuing up to the present. "Although marriages are still contracted for material advantages, it is now popularly believed that the choice of a spouse should be the result of that complex experience called love." The public policy of the Commonwealth undoubtedly calls for this Court to uphold marriage vows; however, "we see no benefit in discouraging or penalizing persons who realize, *before* making these vows, that for whatever reason, they are unprepared to take such an important step."

Given these arguments in favor of abolition as well as the support offered by other jurisdictions and commentators, we now turn to the arguments in favor of its retention. . . . [T]he doctrine of stare decisis compels this Court to retain the action since it is a long-standing remedy and there is no sound reason to eliminate it because it still serves the useful purpose of remedying injury to those who are left standing at the altar. . . .

Stare decisis is a doctrine which has real meaning to this Court. . . . However, when this Court finds a common law cause of action to be anomalous, unworkable or contrary to public policy, it will abolish the action. We believe the cause of action for breach of promise to marry has become an anachronism that has out-lived its usefulness and should be removed from the common law of the Commonwealth. "It is a barbarous remedy, outgrown by advancing civilization and, like other outgrown relics of a barbarous age, it must go." . . . Accordingly, the action for Breach of Promise to Marry is no longer a valid cause of action before the courts of the Commonwealth.

This Court wishes to make clear that it in no way prohibits other remedies, such as claims for breach of contract and intentional infliction of emotional distress, should a party be able to make such a case. As the Supreme Court of Utah noted in *Jackson v. Brown* (1995), any direct "economic losses suffered because of . . . [the defendant's] promise to marry [the plaintiff] (such as normal expenses attendant to a wedding) may be recoverable under a theory of . . . breach of contract. . . . [I]f a proper case is made out, emotional damages resulting from [the defendant's] actions may be remedied by an action for intentional infliction of emotional distress. . . ." While we are removing a cause of action from the common law, we are not eradicating the ability of a party to seek a remedy for such a wrong, but rather we are modifying the form that remedy may take. . . .

III. Application of Law to the Facts of This Case

For several reasons, Ms. Barkes is precluded from recovery from Dr. Gilbert under any contractual theory. First, there were none of the "normal expenses attendant to a wedding" such as a bridal dress, down payment on a reception hall or the like. Ms. Barkes' economic claims were only for the sale of her house and taking early retirement. Neither of these damages are the type of direct wedding-related economic out-of-pocket expenses that are recoverable. Since only direct economic losses of this type can be recovered and there is no proof of any such losses in this case, no recovery is possible. Second, since no wedding date was ever actually set, there is no way Ms. Barkes could recover under any contractual theory because she cannot otherwise affirmatively demonstrate the parties' final and serious intent to enter into marriage. Accordingly, since both conditions would have to be met before Ms. Barkes could state a viable contract claim, there is no way she could maintain any sort of contract action against Dr. Gilbert.

Under the principles of Intentional Infliction of Emotional Distress (IIED), Ms. Barkes is similarly precluded because the record demonstrates that she falls short of proving the elements of this claim. . . . To make out a claim of IIED, the following elements must be proved: (1) the wrongdoer's conduct must be intentional or reckless; (2) the conduct must be outrageous and intolerable in that it offends against generally accepted standards of decency and morality; (3) there must be a causal connection between the wrongdoer's conduct and the emotional distress; and (4) the emotional distress must be severe. . . .

Recklessness in this context requires that the wrongdoer's actions reflect a lack of consideration well in excess of the thoughtlessness that would be evident in most engagements which are broken off. To meet the necessary recklessness threshold, the wrongdoer must engage in conduct which demonstrates total disregard for the other party. The plaintiff must prove conduct that is so insensitive and irresponsible as to rise to the level of being deemed virtually intentional. It must be the conduct which any normal and prudent person would know was likely to cause extreme emotional distress. With respect to the fourth element, there is a fairly high level of emotional distress any time any engagement is broken off. To meet the element of severe emotional distress, however, substantially more than mere sorrow is required.

From the record, it is clear that Ms. Barkes has not alleged facts which could even begin to support a claim for IIED. . . .

What outcome would you expect if the court had retained the BPM cause of action? In that case, what effect on a judgment might there be from the facts that Ms. Barkes took three months to accept the marriage proposal and that the engagement had already lingered over two years when Ms. Barkes sold her home and moved in with Dr. Gilbert?

Does the court draw a clear line between costs that are compensable in a broken engagement case and those that are not? If you became engaged and *bought* a house for you and your spouse to live in, perhaps even though you otherwise would have waited until the market was better for buyers, feeling a pressing need to have a residence large enough for you both, would you consider the transaction costs, relocation costs, or any premium you paid a wedding-related expense? Would the court? How about a down payment on a honeymoon cruise?

Is there symmetry between one person's buying a ring and the other person's (or her family's) incurring wedding-related expenses? The whole situation is highly gendered, so feminists are highly critical of jurisdictions where rings must be returned by the bride and her parents get no recovery for reliance costs. Is there any defense for such a regime? Or for its opposite (i.e., bride keeps ring but groom must help pay for lost deposits)?

Does an engagement today amount to any kind of promise? If so, what is the content of the promise? If it were actually a promise to marry, how does that differ from the wedding vows? Is a marriage itself really a promise of anything today, or just a prediction ("I think I'll want to share a life with you for a very long time, but we'll see . . ."? What would be the point of promising (or threatening) to live with someone for the rest of your life?

D. HOW TO DO IT

State laws prescribe various procedures for a legally valid formal marriage. Typically, the first step is securing a license to marry by filling out paperwork and proving identity and freedom to marry (e.g., by proving divorce from a former spouse) at a local government office. The license is valid for a specified period, such as 60 days, and within that period the couple should go through a ceremony officiated by someone whom the law authorizes to perform weddings. State laws typically authorize judges, private citizens appointed as justices of the peace, and religious leaders to perform weddings. The couple presents their license to the officiating person, and that person then performs the ceremony and afterward fills out a marriage certificate. The officiant or the couple then files the certificate with some government office, usually the same one that issued the license. There are generally no legal requirements as to the content of the ceremony. Once the ceremony, however constructed, is over, Voila!, the couple is legally married and thereafter governed by a large body of legal rules that did not apply to them prior to marriage.

Massachusetts General Laws
Part II. Real and Personal Property and Domestic Relations
Title III. Domestic Relations
Chapter 207. Marriage

§19. Situs; Time; Fees

Persons intending to be joined in marriage in the commonwealth shall, not less than three days before their marriage, jointly cause notice of their intention to be filed in the office of the clerk or registrar of any city or town in the commonwealth, and pay the fee. . . .

§28. Certificate of Intention of Marriage; Delivery; Time

On or after the third day from the filing of notice of intention of marriage, . . . the clerk or registrar shall deliver to the parties a certificate signed by him. . . . Such certificate shall be delivered to the minister or magistrate before whom the marriage is to be contracted. . . .

§38. Situs; Persons Authorized

A marriage may be solemnized in any place within the commonwealth by . . . a duly ordained minister of the gospel in good and regular standing with his church or denomination, including [a Methodist or Catholic deacon and a Jewish cantor or rabbi]; by a justice of the peace . . . ; and [specified members of Spiritual Assembly of the Baha'is, Buddhist community, Unitarian Universalist Association, Ethical Culture Society, Orthodox Islamic religion, Friends or Quakers]. . . . Churches and other religious organizations shall file in the office of the state secretary information relating to persons recognized or licensed. . . .

§39. Justice or Non-Resident Clergymen

. . . [T]he governor may designate any other person to solemnize a particular marriage on a particular date and in a particular city or town. . . .

§48. Solemnization of Marriage Without Authority

Whoever, not being duly authorized by the laws of the commonwealth, undertakes to join persons in marriage therein shall be punished by a fine of not more than five hundred dollars or by imprisonment for not more than one year, or both.

§49. JOINING PERSONS IN MARRIAGE WITHOUT CERTIFICATE

Whoever, being duly authorized to solemnize marriages in the commonwealth, joins in marriage persons who have not complied with the laws relative to procuring certificates of notice of intention of marriage shall be punished by a fine of not more than five hundred dollars.

STATUTORY INTERPRETATION EXERCISE

A couple in Massachusetts, who are brother and sister, has a friend perform a wedding ceremony for them. The friend has no legal authority to perform weddings, and the couple did not obtain a "certificate of notice." The couple has no expectation of having a legal marriage recognized; they just want to have a private wedding ceremony. Has anyone violated Massachusetts law?

Marriage formalities are rarely the subject of court proceedings. They are easy to follow and not burdensome. Various statutory provisions in each state prescribe what should happen when a defect of a procedural (e.g., officiant was not actually authorized to perform weddings) or substantive (e.g., prior marriage not properly terminated) nature is discovered, and they generally aim to avoid harm to parties who acted in good faith.

One question a lawyer might receive from clients is whether they can get themselves qualified to perform weddings. Some people who are neither judges nor religious leaders want to get qualified either because some particular couple thought it would be so wonderful if they could escort the couple to marital paradise or because they want to make some money on the side. As you just saw, Massachusetts law authorizes the Governor to appoint people as one-time officiants. In Virginia, local judges can do the same. What is the state interest in controlling who performs marriages? Why not just have the couple submit another form confirming that they exchanged vows? Is there anything problematic about the fact that a couple's choices might be (depending on who can get the Governor's authorization) between a government-appointed official they have never met before and a religious leader? In this regard, note that religious leaders are not required to marry anyone who requests it; they can refuse anyone and can establish conditions for agreeing (e.g., the Catholic Church generally requires pre-marital counseling and local priests might also require parish membership).

Universal Life Church v. Utah

189 F. Supp. 2d 1302 (D. Utah 2002)

KIMBALL, District Judge.

. . . [T]he Utah Legislature passed during its 2001 legislative session . . . :

30-1-6.1. Ordination by Internet not valid.

Certification, licensure, ordination, or any other endorsement received by a person through application over the Internet or by mail that purports to give that person religious authority is not valid for the purposes of Subsection 30-1-6(1)(a).

. . . §30-1-6 (the "Marriage Solemnization Statute") . . . provides:

> **30-1-6. Who may solemnize marriages—Certificate.**
> (1) Marriages may be solemnized by the following persons only:
> (a) ministers, rabbis, or priests of any religious denomination who are:
> (i) in regular communion with any religious society; and
> (ii) 18 years of age or older;
> (b) Native American spiritual advisors;

In addition, Utah law provides in pertinent part: "If any person not authorized solemnizes a marriage under pretense of having authority . . . he shall be punished by imprisonment in the state prison not exceeding three years." Utah Code Ann. §30-1-14 (1998).

The ULC is headquartered in Modesto, California. It has two tenets: (1) "the absolute right of freedom of religion," and (2) "to do that which is right." . . . The ULC will ordain anyone free, for life, without questions of faith. Anyone can be ordained a ULC minister in a matter of minutes by clicking onto the ULC's website and by providing a name, address, and e-mail address. Anyone can also be ordained by mailing to the ULC a name and address. There is no oath, ceremony, or particular form required. The ULC keeps records of ordinations, but does not keep membership records or records of church rites such as baptisms, weddings, or funerals. One can also order other products to aid in the ministry, including a minister's wallet credentials, blank press passes, a reversible MINISTER/PRESS windshield placard, the Ultimate Wedding Guide book and other clergy packages.

The ULC represents to its ministers that ULC ministers can perform rites and ceremonies, including weddings, and that they can ordain others into the ministry. The only limitation on ordinations is that a minister cannot ordain others without their permission. The ULC requires virtually nothing from its ministers: they are not required to perform any religious ceremonies, to oversee a congregation, to provide religious guidance or counseling, to report religious ceremonies to headquarters, to keep in contact with the ULC other than routine address changes, or to attend any worship services.

Pace was ordained a ULC minister in 1993 by application through the mail. He has had contact with the ULC through sporadic newsletters and reading of-but not participation in-"chat room" dialogue on the Internet. He has performed several marriage ceremonies in Utah as a ULC minister. . . .

Plaintiffs allege that the Challenged Statute violates Plaintiffs' rights to free exercise of religion, . . . equal protection of the laws, and . . . substantive due process . . . , in violation of the United States and Utah Constitutions. The Complaint requests declaratory relief, a preliminary and permanent injunction, attorneys' fees, and costs. . . .

1. Standing

. . . Defendants contend that the statute does not affect Plaintiffs because, regardless of the Challenged Statute, Plaintiffs cannot perform marriages in any event because they are not ministers, priests, or rabbis in "regular communion with any religious society," as required by the Marriage Solemnization Statute. Defendants concede that the Utah Legislature has not defined the above-quoted words, but Defendants offer common dictionary definitions to argue that Pace has never been in "regular communion with a religious society" and that the Legislature did not intend for a "minister" such as Pace to be allowed to perform marriage ceremonies. . . .

Plaintiffs have used the same dictionary as Defendants and have offered other meanings for the word "communion," which they claim encompasses the relationship between Pace and the ULC (i.e., communion is an act or instance of sharing). . . . Plaintiffs contend that Pace is "in regular communion" with the ULC because in his affidavit, he testifies that he is "in regular communion" with his church, and that if Pace and the ULC acknowledge a relationship that is comfortable and satisfactory to each of them and which they define as "regular communion," the discussion ends.

While this court is uncertain about whether Pace's occasional reading of newsletters and chat-room dialogue satisfies the "regular communion" requirement set forth in the Marriage Solemnization Statute, the court need not rule on that issue because the court nonetheless finds that Plaintiffs have standing to contest the constitutionality of the Internet Statute.[2]

. . . The court finds that this case is one of those exceptional cases in which standing exists despite the lack of any actual or threatened prosecution of Plaintiffs. Pace has a personal stake in the outcome sufficient to assure an adversarial presentation of the case, and thus, a case or controversy exists. An "injury in fact" exists because Pace has "alleged an intention to engage in a course of conduct arguably affected with a constitutional interest, but proscribed by statute." . . . Pace specifically stated . . . that he intended to perform wedding ceremonies in August and September. In addition, given the undisputed fact that one of the tenets of the ULC is to act within the law, coupled with the fact that Pace is also an attorney, Pace should not be required to violate the law and risk prosecution in order to seek a determination regarding whether he can continue a practice in which he has engaged for many years without fear of prosecution.

While this case has not been certified as a class action, the court recognizes that a judicial determination regarding the Challenged Statute will impact not only Pace, but also many of the more-than 5,600 ULC ministers in Utah, many of whom received their ordinations through application over the Internet or through the mail. . . .[5]

Moreover, . . . the Challenged Statute appears to directly target the ULC and its ministers. Moreover, the State has not disavowed its intention to enforce the Challenged Statute . . .

a. The Free Exercise Clause

Plaintiffs argue that the State must pursue a course of "neutrality" toward religion, favoring neither one religion over others nor religious adherents collectively over non-adherents. Plaintiffs assert that declaring an act of ordination ineffectual because a church chooses to use the Internet or the mail is an unconstitutional interference with the internal operations of a church. They contend that the Internet Statute takes from churches the ability to decide how to empower a cleric within their religion and that such

2. Thus, the court's decision in this matter expresses no opinion on whether ULC ministers have authority under the Marriage Solemnization Statute to perform marriages in Utah, as that thorny issue is not before the court.

5. The validity of marriages performed by ULC ministers could be called into question if no judicial determination is made regarding the constitutionality of the Internet Statute. The court recognizes that a marriage will not be invalid if it was "consummated in the belief of the parties or either of them that [the person solemnizing their marriage] had authority and that they have been lawfully married." Utah Code Ann. §30-1-5(1) (1998). With the constitutionality of the Challenged Statute now having been called into question, however, it is foreseeable that individuals will continue to use ULC ministers to solemnize their marriages. At the same time, without a judicial determination, and in light of the media attention given to this case, these individuals may face a more difficult burden in establishing that they believed that the ULC minister had authority to marry them, casting a cloud over the validity of such marriages.

minute government management of the operations of a church is excessive entanglement. . . .

The Free Exercise Clause protects beliefs that are religious and sincerely held. Ascertaining the sincerity of a belief generally involves assessing whether an activity is the good faith observance of religious belief. The goal, of course, is "to protect only those beliefs which are held as a matter of conscience."

Nowhere have Plaintiffs demonstrated that being ordained through application over the Internet or through the mail is a religious belief, much less that it is sincerely held. Rather, the Internet and mail application procedures for becoming a minister is merely an administrative convenience to the ULC. Notably, the ULC does not *require* that its ministers be ordained through application through the mail or over the Internet. Indeed, individuals may apply for ordination over the telephone, in person by any other ULC minister, or even by fax. The Challenged Statute does not dictate or control whom the ULC may choose to ordain—it may still ordain whomever it wishes. Moreover, the ULC is not prohibited from ordaining its ministers who send their applications through the Internet or by mail; however, those individuals would not have authority to solemnize marriages in Utah.[10] In addition, the Challenged Statute does not force Plaintiffs to do anything contrary to their beliefs.

Thus, the Internet Statute applies to a secular activity that the State clearly has the power to regulate. It does not violate Plaintiffs' free exercise rights under the First Amendment of the United States Constitution or under Article I, Section 4 of the Utah Constitution.

b. The Due Process Clause

Plaintiffs argue . . . that they have a fundamental liberty and/or property interest in the right to practice their religion (i.e., to perform marriage ceremonies) and to conduct the internal workings of their church, and thus, the Challenged Statute must be scrutinized under a "strict scrutiny" standard. Additionally, they claim that the Challenged Statute is so unfair, capricious, arbitrary, and irrational as to violate substantive due process. . . .

[T]here is no constitutionally protectable liberty or property interest in performing marriage ceremonies. Thus, . . . the Challenged Statute must pass only a deferential rational relationship test. . . . If "any conceivable legitimate governmental interest" supports the contested statute, it "is not 'arbitrary and capricious' and cannot offend substantive due process norms."

While no legislative history is available regarding the purpose of the Challenged Statute, it is conceivable that it bears a rational relation to the State's legitimate purpose of protecting the integrity of marriages. It is clear that states have an absolute right to prescribe the condition upon which marriage shall be created. Indeed, "marriage is a state-conferred legal status, the existence of which gives rise to the rights and benefits reserved exclusively to that particular relationship." The power to regulate the marriage relation "includes the power to determine the requisites of a valid marriage contract and to control the qualifications of the contracting parties, the forms and procedures necessary to solemnize the marriage, the duties and obligations it creates, its effect

10. Indeed, the burden on the ULC is quite minimal given that the Challenged Statute does not pertain to ULC ministers who download the minister application form from the Internet and then fax the completed form to the ULC or telephone the ULC with the required information (i.e., a name and address). Moreover, a close reading of the Challenged Statute does not invalidate the authority of ministers who receive their ordination certificates and other pertinent materials over the Internet, so long as their applications are received by methods other than over the Internet or through the mail.

upon property and other rights, and the grounds for marital dissolution." Accordingly, "'[r]easonable regulations that do not significantly interfere with decisions to enter into the marital relationship may legitimately be imposed.'" *Zablocki v. Redhail*, 434 U.S. 374, 386 (1978)). . . .

Conceivably, the Legislature was concerned that one who so cavalierly becomes a minister might not appreciate the gravity of solemnizing a marriage and might not bring to the ceremony the desired level of dignity and integrity.[14] In addition, it is conceivable that the Legislature could rationally be concerned that an individual's decision to use such a minister might be reflective of a cavalier attitude toward the marriage relationship.[15] It is not the court's role to agree or disagree with the Legislature's methods for achieving its goals; rather, this court is obligated to find the Challenged Statute constitutional unless there is no conceivable rational relationship between the Challenged Statute and the State's interest. . . .

c. The Equal Protection Clause

Plaintiffs claim that the statute violates the Equal Protection Clause because it implicitly allows Native American spiritual advisors to receive ordination over the Internet or by mail while prohibiting certain other ecclesiastics from so receiving their ordination. . . .

This court has ruled that no "fundamental right" is involved in this case. It is not about the right to marry, which is clearly a fundamental right protected by the Constitution. Rather, it is about the right to perform marriage ceremonies. In addition, Plaintiffs do not—and could not—argue that they are a suspect or quasi-suspect class triggering a level of scrutiny more searching than a rational relationship test. Because the Challenged Statute does not make classifications based upon a fundamental right or a suspect class, the statute must pass only a rational relationship test. Under the rational relationship test, Plaintiffs have the "heavy burden of proving that 'the legislative facts on which the classification is apparently based could not reasonably be conceived to be true by the governmental decisionmaker.'" Also, . . . "economic and social legislation generally is presumed valid." A court will not "invalidate a statute because the legislature has not fashioned the classification in question with 'mathematical nicety.'" Further, "[t]he Constitution does not prohibit the legislature from focusing on only part of a problem: 'the reform may take one step at a time, addressing itself to the phase of the problem which seems most acute to the legislative mind.'" . . .

There is no suggestion that Native American spiritual advisors achieve that status by merely sending their name and address over the Internet or through the mail, and thus the Legislature rationally concluded that there was no reason to make the Challenged Statute applicable to Native American spiritual advisors.

As noted above, however, another classification has been created by the Challenged Statute: (1) ministers whose applications were received over the Internet or through the mail, and (2) ministers whose applications were received via fax, telephone, or in person by another ULC minister.[17] The Challenged Statute invalidates the authority of the

14. For example, at the hearing on this matter, counsel for Defendants indicated that there had been a growing problem of individuals ordaining their pets as ULC ministers.

15. The court recognizes that this fear is not borne out by Pace's affidavits concerning the amount of time he spends with couples for whom he intends to perform a marriage ceremony and the thought and preparation that goes into his ceremonies. However, that information is not relevant to the court's analysis.

17. This court makes no determination regarding whether the term "mail" in the Challenged Statute includes or excludes Federal Express, UPS, or any other private delivery service.

individuals in the former group to perform marriages in Utah without risking prosecution, while it does not invalidate the authority of those in the latter group.[18]

With all due respect to the Utah Legislature, this court cannot conceive of any ground upon which such classifications could be rationally related to the State's interest in protecting the integrity of marriages. A state "may not rely on a classification whose relationship to an asserted goal is so attenuated as to render the distinction arbitrary or irrational." If the Legislature was concerned with the casual and effortless manner in which an individual is able to become a ULC minister, there is no rational basis for the differential treatment between (1) ministers who applied via the Internet and mail, and (2) those who applied via fax, telephone, or in person.

The same information—a name and address—is all that is required to become a minister in the ULC, regardless of the manner in which such information is received. It is not disputed that ULC ministers are permitted to submit applications for ordination in methods other than over the Internet or in the mail. Indeed, it is clear that a ULC minister can ordain in person any individual who seeks to be ordained, and even the ULC web site provides a telephone number and a fax number for the ULC. Consequently, there is no plausible connection between the "uniqueness" of the ministers who applied for ordination via the Internet and mail and the purpose of the Internet Statute. The Legislature has relied on a classification whose relationship to a goal is so attenuated as to render the distinction arbitrary and irrational. Accordingly, Plaintiffs have not been accorded equal treatment to those who are virtually identically situated, thus depriving Plaintiffs of their equal protection rights under both the U.S. and Utah Constitutions. . . .

Defendants are permanently enjoined from enforcing the Challenged Statute. . . .

Is it as clear as the court suggests that the statute does not implicate the right to marry, but rather only the right to perform marriages? Might a ULC minister be the only acceptable officiant for some couples? Is the court's freedom of religion analysis adequate? Doesn't the court itself note that the legislature appears to have targeted the ULC specifically? Would it be difficult for the Utah legislature to amend the statute in a way that would satisfy its aims and survive constitutional challenge?

CROSS-CULTURAL PERSPECTIVE:

In some jurisdictions with civil unions or registered partnerships, couples need only register at some government agency; there is no need for an authorized officiant to perform any ceremony. Should we also dispense with the officiating of weddings and just have couples register as married? Or just view marriage as a private contract, perhaps with some default legal rules governing the relationship and its dissolution but without any registering or officiating required? Cf. Mary Ann Case, *Marriage Licenses*, 89 MINN. L. REV. 1758, 1766 (2005) ("the earliest English laws concerning marriage treat it as, in effect, a contract for the purchase of a wife, a purely private transaction, with 'no trace

18. While the court has not ruled that these individuals have authority in any event under the Marriage Solemnization Statute, the fact that the Defendants themselves have highlighted that no ULC minister has ever been prosecuted—or even threatened with prosecution—for lacking the authority to perform a marriage under that Statute creates a presumption that, without being covered by the Challenged Statute, ULC ministers could continue, as they have been, to solemnize marriages without fear of prosecution.

of any such thing as public license or registration; no authoritative intervention of priest or other public functionary. It is purely a private business transaction.'"). In the Muslim world, individualized contract negotiation is the norm for marriage.

David Pearl & Werner Menski, Muslim Family Law

(3d ed. 1998)

6-03 A Muslim marriage is in essence a solemn civil contract between a man and a woman. Middle Eastern writers like Nasir distinguish it from the sacramental concept of Christian marriage, while south Asian authors almost always contrast the Muslim contract of *nikah* with the Hindu concept of marriage as an indissoluble sacrament or *samskara*. . . . It is apparent, however, that a Muslim marriage also has religious elements and is not purely a matter of contractual arrangement between two individuals. Indeed, as a contract before God, it has a character of sanctity.

6-04 In terms of formal requirements, the *nikah is* effected quite simply by the two essential elements of offer and acceptance. The declarations, which must be made conceptually "at the same meeting," are pronounced by the parties themselves, or by an attorney acting on their behalf, or by their guardians when they lack the capacity to contract themselves in marriage. The first speech, from whichever side it emanates, is the offer, and the second speech constitutes the acceptance. . . . [A] proxy marriage, for example over the telephone, is possible in Muslim law.

6-05 Another essential element of a valid Muslim marriage contract, except for Shi'as, is the presence of witnesses. . . . [T]his element of publicity makes the difference between lawful wedlock and fornication. The particulars of this requirement depend on school tradition, but the general rule is that there must be either two males or one male and two females.

6-06 The simple contractual form of marriage is almost always accompanied by religious and customary ceremonials. However . . . : "Those formalities which are usually attendant upon a Muslim marriage, such as the performance of the ceremony in the presence of a religious official like the Imam of the mosque, are matters of customary practice and in no sense legal essentials." However, proof of such forms of celebration of a Muslim marriage may become part of the evidence required to demonstrate the existence of a particular marriage in law. This is important since there may be no written evidence of the simple contractual arrangements, which may have been entirely oral.

6-07 . . . While official registration is considered of paramount importance today, in traditional societies, instead of formal registration, the publicity of the marriage contract serves as an important safeguard. Further, the public celebration of the marriage through feasting and other social rituals leads to public recognition of the married status of the individuals concerned. In this context, certain presumptions of marriage have developed in practice.

6-08 Attempts to introduce registration procedures have met with considerable opposition. . . . [I]n most Muslim countries [today,] facilities exist for registration of marriages, but non-compliance with these merely involves criminal sanctions and does not invalidate the marriage.

6-34 Muslim law permits the proof of marriage on the basis of a prolonged and continuous cohabitation by the parties and thus applies a presumption of marriage. There must be evidence that the man acknowledged the woman as his lawful wife, and equally acknowledged any children by the relationship as being his legitimate children. The presumption does not arise in a case where no lawful marriage could have been solemnised in any event. . . .

Would any legitimate state interest be sacrificed by doing away with the requirement in the United States that some consecrated official "perform" the wedding, rather than the couple simply executing a contract and filing a registration with the state? Would couples take the decision any less seriously? Is some involvement of state officials necessary in the West because family there does not perform the same function as it does in more traditional societies? Does the discussion of publicity in paragraphs 6-05 to 6-07 suggest a possible function that wedding receptions in the United States today might serve? Or is the purpose of the reception just to celebrate a momentous event?

E. RETHINKING MARRIAGE

In the following readings, you are again asked to step back from prevailing practices to rethink fundamental assumptions about a body of family law rules. Specifically, we will consider a "fitness" requirement for marriage, just as we considered a fitness requirement for initial legal parentage, and, on the other hand, abolishing legal marriage altogether, making it a purely private matter.

1. A Fitness Requirement?

As explained in the chapter on parentage, states have been moving toward a legal regime in which parents can be denied a relationship with a newborn baby on the basis of their unfitness to parent, which they might have demonstrated by having previously abused another child, by abusing drugs or alcohol during pregnancy, by committing crimes that land them in jail, by being mentally ill, or by having abandoned other children. The law recognizes that some people, despite a desire to enter into a particular type of family relationship, are not able or willing to behave within the relationship in a way that generates the goods typically associated with that type of relationship, and in fact are likely to cause harm instead. Should the law similarly disqualify some people from entering into legal marriage, on grounds that they are unfit for that type of relationship and likely to generate harm rather than the expected goods of marriage? The prohibitions on same-sex and underage marriage are often justified in such terms. Are there other bases for exclusion that would be strong enough to enact into law?

Think about this issue from the perspective of a taxpayer. Legal marriage entails costs for the state—for example, providing lower tax rates (in some situations), paying survivor social security benefits, and adjudicating divorces. That money comes from general tax revenues, from married and non-married people, so to some extent entails a wealth transfer from single people to married people. Might unmarried taxpayers have cause for complaint if the state includes in this wealth transfer program some people who have a history or characteristics that make it highly unlikely that their marrying would serve the purposes supposed to underwrite state involvement in marriage? Or that in fact make it highly likely that their marrying will have a negative impact on social welfare? Recall the Spanish provision excluding from marriage any person who has previously murdered a spouse. That seems like a sensible idea, doesn't it? Would you go further and disqualify anyone previously convicted of domestic violence against a spouse, at least for some period of time? Or at least require that person to demonstrate in a court or administrative proceeding that he or she has adequately addressed the causes of that past behavior? Someone who has been married previously must produce a divorce decree, so why not require someone with such a previous conviction to produce proof of completing anger management classes? What about serial marriers—should there be a "three strikes" rule: Anyone who has been divorced three times may not marry again? Is it possible rationally to reconcile denying marriage to same-sex couples while freely allowing egregious spouse batterers and thrice divorced people to marry? Are there any other bases for exclusion you could suggest?

2. *The Case for Abolition*

Mary Anne Case, Marriage Licenses

89 Minn. L. Rev. 1758, 1766 (2005)

. . . When the English state finally and definitively asserted control over marriage, it did so through its Established Church. The first systematic reform of English marriage laws, the 1753 Act for the Better Preventing of Clandestine Marriages, popularly known as Lord Hardwicke's Act after the Lord Chancellor who shepherded it through Parliament, represented the apex of the English state's assertion of monopoly control over the formation of marriage. The Act declared null and void all marriages not preceded by the issue of an official ecclesiastical license or by the calling of banns in the Anglican church of the parish where one of the marriage partners had resided for a specified period. It required that marriages be witnessed and set forth detailed requirements for their entry in specially prepared marriage registers. Violation of the Act's provisions by a clergyman was made a felony subject to fourteen years deportation to the colonies, but falsification of a marriage register subjected offenders to the death penalty. Each one of these provisions was designed to remedy perceived abuses in the application of the law of marriage over the preceding century. . . .

At the time Hardwicke's Act first made a marriage license an obligatory precondition for a valid marriage in England, a predominant view of what it was that marriage licensed was contemporaneously set forth by William Blackstone in his Commentaries on the Laws of England. On this view, a marriage license could be seen to have functioned, in ways loosely analogous to a modern dog license, as something like a certificate of ownership of the wife, entitling the husband to her property, her body and its products, including the labor she engaged in for wages and the labor that produced offspring; obliging him to provide for her care and feeding; giving him a cause of action against those who injured her or his interest in her; making him responsible for her actions and giving him the right to control her. She did not have the same rights over and duties to him, although she was obliged to provide him domestic services and sexual access and to share his residence. Just as dog licenses require that the animal wear a collar and tag with its owner's name, so, as late as the 1970s, many U.S. states required by law that a wife take her husband's name; she was obliged to be known after marriage as Mrs. Husband's Name, and customarily always wore a wedding ring. A husband did not ordinarily take his wife's name, or indicate his marital status in his name or title in any way; nor, in much of U.S. society for long periods of history, did husbands tend to wear wedding rings. This asymmetry of roles, duties, and privileges in law, although on the decline since at least the passage of the first Married Women's Property Acts in the mid-nineteenth century, remained . . . very much a part of the legal landscape. . . .

Suzanne A. Kim, Skeptical Marriage Equality

34 Harv. J.L. & Gender 37, 42-47 (2011)

Feminists and gay rights scholars have critiqued marriage both in its historical and contemporary permutations. This critique has largely hinged on marriage as a vehicle for subordinating women and children in a gender-hierarchical structure. Feminist critical efforts have focused on revealing and decreasing the extent to which women's economic, legal, and social power hinges on marriage and on the gender hierarchy within marriage. Gay rights scholars have also focused on the heteronormative discipline that marriage imposes on sexual minorities. . . .

Marriage has fostered this subordination by providing legal cover in the guise of marital privacy for abuses of power within its putative sphere. As described by Martha Fineman, marriage has historically served as the "primary means of protecting and providing for the legal and structurally devised dependency of wives." This dependency occurred through the legally-enforced civil disappearance of wives through coverture. According to Fineman, "[m]arriage has . . . shaped the aspirations and experiences of women and men in ways that have historically disadvantaged women." . . .

From the passage of the Nineteenth Amendment in 1920 to the fundamental reforms of the 1960s onward, marriage has come to be more egalitarian, at least formally. As Twila Perry recounts, the "essentials of marriage," such as the duty of support and duty of services, were formerly distributed along gender lines; legal change rendered these essentials mutual and gender neutral. In addition, the right to determine a family's domicile is held today by each marital partner, rather than solely by the husband. Moreover, reforms in custody presumptions and the advent of no-fault divorce have been lauded for helping to create more formal gender equality in marriage.

Although women's legal status within marriage has improved significantly, marriage still reflects and reinforces gender hierarchy to a significant degree. . . . For example, the practice of women taking their husband's last name upon marriage continues almost universally in this country, despite the elimination of any formal compulsion to do so. Others have written persuasively about the continued gendered division of carework within marriage. Moreover, the phenomenon of women "opting out" of the workforce to care for children highlights the economic vulnerability of women within marriage.

The critique of marriage extends to the privileged status of marriage in family law and policy. Martha Fineman has urged the abolition of marriage as a legal category. She points to the "distort[ing]" effects of marriage, insofar as the "concept of marriage, and the assumptions it carries with it . . . preclude[ ] consideration of other solutions to social problems." Fineman's proposal to reorganize family law around caretaking units aims to provide societal and state support for the inevitable and universal state of dependency more effectively than marriage does.

In critiquing the primacy of marriage as the central organizing principle of family law, Laura Rosenbury has argued that the focus on the marital relationship marginalizes those who are not married and perpetuates "gendered patterns of care." To the extent that the caregiving work that many women perform throughout their lives is only recognized in the context of marriage, women receive inadequate support for the carework that occupies much of their lives. Moreover, [Professor Laura] Rosenbury points to the stigmatization that women who live outside of marriage, either by choice or circumstance, experience due to the primacy of marriage.

Many in the lesbian and gay communities criticize the effort to secure access to marriage for same-sex couples. . . . Some queer theorists critique marriage as a vehicle of the state in regulating intimacy. For example, for Michael Warner, marriage demonstrates the state's sexual discipline and control. Moreover, whether populated and performed by same-sex or opposite-sex couples, marriage is inherently heteronormative; the pursuit of marriage is troublingly normalized and normalizing. The queer theory critique of marriage also focuses on the over-privileging of marriage above other types of affective connection. Warner discusses the "ennobling and . . . demeaning" functions of marriage as part of the problem with marriage, gay or straight:

> To a couple that gets married, marriage just looks ennobling. . . . Stand outside it for a second and you see the implication: if you don't have it, you and your relations are less worthy. Without this corollary effect, marriage would not be able to endow anybody's life with significance. The ennobling and the demeaning go together. Marriage does one only by virtue of the other.

Katherine Franke's critique of marriage focuses similarly on protecting "affective sexual liberty outside of marriage." Franke raises concerns that the same-sex marriage movement threatens this extra-marital space. She has argued that the decision in *Lawrence v. Texas* created a "relative absence of regulation of homosexualities," which should be viewed "as an opportunity rather than as an injury." . . . While Franke acknowledges the benefits of marriage, these benefits come at a cost. She acknowledges the big "payoff" of marriage that requires its participants to submit to a wide range of "regulatory demands": marriage may involve "only two adults, not married to anyone else, who pledge to be monogamous, are financially interdependent in a particular way, and will be bound by a set of nonnegotiable default rules when one or both parties seek to terminate the marriage." Franke argues, accordingly, that "the institution of marriage demands the surrender of a great deal of the liberty rights acknowledged in *Lawrence*, rights that unmarried people enjoy more robustly." . . .

Feminist and gay rights scholars have argued that to advance the cause of same-sex marriage is to promote the primacy of marriage as a central organizing force in family law and to perpetuate a gendered, patriarchal, and oppressive institution. Drawing on Martha Fineman's rejection of marriage as a legal category, Nancy Polikoff has argued that the quest for same-sex marriage is misguided because it diverts attention away from finding more innovative, effective solutions to supporting families and caretaking outside of marriage. Polikoff argues that we should be focusing our collective efforts on valuing all families under the law, not just marital families.

Professor Kim takes the view that the pursuit of same-sex marriage is actually consistent with the aim of deprivileging marriage. She writes:

> The debate on the political left over same-sex marriage generally divides into two modes of thought: "marriage equality" and "marriage skepticism." Marriage equality is based on the notion that the right of access to marriage is a civil right, important for full political participation and social recognition, predicated on the legal and social significance of marriage. Marriage skepticism is based on the idea that marriage is an institution so troubled that the fight for marriage is not worth pursuing. . . .
>
> Thus far, leading efforts to link the concerns of marriage skepticism with those of marriage equality have tended to focus on the ways in which same-sex marriage holds the promise of transforming marriage internally into a more egalitarian institution. . . . The theory of skeptical marriage equality I set forth herein maintains that . . . same-sex marriage, and the quest for marriage equality, may potentially (and counterintuitively) contribute to unsettling the hierarchical relationship between marriage and other forms of intimacy under the law to make way for a more pluralistic landscape of legally recognized family forms. . . . Marriage equality's reconsideration of the sex-based definition of marriage resonates with marriage skepticism's critique of marriage as traditionally constructed. . . . The pursuit of same-sex marriage facilitates the pluralistic goals of the marriage critique by drawing attention to the gender-hierarchical and sexuality norm-enforcing construction of traditional marriage. Marriage equality may also promise to lead to greater pluralism as advocated by marriage skepticism by constituting marriage in a way that redefines marriage away from sex-difference and toward core values that are at stake in marriage, such as commitment and caregiving. A fundamental shift in the socially-privileged status of marriage may pave the way toward more functional understandings of family and intimacy overall.

Id. at 40-41. Supposing that Professor Kim is correct that left advocacy for same-sex marriage can to some degree aid efforts to reform and deprivilege marriage, one might still conclude:

1) Advocacy for same-sex marriage hinders progressive marriage-related reform more than it helps it; and/or
2) the best position for the left and for the gay community to take is a complete rejection of marriage, given its ugly history and its continued service as a vehicle for state-imposed restrictions and stereotypes, and an insistence that the government stop tying public benefits (paid for by all taxpayers) to marital status.

Would anything be lost if we abolished legal marriage? Professor Fineman believes nothing valuable would be. Although social policy discussions suggest that marriage is the necessary and proper means for addressing several compelling societal aims—namely, caring for and nurturing children, addressing dependency, and promoting personal happiness—in fact, marriage is not essential to achieving any of those things. Legal rules for parent-child relationships, better state support for caretaking of dependent persons, and private contracting between adult partners are adequate and preferable for serving these aims. Martha Fineman, *Why Marriage?*, 9 VA. J. SOC. POL'Y & L. 239, 259-271 (2001). Professor Abrams adds that tying public benefits to marriage per se creates an incentive for people to enter into sham marriages and falsify documents. See Kerry Abrams, *Marriage Fraud*, 100 CAL. L. REV. 1 (2012).

Indeed, if the state was not involved in marriage for most of Western history, and if the state in many other countries today is not involved in marriage in any significant way, then how could it be that *legal* marriage is necessary for any social good? Are there important differences between life now and life before the state began establishing legal rules imposing legal rights and responsibilities and state-conferred benefits that would suggest we cannot go back to a regime without legal marriage? Or differences between the United States and countries where marriage is today simply a private contract?

An additional and relatively recent criticism of marriage as practiced in the United States is that, despite any claims about its serving as the foundation upon which a healthy society rests, it actually can have a corrosive effect on social existence. Weddings today frequently have the effect, despite the community nature of the ceremony, of insularizing the married couple. Upon marriage people become less available to friends and families, because so much social and emotional weight is put on the marital relationship now. We expect unmarried friends to be available to us, even if they are living with a lover, but once a marriage occurs we become more reluctant to bother them. Marriage and all its ornaments and trappings suggest that each person in the couple becomes owned or absorbed by the other, and this can have negative consequences for other relationships. See Stephanie Coontz, *Too Close for Comfort*, N.Y. Times, Nov. 7, 2006 ("It has only been in the last century that Americans have put all their emotional eggs in the basket of coupled love. Because of this change, . . . we have also neglected our other relationships, placing too many burdens on a fragile institution and making social life poorer in the process. . . . Until 100 years ago, most societies agreed that it was dangerously antisocial, even pathologically self-absorbed, to elevate marital affection and nuclear-family ties above commitments to neighbors, extended kin, civic duty and religion. . . . In some cases we even cause the breakdown by loading the relationship with too many expectations.")

If you have not yet experienced the loss of friends and siblings to the marital abyss, you soon will. Does this happen because of societal expectations? Or do people today, when they marry, just crave all-consuming companionship with their spouse? Might married people suffer from false consciousness, thinking they want a deeply companionate marriage when any fully autonomous person would never genuinely choose such a thing? Is the public debate about same-sex marriage likely to exacerbate a problem of over-emphasis on the marital relationship?

For arguments in favor of retaining marriage, see Lynn D. Wardle, *The Boundaries of Belonging: Allegiance and the Definition of Marriage*, 25 BYU J. Pub. L. 287 (2011), and Carol Sanger, *A Case for Civil Marriage*, 27 Cardozo L. Rev. 1311 (2006).

Part II

STATE REGULATION OF ESTABLISHED RELATIONSHIPS

"Family privacy" is such a trope in American culture that one might suppose the state, after creating family relationships, fades away and leaves private citizens alone to make of the relationships what they will. Far from it. In the United States, government has always been heavily involved in ongoing family life, but many forms of involvement go unnoticed. As with biology-based creation of parent-child relationships, much of state involvement in ongoing family relationships has been by virtue of statutory law operating over a large number of cases with little or no individualized state decision making. The statutory rules are taken for granted and seem just natural, as if emanating from an extra-legal source. This was once as true of the marital relationship as of the parent-child relationship. The legal regime of "coverture" prior to the mid-nineteenth century was essentially state conferral of extensive powers and rights on husbands and wholesale state removal of powers, rights, and privileges from women. When people married, the state dramatically altered their status with respect to property and other persons, in a way that supported male domination of the household. This was simply natural to our ancestors. Today coverture is gone but state and federal governments still influence the marital relationship in many ways, by direct regulation of inter-spousal conduct and property management, by establishing default rules for dissolution of marriage that turn in part on behavior during the marriage, and by subsidizing (e.g., by reduced taxation) and forcing private employers to subsidize (e.g., family leave and health insurance laws) inter-spousal dependency.

State involvement in the parent-child relationship still involves a near-invisible conferral of extensive powers and rights on one side of the relationship. Creation of a legal parent-child relationship in and of itself means nothing to the life of either party. What determines the nature of any social relationship between parent and child is what the state authorizes parents to do with children after the state creates the legal relationship. States have statutes that tie to legal parent status custodial rights to and great power of control over children. It is only because the state gives legal parents such rights and power that ordinary family life can take place. These laws create exceptions to more general laws that prohibit taking possession of non-consenting persons and that presume self-determination in matters such as education, medical care, and diet. In addition to the general empowerment of parents, there are also numerous more specific rules governing various aspects of children's lives and a great deal of individualized adjudication concerning parents' treatment of children and exercise of their decision-making discretion.

In Part II of this text, the law governing the adult-adult relationship comes first, because it arguably is today a better (albeit imperfect) model than the law governing the parent-child relationship for regulation of an intimate relationship in a way that respects the equal moral worth of both members and that protects equally each person's needs and investment in the relationship.

3

STATE REGULATION OF ADULT INTIMATE RELATIONSHIPS

People marry expecting, or at least hoping, that the marriage will be permanent and bring them greater happiness than they would have without it. The state's interests in marriage are consistent with this aspiration. A healthy partnership without disruption generates positive externalities. People in healthy marriages are on average more productive and reliable, less inclined to engage in risky or harmful behaviors, less needful of medical care or state financial support, and better able to raise healthy and well-adjusted offspring than are single people. An ideal legal regime would therefore facilitate permanent, happy marriages.

To design such an ideal regime, the state might identify, drawing from the social science literature on marriage, the conditions and personal characteristics that tend to make marriages work well and those which tend to strain a relationship. The state might then adopt laws and policies that aim to create good conditions and characteristics and eliminate bad ones. Some things that matter might be beyond the state's power to effect. For example, it is not clear what the state can do about a spouse who has low emotional intelligence. For a very different reason, the state cannot aim to make people more religious, even though religiosity correlates positively with marital happiness and durability. But there is much the state could do, at least if it had unlimited resources. The relevant policy questions really are to what extent it is proper for the state to involve itself in marital life, rather than leaving people "free" to carry on their private lives as they wish, and whether particular forms of involvement are cost-effective. Bear these questions in mind as you study what the current legal regime looks like. That regime includes prohibitions of conduct deemed especially destructive of marriage, rules for ownership and management of property, and some financial supports and protections.

Current laws in the United States reflect successes of the struggle for gender equality and the turn toward individualism of the late twentieth century, cultural phenomena we now take for granted. It is obligatory in a family law course, though, to read about the ugly past, when the rules perpetuated patriarchy and manifested little concern for individual happiness (of wives, at least). Why do that? There is no real danger of returning to that past, and it is not clear that familiarity with it is necessary to identifying current problems in the law. Recalling that marital life used to mean abject subordination for women might even make us complacent about current problems for women that, by comparison, seem slight. Conversely, it might make us overly sensitive to any disparate impact that laws and policies today have for women. If there is value in learning about a past we now reject, perhaps it is as a comparative exercise; after all, American law of 200 years ago bears much resemblance to current law in some non-Western countries. We might learn something about the connection between law and socio-economic conditions, how a particular regime of marriage-related laws can "work" for most people at a given time in given social circumstances even though it would not work well for another society with different circumstances. And studying the past might inspire useful critical reflection on the present; the rate of marital permanence today is drastically lower than it was two centuries ago, and the rate of personal satisfaction in marriage today is not especially high, perhaps even lower than during the regime of "coverture" described below. Why would that be?

Claudia Zaher, When a Woman's Marital Status Determined Her Legal Status: A Research Guide on the Common Law Doctrine of Coverture

94 Law Libr. J. 459 (2002)

Traditional English common law, later adopted by the American colonies, . . . discriminated against married women. The doctrine was called "coverture" or the "unity principle," and it is best described by the great English jurist William Blackstone:

> By marriage, the husband and wife are one person in law: that is, the very being or legal existence of the woman is suspended during the marriage, or at least is incorporated and consolidated into that of the husband; under whose wing, protection, and *cover*, she performs every thing; and is therefore called in our law-french a *feme-covert* . . . under the protection and influence of her husband, her *baron*, or lord; and her condition during her marriage is called her *coverture*. . . .
>
> For this reason, a man cannot grant anything to his wife, or enter into covenant with her: for the grant would be to suppose her separate existence; and to covenant with her, would only to be to covenant with himself. . . .
>
> The husband is bound to provide his wife with the necessaries by law, as much as himself; and, if she contracts debts for them, he is obliged to pay them. . . .
>
> If the wife be injured in her person or her property, she can bring no action for redress without her husband's concurrence, and in his name, as well her own; neither can she be sued. . . . But in trials of any sort they are not allowed to be evidence for, or against, each other: partly because it is impossible their testimony should be indifferent, but principally because of the union of person. . . .
>
> But though our law in general considers man and wife as one person, yet there are some instances in which she is separately considered; as inferior to him, and acting by his compulsion. And therefore all deeds executed, and acts done, by her, during her coverture, are void. . . . She cannot by will devise lands to her husband, unless under special circumstances; for at the time of making it she is supposed to be under his coercion. . . .
>
> These are the chief legal effects of marriage during the coverture; upon which we may observe, that even the disabilities which the wife lies under are for the most part intended for her protection and benefit; so great a favorite is the female sex of the laws of England.

1 William Blackstone, Commentaries 442.

. . . As the common-law tradition developed in England, incorporating and intermingling the legal traditions of the Romans and the Normans with the canon law of the Catholic Church and the Anglo-Saxon traditions, . . . [w]idows and unmarried adult women could own property, collect rents, manage shops, and have standing in court, but by virtue of her marriage, the married woman enjoyed none of these privileges, and her person as well as her personal and real property belonged to her husband.

Under coverture, a wife simply had no legal existence. She became, in the words of the Seneca Falls Declaration of Sentiments, "civilly dead." Any income from property she brought into the marriage was controlled by her husband, and if she earned wages outside the home, those wages belonged to him. If he contracted debts, her property went to cover his expenses. . . . To put it most succinctly, upon marriage the husband and wife became one—*him*. Social norms, as reflected in the law, maintained that this was not only the natural way of things but also God's direct intent, quoting Genesis 3:16: "Your desire shall be for your husband, and he shall rule over you."

The English common law was imported into America, and all American lawyers were trained in the law by studying Blackstone's *Commentaries*, but there were definite conflicts between the imported legal tradition and the realities of the New World. Women were relatively rare and more highly valued in the colonies, and necessity had effected changes in society. . . . Women frequently entered the trades in colonial America and became craftsmen and merchants, but as the frontier moved West, the Eastern colonies became more "cultured," more like England, and coverture reigned again.

In the last half of the nineteenth century, the Industrial Revolution changed American society as men left to go to work away from their homes and their shops and farms. At the same time, Victorian ideals of womanhood were shaping social conventions and manners. . . . [A]lthough the changes altered the stated rationale for coverture, coverture remained firmly entrenched. . . . Women were no longer regarded as the property of their baron/lord/husband. They were viewed as unique individuals but individuals who operated in a "separate sphere." Men were responsible for all public activities and relationships outside the family, and women were responsible for the household and the children and the private world of the home. Since their private sphere was thought to be inferior to the public sphere, they still functioned legally under the cover and protection of their husbands.

. . . [I]t was ultimately the Industrial Revolution that began to dismantle the doctrine. As America became an industrial society, the preeminence of commerce and the stable transition of wealth became highly desirable social values. Married Women's Property Acts were passed in every jurisdiction to further this aim, especially to allow extremely wealthy families to transfer their property through their married daughters, without giving control of the family assets to their daughters' husbands. Once married women were viewed as legal persons who could own, sell, and bequeath property, they slowly began to effect the changes in the law that recognized they were legal persons in other areas of the law, persons who could sue their husbands for divorce or for personal injury, gain custody of their children, and enter professions such as law.

. . . [T]he theory of coverture was never fully realized and . . . there were significant deviations from the purity of the theory in the actual practices of the real world. But the social and legal consequences of the doctrine of coverture were pervasive and have carried over into the present. . . . Pioneering women lawyers were denied admission to the bar because of their married state, reasoning that if a married woman could not enter into a contract, a married woman could not enter into an attorney-client relationship. Before the passage of Title VII of the Civil Rights Act of 1964, women could legally be passed over for promotions in the workplace because it was assumed that they were under the protection and support of their husbands. Married women needed the consent of their husbands to obtain a loan, even a commercial loan for their own successful business. Corporate antinepotism rules usually meant that it was the wife who had to find a new employer. Marital rape was not recognized as a criminal act because of the presumption of a wife's consent to her *baron,* her lord, and interspousal tort immunity meant that a woman had no legal recourse for injuries caused by the negligence of her spouse. . . . Coverture has almost faded from the legal scene, but remnants remain intact.

Imagine that the state suddenly removed from you the rights to own property, to enter into contracts, and to sue people who harm you, and gave legal permission to another adult in your home to whip you for the purpose of controlling your behavior and to have sex with you whenever he or she wanted. That is what once happened to women in America upon marriage and still happens to women in some other countries. Note that in the era of coverture, most people viewed this legal regime not as the result of the brute fact of male power, but as divinely ordained, supported by biblical text, dictated by natural law. Today many people view the plenary power of parents over children in the same way. Is there any way rationally to refute either natural law view? Any way to establish that the natural law argument for coverture was wrong but the natural law argument for parental entitlement is correct?

Now suppose the state suddenly imposed on some other adult (not your parent) a perpetual obligation to support you financially, so that you need not pursue employment outside the home. That might be nice, yes? That was the positive facet of coverture for women, though the obligation was not especially robust. (As we will see, that obligation of support still attends marriage, though now it is a mutual and quite limited obligation.) Was this a good bargain for women? Nearly all women accepted it, and voluntarily so in a formal sense (i.e., not under legal compulsion to marry), though there was certainly parental and societal pressure to enter into it. Do the market conditions Zaher describes explain popular support for coverture law? Gendered role differentiation was prevalent throughout human evolution, so would appear to have been a propitious adaptation historically, but why were there ever laws that *forced* people into gender-based labor sectors?

Kerry Abrams & Peter Brooks, Marriage as a Message: Same-Sex Couples and the Rhetoric of Accidental Procreation

21 Yale J.L. & Human. 1, 8-10 (2009)

. . . Lévi-Strauss argued that the role played by women in marriage was that of gift—and the most precious of gifts, at that, because only women (and not animals or objects) could create the alliances that would result in the mixing of the blood of kinship groups. In feminist theorist Gayle Rubin's gloss on Lévi-Strauss, marriage is responsible both for compulsory heterosexuality (women must be available to be given as gifts) and for gendered division of labor (women and men must be interdependent on each other so that they will perceive a need to marry and perpetuate the system). Thus the sexuality most constrained by marriage is female sexuality, and it should come as no surprise that many cultures punish female sexual transgression more harshly than similar misbehavior by men. Marriage, far from chastening male sexuality, was a way of enabling men to exchange women for sexual and reproductive use. . . . [W]ith the emergence of modern societies and the modern legal system, the subordination of women in marriage became more visible. Upon reflection this is hardly surprising: a system that takes private property very seriously will likely take the ownership of women and children seriously as well, and marriage has been an exemplary facilitator of this kind of ownership.

During the time in which American marriage was being shaped, women in marriage not only were not equal to men but essentially lost their independence and their very identity through coverture. Coverture as a legal matter reflects the objectification of women through marriage. . . . The history of marriage, in legal cases and in imaginative literature from Madame Bovary to Anna Karenina to Middlemarch, largely displays women as oppressed, exploited, abused, and suffocated by marriage. Men may also have felt constricted by its bonds, but they have traditionally been freer to participate in marriage (or not) to their advantage. . . .

Marriage's disproportionately disciplining effect on women can also be detected in the law of adultery. Until the last 200 years (or so), adultery in much of the western world was the crime of having intercourse with a married woman. Sex between an unmarried woman and a married man did not qualify, as sex with a married man would not pollute his family's blood lines and would not result in the attendant disruption of the transmittal of property from one generation to the other. Sex with a married woman, on the other hand, might result in a child who was unrelated to her husband becoming that husband's legal heir. . . . Married men appear to have frequently visited brothels, harbored mistresses, and engaged in extensive extra-marital activity with little social or legal consequence.

This conception of marriage as a formalization of property (woman) transfer underlies the call of some feminists today for abolition or rejection of marriage, as you saw at the end of Chapter 2.

Interestingly, the social custom of wives' adopting their husbands' surname hardened into legal rule only after the end of coverture, perhaps because only then did it become relevant to exercise of public rights and formation of contracts. The legal rule persisted for about a century, until 1970s sex equality jurisprudence made it untenable. The default rule of naming today is that individuals keep their surnames of birth, but still roughly 90 percent of women assume their husbands' last name upon marriage as a complete substitute for their original surnames. See Elizabeth F. Emens, *Changing Name Changing: Framing Rules and the Future of Marital Names*, 74 U. Chi. L. Rev. 761 (2007).

Current law influencing the marital relationship includes laws limiting spouses' behavior toward each other and with respect to third parties; creating financial rights and duties as between spouses and with respect to third parties; and facilitating caretaking. The most familiar laws aim to prevent behavior seriously harmful to a spouse or to a marriage, such as adultery and domestic violence, but many areas of law not typically included in a family law coursebook also influence married life, generally in more subtle ways. A complete account of laws affecting marriage would require volumes. This chapter mostly focuses on topics central to domestic relations practice and family policy. For an historical explanation of how some laws affecting the marital relation came to be included in the canon of family law and others not, see Janet Halley, *What Is Family Law?: A Genealogy, Parts I and II,* Yale J.L. & Human. (2011-12).

A. LIMITS ON BEHAVIOR

Historically, entry into marriage altered one's legal rights, duties, permissions, and liabilities with respect to sex, violence, and caretaking. Try to determine to what extent, if any, that remains true today.

1. Sex

States have attempted both to confine the sexual activity of married people to the marital relationship, for readily understandable reasons, and to restrict the kinds of sexual activity spouses engage in with each other, which is more difficult to understand.

a. Sexual Fidelity to One's Spouse

In a world in which non-marital sex was illegal, marriage was a license to have sex, albeit one very limited in scope (i.e., to one person). Today, anti-fornication laws appear unconstitutional as applied to consenting adults, as the Virginia Supreme Court held in *Martin v. Ziherl.* Marriage therefore does not change the legality of having intercourse with one's partner.

In a majority of states today, marriage also does not change the legality of sex with persons other than one's main partner, because in those states there is no legal prohibition of adultery. Yet infidelity is a primary cause of divorce and of parentage disputes. See Denise Previti & Paul R. Amato, *Is Infidelity a Cause or a Consequence of Poor Marital Quality?*, 21 J. Soc. & Pers. Relationships 217 (2004). Indeed, many people respond to a spouse's infidelity with violence, not just a petition for divorce or paternity testing. Given such harmful consequences, anti-adultery laws should hold up better than anti-fornication laws against constitutional challenge. Why, then, would most state legislatures have eliminated criminal prohibitions of what the Puritan colonists deemed a capital offense? And in states where adultery prohibitions remain in the criminal code, why are prosecutions exceedingly rare?

In over 20 states today, there are still laws ostensibly making it a crime for a married person to have sex with anyone other than his or her spouse. In those states, marriage does drastically shrink one's legal permission with respect to sex partners and creates a significant "family ties burden" that might discourage some people from entering marriage. See Collins, Leib & Markel, *Punishing Family Status*, 88 B.U. L. Rev. 1327 (2008). In most of these states, it is just a misdemeanor, but Michigan purports to take adultery very seriously, especially when committed by a wife.

Michigan Compiled Laws
Chapter 750. Michigan Penal Code
Chapter V. Adultery

750.30. Adultery; Punishment

Sec. 30. Any person who shall commit adultery shall be guilty of a felony; and when the crime is committed between a married woman and a man who is unmarried, the man shall be guilty of adultery, and liable to the same punishment.

A state appellate court judge caused a stir in 2007 by stating that an adultery conviction could result in life imprisonment. But there has been no adultery conviction in Michigan since 1971. If Michigan is a typical state, this means a substantial minority of its residents have committed an unprosecuted felony. See, e.g., Anita L. Vangelisti & Mandi Gerstenberger, *Communication and Marital Infidelity*, *in* The State of Affairs: Explorations in Infidelity and

COMMITMENT (2008) ("[R]esearch has found that . . . 20% to 50% of American women will have sex with someone other than their spouse while they are married."). In what ways would it be problematic to enforce this law today? Suppose you were a prosecutor in a state where adultery is still a crime, and a "cuckolded" spouse reported to you an incident of adultery. What reasons would you have for and against seeking to prosecute? Cf. Michael Sheridan, *Woman Caught Having Sex in Park, Charged with Adultery—in New York,*" N.Y. DAILY NEWS, June 8, 2010 (discussing public lewdness and adultery charges against 41-year-old wife caught having sex with 29-year-old male lover on a picnic table near a playground); Jonathan Turley, *Of Lust and the Law,* WASH. POST, Sept. 5, 2004, p. B01 (describing adultery prosecution—seemingly politically motivated—of town attorney in a small Virginia community).

How to explain the gender asymmetry in the Michigan statute—that is, that male lovers can be prosecuted but not mistresses? Under English common law, a husband's infidelity was not even adultery, it was merely fornication. This was consistent with the etymology of "adultery," which derives from the concept of adulterating the family's bloodline, something a husband's infidelity cannot do. See Peter Nicholas, *The Lavender Letter: Applying the Law of Adultery to Same-Sex Couples and Same-Sex Conduct,* 63 FLA. L. REV. 97, 107 (2011). Minnesota statutes codify this gender-discriminatory rule. See Minn. Stat. §609.36 ("Acts constituting. When a married woman has sexual intercourse with a man other than her husband, whether married or not, both are guilty of adultery and may be sentenced to imprisonment for not more than one year or to payment of a fine of not more than $3,000, or both."). An effort to repeal this law met with stiff resistance from conservative Minnesota legislators.

The supposed harm to husbands from wives infidelity is paternity confusion, which might cause husbands to invest in children who are not their offspring. Yet today, with child support laws making biological fathers financially responsible for all of their offspring, husbands' affairs threaten to divert family resources to children outside the marital family—that is, to children who are not the wives' offspring. Cheating husbands typically also divert resources to their mistresses. Husband infidelity would therefore seem to inflict on a wife a harm similar to that which wife infidelity historically inflicted on a husband—involuntary payment for someone else's offspring. Cf. *Malin v. Loynachan,* 736 N.W.2d 390 (Neb. Ct. App. 2007) (holding that husband's expenditures on mistress during the marriage did not constitute economic misconduct for which he must reimburse the marital estate at divorce) and *Smith v. Smith,* 444 S.E.2d 269 (Va. Ct. App. 1994) (same).

Note that most states treat persons as married even if they are separated; only after divorce is sex with a third party not adultery. Should that particular aspect of adultery law be found unconstitutional? Or simply unwise? Imagine a case in which a woman, after years of terrible physical abuse, works up the courage to move out of the marital home but remains too terrified to petition for divorce, knowing this will enrage her husband. Suppose she forms a new relationship with another man, gaining financial and emotional security for herself and her children as a result. Could the state constitutionally prosecute her for adultery? You might think that would be wrong and highly unlikely, but what constitutional arguments would you make? What about a financial penalty like denying her alimony because of the adultery, which would likely happen in many states? If you think sometimes conduct that technically amounts to adultery is not wrong, or is not properly subject to state-imposed penalty, where would you draw the line?

A question that arises in several family law contexts is whether the state creates harm itself by reacting negatively to conduct that might be inherently innocuous. For example, does treating divorce as a tragedy make it more traumatic for couples and their children? Here we might wonder whether adultery is destructive of marital harmony in large part just because the law says it is a terrible breach of the marital commitment. Perhaps the state should instead encourage people to be more accepting of what seems to be an unstoppable practice, to take a more relaxed attitude toward a spouse's sexual behavior, so that more marriages will survive despite extra-marital flings? Is adultery worse than, for example, secretly losing a lot of money at the horse track? If so, try to articulate why.

American states are not alone, of course, in treating some consensual sex as a crime. There are not many examples in other Western countries, but outside the West there are several. In many Muslim societies, the penalty for a wife's infidelity is death by stoning. See "Afghanistan mother and daughter stoned and shot dead," BBC News (11/11/2011); Saeed Kamali Dehghan & Ian Black, "Iranians still facing death by stoning despite 'reprieve,'" The Guardian (U.K.) (07/08/10) (reporting that twelve women in an Iranian prison awaited death by stoning for alleged adultery); "Man, woman stoned to death in Pakistan," UPI.com (04/02/2008); "Stoning victim 'begged for mercy,'" BBC News (11/04/2008) (reporting that 13-year-old girl in Somalia was charged with adultery after being raped, and "was forced into a hole, buried up to her neck then pelted with stones until she died in front of more than 1,000 people").

Some American colonies also imposed the death penalty for adultery. Why would human males ever react so violently to a woman's sexual activity? This is not just a matter of a woman's partner reacting angrily to her infidelity, and the law excusing his acts of revenge, but also of males collectively policing every woman's intimate life. Is paternity confusion so horrible that it could lead governments to impose the death penalty? Recall that for much of human history people did not even understand the connection between sex and procreation. Is there also a property theft aspect to the offense? Some Islamic societies have also imposed the death penalty for stealing. Penalogical theory posits that the more difficult it is to detect a crime, the more severe the punishment must be in order to achieve optimal deterrence.

In addition to a criminal law response, the state can aim to deter adultery by creating civil law remedies for wronged spouses. Most U.S. states have retained fault grounds for divorce, enabling a victim spouse to exit the marriage more quickly, and in many states serious marital fault like adultery can be a basis for awarding more marital property to the wronged spouse in equitable distribution. Historically, a victim spouse (and more specifically, a cuckolded husband) also could sue the third party in tort, but only a small number of states retain this cause of action today.

Fitch v. Valentine

959 So. 2d 1012 (Miss. 2007)

Randolph, Justice, for the Court.

¶1. Before this Court today is a classic "he said"/"she said"/"the paramour said" case. It commenced when Johnny Valentine filed a civil complaint against Jerry Fitch, Sr. . . . , averring various causes of action, including alienation of affections. Valentine is a plumber, Fitch is a millionaire who owns various businesses, primarily involving oil and real estate.[1] . . .

1. A 1998 financial statement of Fitch revealed a net worth of nearly $22 million.

¶2. Valentine and Sandra Day[2] were married on February 12, 1993. In 1995, the couple had a son together, J.V. In the spring of 1997, Sandra began working as a realtor for the Fitch Realty division of Fitch Oil Company and earned around $400 a week in cash, based upon her commissions. Sandra testified that the adulterous affair with Fitch began in late 1997 or early 1998. . . . Fitch testified to knowing that Sandra was married to Valentine and that the couple had a child together. . . . Fitch testified at his deposition that he did not care if his affair with Sandra might affect her marriage to Valentine.

¶3. Valentine testified that his marriage to Sandra was "normal" prior to late 1998 and early 1999. The couple shared a joint checking account, ate meals together, and engaged in sexual relations "[l]ike normal couples" until that time. In June of 1998, Sandra became pregnant. During the fall of 1998, Valentine suspected Sandra was having an affair, but she denied any such wrongdoing.[4] In February 1999, a daughter, K.V., was presumptively born to the marital union. Valentine testified that, at that time, he believed K.V. was his child. He was present at the hospital for K.V.'s delivery and was listed as K.V.'s father on her birth certificate; and he loved and cared for K.V. According to Valentine, "a few weeks after [K.V.] was born" he began to notice changes in Sandra.

¶4. At trial, Fitch testified that he was aware that K.V. was his child "a month or two after she was born[,]" even though in the divorce proceedings from his wife of thirty-five years, he admitted he knew K.V. was his child three or four days after her birth.

¶5. One night in August 1999, Sandra was not home by 10:30 P.M., and Valentine drove toward Fitch's cabin looking for her. After observing Sandra driving on Highway 4, Valentine flagged her down. Valentine testified that upon being confronted about an affair, Sandra once again denied any wrongdoing and came home with him. Thereafter, Valentine repeatedly requested that Sandra quit her job at Fitch Realty, but she consistently refused to do so. During this time frame, Valentine testified to finding "[t]wo or three hundred here and three or four hundred there, a thousand, $1,100 in different places" around their home. Sandra claimed she made this money at work. Valentine testified that the cash was more than he had previously observed her earning. Sandra's co-worker Susan Fleming testified that, prior to the divorce, Sandra told her that Fitch had given her $8,000 to buy a new Jeep Cherokee, which she acquired soon thereafter.[5]

Fleming also testified that shortly after K.V. was born, Sandra told her that Fitch had purchased a baby bed, high chair, baby seat, baby clothes and other baby items for K.V. Fitch readily admitted to giving money to Sandra between February 1999 and August 1999. Fitch, however, testified that he never paid Sandra to date or marry him, or to entice her away from Valentine.

¶6. On August 28, 1999, Valentine and Sandra separated. In September 1999, DNA testing conclusively excluded Valentine as K.V.'s biological father. Nonetheless, Valentine still offered to raise K.V. as his own child if Sandra would end the adulterous affair with Fitch. Sandra refused.

¶7. Valentine filed for divorce on October 28, 1999, and the divorce decree was entered on November 23, 1999. The decree specifically stated that "[t]he evidence presented in open [c]ourt clearly establishes that [Valentine] is entitled to a divorce on the grounds of *adultery*." (Emphasis added). Prior to the divorce, Valentine testified that Sandra never told him that she did not love him or that she wanted a divorce. He further testified that

2. Now Sandra Fitch, having married Fitch subsequent to her divorce from Valentine.

4. Conversely, Sandra testified that Valentine knew of her affair with Fitch at this time and knew that the child may have been Fitch's.

5. Valentine testified that Sandra came home with a new Jeep Cherokee and he had no idea where she obtained the funds to purchase it.

the marriage failed because Sandra "couldn't resist all the money[,]" and that absent Fitch's interference, the marriage would have remained intact.

¶8. As can be expected, Sandra denied "selling [her] affections" and testified that her affections for Valentine were absent before the adulterous affair with Fitch commenced. According to her testimony, she loved Valentine when they first married. By the time J.V. was born, however, Sandra said the marriage was only "okay." She stated:

> [b]efore his gambling problem, Johnny loved to be with his buddies. He would not come home from work. He would drink. There's been occasions where I've gone looking for Johnny when he was with his buddies, and his remark was, I embarrassed him by coming to where he was to try to get him to come home to be the husband that he should be.[6]

Sandra further testified that, at that time, she "was still, obviously, in love with him. I tried to get him to change and be different, but . . . he didn't." Sandra said the breaking point came in January 1996, when she went to a casino looking for Valentine. She claims to have told him that if he did not leave the casino at that moment then their marriage was over. When he did not leave, Sandra states that "I didn't care if he went every night, and that's when our marriage was over[,]"[7] although she further testified that their sexual relationship did not effectively end until 1997 or 1998. According to Sandra, the couple "separated [on] several occasions about [gambling], and he would promise that he would get help, and he didn't. . . ." Valentine denied having a gambling problem or that the couple ever separated.

¶9. Sandra asserted that the adulterous relationship with Fitch, which she claims to have initiated, was caused by her unhappy marriage to Valentine. Furthermore, while she and Fitch engaged in sex two or three times a week, she maintained that the adulterous sexual activity had no effect on her alleged nonexistent desire to have sex with Valentine.

¶10. On December 21, 1999, Valentine filed suit against Fitch alleging various causes of action, including alienation of affections. . . . Following trial, the jury unanimously found for Valentine and awarded him $642,000 in actual damages and $112,500 in punitive damages against Fitch. . . .

I. Whether the Tort of Alienation of Affections Should Be Abolished. . . .

¶15. The tort of alienation of affections was recognized in Mississippi as early as 1926. In *Camp v. Roberts* (1985), this Court held "[w]here a husband [wife][10] is wrongfully deprived of his rights to the 'services and companionship and consortium of his [her] wife [husband],' he [she] has a cause of action 'against one who has interfered with his [her] domestic relations.'"

Without question, Mississippi's recognition of the tort of alienation of affections places it among the minority of states. (The other states are Illinois, Hawaii, New Mexico, North Carolina, South Dakota, and Utah.) However, in . . . *Bland v. Hill* (Miss. 1999), Justice Smith wisely responded to the "everybody else is doing it, so should I" view, by stating:

6. Valentine denied drinking to an extent that it interfered with his marriage or job, and . . . did not recall Sandra confronting him about going out with his friends.

7. Valentine testified that he did not recall Sandra confronting him about gambling in this, or any other, instance. Despite the claim that Valentine's gambling instigated Sandra's loss of affection, she failed to offer any evidence of gambling debts.

10. The tort of alienation of affections is equally applicable to women as men, avoiding any archaic notion that a wife is the property of her husband.

> [w]hile I agree that it appears society's moral values have changed during modern times, I do not believe Mississippi should get aboard this runaway train. I would also not take away an offended spouse's only legal means to seek redress in our courts for the wrongful conduct of a third party who wilfully and intentionally interferes in and aids in destroying a marriage.[11]

¶16. In retaining the tort, this Court has stated that "the purpose of a cause of action for alienation of affection is the 'protection of the love, society, companionship, and comfort that form the foundation of a marriage. . . .'" "The right sought to be protected is that of consortium." Justice Smith's special concurrence in *Bland* explained the justification and need for continued recognition of the tort of alienation of affections, stating:

> [s]hould an individual be allowed to intrude upon a marriage to such an extent as to cause it to come to an end? Does a spouse have a valuable interest in a marriage that is worthy of protection from the intruding third party? In my view, the answer to both questions is in the affirmative. *The traditional family is under such attack both locally and nationally these days that this Court should not retreat now from the sound view of the tort of alienation of affections espoused by this Court in* Saunders *as entitling a spouse to "protection of the love, society, companionship, and comfort that form the foundation of a marriage."* I do not believe that under the compelling facts of this particular case this Court should hold that the doctrine of alienation of affections has outlived its usefulness as a deterrent protecting the marital relationship of a husband and wife in cases where the facts clearly warrant.

In addition to protecting the marriage relationship and its sanctity, the tort of alienation of affections also provides an appropriate remedy for intentional conduct which causes a loss of consortium. The dissenting opinion in *Helsel* summarized this position, stating:

> [i]n tort cases where a spouse is injured, the other spouse often has a separate claim for loss of consortium. Most of these losses are caused by a defendant's negligence. In alienation of affection—an intentional tort—a defendant's intentional conduct causes the loss. It is inconsistent [if] the law compensates for negligent conduct causing a loss of consortium, but . . . does not compensate for intentional conduct causing the same loss.

Therefore, in the interest of protecting the marriage relationship and providing a remedy for intentional conduct which causes a loss of consortium, this Court declines the invitation to abolish the common law tort of alienation of affections in Mississippi.[12] Alienation of affections is the only available avenue to provide redress for a spouse who has suffered loss and injury to his or her marital relationship against the third party who, through persuasion, enticement, or inducement, caused or contributed to the abandonment of the marriage and/or the loss of affections by active interference. . . .

11. I cannot adopt the position of a majority of states and minimize this activity which the legislature has defined as a crime against public morals and decency, and declared its penalty comparable to similar conduct between a teacher and pupil or a guardian and ward. The Legislature has not seen fit to join the throngs who say these are only "affairs of the heart," "flings," or "stepping out," as a means of attaching validity to such conduct.

12. One dissent suggests that "these suits inevitably do more to hurt families than to help them." I find more persuasive the counter-argument that damage actually arises from the adulterous conduct which first violates, and then destroys, the trust of not only the participants, but also of their respective families. To minimize and cast as theoretical the obvious negative consequences, such as the erosion of the marital relationship and the disruption to family unity ignores these empirical truths. The dissent's fatalistic presupposition that marriages experiencing affairs will "crash and burn," fails to recognize the reality of forgiveness and reconciliation.

IV. Whether the Jury Verdict Was Contrary to the Overwhelming Weight of Evidence

. . . ¶36. The commonly stated elements of the tort of alienation of affections are "(1) wrongful conduct of the defendant; (2) loss of affection or consortium;[15] and (3) causal connection between such conduct and loss." This Court has recognized that persuasion, enticement, or inducement which causes or contributes to the abandonment is a necessary component of "wrongful conduct."

Valentine testified his marriage failed because Sandra "couldn't resist all the money[,]" and, absent Fitch, his marriage would have remained intact. This satisfies the additional element of persuasion, enticement, or inducement, when viewed "in the light most favorable," to Valentine. The key issue is the "causal connection between such conduct and loss." In short, when did the loss of society, companionship, aid, services, support, and the remaining components of loss of affection and consortium occur? Was it before or after Sandra became involved with Fitch? If after, did Fitch's wrongful conduct lead to Sandra's loss of affection or consortium?

Even though the marriage may have been "on the rocks," there is no proof that aid, services, support, or the right to live in the same house and eat at the same table had been lost until after the wrongful conduct. . . . Only after K.V. was born did Valentine begin to notice changes in Sandra. The "loss of affection or consortium," was unquestionably present. After considering the evidence, the jury *unanimously* found for Valentine. . .

V. Whether the Punitive Damage Award Violates Due Process

¶42. Fitch . . . maintains that "the penal component of the award below . . . offends substantive due process insofar as it sanctions punishment for constitutionally permissive conduct." . . . [T]his issue is procedurally barred as no due process challenge to the punitive damage award was raised before the circuit court. . . .

VI. Whether this Court Should Order a Remittitur of the Award in this Case

¶45. As to damages, . . . Valentine lost: his home;[24] physical custody of J.V.;[25] his marriage and the society, companionship, aid, services, support and other components of affection and consortium attached thereto; and K.V., the child he believed to be, and raised as, his daughter. . . . There being no evidence that either "(1) the jury or trier of fact was influenced by bias, prejudice, or passion, or (2) the . . . damages were contrary to the overwhelming weight of the evidence[,]" this Court finds that the circuit court did not abuse its discretion in denying remittitur and the jury verdict should be affirmed.

15. Regarding loss of consortium:

> [t]he interest sought to be protected is personal to the wife [husband] and arises out of the marriage relation. She [He] is entitled to society, companionship, love, affection, aid, services, support, sexual relations and the comfort of her husband [his wife] as special rights and duties growing out of the marriage covenant. To these may be added the right to live together in the same house, to eat at the same table, and to participate together in the activities, duties and responsibilities necessary to make a home. All of these are included in the broad term, 'conjugal rights.' The loss of consortium is the loss of any or all of these rights. . . .

24. He sold his interest in the house to Sandra "because [he] wanted a place for [J.V.] to live."

25. He gave Sandra physical custody of J.V. because "[he] loved [K.V.]. I was not going to split them up and do that to him."

DICKINSON, Justice, Specially Concurring:

¶52. In my view, . . . "[t]here is inherent and fatal contradiction in the term 'alienation of affections.' The alienation belies the affection." . . .

EVOLUTION OF THE ALIENATION OF AFFECTIONS CAUSE OF ACTION

¶53. The tort called alienation of affections originated in the English common law, when wives were considered their husbands' property. A third party who actively interfered with a marriage by persuading a wife to leave her husband was considered to have deprived the husband of his property. . . .

¶54. In order to maintain pure bloodlines and discourage adultery, Teutonic tribes required a wife's lover to compensate the husband for his wife's infidelity, allowing the husband to buy a new wife and ensure the legitimacy of his offspring. The Anglo-Saxons later allowed actions for marital interference on the premise that wives were valuable servants to their husbands. The action was analogous to a master's claim "against one who enticed away his servant, in whose services the master held a quasi-property interest." Thus, . . . a husband could "vindicate" his loss in the marital relationship through an action for alienation of affections, but a wife was not afforded the same right.

¶55. Two centuries ago, in *Hutcheson v. Peck* (N.Y. 1809), the Supreme Court of Judicature of New York applied the common law tort to an action by a husband who sued his wife's father for attempting to alienate his wife's affection. Although at first agreeable to his daughter's marriage, the father-in-law began to question the Plaintiff's ability to provide for his daughter, and changed his mind. He threatened his daughter's husband, going so far as to "strike" him, and then took his daughter into his home and threatened that, if she returned to her husband, he would not support them. In analyzing the claim, the court stated that "[i]f it was the duty of the wife to return to her husband, the defendant did an unlawful act by persuading her to violate that duty. If the wife was unjustifiable in abandoning the plaintiff, the defendant is responsible for having *enticed* and *persuaded* her to abandon him." The court went on to state that, had the defendant "not been instrumental in procuring his daughter to live apart from her husband, and had he gone no further than to receive and support her," the plaintiff would have no recovery. The court then stated, "[v]ery different, however, will be the conclusion, when the parent unlawfully produces the separation by sowing the seeds of discord and hatred; thereby poisoning the sources of domestic harmony and enjoyment." . . .

¶57. . . . In the late nineteenth and early twentieth centuries, the Married Women's Property Acts were passed, giving women the same rights to own property as men. . . . But instead of allowing the tort—along with its wife-as-chattel premise—to fade away, some courts began to justify alienation of affection actions as a means to preserve marriages and discourage interference by third-parties. . . .

¶58. For example, consent was historically prohibited as a defense to alienation actions "based on the legal inferiority of the wife who was deemed incapable of consenting to the injury of her superior, her husband." And even though the cause of action has supposedly moved beyond those outdated roots, consent remains a prohibited defense today. . . . In Mississippi, . . . the legal fiction that the common law tort of alienation of affections preserves a spouse's right to the mind and body of a partner continues to this day, only now it is masked as the means to stabilize the marital union. . . .

¶64. The alienation of affections cause of action has never sufficiently separated from its property-based origins, and the tort is continued because "spousal affection" is characterized as "property" capable of theft. However, that premise is simply illogical. "To posit that one person possesses rights to the feelings of another is an anachronism." Even though courts today do not call the alienated affection "property" or "a possession," that is how it is treated. . . . In the end, the successful plaintiff engages in what is essentially a "sale" of his or her spouse's affections.

¶65. Additionally, "theft" implies the taking of property from an unwilling owner by an outsider. . . . "Human experience is that the affections of persons who are devoted and faithful are not susceptible to larceny no matter how cunning or stealthful."

¶66. Importantly, I do not advocate for the abolition of this tort because I feel defendants in such suits deserve protection, or because I view promiscuity as harmless. I merely find the foundation for such suits—that someone should recover for an injury to "property" which they cannot own—completely erroneous.

¶67. . . . The tort is inherently unplanned, especially where sexual activity is involved, so the idea that the parties would contemplate the possibility of a lawsuit and be deterred is unrealistic. The truth remains that a spouse inclined to engage in an extramarital affair will do so, and even if "a would-be paramour would be thereby dissuaded [by the threat of suit], a substitute is likely to be readily found." . . .

¶68. [T]hese suits inevitably do more to hurt families than to help them. In my view, when a marriage has crashed and burned, the law should not provide an imprimatur to fan the coals of anger and resentment, extending further into the future the time when healing can begin. This is particularly true where children are involved. . . .

¶70. Undeniably, the primary motives in bringing an action for alienation of affections are to gain revenge on the unfaithful spouse and the defendant and to force outrageous settlements. Alienation of affection claims have become prime tools for extortion or blackmail. Such vexatious lawsuits can make contentious divorce proceedings even more bilious. The action can also rearrange the marital assets, making it difficult for a court to properly assess the needs and abilities of the individual spouses. These suits are never used to achieve reconciliation or preserve the marriage; rather, they are fueled by vindictiveness and a desire to destroy reputations and relationships. . . .

¶71. "[T]he action [also] diminishes the plaintiff's dignity and injures his [or her] own reputation through the process of seeking money damages." The intimate details of the marriage, and its breakdown, are revealed for all to see as the parties attempt to assassinate the character of their adversaries. . . . [C]hildren can be required to testify for one parent or another in open court. . . .

¶77. A claim of tortious interference with a contractual relationship is not comparable to a claim of alienation of affections. In contract suits, the aggrieved party can sue both the interferer and the other party to the contract. However, in alienation actions, the "other party" to the "contract" is the spouse . . . who is not subject to suit, as in true contract cases. As the Kentucky Supreme Court pointed out, "[t]his logical asymmetry has prompted the majority of jurisdictions to eliminate these marital torts."

EASLEY, Justice, Dissenting:

. . . ¶96. Prior to trial, Valentine filed a motion in limine to prevent Fitch from introducing any evidence that Valentine and his former wife, Sandra, engaged in and participated in a lengthy adulterous relationship prior to their marriage while Sandra was still married to a prior husband, Tracey Hughey. After Sandra's divorce from her husband, Hughey, she married Valentine. The trial court granted the motion. . . .

¶100. According to Sandra's testimony, she was the initiator of the relationship with Fitch. She testified that she was the one who pursued Fitch and flirted with him. . . .

¶101. Sandra testified that her marriage to Valentine was already over before the relationship began. . . . She stated that Valentine routinely came home drunk, and they had no communication with each other. . . . Valentine would not come home for days, with the longest period being three days. . . . She testified that "[h]e never had anything to say, and then he would expect me to just want to touch . . . he just wanted to have sex with me." . . .

¶104. Fitch testified that . . . Sandra told him that she "did not have a marriage anymore."

¶105. . . . Fitch testified that he never gave Sandra any extravagant gifts [or] any money except for her salary and commissions paid in cash like all his employees. . . .

¶108. . . . [T]he defendant must "directly and intentionally [interfere] with" plaintiff's marriage, thereby inducing the alienation of affections of the plaintiff's spouse. . . .

¶110. Further, Valentine failed to present sufficient evidence of any economic loss to support the award of damages he received. . . . Valentine voluntarily surrendered possession of the marital home to Sandra in the property settlement agreement signed by the parties. Sandra agreed to pay Valentine $32,500 for his interest in the house. . . .

¶115. Valentine introduced no medical bills . . . [and] did not testify that he lost any business during that time. Likewise, Valentine did not testify that he lost any income. . . .

¶116. Therefore . . . the jury's verdict was . . . not based upon legally sufficient evidence to prove a claim of alienation of affections. I would . . . render judgment in favor of Fitch. . . .

Who has the better of the abolition debate? Is the alienation suit a deterrent to adultery? More so or less relative to, for example, a civil suit for assault and battery? Is Justice Dickinson correct that adultery results only when a spouse is predisposed to having an affair, or does it often occur because a spouse happens to meet someone especially attractive to them? If the cause of action does have a deterrent effect, is that a sufficient justification for it? Valentine suffered emotionally, but the core of the damages element is not emotional distress but loss of consortium. Ordinarily compensation is owed for loss of something to which one is entitled, such as possession, occupation, and enjoyment of one's property. Does marriage today create an entitlement to consortium? Morally, if not legally? Or to a monopoly over a spouse's sexuality? If so, how might you estimate the monetary value of that right, in order to set compensation? Cf. Wayne Drash, *Beware Cheaters: Your Lover's Spouse Can Sue You*, CNN.com, Dec. 10, 2009 (stating that "[j]uries in North Carolina have handed out awards in excess of $1 million on multiple occasions" and that Tiger Woods should worry if any of his affairs occurred with married women in states the recognize this cause of action). Justice Dickinson also emphasizes the cheating spouse's volition. Should that be relevant?

Given that loss of consortium is an element of the cause of action, should no action lie if the cheating spouse continues to love, spend time with, help, and have sex with the other spouse? Or so long as the cheating spouse is *willing* to do these things? If the other spouse finds out about the adultery and reacts by refusing the cheater's companionship and affection, can he or she complain of loss of consortium? Perhaps Valentine is responsible for not mitigating his damages by simply accepting that he would have to share his wife, or by not reforming his behavior to draw Sandra back to him. The dissent emphasizes Valentine's responsibility for Sandra's falling out of love. Should that be a valid and adequate defense, or a factor mitigating any financial award, in a divorce action or in a tort suit against the third party? Or should the law push disenchanted spouses to get divorced before they start up with someone new?

The concurrence suggests that allowing this tort cause of action fuels acrimony. Might it instead help the wronged spouse ultimately to overcome the anger, and create a venue other than the divorce proceeding for venting fury? A wronged spouse who recovers handsomely from the third party might thereby become less angry, less inclined to engage in violence, and less inclined to use the infidelity against the other spouse in the divorce. At the same time, the divorce does present an opportunity to recover against the adulterous spouse, in states where marital misconduct is relevant to property distribution, so the concurring judge's concern about asymmetry is misplaced.

If the state does properly penalize adultery in one way or another, it might, as a matter of rational consistency, also penalize other conduct that undermines the marital relationship. Indeed, the social meaning of infidelity is amorphous and for some people very broad, including mere thoughts about being with another partner.

Brenda Cossman, The New Politics of Adultery

15 Colum. J. Gender & L. 274 (2006)

Once restricted to "natural heterosexual intercourse," infidelity now extends to a variety of sexual practices. Indeed, these days, infidelity can occur without sexual contact at all. Computer sex, telephone sex, and email flirtations are all included within the ambit of adulterous relationships that violate the marital relationship. As the definition of infidelity expands, so do its practitioners. In several recent exposés of "the new infidelity," women have increasingly been shown to be equal opportunity cheaters. This expansion of infidelity and infidels has produced a new crisis of adultery; a virtual adultery epidemic has swept the nation. . . .

The legal definition and the underlying harm of adultery have changed considerably over time, from a narrow concern of illegitimate offspring to a much broader violation of marital emotional intimacy. . . . In 1838, the Supreme Court of New Jersey explained. . . . "The heinousness of [adultery] consists in exposing an innocent husband to maintain another man's children, and having them succeed to his inheritance." Indeed, the court pointedly stated that the harm to the husband . . . lay not in "the alienation of the wife's affections, and loss of comfort in her company." . . .

Over time, the double standard was removed, and adultery for the purposes of both criminal and divorce law was redefined as voluntary sexual intercourse between a married man or woman and a person other than the offender's spouse. In recent years, the requirement of sexual intercourse has also begun to change. Some courts have broadened the definition of adultery to include other types of sexual encounters. For example, in 1987, the Fourth Circuit Court of Appeals of Louisiana held that a wife had committed adultery even though she had not had sexual intercourse. The wife admitted that she had slept "in the same bed with another man, that she had touched the other man's sexual organ and that he had touched hers and that they laid on top of each other." . . . Similarly, in 1992, a New Jersey court considered whether lesbian sex amounts to adultery. The court held that, when viewed from the perspective of the injured spouse, an extra-marital relationship is "just as devastating to the spouse irrespective of the specific sexual act performed by the promiscuous spouse or the sex of the new paramour. The homosexual violation of marital vows could be well construed as the ultimate in rejection." . . .

This expansion of the legal definition of adultery . . . reflects the transformation of . . . marriage . . . [to] a relationship about both emotional and sexual intimacy. Pregnancy is no longer the central harm of adultery. . . . [V]irtually any violation of the emotional or sexual exclusivity of marriage can be seen as infidelity. Infidelity experts . . . argue that . . . the transgression comes from the fact that they are sharing more of their "inner self, frustrations and triumphs [with their transgressors] than with their spouses." . . . A Newsweek poll found that forty-five percent of women and thirty percent of men believed that emotional betrayal was actually more upsetting than extra-marital sexual behavior. . . .

A similar shift is apparent in emerging public debates about another "new infidelity," namely, whether viewing Internet pornography and participating in cybersex constitutes adultery. . . . In Dr. Phil's view, watching Internet pornography is disrespectful of one's relationship and may cause "negative emotional harm" to a spouse. "It is not OK behavior. It is a perverse and ridiculous intrusion into your relationship. It is an insult, it is disloyal and it is cheating." . . . As the category expands to include ever more practices and encounters, so too does its potential frequency, thereby contributing to the popular culture's declarations of a new crisis of infidelity. . . . [E]xperts all seem to agree that women's infidelity is on the rise and beginning to equal men's in terms of frequency. According to [a] Newsweek article, "[c]ouples' therapists estimate that among their clientele, the number is close to 30 to 40 percent, compared with 50 percent of men, and the gap is almost certainly closing." . . .

The "discovery" of married women's affairs as the new infidelity is perhaps a bit paradoxical, insofar as the very legal definition of adultery at one time required that the woman be married. . . . As the legal and social definition was slowly broadened to include sexual intercourse between a married person and someone who was not their spouse, however, the . . . stereotype of an affair was more typically one of the married man and "the other woman." When married women did appear in popular culture as adulteresses, the portrayal was most often one of an overly desirous subject, an evil femme fatale. . . . In the "new infidelity," the married adulteress is now the woman next door: she is the suburban housewife or the working mother. As the front inset of the book Undressing Infidelity asks and answers: "who are these cheating women? . . . They are your neighbors, your friends, your coworkers. They go to your gym. They shop at your grocery store. They are the women you see every day who seem to have it all." The bottom line is that the new adulteress is unexceptional. She is everywhere. . . .

[A]n article in the Wall Street Journal announced that "divorce is contagious." By showing that office divorces can break out in what a study in Ohio called "a measles pattern," the research highlights the need for working couples to take steps to "vaccinate their marriages." . . . Dr. Phil writes that to "[i]noculate yourself against infidelity by making sure you're attentive, involved and plugged in to your marriage" is possible. . . . Since infidelities result from a breakdown in the intimacy and communication between the partners, Dr. Phil recommends that individuals "turn towards . . . [their] partner—not away." Spouses must commit themselves to making their marriage a project: "[w]ork on your marriage every single day—not just during the bad times. Wake up each day and ask yourself, 'What can I do today that will make my marriage better?'" In addition to working on the relationship, there is a command of self-improvement: "[t]ake care of yourself. Eat healthy, exercise and look your best. Feeling good about yourself will radiate and your spouse will notice." A marriage inoculated from infidelity is a marriage that begins with self-esteem and individual responsibility.

The new politics of adultery ultimately comes full circle, back to the project of sex in marriage. . . . While the infidelity experts seem to agree that infidelity is not simply about sex, they also seem to agree that couples need to be attentive to their sex lives. . . . Good spouses . . . undertak[e] the hard work of making their relationship work by working on their relationship. . . .

So is there a moral obligation not only to have sex with one's spouse but also to become as good at it as one can be? And to make oneself as sexually attractive as possible? When we study divorce law, we will consider whether a breach of such a duty should factor into the financial aspects of marital dissolution.

Today the Internet makes clandestine extra-marital intimacy extremely easy. One can readily meet potential partners online. Physical separation can make the relationship seem unreal, at least initially, but an emotional connection can form nonetheless. Webcams facilitate virtual physical intimacy that comes close to actual sex. No doubt hundreds of thousands of married men today make frequent visits to their favorite online strippers. Apart from forming relationships online, heavy consumption of pornography is said also to weaken marital bonds.

Patrick F. Fagan, Ph.D., The Effects of Pornography on Individuals, Marriage, Family, and Community

co-published by the Family Research Council (Washington D.C.) and the Marriage and Religion Institute (MARRI)

Key Findings on the Effects of Pornography

THE FAMILY AND PORNOGRAPHY

- Married men who are involved in pornography feel less satisfied with their conjugal relations and less emotionally attached to their wives. Wives notice and are upset by the difference.
- Pornography use is a pathway to infidelity and divorce, and is frequently a major factor in these family disasters.
- Among couples affected by one spouse's addiction, two-thirds experience a loss of interest in sexual intercourse.
- Both spouses perceive pornography viewing as tantamount to infidelity. . . .

THE INDIVIDUAL AND PORNOGRAPHY

- Pornography is addictive, and neuroscientists are beginning to map the biological substrate of this addiction.
- Users tend to become desensitized to the type of pornorgraphy they use, become bored with it, and then seek more perverse forms of pornography.
- Men who view pornography regularly have a higher tolerance for abnormal sexuality, including rape, sexual aggression, and sexual promiscuity.
- Prolonged consumption of pornography by men produces stronger notions of women as commodities or as "sex objects." . . .

Like adultery, heavy porn consumption can be a symptom of marital problems that arise for other reasons, but it can also occur independently and then create problems itself. Even if it is sometimes a result of marital dysfunction rather than the initial cause, is it not an inappropriate response to the dysfunction, just like adultery, and certainly less desirable than counseling? But what can the state do about it? Some non-Western countries criminalize pornography consumption, but that is not an option in the United

States. Does existing constitutional doctrine permit the FCC to shut down online strip clubs? Or permit states to expand their definitions of adultery to include online intimacy? Before acting, the state might want better evidence about the effect of "virtual" sex and relationships. It might well be that this outlet satisfies the sexual or romantic cravings of people who would otherwise go out looking for the real thing, and so actually has a net positive impact on marriage. How would you design a study to test this hypothesis?

b. Sex Within the Marital Relationship

In addition to prohibiting spouses from having sex with a third party, the law in much of the world has historically imposed a legal duty on wives to submit sexually to their husbands. Sex is among the "essentials of marriage" and implicitly consented to by marrying. In Anglo-American law, this understanding was reflected in the exclusion of marital rape from criminal rape provisions. Relatedly, a husband's rights under coverture included the right to determine the marital residence and to cohabit there with his wife, and the state stood ready to force the return of any wife who abandoned the home. Today in the United States, there is no legal obligation to live with or have sex with one's spouse; the only remedy for refusal of sex is to get divorced. Marital rape exceptions no longer exist in the Western world, though the law in some states might treat rape of one's spouse more leniently than rape of someone who is not one's spouse. In at least one non-Western country, the law explicitly establishes a duty of sexual submission for wives. In 2009, the Afghan government passed a law providing that every Shiite man "has the right to have sexual intercourse with his wife every fourth night" and may confine his wives to the home at all times. See Helen Kennedy, *New Afghanistan Law Allows Men to Demand Sex from Wife Every 4 Days*, N.Y. DAILY NEWS, Apr. 3, 2009. The law is not entirely one-sided, however; it also requires every husband to take his wife to bed at least once every four months. Secretary of State Hillary Clinton urged Afghan authorities to repeal the law. Should the United States be condemning another country for having laws reflecting attitudes that prevailed in our own society not so long ago?

As Dr. Phil recognized, one spouse's refusal to have sex can be destructive of the marital relationship, so the state has some interest in preventing people from making this choice. Would it be proper for the state to do *anything* in furtherance of that interest? Reauthorizing rape would clearly be improper, but perhaps the law could compensate a person whose spouse refuses to have sex with him or her for long periods of time—for example, in property distribution upon divorce. Courts have awarded fault-based divorce to a person whose spouse refused to have sex. See, e.g., Ostriker v. Ostriker, 609 N.Y.S.2d 922 (App. Div. 1994) (finding abandonment where husband's rejection of wife's sexual overtures was "willful, continued, and unjustified") And some states' equitable distribution laws include among factors for allocating property the cause of the marital breakdown, which might allow consideration of such refusal. This would create a financial incentive to suppress any aversion one might have to sexual relations with one's spouse. Is that too great an incursion on individuals' sexual autonomy? Less acceptable than a financial consequence for committing adultery? See Twila L. Perry, *The "Essentials of Marriage": Reconsidering the Duty of Support and Services*, 15 YALE J.L. & FEMINISM 1 (2005) (arguing on privacy grounds for elimination of the marital duty of sexual "services").

In seeming contradiction to encouragement of sexual intimacy within marriage, many states have tried to limit the types of sexual conduct married couples enjoy together. Prohibitions on oral and anal sex were once common. See, e.g., Ga. Code Ann., §16-6-2 (prohibiting all persons from engaging in "any sexual act involving the sex organs of one person and the mouth or anus of another"); State v. Smith, 766 So. 2d 501 (La. 2000) (upholding state statute criminalizing oral and anal sex, without a marital exemption); Lovisi v. Slayton, 539 F.2d 349 (4th Cir. 1976) (upholding conviction of married couple for fellatio performed by wife on husband in violation of Virginia's "crime against nature" statute, reasoning in part that presence of a third party diminished the couple's privacy interest). In addition, some states once prohibited dispensation of contraceptives, to married or unmarried people. Such laws shared the potential effect of channeling all sexual conduct by married couples into procreative sex. The motivation might have been to increase the rate of reproduction, or it might have been to discourage recreational sex as immoral. In 1965, however, the U.S. Supreme Court established a right of marital privacy that limits the state's ability to interfere in married couples' intimate activities.

Griswold v. Connecticut

381 U.S. 479 (1965)

Mr. Justice Douglas delivered the opinion of the Court.

Appellant Griswold is Executive Director of the Planned Parenthood League of Connecticut. Appellant Buxton is a licensed physician. . . . They examined the wife and prescribed the best contraceptive device or material for her use. . . .

§53-32 . . . of the General Statutes of Connecticut . . . provides:

> Any person who uses any drug, medicinal article or instrument for the purpose of preventing conception shall be fined not less than fifty dollars or imprisoned not less than sixty days nor more than one year or be both fined and imprisoned.

. . . The appellants were found guilty as accessories and fined $100 each. . . . [A]ppellants have standing to raise the constitutional rights of the married people with whom they had a professional relationship. . . .

The . . . specific guarantees in the Bill of Rights have penumbras, formed by emanations from those guarantees that help give them life and substance. Various guarantees create zones of privacy. The right of association contained in the penumbra of the First Amendment is one. . . . The Third Amendment in its prohibition against the quartering of soldiers "in any house" in time of peace without the consent of the owner is another facet of that privacy. The Fourth Amendment explicitly affirms the "right of the people to be secure in their persons, houses, papers, and effects, against unreasonable searches and seizures." The Fifth Amendment in its Self-Incrimination Clause enables the citizen to create a zone of privacy which government may not force him to surrender to his detriment. The Ninth Amendment provides: "The enumeration in the Constitution, of certain rights, shall not be construed to deny or disparage others retained by the people."

. . . The present case, then, concerns a relationship lying within the zone of privacy created by several fundamental constitutional guarantees. And it concerns a law which, in forbidding the use of contraceptives rather than regulating their manufacture or sale, seeks to achieve its goals by means having a maximum destructive impact upon that relationship. Such a law cannot stand in light of the familiar principle . . . that a "governmental purpose to control or prevent activities constitutionally subject to state regulation may not be achieved by means which sweep unnecessarily broadly and thereby invade the area of protected freedoms." Would we allow the police to search the sacred precincts of marital bedrooms for telltale signs of the use of contraceptives? The very idea is repulsive to the notions of privacy surrounding the marriage relationship.

We deal with a right of privacy older than the Bill of Rights—older than our political parties, older than our school system. Marriage is a coming together for better or for worse, hopefully enduring, and intimate to the degree of being sacred. It is an association that promotes a way of life, not causes; a harmony in living, not political faiths; a bilateral loyalty, not commercial or social projects. Yet it is an association for as noble a purpose as any involved in our prior decisions.

Mr. Justice GOLDBERG, whom THE CHIEF JUSTICE and Mr. Justice BRENNAN join, concurring.

. . . The Court stated many years ago that the Due Process Clause protects those liberties that are "so rooted in the traditions and conscience of our people as to be ranked as fundamental." . . . The inquiry is whether a right involved "is of such a character that it cannot be denied without violating those 'fundamental principles of liberty and justice which lie at the base of all our civil and political institutions". . . .

Mr. Justice Brandeis . . . comprehensively summarized the principles underlying the Constitution's guarantees of privacy:

> . . . The makers of our Constitution undertook to secure conditions favorable to the pursuit of happiness. They recognized the significance of man's spiritual nature, of his feelings and of his intellect. They knew that only a part of the pain, pleasure and satisfactions of life are to be found in material things. They sought to protect Americans in their beliefs, their thoughts, their emotions and their sensations. They conferred, as against the government, the right to be let alone—the most comprehensive of rights and the right most valued by civilized men.

The Connecticut statutes here involved deal with a particularly important and sensitive area of privacy—that of the marital relation and the marital home. This Court recognized in *Meyer v. Nebraska*, that the right "to marry, establish a home and bring up children" was an essential part of the liberty guaranteed by the Fourteenth Amendment. In *Pierce v. Society of Sisters*, the Court held unconstitutional an Oregon Act which forbade parents from sending their children to private schools because such an act "unreasonably interferes with the liberty of parents and guardians to direct the upbringing and education of children under their control." As this Court said in *Prince v. Massachusetts*, the *Meyer* and *Pierce* decisions "have respected the private realm of family life which the state cannot enter." I agree with Mr. Justice Harlan's statement . . . "Of this whole 'private realm of family life' it is difficult to imagine what is more private or more intimate than a husband and wife's marital relations." . . .

My Brother Stewart, while characterizing the Connecticut birth control law as "an uncommonly silly law," would nevertheless let it stand on the ground that it is not for the courts to "substitute their social and economic beliefs for the judgment of legislative bodies, who are elected to pass laws." . . . The logic of the dissents would sanction federal or state legislation that seems to me even more plainly unconstitutional than the statute before us. Surely the Government, absent a showing of a compelling subordinating state interest, could not decree that all husbands and wives must be sterilized after two children have been born to them. . . . While it may shock some of my Brethren that the Court today holds that the Constitution protects the right of marital privacy, in my view it is far more shocking to believe that the personal liberty guaranteed by the Constitution does not include protection against such totalitarian limitation of family size . . .

The State . . . says that preventing the use of birth-control devices by married persons helps prevent the indulgence by some in such extra-marital relations. The rationality of this justification is dubious. . . . But, in any event, it is clear that the state interest in safeguarding marital fidelity can be served by a more discriminately tailored statute, which does not, like the present one, sweep unnecessarily broadly, reaching far beyond the evil sought to be dealt with and intruding upon the privacy of all married couples. . . . The State of Connecticut does have statutes, the constitutionality of which is beyond doubt, which prohibit adultery and fornication. . . . [T]he Court's holding today . . . in no way interferes with a State's proper regulation of sexual promiscuity or misconduct. . . .

Would *Griswold* also preclude application to married couples of laws prohibiting oral and anal sex, if a state such as Georgia ever attempted to enforce them against married people? In recent decades, a number of states have enacted another type of sex regulation applicable to married couples that would not appear to have the purpose or effect of encouraging reproduction, but might discourage recreational sex—namely, prohibitions on sale and/or use of sexual devices, such as vibrators. Several courts have addressed the constitutionality of those laws, generally when challenged by businesses that sell such items. State defenses of such prohibitions in litigations reveal what interests the state supposes it has today in the intimate lives of married couples.

PHE, Inc. v. Earle

517 F.3d 738 (2008)

Reavley, Circuit Judge:

This case assesses the constitutionality of a Texas statute making it a crime to promote or sell . . . any device "designed or marketed as useful primarily for the stimulation of human genital organs." . . . [A] narrow affirmative defense was added to protect those who promoted "obscene devices" for "a bona fide medical, psychiatric, judicial, legislative, or law enforcement purpose." Violating the statute can result in punishment of up to two years in jail. . . . The statute, however, does not prohibit the use or possession of sexual devices for any purpose. . . .

Besides Texas, only three states have a similar obscene-devices statute: Mississippi, Alabama, and Virginia. The Mississippi Supreme Court has upheld its state's statute against First and Fourteenth Amendment challenges. Neither the Alabama nor Virginia supreme court has entertained a challenge to its state's statute, but the Eleventh Circuit has rejected a Fourteenth Amendment challenge to Alabama's statute. On the other hand, while the legislatures of Louisiana, Kansas, and Colorado had enacted obscene-devices statutes, each of their respective state supreme courts struck down its law on Fourteenth Amendment grounds. Likewise, while the Georgia legislature had passed an obscene-device statute, the Eleventh Circuit recently struck it down.

Reliable Consultants, Inc. d/b/a Dreamer's and Le Rouge Boutique operates four retail stores in Texas that carry a stock of sexual devices . . . for off-premise, private use. PHE, Inc. d/b/a Adam & Eve, Inc. . . . sells sexual devices by internet and mail. . . . Reliable and PHE desire to increase their sale of, and advertising for, sexual devices in Texas, and they fear prosecution under the statute if they do so. Reliable and PHE contend that many people in Texas, both married and unmarried, use sexual devices as an aspect of their sexual experiences. For some couples in which one partner may be physically unable to engage in intercourse, or in which a contagious disease, such as HIV, precludes intercourse, these devices may be one of the only ways to engage in a safe, sexual relationship. Others use sexual devices to treat a variety of therapeutic needs, such as erectile dysfunction. Courts scrutinizing sexual-device bans in other states have explained that an "extensive review of the medical necessity for sexual devices" shows that "it is common for trained experts in the field of human sexual behavior to use sexual aids in the treatment of their male and female patients' sexual problems." . . . Supreme Court cases hold that businesses can assert the rights of their customers and that restricting the ability to purchase an item is tantamount to restricting that item's use. . . .

Plaintiffs claim that the right at stake is the individual's substantive due process right to engage in private intimate conduct free from government intrusion. The State proposes a different right for the Plaintiffs: "the right to stimulate one's genitals for non-medical purposes unrelated to procreation or outside of an interpersonal relationship." The Court in *Lawrence* . . . recognized . . . not simply a right to engage in the sexual act itself, but instead a right to be free from governmental intrusion regarding "the most private human contact, sexual behavior." . . . An individual who wants to legally use a safe sexual device during private intimate moments alone or with another is unable to legally purchase a device in Texas, which heavily burdens a constitutional right. . . . Indeed, under this statute it is even illegal to "lend" or "give" a sexual device to another person. . . . The Supreme Court . . . expressly held that "individual decisions by married persons, concerning the intimacies of their physical relationship, even when not intended to produce offspring, are a form of 'liberty' protected by the Due Process Clause of the Fourteenth Amendment. Moreover, this protection extends to intimate choices by unmarried as well as married persons."

The State's primary justifications for the statute are "morality based." The asserted interests include "discouraging prurient interests in autonomous sex and the pursuit of sexual gratification unrelated to procreation and prohibiting the commercial sale of sex." These interests in "public morality" cannot constitutionally sustain the statute after *Lawrence*.[33] . . .

[T]he State asserts that an interest the statute serves is the "protection of minors and unwilling adults from exposure to sexual devices and their advertisement." . . . However, . . . we can divine no rational connection between the statute and the protection of children, and because the State offers none, we cannot sustain the law under this justification. The alleged governmental interest in protecting "unwilling adults" from exposure to sexual devices is even less convincing. The Court has consistently refused to burden individual rights out of concern for the protection of "unwilling recipients." Furthermore, this asserted interest bears no rational relation to the restriction on sales of sexual devices because an adult cannot buy a sexual device without making the affirmative decision to visit a store and make the purchase.

The State argues that if this statute . . . is struck down, it is equivalent to extending substantive due process protection to the "commercial sale of sex." Not so. . . . Following the State's logic, the sale of contraceptives would be equivalent to the sale of sex because contraceptives are intended to be used for the pursuit of sexual gratification unrelated to procreation. This argument cannot be accepted as a justification to limit the sale of contraceptives. . . . Furthermore, there are justifications for criminalizing prostitution other than public morality, including promoting public safety and preventing injury and coercion. . . . The case is not about public sex. It is not about controlling commerce in sex. It is about controlling what people do in the privacy of their own homes because

33. The Eleventh Circuit disagreed in *Williams v. Morgan* (2007). There, the court held that Alabama's interest in "public morality" was a constitutional justification for the state's obscene devices statute. That fails to recognize the *Lawrence* holding that public morality cannot justify a law that regulates an individual's private sexual conduct and does not relate to prostitution, the potential for injury or coercion, or public conduct.

the State is morally opposed to a certain type of consensual private intimate conduct. This is an insufficient justification for the statute after *Lawrence*. . . . Advertisements of the devices could be prohibited if they are obscene . . . as defined by the Supreme Court. . . .

RHESA HAWKINS BARKSDALE, dissenting in part:

. . . [T]he proscribed conduct is *not* private sexual conduct. Instead, for obscene devices, the statute proscribes only the sale or other promotion (such as advertising) of those devices, including, but not limited to, a dildo or artificial vagina. . . . *Lawrence* declined to employ a fundamental-rights analysis, choosing instead to apply rational-basis review. . . . [A]s also held by the Eleventh Circuit, . . . "[t]o the extent *Lawrence* rejects public morality as a legitimate government interest, it invalidates only those laws that target conduct that is *both private and non-commercial*." The Texas statute regulates . . . sale of what it defines as obscene devices. Obviously, such conduct is both public and commercial. Therefore, . . . plaintiffs fail to state a substantive-due-process claim under the Fourteenth Amendment.

Do you agree that non-medically necessary use of genital stimulators (e.g., vibrators) and genital substitutes (e.g., dildos) is comparable to homosexual sodomy, in terms of its centrality to relationships and importance as an aspect of personal liberty? If it is not, then perhaps the law should be subject only to rational basis review. And are the state's justifications really so implausible as the majority suggests? Might the state not justifiably be as concerned about its citizens being over-sexed as it is about its citizens being addicted to alcohol or drugs, because it might diminish productivity? But cf. Laura A. Rosenbury & Jennifer E. Rothman, *Sex In and Out of Intimacy*, 59 EMORY L.J. 809 (2020) (arguing for "a constitutional right to engage in consensual sexual activity without regard to the motives or goals behind the activity," on the grounds that "sex can constitute a vital part of individual identity and self-expression"). Further, does the state not have a legitimate interest in creating a physical and social environment where everyone feels comfortable, an interest that might be undermined by the presence of sex shops? An additional interest, one arguably quite important, is in preserving human dignity. Many people believe, and many scholars have argued, that prostitution is inherently degrading, and for that reason support its criminal prohibition independently of any concern about "promoting public safety and preventing injury and coercion." Could one not reasonably take the same view about, for example, artificial vaginas?

Is the state in a stronger or a weaker position in regulating inter-spousal conduct relative to conduct between people not married to each other? Think about this issue again from the perspective of a taxpayer, especially that of an unmarried taxpayer who is, through various state-conferred financial benefits, subsidizing marriages. Do you not have a stake in how people behave within the marriage, even if they are not harming anyone? Should the state be precluded from trying to induce married people to act in exemplary ways?

Abortion

Another sex-related matter that some states have attempted to regulate is abortion. Most people marry with the expectation of having children, and some husbands might be quite upset to learn that their wives are pregnant but contemplating aborting the child. In many countries of the world, the law requires a husband's consent to a married woman's undergoing an abortion. The U.S. Supreme Court, however, ruled in *Planned Parenthood v.*

Danforth (1976) that states may not require spousal consent to abortion, and ruled in *Planned Parenthood v. Casey* (1992) that they may not constitutionally even require notification of a husband that a wife intends to have an abortion. Here is the Court's analysis of a notification requirement in *Casey*:

Planned Parenthood of Southeastern Pennsylvania v. Casey

505 U.S. 833 (1992)

. . . Section 3209 of Pennsylvania's abortion law provides, except in cases of medical emergency, that no physician shall perform an abortion on a married woman without receiving a signed statement from the woman that she has notified her spouse that she is about to undergo an abortion. The woman has the option of providing an alternative signed statement certifying that her husband is not the man who impregnated her; that her husband could not be located; that the pregnancy is the result of spousal sexual assault which she has reported; or that the woman believes that notifying her husband will cause him or someone else to inflict bodily injury upon her. A physician who performs an abortion on a married woman without receiving the appropriate signed statement will have his or her license revoked, and is liable to the husband for damages.

The District Court . . . made detailed findings of fact regarding the effect of this statute. These included: . . .

> "279. The 'bodily injury' exception could not be invoked by a married woman whose husband, if notified, would, in her reasonable belief, threaten to (a) publicize her intent to have an abortion to family, friends or acquaintances; (b) retaliate against her in future child custody or divorce proceedings; (c) inflict psychological intimidation or emotional harm upon her, her children or other persons; (d) inflict bodily harm on other persons such as children, family members or other loved ones; or (e) use his control over finances to deprive her of necessary monies for herself or her children. . . .
>
> "289. Mere notification of pregnancy is frequently a flashpoint for battering and violence within the family. The number of battering incidents is high during the pregnancy and often the worst abuse can be associated with pregnancy. . . . The battering husband may deny parentage and use the pregnancy as an excuse for abuse. . . .
>
> "290. Secrecy typically shrouds abusive families. Family members are instructed not to tell anyone, especially police or doctors, about the abuse and violence. Battering husbands often threaten their wives or her children with further abuse if she tells an outsider of the violence and tells her that nobody will believe her. A battered woman, therefore, is highly unlikely to disclose the violence against her for fear of retaliation by the abuser. . . .
>
> "291. Even when confronted directly by medical personnel or other helping professionals, battered women often will not admit to the battering because they have not admitted to themselves that they are battered. . . .
>
> "294. A woman in a shelter or a safe house unknown to her husband is not 'reasonably likely' to have bodily harm inflicted upon her by her batterer, however her attempt to notify her husband pursuant to section 3209 could accidentally disclose her whereabouts to her husband. . . .
>
> "295. Marital rape is rarely discussed with others or reported to law enforcement authorities, and of those reported only few are prosecuted. . . .
>
> "296. It is common for battered women to have sexual intercourse with their husbands to avoid being battered. While this type of coercive sexual activity would be spousal sexual assault

> as defined by the Act, many women may not consider it to be so and others would fear disbelief. . . .
>
> 298. Because of the nature of the battering relationship, battered women are unlikely to avail themselves of the exceptions to section 3209 of the Act, regardless of whether the section applies to them."

. . . The vast majority of women notify their male partners of their decision to obtain an abortion. In many cases in which married women do not notify their husbands, the pregnancy is the result of an extramarital affair. Where the husband is the father, the primary reason women do not notify their husbands is that the husband and wife are experiencing marital difficulties, often accompanied by incidents of violence. . . .

Respondents . . . begin by noting that only about 20 percent of the women who obtain abortions are married. They then note that of these women about 95 percent notify their husbands of their own volition. Thus, respondents argue, the effects of §3209 are felt by only one percent of the women who obtain abortions. Respondents argue that since some of these women will be able to notify their husbands without adverse consequences or will qualify for one of the exceptions, the statute affects fewer than one percent of women seeking abortions. For this reason, it is asserted, the statute cannot be invalid on its face.

We disagree with respondents' basic method of analysis. . . . Legislation is measured for consistency with the Constitution by its impact on those whose conduct it affects. . . . [I]n a large fraction of the cases in which §3209 is relevant, it will operate as a substantial obstacle to a woman's choice to undergo an abortion. It is an undue burden, and therefore invalid.

This conclusion is in no way inconsistent with our decisions upholding parental notification or consent requirements. Those enactments, and our judgment that they are constitutional, are based on the quite reasonable assumption that minors will benefit from consultation with their parents and that children will often not realize that their parents have their best interests at heart. We cannot adopt a parallel assumption about adult women.

We recognize that a husband has a "deep and proper concern and interest . . . in his wife's pregnancy and in the growth and development of the fetus she is carrying." With regard to the children he has fathered and raised, the Court has recognized his "cognizable and substantial" interest in their custody. *Stanley v. Illinois* (1972); . . . *Lehr v. Robertson* (1983). If these cases concerned a State's ability to require the mother to notify the father before taking some action with respect to a living child raised by both, therefore, it would be reasonable to conclude as a general matter that the father's interest in the welfare of the child and the mother's interest are equal.

Before birth, however, the issue takes on a very different cast. It is an inescapable biological fact that state regulation with respect to the child a woman is carrying will have a far greater impact on the mother's liberty than on the father's. . . . The Court has held that "when the wife and the husband disagree on this decision, the view of only one of the two marriage partners can prevail. Inasmuch as it is the woman who physically bears the child and who is the more directly and immediately affected by the pregnancy, as between the two, the balance weighs in her favor." This conclusion rests upon the basic nature of marriage and the nature of our Constitution: "[T]he marital couple is not an independent entity with a mind and heart of its own, but an association of two individuals each with a separate intellectual and emotional makeup. If the right of privacy means anything, it is the right of the individual, married or single, to be free from unwarranted governmental intrusion into matters so fundamentally affecting a person as the decision whether to bear or beget a child." *Eisenstadt v. Baird.* The Constitution protects individuals, men and women alike, from unjustified state interference, even when that interference is enacted into law for the benefit of their spouses.

There was a time, not so long ago, when a different understanding of the family and of the Constitution prevailed. In *Bradwell v. State* (1873), three Members of this Court reaffirmed the common-law principle that "a woman had no legal existence separate from her husband, who was regarded as her head and representative in the social state; and, notwithstanding some recent modifications of this civil status, many of the special rules of law flowing from and dependent upon this cardinal principle still exist in full force in most States." Only one generation has passed since this Court observed that "woman is still regarded as the center of home and family life," with attendant "special responsibilities" that precluded full and independent legal status under the Constitution. *Hoyt v. Florida* (1961). These views, of course, are no longer consistent with our understanding of the family, the individual, or the Constitution.

In keeping with our rejection of the common-law understanding of a woman's role within the family, the Court held in *Danforth* that the Constitution does not permit a State to require a married woman to obtain her husband's consent before undergoing an abortion. The principles that guided the Court in *Danforth* should be our guides today. For the great many women who are victims of abuse inflicted by their husbands, or whose children are the victims of such abuse, a spousal notice requirement enables the husband to wield an effective veto over his wife's decision. Whether the prospect of notification itself deters such women from seeking abortions, or whether the husband, through physical force or psychological pressure or economic coercion, prevents his wife from obtaining an abortion until it is too late, the notice requirement will often be tantamount to the veto found unconstitutional in *Danforth.* The women most affected by this law—those who most reasonably fear the consequences of notifying their husbands that they are pregnant—are in the gravest danger.

The husband's interest in the life of the child his wife is carrying does not permit the State to empower him with this troubling degree of authority over his wife. The contrary view leads to consequences reminiscent of the common law. A husband has no enforceable right to require a wife to advise him before she exercises her personal choices. If a husband's interest in the potential life of the child outweighs a wife's liberty, the State could require a married woman to notify her husband before she uses a post-fertilization contraceptive. Perhaps next in line would be a statute requiring pregnant married women to notify their husbands before engaging in conduct causing risks to the fetus. After all, if the husband's interest in the fetus' safety is a sufficient predicate for state regulation, the State could reasonably conclude that pregnant wives should notify their husbands before drinking alcohol or smoking. Perhaps married women should notify their husbands before using contraceptives or before undergoing any type of surgery that may have complications affecting the husband's interest in his wife's reproductive organs. And if a husband's interest justifies notice in any of these cases, one might reasonably argue that it justifies exactly what the *Danforth* Court held it did not justify—a requirement of the husband's consent as well. A State may not give to a man the kind of dominion over his wife that parents exercise over their children. . . .

Which of the Court's points would apply to this situation: A woman who does not want to have children tells her boyfriend that she does want to have children, because she believes he will not marry her otherwise. They marry, and she does not use birth control, because she does not think she can conceal this from her husband. Instead, when she gets pregnant, she has an abortion. The husband assumes there is some problem with their reproductive capacities. The husband has never been abusive toward her. Does the Court say anything to justify prohibiting a state from requiring that a man in that situation receive notification of the intent to abort? Similar situations could involve a wife changing her mind about child bearing after she starts a new career or after she has had one child. To what extent does the Court's reasoning rest on an assumption that cases of that sort are non-existent, few in number, only a minority of cases, or simply not all of the cases in which a wife does not want to disclose an intent to have an abortion?

With respect to the basic right to have an abortion, the Court has avoided discussing the fact that being killed seems to be a worse thing than being forced to continue a pregnancy (though the latter might be quite bad indeed) by positing that the fetus before a certain stage is not a being whose interests matter. The Court cannot do the same with the conflict of interests between husband and wife. The *Casey* decision might be read to imply that being forced to continue a pregnancy is worse than being deprived of an opportunity to procreate and to raise a child. If that is what the Court said, is it correct? In the maltreatment context, the Court has characterized loss of parent status as equivalent to the death penalty. Does the fact of marriage change the calculus at all, or is a husband in no different position than a boyfriend with respect to abortion of his child? Does the fact of marriage also or instead change the normative position of the pregnant woman? Could one plausibly believe that getting married entails a waiver of some portion (though certainly not all) of one's liberty, even with respect to procreation?

The Court places great weight on the possibility of violence or other forms of abuse toward a pregnant wife, in justifying exclusion of husbands from decision making. That is a potentially far-reaching justification, given the great range of things that might anger an abusive husband. What other unilateral decisions by a wife might the state be required to allow, in light of this possibility? Suppose a wife were able to conceal a pregnancy, or to convince her husband that she miscarried, perhaps while he is abroad on military duty or in prison. Should the law authorize her to place the child for adoption without her husband's consent, because it is possible that her husband is abusive? Cf. Lehr v. Robertson, 463 U.S. 248, 262 (1983) (vaguely suggesting that a biological father is constitutionally entitled to "an opportunity . . . to develop a relationship with his offspring.") Or should she be excused if she falsifies his consent to an adoption? Cf. Should wives be excused from any unilateral financial actions they take, or from concealing income or assets to which their husbands would ordinarily have some entitlement, because in some unknown percentage of cases consulting with or disclosing to their husbands could trigger abuse?

A background assumption of the Court's reasoning is that legal protections against domestic abuse are inadequate. The next section describes those protections and assesses their adequacy.

2. *Violence*

Marriage once entailed a license for men to engage in violence toward a woman, including hitting, physically restraining, and raping. Today the criminal law ostensibly treats violence toward a spouse more or less the same as violence toward a stranger, and in addition states have created a special civil proceeding through which individuals can secure orders of protection against a violent partner. Yet the home remains the place where people, especially women and children, are most likely to be victims of violence. Before studying the legal system's response to partner violence, we might try to understand why it occurs.

Martin Daly & Margo Wilson, The Evolutionary Social Psychology of Family Violence

in Handbook of Evolutionary Psychology: Ideas, Issues, and Applications 447-451 (Charles B. Crawford & Dennis L. Krebs eds., 1998)

The marital relationship is a special one from an evolutionary theoretical perspective. Because the well-being of a child contributes similarly to the fitness of both its parents, the resource allocations and other states of affairs that appeal to one parent are likely to have appeal for the other, too. In fact, insofar as reproduction rather than collateral nepotism is the dominant means by which individuals promote their fitness, the fitness linkage, and hence the solidarity of mated couples, is likely to exceed that of blood kin. However, the marital relationship is more fragile than genetic relationships because the correlation between the partners' expected fitnesses can be diminished, or even abolished, if either party becomes less committed to their joint venture.

One challenge to that joint commitment comes from the demands of other family members. Marriage partners have separate kindreds, and each may resent the other's continued nepotistic investment of time, attention, and material resources in collateral kin. This is the evolutionary theoretical gloss on a cross-culturally ubiquitous and widely recognized source of marital friction—in-laws. . . . [W]ife beaters often complain of their wives' excessive attention to collateral kin.

However, . . . the principal motivating factor in a substantial majority of the cases is the husband's discovery or suspicion of his wife's infidelity and/or her intention to desert the marriage. . . . There is considerable evidence that the human male mind construes marriage in large measure as a matter of entitlement to monopolize a woman, and perhaps especially to monopolize her sexuality. . . . As long as we have been a biparentally investing species, wifely infidelity has been an especially potent threat to a husband's fitness because it entails risk that he will . . . invest unwittingly in the upbringing of unrelated children. The asymmetry of this threat is presumably of evolutionary relevance to the fact that the jealousy of men is more focused on the copulatory act than is that of women.

Moreover, female infidelity is universally recognized as a uniquely potent stimulus to violence on the part of normal men, and there is . . . an obvious functional explanation for a rage reaction . . . : A predictably violent response presumably has some chilling effect on the adulterous ardor of both wives and their lovers. . . . [It] does not always succeed in generating effective coercion, however, and when it does not, the violence of spurned men often appears to be dysfunctionally spiteful. . . . In fact, a woman who has recently left her husband has a much higher statistical risk of being killed by him than does a coresiding wife. . . . Uxoricide may seldom serve the interests of the killer, . . . [but] signals of sincerity in threat may have evolved to be hard to fake . . . , with the result that only those who really will follow through with spiteful violence can enjoy a threat's deterrent and coercive benefits. . . .

[W]omen of the greatest reproductive value . . . incur the greatest risk. A woman's reproductive value is maximal soon after puberty, and begins to decline steeply in her 30s. As one would then expect, . . . husbands of young women are likely to be especially jealous, proprietary, and coercive to their wives. . . . [A] young woman is actually increasingly likely to be killed by her husband the *older* he is. . . .

Not surprisingly, de facto unions also entail much higher risks of lethal assault than registered unions, for both partners and at all ages. . . . [A]n exceptionally high incidence of steprelationships is to be found in de facto unions of middle-aged people, and . . . the presence of stepchildren will be a risk factor for violence. . . . [T]he genetic parent must often be motivated to counter stepparental mistreatment, . . . [and any] child of one partner to a marriage who is not the other's child is likely to induce some disparity in the partners' notions of how their joint resources should be allocated. . . .

The common element in all the identified triggers is any diversion of the victim's attention away from her mate and toward others—her kindred, her children from another relationship, and any other actual or potential mate. Adults in intimate relationships, it seems, or at least men in intimate relationships, manifest an inclination to monopolize their mate's attention and resources.

One phenomenon this article does not explain is intensified violence during pregnancy, a time when a man should have less concern about infidelity and a time when violence toward one's female partner is highly counter-productive in terms of reproductive fitness. Can you think of a possible explanation?

Advocates for domestic violence victims have long complained that police, prosecutors, and judges under-react to reports of domestic abuse against women. Part of the explanation for this might be that these state actors have been predominantly male and so sympathetically identify with a man who justifies his violence by referring to one of the universal triggers mentioned above, such as concerns about his wife's or girlfriend's fidelity or devotion to her genetic relatives. Another part of the explanation is likely legitimate concern about the human costs of over-reacting, costs suggested by the following case. The opinion does not provide the underlying facts, so suppose for the sake of analysis that the wife attacked the husband with her fists and incurred a bruise or cut when he pushed her off in self-defense, and that her attorney explained to her that a domestic violence conviction of her husband would help her greatly in property distribution, child custody, and other aspects of their divorce. This case also illustrates the process that typically ensues when a domestic violence complaint is lodged.

State v. Fernando A.

981 A.2d 427 (Conn. 2009)

NORCOTT, J.

. . . The defendant and his wife are involved in divorce proceedings. On October 14, 2007, the defendant was arrested on numerous family violence criminal charges arising from an incident wherein he allegedly had assaulted his wife. Pursuant to §54-63c(b), the police released the defendant that day on the conditions that he not enter the family home and that he avoid contact with his wife pending his first court appearance. At that appearance on October 15, 2007, the trial court . . . issued a criminal protective order as a condition of his pretrial release. Judge Pavia denied the defendant's request for an evidentiary hearing at that time, reasoning that "immediate judicial review of this matter is necessary to protect the safety and well-being of the victim and the family," and that "the need for expeditious assumption of judicial control following a defendant's arrest outweighs the need to minimize risk of error through adversary procedures."

Judge Pavia then continued the case. . . . Subsequently, on October 18, 2007, the defendant appeared before the trial court, Bingham, J., to request an evidentiary hearing to contest the continuation of the criminal protective order. . . . Judge Bingham denied the defendant's request for an evidentiary hearing, reasoning that the procedure for issuing a domestic violence protective order in criminal cases "is similar to a bail hearing, and you're not entitled to a full trial on a bail hearing." . . . On appeal, the defendant contends, inter alia, that the trial court improperly failed to conduct an evidentiary hearing prior to issuing a criminal protective order. . . .

§54-63c(b) . . . authorizes police officers in "family violence crime" cases, after making "reasonable," but unsuccessful, attempts to reach a bail commissioner, to "order the release of such person upon the execution of a written promise to appear or the posting of such bond as may be set by the police officer and may impose nonfinancial conditions of release which may require that the arrested person do one or more of the following: (1) Avoid all contact with the alleged victim of the crime, (2) comply with specified restrictions on the person's travel, association or place of abode that are directly related to the protection of the alleged victim of the crime. . . ." Section 54-63c(b) then provides that: "Any nonfinancial conditions of release imposed pursuant to this subsection shall remain in effect until the arrested person is presented before the Superior Court pursuant to subsection (a) of section 54-1g. *On such date, the court shall conduct a hearing pursuant to section 46b-38c at which the defendant is entitled to be heard with respect to the issuance of a protective order.*" (Emphasis added.)

The text of §54-63c(b) does not specify the nature of the hearing other than describing it as one held "pursuant to section 46b-38c" . . . §46b-38c(a) . . . establishes "family violence response and intervention units in the Connecticut judicial system to respond to cases involving family violence. . . ." Each geographical area of the Superior Court has a "local family violence intervention unit" that is required to: "(1) [a]ccept referrals of family violence cases from a judge or prosecutor, (2) prepare written or oral reports on each case for the court by the next court date to be presented at any time during the court session on that date, (3) provide or arrange for services to victims and offenders, (4) administer contracts to carry out such services, and (5) establish centralized reporting procedures. . . ." Subsection (d) of §46b-38c prescribes only certain limited aspects of the hearing process and provides: "In all cases of family violence, a written or oral report and recommendation of the local family violence intervention unit shall be available to a judge at the first court date appearance. . . ."

§46b-38c(d) does not specify the precise nature of how the hearing shall be conducted, or what the defendant's rights are therein. Because the term "hearing" is "not defined in the statute, . . . we construe the term in accordance with the commonly approved usage of the language . . . as expressed in a dictionary." The word "hearing" is defined alternatively as an "opportunity to be heard, to present one's side of a case, or to be generally known or appreciated," "a listening to arguments" or "a preliminary examination in criminal procedure. . . ." *Merriam-Webster's Collegiate Dictionary* (10th Ed. 1993). Similarly, *Black's Law Dictionary* (7th Ed. 1999) defines "hearing" as a "judicial session, usu[ally] open to the public, held for the purpose of deciding issues of fact or of law, *sometimes with witnesses testifying.* . . ." (Emphasis added.) Resorting to these dictionary definitions does not answer conclusively the question of whether a hearing under §54-63c(b) must be evidentiary in nature. The statute is, therefore, ambiguous, and we may consult extratextual sources in resolving this issue.

The legislative history of . . . §54-63c(b) indicates only that the statute was enacted to authorize police officers, in the event that "reasonable efforts" to locate a bail commissioner failed, to impose nonfinancial conditions of release pending the defendant's first appearance before the trial court. . . . [This] would avoid the unnecessary detention of defendants, while providing additional and formal protection for complainants pending the defendant's first court appearance. . . .

Moreover, our construction of §46b-38c(d) necessarily is informed by the various exigencies faced by a trial court considering whether to grant a criminal protective order in a family violence case. . . . [T]he legislature did not intend for §§ 54-63c(b) and 46b-38c to entitle a defendant to an evidentiary hearing beyond consideration of the parties' arguments and the family services report prior to the *initial* issuance of a criminal protective order at arraignment, which may well occur within hours of the alleged incident of family violence. This reflects the potential need for immediate judicial intervention to restore order and safety in the home . . . [and] legislative recognition of the heavy flow of judicial business . . . during arraignment sessions. . . .

We agree, however, with the defendant's claims that the extended effects of that initial emergency order may well cause a defendant significant pretrial deprivations of family relations and/or property.[18] . . .

[A]fter a criminal protective order has been issued at arraignment, a defendant is entitled, upon his request made at that time, to a more extensive hearing to be held within a reasonable period of time about the continued necessity of that order. At that second hearing, the state bears the burden of proving, by a fair preponderance of the evidence, the continued necessity of the criminal protective order in effect since the defendant's arraignment.[20]

With respect to the type of proof required at this subsequent hearing, we further conclude that, inasmuch as the legislature has not required the introduction of evidence that conforms strictly with the rules of evidence; the state may, consistent with the defendant's federal due process rights, proceed by proffer, supported by reliable hearsay evidence, and the trial court retains the discretion to determine whether testimony from the complainant or other witnesses is necessary for the order to continue.[21] . . .

18. It is undisputed that criminal protective orders may have a significant impact on a defendant's fundamental constitutional rights. See . . . *People v. Forman*, supra, 546 N.Y.S.2d 755 ("Each of the temporary orders of protection restrict [the] defendant's liberty to go where he pleases—he may not go to the home, place of business or place of employment of his wife, as well as his associational liberty in relation to his wife. . . . The orders also exclude him from real property in which [the] defendant otherwise shares ownership and a right to possession."); Moore v. Moore, 376 S.C. 467 (2008) (subject of civil protective order faces, inter alia, "immediate loss of his children . . . and possession of the marital residence," as well as "future ramifications" with "long-term impact" on marital litigation). Moreover, by imposing what some commentators have referred to as "de facto divorce," albeit without the benefit of property division and procedures attendant to the dissolution context, the protective order further compounds the financial difficulties attendant to being tried on criminal charges. See J. Suk, "Criminal Law Comes Home," 116 Yale L.J. 2, 42, 50 (2006).

20. We emphasize that this subsequent hearing should not be a minitrial on the underlying criminal charges, or, put differently, the state is not required to prove the elements of those crimes charged by a preponderance of the evidence. Indeed, only those defendants charged with crimes punishable by death or life imprisonment have a right to a probable cause hearing in Connecticut. Thus, once probable cause has been established for the defendant's arrest . . . the state's burden is limited to proving by a preponderance of the evidence the necessity of the criminal protective order as a regulatory means for protecting the complainant and other members of the defendant's household. The defendant remains free, however, to adduce his own evidence tending to negate the necessity for the criminal protective order or portions thereof, evidence that may well pertain to the merits of the underlying criminal charges.

21. . . . Indeed, other courts have . . . concluded that a defendant is not constitutionally entitled to an evidentiary hearing with the right to confront and to cross-examine the complainant prior to the issuance of a criminal protective order in a domestic violence case. . . .

The defendant may, however, upon the trial court's acceptance of his proffer of relevant evidence regarding the continued necessity of the protective order, testify or present witnesses on his own behalf, and may cross-examine any witnesses whom the state might elect to present against him.[22] . . .

Accordingly, on remand, the defendant is entitled to the opportunity to request, and to receive, an evidentiary hearing as described in the preceding paragraph about the continued necessity of the criminal protective order. . . .

When someone alleges violence on the part of someone who is not a member of the same household, a stay-away order is unlikely to cause any hardship during the wait for an evidentiary hearing. But imagine what it would be like if you walked out of your family law class and a police officer waiting outside told you that you were prohibited until further notice from returning home and from contacting the people you live with. Particularly if those people included your children, the sudden and indefinite rupture of the relationship could be quite traumatic. See David Michael Jaros, *Unfettered Discretion: Criminal Orders of Protection and Their Impact on Parent Defendants*, 85 IND. L.J. 1445 (2010). Combined with needing to find another place to live and not having access to your belongings, this order could cause great suffering. Thus, despite serious concern about a complainant's being in real danger, police and judges might be reluctant to act absent quite clear physical evidence or corroborating witnesses.

That said, under-reporting of actual violence appears to be a much greater problem than that of false reports. One reason for under-reporting is that some domestic violence victims perceive the legal system's response to be too blunt, providing either no protection or complete severance of the relationship. Professor Goldfarb presents an overview of the American legal system's response to domestic violence, which has evolved from indifference to rather aggressive intervention, and she argues that an intermediate or more nuanced approach would in many cases better serve women's interests and autonomy.

Sally F. Goldfarb, Reconceiving Civil Protection Orders for Domestic Violence: Can Law Help End the Abuse Without Ending the Relationship?

29 Cardozo L. Rev. 1487, 1492 (2008)

. . . By a conservative estimate, nearly two million women are physically assaulted, stalked, and/or raped by their partners every year. . . . One quarter of all American women have been victims of domestic violence. . . . Assaults inflicted on women by their partners range from hitting and pushing to kicking, burning, choking, and the use of weapons. Abuse often starts or intensifies during pregnancy. . . . In addition to the physical and psychological harm . . . [a]busive partners prevent women from obtaining education, employment, and economic independence. Violence in the home is responsible for forcing many women and children into homelessness. A large number of women in prison were compelled to commit crimes by abusive partners. Being a victim

22. Should the trial court . . . deem it necessary for the complainant or children to testify, we note that such testimony may be taken and the witness cross-examined in a manner intended to address concerns . . . about the potential intimidation of testifying complainants and children.

of domestic violence can cause women to lose custody of their children. Perhaps the most profound effect of domestic violence is that it deprives women of the opportunity for equality within relationships and in society. . . .

The American legal system has traditionally been unresponsive to the needs of battered women. Although a law forbidding wife abuse was enacted in the Massachusetts Bay Colony as early as 1641, civil and criminal penalties for domestic violence remained rare throughout most of the nation's history. Police customarily refused to arrest batterers. Instead, they either let violent incidents take their course or employed ineffective methods like informal mediation or ordering the offender to "walk around the block and cool off." If an arrest did occur, prosecutors typically declined to pursue criminal charges. When cases came to court, judges routinely denied relief, viewing domestic violence as a family matter to be worked out by the parties themselves. These traditional patterns endured into the 1970s, and in some cases beyond.

This policy of non-intervention had different justifications at different times. Initially, it was a natural outgrowth of the common law rule of coverture. . . . Since "the husband and wife are one person in law," a legal action by one against the other is a logical impossibility. Coverture thus lent support to interspousal tort immunity, which forbids civil suits by one spouse against the other, and the marital rape exemption, which ordains that a man's rape of his wife is not a crime. Furthermore, because marital unity made the husband legally responsible for his wife's actions, coverture conferred on him the power of "domestic chastisement"—that is, the right to use physical force to punish his wife and control her behavior. . . .

During the middle of the nineteenth century, with the emergence of the ideal of affectionate companionship in marriage, the common law rule permitting husbands to inflict corporal punishment on their wives came to seem both antiquated and indefensible. Judges consequently became less willing to rely on the right of chastisement. However, a new rationale for the law's laissez-faire approach to domestic violence arose . . . : the concept of family privacy. According to the family privacy ideology, legal intervention in the family is inevitably destructive, and family members must be left free to resolve their differences without the damage that would be inflicted on their relationship if the law were to invade the private domestic sphere. . . .

Some police, prosecutors, and judges remain reluctant to interfere in cases of violence within the family. However, . . . [there is] a new, increasingly dominant trend toward vigorous legal intervention in cases of domestic violence—specifically, legal intervention with the aim of extricating women from relationships with abusive men. This trend began to appear in the 1970s and has accelerated in recent years. . . . The work of psychologist Lenore Walker was particularly influential. Walker described domestic violence as a cycle, consisting of a tension-building phase, followed by an acute battering incident, and a honeymoon phase, during which the abuser is kind, loving, and contrite. Walker also drew on the research of experimental psychologist Martin Seligman, who showed that dogs subjected to random electrical shocks would eventually stop trying to escape; she concluded that battered women . . . suffer from "learned helplessness" that renders them incapable of acting in their own self-interest. Walker's theories have been extensively critiqued. Nevertheless, they gained rapid acceptance, especially among judges, juries, and others who were seeking an explanation for battered women's seemingly inexplicable behavior, including their failure to leave the abuser. . . .

[S]upport grew for aggressive legal interventions. . . . New approaches adopted in many jurisdictions include mandatory arrest policies, which require police to arrest anyone who they have probable cause to believe has committed domestic violence, and "no-drop" prosecution policies, which prevent prosecutors from complying with a victim's request to drop charges against the abuser. Civil protection orders became available in every state; in most cases, they forbid the abuser to live with, contact, or approach the victim. The movement toward stricter enforcement of domestic violence laws gained an important federal imprimatur in 1994 with the enactment of the Violence Against Women Act, which included federal funding to support policies that mandate or encourage arrest for domestic violence offenses, as well as measures designed to improve the availability and impact of protection orders. . . . [A]ctors in the legal system—including judges, legislators, prosecutors, and police—increasingly see their role as assisting a battered woman to separate from her abuser, against her will if necessary. . . . Under this new paradigm, every victim should leave her abuser, and if she turns to the legal system at all, she should cooperate with its efforts to remove her from the relationship. . . .

Missing from this picture is a recognition that battered women should have the choice to remain in a relationship and obtain the legal system's assistance to end the violence. . . . Women have many reasons for staying with or returning to violent partners, including financial dependency, fear of retaliation, social isolation, community pressure, and concern about losing custody of children. A common reason for not leaving is that the woman has a deep emotional bond with her partner and wants to preserve and improve the relationship. . . . [A]busive relationships are often multidimensional, with episodes of abuse occurring in a context that also includes positive attributes like mutual emotional commitment, companionship, intimacy, and sharing. Battered women's feelings about their relationships frequently include hope for the future and a willingness to forgive. . . . This aspiration should not be dismissed as naïve or misguided. Many women have succeeded in remaining in their relationships and putting an end to violence, and with the assistance of the legal system, many more might be able to do so. . . .

An understanding that battered women exercise agency under conditions of oppression leads to the conclusion that a victim is entitled to make vital choices about her own situation (including whether or not to continue a relationship), while at the same time receiving support to overcome the constraints under which she lives. Indeed, empowerment through decision-making is an important step in women's psychological recovery from the effects of domestic violence. The power to decide whether to stay or leave is particularly central to establishing a battered woman's autonomy. If the law denies women the power to make that decision, it replicates the domination exercised by the abuser. . . .

Civil protection orders have emerged as the most frequently used and, in the view of many experts, the most effective legal remedy against domestic violence. . . . Among the most common features of protection orders are provisions . . . ordering the offender to refrain from contacting the victim, to remain a specified distance away from her and places that she frequents, and to vacate a home shared with the victim. . . . In some jurisdictions, they are mandatory by law or judicial custom. . . . Indeed, the term "stay-away order" is sometimes used as a synonym for protection order. . . . In addition . . . , the relief granted may include such measures as a prohibition on further abuse, child custody and visitation, spousal support and child support, monetary compensation, a ban on possession of firearms and other weapons, mandatory counseling for the batterer, and other relief deemed appropriate by the court. . . .

In many respects, a civil protection order may be more advantageous to the victim than criminal prosecution of the abuser. Many women do not want to have their partners arrested and sent to jail; they view the types of relief offered in a protection order as more likely to benefit themselves and their children. Women of color may be especially hesitant to expose their partners to the criminal justice system, which has historically discriminated against members of minority groups. For immigrants, an additional disincentive for becoming involved with the criminal justice system is the fact that a criminal conviction can lead to deportation. . . . In addition, protection orders are available for minor crimes that are unlikely to result in meaningful criminal penalties, and crimes for which it would be difficult to obtain a conviction because of evidentiary problems. . . .

[I]n most cases where the victim and abuser have children in common, the court permits ongoing contact between the abuser and the children. Batterers often use their access to the children to perpetrate further violence against the mother—for example, when exchanging the children for visitation periods. . . . In addition, battered women face the danger of separation assault. . . . Women are most at risk after ending, or while trying to end, an abusive relationship. . . .

[A] stay-away order can impose other types of harm on the victim. These include loss of access to the abuser's income and resulting impoverishment, loss of his child care assistance leading to the victim's inability to keep a job, and loss of support from extended family and community. Separation also inflicts the emotional loss attendant on ending an intimate relationship and breaking up a family.

Further problems arise if the woman wants to reconcile or even just communicate with her partner. Voluntary contact between the victim and offender following issuance of a protection order is common. If the abuser has been prohibited from having contact with the victim, any future communication between the parties—even if the victim initiated it—can lead to a finding that he has violated the order and subject him to criminal penalties. . . . [S]ome courts have penalized victims for engaging in conduct that violates the terms of the order. . . . Thus, an order that was designed as a shield to protect the victim can end up being used as a sword to punish her. . . . Most importantly, the prevalence of stay-away provisions deters many women from applying for civil protection orders and prevents many women who have gotten temporary orders from completing the process of receiving a final order. For women who are not ready to separate from an abusive partner, not getting a protection order may seem preferable to getting an order that prohibits ongoing contact. Currently, the majority of women who are eligible for protection orders do not obtain them. Those who do obtain them often wait until the violence has persisted for a long time and progressed to a severe level. . . .

The option of obtaining a protection order that authorizes an ongoing relationship between the parties but sets limits on the abuser's behavior provides a valuable alternative. . . . [T]he orders can help change the batterer's behavior. One lawyer reported that . . . "it gives a little bit of the power back to her" and "says that [domestic violence] is not acceptable." Another said that "it is a way to hold the batterer accountable for his actions. . . . [H]e is on notice that the next time he 'loses control' he will be arrested." . . . [A] common theme among the lawyers interviewed was that such orders are better than nothing. For instance, when there is insufficient evidence to win a full stay-away order, . . . [or] if a victim has a stay-away order that she no longer wants to maintain, dropping the stay-away provisions and keeping the remainder of the order in effect offers more protection than vacating the order in its entirety . . . [and] is less likely to leave the batterer feeling that he has "won" and is free to resume his abusive behavior. . . . And for victims who would be unwilling to enter the legal system if stay-away orders were the only option, an order permitting ongoing contact—even if less than ideal—provides a crucial alternative. . . .

To operate effectively, an order . . . should be custom-tailored to express the victim's preferences regarding the parties' future interactions. . . . For example, a limited order might indicate that the abuser may approach the victim in public but not at home, or that he may contact her by telephone but not in person. Alternatively, the order could prohibit future abusive conduct, but place no limitations whatsoever on contact. . . . As the batterer's behavior or the victim's needs change, the victim should have the opportunity to modify the order by adding, deleting, or altering provisions restricting contact between the parties, or even by converting the limited order into a full stay-away order if the victim wishes. The order must also list the types of abusive behavior that are forbidden. In many instances, when batterers stop physically assaulting their partners, their reliance on nonphysical abuse begins or increases. Therefore, in addition to prohibiting physical assault, it is essential that protection orders also prohibit stalking, harassment, threats, damage to property and pets, and other forms of psychological abuse.

Professor Goldfarb emphasizes victims' autonomy and preferences. Supposing there might often be a conflict between those things and what is best for society—in particular, if protective orders allowing for continued contact are more costly for police to enforce and are less effective in stopping violence, why should the legal system favor the victim over collective interests? In other realms, the state prevents people from putting their own health and safety at risk in part to avoid imposing on the rest of society costs such as uninsured medical costs and dependence on welfare. Why not in this realm? Do you, as a taxpayer, have an obligation to subsidize domestic violence victims' preference for a more nuanced (and costly) state response to their predicament? If so, do you also have an obligation to help pay for marriage-preserving services for couples experiencing domestic violence, such as anger management classes and couples counseling? By way of comparison, consider that taxpayers do pay for rehabilitation of abusive parents. Do we collectively owe the same obligation to adult abuse victims as we owe to abused children? Cf. Aya Gruber, *The Feminist War on Crime*, 92 IOWA L. REV. 741 (2007) (arguing that emphasis on criminal law enforcement against batterers diverts attention from society's collective responsibility for the unequal power, opportunities, and financial resources between the sexes that is a partial cause of the epidemic of violence against women).

Comparison with the parent-child relationship raises an additional question: Given that parents are legally permitted to hit their children for disciplinary purposes—that is, to exercise a "power of 'domestic chastisement'" with children, and that the vast majority of Americans accept this, why should the law not accept an adult's hitting another adult with whom there is a family relationship? What exactly explains the difference in attitudes with respect to violence in the two types of relationship? Is there a difference in the vulnerability, culpability, or moral status of the persons hit? Is there a difference in the motivation of the people doing the hitting that makes a moral difference? Try to identify the precise factual differences between the two situations and then to explain why those factual differences are determinative of the normative issue of whether the law should permit the violence. Not every difference amounts to a justification. Compare, for example, a mother slapping her son for saying she is stupid and a wife slapping her husband for saying she is stupid. Another interesting comparison might be between a father who hits his child on the buttocks with a belt for breaking one of the father's prized possessions, and a husband doing the same to his wife for the same reason.

In addition to having legal permission to beat their wives for chastisement purposes, husbands historically were deemed entitled to have sexual access to their wives.

Jill Elaine Hasday, Contest and Consent: A Legal History of Marital Rape

88 CAL. L. REV. 1373 (2000)

. . . At common law, husbands were exempt from prosecution for raping their wives. Over the past quarter century, this law has been modified somewhat, but not entirely. A majority of states still . . . criminalize a narrower range of offenses if committed within marriage, subject the marital rape they do recognize to less serious sanctions, and/or create special procedural hurdles for marital rape prosecutions. . . .

[A] husband's conjugal rights became the focus of public controversy almost immediately after the first organized woman's rights movement coalesced in 1848. Over the course of the next half century, feminists waged a vigorous, public, and extraordinarily frank campaign against a man's right to forced sex in marriage. . . . [L]eading nineteenth-century feminists argued—in public, vociferously, and systematically—that economic and political equality, including even the vote, would prove hollow, if women did not win the right to set the terms of marital intercourse. Indeed, feminists explained a woman's lack of control over her person as the key foundation of her subordination. This claim was acutely gender-specific, grounded in the argument that women needed to control the terms of marital intercourse in order to regulate the portion of their lives they would have to devote to raising children. Convinced that women's subordination was ultimately rooted in the structure of marital relations, feminists demanded both the right to refuse and viable socioeconomic alternatives to submission. . . .

States willing to augment the property rights of married women in the middle of the nineteenth century, or to ratify woman suffrage in the early twentieth century, were emphatically unwilling to subject husbands to prosecution for marital rape. At least in this arena where sexual and reproductive relations were so directly implicated, authoritative legal sources proved staunchly opposed to the notion of incorporating into the law a vision of marriage as a potentially disharmonious, abusive, even dangerous site of human interaction, in which wives might need and deserve legal rights against their husbands. . . . [O]ne of the most striking aspects of the modern defense of the marital rape exemption . . . is that it assumes the aligned interests of husband and wife. The exemption's contemporary defenders argue that the rule's continued existence protects marital privacy and promotes marital harmony and reconciliation, leaving both husband and wife better off. . . . [P]roponents do not acknowledge that a marital rape exemption might cause wives harm. . . .

In the nineteenth century, the harm that a husband's right to marital rape inflicted upon wives was freely and explicitly acknowledged as a social matter. . . . The modern defense of the marital rape exemption, in contrast, obscures and denies the harm that the rule inflicts upon women. This has been a crucial tactic because the injury that marital rape causes is far harder to defend, and the absence of legal remediation far harder to justify, in a nation now explicitly committed to women's legal equality. . . .

Professor Hasday explains that the justification for a marital exception to rape law originally was that women gave global consent to sex when they married. But what would have *motivated* judges and later legislators to impute to wives such consent to forced sex and thus to create this exception? Has it been so common historically for husbands to overpower their wives physically and force them to have intercourse that many men would have supported, or even demanded, legal accommodation? Hasday's research suggests that instead what husbands wanted, and what resulted from the law and social norms imputing to wives a duty of sexual submission, was for wives always to submit *willingly* (even if sometimes unhappily) to their husbands' sexual desires.

Jill Elaine Hasday, Contest and Consent: A Legal History of Marital Rape

88 Cal. L. Rev. 1373 (2000)

. . . I was able to locate no nineteenth-century prosecutions of a husband for raping his wife. The existence of the exemption made such attempts patently futile. . . . The studies of women's sexual experiences in marriage that do exist, however, suggest a widespread desire among women to control the terms of marital intercourse, a widespread recognition that they did not have the right to exercise this control, and a widespread experience of harm caused by unwanted sex in marriage.

Katharine Bement Davis's Factors in the Sex Life of Twenty-Two Hundred Women (1929) is the most systematic and rigorous examination of women's experience of sex in marriage during this approximate period. . . . The women Davis surveyed repeatedly made clear that they had entered into marriage with the expectation that their husbands had the right to control the terms of marital intercourse, although they were hardly enthusiastic about that husbandly prerogative. . . . As one wife in this cohort explained, " 'My mother taught me what to expect. The necessity of yielding to her husband's demands had been a great cross in her own life.' " Davis's questioning about whether the women had been " 'attracted or repelled by the way in which married sex relations came into [their] experience' " generated even more revealing responses. Nearly a quarter (223) of the first thousand women to respond "replied 'neither.' "

> Of these, 173 said that they "took it as a matter of fact"—something that every married woman had to go through with, regardless of her feelings. The other 50 qualified the "neither" with the following adjectives: Amused, 1; astonished, 8; bewildered, 3; disappointed, 7; frightened, 8; indifferent, 8; indignant, 1; interested, 5; relieved (that it was no worse), 1; resigned, 3; shocked, 1; sorry, 1; stunned, 1; submissive, 2.

Davis's work also suggests that women's marital happiness in this period importantly turned on how a husband chose to wield his authority over marital intercourse—whether a husband actually exercised his admitted rights or restrained himself voluntarily. . . .

Dr. Clelia Duel Mosher's earlier, if significantly smaller and less systematic, survey of married women's sexual lives . . . [was] conducted between 1892 and 1920. . . . Mosher's subjects repeatedly explained that they wished to limit marital intercourse to those occasions when it was agreed to by wife and husband alike. . . . "[E]verything to be absolutely mutual," they typically responded. "When desired by both." "No habit at all, but the most sensitive regard of each member of the couple for the personal feeling and desires and health of the other." . . . Some women happily reported that their husbands had agreed to mutuality. . . . Many other women in Mosher's study, however, indicated that they were routinely obliged to submit to unwanted sex. . . . One of these respondents described "having intercourse on an average of once a week," although sexual relations were "[v]ery painful" for her because of injuries sustained in pregnancy and childbirth. Another explained that she had engaged in marital intercourse when she "often felt averse to it". . . . Some reported deep disappointment and dissatisfaction in marriage. One woman had repeatedly been subject to much more frequent intercourse than she desired. Although she felt "[m]ore alive mentally & physically" after sexual climax, she concluded nonetheless that her sexual experience in marriage had been "[n]ot agreeable" and that "men ha[d] not been properly trained." A second woman in the same position wrote, more emphatically, of the "[s]hock and destruction of all ideals: When a pure woman is treated by her husband as he has treated the prostitute he has been to before marriage, it becomes loathsome." . . .

This understanding about a husband's right to marital intercourse may have had non-legal sources. But it was certainly given enormous strength and realism by the fact that the criminal law categorically refused to entertain claims based on forced sex in marriage, especially when combined with the legal and socioeconomic obstacles to securing a divorce based on marital rape. . . .

No experience Professor Hasday describes would today provide a basis for a rape charge, regardless of the marital status of the persons involved. Her exhaustive research uncovered no evidence of any instances in which husbands did what we would characterize as rape—that is, physically restraining and forcing penetration over objection, or threatening harm if a wife did not submit. Although there must have been some such instances, they might have been as rare as marital rape is today. The real effect of the marital exception to rape law might therefore have been to serve as a vague background threat that helped, along with societal and religious expectations, to induce wives to acquiesce to husbands' sexual advances. It was wise to accept sex, because refusing might, in addition to causing scorn by family or community and violating religious duties, cause a husband to extract sex violently, and one would have no recourse if he did.

Was husbands' expectation of wives' acquiescence to sex unreasonable? From an evolutionary perspective, sexual exclusivity is not natural for males, but in modern society men agree to it when they marry, because the law of marriage demands it. Are men not entitled to expect in return a certain frequency of intercourse? In an era when divorce was nigh impossible, what might have been the effect on marriage rates if men knew a wife could refuse to have sex with him but he would for the rest of his life remain constrained by adultery and fornication laws not to have sex with any other woman and he would remain obligated to support his wife financially? Of course, women, too, agree to sexual exclusivity when they marry, and for some this might be a sacrifice, so we might impute to both husbands and wives a duty to submit to the desires of the other, to have sex even when not "in the mood," or at least not to deprive the other for long periods. What, if anything, is wrong with this line of reasoning?

What recourse is there today for a victim of violence within an intimate relationship, in addition to or instead of exiting the relationship? Today, any violence toward a spouse that is not self-defense is criminal, even if in some cases it is deemed a lesser offense than similar conduct toward a non-intimate. See, e.g., S.C. Code Ann. §§ 16-3-615 and -652 (ten-year maximum sentence for aggravated sexual battery against a spouse, 30-year maximum for aggravated sexual battery against anyone else). It is also a basis for a civil protective order. We will look first at remedies the victim controls.

a. Private Remedies

As Professor Goldfarb explains, civil domestic abuse laws enable a victim to seek protection without a criminal action against the perpetrator. They generally cover a quite broad range of relationships and conduct, enable many people in addition to the victim to initiate legal proceedings, and authorize a great variety of remedies.

McKinney's Consolidated Laws of New York
Family Court Act
Article 8. Family Offenses Proceedings

§812. PROCEDURES FOR FAMILY OFFENSE PROCEEDINGS

1. Jurisdiction. The family court and the criminal courts shall have concurrent jurisdiction over . . . disorderly conduct, harassment . . . , sexual misconduct, forcible touching, stalking . . . , criminal mischief, menacing . . . , reckless endangerment, criminal obstruction of breathing or blood circulation, strangulation . . . , assault in the second degree, assault in the third degree or an attempted assault between spouses or former spouses, or between parent and child or between members of the same family or household. . . . For purposes of this article, "members of the same family or household" shall mean the following:

(a) persons related by consanguinity or affinity;

(b) persons legally married to one another;

(c) persons formerly married to one another regardless of whether they still reside in the same household;

(d) persons who have a child in common regardless of whether such persons have been married or have lived together at any time; and

(e) persons who are not related by consanguinity or affinity and who are or have been in an intimate relationship regardless of whether such persons have lived together at any time. Factors the court may consider in determining whether a relationship is an "intimate relationship" include but are not limited to: the nature or type of relationship, regardless of whether the relationship is sexual in nature; the frequency of interaction between the persons; and the duration of the relationship. Neither a casual acquaintance nor ordinary fraternization between two individuals in business or social contexts shall be deemed to constitute an "intimate relationship." . . .

§822. PERSON WHO MAY ORIGINATE PROCEEDINGS

(a) Any person in the relation to the respondent of spouse, or former spouse, parent, child, or member of the same family or household;

(b) A duly authorized agency, association, society, or institution;

(c) A peace officer, acting pursuant to his special duties, or a police officer;

(d) A person on the court's own motion.

§841. ORDERS OF DISPOSITION

At the conclusion of a dispositional hearing . . . , the court may enter an order:

(a) dismissing the petition, if the allegations of the petition are not established; or

(b) suspending judgment for a period not in excess of six months; or

(c) placing the respondent on probation for a period not exceeding one year, and requiring respondent to participate in a batterer's education program designed to help end violent behavior, which may include referral to drug and alcohol counseling . . . ; or

(d) making an order of protection in accord with section 842 of this part; or

(e) directing payment of restitution in an amount not to exceed ten thousand dollars. . . .

§842. Order of Protection

An order of protection . . . shall set forth reasonable conditions of behavior to be observed for a period not in excess of 2 years by the petitioner or respondent or for a period not in excess of 5 years upon (i) a finding . . . of aggravating circumstances . . . or (ii) a . . . violation of a valid order of protection. . . . Any order of protection . . . may require the petitioner or the respondent:

(a) to stay away from the home, school, business or place of employment of any other party, the other spouse, the other parent, or the child, and to stay away from any other specific location designated by the court . . . ;

(b) to permit a parent . . . to visit the child at stated periods;

(c) to refrain from committing a family offense . . . or any criminal offense against the child or against the other parent or against any person to whom custody of the child is awarded, or from harassing, intimidating or threatening such persons;

(d) to permit a designated party to enter the residence during a specified period of time in order to remove personal belongings . . . ;

(e) to refrain from acts of commission or omission that create an unreasonable risk to the health, safety or welfare of a child;

(f) to pay the reasonable counsel fees and disbursements involved in obtaining or enforcing the order of the person who is protected by such order . . . ;

(g) to require the respondent to participate in a batterer's education program designed to help end violent behavior, which may include referral to drug and alcohol counseling . . . ;

(h) to provide, either directly or by means of medical and health insurance, for expenses incurred for medical care and treatment arising from the incident or incidents forming the basis for the issuance of the order.

(i) to refrain from intentionally injuring or killing, without justification, any companion animal the respondent knows to be owned, possessed, leased, kept or held by the petitioner or a minor child residing in the household.

(j) to observe such other conditions as are necessary to further the purposes of protection.

The court may also award custody of the child, during the term of the order of protection to either parent, or to an appropriate relative within the second degree. . . .

The court may also upon the showing of special circumstances extend the order of protection for a reasonable period of time.

[T]he court may in addition . . . issue an order for temporary child support . . .

STATUTORY INTERPRETATION QUESTIONS

1. Would these provisions apply if a fellow law student living with you were to hit you?
2. If you had a brother and heard he was beating his wife, could you originate a family offense proceeding against him? What if it were the victim who was your sibling?

Respondents have advanced various constitutional objections to imposition of protective orders, generally without success. See, e.g., Crespo v. Crespo, 972 A.2d 1169 (N.J. Super. Ct. App. Div. 2009) (rejecting due process challenge to preponderance evidentiary standard and second amendment challenge to prohibition on firearms possession). Some advocates for abuse victims, on the other hand, complain that the scope of protection is too narrow, because most states do not define domestic abuse so as to include non-physical forms of harm, such as malicious use of economic control and emotional abuse. As with infidelity, abuse can take on more subtle forms, and emotional impact might be more damaging in the long run than physical harm, so again we might ask whether the state should target a broader range of conduct, not just the stereotypical form of the offense.

An additional private remedy for someone whose spouse physically harms them is to sue in tort, just as one might do if a stranger acted violently and caused one harm. Under coverture such a suit against a husband was impossible, as wives were disabled from bringing suit in their own name and a husband and wife were viewed as one person under law. Today there is no categorical barrier to financial recovery from an abusive spouse, yet such suits are fairly rare. Does the law take account of the fact that victims will often be too frightened to bring suit for a substantial period after the abuse ends?

Michele Noel Pugliese v. The Superior Court of Los Angeles County

53 Cal. Rptr. 3d 681, 146 Cal. App. 4th 1444 (2007)

CHAVEZ, J.

. . . Michele and Dante were married in January 1989. Michele filed a petition for dissolution of that marriage on April 22, 2002. On April 2, 2004, Michele sued Dante for assault, battery, intentional infliction of emotional distress and violation of civil rights. Michele alleged Dante had engaged in a pattern of domestic abuse, both physical and mental, which began within a few months of the marriage. Although the physical acts allegedly ceased in April 2001, Michele claims the emotional abuse continued until April 2004. . . .

Spouses are permitted to pursue appropriate civil remedies against each other, including lawsuits asserting the tort of domestic violence. Civil Code section 1708.6, subdivision (a) provides: "A person is liable for the tort of domestic violence if the plaintiff proves both . . . : (1) The infliction of injury upon the plaintiff resulting from abuse, as defined in . . . the Penal Code. (2) The abuse was committed by the defendant, a person having a relationship with the plaintiff as defined in . . . the Penal Code."[2]

2. Penal Code section 13700 provides . . . : "'Domestic violence' means abuse committed against an adult or a minor who is a spouse, former spouse, cohabitant, [or] former cohabitant. . . ."

The time for commencement of an action . . . is governed by Code of Civil Procedure section 340.15, which provides:

> "(a) In any civil action for recovery of damages suffered as a result of domestic violence, the time for commencement of the action shall be the later of the following:
>
> "(1) Within three years from the date of the last act of domestic violence by the defendant against the plaintiff.
>
> "(2) Within three years from the date the plaintiff discovers or reasonably should have discovered that an injury or illness resulted from an act of domestic violence by the defendant against the plaintiff.
>
> "(b) As used in this section, 'domestic violence' has the same meaning as defined in Section 6211 of the Family Code."

Family Code section 6211 defines "domestic violence" as "abuse perpetrated against . . . [a] spouse or former spouse." "Abuse" is defined as any of the following: "(a) Intentionally or recklessly to cause or attempt to cause bodily injury. (b) Sexual assault. (c) To place a person in reasonable apprehension of imminent serious bodily injury to that person or to another. (d) To engage in any behavior that has been or could be enjoined pursuant to Section 6320."[3]

. . . Thus, spouses and ex-spouses are entitled to allege, as did Michele, causes of action for assault, battery and intentional infliction of emotional distress . . . governed by the two-year statute of limitations set forth in Code of Civil Procedure section 335.1. Michele alleges the last physical act of abuse occurred in April 2001. Thus, her assault and battery causes of action are barred by Code of Civil Procedure section 335.1. As for Michele's intentional infliction of emotional distress claim, she alleges the last act of emotional abuse occurred in April 2004, less than two years prior to the filing of the complaint. Thus, her intentional infliction of emotional distress claim was timely filed. . . .

Although the assault and battery causes of action are barred by the applicable statute of limitations, the complaint, taken as a whole, alleges a violation of Civil Code section 1708.6. Michele claims that during the period June 1989 to April 2004, Dante shoved, pushed, kicked, hit, slapped, shook, choked and sexually abused her. She also alleges he pulled her hair, pinched and twisted her flesh, threatened to kill her, threatened her with bodily harm, confined her in the family car while driving erratically and drunkenly and infected her with sexually transmitted diseases. Clearly, Michele has alleged that Dante intentionally or recklessly caused or attempted to cause her bodily injury, sexually assaulted her, placed her in reasonable apprehension of imminent serious bodily injury and engaged in behavior that could have been enjoined pursuant to Family Code section 6320. We therefore conclude Michele has set forth a cognizable claim for domestic violence. Accordingly, the 3-year limitations period set forth in section 340.15 applies. Because Michele alleges the last physical act of abuse occurred in April 2001 and the last act of emotional abuse occurred in April 2004, and because the complaint was filed within three years of these dates, Michelle' Civil Code section 1708.6 domestic violence claim was timely filed.

3. Section 6320 permits a court to enjoin a party from "molesting, attacking, striking, stalking, threatening, sexually assaulting, battering, harassing, telephoning, including, but not limited to, annoying telephone calls . . . , destroying personal property, contacting, either directly or indirectly, by mail or otherwise, coming within a specified distance of, or disturbing the peace of the other party. . . ."

Michele contends she is entitled to seek damages for acts of domestic abuse occurring beyond the three-year limitations period set forth in Code of Civil Procedure section 340.15, subdivision (a). We agree. . . . Code of Civil Procedure section 335.1, the statute setting forth the limitations period for assault and battery between *nondomestic* partners, views each incident of abuse separately and the limitations period commences at the time the incident occurs. By contrast, section 340.15 provides that domestic violence lawsuits must be commenced within three years "from the date of the *last act* of domestic violence. . . ." The words "last act" are superfluous if they have no meaning. By adding these words, we believe the Legislature adopted by statute the continuing tort theory, thus allowing domestic violence victims to recover damages for all acts of domestic violence occurring during the marriage, provided the victim proves a continuing course of abusive conduct and files suit within three years of the "last act of domestic violence."[7]

. . . Dante concludes the situation at hand is precisely the sort in which statutes of limitations must be strictly enforced; otherwise he will be forced to combat evidence that has long since faded in amount, potency, reliability, and relevance. While we recognize the difficulty a spouse or ex-spouse may have in defending against domestic violence cases, the continuing tort doctrine seems especially applicable in such cases. . . . Most domestic violence victims are subjected to "an *ongoing* strategy of intimidation, isolation, and control that extends to all areas of a woman's life, including sexuality; material necessities; relations with family, children, and friends; and work." Pursuing a remedy, criminal or civil, while in such an environment defies the abuser's control, thus exposing the victim to considerable risk of violence. . . .

In adopting Civil Code section 1708.6, our Legislature declared: "(a) Acts of violence occurring in a domestic context are increasingly widespread. (b) These acts merit special consideration as torts, because the elements of trust, physical proximity, and emotional intimacy necessary to domestic relationships in a healthy society make participants in those relationships particularly vulnerable to physical attack by their partners. (c) It is the purpose of this act to enhance the civil remedies available to victims of domestic violence in order to underscore society's condemnation of these acts, to ensure *complete* recovery to victims, and to impose significant financial consequences upon perpetrators."

Clearly our Legislature, like the authors of the VAWA, understood that domestic violence encompasses a series of acts, including assault, battery and intentional infliction of emotional distress, and that when these acts are coupled with an oppressive atmosphere of control, the continuing tort of domestic violence results. . . .

Is there some other way for the state to secure compensation for victims? In some states, but not all, divorce courts can use property distribution as a means of compensation. But that, too, would depend on victims feeling secure enough to make allegations and request a monetary award against the perpetrator, and it would depend on there being sufficient marital assets to provide compensation. Should there also be state-funded "domestic violence relief funds" similar to the hurricane relief funds many governments have? Or would that create a danger of collusion, a moral hazard that might explain why

7. We can envision facts which may lead a court to exclude references to prior acts of domestic violence and to bar recovery for these acts. However, here it is alleged the acts of physical violence . . . continued . . . without any break in the cycle. . . .

insurance companies do not offer private policies insuring against damage from domestic violence?

Would it make more sense to have a "lack of capacity" exception to statutes of limitations, just as there is a "lack of knowledge" exception in some cases, rather than have the "continuing tort" rationale this court invokes? Is it clear that the equities relating to delay in filing suit are different for domestic violence than they are in connection with other torts? Is assault by a non-intimate typically less traumatic, or less likely to create fear of recurrence?

b. Criminal Prosecution

Domestic violence is still most often handled outside the criminal law system, even when the conduct clearly constitutes a crime. When prosecutors do charge an abuser, they might invoke the standard code provisions for assault and battery, kidnapping, sexual assault, etc., or in some states there might be special criminal code provisions governing violence toward a household member. Not long ago, the classification system and sentences typically were more lenient for domestic violence, but states have largely eliminated such distinctions. Leniency might today instead result simply from prosecutors' discretion whether to file charges. States have tried a number of policy reforms to increase the rate of prosecution. In this realm, too, scholars debate the proper balance between protecting and respecting the choices of victims. Victims generally have much less control over the criminal law response than over the civil law response.

Leigh Goodmark, Autonomy Feminism: An Anti-Essentialist Critique of Mandatory Interventions in Domestic Violence Cases

37 Fla. St. U. L. Rev. 1 (2009)

. . . In the criminal system, the best examples of policy initiatives that deprive women who have been battered of meaningful choices are mandatory arrest laws and "no-drop" prosecution policies. . . . [M]andatory arrest policies . . . require the officer to make an arrest whenever the officer has probable cause to believe that an act of domestic violence has been committed. Mandatory arrest laws were thought to solve the . . . problem [of] the perpetrator who gets warning after warning from police but is never arrested, and who, as a result, feels secure in his ability to continue to harass, threaten, and abuse his partner free from state sanction. Frustrated with years of police inaction in the face of severe violence, advocates for women who had been battered saw police discretion as a crucial weakness in the criminal justice system, particularly because police were trained to use that discretion to avoid arrest whenever possible. Remove the discretion, the thinking went, and domestic violence would be treated just as seriously as any other crime. Moreover, mandatory arrest laws would prevent police from citing discretion when choosing to credit the stories of abusers who said that their wives were simply overwrought, when ordering women who had been battered to leave their own homes, or when blaming the victim for provoking the attack.

Mandatory arrest laws were thought to serve as a deterrent to individual abusers, sending the message that domestic violence was criminal activity warranting the intervention of the justice system. . . . These laws would give women who had been battered a respite from the abuse without requiring them to affirm that they wanted to pursue charges, eliminating the potential for pressure and coercion by abusers regarding the decision about whether to arrest. On a societal level, proponents believed mandatory arrest laws would remove domestic violence from the privacy of the home and subject it to the harsh light of community scrutiny. . . . The shift from private to public resolution of domestic violence reflected the belief that women who had been battered wanted domestic violence to be brought into the public sphere and that they would welcome state intervention and protection. . . .

While arrest proved to deter future violence in some locations, in others there was no deterrent effect. Even worse, some evidence indicated that arrest contributed to increases in future violence. . . . Sherman's studies found that those who were married and employed had a greater stake in conformity and therefore were more likely to be deterred by arrest. Race also factored into the deterrent effect of arrest. In cities with large African American populations, arrest was positively correlated with future violence, suggesting that arrest policies endangered African American women. . . .

Mandatory arrest laws got a further boost from the Violence Against Women Act of 1994. This Act required states to certify that they had adopted either pro- or mandatory arrest policies in order to be eligible for federal funding under the Grants To Encourage Arrests program—a program that provided $120 million over three years to state and local police departments. . . . Today, every state has some form of pro-arrest policy and, as of 2004, at least twenty states and the District of Columbia mandated arrest in cases involving domestic violence. . . .

Just as police officers historically had used their discretion to refuse to arrest perpetrators of domestic violence, prosecutors had also routinely chosen not to pursue cases against the few perpetrators of violence who police had actually arrested. Ironically, prosecutors' failure to pursue cases involving domestic violence has been cited as yet another reason police declined to make arrests. Scholars have posited a number of reasons for the low rate of prosecution in domestic violence cases: the lack of evidence, the patriarchal views of prosecutors, skepticism about the seriousness of the crimes involved, and prosecutors' perceptions that judges were not interested in entertaining such cases. The justification most frequently offered . . . was their inability to rely on their star witnesses—the wives and girlfriends of the men they were prosecuting. . . . The failure of women who had been battered to participate in prosecutions was widely attributed to the victims' fear of repercussions at the hands of their abusers, a credible fear given that, even after successful prosecution, sentences for domestic violence offenses were ridiculously light and jail time was rarely imposed in misdemeanor cases. . . .

The success of victimless prosecution hinges on the willingness of police officers to respond to cases involving domestic violence differently and more thoroughly than they would ordinary assault cases. Police officers were trained to carefully investigate crime scenes, make detailed reports, and collect evidence that would allow prosecutors to pursue cases even when the victims were unwilling to testify—much as police would investigate homicide cases. Prosecutors relied on physical evidence, photographs of both the victim and the perpetrator (to show his demeanor at the time of arrest and any injuries, defensive or otherwise), 9-1-1 tapes, statements made to police, medical records, and other witness statements to secure convictions in cases that would have been impossible to successfully prosecute without such careful attention to gathering evidence.

Victimless prosecution allowed prosecutors to circumvent the wishes of the victim. . . . Victimless prosecution also enabled prosecutors to undermine the testimony of victims who appeared on behalf of their partners, impeaching them with prior inconsistent statements to police, or confronting them with photographs of injuries and their own words on 9-1-1 tapes. Despite the implementation of these increasingly sophisticated methods of preparing domestic violence cases, prosecutorial reluctance to bring domestic violence cases and victim unwillingness to testify continued to hamper successful prosecutions. The adoption of no-drop prosecution was meant to address both of these issues. No-drop means . . . prosecutors would not dismiss criminal charges in otherwise winnable cases simply because the victim was not interested in, or was even adamantly opposed to, pursuing the case.

Advocates of no-drop prosecution strategies . . . argue that . . . the purpose of the criminal system is not to bend to the wishes of individual victims, but rather to punish offenders and to deter others from committing similar crimes. The role of the prosecutor . . . is to reinforce the state's conception of the boundaries of acceptable behavior by ensuring compliance with the laws that define and regulate what individuals are and are not permitted to do. . . . The second justification proffered for no-drop prosecution is victim safety. Prosecuting those who commit domestic violence increases safety both for the individual victim by removing the immediate threat to her, and for future victims of the same perpetrator. The victim's inability to thwart the process is a particularly important guarantor of her safety. Because the victim no longer has the ability to stop the prosecutor from bringing the case to court, her abuser has no motivation to pressure her to do so. . . . The final justification for no-drop prosecution policies was, ironically, victim empowerment. Women who had been battered, the argument went, would derive strength and validation from the experience of participating in the prosecution. This argument assumed successful prosecution of the case and positive treatment of the victim throughout the process. . . .

In "soft" no-drop jurisdictions, victim testimony is not compelled; instead, prosecutors work with women who have been battered to help them feel comfortable with the system and offer them resources and support that will make compliance with the prosecutor's requests to assist in the prosecution possible. If the woman who has been battered is ultimately unwilling, unable, or uninterested in assisting prosecutors, she will not be forced to do so (although the services and support the woman may be relying on may no longer be available if she chooses not to cooperate with prosecutors). . . . In a hard no-drop jurisdiction, when a victim is unwilling to appear voluntarily, prosecutors might subpoena her to testify or, in the most extreme cases, issue a warrant for her arrest and/or have her incarcerated in order to compel her testimony. Law professor Cheryl Hanna, a former prosecutor, explains the necessity for such actions: ". . . If both the perpetrator and victim are aware that the prosecutor will not follow through on the threat to force the victim's compliance, there is little incentive for the perpetrator to refrain from pressuring the victim to withdraw her support for prosecution and even less for the reluctant victim to comply voluntarily."

At their core, these policies reflect a struggle over who will control the woman who has been battered—if the state does not exercise its control over her by compelling her testimony, the batterer will, by preventing her from testifying. Hard no-drop policies express the state's belief that it has a superior right to intervene on behalf of the woman who has been battered in service of both the woman's needs and the state's objectives. . . .

Some philosophers have questioned whether women who have been battered are ever capable of acting autonomously. They argue that battering is inherently coercive, creating a context that precludes women who have been battered from being able to exercise free will. . . . Ruth Jones has gone so far as to suggest that courts should appoint guardians for women who have been coercively controlled because their judgment has been so impaired and their autonomy so extinguished as to render them incapable of protecting themselves or separating from their partners. . . .

This formulation ignores the legitimate autonomous choices that some women make to remain with abusive partners. . . . The lives of many women who have been battered are not always at risk. . . . The exercise of autonomy does not require unfettered or entirely consistent choice. . . . Kathryn Abrams argues that self-direction may exist even when others fail to see it. . . .

Paternalism reflects a lack of respect for autonomy and for the individual as a person. . . . [R]estoring power to women who have been battered should be a priority when crafting domestic violence law and policy. . . . For Schechter, empowerment is

> [A] process through which women, experts about their own lives, learn to know their strength. "Empowerment" combines ideas about internalizing personal and collective power and validating women's personal experiences as politically oppressive rather than self-caused or "crazy." . . .

Researchers . . . have found that empowering court experiences predict long-term improvements in depression and quality of life for women who have been battered. . . . Too often, though, . . . choices have been constrained by what service providers, advocates, and policy makers deem acceptable alternatives . . . In "giving" the woman options, certain possibilities, like engaging in mediation or dropping criminal charges, may never come up for discussion. If those options are raised, they are presented in a manner meant (consciously or unconsciously) to dissuade the woman from seeing them as viable alternatives. . . . But empowerment must mean more than simply substituting advocates or the state for the abusive partner as the arbiter of choices for women who have been battered. Empowerment should be read as . . . enabling the woman who has been battered . . . to define the options for herself . . .

Can the choice between protective policies and empowerment be decided on the basis of one approach being respectful of women and the other not? Is "paternalism" inherently disrespectful of people? Is it so in relation to children? With adults who have been competent but who become mentally incompetent because of injury or old age? What policies might empower domestic violence victims against both abusers and the state?

One consequence of mandatory arrest and prosecution policies is that the criminal law response to domestic violence is no longer within the control of the victim, and courts routinely issue no-contact protective orders in criminal proceedings. Professor Suk points out that by means of these orders the state effectively forces couples to divorce, by prohibiting all the normal incidents of married life.

Jeannie Suk, Criminal Law Comes Home

116 Yale L.J. 2, 13-14 (2006)

. . . Many states have statutorily authorized or mandated issuance of the criminal protection order as a condition of bail or pretrial release. Criminal protection orders remain in effect while prosecution is pending and can become more permanent as part of a criminal sentence. Whereas the civil protection order is sought voluntarily by the victim, the criminal protection order is sought and issued by the state in the public interest. The practice . . . shifts the decision to exclude an alleged abuser away from the victim and to the state.

The protection order . . . criminalizes conduct that is not generally criminal—namely presence at home. . . . Presence at home is a proxy for domestic violence (DV). . . . The advantages of using presence at home as a proxy are evidentiary and preventive. . . . A violation of a protection order is far easier to prove than the target crime of DV. The testimony of the victim is generally less important. No physical injury need be shown. The existence of the protection order and the defendant's presence in the home, to which the arresting officer can usually bear witness, are sufficient to establish violation of the protection order. With a "no-contact" order, all that may need to be shown is that the defendant made a phone call to the protected party. . . . Furthermore, using presence at home as a proxy is designed to prevent conduct that, though innocent itself, can lead to the target crime. . . . Prohibiting a person's presence at home via the protection order reduces the likelihood that he will have the opportunity to engage in DV. . . . Finally, in excluding the abuser from the home, the protection order identifies the home itself as a dangerous place where the presence of the abuser causes fear in the victim. This reflects a theory of DV as operating often without actual violence but with the terrifying and inconsistent uses of the threat of violence to control the victim. . . .

Prosecutors' deployment of protection orders in the normal course of misdemeanor DV prosecution amounts in practice to state-imposed de facto divorce. . . . The vast majority of DV cases involve charges of misdemeanor or lesser severity. . . . By definition, misdemeanors do not involve serious physical injury. Many DV misdemeanor cases charged in criminal court do not allege physical harm. The harm alleged may instead be psychological, financial, or to property. Common charges . . . include criminal mischief (damaging property), larceny, criminal contempt (violation of a protection order), and harassment (a violation, not a crime). . . .

The uniform application of a mandatory protocol in every case represents the prosecutorial response to a paradigm story in which DV victims can turn into murder victims overnight. . . . The enforcement protocol [in Manhattan] consists of the following practices. Police officers must make an arrest if there is reasonable cause to believe that a DV crime, including violation of a protection order, has been committed. . . . Once a DV arrest is made, the D.A.'s Office has a no-drop prosecution policy, according to which the decision to charge and prosecute does not hinge on the victim's willingness to cooperate. . . . At the arraignment of any defendant charged with a DV crime, the D.A.'s Office's mandatory practice involves asking the criminal court to issue a temporary order of protection (TOP) as a condition of bail or pretrial release. The order of protection, issued on a standard form for a "family offense," normally prohibits any contact whatsoever with the victim, including phone, e-mail, voice-mail, or third-party contact. Contact with children is also banned. The order excludes the defendant from the victim's home, even if it is the defendant's home. It also bans the defendant from the victim's school, business, and place of employment. . . . The prosecutor generally requests a full stay-away order even if the victim does not want it.

The criminal court routinely issues the order of protection at arraignment, the defendant's first court appearance. The brief, formulaic, and compressed nature of arraignments in criminal court, which run around the clock to ensure that all defendants are arraigned within twenty-four hours of arrest, means that courts often issue orders with little detailed consideration of the particular facts. DV orders are generally requested and issued as a matter of course.

When the protection order goes into effect, the defendant cannot go home or have any contact with the victim (usually his wife) and his children. If the defendant does go home or contact the protected parties, he could be arrested, prosecuted, and punished for a fresh crime. This is so even if the victim initiates contact or invites the defendant to come home. Police officers then make routine unannounced visits to homes with a history of domestic violence. If a defendant subject to a protection order is present there, he is arrested. . . . The protection order remains in effect while the case is ongoing. . . .

[T]he protection order shifts the very goal of pursuing criminal charges away from punishment to control over the intimate relationship in the home. . . . Punishment as a goal can be put on the backburner because separation is a more direct and achievable way to stop or prevent violence. . . . Of course prosecutors prefer to see criminal defendants tried, convicted, and punished with imprisonment. But the difficulty of trying DV cases because of the reluctance of victims to cooperate leads prosecutors to look to plea bargains imposing alternatives to imprisonment. The protection order is the most significant tool. . . . [T]he prosecutor offers the defendant a plea bargain consisting of little or no jail time (or time served) and a reduction of the charge, or even an adjournment in contemplation of dismissal, in exchange for the defendant's acceptance of a final order of protection prohibiting his presence at home and contact with the victim. . . . The offer is particularly attractive for a defendant who has remained in jail since arraignment pending disposition of his case; if he agrees he will be released. . . .

The full and final order of protection prohibits contact between the parties, and violation of the order constitutes commission of a fresh crime. It is unlawful for the party subject to the order to see or to speak to his spouse, or to go to the home in which they reside together. Even a phone call, letter, or e-mail risks arrest and criminal charges. Regardless of whether parties are formally married, it is therefore criminal for them to continue, in any substantive way, their marital, domestic, or intimate relationship. . . . Spouses can surely remain legally married even as they obey all the prohibitions of the order, but cannot live or act like they are married. . . . Furthermore, the separation is not accompanied by the actual family law divorce regime of property division, alimony, child custody, and support. Ordinarily the order of protection makes no mention of alimony, child custody, visitation, or support. . . . But de facto divorce does entail de facto arrangements regarding custody, visitation, and support—that is, no custody, no visitation, and no support. Thus in the imposition of de facto divorce, criminal law becomes a new family law regime. But because it is criminal law regulation, the parties cannot contract around the result except by risking arrest and punishment of one of them. . . .

Indeed, the order goes much further than would ordinary divorce, prohibiting any contact, even by express permission of the protected party. It is super-divorce. . . . Unlike actual divorce, in which a general principle of autonomy governs so that one or both parties in the marriage must initiate it, here the separation is forced by the state. . . .

As a product of the plea bargain, de facto divorce goes into effect without the benefit of traditional criminal process or proof of the crime. The arrest may have come at the behest of neighbors rather than the victim herself. Or the victim may have called the police to seek specific intervention in that moment. But as a result of the initial arrest and through the operation of mandatory arrest and no-drop prosecution policies, the relationship can be, for practical purposes, dissolved by the force of the criminal law. . . .

At least one state court has addressed the constitutional dimensions of state-imposed de facto divorce. State v. Ross was a 1996 Washington case in which a criminal sentence after the defendant's trial and conviction for felony harassment and assault included a no-contact order. Between the defendant's trial and his sentencing, the defendant and the victim married, in violation of a temporary no-contact order that had been in effect since criminal charges were filed. As part of the defendant's sentence, the court ordered that the convicted felon have no contact for ten years with his wife, who opposed the order. The defendant challenged that no-contact order as nullifying his marriage and thereby violating his right to marry. The Washington appellate court upheld the sentence. The court acknowledged that the no-contact order interfered with the fundamental right to marry. But against this right, the court weighed the state's "compelling interest in preventing future crimes." . . . The less intrusive alternative of DV treatment alone was inadequate. . . .

Of course, incarceration effectively separates a prisoner from his spouse and family. But . . . prisoners are normally allowed to have some contact through which they can maintain their relationships. For example, they can write and receive letters, make phone calls, and have visitors, all of which would be criminal under a no-contact order. Thus, even incarceration, which undoubtedly burdens the relationship, does not seek to end it. By contrast, the no-contact order intends the termination of the relationship. . . . One would need to take a strong view of gendered coercion in intimate relationships generally to rationalize a world in which this kind of state control is regularly triggered by misdemeanor arrests not involving serious physical injury, particularly as the category of nonviolent conduct that constitutes DV expands.

Could the problem Professor Suk identifies be addressed by precluding plea bargaining in domestic violence cases, thus insuring that judges, the only actors in the prosecution pipeline who appear to have retained discretion and who operate in public view, review every case and choose the best remedy, in light of each couple's situation? Or would the litigation costs generated by that approach exceed the benefits gained from preserving those marriages in which dysfunction can be cured or simply managed?

An additional criticism of state domestic violence practices is that they have a disparate impact on minority race families—that is, police are more willing to intrude into minority race households than into white households and prosecutors are more inclined to prosecute men of minority race than white men. See, e.g., Aya Gruber, *The Feminist War on Crime*, 92 Iowa L. Rev. 741 (2007). The same complaint is made of child protection intervention; many scholars lament the substantial "race disproportionality" in the foster care system and charge the state actors involved with racial bias. What is the proper response to the undeniable fact that the state disproportionately charges black adults with both domestic violence and child abuse? Compare Cheryl Hanna, *No Right to Choose: Mandated Victim Participation in Domestic Violence Prosecutions*, 109 Harv. L. Rev. 1850, 1881-1882 (1996) (arguing that the proper response is not to forbear from prosecuting minority-race defendants but rather to prosecute white abusers more aggressively) with Elizabeth Bartholet, *The Racial Disproportionality Movement in Child Welfare: False Facts and Dangerous Directions*, 51 Ariz. L. Rev. 871 (2009) (showing that "a powerful group of players in the child welfare policy arena . . . characterize as overrepresentation the fact that black children are represented in the foster care system at a higher rate than white children . . . [and] call for solutions which would reduce the rate at which black children are removed from their parents for maltreatment and increase the rate at which those removed to foster care are reunified with their parents," and demonstrating that this position rests on mistaken assumptions and an unjustifiable focus on adults' interests rather than on children's welfare).

One might wonder whether rules removing discretion from state actors make state agencies and their employees more vulnerable to tort suits if they fail to do what the law requires and someone is revictimized as a result? Consider whether the Supreme Court decision below, rejecting a tort suit against local officials who failed to act to enforce a protective order, would have come out differently if the municipality sued in this case had had truly mandatory arrest policies.

Town of Castle Rock, Colorado v. Gonzales

545 U.S. 748 (2005)

Justice SCALIA delivered the opinion of the Court.

. . . Respondent alleges that . . . police officers . . . failed to respond properly to her repeated reports that her estranged husband was violating the terms of a restraining order. The restraining order had been issued by a state trial court several weeks earlier in conjunction with respondent's divorce proceedings. The original form order . . . commanded him not to "molest or disturb the peace of [respondent] or of any child," and to remain at least 100 yards from the family home at all times. . . . The preprinted text on the back of the form included the following **"WARNING"**:

> "**A KNOWING VIOLATION OF A RESTRAINING ORDER IS A CRIME**. . . . A VIOLATION WILL ALSO CONSTITUTE CONTEMPT OF COURT. **YOU MAY BE ARRESTED** WITHOUT NOTICE IF A LAW ENFORCEMENT OFFICER HAS PROBABLE CAUSE TO BELIEVE THAT YOU HAVE KNOWINGLY VIOLATED THIS ORDER."

The preprinted text on the back of the form also included a **"NOTICE TO LAW ENFORCEMENT OFFICIALS,"** which read in part:

> "YOU SHALL USE EVERY REASONABLE MEANS TO ENFORCE THIS RESTRAINING ORDER. YOU SHALL ARREST, OR, IF AN ARREST WOULD BE IMPRACTICAL UNDER THE CIRCUMSTANCES, SEEK A WARRANT FOR THE ARREST OF THE RESTRAINED PERSON WHEN YOU HAVE INFORMATION AMOUNTING TO PROBABLE CAUSE THAT THE RESTRAINED PERSON HAS VIOLATED OR ATTEMPTED TO VIOLATE ANY PROVISION OF THIS ORDER AND THE RESTRAINED PERSON HAS BEEN PROPERLY SERVED WITH A COPY OF THIS ORDER OR HAS RECEIVED ACTUAL NOTICE OF THE EXISTENCE OF THIS ORDER."

On June 4, 1999, the state trial court modified the terms of the restraining order and . . . gave respondent's husband the right to spend time with his three daughters (ages 10, 9, and 7) on alternate weekends, for two weeks during the summer, and, "'upon reasonable notice,'" for a midweek dinner visit "'arranged by the parties'"; the modified order also allowed him to visit the home to collect the children for such "parenting time."

According to the complaint, at about 5 or 5:30 P.M. on Tuesday, June 22, 1999, respondent's husband took the three daughters while they were playing outside the family home. No advance arrangements had been made for him to see the daughters that evening. When respondent noticed the children were missing, she suspected her husband had taken them. At about 7:30 P.M., she called the Castle Rock Police Department, which dispatched two officers. The complaint continues: "When [the officers] arrived . . . , she showed them a copy of the TRO and requested that it be enforced and the three children be returned to her immediately. [The officers] stated that there was nothing they could do about the TRO and suggested that [respondent] call the Police Department again if the three children did not return home by 10:00 P.M."

At approximately 8:30 P.M., respondent talked to her husband on his cellular telephone. He told her "he had the three children [at an] amusement park in Denver." She called the police again and asked them to "have someone check for" her husband or his vehicle at the amusement park and "put out an [all points bulletin]" for her husband, but the officer with whom she spoke "refused to do so," again telling her to "wait until 10:00 P.M. and see if" her husband returned the girls.

At approximately 10:10 P.M., respondent called the police and said her children were still missing, but she was now told to wait until midnight. She called at midnight and told the dispatcher her children were still missing. She went to her husband's apartment and, finding nobody there, called the police at 12:10 A.M.; she was told to wait for an officer to arrive. When none came, she went to the police station at 12:50 A.M. and submitted an incident report. The officer who took the report "made no reasonable effort to enforce the TRO or locate the three children. Instead, he went to dinner."

At approximately 3:20 A.M., respondent's husband arrived at the police station and opened fire with a semiautomatic handgun he had purchased earlier that evening. Police shot back, killing him. Inside the cab of his pickup truck, they found the bodies of all three daughters, whom he had already murdered.

On the basis of the foregoing factual allegations, respondent brought an action under 42 U.S.C. §1983 claiming that the town violated the Due Process Clause because its police department had "an official policy or custom of failing to respond properly to complaints of restraining order violations" and "tolerate[d] the non-enforcement of restraining orders by its police officers."[3] The complaint also alleged that the town's actions "were taken either willfully, recklessly or with such gross negligence as to indicate wanton disregard and deliberate indifference to" respondent's civil rights.

II

The Fourteenth Amendment to the United States Constitution provides that a State shall not "deprive any person of life, liberty, or property, without due process of law." In 42 U.S.C. §1983, Congress has created a federal cause of action for "the deprivation of any rights, privileges, or immunities secured by the Constitution and laws." Respondent claims the benefit of this provision on the ground that she had a property interest in police enforcement of the restraining order against her husband; and that the town deprived her of this property without due process by having a policy that tolerated non-enforcement of restraining orders. . . .

[W]e left a similar question unanswered in DeShaney v. Winnebago County Dept. of Social Servs., 489 U.S. 189 (1989), another case with "undeniably tragic" facts: Local child-protection officials had failed to protect a young boy from beatings by his father that left him severely brain damaged. We held that the so-called "substantive" component of the Due Process Clause does not "requir[e] the State to protect the life, liberty, and property of its citizens against invasion by private actors." We noted, however, that the petitioner had not properly preserved the argument that—and we thus "decline[d] to

3. Three police officers were also named as defendants in the complaint, but the Court of Appeals concluded that they were entitled to qualified immunity . . .

consider" whether—state "child protection statutes gave [him] an 'entitlement' to receive protective services in accordance with the terms of the statute, an entitlement which would enjoy due process protection."

The procedural component of the Due Process Clause does not protect everything that might be described as a "benefit": "To have a property interest in a benefit, a person clearly must have more than an abstract need or desire" and "more than a unilateral expectation of it. He must, instead, have a legitimate claim of entitlement to it." Such entitlements are, "'of course, . . . not created by the Constitution. Rather, they are created and their dimensions are defined by existing rules or understandings that stem from an independent source such as state law.'" . . . Our cases recognize that a benefit is not a protected entitlement if government officials may grant or deny it in their discretion.

The critical language in the restraining order came not from any part of the order itself . . . , but from the preprinted notice to law-enforcement personnel that appeared on the back of the order. That notice effectively restated the statutory provision describing "peace officers' duties" related to the crime of violation of a restraining order. At the time of the conduct at issue in this case, that provision read as follows:

> "(a) Whenever a restraining order is issued, . . . [a] *peace officer shall use every reasonable means to enforce a restraining order.*
>
> "(b) *A peace officer shall arrest, or, if an arrest would be impractical under the circumstances, seek a warrant for the arrest of a restrained person* when the peace officer has information amounting to probable cause that . . . [t]he restrained person has violated or attempted to violate any provision of a restraining order. . . .
>
> "(c) . . . *A peace officer shall enforce a valid restraining order whether or not there is a record of the restraining order in the registry.*" Colo. Rev. Stat. §18-6-803.5(3).

. . . We do not believe that these provisions of Colorado law truly made enforcement of restraining orders *mandatory.* A well established tradition of police discretion has long coexisted with apparently mandatory arrest statutes.

> "In each and every state there are long-standing statutes that, by their terms, seem to preclude nonenforcement by the police. . . . However, for a number of reasons, including their legislative history, insufficient resources, and sheer physical impossibility, it has been recognized that such statutes cannot be interpreted literally. . . . [T]hey clearly do not mean that a police officer may not lawfully decline to . . . make an arrest. As to third parties in these states, the full-enforcement statutes simply have no effect, and their significance is further diminished." 1 ABA Standards for Criminal Justice 1-4.5, commentary, pp. 1-124 to 1-125 (2d ed. 1980).

The deep-rooted nature of law-enforcement discretion, even in the presence of seemingly mandatory legislative commands, is illustrated by Chicago v. Morales, 527 U.S. 41 (1999), which involved an ordinance that said a police officer "'shall order'" persons to disperse in certain circumstances. This Court rejected out of hand the possibility that "the mandatory language of the ordinance . . . afford[ed] the police *no* discretion." It is, the Court proclaimed, simply "common sense that *all* police officers must use some discretion in deciding when and where to enforce city ordinances."

Against that backdrop, a true mandate of police action would require some stronger indication from the Colorado Legislature than "shall use every reasonable means to enforce a restraining order" (or even "shall arrest . . . or . . . seek a warrant"). . . . It is hard to imagine that a Colorado peace officer would not have some discretion to determine that—despite probable cause to believe a restraining order has been violated—the circumstances of the violation or the competing duties of that officer or his agency counsel decisively against enforcement in a particular instance.[8] The practical necessity for discretion is particularly apparent in a case such as this one, where the suspected violator is not actually present and his whereabouts are unknown.

The dissent correctly points out that, in the specific context of domestic violence, mandatory-arrest statutes have been found in some States to be more mandatory than traditional mandatory-arrest statutes. The Colorado statute mandating arrest for a domestic-violence offense is different from but related to the one at issue here, and it includes similar though not identical phrasing. See Colo. Rev. Stat. §18-6-803.6(1) ("When a peace officer determines that there is probable cause to believe that a crime or offense involving domestic violence . . . has been committed, the officer shall, without undue delay, arrest the person suspected of its commission. . . ."). Even in the domestic-violence context, however, it is unclear how the mandatory-arrest paradigm applies to cases in which the offender is not present to be arrested. As the dissent explains, much of the impetus for mandatory-arrest statutes and policies derived from the idea that it is better for police officers to arrest the aggressor in a domestic-violence incident than to attempt to mediate the dispute or merely to ask the offender to leave the scene. Those other options are only available, of course, when the offender is present at the scene. . . . Colorado's restraining-order statute appears to contemplate a similar distinction, providing that when arrest is "impractical"—which was likely the case when the whereabouts of respondent's husband were unknown—the officers' statutory duty is to "seek a warrant" rather than "arrest." §18-6-803.5(3)(b).

Respondent does not specify the precise means of enforcement that the Colorado restraining-order statute assertedly mandated—whether her interest lay in having police arrest her husband, having them seek a warrant for his arrest, or having them "use every reasonable means, up to and including arrest, to enforce the order's terms."[9]

Such indeterminacy is not the hallmark of a duty that is mandatory. Nor can someone be safely deemed "entitled" to something when the identity of the alleged entitlement is vague. The dissent . . . contends that the obligations under the statute were quite precise: either make an arrest or (if that is impractical) seek an arrest warrant. The problem with this is that the seeking of an arrest warrant would be an entitlement to nothing but procedure—which we have held inadequate even to support standing, much less can it be the basis for a property interest. After the warrant is sought, it remains within the discretion of a judge whether to grant it, and after it is granted, it remains within the discretion of the police whether and when to execute it.[11] Respondent would have been assured nothing but the seeking of a warrant. This is not the sort of "entitlement" out of which a property interest is created.

8. Respondent in fact concedes that an officer may "properly" decide not to enforce a restraining order when the officer deems "a technical violation" too "immaterial" to justify arrest. . . .

9. Respondent characterizes her entitlement in various ways. See Brief for Respondent 12 ("'entitlement' to receive protective services"); *id.*, at 13 ("interest in police enforcement action"); *id.*, at 14 ("specific government benefit" consisting of "the government service of enforcing the objective terms of the court order protecting her and her children against her abusive husband"); *id.*, at 32 ("[T]he restraining order here mandated the arrest of Mr. Gonzales under specified circumstances, or at a minimum required the use of reasonable means to enforce the order").

11. The dissent asserts that the police would lack discretion in the execution of this warrant, but cites no statute mandating immediate execution. The general Colorado statute governing arrest provides that police "may arrest" when they possess a warrant "commanding" arrest.

Even if the statute could be said to have made enforcement of restraining orders "mandatory" because of the domestic-violence context of the underlying statute, that would not necessarily mean that state law gave *respondent* an entitlement to *enforcement* of the mandate. Making the actions of government employees obligatory can serve various legitimate ends other than the conferral of a benefit on a specific class of people. See, *e.g.*, Sandin v. Conner, 515 U.S. 472 (1995) (finding no constitutionally protected liberty interest in prison regulations phrased in mandatory terms, in part because "[s]uch guidelines are not set forth solely to benefit the prisoner"). The serving of public rather than private ends is the normal course of the criminal law because criminal acts, "besides the injury [they do] to individuals, . . . strike at the very being of society; which cannot possibly subsist, where actions of this sort are suffered to escape with impunity." 4 W. Blackstone, Commentaries on the Laws of England 5 (1769). This principle underlies, for example, a Colorado district attorney's discretion to prosecute a domestic assault, even though the victim withdraws her charge. . . .

If she was given a statutory entitlement, we would expect to see some indication of that in the statute itself. . . . It said that a "protected person shall be provided with a copy of [a restraining] order" when it is issued, that a law enforcement agency "shall make all reasonable efforts to contact the protected party upon the arrest of the restrained person," and that the agency "shall give [to the protected person] a copy" of the report it submits to the court that issued the order. Perhaps most importantly, the statute spoke directly to the protected person's power to "initiate contempt proceedings against the restrained person if the order [was] issued in a civil action or request the prosecuting attorney to initiate contempt proceedings if the order [was] issued in a criminal action." The protected person's express power to "initiate" civil contempt proceedings contrasts tellingly with . . . the complete silence about any power to "request" (much less demand) that an arrest be made.

Even if we were to think otherwise concerning the creation of an entitlement by Colorado, it is by no means clear that an individual entitlement to enforcement of a restraining order could constitute a "property" interest for purposes of the Due Process Clause. Such a right would not, of course, resemble any traditional conception of property. Although that alone does not disqualify it from due process protection . . . , the right to have a restraining order enforced does not "have some ascertainable monetary value," as even our "*Roth*-type property-as-entitlement" cases have implicitly required.[12]

Perhaps most radically, the alleged property interest here arises *incidentally*, not out of some new species of government benefit or service, but out of a function that government actors have always performed—to wit, arresting people who they have probable cause to believe have committed a criminal offense. The indirect nature of a benefit was fatal to the due process claim of the nursing-home residents in O'Bannon v. Town Court Nursing Center, 447 U.S. 773 (1980). We held that, while the withdrawal of "direct benefits" (financial payments under Medicaid for certain medical services) triggered due process

12. The dissent suggests that the interest in having a restraining order enforced does have an ascertainable monetary value, because one may "contract with a private security firm . . . to provide protection" for one's family. . . . Respondent probably could have hired a private firm to guard her house, to prevent her husband from coming onto the property, and perhaps even to search for her husband after she discovered that her children were missing. Her alleged entitlement here, however, does not consist in an abstract right to "protection," but (according to the dissent) in enforcement of her restraining order through the arrest of her husband, or the seeking of a warrant for his arrest, after she gave the police probable cause to believe the restraining order had been violated. A private person would not have the power to arrest under those circumstances because the crime would not have occurred in his presence. And, needless to say, a private person would not have the power to obtain an arrest warrant.

protections, the same was not true for the "indirect benefit[s]" conferred on Medicaid patients when the Government enforced "minimum standards of care" for nursing-home facilities. "[A]n indirect and incidental result of the Government's enforcement action . . . does not amount to a deprivation of any interest in life, liberty, or property." . . .

III

We conclude, therefore, that respondent did not, for purposes of the Due Process Clause, have a property interest in police enforcement of the restraining order against her husband. . . . In light of today's decision and that in *DeShaney*, the benefit that a third party may receive from having someone else arrested for a crime generally does not trigger protections under the Due Process Clause, neither in its procedural nor in its "substantive" manifestations. This result reflects our continuing reluctance to treat the Fourteenth Amendment as "'a font of tort law,'" but it does not mean States are powerless to provide victims with personally enforceable remedies. . . .

Justice STEVENS, with whom Justice GINSBURG joins, dissenting.

. . . Three flaws in the Court's rather superficial analysis of the merits highlight the unwisdom of its decision to answer the state-law question *de novo*. First, the Court places undue weight on the various statutes throughout the country that seemingly mandate police enforcement but are generally understood to preserve police discretion. As a result, the Court gives short shrift to the unique case of "mandatory arrest" statutes in the domestic violence context; States passed a wave of these statutes in the 1980's and 1990's with the unmistakable goal of eliminating police discretion in this area. Second, the Court's formalistic analysis fails to take seriously the fact that the Colorado statute at issue in this case was enacted for the benefit of the narrow class of persons who are beneficiaries of domestic restraining orders, and that the order at issue in this case was specifically intended to provide protection to respondent and her children. Finally, the Court is simply wrong to assert that a citizen's interest in the government's commitment to provide police enforcement in certain defined circumstances does not resemble any "traditional conception of property"; in fact, a citizen's property interest in such a commitment is just as concrete and worthy of protection as her interest in any other important service the government or a private firm has undertaken to provide.

. . . [T]he Colorado Legislature used the term "shall" advisedly in its domestic restraining order statute. . . . [I]t is hard to imagine what the Court has in mind when it insists on "some stronger indication from the Colorado Legislature." . . . [O]ther state courts interpreting their analogous statutes have not only held that they eliminate the police's traditional discretion to refuse enforcement, but have also recognized that they create rights enforceable against the police under state law. [Citing decisions in Oregon, Tennessee, New Jersey, and Washington.] To what extent the Colorado Supreme Court would agree with the views of these courts is, of course, an open question, but it does seem rather brazen for the majority to assume that the Colorado Supreme Court would repudiate this consistent line of persuasive authority from other States. . . .

Regardless of whether the enforcement called for in this case was arrest or the seeking of an arrest warrant (the answer to that question probably changed over the course of the night as the respondent gave the police more information about the husband's whereabouts), the crucial point is that, under the statute, the police were *required* to provide enforcement; *they lacked the discretion to do nothing*. Suppose a State entitled every citizen whose income was under a certain level to receive health care at a state clinic. The provision of health care is not a unitary thing—doctors and administrators must decide what tests are called for and what procedures are required, and these decisions often involve difficult applications of judgment. But it could not credibly be said that a citizen lacks an entitlement to health care simply because the content of that entitlement is not the same in every given situation. . . .

Police enforcement of a restraining order is a government service that is no less concrete and no less valuable than other government services, such as education. . . . Colorado law *guaranteed* the provision of a certain service, in certain defined circumstances, to a certain class of beneficiaries, and respondent reasonably relied on that guarantee. . . . At the very least, due process requires that the relevant state decisionmaker *listen* to the claimant and then *apply the relevant criteria* in reaching his decision. The . . . process she was afforded by the police constituted nothing more than a "'sham or a pretense.'" . . . Accordingly, I respectfully dissent.

This decision obviously raises broad questions about criminal law enforcement. What is of particular relevance for family law is whether the decision leaves victims of domestic violence less able to rely on police. The Court essentially said that mandatory arrest laws do not mean what they say and that abuse victims with protective orders have no recourse under federal law if local police do nothing when violations occur. In most states, there would also be no recourse under state law. Some abuse victims might actually be made worse off by a mandatory policy that is not really mandatory, if the law on the books induces them to incur the risks attendant to seeking a protective order but then police react to violation reports with the same passivity that motivated passage of the VAWA.

In contrast to the negative-rights conception of constitutional protections in the United States, as reflected in *Castle Rock* and *DeShaney*, regional and international authorities outside the United States have imputed to states a positive obligation under human rights treaties and conventions, such as the European Convention on Human Rights (ECHR), to protect citizens from private violence. In *Yildirim v. Austria* (2007), the enforcement committee for the Convention on Elimination of Discrimination Against Women found Austria responsible for the death of a woman killed by her husband, because it did not detain him after learning that he had threatened and harassed her. Likewise, in *Goekce v. Austria* (2007), the same committee held Austria liable for the death of a woman at the hands of her husband, where officials had repeatedly intervened in the couple's fights and had issued restraining orders against the husband but knew their measures were not entirely effective and that the husband had recently purchased a handgun, and they failed to respond to an emergency call by the victim. In *Opuz v. Turkey* (2009), the European Court of Human Rights held that Turkey's failure to protect a woman against her husband's killing her constituted sex discrimination in violation of Article 14 of the ECHR, where officials knew of the husband's history of causing his wife and her mother serious bodily harm, responded lackadaisically and leniently, and released him from prison after he killed his mother-in-law and continued to threaten his then ex-wife, while his appeal was pending. See Monica Hakimi, *State Bystander Responsibility*, 21 EUR. J. INT'L L. 341, 379-383 (2010) (analyzing those three decisions). And in *Bevacqua and S. v. Bulgaria*, App. No. 71127/01, Eur. Ct. H.R. (2008), the European human rights court held that failure to protect a woman from her husband's violence contravened the command of respect for private and family life in Article 8 of the ECHR. The court stated that there are "positive obligations inherent in effective 'respect' for private and family life. . . . Children and other vulnerable individuals . . . are entitled to effective protection . . . [and] the concept of private life includes a person's physical and psychological integrity."

Does it seem reasonable to impose liability in those circumstances? Note that the European human rights court, like the U.S. Supreme Court, has recognized that unwarranted state intrusion into the family under the banner of protecting against abuse can also constitute a violation of rights to privacy and family life. Does imposing both positive and negative obligations on the state put it in an impossible bind? Or does the ECHR concept of "margin of appreciation," under which states are expected simply to act reasonably within a substantial range of latitude, allow for the two types of obligations to co-exist unproblematically? Is there a similar concept in American constitutional doctrine that could do so as well?

Some victims of partner violence might conclude from a decision like *Castle Rock* that they will be safe only if they take upon themselves the task of disabling their abusers. But doing so could subject them to criminal charges. In cases charging domestic abuse victims with assault or murder, many claim self-defense and attempt to introduce expert evidence of Battered Women's Syndrome (BWS), or "learned helplessness." Courts were initially skeptical about such evidence and the theory purporting to make it relevant, but today most accept BWS evidence. See, e.g., People v. Hartman, 883 N.Y.S.2d 361 (2009); State v. B.H., 870 A.2d 273 (N.J. 2005); State v. Edwards, 60 S.W.3d 602 (Mo. App. 2001). There remains some divergence among states regarding to which precise questions such evidence is relevant or to which specific questions an expert may testify—for example, the nature of the syndrome as opposed to whether a particular defendant suffered from it. A few states have codified a rule authorizing such evidence for particular purposes. See, e.g., Ariz. Rev. Stat. §13-415 ("If there have been past acts of domestic violence . . . against the defendant by the victim, the state of mind of a reasonable person under [justification and self-defense statutes] shall be determined from the perspective of a reasonable person who has been a victim of those past acts of domestic violence.").

Evidence of BWS or learned helplessness is also often relevant in prosecution of batterers, when they challenge the credibility of the victim by suggesting that if she really were a victim of violence she would have separated from the defendant, or when victims recant accusations against batterers.

State v. Haines

860 N.E.2d 91 (Ohio 2006)

PFEIFER, J.

. . . Haines and Bohley met on December 26, 1997. By July 1998, they had begun living together in the home of Haines's brother, Ryan, and in January 2000, they moved into a condominium that Bohley had purchased. Bohley described the relationship as rocky and testified that Haines did not allow her to have friends or much freedom. She had to wear a pager so that he could always reach her. Haines timed how long Bohley's trip between home and work should take and required her to phone him upon leaving for work and arriving at work. If she was late, he would get very angry, and a fight would ensue. Bohley was called into her boss's office at least three times because her telephone arguments with Haines disrupted her work. Haines also demanded constant contact regarding Bohley's whereabouts outside of work. Bohley said that she complied in order to avoid arguments. On May 6, 2001, Bohley and Haines became engaged.

On October 8, 2001, Bohley went to police to report an incident of domestic violence that had occurred on October 4, 2001. Haines was convicted of a domestic violence charge and served 18 days in jail. Bohley ended their engagement and got a temporary protection order against Haines. . . . Bohley . . . was soon seeing Haines again. His 18-day jail term was work-release (Haines spent only evenings in jail), and Bohley would visit him during the day. Later, Haines served a period of house arrest at his brother's home, and Bohley visited him there, too, occasionally spending the night and engaging in sexual relations. Bohley never removed all of Haines's possessions from her home, and by late January 2002, they were again living together in Bohley's condominium. . . .

Easter Sunday, March 31, 2002, Bohley found a card to Haines from another woman when she was putting away some of his belongings; she went outside to confront him about it. Haines suggested that they go inside the house to discuss the matter, and Bohley complied. When then were both inside, Haines locked the door and the deadbolt. Haines told Bohley that he would be moving out, but only when he wanted to, and that it could take a year for him to do so. Bohley said that she would no longer be sleeping with him in the same bed, which infuriated Haines. Haines picked up a piece of baseboard left from a remodeling project and struck Bohley on the arms and legs. He then began breaking objects in the house. Bohley tried to escape by running through a sliding glass door, but she was unable to break the glass. In an effort to divert Haines's attention, Bohley slit her wrist with a piece of broken glass. She drew blood, and Haines did show some concern and helped her wrap the wrist.

After helping Bohley with her wrist, Haines told her that he was going to show her what it was like to be in jail and ordered her into her condominium's crawlspace. His jail sentence had become a consistent theme in their relationship, and he said that he would make her stay in the crawlspace for 18 days. Bohley entered the crawlspace, which was about three feet high and had a lid, feeling that she had no other choice. The lid had a hole in it, and Haines ordered Bohley to keep her finger through the hole at all times so that he could be sure she was not trying to escape. Haines screwed eight screws into the lid once she was inside. Periodically, he checked to see if her finger was still in the hole, and then released her after 30 to 45 minutes. Haines was upset and crying when he released Bohley and asked her to pray with him. She prayed with him and told him she forgave him, in order to appease him.

After the prayer, Haines told Bohley that they were going to take an Easter gift to his daughter. While driving home from making that delivery, Haines became agitated again, and when they arrived back home, Bohley refused to leave the vehicle. Haines told her that she could trust him and that he would not hurt her if she went inside the house, so Bohley reluctantly accompanied him inside. Once inside, he locked the doors and told her that she was going to die that night. Bohley screamed, and Haines covered her mouth and nose. He punched and then kicked Bohley in the ribs and stepped on her ankle. After that, they went to bed. The next day, Bohley told Haines's family members what had happened the night before. That evening, Haines and Bohley met with his father to discuss the situation. They all agreed that Haines should move out of Bohley's condominium.

Upon cross-examination regarding the March 31 incident, Bohley testified that she and Haines had engaged in sexual relations that evening. She also testified that she had gone to the emergency room on April 5 to have her painful ribs checked, but that she had lied to the people caring for her about the cause of her injury, claiming that she had fallen over a fence while rollerblading. Haines's counsel also elicited testimony from Bohley on cross-examination that she did not tell any of her co-workers or any doctors what had happened on March 31, 2002, and that she did not report that incident to police until after the April 18 incident.

Despite the earlier agreement that Haines would move out, he did not, and the situation deteriorated. In the early evening of April 17, 2002, Haines and Bohley engaged in what she called "abnormal" sexual relations involving the Internet, which Bohley said Haines knew disgusted her. Haines immediately left the house for a couple of hours. When he returned at about 10:30, he was upset. He blamed Bohley for his jail term and wanted her to apologize. For self-preservation, she told him what he wanted to hear. Haines twisted her wrist and stuck his fingers in her eyes. He ripped her nightgown and got a belt from the closet, commenting that he was going to hit her like a child with the belt because that was the only way she would understand that what she had done was wrong. He told he to lie on her stomach, and he hit her five times on the buttocks with the belt. Haines became concerned that Bohley might tell someone what had happened and began swinging the belt again with more force. He hit her multiple times in the shoulder and arm. He then cried out that Bohley had ruined his life, and she comforted him in an effort to defuse the situation. He took some sleeping pills, but before he fell asleep, he told her to keep her hand on him at all times so that he would know whether she was trying to get away. He allowed her to go to the bathroom, but warned her to not try to go downstairs.

The next morning, Haines refused to allow Bohley to go to work. Fearing that her work colleagues would be concerned by her absence, Haines directed Bohley to phone the office and leave a message. As she made the call, Haines held his fist against her face. Soon after, Haines ordered Bohley to place another call to work, begging to not be fired. Haines held a knife to her throat as she made that call. During her initial call to work, Bohley left a message using a pre-arranged code-phrase, "Red Eye Printing," to indicate to her co-workers that she was in trouble. On her message, she asked her co-workers to check the "Red Eye Printing" envelope on her desk. The co-workers opened the envelope, which contained a document that gave instructions to call the police. Bohley's co-workers called police, and officers arrested Haines at the condominium.

The state called as its last witness in its case-in-chief Dr. James Eisenberg, a board-certified forensic psychologist. . . . Dr. Eisenberg testified about battered-woman syndrome, stating that "it refers to a woman . . . that is the subject of repeated psychological, physical, or sexual abuse by one's partner. The syndrome itself speaks to the individuals who remain in relationships in spite of those beatings." He explained the syndrome's three-part process—the tension stage, the acute battering stage, and the stage of contrition. He stated that the batterer exerts extreme control over the woman's entire life, leading to her isolation. He explained that a woman in a relationship with a batterer sees the world "through a very small opening and all that she sees is this guy. . . . The threat is always there, whether you leave or whether you stay. . . . [She thinks], If I leave he's gonna beat me. If I stay he's gonna beat me. Let me just—let's just get it out."

Eisenberg spoke mostly in generalities about battered-woman syndrome and its symptoms. Toward the end of his direct examination, however, the following exchange occurred:

Q. Now, Doctor, in this particular case, are you familiar with some of the facts and circumstances surrounding the criminal charges in this case?
A. Yes.

Q. All right. And as a result of that, do you have an opinion, within a reasonable degree of forensic certainty, as to whether or not you see any features of the investigation of this case that would parallel a Battered Woman's Syndrome?
Mr. M. DiCello: Objection.
Judge Lucci: Overruled.
A. Yes.
Q. Okay. And what is—is that opinion within a reasonable degree of forensic certainty?
A. Yes.
Q. And what is that opinion?
A. My opinion is that, as I understand the facts of the case, and again I'm not a fact finder, but as I understand the facts of the case in front of us, and from my review of the records, it's very consistent with what we see in a Battered Woman's Syndrome scenario."

The jury returned a verdict convicting Haines of all seven counts with which he was charged—kidnapping, abduction, and domestic violence relating to the March 31, 2002 incident; kidnapping, abduction, and domestic violence relating to the incident of April 17, 2002; and one count of kidnapping relating to the events of the morning of April 18, 2002. . . . Haines sought reversal on all counts due to the trial court's admission of Eisenberg's testimony regarding battered-woman syndrome, arguing that such evidence was "irrelevant, prejudicial, inflammatory, and prohibited. . . ."

In *State v. Koss* (1990), this court first recognized the admissibility of expert testimony regarding battered-woman syndrome. In that case, the defendant had killed her husband, and the testimony regarding battered-woman syndrome was offered by the defendant in support of her affirmative defense of self-defense. . . . In allowing the admission of expert testimony regarding the battered-woman syndrome in *Koss*, this court "[did] not establish a new defense or justification." Rather, such testimony was allowed as evidence to prove one element of self-defense. "In Ohio, to prove self-defense it must be established that the person asserting this defense had '. . . a *bona fide belief* that he [she] was in imminent danger of death or great bodily harm and that his [her] only means of escape from such danger was in the use of such force.'" *Koss* recognized that since Ohio has a subjective test to determine whether a defendant properly acted in self-defense, the defendant's state of mind is a crucial issue. . . . The court concluded:

> "Expert testimony regarding the battered woman syndrome can be admitted to help the jury not only to understand the battered woman syndrome but also to determine whether the defendant had reasonable grounds for an honest belief that she was in imminent danger when considering the issue of self-defense. Expert testimony on the battered woman syndrome would help dispel the ordinary lay person's perception that a woman in a battering relationship is free to leave at any time. The expert evidence would counter any "common sense" conclusions by the jury that if the beatings were really that bad the woman would have left her husband much earlier. Popular misconceptions about battered women would be put to rest, including the beliefs that the women are masochistic and enjoy the beatings and that they intentionally provoke their husbands into fits of rage."

. . . R.C. 2901.06 . . . recognizes the value of battered-woman-syndrome testimony and sets forth that it may be employed in self-defense cases. . . . R.C. 2945.392 . . . allows battered-woman-syndrome testimony to be admitted by a defendant who pleads not guilty by reason of insanity. *Koss* and R.C. 2901.06(A) establish that battered-woman-syndrome testimony meets the requirements of Evid. R. 702 in regard to scientific validity and the requirement of specialized knowledge. Neither *Koss* nor R.C. 2901.06 nor R.C. 2945.392 limits the use of such testimony to self-defense or insanity cases. *Koss* and the statutes do recognize that testimony on the syndrome is properly admitted pursuant to Evid. R. 702 as expert testimony that can assist the trier of fact in search of the truth. *Koss*, 49 Ohio St. 3d at 216, 551 N.E.2d 970. But admissibility under Evid. R. 702 is only part of the picture. . . .

Further consideration is especially needed when the testimony is not offered by a defendant, but by the state against a defendant. . . . [T]he courts in an overwhelming majority of jurisdictions that have considered the issue have held that such evidence is admissible under the proper circumstances. . . . Relevance under Evid. R. 401 is the first hurdle to clear. "Generally, battered woman syndrome testimony is relevant and helpful when needed to explain a complainant's actions, such as prolonged endurance of physical abuse accompanied by attempts at hiding or minimizing the abuse, delays in reporting the abuse, or recanting allegations of abuse." Such seemingly inconsistent actions are relevant to a witness's credibility. "Because the victim's credibility can be attacked during cross-examination of the victim or even during opening statements, the prosecution need not wait until rebuttal to present expert testimony on battered woman syndrome. Rather, such testimony may be presented as rehabilitative evidence during the state's case-in-chief."

In this case, Bohley's behavior after incidents of alleged abuse was a focus of Haines's cross-examination. . . . Haines attempted to demonstrate that Bohley would become intimate with Haines after he allegedly abused her, that she broke off their relationship only temporarily, that she did not report the abuse, and that she gave differing explanations regarding some of her injuries. . . . [E]xpert testimony on battered-woman syndrome could address those supposed anomalies. But . . . it cannot be considered relevant if there is no evidence that the victim suffers from battered-woman syndrome. . . . "[T]he party seeking to introduce battered woman syndrome evidence must lay an appropriate foundation substantiating that the conduct and behavior of the witness is consistent with the generally recognized symptoms of the battered woman syndrome. . . ." [Quoting State v. Stringer, 897 P.2d 1063 (Mont. 1995).]

Evidence generally establishing the cycles of a battering relationship is an appropriate foundation. . . . "The battering relationship itself is often described as cyclical in nature, with three distinct phases: tension building, confrontation, and contrition. During the 'tension building' phase, the woman is generally compliant, often feeling as though she deserves the abuse. Once the tension reaches a boiling point, the batterer will erupt uncontrollably, committing a violent act. Next, in an abrupt about-face, the abuser will exhibit seemingly intense love and affection towards his victim. The victimized women are then led to believe that the violence was an isolated incident and that it will not continue. This cycle of violence may leave the victim with feelings of learned helplessness, low self-esteem, depression, minimization techniques, self-isolation, and passivity." . . . "'[I]n order to be classified as a battered woman, the couple must go through the battering cycle at least twice. Any woman may find herself in an abusive relationship with a man once. If it occurs a second time, and she remains in the situation, she is defined as a battered woman.'" *Koss*, 49 Ohio St. 3d at 216. The evidence against Haines generally established the cycles of a battering relationship. . . .

Even when its relevance is shown through a proper foundation, a court must carefully weigh whether the expert testimony violates Evid. R. 403(A), which states, "Although relevant, evidence is not admissible if its probative value is substantially outweighed by the danger of unfair prejudice, of confusion of the issues, or of misleading the jury." An expert witness who diagnoses a victim as a battered woman essentially concludes that the defendant is a batterer. In a case where the underlying charges involve domestic violence, such a conclusion by an expert witness is prejudicial to the defendant and usurps the jury's role as finder-of-fact. A diagnosis can prejudice a defendant further because the expert is presenting a conclusion regarding the victim's credibility, which again is a conclusion to be made by the jury. In cases where domestic violence is not the underlying charge, but battered-woman-syndrome testimony is offered to explain the conflicting statements or activities of a witness, a defendant can again be prejudiced by being labeled as a batterer. Thus, courts must carefully balance the admission of expert testimony on battered-woman syndrome under Evid. R. 403.

An acceptable balance is best achieved through a tailoring of the expert's testimony. . . . The rule in most jurisdictions is that general testimony regarding battered-woman syndrome may aid a jury in evaluating evidence and that if the expert expresses no opinion as to whether the victim suffers from battered-woman syndrome or does not opine on which of her conflicting statements is more credible, such testimony does not interfere with or impinge upon the jury's role in determining the credibility of witnesses. . . . The best way to approach this is by . . . limit[ing] their testimony to the general characteristics of a victim suffering from the battered woman syndrome. The expert may also answer hypothetical questions regarding specific abnormal behaviors exhibited by women suffering from the syndrome, but should never offer an opinion relative to the alleged victim in the case." Trial courts should tailor the scope of the state's questioning and should also ensure that jurors are instructed as to the limits of the expert's testimony.

The trial court failed to do so in this case, and the direct examination of the battered-woman-syndrome expert crossed the line. The prosecutor asked Dr. Eisenberg, "[D]o you have an opinion, within a reasonable degree of forensic certainty, as to whether or not you see any features of the investigation of this case that would parallel a Battered Woman's Syndrome?" . . . The prosecutor's question essentially solicited a diagnosis, and the doctor's response provided one. A reasonable juror would conclude that Eisenberg believed that Bohley suffered from battered-woman syndrome. Such testimony went beyond the providing of a context for a witness's testimony into the area of determining credibility. The testimony also went to the very question that the jury was asked to answer—whether Haines committed domestic violence against Bohley—and answered it. Defendant's counsel then elicited more testimony from Eisenberg that called for a specific diagnosis of Bohley as well as a discussion of further facts about her. . . .

The state argues that the bulk of the battered-woman-syndrome testimony that addresses Bohley's specific case was brought to light by Haines. However, the key testimony solicited by the state thrust Haines into the situation where he had to defend himself against a diagnosis. The evidence admitted in cross-examination did not change the fact that Eisenberg's testimony on direct examination was prejudicial. . . .

Counts One through Three relate to the incident on March 31, 2002. The evidence regarding that incident is almost entirely based upon Bohley's testimony and therefore relies on her credibility. Bohley did not report that incident to the police for weeks. She continued to reside with Haines after it occurred. There is a reasonable probability that evidence concerning her credibility might have contributed to the jury's verdict on those counts—a juror might question Bohley's response to the abuse and then find a consistent explanation for it in Eisenberg's testimony. We thus find that the trial court's error in admitting Eisenberg's testimony attributing battered-woman syndrome to Bohley was not harmless as to Counts One through Three.

The evidence concerning the counts relating to the incident of April 17-18 was more varied. The jury saw photographs of Bohley's injuries, heard testimony from her co-workers regarding her telephone calls to her office on the morning of April 18, and heard testimony from the police officers responding to the scene. Jurors were not confronted with questions about why Bohley had not reported the incident, as they were with the March 31, 2002 incident. Thus, we find Eisenberg's testimony harmless beyond a reasonable doubt on Counts Four through Six; there is not a reasonable possibility that his testimony contributed to those convictions. Thus, we affirm in part and reverse in part. . . .

Is it not common for experts in various fields (physics, chemistry, forensics, behavioral science, etc.) to testify as to whether the facts of the particular case are consistent with a particular common phenomenon? Why is that so problematic in this context? On cross-examination, opposing counsel can press the expert to acknowledge that another explanation for the alleged victim's behavior is simply that no abuse actually occurred, that the victim is lying. On the other hand, why is an expert needed to explain victims' mindset and thought process when the victims can testify themselves about why they returned to an abuser? Is the syndrome so bizarre that jurors will not believe the victim absent corroborating expert testimony? Is it so difficult to understand a woman's belief that an abuser will become enraged if she tries to leave and will track her down wherever she goes?

Cultural Defense?

Should the law of domestic violence also take into account an unusual (but not psychotic) mindset *of the perpetrator*? A final question to consider with respect to domestic violence is one that will arise also in Chapter 4 with respect to child abuse or neglect—namely, whether greater tolerance or leniency should be given to people who are from another culture or religious community with different norms for behavior in family relationships.

S.D. v. M.J.R.

2 A.3d 412 (N.J. Super. Ct. App. Div. 2010)

PAYNE, J.A.D.

Plaintiff, S.D., appeals from the denial of a final restraining order following a finding of domestic violence. . . . S.D. and defendant, M.J.R., are citizens of Morocco and adherents to the Muslim faith. They were wed in Morocco in an arranged marriage on July 31, 2008, when plaintiff was seventeen years old. The parties did not know each other prior to the marriage. On August 29, 2008, they came to New Jersey as the result of defendant's employment in this country as an accountant. They settled in Bayonne, where they were joined one month later by defendant's mother.

As plaintiff described it at trial, the acts of domestic abuse that underlie this action commenced on November 1, 2008, after three months of marriage. On that day, defendant requested that plaintiff, who did not know how to cook, prepare three Moroccan dishes for six guests to eat on the following morning. Plaintiff testified that she got up at 5:00 A.M. on the day of the visit and attempted to make two of the dishes, but neither was successful. She did not attempt the third. At 8:00 A.M., defendant arrived at the couple's apartment with his guests. He went into the kitchen, but nothing had been prepared. Defendant, angry, said to plaintiff, "I'm going to show you later on, not now, I'm not going to talk to you right now until the visitors leave." Approximately two hours later, the visitors departed. According to plaintiff:

> At that time I was sitting in my room. I was afraid. I was afraid, what is he going to do to me? So I started to read some of our holy book the Koran and the visitors left around 10 o'clock A.M. and he said to me, now I'm going to start punishing you. So he started to pinch me all over my body. He would go—the pinching he would do it like a sensation with his fingers over circulation in my flesh, then he'd pull his fingers out. I felt he was enjoying hurting me.

When asked to describe specifically where defendant was pinching, plaintiff responded that the pinching took place on her breasts, under her arms, and around her thighs; that the pinches left bruises. . . . The punishment continued for approximately one hour, during which time plaintiff was crying. Plaintiff testified that, while administering the punishment, defendant said "I am doing all that to correct you. You have to learn to do something." Nonetheless, plaintiff stated that she "kept all this inside of [her] and we started to live again together, normal life."

An additional incident took place on November 16, 2008. At approximately 3:00 P.M., defendant announced that he planned to have guests who were to arrive at approximately 9:00 or 10:00 that night, and he asked plaintiff to prepare a supper for them. Plaintiff responded that she did not know how to cook. Defendant then left the apartment, returning at 6:00 with his mother and stating that she would do everything. The mother-in-law refused plaintiff's offers of help, so plaintiff went to her room. At some time thereafter, plaintiff, in anger and frustration, pushed papers that defendant had placed on a desk in the bedroom to the floor.

Plaintiff stated that the guests left at approximately midnight, and that defendant came into the bedroom between twelve and one.

> When he came in and he saw everything on the floor—so he entered and he came toward me and he took all my clothes off me. It was very cold day. I had two pants on. He said, what, you think you're going to escape my punishment to you? Let's see what we're going to do now. After that he took off all my clothes. . . . Even my underwear wasn't on. So I felt I was an animal, like an animal. So he said first of all, you better go and pick [up] everything from the floor. Then he said, now we're going to start punishing you. Then he started to pinch my private area. And he was pinching my tits or my chest area. I was crying.

Additionally, plaintiff testified that defendant pulled her pubic hair. Plaintiff stated that her vaginal area was very, very red and that it was hurting. Although she attempted to leave, defendant had locked the door. As a consequence, she attempted to lie on the other side of the bed. Plaintiff testified:

> He said to me, no, you cannot go and sleep on the side of the bed. You're still my wife and you must do whatever I tell you to do. I want to hurt your flesh, I want to feel and know that you're still my wife. After that—he had sex with me and my vagina was very, very swollen and I was hurting so bad.

The judge then asked: "You told him that you did not wish to have . . . intercourse, is that correct?" Plaintiff responded: "Of course because I was—I had so much pain down there." According to plaintiff, the entire episode took approximately two to three hours.

On the following morning, plaintiff asked defendant why he had done what he did. As she reported it, defendant responded

> [by] mak[ing] like a list and he would read the list and he started to say, okay, now you don't know how to cook, but there's other stuff you're going to do in the house, around the house. And when I come back from work, I will see—look at the list and see what you did and what you didn't do. Whatever you didn't do, I'm going to punish you the same way I punished you for the stuff that you didn't do before.

An additional incident occurred on November 22, 2008. That morning, following an argument with her mother-in-law, plaintiff locked herself in her bedroom. Defendant, having been refused entry, removed the latch from the door, entered the bedroom, and engaged in nonconsensual sex with plaintiff. Although plaintiff's mother-in-law and sister-in-law were in the apartment, and although plaintiff was crying throughout the episode, neither came to her assistance.

Defendant and his relatives then left the apartment, and plaintiff started to break everything in the bedroom, including one of its two windows. After defendant returned with his mother at approximately 4:00 P.M., plaintiff attempted to leave the apartment. However, defendant pulled her back into the bedroom and assaulted her by repeatedly slapping her face, causing her lip to swell and bleeding to occur. He then left the room, and plaintiff escaped without shoes or proper clothing through the unbroken window.

Once outside, plaintiff encountered a Pakistani woman from whom she requested shoes. Seeing plaintiff's condition, the woman called the police, who arrived shortly thereafter, along with an ambulance. Plaintiff was taken to Christ Hospital in Jersey City, where her injuries were treated, photographs were taken, and an attempt was made by detectives from the Hudson County Prosecutor's Office to interview her. However, she was too distraught to speak with them at length.

Four of the photographs of plaintiff's body . . . depict bruising to both of plaintiff's breasts and to both of her thighs, as well as her swollen, bruised and abraded lips. . . . [T]he remaining photographs disclosed injuries to plaintiff's left eye and right cheek. . . . Additional police testimony established that there were stains on the pillow and sheets of plaintiff's and defendant's bed that appeared to be blood. On the day of this episode, a domestic violence complaint was filed, and a temporary restraining order was issued. However, the action was later dismissed for lack of prosecution.

Following the November 22 incident, plaintiff took up residence with a Moroccan nurse from Christ Hospital, and she remained with her until January 15, 2009. On December 22, she was determined to be pregnant. Following a meeting between plaintiff, defendant, the nurse, and the Imam of the mosque at which plaintiff and defendant worshiped, the couple was persuaded to reconcile on the condition that defendant stop mistreating and cursing at plaintiff, that they move back to Morocco at the conclusion of defendant's employment, and that defendant obtain an apartment where the couple could live away from his mother. Plaintiff and defendant moved together into an apartment in Jersey City on January 15, 2009. Defendant's mother lived elsewhere.

However, on the night of the reconciliation, defendant again engaged in nonconsensual sex three times, and on succeeding days plaintiff stated that he engaged in further repeated instances of nonconsensual sex. According to plaintiff, during this period, she was deprived of food, she lacked a refrigerator and a phone, and she was left by her husband for many hours, alone. She responded to her plight by breaking dishes, and on January 18, defendant called plaintiff's parents in Morocco, informed them that plaintiff was "in very bad condition," and asked them to send $600 for a ticket back to Morocco. On January 22, 2009, defendant took plaintiff to a restaurant for breakfast. Upon their return to the apartment, defendant forced plaintiff to have sex with him while she cried. Plaintiff testified that defendant always told her

> this is according to our religion. You are my wife, I c[an] do anything to you. The woman, she should submit and do anything I ask her to do.

After having sex, defendant took plaintiff to a travel agency to buy a ticket for her return to Morocco. However the ticket was not purchased, and the couple returned to the apartment. Once there, defendant threatened divorce, but nonetheless again engaged in nonconsensual sex while plaintiff cried. Later that day, defendant and his mother took plaintiff to the home of the Imam and, in the presence of the Imam, his wife, and defendant's mother, defendant verbally divorced plaintiff.[2]

Plaintiff remained at the Imam's house until January 25, 2009, at which time she filed a complaint in municipal court against defendant and obtained a temporary restraining order. A complaint was also filed in Superior Court on January 29, 2009, and an additional temporary restraining order was issued. The two actions were merged for trial in the Superior Court. . . . [A] parallel criminal action was also pending.

Defendant did not testify at the domestic violence trial. However, his mother did so, stating in connection with the November 16 incident that defendant did not complain about plaintiff's lack of cooking skills, and she did not hear evidence of discord between the two. With respect to the November 22 incident, the mother testified that after defendant opened the door with a screwdriver, plaintiff hit him and pulled his beard. Plaintiff also allegedly stated that she was going to destroy the family. The mother stated that the reason defendant wished to go into the room was to get his jacket and health insurance information, needed in order to take the mother to the doctor. Upon their return, they found plaintiff asleep, and she refused to leave her room when guests came over. Neither she nor defendant knew that plaintiff had left the house through the bedroom window.

The mother testified additionally regarding the events of January 22, 2009. She stated that, on that day, she pulled up in front of the couple's apartment and opened the car door to permit defendant to sit in the front and plaintiff to sit in the back seat. When defendant announced that he was going to the Imam to procure a divorce, plaintiff commenced to grab defendant's hair and beard and to "beat" him. According to the mother, defendant then took the car, while she and plaintiff walked to the Imam's house. During their walk, plaintiff allegedly stated that she was going to "destroy" defendant for divorcing her, and that she did not care if she were destroyed in the process, as well. When they arrived at the Imam's house, the mother heard plaintiff say that she loved defendant, that she did not wish a divorce, and that she would do anything for him. She did not hear plaintiff complain about nonconsensual sex. The mother stated that, after the divorce, on January 24, she received a phone call from plaintiff, during which plaintiff accused the family of having no decency and stated that the mother was an old, ugly woman. . . .

2. The Imam testified that defendant divorced plaintiff on January 24, 2009, and called him to announce the fact shortly thereafter. Because plaintiff was pregnant, the divorce would not become effective until the child was delivered. If she had not been pregnant, the divorce would have become effective after three months if plaintiff's husband did not reconcile with her.

The Imam testified that defendant sought to divorce plaintiff because she threatened to go to the police, but that she never mentioned to him being forced to engage in nonconsensual sex. According to the Imam, although defendant sought a divorce, plaintiff opposed it. The Imam testified additionally that arrangements were made for plaintiff's return to Morocco, but when he and his wife sought to take her to the airport, she refused. . . . [T]he Imam testified regarding Islamic law as it relates to sexual behavior. The Imam confirmed that a wife must comply with her husband's sexual demands, because the husband is prohibited from obtaining sexual satisfaction elsewhere. However, a husband was forbidden to approach his wife "like any animal." The Imam did not definitively answer whether, under Islamic law, a husband must stop his advances if his wife said "no." . . .

The judge found . . . that plaintiff had proven by a preponderance of the evidence that defendant had engaged in harassment and assault. He . . . did not find sexual assault or criminal sexual conduct to have been proven. He stated:

> This court does not feel that, under the circumstances, that this defendant had a criminal desire to or intent to sexually assault or to sexually contact the plaintiff when he did. The court believes that he was operating under his belief that it is, as the husband, his desire to have sex when and whether he wanted to, was something that was consistent with his practices and it was something that was not prohibited.

. . . [T]he judge found that defendant did not act with a criminal intent when he repeatedly insisted upon intercourse, despite plaintiff's contrary wishes.

Having found acts of domestic violence consisting of assault and harassment to have occurred, the judge turned to the issue of whether a final restraining order should be entered. He found such an order unnecessary, . . . characteriz[ing] November as a "bad patch" in the parties' marriage and plaintiff's injuries as "not severe." The judge then stated:

> [T]his is a case where there is no history of domestic violence. In fact, they have been—they were together for only three months. Then the bad patch was three weeks, and then another week. And then—and then, the record indicates that this defendant has filed for a divorce. . . . The parties are living separate and apart now. This defendant's visa expires in July, I believe.[5]

The judge therefore found that the parties had no reason to be together again, but immediately thereafter, he noted that their baby was expected in August and "[t]hat will require that the parties be in contact presumably." . . . Nonetheless, the judge cautioned defendant not to have any contact with plaintiff. . . . As a final matter, the judge recognized the pendency of a criminal action against defendant, and indicated its existence constituted an additional basis for the judge's ruling denying a final restraining order, since he assumed that a no-contact order had been entered as a condition of bail. . . .

III

The New Jersey Prevention of Domestic Violence Act (PDVA) . . . requires that . . . the judge shall consider, . . . in making his dual decisions whether to find the occurrence of

5. The judge indicated that plaintiff's visa status was unclear, because she was seeking to stay in the United States as a victim of domestic violence.

domestic violence and whether to issue a final restraining order, "(1) [t]he previous history of domestic violence between the plaintiff and defendant, including threats, harassment and physical abuse; (2) [t]he existence of immediate danger to person or property;" and other factors . . .

N.J.S.A. 2C:14-2c provides that "[a]n actor is guilty of sexual assault if he commits an act of sexual penetration with another person" under several circumstances, including when "[t]he actor uses physical force or coercion, but the victim does not sustain severe personal injury." To establish physical force . . . , the plaintiff does not have to prove force in addition to "that necessary for penetration so long as the penetration was accomplished 'in the absence of what a reasonable person would believe to be affirmative and freely-given permission.'" Testimony by plaintiff at trial adequately established the absence of freely given permission. *N.J.S.A.* 2C:14-3b provides that "[a]n actor is guilty of criminal sexual contact if he commits an act of sexual contact with the victim under any of the circumstances set forth in section 2C:14-2c." . . . Neither the sexual assault statute nor the criminal sexual contact statute specifies the mental state that must be demonstrated in order to establish the defendant's criminal intent. . . . *N.J.S.A.* 2C:2-2c(3) establishes the principle that criminal statutes that do not designate a specific culpability requirement should be construed as requiring knowing conduct. Defendant's conduct in engaging in nonconsensual sexual intercourse was unquestionably knowing, regardless of his view that his religion permitted him to act as he did.

As the judge recognized, the case thus presents a conflict between the criminal law and religious precepts. . . . In Reynolds v. United States, 98 U.S. 145 (1878), the Supreme Court considered an appeal from a Mormon's conviction under a Congressionally passed bigamy statute applicable to the Utah territory. . . . In affirming the conviction, the Court [said]: . . . "Laws are made for the government of actions, and while they cannot interfere with mere religious belief and opinions, they may with practices. . . . Can a man excuse his practices to the contrary because of his religious belief? To permit this would be to make the professed doctrines of religious belief superior to the law of the land, and in effect to permit every citizen to become a law unto himself. Government could exist only in name under such circumstances. . . . Ignorance of a fact may sometimes be taken as evidence of a want of criminal intent, but not ignorance of the law. . . . [W]hen the offense consists of a positive act which is knowingly done, it would be dangerous to hold that the offender might escape punishment because he religiously believed the law which he had broken ought never to have been made. . . ."

Over the years, the United State Supreme Court's treatment of Free Exercise Clause cases has changed. . . . However, in Employment Div., Dep't of Human Res. of Oregon v. Smith, 494 U.S. 872 (1990), the Supreme Court held that the Free Exercise Clause did not require Oregon to exempt the sacramental ingestion of peyote by members of the Native American Church from Oregon's criminal drug laws. The Court determined that such valid, generally applicable, and neutral laws may be applied to religious exercise even in the absence of a compelling governmental interest. In doing so, the Court held that "[t]he only decisions in which we have held that the *First Amendment* bars application of a neutral, generally applicable law to religiously motivated action have involved not the *Free Exercise Clause* alone, but the *Free Exercise Clause* in conjunction with other constitutional protections." . . . The Court concluded:

> The government's ability to enforce generally applicable prohibitions of socially harmful conduct, like its ability to carry out other aspects of public policy, "cannot depend on measuring the effects of a governmental action on a religious objector's spiritual development."

> To make an individual's obligation to obey such a law contingent upon the law's coincidence with his religious beliefs, except where the State's interest is "compelling"—permitting him, by virtue of his beliefs, "to become a law unto himself,"—contradicts both constitutional tradition and common sense.

. . . Because it is doubtlessly true that the laws defining the crimes of sexual assault and criminal sexual contact are neutral laws of general application, and because defendant knowingly engaged in conduct that violated those laws, the judge erred when he refused to recognize those violations as a basis for a determination that defendant had committed acts of domestic violence. . . . [W]e note, as well, the Legislature's recognition of the serious nature of domestic violence.

IV

Following a finding that a defendant has committed a predicate act of domestic violence, the judge is required to consider whether a restraining order should be entered that provides protection to the victim. . . . "Although this second determination—whether a domestic violence restraining order should be issued—is most often perfunctory and self-evident, the guiding standard is whether a restraining order is necessary . . . to protect the victim from an immediate danger or to prevent further abuse." . . . We construe the judge's characterization of the violence that took place as a bad patch in the parties' marriage and plaintiff's injuries as not severe as manifesting an unnecessarily dismissive view of defendant's acts of domestic violence. Although it is true that the November episodes spanned only three weeks, that period constituted approximately one-fourth of the parties' marriage. Moreover, we find it significant . . . that the violence resumed on the very first night of the parties' reconciliation, and after defendant had assured the Imam that he would not engage in further such acts. . . .

We find it inappropriate, when restraints are civilly required, for a Family Part judge to rely on restraints issued in a parallel criminal proceeding. This is particularly the case because the need to protect the victim-spouse may outlive the termination of the criminal action. As a final matter, we find that the judge failed to give sufficient measured consideration to the imminence of the birth of the couple's child—an event that the judge acknowledged would bring the two into contact and almost inevitably be a source of conflict. . . . [T]he judge was mistaken . . . not to issue a final restraining order. . . .

Was there any downside to issuing a protective order that could explain the trial court's decision not to do so? What costs could it have for the husband if he was already separated from his wife?

The court relied on the U.S. Supreme Court decision in *Emp't Div. v. Smith* establishing that the state generally need not create religious exceptions to laws of general applicability. In *Smith*, the majority suggested that this rule does not apply to parenting cases—that is, to parental free exercise challenges to laws governing child rearing, such as education, medical neglect, or physical abuse laws. Thus, if some U.S. state were to pass a law banning corporal punishment, without exception, a court might conclude, despite the generality and religion-neutrality of the law, that this violates a First Amendment right of parents whose religion commands them to discipline their children in this way. Is there a principled basis for distinguishing between the two types of relationships in this context—that is, for saying that states must sometimes grant exemptions to parents whose religious views conflict with mainstream child-rearing norms but need not grant exemptions to spouses whose religious views conflict with mainstream norms of inter-spousal conduct?

What About Male Victims?

As with infidelity, some complain of too little recognition that many women, too, are guilty of domestic violence. Indeed, this section on domestic violence has thus far presented the issue as if only men engage in violence toward partners. The neglect of male victims occurs not only in textbooks and legal scholarship, but also in public policy. Have you ever heard of a shelter for battered men or seen a billboard depicting a male victim and providing a phone number to call for assistance? Let us see if there is any rational justification for the highly gendered nature of discourse and advocacy relating to domestic violence.

Linda Kelly, Disabusing the Definition of Domestic Abuse: How Women Batter Men and the Role of the Feminist State

30 Fla. St. U. L. Rev. 791 (2003)

. . . [L]eading sociologists have repeatedly found that men and women commit violence at similar rates. However, . . . female violence is not recognized within the extensive legal literature on domestic violence. . . . [The] refusal to react is a product of the feminist control over the issue of domestic violence. Female violence presents both a threat to feminist theory as well as to the practice of domestic violence law. . . . [T]he feminist definition of domestic violence has skewed arrest and prosecution philosophies, resulting primarily in having only male batterers criminally pursued. . . . [R]ehabilitative programs are geared toward treating domestic violence as the byproduct of a patriarchal society, thereby only producing programs which address male violence. Similarly, the services for domestic violence victims, in particular, the availability of shelters, have also been shaped by the feminist definition of domestic violence. . . .

[Early] surveys consistently reported that *women not only use violence at rates similar to men, but that women match, and often exceed, husbands in the frequency with which they engage in violent behavior.* . . . Combining the data collected . . . to create a "Severe Violence Index," *wives were found to engage in more severe acts of violence than husbands.* . . . [C]omparison of the 1975, 1985 and 1992 studies also reveals an important trend. . . . In comparing the 1975 and 1985 results, researchers observed that while the male use of severe physical violence had declined 21%, the female use of such violence remained virtually constant. In the 1992 results, researchers again found that while severe assaults by wives remained fairly steady, the rate of severe abuse perpetrated by husbands decreased between 1985 and 1992 by almost 37%. . . .

Criticisms have ranged from personally attacking the researchers, to more academic efforts directed at attacking the work itself by denying the validity of the reports, to an outright defense of the violent behavior of women or otherwise minimizing its significance. . . . Perhaps the most physically and personally intimidating behavior was directed at Suzanne Steinmetz, who had first brought the issue to the public's attention. . . . Verbal threats were launched against her and her children—at home and in public. Threatening phone calls were made to Steinmetz and the sponsors of her speaking engagements in order to prevent Steinmetz from further publicizing her work. On one occasion, a bomb threat was called into an ACLU meeting at which Steinmetz was scheduled to speak. Professionally, Steinmetz was also threatened. In an attempt to prevent her from receiving tenure, every female faculty member at the University of Delaware was lobbied by individuals calling on behalf of the women's rights movement. Academicians also became involved in the personal attack, deriding her work as anti-feminist and simply biased to its funding source. Other social scientists committed to the study of husband abuse and family violence were similarly mistreated. Such tactics seem to have proven effective. Both researchers who were involved in the early projects, and even those who might have become involved, admit that they now choose to give the topic of battered men "wide berth." . . .

For those interested in discrediting the assertion that men and women both act violently, a bolder move is to not only accept the female use of violence, but to defend it . . . as self-defense—a lifesaving reaction of women who are being physically attacked by their male partners. . . . [H]owever, . . . while in approximately 50% of cases both spouses are reported to act violently, in the remaining 50% only one spouse is reported to ever use domestic violence. . . . [W]hile the husband is the sole perpetrator in one half of such cases, the wife is the sole perpetrator in the remaining half. Moreover, . . . men and women report initiating violence at similar rates. . . .

When the severity of a woman's violent behavior is greater than her spouse's, it is suggested that a woman's lack of training in less violent reactions may excuse her behavior. . . . Others have [argued] . . . that women's use of violence is warranted when men engage in "unwanted sexual advances, belittling of . . . [women], verbal intimidation, [and] drunken frenzy." In this vein, the question changes from, "[W]ho began [the] hitting?" to, "[W]ho began the argument?" . . . [T]he implication is that because male anger carries the threat of greater harm, acts of female violence cannot only be condoned as a preventive defense, but can also be overlooked. . . .

[T]he greater physical strength of men as compared to women provides the most plausible explanation for disregarding female violence. Male violence produces injury at *six* times the rate of female violence. . . . [W]omen suffer greater physical and psychological harm when physically assaulted. When measuring physical injury via the three categories of the need for medical care, time off from work, and time spent bedridden, women rank higher in every category. In terms of psychological injuries, while abused men and women consistently display psychosomatic symptoms, abused women suffer greater depression and stress levels than abused men. . . . [T]he differing rates of injury also supply an argument for dismissing the statistical parity between the genders in their use of violence. Men are seen to possess the "single beating" advantage, as the mere threat of causing injury allows men to control women without physically having to raise a hand after the first beating. . . .

A number of important practical and theoretical justifications militate against ignoring female violence. First, notwithstanding the "damage differential," . . . there appears to be no basis for the traditional belief that women are either born or bred to be less physically aggressive than men. . . . Second, focusing on the injury, rather than the assault, contradicts the understood campaign against wife-beating which has been to end wife abuse per se, not just the violence which produces injury. . . . A third argument for resisting the effort to deny, defend, or minimize female abuse of men lies in recognizing that . . . failure to stigmatize or even acknowledge the female abuse of men allows and encourages its continuation. . . . [F]ourth, . . . female violence must be addressed in order to protect women, as a man provoked by a violent female has the potential to inflict greater injury. . . . [F]ifth . . . witnessing either husband-beating or wife-beating as a child is equally likely to breed a predisposition toward intimate violence. Finally, a wider look at family violence . . . will also allow a greater emphasis to be placed on the socio-cultural factors which teach violent tendencies. Male-blaming can no longer be relied upon as the single explanation for the ills of society. . . .

What then is the harm in targeting, discussing, or even revealing the abuse of men by women? . . . Why does the denial continue? . . . Domestic violence represents the prized gemstone of feminist theory's fundamental message that our legal, social, and cultural norms are fashioned in a manner which permit men to engage in a constant and pervasive effort to oppress women by any and every available means. A successful challenge to the patriarchal definition of domestic violence may thus undermine feminism itself. To remain true to feminist theory, no aspect of male-female relations can be considered without first accepting the male as all powerful and the female as powerless. . . . Defining domestic violence beyond the threat to women is seen in and of itself as a threat to women's lives. . . .

For real-world domestic violence advocates, . . . competition for adequate attention and funding is terrific. . . . By limiting the definition of domestic violence to male violence, domestic violence advocates have been able to frame the issue in a manner narrow and sympathetic enough for it to remain high on the public agenda. . . . [T]he "helpless victim" stereotype remains very much a part of the common understanding of domestic violence and . . . when it comes to funding, battered women advocates are willing to promote a stereotype which, in other contexts, is readily recognized as inaccurate. . . .

At least one author has argued that the treatment of female violence by feminists—be it to deny, defend, or minimize—is . . . purely an act of revenge. Angry over a history of domination, feminists have discredited female violence in order to give women a secret way to strike back. . . .

What do you think would really be the societal response to widespread recognition of female violence against male partners? Would it undermine the cause of equality for women? Would it diminish public financial support for domestic violence shelters? What affect might it have on men to hear public condemnation of violence by women against men? Might it help impress on them the message that no violence is acceptable?

As Professor Kelly briefly notes, in addition to protecting men from harm, stricter enforcement of domestic violence laws against female abusers would likely reduce violence against women in individual cases. Imagine that you are a husband and that your wife, when angry at you, tends to throw things at you or to hit you, instead of just vocalizing her feelings. You might not feel endangered by this, if you are significantly bigger and stronger than your wife, depending on what she is throwing or how hard and where she is hitting. But in any case, it is likely to be quite bothersome, and you find yourself unable simply to accept it. What are your options for stopping it? If you call the police and they respond with skepticism, inaction, and even derision, then your only other options would seem to be striking back or exiting the relationship, and presumably the state does not want to encourage either of those options. Why would any woman initiate violence in this way against a bigger, stronger male partner? Is the psychology likely the same as with a man who initiates violence against a woman?

Is it likely that any men are rendered helpless by a female partner's abuse, unable to stop the violence but also too terrified to try to leave? There have been a couple of reported cases in which a male claiming to be a victim of domestic violence has asked to introduce evidence of a Battered Man's Syndrome, to support a self-defense argument against prosecution for murdering his female partner. See People v. Grayson, 2002 WL 31151641 (Cal. App. 3d); Chester v. State, 471 S.E.2d 836 (Ga. 1996). In same-sex relationships, the partners are more likely to be of similar size and strength, and gendered attitudes might be less likely to play a role. For discussion of this topic, see Adele M. Morrison, *Queering Domestic Violence to "Straighten Out" Criminal Law: What Might Happen When Queer Theory and Practice Meet Criminal Law's Conventional Responses to Domestic Violence*, 13 S. Cal. Rev. L. & Women's Stud. 81 (2003); Nancy J. Knauer, *Same-Sex Domestic Violence: Claiming a Domestic Sphere While Risking Negative Stereotypes*, 8 Temp. Pol. & Civ. Rts. L. Rev. 325 (1999).

ADVOCACY CHALLENGE

Conceptualize a television spot or billboard aimed at eradicating partner abuse, while not saying anything that could be viewed as opposition to corporal punishment of children. Could you include any general statements about violence, family life, or love? *Cf.* Or. Rev. Stat. §106.041(4) ("A marriage license must contain the following statement: 'Neither you nor your spouse is the property of the other. The laws of the State of Oregon affirm your right to enter into marriage and at the same time to live within the marriage free from violence and abuse.'").

3. Caretaking

The rules relating to behavior during marriage addressed thus far have principally imposed negative duties—in particular, not to have sexual relations with anyone other than one's spouse and not to act violently toward one's spouse. Marriage does also entail some positive duties between spouses. The next section addresses the duty of financial support, but is there any legal obligation to do anything else for one's spouse, besides pay for basic needs? A duty to have sex no longer exists for either spouse, so the state will not attempt to force a spouse to have sex nor permit one spouse to force the other to have sex. The only recourse today for someone dissatisfied with the sexual aspect of marriage is to secure an annulment or divorce. Likewise with a duty to perform housework or paid labor. Though under coverture a husband could force his wife to do housework by beating her, today someone dissatisfied with the contribution his or her spouse makes to the household can only plead for more assistance or exit the relationship.

In many states, the law does create indirect pressure on spouses to do the things, such as sex and contributing to the functioning of the household, ordinarily expected in a marriage, through its rules for financial aspects of divorce. For example, in many states important considerations in equitable distribution of marital property are the contribution—material and non-material—each spouse has made to acquisition of the property and, conversely, the cause of the marital dissolution. Refusal to do normal things spouses are expected to do could be relevant to either. But there is no direct legal command of the sort Afghanistan has to offer oneself sexually to one's spouse, nor does any written law say that spouses must expend effort for the good of the household. The reasons why no such laws exist might be obvious, but try to articulate what they are. If the main reason is difficulty of enforcement, might anything be gained by a state's enacting a statute announcing certain positive duties of spouses without creating any mechanism for enforcement? Or is providing easy exit the only or best thing the state can do to promote commitment to marital responsibilities?

There are a couple of explicit positive legal duties in special circumstances. You were probably not previously aware that married people have a legal duty to rescue their spouse in life-threatening situations. Philosopher Bernard Williams famously quipped that rescuing one's drowning spouse because one has a duty to do so "is to have one thought too many." But the common law of many U.S. states has imposed such a duty. See Collins, Leib & Markel, *Punishing Family Status*, 88 B.U. L. Rev. 1327, 1336 (2008) ("if a defendant 'realizes (or culpably fails to realize) his wife is in danger, realizes (or culpably fails to realize) that he can rescue her with minimal risk and/or sacrifice, and realizes (or culpably fails to realize) that she is his wife,' then he can be criminally liable for homicide" if he does not attempt to rescue her). The reported cases suggest that needing immediate medical attention is the most common such situation.

We generally do not think of spouses as needing ongoing caretaking, because when we think of married couples we tend to think of two competent, autonomous adults. But most humans do lose capacities for self-care at some point, and most of them are married when that happens. Do their spouses have any legal obligation to care for them then, or are love and a sense of moral obligation the only real motivators? As noted above, the "duty to rescue" kicks in when a spouse is in immediate need of medical attention, and so one would seem to have a duty to secure assistance for a spouse whose incompetence creates a danger of imminent physical harm to himself or herself. Some states' statutes speak directly of a duty to secure medical assistance. See, e.g., Idaho Code Ann. §18-401 ("Every person who . . . willfully abandons and leaves a spouse in a destitute condition, or who refuses or neglects to provide such spouse with necessary food, clothing, shelter, or medical attendance, unless by the spouse's misconduct he or she is justified in abandoning him or her; [s]hall be guilty of a felony and shall be punishable by a fine . . . or by imprisonment for not to exceed fourteen years, or both."); Ariz. Rev. Stat. §13-3611 (criminalizing failure "to provide the spouse with necessary food, clothing, shelter or medical attendance"). Others speak instead of paying for the medical care of a spouse if the spouse is not able himself or herself to pay, as an aspect of the duty of financial support discussed in Section II below.

What about ongoing physical care and attention? Typically, a court appoints a guardian for an adult who becomes incompetent, and capable spouses generally receive priority in appointment. But accepting that role is optional for a spouse. If and when someone does accept a guardian role with respect to a spouse, then the normal positive duties of care of a guardian apply. These include managing the ward's affairs: "They can be required to defend their wards from civil suits, from criminal prosecution, and to enter and sever contracts and agreements on their ward's behalf to provide for the ward's well-being." Mark Schwarz, Note, *The Marriage Trap: How Guardianship Divorce Bans Abet Spousal Abuse*, 13 J.L. & Fam. Stud. 187, 197 (2011). In addition, even in the absence of a guardian appointment, if one assumes the role of primary caretaker with respect to an incompetent spouse, rather than immediately placing one's spouse in the care of others, then one takes on a number of positive legal duties as to the spouse's basic physical needs. For example, Florida statutes define "caregiver" as "a person who has been entrusted with or has assumed responsibility for the care or the property of an elderly person or disabled adult," including "relatives, court-appointed or voluntary guardians, adult household members, neighbors . . . ," and treat as a felony a "caregiver's failure or omission to provide an elderly person or disabled adult with the care, supervision, and services necessary to maintain the elderly person's or disabled adult's physical and mental health, including, but not limited to, food, nutrition, clothing, shelter, supervision, medicine, and medical services that a prudent person would consider essential for the well-being of the elderly person or disabled adult; or . . . to make a reasonable effort to protect an elderly person or disabled adult from abuse, neglect, or exploitation by another person." Fla. Stat. §§825.101(2), 825.102(3). This is similar to the legal definition of child neglect by a parent.

In contrast to the law of parental obligation, however, there is no exception to the general "act in the ward's best interests" obligation of guardianship or caretaking arising from the religious beliefs of a spousal guardian or caretaker (as opposed to the religious beliefs of the ward when competent). See, e.g., Minn. Stat. §609.233 ("A caregiver . . . who intentionally neglects a vulnerable adult . . . is guilty of a gross misdemeanor. . . . A vulnerable adult is not neglected for the sole reason that . . . a caregiver in good faith selects and depends upon spiritual means or prayer for treatment or care of disease or remedial care of the vulnerable adult in lieu of medical care, provided that this is consistent with the prior practice or belief of the vulnerable adult or with the expressed intentions of the vulnerable adult"). As we will see in Chapter 4, there is a partial exemption from the normal responsibilities of child rearing for parents whose own religious beliefs conflict with those responsibilities. Should a spousal guardian or caretaker be legally entitled to act contrary to what the state believes is best for the incompetent spouse if the guardian has a religious motivation for doing so, regardless of what the incompetent spouse's religious beliefs are or were? In a situation sharing features both with guardianship of a spouse (namely, the ward was an adult) and with parenting (namely, the ward was the guardian's offspring), the U.S. Supreme Court in Cruzan v. Dir., Mo. Dep't of Health, 497 U.S. 261 (1990), rejected a claim by parents of a woman in a persistent vegetative state that they, the parents, had a right under the First Amendment to decide in accordance with their own religious beliefs that their daughter's life support would be removed. The Court stated that only the incompetent adult herself could have any rights at stake, rights to what she previously chose for herself or to what was in her best interests. Can you articulate an argument for extending that principle to the spousal guardianship context that would not also require rejecting the doctrine of parental free exercise entitlement to refuse medical care for a child?

B. FINANCES

Whatever else it might be, marriage is a financial contract; the parties implicitly agree to be governed by certain rules regarding their property by which they otherwise would not be governed—default rules created by statute or judicial decision and/or rules the husband and wife themselves establish in a pre-marital agreement. This section presents a few of the default rules, some of which cannot be avoided by private contract.

1. *The Support Duty*

Under the coverture regime, husbands were legally liable for the support of their wives, who were themselves legally incapable of contracting with providers of goods and services and also generally not in control of any property. Since the elimination of the legal disabilities of coverture, a small number of states have eliminated the support duty, viewing it as an anachronism. See, e.g., Emanuel v. McGriff, 596 So. 2d 578 (Ala. 1992); Condore v. Prince George's Cnty., 425 A.2d 1011 (Md. 1981). But the duty remains in most states, now in gender-neutral form.

Virginia Code
Title 20. Domestic Relations
Chapter 5. Desertion and Nonsupport

§20-61 Desertion or Nonsupport of Wife, Husband . . . in Necessitous Circumstances

Any spouse who without cause deserts or willfully neglects or refuses or fails to provide for the support and maintenance of his or her spouse, . . . the spouse . . . being then and there in necessitous circumstances, shall be guilty of a misdemeanor and upon conviction shall be punished by a fine of not exceeding $500, or confinement in jail not exceeding twelve months, or both, or on work release employment . . . ; or in lieu of the fine or confinement . . . he or she may be required by the court to suffer a forfeiture of an amount not exceeding . . . $1,000 and the fine or forfeiture may be directed by the court to be paid in whole or in part to the spouse. . . .

§20-64 Proceedings Instituted by Petition

Proceedings under this chapter may be instituted upon petition . . . by the spouse . . . or by any state or local law-enforcement officer or by the Department of Social Services upon information received, or by any other person having knowledge of the facts. . . .

§20-72 Probation on Order Directing Defendant to Pay and Enter Recognizance

[I]nstead of imposing the penalties hereinbefore provided, or in addition thereto, the judge, . . . shall have the power to make an order, directing the defendant to pay a certain sum or a certain percentage of his or her earnings periodically, either directly or through the court to the spouse. . . .

§55-37 Spouse not Responsible for Other Spouse's Contracts, etc.; Mutual Liability for Necessaries; Responsibility of Personal Representative

Except as otherwise provided in this section, a spouse shall not be responsible for the other spouse's contract or tort liability to a third party, whether such liability arose before or after the marriage. The doctrine of necessaries as it existed at common law shall apply equally to both spouses, except where they are permanently living separate and apart, but shall in no event create any liability between such spouses as to each other. . . .

Is there an inconsistency in Virginia between Title 20 and Title 55 as to one spouse's liability to the other for failure to provide needed support? In any event, suits by a dependent spouse against a primary-earner spouse who has deserted have been common and generally successful, notwithstanding the language of §55-37. As we will see in Chapter 6, today states have special code sections authorizing courts to order spousal support during the separation period that typically precedes a divorce, so a dependent spouse would typically invoke that authorization rather than the non-support provision. What has been extremely rare is for a dependent spouse to bring legal action for non-support while still cohabiting with the primary-earner, though economic abuse of a spouse is a significant phenomenon. The most common cause of action resting on the spousal support duty is a suit by third-party providers of medical care, which usually arises when spouses are separated or after the spouse who received services has died.

Southern New Hampshire Medical Center v. Hayes

992 A.2d 596 (N.H. 2010)

DUGGAN, J.

. . . Anthony and Karen Hayes married in 1977. In July, August, October and November 2006, Karen, who did not have health insurance, received emergency medical treatment at SNHMC for complications stemming from alcoholism, leaving a balance due of $85,238.88. . . . While Karen's medical records indicate that she was living with Anthony, Anthony disputes this, asserting that he and Karen "did not live as husband and wife for the past seven to eight years. . . ." Anthony testified that sometimes Karen was admitted to SNHMC after being "taken out of hotels, motels, and other people's houses."

SNHMC filed suit against the Hayeses, and successfully sought a real estate attachment on two unencumbered parcels owned jointly by the Hayeses . . . [while] Karen and Anthony were still married. The Hayeses were divorced in January 2007 pursuant to a stipulated agreement. Under the terms of the divorce, . . . "Karen [was] responsible for paying the debt to [SNHMC] as well as any other medical debts or bills." Karen received one automobile valued at $1,200, her bank account with a balance of $0.00, and all of her debts. Anthony received the marital properties subject to SNHMC's attachment. . . .

The ancient common law doctrine of necessaries imposed liability on husbands for "essential goods and services provided to [their wives] by third parties" if they failed to provide their wives "with such necessaries." Necessaries included "necessary food, drink, washing, physic, instruction, and a suitable place of residence, with such necessary furniture as is suitable to her condition." *See* Morrison v. Holt, 42 N.H. 478 (1861) (legal expenses not necessaries unless husband's conduct rendered expenses necessary to secure wife's personal protection or safety). This doctrine originated as a result of draconian legal restrictions on the rights of married women to "contract, sue, or be sued individually" or exercise control over their property or financial affairs. A married woman's contracts "'were absolutely void,—not merely voidable, like those of infants and lunatics.'" "[U]pon marriage a woman forfeited her legal existence and became the property of her husband," as, in the eyes of the law, a husband and wife were considered one legal entity. In return for his responsibility for his wife's support and liability for her torts, a husband was entitled to her "society." . . . The husband was "the sole owner of the family wealth," and the wife was "viewed as little more than a chattel in the eyes of the law." Accordingly, the law of necessaries "attempted to obviate some of the victimization which coverture would otherwise have permitted" by "providing a common-law mechanism by which the duty of support could be enforced." . . .

[A] husband whose wife "eloped" would not be liable for her necessaries. . . . Key to the determination of "elopement" was whether the wife had left her husband, committed adultery and also remained beyond his control.

"In modern America, 'no longer is the female destined solely for the home and the rearing of the family, and only the male for the marketplace and the world of ideas.'" "The modern marital relationship is viewed by law as a partnership of equality. . . ." Undoubtedly, married women today have an "unrestricted right to contract," and RSA 546-A:2 (2007) "imposes a gender-neutral obligation of spousal support." The doctrine of necessaries has been characterized as "an anachronism that no longer fits contemporary society," and some courts have abolished it. *See, e.g., Emanuel v. McGriff* (Ala. 1992); *Condore v. Prince George's Cty.*, 289 Md. 516 (1981). In New Hampshire, however, the doctrine endures: we extended it to apply to all married individuals, regardless of gender, and many courts have similarly extended the doctrine to apply to both husbands and wives. *See, e.g.*, North Ottawa Community Hosp. v. Kieft, 457 Mich. 394 (1998). . . .

> In order to establish a *prima facie* case against one spouse for the value of [services or goods] provided to the other spouse, the . . . provider must show that (1) [services or goods] were provided to the receiving spouse, (2) [they] were necessary for the health and well-being of the receiving spouse, (3) the person against whom the action is brought was married to the receiving spouse at the time the [services or goods] were provided, and (4) payment for the necessaries has not been made.

Wesley Long Nursing Center, Inc. v. Harper (N.C. Ct. App. 2007); *see also* Queen's Medical Center v. Kagawa, 88 Hawai'i 489 (1998); Trident Regional Medical Center v. Evans, 317 S.C. 346 (1995). . . . We note that, for the purposes of the necessaries doctrine, hospitals and other medical providers are uniquely situated and, therefore, uniquely likely to seek the application of this doctrine, as, unlike other creditors, medical providers may not turn away patients who require treatment. . . .

We conclude that "elopement" is no longer a defense to the doctrine of necessaries. . . . Such a defense does not comport with the modern status of marriage. We have "rejected such antiquated and obsolete notions concerning women. . . ." Given that the "historical purposes underlying the [elopement] exception to the necessaries doctrine are incompatible with current mores and laws governing modern marital relationships . . . ," we find that the elopement exception "has no place in the common law." Rather, we conclude that, under the third prong of the *prima facie* case that we have outlined above, the creditor—in this case, the hospital—must show more than the legal fact of marriage to demonstrate that the parties are "married" for the purposes of liability under the necessaries doctrine. . . . The non-debtor spouse's liability under the necessaries doctrine depends on a mutual expectation that the spouses will share assets, expenses, and debts. Accordingly, factors to consider in determining whether the marriage is no longer viable for the purposes of the necessaries doctrine might include whether the parties were separated, when they separated, whether they are living apart, and whether they share their living expenses and debt. If a marriage has broken down to the extent that spouses are no longer sharing assets or debts, it makes little sense to hold a non-debtor spouse liable for the medical expenses of the other. *But see Kagawa* (Haw. 1998) (non-debtor spouse liable for necessaries until divorce finalized); *Bartrom* (Ind. 1993) (holding that "duty of spousal support continues at least until the marriage relationship is dissolved"). . . . Because we hold today that "elopement" is not an affirmative defense, we reverse and remand to the trial court for a new trial on the merits. . . .

Under the doctrine of necessaries, "a husband or wife is not liable for necessary medical expenses incurred by his or her spouse unless the resources of the spouse who received the services are *insufficient* to satisfy the debt." Accordingly, "the spouse who receives the necessary goods or services is primarily liable for payment," and "the other spouse is secondarily liable." . . . However, . . . SNHMC demonstrated that Karen's estate could not satisfy the debt to SNHMC.

HICKS, J., concurring specially.

. . . Without the underlying legal disability of the wife, the common law justification for binding her husband to her contracts for necessaries disappears. . . . There is, in fact, some indication that "the modern[, gender-neutral] doctrine seems to result in *less* available credit for needy spouses." . . . "In truth, extension of the doctrine serves creditors' rights, not spousal support rights."

Do you suppose many people are aware of the necessaries doctrine when they get married or when they do estate planning? What unanticipated and unfair consequences might result from a lack of awareness? Does the rule benefit married people themselves, or only providers of goods and services such as the medical facility in this case, as the concurring judge suggests?

If people were generally aware of this rule, what effect might it have on a person with multiple serious medical problems who wishes to marry? Could it induce some married couples to divorce, if one spouse develops serious medical problems likely to generate large bills not covered by insurance? See Andrea B. Carroll, *Incentivizing Divorce,* 30 CARDOZO L. REV. 1925 (2009).

If the necessaries doctrine is at all justifiable, why should it matter whether the couple still cohabits and acts like a married couple for purposes of joint liability, given that they enjoy benefits tied to marriage like health insurance coverage and joint tax filing status unless and until they formally divorce? Moreover, if spouses' actual intention as to sharing debts is irrelevant to liability for necessaries when they are happily married and cohabiting, why should it matter during a period when they are moving toward dissolution? Compare the Connecticut statute below, which treats separation without reference to the parties' intentions. In any state where separation matters, is it right to put the burden on the creditor to establish that the defendant was married and not separated, or "really married" despite separation, to the primary debtor?

In one of the out-of-state cases cited, Wesley Long Nursing Ctr. v. Harper, 653 S.E.2d 256 (N.C. App. (2007)), the court held that the widower husband was equally, not secondarily, liable for his deceased wife's end-of-life medical bills. A creditor might find it easier for one reason or another to bring suit against the non-debtor spouse, and that spouse would then have the burden of joining the debtor spouse or her estate in the suit. Is it fair to impose that burden on the debtor's spouse? More efficient?

Why do most states limit the support obligation to spouse and children? In a few states and in many other countries, people ostensibly have a legal obligation to support other family members who are destitute as well, principally their parents. See, e.g., Cal. Fam. Code §4400 ("an adult child shall, to the extent of his or her ability, support a parent who is in need and unable to maintain himself or herself by work"); Conn. Gen. Stat. §53-304 (duty to support parent in need who is under age 65); Ind. Code §35-46-1-7 9 (failure to support parent in need is a misdemeanor); Ohio Rev. Code Ann. §2919.21(A)(3) (failure "to provide adequate support to . . . aged or infirm parent . . . unable to provide adequately for the parent's own support"). In Spain, adults owe a support duty even to their siblings.

Civil Code of Spain, Chap. V, Title VI, Art. 143. In China, traditionally a wife has been expected to care for her husband's parents. How might American society change if adults were required to support their siblings, their parents, and even their spouse's parents?

Implicit in the common-law necessaries doctrine is an assumption that spouses are not liable for debts their spouses independently incur for things other than necessaries. Professor Reilly writes: "In many situations, whether a married person is financially responsible for her spouse's debt is a simple question of personal liability under contract or other law. Suppose one spouse wants to buy a motorcycle on credit. If the other spouse co-signs the loan, both spouses are directly liable to the creditor, even though only one of them rides the motorcycle and even though they think of the loan as solely his responsibility. In some situations, one spouse becomes liable for the other not by consent but rather by imputation. Suppose a married person defrauds a business associate and becomes liable in tort. If the tortfeasor acted as agent for the other spouse or on behalf of their marital partnership, then the other spouse is liable by imputation." Marie T. Reilly, *In Good Times and in Debt: The Evolution of Marital Agency and the Meaning of Marriage*, 87 Neb. L. Rev. 373, 374 (2008). Should one spouse be responsible for paying the bills of the other spouse who runs up credit card bills without the other's knowledge? The rule of spousal liability is more expansive in a few separate property states.

Connecticut General Statutes
Title 46B. Family Law, Chapter 815E. Marriage

§46B-37. Joint Duty of Spouses to Support Family. Liability for Purchases and Certain Expenses. Abandonment

(a) Any purchase made by either a husband or wife in his or her own name shall be presumed, in the absence of notice to the contrary, to be made by him or her as an individual and he or she shall be liable for the purchase.

(b) Notwithstanding the provisions of subsection (a) of this section, it shall be the joint duty of each spouse to support his or her family, and both shall be liable for:

(1) The reasonable and necessary services of a physician or dentist;

(2) hospital expenses rendered the husband or wife or minor child while residing in the family of his or her parents;

(3) the rental of any dwelling unit actually occupied by the husband and wife as a residence and reasonably necessary to them for that purpose; and

(4) any article purchased by either which has in fact gone to the support of the family, or for the joint benefit of both.

(c) Notwithstanding the provisions of subsection (a) of this section, a spouse who abandons his or her spouse without cause shall be liable for the reasonable support of such other spouse while abandoned.

(d) No action may be maintained against either spouse under the provisions of this section, either during or after any period of separation from the other spouse, for any liability incurred by the other spouse during the separation, if, during the separation the spouse who is liable for support of the other spouse has provided the other spouse with reasonable support.

STATUTORY INTERPRETATION QUESTION

Suppose a private nursing home accepts a patient and later learns that Medicaid will not cover all, or perhaps any, of the patient's bill (perhaps, for example, because the patient transferred substantial assets to her offspring just before entering the home). Can the patient's spouse be held liable for any unpaid portion of the bill under this statute? Cf. Wilton Meadows Ltd. P'ship v. Coratolo, 14 A.3d 982 (Conn. 2011) (holding that nursing home expenses do not come within the meaning of "article" in (b)(4)).

Though clauses (1) and (2) of paragraph (b) might operate when spouses are estranged (subject to the limitation of paragraph (d) for separated spouses), clauses (3) and (4), which go beyond the traditional conception of "necessaries," would seem to operate only when husband and wife are peaceably cohabiting, so whom do they protect? In Yale Univ. Sch. of Med. v. Scianna, 701 A.2d 65 (Conn. Super. 1997), the court clarified that paragraph (d) applies not only to protect a supporting spouse when a dependent spouse is the debtor, but also when a supporting spouse incurs liability and the creditor sues the dependent spouse.

See also North Shore Cmty. Bank & Trust Co. v. Kollar, 304 Ill. App. 3d 838 (1999) (noting that concept of "family expenses," for which both spouses are liable under the Illinois Rights of Married Persons Act, can include hospital and other medical care, funeral services, utilities, clothing including furs and jewelry, rent, and maid service; stating: "The purpose of the Act is to protect creditors."; but holding that the concept does not include a bank loan, regardless of how the borrowed money is used); Colo. Rev. Stat. §14-6-110 ("The expenses of the family and the education of the children are chargeable upon the property of both husband and wife, or either of them, and in relation thereto they may be sued jointly or separately.").

Community property states generally make the spouses' community property (i.e., anything earned by either of them during the marriage) liable for the debts of either spouse incurred during the marriage, with some exceptions. California even makes some community property (see if you can figure out which) liable for either spouse's *pre*-marital debts.

West's California Family Code
Division 4. Rights and Obligations During Marriage
Part 2. Characterization of Marital Property

§910. Community Estate; Liability for Debts

(a) Except as otherwise expressly provided by statute, the community estate is liable for a debt incurred by either spouse before or during marriage, regardless of which spouse has the management and control of the property and regardless of whether one or both spouses are parties to the debt or to a judgment for the debt. . . .

(b) "During marriage" . . . does not include the period during which the spouses are living separate and apart before a judgment of dissolution of marriage or legal separation. . . .

§911. Earnings of Married Persons; Liability for Premarital Debts

(a) The earnings of a married person during marriage are not liable for a debt incurred by the person's spouse before marriage. After the earnings of the married person are paid, they remain not liable so long as they are held in a deposit account in which the person's spouse has no right of withdrawal and are uncommingled with other property in the community estate, except property insignificant in amount. . . .

§913. Separate Property of Married Person; Liability for Debt

(a) The separate property of a married person is liable for a debt incurred by the person before or during marriage.

(b) Except as otherwise provided by statute:

(1) The separate property of a married person is not liable for a debt incurred by the person's spouse before or during marriage.

(2) The joinder or consent of a married person to an encumbrance of community estate property to secure payment of a debt incurred by the person's spouse does not subject the person's separate property to liability for the debt unless the person also incurred the debt.

§914. Personal Liability for Debts Incurred by Spouse; Separate Property Applied to Satisfaction of Debt

(a) Notwithstanding Section 913, a married person is personally liable for the following debts incurred by the person's spouse during marriage:

(1) A debt incurred for necessaries of life of the person's spouse while the spouses are living together. . . .

§915. Child or Spousal Support Obligation not Arising out of Marriage; Reimbursement of Community

(a) For the purpose of this part, a child or spousal support obligation of a married person that does not arise out of the marriage shall be treated as a debt incurred before marriage, regardless of whether a court order for support is made or modified before or during marriage and regardless of whether any installment payment on the obligation accrues before or during marriage.

(b) If property in the community estate is applied to the satisfaction of a child or spousal support obligation of a married person that does not arise out of the marriage, at a time when nonexempt separate income of the person is available but is not applied to the satisfaction of the obligation, the community estate is entitled to reimbursement from the person in the amount of the separate income, not exceeding the property in the community estate so applied. . . .

Section 910 is a very broad statement of community property liability for debts. Make a list of the types of debts it could include. Cf. In re Marriage of Leni, 144 Cal. App. 4th 1087 (Cal. App. 3 Dist. 2006) (holding that husband was not obliged when marriage dissolved to reimburse community for funds he used to care for his infirm mother, because husband's statutory obligation to support his mother was a "debt" for which the community was liable); Smaltz v. Smaltz, 82 Cal. App. 3d 568 (1978) (holding under statute in effect at that time that spouses' community property, including earnings of the wife, was liable for the husband's alimony obligation to his prior wife). Now make a list of the circumstances covered by the "except as otherwise provided" qualification. What exceptions do other code provisions make from this broad rule?

Based on these two lists, how would you counsel a client contemplating marriage? Imagine the client has a well-paying job and plans to marry a law student. Then reverse the roles. Add a prior divorce with resulting spousal and/or child support obligations for one of the parties. What kinds of personal circumstances are most worrying, in light of this liability rule? Is holding "the community" liable for the pre-marital debts of each spouse likely ever to affect anyone's decision about getting married?

STATUTORY INTERPRETATION QUESTIONS:

1. Does the California code require a debtor spouse to use his or her separate property to satisfy debts before community property is liable on the debts? Should it?

2. Suppose a couple is living in San Francisco, but then the wife takes a job in Los Angeles, buys a house there, spends most of each month there, and defaults on the mortgage, and then her husband decides he wants a divorce. Can the mortgage holder seek payment from money the husband earned and saved after his wife started the job in Los Angeles?

Spouses Who Are Not Cohabiting

As with the duty of sexual fidelity, clients contemplating divorce should be aware that liability for a spouse's debts might exist even following separation. The California statute above effects a contrary rule, terminating the liability of the community estate when spouses commence living separate and apart, though you have just seen that its meaning is not entirely clear. As reflected in the *Hayes* decision above, New Hampshire also exempts a spouse from liability in some circumstances following physical separation. In states where marital duties presumptively continue until a divorce decree issues, clients might wonder whether they can terminate the duties by agreement. Whether and to what extent a separation agreement can determine liability for debts to third parties is rather complex and state specific. In practice, one would become familiar with the particular rules where one practices. For a useful secondary source, see Andrea B. Carroll, *Incentivizing Divorce*, 30 Cardozo L. Rev. 1925 (2009).

A more common purpose of separation agreements is to establish post-separation maintenance for a dependent spouse. The agreement can impose a temporary support obligation just for the time between separating and a divorce decree, or it can settle the matter for good. In the absence of agreement, a spouse can petition a court for temporary support, to last until the time of divorce or until one or both parties successfully petition for termination or modification of the obligation. We return to this topic in Chapter 6.

2. *Property Ownership and Management*

Alicia Brokars Kelly, Money Matters in Marriage: Unmasking Interdependence in On-going Spousal Economic Relations

47 U. Louisville L. Rev. 113 (2008)

. . . For several decades now, as a vaguely stated ideal, marriage as a partnership has enjoyed widespread acceptance in American society and law. In significant ways, it has already been integrated nationwide into property distribution law governing termination of marriage by divorce or upon death. . . . However, except in the nine community property states, the theory has been strangely absent in modern intact marriage law. . . . [P]artnership theory views marriage as a sharing relationship and recognizes that both spouses meaningfully contribute economic and non-economic resources, although perhaps in different ways. . . . [It] logically follows . . . that wealth accumulated from labor during the relationship is presumed to be jointly owned. . . .

A significant part of the appeal of partnership marriage . . . is its reflection of the common understanding of the goals and operation of marriage held by couples themselves. . . . Notwithstanding dauntingly high divorce rates, couples entering marriage commonly see the relationship as an open-ended and serious commitment to a shared life, and they optimistically expect to stay together. . . . Research demonstrates that extensive sharing is viewed as a centrally important goal for marriage. . . . [H]esitance to share money is often interpreted as a lack of commitment to the relationship and a violation of mutual trust. . . . Couples don't necessarily combine all financial assets (although that is common); some money may be put in a communal pot and some kept separate. . . . [But] money in marriage is widely (although not always completely) shared, and spouses generally think of themselves as a joint financial team. . . .

Yet overwhelmingly, intact marriage law rejects this sharing orientation and, perversely, expresses the opposite view—it treats spouses as if they were single, as if their economic relations were unchanged by marriage. Holding on to an antiquated common law system, in the dominant law today governing spousal economic relations during marriage, formal legal title to wealth still matters very much. This hyper-individualistic view is most strongly evident in the majority approach to property ownership in marriage—in the aptly named "separate property" states. . . . The law of forty-one states provides that formal title confers legal ownership and power over property during an ongoing marriage. Usually, title is established with earnings from the employment market. The default rule in separate property states assumes that property is earned and owned individually during marriage, just as it is for single persons. As the owner, the titled spouse has the power to control and dispose of property without the consent of, or even notice to, the other spouse.

Separate property states will recognize a couple's choice to share wealth if they make that choice explicitly in a formal document of title reflecting joint ownership of a particular asset. . . . Joint bank accounts are very common and are particularly important, as they serve as a funnel for family money. Nonetheless, in separate property states, . . . [a]lthough joint accounts give accountholders access to funds, subject to various presumptions that differ from state to state, ownership of money in the account is based on who contributed it. . . . With the notable exception of tenancy by the entireties ownership, an individual-contributions approach generally establishes ownership for other jointly titled assets as well, such as real estate and stock accounts. The cumulative result is that individual ownership of property based on market wages is the prevailing model. . . .

For couples who are not in need of direct legal intervention in a dispute, the state of the law might seem an abstraction that plays no active role in their relationship. Yet even happy couples may feel the influence of law. . . . Whether we agree with law or not, law sends messages. . . . The messages embedded in the majority approach to marital property law are that spouses are solitary individuals unchanged by marriage and that individual market earnings and formal title control ownership. . . . The message for caregivers? Unpaid family work, still performed predominantly by women, is accorded zero value—even as it relates to wealth distribution within the family. . . . Renouncing the community orientation widely held by married couples, the dominant model of intact marriage law is solitary achievement based on market standards. . . .

This approach undermines family life in a number of critical ways. By devaluing community, law diminishes the autonomy of spouses who commit to sharing and interdependence as important values embraced and reflected in married life. . . . Also crucial, the market and family work interface produced by the separate property approach reproduces and perpetuates gender inequality. . . . Moreover, the regime creates an incentive to engage in self-interested, individually-based market work. It penalizes interdependent sharing for spouses who do not conform to the market model, counseling against doing it. . . . [T]he caregiving spouse's access to most of the family wealth depends solely on the willingness of the market spouse to share it. . . . It might erode a woman's sense of independence and perhaps her sense of self-worth . . .

But married couples experience the law's impact more overtly when they engage in transactions with third parties, or if spouses seek legal resolution of a dispute. Consider this example. . . . Imagine a typical couple in modern times, where the husband works full-time and the wife works part-time in the employment market. They have two school-age children, and the wife performs a disproportionate share of the care work for the family. . . . The couple has a joint bank account into which both parties contribute their wages and from which ordinary family expenses are paid. Although the joint bank account is managed by both spouses, the husband manages the modest accumulated family wealth, including the stock accounts, which, for ease of management, are titled solely in the husband's name. The husband has an adult brother with whom he is close, but who has always struggled financially. Although the wife cares for her brother-in-law, she thinks he is irresponsible with money. Without telling his wife, suspecting she would not approve, the husband gives his brother $5,000 from the couple's stock account as a gift. A year later, the wife discovers the gift. . . .

The husband is considered the owner of the stock accounts simply because his name is on them. He has complete legal power over the resource, without any obligation to seek consent of the non-titled spouse or any obligation of disclosure. . . . Unless her husband repents, the wife is stuck with his decision even if she strongly disagrees with it and is left without an acceptable alternative. She could seek a divorce. Encouraging divorce is not a desirable policy in general, but particularly so in a situation like this one where the couple may want to stay together and resolve the disagreement. Additionally, it is unlikely that she would be able to obtain a remedy in divorce proceedings, because the law of intact marriage generally governs transfers made during marriage—the titled spouse's unilateral power to act would be affirmed. . . .

Under the doctrine of necessaries, the untitled spouse, in theory, is allowed to pledge the other spouse's credit to purchase a necessary. A creditor—but not a spouse—has the right to sue to enforce the duty and collect the debt. . . . This option could be a means for an untitled spouse to stake a claim for her financial interests and for decision-making power in the marriage. . . . Predictably, this would fuel animosity between the spouses and could just bring the merchant into a couple's standoff. Moreover, the conduct would violate marital norms of interdependent sharing, cooperation, and trust. . . . Sensibly, merchants are very unlikely to voluntarily risk involvement by extending credit to the wife. . . .

The nine community property states have explicitly committed to the general ideal of marriage as a partnership, both in ongoing marriage and upon dissolution. . . . The law . . . provid[es] that spouses collectively own earnings that are produced in marriage, along with accumulated assets. . . . A partnership model affirms and facilitates interdependent sharing in marriage. Simultaneously, it recognizes the importance of caregiving and household work by according this work concrete economic value and an enforceable ownership entitlement. Further, shared and equal ownership promotes an equality-of-status ideal regardless of gender, and this, in turn, helps safeguard individual autonomy within marriage. . . .

Whether the benefits of an equal-ownership regime will be realized, however, also depends on the degree to which each spouse is accorded control over shared financial resources. Formal ownership is not enough. . . . Three different formally gender-neutral management systems exist today in community property states: (1) sole management, where legal control follows legal title; (2) unilateral management by either spouse, where each has power to act alone and without notice to the non-acting spouse; and (3) joint management, where mutual agreement is required.

The sole management approach mirrors the separate property system and thus generally vests control in the hands of the earner, leaving out the untitled spouse. The unilateral management approach has some appeal because it seems to provide an avenue for financial autonomy for each individual spouse. It is also easy to implement, because either spouse can act alone. However, as commentators have pointed out, this rule masks the greater power of the usually male dominant earner. As a practical matter, the commercial world will generally deal with the titled spouse; the untitled spouse will not be given authority, nor will her consent be voluntarily solicited. Within marriage, a more powerful spouse can make independent decisions that the management regime will validate. Additionally, like the separate property approach, both sole and unilateral management expose the market-disadvantaged spouse to the possibility that she will lose access to wealth she is (or should be) legally entitled to share, either because the wealth is transferred away or monopolized by a dominant spouse. This demonstrates how uniquely vulnerable spouses are in both separate property and community property systems, because one spouse often has power over the wealth of both of them, not just over an "individual share." Yet the fact of shared wealth is ignored, and is replaced with the fiction of an individual actor.

In contrast, the consensus decision-making system (as one commentator characterizes the joint management system) is compelling. Similarly attractive is tenancy by the entireties (available in only a subset of separate property states), because it has the same feature of shared control. . . . Shared control offers valuable protection against a mismanaging spouse, while also cultivating relational and individual benefits. Not surprisingly, having to reach agreement is a more demanding process than unilateral decision making, and may well trigger or reveal conflict. Yet research suggests that sharing control over money is good for marriage. . . . A recurrent collaborative decision-making process marks and augments the communal experience, and at the same time encourages each spouse to find his or her individual voice. . . . If a wife is given meaningful legal control over wealth, a door is left open for her to participate and express preferences in financial decisions and perhaps to shift consumption accordingly.

The robust advantages of joint consent, however, come with limitations. As noted, the sole and unilateral management options . . . do facilitate commercial transactions and everyday consumption. . . . [I]t is also likely that a sphere of autonomous decision making may be beneficial to spouses, "as it both preserves the ability of each spouse to act in the world as an individual and furthers trust by providing for spouses to demonstrate their genuine concern for one another." For some decisions, then, particularly those related to everyday consumption and managing a business, a spouse should be granted individual control in the commercial world. In these situations, unilateral control by either spouse is far preferable to sole management.

Undoubtedly taking into account some of these benefits and limitations, community property states have adopted a combination of management approaches that vary and depend on the nature of the transaction. Nonetheless, one approach dominates. The default rule in eight of the nine states is unilateral management, where "either" spouse can act. Texas is the loner, attaching sole management power to a broad class of assets that includes income, so that an earner is the manager as if he were single. . . .

There is a pattern of exceptions to the unilateral management rule among the community property states. Management powers follow title documents in three states. . . . Sole or primary management is the rule for community businesses in several states. Joint consent is commonly required for transfers of real estate, with three states also requiring agreement to purchase realty. Personal property (such as money and stock accounts) is not generally governed by joint management, although some states have limitations on unilateral gifts and on transfers of household furniture or personal effects. To mitigate the potential adverse effects of the unilateral management system, some states authorize remedies if control is co-opted by one spouse. States may allow an order for an accounting, for a spouse to add her name to the title of an asset, or for an action against a spouse for waste with the possibility of separating assets and debts. . . .

To make the equal-ownership rule meaningful, law must commit to a consensual-management model as the ideal. Requiring joint consent recognizes interdependence in marriage—providing protection to a vulnerable spouse at the same time it facilitates the couple relationship by encouraging communication and collaboration. . . . Aside from financial interests, joint consent must also be required if the transaction would seriously affect either spouse personally. Accordingly, default rules must require mutual agreement for transfers relating to realty (for encumbrances, sales, and purchases), including not only the family home and personal effects, but also for other major personal property transactions, such as the sale and purchase of securities and gifts that are not de minimis. "Major transactions" include transfers involving formal documents of title. . . . Whether a transaction is major could be further defined using either a flexible standard allowing for a fact-intensive analysis that examines the financial interests at stake relative to the financial status of the family, or using a more rigid rule defining "major" as a definitive dollar amount such as $1000, $2500, or $5000. . . .

During an ongoing marriage, the entitlement to share earnings and other marital property will be operationalized primarily through internal spousal negotiation and through spousal interactions in commerce. The option to seek legal intervention, however, must be available during an ongoing relationship if needed for dispute resolution. As a supplement to traditional litigation during an intact marriage, an alternative dispute resolution forum such as mediation is desirable, as it would provide an opportunity for discussing and resolving spousal disagreements in a cooperative setting. Alternatively, a generous statute of limitations is needed so that contested issues can also be raised upon death or divorce rather than during an ongoing marriage, thus mitigating the serious concern about damage to an intact marital relationship. . . .

Management rules are more salient in community property states, because there ownership regularly diverges from title. The nine community property states are Arizona, California, Idaho, Louisiana, Nevada, New Mexico, Texas, Washington, and Wisconsin. But such rules are also needed in common-law property states to determine who has what power with respect to jointly owned property. They are generally much the same, with an equal management rule applying to ordinary personal property, such as money in a bank account or household belongings, and a joint management rule applying to larger assets with title documents, such as a house or car.

The idea of creating a mechanism for married couples to mediate or have a third party resolve their financial disagreements is intriguing. In some non-Western cultures, it is common for spouses to bring a dispute to community leaders for resolution. Professor Oldham summarizes reasons in favor of doing so: "Some commentators . . . question the paternalism of refusing such a remedy. Others note that if a legal remedy is not provided, one spouse can still employ nonlegal methods to resolve a dispute, such as nagging, ceasing to perform household duties, withholding sex, threatening to separate, or committing violence; it is not clear that such dispute resolution methods are superior to judicial proceedings. . . . Even if few couples actually avail themselves of the remedy, its existence may encourage some recalcitrant spouses to obey the dictates of equal management." J. Thomas Oldham, *Management of the Community Estate During an Intact Marriage*, 56 LAW & CONTEMP. PROBS. 99 (1993). What considerations count against having state actors resolve or help marital disputes or give redress to someone whose spouse recklessly mismanaged their assets?

What is a fair distribution of wealth within marriage and at divorce is an immensely complicated issue. It is difficult from any perspective to explain why housework and/or child care are of equal financial value to any particular paid employment (and why their value would vary based on the income of the primary breadwinner). Then there is the policy question of whether the state should, by creating various protections for primary homemakers, facilitate dropping out of the paid workforce, or should instead encourage every person, married or not, to be as financially productive as possible. In addition, though Professor Kelly usefully identifies some values arising from mandatory joint decision making, how can we calculate whether those values outweigh the efficiency loss she acknowledges? That loss can include extra time in discussing proposed transactions and in having the second spouse meet with other parties and complete documents (imagine, for example, someone heavily invested in the stock market needing spousal approval for every trade). It can also include lost economic opportunities, if businesses prefer not to deal with married people as a result of such a joint-management rule. Her proposed regime might also generate resentment on the part of primary breadwinners, and that could produce marital conflict counteracting any gain in marital quality from cooperation. There is also the potential impact on marriage rates if the content of the default rules changes in a way disadvantageous or burdensome to wealthier people. Some might choose not to marry a lower-income partner. Others might insist on pre-nups as a result, to contract around the new default rules, and that might color the nature of the marriage in an adverse way. Notably, a pre-nuptial agreement waiving the equal ownership and joint management rules is not likely to alleviate the inefficiency problems with those rules, because businesses do not want to examine and rely on such agreements.

Professor Kelly's equal ownership proposal amounts more or less to extending the community property law that already exists in some states, into the great majority of states that have not adopted it. It is also an extension into the ongoing marriage of more or less the equitable ownership rule that the law applies even in "separate property states" if and when divorce occurs; equitable distribution law treats property acquired by either spouse's labor during the marriage as marital property to which both spouses have a claim. In addition, as she notes, most couples in separate property states put most of their property into joint ownership form, and with an equal/unilateral management rule the property is for all intents and purposes jointly owned. It is only if a spouse who was the predominant or sole contributor dies that there might be some question about the non-contributing spouse's share, and even then most states apply a presumption with spouses that the contributing spouse did intend true joint ownership. So the equal ownership proposal is far from radical. Her joint-management proposal might have a greater impact on couples' daily lives. Were you convinced it would be on the whole a positive one?

It is important to note also that married persons in community property states can own separate property—essentially anything not *earned during* the marriage, including property owned prior to the marriage and property acquired during marriage by gift or inheritance. This is reflected in §770 of the California statute below. (These types of property are also generally excluded from the marital property pie subject to division in common-law property states.) In addition, as §850 below indicates, couples in community property states can elect to convert ("transmute") community property into the separate property of one spouse at any time.

West's California Family Code
Division 4. Rights and Obligations During Marriage

Part 2. Characterization of Marital Property

§760. Community Property Defined

Except as otherwise provided by statute, all property, real or personal, wherever situated, acquired by a married person during the marriage while domiciled in this state is community property.

§751. Community Property; Interests of Parties

The respective interests of the husband and wife in community property during continuance of the marriage relation are present, existing, and equal interests.

§770. Separate Property of Married Person

(a) Separate property of a married person includes all of the following:

(1) All property owned by the person before marriage.

(2) All property acquired by the person after marriage by gift, bequest, devise, or descent.

(3) The rents, issues, and profits of the property described in this section.

(b) A married person may, without the consent of the person's spouse, convey the person's separate property.

§752. Separate Property; Interest of Parties

Except as otherwise provided by statute, neither husband nor wife has any interest in the separate property of the other.

§753. Exclusion of Spouse from Other's Dwelling

Notwithstanding Section 752 . . . , neither spouse may be excluded from the other's dwelling.

§850. Transmutation by Agreement or Transfer

. . . [M]arried persons may by agreement or transfer, with or without consideration . . . :

(a) Transmute community property to separate property of either spouse.

(b) Transmute separate property of either spouse to community property.

(c) Transmute separate property of one spouse to separate property of the other spouse.

§852. Requirements

(a) A transmutation of real or personal property is not valid unless made in writing by an express declaration that is made, joined in, consented to, or accepted by the spouse whose interest in the property is adversely affected. . . .

(c) This section does not apply to a gift between the spouses of clothing, wearing apparel, jewelry, or other tangible articles of a personal nature that is used solely or principally by the spouse to whom the gift is made and that is not substantial in value taking into account the circumstances of the marriage.

§1100. Community Personal Property; Management; Restrictions on Disposition

(a) Except as provided in subdivisions (b), (c), and (d) and Sections 761 and 1103, either spouse has the management and control of the community personal property, . . . with like absolute power of disposition, other than testamentary, as the spouse has of the separate estate of the spouse.

(b) A spouse may not make a gift of community personal property, or dispose of community personal property for less than fair and reasonable value, without written consent of the other spouse. This subdivision does not apply to gifts mutually given by both spouses to third parties and to gifts given by one spouse to the other spouse.

(c) A spouse may not sell, convey, or encumber community personal property used as the family dwelling, or the furniture, furnishings, or fittings of the home, or the clothing or wearing apparel of the other spouse or minor children which is community personal property, without the written consent of the other spouse.

(d) Except as provided in subdivisions (b) and (c), and in Section 1102, a spouse who is operating or managing a business or an interest in a business that is all or substantially all community personal property has the primary management and control of the business or interest. Primary management and control means that the managing spouse may act alone in all transactions but shall give prior written notice to the other spouse of any sale, lease, exchange, encumbrance, or other disposition of all or substantially all of the personal property used in the operation of the business (including personal property used for agricultural purposes), whether or not title to that property is held in the name of only one spouse. . . . A failure to give prior written notice shall not adversely affect the validity of a transaction nor of any interest transferred.

(e) Each spouse shall act with respect to the other spouse in the management and control of the community assets and liabilities in accordance with the general rules governing fiduciary relationships which control the actions of persons having relationships of personal confidence as specified in Section 721, until such time as the assets and liabilities have been divided by the parties or by a court. This duty includes the obligation to make full disclosure to the other spouse of all material facts and information regarding the existence, characterization, and valuation of all assets in which the community has or may have an interest and debts for which the community is or may be liable, and to provide equal access to all information, records, and books that pertain to the value and character of those assets and debts, upon request.

§1101. Claim for Breach of Fiduciary Duty; Court Ordered Accounting; Addition of Name of Spouse to Community Property; Consent of Spouse Not Required

(a) A spouse has a claim against the other spouse for any breach of the fiduciary duty that results in impairment to the claimant spouse's present undivided one-half interest in the community estate. . . .

(b) A court may order an accounting of the property and obligations of the parties to a marriage and may determine the rights of ownership in, the beneficial enjoyment of, or access to, community property, and the classification of all property of the parties. . . .

(c) A court may order that the name of a spouse shall be added to community property held in the name of the other spouse alone or that the title of community property held in some other title form shall be reformed to reflect its community character, except . . . :

(1) A partnership interest held by the other spouse as a general partner.

(2) An interest in a professional corporation or professional association.

(3) An asset of an unincorporated business if the other spouse is the only spouse involved in operating and managing the business.

(4) Any other property, if the revision would adversely affect the rights of a third person. . . .

(e) In any transaction affecting community property in which the consent of both spouses is required, the court may, upon the motion of a spouse, dispense with the requirement of the other spouse's consent if both of the following requirements are met:

(1) The proposed transaction is in the best interest of the community.

(2) Consent has been arbitrarily refused or cannot be obtained due to the physical incapacity, mental incapacity, or prolonged absence of the nonconsenting spouse.

(f) Any action may be brought under this section without filing an action for dissolution of marriage, legal separation, or nullity, or may be brought in conjunction with the action or upon the death of a spouse.

(g) Remedies for breach of the fiduciary duty by one spouse, including those set out in Sections 721 and 1100, shall include, but not be limited to, an award to the other spouse of 50 percent, or an amount equal to 50 percent, of any asset undisclosed or transferred in breach of the fiduciary duty plus attorney's fees and court costs. . . .

§1102. Community Real Property; Spouse's Joinder in Conveyances

(a) Except as provided in Sections 761 and 1103, either spouse has the management and control of the community real property, . . . but both spouses . . . must join in executing any instrument by which that community real property or any interest therein is leased for a longer period than one year, or is sold, conveyed, or encumbered.

(b) Nothing in this section shall be construed to apply to a lease, mortgage, conveyance, or transfer of real property or of any interest in real property between husband and wife.

(c) Notwithstanding subdivision (b): . . .

(2) The sole lease, contract, mortgage, or deed of either spouse, holding the record title to community real property to a lessee, purchaser, or encumbrancer, in good faith without knowledge of the marriage relation, shall be presumed to be valid. . . .

Imagine yourself operating under the management rules laid out here. Does the joint management aspect seem overly broad, or would you include even more things? For example, should there be a minimum value on gifts of community property that require joint consent? Should a parent need the other's written consent to bring some of their children's clothes to a consignment shop? What are the problematic cases about which the legislature was concerned? The case below illustrates the problems that can arise for third parties in larger transactions.

Rackmaster Systems v. Maderia

193 P.3d 314 (Ariz. Ct. App. 2008)

WEISBERG, Judge.

Patrick and Jane Maderia, husband and wife, appeal from the superior court's ruling . . . that Rackmaster Systems, Inc., of Bloomington, Minnesota could garnish an Arizona bank account belonging to both Patrick and Jane to satisfy a Minnesota judgment Rackmaster had obtained solely against Patrick. . . .

As president and Chief Executive Officer of TriStar International, Inc., an Arizona corporation, Patrick signed a credit agreement in 2001 with Rackmaster that stated: "Signature of this application constitutes a personal guarantee should this account become delinquent." Jane did not sign the credit application. TriStar defaulted on its obligation, and Rackmaster filed suit in Minnesota against TriStar, Patrick, and another entity. Jane was not named. . . . A Minnesota court entered a default judgment solely against Patrick in the amount of $23,110.98. In 2003, Rackmaster filed in Maricopa County [Arizona] Superior Court an affidavit of foreign judgment . . . and an application for a writ of garnishment, all of which named only Patrick. . . .

At the hearing, Patrick argued that he and Jane had been married and were residents of Arizona when the Minnesota court entered judgment against him, that their bank account was community property, and that Jane had never been named or served in the garnishment matter. Rackmaster asserted that the Minnesota judgment arose from a community pursuit, was a community debt, and was entitled to full faith and credit. Rackmaster conceded that the garnished account was community property but cited Arizona Revised Statute section 25-215(C), which provides that "[t]he community property is liable for a spouse's debts incurred outside of this state during the marriage which would have been community debts if incurred in this state."[2] . . .

In enacting statutes governing community property, the Arizona legislature has determined that, in most circumstances, either spouse can control and encumber the assets of the marital community. For example, A.R.S. §25-214(B) states: "The spouses have equal management, control and disposition rights over their community property and have equal power to bind the community." Furthermore, in most circumstances, A.R.S. §25-215(D) allows one spouse to contract debts for the community. However, it limits such power by providing in part that: "*Except as prohibited in §25-214*, either spouse may contract debts and otherwise act for the benefit of the community." . . . A.R.S. §25-214(C)(2) . . . states that

2. All property acquired by either spouse during marriage is presumed to be the community property of both. In addition, debts incurred during marriage by either spouse are presumed to be community debts, and one who asserts otherwise must produce clear and convincing proof to overcome the presumption.

when the instrument is a guaranty, the community will be bound only upon the signatures of both spouses.[5] . . .

[T]he purpose of A.R.S. §25-214(C) "is to protect one spouse against obligations undertaken by the other spouse without the first spouse's knowledge and consent" and . . . this purpose "would be frustrated if the husband . . . were able to charge the wife's interest in the community with the debts he guaranteed." Thus, whether the guaranty benefitted the community is beside the point. . . .

[T]here is no reason to reach a different conclusion when the creditor seeking to enforce a guaranty given by one Arizona spouse brings an out-of-state judgment to Arizona that if enforced would infringe the interest of the other spouse in community property. . . . "It makes no sense to allow a spouse to jeopardize the other spouse's property rights by going to another state and making a unilateral guarantee affecting that property." . . . Because the legislature clearly intended that A.R.S. §25-214(C)(2) protect the substantive rights of the non-signing spouse, we conclude that it is a substantive law that bars collection of the guaranteed debt from the community's property. . . .

In one sense, the Minnesota company is made no worse off by this decision than it would have been if the Maderias were Minnesota residents, because there, too, the wife's assets would not have been susceptible to garnishment for the husband's debts. Minnesota is a common-law property state, and so there, spouses are not liable for each other's debts (except for necessaries). See Minn. Stat. §519.05. On the other hand, if the Maderias lived in Minnesota, Patrick's income would be all his property, not half his wife's, so the entirety of his income would be subject to garnishment. If all the money in a joint bank account came from his income, a court would likely treat it as all his property.

In other contexts, failure to involve a spouse in a transaction invalidates the transaction. That spouse might seek to have the transaction undone in the context of a divorce action, if it is disadvantageous to him or her. However, although the purpose of the rule is to protect married individuals' property interests against misconduct or waste by their spouses, most of the reported cases in this area involve intact couples together trying to invalidate a transaction, on the grounds that one of them did not sign off on it, because it turned out to be a bad deal for both of them.

For example, in *Jesse v. Sanders* (Ariz. App. Div. 1 2007), a wife had signed an agreement to purchase several properties and had put money in escrow, but when she could not secure financing she tried to invalidate the agreement and get her money back, on the grounds that her husband had not signed. She might have succeeded, except that her

5. Section 25-214(C) states:

> Either spouse may separately acquire, manage, control or dispose of community property or bind the community, *except that joinder of both spouses is required in any of the following cases*:
>
> 1. Any transaction for the acquisition, disposition or encumbrance of an interest in real property other than an unpatented mining claim or a lease of less than one year.
> 2. Any transaction of *guaranty*, indemnity or suretyship.
> 3. To bind the community, irrespective of any person's intent with respect to that binder, after service of a petition for dissolution of marriage, legal separation or annulment if the petition results in a decree of dissolution of marriage, legal separation or annulment.

husband was deemed to have ratified the agreement by participating in the transaction in various ways other than signing—for example, by co-signing one of the checks to the escrow agent. In Geronimo Hotel & Lodge v. Putzi, 728 P.2d 1227 (Ariz. 1986), a husband had signed a lease as to a parcel of land he and his wife owned, but he later decided he did not want to lease the property. The lease per se was straightforwardly unenforceable, because the wife had neither signed nor ratified. The court explained: "Unlike a guarantee, a lease agreement cannot be performed by the signing spouse without the nonsigning spouse's consent." In that case, however, the husband had included a warranty in the lease, and the court, following the lead of Washington State courts, held that "contract provisions such as warranties that can be performed by the signing spouse without injuring the community should be enforceable against the signing spouse." The husband could therefore be found in breach of contract and liable for damages to the would-be tenant to the extent his separate property would allow. As a result of this ruling, businesses and others dealing with people who might be married gain some protection by insisting on a warranty clause. Is the other spouse really protected if all of the signing spouse's separate property is at risk? Of course, businesses can also simply ask whether the person they are dealing with is married, and if so whether the property at issue is community property, and if it is they can insist that both spouses sign the contract.

As to community property or jointly owned assets governed by an equal management rule, married persons receive little protection against unilateral action by a spouse. In theory, spouses have a fiduciary duty to one another, but courts do not welcome suits for breach of that duty. The only recourse might be in the context of a divorce action, but even there one generally must show intentional squandering or improper transfer of assets, not just mismanagement. For example, in Hague v. Hague, 427 N.W.2d 154 (Wis. Ct. App. 1988), a wife argued that the entirety of debts arising from speculative purchase of race horses by the husband should be allocated to the husband in their divorce proceeding, claiming that he had concealed the activity from her. The court rejected her argument, however, because she had not shown that her husband "intentionally squandered or destroyed marital property." The court also noted, by way of justification for the outcome, that "had the investments continued to be profitable under the same circumstances, [husband] would have had no right to claim the proceeds solely as his own." Is that symmetry rationale convincing, or would it be fair and preferable to require a spouse engaged in speculative investing to share any gains but bear the entire downside risk? If the wife had been aware of the husband's investments in horses during the marriage, would it not be better for her to be able to go to a court and obtain an order enjoining him from making the investments, rather than leaving her with divorce as the only recourse?

Migrating Couples

When couples move from one type of state (i.e., community property or common-law property) to the other, this does not change the character of assets acquired before the move. If, for example, a couple moved from California to Massachusetts, any community property they own remains such regardless of how it is nominally titled and without need for retitling. See Mass. Gen. Laws ch. 209 §29. Thus, in a subsequent divorce, each spouse's share of a community asset should be allocated to him or her, rather than being lumped together for distribution purposes with marital property acquired in the common law property state. If one spouse died, his or her share of a community asset would be in the estate, but the surviving spouse's share would not be, again regardless of title. Conversely, if a couple moved from Massachusetts to California, this would not convert any separately titled property earned during the marriage but before the move into community property.

As to any property acquired by effort *after* a couple's move in one direction or the other, the laws of the new state of residence govern. Thus, suppose an employer relocates a married employee from Massachusetts to California, and suppose that before and after the relocation the employee-spouse directs all her income into a bank account solely in her name. Income earned while she was a Massachusetts resident was and would remain entirely hers during the remainder of the marriage, but income earned after the move to California would be community property and hence only half hers. A portion of the money in her bank account would thereafter belong to her husband.

All of this presupposes that the couple has not entered into an agreement dictating a different treatment of their property and earnings, which couples are free to do in both community property and common-law property states.

3. *External Support*

So far in this section we have studied the financial relationship between spouses. Naturally, outside financial influences can also shape married life. Various financial benefits or burdens can attach simply to being married, which could strengthen or strain a couple's relationship, or to particular choices a couple might make, which could alter the decisions they make about their lives. Private entities can exert such influence. Parents and other family members might offer or withdraw financial assistance—in the form of inter vivos gifts or will bequests—as a result of a person's getting married, having a child, taking or leaving a job, relocating, etc. Employer-provided benefits, such as health insurance coverage for employees' family members, can make married life more comfortable and can make it easier for an employee's spouse to forego employment outside the home and for the couple to have children. Conversely, employers can strain employees' marriages and discourage child-bearing by imposing extreme work demands. Does it "take a whole village" to nurture a marriage?

In this section we look at what further efforts the state might make to support marriages and the freedom of married couples to live in the way they find most satisfying. The legal rules we have seen thus far in this chapter aim to prevent conduct by spouses that can seriously damage a marriage, such as adultery, inter-spousal violence, deprivation of basic physical needs, and illicit alienation of a spouse's property. But there are more minor things that can undermine a marriage, and the state could aim to optimize conditions for marital life rather than just ensure minimally acceptable conditions. With respect to the parent-child relationship, as we will see, the state arguably goes beyond the minimum, providing education, health care, day care subsidies, respite care and special educational services for children with special needs, extensive rehabilitative services for parents whose relationships with their children become dysfunctional, etc. To what extent do government policies materially support marriage and married couples' choices?

Financial Support

As noted in Chapter 2, federal tax policy supports and thereby encourages a form of married life in which one spouse (typically the wife) works principally as a homemaker, insofar as couples with greatly disparate incomes are better off tax-wise than they were collectively before marrying (if they had the same incomes then), whereas there is a "marriage penalty" for couples with roughly equal incomes. Thus, tax policy might be viewed as supporting not marriage per se, but rather traditional marriage. Looked at another way, the government aims to help all marriages succeed by providing financial support where it is needed, and it directs its support to those marriages thought to need it the most. One might suppose that couples with two incomes on average need less external financial support than couples with just one income. But see Martha T. McCluskey, *Taxing the Family Work: Aid for Affluent Husband Care*, 21 COLUM. J. GENDER & L. 109 (2011) (explaining that joint filing in practice principally benefits high-income single-earner couples and not so much lower-income single-earner couples).

In addition, there are direct government payments to people based on marital status. The military provides many benefits to spouses of employees, such as housing, medical care, and post-retirement payments. Social Security provides benefits to spouses of retired and disabled former workers.

There are also government welfare programs in which some married couples might participate. None are directed just at married people and almost all are limited to the poorest households, so they disproportionately serve single people. But for very-low-income married couples, subsidies for child rearing—for example, Temporary Assistance for Needy Families, the Child Care and Development Fund, the Children's Health Insurance Program, and the National School Lunch Program—do make it easier to choose to have children. In addition, some state support for child rearing is not limited to poorer families. Special education funding, tax exemptions for dependents, and many state educational and recreational programs are available to children of upper-income parents as well as poor parents. So for all married couples there is at least some government subsidy that facilitates a choice to have children.

Promoting Marriage Skills

Money is certainly relevant to marital happiness and endurance; financial strain is a primary cause of marital discord. But marriages need much more than money to succeed; the rich are not known for their marital success. Marital satisfaction depends very much on spouses' "providing emotional support, demonstrating affection, being sensitive, showing empathy, and giving comfort." Researchers have found that "dimensions of emotional expression provide the best correlates of marital satisfaction"—specifically, creating positive affect in daily interactions, being responsive to a spouse's desire for connection, demonstrating attentiveness to a spouse's experience, and showing fondness and admiration. They have also observed that males have lower emotional intelligence ("ability to identify and manage their own and other's emotions") and are socialized in such a way that on average they engage in the positive relationship behaviors just listed less than women do. Wall et al., *Husbands' Characteristics and Marital Friendship Behaviors: The Influence of Family Expressiveness, Gender Role Conflict, and Emotional Intelligence*, *in* Amato et al., VISION 2004: WHAT IS THE FUTURE OF MARRIAGE? 9-10 (2004).

Strategies for facilitating healthier marriages could therefore include marital education and counseling to encourage relationship-strengthening behaviors, and in recent decades private organizations have developed many kinds of marriage enhancement programs, as people have become increasingly open to outside assistance. Strategies might also include efforts to alter the socialization of boys, to foster emotional intelligence and expressiveness in them. Should the state be involved in such efforts?

Chapter 2 discussed efforts some states have made to promote pre-marital education. Government support of programs for couples during marriage has also been developing. The federal Personal Responsibility and Work Opportunity Reconciliation Act (PRWORA) of 1996 created the TANF funding program, and states may use TANF funds for programs to strengthen marriages, in order to reduce the number of children raised in single-parent homes. Professor Maldonado notes that "Oklahoma set aside $10 million in TANF funds for a marriage initiative that seeks to reduce the state's divorce rate and also provides marriage education workshops. . . . Arizona earmarked $1 million in TANF funds for marriage skills workshops, including a marriage handbook, and vouchers for low-income parents to use to attend marriage-skills training courses. Utah used TANF funds for a marriage-education video, marriage-enrichment materials, vouchers for counseling for low-income couples, and an annual marriage conference." Solangel Maldonado, *Illegitimate Harm: Law, Stigma, and Discrimination Against Nonmarital Children*, 63 FLA. L. REV. 345 (2011). Some studies of such programs have concluded that they are successful in improving couple communication and increasing marital satisfaction. See M. Robin Dion, *Healthy Marriage Programs: Learning What Works*, 15 FUTURE OF CHILDREN 139 (2005).

As noted in Chapter 2, some scholars have criticized government funding aimed at pushing single people into marriage. In addition, some have raised concern about government marriage preservation policies that are insufficiently sensitive to the problem of domestic violence. But helping healthy existing marriages survive might appear to be an unassailable undertaking. Some scholars nevertheless question whether the government should be attempting to influence private life and raise concerns about a hidden political agenda. For example, Professor Gustafson writes: "The boundary between politics and religion is fuzzy when it comes to the federal marriage promotion funding. Much of the federal grant money drawn from the Healthy Marriage and Fatherhood Initiative grants is flowing to faith-based organizations . . . [and] some of the organizations . . . are pushing for legislative reforms . . . to abolish no-fault divorce laws. . . . The design of the Healthy Family Initiative and Fatherhood Initiative simply expands government reach even further in an effort to regulate the fundamental choices and daily lives of individuals." Kaaryn Gustafson, *Breaking Vows: Marriage Promotion, the New Patriarchy, and the Retreat from Egalitarianism*, 5 STAN. J. CIV. RTS. & CIV. LIBERTIES 269, 291-296 (2009). If you were a legislator, would you support a program providing counseling vouchers to married couples? If so, would you allow recipients to use the vouchers for counseling provided by religious organizations? Would you require that counselors accepting vouchers respond in a particular way to evidence of domestic violence—for example, prohibiting them from urging wives to be more submissive or requiring them to admonish abusers that use of physical force to control a spouse is never acceptable, regardless of their religious beliefs?

Trying to teach adults to express their feelings more and in a healthier way, and to communicate better more generally, might be less effective than training people to do this starting in childhood. Would you support a new state policy to promote emotional intelligence and expressiveness through the elementary school curriculum in public schools, with a special emphasis on training boys to be more attentive to and able to discuss feelings? The prevailing approach in schools today appears to be the opposite, to eliminate any potential cause of inter-personal disagreement—for example, by means of school uniforms and removal of sensitive subjects from the curriculum—and to punish participants in conflicts rather than facilitate problem solving and reconciliation through dialogue.

Employment Regulation

An additional way government might aim to strengthen marriages is by ensuring that couples can spend substantial time together. Neither money nor communication ability is of much use if married people are overwhelmed with work demands. On the other hand, having too little work can strain a marriage. This is true not only when a couple has too little income to support the lifestyle they seek, but also when either spouse is unable to realize her or his work aspirations. And then there is the fairness issue—that is, whether a couple perceives the division of paid and unpaid work between them as fair. An ideal state of affairs, in terms of optimizing conditions for marital success, might be one in which both spouses in a marriage are in every sense able to engage in paid employment as much as each wishes while also being able and inclined to devote substantial time to their relationship and to family responsibilities. To what extent does the law promote such an ideal?

Julie C. Suk, Are Gender Stereotypes Bad for Women? Rethinking Antidiscrimination Law and Work-Family Conflict

110 Colum. L. Rev. 1 (2010)

In the United States, the work-family conflict has historically been framed as a problem for equality and antidiscrimination law. . . . [T]he two main federal statutory frameworks that address work-family conflict [are] the Family and Medical Leave Act (FMLA) and Title VII of the Civil Rights Act. . . . [O]ne of the stated goals of the FMLA is to "promote the goal of equal employment opportunity for women and for men." . . . [I]t entitles covered employees to twelve weeks of unpaid leave annually to care for a newborn baby or adopted child, an ill family member, or their own serious health condition. The employee is entitled to be restored to the same job upon return, or to a job with equivalent pay, benefits, and other terms and conditions of work. The federal statute does not distinguish between maternity and paternity leave. . . .

Legal scholars have criticized the FMLA for being too limited. . . . First, the statute defines "eligible employee" in a way that excludes many American employees from coverage. To be eligible, an employee must work for an employer who employs at least fifty people within a seventy-five mile radius of the workplace. Furthermore, to be entitled to leave, an employee must have worked for the same employer for 1,250 hours in the previous year. This effectively excludes part-time workers, even those who work up to twenty-five hours a week. . . . 89.2% of U.S. employers are not covered by the FMLA, and only 58.3% of American workers work for covered employers. And due to the minimum hour provision, even fewer of those workers are actually covered. Second, the FMLA is underutilized by covered employees because the leave guaranteed by the statute is unpaid. Only sixteen percent of employers offer full pay during periods of maternity-related leave, and many employees who are covered by the FMLA do not take the leave to which they are entitled. The most common reason for not taking available leave is the inability to afford it. . . .

Title VII's prohibition of discrimination on the basis of sex has historically played the central role in enabling women to obtain maternity leave. . . . [T]he Pregnancy Discrimination Act of 1978 (PDA) . . . amended Title VII to clarify that discrimination "because of sex" included discrimination "on the basis of pregnancy." . . . It also made clear that the exclusion of pregnancy from sickness and disability programs violated Title VII. . . . As a result of the PDA, some fifty-two percent of female employees in large enterprises now receive some wage replacement during maternity leave under their employer's temporary disability insurance plan. . . . From 1992 to 2007, charges filed by individuals alleging pregnancy discrimination increased by sixty-five percent . . . largely fueled by charges filed by women of color. . . . Recent pregnancy discrimination settlements have required employers to grant seniority credit to women for time spent on pregnancy or maternity leave. . . .

Recent litigation has given rise to a new legal theory of discrimination on the basis of sex: "family responsibilities discrimination" (FRD). When an employee, male or female, is treated adversely because of his or her family responsibilities, such practices can constitute FRD in violation of Title VII. . . . [T]he EEOC in 2007 . . . issued an Enforcement Guidance on "Unlawful Disparate Treatment of Workers with Caregiving Responsibilities." . . . The concept of FRD has its origins in a 1971 Supreme Court case holding that an employer could incur Title VII liability by rejecting female job applicants because they have preschool age children. . . . FRD cases have a greater than fifty percent win rate, a rate significantly higher than the 1.6% win rate in race and gender employment discrimination cases. . . .

[I]n her influential book UNBENDING GENDER: WHY FAMILY AND WORK CONFLICT AND WHAT TO DO ABOUT IT, Joan Williams argued that . . . the work-family conflict is a consequence of designing the workplace around masculine norms. Employers tend to envision an ideal worker who is able to work full-time, move when the job requires it, and take little time off. This ideal is "masculine" because the role relies on the worker's access to a stay-at-home spouse who raises the children. . . . Williams' second account is the "maternal wall" theory of FRD. The "maternal wall" refers to the hostility women experience when they return to work after having a baby. . . . [E]mployers presume that a mother, particularly a mother of a young child, will have more family responsibilities than other workers and will prioritize those responsibilities over her work. Based on [this], women with young children are passed over for promotions and other opportunities. . . . In practice, the "maternal wall" theory, rather than the "masculine ideal worker" theory, has dominated FRD litigation under Title VII. . . .

Although women bring the vast majority of claims alleging discrimination on the basis of caregiving responsibilities, men have also successfully brought claims. . . . Gender stereotypes include the assumption that . . . men are not caregivers and are therefore lying if they demand the parental or family care leave to which they are statutorily or otherwise entitled. . . .

[P]olitical debates about legislative and regulatory reform of family and medical leave are going nowhere. . . . [E]mployers and industry groups tend to oppose any expansion of family and medical leave, especially paid leave, on the grounds that existing FMLA entitlements are already too burdensome and costly. . . . [E]mployers' most serious complaint about the FMLA arises in opposition to intermittent leave, most often taken to care for an employee's own illness, rather than to care for babies or other family members. . . . FMLA functions primarily as a national unpaid sick leave policy, rather than as a source of pregnancy, maternity, or paternity leave. . . . [C]osts arise from the unpredictability of both the timing and the length of the leave. For childbirth and newborn care, by contrast, employers usually have advance notice of at least thirty days, and the leave is usually taken for a predictable, set period of time. . . . Second, medical leave for an employee's own illness raises the potential for abuse and the accompanying suspicion of abuse, which do not exist in the context of childbirth and newborn-care leave. . . . Nonetheless, organizations devoted to the interests of women and families tend to be as ardent in support of existing medical leave rights under the FMLA as they are in support of rights that directly affect work-family balance. . . .

The European approach demonstrates that it is possible to be generous with maternity and parental leave without being equally generous with medical leave. . . . A 1992 EU directive . . . required at least fourteen weeks of maternity leave . . . [which] "must include compulsory maternity leave of at least two weeks allocated before and/or after confinement . . ." [and] measures to ensure that pregnant workers can receive paid time off of work for prenatal care. Furthermore, . . . the directive requires member states to adopt laws protecting employees from dismissal from the beginning of their pregnancy until the end of their maternity leave, except in "exceptional cases not connected with their condition." . . .

Sweden has pursued the explicit purpose of bringing about a more equitable division of labor within families and homes. . . . The Parental Leave Act provides for maternity leave for female employees in connection with childbirth or breastfeeding, but paid parental leave is available to both mothers and fathers. The maternity leave consists of job-protected leave for fourteen weeks, seven of which may be used prior to the due date. . . . The Parental Leave Act enables Swedish parents to take "full leave for the care of a child until the child reaches eighteen months, irrespective of whether the parent receives parental benefit." The parental benefit is paid by the state, pursuant to the National Insurance Act, for up to 480 days that a parent forgoes gainful employment to look after a child. The 480 days of pay are allocated per child, to be shared by the parents. Thus, in a two-parent household, each parent is entitled to 240 days of the benefit. One parent may transfer all but sixty days of his or her allocation to the other parent. In other words, if only the mother takes leave, the family's total allocation of parental benefits in connection with care for one child is reduced to 420 days, and the father's sixty days of leave are lost to the family. Furthermore, as of July 2008, there is a "gender equality bonus" in the form of a tax rebate, with greater rebates for parents who share the leave as evenly as possible. The Parental Leave Act also makes it possible for parents to reduce their working hours during the period that they receive the parental benefit, with a proportionate reduction of the benefit. . . .

Every child who lives in Sweden is entitled to a child allowance beginning the month after birth. The allowance . . . is paid monthly until the child reaches the age of sixteen. The Swedish government also provides a childcare allowance for parents who care for sick or disabled children in their homes. . . . Like France, the Swedish state provides extensive support for daycare and early childhood education. . . . Every child over the age of one year is legally entitled to public childcare and preschool. . . . Over half of all preschool employees have university degrees in preschool education. . . .

Like France, Sweden has a sick leave regime that is separate from its family leave regime. . . . In Sweden, the law effectively allows workers to take paid sick leave for up to seven days whenever they deem it necessary, since employers can only require medical certification for absences lasting longer than a week. The first day of sick leave is unpaid, but the next fourteen days are paid by the employer at a rate of eighty percent of the employee's wages. . . . The employer's obligation to pay ends after two weeks. At that point, the worker is entitled to the government's sickness benefit, equal to eighty percent of the employee's usual wages. . . . Ten percent of the Swedish work force is on sick leave at any given time. A[] study included survey data in which more than sixty percent of employees said they had taken sick leave when they were not really sick and felt there was nothing wrong with doing so. . . . But, because sick leave and family leave are completely separate legal entitlements with separate administrative regimes, controversies about sick leave excess do not cast doubt on the legitimacy of Sweden's generous and ever-expanding family-friendly policies. . . .

In the United States, mandatory maternity leave constitutes discrimination on the basis of sex, violating Title VII and the Constitution. . . . Indeed, one widespread practice to which the PDA offered a remedy was employers' policies forcing women to take unpaid leaves of absence after they announced their pregnancies. . . . In the U.S., it is assumed that restricting women's choice about the length of maternity leave undermines their equality. But . . . [w]hen maternity leave is optional, employers can pressure all women to take shorter leave, or hire only those women they believe will take shorter leave. . . . [W]hile France, Sweden, and all other EU countries require women to take maternity leave for at least two weeks, none of these regimes require men to take paternity leave. . . . [Yet] France and Sweden boast higher rates of female labor market participation and smaller gender wage gaps [than the U.S.]. These outcomes challenge the American wisdom that all gender stereotypes are bad for women. . . .

What explains the greater persistence of gendered work versus family responsibilities divisions in the United States?

Katharine K. Baker, The Stories of Marriage

12 J.L. & Fam. Stud. 1 (2010)

. . . [O]ne of the advantages of marriage is that it allows for a division of labor and an allocation of roles within households. This role division provides stability for the household, for the individuals within it and for society as a whole. In the vast majority of households, this role division is also gendered. As Sarah Berk showed in her classic book, The Gender Factory, standard economic explanations for how and why unpaid work might be divided in a household cannot explain the social reality of how work is divided in households. Gender can. Gender predicts who does what, how much each married partner does and why husbands and wives do not negotiate more over who does what or how much. Couples do not fight over what jobs they will do because the allocation is so patterned into who they are as gendered selves. And the more those gendered work patterns are replicated, the more entrenched gender roles become.

Thus, the home and the marriages that define it not only reflect gender, they create it. . . . Marriage increases the amount of domestic work that women do and decreases the amount that men do. Married women, regardless of whether they also work outside the home, do much more household work than their husbands. . . . Marriage, particularly marriages with children, decrease women's commitment to paid work and increase their commitment to unpaid work. A strong majority of married mothers work outside the home, but . . . mothers average 67% of the unpaid work in a household, while fathers average 64% of the paid hours for a household. Mothers do twice as much child care as fathers. . . . Women with the strongest commitment to paid labor . . . still reported working almost 500 fewer hours per year than men. . . .

Most women who currently make the choice to do less paid work were raised during what might be described as a time of maximum gender equality, with all the benefits that Title VII, Title IX, and constitutional gender equality doctrine afforded them. . . . One study found that . . . "[e]ven wives with graduate and professional degrees do not usually work full time if their husband's income exceed[s] $75,000." . . . The labor supply curve for married women is very elastic, yet it is starkly inelastic for married men. If anything, marriage increases men's commitment to the paid labor force because if their wives choose not to do paid work or do less of it, married men do more of it. Thus, marriage propels men into the paid labor force, even as it offers women a path out of it.

Neither men nor women seem particularly upset by this differential response to marriage. Despite their spending significantly different amounts of time on paid and unpaid work, married mothers and fathers report "feeling very successful in balancing work and family life." Married fathers are more likely than married mothers to report making sacrifices in family time for the sake of their job, but they are also slightly more likely to report making sacrifices in their job for the sake of the family. . . . Married mothers, who work the fewest paid hours, are the most content with their role balance.

The gendered differential in time allocation and married parents' satisfaction with it does not conform particularly well with what parents say they believe about a gendered division of work. Of people born between 1965 and 1981, 82% believe that "both parents should be equally involved in care giving." . . . Also interesting, is the correlation between belief in gender egalitarianism and gendered work patterns. Education level is highly correlated with belief in gender equality, as is income level. Yet, the more wealth a married couple has, the more profound their gender specialization tends to be. What can account for a feeling of success if one's behavior so clearly deviates from one's beliefs about gender equity?

One answer may be capaciousness in the term "equality." It is not precisely clear what people mean when they say that both parents should share equally. Perhaps people mean that the investment in caretaking should be comparable, or equal-on-major-decision-making, or at least close. . . . Another reason . . . is that they underestimate the importance of gender in their own lives. Women may feel like they have successfully negotiated a paid/unpaid balance even though they do twice as much unpaid work as their spouses because norms of motherhood encourage them to do so much unpaid work. . . . Men may feel comfortable doing so much less unpaid work in the home because masculinity norms strongly encourage them to participate in the workforce. . . . "[B]readwinning has remained the great unifying element in fathers' lives. Its obligations . . . shape their sense of self, manhood and gender." . . .

The importance of gender roles is evident in the incidence of marriage as well. Data collected on those who do not marry suggests that marital gender roles are more robust than marriage itself. Women who are likely to earn equal to or more than their husbands are much less likely to marry. This phenomenon is most profound at either end of the income scale. Studies of unmarried poor women indicate that though many of these women want to marry and have turned down marriage proposals from men, they remain single because they cannot find a suitable spouse. A suitable spouse, for them, would be one who would remain faithful, stay employed, and provide for the family. . . . High-earning women have a related problem. One study found that for women between the ages of forty and forty-four, the percentage who have never married increases with education for every year beyond one year of college. This may be because, like poor women, high-earning women seek men who can perform the traditional provider role and the more women provide for themselves, the higher the standard they will set for their prospective spouses. Alternatively, it may be that men do not want to relinquish the traditional marital role and, therefore, prefer not to marry women who might earn as much as them. It may be both. . . .

The prevalence of gendered marital roles is often thought to be beyond the law's reach. The law—and many people—view the marital relationship as a private one, entitled to a norm of non-interference. An individual couple's decision to specialize along gender lines probably feels personal to them and a function of their unique attributes as a couple. . . . Legal attempts to interfere with a couple's allocation of marital roles would probably strike many as impermissibly invasive. Yet the gender patterns that continue to reproduce themselves in these seemingly private relationships have indisputable social force. . . . [B]y facilitating gender differentiation, the social institution of marriage helps reify gender roles. . . .

It is relatively straightforward determining the relative involvement of men and women in paid labor. Less straightforward is determining how much men and women engage in unpaid labor for the good of the family, because that concept is rather vague and there are a great variety of things that might be considered labor of a sort for the family. Most studies attempting to quantify the relative devotion of husbands and wives to unpaid labor ask couples about a limited set of activities, such as cleaning the house, preparing meals, and getting the children dressed. Bias might cause them to leave out some tasks more likely to be performed by one gender or the other—for example, managing investments, planning travel, and making repairs. Would a more accurate picture of unpaid labor emerge if researchers instead asked how much time each spouse spends on leisure activities, such as watching television, talking with friends, sleeping, and exercising? Would it be easy to define what counts as a leisure activity?

Is it an appropriate role of the state to seek to eliminate gendered attitudes and to change people's preferences about family life? Should state policies and laws affecting marital relationships be based on what people choose, what people say they want, what the government or scholars think people really want at a deeper level, or what policy makers think is best for the future of our society regardless of what people today want? Are happiness and endurance the wrong criteria of a "good" marriage? Surprisingly, a 2007 study showed that desire for full-time work actually declined substantially among mothers in the preceding decade, and the percentage of stay-at-home mothers who believed that not working at all outside the home was ideal for them rose substantially. The survey also found that 41 percent of the general population viewed the trend toward more mothers working outside the home as a bad thing for society, and only 22 percent viewed it as a good thing. Forty-two percent said the ideal situation for children is that their mothers not work outside the home. See *Fewer Mothers Prefer Full-Time Work*, Pew Research Center Report (2007).

In another writing, Professor Baker acknowledges the biological explanation for gendered employment/homecare patterns that many people invoke, but questions whether contemporary public policy should rest on evolutionary history.

Katharine K. Baker, The Problem with Unpaid Work

4 U. St. Thomas L.J. 599, 601-605 (2007)

Evolutionary biology provides a very straightforward explanation for why women and men devote different amounts of energy to unpaid caretaking. . . . A mother, at least a mammalian mother, invests much more in every gamete than does a father because much more energy goes into making one egg than one sperm. A mother, at least a mother in any species that fertilizes and gestates internally, must also invest substantially in feeding and protecting the embryo before it is ever born. . . . At birth, biology and numerous cultural adages tell us that because fertilization happens internally, a male can never be completely sure that he is the father of a child. Because he can never be sure that any given child does carry his genetic material, he is less likely to invest in a born child than is a mother who, because she gave birth to the baby, knows that the child carries her genetic material. . . . In addition, human mothers used to always, and now usually, nurse infants. The process of nursing requires the mother to spend huge amounts of time with the child; it helps the mother feel close to the child, and it soothes the child. The child becomes used to being soothed by the mother. The mother develops child-specific expertise that makes her particularly good at soothing the child. Once the mother clearly has greater child-specific expertise, it often seems more efficient for her to care for the child because she is simply better at it than is someone who has not had the opportunity to nurse and bond with the child. Thus, biology provides an uncomplicated and well-known narrative that can readily explain why women are more likely to take care of children than are men.

The biological story also fleshes out why men may be more likely to engage in paid work. Men further their own genetic goals by demonstrating their own success or potential for success. Men are attractive to women when they appear to be able to provide ample resources for offspring. The more a man demonstrates his prowess vis-à-vis other men, the more a woman will feel confident of that man's ability to protect her and her offspring. Thus, . . . men care about resources and status; women care about babies.

There may be much to criticize in this highly abbreviated biological account, and there are very sound reasons not to use evolutionary biology too comprehensively when describing how human beings behave today. Nonetheless, I think it is important to acknowledge the biological explanation of the gendered division of familial work because so many people believe it is relevant. Ask any parent shortly after the birth of his or her first child whether he or she thinks there is a biological component to attachment and, in my experience, both men and women will say (usually in hushed tones) "yes." Very successful, professional women who seem to defy many biological norms often invoke biology to explain their choices to opt out of, or cut back substantially from, their paid labor. People speak reluctantly about biology either because they have been taught to believe that biology is not destiny or because they think it defeatist to assume that biology plays such a strong role in determining our predispositions. Nonetheless, the biological explanation continues to surface.

This reticence people display for the biological argument is understandable given the historical misuse of biology, but the reluctance is misplaced. The fact of biological predisposition in no way condones the propriety or inevitability of biological roles. . . . [T]he fact that caretaker and provider roles may be rooted in biological differences in no way suggests that we must continue to let those roles map onto lived differences. After all, biological predisposition may explain many things—rape, sexual harassment, child abuse—and virtually no one uses that predisposition to justify those activities. The law's job, and society's job, is to structure laws and norms that we endorse as good, fair and beneficial regardless of whether we have to buck biological predisposition to do so.

The problem is ascertaining what we think of as good, fair and beneficial when it comes to the division of unpaid work. Unlike rape, sexual harassment and child abuse, which are all wrong according to anyone's moral code, the disproportionate division of household labor is not so obviously wrong. Women do not work that much more than men; they just work at different jobs. It may be wrong that men get market wages for their work when women do not, though . . . many women do get paid by their husbands for the work they perform in the house. Other women, at least women in other countries, get state subsidies for the work they do in the household. Thus, much of women's unpaid work is compensated, just not by the market. This makes it particularly hard to identify the wrong in the disproportionate distribution of unpaid work. . . .

Experience in Sweden and some studies of couples in the United States show that wives' employment and husbands' assumption of greater responsibility for child rearing increase marital stability and wives' happiness, though they might not alter the quality of the marital relationship. See, e.g., Schoen et al., *Wives' Employment and Spouses' Marital Happiness*, 27 J. FAM. ISSUES 506 (2006). The greater gender equality in paid work and assumption of family responsibilities in Sweden appears to be a result not just of the legal rules for parental leave that Professor Suk described, but also of a broader and conscious societal effort to redefine masculinity. See Katrin Bennhold, *In Sweden, the Men Can Have It All*, N.Y. TIMES, June 9, 2010 (describing changes in advertising and in the books used in schools, to eliminate gender stereotypes, and noting that "85 percent of Swedish fathers take parental leave. Those who don't face questions from family, friends and colleagues."). Can and should governments in the United States undertake a project of redefining masculinity? Professors Williams and Tait suggest that economic forces might have this effect, as the transformation from a manufacturing to a service economy and the disproportionate loss of manufacturing jobs during the recent recession have severely reduced the number of traditional male jobs and elevated the unemployment rate for men, thereby undermining "critical psychological components of manhood and, equally important, deeply ingrained ideas about male dominance in the job market." As "women became privileged earners and competitive labor-market players, men became ineffective, unemployed, and feminized targets of workplace hostility and discrimination." Joan Williams & Allison Tait, *"Mancession" or "Momcession"? Good Providers, A Bad Economy, and Gender Discrimination*, 86 CHI.-KENT L. REV. 857, 862-863 (2011).

Though wives on average do more housework (as defined by researchers) than husbands (17 hours vs. 13 hours per week according to this study), husbands on average do more housework than single men (13 hours vs. 8 hours). See *Exactly How Much Housework Does a Husband Create?*, sciencedaily.com, Apr. 8, 2008. So men should not, and perhaps do not, get married thinking this will reduce their housework burden. Women also do more housework after marriage than before (17 hours vs. 12 hours). The addition of children likely explains much, if not all, of the greater collective time commitment to housework after marriage.

An additional critique of existing employment policy and law is that they reflect a class and race bias. Professor Dowd articulates this concern and also identifies additional areas of the law, not typically thought of as connected to family policy, that impact family life.

Nancy Dowd, Bringing the Margin to the Center: Comprehensive Strategies for Work/Family Policies

73 U. Cin. L. Rev. 433 (2004)

. . . Equality principles require that work/family policy and strategies also pay close attention to race and class inequalities as well as the more common attention to gender inequality. . . . The core insight of intersectionality and antiessentialist feminist legal theory is that gender does not operate in isolation, but rather is significantly differentiated based on its intersections with other important social identifiers that translate into individual and group privileges and inequalities. Most significantly, gender interacts with race and class. Women's social position and issues across those intersections are different: the work/family issues of middle-class white women are not the same as middle-class women of color; the challenges for working-class women of color are not the same as those of working-class white women. Intersectionality also points to the interaction of privilege and markers for discrimination and inequality. For example, gender analysis alone tends to presume male privilege. Intersectionality exposes the trumping of male privilege in some respects for men of color, and the presence of privilege among upper-class white women. . . .

Race is the core inequality—although not the only one—that we should keep in mind in addressing work/family issues from a feminist, hence gendered, lens. . . . When we identify the familiar gender patterns of work and distribution of family responsibilities and the needs of children for family care, we need to ask: "Where is the racism in this? Where are the racial patterns and inequalities in this?" . . . Work/family should not be seen as a "gender" issue, where gender becomes code for "white" and "middle or upper class." . . . This is particularly important in work/family policy since historically and presently, privileged, predominantly white women have advanced while being complicit in the ongoing subordination of women of color. . . . Those with the strongest voices, who more typically are at the center of the room, often tend to be those who can count on privilege to remove some barriers and problems, as well as insure that their voices are heard. Bringing the margin to the center requires that those most marginalized be identified and not spoken for, but listened to and empowered . . . so that their needs, their voice, can be heard and that those needs be made the center of policy and strategy, the first priorities to be achieved. It requires that the process of coalition building be one of giving up power and privilege in order to achieve equality. . . .

Welfare policies, for example, remain stingy and punitive, reflecting an assumption that the poor are responsible for their poverty, while efforts to help the middle class are cast as essential supports to the bedrock families on which our country depends. . . . Housing and education, along with jobs, have been the bulwark of persistent racial inequality. Housing segregation has remained constant, and has even increased in some areas, significantly contributing to ongoing educational inequality. . . . If policy continues to be class defined (e.g., unpaid family leave, minimal support for quality childcare or universal preschool, lack of universal healthcare, lack of universal, quality, affordable after-school care), then work/family conflict will persist or even increase for low-income families, while it may be eased for middle-class families. The burden of that class-defined policy falls directly on children, and disproportionately on children of color. . . .

Is the Family and Medical Leave Act's mandate of unpaid leave effectively a requirement that employers hold jobs open for wealthy white wives while they have babies?

Other Determinants of Marital Happiness

Think of all the things that might make you fall in love with and want to share a life with another person. It stands to reason that the disappearance of any of those things would diminish your enthusiasm for the relationship. Some laws and policies discussed above might address that concern with respect to some characteristics, such as income, communication, and parenting inclination. As to some common aspects of mate attractiveness, though, it is socially difficult even to have a discussion, let alone to propose public policies aimed at preserving them. For example, would you feel comfortable having a conversation in class about changes in men's and women's physical attractiveness in middle age, about whether spouses have a personal responsibility to make themselves fit and well dressed, and about whether the state should do anything to encourage married people to improve their appearance? Cf. Meltzer et al., *Marriages Are More Satisfying When Wives Are Thinner Than Their Husbands*, 2 Soc. Psychol. & Personality Sci. 416-424 (2011). What about physical or mental health problems that could have been avoided, either of which could severely strain a marriage? As noted at the beginning of the chapter, divorce law has the potential to influence behavior during marriage, by making particular benefits at divorce hinge on such behavior. Should the things just mentioned factor into property distribution at divorce?

4

STATE REGULATION OF THE PARENT-CHILD RELATIONSHIP

Parent-child relationships resemble marital relationships in several ways that might support an assumption that similar legal rules should govern the two relationships. Both relationships usually entail living in the same household and cooperating to ensure it operates satisfactorily. As such, both create opportunities for mutually gratifying closeness and for intense conflict. People derive important emotional and psychological benefits from being in either relationship when it functions properly—that is, from being a spouse, an offspring, or a parent. Usually there is between the parties to both relationships a physical asymmetry and an asymmetry of financial contribution to the household. In part because of the former, one party in each relationship is at greater risk than the other of incurring physical injury. In part because of the latter, generally one party in each type of relationship controls most of the resources and the other party is dependent on the other for provision of material goods. In both types of relationships, it is possible that one party will at some time be completely dependent, because of physical or mental limitations, but typically for a substantial portion of both relationships both parties are largely self-sufficient.

As to both relationships, entrance entails opportunity costs—that is, forming the relationship with one particular person can limit opportunities for having that kind of relationship with other persons. This cost, though, varies considerably across the various roles. It seems greatest for children; the law traditionally has limited to two the number of parents one may have, parents can monopolize children's upbringing, and it is rare for legal parents to be replaced. The opportunity cost seems least for parents; time and resources for child bearing and rearing are limited, but the law imposes no numerical limit on how many children one can be legal parent to at the same time. In between are spouses; the law limits people to one marital partner at a time, and one's attractiveness as a mate declines with each marriage one enters and exits, but a married person can unilaterally dissolve the relationship at any time and will likely be able then to enter into a new one. As to both parenthood and marriage, there might be some difference between the sexes; women must invest more of their time and bodies than men do into having children, and women might experience a greater attractiveness cost with successive marriages than men do, especially if they have children in the marriage and assume primary custody after dissolution.

When a business or personal relationship entails high opportunity costs for a person, we expect them to be more circumspect in choosing a partner and to demand stronger protection of their interests in the relationship. The social science literature supports the circumspection-in-choosing hypothesis insofar as it shows females to be more selective in choosing a mate and more concerned to avoid unwanted pregnancy. Protections of women during marriage have arisen in the United States only relatively recently, but there are now laws that proscribe all violence in marriages; rules of shared ownership of income during marriage in community property states; and, in other states, divorce laws that give dependent spouses a claim on family resources in the event of a dissolution. In contrast, we saw in Chapter 1 that there is no circumspection by or in behalf of children with respect to entering a parent-child relationship; the law forces nearly all children to enter into this legal and social relationship with their biological parents regardless of how unfit for the relationship those persons are. In contrast, women have complete legal freedom to avoid a parent-child relationship—by not having sex, by aborting, or by relinquishing a child at birth. Men can avoid a parent-child relationship by avoiding conception and sometimes even after conception occurs, if the birth mother aborts or consents to adoption. In this chapter we will examine what protections the law confers on children and parents during a parent-child relationship. As we did with the marital relationship, we will also consider in this chapter to what extent the state aims to facilitate optimal relationships rather than just to prevent very destructive behavior and choices.

Before beginning, we should also articulate what is inherently different about a parent-child relationship relative to a marital relationship. By "inherently" I mean part of the concept of the relationship as a distinctive type of relationship; this is something other than the particular rules that a society happens to have attached to the relationship. One distinctive inherent aspect of the parent-child relationship is that it begins as a vertical, caretaking relationship. A marriage can become that if one spouse becomes incapacitated, but most never do, and it almost never begins that way. Marriage is today paradigmatically a horizontal, cooperative relationship between persons of equal capacity. Because the relationship between parents and minor children is inherently a hierarchical, caretaking one, the rules governing each member of the relationship are different. In contrast, the rules governing marriage are for the most part the same for both spouses (one important exception being control over reproduction).

Another inherent difference is that the marital relationship entails sexual intimacy and the freedom to engage in reproduction if the parties wish, whereas the law criminalizes such behavior in parent-child relationships. Can you think of any other inherent differences? In studying the law governing ongoing parent-child relationships, we will frequently refer to these various similarities and differences in the nature of the two relationships in order to assess the law's appropriateness.

A. COHABITATION

Perhaps the most important legal regulation of the parent-child relationship is that determining whether the parent and child live together. Different rules apply in the case of minor children depending on whether the parent wishes to live with the child.

1. *When Parents Do Not Wish to Live with a Child*

A parent who does not wish to live with a minor child is in the same legal position as a married person who does not wish to live with a spouse—that is, complete freedom not to cohabit. The law no longer forces a wife to return to her husband if she leaves the marital residence. Likewise, if a parent chooses not to live with his or her minor child, the state will not override that choice. Neglect laws discussed below prohibit parents from abandoning a child in circumstances where their basic needs will not be met, but the law allows for a parent to leave a child entirely in the care of the other parent or of any other adult capable of caring for the child, subject only to a financial support obligation.

As to the relationship between a parent and an adult child, of course both are free to refuse cohabitation so long as both are competent and self-sufficient. When elderly parents become incompetent and need a live-in caretaker, a court may appoint a guardian for them, and the guardian has the power to decide the ward's residence. As noted in Chapter 3, first priority in guardianship is given to someone nominated by the incompetent adult, and in the absence of such a designation to that adult's spouse, if there is a spouse who is able and desirous of the role. Next in line ordinarily are offspring. Cf. Fla. Stat. §744.312 (requiring that courts "give preference to the appointment of a person who: (a) Is related by blood or marriage to the ward . . ."). There could be cases, therefore, in which parents are forced to live with an offspring against their will. In theory, that should only occur if that is in the parent ward's best interests, and if it were clearly not, another interested party could petition a court to override the guardian's decision and change the parent's residence.

2. *When Parents Do Wish to Live with a Child*

When a parent does wish to live with a child, the rules vary depending on whether the parent is cohabiting with the other parent, if there is one.

a. When Parents' Relationship Is Intact or There Is Only One Parent

Legal parents have a presumptive right to custody of their children, so when parents live with each other there is typically no dispute about who will have custody of their children; the parents do jointly. The same is true when a child has only one legal parent, as might be true if one biological parent is unknown, permanently absent, or dead; there is generally no doubt that she or he will be the child's custodian. There are two significant exceptions: First, sometimes parents leave a child in the care of a non-parent for an extended period, the non-parent seeks guardianship of the child, and a court refuses the legal parent's requests for return of custody. See, e.g., In re Guardianship of Nicholas P., 2011 WL 2548590 (N.H. 2011) (awarding guardianship to child's adult half-brother after mother abandoned the home and father died); Ortiz v. Winig, 920 N.Y.S.2d 441 (App. Div. 2011) (refusing father's request to regain custody from grandparent). Second, the state must sometimes assume custody of a child because of parental abuse or neglect. Section II of this chapter presents the legal standards for abuse and neglect, and we will see that it is not sufficient for a state actor to find that it would be in a child's best interests to be removed from parental custody; the state must show fairly serious misconduct and danger to the child. In contrast, a spouse can move out of the marital home based on a conclusion that it would be in her best interests.

b. When Parents' Relationship Has Dissolved

This situation gives rise to a major component of family law practice. The percentage of children who spend their entire minority living with both parents has declined steadily in the past half century. As of 2009, the percentage of newborns whose biological parents are not married to each other at the time of birth has risen to 41 percent, and most of those parent sets are not cohabiting. Further, among parents who are married and cohabiting when children are born, a substantial minority will divorce before the children are grown. Thus, roughly half of all children born in the United States will spend much of their childhood living with just one parent or moving back and forth between parents. The legal rules for assigning custody as between non-cohabiting parents are thus exceedingly important, influencing this most basic aspect of life for an enormous number of children.

This does not mean that for most children whose parents have split there will be a battle for their custody in court. Many parents who do not live together simply create their own arrangement without court involvement. Others draft a written agreement embodying a parenting plan they decide on themselves and simply submit the agreement to a court for approval and incorporation into an order. Many jurisdictions now require parents to attend custody mediation to try to reach an agreement before they may go to court for a custody trial. However, a significant percentage of estranged parents do litigate custody, typically in the course of divorce or paternity proceedings, and the legal rules set forth in statutes to govern such disputes and the courts' elaboration of those rules also guide parents and their attorneys who craft agreements and guide judges in deciding whether to approve such an agreement.

"Custody" actually refers to two distinct aspects of the parental role. Physical custody is possession, having the child live in your house. Legal custody is decision-making power. A court order should address each of those, and it is common for the order to assign them somewhat differently. Joint legal custody is the norm, whereas joint physical custody is less common than is an award of "primary custody" or "sole custody" to one parent and visitation to the other. The materials below flesh out these concepts.

(1) The Basic Standard

As does the law of guardianship appointment, child custody law ostensibly makes what is best for the dependent person the sole, ultimate standard of decision. In theory, judges must do a best-interests assessment even when parents submit an agreement as to custody and should reject an agreement they deem contrary to the child's welfare. See, e.g., Ga. Code Ann. §19-9-5. Indiana's custody statute is typical, setting out this standard and then numerous non-exclusive factors to guide the court's thinking about what is best for the child:

Indiana Code
Title 31, Article 17. Family Law: Custody and Visitation Rights
Chapter 2. Actions for Child Custody and Modification of Custody Orders

§31-17-2-8 Custody Order

The court shall determine custody and enter a custody order in accordance with the best interests of the child. In determining the best interests of the child, there is no presumption favoring either parent. The court shall consider all relevant factors, including the following:

(1) The age and sex of the child.

(2) The wishes of the child's parent or parents.

(3) The wishes of the child, with more consideration given to the child's wishes if the child is at least fourteen (14) years of age.

(4) The interaction and interrelationship of the child with:

(A) the child's parent or parents;

(B) the child's sibling; and

(C) any other person who may significantly affect the child's best interests.

(5) The child's adjustment to the child's:

(A) home;

(B) school; and

(C) community.

(6) The mental and physical health of all individuals involved.

(7) Evidence of a pattern of domestic or family violence by either parent. . . .

In some other states, statutory language articulating the overarching standard is not so straightforward. Texas and Virginia custody statutes, for example, direct courts to give "primary consideration" to the best interests of the child. Tex. Fam. Code Ann. §153.002; Va. Code Ann. §20-124.2. What does that mean? Does it mean that considerations unrelated to the child's well being can properly influence decisions? Could such other considerations even override the child's interests?

The best-interests standard is quite vague, and many scholars and practitioners have complained that it gives judges too much discretion. Such discretion makes outcomes unpredictable, critics say, and that fosters more destructive litigation. Such discretion also creates unacceptable risk that judges will act out of personal bias—for example, against parents who do not fit gender stereotypical norms, rather than remaining focused on what is truly best for a child. Legislators have added lists of factors in an effort to make judgments more objective and consistent, but that does not satisfy many of the critics. Do you think the factors in the Indiana statute leave substantial room for biased decision making?

(2) Presumptions

In a further effort to make custody decisions predictable, consistent, and less affected by judicial bias, states have over time adopted various presumptions as to custody. For a thorough historical account, see Mary Ann Mason, From Father's Property to Children's Rights: A History of Child Custody in America (1994). The evolution of gender-based presumptions reflects the history of family life and the rights of women in America. Prior to the nineteenth century, Anglo-American law generally applied a presumption of paternal custody, consistent with the ancient view of family members as a father/husband's property. This rule and underlying view persist in some patriarchal Third World cultures. See, e.g., Bolaji Owasanoye, *The Regulation of Child Custody and Access in Nigeria,* 39 Fam. L.Q. 405, 420-423 (2005) (discussing custody rules under customary law and under Muslim law in Nigeria).

Before industrialization, most fathers and mothers in the United States worked in or near the home, so fathers could oversee child rearing. Industrialization changed family life for most American families, causing fathers to leave home to work in factories for much of each day, which in turn increased mothers' control of the household and role in raising children. In addition, as with wives, children's status in popular perspective rose in the late nineteenth century, such that the official line was that they were no longer to be regarded as a father's property, but instead as persons in their own rights with basic rights to protection of their welfare. Accordingly, courts in this period adopted a maternal preference, sometimes called a "tender years" presumption, under which children, at least when young, should go with the mother following a divorce, unless the mother was unfit to parent. Courts explained that younger children need their mother's care above all else.

The maternal preference continued until equal protection doctrine in the late twentieth century made it untenable. As recently as 1978, in *J.B. v. A.B.* (1978), the Supreme Court of Appeals of West Virginia applied a maternal-preference rule, overturning a custody award to a husband. Though the trial court had found that "the child received from both parents the type of affection and care which this society expects of competent parents," the state's high court held that custody should be awarded to a mother unless she is truly unfit as a parent. The court explained that women "develop certain attitudes such as surpassing patience and a high tolerance for a close, grating, aesthetically unpleasant, and frequently oppressive, yet nonetheless absolutely indispensable physical relationship with children." The court also referred to "the familiar rationale that the mother is the natural custodian of her young, and that her love for her child is irreplaceable." Further:

> From a strictly biological perspective, children of the suckling age are necessarily accustomed to close, physical ties with their mothers, and young children, technically weaned, are accustomed to the warmth, softness, and physical affection of the female parent. The welfare of the child seems to require that if at all possible we avoid subjecting children to the trauma of being wrenched away from their mothers, upon whom they have naturally both an emotional and physical dependency.

Are the court's gendered empirical assumptions clearly false or implausible? Regardless, the U.S. Supreme Court's sex equality jurisprudence rendered a gendered custody presumption constitutionally problematic. And so most states substituted a "primary caretaker" presumption that still prevails, being either explicit in state legal rules or simply evident in practice. In the leading case of *Garska v. McCoy* (1981), the West Virginia Supreme Court of Appeals ventured a test for determining which parent has been the primary caretaker:

> While it is difficult to enumerate all of the factors which will contribute to a conclusion that one parent was the primary caretaker parent, nonetheless, there are certain obvious criteria to which a court must initially look. . . . [T]he trial court shall determine which parent has taken primary responsibility for, inter alia, the performance of the following caring and nurturing duties of a parent: (1) preparing and planning of meals; (2) bathing, grooming and dressing; (3) purchasing, cleaning, and care of clothes; (4) medical care, including nursing and trips to physicians; (5) arranging for social interaction among peers after school, i.e. transporting to friends' houses or, for example, to girl or boy scout meetings; (6) arranging alternative care, i.e. babysitting, day-care, etc.; (7) putting child to bed at night, attending to child in the middle of the night, waking child in the morning; (8) disciplining, i.e. teaching

> general manners and toilet training; (9) educating, i.e. religious, cultural, social, etc.; and, (10) teaching elementary skills, i.e., reading, writing and arithmetic.

What definition of "care" underlies this list? Is it "demonstrating concern about or responsibility for"? Or is it "directly attending to"? What definition should be used? Is there any way to care for a child in the first sense that is not reflected in the list?

There is considerable controversy today about whether application of such a presumption is appropriate. Fathers' rights groups argue that the primary caretaker rule is not in fact gender neutral, and that in any event judges harbor a strong bias against father custody. Arguing for the crucial importance of father involvement in children's lives and pointing to statistics showing most fathers drop out of their children's lives within a few years after divorce, these groups have succeeded in some states at some times in getting legislatures to adopt an explicit or implicit presumption in favor of joint legal and physical custody—that is, equal decision-making power and roughly equal division of time between the parents' respective households. See, e.g., 750 Ill. Comp. Stat. 5/-602.1(b) (stating that if either parent requests joint custody, "the court shall initially request the parents to produce a Joint Parenting Agreement" and "may order mediation," and providing: "In the event the parents fail to produce a Joint Parenting Agreement, the court may enter an appropriate Joint Parenting Order . . .").

Some women's organizations, though, have opposed court-ordered joint custody, taking the position that joint custody is appropriate only when both parents agree to it. Feminist scholars have been ambivalent; they approve of fathers' assuming equal responsibility for child rearing, but they sympathize with mothers who want sole custody after sacrificing a great deal to be the primary caretaker of children in the early years; they harbor suspicions about fathers' motives for suddenly wanting to play an equal role in a child's life (e.g., that they are just trying to reduce their child support obligation); and they fear forced co-parenting will foster conflict and potentially violence toward mothers.

Participants in the legal system have seen many cases in which equal parenting time did not work well, because of the difficulty for children of having their life split between two households, and also cases in which shared custody gradually morphs into maternal sole custody, because fathers' initial enthusiasm wanes. They have also seen cases where it works well enough for the children and succeeds in preserving the children's bond with both parents, making it worth the costs involved. Much depends on where the parents live in relation to each other—for example, in the same school district or not—and how well the parents cooperate to maintain a normal routine for a child despite the dual living situation—for example, bringing over Suzie's violin because she forgot to take it when mom picked her up. The prevailing rule in the United States today is that courts can award joint physical and/or legal custody but there is no presumption for or against it; courts are to decide on a case-by-case basis whether it is in the child's best interests. See, e.g., Ga. Code Ann. §19-9-3; Mass. Gen. Laws ch. 208, §31. In contrast, shared physical custody appears to be the norm in Sweden and France, whereas several countries, such as Japan, do not even allow for such a sharing of custody. See D. Marianne Blair & Merle H. Weiner, *Resolving Parental Custody Disputes—A Comparative Exploration*, 39 FAM. L.Q. 247, 264-265(2005).

In practice, joint legal custody is routine today in divorce actions and, though problematic, has not been as controversial. It is less common in paternity actions, which typically involve an infant who has never lived with the father. Joint physical custody is still the result in only a minority of all cases. It is still true that in the great majority of cases, mothers get primary physical custody and fathers get just visitation rights.

The most recent legal innovation is a presumption that the custody allocation should approximate the division of child care that the parents adopted on their own prior to the filing of a custody petition. The American Law Institute proposed this rule in 2000, inspired by Professor Elizabeth Scott's 1992 article, *Pluralism, Parental Preference, and Child Custody,* 80 Cal. L. Rev. 615. West Virginia was again the first to experiment with a new idea for custody presumptions. Its custody statute now creates a presumption that courts will "allocate custodial responsibility so that the proportion of custodial time the child spends with each parent approximates the proportion of time each parent spent performing caretaking functions for the child prior to the parents' separation or, if the parents never lived together, before the filing of the action." W. Va. Code §48-9-206. The presumption can be overcome by showing that approximation would be "manifestly harmful to the child" or would interfere with one of various objectives, including ensuring that the child has an opportunity to maintain a relationship with both parents, respecting the wishes of an adolescent or a prior agreement of the parents, keeping siblings together, facilitating a parent's relocation, and avoiding an outcome that is "extremely impractical" for the parents.

Whatever the approximation rule might add to predictability and objectivity, no other state has adopted it. Which aspects of the rule might be sufficiently vague to undermine these aims? What about the very term "approximate"? If a court concluded that mother did 80 percent of child care during the marriage and awarded her 60 percent of custodial time as an approximation, would that clearly be a misapplication of the rule? For a critique of the rule, see Richard A. Warshak, *Parenting by the Clock: The Best-Interest-of-the-Child Standard, Judicial Discretion, and the American Law Institute's "Approximation Rule,"* 41 U. Balt. L. Rev. 83 (2011).

The following case exemplifies the struggle states have gone through in deciding what stance to take toward court-ordered shared parenting following parents' break-up.

In re Marriage of Hansen

733 N.W.2d 683 (Iowa 2007)

Appel, Justice.

. . . Lyle and Delores were married on September 4, 1987. The marriage lasted approximately eighteen years. At the time of trial, Lyle was forty-five years of age and Delores was forty-six. Two children were born of the marriage, Miranda, who was twelve years old at the time of the district court proceedings, and Ethan, who was eight.

At all times prior to the filing of the divorce petition, Delores was the primary caregiver. Lyle, alternatively, was the main breadwinner. . . . Delores attended parent teacher conferences on a regular basis, while Lyle did not. The vast majority of the time, it was Delores who helped the children with their homework. . . . Lyle missed important childhood events because of social activities or work-related assignments. When the children were in infancy, Delores opened a day care center in their home. Later, when family finances became an issue, she held full-time employment outside the home. After the parties' separation, however, Lyle has become more involved in the lives of the children.

The record developed at trial reveals serious marital stress. The record demonstrates a history of recurrent arguments, excessive consumption of alcohol, allegations of infidelity and sexual misconduct, and allegations of domestic abuse. Unfortunately, at least some of these contretemps were in front of the children. It was not a pleasant proceeding. . . .

The record further reveals that Delores tended to acquiesce to Lyle when there were disagreements. For example, when Delores was pregnant with Miranda, she wanted to attend child-birthing classes, but Lyle stated that *he* had already undergone training and that, as a result, the classes were not needed. When Delores began operating a child care center out of their home, Lyle insisted on reviewing applicant backgrounds and controlled which children could utilize the service. He further demanded that parents or custodians pick up their children by 5:00 P.M. sharp. Delores did not agree with these practices, but felt she had no choice but to acquiesce. In addition, Delores asked Lyle if he would participate in marital counseling, but he refused, stating that he did not believe in counseling. Delores testified that she agreed to temporary joint physical care prior to trial only because she did not feel she could stand up to her husband. Delores expressed concern that if she disagrees with Lyle, he becomes angry and intimidating.

The parties appear to have different approaches to child rearing. Delores wants the children to be active in the Methodist church and other extracurricular activities. . . . Lyle did not encourage these kinds of activities. . . . Lyle believed that discipline needed to be more severe than Delores was willing to impose. . . . [T]here are some things that he might let the children do that Delores might not, and vice versa.

At trial, Lyle expressed concern that Delores will expose their children to her family, which he finds highly dysfunctional. Delores testified that her father abused her as a child, but they have reconciled sufficiently to maintain an ongoing relationship. . . . [O]ther members of Delores' family have been convicted of child endangerment and drug offenses. Delores counters that when the children visit her family, it is always under her supervision.

Prior to trial, the parties were apparently able to work out the scheduling issues inherent in a joint physical care arrangement. There was not always agreement, however, on matters related to the children. For instance, when one child experienced unexpected academic difficulties, Delores believed professional counseling would be of help. Lyle disagreed, once again stating that he did not believe in professional counseling. Delores acquiesced. . . . On another occasion, the kids called their mother and asked to be picked up because Lyle was angry that they had not cleaned their rooms, and had slammed the kitchen door, breaking its glass pane. Moreover, Delores testified that Miranda told her she desired a more stable living arrangement with a home base.

While much of the record in this case is unattractive, it is clear that both Lyle and Delores love their children. They are both capable of making substantial contributions to their lives. The record further reveals that the children are bright and generally well-adjusted.

With respect to financial matters, . . . Lyle was earning $46,300 per year as a detective for the City of Washington Police Department. Delores was employed as a bank teller, earning $18,900 per year. Delores has only a high school education and little prospect in Washington, Iowa, for substantial increase in income. . . .

The district court granted "joint legal custody" and "joint physical care" of the minor children to Lyle and Delores. . . . "[P]hysical care" would alternate between Lyle and Delores for six-month periods . . . , with liberal visitation for the spouse not currently having physical care. . . . [T]he court ordered that each parent "shall permit the child(ren) to continue the activities after a physical care change." Because Delores was awarded physical care for the first six-month period, the effect of the court order was that her choices of extracurricular activities would be binding on Lyle. The district court additionally ordered that Delores "shall select the church affiliation for the children." The district court ordered that Delores be present when the children visited her family.

The court further ordered that if a party moved from the Washington School District, the nonmoving party shall become the physical custodian until further order of the court.

Lastly, the district court decision contained the following language in bold print:

> **This custody arrangement is predicated on the court's belief that the parties are able to communicate regarding the best interests of their children. Failure to communicate in a positive manner may constitute a basis for modification of this decree. . . .**

At the outset, it is important to discuss the differences between joint legal custody and joint physical care. "Legal custody" carries with it certain rights and responsibilities, including but not limited to "decisionmaking affecting the child's legal status, medical care, education, extracurricular activities, and religious instruction." When joint legal custody is awarded, "neither parent has legal custodial rights superior to those of the other parent." A parent who is awarded legal custody has the ability to participate in fundamental decisions about the child's life.

On the other hand, "physical care" involves "the right and responsibility to maintain a home for the minor child and provide for routine care of the child." If joint physical care is awarded, "both parents have rights to and responsibilities toward the child including, but not limited to, shared parenting time with the child, maintaining homes for the child, [and] providing routine care for the child. . . ." The parent awarded physical care maintains the primary residence and has the right to determine the myriad of details associated with routine living, including such things as what clothes the children wear, when they go to bed, with whom they associate or date, etc. If joint physical care is not warranted, the court must choose a primary caretaker who is solely responsible for decisions concerning the child's routine care. Visitation rights are ordinarily afforded a parent who is not the primary caretaker.

For decades, Iowa appellate courts have disfavored joint physical care arrangements in dissolution cases as not in the best interest of children. In *In re Marriage of Burham* (Iowa 1979), this court . . . [explained] that divided custody is destructive of discipline, induces a feeling of not belonging to either parent, and in some instances can permit one parent to sow seeds of discontent concerning the other. . . . [Later] cases have generally emphasized . . . stability and continuity. . . . The Iowa legislature has shown recent interest in joint physical care as a potential alternative in dissolution cases. . . . In 1997, the legislature . . . stated that a district court "may consider" joint physical care upon the application of either party. . . . In 2004, the legislature again . . . amend[ed] Iowa Code section 598.41(5) to read, in relevant part:

> If joint legal custody is awarded to both parents, the court may award joint physical care to both joint custodial parents upon the request of either parent. . . . If the court denies the request for joint physical care, the determination shall be accompanied by specific findings of fact and conclusions of law that the awarding of joint physical care is not in the best interest of the child.

. . . [T]he 1997 and 2004 legislation did not create a presumption in favor of joint physical care. . . . With respect to joint [legal] custody, the legislature has declared that if the court does not grant joint [legal] custody, it shall "cite clear and convincing evidence" that joint custody is unreasonable and not in the best interests of a child. Iowa Code §598.41(2)(*b*). No similar language appears in the joint physical care provisions of Iowa law. . . . The amendments only require the courts to consider and explain the basis of decisions to deny physical care. . . . [W]e nonetheless believe that the notion that joint physical care is strongly disfavored except in exceptional circumstances is subject to reexamination in light of changing social conditions and ongoing legal and research developments. Increasingly in Iowa and across the nation, our family structures have become more diverse. While some families function along traditional lines with a primary breadwinner and primary caregiver, other families employ a more undifferentiated role for spouses or even reverse "traditional" roles. A one-size-fits-all approach in which joint physical care is universally disfavored is thus subject to serious question given current social realities.

In addition, the social science research related to child custody issues is now richer and more varied than it was in the past. In the past, many scholars and courts rejected joint physical care based on . . . attachment theory [that] emphasize[s] the need to place children with a single "psychological parent" with whom the children had bonded. Joseph Goldstein, Anna Freud, & Albert J. Solnit, *Beyond the Best Interests of the Child* 98 (1979). . . . [A] substantial body of scholarly commentary now challenges the blanket application of the monotropic psychological parent attachment theory. . . . They cite a wide range of studies to suggest that children may be better off with joint physical care than other arrangements. . . . [T]here are substantial questions of definition and methodology. Such criticisms include: samples that only examine parents who voluntarily choose joint custody, the use of small and homogenous groups, the skewing of samples toward middle class parents with higher incomes and education, the lack of control groups, and the lack of distinction between "joint custody" arrangements and traditional sole custody with visitation, and the failure to differentiate the effects of preexisting parental characteristics from the effects of custody type. . . . An exhaustive review commissioned by the Washington State Supreme Court Gender and Justice Commission and the Domestic Relations Commission examined the many studies related to child custody issues. The review concluded that the available research did not reveal any particular post-divorce residential schedule to be most beneficial to children. . . .

While it seems clear that children often benefit from a continuing relationship with both parents after divorce, the research has not established the amount of contact necessary to maintain a "close relationship." Preeminent scholars have noted that "surprisingly, even a fairly small amount of close contact seemed sufficient to maintain close relationships, at least as these relationships were seen from the adolescents' perspective." There is thus growing support for the notion that the quality, and not the quantity, of contacts with the non-custodial parent are the key to the wellbeing of children. Quality interaction with children can, of course, occur within the framework of traditional visitation and does not occur solely in situations involving joint physical care.

At present, the available empirical studies do not provide a firm basis for a dramatic shift that would endorse joint physical care as the norm in child custody cases. Nonetheless, in light of the changing nature of the structure of families and challenges to the sweeping application of psychological parent attachment theory, we believe the joint physical care issue must be examined in each case on the unique facts and not subject to cursory rejection based on a nearly irrebuttable presumption found in our prior cases. . . . Physical care issues are not to be resolved based upon perceived fairness to the *spouses*, but primarily upon what is best for the *child*. The objective of a physical care determination is to place the children in the environment most likely to bring them to health, both physically and mentally, and to social maturity.

We recognize that the "best interest" standard is subject to attack on the ground that it is no standard at all, that it has the potential of allowing gender bias to affect child custody determinations, and that its very unpredictability increases family law litigation. On the other hand, the advantage of the standard is that it provides the flexibility necessary to consider unique custody issues on a case-by-case basis. We believe the best approach to determining difficult child custody matters involves a framework with some spine, but the sufficient flexibility to allow consideration of each case's unique facts. . . .

In considering whether to award joint physical care where there are two suitable parents, stability and continuity of caregiving have traditionally been primary factors. Stability and continuity factors tend to favor a spouse who, prior to divorce, was primarily responsible for physical care. . . . As noted by a leading scholar, "past caretaking patterns likely are a fairly reliable proxy of the intangible qualities such as parental abilities and emotional bonds that are so difficult for courts to ascertain." While no post-divorce physical care arrangement will be identical to predissolution experience, preservation of the greatest amount of stability possible is a desirable goal. . . . Conversely, however, long-term, successful, joint care is a significant factor in considering the viability of joint physical care after divorce.

Stability and continuity concepts have been refined in the recent literature and expressed in terms of an approximation rule. . . . Iowa Code section 598.41(3) and our case law requires a multi-factored test where no one criterion is determinative. Any wholesale adoption of the approximation rule would require legislative action. Nonetheless, we believe that the approximation principle is a factor to be considered by courts in determining whether to grant joint physical care. By focusing on historic patterns of caregiving, the approximation rule provides a relatively objective factor for the court to consider. The principle of approximation also . . . recognizes the diversity of family life. . . .

There may be circumstances, of course, that outweigh considerations of stability, continuity, and approximation. For example, if a primary caregiver has abandoned responsibilities or had not been adequately performing his or her responsibilities because of alcohol or substance abuse, there may be a strong case for changing the physical care relationship. In addition, the quality of the parent-child relationship is not always determined by hours spent together or solely upon past experience. . . .

A second important factor to consider in determining whether joint physical care is in the child's best interest is the ability of spouses to communicate and show mutual respect. A lack of trust poses a significant impediment to effective co-parenting. Evidence of controlling behavior by a spouse may be an indicator of potential problems. Evidence of untreated domestic battering should be given considerable weight in determining custody and gives rise to a presumption against joint physical care.

Third, the degree of conflict between parents is an important factor in determining whether joint physical care is appropriate. Joint physical care requires substantial and regular interaction between divorced parents on a myriad of issues. Where the parties' marriage is stormy and has a history of charge and countercharge, the likelihood that joint physical care will provide a workable arrangement diminishes. It is, of course, possible that spouses may be able to put aside their past, strong differences in the interest of the children. Reality suggests, however, that this may not be the case. . . . [T]here is evidence that high levels of child contact with a nonresidential father are beneficial to children in low conflict families, but harmful to children in high conflict families. . . . Even a low level of conflict can have significant repercussions for children. . . .

Because of the perceived detrimental impact of parental conflict on children, some commentators have urged that joint physical care should be encouraged only where both parents voluntarily agree to it. *See* Or. Rev. Stat. §107.169(3) (2007) (joint custody only upon agreement of parents); Vt. Stat. tit 15, §665(a) (2007) ("When parents cannot agree to divide or share parental rights and responsibilities, the court shall award parental rights and responsibilities primarily or solely to one parent."). Iowa Code section 598.41(5)(*a*), however, requires the court to consider joint physical care upon the request of either party. While we, therefore, reject the notion that one spouse has absolute veto power over whether the court grants joint physical custody, the lack of mutual acceptance can be an indicator of instability in the relationship that may impair the successful exercise of joint physical care. *See* Iowa Code §598.41(3)(*g*) (court should consider whether one or both spouses agree or are opposed).

A fourth important factor . . . is the degree to which the parents are in general agreement about their approach to daily matters. . . . The greater the amount of agreement between the parents on child rearing issues, the lower the likelihood that ongoing bitterness will create a situation in which children are at risk of becoming pawns in continued post-dissolution marital strife. . . .

The above factors present important considerations, but no iron clad formula or inflexible system of legal presumptions.

Once it is decided that joint physical care is not in the best interest of the children, the court must next choose which caregiver should be awarded physical care. The parent awarded physical care is required to support the other parent's relationship with the child. In making this decision, the factors of continuity, stability, and approximation are entitled to considerable weight. The court should be alert, however, to situations where the emotional bonds between children and a parent who has not been the primary caregiver are stronger than the bonds with the other parent. In making decisions . . . , courts must avoid gender bias. . . .

In light of the above principles, and after our de novo review of the entire record, we agree with the court of appeals that joint physical care is not in the best interest of the children under the unique facts presented in this case. For most of the marriage, Delores has been the primary caregiver. The concepts of continuity, stability, and approximation thus cut strongly against joint physical care as a quality alternative least disruptive to the children and most likely to promote their long-term physical and emotional health. The record also shows that the parties have significant difficulties in communication. . . . Further, the divorce proceedings demonstrated considerable mutual distrust and a high level of conflict between the parties, complete with allegations of sexual improprieties and domestic abuse. It is noteworthy that while Lyle disputed most of the alleged incidents of physical abuse, he admitted that he and Delores engaged in "pushing matches." Furthermore, there was substantial evidence in the record that Lyle has a controlling personality that could extend into the post-divorce world. . . . The record also demonstrates differences in parenting styles. . . . Over the long haul, we believe there is a high potential for conflict if joint physical care continued. . . .

The district court's order alternating physical custody on six-month intervals may have also been designed to lessen potential friction between the parties. There was no evidence in the record to suggest that the alternate six-month arrangement was designed to accommodate work schedules of the parties or was based on some other logistical factor. Like the court of appeals in this case, a number of appellate courts have invalidated similar arrangements. *Ireland v. Ireland* (Mo. Ct. App. 1996) (invalidating change of custody every two months); *In re Custody of D.M.G.*, 287 Mont. 120 (1998) (reversing two-year alternating custody order); *Reavis v. Reavis* (Wyo. 1998) (reversing two-month alternate custody). As noted by the Washington Supreme Court, orders which provide for alternating residence of the child for substantially equal intervals can result when the parties and the courts are searching to avoid underlying disputes. . . . We conclude that the best interest of the children will be advanced by awarding physical care to Delores rather than to award joint physical care.

At the same time, Lyle has an important role to play in his children's lives. No one questions his devotion to them and their need for his guidance and support. A responsible, committed, nonresident parent, with good parenting skills, has the potential to engage in a high-quality relationship with his or her child and to positively impact the child's adjustment. Because the district court ordered the parties to share joint legal custody, Lyle will continue to be involved in major decisionmaking for his children. In order to promote the desirable level of physical contact, on remand, the district court should establish liberal visitation for Lyle, which includes visitation every other weekend, commencing at 6:00 P.M. on Friday night and concluding at 6:00 P.M. Sunday evening and every Wednesday night commencing at 6:00 P.M. and ending at 8:00 A.M. Thursday morning. Lyle shall have visitation on his birthday and Father's Day every year. Delores, conversely, shall have physical custody of the children on her birthday and Mother's Day each year. In addition, Lyle shall have visitation on every other holiday including New Year's Day, Easter, Memorial Day, Fourth of July, Labor Day, Thanksgiving Day, Christmas Eve, Christmas, New Year's Eve. Holiday visitation shall be from 9:00 A.M. to 9:00 P.M. Lyle shall have visitation on the children's birthdays on odd numbered years, while Delores shall have even numbered years. In addition, Lyle shall have visitation of the children in the summer for a total of four weeks at two two-week intervals. These two-week intervals shall be separated by at least one week. Lyle shall give Delores written notice no later than April 15 of each year of the times at which he wishes to exercise these vacation periods. During one of those two-week intervals, Lyle shall have uninterrupted visitation. Delores is also entitled to exercise one two-week period of visitation exclusive of Lyle's rights each summer. Delores shall provide Lyle written notice no later than April 30 of each year of the weeks she has selected. Each party is further entitled to uninterrupted visitation during alternating spring breaks. Delores shall have visitation in even numbered years and Lyle shall have visitation in odd numbered years. Finally, the parties shall alternate visitation during Christmas break. In odd numbered years, Delores shall have visitation the first half and Lyle the second. The reverse is true in even numbered years. Lyle is further entitled to any additional visitation that can be agreed upon by the parties.

Dividing up a child's life is usually a sad thing for everyone, and often frightening for the child and at least one of the parents as well. Litigation brings unfamiliar and often aggressive lawyers into a difficult family situation, usually including a lawyer or other representative for the child, who must meet with the child to discuss the parents' dispute. Yet the court devoted no attention to the policy aim of discouraging custody litigation.

The Iowa court suggests a case-sensitive approach, based largely on past parenting tendencies. What connection is there exactly between having performed these functions in the past and the child's well being in the future? Are parenting tendencies likely to remain the same after divorce? Or does the fact of being married to a co-parent ordinarily influence people's decisions about how they divide their time between earning money and spending time with their children? We might also wonder how likely it is that both parents' work demands will remain the same after they end their relationship, especially if one was financially dependent on the other during the relationship. Is a backward-looking rule like "primary caretaker" or "approximation" that aims to preserve the status quo likely to produce sensible results in any case in which parents' circumstances or preferences will change substantially?

Is the court clear about the connection between joint physical custody and parental conflict? The Iowa Supreme Court spelled out an elaborate visitation schedule for the non-custodial parent, prescribing a typical arrangement. It involves a lot of transitions from one household to the other, possibly more than the children had under a joint physical custody regime. Transitions are principally when conflicts occur. The court is also rather sanguine about the award of joint legal custody—that is, of equal power as to major life decisions, yet such larger decisions are also a primary source of conflict. Would there likely be significantly more conflict if the court shifted, say, 20 percent of the children's time to the father? Does the amount of time the court did allot for visitation seem adequate for maintenance of a strong parent-child relationship? Is it troubling that the state is micro-managing family life in this way?

In short, there is no consensus today on what presumption, if any, courts should apply in custody disputes. There is near-universal agreement that having judges make highly subjective decisions as to the future family life of children whom they likely never meet is worrisome. But there is no single, obviously superior alternative.

(3) Role of Local Norms and Progressive Social Policies

The *Hansen* court referred to changing societal practices and attitudes, which raises the general question: Should state decision making about parent-child relationships reflect present social circumstances, including prevailing prejudices and expectations, which might appear unfair to some group of people, or should progressive societal aims control or at least influence such decision making? This subsection raises this general question in the specific contexts of gender and race equality.

Chapter 3 discussed state encouragement of more equal division of child care between fathers and mothers, and we saw that the United States lags behind many other countries in this respect. The motivation for this encouragement does not appear directly related to children's well being, but rather derives from the progressive aim of gender equality for adults; shared parenting makes women freer to pursue careers after having children and helps break down patriarchal norms in the workplace. Professor Sanger explains that gender-stereotyped societal expectations about who raises children are a double-edged sword for women in custody litigation. They can help secure custody for women who conform to the model of domesticated mother, but they might also produce unjustifiably bad results for women who do not so conform. Judges might condemn career-minded women and punish them by denying custody. See Carol Sanger, *Separating from Children*, 96 Colum. L. Rev. 375 (1996).

Many other cultures are more comfortable with a clear gender divide in child rearing responsibility, and some have strong custody preferences for either mothers or fathers. Legal systems applying an assumption of maternal custody adhere to empirical beliefs about what is best for children of the sort that the West Virginia Supreme Court expressed in *J.B. v. A.B.* (1978) (described above). With international marriages increasingly common, this creates a danger for American parents after divorce, that their relationship with their children could be severed if their ex-spouse takes their children to his or her country of origin and the legal system there is hostile to the American parents' assertion of rights. For example, many American fathers who married and then divorced a woman from Japan, after they had children, have been completely deprived of a relationship with their children because their ex-wives travelled to Japan with the children and did not return, and Japanese authorities will not take action. In Japan, the legal and societal expectation is that a father will have no connection with the children after a divorce. See Michael Inbar, *U.S. Dad Jailed in Japan in Child Custody Battle*, MSNBC.com, Sept. 30, 2009.

Conversely, in some Muslim cultures, there is a norm of paternal ownership of children, as there once was in the United States. American women who have married a man from another country where Muslim family law governs must worry that he will take the children to his native country and not return. They might experience great difficulty in getting authorities in the father's country to help them. Conversely, men in those countries might have difficulty getting a custody order of their own country enforced if the child ends up in the United States. See, e.g., Christina Pazzanese, *Massachusetts Appeals Court Rejects Foreign Custody Decree*, MASS. LAW. WKLY., Dec. 2, 2010 (discussing local court decision to ignore Lebanese court's custody award to father, because rather than a best-interests test, the court applied a rule that the father receives custody unless he is unwilling or unfit); Amin v. Bakhaty, 798 So. 2d 75 (La. 2001) (refusing to enforce Egyptian custody order). But see Hosain v. Malik, 284, 671 A.2d 988 (Md. Ct. Spec. App. 1996) (holding that Maryland court should uphold foreign custody decree if "the best interest of the child standard was applied as a Pakistani court would have applied it utilizing the customs and mores indigenous to that society"). The norm of paternal custody in those countries has its own child welfare justification; children's access to vital goods and services in such patriarchal societies is very much dependent on their fathers.

Another example of societal prejudice affecting children's relationships with their parents is the prejudice against interracial marriage, which used to trigger great community hostility throughout the United States and still does so today in some localities. In *Palmore v. Sidoti* (1989), the U.S. Supreme Court held that it violated the Equal Protection Clause of the federal Constitution for trial courts to make such racist attitudes determinative as to with which parent a child should primarily live, even if there is evidence that a child is suffering from stigmatization and even violence as a result of his mother's remarrying to someone of another race. Some lower courts have extended to the same-sex partner context the general principle of *Palmore* that the state should not "give effect" to societal prejudices in custody decision making. Does this amount to forcing children to bear the burden of carrying American society into a more tolerant future? Is there some other way to serve this progressive aim that does not sacrifice the welfare of today's children?

A newer question facing courts is whether the race of each parent in an interracial relationship should factor into custody decision making regarding their bi-racial children.

In re Marriage of Gambla & Woodson

853 N.E.2d 847 (Ill. App. Ct. 2006)

Justice GILLERAN JOHNSON delivered the opinion of the court:

. . . The parties were married on May 11, 2002, in Atlanta, Georgia. Christopher is Caucasian, and Kimberly is African-American. Shortly after they married, the parties moved to Illinois, along with Che Woodson, Kimberly's then six-year-old son from a previous marriage. One child was born to the parties' marriage: Kira Marie, born on

October 19, 2002. On May 13, 2003, Christopher filed a petition for dissolution of marriage in which he sought sole custody of Kira. On May 14, 2003, Kimberly filed a counter-petition for dissolution of marriage in which she also sought sole custody of Kira. Between May 31, 2005, and July 5, 2005, the trial court conducted 15 days of trial, at which the parties, one court-appointed expert, three experts retained by Kimberly, and several character witnesses testified. . . .

Christopher argues that the trial court failed to consider all of the requisite statutory factors and improperly considered the fact that Kira is biracial. In a custody dispute, the primary consideration is the best interest and welfare of the child. 750 ILCS 5/602 (West 2004). . . . There is a strong and compelling presumption that the trial court, the entity closest to the litigation, has made the proper custody decision. . . . A custody determination inevitably rests on the parties' temperaments, personalities, and capabilities and the witnesses' demeanor.

Section 602(a) of the Illinois Marriage and Dissolution of Marriage Act (Act) provides that the court shall consider all relevant factors, including: "(1) the wishes of the child's parent or parents as to his custody; (2) the wishes of the child as to his custodian; (3) the interaction and interrelationship of the child with his parent or parents, his siblings and any other person who may significantly affect the child's best interest; (4) the child's adjustment to his home, school and community; (5) the mental and physical health of all individuals involved; (6) the physical violence or threat of physical violence by the child's potential custodian, whether directed against the child or directed against another person; (7) the occurrence of ongoing abuse . . . ; and (8) the willingness and ability of each parent to facilitate and encourage a close and continuing relationship between the other parent and the child." The factors . . . are not exclusive. . . .

As to the first factor, the trial court found that both Christopher and Kimberly desired sole custody of Kira and that their desires were well-intended. The trial court . . . found that because Kira was only two years old, she could not express her feelings as to with which parent she desired to live. The trial court noted, however, that by the accounts of all the witnesses, Kira loves both parents and is happy spending time with each of them.

Third, . . . the trial court found that Kira has a loving relationship with each parent, as well as with Che and her grandparents, uncles, aunts, and cousins. This third factor is very significant here, as the evidence in this case reveals a close relationship between Kira and Che, who resides with Kimberly. Fourth, . . . the trial court found no indication that Kira had any difficulty in her father's home or her mother's home. . . .

As to the fifth factor, . . . the trial court found that neither Christopher nor Kimberly suffered from any mental or physical maladies that would preclude them from parenting Kira. . . . Dr. Hatcher and Dr. Hynan reported that Kimberly had some psychological difficulties. However, there was inconsistency in Dr. Hatcher's testimony, as he at one point described Kimberly's elevation as merely a "mild clinical elevation." Furthermore, Dr. Thomas and Dr. Alexander believed that Dr. Hatcher and Dr. Hynan may have failed to take into account pertinent outside factors in scoring Kimberly's personality tests. The trial court apparently found Dr. Hatcher's and Dr. Hynan's testimony to be slightly impeached, which the trial court was certainly entitled to do. . . .

As to the sixth and seventh factors, the trial court found no evidence of physical violence or ongoing abuse. Although Christopher in his testimony alluded to some acts of physical violence by Kimberly, the trial court found otherwise. . . . Finally, the trial court considered the willingness and ability of each party to facilitate and encourage a close and continuing relationship between Kira and the other parent. With regard to this factor, the trial court found that both parents needed improvement. . . .

With the parties being equal as to all of the above statutory factors, the trial court looked to other relevant factors. One factor was the fact that Kira is both African-American and Caucasian and that, as an African-American woman, Kimberly could provide Kira with a "breadth of cultural knowledge" as to her African-American heritage. The trial court noted that Kira would have to learn to exist as a biracial woman in a society that is sometimes hostile to such individuals and that Kimberly would be better able to provide for Kira's emotional needs in this respect. The trial court believed that this factor tipped the scale slightly in Kimberly's favor, and it awarded Kimberly sole custody of Kira. . . .

The cold reality is that no one can put blindfolds on in this case. Christopher is Caucasian, Kimberly is African-American, and Kira is biracial. Illinois case law provides that race may be considered, but that it may not outweigh all of the other relevant factors. . . . For example, in *In re Custody of Russell* (1979), the Appellate Court, Fifth District, reviewed a custody determination where the trial court had awarded custody of the parties' minor son to the father over the mother. In making its determination, the trial court had relied in part on the fact that the mother faced potential social problems due to her interracial marriage to an African-American man. However, the trial court also considered a handful of other factors, such as the mother's emotional problems, the instability of the mother's marriage, and the fact that the mother did not have concrete child care plans in place. In affirming the trial court, the *Russell* court reasoned:

> We have no doubt, after reviewing the record, that the court took into consideration all relevant factors and did not allow the matter of race alone to overweigh all other considerations and did not regard the racial factor as decisive. Instead, the court simply acknowledged that social pressures could develop that would be difficult or detrimental for [the child]."

Illinois case law is in line with a United States Supreme Court case, Palmore v. Sidoti, 466 U.S. 429 (1984). In *Palmore*, the Supreme Court reviewed an award of custody of a Caucasian child to the Caucasian father over the Caucasian mother, who had remarried an African-American man. The Supreme Court determined that the custody award was unconstitutional, not because the trial court considered race, but because the trial court considered *solely* race. Indeed, the Supreme Court was careful to premise its holding with the following statement: "But that court was entirely candid and made no effort to place its holding on any ground other than race."

Volumes of cases from other jurisdictions have interpreted *Palmore* as not prohibiting the consideration of race in matters of child custody. . . . [Look closely at the citations that follow. Do all support the foregoing statement?—Ed.] See, *e.g., J.H.H. v. O'Hara* (8th Cir. 1989) (declining to read *Palmore* as "a broad proscription against the consideration of race in matters of child custody"); *Drummond v. Fulton County Department of Family & Children's Services* (5th Cir. 1977) (*en banc*) (determining that use of race as merely one factor in making adoption decisions is constitutional), *cert. denied*, 437 U.S. 910 (1978); *Tallman v. Tabor* (E.D. Mich. 1994) (holding that race can be considered in determining custody so long as race is not the sole consideration); *In re Davis*, 502 Pa. 110 (1983) (holding that trial court should have considered race as a factor in making foster placement decision); Farmer v. Farmer, 439 N.Y.S.2d 584, 588 (1981) (stating that "the general rule appears to be that race is simply one factor among many others which should be considered in determining what is in the child's best interest"). Indeed, it appears that so long as race is not the sole consideration for custody decisions, but only one of several factors, it is not an unconstitutional consideration. The dissent grossly misinterprets the holding of *Palmore* and ignores its progeny.

In this case, Kira's racial status did play a role in the trial court's decision to award custody to Kimberly. However, . . . many components besides race . . . factored into the trial court's decision. The trial court heard evidence from Kimberly as to how she would teach Kira about African-American culture. In particular, Kimberly hoped to teach Kira about African-American expressions, the African-American way of moving, African-American celebrations, and African-American family relationships. Kimberly also wanted to teach Kira how to cope with being a woman of color. However, the ability to provide Kira with an atmosphere rich in traditions from her African-American heritage was not the sole factor nor the primary factor considered by the trial court. In fact, the trial court stated that it did not believe in a "broad stroke" approach that would award custody to Kimberly solely because she is African-American. The trial court carefully considered and appropriately weighed the eight requisite statutory factors, along with Kira's cultural background. . . .

Finally, the dissent criticizes this decision, claiming it is based on a slanted presentation of "pseudo-facts" and speculation. However, none of the facts that the dissent recites as being overlooked would merit a different result. . . . Furthermore, any "speculations" that the dissent refers to are actually logical inferences drawn from facts recited. . . . [T]he trial court was faced with two good parents, each of whom is capable of raising Kira. . . . Giving the trial court due deference, a reasonable person cannot possibly find that the trial court's custody determination is against the manifest weight of the evidence.

The trial court decision in this case was actually not different from that of the trial court in *Palmore*, in terms of the role race played. In *Palmore* as well, the trial court had considered all prescribed custody factors, had found that the parents were not readily distinguishable based on those factors, and then concluded that problems associated with the mother's new relationship tipped the balance toward the father. Those problems were not just that the relationship was interracial and for that reason likely to trigger societal hostility, but also that it initially involved non-marital cohabitation and the court had treated this, as many courts still do today (see below), as immoral and an indication of the mother's propensity to put her own desires before the well being of her child. 466 U.S. at 431. Moreover, the trial court decision in *Palmore* was not based on the race of either parent (both were white), but rather on the consequences for the child of the mother's relationship choice. Thus, it was arguably *less* true in *Palmore* than in this case that the trial court based its decision solely on race. Yet the Supreme Court held in *Palmore* that the trial court had acted unconstitutionally. In *Gambla*, one parent clearly suffers an important loss solely because of his race. Is that not more clearly at odds with the command of the Equal Protection Clause? The Court in *Palmore* stated that the "core purpose of the Fourteenth Amendment was to do away with all governmentally imposed discrimination based on race." Id. at 432. And does the court in *Gambla* not also "give effect" to racist attitudes in society, letting them dictate that a non-white child should stay with a non-white parent? Cf. id. at 433 ("Private biases may be outside the reach of the law, but the law cannot, directly or indirectly, give them effect.").

If the child were very light-skinned, would it be appropriate for the court to favor the white father, based on an assumption that the child would suffer socially if in the custody of a mother who appeared to be of a different race, or based on an assumption that the father could better facilitate the child's negotiation of white culture? If you were the trial court judge, would you be inclined to split the baby and grant the parents joint custody?

For further discussion of custody disputes involving bi-racial children, see, e.g., Cynthia R. Mabry, *The Browning of America—Multicultural and Bicultural Families in Conflict: Making Culture a Customary Factor for Consideration in Child Custody Disputes,* 16 WASH. & LEE J. C.R. & SOC. JUST. 413 (2010); David D. Meyer, Palmore *Comes of Age: The Place of Race in the Placement of Children,* 18 U. FLA. J.L. & PUB. POL'Y 183 (2007)

(4) FAULT VS. DISABILITY

A universal custody consideration is the relative ability and demonstrated willingness of the parents to care for a child. All else being equal, a parent who consistently chooses to pursue his or her own pleasures instead of providing for a child's needs will be disfavored in a custody determination. But what if a parent is committed but less capable because of a disability or medical condition? Advocates for persons with disabilities have argued that the state should provide such persons reasonable assistance with parenting. But even with assistance, some persons might be less able to care for a child because of a disability, such as paralysis or mental illness. Is it wrong to "punish" a parent for such unchosen circumstances by denying custody? What about a terminal illness? A North Carolina custody decision made headlines because the judge's primary basis for awarding custody of an 11-year-old girl and 6-year-old boy to their father, who lived in Illinois, was that the mother had stage 4 breast cancer. See Courtney Hutchison, *Judge Cites Mom's Breast Cancer in Denying Custody of Children,* ABC News.com, May 11, 2011.

(5) RELIGIOUS TEACHINGS, PRACTICES, AND CHILD-REARING DECISIONS

Courts are divided on the permissibility of considering adverse secular effects on a child from a parent's religious speech, conduct, or child-rearing choices. Any court would count against a parent non-ideological speech that adversely affects a child, such as comments derogatory of the other parent; many custody statutes explicitly direct courts to consider the extent to which each parent supports the child's relationship with the other. However, courts generally require a greater showing of harm to a child when parental speech is religiously grounded, and so rarely impose restrictions on religious expression. For example, in Shepp v. Shepp, 906 A.2d 1165 (Pa. 2006), the Supreme Court of Pennsylvania overturned a lower court order instructing a non-custodial father not to impress his fundamentalist Mormon belief in polygamy on his daughter. The father had previously instructed his step-daughter, "that she would go to hell if she did not believe in polygamy." The court subjected the custody and visitation order to strict scrutiny and concluded: "Where . . . there is no finding that discussing such matters constitutes a grave threat of harm to the child, there is insufficient basis for the court to infringe on a parent's constitutionally protected right to speak to a child about religion as he or she sees fit."

It might seem obvious that "penalizing" parents for their religious expression by counting it against them in a custody decision infringes the parents' First Amendment rights, and some scholars so maintain. See Eugene Volokh, *Parent-Child Speech and Child Custody Speech Restrictions,* 81 N.Y.U. L. REV. 631 (2006). But comparison with expression between adults might suggest otherwise. Significantly, the mother in *Shepp* stated that the father's belief in polygamy was the reason she sought a divorce from him. Yet, of course, the Pennsylvania high court nowhere suggested that granting her the divorce violated the husband's First Amendment rights, unjustifiably imposing a "penalty" on him for engaging in protected speech, nor that the mother had somehow wronged him for causing him to suffer in his relationship *with her* because of his religious expression. In our dealings with other adults, we just accept that we have no right against adverse effects on our relationships with them as a result of their reacting negatively to what we say to them, regardless of the religious or non-religious nature of that speech. If we view a court deciding child custody, charged with doing what is best for the child, as essentially a proxy decision maker for the child, should we not similarly say that parents have no right against adverse effects on their relationship with their children as a result of the children's proxy reacting to what parents say to the children? See James G. Dwyer, *Parents' Self-Determination and Children's Custody: A New Analytical Framework for State Structuring of Children's Family Life*, 54 ARIZ. L. REV. 79 (2012) (making that argument).

Parents' religious beliefs can also affect their parenting choices. Should parents be at a disadvantage in a custody dispute if they are religiously opposed to medical care or to mainstream education? Or if their religious practices threaten their own health and safety, as, for example, by handling snakes, which could make it difficult or impossible to care for their children? Most courts in the United States have taken the approach of counting religiously motivated conduct against a parent in an initial custody award, or of imposing restrictions on a parent's behavior when with the child, only if the other parent shows the practices have already caused harm to the child. Out of solicitude for parents' religious liberty, courts will not base decisions on a prediction of harm from religious practices, even though they do so with respect to harm from non-religious parental conduct such as smoking and alcohol or drug abuse.

For example, in Harrison v. Tauheed, 2010 WL 2791564, the Court of Appeals of Kansas held that a trial court could not constitutionally consider in a custody decision that the mother would, because of her religious beliefs, refuse medical care for the child, in the absence of a showing that this disposition of the mother had already harmed the child. The court held the same as to the mother's practice of requiring the five-year-old child to go door-to-door proselytizing with her for five hours at a time. In Quiner v. Quiner, 59 Cal. Rptr. 503 (Cal. Ct. App. 1967), a California appellate court overturned a trial court award of custody to a father, despite agreeing that this decision was likely in the child's best interests, because an important factor in the trial court's decision was that the mother had brought the child to religious meetings at which women were not permitted to speak. The appellate court held that this violated the Free Exercise rights of the mother. The American Law Institute (ALI) has advocated a stringent test for basing custody decisions on parents' religious practices, urging courts not to consider such practices at all "except to the minimum degree necessary to protect the child from severe and almost certain harm." A.L.I., Principles of the Law of Family Dissolution: Analysis and Recommendations §2.12 (2002). The European Court of Human Rights adopted a similar position in a case resembling Harrison v. Tauheed. See Hoffman v. Austria, 225 Eur. Ct. H.R. (ser. A) 45 (1993) (holding that award of custody to father based in part on mother's opposition to blood transfusions as a Jehovah's Witness violated her rights under the ECHR to respect for family life and against discrimination based on religious belief).

Again we might ask why the rule for courts' deciding about children's family relationships should be so different from adults' deciding about their own family relationships. An adult who does not want to continue an intimate partnership with another adult because the other insists she join in long days of proselytizing or attend sex-segregated meetings is morally and legally free to discontinue it, unconstrained by any right of the other adult. Why should a court deciding in behalf of a child not be equally free?

On the other hand, Volokh and some family law scholars advance a kind of "equal treatment for divorced parents" argument. They maintain that courts should not be able to curtail the religious freedom of parents whose relationship has dissolved to a greater extent than they may when parents are cohabiting in an intact relationship. And they note that the state does not presume to remove children from intact families simply because the parents have religious beliefs opposed to medical care or to gender equality. A Wisconsin court adopted this reasoning also, in holding that a trial court had violated a mother's free exercise rights by awarding custody to the father on the grounds that the mother, who had converted to the Amish faith, would deny a high school education to their daughter. Adrian v. Petty, 302 Wis. 2d 260 (Wis. Ct. App. 2007). Can you put forth any reasons why different treatment might be justified in the two situations—that is, why divorce might properly license the state incidentally to infringe parents' religious liberty (by making relevant to a custody decision religious beliefs that might someday lead to harm or religious practices that threaten only more subtle detriment) to a greater extent than it does when parents are cohabiting? Does the New Hampshire court in the case below provide adequate reasons?

In re Kurowski

20 A.3d 306 (N.H. 2011)

Lynn, J.

. . . The parties were divorced in 1999 in Massachusetts, at which time they stipulated to joint legal custody of daughter who was an infant. At all times relevant to this appeal, daughter has resided primarily with mother. In 2002, . . . mother moved to this state with daughter. At the time of this move, daughter was about three years old. In October 2002, the parties stipulated to a routine residential responsibility schedule that gave father time with daughter one evening per week and on alternate weekends . . . They also agreed to "consult with one another with respect to the educational plans for said child." . . .

Daughter attended a private school for kindergarten and mother decided to home school her for first grade. In 2005, father filed a contempt motion in which he alleged that mother had unilaterally decided to home school daughter. He also related his concern that daughter's home schooling was based upon mother's religious practice, which had the effect of isolating daughter from her peers. . . . [D]aughter spent time exclusively with children who are part of her mother's church and religion, causing her to be uncomfortable in his family environment, and [father] expressed his desire that daughter . . . experience diversity and improve her ability to accept differences in his home. . . .

In January 2007, father filed a motion for modification [and] alleged: "At her mother's insistence, and against [his] wishes, [daughter] is home-schooled through a program that is affiliated with a church that both [mother] and [daughter] attend on a regular basis"; daughter is withdrawn during his parenting time and has difficulty integrating with his new wife and new child . . . He requested that the court appoint a guardian ad litem to represent daughter's best interests. . . . He . . . sought both to compel daughter's enrollment in public school and to expand his routine parenting time. . . .

On September 24, 2008, the parties and the GAL . . . agreed to joint decision-making on all major decisions, including daughter's education and religious training. They also agreed to expand father's routine parenting time. . . . With respect to daughter's schooling, the plan . . . stated: ". . . there shall be a meeting in January, 2010, when [daughter] is completing fifth grade, to discuss [daughter's] transition to public school, unless the parents agree she should continue home schooling at that time." . . .

In January 2009, daughter began attending three classes at public school to augment her home school education. In February 2009, mother moved to modify the 2008 Parenting Plan alleging that daughter was experiencing "extreme difficulty" and that her "emotional and mental health have been negatively impacted by the increased time with [father]." . . . On July 14, 2009, the trial court issued an order . . . that daughter would attend public school in the 2009–2010 academic year . . . applying the best interests standard. . . .

The United States Constitution protects the fundamental right of parents to make decisions concerning the custody, care and control of their children, including a child's education and religious upbringing. *See Troxel v. Granville* (2000) (parenting rights protected under Due Process Clause of Fourteenth Amendment); *Wisconsin v. Yoder* (1972) (Free Exercise Clause of the First Amendment, and the traditional interest of parents, protect rights of parents to make decisions concerning the religious upbringing of their children); *Pierce v. Society of Sisters* (1925). . . . [T]here is a presumption that fit parents act in the best interests of their children, *Troxel*.

Mother cites several cases in support of her contention that the trial court's school placement decision is subject to strict scrutiny. However, . . . in none of the cited cases was a court resolving a dispute between two parents with equal constitutional parenting rights and decision-making authority regarding their child's education and religious training. . . . Each parent was equally entitled to the presumption that his or her respective decision was consonant with daughter's best interests. Yet, . . . they ultimately reached an impasse. . . . The legislature established a procedure for courts to resolve disputes between parents . . . guided by the best interests standard. . . . [T]he best interests standard "does not and cannot abrogate a fit parent's constitutional right to direct the upbringing of his or her child." However, in the context of a divorce, the . . . trial court's decision is not subject to strict scrutiny review. . . . Our decision is consistent with that of many other courts. *See Jordan v. Rea* (Ariz. App. 2009) (father's religious objection cannot be the basis of precluding superior court from determining what educational placement is in the child's best interest); *Yordy v. Osterman* (Kan. 2007) (trial court has authority to decide between secular and religious schools, based on best interest of child, where parents with joint legal custody cannot agree). . . .

The GAL testified that she had researched the subject of adolescent brain development. . . . She stated that "the literature" explains that "the repeated stimulation of brain connections causes areas of the brain to become strengthened, while not using areas of the brain causes them to wither away . . . [and] [t]hat . . . raises the question about whether a child should be engaged in activities which promote active brain development and active brain skill development." She also testified that she was "not an expert in brain science." . . . [S]he also testified to . . . the strong alignment of daughter's beliefs with her mother's, daughter's limited opportunity in her home school experience to face situations that will be socially challenging to her, her hindered ability to consider and discuss disparate points of view with others who do not share her position, and her tenuous relationship with her father. . . . [D]aughter's home school experience consisted of performing school work at home, taking private music lessons, and attending a monthly theater class and weekly classes in art, Spanish and physical education at a public school in Meredith. . . . [T]he curriculum . . . , approved by the school district, was "comparable to the public school curriculum at the same age, except for the bible class." . . .

The trial court found that "[daughter] is generally likeable and well liked, social and interactive with her peers, academically promising, and intellectually at or superior to grade level." It also determined that daughter "is doing very well academically and scores above-average in most classes when compared with the national average for children of her class and age group," that she fulfills the public school requirements for theatre and music, and that she engages in many social activities that are not related to her church or faith. Noting that the relative academic merits of daughter's home schooling as compared to public schooling were not disputed by the parties, the trial court stated that "the debate centers on whether enrollment in public school will provide [daughter] with an increased opportunity for group learning, group interaction, social problem solving, and exposure to a variety of points of view." It identified the guideposts it utilized to resolve the dispute:

> the Court is guided by the premise that education is by its nature an exploration and examination of new things, and by the premise that a child requires academic, social, cultural, and physical interaction with a variety of experiences, people, concepts, and surroundings in order to grow to an adult who can make intelligent decisions about how to achieve a productive and satisfying life.

The trial court remarked that it considered the impact that daughter's religious convictions had on her "interaction with others, both past and future."

Ultimately, . . . the trial court concluded that "it would be in [daughter's] best interests to attend public school." The trial court declined "to impose any restrictions on either party's ability to provide [daughter] with religious training or to share with [daughter] their own religious beliefs." Also, . . . it emphasized that the parties had the "authority to agree to continue the hybrid approach they have been using (home school plus some public school classes), and authority to agree that [daughter] attend a Christian school or other school with a religious educational program" . . .

When applying the best interests standard to decide a parenting rights and responsibilities matter, the trial court may consider a parent's religious training of his or her child solely in relation to the welfare of the child. The trial court can restrict a parent's religious training of his or her child only if substantial evidence shows that the child's welfare was in fact jeopardized by that religious training. . . . In its order, the trial court referred to . . . : the GAL's account of daughter's interaction with her counselor in which daughter "appeared to reflect her mother's rigidity on questions of faith"; the GAL's concerns about the impact of daughter's religious beliefs on her relationship with her father; the father's desire to expose daughter to different viewpoints to decrease his daughter's "rigid adherence" to her mother's religious beliefs; and mother's acknowledgement of the strength of her and daughter's religious beliefs. The trial court also remarked that daughter's strong adherence to religious convictions that align with her mother's beliefs likely was the effect of "spend[ing] her school time with her mother and the vast majority of all of her other time with her mother." [I]t had "not considered the merits of [daughter's] religious beliefs, but considered only the impact of those beliefs on her interaction with others, both past and future." . . . "Evidence of some of the specific tenets of [mother's] faith [was] only admitted because of statements and behaviors of [daughter] suggesting that [daughter's] application of the logical consequences of those tenets was impacting her feelings toward her father and might impact her development in other areas"; and "The evidence about faith is only relevant because [daughter] was unhappy that her father does not love her enough to want to spend eternity with her by adopting her faith. . . ." The record supports these statements.

Specifically, evidence was presented that daughter exhibited difficulty interacting with others, particularly her father, when they did not agree with her religious convictions. For example, the GAL testified to a situation in which daughter became angry with her therapist when the therapist did not read certain religious materials provided by daughter and "closed down in the [therapy] session." Father testified regarding some conversations he tried to have with daughter about her religious beliefs, and explained "if somebody doesn't believe in [daughter's] religion, if somebody does something differently from what she has been told by her mom is either right or wrong, based on this religion, she has a real, real hard time with it." He also testified, "if there's ever anything that goes against what she believes in, she doesn't really know how to respond and she automatically thinks that somebody's attacking her or somebody is going up against her," and, "when you have a serious discussion with [daughter] . . . when you question her beliefs, or you present another idea to her about a religious belief, she doesn't know what to do. She clams up. She turns away. You know, she just really can't go any further."

In its order, the trial court did not express a belief that daughter needed to be exposed to other religions that were contrary to or different from the beliefs of her parents. Instead, it considered the importance of daughter having the ability to openly communicate with others who have a different viewpoint on a subject matter, whether or not the topic is religious in nature. It also considered the benefits of group learning, group interaction, social problem solving and exposure to a variety of points of view. We reject mother's contention that the trial court expressed disapproval of her actions in encouraging daughter to share her religious views. Rather, the trial court found that daughter's firm religious convictions likely stemmed from the amount of time she spends with her mother, considering that daughter primarily resided with, and had been primarily educated by, her mother. The trial court did not express disfavor regarding the religious nature of daughter's beliefs or disapproval regarding her vigorous defense of her religious beliefs. Nor did the court criticize the merits of mother's and daughter's religious convictions. . . .

Accordingly, we conclude that the trial court properly considered daughter's religious beliefs only in the context of her welfare when resolving the school placement dispute between the parents. . . . [Its] references to the nature of education and foundational skills necessary for a child to become a productive and satisfied adult were not inconsistent with RSA 193-E:2 or RSA 193-A:4, I. RSA 193-E:2 sets forth the criteria for an adequate education provided through the public school system, including "[s]kills for lifelong learning . . . to enable them to learn, work, and participate effectively in a changing society." Also, the legislature declared that public elementary and secondary education shall provide "all students with the opportunity to acquire the knowledge and skills necessary to prepare them for successful participation in the social, economic, scientific, technological, and political systems of a free government, now and in the years to come." . . . The court's order refers to such factors as group learning, social problem solving, exploration and examination of new things, and academic, social, cultural and physical interaction with a variety of experiences, people, concepts and surroundings, as well as securing foundational skills necessary to become a productive and satisfied adult. These criteria are in accord with the factors set forth in RSA 461-A:6, I, including "[t]he relationship of the child with each parent," "[t]he child's developmental needs," and "[t]he quality of the child's adjustment to the child's school and community and the potential effect of any change," as well as "[a]ny other additional factors the court deems relevant." We conclude that mother has failed to demonstrate that the parameters used by the trial court to guide its decision constituted legal error or an unsustainable exercise of discretion.

Finally, . . . neither its order nor the record reveals that the trial court exhibited a presumptive bias in favor of public schooling. . . . [D]aughter learned many of her academic subjects . . . primarily by watching recorded lessons by herself on a computer at home, completing worksheets or workbooks and asking her mother questions as needed. . . . [T]here was no interactive quality between daughter and the person providing instruction in the recorded lesson. . . . This process encompassed approximately three to three and one-half hours per day, and there was evidence that daughter was "bored" with, and "lonely" in, this educational environment. Regarding her public school classes, there was evidence that daughter actively participated and adapted well. . . . The trial court noted the GAL's conclusion that [her] "interests . . . would be best served by . . . be[ing] challenged to solve problems presented by a group learning situation and by the social interactivity of children of her age. . . .

We emphasize that the trial court did not need to decide that home schooling was somehow deficient or detrimental to daughter in order to determine that her placement in public school was consonant with her best interests. Nor does the fact that the trial court reasonably could have reached a different decision based upon the evidence before it mean that its decision constitutes an unsustainable exercise of discretion. . . . [T]he evidence provides an objective basis sufficient to sustain the trial court's discretionary judgment that it was in daughter's best interests to attend public school. . . .

Implicit in the trial court's reasoning was that there is something developmentally defective about an adolescent who adheres to particular religious beliefs rigidly and cannot have a calm, reasoned, respectful dialogue with people who hold different beliefs. Do you suppose courts or other government bodies would ever say such a thing about adults? Is unquestioning religious faith a clear indication of a deficient education? Looked at from another direction, is a child's interest in becoming morally autonomous a sufficient basis for state limitation of schooling options? And if it is, if children need exposure to ideological diversity, then why do states not require it for all children, regardless of whether their parents are battling for their custody? One could, after all, respond to equal treatment argument above by contending that the state should intervene more into intact families than it currently does, to avoid the same sorts of harms arising from parents' religious beliefs that courts sometimes use a custody decision between parents to avoid. Should an advocate for children be able to challenge state toleration of fundamentalist religious homeschooling? As we will see below, all states now empower parents to keep their children at home for schooling and most leave home schools virtually unregulated.

(6) Children's Wishes

The *Kurowski* opinion gives little attention to the daughter's wishes. Would a better fallback, when parents disagree, be the preference of the child, at least if the child has reached a certain age, rather than a judge's view of what is best for her? State custody laws typically direct courts to give some weight, perhaps even decisive weight, to the wishes of adolescents as to with which parent they primarily live. Most commonly, children 14 or older get to choose their living arrangement, unless a parent can show that this is clearly contrary to their welfare. See, e.g., Ga. Code Ann. §19-9-3(5), (6) ("In all custody cases in which the child has reached the age of 14 years, the child shall have the right to select the parent with whom he or she desires to live. The child's selection for purposes of custody shall be presumptive unless the parent so selected is determined not to be in the best interests of the child. . . . In all custody cases in which the child has reached the age of 11 but not 14 years, the judge shall consider the desires and educational needs of the child in determining which parent shall have custody.").

What are the pros and cons of putting this choice to a 14-year-old? Or of just soliciting the child's preferences? Illinois's custody statute requires courts to consider the child's wishes without limitation as to the child's age, but not necessarily to make those wishes decisive. See 750 Ill. Comp. Stat. 5/602(a)(2). Imagine yourself in the role of a guardian ad litem speaking with an eight-year-old client about the custody decision. Then imagine yourself a parent whose children are going to be asked by a guardian ad litem and perhaps directly by the judge with whom they want to live. What concerns would you have in either situation?

(7) Parents' New Relationships

The Indiana custody statute directs courts deciding custody to consider the "interaction and interrelationship of the child with . . . any other person who may significantly affect the child's best interests." One frequent source of custody litigation is one parent's feelings about the other's new spouse or partner. We will see below that courts in some states will order parents not to expose a child to a "meretricious" relationship, but in other states courts are disinclined to pass moral judgment on non-marital intimate relationships. And if a parent remarries, immorality of the new adult's presence is not part of the equation. The unhappy parent might nevertheless invoke such a statutory provision as invitation to consider the impact of the new partner's presence, and could point to research showing that step-parents are a common source of stress, depression, and even abuse in a child's life. See, e.g., Judith Wallerstein & Julia M. Lewis, *Sibling Outcomes and Disparate Parenting and Stepparenting After Divorce: Report from a 10-Year Longitudinal Study*, 24 Psychoanalytic Psychol. 445-458 (2007). However, courts generally do not rely on statistical averages or patterns, but instead require some evidence about the individual situation before them. Evidence that a particular child's relationship with a step-parent is marked by great conflict could influence a custody decision.

(8) Non-Custodial Parent Visitation

When one legal parent receives primary or sole custody, the other is generally entitled to significant visitation absent a finding of unfitness. For example, Arizona statutes state: "A parent who is not granted custody of the child is entitled to reasonable parenting time rights to ensure that the minor child has frequent and continuing contact with the noncustodial parent unless the court finds, after a hearing, that parenting time would endanger seriously the child's physical, mental, moral or emotional health." Ariz. Rev. Stat. §25-408. See also 750 Ill. Comp. Stat. 5/607 (same). This is a modern rule and practice reflecting two late-twentieth-century developments: one, a conclusion among child developmental theorists that preserving children's relationships with non-custodial parents is good for their health and happiness and, two, strong public policies in favor of having non-custodial parents rather than the state supply financial support to custodial parents. The two developments reinforced each other; non-custodial parents are inclined to stay more involved in their children's lives when they are paying support and are more inclined to comply with support orders when they have a relationship with the child. See William V. Fabricius & Sanford L. Braver, *Non-Child Support Expenditures on Children by Nonresidential Divorced Fathers,* 41 FAM. CT. REV. 321 (2003) (finding that "more time spent together does cause fathers to spend more money" and to "assume more financial responsibilities that by law are those only of custodial parents").

Non-custodial parents have this right to contact, so long as they are not unfit, regardless of their children's wishes and regardless of whether it is in the children's best interests. Moreover, because a common factor in awarding custody is whether a parent is inclined to encourage the child's relationship with the other parent, attorneys typically advise primary caretakers not to oppose visitation for the other parent unless there is clear evidence of danger to the child. See, e.g., Ga. Code Ann. §19-9-3(3) ("In determining the best interests of the child, the judge may consider . . . [t]he willingness and ability of each of the parents to facilitate and encourage a close and continuing parent-child relationship between the child and the other parent, consistent with the best interest of the child."); 750 Ill. Comp. Stat. 5/602(a)(8) (same).

This right of the non-custodial parent to visitation is one that they are free to waive; a court will not order a parent to spend time with a child, though it might increase a child support award if the non-custodial parent fails to take advantage of visitation opportunities, on the grounds that the custodial parent is carrying a greater child rearing burden as a result. Assuming that the non-custodial parent is fit, and therefore must be awarded some visitation if he requests it, courts will determine the specific schedule of visitation based on the best interests of the child. Issues that frequently arise in litigation over visitation include: a) whether the visitation should be supervised, because the custodial parent distrusts the non-custodial parent for some reason; b) what courts should do when the child and/or custodial parent obstructs ordered visitation; c) whether the court should impose restrictions on the non-custodial parent's behavior during visitation; and d) whether custodial parents may relocate with the child. We will look at the first two of these here, and at limits on behavior and relocation in the next section of the chapter.

Supervised Visitation

Custodial parents sometimes ask that a non-custodial parent have no visitation or, in the alternative, only visitation under supervision. They argue that the non-custodial parent poses a danger to the child if left unsupervised. Often the custodial parent is content to have a family member supervise, so might ask that visitation occur in the home of grandparents while the grandparents are present. In other cases, they request court-ordered professional supervision of custodial time.

All states have now institutionalized formal supervision, creating or contracting with agencies that can provide this service, and they are increasingly developing detailed standards for the operations of such agencies. See Elizabeth Barker Brandt, *Concerns at the Margins of Supervised Access to Children,* 9 J.L. & FAM. STUD. 201, 207 (2007); Nat Stern & Karen Oehme, *A Comprehensive Blueprint for a Crucial Service: Florida's New Supervised Visitation Strategy,* 12 J.L. & FAM. STUD. 199 (2010). With formal supervision, a non-custodial parent typically must go to the agency offices and meet with his or her child only in a designated room at the agency, with an agency employee present. The employee might simply observe and take notes or might become involved in the parent-child interactions in a therapeutic and educational role. In any case, the agency is evaluating the parent and might testify or submit a report in litigation.

Regardless of how supervision is structured, non-custodial parents generally do not like it and often protest that it is unnecessary and offensive. Formal supervision is quite unnatural and typically makes non-custodial parents uncomfortable. Formal supervision is also costly. Courts therefore have reason to refuse custodial parents' requests for it. When courts do order supervision, they frequently prefer that someone more knowledgeable about the non-custodial parent's mental condition and behavior—such as the supervisor or the other parent—make subsequent judgments about when and how such visitation will occur and when supervision will end. But that, too, rankles non-custodial parents.

Pratt v. Pratt

56 So. 3d 638 (Ala. Civ. App. 2010)

MOORE, Judge.

. . . [M]other had developed health problems following the birth of the parties' three children that caused her lethargy and other disabling symptoms, which sometimes prevented her from properly caring for the children. The mother used narcotic and other medications to treat those health problems, resulting in what one expert considered a substance-abuse problem, which another expert described as an "iatrogenic addiction."[1]

The mother appeared to overcome those problems after the parties separated, which allowed her to start working as a nurse and permitted her to exercise custody of the children uneventfully for a period. However, in early December 2008, the mother experienced a seizure-like episode and lost consciousness late at night while at her home in Montgomery with the children and her father. Following that episode, the father obtained custody of the children while the mother remained hospitalized.

Upon her discharge several days later, the mother's treating physicians, who did not definitively diagnose the cause of the episode but suspected it may have arisen from the mother's medically unsupervised attempt to withdraw from all of her medications, recommended that the mother cease using narcotic medications; however, at the time of trial, the mother continued to use narcotic medications prescribed by her pain-management physician. Some evidence suggested that the mother had also obtained prescription medications from other physicians without coordinating with her primary doctor. All the expert testimony on the subject recommended that, due to her unresolved health and prescription-drug-use problems, the mother should have supervised visitation with the children.

The trial court entered its judgment of divorce on June 24, 2009. In that judgment, the trial court . . . awarded the parties joint legal custody of the children, awarded the father primary physical custody of the children, and awarded the mother supervised visitation. In reference to the mother's supervised visitation, the judgment stated:

> "3. . . . The [mother] shall have supervised visitation with the children and said visitation shall be supervised by Roger and Gloria Burk. The counselor, Laurie Mattson Shoemaker, shall prepare guidelines to be given to the supervisors for the supervised visitation.

1. "Iatrogenic" is defined to mean "induced inadvertently by a physician or surgeon or by medical treatment or diagnostic procedures."

> "4. The schedule of supervised visitation may be upon agreement of the parties, however, said visitation shall occur no less than once every two weeks, beginning June 26, 2009. The location and length of visits are at the discretion of the [father] and the supervising party, however, each visit should last at least two hours and should be held in as 'home-like' a setting as possible, so that the children feel comfortable." . . .

. . . [T]he mother contends that the trial court should have protected the children by using means other than supervised visitation that would be less intrusive on the parent-child relationship. . . . In exercising its discretion over visitation matters, "'[t]he trial court is entrusted to balance the rights of the parents with the child's best interests to fashion a visitation award that is tailored to the specific facts and circumstances of the individual case.'" A noncustodial parent generally enjoys "reasonable rights of visitation" with his or her children. However, those rights may be restricted in order to protect children from conduct, conditions, or circumstances surrounding their noncustodial parent that endanger the children's health, safety, or well-being. In fashioning the appropriate restrictions, out of respect for the public policy encouraging interaction between noncustodial parents and their children, the trial court may not use an overbroad restriction that does more than necessary to protect the children. . . . The mother argues that, in this case, the trial court could have adequately addressed its safety concern for the children by simply ordering that she refrain from using prescription drugs.

In *Jackson v. Jackson* (Ala. Civ. App. 2007), a plurality of this court concluded that a mother, who was accused of having in the past occasionally used marijuana for recreational use outside the presence of her children, should have been allowed unsupervised visitation subject to a prohibition against exposing the children to any illegal drug use. However, . . . mother in this case uses narcotic and other prescription medications daily, which use has adversely affected her ability to parent the children in the past and the cessation of which may have caused or contributed to her prior "black-out" episode while in her home with the children. In *Ratliff, supra*, we found it unreasonable to restrict a mother from using prescription drugs designed to control her mental-health problems while visiting with her children because such a restriction could actually endanger the children. For that same reason, we conclude that the trial court in this case could not have merely ordered the mother to refrain from using her prescription medications while visiting with the children. . . .

The mother next contends that the manner in which the trial court structured its award of supervised visitation granted the father so much discretion over her right to visitation that the father, in essence, may effectively veto that right. Although the trial court specified that the mother was to receive, at a minimum, two hours of visitation every two weeks, the trial court did not specify the location or the length of the mother's visits. Rather, the trial court granted the father and the visitation supervisors the exclusive discretion to determine the location of the visitation and whether the mother's visits should be extended beyond the minimum two-hour period. Additionally, although the trial court's judgment did not expressly grant the father the right to dictate the time at which the mother's visits are to be held, the judgment places considerable discretion in the father by requiring his agreement as to the timing of the visitation. . . .

Although Alabama law originally found no problem with vesting a custodial parent with complete discretion over the visitation of the noncustodial parent, over time our appellate courts began to recognize that divorced parties often disagree regarding visitation matters, and that a custodial parent should not be allowed to unilaterally limit or restrict the noncustodial parent's visitation. This court eventually held that a visitation order awarding "'reasonable visitation with the minor children at the discretion of the [custodial parent]'" generally should not be allowed because it authorizes the custodial parent to deny visitation altogether, which would not be in the best interests of the children. Since [that] decision . . . , this court has repeatedly held that a judgment awarding visitation to be supervised by the custodian of the child, without establishing a minimal visitation schedule for the noncustodial parent, impermissibly allows the custodian to control all visitation. *See also J.J. v. J.H.W.* (Ala. Civ. App. 2008) (court's judgment conditioning mother's right to visitation on dates and times children visited with maternal grandparents impermissibly deprived mother of right to specific visitation by granting maternal grandparents complete control over whether any visitation occurred). Based on the above-cited cases, an order of visitation granting a custodian so much discretion over a visitation schedule that visitation could be completely avoided if the custodian so desired should be deemed to be an award of no visitation and to be in violation of the rights of the noncustodial parent.

This court, however, has affirmed awards of unspecified visitation based on the agreement of the parties when the trial court also provides that, in the event of disagreement, "standard visitation" or some other specified visitation would be imposed. Thus, a judgment awarding visitation that guarantees the noncustodial parent a specified visitation schedule, while granting the custodian discretion to allow for additional visitation, does not necessarily violate the rights of the noncustodial parent. The propriety of the judgment depends on whether the noncustodial parent has a sufficient, specified visitation schedule to rely upon, independent of the custodial parent's discretion. . . .

. . . [I]n this case, we agree with the mother that the visitation schedule is unduly vague and that it, in fact, fails to provide her with any schedule at all. . . . [T]he mother has no recourse should the father elect to schedule those visits at a time and location prohibitive for the mother. . . . We also reiterate that "'[t]he *trial court* is entrusted to balance the rights of the parents with the child's best interests to fashion a visitation award.'" That judicial function may not be delegated to a third party. *See, e.g., M.R.J. v. D.R.B.* (Ala. Civ. App. 2009) (reversing as an improper delegation of judicial authority a trial court's visitation judgment in which the mother's visitation was at the sole discretion of the child's guardian ad litem). A trial court is not empowered to delegate its judicial functions even to another governmental agency. *Hall v. Hall* (Ala. Civ. App. 1998) (a trial court cannot delegate the decision whether to terminate father's supervised visitation to those who would decide whether father would be prosecuted for sexual abuse). *See also Sloand v. Sloand* (N.Y. App. Div. 2006) (reversing as an improper delegation of judicial authority that portion of the order delegating to the child's therapist the authority to expand or reduce mother's access to child).

The trial court's visitation award, as written, vests the father and the visitation supervisors with nearly complete discretion in determining when, where, and how the mother exercises her current visitation rights; it also grants a third party the right to decide when and if the mother's visitation rights should be expanded. Because those are nondelegable determinations for the trial court, we reverse those portions of the trial court's judgment and remand the cause for the trial court to establish a sufficiently specific visitation order for the mother. . . . [In addition,] the trial court exceeded its discretion by improperly delegating its judicial authority to the children's counselor to specify the conditions governing the mother's supervised visitation. . . .

The trial court in this case found the mother's struggle with medications reason not only for supervision of visitation but also for severe limitation of the amount of visitation. What reason did the court have for the latter? Why not order a lot of supervised visitation, especially where the concern is not that a parent will abuse a child but rather might become incapacitated for a time? Should it matter to the court's decision that the mother's condition was "iatrogenic"? In other words, should parental fault matter? Was this mother at all at fault? Cf. D.M.B.T. v. M.A.T., 2011 WL 1880372 (La. Ct. App. 2011) (approving order of supervision where HIV-positive father failed to take precautions to prevent transmission of bodily fluids to children, as evidenced by his biting one child on the butt (but not breaking the skin) while roughhousing).

In most cases resulting in supervision, the non-custodial parent has previously harmed the child by conduct or speech or has demonstrated a propensity to dangerous conduct. See, e.g., Ex parte Thompson, 51 So. 3d 265 (Ala. 2010) (holding that mother's request for supervision should be granted because of "undisputed evidence of [father's] inappropriate sexual arousal when the child, then two years old, sat on his lap, of [father's] abuse of drugs and alcohol, of his repeated attempts at rehabilitation and subsequent relapses, and of three alcohol-related arrests in a very short period, as well as his admission that he continues to drink alcohol and the fact that he has exhibited rage and inappropriate violent conduct in the presence of the minor child"); Cannon v. Cannon, 280 S.W.3d 79 (Mo. 2009) (upholding order that father's visits with his biological son and daughter must be supervised because father had previously raped his step-daughter).

Non-Cooperation with Visitation Orders

What recourse does a non-custodial parent have if s/he wants to spend time with the child but the custodial parent does not comply with a visitation order? What if the reason is that the child does not want to visit a parent? Some states address this common problem by authorizing a change of custody or a charge of contempt if a custodial parent acts improperly. See, e.g., Va. Code Ann. §20-108 ("The intentional withholding of visitation of a child from the other parent without just cause may constitute a material change of circumstances justifying a change of custody in the discretion of the court."); Va. Code Ann. §20-124.2 ("The court shall have the continuing authority . . . to make any additional orders necessary to effectuate and enforce any [prior] order . . . including the authority to punish as contempt of court any willful failure of a party to comply with the provisions of the order."). But courts are supposed to avoid issuing orders that are contrary to a child's interests, so endeavoring to create incentives for parental compliance often creates a conundrum.

In re Paternity of M.P.M.W.

908 N.E.2d 1205 (Ind. Ct. App. 2009)

Kirsch, Judge.

. . . Mother and Father have never been married, but have a child together, M.P.M.W., who was born on April 8, 2002. On September 20, 2005, Father filed a petition alleging paternity of M.P.M.W., and Mother admitted Father was the biological father of M.P.M.W. Mother was granted primary physical custody. Because Father and M.P.M.W. had not had a relationship prior to the filing of the paternity petition, a gradual schedule of unsupervised visitations was established.

In January 2007, Father filed a motion for contempt and petition for change of custody against Mother because she had withheld visitation rights. Father then filed another motion for contempt, and the trial court issued an order, finding Mother in contempt, issuing a writ for her arrest, and taking sentencing under advisement until Mother appeared in court. Father was also awarded sole custody with no visitation granted for Mother. In July 2007, the writ was served, and Mother was taken into in custody. Father filed a petition for change of custody, and after Mother was released from custody, she was allowed to have supervised visitation with M.P.M.W.

Over the next several months, Mother filed at least seven motions for contempt against Father regarding visitation. At one point, the trial court entered an order stating that law enforcement had the authority to require Father to turn M.P.M.W. over to Mother for summer visitation and modifying custody back to Mother. On September 24, 2008, the trial court issued an order finding Father to be in contempt of court for failing to notify Mother that he was taking M.P.M.W. out of state and for failing to timely turn the child over to Mother for summer visitation. Father received a 30-day suspended sentence on each offense for a total of sixty days suspended. The trial court also sentenced Mother for her previous finding of contempt to two years to be suspended on the condition that she not violate any of the trial court's orders in the future. The trial court also ordered that Father be awarded primary physical custody of M.P.M.W. Mother now appeals. . . .

Under Indiana Code section 31-17-2-21, a trial court may not modify a child custody order unless modification is in the child's best interests and a substantial change has occurred. Generally, cooperation or lack thereof is not appropriate grounds for switching custody. Were a court to consider such in its determination of a custody modification, it would impermissibly punish a parent for noncompliance with a custody agreement.

Here, although the trial court did include language regarding punishing Mother for violating the trial court's previous order and absconding the state with M.P.M.W., it also noted the following factors that led to its decision that a substantial change in circumstances had occurred and that it was in the best interest of M.P.M.W. that Father be awarded custody:

> The Mother absconded with the child to the State of Michigan and deprived the Father and their daughter of their relationship.
>
> The Mother dyed the hair of her child while in Michigan presumably to avoid being found.
>
> The Mother withdrew the child from daycare and didn't re-enroll the child while in Michigan.
>
> The Mother skipped a dentist appointment by going to Michigan.
>
> The child's teeth were in an extremely deplorable condition when this took place and later the child had to have oral surgery due to the condition of her teeth. The court attributes the child's dental problems, in part, to the neglect of the Mother. The child confirmed this when speaking with the court by indicating and demonstrating that she would eat handfuls of sugar at a time and rarely brushed her teeth while at the Mother's home.
>
> The Mother has reported the Father to Child Protective Services on more than one occasion without merit and as the court previously ruled this includes the allegation whereby the Father was watching an X-rated [movie] while in bed with the child. Again, the child confirmed to the court that this was a lie. The manner in which the child did this, by walking over to the judge and cupping her mouth and whispering that she lied added credibility to this statement.
>
> The child's immunizations were not kept up to date by the Mother.

We therefore conclude that the trial court based its decision on proper considerations, and it did not err in its decision to modify custody to Father. . . .

Civil contempt is failing to do something that a court in a civil action has ordered to be done for the benefit of an opposing party. A party who has been injured or damaged by the failure of another to conform to a court order may seek a finding of contempt. Whether a party is in contempt is a matter left to the discretion of the trial court. . . . It lies within the inherent power of the trial court to fashion an appropriate punishment for the disobedience of its order. Unlike criminal indirect contempt, the primary objective of a civil contempt proceeding is not to punish the contemnor but to coerce action for the benefit of the aggrieved party. . . . Here, the trial court found . . . :

> The Mother's many attempts to keep the Father from establishing custody and then undermining his right to be a part of his daughter's life cannot go unnoticed. By having a lengthy suspended sentence the Mother should appreciate the fact that if she absconds again with the child this court has a great ability to punish her to the fullest extent of the law. . . . This court will not tolerate any more dictatorial practices. . . .

When a suspended sentence for civil contempt is conditioned upon compliance with a trial court's orders, this court has previously held that the suspended sentence is not punitive in nature because it is intended to coerce the party to abide by the trial court's orders and affords an opportunity for the party to purge itself of the contempt. . . . [However, the] majority of cases where a suspended sentence has been found to be a proper sanction for a civil contempt violation have involved shorter periods of imprisonment. . . . [T]he two-year sentence in the present case, which falls within the sentencing range for a Class C felony, went beyond coercing action of a party and became punitive. Further, Mother's sentence did not offer an opportunity for her to purge herself of the contempt. Unlike a contempt sanction conditioned on the payment of money or the accomplishment of a single task, this contempt sentence here cannot be purged. We therefore conclude that Mother's sentence was punitive in nature and vacate her two-year suspended sentence and remand to the trial court for resentencing. . . .

If the mother did continue to violate court orders and the court ordered her imprisoned, that could certainly impact the child detrimentally. Are there any ways to compel parental compliance with a custody/visitation order that are not likely indirectly to impact the child adversely? Only when the parents are wealthy enough to pay a fine without the child suffering? In *M.P.M.W.*, it seems clear the parents are at fault for the non-compliance with the parenting plan. More difficult are cases in which children are opposed to the visitation.

In re Marriage of Rideout

77 P.3d 1174 (Wash. 2003)

ALEXANDER, C.J.

. . . Christopher Rideout filed a petition . . . seeking dissolution of his marriage to Sara Rideout. During the course of the Rideout's marriage, a son, Christopher (Kit) (birth date 7/23/1989), and a daughter, Caroline (birth date 8/1/1987), were born to the Rideouts. . . . On August 25, 1997, the superior court entered a decree dissolving the Rideout's marriage and approving a permanent parenting plan.

The plan provided that Sara was to have the children "the majority of the time," except that Christopher and Sara would alternate weekends with the children. Concerning the summer residence of the children, the parenting plan provided that Kit and Caroline would reside with Sara except for a four-week period when the children were to be with Christopher. Christopher's summer residential time was to be taken in "one or two blocks of time, at the father's option." . . . Transportation of the children for all scheduled residential times was to be provided by "the parent receiving the child(ren)." The parenting plan also provided that Christopher was to have residential time with Caroline on her birthday in "odd" years. . . .

Beginning on June 18, 2000, Christopher left several telephone messages for Sara in which he set forth the dates he wished to exercise his summer residential time with their children. Specifically, he indicated that he had requested "four weeks of visitation with both of my children beginning on July 14, 2000, and continuing for four consecutive weeks." He said that during the third and fourth week of the residential time they would be "out of town" for a family reunion in Idaho. July 14, 2000, was also the first day of a weekend on which Christopher was entitled to residential time with the children, pursuant to the alternate weekend residential time provision of the parenting plan. Christopher followed his telephone calls with a July 11, 2000, letter to Sara, in which he reiterated the dates he wished to have the children with him that summer. Christopher's attorney also sent Sara a letter on July 14, 2000, in which he specified the same dates. . . .

On July 14, 2000, Christopher went to Sara's home to pick up the children for his weekend and summer residential time. Neither Sara nor the children were then at the home. Later that day, Kit called his father who then went back to Sara's house in order to pick him up. When Christopher was at Sara's house collecting Kit, he was told that Caroline was horseback riding and that she would be delivered to Christopher's home later that day. However, Sara telephoned Christopher that day to tell him that Caroline was going to be staying with her instead of going with Christopher. The following day, Christopher again went to Sara's house in an effort to obtain Caroline. Sara's boyfriend answered the door and declined to supply Christopher with any information regarding Caroline's whereabouts.

On July 18, 2000, Christopher sought an order from the Thurston County Superior Court establishing specific dates for his summer residential time. In response, Sara filed a declaration in which she stated that "Chris[topher] Rideout is taking me to court, but his dispute is with our daughter. Since she is still a minor, she is at a great disadvantage in this dispute and I get dragged into the middle of it no matter how hard I try to stay out." On July 27, 2000, the superior court entered an order which provided that Christopher was to have residential time with Caroline from July 27, 2000, through August 24, 2000. The order also required Sara to transport Caroline to Christopher's house at 4:00 P.M. on that day. Sara did not deliver the child to Christopher as she had been ordered. . . .

Christopher brought a motion for an order holding Sara in contempt of court. . . . An order to show cause why Sara should not be held in contempt was then served on her. Sara responded . . . that Caroline did not want to spend time with her father, indicating that "I have tried every method of persuasion available to me to encourage my daughter to visit with her father[, but] Caroline adamantly refuses to go visit him."

On August 3, 2000, . . . Christopher filed a second motion for contempt against Sara. . . . A show cause hearing on both show cause orders was held. . . . Christopher's declarations described a pattern of behavior by Sara during the summers of 1998, 1999, and 2000 in which Sara allegedly failed to comply with the parenting plan insofar as it provided for Christopher's summer and alternate weekend residential time with Caroline. . . .

. . . [I]n the summer of 1998, he planned to take Caroline and Kit with him on vacation during a portion of his four weeks of summer residential time with the children.

Christopher indicated that shortly before they were to leave for the vacation, Sara called him to say that Caroline would not be going on vacation with him and that he could come over to her home and "drag Caroline out." Christopher claimed that, as a consequence, he "[r]eluctantly . . . forfeited a week and a half [of his summer residential time]."

In . . . summer of 1999, as he was planning to leave on a two-week trip with the children, Sara called Christopher to say that Caroline was ill. Christopher indicated that he waited two days for Caroline to recover from her illness, but was then informed by Sara that Caroline was still ill. Again, Christopher had a shortened summer residential time with Caroline.

Sara presented a declaration, purportedly written by Caroline on July 25, 2000, expressing . . . that she called her father . . . "hoping to negotiate a plan involving the rest of [the] summer." She indicated that Christopher told her that "all of the 'hassle' about the parenting plan was [her] fault." She further stated that "I don't want to spend four weeks with my father this summer." In response, Christopher presented a declaration, in which he indicated that he was "confident that this declaration is not a free expression of my daughter." . . .

[T]he court commissioner [found] . . . :

> 10. The mother has overly involved the minor daughter in this action, including facilitating the daughter's signing a statement which was filed in this action.
>
> 11. Ms. Rideout is an intelligent, competent, and capable parent with the ability to cause her thirteen year old to comply [with] the court's orders. . . .
>
> 16. The fact that the daughter does not live on her own and has lived in the home of the mother is evidence that the mother could have caused the daughter to visit her father. . . .

The commissioner also concluded that:

> 3. Although the mother failed to comply with the terms of the parenting plan by not allowing for every other weekend visitation, her actions do not rise to the level of bad faith.
>
> 4. . . . [However, a] finding of contempt, warranted by bad faith, should be entered for the mother's refusal or failure to comply with the terms of the court's order of July 27, 2000.

The court commissioner held, finally, that Sara was in contempt of the court . . . He then entered judgment against Sara for "$100 per day" from "July 27, 2000 through August 16, 2000." Although Christopher had requested an award of attorney fees and costs in the amount of $3,349.32, the commissioner ordered Sara to pay the lesser sum of $892.50. . . . [A] superior court judge . . . entered an additional finding of fact that "[n]othing, prior to July 27, 2000, indicated that the child was reluctant to . . . visit her father."

. . . [A] parent who refuses to comply with duties imposed by a parenting plan is considered to have acted in "bad faith." RCW 26.09.160(1). Parents are deemed to have the ability to comply with orders establishing residential provisions and the burden is on a noncomplying parent to establish by a preponderance of the evidence that he or she lacked the ability to comply with the residential provisions of a court-ordered parenting plan or had a reasonable excuse for noncompliance. . . . Sara does not dispute the fact that she did not comply with that order. Rather, she contends that her failure to comply was not in bad faith because she tried, albeit unsuccessfully, to persuade Caroline to visit her father at the time specified. The trial court did not accept that explanation. . . . [T]he findings are supported by substantial evidence.

The more fundamental question before us is whether a contempt order is appropriate when a child refuses to attend a court-ordered residential time because the parent charged with facilitating that visit has, as the trial court found, either acquiesced in or encouraged the child's refusal to visit? After examining relevant case law from other states,[6] the Court of Appeals answered that question in the affirmative. . . .

Sara not only contributed to Caroline's resistance to residential time with her father, but failed to make reasonable efforts to require Caroline to visit Christopher as required by the parenting plan and the trial court's order for residential time. . . . Although Sara portrayed herself as a powerless bystander . . . , she side-stepped her responsibilities as a parent. . . . Whether they like it or not, parents, like Sara, have an obligation to attempt to overcome the child's resistance to the residential time in order to ensure that a child's residential time with the other parent takes place. Sara . . . was obligated to make good faith efforts to require Caroline to do so. . . . [W]hile a parent should not be punished for the actions of a truly recalcitrant child, punishment is appropriate when the parent is the source of the child's attitude or fails to overcome the child's recalcitrance when, considering the child's age and maturity, it is within that parent's power to do so. . . .

In sum, we hold that where a child resists court-ordered residential time and where the evidence establishes that a parent either contributes to the child's attitude or fails to make reasonable efforts to require the child to comply with the parenting plan and a court-ordered residential time, such parent may be deemed to have acted in "bad faith." . . . RCW 26.09.160(1) provides. . .:

> An attempt by a parent . . . to refuse to perform the duties provided in the parenting plan, . . . shall be deemed bad faith and shall be punished by the court by holding the party in contempt of court and by *awarding to the aggrieved party reasonable attorneys' fees and costs incidental in bringing a motion for contempt of court.*

In addition, RCW 26.09.160(2)(b)(ii) provides:

> (b) If . . . the parent, in bad faith, *has not complied with the order establishing residential provisions for the child,* the court shall find the parent in contempt of court. Upon a finding of contempt, the court shall order: . . .
>
> (ii) The parent to pay, to the moving party, *all court costs and reasonable attorneys' fees incurred as a result of the noncompliance,* and any reasonable expenses incurred in locating or returning a child. . . .

6. *See, e.g., MacIntosh v. MacIntosh* (Ind. Ct. App. 2001) (Where the court rejected the notion that a child's resistance may excuse a missed visitation.); *Hartzell v. Norman T.L.* (Ind. Ct. App. 1994) ([A]n adolescents refusal to cooperate with scheduled visitation cannot divest a dissolution court of its authority to enforce its visitation orders.); Hancock v. Hancock, 122 N.C. App. 518 (1996) (Where the court held that where "the custodial parent does not prevent visitation but takes no action to force visitation when the child refuses to go," a contempt order is inappropriate because the parent's action is not willful.); Smith v. Smith, 70 Ohio App. 2d 87 (1980) (Where the court, focusing on the young age of the children (five- and eight-years-old), and reasoning that they were too young to make an affirmative and independent choice not to visit their father, upheld a contempt order against the mother who argued that her children refused to visit their father despite her encouragement to them to do so. The court reasoned that, given the age of the children, the mother had to do more than simply encourage them to visit their father.); Commonwealth ex rel. Ermel v. Ermel, 322 Pa. Super. 400 (1983) (after finding that the daughter's "'negative attitude' toward her father [was] a direct result of [her mother's] conduct," the court upheld a contempt order where an 11-year-old girl refused to visit her father).

Sara . . . must, therefore, pay Christopher's attorney fees and costs for his appeal to the Court of Appeals . . . [and] for his appeal to this court. . . .

The statute places on the non-compliant parent the burden of showing by a preponderance of evidence that he or she did not have the ability to comply. What sort of evidence might be used to meet that burden? During the summer of 1998 episode, the mother invited the father to come to her house and drag the daughter out, but apparently he declined to do that. If dragging is necessary to get a child to go on visitation, which parent should have the responsibility to do it, the custodial or non-custodial parent? Does the description of the summer 2000 episode suggest mother could have done something more, besides dragging, to increase the likelihood Caroline would go with her father? See also Brown v. Erbstoesser, 928 N.Y.S.2d 92 (App. Div. 2011) (rejecting request by custodial mother and teen siblings for modification of visitation order so that visitation would be at sole discretion of the children).

The court did not mention that the statute authorizes even more severe penalties—namely, jail time. When, if ever, is incarceration a proper response to a parent's thwarting of the other parent's visitation with a child? Cf. Adrian v. Petty, 302 Wis. 2d 260 (Wis. Ct. App. 2007) (overturning five-day jail sentence for contempt, which had been based on mother's not producing daughter for visitation with father, in part because mother claimed daughter had run away and father had not disproven this). See also Judith G. McMullen, *"You Can't Make Me!": How Expectations of Parental Control Over Adolescents Influence the Law,* 35 Loy. U. Chi. L.J. 603 (2004) (arguing that "while current evidence may justify a presumption of parental control over and responsibility for the behavior of older children, that presumption should be rebuttable because current evidence also shows that even diligent parental efforts cannot achieve complete control").

(9) Modification of Custody or Visitation

The Massachusetts rule for subsequent modification of a parenting plan is typical: "Upon a complaint . . . by either parent or by a next friend on behalf of the children . . . , the court may make a judgment modifying its earlier judgment as to the care and custody of the minor children of the parties provided that the court finds that a material and substantial change in the circumstances of the parties has occurred and the judgment of modification is necessary in the best interests of the children." Mass. Gen. Laws. Ann. ch. 208, §28. We will study the concept of substantial change of circumstances further below in connection with both relocation and child support. Relocation is a commonly asserted change of circumstances, and a change in custody is usually accompanied by a change in child support.

(10) Effects of Partnership Dissolution on Children

Divorce is typically a traumatic event in the lives of the adults involved, and the impact on them can generate social costs as well—for example, lost work productivity, health care needs, and police enforcement of criminal laws and protective orders. Not much attention is paid in public debate or social science research to dissolution of non-marital partnerships, but surely that can also be traumatic for the adult partners. Most complaints about the prevalence of divorce, however, focus on the impact it has on children. Do you think policy makers would or should stop worrying about divorce rates if it were the case that children did not suffer in any significant way?

There has been a great deal of social science research on the effects of divorce on children, with substantial variation in the degree of negative effect found, and with much debate about the validity of measures used and of conclusions drawn from the evidence gathered. Below is an excerpt from a well-received meta-analysis of numerous studies done in recent decades.

Alison Clarke-Stewart & Cornelia Brentano, Divorce: Causes and Consequences

106-129, 133, 139, 146-150, 174-175 (Yale Univ. Press 2006)

. . . [N]early half of the children born to married parents in this country go through a divorce experience before they are eighteen—about one million children each year. For these children, even more than for their parents, divorce can be an extraordinarily difficult experience. For adults, a divorce may offer advantages—pursuit of a new career, a new hobby, a new spouse, or a new lover. . . . But children see no benefit in divorce. . . . Reactions vary with age, but across the board, children experience feelings of confusion and betrayal as they watch their family fall apart and feel neglected while their parents struggle with their own problems. . . . Compared with children in intact families, children from divorced families are more likely to have conduct problems and show signs of psychological maladjustment; they have lower academic achievement, more social difficulties, and poorer self-esteem. . . . Their parents rate them as being less healthy, and the children themselves report more physical symptoms. . . . [E]motional costs include embarrassment, fear of abandonment, grief over loss, irrational hope of reconciliation, worry about their parents' well-being, anxiety about divided loyalties, and uncertainty about romantic relationships. . . . In one study of college students, . . . researchers found that those who had experienced their parents' divorce . . . harbored painful feelings. . . . Three-quarters of them said that they felt they would have been a different person if their parents had not gotten divorced. . . .

Infants and Preschool Children React to the News

. . . [E]ven infants are vulnerable because they . . . survive and thrive at the whim of the environment. . . . [S]tudies suggest that divorce affects infants' and toddlers' emotional relationships with their mother—perhaps reflecting the mother's own emotional problems. Children who are a little older are likely to find divorce bewildering. . . . They don't know what the words "separation" and "divorce" mean. They don't understand why Daddy is leaving, why Mommy is crying. . . . For them, love is *being with* the person. At this age children are frightened when the parent leaves—afraid of being left alone, anxious about being abandoned. If Daddy has left, who is to say that Mommy won't stop loving them and leave too? Compared with older or younger children, these children are most distressed. . . . In their play and conversations, these children made it clear they were concerned with making home safe from monsters, beasts, and baby kidnappers. . . . Lawyers were sometimes described as pirates, vampires, or wolves who scared children and stole from parents.

Preschool children have more difficulty accepting the permanence of the divorce and giving up hope for reconciliation than older ones. . . .

[I]t is not uncommon for parents to separate and reconcile and separate again before they ultimately get a divorce. From the child's point of view, this is even more confusing than one break, and certainly it is more difficult for the parent to explain. . . . The stress of divorce may lead young children to regress . . . . Their play behavior with peers is less mature; they stare at the other children instead of joining in the play. . . . [T]hey treat a stick merely as a stick rather than pretending that it is a witch's broom or magic wand. They are whiny, act out, and have temper tantrums. They have nightmares about monsters. . . . They suck their thumbs, . . . cling to their mothers. . . . They wet their beds . . . Some of the boys even act like girls. . . . [T]eachers say that they are more dependent, can't concentrate on tasks. . . .

Preschoolers may also feel guilty and responsible, as if the divorce is their fault. . . . They reason as follows: a person who doesn't like someone goes away; Daddy went away, so Daddy doesn't like me, so it was my fault. . . . They make up stories about seeing Daddy or talking to him on the phone. . . . Preschool children don't have a good sense of time, so a week is forever. They don't understand blood ties, so they think the departed parent may find another son or daughter to replace them. They are afraid that the parent will forget about them when they're gone. As one child put it, "When I'm with one parent, I always think the other one is dead." . . . For most children, however, the effects are relatively short-lived as they come to understand and accept the realities of their new family arrangements. . . .

School-Age Children Understand But Still Suffer

School-age children (six- to eleven-year-olds) understand better what the words "separation" and "divorce" mean, but they may be just as shocked and just as worried as younger children. . . . These older children, too, experience grief and sadness. . . . They are particularly affected by the loss of their father, expressing longing for him and grieving openly, wishing they could spend more time with him . . . . Older school-age children (nine- to eleven-year-olds) are not as likely to express their grief and sadness. Their most common reaction is anger, as they blame one parent for the divorce and for the other parent's suffering and lash out, openly expressing their animosity and even hatred. . . . [C]hildren in this age group expressed anger about moving away from their friends and having less money for things they needed, anger about their parents' suffering and their own deteriorating relations with their parents, and anger about practical problems with custody such as being shuttled back and forth between two homes. Many children in this age group also ruminate about the divorce . . . [and] have problems in school. . . . They were less regular in their school attendance, less popular and socially competent, and more likely to be referred to a psychologist or placed in special education. Compared with children from intact families, they were rated by teachers as being more aggressive and disobedient and lacking self-control. . . . Furthermore, these children may suffer from psychosomatic symptoms of stress—headaches, vomiting, dizziness, sleep problems, inability to concentrate. Again, it is important to note that not all children have these negative reactions; these differences reflect group averages . . .

Personal Story: "My parents separated when I was in the fifth grade. In retrospect, . . . I realize how miserable they were and how much they fought. But regardless of how unhappy they were, I did not want them to divorce. Years later, I came to realize that my parents' divorce was the best thing they could have done for our family. But at the time, I was devastated . . . . Not only was I terribly hurt, I was embarrassed. . . . My parents' separation was the most devastating event in my life. . . . I was sick for weeks; all I did was sleep and vomit. . . ."

Young Adolescents Are Anguished

. . . Early adolescence is a vulnerable time at best—a time of shaky self-esteem and autonomy issues. When their parents divorce, young adolescents often overreact with unrealistic anguish and anxiety. In their adolescent egocentrism they can see only their own needs and they feel that the world's eyes are on them. So they lash out at their parents, "How could you do this to me?" . . . Rarely do they understand their parents' perspective. . . .

To make matters worse, their parents often give these young adolescents added household and child-care responsibilities and urge them to take on odd jobs to make some extra money. . . . [T]he entire divorce experience can lead young adolescents to have a sense of "false maturity." They identify with the custodial parent and take on the role of the departed parent: an adolescent son becomes the man around the house; and an adolescent girl becomes the parent's confidant. Often, they have to listen as their parents unload their feelings of misery and frustration. . . . Being cast into a role for which they are not ready may lead young adolescents to be depressed. . . . They cannot hide behind the confusion of the preschool child or erupt into the angry outbursts of the school-age child. . . . They are angry about their lack of control and may engage in risky behaviors, such as sex, drugs, and alcohol. . . . Remember, though, that we are talking about increases in the *likelihood* of these problems for children of divorce; not all young adolescents experience these difficulties.

Older Adolescents Get in Trouble

Older adolescents (fifteen- to eighteen-year-olds) may not experience their parents' divorce to be as earth shattering as it is for younger ones, because their egos are more mature. They are more involved in their own activities, more independent of their parents. Nevertheless . . . [t]hey may feel abandoned, anxious, and depressed. . . . They may have problems sleeping and eating and focusing on their work or studies. . . . [A]dolescents developing identity can be thrown into chaos and their self-confidence may be undermined. . . . Studies show that adolescents from divorced families get lower grades, do more poorly on achievement tests, and have lower educational aspirations . . . [and] are twice as likely to drop out of school as those from intact families. . . . [T]hey are more aggressive and antisocial. . . . They say that they have committed more delinquent acts—shoplifting, damaging school property, running away from home, getting drunk in a public place, fighting, stealing, being stopped or picked up by police . . . . They were more likely . . . to have sex—more than twice as likely if they were girls and four times as likely if they were boys. They were more likely to smoke and to use other drugs. . . . [T]hey are twice as likely to feel hopeless (30 percent versus 14 percent) or to think of ending their lives (16 percent versus 8 percent) as adolescents whose parents are happily married.

Young Adults Are Not Immune

Even when the "children" are young adults, no longer living at home, they . . . are sad and concerned about the well-being of their parents, especially their mothers, for several years. . . . They may feel the demand to "parent" their parents . . . . Even years later, . . . [they] tend to be more depressed . . . . They are more likely to break up with their live-in partner and . . . are more likely to be unemployed . . . to live in subsidized housing and to be on welfare.

Personal Story: "My grades at college during the quarter when my parents split up were the worst I've ever gotten. I couldn't concentrate on schoolwork at all. I went to a lot of parties and drank to get drunk. When I was drunk, I did not have to worry about my parents' divorce. I had horrible insomnia and rarely got to sleep before three in the morning. When I did sleep I would have nightmares and wake up with my shoulders so tense they hurt. During finals week, I got strep throat and mononucleosis. I missed all my finals, flew home, and spent five weeks in bed. I lost twenty pounds and almost did not go back to school in winter quarter."

How Large Are Divorce Effects?

. . . [T]he long-term effects of divorce should not be exaggerated. . . . [T]he majority of children appear to be developing within the normal range—without identifiable psychosocial scars or other adverse consequences—even when the process of marital dissolution was painful for them. . . . Nevertheless, . . . [d]ivorce has a stronger effect on problem behavior and psychological distress than race, birth order, moving, having a new sibling, experiencing the illness or death of a significant family member, being ill, or having parents with little education. The association is larger than the link between smoking and cancer. . . . [S]ome individuals experience brief decrements in well-being while others never recover fully; some differences diminish over the first couple years after the divorce; others persist for a long time. . . . In some ways, children get over divorce faster than their parents. . . . Children's fear, grief, shock, confusion, disbelief, and desire for parental reunion fade quickly. . . . Children's behavior problems, especially aggressive behavior, also drop sharply after the first year or so. . . . One feeling that may not diminish over time, however, is anger . . . at the parent who had left them. . . . Effects on boys' academic achievement (grades and tests) did not diminish over the five years after divorce in one study . . . . [A]nxiety and depression also may persist. In Wallerstein's study, five and ten years after divorce, about one-third of the children who were preschoolers or school age when their parents divorced were still depressed and spoke wistfully of life in an intact family. . . . [T]hey expressed a new sense of powerlessness and a yearning for their father and they were afraid of disappointment in love relationships. These emotional longings are sometimes expressed in early sexual activity and pregnancy. . . . [T]he risk of childbearing before age twenty is about 30 percent for adolescents from divorced families versus only 15 percent for adolescents in two-parent families. . . . One-quarter of the adolescents whose parents divorced six years earlier had clinically significant mental disorders. . . .

Growing up in a divorced family can also hurt young people's hope for educational and occupational success. . . . The majority of divorced fathers do not provide support for higher education. . . . When they have a romantic relationship, it is likely to be more insecure, conflicted, and unhappy than the relationships of adults from intact families. . . . Wallerstein found that twenty-five years after their parents' divorce only 60 percent of the children . . . had married, compared with 84 percent in the general population. . . . The individuals who had not married . . . had no idea what a loving relationship should look like. . . . They held out for the perfect mate, and once they were convinced they had found him or her, they leaped into marriage and then were let down as their romantic expectations gave way to bitter disillusionment. . . . Anxiety about relationships is a constant, damaging theme in the lives of these young adults. . . . Parental divorce doubles the odds of offspring divorce. On average, children from divorced families died four years earlier than those from intact families. . . .

Personal story: "There were two positive consequences of my parents' divorce for me. I discovered my own strength by living through this most difficult experience and surviving the loss of my father, and I developed a close bond with my mother from sharing the experience. She and I have become best friends."

Personal story: "I remember walking alongside a white wooden fence on the way home from the grocery store with my mom when I was seven years old. I asked her why she and Dad were getting a divorce. She quickly replied, "'It's none of your business. I'll tell you when you are older.'"

Personal story: "Six months after the divorce my mom was still devastated. Dinner used to be family time with the four of us sitting around the table—my mom, my dad, my brother, and me. Now my mom would look at my father's empty seat and cry. My brother and I did not understand, and we would say something insensitive like, 'Are you going to cry again?' or 'Where is Daddy?' We were the most important thing in Mom's life, but she was always so sad and tired."

Marital Discord versus Marital Disruption

Knowing that parents who divorce have conflicts even before they separate raises a question: which is worse for the child, the conflict or the divorce? First, one might ask, do parents protect their children from the arguments? . . . One research team [found] . . . that when children were there, the parents' emotions were *more* negative and they were *more* apt to engage in verbal attacks and insults and less likely to talk calmly or display affection. . . . Not surprisingly, then, research consistently shows that marital conflict has bad consequences for children. . . . More emotional and behavior problems and less self-esteem than children in harmonious families. . . . In one study, researchers found that . . . when parents were jealous, moody, critical, domineering, and got angry easily, their offspring carried on the tradition in their own marital relationships. When parents were violent, their offspring were also. . . . Conflicts centering on the child are also particularly destructive. . . .

But which is worse, conflict or divorce? The answer seems to depend on the study. Conflict has been found to be worse for children's behavior problems, well-being, and achievement and for adults' life satisfaction. However, divorce has been found to be worse for children's perceived competence, problem behavior, and psychological distress and for adults' marital and relationship instability, relationships with father, and educational attainment. There is no clear pattern; both conflict and divorce are bad. Another question that arises is whether marital conflict is the reason that divorce affects children negatively. The most recent studies indicate that conflict accounts for about 15 percent of the effect of divorce on children's well-being. In other studies, conflict did not account for increases in behavior problems in children or lower educational attainment of adolescents with divorced parents. . . .

Often, unhappy parents ask whether it is better to stay together, even in an unharmonious marriage, "for the sake of the children." . . . There is research that supports the view that children are better off if their parents divorce rather than staying married—*if* the parents are in conflict before the divorce. . . . [However, w]hen divorce did not end the parents' conflict, offspring in divorced families had more problems than those in high-conflict families that stayed together; when divorce did end conflict, children in divorced families were better off. . . . [T]erminating a conflicted marriage is beneficial for children if it ends their stress. . . . But what if the couple is not in overt conflict? What if they just drift apart . . . ? Multiple studies show that children in low-conflict families are worse off if their parents split up than if they stay together. . . . Divorce after a low-discord marriage is especially distressing to children because they see no obvious reason for it. . . . [A] majority of recent divorces are not preceded by an extended period of overt and intense marital conflict. . . . If they can keep their unhappiness hidden from their children, it is better for the children if they stay together. . . .

WHAT HELPS CHILDREN ADJUST?

Qualities such as being smart and having an easy temperament and an optimistic outlook help children negotiate divorce more successfully. Being blessed with parents who are economically stable and psychologically healthy is also a great boon. . . . When parents are involved in their children's activities, express warmth and affection, and provide appropriate supervision and guidance as well as authoritative discipline, children are buffered from the adversities of divorce. . . . Another helpful factor is children's continuing contact with a noncustodial father, but regular contact of high quality and a positive father-child relationship matter more than the mere frequency of visits. Contact with Dad is more likely to have a positive effect if the parents get along. Parents shielding children from parental conflict and developing a cooperative coparenting strategy help the children cope effectively. Children also find the adjustment to divorce easier if they experience fewer stressors, such as relocation, litigation, and changes in custody. A network of supportive neighbors, friends, relatives, classmates, and even an adult mentor can help ease children's transition through divorce, and professionals can provide school programs, therapy, and advice to help them navigate the postdivorce terrain. What would be the pros and cons?

What implications might this empirical information have for public policy? For practice as a divorce attorney or as a guardian ad litem for children in disputed custody cases? Did this account of the research leave any important empirical questions unanswered? To what extent would you suppose the effects of divorce on children change from one era to the next? Is it likely easier for children to deal with now than it was a few decades ago, when divorce was less common and triggered stronger familial and societal disapprobation? How many of your classmates do you suppose have divorced parents?

On the impact that divorce can have on sibling relationships, see Shumaker, Miller, Ortiz & Deutsch, *The Forgotten Bonds: The Assessment and Contemplation of Sibling Attachment in Divorce and Parental Separation*, 49 FAM. CT. REV. 46 (2011).

(11) RETHINKING CUSTODY DECISION MAKING

There is widespread agreement that it is generally best for non-cohabiting parents to come up with their own parenting plan. There is some concern about a financially vulnerable spouse giving up too much in custody bargaining in order to secure more financial security, and some concern about spouses who have been victims of domestic violence being further abused in the negotiation process, but otherwise it seems the best outcomes are likely if the parents agree to a division of time and responsibility.

There is substantial disagreement, though, about how custody should be decided when parents do not agree. Is a judge the best person to make what is essentially a child rearing decision? Or is a judge needed only if you assume there are relevant legal considerations other than simply what is the best for the child in this inevitably sub-optimal situation? If custody decision making were exclusively a matter of doing the best thing for the child, would it be better to create a distinct office, a Public Guardian perhaps, staffed by child development and family counseling professionals, and give them definitive authority to determine the custody arrangement?

An alternative practical arrangement that courts never consider, but which the rare couple has adopted, is to have the child reside in one home and have the parents rotate in and out, in order to create more stability for the child. Assuming a particular couple can afford to make this work (it might require three residences—one for the child and another for each parent to live in when not with the child), should courts consider ordering it? What arguments could you make against such an order if you represent a parent? What position would you take as a guardian ad litem for a child?

B. LIMITS ON BEHAVIOR

We saw that legal marriage alters what the law permits or requires adults to do, in terms of sexual behavior and caretaking; triggers application of a special set of rules pertaining to violence; and gives rise to certain state-created financial benefits and burdens. With respect to the parent-child relationship, sex is not supposed to be part of the relationship, and the law reflects this by prohibiting any sexual conduct by parents with their children. But otherwise the law confers on parents extensive privileges and powers, and by means of those privileges and powers parents exert considerable control over the behavior of children, rendering state intervention to protect parents mostly unnecessary.

The more important sex-related legal rule pertaining to marriage was actually not about spouses' conduct with each other but rather about fidelity, and it is worthwhile to consider whether there is or should be any legal rule imposing some form of fidelity on parents or children, so Section II.A does that. In addition, we might ask whether there is a legally enforceable expectation that a person who enters a parent-child relationship, as parent or child, will engage in the behaviors ordinarily constitutive of the assumed role, something comparable to the expectation—today enforceable only by threat of terminating the relationship—that spouses will do the things ordinarily constitutive of a marriage, such as contributing to household maintenance and finances. Violence and caretaking by parents are salient issues in the parent-child context, just as they were in the marital context, and this Section covers these topics as well.

1. Fidelity

Prohibitions on polygamy and adultery aim to make marriage an exclusive intimate partnership. A married person is expected to have only the one mate-like relationship. Becoming intimate with someone other than one's spouse violates a legal and, in the eyes of most people, sacred moral obligation. The situation is quite different, and more complex, with parent-child relationships. We will first consider expectations with respect to a child.

a. Exclusivity of the Parental Role

The law historically has limited the number of legal parent-child relationships a child can be in at a given time to two—that is, with one mother and one father—and have given legal protection only to those relationships. Many scholars have critiqued this confining conception of parenting as inconsistent with the varied nature of caretaking for children. See, e.g., Sacha M. Coupet, *"Ain't I a Parent?": The Exclusion of Kinship Caregivers from the Debate over Expansions of Parenthood,* 34 N.Y.U. Rev. L. & Soc. Change 595 (2010); Katharine K. Baker, *Bionormativity and the Construction of Parenthood,* 42 Ga. L. Rev. 649 (2008); Laura T. Kessler, *Community Parenting,* 24 Wash. U. J.L. & Pol'y 47 (2007); Nancy E. Dowd, *Multiple Parents/Multiple Fathers,* 9 J.L. & Fam. Stud. 231 (2007); Melanie B. Jacobs, *My Two Dads: Disaggregating Biological and Social Paternity,* 38 Ariz. St. L.J. 809 (2006). See also Laura A. Rosenbury, *Between Home and School,* 155 U. Pa. L. Rev. 833 (2007) (criticizing the law's failure to address the importance to children's development of the time they spend neither with parent figures nor in school).

As we saw in Chapter 1, in the Supreme Court's *Michael H.* paternity-law decision, the plurality rejected the argument that the child was entitled to protection of her relationships with both of the men who had co-parented her, along with her mother. Today, the law in some states allows for some flexibility in the gender of a child's two parents. See, e.g., Elisa B. v. Superior Court, 33 Cal. Rptr. 3d 46 (Cal. 2005) (treating both members of a lesbian couple as legal parents under Uniform Parentage Act, in order to impose a child support order on one). But still there is almost universally a limit of two legal parents per child.

This numerical limitation on *legal* parent-child relationships is analogous to anti-polygamy laws. There is, however, no legal limit on children having parent-child-like *social* relationships with persons other than legal parents—that is, being cared for or even in the custody of non-parents. There is no criminal prohibition analogous to adultery laws proscribing interactions with outsiders that resemble the legally recognized relationship. Indeed, society has always expected adults other than parents to assist with child rearing, including grandparents, aunts and uncles, and neighbors. "It takes a village" is now a cliché in public policy discussions and in social discourse.

What the law does do, however, is give parents extensive control over children's relational lives, so that parents generally can completely monopolize a child's care and associations if they wish, ensuring that all of a child's attention and affection are directed to them. They may take a child to live in a trailer in the middle of the Wyoming prairie and never allow exposure to the outside world. The state would not treat this as a form of child abuse or neglect; the law does not impose on legal parents a duty to afford children any particular level of socialization. Maltreatment law at most requires that at least one person provides some minimum amount of emotional nurturance for a child, and a parent could choose to be the only person who provides any. The law bolsters this parental control over children's relational lives with rules analogous to the ancient crime of spousal seduction and civil causes of action against any person with whom one's spouse commits adultery. There are criminal prohibitions on child abduction and kidnapping, and there are civil causes of action for intentional interference with custodial rights and intentional infliction of emotional distress that a parent can use against someone who takes a child away. See, e.g., Wyatt v. McDermott, 2012 WL 1377362 (Va.) (affirming existence of common law action for tortious interference with parental rights); Stewart v. Walker, 5 So. 3d 746 (Fla. Dist. Ct. App. 4th Dist. 2009) (extending cause of action for IIED to apply against a custodial parent who relocates a child without permission).

One potential limitation on parents' control over this aspect of children's lives is statutory authorization of courts to order visitation between children and non-parents. Short visits would not be equivalent to the custody and primary caretaking that typically characterizes parenting, but these statutes also allow for orders of overnight and longer visits, and some even for shared custody. Most states have limited the opportunity to petition for visitation to grandparents, but some have opened the door much wider, authorizing any non-parent to petition for court-ordered visitation over the objection of a custodial parent and simply requiring that the court find visitation to be in the child's best interests. See, e.g., Va. Code §20-124.2(B) ("The court shall give due regard to the primacy of the parent-child relationship but may upon a showing by clear and convincing evidence that the best interest of the child would be served thereby award custody or visitation to any other person with a legitimate interest."). One such broad visitation statute became the subject of a U.S. Supreme Court decision, and that decision caused many states to scale back their third-party visitation statutes, bolstering the power parents have to exclude other potential caregivers.

Troxel v. Granville

530 U.S. 57 (2000)

O'Connor, J. announced the Court's judgment and delivered an opinion, in which The Chief Justice and Justices Ginsburg and Breyer join.

. . . Tommie Granville and Brad Troxel shared a relationship that ended in June 1991. The two never married, but they had two daughters, Isabelle and Natalie. Jenifer and Gary Troxel are Brad's parents, and thus the paternal grandparents of Isabelle and Natalie. After Tommie and Brad separated in 1991, Brad lived with his parents and regularly brought his daughters to his parents' home for weekend visitation. Brad committed suicide in May 1993. Although the Troxels at first continued to see Isabelle and Natalie on a regular basis after their son's death, Tommie Granville informed the Troxels in October 1993 that she wished to limit their visitation with her daughters to one short visit per month.

In December 1993, the Troxels . . . [filed] a petition to obtain visitation rights with Isabelle and Natalie . . . under . . . Wash. Rev. Code 26.10.160(3), [which] provides: "Any person may petition the court for visitation rights at any time including, but not limited to, custody proceedings. The court may order visitation rights for any person when visitation may serve the best interest of the child whether or not there has been any change of circumstances." . . . [T]he Troxels requested two weekends of overnight visitation per month and two weeks of visitation each summer. Granville did not oppose visitation altogether, but instead asked the court to order one day of visitation per month with no overnight stay. In 1995, the Superior Court . . . entered a visitation decree ordering visitation one weekend a month, one week during the summer, and four hours on both of the petitioning grandparents' birthdays. Granville appealed, during which time she married Kelly Wynn. . . . Granville's husband formally adopted Isabelle and Natalie.

II

The demographic changes of the past century make it difficult to speak of an average American family. The composition of families varies greatly from household to household. While many children may have two married parents and grandparents who visit regularly, many other children are raised in single-parent households. . . . Understandably, in these single-parent households, persons outside the nuclear family are called upon with increasing frequency to assist in the everyday tasks of child rearing. In many cases, grandparents play an important role. For example, in 1998, . . . 5.6 percent of all children under age 18—lived in the household of their grandparents. . . .

Because grandparents and other relatives undertake duties of a parental nature in many households, States have sought to ensure the welfare of the children therein by protecting the relationships those children form with such third parties. The States' nonparental visitation statutes are further supported by a recognition, which varies from State to State, that children should have the opportunity to benefit from relationships with statutorily specified persons—for example, their grandparents. The extension of statutory rights in this area to persons other than a child's parents, however, . . . can place a substantial burden on the traditional parent-child relationship. . . .

The Fourteenth Amendment provides that no State shall "deprive any person of life, liberty, or property, without due process of law." We have long recognized that [this] "guarantees more than fair process." The Clause also includes a substantive component that "provides heightened protection against government interference with certain fundamental rights and liberty interests."

The liberty interest at issue in this case—the interest of parents in the care, custody, and control of their children—is perhaps the oldest of the fundamental liberty interests recognized by this Court. More than 75 years ago, in *Meyer v. Nebraska* (1923), we held that the "liberty" protected by the Due Process Clause includes the right of parents to "establish a home and bring up children" and "to control the education of their own." Two years later, in *Pierce v. Society of Sisters* (1925), we again held that the "liberty of parents and guardians" includes the right "to direct the upbringing and education of children under their control." We explained in *Pierce* that "the child is not the mere creature of the State; those who nurture him and direct his destiny have the right, coupled with the high duty, to recognize and prepare him for additional obligations." We returned to the subject in *Prince v. Massachusetts* (1944), and again confirmed that there is a constitutional dimension to the right of parents to direct the upbringing of their children. "It is cardinal with us that the custody, care and nurture of the child reside first in the parents, whose primary function and freedom include preparation for obligations the state can neither supply nor hinder."

In subsequent cases also, we have recognized the fundamental right of parents to make decisions concerning the care, custody, and control of their children. See, *e.g.*, *Wisconsin v. Yoder* (1972); *Quilloin v. Walcott* (1978); *Parham v. J. R.* (1979) [parental right to commit children to mental health facility]; *Santosky v. Kramer* (1982) [state must prove unfitness by clear and convincing evidence to terminate parental rights]. In light of this extensive precedent, it cannot now be doubted that the Due Process Clause of the Fourteenth Amendment protects the fundamental right of parents to make decisions concerning the care, custody, and control of their children.

Section 26.10.160(3), as applied to Granville and her family in this case, unconstitutionally infringes on that fundamental parental right. The Washington nonparental visitation statute is breathtakingly broad. According to the statute's text, "*any person* may petition the court for visitation rights *at any time*," and the court may grant such visitation rights whenever "visitation may serve *the best interest of the child*." That language effectively permits any third party seeking visitation to subject any decision by a parent concerning visitation of the parent's children to state-court review. Once the visitation petition has been filed in court and the matter is placed before a judge, a parent's decision that visitation would not be in the child's best interest is accorded no deference. §26.10.160(3) contains no requirement that a court accord the parent's decision any presumption of validity or any weight whatsoever. Instead, the Washington statute places the best-interest determination solely in the hands of the judge. Should the judge disagree with the parent's estimation of the child's best interests, the judge's view necessarily prevails. Thus, in practical effect, in the State of Washington a court can disregard and overturn *any* decision by a fit custodial parent concerning visitation whenever a third party affected by the decision files a visitation petition, based solely on the judge's determination of the child's best interests. . . .

. . . [T]he record reveals that the Superior Court's order was based on precisely the type of mere disagreement we have just described and nothing more. The Superior Court's order was not founded on any special factors that might justify the State's interference with Granville's fundamental right to make decisions concerning the rearing of her two daughters. To be sure, this case involves a visitation petition filed by grandparents soon after the death of their son—the father of Isabelle and Natalie—but the combination of several factors here compels our conclusion that §26.10.160(3), as applied, exceeded the bounds of the Due Process Clause.

First, the Troxels did not allege, and no court has found, that Granville was an unfit parent. That aspect of the case is important, for there is a presumption that fit parents act in the best interests of their children. As this Court explained in *Parham*:

> Our constitutional system long ago rejected any notion that a child is the mere creature of the State and, on the contrary, asserted that parents generally have the right, coupled with the high duty, to recognize and prepare [their children] for additional obligations. . . . The law's concept of the family rests on a presumption that parents possess what a child lacks in maturity, experience, and capacity for judgment required for making life's difficult decisions. More important, historically it has recognized that natural bonds of affection lead parents to act in the best interests of their children.

Accordingly, so long as a parent adequately cares for his or her children (*i.e.*, is fit), there will normally be no reason for the State to inject itself into the private realm of the family to further question the ability of that parent to make the best decisions concerning the rearing of that parent's children.

The problem here is not that the Washington Superior Court intervened, but that when it did so, it gave no special weight at all to Granville's determination of her daughters' best interests. More importantly, it appears that the Superior Court applied exactly the opposite presumption. . . . [T]he Superior Court judge explained:

> . . . I think . . . it is normally in the best interest of the children to spend quality time with the grandparent, unless . . . there are some issues or problems involved wherein the grandparents, their lifestyles are going to impact adversely upon the children. That certainly isn't the case here from what I can tell.

The judge's comments suggest that he presumed the grandparents' request should be granted unless the children would be "impacted adversely." In effect, the judge placed on Granville, the fit custodial parent, the burden of *disproving* that visitation would be in the best interest of her daughters. . . . The decisional framework employed by the Superior Court directly contravened the traditional presumption that a fit parent will act in the best interest of his or her child. In that respect, the court's presumption failed to provide any protection for Granville's fundamental constitutional right to make decisions concerning the rearing of her own daughters. Cf., *e.g.*, Cal. Fam. Code §3104(e) (rebuttable presumption that grandparent visitation is not in child's best interest if parents agree that visitation rights should not be granted); Me. Rev. Stat., Tit. 19A, §1803(3) (court may award grandparent visitation if in best interest of child and "would not significantly interfere with any parent-child relationship or with the parent's rightful authority over the child"); Minn. Stat. §257.022(2)(a)(2) (similar); Neb. Rev. Stat. §43-1802(2) (similar); R.I. Gen. Laws

§15-5-24.3(a)(2)(v) (grandparent must rebut, by clear and convincing evidence, presumption that parent's decision to refuse grandparent visitation was reasonable); Utah Code §30-5-2(2)(e) (same); Hoff v. Berg, 595 N.W.2d 285 (N. D. 1999) (holding North Dakota grandparent visitation statute unconstitutional because State has no "compelling interest in presuming visitation rights of grandparents to an unmarried minor are in the child's best interests and forcing parents to accede to court-ordered grandparental visitation unless the parents are first able to prove such visitation is not in the best interests of their minor child").

In an ideal world, parents might always seek to cultivate the bonds between grandparents and their grandchildren. Needless to say, however, our world is far from perfect, and in it the decision whether such an intergenerational relationship would be beneficial in any specific case is for the parent to make in the first instance. And, if a fit parent's decision of the kind at issue here becomes subject to judicial review, the court must accord at least some special weight to the parent's own determination.

Finally, we note that there is no allegation that Granville ever sought to cut off visitation entirely. . . . In the Superior Court proceedings Granville did not oppose visitation but instead asked that the duration of any visitation order be shorter than that requested by the Troxels. . . . The Superior Court gave no weight to Granville's having assented to visitation even before the filing of any visitation petition. . . . The court instead rejected Granville's proposal and settled on a middle ground, ordering one weekend of visitation per month, one week in the summer, and time on both of the petitioning grandparents' birthdays. Significantly, many other States expressly provide by statute that courts may not award visitation unless a parent has denied (or unreasonably denied) visitation to the concerned third party. See, *e.g.*, Miss. Code §93-16-3(2)(a); Ore. Rev. Stat. §109.121(1)(a)(B); R.I. Gen. Laws §15-5-24.3(a)(2)(iii)-(iv) (court must find that parents prevented grandparent from visiting grandchild and that "there is no other way the petitioner is able to visit his or her grandchild without court intervention"). . . .

. . . [T]he combination of these factors demonstrates that the visitation order in this case was an unconstitutional infringement on Granville's fundamental right to make decisions concerning the care, custody, and control of her two daughters. The Superior Court failed to accord the determination of Granville, a fit custodial parent, any material weight. In fact, the Superior Court made only two formal findings in support of its visitation order. First, the Troxels "are part of a large, central, loving family, all located in this area, and the [Troxels] can provide opportunities for the children in the areas of cousins and music." Second, "the children would be benefitted from spending quality time with the [Troxels]. . . ." These slender findings, in combination with the court's announced presumption in favor of grandparent visitation and its failure to accord significant weight to Granville's already having offered meaningful visitation to the Troxels, show that this case involves nothing more than a simple disagreement between the Washington Superior Court and Granville concerning her children's best interests.

The Superior Court's announced reason for ordering one week of visitation in the summer demonstrates our conclusion well: "I look back on some personal experiences. . . . We always spent as kids a week with one set of grandparents and another set of grandparents, [and] it happened to work out in our family that [it] turned out to be an enjoyable experience. Maybe that can, in this family, if that is how it works out." As we have explained, the Due Process Clause does not permit a State to infringe on the fundamental right of parents to make childrearing decisions simply because a state judge believes a "better" decision could be made. Neither the Washington nonparental visitation statute generally—which places no limits on either the persons who may petition for visitation or the circumstances in which such a petition may be granted—nor the Superior Court in this specific case required anything more. Accordingly, we hold that §26.10.160(3), as applied in this case, is unconstitutional.

Because we rest our decision on the sweeping breadth of §26.10.160(3) and the application of that broad, unlimited power in this case, we do not consider . . . whether the Due Process Clause requires all nonparental visitation statutes to include a showing of harm or potential harm to the child as a condition precedent to granting visitation. We do not, and need not, define today the precise scope of the parental due process right in the visitation context. In this respect, we agree with Justice Kennedy that the constitutionality of any standard for awarding visitation turns on the specific manner in which that standard is applied and that the constitutional protections in this area are best "elaborated with care." Because much state-court adjudication in this context occurs on a case-by-case basis, we would be hesitant to hold that specific nonparental visitation statutes violate the Due Process Clause as a *per se* matter. . . .

Justice SOUTER, concurring in the judgment.

. . . [B]ecause the state statute authorizes any person at any time to request (and a judge to award) visitation rights, subject only to the State's particular best-interests standard, the state statute sweeps too broadly and is unconstitutional on its face. Consequently, there is no need to decide whether harm is required or to consider the precise scope of the parent's right or its necessary protections. . . . *Meyer*'s repeatedly recognized right of upbringing would be a sham if it failed to encompass the right to be free of judicially compelled visitation by "any party" at "any time" a judge believed he "could make a 'better' decision" than the objecting parent. . . .

The strength of a parent's interest in controlling a child's associates is as obvious as the influence of personal associations on the development of the child's social and moral character. Whether for good or for ill, adults not only influence but may indoctrinate children, and a choice about a child's social companions is not essentially different from the designation of the adults who will influence the child in school. Even a State's considered judgment about the preferable political and religious character of schoolteachers is not entitled to prevail over a parent's choice of private school. *Pierce v. Society of Sisters* (1925). It would be anomalous, then, to subject a parent to any individual judge's choice of a child's associates from out of the general population merely because the judge might think himself more enlightened than the child's parent. . . .

Justice THOMAS, concurring in the judgment.

. . . *Pierce* holds that parents have a fundamental constitutional right to rear their children, including the right to determine who shall educate and socialize them. . . . I would apply strict scrutiny to infringements of fundamental rights. Here, the State of Washington lacks even a legitimate governmental interest—to say nothing of a compelling one—in second-guessing a fit parent's decision regarding visitation with third parties. . . .

Justice STEVENS, dissenting.

. . . [A] facial challenge should fail whenever a statute has "a 'plainly legitimate sweep.'" Under the Washington statute, there are plainly any number of cases—indeed, one suspects, the most common to arise—in which the "person" among "any" seeking visitation is a once-custodial caregiver, an intimate relation, or even a genetic parent. Even the Court would seem to agree that in many circumstances, it would be constitutionally permissible for a court to award some visitation of a child to a parent or previous caregiver in cases of parental separation or divorce, cases of disputed custody, cases involving temporary foster care or guardianship, and so forth. . . .

The second key aspect of the Washington Supreme Court's holding—that the Federal Constitution requires a showing of actual or potential "harm" to the child before a court may order visitation continued over a parent's objections—finds no support in this Court's case law. . . . [W]e have never held that the parent's liberty interest in this relationship is so inflexible as to establish a rigid constitutional shield, protecting every arbitrary parental decision from any challenge absent a threshold finding of harm. The presumption that parental decisions generally serve the best interests of their children is sound, and clearly in the normal case the parent's interest is paramount. But even a fit parent is capable of treating a child like a mere possession.

Cases like this do not present a bipolar struggle between the parents and the State over who has final authority to determine what is in a child's best interests. There is at a minimum a third individual, whose interests are implicated in every case to which the statute applies—the child. . . . [P]arental liberty interests . . . have never been seen to be without limits. . . . These limitations have arisen, not simply out of the definition of parenthood itself, but because of this Court's assumption that a parent's interests in a child must be balanced against the State's long-recognized interests as *parens patriae* and, critically, the child's own complementary interest in preserving relationships that serve her welfare and protection.

While this Court has not yet had occasion to elucidate the nature of a child's liberty interests in preserving established familial or family-like bonds, it seems to me extremely likely that, to the extent parents and families have fundamental liberty interests in preserving such intimate relationships, so, too, do children have these interests, and so, too, must their interests be balanced in the equation. At a minimum, our prior cases recognizing that children are, generally speaking, constitutionally protected actors require that this Court reject any suggestion that when it comes to parental rights, children are so much chattel. The constitutional protection against arbitrary state interference with parental rights should not be extended to prevent the States from protecting children against the arbitrary exercise of parental authority that is not in fact motivated by an interest in the welfare of the child.

This is not, of course, to suggest that a child's liberty interest in maintaining contact with a particular individual is to be treated invariably as on a par with that child's parents' contrary interests. Because our substantive due process case law includes a strong presumption that a parent will act in the best interest of her child, it would be necessary, were the state appellate courts actually to confront a challenge to the statute as applied, to consider whether the trial court's assessment of the "best interest of the child" incorporated that presumption. Neither would I decide whether the trial court applied Washington's statute in a constitutional way in this case, although, as I have explained, I think the outcome of this determination is far from clear. For the purpose of a facial challenge like this, I think it safe to assume that trial judges usually give great deference to parents' wishes, and I am not persuaded otherwise here.

But presumptions notwithstanding, we should recognize that there may be circumstances in which a child has a stronger interest at stake than mere protection from serious harm caused by the termination of visitation by a "person" other than a parent. The almost infinite variety of family relationships that pervade our ever-changing society strongly counsel against the creation by this Court of a constitutional rule that treats a biological parent's liberty interest in the care and supervision of her child as an isolated right that may be exercised arbitrarily. It is indisputably the business of the States, rather than a federal court employing a national standard, to assess in the first instance the relative importance of the conflicting interests that give rise to disputes such as this. Far from guaranteeing that parents' interests will be trammeled in the sweep of cases arising under the statute, the Washington law merely gives an individual—with whom a child may have an established relationship—the procedural right to ask the State to act as arbiter, through the entirely well-known best-interests standard, between the parent's protected interests and the child's. It seems clear to me that the Due Process Clause of the Fourteenth Amendment leaves room for States to consider the impact on a child of possibly arbitrary parental decisions that neither serve nor are motivated by the best interests of the child. Accordingly, I respectfully dissent.

Justice SCALIA, dissenting.

In my view, a right of parents to direct the upbringing of their children is among the "unalienable Rights" with which the Declaration of Independence proclaims "all Men . . . are endowed by their Creator." And in my view that right is also among the "other [rights] retained by the people" which the Ninth Amendment says the Constitution's enumeration of rights "shall not be construed to deny or disparage." The Declaration of Independence, however, is not a legal prescription conferring powers upon the courts; and the Constitution's refusal to "deny or disparage" other rights is far removed from affirming any one of them, and even farther removed from authorizing judges to identify what they might be, and to enforce the judges' list against laws duly enacted by the people. Consequently, while I would think it entirely compatible with the commitment to representative democracy set forth in the founding documents to argue, in legislative chambers or in electoral campaigns, that the state has *no power* to interfere with parents' authority over the rearing of their children, I do not believe that the power which the Constitution confers upon me *as a judge* entitles me to deny legal effect to laws that (in my view) infringe upon what is (in my view) that unenumerated right.

Only three holdings of this Court rest in whole or in part upon a substantive constitutional right of parents to direct the upbringing of their children—two of them from an era rich in substantive due process holdings that have since been repudiated. See *Meyer v. Nebraska* (1923); *Pierce v. Society of Sisters* (1925); *Wisconsin v. Yoder* (1972). The sheer diversity of today's opinions persuades me that the theory of unenumerated parental rights underlying these three cases has small claim to *stare decisis* protection. A legal principle that can be thought to produce such diverse outcomes in the relatively simple case before us here is not a legal principle that has induced substantial reliance. While I would not now overrule those earlier cases (that has not been urged), neither would I extend the theory upon which they rested to this new context.

Judicial vindication of "parental rights" under a Constitution that does not even mention them requires not only a judicially crafted definition of parents, but also—unless, as no one believes, the parental rights are to be absolute—judicially approved assessments of "harm to the child" and judicially defined gradations of other persons (grandparents, extended family, adoptive family in an adoption later found to be invalid, long-term guardians, etc.) who may have some claim against the wishes of the parents. If we embrace this unenumerated right, I think it obvious . . . that we will be ushering in a new regime of judicially prescribed, and federally prescribed, family law. I have no reason to believe that federal judges will be better at this than state legislatures; and state legislatures have the great advantages of doing harm in a more circumscribed area, of being able to correct their mistakes in a flash, and of being removable by the people.

Justice KENNEDY, dissenting.

. . . While it might be argued as an abstract matter that in some sense the child is always harmed if his or her best interests are not considered, the law of domestic relations, as it has evolved to this point, treats as distinct the two standards, one harm to the child and the other the best interests of the child. . . . On the question whether one standard must always take precedence over the other in order to protect the right of the parent or parents, "our Nation's history, legal traditions, and practices" do not give us clear or definitive answers. The consensus among courts and commentators is that at least through the 19th century there was no legal right of visitation; court-ordered visitation appears to be a 20th-century phenomenon. . . . To say that third parties have had no historical right to petition for visitation does not necessarily imply . . . that a parent has a constitutional right to prevent visitation in all cases not involving harm. True, this Court has acknowledged that States have the authority to intervene to prevent harm to children, but that is not the same as saying that a heightened harm to the child standard must be satisfied in every case in which a third party seeks a visitation order.

It is also true that the law's traditional presumption has been "that natural bonds of affection lead parents to act in the best interests of their children." . . . My principal concern is that the holding seems to proceed from the assumption that the parent or parents who resist visitation have always been the child's primary caregivers and that the third parties who seek visitation have no legitimate and established relationship with the child. That idea, in turn, appears influenced by the concept that the conventional nuclear family ought to establish the visitation standard for every domestic relations case. As we all know, this is simply not the structure or prevailing condition in many households. For many boys and girls a traditional family with two or even one permanent and caring parent is simply not the reality of their childhood. This may be so whether their childhood has been marked by tragedy or filled with considerable happiness and fulfillment.

Cases are sure to arise—perhaps a substantial number of cases—in which a third party, by acting in a caregiving role over a significant period of time, has developed a relationship with a child which is not necessarily subject to absolute parental veto. See . . . *Lehr v. Robertson* (1983) ("'The importance of the familial relationship, to the individuals involved and to the society, stems from the emotional attachments that derive from the intimacy of daily association, and from the role it plays in 'promoting a way of life' through the instruction of children . . . as well as from the fact of blood relationship.'"). Some pre-existing relationships, then, serve to identify persons who have a strong attachment to the child with the concomitant motivation to act in a responsible way to ensure the child's welfare. . . . [T]hose relationships can be so enduring that ". . . depriving the child of the relationship could cause severe psychological harm to the child," and harm to the adult may also ensue. . . . States may be entitled to consider that certain relationships are such that to avoid the risk of harm, a best interests standard can be employed by their domestic relations courts in some circumstances.

Indeed, contemporary practice should give us some pause before rejecting the best interests of the child standard in all third-party visitation cases. . . . The standard has been recognized for many years as a basic tool of domestic relations law in visitation proceedings. Since 1965 all 50 States have enacted a third-party visitation statute of some sort. Each of these statutes, save one, permits a court order to issue in certain cases if visitation is found to be in the best interests of the child. . . . [T]he statutes also include a variety of methods for limiting parents' exposure to third-party visitation petitions and for ensuring parental decisions are given respect. Many States limit the identity of permissible petitioners by restricting visitation petitions to grandparents, or by requiring petitioners to show a substantial relationship with a child, or both. . . . [S]ome permit visitation petitions when there has been a change in circumstances such as divorce or death of a parent, and some apply a presumption that parental decisions should control. Georgia's is the sole State Legislature to have adopted a general harm to the child standard, and it did so only after the Georgia Supreme Court held the State's prior visitation statute invalid under the Federal and Georgia Constitutions.

In light of the inconclusive historical record and case law, as well as the almost universal adoption of the best interests standard for visitation disputes, I would be hard pressed to conclude the right to be free of such review in all cases is itself "'implicit in the concept of ordered liberty.'" In my view, it would be more appropriate to conclude that the constitutionality of the application of the best interests standard depends on more specific factors. In short, a fit parent's right vis-à-vis a complete stranger is one thing; her right vis-à-vis another parent or a *de facto* parent may be another. . . . [F]amily courts in the 50 States confront these factual variations each day, and are best situated to consider the unpredictable, yet inevitable, issues that arise. . . .

. . . [A] domestic relations proceeding in and of itself can constitute state intervention so disruptive of the parent-child relationship that the constitutional right of a custodial parent to make certain basic determinations for the child's welfare becomes implicated. The best interests standard has at times been criticized as indeterminate, leading to unpredictable results. If a single parent who is struggling to raise a child is faced with visitation demands from a third party, attorney's fees alone might destroy her hopes and plans for the child's future. Our system must confront more often the reality that litigation can itself be so disruptive that constitutional protection may be required; and I do not discount the possibility that in some instances the best interests of the child standard may provide insufficient protection to the parent-child relationship. We owe it to the Nation's domestic relations legal structure, however, to proceed with caution. . . .

Who makes a decision about a child's life, what the substantive basis for that decision should be, and by what process the decision should be made are three distinct questions. The Washington statute gave state courts the ultimate authority to make decisions about visitation, and it made the child's best interest the substantive basis of decision. The trial court in this case appeared to follow a process of presuming court-ordered visitation with grandparents would be in the children's best interests and imposing on the children's mother the burden of rebutting that presumption. The plurality clearly stated that applying that presumption violated the constitutional right of parents. Did the plurality say anything about courts being the decision maker or about "best interests" being the basis of decision? What position on each of these three questions do the other opinions take?

Did any of the Justices who believed the Washington statute, or its application in this case, unconstitutional base that conclusion clearly and solely on a determination that the statutory rule itself did not generally serve children's well being—i.e., that giving courts that much discretion was bad for children? Or does concern for the self-regarding interests and supposed entitlement of parents play a determinative role in their thinking?

Is the practical effect of invalidating such a statute to reduce "state intervention in the family"? Or does it just create a different sort of state intervention into children's lives—that is, one that assigns more extensive power over their lives to one actor (a parent) rather than another (a court)?

The plurality declined to decide whether states must apply a harm standard—that is, must require a showing of harm to a child in the absence of court-ordered visitation. What is the difference between that standard and a best-interests rule? Justice Kennedy recognized that this is a pertinent question, but does he answer it?

It is unusual to give one person control over another's social relationships. We might say married people have a "right" that their spouses not enter into a sexual or romantic relationship with another person, a right based on an assumption that such a relationship is destructive of the marriage, but in no sense are married people entitled to prevent their spouses from merely socializing with others. In fact, we might view such controlling behavior as abuse. You would certainly find it strange, indeed offensive, if the state gave someone else a right to decide with whom you may associate—suppose, for example, that the law still accorded your parents power to determine whether you visit your grandparents. We autonomous adults, regardless of what family relationships we might have, are entitled (probably as a matter of constitutionally protected liberty) to decide with whom we visit, based on our judgment of what is in our best interests. Guardians for incompetent adults exercise control over their wards' daily life, but the law does not confer discretion on guardians based on any assumption that they are entitled to it, and no court would view legal limitations on their discretion as infringement of their rights.

Why, then, is *Troxel* a case about parents' rights, rather than about the rights of children? If the claim were properly presented to them, the Court might have held that a) a constitutional right of the children themselves is controlling and b) that the substance of the right is that children are entitled to visit with third parties who want to visit them, even over the objection of their parents, if and to the extent that visiting would be in their best interests. It might have held further that c) courts may enforce this right if parents act contrary to it. In addition, though, the Court might wisely have held that d) children are entitled to have courts give special weight to their parents' view of what is in their best interests. If the Court had said all these things instead, would the outcome of the case be any different? Is that a coherent way of looking at the conflict? Is it a preferable way? Cf. Anne C. Dailey, *Children's Constitutional Rights*, 95 MINN. L. REV. 2099 (2011) (critiquing bias against recognizing rights of children arising from mistaken reliance on an exclusively choice-based conception of rights); JAMES G. DWYER, THE RELATIONSHIP RIGHTS OF CHILDREN (2006) (presenting a theory of children's constitutional and moral rights in connection with family relationships).

Note that even Justice Stevens, who alone considered that the children might have some right at stake, was unwilling to say that such a right supplanted or trumped the supposed right of parents. He denied that "a child's liberty interest in maintaining contact with a particular individual is to be treated invariably as on a par with that child's parents' contrary interests." Instead he appears to recommend a balancing of children's interests against parents' interests, and to suggest that sometimes the parents' interests will trump those of a child. Is such a balancing appropriate? If so, what interests of parents might weigh in the balance? Just one in having control for its own sake?

The reality is that one rarely sees reference to rights of children vis-à-vis parents in statutes or court decisions in the United States. Statutes express limits on parental freedom simply as commands that parents do or not do certain things, and courts generally treat legal conflicts over childrearing as contests between parents' rights and state authority. In contrast, legislatures and courts in most other Western nations speak frequently and forcefully of children's rights. For example, the Family Code of the Russian Federation has an entire chapter of "*Rights of Minor Children.*" It contains articles announcing a right of children "to live and to be nurtured in a family," "to know his parents," to have "their concern," "to reside with parents except when this is contrary to their interests," "to nurturing by parents, ensuring of their interests, comprehensive development, and respect of their human dignity," "defence against abuses on the part of parents (or persons replacing them)," "to express their opinion when deciding any question in the family affecting their interests," and "to receive maintenance from their parents and other members of the family."

Other Western nations are also more likely to refer explicitly to parental obligations and to characterize parental power over children as "authority" rather than "a right" or entitlement on their part. For example, the Russian family code states that parents "shall be obliged to nurture their children. . . . They shall be obliged to be concerned about the health and the physical, mental, spiritual, and moral development of their children" and "shall be obliged to ensure the receipt by children of a basic general education." The Civil Code of Spain, in "Title VII—Of Parent-Child Relations," states: "Parental authority shall always be exercised for the benefit of the children, in accordance with their personality, and comprises the following duties and powers: 1. Supervise the children, have them in the parents' company, support them, educate them, and provide them with a wholesome upbringing. 2. Represent them and administer their property."

Non-Western nations, too, increasingly include references to the rights of children and the duties of parents in their codes, prompted in large part by the United Nations Convention on the Rights of the Child, to which every government on earth other than that of the United States has become a signatory. See Christian Salazar Volkmann, *30 Years After the War: Children, Families, and Rights in Vietnam*, 19 INT'L J.L. POL'Y & FAM. 23 (2005).

Does terminology matter? Does it matter who is viewed as having rights? If so, why do you suppose American law speaks less of children's rights and parental duty than does the law in other countries, and instead speaks more of parental right? In practice, the legal system in the United States is actually much more protective of children than that in some countries that include grand pronouncements about the rights of children and the responsibilities of parents. Child protection agencies in the former Soviet Union countries, for example, are characteristically indifferent to reports of abuse that they receive from doctors, teachers, and others.

Because of the division among the Justices in *Troxel* and the lack of clarity in the plurality opinion as to what is constitutionally required beyond a presumption of sound parental decision making, there remains substantial variety among states in the content of their third-party statutes and the constitutional tests courts apply to those statutes. State legislatures for the most part did not change who may petition for visitation after *Troxel*, but many courts modified the substantive rule of decision on such petitions.

Sonya C. Garza, The *Troxel* Aftermath: A Proposed Solution for State Courts and Legislatures

69 La. L. Rev. 927, 940-942 (2009)

. . . After *Troxel*, the majority of states waited for the challenges to visitation statutes to play out in court. . . . 21 states found their third-party visitation statutes to be constitutional.[100] Only six states found their third-party statutes facially unconstitutional.[101] Nine states found their third-party statutes unconstitutional as applied, and fourteen states made no

100. Alabama, Alaska, Arizona, Indiana, Kentucky, Louisiana, Maine, Massachusetts, Minnesota, Mississippi, Missouri, Montana, New Hampshire, New Mexico, New York, Oregon, Pennsylvania, Texas, Virginia, West Virginia, and Wisconsin all found their statutes to be constitutional.

101. Only California, Florida, Illinois, Iowa, Michigan, and Washington found their statutes to be unconstitutional on their face.

court determination regarding their third-party visitation statutes.[102] . . . The variety among the individual third-party visitation statutes is even more apparent after *Troxel.* While most states limit third-party visitation to grandparents, many include great-grandparents, stepparents, siblings, and third parties who have a significant relationship with the child. . . .[103] Further, some states . . . use the common law doctrines of de facto parenthood, in loco parentis, or psychological parenthood. . . .[105]

Most statutes use a "best interests of the child" standard in third-party visitation cases.[106] Michigan provides that an affidavit from both parents will serve as grounds for a dismissal of a third-party petition for visitation. . . . Many states began imposing additional requirements if parents are in an intact marriage. . . . [However,] many jurisdictions continue to allow third-party visitation petitions to be filed at any time. . . .[121] Many states require a harm determination in addition to determining the best interests of the child,[128] others include harm as one of many best interests factors.[129] . . . In Illinois, the party filing must prove that the parent's actions and decision regarding visitation times are harmful to the child's mental, physical, or emotional health.[139]

What motivations, commendable or condemnable, might any parents have for cutting off a child's relationship with grandparents or other family members? What motivations could a grandparent, aunt, uncle, etc., have for asking a court to order visitation over a parent's objection? Should an existing relationship or past caretaking of the child at issue be a prerequisite for petitioning? Or is the potential for a relationship valuable enough to justify judicial involvement in such intra-familial battles?

De Facto Parents

The grandparents in *Troxel* had spent substantial time with the children but never lived with them. The plurality suggested this was significant to its holding that state courts must at least apply a presumption in favor of the preference of the custodial parent as to whether and to what extent third-party visitation would be beneficial to a child. The

102. Arkansas, Connecticut, Kansas, Maryland, New Jersey, Oklahoma, South Carolina, South Dakota, and Vermont all found their statutes unconstitutional as applied.

103. Alaska, California, Connecticut, Delaware, Hawaii, Louisiana, Virginia, and Wisconsin have broad visitation statutes that permit visitation to third parties more generally.

105. Alabama, Colorado, Delaware, Georgia, Hawaii, Idaho, Nebraska, Nevada, North Carolina, North Dakota, Ohio, Rhode Island, Tennessee, Utah, and Wyoming have no court determinations regarding their third party visitations statutes.

106. See Ariz. Rev. Stat. Ann. §25-409 (2007); Conn. Gen. Stat. Ann. §46b-59; Fla. Stat. Ann. §39.509 (West 2003); La. Civ. Code Ann. art. 136(b); S.D. Codified Laws §25-4-52 (2004); Vt. Stat. Ann. tit. 15, §1011 (1989); W. Va. Code Ann. §48-10-501 (West 2002); Dodd v. Burleson, 932 So. 2d 912 (Ala. Civ. App. 2005); Fairbanks v. McCarter, 622 A.2d 121 (Md. 1993).

121. Ariz. Rev. Stat. Ann. §25-409 (West 2007); Cal. Fam. Code Ann. §3104(b); Haw. Rev. Stat. Ann. §571-46 (LexisNexis Supp. 2007); Kan. Stat. Ann. §60-1616 (2005); Ky. Rev. Stat. Ann. §405.021 (West 2006); Me. Rev. Stat. Ann. tit. 19-A, §1803 (Supp. 2008); Md. Code. Ann. Fam. Law §9-102 (West 2006); S.D. Codified Laws §25-4-52 (2004); Vt. Stat. Ann. tit 15, §1011 (1989); Va. Code Ann. §16.1-278.15 (2001); W. Va. Code §48-10-501 (2002); Wis. Stat. Ann. §54.56 (West 2008).

128. See Ark. Code Ann. §9-13-103; Conn. Gen. Stat. Ann. §46b-59 (West 2004); Del. Code. Ann. tit. 10, §1031 (West 2006); Ga. Code Ann. §19-7-3 (West 2003); Doe v. Doe, 172 P.3d 1067 (Haw. 2007); Scott v. Scott, 80 S.W.3d 447 (Ky. Ct. App. 2002).

129. Ark. Code Ann. §9-13-103.

139. 750 Ill. Comp. Stat. Ann. 5/607 (West 2009).

Court might conclude that when a person who is not a legal parent has served in a custodial or "de facto parent' role, it is constitutionally permissible (or even requisite) for state courts to presume that continued contact would be in a child's best interests. See Solangel Maldonado, *When Father (or Mother) Doesn't Know Best: Quasi-Parents and Parental Deference After* Troxel v. Granville, 88 Iowa L. Rev. 865 (2003) (arguing for that interpretation). We saw in the context of parentage law that in recent years some courts have treated serving in a de facto co-parent role as a basis for attributing parental status. Here we examine to what extent past caretaking can instead support a request simply for court-ordered visitation against the wishes of a custodial parent.

In recent years, there has been an explosion of that sort of "third party visitation" request. This is in part a reflection of the multiple marrying phenomenon, which has produced an increasing number of step-parents who have bonded with step-children. Further, it has long been the case that grandparents of babies born to immature parents tend to take on the primary caretaker role with respect to the grandchildren. In addition, same-sex couples are increasingly having children, and though the non-biological parent is unable to adopt in most states, that person is typically viewed by everyone from the outset of the child's life as the child's second parent. In any of these contexts, it can be the case that an adult with whom a child has bonded cannot claim legal parent status and a legal parent tries suddenly to separate the child from that person completely.

Latham v. Schwerdtfeger

802 N.W.2d 66 (Neb. 2011)

Miller-Lerman, J.

. . . Teri A. Latham and . . . Susan Rae Schwerdtfeger, . . . met in college and moved in together in 1985. At that time, the parties began sharing their finances. After several years of living together, the parties discussed having a child. They ruled out adoption, and instead, it was decided that Schwerdtfeger would be the birth parent of the child. The parties chose a sperm donor, and after several unsuccessful attempts at artificial insemination, Schwerdtfeger underwent in vitro fertilization, which was successful. The cost of these procedures was shared by both parties.

Both parties attended doctors' appointments, and both parties were present at the birth of P.S. The parties are not married. Latham took maternity leave to care for Schwerdtfeger and the baby. After the birth, Latham continued her role as coparent, helping to raise the minor child and supporting him both emotionally and financially. Latham claims that P.S. identified her as "Mom" and that she would assist P.S. in getting ready for school, was involved in disciplining P.S., took P.S. to medical appointments, and helped him with his homework.

In 2005, Latham and Schwerdtfeger separated, and Latham moved out of the family home in 2006. Latham claims that even though she was not living in the home, she continued her role as coparent to the minor child . . . [but] that beginning in 2007, Schwerdtfeger began to arbitrarily cut down on Latham's parenting time with P.S. . . . On December 14, 2009, Latham filed a complaint for custody and visitation. . . .

Standing requires that a litigant have such a personal stake in the outcome of a controversy as to warrant invocation of a court's jurisdiction and justify exercise of the court's remedial powers on the litigant's behalf. To have standing, a litigant must assert the litigant's own rights and interests. . . . "In the area of child custody, principles of standing have been applied with particular scrupulousness. . . ." *J.A.L. v. E.P.H.* (Pa. Super.

1996). . . . Latham is neither a biological nor an adoptive parent. . . . [T]here is no explicit statutory basis to support her claim of standing. . . . [But] the Legislature did not intend that statutory authority be the exclusive basis of obtaining court-ordered visitation. . . . [W]e have long applied the common-law doctrine of *in loco parentis* to afford rights to nonparents where the exercise of those rights is in the best interests of the child. . . . We have explained . . . :

> a person standing *in loco parentis* to a child is one who has put himself or herself in the situation of a lawful parent by assuming the obligations incident to the parental relationship, without going through the formalities necessary to a legal adoption, and the rights, duties, and liabilities of such person are the same as those of the lawful parent.

In *Hickenbottom v. Hickenbottom* (1991), we determined that the doctrine of in loco parentis, although not enumerated in the statutes, is a proper consideration when determining stepparent visitation with due consideration to the best interests of the child. Similarly, in *Weinand v. Weinand*, we explained that in the absence of a statute, child support may properly be imposed in cases where a stepparent has voluntarily taken the child into his or her home and acted in loco parentis. In *State on behalf of Combs v. O'Neal* (2003), the Nebraska Court of Appeals affirmed an order granting custody of a minor to the grandmother based on the doctrine of in loco parentis, notwithstanding a claim of parental preference urged by the biological father. Other courts have applied similar reasoning and determined that standing exists and custody and visitation may be considered although not explicitly provided for in statutes. See, e.g., *T.B. v. L.R.M.* (Pa. 2001); *In re Parentage of L.B.* (Wash. 2005) (stating ". . . statutes often fail to contemplate all potential scenarios which may arise in the ever changing and evolving notion of familial relations"); *Custody of H.S.H.-K.* (Wis. 1995). . . .

Because we have not used the doctrine in a case such as the one presently before us, we turn to other jurisdictions that have. . . . See *Mullins v. Picklesimer* (Ky. 2010) (stating "[s]everal of our sister states have found that the nonparent has standing to seek custody and visitation of the child when the child was conceived by artificial insemination with the intent that the child would be co-parented by the parent and her partner") (cases collected). As other courts have done, we have also considered scholarly articles in this area. . . . The courts that have applied the doctrine of in loco parentis in cases such as ours have looked to the purpose of the doctrine and noted that the focus . . . "should be on what, if any, bond has formed between the child and the non-parent." *Bethany v. Jones* (Ark. 2011). In *J.A.L. v. E.P.H.* (Pa. Super. 1996), the court explained:

> The in loco parentis basis for standing recognizes the need to guard the family from intrusions by third parties and to protect the rights of the natural parent must be tempered by the paramount need to protect the child's best interest. Thus, while it is presumed that a child's best interest is served by maintaining the family's privacy and autonomy, that presumption must give way where the child has established strong psychological bonds with a person who, although not a biological parent, has lived with the child and provided care, nurture, and affection, assuming in the child's eye a stature like that of a parent. . . .

The court in *J.A.L.* went on to state . . . that because "a wide spectrum of arrangements [have filled] the role of the traditional nuclear family, flexibility in the application of standing principles is required in order to adapt those principles to the interests of each particular child." . . .

In *Bethany v. Jones, supra,* the Arkansas Supreme Court determined that the doctrine of in loco parentis applied because the focus of the in loco parentis analysis is on the relationship between the nonparent adult and the child, not on the relationship between the biological parent and the nonparent adult. . . . Similarly, in *In re Custody of H.S.H.-K.* (Wis. 1995), the Wisconsin Supreme Court . . . determined that a trial court may determine whether visitation with the nonbiological parent is in the best interests of a child, if the individual could establish that she had a parent-like relationship with the child and that there was a triggering event by which the biological parent substantially interfered with the parent-like relationship.

We agree with the reasoning of these courts and conclude . . . that the doctrine of in loco parentis applies to this case. . . . The primary determination in an in loco parentis analysis is whether the person seeking in loco parentis status assumed the obligations incident to a parental relationship. Application of the doctrine protects the family from allowing intervention by individuals who have not established an intimate relationship with the child while at the same time affording rights to a person who has established an intimate parent-like relationship with a child, the termination of which would not be in the best interests of the child. . . . [T]here is no reason to exclude this case from the benefits of the doctrine afforded to stepparents and grandparents who have created similar relationships with a minor child. . . .

The facts taken in a light most favorable to Latham show that she was involved in the decision to conceive the minor child, was present at his birth, spent the first 4 years of his life in the home with him, and took part in parental duties such as feeding, clothing, and disciplining him. When the parties separated, the facts of Latham's involvement and relationship with the minor child become less clear. But viewing the facts in this record in a light most favorable to Latham, for at least 1½ years after the separation, she had regular visits with the minor child three to five times per week and participated in his extracurricular activities. Latham and Schwerdtfeger shared their finances through the summer of 2007. Therefore, Latham continued to assist in supporting P.S. financially until that time. It appears that Latham's visitations with P.S. diminished in 2007 and 2008 and that Latham had, on average, visitation with P.S. two times a week. Recently, visitation between Latham and P.S. has evidently become nonexistent. The amount of visitation Latham has been afforded does not appear to reflect a lack of desire on her part to be an active part of P.S.' life; rather, that fact appears to be the result of the relationship between the parties and a result of Schwerdtfeger's apparent decision to end Latham's visitation with P.S. . . .

The relationship between Latham and Schwerdtfeger, however, is not the deciding factor. The record is clear that Schwerdtfeger consented to Latham's performance of parental duties. Schwerdtfeger encouraged Latham to assume the status of a parent and acquiesced as Latham carried out day-to-day care of P.S. Latham did not assume a parenting role against the wishes of Schwerdtfeger. It has been observed that "a biological parent's rights do not extend to erasing a relationship between her partner and her child which she voluntarily created and actively fostered simply because after the parties' separation she regretted having done so." *T.B. v. L.R.M.* (Pa. 2001).

There are material questions of fact concerning the amount of time Latham spent with P.S. and the nature and extent of the relationship between Latham and P.S. after Latham and Schwerdtfeger separated. . . . Accordingly, we reverse the ruling granting summary judgment in favor of Schwerdtfeger and the order of dismissal, and remand for further proceedings consistent with this opinion.

If the relationship between the adults is irrelevant or "not the deciding factor," then why is the biological parent's encouragement of a relationship with the child relevant? Is that relevant only if the decision were to rest on a finding of a contractual relationship between the adults? Or if the decision needs to be equitable to the biological parent as well as in the child's best interests?

The court's focus is on standing, rather than on the substantive rule for granting visitation or custody to a non-parent. As to primary custody of a child, some states confer standing to petition to persons who have acted in loco parentis but still apply a presumption in favor of the biological/legal parent in deciding the merits of the petition. See, e.g., Jacob v. Shultz-Jacob, 923 A.2d 473 (Pa. Super. Ct. 2007) ("standing established by virtue of in loco parentis status does not elevate a third party to parity with a natural parent in determining the merits of custody dispute. Rather, . . . 'where the custody dispute is between a biological parent and a third party, . . . the parents have a prima facie right to custody which will be forfeited only if convincing reasons appear that the child's best interest[s] will be served by an award to the third party. Thus, even before the proceedings start, the evidentiary scale is tipped, and tipped hard, to the [biological] parents' side.'").

On the other hand, when biological parents have challenged conferral of custody or visitation on de facto parents as unconstitutional, they have usually failed. See, e.g., Smith v. Guest, 16 A.3d 920 (Del. 2011) (upholding against constitutional challenge application of state de facto parent rule to award joint custody to former lesbian partner); Kulstad v. Maniaci, 220 P.3d 595 (Mont. 2009) (upholding constitutionality of statute authorizing award of a "parental interest" to a non-parent when "the natural parent has engaged in conduct that is contrary to the child-parent relationship; and the nonparent has established with the child a child-parent relationship . . . and it is in the best interests of the child to continue that relationship"); SooHoo v. Johnson, 731 N.W.2d 815 (Minn. 2007) (upholding constitutionality of statute authorizing award of visitation to a non-parent "who resided in a household with a child for two or more years," in case involving former lesbian partner).

What effect on such cases might there be from the progressive extension of marriage and adoption rights to same-sex partners? Will such partners be denied standing if they have not done everything possible to formalize their relationships before their family life falls apart? In *Debra H. v. Janice R.*, the New York Court of Appeals ruled that because adoption is now available to same-sex partners, it would uphold a prior ruling establishing that non-parents do not have standing to petition for visitation. 930 N.E.2d 184 (2010). The Nebraska Supreme Court in *Latham* neglected to cite *Debra H.* and rulings in other states that have dismissed petitions by former same-sex partners for lack of standing. For example, in In re Mullen, 953 N.E.2d 302 (Ohio 2011), the Ohio Supreme Court held that although "a parent may voluntarily share with a nonparent the care, custody, and control of his or her child through a valid shared-custody agreement," absent clear evidence of such an agreement a former partner lacks standing to petition for shared custody. See also Janice M. v. Margaret K., 948 A.2d 73 (Md. 2008) (holding that Maryland does not recognize de facto parent status and that former partner must show exceptional circumstances to overcome legal mother's right to deny her visitation).

A long-running and highly publicized custody battle between former lesbian partners, the *Miller-Jenkins* case, was unusual insofar as the partners had formed a civil union in Vermont. Vermont law treats parties to a civil union the same as married persons, and the non-biological mother (Jenkins) therefore was equivalent to a step-parent. Vermont had applied the in loco parentis doctrine to predicate standing for step-parents to seek custody, so Vermont courts concluded that the same should be true for a former civil union partner who acted as a parent and that Ms. Jenkins should have visitation with the child.

See Miller-Jenkins v. Miller-Jenkins, 912 A.2d 951 (Vt. 2006). However, the biological mother (Miller) moved to Virginia after their breakup, declared herself a born-again Christian, and resolved to shield her child from what she now regarded as the immoral lesbian lifestyle. She attempted to get Virginia courts to enter a contrary ruling denying contact to Jenkins, but ultimately Virginia courts ruled that Virginia must respect the jurisdiction and ruling of the Vermont courts. See Miller-Jenkins v. Miller-Jenkins, 661 S.E.2d 822 (Va. 2008). Ms. Miller then simply refused to comply with the Vermont order, and when Vermont courts responded by ordering a change of custody to Jenkins, Miller fled to Nicaragua with the girl. Should she ever return to the United States, she will face criminal kidnapping charges. See Erik Eckholm, *Pastor Is Accused of Helping to Kidnap Girl at Center of Lesbian Custody Fight*, N.Y. TIMES, Apr. 24, 2011.

In such situations involving same-sex partners, there are typically only the two partners seeking to play a role in the child's life. Extending standing to petition for custody in those cases thus does not reflect a judicial willingness to multiply parental figures beyond two. When there are two legal parents who are fit and involved in a child's life, courts are highly resistant to adding a third custodian and, as reflected by *Troxel* and its aftermath, are also disinclined to award mere visitation rights to a third adult. The law thus protects parents against diffusion of their children's time and attention among many adults; with exceedingly rare exception, the law will not confer the same status on more than two of them, and the law gives them presumptive plenary power to exclude other persons entirely from their children's lives.

Should nannies and other paid caregivers sometimes receive recognition as de facto parents? For an argument in support, see Pamela Laufer-Ukeles, *Money, Caregiving, and Kinship: Should Paid Caregivers Be Allowed to Obtain De Facto Parenting Status?*, 74 MO. L. REV. 25 (2009).

b. Exclusivity of the Child's Role

In stark contrast to the law's traditional hostility to multiplication of the parental role, there has never been in the United States a legal limit on the number of offspring a parent can have, and the law is hostile to restrictions on a person's freedom to multiply their parental status. Yet a parent's repeated procreation or adoption of children clearly can adversely affect an existing child. Most people believe that it is good for a child to have siblings, but siblings are competitors for parental resources (time and money), and at some point any marginal social benefit from an additional sibling might be outweighed for existing children by the additional burden on resources that a new child represents. This is especially so when the later child is in a different household, as after a parent changes intimate partners. In addition, the law makes little effort, for the sake of children, to limit the attention parents give to other adults. At the extreme, the state might charge parents with neglect if an adult relationship or other distraction prevents parents from meeting children's basic needs. But otherwise parents are completely free to divert their attention away from one child and toward other children or other adults. In other words, the law does not recognize what might be termed "parental infidelity."

This is so even though most people probably would assent to the principle that someone who is a parent should take on additional relationships (by procreating or marrying) only if this makes his or her existing children better off, or at least not worse off. One might view as a reflection of this principle the state law that the U.S. Supreme court struck down in *Zablocki v. Redhail*, excerpted in Chapter 2, a law denying child support delinquents the ability to get married. Another reflection of it exists in current law in some states, discussed below in Section V, refusing to reduce an existing child support obligation on the grounds that the obligor has remarried or procreated again and so now has more dependents. See Adrienne Jennings Lockie, *Multiple Families, Multiple Goals, Muliptle Failures: The Need for "Limited Equalization" as a Theory of Child Support*, 32 HARV. J.L. & GENDER 109 (2009). More direct efforts to prevent additional procreation by persons incapable of caring for any children—for example, providing free Norplant to female drug addicts and making return of children in foster care dependent on a mother's not getting pregnant again—have triggered vehement protest in some quarters and have mostly been discontinued. But the protest is a reaction to infringement of women's autonomy and not a rejection of this principle that people should first take care of the children they already have. Thus, the notion that one has a duty of "fidelity" to one's offspring is not entirely foreign to us. Yet apart from the refusal of some states to reduce a child support obligation for the sake of later children, the law does not now force or even encourage parents to respect such a duty. In fact, the state arguably fosters "infidelity" by conferring on parents additional financial benefits for having more children (e.g., tax exemptions and credits), benefits that fall far short of compensating existing children for the diversion of parental attention and resources that the additional children occasion.

2. *Violence*

As with intimate relationships between adults, the criminal and civil codes of every state contain general prohibitions on violence in parent-child relationships.

a. Children's Violence Toward Parents

Whereas states have created special legal rules for violence between spouses and for violence by parents against children, rules whose tendency is to treat such violence between family members as less severe than violence toward strangers, U.S. states have no special criminal code provisions relating to violence by children toward parents. Instead, general criminal statutory provisions, such as regular assault and battery, apply. If prosecutors bring legal action against a minor for violence toward a parent, it is likely to be a delinquency petition in juvenile court, though in severe cases they will seek to prosecute in adult court. In addition, parents and certain government agencies can initiate a CHINS (Children In Need of Supervision) proceeding against a violent child and ask a court to place the child in detention or under supervision of a probation officer. See, e.g., Wash. Rev. Code §13.32A.190; In re Nelly O., 381 N.Y.S.2d 66 (App. Div. 1976).

When adult offspring commit violence toward a parent, parents or someone acting in their behalf can, in addition to seeking criminal prosecution, file a domestic violence petition and request a protective order against the offspring. As noted in Chapter 3, civil domestic abuse laws now reach broadly to cover many family relationships, not just spouses or intimate partners.

b. Parental Violence Toward Children

While leaving minor children's violence toward parents covered by general criminal code provisions, states throughout the United States have created special offenses with lesser penalties for violence by parents toward minor children, such as "criminal child abuse," "abuse of a family or household member," and "endangering the welfare of a minor." See, e.g., Colo. Rev. Stat. §18-6-401(1)(a) ("A person commits child abuse if such person causes an injury to a child's life or health, or permits a child to be unreasonably placed in a situation that poses a threat of injury to the child's life or health, or engages in a continued pattern of conduct that results in malnourishment, lack of proper medical care, cruel punishment, mistreatment, or an accumulation of injuries that ultimately results in the death of a child or serious bodily injury to a child.").

In addition, states explicitly authorize some violence toward minor children, ordinarily in a statutory defense to any of the above charges. Typical language authorizes "reasonable and appropriate physical force" that the adult reasonably believes necessary "to maintain discipline" or "to promote the welfare" of the child. See, e.g., Minn. Stat. §609.06 ("reasonable force may be used . . . by a parent . . . or other lawful custodian of a child . . . to restrain or correct such child"); Ariz. Rev. Stat. §13-403; Colo. Rev. Stat. §18-1-703; Conn. Gen. Stat. §53a-18; N.Y. Penal Law §35.10. Most statutes leave "reasonable" for judges to define *ex post* in child abuse hearings, but the Delaware legislature has offered parents *ex ante* guidance:

> The force shall not be justified if it includes . . . : Throwing the child, kicking, burning, cutting, striking with a closed fist, interfering with breathing, use of or threatened use of a deadly weapon, prolonged deprivation of sustenance or medication, or doing any other act that is likely to cause or does cause physical injury, disfigurement, mental distress, unnecessary degradation or substantial risk of serious physical injury or death.

Del. Code Ann. tit. 11, §468(c).

Does that leave much room for physical chastisement, especially given the proscription of acts that cause mental distress? Is it preferable to give judges broad discretion in determining reasonableness rather than categorically excluding certain actions by statute? The following case presumably would come out differently under Delaware law.

State v. Roman

199 P.3d 57 (Haw. 2008)

Opinion of the Court by Moon, C.J.

. . . Minor . . . liv[ed] with his mother and his mother's boyfriend (Roman) in Roman's house. . . . Roman had planned to prepare tacos for Mother's Day dinner. . . . Roman instructed Minor to grate cheese for the tacos; however, Minor remained "laying on a futon watching television" and did not perform the requested task. According to Minor, Roman "asked me again [to grate the cheese]—the second time he asked me, I went to go do it[;] he told me I was doing it wrong and to go lay down or sit down." Minor went and sat in the living room; Roman then left his house to run an errand. Forty-five minutes to an hour later, Roman returned and started yelling at Minor because he did not grate the cheese correctly. . . .

> *Q.* [By the Prosecution:] So after [Roman] came into the house and he was yelling at you, what did he do next?
>
> *A.* [By Minor:] Um, he, he, um, he [(Roman)] started coming towards me then he started kicking me in my back.

Q. He kicked you in your back?
A. Yep.
Q. Can you tell me where on your back?
A. My lower back. . . .
Q. And how many times did he kick you?
A. Couple. . . .
Q. Okay. What happened after that?
A. Then I got up and then he started yelling at me some more and he whacked me couple times.
Q. When you say he whacked you, what does that mean?
A. He hit me with his hand.
Q. Was it an open hand?
A. I don't remember.
Q. Where did he hit you?
A. My face.
Q. How many times?
A. A couple. . . .

Mother tried to intervene, but was struck by Roman. Thereafter, Roman called the police to report the incident that he had hit Minor and Mother. Minor stated that, after the incident, he went to stay with his father; while at the father's home, his step-mother called the police to "make a statement because [Minor] had a mark on [his] face." . . . Minor stated that it was "a lump and was red." Minor also stated that, during the course of that evening, Roman had consumed about a case of beer.

On cross-examination, defense counsel questioned Minor. . . .

Q. Did you used to go out in the yard and beat the trees with a stick?
A. Yes. . . .
Q. Did you used to kill chickens?
A. Yes.
Q. And did you take a glue stick, a hot glue stick, to a friend's arm to burn him?
A. Yes, 'cause he burnt me. . . .

Officer Bolos testified that . . . he spoke with Roman and Mother, who told him that they had been arguing. . . . Officer Matsumoto stated that, when she arrived at the residence,

> [Minor] was in the garage area. Apparently he was upset. I observed that his facial area was red but there was no bruising. . . . I asked him if, uh, if he needed any kind of medical assistance, uh, or anything, he said, no, he didn't.

Officer Matsumoto did not notice any swelling to Minor's face. . . . Officer Saludares also testified that . . . Minor "had some redness on his face" and "scratches on his front neck area." . . .

Q. [By the Prosecution:] What was [Minor's] demeanor?
A. [By Officer Saludares:] [Minor] spoke to me in a quieter lower tone, appeared to be a little afraid. Just trying to think of a way to describe it but afraid in a way. Not comfortable.
Q. Was he afraid of you?

A. No.
Q. What made you think he was afraid?
A. Um, from what he told me, the incident that occurred that night and, uh, just his demeanor, the way that he spoke to me having a, a-when he was talking about the incident that night.
Q. Was he upset?
A. Yes, a little.
Q. What was he telling you about the incident that night?
A. Um, he informed me that, um, his mother's boyfriend had arrived home that night, he was intoxicated, at which time he had, uh, began yelling and swearing at [Minor] and had kicked him in his lower back area as well as began to choke him on the front of his neck area. . . .

Roman testified that he and Mother had been "boyfriend/girlfriend" since 1995 and that he treated Minor "like a step son." . . . According to Roman,

> . . . I had gone to the store, I had purchased what was necessary, I came back, after which I had to leave again but not until I had asked [Minor] if he could please grate the cheese and shred some lettuce. . . . Well, . . . he was laying down in front of the television with his walkman just blaring and I didn't talk to [Minor] when I returned. I walked into the house and I walked over to the refrigerator and I looked into the ice box and I seen that the lettuce nor the cheese or any of that had even been touched. It was still in the original containers. . . . I started calling [Minor]. . . . He did not respond because the stereo on his head was so loud. . . . I walked . . . [toward] him and I said, [Minor], and he turned and he looked at me and—. . . . You know, I said, [Minor], what about the cheese and he just kept staring at me, just staring, he just kept looking at me. . . . I walked up to him, I kicked him in his okole. . . . He spun around, he spun to his feet, uh, I had no idea what was on his mind . . . [and he stood there with a] clenched fist. Um, honestly, I felt at that point that I had fully lost all control of [Minor] as far as being a friend and a member of the family. . . .
>
> I started yelling at him and he kept looking at me, he kept looking at me and I finally said, [Minor], hey, what is this, I mean, you want to hit me, go ahead and hit me, and he stepped forward towards me and I slapped him. Your Honor, I slapped him across the cheek. . . . There was absolutely no response from him. . . . And at that point, I said, no, I think this should be recorded so I made a phone call to the . . . [p]olice [d]epartment and I told them of the incident that had happened and if they could send some officers up as soon as possible. . . .

Roman further testified that he "wanted to be noticed as the head of the household which has never happened with [Minor] for many, many years, which is why I never did physically, let me restate this, slap, hit, I have never even punished [Minor] in all the years that he was with me." . . . On cross-examination, Roman conceded that he drank a six pack between 2:00 P.M. and 6:30 P.M. on the day of the incident. The prosecution, thereafter, asked Roman:

Q. Isn't it true you attempted to choke him?
A. I held him back at one point because I wasn't sure exactly what was on his mind[.]
Q. . . . [I]sn't it true that [Minor's] mother had to intervene and pull you off of [Minor]?
A. No.
Q. Isn't it true that you called the police and you said, I just hit my girlfriend and my stepson?

A. Yes.
Q. And you said you did it because you, you were going to diffuse the situation?
A. I was trying to so—
Q. You were trying to diffuse the situation by kicking and slapping [Minor]?
A. No, no, no. I diffused the situation of the entire incident that happened. . . .
Q. Isn't it true that [Minor] attempted to grate the cheese and you went and told him that he wasn't doing it right and you told him to go and sit down? . . .
A. He never was grating the cheese so why should I tell him to sit down?

On redirect examination, defense counsel asked Roman "why did [he] make the statement that [he] had just hit [his] wife or [his] girlfriend and [Minor]," to which Roman responded:

> 'Cause in my heart of hearts, I wanted this ended and I wanted it ended with the police and I wanted them to be there as witnesses for me of what I am trying to do in this situation that I believe it's time he leave the house and go live with his father, which is what the boy wanted to do for year—about a year before this because there is no discipline at the father's house.

During closing arguments, the prosecution contended that:

> . . . [W]hen his mother disciplines him, she spanks him on his rear end. She doesn't kick him in the back, she doesn't slap him in the face. Also, . . . he attempted to grate the cheese, [Roman] didn't like the way he did, [Roman] told him to go and sit down, he did exactly what he was told to do so I don't see any misconduct on the part of the child here.

Defense counsel, however, argued that:

> . . . At 17 years old, it's pretty hard to spank a child on the bottom. Mr. Roman was the man of the household, the head of the house, in essence, the parent. The [m]other was sleeping, he had asked the son to help with the meal. The son was defiant, refused to do what he was being asked. . . . [H]ad Mr. Roman intended to hurt him, there would have been much more than a welt showing up. . . .

Subsequently, the family court orally announced its factual findings—specifically that:

> . . . Alfred Roman is a fairly large person and his manner and demeanor is quite masculine and I think he has that sense of being in charge sort [sic] to speak. . . . [Minor], uh, had some emotional problems, whether they're related to the divorce or not, the [c]ourt doesn't know that, but he . . . had to be treated, perhaps, as a special needs type of person and, therefore, uh, was someone whose guidance and discipline had to take a different [indiscernible]. . . . Um, *the incident that transpired,* uh, *was not, in the [c]ourt's estimation, an incident where there was misconduct on the part of [Minor]. . . . we're . . . not dealing with someone who has done something wrong, we're dealing with something, somebody who has not done something as requested for this special day.* In other words, . . . *we're not in a situation where we're correcting misbehavior but we're trying to take control of the situation where we're not having cooperation.* Uh, . . . *at one point there was a kick, uh, that was to get attention, and at another point, there was a slap, uh, and that was, as the [c]ourt understands . . . a reaction to what was deemed to be defiance. . . . We know that at this point there was a high level of emotion. [Minor] was kicked, he stood up, he stared at Mr. Roman, he had his fists clenched, and Mr. Roman, uh, was also at a high pitch of emotion and took this to be a defiant child, probably with the head phones still on and blaring, and not giving heed to what Mr. Roman had expected and, uh, there was such a fever of emotion that Mr. Roman even said words to the effect that if you like, you*

> *can hit me or something to that effect, inviting a confrontation.* . . . [A]nd at this point, we have, uh, Mother who is on the scene, and, uh, becoming part of what I'll relate to as a fracas . . . and the [c]ourt is satisfied this confrontation involved three people, that it was physical, that there was a point that Mr. Roman put his hands on [Minor]'s neck, and there was a point where [Mother] also physically was man handled or struck by Mr. Roman.

The family court, thereafter, ruled that the parental discipline defense did not apply [and] found Roman guilty of abuse of family or household members. . . . The family court sentenced Roman to, *inter alia*, two years probation and fifteen days imprisonment, thirteen days of which would be stayed pending the probationary period.[8] . . .

His conviction required proof beyond a reasonable doubt that: (1) he physically abused Minor; (2) he did so intentionally, knowingly or recklessly; and (3) Minor was a present or former family or household member of Roman's. *See* HRS §709-906(1). Roman, however, believes that his use of force upon Minor was justified pursuant to the parental discipline defense under HRS §703-309(1), which provides:

The use of force upon or toward the person of another is justifiable under the following circumstances:

> (1) The actor is the parent or guardian or other person similarly responsible for the general care and supervision of a minor, or a person acting at the request of the parent, guardian, or other responsible person, and:
>
> (a) The force is employed with due regard for the age and size of the minor and is reasonably related to the purpose of safeguarding or promoting the welfare of the minor, including the prevention or punishment of the minor's misconduct; and
>
> (b) The force used is not designed to cause or known to create a risk of causing substantial bodily injury,[9] disfigurement, extreme pain or mental distress, or neurological damage.

. . . [T]he parental discipline defense was available to Roman "so long as *some* evidence was adduced, *no matter how weak, inconclusive, or unsatisfactory it might be,* which was probative of [the aforementioned elements]." Here, . . . the family court erred in failing to apply the defense "because Roman's testimony, however weak, inconclusive, or unsatisfactory, was probative of the fact that (a) Roman had parental authority over Minor, (b) the force at issue was employed with due regard for Minor's age and size, and (c) the force was reasonably proportional to the misconduct being punished and reasonably believed necessary to protect the welfare of the recipient."

. . . [T]he burden then shifted to the prosecution to prove beyond a reasonable doubt that Roman's conduct did not come within the scope of parental discipline as prescribed in HRS §703-309(1). . . . "These required factors are obviously general in nature and, by their very terms, place a large amount of discretion with the courts . . . [T]he *permissible*

8. The family court also ordered Roman to (1) undergo a domestic violence intervention program; (2) submit to an alcohol abuse assessment, follow recommended treatment, and be subject to any requested random urinalysis screening for drugs and/or alcohol; and (3) not possess or consume alcohol during his probation period.

9. HRS §707-700 (1993) defines "substantial bodily injury" as bodily injury which causes:

> (1) A major avulsion, laceration, or penetration of the skin;
> (2) A chemical, electrical, friction, or scalding burn of second degree severity;
> (3) A bone fracture;
> (4) A serious concussion; or
> (5) A tearing, rupture, or corrosive damage to the esophagus, viscera, or other internal organs.

degree of force will vary according to the child's physique and age, the misconduct of the child, the nature of the discipline, and all the surrounding circumstances. . . ."

. . . Although he was a minor at age seventeen, Minor was hardly a child. . . . [T]he family court apparently believed that Minor's failure to grate the cheese as Roman requested, or failure to grate the cheese to Roman's satisfaction, was essentially an issue of "not having cooperation" as opposed to "misbehavior" or misconduct. . . . Curiously, however, the family court also described Minor as a "defiant child," based on Minor's "st[anding] up" and "star[ing]" at Roman with "his fists clenched," and that Roman's conduct in slapping Minor was a "reaction to the boy's defiance." . . . In our view, not cooperating with a defiant attitude and demeanor is "misbehavior," *i.e.*, misconduct, on the part of Minor as such behavior shows disrespect for parental authority. It seems natural that Roman, as one of the persons responsible for the general care and supervision of Minor, would view Minor's attitude and demeanor as misconduct that warranted discipline. . . . Roman's discipline caused a little soreness in his lower back and redness and a small lump on his cheek for an unknown duration. There was no evidence of bruising or swelling; nor did Minor require medical attention. Further, there was no evidence to indicate any detriment to Minor's overall well-being or physical, emotional or psychological state.

Thus, considering the totality of the facts and circumstances, the force employed by Roman (1) was reasonably proportionate to Minor's defiant behavior towards Roman and (2) was reasonably believed to be necessary to discipline Minor for his defiant attitude and demeanor. Moreover, the degree of force used was "not designed to cause or known to create a substantial risk of causing bodily injury, disfigurement, extreme pain or mental distress, or neurological damage."

The discipline used by Roman was slightly less than that used by the defendant-father upon his seventeen-year-old daughter in State v. Kaimimoku, 9 Haw. App. 345 (1992). . . . Specifically, the father slapped his daughter on the face and punched her shoulder, leaving a scratch and a bruise, and causing some pain of unknown duration. On appeal, the ICA reversed the father's conviction, finding that the force used was within the bounds afforded to the father as a parent. Likewise, in State v. Deleon, 72 Haw. 241 (1991), the defendant-father's conviction of abuse of a family or household member was reversed on appeal even though . . . the father struck his fourteen-year-old daughter with a folded belt six to ten times above her knees, causing pain lasting for an hour and a half, and bruises lasting for about a week. . . .

In contrast, the ICA in State v. Tanielu (Haw. App. 1996),

> agreed with the trial court that the "viciousness of the attack . . . severed any relationship between the use of force and the welfare of [the d]aughter. . . ." In that case, the defendant kicked his fourteen-year-old daughter in the shin, slapped her six to seven times, punched her in the face five to ten times, stomped on her face, and pulled her ears after discovering that she, *inter alia,* violated his orders not to see her verbally and physically abusive eighteen-year-old boyfriend. . . .

Similarly, in *Crouser,* the defendant punished his girlfriend's fourteen-year-old daughter because she forged a school progress report by (1) hitting her across both sides of her face, (2) knocking her to the floor, (3) throwing her on the bed, and (4) hitting her bare buttocks with a plastic bat to the point where the bat broke. The daughter testified that she had a hard time sitting and felt dizzy for an hour or so, and her bottom was bruised, had a deep reddish-purple color, and hurt for a couple of weeks after the incident. This court affirmed the defendant's conviction of abuse of a family or household member because the force inflicted upon the daughter exceeded the permissible level of discipline.

Based upon the foregoing . . . , we do not believe Roman's discipline was excessive in light of Minor's age, his misconduct, and the comparatively mild physical force used by Roman. . . . The discipline used by Roman was reasonably proportionate to Minor's misconduct, *i.e.*, his defiant attitude and demeanor, and the discipline was necessary to punish Minor's misconduct. Therefore, . . . the prosecution failed to disprove Roman's parental discipline defense beyond a reasonable doubt. . . . [W]e vacate the . . . judgment . . .

Is it implicit in the position that the boy's attitude after being kicked amounted to misconduct that minors should accept a kick in the back by a parent figure, without protest, as appropriate or as the adult's prerogative? If so, do you agree? Is Delaware wrong to exclude kicking categorically as unreasonable and unnecessary?

The mother's large boyfriend did not testify that he felt physically threatened by the boy, and he abandoned a self-defense defense in the lower court. The evidence also did not show that the boy refused to do what he was asked to do, so behavior modification was not really an issue. The Hawaii courts therefore viewed the assaults just as attitude-correction. The attitude was in part a product of being kicked and in part dislike of mom's boyfriend and resentment of his presence in the home. Is it wrong for young people to have and display such feelings, such that punishment is in order? Is hitting them in the face necessary or even likely to improve their attitude?

Change the facts of the case such that it was the mother who grated the cheese inadequately, tuned out with a Walkman, and got angry when kicked in the back by the boyfriend. Suppose she was a chronically moody person and the boyfriend was tired of her negativity, laziness, and selfishness. Would it be reasonable for the boyfriend to kick her to get her attention and then hit her in the face a couple of times to get the message through to her that she needs to change her attitude? Should the analysis be different if they are married? If you think a boyfriend should exit the relationship if he can no longer tolerate a girlfriend's attitude, rather than trying to change her with kicking, choking, and hitting in the face, should you similarly think the boyfriend in this case should have just moved out if he could not find a non-violent way to improve the boy's attitude?

If you think the outcome wrong in the *Roman* case, what change in the boy's behavior might change your mind? What if the boy always refused to do anything Roman asked him to do? Would hitting then be appropriate? What if the boy always responded with "F— you" whenever Roman spoke to him? Or if the boy used beer or marijuana to tune out instead of a Walkman?

As with partner violence, states have also created special civil proceedings to handle reports of violence by parents toward children. Civil child abuse laws address a broader range of acts, but these too contain an authorization of some violence toward children.

Illinois Compiled Statutes
Chapter 705, Act 405. Juvenile Court Act of 1987
Article II. Abused, Neglected or Dependent Minors

405/2-3. Neglected or Abused Minor

. . . (2) Those who are abused include any minor under 18 years of age whose parent or immediate family member, or any person responsible for the minor's welfare, or any person who is in the same family or household as the minor, or any individual residing in the same home as the minor, or a paramour of the minor's parent:

(i) inflicts, causes to be inflicted, or allows to be inflicted upon such minor physical injury, by other than accidental means, which causes death, disfigurement, impairment of physical or emotional health, or loss or impairment of any bodily function;

(ii) creates a substantial risk of physical injury to such minor by other than accidental means which would be likely to cause death, disfigurement, impairment of emotional health, or loss or impairment of any bodily function;

(iii) commits or allows to be committed any sex offense against such minor . . . ;

(iv) commits or allows to be committed an act or acts of torture upon such minor; or

(v) inflicts excessive corporal punishment;

(vi) commits or allows to be committed the offense of involuntary servitude, involuntary sexual servitude of a minor, or trafficking in persons for forced labor or services . . . upon such minor; or

(vii) allows, encourages or requires a minor to commit any act of prostitution. . . .

Authorization of violence is implicit in this civil abuse definition insofar as it treats a physical attack on a child as abusive only when it is "excessive." In the civil codes of some other states, the authorization is explicit. For example, Indiana's civil code chapter on child abuse contains a section clarifying that "[t]his chapter does not . . . [l]imit the right of a parent, guardian, or custodian of a child to use reasonable corporal punishment when disciplining the child." Ind. Code §31-34-1-15.

If you were a judge called upon to give meaning to terms like "excessive" or "reasonable," in a criminal or a civil proceeding, how would you do it? By thinking about your own childhood? By looking to standards in your community? If community standards, how would you determine this? By conducting a survey? A survey of only adults or also/instead of children? Or would you attempt to define these terms by conceptual analysis, abstracted from the beliefs that people happen to have at this particular time in this particular country? Does the statutory definition of abuse provide any guidance?

In a few states, civil domestic violence statutes, enacted principally to protect adults from partner violence, are written broadly enough to encompass child victims, and those statutes contain no exception to the proscription of and availability of protective orders against "violence." See, e.g., Katherine B.T. v. Jackson, 640 S.E.2d 569 (W. Va. 2006) (holding that minor could file under state's domestic violence laws for protective order against mother who choked and punched him). Courts in those states have yet to resolve the seeming inconsistency between domestic violence laws and child abuse laws.

The appropriateness of legal authorization of some violence toward children is currently a topic of much debate among legal scholars, children's rights advocates, and child development experts. Here is one presentation of the case for abolition:

Elizabeth T. Gershoff & Susan H. Bitensky, The Case Against Corporal Punishment of Children

Psychol. Pub. Pol'y & L. (2007)

. . . The academic debate is largely divided into those who argue that corporal punishment in some circumstances is effective and sometimes necessary to discipline children and those who assert that there is very little benefit and rather a substantial risk of harm from using corporal punishment on children. The debate also continues among the public, with popular press newspapers and magazines continuing to publish articles each year regarding the debate about pros and cons of using corporal punishment with children. In 2006 alone, articles appeared in *American Baby, Men's Health, The New York Times, Parenting, Time,* and *USA Today,* among many other similar publications.

What may come as . . . a surprise to Americans is that . . . outside the United States . . . , authoritative bodies, charged with interpreting treaties, have deemed the practice to be a violation of international human rights law and have urged nations to institute domestic bans on it (United Nations: Committee on the Rights of the Child, 2006; Council of Europe, Parliamentary Assembly, 2005; Council of Europe, Commissioner for Human Rights: Hammarberg, 2006; United Nations Study on Violence Against Children: 2006). In 2007 alone, Chile, the Netherlands, New Zealand, Portugal, Spain, Uruguay, and Venezuela adopted legal bans of all corporal punishment of children, be it by parents, teachers, or other caregivers, bringing the number of countries with total bans to 23. An additional 91 of the world's 231 countries and principalities have banned corporal punishment of children by teachers or school administrators.

For purposes of this article, we define corporal punishment as the use of physical force, no matter how light, with the intention of causing the child to experience bodily pain so as to correct or punish the child's behavior. Such physical force typically includes hitting children either with a hand or with an object. In the U.S., corporal punishment is known by a variety of euphemisms, including spank, smack, slap, pop, beat, paddle, punch, whup/whip, and hit . . . .

Corporal punishment remains a common child rearing practice in the United States. In a nationally representative survey of almost 1,000 parents of 1- and 2-year-olds, 63% reported using physical punishment (Regalado et al., 2004). A smaller survey of parents of 1- and 2-year-olds found a very similar rate of corporal punishment, at 65% (Socolar, Savage, & Evans, 2007). We analyzed data from a nationally representative longitudinal study of over 21,000 children and found that by the time these children reached the fifth grade in 2003, 80% had been corporally punished by their parents. Similarly, most of the adolescents in a recent study reported having been slapped or spanked (85%), and half reported having been hit with a belt or similar object (51%; Bender et al., 2007). . . . Although less common than in homes, corporal punishment continues to be used in schools as well; in the 2004-2005 school year, corporal punishment was administered to a total of 272,028 school children across the nation (Office for Civil Rights, 2007). . . .

Gershoff (2002) reviewed 88 studies that had been conducted over a period of 62 years and calculated average effect sizes for the associations of corporal punishment with 11 child outcomes. We complement the Gershoff findings with summaries of the findings from more recently published research.

Does Corporal Punishment Promote Child Obedience and Reduce Problem Behavior?

. . . The primary goal of any socialization should be to promote children's internalization of the reasons for behaving appropriately rather than to behave solely to avoid punishment. The research to date indicates that physical punishment does not promote long-term, internalized compliance. In contrast to the findings on immediate compliance, the findings regarding corporal punishment as a predictor of moral internalization are more consistent, with 85% of the studies included in the Gershoff meta-analysis reporting corporal punishment to be associated with less moral internalization and long-term compliance. Similarly, the more children receive physical punishment, the less likely they are to express empathy for others.

Parents report that one of the main instances in which they use corporal punishment is when their children have behaved aggressively, such as hitting a younger sibling, or antisocially, such as stealing money from parents. Yet there are many reasons to suspect that physical punishment may increase, rather than decrease, children's aggression and antisocial behavior, including that it models the use of force to achieve desired ends and increases the likelihood that children will make hostile attributions that, in turn, increase the likelihood that they will behave inappropriately in social interactions (Dodge, 1986; Weiss, Dodge, Bates, & Pettit, 1992). . . .

In Gershoff's meta-analysis of 27 studies, every one of the studies found corporal punishment was associated with more, not less, child aggression. Of the 13 studies included in a meta-analysis of the association of corporal punishment to child antisocial behavior, 12 found more corporal punishment was associated with more antisocial behavior. In both cases, the size of the association was moderate. Similarly, in recent studies of children around the globe, corporal punishment has been associated linearly with more physical aggression (Canada: Pagani et al., 2004; China: Nelson, Hart, Yang, Olsen, & Jin, 2006; China, India, Italy, Kenya, Philippines, and Thailand: Gershoff et al., 2007; Lansford et al., 2005; Singapore: Sim & Ong, 2005), verbal aggression (Canada: Pagani et al., 2004), physical fighting and bullying (United States: Ohene, Ireland, McNeely, & Borowsky, 2006), antisocial behavior (U.S.: Grogan-Kaylor 2005), and behavior problems generally (Norway: Javo, Heyerdahl, & Rudmin, 2004; U.S.: Bender et al., 2007; Kerr et al. 2004). . . .

How Do We Know That Parental Corporal Punishment Causes Increased Child Defiance and Problem Behavior?

. . . Because experiments assigning children to parents who spank or not or assigning parents to spank or no-spank conditions are both unfeasible and unethical, . . . the field's overall reliance on correlational studies of corporal punishment has left open the possibility that the causal pathway may not be entirely (or at all, by some accounts) from parent to child as is typically assumed. Two primary alternative hypotheses . . . [are] that this association . . . is the result of difficult children eliciting corporal punishment from their parents rather than of parents' use of corporal punishment causing children to be aggressive . . . [and] that a third variable altogether, namely, shared genetics, predicts both parental corporal punishment and child problem behavior. . . .

The Child Effect Alternative Hypothesis.

. . . Some support for . . . this alternative hypothesis comes from experiments in which both familiar and unfamiliar adults behaved more harshly with children who were difficult. Furthermore, parents use punishments generally and corporal punishment in particular more for misbehaviors involving aggression. . . . [However,] . . . analyses continue to find that corporal punishment predicts later problem behavior even after initial levels of such behaviors and race, gender, and family socioeconomic status have been controlled (e.g., Grogan-Kaylor, 2004, 2005; Gunnoe & Mariner, 1997; Singer, Singer, & Rapaczynski, 1984; Weiss et al., 1992). . . .

Yet such studies do not directly test whether child behavior problems predict parent corporal punishment in the future, which would be needed to entirely rule out the possibility that a child-to-parent direction of effect is at work. A second line of research addresses this possibility by comparing parent- with child-effect pathways using cross-lagged structural equation models. Cross-lagged models simultaneously estimate predictive paths from parental corporal punishment to child behavior and vice versa. Two such studies do confirm the presence of a child effect on the frequency with which parents use harsh (including corporal) punishment, while a third did not find a child effect on harsh punishment. In contrast, all three of these studies also found strong parent effects on later child behavior problems. . . .

A very strong test of parent versus child effects comes from a recent evaluation of a parent-training program that included reduction of corporal punishment as a goal. The study examined change in parents' use of corporal punishment as a mediator of the impact of parent training on children's externalizing problem behaviors. Crucially . . . , the model explicitly tested whether the parent training reduced child externalizing behavior problems by reducing parents' use of corporal punishment (a parent effect) after controlling for child effects at baseline and across time. Research with over 500 families revealed that significant reductions in children's externalizing behavior problems were a direct result of decreases in parents' reliance on corporal punishment as a result of program participation. These analyses present strong support for a causal link between parents' use of corporal punishment and children's subsequent behavior problems.

THE SHARED GENETICS ALTERNATIVE HYPOTHESIS.

. . . Proponents of this hypothesis argue that a shared genetic predisposition to be aggressive could result in both parents and children being easily frustrated and aggressive, which is manifest as harsh discipline by the parent and aggressive and problem behaviors in the child. . . . Using cross-sectional data from a sample of adopted children and their adoptive and biological parents, Ge and colleagues (1996) found that after controlling for genetic risk (indexed as psychiatric disorder in their biological parents), there were significant bidirectional effects between mothers' use of harsh and inconsistent discipline (including corporal punishment) and children's antisocial behavior; each significantly predicted the other. For fathers, only a child effect was found, such that the child's antisocial behavior predicted fathers' use of harsh and inconsistent discipline but not vice versa. The fact that both parent and child effects were identified in a sample of parents and children who were not genetically related appears to undercut the shared genetics explanation.

A second study, by O'Connor et al. (1998) replicated the Ge et al. study using longitudinal data. Although O'Connor et al. confirmed that children at genetic risk did evoke more negative parenting from their adoptive parents, adoptive parents' use of negative parenting continued to predict children's problem behaviors even after the genetic risk had been partialed out. Taken together, these studies demonstrate that although there is a child genetic effect that evokes corporal punishment from parents, there is an equally strong effect of corporal punishment on the development of nongenetically related children's behavior problems. . . .

In a study of twins and their parenting of their own children, Lynch et al. (2006) found that when adult twins differed in their use of harsh physical punishment with their own biological children, the twin who used more harsh physical punishment had children with more externalizing, internalizing, and drug and alcohol abuse symptoms. Thus, when shared genetics are controlled, harsh physical punishment predicts greater symptomatology in children. . . .

ADDITIONAL EVIDENCE AGAINST BOTH ALTERNATIVE HYPOTHESES.

. . . Both hypotheses assume an affective or uncontrolled, rather than a cognitive and planned, component to parents' use of corporal punishment. . . . [However,] parents themselves report using more corporal punishment with the intention that it will improve their children's behavior, not out of a short-term frustration with inappropriate child behavior or a genetically driven aggressive response to child misbehavior. . . .

DOES CORPORAL PUNISHMENT PUT CHILDREN AT RISK FOR UNINTENDED NEGATIVE OUTCOMES?

In addition to failing to achieve parents' intended goals, physical punishment also has been found to put children at risk for a range of unintended consequences or side effects. . . .

IMPAIRED MENTAL HEALTH.

[Studies] . . . have confirmed across multiple countries the association of corporal punishment with impairments in children's mental health, including anxiety and depression (Hungary: Csorba et al., 2001; U.S.: Bender et al., 2007; Eamon, 2001; Rodriguez, 2003), alcohol and drug use (Hong Kong: Lau et al., 2005), and general psychological maladjustment (Jamaica: Steely & Rohner, 2006). . . . Frequency of corporal punishment has been found to predict self-reported psychological distress among 10-16-year-olds, even at low rates of corporal punishment (Turner & Finkelhor, 1996). In children as young as 1 year old, toddlers who experience frequent corporal punishment show elevated levels of the stress hormone cortisol in reaction to an anxiety-provoking interaction involving their mothers (Bugental, Martorell, & Barraza, 2003). . . . [A] large body of research . . . has linked the experience of physical assault substantiated as abuse with lasting impairments in children's neurobiological stress systems. There is also some evidence that the associations of corporal punishment with impaired mental health persist into adulthood. Corporal punishment was associated with deteriorated mental health in eight studies included in Gershoff's meta-analysis. Subsequent studies continue to find that mental health problems such as increased depressive symptoms in adulthood are predicted by levels of corporal punishment experienced as a child.

ERODED PARENT-CHILD RELATIONSHIP QUALITY.

. . . Children are motivated to avoid painful experiences, and if they see their parents as sources of pain (as delivered via physical punishment), they will attempt to avoid their parents, which in turn will erode feelings of trust and closeness between parent and child. Such concerns have in fact been borne out in research findings, with 13 out of 13 studies finding corporal punishment to be associated with eroded parent-child relationship quality.

ADULT AGGRESSION AND ANTISOCIAL BEHAVIOR.

Children can carry the lessons they have learned about the acceptability of aggression as a problem-solving measure and as a method of controlling others' behavior into their own adulthoods. Children who have experienced corporal punishment are more likely to report having hit a dating partner than children who have not been physically punished (Straus, 2004). The more men and women report having been physically punished as a child, the more they report using verbal and physical aggression and ineffective problem-solving behaviors with their spouses (Cast, Schweingruber, & Berns, 2006). An increased likelihood that individuals who were physically punished in childhood will perpetrate violence as adults on their own family members [including their own children] was found in Gershoff (2002).

ALTERNATIVE EXPLANATIONS.

There are no clear alternative explanations for this set of unintended consequences of parental corporal punishment. The child effect alternative hypothesis . . . makes little sense for the link with child mental health conditions; it seems unlikely that a child's symptoms of anxiety or depression would make a parent so frustrated or angry as to increase the parent's use of physical punishment or any other forms of discipline. Rather, longitudinal research has found that parents use less, not more, power assertion with anxious and fearful children (Kochanska, Aksan, & Joy, 2007). They do so with good reason: Discipline techniques high in power assertion, including corporal punishment, have been found to substantially undermine moral internalization among children high in fearfulness or anxiety (ibid.). . . . Regarding the parent-child relationship, it is possible that a parent who does not have a close, warm, or trusting relationship with his or her child will be more likely to use corporal punishment out of frustration, resentment, or ill will. Unfortunately, no studies have examined this. . . .

A protracted version of the child effect hypothesis could be developed for the association between childhood experiences of corporal punishment and aggression and problem behavior in adulthood. . . . Some evidence to support this alternative hypothesis comes from a longitudinal study of the development of aggression. . . .

ARE CHILDREN WHO ARE PHYSICALLY PUNISHED MORE LIKELY TO BE PHYSICALLY ABUSED?

A particularly troubling aspect of corporal punishment and one that underlies much of the current policy and advocacy surrounding it is its association with physical abuse. . . . [M]ost incidents of physical abuse take place within a punishment context. . . . Abusive parents in the United States themselves reveal that as many as two-thirds of their abusive incidents began as attempts to change children's behavior or to teach them a lesson (Coontz & Martin, 1988; Gil, 1973; Kadushin & Martin, 1981). The fact that parents in treatment for past substantiated abuse spank their children significantly more often than parents without history of abuse (Whipple & Richey, 1997) suggests that physical abuse is more likely among parents who use corporal punishment frequently. . . .

Gershoff found a very strong and consistent (in 10 out of 10 studies examined) relation between parents' use of corporal punishment and the likelihood that the parent would physically injure the child or be reported to a child protective services agency. Having experienced corporal punishment at the hands of their parents (such as pinching, shaking, or spanking) puts children at 7 times greater risk of undergoing severe violence (such as punching, kicking, or hitting with an object; Clément et al. 2000) and make them more than 2 times as likely to suffer an injury requiring medical attention (Crandall, Chiu, & Sheehan, 2006) compared with children who have not experienced corporal punishment. . . . In an analysis of child deaths from maltreatment in the 30 wealthy nations that are members of the Organisation for Economic Cooperation and Development, UNICEF called corporal punishment "the most common form of violence in the industrialized world." It went on to call resolutely for a global ban on corporal punishment as a way to drastically decrease fatal violence against children.

International Human Rights Law Regarding Corporal Punishment of Children

While the effects and effectiveness of corporal punishment on children continue to be debated in academia, the rest of the world has moved ahead to accord corporal punishment of children the status of a human rights violation. The Commissioner for Human Rights of the Council of Europe condemned corporal punishment in a recent statement, observing that

> Children have had to wait until last to be given equal legal protection from deliberate assaults—a protection the rest of us take for granted. It is extraordinary that children, whose developmental state and small size is acknowledged to make them particularly vulnerable to physical and psychological injury, should be singled out for less protection from assaults on their fragile bodies, minds and dignity. (Hammarberg, 2006, paras. 4-5)

. . . The view of the international lawmaking community overwhelmingly is that corporal punishment of children violates international human rights law (Bitensky, 2006). This principle of law implicitly stems from at least seven multilateral human rights treaties: the United Nations Convention on the Rights of the Child ([Children's Convention] 1989); the International Covenant on Civil and Political Rights ([ICCPR] 1966); the International Covenant on Economic, Social and Cultural Rights ([ICESCR] 1966); the Convention Against Torture and Other Cruel, Inhuman or Degrading Treatment or Punishment ([Torture Convention] 1984); the American Convention on Human Rights ([American Convention] 1969); and the two European Social Charters (European Social Charter, 1961; European Social Charter [Revised], 1996).

Of the above treaties, the United States has ratified and therefore is a party to the ICCPR (1966) and the Torture Convention (1984), making them "the supreme Law of the Land" under the U.S. Constitution (art. VI, para. 2). Counterintuitive though it may appear, such an exalted characterization does not avail children much in terms of vesting them with a mandatory right to protection against corporal punishment. Caveats and complications abound. The federal government has made reservations to some of the pertinent provisions of these conventions so as to effectively inhibit the provisions' present application to corporal punishment of children in the United States. Legal technicalities concerning non-self-executing treaties also make the conventions, in the absence of implementing legislation, unenforceable in American courts. Congress has as yet not enacted legislation to implement ICCPR or Torture Convention provisions germane to the issue of corporal punishment of children. However, the lack of domestic judicial enforceability does not negate the legal duty of both the government and the private sector to adhere to both international conventions, and adherence to the provisions of the conventions is monitored internationally by United Nations committees. Because these committees have no power of compulsion, the arrangement is essentially one of an honor system, in which the government and private actors may avoid compliance without serious repercussions.

Although the United States has not ratified the Children's Convention (1989), the ICESCR, or the American Convention, it has signed these three treaties. Mere signature does imply intention to ratify but, by itself, does not suffice to make the United States a party to these treaties. Nevertheless, signature does still impose certain legal obligations on the signatory nation. It is well established that signing a treaty requires a nation "to refrain from acts which would defeat the object and purpose of the treaty . . . until it shall have made its intention clear not to become a party to the treaty." . . .

The Children's Convention is unique in being the first international treaty to focus solely on the physical, social, cultural, political, and civil rights of children. . . . The Children's Convention has been ratified by 192 countries around the world. . . . The Children's Convention (1989) created the Committee on the Rights of the Child to monitor states parties' compliance with its terms. The committee recently issued General Comment No. 8, which forcefully declared that

> There is no ambiguity: "all forms of physical or mental violence" does not leave room for any level of legalized violence against children. Corporal punishment and other cruel or degrading forms of punishment are forms of violence and the State must take all appropriate legislative, administrative, social and educational measures to eliminate them. . . .

THE LEGAL STATUS OF CORPORAL PUNISHMENT OF CHILDREN IN THE UNITED STATES

. . . Corporal punishment by parents is permitted in 49 states by statute or court decision. . . . This legal standing of corporal punishment reflects public opinion that children are in essence the property of their parents and that parents have the right to raise them as they choose (Belsky, 1993; Pollard, 2003). The U.S. Supreme Court . . . has not yet considered whether parents have a fundamental constitutional right to use corporal punishment with their children. . . . The Supreme Court has, however, considered the constitutionality of corporal punishment administered by public school personnel at the elementary and secondary levels. The high Court held by a 5-to-4 margin that this punishment, regardless of its severity, cannot violate the Eighth Amendment prohibition of cruel and unusual punishments (*Ingraham v. Wright*, 1977). In that case, two junior high school students were hit by their school principal on the buttocks and arms with a wooden paddle 2 feet long, 3 to 4 inches wide, and half an inch thick. The result was that one child developed a hematoma requiring medical attention and was unable to function normally for several days, while the other child lost full use of an arm for a week.

The Court . . . averred that students, unlike prisoners, have no need of the amendment in view of the benign nature of elementary and secondary schools . . . and contended that there is no national groundswell of opinion against this form of punishment. . . . 28 states and the District of Columbia now ban corporal punishment of students in the public schools. Many of the remaining 22 states empower their local school districts to prohibit the practice, and a large number have opted for prohibition; these include districts in some of the largest cities in the country. . . . In addition, many national professional organizations concerned with children's physical and mental welfare and well-being have called for bans on corporal punishment in schools, including the American Academy of Pediatrics, the American Bar Association, the American Civil Liberties Union, the American Psychological Association, the National Association of Elementary School Principals, the National Association of School Psychologists, the National Association of Social Workers, the National Association for State Boards of Education, and the National Education Association (Center for Effective Discipline, 2007b). . . .

Consider that in 1992, the Court ruled that use of excessive physical force against a prisoner may constitute an Eighth Amendment violation even though his bodily injuries are minor (*Hudson v. McMillian*, 1992). This put the Court in the awkward position of upholding the constitutionality of injury-causing force against children in public schools while striking down the use of a similar level of force against adults in penal institutions. . . . Most states . . . bar foster parents from using this form of discipline. . . . Most states do not tolerate corporal punishment in nonresidential care facilities such as child care. Well over half of the states prohibit corporal punishment of juvenile delinquents when detained or jailed by law enforcement. . . .

Parental corporal punishment that exceeds the reasonableness standard is generally categorized as physical child abuse. . . . [W]hat is deemed reasonable varies from state to state; indeed, it often varies within a state according to the predilections and acumen of the judges faced with applying the standard during litigation. Compare, for example, *In re Miles* (Ohio Ct. App. 2002) (refusing to find child abuse in relation to parent allowing her fiancé to bite her 9-year-old's face, leaving marks from both his upper and lower teeth, as a reprimand for the child's having done the same to a sibling) and *City of Shaker Heights v. Wright* (Ohio Ct. App. 1996) (finding no liability for child endangering, but only legal corporal punishment instead, where father whipped his 10-year-old with a belt so as to produce welts on the child's legs, the scarring of which lasted for 6 months) with *In re K. B.* (Ohio Ct. App. 2003) (ruling that there was child abuse where toddler was spanked with such substantial force as to result in several bruises on her cheek, abdomen, back, and arm) and *State v. Howard* (Ohio Ct. App. 1999) (holding father guilty of domestic violence and child abuse for striking his 12-year-old son at least twice on the back and head with a broom handle, thereby causing a 3- to 4-inch reddish mark to appear on the child's back). This lack of uniformity makes it difficult, if not impossible, for parents and caregivers to gauge when their behavior might cross the wavering line from the legal to the illegal.

The Legal Status of Corporal Punishment of Children in Selected Other Countries

There is without doubt a growing momentum among countries to enact legal bans on all forms of corporal punishment. . . . The Parliamentary Assembly of the Council of Europe recently adopted Recommendation 1666, in which it stated, "The Assembly considers any corporal punishment of children is in breach of their fundamental right to human dignity and physical integrity. . . . The social and legal acceptance of corporal punishment of children must be ended" The Parliamentary Assembly went on to call for a coordinated campaign against corporal punishment in all member countries (of which there are 45) and to make Europe "a corporal punishment-free zone for children" (Council of Europe, Parliamentary Assembly, 2005).

To date, 23 countries have instituted universal bans on corporal punishment of children: Sweden (in 1979), Finland (in 1983), Norway (in 1987), Austria (in 1989), Croatia (in 1994), Cyprus (in 1994), Denmark (in 1997), Latvia (in 1998), Bulgaria (in 2000), Germany (in 2000), Israel (in 2000), Iceland (in 2003), Romania (in 2004), Ukraine (in 2004), Hungary (in 2005), Greece (in 2006), the Netherlands (in 2007), New Zealand (in 2007), Portugal (in 2007), Spain (in 2007), Chile (in 2007), Uruguay (in 2007), and Venezuela (in 2007; Global Initiative, 2007b). The latter three bans are significant because they are the first universal bans on corporal punishment of children in the Western hemisphere. We describe Sweden's ban in depth here both because it is the first and because it remains the most studied of the bans.

The First Country to Institute a Universal Ban: Sweden

[In] Sweden . . . , corporal punishment . . . was widely practiced by parents at least until the 1950s. As in the United States, much of the support for corporal punishment as a component of child rearing in Sweden was rooted in religious beliefs and literal interpretations of religious texts. . . . In 1957, Sweden eliminated the criminal defense to corrective assault of a child (i.e., corporal punishment). Then, in 1966, the exemption for mild corporal punishment was removed from the civil code. The effect of these two reforms was to make the hitting of children a criminal assault equivalent to a prosecutable assault of an adult. At this time, one half of the Swedish population still believed that corporal punishment was necessary in child rearing (Durrant, 2003), reflecting the fact that the government based these decisions on social science research findings and human rights principles, not on popular opinion.

The stage for a complete ban on corporal punishment was set in the early 1970s when public outrage at a few high-profile cases of child physical abuse, including one in which a father was acquitted of assault because he claimed to be disciplining the child, led to the creation of the Children's Rights Commission in 1977. This commission, made up of lawyers, psychologists, psychiatrists, and politicians, issued a report arguing that a ban on corporal punishment was necessary to promote children's healthy development, to prevent abuse, and to teach the public that all violence against children is unacceptable. In direct response to this report, the Swedish parliament amended the country's civil law code to explicitly prohibit corporal punishment of children by all adults. . . . [I]t now reads, "Children are entitled to care, security, and a good upbringing. Children are to be treated with respect for their person and individuality and may not be subjected to physical punishment or any other injurious or humiliating treatment." . . .

The Swedish government pursues a policy of prosecutorial restraint . . . , trusting instead to the gradual pedagogical effect of the civil ban working in tandem with the possibility (however remote) of criminal prosecution. . . . [T]he government began a universal campaign to educate the public about the civil code ban. The main thrust of the campaign was the distribution of booklets that advise parents about the rationale for the law, the reasons for avoiding corporal punishment, and suggestions for alternative approaches to resolving parent-child conflict. . . . In an effort to extend this education to children directly, information about the new law appeared on milk cartons for 2 months after the law passed, and the law was discussed in family life classes in Swedish schools. The education campaign was amazingly successful, with 99% of the public aware of the law after only 2 years, an unprecedented level of public awareness of any law throughout the industrialized world.

The ban appears to have been successful both in changing attitudes about corporal punishment as an acceptable discipline practice and in changing the incidence of it. The percentage of adults who profess positive attitudes toward spanking has declined from over 50% in the 1970s before the ban to close to 10% in 2000 (Janson, 2005). Even more impressive is the low support for corporal punishment among children after the ban. In a 1994-1995 survey, among both respondents who were 18 to 34 years old (and, thus, children when the ban went into effect) and respondents who were then 13- to 15-year-old children (born after the 1979 ban), only 6% approved of the use of mild forms of corporal punishment (Durrant, 2003). Use of corporal punishment has also declined dramatically, although it has not disappeared: Whereas 51% of all preschool children had experienced corporal punishment in 1980, only 8% had by 2000 (Janson, 2005). In the 2 decades after the ban, child injuries from assaults also decreased (Durrant, 1999). . . . Detractors of the ban argued that it would result in an increase in youth violence and delinquency, worrying that parents who do not use corporal punishment would be too permissive. On the contrary, youth involvement in theft, drug use, and drug trafficking declined following the ban (Durrant, 2000). Youth suicide also declined (Durrant, 2000). . . .

PROGRAM AND POLICY STRATEGIES TO REDUCE CORPORAL PUNISHMENT OF CHILDREN IN THE U.S.

Both the social science and legal arguments point to a similar conclusion: The risks of corporal punishment outweigh any perceived benefits to children or to parents. . . . To have all Americans embrace the goal of . . . eliminating corporal punishment of children, a multilayered strategy of interventions is necessary. . . .

STRATEGY 1: UNIVERSAL PREVENTION—EDUCATION CAMPAIGN ON EFFECTIVE DISCIPLINE . . .

STRATEGY 2: TARGETED INTERVENTIONS FOR NEW PARENTS, PRE-PARENTS, AND AT-RISK PARENTS . . .

STRATEGY 3: EDUCATION FOR PROFESSIONALS WHO WORK WITH CHILDREN AND FAMILIES . . .

STRATEGY 4: REFORMING FEDERAL AND STATE LAWS REGARDING CORPORAL PUNISHMENT . . .

Were you surprised at the number of jurisdictions that legally prohibit spanking children? At some of the particular countries that have done so? What explanation would you offer for American intransigence on the issue of parental freedom to corporally punish children when so many other countries have eliminated it? For one theory, pointing to the Puritan and Protestant influences on formation of American culture, and to the link many people make between corporal punishment of children and religious freedom, see Tamar Morag, *Religious Tradition and the Corporal Punishment of Children: A Comparison of the American and Israeli Legal Systems*, 25 INT'L J.L. POL'Y & FAM. 338 (2011).

Taking into account the arguments for and against corporal punishment in the article above, the responsibilities parents bear for their children's well being, and recent recognition of children as equal persons under the law, which of the following (or some variation on one of them) is the most appropriate legal rule?

1. Parents may never intentionally hit a child.
2. Parents may intentionally hit a child only when absolutely necessary to advance the child's well being, and only with the least severity that will be effective.
3. Parents may intentionally hit a child only when this will be more effective than alternative means of correcting behavior.
4. Parents may intentionally hit a child whenever this will be effective at correcting behavior, so long as they do not inflict lasting injury.
5. Parents may hit a child whenever they wish, but may not cause severe injury.

If you favor any rule other than #1, consider again whether you would favor a rule with the same wording except that "parents" were replaced with "husbands" or "one spouse" and "a child" were replaced with "a wife" or "the other spouse." If not, try to articulate a justification for the different treatment of children and spouses. Would you reach a different conclusion as to situations in which a spouse has lost mental faculties in such a way that others say he or she "acts like a child"? If you do not conclude that an immediate change in the law as to hitting children is called for, do you think the state should undertake any other measures to reduce parental use of corporal punishment, such as a media campaign to educate parents about alternatives? For recent analysis of corporal punishment from multiple disciplinary perspectives, see Symposium: *Corporal Punishment of Children*, 73(2) LAW & CONTEMP. PROBS. (2010).

Should the analysis of corporal punishment be different in the schooling context? Does it depend on whether schools require parental authorization to paddle students? A majority of states prohibit it in schools, but roughly 20, almost all southern states, still allow it. The Supreme Court upheld such laws against constitutional challenge by a group of junior high school students in Ingraham v. Wright, 430 U.S. 651 (1977). Congresswoman Carolyn McCarthy has repeatedly introduced legislation at the federal level to ban the practice in schools, but so far without success. See Ending Corporal Punishment in Schools Act, H.R. 3027, 112th Cong. (2011). Given that a majority of states prohibit school spanking, why would not a majority of congresspersons support this bill?

Would any of the points in the Gershoff and Bitensky article also apply to other aspects of child rearing, such as other forms of discipline (e.g., parental rejection or shouting), education (e.g., bad private schooling or homeschooling), or violations of bodily integrity (e.g., circumcising or piercing babies)? Are the identified harms of corporal punishment greater than those that might result from verbal denigration or from educational deprivation? Is there an experiential difference between a parent or teacher spanking a child and a parent or teacher telling a child that she is wicked, sinful, and destined for an eternity in hell? Or teaching girls that they are inherently inferior to boys? Should the law prohibit teachers and parents from doing those things? Or should the law just accept that childhood inevitably entails some denigration and suffering?

A recent case in Oregon raised the question whether the standards of physical treatment should vary based on parents' subcultural norms or religious beliefs, a question that also arises, as we saw in Chapter 3, in the partner abuse context:

Miriam Jordan, Abuse Case Sparks a Clash over Limits of Tough Parenting

Wall St. J., Jan. 22, 2011

SALEM, Ore.— . . . Here in one of America's most progressive states, authorities are grappling with a vexing problem: how to accommodate an immigrant community that is large but reclusive, heavy users of public assistance but openly anti-government. Oregon is now home to about 150,000 evangelical Christians from the former Soviet Union. . . . The group, which hails largely from the Ukraine, subscribes to a literal interpretation of the Bible, including corporal punishment. Compared to newcomers from Vietnam, Bhutan and elsewhere, the Slavic Christians have assimilated "less than other groups." . . . Integrating recent immigrants who buck mainstream culture is a problem in pockets around the nation. In Massachusetts and New York, some parents from African nations have forced daughters to undergo female circumcision—a painful cutting of the genitalia that has been banned in the U.S. . . .

Mr. and Mrs. Kozlov [are] evangelical Baptists who came to the U.S. in 2003 from the Ukraine. "Their kids were trying to do what they saw other kids do, and they were getting in massive trouble with their parents for that," says Hannah Tipton, a court-appointed special advocate for the Kozlov children. At the time of his arrest, Oleksandr Kozlov, 42, was jobless and collecting unemployment benefits. He had worked in a factory that made the leather straps he allegedly used in several beatings. His 40-year-old wife, Lyudmila, stayed at home taking care of the children. Life revolved around the small Russian-speaking Evangelical Christian Baptist Church of Salem, one of several Slavic Christian congregations in the area. They had virtually no contact with Americans, according to social workers and other community members. Dmitriy Kozlov was in bed one morning in

July 2009 when his mother spotted a temporary tattoo on his right arm, he testified in court. He said she grabbed an iron and began lashing his arm with the electrical cord, leaving multiple bruises. A few days later, Mrs. Kozlov noticed that her oldest child, Tatyana, 15, and her second daughter, Yekaterina, 13, had trimmed their hair without permission while she had been in the hospital giving birth to her seventh child. Mrs. Kozlov whipped the teenagers, leaving extensive bruises on their arms, backs and legs, Tatyana testified in court.

"Tired of our parents hitting us," as she said in court, the three oldest Kozlov children hatched a plan. One July evening, when their father was out and their mother was asleep, they snuck out of the house, found a pay phone and made that 911 call. The next day, police and social workers took into protective custody the other four Kozlov children, including baby Lilya, then eight days old. Mr. and Mrs. Kozlov were arrested and held on charges of criminal mistreatment. . . . On Russian-language websites and blogs, the removal of the children from their parents was depicted as the U.S. destroying a family and a violation of human rights. . . . Hundreds of Russian-speaking Baptists, including some from California and Washington, descended on Salem. . . . They marched on the state Capitol. . . . They held vigils outside Marion County's courthouse. . . . Their signs read, "Don't Destroy Our Families". . . . Kozlov supporters said corporal punishment was a parental duty condoned by the Bible. . . .

On August 19, 2009, roughly 750 Slavic Christians packed the First Slavic Baptist church for a forum on U.S. law and parental rights. For three hours, members put questions to the district attorney, state child-welfare officials and law-enforcement officers with the help of a Russian-language interpreter. Among the questions . . . : "How can I keep my child from smoking if I can't beat him or her?" "What are parents supposed to do when a child, particularly a teenager, is disobedient?" "The difference between discipline and abuse is lasting injury," . . . an official with the Department of Human Services told the audience. Oregon authorities, too, wanted to learn about this newly vocal community. . . . [A] Pentecostal refugee from Russia . . . spoke about the perilous life in the Soviet Union of those who secretly practiced their religion. "In some families, parents and children were separated because parents taught the Bible,". . . . "Children were placed in foster care to forget about God, the Bible and how to pray. . . ." The Slavic Christians saw the Kozlov case . . . "through the eyes of persecution they suffered in the past."

Hoping the Kozlov family could be reunited, Oregon officials in September appointed a Russian psychologist in Portland to evaluate them and offer counseling. The attempts proved futile. "They didn't want to talk about being better parents. They would say, 'Bible says it's O.K. to spank children,'" says Olga Parker, the psychologist. Mrs. Parker, who interviewed six of the Kozlov children, later testified in court that none of them wanted to return home. . . . Six out of the seven Kozlov children testified. . . . Tatyana, the eldest, testified that all the children in her family had been beaten, except the baby. The 14-year-old Dmitriy testified that he was once "whipped" so badly with a leather strap by his father that he had to skip school to allow the injuries to heal. During one hearing, Mrs. Kozlov interrupted to dispute her children's allegations. Over the judge's protests, she warned the children that God would punish them for what they said. . . . In their closing arguments, the Kozlovs again cited the Bible as justification for their actions. "The law of God is in disciplining children. It's not any less than the law of the United States," Mr. Kozlov said.

On Dec. 4, the jury found Mr. and Mrs. Kozlov each guilty of nine counts of criminal mistreatment. Five days later, the judge sentenced them each to seven years and three months. All seven children were placed in foster care with relatives in Virginia. . . . On Sept. 23, Mr. and Mrs. Kozlov shuffled into a courtroom in Salem, shackled and in prison garb for a hearing on the state's motion to terminate their parental rights. . . . The judge terminated the Kozlov couple's parental rights to the three youngest children, freeing them for adoption by relatives. The four older children will remain in foster care. . . .

Was criminal prosecution and termination of parent-child relationships the appropriate response in this case? What if the parents had expressed willingness to change their discipline practices? Should answers to questions like this be different in the parent-child context than in the partner abuse context?

Parental Procurement of Genital-Altering Surgery

Parents generally do not go out of their way to procure services for their children that the children do not need and that are actually, at least as a matter of short-term well being, harmful to them. A widespread exception concerns children's sexual organs. Many cultures have had a practice of damaging young children's sexual organs in one way or another, one obvious purpose of which is to stifle sexuality. Parents and mates have a genetic and financial interest in favor of controlled and orderly rather than random reproduction. It would be odd for any culture to select the genitals as a site of ritual physical alteration if sexuality were not a central concern.

The article above mentions female genital mutilation (FGM), a cultural and religious practice that has been common in many non-Western countries but treated as criminal child abuse and a human rights violation throughout the Western world. See, e.g., Colo. Rev. Stat. §18-6-401(1)(b) ("a person commits child abuse if such person excises or infibulates, in whole or in part, the labia majora, labia minora, vulva, or clitoris of a female child. A parent, guardian, or other person legally responsible for a female child or charged with the care or custody of a female child commits child abuse if he or she allows the excision or infibulation. . . . Belief that the conduct described . . . is required as a matter of custom, ritual, or standard practice or consent to the conduct by the child on whom it is performed or by the child's parent or legal guardian shall not be an affirmative defense . . ."); 18 U.S.C. §116 ("whoever knowingly circumcises, excises, or infibulates the whole or any part of the labia majora or labia minora or clitoris of another person who has not attained the age of 18 years shall be fined under this title or imprisoned not more than 5 years, or both. . . . [N]o account shall be taken of the effect on the person on whom the operation is to be performed of any belief on the part of that person, or any other person, that the operation is required as a matter of custom or ritual"); Declaration on the Elimination of Violence Against Women, G.A. Res. 48/104, art. 2, U.N. Doc. A/RES/48/49 (1993).

In potential contrast to the latter part of the Colorado and federal statutory provisions, however, California law contains a general cultural defense to child maltreatment: "Cultural and religious child-rearing practices and beliefs which differ from general community standards shall not in themselves create a need for child welfare services unless the practices present a specific danger to the physical or emotional safety of the child." Cal. Welf. & Inst. Code §16509. Suppose an immigrant community in California followed a practice of removing some portion of girls' labia, with trained surgeons operating in sanitary conditions and with anesthetics, and prosecutors charged the surgeons and parents with criminal child abuse. How would you as prosecutor or judge respond when they assert this cultural defense? Is there any danger to the girls' safety? Would it change your position if studies showed that removing a girl's labia reduces the risk of urinary tract and other infections and of cancer in that part of her anatomy? Defenders of FGM cite hygiene as a reason for the practice. See OFFICE OF THE HIGH COMMISSIONER FOR HUMAN RIGHTS, FACT SHEET NO. 23: HARMFUL TRADITIONAL PRACTICES AFFECTING THE HEALTH OF WOMEN AND CHILDREN (1987). Does it matter that many women in that cultural community would strongly defend the practice? Suppose some other immigrant group had a practice of removing pubescent girls' breasts, motivated by religious belief but also citing effectiveness in preventing breast cancer. Would you view that as child abuse?

In stark contrast to the prevailing view in the world today about the inviolability of girls' genitals, Americans have always accepted the Jewish practice of amputating baby boys' foreskins, and in the late nineteenth century, non-Jewish Americans began circumcising their boys in large numbers. Christians did so at the urging initially of John Kellogg, who in addition to being the inventor of Corn Flakes was a medical doctor and a Seventh Day Adventist. Kellogg believed sexual desire the greatest threat to civilization and salvation. He argued that circumcision (along with a bland and meatless diet, hand binding, wire sutures on the foreskin, and cages on the genitals) would reduce the practice of masturbation, "the solitary vice," which he believed a greater abomination than fornication. In a book he reportedly authored while on his honeymoon, Kellogg wrote: "A remedy which is almost always successful in small boys is circumcision. . . . The operation should be performed by a surgeon without administering an anæsthetic, as the brief pain attending the operation will have a salutary effect upon the mind, especially if it be connected with the idea of punishment, as it may well be in some cases." JOHN HARVEY KELLOGG, *Treatment for Self-Abuse and its Effects, in* PLAIN FACTS FOR OLD AND YOUNG (1888) 295. Equally concerned about unrestrained female sexuality, he further wrote: "In females, the author has found the application of pure carbolic acid to the clitoris an excellent means of allaying the abnormal excitement. . . ." Id. at 296.

Medical researchers added support by positing various health benefits from circumcision, with new benefits proposed when earlier ones were disproved. In the late twentieth century, however, the American Academy of Pediatrics and other major medical organizations announced that male circumcision is not justifiable on medical grounds. The rate of circumcision in America peaked in the United States in the early 1970s, at roughly 70 percent, and has declined since then to around 50 percent. The practice has never been common among non-Jews in European countries; there, circumcision rates have always been under 10 percent. Yet those who advocate forcefully for prohibition of circumcision in the United States are generally regarded as a fringe element, as anti-Semitic, and/or as perversely preoccupied with penises. In 2011, two independent efforts in California to secure local bans on male circumcision (with an exception for medical necessity) by ballot initiative provoked charges of anti-Semitism. See Jennifer Medina, *In Santa Monica, Circumcision Opponent Abandons Efforts,* N.Y. TIMES, June 8, 2011; Maria L. LaGanga, *Foes Sue to Get Circumcision Ban Taken Off S.F. Ballot,*" L.A. TIMES, June 23, 2011. Ultimately, the state legislature passed and Governor Brown signed a law prohibiting local governments from banning circumcision. See Nathan Koppel, *California Governor Snips Male-Circumcision Measure,* WALL ST. J., Oct. 3, 2011.

Most Americans take the position that circumcision of boys (but not circumcision, labia removal, clitoridectomy, or infibulation with girls) should be left to parental choice. Even medical organizations, despite rejecting circumcision as a medical practice, have declined to argue for prohibition as they have done with female genital alteration. Whereas most Europeans view the practice as barbaric, Americans see male circumcision as simply a custom, a cultural practice, even when done without religious significance, one sufficiently innocuous that it should be permitted even if it is not justifiable on medical grounds. Probably most would simply prefer not to discuss it. Might it be difficult psychologically for circumcised men to view their genitalia as damaged or to believe that their parents consented to something harmful to them?

There have been many malpractice cases against doctors and mohels who caused more than the normal damage in the process of performing circumcisions, but little litigation aimed at preventing circumcisions. In Fishbeck v. State, 115 F.3d 580 (8th Cir. 1997), a federal appellate court rejected on standing grounds an equal protection challenge to a state law that prohibited female circumcision but not male circumcision. In Marriage of Boldt, 176 P.3d 388 (Or. 2008), the Oregon Supreme Court addressed a dispute between a custodial father who converted to Judaism and wanted to circumcise his 12-year-old son and a non-custodial mother who was opposed to circumcision. The court noted that "the decision to circumcise a male child is one that generally falls within a custodial parent's authority, unfettered by a noncustodial parent's concerns or beliefs—medical, religious or otherwise," but remanded the case for a determination of the child's wishes, suggesting that if the child agreed with the mother then it might be appropriate to transfer primary custody to the mother.

Genital "mutilation" or alteration can take many forms, ranging in severity, for both girls and boys. Westerners generally take the view that no form of cutting is permissible with infant girls' genitals. In 2010, the American Academy of Pediatrics triggered public outcry by expressing the view that the law should tolerate a "ritual nick" of girls' genitals, without removing any tissue, which would be "not physically harmful and . . . much less extensive than routine newborn male genital cutting." The AAP argued that legalizing this alternative might prevent some parents from taking their girls outside the United States to undergo a more severe form of genital cutting. But anti-FGM activists objected that girls have a fundamental right against absolutely any such violation of their persons. See AAP Committee on Bioethics, *Ritual Genital Cutting of Female Minors*, 125(5) PEDIATRICS 1088-1093 (2010); Pam Belluck, *Group Backs Ritual "Nick" as Female Circumcision Option*, N.Y. TIMES, May 6, 2010.

Is it possible to have a rationally consistent position on genital integrity that opposes all forms of genital cutting with girls, or anything more than a "ritual nick," but endorses parental power to consent to surgical removal of boys' foreskins? If you hold those two positions, try to articulate a general normative principle that supports both. If, for example, you were inclined to argue that parents should be permitted to have their boys circumcised if this would have any health benefit for the boys, then presumably you should accept legalization of a comparable practice with girls if it would have any health benefit for them. So a principle that "parents may have their babies' genitalia surgically altered if this would provide any health benefit" would not work here to reconcile the two views. Contrariwise, if you were inclined to argue that girls have a right of bodily integrity such that only an immediate medical necessity could justify surgical alteration of their genitalia, then presumably you should attribute that same right to boys. And so a principle of "parents may have their children's genitalia surgically altered only if there is an immediate medical need to do so" likewise would not work. Is there some other principle that could explain and justify the current gender asymmetry in the law relating to genital alteration? Cf. Isabelle R. Gunning, *Global Feminism at the Local Level: Criminal and Asylum Laws Regarding Female Genital Surgeries*, 3 J. GENDER RACE & JUST. 45, 51 (1999) ("I cannot help but wonder if the thought of rabbis, hospitals, and medical doctors on trial or the image of white parents being imprisoned as torturers and child abusers for their misguided and damaging religious and cultural beliefs is more horrifying to westerners than the sight of misguided African parents (mothers in particular) being tried and imprisoned for their "own good.").

In assessing the appropriateness of allowing male circumcision, consider also other things parents might wish to do to a child's body as a matter of cultural tradition, things which might even entail some beneficial secular side effects but which are not done in mainstream society. How does circumcision compare to, for example, the Hindu ceremony of Chudakarana, which involves shaving the hair off of a girl's head, something which would lessen the likelihood of having lice but which non-Hindu parents would never do to their daughters? Cf. Sagar v. Sagar, 781 N.E.2d 54 (Mass. App. Ct. 2003) (ruling in a dispute between divorcing parents that Chudakarana should not be performed "until the child is of sufficient age to make that determination herself, absent a written agreement between the parties."). How does it compare to piercing the ears of a newborn child, as some parents do, which would seem not to entail any benefits for a child? What if a parent who had pierced her tongue or nose decided she wished her child to have the same, so they would look more alike?

Physical Abuse of a Fetus

When does a human being become a person protected by criminal prohibitions of and civil child protective proceedings? In reaction to epidemic use of crack cocaine, methamphetamines, and other non-medical drugs and to studies demonstrating the short- and long-term harm done to children by exposure to those drugs in utero, local actors have attempted to apply such laws to pregnant drug abusers. A few prosecutors have brought charges of criminal child abuse, reckless endangerment, and other crimes. Child protection agencies occasionally take custody of such babies at birth and charge mothers with child maltreatment or treat the babies as in need of supervision because of the mothers' continuing drug use. Federal law now requires states to mandate that birthing facilities report to a child protection agency detection of illegal drugs or alcohol in a blood test of newborns, though there is no legal mandate that such facilities perform such tests.

Child protection interventions based on mothers' present inability to care for a child are generally successful, when the agency can demonstrate that inability to a court. But efforts by these agencies and by prosecutors to charge mothers with abuse based on conduct while pregnant have had much less success in the absence of explicit legislative authorization. These state actors argue that U.S. Supreme Court precedent treats third semester fetuses as "persons," that conduct during pregnancy causes harm in the future to the child after birth and the time delay should not matter, and that it is anomalous to prosecute third parties for harming a fetus (e.g., by assault on a pregnant woman or by reckless driving that causes an accident, which in turn causes death of a fetus) but not to prosecute a mother for doing so. One state high court has agreed to treat an unborn child as a "child" within the meaning of a criminal child maltreatment law. See State v. McKnight, 576 S.E.2d 168 (S.C. 2003) (upholding conviction for homicide by child abuse based on illegal drug use during pregnancy); Whitner v. State, 492 S.E.2d 777 (S.C. 1997), *cert. denied*, 523 U.S. 1145 (1998) (holding that woman could be prosecuted for endangering fetus by prenatal substance abuse). See also Ankrom v. State, — So. 3d — (Ala. Crim. App. 2011) (upholding conviction for "chemical endangerment of a child" based on drug ingestion during viability stage of pregnancy); 705 Ill. Comp. Stat. 405/2-3(1)(c) (treating as neglected "any newborn infant whose blood, urine, or meconium contains any amount of a controlled substance").

The vast majority of courts, though, have refused, concluding that legislative intent behind the criminal or civil child abuse laws was most likely otherwise and so that the legislature would have to amend the governing statutes in order to bring conduct affecting a fetus within the ambit of these laws. See, e.g., State v. Cervantes, 223 P.3d 425 (Or. Ct. App. 2009) (woman cannot be charged for recklessly endangering another person based on methamphetamine ingestion during pregnancy); State v. Geiser, 763 N.W.2d 469 (N.D. 2009) (holding that an unborn child is not a child within meaning of child endangerment statute); State v. Armstard, 991 So. 2d 116 (La. Ct. App. 2008), *writ denied,* 998 So. 2d 89 (La. 2009) (mother cannot be charged with cruelty to a juvenile based on drug transmission through umbilical cord immediately after birth); State v. Wade, 232 S.W.3d 663 (Mo. Ct. App. 2007) (dismissing child endangerment complaint); State v. Kilmon, 905 A.2d 306 (Md. 2006) (dismissing charge of reckless endangerment); State v. Aiwohi, 109 Hawai'i 115, 123 P.3d 1210, 1214 (Haw. 2005) (rejecting charge based on manslaughter statute). In *Kilmon,* the Maryland Court of Appeals reasoned that if "the statute is read to apply to the effect of a pregnant woman's conduct on the child she is carrying, it could well be construed to include not just the ingestion of unlawful controlled substances but a whole host of intentional and conceivably reckless activity that could not possibly have been within the contemplation of the Legislature—everything from becoming (or remaining) pregnant with knowledge that the child likely will have a genetic disorder that may cause serious disability or death, to the continued use of legal drugs that are contraindicated during pregnancy, to consuming alcoholic beverages to excess, to smoking, to not maintaining a proper and sufficient diet, to avoiding proper and available prenatal medical care, to failing to wear a seat belt while driving, to violating other traffic laws in ways that create a substantial risk of producing or exacerbating personal injury to her child, to exercising too much or too little, indeed to engaging in virtually any injury-prone activity that, should an injury occur, might reasonably be expected to endanger the life or safety of the child. Such ordinary things as skiing or horseback riding could produce criminal liability." 905 A.2d at 311. Is that slippery slope argument persuasive? Why do you suppose state legislatures have not amended their criminal and civil statutes to clarify whether unborn children are included in the laws' protections?

There is a large feminist literature hostile to any legal penalties predicated on pregnancy. See, e.g., Lynn M. Paltrow, *Pregnant Women, Junk Science, and Zealous Defense,* 34 CHAMPION 30 (May 2010); Linda C. Fentiman, *In the Name of Fetal Protection: Why American Prosecutors Pursue Pregnant Drug Users (And Other Countries Don't),* 18 COLUM. J. GENDER & L. 647 (2009); Michele Goodwin, *Prosecuting the Womb,* 76 GEO. WASH. L. REV. 1657 (2008) April L. Cherry, *The Detention, Confinement, and Incarceration of Pregnant Women for the Benefit of Fetal Health,* 16 COLUM. J. GENDER & L. 147 (2007); Jane C. Murphy, *Legal Images of Motherhood: Conflicting Definitions from Welfare "Reform," Family, and Criminal Law,* 83 CORNELL L. REV. 688 (1998); Dorothy E. Roberts, *Punishing Drug Addicts Who Have Babies: Women of Color, Equality, and the Right of Privacy,* 104 HARV. L. REV. 1419 (1991).

Non-Physical Abuse

The Illinois definition of child abuse above includes infliction of physical injury and any sexual conduct. Illinois appears not to prohibit verbal abuse or other conduct that causes no physical injury but that causes psychological or emotional injury. Yet the greater, more lasting component of the harm from physical or sexual abuse is usually a psychological and emotional one. Thus, most other states recognize that children can incur similar harm from verbal attacks or exposure to disturbing events, and so include emotional and/or psychological abuse in their statutory definitions. Child protection agencies predominantly react to reports of physical neglect or abuse, but they do occasionally intervene when the parental conduct triggering a report is solely or primarily parental denigration or repeated verbal assaults on a child. Intentionally exposing children to conduct or events that are disturbing for them, such as pornography or dog-fighting, could also lead to an abuse charge, though that is fairly rare.

What if parental speech or exposure to disturbing events is a component of parents' exercise of religion? For example, some parents and private schools belonging to particular faiths in the United States teach girls that they are inferior beings and put on earth to serve men. Could such teaching cause emotional or psychological "harm" to girls? If so, should those parents have a stronger claim against state interference with their speech than do parents who say the same thing to their daughters without the religious motivation or support?

Exposure to traumatizing events can also occur in a religious context. Some religions' services involve such dramatic activities as snake handling, exorcism, or animal sacrifice.

New Jersey Division of Youth and Family Services v. Y.C.

2011 WL 2304147 (N.J. Super. Ct. App. Div.)

PER CURIAM.

. . . DYFS case worker, Kenrick Lawrence . . . testified that . . . A.C. reported to a school official "that she witnessed an animal sacrifice [in which] chickens, [a] goat, and a snake [were] killed . . . [a]nd she got poked by a needle on her body." The school official reported observing a series of "pin marks" on the child's "toes, feet, hand, back/shoulder area, and forehead." . . . [W]hen Lawrence interviewed her without her mother [Y.C.] present, the child told him "that she went to her godfather's house in Passaic where she observed animal sacrifice. She got poked with a needle all over her body. And she was forced to eat the heart of a chicken."

The child told Lawrence that she saw a goat and some chickens being beheaded, and she saw a dead snake. A.C. told Lawrence that she was fearful and crying during the ceremony and that the needles caused pain. Lawrence observed "puncture marks" on her legs, feet, and shoulders. . . . [A] female co-worker . . . found "ten symmetrical marks on the child's body." . . . The doctor found a mark on the child's forehead, "several marks on the front of her shoulders, marks on her shoulder blades, marks on the backs of her calves, marks on the insides of her wrists, and marks on her feet." . . .

Lawrence immediately re-interviewed Y.C., who told him that she was Catholic, that the child did not have a godfather, and that she did not "believe in rituals." She insisted that the marks on the child were from skates and fights with other children. Because Y.C. did not offer a credible explanation for the marks all over the child's body, DYFS removed the child from the home on an emergency basis. The child was initially placed with a maternal aunt and was later placed with her father, who did not live with Y.C.[2]

2. As a result of this incident, criminal charges were also filed against Y.C.

Seventy-two hours after the removal, . . . Y.C. admitted attending a "ceremony" with A.C. She stated that the ceremony was "a form of protection." Y.C. clarified that the adults who participated in the ceremony were not relatives of hers or the child, but were persons she found "on the [i]nternet." Y.C. said she told the child that the leader of the ritual was her "godfather," because that was his title in the ceremony. . . . She stated that she intended to enlist in the armed services, and that the ceremony was intended to "keep her daughter safe while she was gone." . . . DYFS believed the ceremony was a "Santeria ritual." However, there was no testimony or other evidence that Y.C. was an adherent of Santeria. . . . Therefore, we will not consider Y.C.'s First Amendment claims raised for the first time on this appeal. . . .

Title 9 defines an abused or neglected child as:

> a child whose physical, mental, or emotional condition has been impaired or is in imminent danger of becoming impaired as the result of the failure of his parent or guardian, as herein defined, to exercise a minimum degree of care . . . (b) in providing the child with proper supervision or guardianship, by unreasonably inflicting or allowing to be inflicted harm, or substantial risk thereof. . . .

In determining whether a child has been abused or neglected in violation of the statute, the parent's intent is irrelevant. Rather, the focus is on the harm to the child. . . . "[A] guardian fails to exercise a minimum degree of care when he or she is aware of the dangers inherent in a situation and fails adequately to supervise the child or recklessly creates a risk of serious injury to that child." . . .

Watching a stranger slit a goat's throat and strangle live chickens would understandably be terrifying to a young child.[3] Offering the chicken's heart to the child to eat would also naturally be traumatic, as would having strange adults stick her with needles all over her body. Additionally, the risk of blood-borne diseases posed by needle punctures should have been obvious to Y.C. She subjected the child to physical pain, emotional trauma, and the risk of very serious physical harm. We therefore find no error in the judge's conclusion that Y.C. committed abuse and neglect. . . .

Is there any real doubt that the ceremony was religious, or that the mother's motivation was religion-like? The court's emphasis on the mother's initial denial of a "religious" motivation suggested a possibly different outcome if the mother consistently claimed a religious defense. Should there be? Or is parental intent truly irrelevant? Should the outcome be the same if there was no poking?

Another intense religious practice is casting out demons, which some religious groups do with children as well as adults. See, e.g., Pleasant Glade Assembly of God v. Schubert, 264 S.W.3d 1 (Tex. 2008) (holding that church and its officials were entitled to free exercise protection from liability for emotional damages to 17-year-old girl caused by "laying hands" on her to combat "evil forces"). Are there more mainstream religious teachings or ceremonies that are also frightening or psychologically damaging to children? How about teaching little children that they will go to hell if they commit sins? Or causing a gay adolescent to believe his nature is a moral abomination? Or bringing up girls to believe they are inherently inferior creatures? The lasting consequences for the girl in

3. As previously noted, this case does not present First Amendment issues, and our decision should not be read as opining on the practices of any religion. . . .

Y.C. seemed to be mostly nightmares and fear of speaking with her mother about the ceremony. Could even some normal, non-religious instruction of a child cause nightmares—for example, warning about the dangers of talking to strangers. If you think such instruction nevertheless justified, perhaps because the benefits you perceive outweigh any negative psychological impact, should the benefits the mother perceived in this case outweigh the fear her child experienced, in a determination of whether the law should outlaw the practice? In other words, whose view of benefits should control legally? Is there a rational, objective way to draw the line between circumstances in which the parents' view should control and circumstances in which the state's view should control?

Can parents harm children by pinning a bizarre name on them? Celebrities are notorious for doing so. Consider, for example, Knox and Pax Pitt-Jolie, Zuma Nesta Rock Stefani-Rossdale, Jason Lee's son Pilot Inspektor, Apple Paltrow-Martin, Prince Michael II Jackson, Hud and Spec Wildhorse Mellencamp, Dweezil and Diva Thin Muffin and Moon Unit Zappa, and Bob Geldof's daughters Fifi Trixabelle, Peaches Honeyblossom, and Little Pixie. Could it get any worse? How about Jermaine Jackson's son Jermajesty or Rob Morrow's son Tu? In the United States, there is virtually no legal constraint on naming of children. Several European countries, in contrast, have child-naming laws. For example, German law dictates that a child's first name must reflect the sex of the child and must not endanger the "well-being of the child." Some countries publish a long list of acceptable names and a long list of unacceptable names. See *What Can You Name Your Child?*, BBCnews.com, Aug. 10, 2007 (reporting New Zealand's preclusion of names beginning with numbers, which caused one set of parents to give up 4Real and instead name their baby Superman). Children can petition to change their name when they are older, but should the law spare them from early years of being called Pilot Inspektor? Why does it not do so now?

The Civil Protection Process

The following case excerpt describes the agency and court response to child abuse. Think about whether the process moves too slowly or too quickly, whether it is likely to generate more false positives or false negatives, whether it is overly protective of parents or of children, and how it differs from the process for responding to partner violence. We might think of the state child protection agency as a proxy for an abused child, initiating a civil protective proceeding in behalf of the child, in the way that an adult abuse victim ordinarily does for herself, and then ask whether any differences between civil child protection and civil domestic violence proceedings are entirely explainable and justified by differences between child and adult victims of violence.

Nicholson v. Scoppetta

344 F.3d 154 (2d Cir. 2003)

KATZMANN, Circuit Judge.

Few matters are closer to the core of a State's essential function than the protection of its children against those who would, intentionally or not, do them harm. . . . The State of New York has the power to monitor and protect against abuse or neglectful treatment of the State's children. . . . In New York City, a city agency known as the Administration for Children's Services ("ACS") bears primary responsibility for child protection. . . . ACS is . . . supervised by a state agency, the Office of Children and Family Services ("OCFS").

Most of ACS's activity begins with a reference from the State Central Register for Child Abuse and Maltreatment ("SCR"), a division of OCFS. SCR maintains a telephone hotline with a toll-free number, staffed around the clock, for reports of child abuse, neglect, or maltreatment. Although anyone with pertinent information can contact the SCR, certain individuals, such as health care professionals, school officials, social service workers, day care center employees, and law enforcement personnel are required by law to report suspicions of abuse or neglect. SCR screens reports it receives to ensure that the allegations and identifying information are sufficient to begin an investigation. If the report passes this initial screening, SCR transmits the report as well as any background information to a field office in the county where the child is located. . . .

When an ACS field office receives a report from SCR, an applications worker forwards it to a supervisor, who then assigns a caseworker to investigate. . . . By statute, ACS must complete its investigations of complaints referred by SCR within sixty days. At the conclusion of the investigation, ACS must determine whether there is "credible evidence" to support the allegations. If ACS concludes there is such evidence, it declares the report "indicated." Otherwise, it must declare the report "unfounded." . . . During the course of its investigation (or, if the report is "indicated," following an investigation), ACS may commence child protective proceedings in Family Court against a parent or guardian[2] . . . by filing an "Article 10 petition." . . .

Once ACS has filed a petition, the Family Court must hold a preliminary hearing "as soon as practicable," in order to determine whether the child's interests require protection pending a final order of disposition. The court has the power to order "removal" of the child—that is, placement of the child in the protective custody of someone other than the custodial parent or guardian. However, the court may only order removal if it is necessary to avoid "imminent risk to the child's life or health." "In determining whether removal . . . is necessary . . . the court shall consider . . . whether reasonable efforts were made prior to the date of the hearing . . . to prevent or eliminate the need for removal." Further, before ordering removal, the court must find that the imminent risk to the child could not be eliminated by instead exercising its power to issue a "temporary order of protection," directing the removal of a person or persons other than the child from the residence. . . .

If ACS determines that there is not enough time to file a petition and hold a preliminary hearing, it is authorized to seek, and the Family Court to issue, a preliminary order of removal. The court again must consider available alternative protective services, including the removal of threatening persons from the residence, in deciding whether to issue such an order. Additionally, if ACS "has reasonable cause to believe" that there is not even time to obtain this expedited preliminary order, it may remove a child from the parent or guardian without any court order. If ACS removes a child without a court order it must file a petition "forthwith," ideally within twenty-four hours, and in any event within no more than three business days. ACS must also "make every reasonable effort to communicate immediately with the child's parent," and the parents of a child removed without a court order have the right to apply for a court hearing to secure the child's return. This hearing must take place within three days of the parent's application, absent "good cause shown." . . .

Instead of returning full custody of a removed child to a parent, the Family Court may parole the child to the parent pending the outcome of the proceedings. Testimony below suggested that parole is common. A paroled child returns to live with the parent, but subject to broad supervision by ACS. For instance, ACS may demand the right to make

2. ACS can also refer cases to the District Attorney for investigation and possible criminal prosecution.

unannounced home visits, or that the parents participate in counseling, relocation, or other services.

After provisional arrangements for the child have been addressed, the court proceedings move to the fact-finding stage. The court first must determine whether the child has been abused or neglected. An abused child is one whose parent or guardian creates or allows a "substantial risk of," or actually inflicts, "physical injury to such child by other than accidental means," where such injury in turn would likely "cause death or serious or protracted disfigurement, or protracted impairment of physical or emotional health or protracted loss or impairment of the function of any bodily organ." Abuse also includes various forms of sexual abuse. . . .

Notably, the court must find that there is abuse or neglect by a preponderance of the evidence. The court cannot rely on the mental or emotional state of the child as a basis for its finding unless it concludes that the child's mental or emotional impairments are "clearly attributable to the unwillingness or inability of the respondent to exercise a minimum degree of care toward the child." The court can use "competent opinion or expert testimony" to make this determination, and can order that a child "be made available for examination by a physician, psychologist or social worker."

If the fact-finding hearing results in a finding of abuse or neglect, a "dispositional hearing," at which the ultimate placement of the child is determined, follows. The court has wide latitude to decide the appropriate placement of the child, and its options include placing the child in foster care for renewable one-year periods. The court may also, ultimately, decide to terminate the rights of the original custodial parent or guardian and place the child permanently elsewhere.

As the court notes, several groups of professionals are mandatory child maltreatment reporters. A large percentage of reports to child protection agencies originate with teachers, because they typically have more contact with a maltreated child than anyone else besides the child's parents. Would it be a good state policy to have teachers or counselors in schools routinely ask children whether their parents beat them or maltreat them in other ways?

We saw in Chapter 3 that some scholars believe women who are victims of domestic violence should retain control over the legal system's response to their situation. Are there any circumstances in which one could plausibly make a similar argument about child abuse, that the child victim should have some or complete control over whether any legal action is taken, and if so what form that takes? What are the pros and cons of giving children some decision-making power in maltreatment cases?

Right to State Protection

The U.S. Supreme Court, in *Town of Castle Rock v. Gonzales,* held that adult domestic violence victims have no basic constitutional right to state protection against such private harm. The Court mentioned its prior decision—DeShaney v. Winnebago County Department of Social Services, 489 U.S. 189 (1989)—reaching a similar conclusion as to children who incur harm from abuse by their parents. The state negligence in *Gonzales* arguably was confined to one night. That in *DeShaney* continued for over two years, with child protection workers repeatedly finding Joshua DeShaney beaten by his father and repeatedly returning Joshua to his father without taking adequate steps to ensure the boy's safety.

Ultimately, Joshua ended up in a coma and with permanent, severe brain damage. His mother sued for compensation from the state based on a claim that the state's actions violated a substantive due process right of Joshua, but a majority of the Court could see only inaction by the state. The Court held that the state can only be liable when it takes affirmative action that harms a child or when it fails to protect a child from a state-created danger or from harm while the child is in state custody. Several lower courts have accordingly found the state liable when children incur harm at the hands of foster parents. See, e.g., K.J. ex rel. Lowry v. Div. of Youth & Fam. Servs., 363 F. Supp. 2d 728 (D.N.J. 2005). But with respect to legal parents, the state now is assumed to have no duty to select them with care, to protect any child from harm by them, nor to keep a child out of parents' custody after finding that they have brutally abused the child.

Apart from the specific differences between these two particular cases, *Gonzales* and *DeShaney*, is there any reason to differentiate between adult victims and child victims with respect to whether the state has a constitutional obligation to protect individuals from harm by private parties? Recall the argument at the end of Chapter 1 that the state is just as involved in placing children with custodians when it assigns legal parenthood and custody to biological parents as it is when it selects adoptive or foster parents for a child. It was not natural law that conferred legal parent status and custody on Randy DeShaney when Joshua was born. It was a Wisconsin state statute, a state-created controlling rule, that was indifferent to Randy's fitness to parent, imposing on Joshua a state decision that could in no way be characterized as a surrogate or imputed choice in his behalf (and so is not analogous to state recognition of two adults' choice to marry). And it was Wisconsin law and legal actors that continued that status and custody despite proof of Randy's horribly abusive treatment of Joshua, which one might view as comparable to state actors charged with responding to partner violence repeatedly returning a battered wife to her husband without her consent and refusing to allow her a divorce from him. Does it implicate the state even further in parental violence toward children that it explicitly authorizes parents to hit their children, in statutes and court decisions relating to corporal punishment? Similarly, was the state in part responsible for violence toward wives in the era of coverture, insofar as it not only refused to allow wives to bring a complaint against an abusive husband but also explicitly authorized physical "chastisement"? If so, is it not also partly responsible for the physical abuse of children?

As noted in Chapter 3, some courts outside the United States have held in the context of partner abuse that human rights charters confer on individuals a right to state protection against private harm. The European Court of Human Rights has also held that the state violates children's rights under the European Convention on Human Rights when it fails to respond reasonably to clear warning signs of parental abuse of a child. See Z and Others v. United Kingdom, 34 Eur. H.R. Rep. 97 (2002) (finding a violation of Article 3's prohibition of "torture or inhuman or degrading treatment of punishment," where a social service agency took no action in response to numerous complaints about certain children's living situation, reasoning that Article 3 "requires States to take measures designed to ensure that individuals within their jurisdiction are not subjected to . . . such ill-treatment administered by private individuals.").

3. Caretaking

We saw in Chapter 3 that spouses generally have no legal duty to provide daily physical care for a spouse, even if the spouse becomes disabled in some way, and a married person cannot legally force his or her spouse to have sex or do housework. At most, divorce law creates an incentive for married people to fulfill the usual expectations for contributing to a marriage and household, insofar as property distribution and alimony rules in some states take into account behavior during the marriage.

In parent-child relationships, minor children have no legal obligation to take physical care of their parents, and parents cannot force their children to undertake paid employment outside the household. But parents generally have the practical ability to force children to contribute in various ways to the functioning of the household. Parents can use their control over family wealth and other aspects of home life to manipulate children into doing chores, and parents are legally empowered to punish children in various ways for non-compliance with parental commands. There is tremendous variety among parents as to how much and what form of contribution they demand of children, but probably most adolescents are expected to help with house cleaning, yard work, and errands, and many feel constrained to bring in some income. So the parent-child relationship is not entirely a one-way street in terms of family-related responsibilities.

Nevertheless, there is a marked asymmetry in allocation of positive duties in parent-child relationships; much more is expected of parents than of minor children (this generally reverses when offspring become adults and parents are elderly). The parent's situation is similar to that of someone whose spouse becomes incapable of self-care. Parents have an explicit legal duty to provide basic financial support to their children, and parents who choose to be physical custodians of a child also have a legal duty to provide adequate physical care and supervision, and to secure certain goods and services for the child, such as medical care. What might most distinguish the parental role from that of a guardian for an incompetent spouse, in terms of legal duties, is that a parent must secure schooling for a child. This educational duty, however, really does not demand much of parents, because the state provides schooling and transportation without charge to parents. Parents can fully discharge the duty simply by making sure their child gets out of the house in the morning in time to get on the bus. State neglect laws spell out the specific components of the care required of parents:

Illinois Compiled Statutes
Chapter 705, Act 405. Juvenile Court Act of 1987
Article II. Abused, Neglected or Dependent Minors

405/2-3. Neglected or Abused Minor

(1) Those who are neglected include:

(a) any minor under 18 years of age who is not receiving the proper or necessary support, education as required by law, or medical or other remedial care recognized under State law as necessary for a minor's well-being, or other care necessary for his or her well-being, including adequate food, clothing and shelter, or who is abandoned by his or her parents or other person responsible for the minor's welfare, except that a minor shall not be considered neglected for the sole reason that the minor's parent or other person responsible for the minor's welfare has left the minor in the care of an adult relative for any period of time; or

(b) any minor under 18 whose environment is injurious to his or her welfare; or

(c) any newborn infant whose blood, urine, or meconium contains any amount of a controlled substance . . . ; or

> (d) any minor under the age of 14 years whose parent . . . leaves the minor without supervision for an unreasonable period of time without regard for the mental or physical health, safety, or welfare of that minor; . . .
>
> Whether the minor was left without regard for the mental or physical health, safety, or welfare of that minor or the period of time was unreasonable shall be determined by considering the following factors, including but not limited to:
>
> (1) the age of the minor;
> (2) the number of minors left at the location;
> (3) special needs of the minor . . . ;
> (4) the duration of time in which the minor was left without supervision;
> (5) the condition and location where the minor was left without supervision;
> (6) the time of day or night when the minor was left without supervision;
> (7) the weather conditions . . . ;
> (8) . . . the physical distance the minor was from the parent or guardian at the time the minor was without supervision;
> (9) whether the minor's movement was restricted . . . ;
> (10) whether the minor was given a phone number of a person or location to call in the event of an emergency and . . . was capable of making an emergency call;
> (11) whether there was food and other provision left for the minor;
> (12) whether any of the conduct is attributable to economic hardship or illness and the parent . . . made a good faith effort to provide for the health and safety of the minor;
> (13) the age and physical and mental capabilities of the person or persons who provided supervision for the minor;
> (14) whether the minor was left under the supervision of another person;
> (15) any other factor that would endanger the health and safety of that particular minor.
>
> A minor shall not be considered neglected for the sole reason that the minor has been relinquished in accordance with the Abandoned Newborn Infant Protection Act.

Do the legal responsibilities indicated in this statute appear very demanding? Does the state make sufficiently clear for parents what is expected of them?

Note that one parent can leave a child in the care of the other parent and never care for the child, yet not be considered neglectful. A court will order such a parent to pay child support, if the other parent or the state welfare office petitions for child support. But so long as an absent parent pays any child support award, he cannot be considered neglectful under this statute. Yet he can return at any time and demand visitation rights.

Neglect is the most common form of proven child maltreatment, and the most common forms of neglect are an unsuitable home environment and lack of supervision. The former typically involve extremely unsanitary conditions (almost always including pet feces) and also a shortage of food, clean clothing, and sleeping space, and the conditions typically result from a combination of poverty plus parental substance abuse, mental illness, and/or mental disability. Failure-to-supervise situations often arise from the same parental dysfunctions, but sometimes occur only because parents are unable to secure alternative child care while they work or perform necessary household tasks. Both types of cases raise a basic question about the appropriateness of imposing a particular norm of living on all families. Many critics of the child protection system charge that the imposed norms reflect class and cultural bias. Do you perceive such bias in any of the following cases?

a. Failure to Maintain a Suitable Living Environment

Bailey v. City of Alexandria Department of Human Services

Court of Appeals of Virginia (2007)

Per Curiam.

Barbie Bailey (mother) appeals the trial court's decision terminating her residual parental rights to her minor child, L.B, born on January 24, 1996. . . .

[In] 2001, due to lack of supervision of her children, a filthy home, and the children's poor hygiene, DHS began providing voluntary services to mother. These services included home-based counseling, individual therapy, mental health therapy, and an in-home aide to teach mother how to clean and organize her home and her four children. While mother initially cooperated, problems persisted and, due to mother's sporadic compliance, DHS filed an Abuse and Neglect Petition in October 2002. . . . [The Juvenile & Domestic Relations] court entered a Preliminary Child Protective Order, directing mother to complete a mental health evaluation, follow all treatment recommendations, cooperate with all home-based services, ensure proper hygiene of her children at all times, and cooperate with school officials to ensure her children's academic success.

In August 2003, DHS filed another Abuse and Neglect Petition . . . because mother was not cooperating with services. She had stopped seeing the home-based counselor, her home was filthy again-with food ground into the carpet, the door ripped off the hinges, holes in walls, and the children smelling of urine and feces. On October 3, 2003, . . . J & DR court entered another protective order.

On September 9, 2004, L.B. and mother's other children were removed from her care under an Emergency Removal Order. At that time, Michelle Mintling, the social worker assigned to the case, made an unannounced visit to mother's home after being alerted that L.B. had not attended school that term. . . . Mother's home was cluttered to the point of posing a safety hazard to the children—no sheets on the beds; dirty mattresses; broken beds piled high with clothing; rooms smelling of urine; bowls of dried food in the children's rooms; dirty dishes in the sink; filthy walls and carpets, which had been painted five months earlier; and the front door, which had been broken in twice, no longer locked. Mintling found L.B., who was eight years old, home alone with an unknown adult male, rather than in school. L.B. was crying because she did not have any shoes and, therefore, could not go to school. That morning mother had tested positive for marijuana and opiates. . . . While Mintling was at the house, at least six young men came and went from the home as if they lived there. The extent of the damage to mother's home, which was worse than Mintling had seen in 2001, caused mother to be evicted.

Starting in September 2004, DHS continued to offer an array of services to mother, including up to 140 hours per month of home-based counselor services to assist mother in learning the daily responsibilities of being a parent, to teach her about the effect of her behavior on her children, and to assist her with obtaining employment. . . .

December 15, 2004, the J & DR court transferred custody of L.B. to DHS under a foster care plan . . . , with the goal of return to parent and concurrent goal of relative placement. . . . [M]other was given target duties to complete a substance abuse evaluation, obtain a referral to drug court programs, seek a mental health evaluation, follow treatment recommendations of mental health and the drug court, find and maintain employment, find and maintain appropriate housing which could accommodate her children, demonstrate her ability to keep her housing clean, and free of any health and/or safety hazards, attend and participate in a family group conference to determine her relatives' interest and availability to assist her and her children, complete a parent fitness assessment, follow any recommendations related to her role as a parent, maintain regular visits with her children, attend school meetings and events related to the children, and maintain contact with her DHS social worker. DHS agreed to continue to provide services to mother to assist her in meeting those goals. . . .

[M]other was supposed to submit five applications per week for a job, but initially failed to do so. Mother waited ten and one-half months to have her evaluation for drug court and appeared intoxicated on some of Schlegel's visits. Mother failed to find appropriate housing and continued to demonstrate that she could not maintain a home in proper condition.

In May 2005, DHS filed a Foster Care Service Plan Review with the goal of return to parent. . . . At that time, mother was receiving outpatient substance abuse treatment, had recently started drug court, and was meeting with a mental health counselor and a home-based counselor. However, issues remained. Mother had not yet obtained appropriate housing or regular employment; she tended to minimize her substance abuse issues; she reported to her substance abuse evaluation, her probation officer, and for visitation with her children under the influence of alcohol; and she could not consistently control her anger and avoid emotional outbursts.

In October 2005, the J & DR Court . . . amend[ed] the target date for returning L.B. to mother from December 31, 2005 to April 27, 2006. . . . As of that time, L.B. had been in foster care for approximately one year and mother had been receiving services for almost four years. The court approved a plan with the goal of return to parent, concurrent with relative placement. That plan identified the main barrier to reunification as being that mother had to establish suitable housing and demonstrate that she could maintain an orderly and safe home environment.

On March 29, 2006, DHS filed another Foster Care Service Plan with the goal of return to parent and concurrent goal of relative placement. That plan acknowledged mother's progress with her substance abuse and parenting issues and that she had obtained housing and part-time employment, but noted that the situation was still not sufficiently improved to allow L.B. to return home permanently. At that time, L.B. had some trial visits with mother on weekends. . . .

From April 13, 2006 to April 16, 2006, L.B., along with her siblings, returned home for a trial visit, for the first time since L.B.'s removal from mother's care eighteen months earlier. Prior to the return, mother executed a safety plan in which she agreed to continue all services, ensure the children had adequate adult supervision, and keep them away from bad influences. Mother assured Morrow that she had taken time off from work and would be home while the children visited. Later, mother admitted to Morrow that she had lied and did not take time off from work to be home to supervise the children. Morrow learned that mother was either not present or was asleep during much of the visit and that the children awoke in the morning with no adult supervision. Morrow learned that mother had allowed the three older children to spend the night away from the house and was unaware of when they returned. In addition, mother admitted that she allowed her son to go on the roof and did not perceive that as a safety issue. Mother admitted she was overwhelmed by the children's visit, and Morrow learned that mother wanted to slow down the reunification process and extend the children's time in foster care.

When [social worker] Schlegel visited the home on April 17, 2006, it was in "shocking condition[ ]," with clumps of hair and garbage strewn about and with nowhere to sit on cluttered couches. Mother would not allow Schlegel to see the bedrooms. Schlegel learned that despite his history of violence and a court order prohibiting contact, the children's father was permitted contact with them. Schlegel acknowledged that over the three years she had worked with mother, mother had made personal progress in the areas of substance abuse and obtaining employment and housing, but that she had not made progress with her ability to parent. Schlegel opined as an expert in family counseling, that based on her training and experience and the time spent with mother and her family, mother could not be an effective parent to her children.

On April 19, 2006, Deputy Steven Hajdasz responded to mother's home regarding a narcotics complaint. When Hajdasz arrived, he found a juvenile male, who did not live in the home, but who was able to enter the unlocked home. Hajdasz also found an adult male at the home. Mother was not at home. The juvenile obtained from inside the house a "homemade bong," which he gave to Hajdasz.

On April 20, 2006, when Sonja Stephens, mother's probation officer,[4] made an unannounced visit to mother's home, Stephens found the carpet stained, boxes stacked in the house, dishes in the sink, open box cutters in more than one room, mattresses without sheets, laundry strewn about the house, and food in the bedrooms. Stephens stated that the house was filthy, worse than other homes she had inspected as a probation officer.

At the next hearing in April 2006, DHS requested . . . a goal of adoption for L.B. . . . , ten at the time of trial. . . . Since L.B.'s removal from mother's care in September 2004, L.B. had been in mother's care less than ten days.

Based upon this record, the circuit court terminated mother's residual parental rights to L.B. . . . The trial judge found that mother did not have the ability to maintain a safe environment for her children. . . . [W]e affirm the trial court's decision.

Presumably, none of us lives in a house of the sort described in the case and never has. Focusing for a moment just on the cleanliness and orderliness aspect of the neglect, should we be reluctant to pass judgment on a parent's standards for home environment? After all, other parents with perfectly neat houses do other things that create some risk of sickness or injury, right? Is there necessarily greater danger from urine and feces smeared about than from, for example, second-hand smoke?

Considering the entire picture in this case, few would criticize DHS for intervening in some fashion. But could one plausibly maintain that DHS should never have removed the children? Or that DHS should have done more to assist the mother? Or that there was a better alternative to termination for L.B.? An operative assumption of child protection agencies is that parents must be reformed so that they will no longer need assistance in caring for their children. Should the state instead accept that some people on whom it has chosen to confer legal parent status need help with child rearing permanently, and provide whatever help is needed so that the children do not have to suffer separation from their parents? On the other hand, could one plausibly argue that DHS

4. Mother had been convicted of embezzlement and was on probation.

did too much for this mother, at the expense of the children's well being and/or taxpayers' money?

Parents whose house is tidy and well-stocked with food, clothing, and other necessities might nevertheless be charged with creating an environment injurious to their children if they permit activities in the home that the state deems harmful to children, such as sexual activity or manufacture of drugs. See, e.g, Colo. Rev. Stat. §18-6-401(1)(c).

b. Failure to Supervise

The duty to provide a safe and sanitary home environment is ostensibly uniform across communities, though different localities might have different notions of what is minimally acceptable. In contrast, and as reflected in the Illinois statute above, the content of the duty to supervise for the safety of a child necessarily varies according to the larger community environment, because the need for supervision depends on what dangers are present in a particular environment. A nine-year-old who walks alone in the evening to a friend's house a half mile away might be in great danger in a crime- and drug-infested urban area but in little danger in a white-picket-fence suburb. Is it unfair to parents who live in unsafe neighborhoods to impose on them a greater duty of supervision? Does it effectively punish them for other people's vices?

The type of failure-to-supervise cases more often reported in the press are atypical ones involving seemingly normal mothers who leave their children unattended while they run to perform some household-related task, such as buying groceries, or to do something enjoyable for themselves. See, e.g., *Mom Left Kids in Car While She Worked*, WSBTV.com (Georgia), Aug. 31, 2011;*Mom Left Kids In Hot Car, Beat Good Samaritan*, TheINDYchannel.com, Jan. 12, 2011 (grocery store visit); Allison Oswalt, *Tempe Police: Mom Left Kids in Car to Attend Party*, ARIZ. REPUBLIC, May 17, 2011; Associated Press, *Mom Left Kids in Car for Black Friday Shopping*, PROVIDENCE J., Nov. 26, 2010; Amy L. Edwards, *Mom Left 3 Kids in Hot Car While Visiting Boyfriend in Jail*, ORLANDO SENTINEL, Aug. 24, 2010; Associated Press, *Mom Left Kids in Car While Tanning*, azcentral.com, Jan. 7, 2010. These incidents interest us because they call into question state and societal expectations for mothers (Are they to be shackled to their children at all times? Why do they not receive more help with child care so they can have their own enjoyments?); our own standards of care as parents (Would I leave my children in the car while I run in to the store for milk?); and how safe the world really is for children (Do we exaggerate the danger of predators lurking everywhere?). For nuanced analysis of the maternal experience of, and social norms regarding, mothers' physical care of children, see Carol Sanger, *Separating from Children*, 96 COLUM. L. REV. 375 (1996).

Parents have a duty to supervise not only for the sake of children's safety. The law also imposes on parents a duty to supervise that is owed to the public, and in some circumstances states impose on parents liability for harms their children cause to others. At common law, there was no general parental liability for children's torts, though parents might be held liable if the child was acting as the parent's agent or if the parent negligently helped to create the situation in which the child caused harm. But as part of a general reaction to youth crime in the late twentieth century, many states passed parental responsibility statutes, imposing liability for negligent supervision when youths engage in "willful or malicious acts" that cause damage to person or property. See Leslie J. Harris, *Making Parents Pay*, 31 FAM. ADVOC. 38 (Winter 2009) (describing history of parental responsibility laws, citing statutes across the United States, and noting that tort suits and criminal prosecutions of parents for damage caused by offspring remain rare despite these new laws). Here is one example:

West's Code of Georgia Annotated
Title 51. Torts, Chapter 2. Imputable Negligence

§51-2-3. Liability of Parent or Guardian for Willful Torts by Minor Children

(a) Every parent or guardian having the custody and control over a minor child or children under the age of 18 shall be liable in an amount not to exceed $10,000 plus court costs for the willful or malicious acts of the minor child or children resulting in reasonable medical expenses to another, damage to the property of another, or both reasonable medical expenses and damage to property. . . .
(b) The intent of the General Assembly in passing this Code section is to provide for the public welfare and aid in the control of juvenile delinquency, not to provide restorative compensation to victims of injurious or tortious conduct by children.

Ventres v. Renny

2009 WL 160432 (N.J. Super. App. Div.)

Per Curiam.

. . . Defendants Thomas Renny and Denise D'Meo are the owners of a dirt bike operated by their minor son Justin Renny on a public street at 11:30 p.m. Justin was driving the dirt bike, which had no lights or reflectors, without an operator's license. Defendants purchased the dirt bike for Justin's use on dirt bike trails. The vehicle was not stored at defendants' home, but rather in the garage of Mike Korn, Justin's friend. Bike trails were located in a wooded area behind Korn's home. On the night of the incident, defendants allowed Justin to spend the night with a different friend. . . . Justin did not obtain express permission from his parents to operate the dirt bike on the night of the accident. However, Justin knew the bike's location and the access code to the Korn's garage, and apparently the ignition keys were kept with the dirt bike.

While operating the dirt bike on the street, Justin collided with plaintiff's Mustang. Both he and Michella [plaintiff] suffered injuries. The police cited Justin for several motor vehicle violations, including careless driving, driving an unlicensed vehicle, and driving an uninsured motor vehicle. . . . The costs to repair the automobile's damage, including the impound fee, totaled $3,986.83, and Michella's unpaid medical bills were $1,050.50. . . .

What we must determine is whether defendants, as the vehicle owners, are vicariously liable for plaintiff's damages, caused by the their son's use of the vehicle. First, we note defendants' status as the vehicle's owners alone does not trigger liability. Generally, New Jersey common law imposing vicarious liability provides, "the owner of a motor vehicle is not liable for the negligence of the operator of the vehicle, unless the operator is acting as the owner's agent or employee." . . . If one uses the vehicle of another, a rebuttable presumption of agency is raised. So too, a familial relationship may suggest agency. However, standing alone, "[t]he mere existence of the relationship of parent and child does not render a parent liable for his child's torts." . . . [T]he facts surrounding the relationship must be carefully examined.

In *Doran*, the father's adult daughter had general permission to use the family car. On the day of the accident, the daughter took the vehicle to go riding with friends without her father's express permission, as he was out of town. The court concluded the daughter's action of using the vehicle for pleasure was not done on behalf of her father. In *Missell v. Hayes*, the son drove his mother, sister and friends in his father's automobile. The fact the father's immediate family and guests occupied the vehicle evinced "that the automobile was being used in the father's affairs or business." . . . In *Marriner*, the automobile owner-parents were not liable for injuries to a third-party when their son took the vehicle to push a friend's disabled vehicle during a storm after he was expressly told not to do so. The Court concluded no agency relationship existed, as the son defied the express direction of his mother. . . . [I]n *Willett v. Ifrah* (N.J. App. Div. 1997), . . . a father purchased an automobile for his son to drive to and from school. . . . This court concluded no agency relationship existed at the time of the accident because the son had total control of the car and was not using it for any "family purpose." . . .

[D]efendants acknowledged Justin operated the dirt bike on dirt trails with defendants' permission. . . . Nevertheless, on the night of the accident, Justin used the vehicle on a public roadway without informing his parents. Other than the presumption of agency due to a familial relationship, these facts cannot support a finding . . . Justin used the dirt bike on the night of the accident as an agent of his parents.

Defendants may still be liable if they themselves engaged in negligent acts. In *Doran*, the Court . . . stated:

> If the machine had been bought for his children's use, and it was in its nature or use a menace to the safety of others, then . . . it might well be that liability would arise by reason of the father's entrusting a dangerous machine or agency to the hands of an inexperienced or incompetent person. Such a liability does not rest upon the negligence of the servant, but upon the father's negligence in permitting his child to use a dangerous machine. In the one the gist of the action is the negligence of the servant imputed to the master; in the other, the negligence of the father. . . . [T]he parent may be liable for an injury which may be caused directly by the child, where by his negligence he made it possible for the child to cause the injury complained of, and probable that the child would do so, this liability is based upon the rules of negligence rather than the relation of parent and child.

Thus, a parent retains an obligation to exercise reasonable care to control a minor child to avoid the creation of an unreasonable risk of bodily harm to others, "if the parent (1) knows or has reason to know that he has the ability to control his child, and (2) knows or should know of the necessity and opportunity for exercising such control" when dealing with a dangerous instrumentality.

The scope of a parent's obligation to control a minor child when faced with third-party claims is limited by the doctrine of parental immunity. The doctrine excludes liability only in circumstances implicating "customary child-care issues or a legitimate exercise of parental authority or supervision." While parents should be able to raise their children autonomously and free from scrutiny by the courts, the parental immunity doctrine does not apply in circumstances where the actions of a parent are willful or wanton as determined by the totality of the circumstances. . . . For behavior to fall within the definition of willful and wanton, which has been "defined as an intermediary position between simple negligence and the intentional infliction of harm," "a parent must be conscious . . . that injury will likely or probably result from his conduct, and with reckless indifference to the consequences, [the parent] consciously and intentionally does some wrongful act or omits to discharge some duty which produces the injurious result."

Additionally, conduct other than parental decision-making falls beyond the veil of immunity. Thus, the acts of a parent claiming immunity should "'fall[ ] within the realm of activities which partake of the everyday exigencies of regular household existence[.]'" "[I]f a parent's conduct does not implicate legitimate child-rearing issues, but simply places a third-party negligently at risk, then there would be no immunity."

Here, we conclude defendants are not shielded by parental immunity based on the conduct at issue. Unlike the injuries in *Foldi*, resulting from interaction with a family dog, or those in *Buono*, involving bike riding, plaintiff's injuries resulted from the defendants' son's operation of a small motorcycle. Use of a motor vehicle implicates state regulation for operation. Thus, it is not an area confined to the bailiwick of the free exercise of parental "discipline, care and control." A motor vehicle should not pose a danger to others, unless it is handled by an incompetent person in which case it may become highly dangerous and a public menace. Defendants purchased the dirt bike for and provided access to Justin, knowing he was not old enough to obtain even a provisional operator's license. State licensure laws mandate motor vehicle operators obtain behind-the-wheel instruction, and satisfactorily pass a written examination, as well as a road test and procure a vision test, to ensure the safe operation of the motor vehicle. Further, defendants failed to separately secure the keys to limit Justin's access to the dirt bike. Justin's age reflects his limited maturity requiring supervised access to the dirt bike be secured. Viewing the totality of the circumstances, we conclude defendants' actions and omissions extend beyond the "special situations that involve the exercise of parental authority and customary child care," making parental immunity inapplicable. Thus, defendants' conduct may provide a basis for liability. . . .

The facts presented also implicate possible strict liability pursuant to *N.J.S.A.* 2A:53A-15, which provides:

> A parent, guardian or other person having legal custody of an infant under 18 years of age who fails or neglects to exercise reasonable supervision and control of the conduct of such infant, shall be liable in a civil action for any willful, malicious or unlawful injury or destruction by such infant of the real or personal property of another.

The court must review the circumstances of the accident to discern whether Justin's actions of operating an unregistered motor vehicle on a public thoroughfare at 11:30 P.M. without the benefit of lights or an operator's license violated the statute. If the court makes that finding, it must also examine whether defendants failed to exercise reasonable supervision and control of their son's conduct to discern whether statutory liability results. We . . . remand this matter for a new trial consistent with this opinion.

As the opinion suggests, there are a lot of cases involving car accidents caused by teens. Ordinarily in those cases the teens had a valid driver's license and general permission to use a family car or their own car. Despite the well-known high rate of car accidents in this age group, the law deems it not negligent to supply one's 16-year-old with a car to drive, absent special circumstances implicating the parent to a greater extent in a teen's bad driving. Here the court places much weight on the fact that it was illegal for the youth to be operating the motor bike.

Many parents also give much younger children dangerous toys and allow the children to use the toys without supervision. They usually do not incur liability for harm the toys cause when their children are playing with friends.

Bastian v. McGannon

2008 WL 833997 (Ohio Ct. App.)

WHITMORE, Judge.

. . . J.B. suffered a permanent injury to his right eye when another child shot a Red Ryder B.B. gun ("BB gun"), and the shot struck J.B.'s eye. Prior to J.B. being shot, J.B. and M.M. were playing with the BB gun in M.M.'s backyard. The two took turns shooting at each other with the BB gun, one person firing and the other running. Although M.M.'s father was at home during these events, he did not intervene and stop the boys. Sometime after the boys started their shooting game, C.L. and several other neighborhood girls walked into M.M.'s backyard to look for a neighbor's cat. J.B. accidentally shot one of the girls while she was looking, hitting her just below the hairline. Subsequently, J.B., M.M., and C.L. climbed onto the elevated deck surrounding M.M.'s swimming pool. While the children were on the deck, J.B. sustained the injury to his right eye. . . .

"Where individuals engage in recreational or sports activities, they assume the ordinary risks of the activity and cannot recover for any injury unless it can be shown that the other participant's actions were either reckless or intentional[.]" If successfully proven, the doctrine of primary assumption of risk . . . "relieves a recreation provider from any duty to eliminate the risks that are inherent in the activity . . . because such risks cannot be eliminated." The determining factor in such cases is the conduct of the defendant, "not the participant's or spectator's ability or inability to appreciate the inherent dangers of the activity." Furthermore, "the reckless/intentional standard of liability applies regardless of whether the activity was engaged in by children or adults, or was unorganized, supervised, or unsupervised."

In determining whether the primary assumption of the risk doctrine bars an injured party's recovery, a court essentially engages in a three part analysis. First, the court must determine whether the plaintiff was a participant or spectator in a recreational activity. If the plaintiff was either a participant or spectator, the court then must determine whether the defendant was a participant in the recreational activity. Finally, if the defendant was also a participant, then the court must look to his conduct and determine whether he acted recklessly or intentionally under the particular facts of the case. In cases involving children, . . . a court must not delve into the scope of the child's consent to an activity based on what the child understood the rules of the recreational activity to be. Once the court determines that the children were engaging in a recreational activity, the court's focus must shift to the alleged reckless or intentional nature of the defendant's conduct. . . .

A number of activities have qualified as "recreational activities." See *id.* (performing recreational activity analysis where minor child hit another in the eye with a nail while hammering the nail into a chair); *Marchetti, supra* (performing recreational activity analysis where children were playing modified game of "kick the can"). The determination that an activity is a "recreational activity" does not depend upon the existence of well-defined or verbalized rules.[1] . . . Indeed, the Ohio Supreme Court has stated that "typical backyard play . . . falls within the definition of recreational activity." . . .

While J.B. and M.M.'s BB gun game likely constituted a recreational activity, J.B.'s affidavit indicates that J.B. and M.M. ended the game prior to J.B. getting shot. If the activity truly ended prior to J.B.'s injury, then he was not a participant in a recreational activity at the time of his injury. Second, . . . J.B. stated that C.L. was not a part of the game that he and M.M. were playing. While the victim of a recreational activity may be either a participant or a spectator, the alleged wrongdoer must be a participant in the activity. Therefore, if C.L. was not a participant in the game and she shot J.B., then the primary assumption of the risk doctrine would not bar J.B.'s claim. Related to this last point, there is also a genuine issue of material fact as to who shot J.B. Several of the children indicated that C.L. shot J.B., but C.L. denied doing so. C.L. stated that M.M. shot J.B., and J.B. admitted in his deposition that he did not know whether M.M. or C.L. shot him. . . .

Furthermore, the record that is before this Court does not contain any facts that would support a finding that McGannon knew of any alleged reckless or negligent tendencies that M.M. might have had. See *Hau v. Gill* (1999), 9th Dist. (listing the elements of negligent supervision, including that the parent must have known about the child's reckless or negligent tendencies). . . .

[Finally,] the Bastians argue that McGannon provided M.M. with access to the BB gun and that a BB gun is a firearm pursuant to R.C. 2923.21(A)(3) (prohibiting a person from improperly furnishing a firearm to a minor). [However, they] rely on evidence outside of the record to support their claim that McGannon negligently stored the BB gun. . . . [W]e cannot consider evidence which is outside of the trial court record. . . .[2]

How is it possible that Ohio has never decided whether a BB gun is something that must be stored safely? Or that in Ohio parents can give their children BB guns and have no legal obligation to supervise their use of the gun absent knowledge that their child has "reckless or negligent tendencies"? Are there any young boys who do not have reckless and negligent tendencies? See also Herzberg v. Am. Nat'l Prop. & Cas. Co., 2005 WL 3435742 (Ohio Ct. App.) (finding no parental liability for injury to woman who fell while running away from a birthday boy squirting her with a "Super Soaker" water gun, because there was no evidence the father "knew or should have known that injury could result from his son's use of the water gun").

c. Failure to Protect

Another common form of neglect, similar to a failure to supervise, is "failure to protect." In some states, such as Illinois, this is expressed in definitions of abuse as "allowing injury to be inflicted" or "allowing another person to commit abuse of a child." In some others, statutes explicitly identify failure to protect as a form of neglect. It is better viewed

1. However, the existence of rules as well as "the nature of the sport involved, the . . . regulations which govern the sport, the customs and practices which are generally accepted and which have evolved with the development of the sport" are items that a court should consider when determining whether a defendant's conduct was reckless or intentional.

2. We note that [this] raises a novel issue of law for this Court. Namely, whether a BB gun constitutes a firearm pursuant to R.C. 2923.21(A)(3). . . .

as neglect—a breach of a positive duty, harming by inaction. Child protection agencies frequently charge one parent (typically the mother) with failure to protect at the same time that it charges the other parent or another adult in the household (typically the mother's husband or boyfriend) with abuse for repeatedly beating or sexually abusing a child. A parent who is aware of such abuse is expected to take immediate steps to prevent its recurrence, by discontinuing the cohabitation or by notifying state officials. In recent years there have also been wholesale removals of children from insular religious communities where sex with minors was common, based in part on failure to protect charges against parents. See Myers v. Ark. Dep't of Hum. Servs., 2011 Ark. 182 (Ark. 2011) (rejecting free exercise challenge to removal of children from Tony Alamo followers in Arkansas); In re Tex. Dep't of Fam. & Prot. Servs., 255 S.W.3d 613, 615 (Tex. 2008) (holding that emergency removal of 468 children from Yearning For Zion Ranch was not necessary, and ordering that children be returned to parents while the child protection agency further investigated and pursued maltreatment charges).

A quite controversial form of failure-to-protect intervention is charging a parent (typically a mother) who is a victim of domestic violence with exposing her child to that violence. Of course, state actors will also charge the perpetrator of violence with child maltreatment for abusing a child's parent in front of the child. For example, in Matter of Kiara C., 926 N.Y.S.2d 566 (App. Div. 2011), a New York intermediate court upheld a family court finding that a father had created "imminent risk of impairing the child's physical, mental, or emotional condition" when he "slapped the mother while the mother was holding the child, who was only a few weeks old." No one objects to that sort of charge. There are also occasional cases in which a custodial mother is herself violent toward a partner, usually triggering reciprocal violence toward her, all in front of her child, and it is relatively uncontroversial to charge the mother in such cases with child neglect. See, e.g., Matter of Kaleb U., 908 N.Y.S.2d 773 (App. Div. 2010) (mother tended to get drunk and engage in erratic and violent behavior toward fiancé).

But child protection agencies also sometimes remove children from the custody of mothers who are subject to partner abuse, based on a failure-to-protect rationale. In extreme cases, the state will even terminate a parent-child relationship because the parent has repeatedly exposed the child to violence by entering into abusive intimate relationships. See, e.g., In re J.J.S., 272 S.W.3d 74 (Tex. App.—Waco, 2008) (mother lived with a series of abusers, sometimes engaged in partner violence herself, and failed to protect child from sexual abuse). There is little dispute that children suffer psychologically and emotionally from witnessing violence, and especially from witnessing violence against a parent. However, advocates for battered women object to what looks like "punishing the victim" and to separating children from mothers who are otherwise adequate caregivers based on other persons' unlawful conduct. A federal court lawsuit challenging New York City's practice of routine removal of children from abused mothers forced the City to be more discriminating in choosing to separate children from parents. The federal court certified to the New York Court of Appeals certain questions of statutory interpretation.

Nicholson v. Scoppetta

820 N.E.2d 840 (N.Y. 2004)

KAYE, Chief Judge.

. . . Plaintiffs alleged that New York City Administration for Children's Services (ACS), as a matter of policy, removed children from mothers who were victims of domestic violence because, as victims, they "engaged in domestic violence." . . . That policy, and its implementation—according to plaintiff mothers—constituted, among other wrongs, an unlawful interference with their liberty interest in the care and custody of their children in violation of the United States Constitution. . . .

In January 2002, the [federal] District Court . . . found that ACS unnecessarily, routinely charged mothers with neglect and removed their children . . . without ensuring that the mother had access to the services she needed, without a court order, and without returning these children promptly after being ordered to do so by the court;[2] that ACS . . . practice was to separate mother and child when less harmful alternatives were available; . . . and that none of the reform plans submitted by ACS could reasonably have been expected to resolve the problems within the next year. . . .

On appeal, the Second Circuit held that . . . resolution of uncertain issues of New York statutory law would avoid, or significantly modify, the substantial federal constitutional issues presented . . . . We accepted certification and now proceed to answer those questions.

CERTIFIED QUESTION NO. 1: NEGLECT

> "Does the definition of a 'neglected child' under N.Y. Family Ct. Act §1012(f), (h) include instances in which the sole allegation of neglect is that the parent or other person legally responsible for the child's care allows the child to witness domestic abuse against the caretaker?"

Family Court Act §1012(f) is explicit in identifying the elements that must be shown to support a finding of neglect. As relevant here, it defines a "neglected child" to mean:

> "a child less than eighteen years of age
>
> "(i) whose physical, mental or emotional condition has been impaired or is in imminent danger of becoming impaired as a result of the failure of his parent or other person legally responsible for his care to exercise a minimum degree of care. . . .
>
> "(B) . . . , by unreasonably inflicting or allowing to be inflicted harm, or a substantial risk thereof. . . ."

. . . The first statutory element requires proof of actual (or imminent danger of) physical, emotional or mental impairment to the child. . . . Imminent danger . . . must be near or impending, not merely possible. In each case, additionally, there must be a link or causal connection between the basis for the neglect petition and the circumstances that allegedly produce the child's impairment or imminent danger of impairment. . . . The statute specifically defines "[i]mpairment of emotional health" and "impairment of mental or emotional condition" to include

> "a state of substantially diminished psychological or intellectual functioning in relation to, but not limited to, such factors as failure to thrive, control of aggressive or self-destructive impulses, ability to think and reason, or acting out or misbehavior, including incorrigibility, ungovernability or habitual truancy."

2. The District Court cited the testimony of a child protective manager that it was common practice in domestic violence cases for ACS to wait a few days before going to court after removing a child because "after a few days of the children being in foster care, the mother will usually agree to ACS's conditions for their return without the matter ever going to court."

Under New York law, "such impairment must be clearly attributable to the unwillingness or inability of the respondent to exercise a minimum degree of care toward the child." Here, the Legislature recognized that the source of emotional or mental impairment—unlike physical injury—may be murky, and that it is unjust to fault a parent too readily. . . .

Notably, the statutory test is "*minimum* degree of care"—not maximum, not best, not ideal—and the failure must be actual, not threatened. Courts must evaluate parental behavior objectively: would a reasonable and prudent parent have so acted, or failed to act, under the circumstances then and there existing. The standard takes into account the special vulnerabilities of the child, even where general physical health is not implicated (*see Matter of Sayeh R.* (1997) [mother's decision to demand immediate return of her traumatized children without regard to their need for counseling and related services "could well be found to represent precisely the kind of failure 'to exercise a minimum degree of care' that our neglect statute contemplates"]). . . .

[W]hat course of action constitutes a parent's exercise of a "minimum degree of care" may include such considerations as: risks attendant to leaving, if the batterer has threatened to kill her if she does; risks attendant to staying and suffering continued abuse; risks attendant to seeking assistance through government channels, potentially increasing the danger to herself and her children; risks attendant to criminal prosecution against the abuser; and risks attendant to relocation. Whether a particular mother in these circumstances has actually failed to exercise a minimum degree of care is necessarily dependent on facts such as the severity and frequency of the violence, and the resources and options available to her. . . .

When "the sole allegation" is that the mother has been abused and the child has witnessed the abuse, [the requisite] showing has not been made. This does not mean, however, that a child can never be "neglected" when living in a household plagued by domestic violence. Conceivably, neglect might be found where a record establishes that, for example, the mother acknowledged that the children knew of repeated domestic violence by her paramour and had reason to be afraid of him, yet nonetheless allowed him several times to return to her home, and lacked awareness of any impact of the violence on the children, or where the children were exposed to regular and continuous extremely violent conduct between their parents, several times requiring official intervention, and where caseworkers testified to the fear and distress the children were experiencing as a result of their long exposure to the violence.

In such circumstances, the battered mother is charged with neglect not because she is a victim of domestic violence or because her children witnessed the abuse, but rather because a preponderance of the evidence establishes that the children were actually or imminently harmed by reason of her failure to exercise even minimal care in providing them with proper oversight.

CERTIFIED QUESTION NO. 2: REMOVALS

Next, we are called upon to . . . decide whether emotional injury from witnessing domestic violence can rise to a level that establishes an "imminent danger" or "risk" to a child's life or health, so that removal is appropriate either in an emergency or by court order. . . . [W]e acknowledge the Legislature's expressed goal of "placing increased emphasis on preventive services designed to maintain family relationships rather than responding to children and families in trouble only by removing the child from the family." We further acknowledge the legislative findings . . . that

> ". . . [a]buse of a parent is detrimental to children whether or not they are physically abused themselves. Children who witness domestic violence are more likely to experience delayed development, feelings of fear, depression and helplessness and are more likely to become batterers themselves."

. . . New York has long embraced a policy of keeping "biological families together." Yet "when a child's best interests are endangered, such objectives must yield to the State's paramount concern for the health and safety of the child." . . .

Not every child exposed to domestic violence is at risk of impairment. A fortiori, exposure of a child to violence is not presumptively ground for removal, and in many instances removal may do more harm to the child than good. Part 2 of article 10 of the Family Court Act sets forth four ways in which a child may be removed from the home in response to an allegation of neglect (or abuse) related to domestic violence: (1) temporary removal with consent; (2) preliminary orders after a petition is filed; (3) preliminary orders before a petition is filed; and (4) emergency removal without a court order. . . .

[T]he sections of part 2 of article 10 create a "continuum of consent and urgency and mandate a hierarchy of required review" before a child is removed from home. . . . [W]here the circumstances are not so exigent, the agency should bring a petition and seek a hearing *prior to* removal of the child. . . . For example, in *Matter of Adam DD.* (3d Dept. 1985), . . . respondent mother had told her son on several occasions that she intended to kill herself. . . . The parent's repeated threats of suicide caused emotional harm that could be akin to the experience of a child who witnesses repeated episodes of domestic violence perpetrated against a parent. In this circumstance, the agency did not immediately remove the child, but proceeded with the filing of a petition and a hearing. . . .

In order to justify a finding of imminent risk to life or health, the agency need not prove that the child has suffered actual injury. Rather, the court engages in a fact-intensive inquiry to determine whether the child's emotional health is at risk. . . . [However, the] plain language of the section and the legislative history supporting it establish that a blanket presumption favoring removal was never intended. The court *must do more* than identify the existence of a risk of serious harm. Rather, a court must weigh, in the factual setting before it, whether the imminent risk to the child can be mitigated by reasonable efforts to avoid removal . . . such as issuing a temporary order of protection or providing services to the victim. The Committee Bill Memorandum supporting this legislation explains the intent that "[w]here one parent is abusive but the child may safely reside at home with the other parent, the abuser should be removed. This will spare children the trauma of removal and placement in foster care." . . .

If the agency believes that there is insufficient time to file a petition, the next step on the continuum should not be emergency removal, but ex parte removal by court order. . . . Just as in a [preliminary removal order] inquiry, the court must consider . . . whether reasonable efforts were made prior to the application to prevent or eliminate the need for removal from the home; and whether imminent risk to the child would be eliminated by the issuance of a temporary order of protection directing the removal of the person from the child's residence. . . . [E]mergency removal is appropriate where the danger is so immediate, so urgent that the child's life or safety will be at risk before an ex parte order can be obtained. . . . "It is not required that the child be injured in the presence of a caseworker nor is it necessary for the alleged abuser to be present at the time the child is taken from the home. It is sufficient if the officials have persuasive evidence of serious ongoing abuse and, based upon the best investigation reasonably possible under the circumstances, have reason to fear imminent recurrence." . . . [The section authorizing emergency removal] . . . concerns, moreover, only the very grave circumstance of danger to life or health. While we cannot say . . . the possibility can *never* exist, in the case of emotional injury—or, even more remotely, the risk of emotional injury—caused by witnessing domestic violence, it must be a rare circumstance in which the time would be so fleeting and the danger so great that emergency removal would be warranted. . . .

Does the court of appeals' interpretation of the statute strike an appropriate balance among relevant interests? What are the relevant interests? Does it really follow "a fortiori" from the premise that "[n]ot every child exposed to domestic violence is at risk of impairment" that "exposure of a child to violence is not presumptively ground for removal"? What if 90% are at risk? If it does follow, what circumstances do you think *would* give rise to a presumption?

Should it matter whether a parent charged with neglect is blameworthy? Is a parent blameworthy if she remains with an abuser out of fear for herself—that is, that she will be killed if she tries to leave? What if an abuse victim who feels unable to leave her abuser could send her child to live with another parent or a grandparent but chooses not to do so, because of her own emotional needs?

d. Educational Neglect

Failure to ensure that children receive schooling and medical care often amounts to true neglect—that is, it occurs because of parental indifference or incapacity. There is rarely any dispute in truancy cases that the parents' inaction constitutes a breach of parental duty and justifies child protection intervention. Free public schooling and transportation to school are available to all. Social services agencies will help any poor parent try to find medical care, and if it is simply not possible to find any then the state will not charge the parents with neglect. Legal challenges to findings of neglect instead have arisen when parents objected in principle to the state's view of what schooling or health care children should receive, and usually parents have asserted a First Amendment right of religious freedom to bolster their claim that they are entitled to raise their children as they see fit. Many legislators share the view of these parents that their constitutional right of religious freedom includes such a power, and many simply want to avoid such highly charged litigation. As a result, most states have modified their laws to accommodate "religious objectors." How would you describe the content of parental power over children's schooling in Texas?

Vernon's Texas Education Code
Title 2. Public Education
Subtitle E. Students and Parents
Chapter 25, Subchapter C. Operation of Schools and School Attendance

§25.085. COMPULSORY SCHOOL ATTENDANCE

. . . (b) Unless specifically exempted by Section 25.086, a child who is at least six years of age, . . . and who has not yet reached the child's 18th birthday shall attend school. . . .

§25.086. EXEMPTIONS

(a) A child is exempt from the requirements of compulsory school attendance if the child:

(1) attends a private or parochial school that includes in its course a study of good citizenship; . . .

There are no further substantive requirements for operating a private school in Texas. Thus, if parents enroll their child in any sort of program that provides any sort of instruction about good citizenship (as the program operators interpret that), they have fully fulfilled their legal obligation with respect to schooling, even if the program teaches nothing else. In most other states, statutes command that private schools and home schools teach the core subjects that public schools teach, but they generally do not spell out particular curricular requirements beyond this nor demand any proof of student educational progress in any of these subjects. This stands in sharp contrast to states' extensive regulation of public school curricula, down to specifying the texts that will be used, and the standardized testing that now dominates schooling for the 90 percent of American children who attend public schools. It is also quite different from the norm in Europe, which is to require all schools, including private religious schools, to comply with the same curricular and academic standards. See NORMAN DOE, LAW AND RELIGION IN EUROPE: A COMPARATIVE INTRODUCTION (2011), 202. What explains the difference? Why do state legislators in the United States largely leave private schools free to do whatever they want, with no state supervision or protection against educational deprivation?

One common explanation is that market forces will drive private schools to provide the best possible education; private schools compete in a way that public schools generally do not for parents' choice. Two assumptions, usually unstated, underlying this explanation are 1) that most, if not all, parents are capable of evaluating the quality of education provided by different schools and 2) that all parents who choose private schools want good schooling for their children. The first assumption arguably underestimates the complexity of education and overstates the average person's understanding of children's intellectual development and how to promote it. Do you feel capable of reliably evaluating the relative quality of the private schools in your area? On what basis would you compare them? Bear in mind that private schools are not required to administer standardized tests and that most choose not to do so, so you would not have average scores to rely on for comparison, whatever value such scores might have.

As to the second assumption, it does seem plausible to suppose that any parents who willingly make the effort and incur the expense of securing private schooling for their children are not indifferent, but on the contrary have above-average concern for their children's schooling. What is problematic about the second assumption is rather the ambiguity of "good." If it means "good as the state sees it"—that is, fulfilling well what the state regards as the objectives of schooling, then the assumption is plainly false, for a significant percentage of parents reject many of the aims of secular education. They view those aims as irrelevant or even antithetical to the parents' overriding goal of ensuring ideological conformity. Some parents want their children to read, so that they can read religious texts, but not to learn the sort of science or history that most schools (public and private) teach. Some parents "shop" for a school that will stifle independent and critical thinking instead of promoting it, discourage children from pursuing college education, and reinforce gendered role expectations. If instead "good" means "good as parents see it," then there is a disconnect between the second assumption and the conclusion that the market will produce what state regulation otherwise would aim to produce, again because of parents who hold illiberal conceptions of the good.

Some states' statutes make clear that legislators are aware there are such parents who are radically opposed to education "as the state sees it." Virginia law, for example, categorically exempts religious-objector parents from the duty to provide an education to their children. Va. Code Ann. §22.1-254 provides: "A school board shall excuse from attendance at school . . . [a]ny pupil who, together with his parents, by reason of bona fide religious training or belief is conscientiously opposed to attendance at school."

Thus, with respect to parents whose beliefs about what is best for their children's development diverges widely from mainstream beliefs reflected in public school academic standards and in the curricula of most private schools, the market explanation/argument for non-regulation has little force. Instead, defenders of non-regulation might appeal to the widely accepted notion of parental entitlement, a notion that is (ironically?) more appealing to many people when parents oppose mainstream educational norms out of religious conviction rather than based on having theoretical and empirical support for alternative modes of secular education—that is, in those situations when it is simply nonsensical to appeal to a "parents know best" principle.

The notion of parental entitlement to depart from mainstream norms enjoys some support from the U.S. Supreme Court's interpretation of the First and Fourteenth Amendments. Read the decisions below carefully and try to define precisely the scope of parents' constitutional right to control their children's education, so you can judge whether it does in fact entitle parents to do what the state (including the reviewing court) believes to be contrary to children's interests, and does forestall states from imposing on any private or home schools curricular requirements, minimum academic achievement standards, testing mandates, or restrictions on the way teachers treat pupils (e.g., gender discrimination). Pay attention also to language suggesting what standard of judicial review applies when parents assert their constitutional rights against school laws.

The Court first addressed to what extent states may restrict the content of private school instruction, then whether states must allow for private schooling at all as an alternative to public schooling, and then whether states must altogether exempt some religious objectors from the parental duty to enroll children in school. Along the way, the Court also considered the scope of parents' freedom to involve their children in religious proselytizing. The first two questions actually arose in challenges to state law brought not by parents but rather by teachers or schools asserting rights to enter contracts or carry on a business, during the *Lochner* era of commercial substantive due process.

Meyer v. Nebraska

262 U.S. 390 (1923)

Mr. Justice McReynolds delivered the opinion of the Court.

[W]hile an instructor in Zion Parochial School [plaintiff] unlawfully taught the subject of reading in the German language to Raymond Parpart, a child of 10 years, who had not attained and successfully passed the eighth grade. . . . "An act relating to the teaching of foreign languages in the state of Nebraska," approved April 9, 1919, [states]:

> Section 1. No person . . . shall, in any private, denominational, parochial or public school, teach any subject to any person in any language than the English language.

> Sec. 2. Languages, other than the English language, may be taught as languages only after a pupil shall have attained and successfully passed the eighth grade. . . .
> Sec. 3. Any person who violates . . . this act shall be deemed guilty of a misdemeanor and upon conviction, shall be subject to a fine . . . or be confined in the county jail. . . .

The Supreme Court of the state . . . [stated]:

> . . . The Legislature had seen the baneful effects of permitting foreigners, who had taken residence in this country, to rear and educate their children in the language of their native land. The result of that condition . . . was to educate them so that they must always think in that language, and, as a consequence, naturally inculcate in them the ideas and sentiments foreign to the best interests of this country. . . .

[T]he Fourteenth Amendment [provides]: "No state . . . shall deprive any person of life, liberty or property without due process of law." . . . [T]he liberty thus guaranteed . . . denotes not merely freedom from bodily restraint but also the right of the individual to contract, to engage in any of the common occupations of life, to acquire useful knowledge, to marry, establish a home and bring up children, to worship God according to the dictates of his own conscience, and generally to enjoy those privileges long recognized at common law as essential to the orderly pursuit of happiness by free men. [Citation to *Slaughter-House Cases, Lochner v. New York,* and numerous other business regulation cases.] The established doctrine is that this liberty may not be interfered with, under the guise of protecting the public interest, by legislative action which is arbitrary or without reasonable relation to some purpose within the competency of the state to effect. . . .

Corresponding to the right of control, it is the natural duty of the parent to give his children education suitable to their station in life; and nearly all the states, including Nebraska, enforce this obligation by compulsory laws. Practically, education of the young is only possible in schools conducted by especially qualified persons who devote themselves thereto. The calling always has been regarded as useful and honorable, essential, indeed, to the public welfare. Mere knowledge of the German language cannot reasonably be regarded as harmful. Heretofore it has been commonly looked upon as helpful and desirable. Plaintiff in error taught this language in school as part of his occupation. His right thus to teach and the right of parents to engage him so to instruct their children, we think, are within the liberty of the amendment. . . .

It is said the purpose of the legislation was to promote civic development . . . [and] that the foreign born population is very large, that certain communities commonly use foreign words, follow foreign leaders, move in a foreign atmosphere, and that the children are thereby hindered from becoming citizens of the most useful type and the public safety is imperiled. That the state may do much, go very far, indeed, in order to improve the quality of its citizens, physically, mentally and morally, is clear; but the individual has certain fundamental rights which must be respected. . . . Perhaps it would be highly advantageous if all had ready understanding of our ordinary speech, but this cannot be coerced by methods which conflict with the Constitution—a desirable end cannot be promoted by prohibited means.

For the welfare of his Ideal Commonwealth, Plato suggested a law which should provide:

> "That the wives of our guardians are to be common, and their children are to be common, and no parent is to know his own child, nor any child his parent. . . . The proper officers will take the offspring of the good parents to the pen or fold, and there they will deposit them with certain nurses who dwell in a separate quarter. . . ."

In order to submerge the individual and develop ideal citizens, Sparta assembled the males at seven into barracks and intrusted their subsequent education and training to official guardians. . . . [I]t hardly will be affirmed that any Legislature could impose such restrictions upon the people of a state without doing violence to both letter and spirit of the Constitution.

The desire of the Legislature to foster a homogeneous people with American ideals prepared readily to understand current discussions of civic matters is easy to appreciate. Unfortunate experiences during the late war and aversion toward every character of truculent adversaries were certainly enough to quicken that aspiration. But the means adopted, we think, exceed the limitations upon the power of the state and conflict with rights assured to plaintiff in error. The interference is plain enough and no adequate reason therefor in time of peace and domestic tranquility has been shown.

The power of the state to compel attendance at some school and to make reasonable regulations for all schools, including a requirement that they shall give instructions in English, is not questioned. Nor has challenge been made of the state's power to prescribe a curriculum for institutions which it supports. Those matters are not within the present controversy. . . . No emergency has arisen which renders knowledge by a child of some language other than English so clearly harmful as to justify its inhibition with the consequent infringement of rights long freely enjoyed. We are constrained to conclude that the statute as applied is arbitrary and without reasonable relation to any end within the competency of the state.

As the statute undertakes to interfere only with teaching which involves a modern language, leaving complete freedom as to other matters, there seems no adequate foundation for the suggestion that the purpose was to protect the child's health by limiting his mental activities. It is well known that proficiency in a foreign language seldom comes to one not instructed at an early age, and experience shows that this is not injurious to the health, morals or understanding of the ordinary child. The judgment of the court below must be reversed. . . .

This is the first Supreme Court decision attributing to parents a Fourteenth Amendment right to control children's upbringing. Announcement of the right does not respond to any claim of the parties, is arguably dictum, does not follow any analysis of text or framers' intent, draws normative purchase by hyperbolic comparison with Plato's Republic, and suggests that the right is effective only against restrictions on parental freedom that do nothing to advance children's interests. Yet courts at all levels continue to cite *Meyer* as the doctrinal source, along with *Pierce* (below) of parents' power to resist state interference with their child-rearing behavior and choices. Note that the same Justice who wrote the *Meyer* opinion also authored the next:

Pierce v. Society of Sisters of the Holy Names of Jesus and Mary and Hill Military Academy

268 U.S. 510 (1925)

Mr. Justice McReynolds delivered the opinion of the Court.

. . . The challenged act, effective September 1, 1926, requires every parent, guardian, or other person having control or charge or custody of a child between 8 and 16 years to send him "to a public school for the period of time a public school shall be held during the current year" in the district where the child resides; and failure so to do is declared a misdemeanor. . . . The manifest purpose is to compel general attendance at public schools by normal children, between 8 and 16, who have not completed the eighth grade. And without doubt enforcement of the statute would seriously impair, perhaps destroy, the profitable features of appellees' business and greatly diminish the value of their property.

Appellee the Society of Sisters . . . has long devoted its property and effort to the secular and religious education and care of children. . . . In its primary schools . . . are taught the subjects usually pursued in Oregon public schools during the first eight years. Systematic religious instruction and moral training according to the tenets of the Roman Catholic Church are also regularly provided. . . . The business is remunerative—the annual income from primary schools exceeds $30,000. . . . [T]he Society's bill alleges that the enactment conflicts with the right of parents to choose schools where their children will receive appropriate mental and religious training, the right of the child to influence the parents' choice of a school, the right of schools and teachers therein to engage in a useful business or profession, and is accordingly repugnant to the Constitution and void.

Appellee Hill Military Academy is . . . engaged in owning, operating, and conducting for profit an elementary, college preparatory, and military training school for boys between the ages of 5 and 21 years. . . . The elementary department is divided into eight grades, as in the public schools; the college preparatory department has four grades, similar to those of the public high schools; the courses of study conform to the requirements of the state board of education. . . . The Academy's bill . . . alleges that the challenged act contravenes the corporation's rights guaranteed by the Fourteenth Amendment. . . .

No answer was interposed in either cause. . . .

No question is raised concerning the power of the state reasonably to regulate all schools, to inspect, supervise and examine them, their teachers and pupils; to require that all children of proper age attend some school, that teachers shall be of good moral character and patriotic disposition, that certain studies plainly essential to good citizenship must be taught, and that nothing be taught which is manifestly inimical to the public welfare. . . .

Appellees are engaged in a kind of undertaking not inherently harmful, but long regarded as useful and meritorious. Certainly there is nothing in the present records to indicate that they have failed to discharge their obligations to patrons, students, or the state. And there are no peculiar circumstances or present emergencies which demand extraordinary measures relative to primary education.

Under the doctrine of *Meyer v. Nebraska*, we think it entirely plain that the Act of 1922 unreasonably interferes with the liberty of parents and guardians to direct the upbringing and education of children under their control. As often heretofore pointed out, rights guaranteed by the Constitution may not be abridged by legislation which has no reasonable relation to some purpose within the competency of the state. The fundamental theory of liberty upon which all governments in this Union repose excludes any general power of the state to standardize its children by forcing them to accept instruction from public teachers only. The child is not the mere creature of the state; those who nurture him and direct his destiny have the right, coupled with the high duty, to recognize and prepare him for additional obligations.

Appellees are corporations, and therefore, it is said, they cannot claim for themselves the liberty which the Fourteenth Amendment guarantees. Accepted in the proper sense, this is true. *Northwestern Life Ins. Co. v. Riggs*; *Western Turf Association v. Greenberg*. But they have business and property for which they claim protection. . . . And this court has gone very far to protect against loss threatened by such action. . . . Generally, it is entirely true . . . that no person in any business has such an interest in possible customers as to enable him to restrain exercise of proper power of the state upon the ground that he will be deprived of patronage. But the injunctions here sought are not against the exercise of any proper power. Appellees asked protection against arbitrary, unreasonable, and unlawful interference with their patrons. . . . Their interest is clear and immediate, within the rule approved in . . . cases where injunctions have issued to protect business enterprises against interference with the freedom of patrons or customers.

The opinion focuses primarily on rights of businesses against state interference but says more about parents' right of control than *Meyer* did. Of course, in the *Pierce* litigation, attorneys thought to assert a right of parents, precisely because *Meyer* had announced such a right two years earlier. And Justice McReynolds could cite his own dictum in *Meyer* as doctrinal support for the existence of this unenumerated constitutional right. That is how the parental constitutional right of control over child rearing came into existence. Not in *Meyer*, *Pierce*, or any decision since has the Court searched for a textual or originalist basis for the right.

Do you find any hyperbole in Justice McReynolds language in his *Pierce* opinion? If you attended public schools, do you believe the state standardized you and that you were made a "creature of the state"? Should the state be concerned about some parents trying to standardize their children in their own way?

One of the most interesting passages in the opinion is the statement that parents "have the right, coupled with the high duty, to recognize and prepare [the child] for additional obligations." What are the additional obligations for which parents have a duty to prepare children? Additional to what? If it means religious obligations, is it proper for the Supreme Court to declare that parents have this duty? Relatedly, does "high duty" mean religious duty? If so, does it make sense to tie a legal right to a religious duty? And what does it even mean for a right to be "coupled with" a duty? Does it mean the right follows from the duty in some sense? If so, in what sense? That the right depends on and therefore is only as extensive as the duty? If so, and if only legal duties give rise somehow to legal rights, does that make any rights superfluous, because the state naturally will allow parents to fulfill their legal duties? Or can a legal right follow from a religious duty, in the sense of being a logically necessary corollary to it?

Perhaps the most peculiar words of the *Pierce* opinion are the Society's assertion that the law at issue violated "the right of the child to influence the parents' choice of a school." What does that mean? Is this a commonly recognized right? Justice McReynolds did not say anything about children having that right or any other rights. What should be the content of any constitutional rights of children in connection with their schooling?

A third Supreme Court decision about private school regulation in the 1920s, rarely mentioned, was Farrington v. Tokushige, 273 U.S. 284 (1927). Justice McReynolds again wrote for the Court and invalidated the regulations. The decision likely receives little attention because the challenged laws were those of a territory, Hawaii, not a state, and so the Court applied the Fifth Amendment; because the laws applied only to private foreign language schools; and because the Court's analysis was vague, seeming to suggest that the regulations on the whole were obviously impermissible under *Meyer* and *Pierce* because they effectively amounted to state takeover of the schools without justification: "They give affirmative direction concerning the intimate and essential details of such schools, intrust their control to public officers, and deny both owners and patrons reasonable choice and discretion in respect of teachers, curriculum and textbook."

None of Justice McReynolds's parents' rights opinions of the 1920s mentioned parents' religious freedom explicitly. In 1944, the Court for the first time considered whether parents sometimes also have a right under the First Amendment Free Exercise Clause. *Prince*, below, could be viewed as being about training a child for "additional obligations," but it ostensibly was about parents' duty to protect children from dangers to their health and safety and so is more often cited in cases involving other forms of child neglect, especially medical neglect. *Prince* is also unusual and important because it is the only Supreme Court decision in which the state won, apart from a 1968 summary affirmance, in *Jehovah's Witnesses v. King County Hospital*, of a trial court order to give a blood transfusion to a child of Jehovah's Witness parents.

Prince v. Commonwealth of Massachusetts

321 U.S. 158 (1944)

Mr. Justice RUTLEDGE delivered the opinion of the Court.

. . . Sarah Prince appeals from convictions for violating Massachusetts' child labor laws. . . . [S]he was the aunt and custodian of Betty M. Simmons, a girl nine years of age. . . . Massachusetts' comprehensive child labor law . . . provide[s] . . . :

> "No boy under twelve and no girl under eighteen shall sell, expose or offer for sale any newspapers, magazines, periodicals or any other articles of merchandise of any description, or exercise the trade of bootblack or scavenger, or any other trade, in any street or public place. . . .
>
> "Any parent . . . who compels or permits such minor to work in violation of any provision . . . shall for a first offence be punished by a fine . . . or by imprisonment. . . ."

Mrs. Prince, living in Brockton, is the mother of two young sons. She also has legal custody of Betty Simmons who lives with them. The children too are Jehovah's Witnesses and both Mrs. Prince and Betty testified they were ordained ministers. The former was accustomed to go each week on the streets of Brockton to distribute "Watchtower" and "Consolation." . . . [One] evening, as Mrs. Prince was preparing to leave her home, the children asked to go. She at first refused. Childlike, they resorted to tears and, motherlike, she yielded. Arriving downtown, Mrs. Prince permitted the children "to engage in the preaching work with her upon the sidewalks." That is, with specific reference to Betty, she and Mrs. Prince took positions about twenty feet apart near a street intersection. Betty held up in her hand, for passersby to see, copies of "Watch Tower" and "Consolation." From her shoulder hung the usual canvas magazine bag, on which was printed "Watchtower and Consolation 5¢ per copy." . . . Mrs. Prince and Betty remained until 8:45 P.M. . . . [T]estimony, by Betty, her aunt and others, was offered . . . to show that Betty believed it was her religious duty to perform this work and failure would bring condemnation "to everlasting destruction at Armageddon."

Appellant does not stand on freedom of the press. Regarding it as secular, she concedes it may be restricted as Massachusetts has done. Hence, she rests squarely on freedom of religion under the First Amendment, applied by the Fourteenth to the states. She buttresses this foundation, however, with a claim of parental right as secured by the due process clause of the latter Amendment.[8] Cf. *Meyer v. Nebraska.* These guaranties, she thinks, guard alike herself and the child in what they have done. Thus, two claimed liberties are at stake. One is the parent's, to bring up the child in the way he should go, which for appellant means to teach him the tenets and the practices of their faith. The other freedom is the child's, to observe these; and among them is "to preach the gospel . . . by public distribution" of "Watchtower" and "Consolation," in conformity with the scripture: "A little child shall lead them." . . .

The parent's conflict with the state over control of the child and his training is serious enough when only secular matters are concerned. It becomes the more so when an element of religious conviction enters. Against these sacred private interests, basic in a democracy, stand the interests of society to protect the welfare of children, and the state's assertion of authority to that end, made here in a manner conceded valid if only secular things were involved. The last is no mere corporate concern of official authority. It is the interest of youth itself, and of the whole community, that children be both safeguarded from abuses and given opportunities for growth into free and independent well-developed men and citizens. . . .

Previously in *Pierce v. Society of Sisters,* this Court had sustained the parent's authority to provide religious with secular schooling, and the child's right to receive it, as against the state's requirement of attendance at public schools. And in *Meyer v. Nebraska,* children's rights to receive teaching in languages other than the nation's common tongue were guarded against the state's encroachment. It is cardinal with us that the custody, care and nurture of the child reside first in the parents, whose primary function and freedom include preparation for obligations the state can neither supply nor hinder. *Pierce.* And it is in recognition of this that these decisions have respected the private realm of family life which the state cannot enter.

But the family itself is not beyond regulation in the public interest, as against a claim of religious liberty. *Reynolds v. United States.* And neither rights of religion nor rights of parenthood are beyond limitation. Acting to guard the general interest in youth's well being, the state as parens patriae may restrict the parent's control by requiring school attendance, regulating or prohibiting the child's labor, and in many other ways. Its authority is not nullified merely because the parent grounds his claim to control the child's course of conduct on religion or conscience. Thus, he cannot claim freedom from compulsory vaccination for the child more than for himself on religious grounds.[12] The right to practice religion freely does not include liberty to expose the community or the child to communicable disease or the latter to ill health or death. The catalogue need not be lengthened. It is sufficient to show what indeed appellant hardly disputes, that the state has a wide range of power for limiting parental freedom and authority in things affecting the child's welfare; and that this includes, to some extent, matters of conscience and religious conviction.

But it is said the state cannot do so here. This, first, because when state action impinges upon a claimed religious freedom, it must fall unless shown to be necessary for or conducive to the child's protection against some clear and present danger. . . . The child's presence on the street, with her guardian, distributing or offering to distribute the

8. The due process claim, as made and perhaps necessarily, extends no further than that to freedom of religion, since in the circumstances all that is comprehended in the former is included in the latter.

12. Jacobson v. Massachusetts, 197 U.S. 11.

magazines, it is urged, was in no way harmful to her, nor in any event more so than the presence of many other children at the same time and place, engaged in shopping and other activities not prohibited. . . . And, finally, it is said, the statute is, as to children, an absolute prohibition, not merely a reasonable regulation, of the denounced activity.

Concededly a statute or ordinance identical . . . except that it is applicable to adults or all persons generally, would be invalid. But the mere fact a state could not wholly prohibit this form of adult activity, whether characterized locally as a "sale" or otherwise, does not mean it cannot do so for children. Such a conclusion granted would mean that a state could impose no greater limitation upon child labor than upon adult labor. Or, if an adult were free to enter dance halls, saloons, and disreputable places generally, in order to discharge his conceived religious duty to admonish or dissuade persons from frequenting such places, so would be a child with similar convictions and objectives, if not alone then in the parent's company, against the state's command.

The state's authority over children's activities is broader than over like actions of adults. This is peculiarly true of public activities and in matters of employment. A democratic society rests, for its continuance, upon the healthy, well-rounded growth of young people into full maturity as citizens, with all that implies. It may secure this against impeding restraints and dangers, within a broad range of selection. Among evils most appropriate for such action are the crippling effects of child employment, more especially in public places, and the possible harms arising from other activities subject to all the diverse influences of the street. It is too late now to doubt that legislation appropriately designed to reach such evils is within the state's police power, whether against the parents claim to control of the child or one that religious scruples dictate contrary action.

It is true children have rights, in common with older people, in the primary use of highways. But even in such use streets afford dangers for them not affecting adults. And in other uses, whether in work or in other things, this difference may be magnified. This is so not only when children are unaccompanied but certainly to some extent when they are with their parents. . . . [P]resence of the child's guardian . . . may lessen the likelihood that some evils the legislation seeks to avert will occur. But it cannot forestall all of them. The zealous though lawful exercise of the right to engage in propagandizing the community, whether in religious, political or other matters, may and at times does create situations difficult enough for adults to cope with and wholly inappropriate for children, especially of tender years, to face. Other harmful possibilities could be stated, of emotional excitement and psychological or physical injury.

Parents may be free to become martyrs themselves. But it does not follow they are free, in identical circumstances, to make martyrs of their children before they have reached the age of full and legal discretion when they can make that choice for themselves. Massachusetts has determined that an absolute prohibition, though one limited to streets and public places and to the incidental uses proscribed, is necessary to accomplish its legitimate objectives. Its power to attain them is broad enough to reach these peripheral instances in which the parent's supervision may reduce but cannot eliminate entirely the ill effects of the prohibited conduct. We think . . . the power of the state to control the conduct of children reaches beyond the scope of its authority over adults, as is true in the case of other freedoms, and the rightful boundary of its power has not been crossed in this case.

In so ruling we dispose also of appellant's argument founded upon denial of equal protection. It falls with that based on denial of religious freedom, since in this instance the one is but another phrasing of the other. Shortly, the contention is that the street, for Jehovah's Witnesses and their children, is their church, since their conviction makes it so;

and to deny them access to it for religious purposes as was done here has the same effect as excluding altar boys, youthful choristers, and other children from the edifices in which they practice their religious beliefs and worship. The argument hardly needs more than statement, after what has been said, to refute it. . . . [T]here is no denial of equal protection in excluding their children from doing there what no other children may do.

Our ruling does not extend beyond the facts the case presents. We neither lay the foundation "for any (that is, every) state intervention in the indoctrination and participation of children in religion" which may be done 'in the name of their health and welfare' nor give warrant for "every limitation on their religious training and activities." The religious training and indoctrination of children may be accomplished in many ways, some of which, as we have noted, have received constitutional protection through decisions of this Court. These and all others except the public proclaiming of religion on the streets, if this may be taken as either training or indoctrination of the proclaimer, remain unaffected by the decision.

Mr. Justice MURPHY, dissenting.

This attempt by the state of Massachusetts to prohibit a child from exercising her constitutional right to practice her religion on the public streets cannot, in my opinion, be sustained. . . . It is undisputed . . . that she did this of her own desire. . . . She testified that she was motivated by her love of the Lord and that He commanded her to distribute this literature; this was, she declared, her way of worshipping God. . . .

Religious training and activity, whether performed by adult or child, are protected by the Fourteenth Amendment against interference by state action, except insofar as they violate reasonable regulations adopted for the protection of the public health, morals and welfare. . . . [T]he human freedoms enumerated in the First Amendment and carried over into the Fourteenth Amendment are to be presumed to be invulnerable and any attempt to sweep away those freedoms is prima facie invalid. . . . The burden was therefore on the state of Massachusetts to prove the reasonableness and necessity of prohibiting children from engaging in religious activity of the type involved in this case. . . .

The great interest of the state in shielding minors from the evil vicissitudes of early life does not warrant every limitation on their religious training and activities. The reasonableness that justifies the prohibition of the ordinary distribution of literature in the public streets by children is not necessarily the reasonableness that justifies such a drastic restriction when the distribution is part of their religious faith. If the right of a child to practice its religion in that manner is to be forbidden by constitutional means, there must be convincing proof that such a practice constitutes a grave and immediate danger to the state or to the health, morals or welfare of the child. . . .

The state, in my opinion, has completely failed to sustain its burden. . . . [T]here is not the slightest indication . . . that children engaged in distributing literature pursuant to their religious beliefs have been or are likely to be subject to any of the harmful "diverse influences of the street." . . . And the fact that the zealous exercise of the right to propagandize the community may result in violent or disorderly situations difficult for children to face is no excuse for prohibiting the exercise of that right. . . .

From ancient times to the present day, the ingenuity of man has known no limits in its ability to forge weapons of oppression for use against those who dare to express or practice unorthodox religious beliefs. . . . Jehovah's Witnesses are living proof of the fact that even in this nation, . . . the right to practice religion in unconventional ways is still far from secure. Theirs is a militant and unpopular faith, pursued with a fanatical zeal. They have suffered brutal beatings; their property has been destroyed; they have been harassed at every turn by the resurrection and enforcement of little used ordinances and statutes. . . . We should therefore hesitate before approving the application of a statute that might be used as another instrument of oppression. . . .

How appealing is the claim that a nine-year-old child has a constitutional right of religious freedom? What implications might it have in other contexts? Does the *Prince* majority adequately respect Betty Simmons and her choices?

Despite clear reference to rights of children in the majority and dissenting opinions, *Prince* is typically cited only as a case about parents' rights. Try to figure out exactly what the majority was saying about parents' rights—in particular, whether the rights are stronger when parents act out of religious conviction and what level of scrutiny applies to laws infringing "parental free exercise rights." For guidance on those questions, courts today mostly look to the Court's later decision in *Yoder*, below; they cite *Prince* principally for its hyperbolic "martyr" language and for its specific statements about child labor and vaccination.

Yoder is the Court's strongest statement to date of parental child-rearing rights. As you read the case, imagine that the Court is instead addressing the desire of Amish husbands to control their wives' education or exposure to the outside world, and as usual ask whether factual differences between a wife and a 15-year-old daughter justify treating the two differently with respect to a husband/father's demand for a constitutional entitlement to control, as against state efforts to ensure opportunity-enhancing education. And note that although the statute Amish parents violated requires parents to "cause their children to attend" a school, the parents demanded not simply exemption from responsibility for enrolling their children and getting them out the door in the morning, but also power to prevent anyone else from doing those things, including the children themselves.

Wisconsin v. Yoder

406 U.S. 205 (1972)

Mr. Chief Justice BURGER delivered the opinion of the Court.

Respondents Jonas Yoder and Wallace Miller are members of the Old Order Amish religion, and respondent Adin Yutzy is a member of the Conservative Amish Mennonite Church. Wisconsin's compulsory school-attendance law required them to cause their children to attend public or private school until reaching age 16 but the respondents declined to send their children, ages 14 and 15, to public school after they complete the eighth grade.[1] The children were not enrolled in any private school, or within any recognized exception to the compulsory-attendance law.

On complaint of the school district administrator for the public schools, respondents were charged, tried, and convicted of violating the compulsory-attendance law and were fined the sum of $5 each. Respondents defended on the ground that the application of the compulsory-attendance law violated their rights under the First and Fourteenth Amendments.[4] The trial testimony showed that respondents believed, in accordance

1. The children, Frieda Yoder, aged 15, Barbara Miller, aged 15, and Vernon Yutzy, aged 14, were all graduates of the eighth grade of public school.

4. The First Amendment provides: "Congress shall make no law respecting an establishment of religion, or prohibiting the free exercise thereof. . . ."

with the tenets of Old Order Amish communities generally, that their children's attendance at high school, public or private, was contrary to the Amish religion and way of life. They believed that by sending their children to high school, they would not only expose themselves to the danger of the censure of the church community, but . . . also endanger their own salvation and that of their children.

The history of the Amish sect . . . [began] with the Swiss Anabaptists of the 16th century who rejected institutionalized churches and sought to return to the early, simple, Christian life de-emphasizing material success, rejecting the competitive spirit, and seeking to insulate themselves from the modern world. As a result of their common heritage, Old Order Amish communities today are characterized by a fundamental belief that salvation requires life in a church community separate and apart from the world and worldly influence. This concept of life aloof from the world and its values is central to their faith.

A related feature of Old Order Amish communities is their devotion to a life in harmony with nature and the soil, as exemplified by the simple life of the early Christian era that continued in America during much of our early national life. Amish beliefs require members of the community to make their living by farming or closely related activities. The Old Order Amish religion pervades and determines the entire mode of life of its adherents. Their conduct is regulated in great detail by the Ordnung, or rules, of the church community. Adult baptism, which occurs in late adolescence, is the time at which Amish young people voluntarily undertake heavy obligations, not unlike the Bar Mitzvah of the Jews, to abide by the rules of the church community.

Amish objection to formal education beyond the eighth grade is firmly grounded in these central religious concepts. They object to the high school, and higher education generally, because the values they teach are in marked variance with Amish values and the Amish way of life; they view secondary school education as an impermissible exposure of their children to a "worldly" influence in conflict with their beliefs. The high school tends to emphasize intellectual and scientific accomplishments, self-distinction, competitiveness, worldly success, and social life with other students. Amish society emphasizes informal learning-through-doing; a life of "goodness," rather than a life of intellect; wisdom, rather than technical knowledge, community welfare, rather than competition; and separation from, rather than integration with, contemporary worldly society.

Formal high school education beyond the eighth grade is contrary to Amish beliefs, not only because it places Amish children in an environment hostile to Amish beliefs with increasing emphasis on competition in class work and sports and with pressure to conform to the styles, manners, and ways of the peer group, but also because it takes them away from their community, physically and emotionally, during the crucial and formative adolescent period of life. During this period, the children must acquire Amish attitudes favoring manual work and self-reliance and the specific skills needed to perform the adult role of an Amish farmer or housewife. They must learn to enjoy physical labor. Once a child has learned basic reading, writing, and elementary mathematics, these traits, skills, and attitudes admittedly fall within the category of those best learned through example and "doing" rather than in a classroom. And, at this time in life, the Amish child must also grow in his faith and his relationship to the Amish community if he is to be prepared to accept the heavy obligations imposed by adult baptism. In short, high school attendance with teachers who are not of the Amish faith—and may even be hostile to it—interposes a serious barrier to integration of the Amish child into the Amish religious community.

The Amish do not object to elementary education through the first eight grades as a general proposition because they agree that their children must have basic skills in the "three R's" in order to read the Bible, to be good farmers and citizens, and to be able to deal with non-Amish people when necessary in the course of daily affairs. They view such a basic education as acceptable because it does not significantly expose their children to wordly values or interfere with their development in the Amish community during the crucial adolescent period. While Amish accept compulsory elementary education, wherever possible they have established their own elementary schools in many respects like the small local schools of the past. In the Amish belief higher learning tends to develop values they reject as influences that alienate man from God.

Dr. Hostetler testified that compulsory high school attendance could not only result in great psychological harm to Amish children, because of the conflicts it would produce, but would also, in his opinion, ultimately result in the destruction of the Old Order Amish church community as it exists in the United States today. Dr. Donald A. Erickson, an expert witness on education, showed that the Amish succeed in preparing their high school age children to be productive members of the Amish community. He described their system of learning through doing the skills directly relevant to their adult roles in the Amish community as 'ideal' and perhaps superior to ordinary high school education. The evidence also showed that the Amish have an excellent record as law-abiding and generally self-sufficient members of society.

I

There is no doubt as to the power of a State, having a high responsibility for education of its citizens, to impose reasonable regulations for the control and duration of basic education. Providing public schools ranks at the very apex of the function of a State. Yet even this paramount responsibility was, in *Pierce*, made to yield to the right of parents to provide an equivalent education in a privately operated system. . . . As that case suggests, the values of parental direction of the religious upbringing and education of their children in their early and formative years have a high place in our society. See also *Meyer v. Nebraska* (1923). Thus, a State's interest in universal education, however highly we rank it, is not totally free from a balancing process when it impinges on fundamental rights and interests, such as those specifically protected by the Free Exercise Clause of the First Amendment, and the traditional interest of parents with respect to the religious upbringing of their children so long as they, in the words of *Pierce*, "prepare (them) for additional obligations."

It follows that in order for Wisconsin to compel school attendance beyond the eighth grade against a claim that such attendance interferes with the practice of a legitimate religious belief, it must appear either that the State does not deny the free exercise of religious belief by its requirement, or that there is a state interest of sufficient magnitude to override the interest claiming protection under the Free Exercise Clause. Only those interests of the highest order and those not otherwise served can overbalance legitimate claims to the free exercise of religion. However strong the State's interest in universal compulsory education, it is by no means absolute to the exclusion or subordination of all other interests.

II

A way of life, however virtuous and admirable, may not be interposed as a barrier to reasonable state regulation of education if it is based on purely secular considerations; to have the protection of the Religion Clauses, the claims must be rooted in religious belief. Although a determination of what is a "religious" belief or practice entitled to constitutional protection may present a most delicate question, the very concept of ordered liberty precludes allowing every person to make his own standards on matters of conduct in which society as a whole has important interests. Thus, if the Amish asserted their claims because of their subjective evaluation and rejection of the contemporary secular values accepted by the majority, much as Thoreau rejected the social values of his time and isolated himself at Walden Pond, their claims would not rest on a religious basis. Thoreau's choice was philosophical and personal rather than religious, and such belief does not rise to the demands of the Religion Clauses.

That the Old Order Amish daily life and religious practice stem from their faith is shown by the fact that it is in response to their literal interpretation of the Biblical injunction from the Epistle of Paul to the Romans, "be not conformed to this world. . . ." Moreover, for the Old Order Amish, religion is not simply a matter of theocratic belief. As the expert witnesses explained, the Old Order Amish religion pervades and determines virtually their entire way of life, regulating it with the detail of the Talmudic diet through the strictly enforced rules of the church community. The respondents' religious beliefs and attitude toward life, family, and home have remained constant—perhaps some would say static—in a period of unparalleled progress in human knowledge generally and great changes in education. Their religious beliefs and what we would today call 'life style' have not altered in fundamentals for centuries. Their rejection of telephones, automobiles, radios, and television, their mode of dress, of speech, their habits of manual work do indeed set them apart from much of contemporary society; these customs are both symbolic and practical.

As the society around the Amish has become more populous, urban, industrialized, and complex, particularly in this century, government regulation of human affairs has correspondingly become more detailed and pervasive. The Amish mode of life has thus come into conflict increasingly with requirements of contemporary society exerting a hydraulic insistence on conformity to majoritarian standards. So long as compulsory education laws were confined to eight grades of elementary basic education imparted in a nearby rural schoolhouse, with a large proportion of students of the Amish faith, the Old Order Amish had little basis to fear that school attendance would expose their children to the worldly influence they reject. But modern compulsory secondary education in rural areas is now largely carried on in a consolidated school, often remote from the student's home and alien to his daily home life. Secondary schooling, by exposing Amish children to worldly influences in terms of attitudes, goals, and values contrary to beliefs, and by substantially interfering with the religious development of the Amish child and his integration into the way of life of the Amish faith community at the crucial adolescent stage of development, contravenes the basic religious tenets and practice of the Amish faith, both as to the parent and the child.

The impact of the compulsory-attendance law on respondents' practice of the Amish religion is not only severe, but inescapable, for the Wisconsin law affirmatively compels them, under threat of criminal sanction, to perform acts undeniably at odds with fundamental tenets of their religious beliefs. It carries with it precisely the kind of objective danger to the free exercise of religion that the First Amendment was designed to prevent. Compulsory school attendance to age 16 for Amish children carries with it a very real threat of undermining the Amish community and religious practice as they exist today; they must either abandon belief and be assimilated into society at large, or be forced to migrate to some other and more tolerant region.[9]

9. . . . Forced migration of religious minorities was an evil that lay at the heart of the Religion Clauses.

III

Wisconsin concedes that under the Religion Clauses religious beliefs are absolutely free from the State's control, but it argues that "actions," even though religiously grounded, are outside the protection of the First Amendment. But our decisions have rejected the idea that religiously grounded conduct is always outside the protection of the Free Exercise Clause. It is true that activities of individuals, even when religiously based, are often subject to regulation by the States in the exercise of their undoubted power to promote the health, safety, and general welfare. . . . See, e.g., *Prince v. Massachusetts* (1944). But to agree that religiously grounded conduct must often be subject to the broad police power of the State is not to deny that there are areas of conduct protected by the Free Exercise Clause of the First Amendment and thus beyond the power of the State to control, even under regulations of general applicability. A regulation neutral on its face may, in its application, offend the constitutional requirement for governmental neutrality if it unduly burdens the free exercise of religion. The Court must not ignore the danger that an exception from a general obligation of citizenship on religious grounds may run afoul of the Establishment Clause, but that danger cannot be allowed to prevent any exception no matter how vital it may be to the protection of values promoted by the right of free exercise.

Where fundamental claims of religious freedom are at stake, . . . we must searchingly examine the interests that the State seeks to promote. The State notes . . . that some degree of education is necessary to prepare citizens to participate effectively and intelligently in our open political system if we are to preserve freedom and independence. Further, education prepares individuals to be self-reliant and self-sufficient participants in society.

We accept these propositions. However, . . . an additional one or two years of formal high school for Amish children in place of their long-established program of informal vocational education would do little to serve those interests. . . . [T]he value of all education must be assessed in terms of its capacity to prepare the child for life. It is one thing to say that compulsory education for a year or two beyond the eighth grade may be necessary when its goal is the preparation of the child for life in modern society as the majority live, but it is quite another if the goal of education be viewed as the preparation of the child for life in the separated agrarian community that is the keystone of the Amish faith.

The State attacks respondents' position as one fostering "ignorance" from which the child must be protected by the State. . . . [T]his argument does not square with the facts disclosed in the record. Whatever their idiosyncrasies as seen by the majority, . . . the Amish community has been a highly successful social unit within our society, even if apart from the conventional "mainstream." Its members are productive and very law-abiding members of society; they reject public welfare in any of its usual modern forms. The Congress itself recognized their self-sufficiency by authorizing exemption of such groups as the Amish from the obligation to pay social security taxes.[11]

We must not forget that in the Middle Ages important values of the civilization of the Western World were preserved by members of religious orders who isolated themselves from all worldly influences against great obstacles. There can be no assumption that today's majority is "right" and the Amish and others like them are "wrong." A way of life that is odd or even erratic but interferes with no rights or interests of others is not to be condemned because it is different.

11. The record in this case establishes without contradiction that the Green County Amish had never been known to commit crimes, that none had been known to receive public assistance, and that none were unemployed.

The State, however, supports its interest in providing an additional one or two years of compulsory high school education to Amish children because of the possibility that some such children will choose to leave the Amish community, and that if this occurs they will be ill-equipped for life. . . . However, on this record, that argument is highly speculative. There is no specific evidence of the loss of Amish adherents by attrition, nor is there any showing that upon leaving the Amish community Amish children, with their practical agricultural training and habits of industry and self-reliance, would become burdens on society because of educational shortcomings. . . . To the contrary, not only do the Amish accept the necessity for formal schooling through the eighth grade level, but continue to provide what has been characterized by the undisputed testimony of expert educators as an "ideal" vocational education for their children in the adolescent years. There is nothing in this record to suggest that the Amish qualities of reliability, self-reliance, and dedication to work would fail to find ready markets in today's society. . . . [N]or is there any basis in the record to warrant a finding that an additional one or two years of formal school education beyond the eighth grade would serve to eliminate any such problem that might exist.

Insofar as the State's claim rests on the view that a brief additional period of formal education is imperative to enable the Amish to participate effectively and intelligently in our democratic process, it must fall. . . . When Thomas Jefferson emphasized the need for education as a bulwark of a free people against tyranny, there is nothing to indicate he had in mind compulsory education through any fixed age beyond a basic education. Indeed, the Amish communities singularly parallel and reflect many of the virtues of Jefferson's ideal of the "sturdy yeoman" who would form the basis of what he considered as the ideal of a democratic society. Even their idiosyncratic separateness exemplifies the diversity we profess to admire and encourage.

The requirement for compulsory education beyond the eighth grade is a relatively recent development in our history. Less than 60 years ago, the educational requirements of almost all of the States were satisfied by completion of the elementary grades, at least where the child was regularly and lawfully employed.[15]

We should also note that compulsory education . . . laws reflected the movement to prohibit most child labor under age 16 that culminated in the provisions of the Federal Fair Labor Standards Act of 1938. . . . Wisconsin's interest in compelling the school attendance of Amish children to age 16 emerges as somewhat less substantial than requiring such attendance for children generally. For, while agricultural employment is not totally outside the legitimate concerns of the child labor laws, employment of children under parental guidance and on the family farm from age 14 to age 16 is an ancient tradition that lies at the periphery of the objectives of such laws. There is no intimation that the Amish employment of their children on family farms is in any way deleterious to their health or that Amish parents exploit children at tender years. Moreover, employment of Amish children on the family farm does not present the undesirable economic aspects of eliminating jobs that might otherwise be held by adults.

IV

Finally, the State, on authority of *Prince v. Massachusetts*, argues that a decision exempting Amish children from the State's requirement fails to recognize the substantive right of the

15. Even today, an eighth grade education fully satisfies the educational requirements of at least six States. See [statutes in Arizona, Arkansas, Iowa, Mississippi, South Dakota, and Wyoming] [this is not true today, of course].

Amish child to a secondary education, and fails to give due regard to the power of the State as *parens patriae* to extend the benefit of secondary education to children regardless of the wishes of their parents. . . . This case is not one in which any harm to the physical or mental health of the child or to the public safety, peace, order, or welfare has been demonstrated or may be properly inferred.

Contrary to the suggestion of the dissenting opinion of Mr. Justice Douglas, our holding today in no degree depends on the assertion of the religious interest of the child as contrasted with that of the parents. It is the parents who are subject to prosecution here for failing to cause their children to attend school, and it is their right of free exercise, not that of their children, that must determine Wisconsin's power to impose criminal penalties on the parent. The dissent argues that a child who expresses a desire to attend public high school in conflict with the wishes of his parents should not be prevented from doing so. There is no reason for the Court to consider that point since it is not an issue in the case. The children are not parties to this litigation. The State has at no point tried this case on the theory that respondents were preventing their children from attending school against their expressed desires. . . .[21] The State's position from the outset has been that it is empowered to apply its compulsory-attendance law to Amish parents in the same manner as to other parents—that is, without regard to the wishes of the child. . . .

Our holding in no way determines the proper resolution of possible competing interests of parents, children, and the State in an appropriate state court proceeding in which the power of the State is asserted on the theory that Amish parents are preventing their minor children from attending high school despite their expressed desires to the contrary. Recognition of the claim of the State in such a proceeding would, of course, call into question traditional concepts of parental control over the religious upbringing and education of their minor children recognized in this Court's past decisions. It is clear that such an intrusion by a State into family decisions in the area of religious training would give rise to grave questions of religious freedom comparable to those raised here and those presented in *Pierce v. Society of Sisters*.

The State's argument proceeds without reliance on any actual conflict between the wishes of parents and children. It appears to rest on the potential that exemption of Amish parents from the requirements of the compulsory-education law might allow some parents to act contrary to the best interests of their children by foreclosing their opportunity to make an intelligent choice between the Amish way of life and that of the outside world. The same argument could, of course, be made with respect to all church schools short of college. There is nothing in the record or in the ordinary course of human experience to suggest that non-Amish parents generally consult with children of ages 14-16 if they are placed in a church school of the parents' faith.

Indeed it seems clear that if the State is empowered, as *parens patriae*, to "save" a child from himself or his Amish parents by requiring an additional two years of compulsory formal high school education, the State will in large measure influence, if not determine, the religious future of the child. Even more markedly than in *Prince*, therefore, this case involves the fundamental interest of parents, as contrasted with that of the State, to guide the religious future and education of their children. The history and culture of Western civilization reflect a strong tradition of parental concern for the nurture and upbringing

21. The only relevant testimony in the record is to the effect that the wishes of the one child who testified corresponded with those of her parents. Testimony of Frieda Yoder [was] to the effect that her personal religious beliefs guided her decision to discontinue school attendance after the eighth grade. The other children were not called by either side.

of their children. This primary role of the parents in the upbringing of their children is now established beyond debate as an enduring American tradition. [Quoting *Pierce.*] . . . The duty to prepare the child for "additional obligations," referred to by the Court, must be read to include the inculcation of moral standards, religious beliefs, and elements of good citizenship. *Pierce,* of course, recognized that where nothing more than the general interest of the parent in the nurture and education of his children is involved, it is beyond dispute that the State acts "reasonably" and constitutionally in requiring education to age 16 in some public or private school meeting the standards prescribed by the State.

However read, the Court's holding in *Pierce* stands as a charter of the rights of parents to direct the religious upbringing of their children. And, when the interests of parenthood are combined with a free exercise claim of the nature revealed by this record, more than merely a "reasonable relation to some purpose within the competency of the State" is required to sustain the validity of the State's requirement under the First Amendment. To be sure, the power of the parent, even when linked to a free exercise claim, may be subject to limitation under *Prince* if it appears that parental decisions will jeopardize the health or safety of the child, or have a potential for significant social burdens. But in this case, the Amish have introduced persuasive evidence undermining the arguments the State has advanced to support its claims in terms of the welfare of the child and society as a whole. The record strongly indicates that accommodating the religious objections of the Amish by forgoing one, or at most two, additional years of compulsory education will not impair the physical or mental health of the child, or result in an inability to be self-supporting or to discharge the duties and responsibilities of citizenship, or in any other way materially detract from the welfare of society. . . . [W]e cannot accept a *parens patriae* claim of such all-encompassing scope and with such sweeping potential for broad and unforeseeable application as that urged by the State.

V

For the reasons stated we hold, with the Supreme Court of Wisconsin, that the First and Fourteenth Amendments prevent the State from compelling respondents to cause their children to attend formal high school to age 16.[22] Our disposition of this case, however, in no way alters our recognition of the obvious fact that courts are not school boards or legislatures, and are ill-equipped to determine the "necessity" of discrete aspects of a State's program of compulsory education. This should suggest that courts must move with great circumspection in performing the sensitive and delicate task of weighing a State's legitimate social concern when faced with religious claims for exemption from generally applicable education requirements. It cannot be overemphasized that we are not dealing with a way of life and mode of education by a group claiming to have recently discovered some "progressive" or more enlightened process for rearing children for modern life.

22. What we have said should meet the suggestion that the decision of the Wisconsin Supreme Court recognizing an exemption for the Amish from the State's system of compulsory education constituted an impermissible establishment of religion. Accommodating the religious beliefs of the Amish can hardly be characterized as sponsorship or active involvement. The purpose and effect of such an exemption are not to support, favor, advance, or assist the Amish, but to allow their centuries-old religious society, here long before the advent of any compulsory education, to survive free from the heavy impediment compliance with the Wisconsin compulsory-education law would impose. Such an accommodation "reflects nothing more than the governmental obligation of neutrality in the face of religious differences, and does not represent that involvement of religious with secular institutions which it is the object of the Establishment Clause to forestall."

Aided by a history of three centuries as an identifiable religious sect and a long history as a successful and self-sufficient segment of American society, the Amish in this case have convincingly demonstrated the sincerity of their religious beliefs, the interrelationship of belief with their mode of life, the vital role that belief and daily conduct play in the continued survival of Old Order Amish communities and their religious organization, and the hazards presented by the State's enforcement of a statute generally valid as to others. Beyond this, they have carried the even more difficult burden of demonstrating the adequacy of their alternative mode of continuing informal vocational education in terms of precisely those overall interests that the State advances in support of its program of compulsory high school education. In light of this convincing showing, one that probably few other religious groups or sects could make, and weighing the minimal difference between what the State would require and what the Amish already accept, it was incumbent on the State to show with more particularity how its admittedly strong interest in compulsory education would be adversely affected by granting an exemption to the Amish.

Nothing we hold is intended to undermine the general applicability of the State's compulsory school-attendance statutes or to limit the power of the State to promulgate reasonable standards that, while not impairing the free exercise of religion, provide for continuing agricultural vocational education under parental and church guidance by the Old Order Amish or others similarly situated. The States have had a long history of amicable and effective relationships with church-sponsored schools, and there is no basis for assuming that, in this related context, reasonable standards cannot be established concerning the content of the continuing vocational education of Amish children under parental guidance, provided always that state regulations are not inconsistent with what we have said in this opinion.

Mr. Justice DOUGLAS, dissenting in part.

The Court's analysis assumes that the only interests at stake in the case are those of the Amish parents on the one hand, and those of the State on the other. . . . Respondents' motion to dismiss in the trial court expressly asserts, not only the religious liberty of the adults, but also that of the children, as a defense to the prosecutions. . . . If the parents in this case are allowed a religious exemption, the inevitable effect is to impose the parents' notions of religious duty upon their children. As the child has no other effective forum, it is in this litigation that his rights should be considered. And, if an Amish child desires to attend high school, and is mature enough to have that desire respected, the State may well be able to override the parents' religiously motivated objections.

Our opinions are full of talk about the power of the parents over the child's education. And we have in the past analyzed similar conflicts between parent and State with little regard for the views of the child. Recent cases, however, have clearly held that the children themselves have constitutionally protectible interests. These children are "persons" within the meaning of the Bill of Rights. We have so held over and over again. On this important and vital matter of education, I think the children should be entitled to be heard. While the parents, absent dissent, normally speak for the entire family, the education of the child is a matter on which the child will often have decided views. He may want to be a pianist or an astronaut or an oceanographer. To do so he will have to break from the Amish tradition.[2]

2. A significant number of Amish children do leave the Old Order. Professor Hostetler notes that "(t)he loss of members is very limited in some Amish districts and considerable in others." In one Pennsylvania church, he observed a defection rate of 30%. Rates up to 50% have been reported by others.

It is the future of the student, not the future of the parents, that is imperiled by today's decision. If a parent keeps his child out of school beyond the grade school, then the child will be forever barred from entry into the new and amazing world of diversity that we have today. The child may decide that that is the preferred course, or he may rebel. It is the student's judgment, not his parents', that is essential if we are to give full meaning to what we have said about the Bill of Rights and of the right of students to be masters of their own destiny.[3] If he is harnessed to the Amish way of life by those in authority over him and if his education is truncated, his entire life may be stunted and deformed.

In Reynolds v. U.S. (1878), the Supreme Court recognized that a reclusive community might practice polygamy "without appearing to disturb the social condition of the people who surround it," but nevertheless had no doubt that the government could prohibit them from doing so. As justification, the Court explained that "polygamy leads to the patriarchal principle, and which, when applied to large communities, fetters the people in stationary despotism." The Court held that religious belief does not entitle anyone to an exception to anti-polygamy legislation, because "[t]o permit this would be to make the professed doctrines of religious belief superior to the law of the land, and in effect to permit every citizen to become a law unto himself." Is the Amish claim to an exception from laws against uneducated children stronger or weaker than an FLDS claim to an exception from laws against multiple marriage? Professors Ristroph and Murray argue that *Reynolds* and *Yoder* are consistent insofar as they both reinforce a particular state-preferred norm of marital family life. See Alice Ristroph & Melissa Murray, *Disestablishing the Family,* 119 YALE L.J. 1236 (2010). What is the content of that norm?

What moral presuppositions appear to underlie the *Yoder* majority's reasoning? Does it view children as "mere creatures" of their parents or of the Amish community? Abraham Lincoln said: "Those who deny freedom to others deserve it not for themselves." Is it ironic that parents would assert a First Amendment right to prevent their children from being exposed to competing ideas and ways of life?

Is it any clearer in this decision for what "additional obligations" parents have a duty to prepare children, or whether the duty is a legal one or rather a self-imposed moral one? The Court repeatedly put forward this passage, with its opaque invocation of a right-duty connection, as its primary, if not sole, support for the unenumerated parental right. Yet the existence of the right is hardly plain; it was so unfamiliar in 1923 that the school teacher in *Meyer* did not think to assert it, and Justice Scalia suggested in *Troxel* that he would vote to overturn this doctrine. Would you expect more of an effort by the Court to support the right?

Is the majority inconsistent as to the importance of ninth and tenth grade? Responding to the parents' desire to ensure continued adherence to the Amish faith and way of life, the majority treats those two years as crucial; requiring that the children attend school for those two years seriously threatens the Amish community's survival. Responding to the state's desire to ensure an open future, the majority dismisses the two extra years as inconsequential. Is Justice Burger correct about either assumption? He cited no empirical studies of children's moral and intellectual development in either instance.

3. There is substantial agreement among child psychologists and sociologists that the moral and intellectual maturity of a 14-year-old approaches that of an adult. The maturity of Amish youth, who identify with and assume adult roles from early childhood, is certainly not less than that of children in the general population.

The age span for compulsory schooling has expanded in most U.S. states in recent decades, as the sorts of jobs for which a high school dropout is qualified have shrunk. A slim majority of states sets the age at 16, but many, including Wisconsin, have raised it to 18. See Wis. Stat. §118.15. Yet 35 years after *Yoder*, a Wisconsin appellate court held that it was improper to base a transfer of custody to a non-Amish father from a mother who converted to the Amish faith on the fact that the mother would deny a high school education to their daughter, and the court based this holding in part on the *Yoder* decision and in part on an assertion that the child would not be harmed by failing to complete high school. Adrian v. Petty, 302 Wis. 2d 260 (Wis. Ct. App. 2007).

Justice Douglas obviously is more focused on the interests of the children involved, but his recommendation places great weight on the Amish youths' expressed preferences, rather than the state's judgment about their interests. If this were a case about husbands' control over wives, presumably the entire Court would have said that the wishes of the wives are important, and in fact decisive. Is it realistic, though, with respect to wives or adolescent children in authoritarian, reclusive religious communities to suppose they can express autonomous preferences? Are the youths' stated views likely to coincide with their interests as the state saw them and as Justice Douglas described them—that is, with their having an "open future"? Is there any basis in the Constitution for Douglas's position? Are children entitled to some degree of openness in their future? If so, why must it be that which mainstream society offers rather than that offered within their community of birth? By way of comparison, how open is the future of children born into the worst American ghettos? Or is the right of children simply to choose or to have the best of what is available to them?

The reasoning of the European Court of Human Rights in a somewhat similar case, Konrad v. Germany, provides an illuminating contrast. The case did not involve a reclusive community like the Amish, but rather a single fundamentalist Christian family in which parents opposed the messages and influences of public schooling, and so the holding in favor of the state is not much different from that of lower courts in the United States rejecting extension of the *Yoder* holding beyond the Amish. But the decision's emphasis on the rights of children is unlike what one generally finds in U.S. court decisions.

Konrad v. Germany

35504/03 Eur. Ct. H.R. (2006)

The applicants belong to a Christian community which is strongly attached to the Bible and reject the attendance of private or State schools for religious reasons. The applicant parents find that school education does not suit their beliefs since sex education is taught, mythical creatures such as witches and dwarfs appear in fairy tales during school lessons, and physical and psychological violence among pupils at school is on the increase. They educate their children at home in accordance with the syllabus and materials of the "Philadelphia School," an institution based in Siegen which is not recognised as a private school by the State. The institution specialises in assisting devout Christian parents in educating their children at home. The school's syllabus contains both books and materials which are used by State or private schools and materials specially prepared to support the education of religious beliefs. Teaching by parents is supervised by staff trained by the Philadelphia School. The teaching is supplemented by occasional gatherings of parents, children and staff members.

The applicant parents applied for their children to be exempted from compulsory primary school attendance and for permission to educate them at home. . . . [T]he Offenburg Education Office rejected the application. . . . The relevant provisions of [German] Law are:

> Article 6
>
> . . . 2. The care and upbringing of children is the natural right of parents and a duty primarily incumbent upon them. The State shall supervise them in the performance of this duty. . . .
>
> Article 7
>
> 1. The entire school system shall be under the supervision of the State.
>
> 2. Parents and guardians shall have the right to decide whether children should receive religious instruction.
>
> 3. Religious instruction shall form part of the regular curriculum in State schools, with the exception of non-denominational schools. Without prejudice to the State's right of supervision, religious instruction shall be given in accordance with the tenets of the religious community concerned. . . .
>
> 4. The right to establish private schools shall be guaranteed. Private schools that serve as alternatives to State schools shall require the approval of the State and shall be subject to the laws of the *Länder*. Such approval shall be given where private schools are not inferior to State schools in terms of their educational aims, their facilities, or the professional training of their teaching staff, and where segregation of pupils according to the means of their parents will not be encouraged thereby. . . .

The relevant provisions of the Baden-Württemberg School Act are the following:

> Section 72—Compulsory school attendance: pupils' obligations
>
> (1) Compulsory school attendance shall apply to all children and juveniles who are permanently resident . . . in the *Land* of Baden-Württemberg. . . .
>
> (4) . . . The school supervisory authority shall decide on any exemption. . . .
>
> Section 76—Compliance with compulsory school attendance
>
> (1) . . . Alternative tuition instead of primary-school attendance may only be granted in exceptional circumstances. . . .

The applicants complained under . . . the [European Human Rights] Convention . . . of the refusal to allow the applicant parents to educate their children at home in conformity with their own religious beliefs . . .

1. . . . Article 2 [of the EHRC] . . . provides:

> No person shall be denied the right to education. In the exercise of any functions which it assumes in relation to education and to teaching, the State shall respect the right of parents to ensure such education and teaching in conformity with their own religious and philosophical convictions.

The applicant parents submitted that it was their duty to educate their children in accordance with the Bible and Christian values. They inferred from numerous quotations from the Bible that their children's education was an obligation on them which could not easily be transferred to third persons. . . . Their children's attendance of a primary school would inevitably lead to grave conflicts with their personal beliefs as far as syllabus and teaching methods were concerned. Compulsory school attendance would therefore severely endanger their children's religious education, especially regarding sex education and concentration training (as provided in some schools), which in their view amounted to esoteric exercises. . . . As the applicants belonged to a religious minority, there were no private schools which suited their convictions. Moreover, the applicants pointed out that home education was permitted in the United States, Canada, Switzerland, Austria and Norway. Countries such as Denmark, Finland and Ireland provided for home education in their constitution. . . .

Article 2 . . . recognises the role of the State in education as well as the right of parents . . . It aims at safeguarding pluralism in education, which is essential for the preservation of the "democratic society." . . . In view of the power of the modern State, it is above all through State teaching that this aim must be realised.

Furthermore, the second sentence of Article 2 must be read together with the first, which enshrines the right of everyone to education. It is on to this fundamental right that is grafted the right of parents to respect for their religious and philosophical convictions. Therefore, respect is only due to convictions on the part of the parents which do not conflict with the child's right to education, the whole of Article 2 of Protocol No. 1 being dominated by its first sentence. This means that parents may not refuse a child's right to education on the basis of their convictions.

The Court notes that, in the present case, the applicant parents also filed their complaints on behalf of the applicant children. Therefore, it cannot be formally said that the applicant parents are seeking to impose their religious convictions against their children's will. Nevertheless, the Court agrees with the finding of the Freiburg Administrative Court that the applicant children were unable to foresee the consequences of their parents' decision to opt for home education because of their young age. As it would be very difficult for the applicant children to take an autonomous decision for themselves at that age, the Court considers that the above principles apply to the present case. . . .

While some countries permit home education, other States provide for compulsory attendance of State or private schools. . . . German authorities and courts have . . . stressed the fact that not only the acquisition of knowledge but also integration into and first experiences of society are important goals in primary-school education. The German courts found that those objectives could not be met to the same extent by home education, even if it allowed children to acquire the same standard of knowledge as provided by primary-school education. The Court considers that this presumption is not erroneous and falls within the Contracting States' margin of appreciation in setting up and interpreting rules for their education systems. The Federal Constitutional Court stressed the general interest of society in avoiding the emergence of parallel societies based on separate philosophical convictions and the importance of integrating minorities into society. The Court regards this as being in accordance with its own case-law on the importance of pluralism for democracy (see *Refah Partisi and Others v. Turkey* (1998)).

Moreover, . . . the applicant parents were free to educate their children after school and at weekends. Therefore, the parents' right to education in conformity with their religious convictions is not restricted in a disproportionate manner. . . . It follows that this complaint must be rejected as manifestly ill-founded. . . .

2. The applicants also complained that the refusal . . . amounted to a violation of . . . Article 8 of the Convention, which provides:

> 1. Everyone has the right to respect for his private and family life, his home and his correspondence.

> 2. There shall be no interference by a public authority with the exercise of this right except such as is . . . necessary in a democratic society in the interests of national security, public safety or the economic well-being of the country, for the prevention of disorder or crime, for the protection of health or morals, or for the protection of the rights and freedoms of others.

Moreover, the applicants complained of a violation of their freedom of thought, conscience and religion, as guaranteed by Article 9 of the Convention, which provides:

> 1. Everyone has the right to freedom of thought, conscience and religion; this right includes freedom to change his religion or belief and freedom, either alone or in community with others and in public or private, to manifest his religion or belief, in worship, teaching, practice and observance.
>
> 2. Freedom to manifest one's religion or beliefs shall be subject only to such limitations as are . . . necessary in a democratic society in the interests of public safety, for the protection of public order, health or morals, or for the protection of the rights and freedoms of others.

The Court finds that any interference with the applicants' rights under either of these provisions would, for the reasons stated above, be justified . . . in view of the public interest in ensuring the children's education. Therefore, this part of the application is likewise manifestly ill-founded. . . .

3. . . . The Court notes a difference of treatment between the applicant children and other children who have obtained an exemption from compulsory school attendance "in exceptional circumstances". . . . However, . . . such "exceptional circumstances" had been recognised by the school supervisory authorities only in cases in which children were physically unfit to attend school or in which the parents had to move around the country for professional reasons. Such exemptions were granted by the school supervisory authorities because the limited feasibility of school attendance would have caused undue hardship for those children. Those exemptions were hence granted for merely practical reasons, whereas the applicants sought to obtain an exemption for religious purposes. Therefore, the Court finds that the above distinction justifies a difference of treatment. . . .

Other European countries that do not allow homeschooling include Greece and Spain, whose cultures are significantly different from Germany's. What is common among them that might explain their shared aversion to homeschooling?

The U.S. Constitution does not enumerate a right of children to education. What resistance would you expect to a proposed amendment to add language like that in Article 2 of the European Convention? Some state constitutions do declare a right to education, but who would assert that right in behalf of a child whose parents want to keep them home and give them only religious instruction? What has been proposed at the federal level is instead a constitutional amendment to strengthen protection for parents whose beliefs or preferences conflict with child welfare laws. In the 2007-2008 session of Congress, H.J. Res. 97 died in subcommittee. It would have amended the Constitution to say: "The liberty of parents to direct the upbringing and education of their children is a fundamental right." and "Neither the United States nor any State shall infringe upon this right without demonstrating that its governmental interest as applied to the person is of the highest order and not otherwise served." This would impose strict scrutiny when parents assert religious (or even non-religious) objections to laws limiting their power over children's lives, whereas after Employment Division v. Smith, 494 U.S. 872 (1990), only rational basis review applies when people assert religious objections to laws that limit their power over their own lives but that do not infringe some other, fundamental right. Is that backwards? Should not a free exercise claim be stronger when opposed to a law restricting self-determining freedom than when opposed to a law restricting control over another person's life?

Homeschooling in the United States Today

Kimberly A. Yuracko, Education off the Grid: Constitutional Constraints on Homeschooling

96 Cal. L. Rev. 123, 124-129, 156-157 (2008)

. . . Homeschooling was common in the United States before the nineteenth century, but by the early 1980s the practice was illegal in most states. . . . Today, homeschooling is legal in all states. Estimates of the number of children currently homeschooled range from 1.1 to 2 million. The 1.1 million estimate represents 2.2 percent of the school-age population in the country. . . . [T]he number of children receiving their education through homeschooling is growing at a rate of ten to twenty percent per year.

The modern homeschool movement arose in the 1950s and was originally dominated by liberals and educational progressives. . . . Many believed that traditional schools were rigid and intellectually stifling. . . . By the early 1990's, however, homeschooling had expanded and divided into two distinct movements: one secular and the other conservative Christian. . . . The Christian homeschooling movement came to dominate its secular counterpart in size, profile and political influence. In other words, while homeschoolers themselves continue to be a diverse lot, the homeschooling movement has become defined and driven by its conservative Christian majority.

At the heart of the Christian homeschooling movement is the Home School Legal Defense Association (HSLDA). HSLDA's commitment to ensuring parents' unfettered right to homeschool flows from two core ideological beliefs. The first is a belief in parental control—indeed ownership—of children. . . . The second is a belief in the need for Christian families to separate and shield their children from harmful secular social values . . . : "the acceptability of homosexuality as an alternative lifestyle; the acceptability of premarital sex as long as it is 'safe'; the acceptability of relativistic moral standards." . . . For the last two decades HSLDA has opposed virtually all state oversight and regulation of homeschooling. . . . [F]ormer U.S. Representative Bill Godling from Pennsylvania, the former chair of the House Committee of Education and the Workforce, called homeschoolers "the most effective educational lobby on Capitol Hill." . . . HSLDA has devoted its resources to challenging teacher certification requirements for homeschool teachers, subject matter requirements for homeschools, testing requirements for homeschooled children, and home inspection visits of homeschools. . . . [T]en states . . . do not even require homeschooling parents to notify the state of their intent to homeschool. . . .

A review of popular Christian homeschooling curricula, books and websites reveals an ideology of female subservience and rigid gender role differentiation. Prominent homeschool curricula, for example, emphasize that girls should be subordinate to their fathers and later their husbands. Vision Forum Ministries, a group founded by a leading homeschool advocate and influential among Christian homeschoolers, posts articles on its website asserting that women belong exclusively in the private domestic sphere. Several articles assert that women should not work outside the home, with one contending that "God does not allow women to vote." Not surprisingly, this ideology of constraint also has something to say about girls' education. In So Much More, for example, a book written by two homeschooled sisters and currently popular in the Christian homeschool community, the authors argued that college is dangerous for young women because it diverts them from their God-ordained role as helpmeets for their fathers and husbands. Under existing laws, it is impossible to know how often and to what extent such beliefs lead to significantly inferior substantive educations for homeschooled girls. . . .

Though *Yoder* essentially established a right of Amish parents to home school their children in their own way, the Court was careful to limit its holding just to schooling after eighth grade and to long-standing separatist religious communities. In a few subsequent cases, members of other religious groups cited *Yoder* in support of claims to home school their children free of any state oversight, but lower courts read *Yoder* as establishing a right to exemption from compulsory schooling only for the Amish and Mennonites. Yet every state today authorizes all parents to keep children of all ages entirely out of schools and instead to provide instruction at home, and most states leave home schools virtually unregulated. Why would legislators choose to do this?

In most states, the authorization to home school is explicit in statutes. E.g., Del. Code Ann. tit. 14, §2703A ("For purposes of this chapter, a "homeschool" shall be considered a non-public school."). In others, courts have read this authorization into the law. For example, the Texas statute above does not refer to homeschooling per se, but the Texas Supreme Court has held that the exemption for "private school" includes a home school. And Texas law has no requirements relating to home schools. This is true also in Virginia for parents who home school for religious reasons, by virtue of the statutory provision noted above excusing religious objectors altogether from the schooling requirement, and the state generally does not demand proof of religious belief. In most other states as well, there is no real regulation of home schools; parents might fulfill their duty relating to education simply by notifying the state education department of their intention to home school. Many states do require that home-school instructors have some minimal qualification, but this might be nothing more than a high school diploma. Only a minority of states make a real effort to ensure that home-schooled students progress academically, for example, by requiring home instructors to administer standardized tests or to submit curricula or pupil portfolios to education officials. See Courtenay E. Moran, *How to Regulate Homeschooling: Why History Supports the Theory of Parental Choice*, 2011 Ill. L. Rev. 1061 (2011).

Thus, the duty that most distinguishes the parental role from that of a guardian for an incompetent adult, the duty to secure an education, is in most states slight or nonexistent. Parents need not send their children to a "school," and regardless of whether they send their children to a school or instead purport to home school, states impose no real requirements for what transpires in the chosen school. Professor Yuracko maintains that this violates a basic right of children to a minimally adequate education, a right arguably enshrined in state constitutional mandates that all children have access to an education and in the federal constitution's Fourteenth Amendment Due Process Clause. See Yuracko, *supra,* 96 Cal. L. Rev. at 135-142.

In 2008, a California intermediate court shocked the education world by ruling that California law did not permit homeschooling except by parents who are state-certified teachers, and that this did not violate parents' rights. However, the court later reversed itself. The later opinion reveals that homeschooling presents danger for interests of children in addition to the educational ones that Professor Yuracko identifies. It also sets out the regulatory scheme in one of the most regulation-heavy U.S. states.

Jonathan L. v. Superior Court

165 Cal. App. 4th 1074 (Cal. Ct. App. 2008)

Croskey, J.

. . . The family in this case had a history of dependency court proceedings involving charges of physical abuse, neglect, and failure to prevent sexual abuse. After the two youngest children were declared dependent due to the abuse and neglect of their siblings, their attorney sought an order that they be sent to private or public school, rather than educated at home by their mother, so that they would be in regular contact with mandatory reporters of abuse and neglect. The dependency court declined to issue such an order, primarily based on its view that parents have an absolute constitutional right to home school their children. The children's counsel sought relief in this court. . . .

We filed our original opinion . . . granting the petition on the bases that: (1) California statutory law does not permit home schooling; and (2) this prohibition does not violate the U.S. Constitution. We subsequently granted the father's petition for rehearing. . . .

The intervention began in 1987, when father physically abused his eldest daughter. She was not adjudicated dependent, however, as she went to live with her mother in order to avoid further abuse from father. Father next physically abused a second daughter. She was declared dependent due to physical abuse and taken from parents' custody. Father continued his abusive behavior, and, in the instant proceeding, Rachel was declared dependent due to physical abuse by him. Throughout this time, mother was aware of the physical abuse, yet failed to protect the children.[5] . . . Jonathan and Mary Grace . . . were declared dependent in the instant case due to the abuse of their siblings.

Throughout the instant dependency proceeding, the parents have been uncooperative. When Jonathan and Mary Grace were ordered detained, mother fled and attempted to hide the children from the authorities. When . . . parents were directed to allow the social workers and the attorney appointed for the children to interview the children without parents being present and to visit the children in the home . . . , parents limited the social workers' access . . . and coached the children not to talk. . . .

. . . Rachel, who was home schooled by mother, believed she should attend public school. DCFS amended the petition to allege that Rachel was dependent on the additional basis that parents' refusal to send her to public school placed her at risk of serious

5. Additionally, a previous dependency proceeding was based on the sexual abuse of one of the parents' daughters. Leonard C., a frequent visitor to the household, was considered a possible perpetrator of the abuse and parents were directed not to allow him in the home. The parents complied, but once the petition had been dismissed, parents allowed Leonard C. to return, whereupon he sexually abused Rachel. The parents' failure to protect Rachel from this sexual abuse was another basis for her dependency.

emotional damage. . . . All eight of the family's children have been home schooled. Mother, who had completed 11th grade, was the primary teacher. The children worked from "education packs," which were prepared educational materials in different subjects. Mother would give the children assignments from their workbooks, and they would read in the book and fill out the necessary worksheets.[7] If the children needed help with a particular assignment, they would ask mother, who would further explain to them. Sometimes the older children helped the younger ones with their work. . . .

The children were home schooled through Sunland Christian School. Sunland is a private school that teaches via independent study in the students' homes. . . . Sunland interviews and supervises all parents to make certain that they are capable of teaching. Sunland requires the parents to teach for at least 3 hours per day for 175 days per year, although "[t]he parent/teacher is required to continue the school day until the appropriate amount of work is completed per student." . . . One of Rachel's older sisters had graduated from Sunland and intended to attend college. Another sister had completed Sunland but failed to graduate, receiving only a certificate of completion. . . . Rachel's most recent scores on a standardized test . . . indicated that she was achieving at or near grade level in some subjects, and substantially below grade level in others.

1. CALIFORNIA LAW REGARDING HOME SCHOOLING

California Constitution . . . provides, "A general diffusion of knowledge and intelligence being essential to the preservation of the rights and liberties of the people, the Legislature shall encourage by all suitable means the promotion of intellectual, scientific, moral, and agricultural improvement." The state is responsible for educating all California children.[17] Education plays an indispensable role in the modern state. "This role, we believe, has two significant aspects: First, education is a major determinant of an individual's chances for economic and social success in our competitive society; second, education is a unique influence on a child's development as a citizen and his participation in political and community life." It is "the lifeline of both the individual and society."

In addition to the political and economic contributions of education, there is also a social dimension to the state's interest in education. "[E]ducation serves as a 'unifying social force' among our varied population, promoting cohesion based upon democratic values. The public schools bring together members of different racial and cultural groups and, hopefully, help them to live together '"in harmony and mutual respect."'" "In addition to the particular skills taught, group activities encourage active participation in community affairs, promote the development of leadership qualities, and instill a spirit of collective endeavor. These results are directly linked to the constitutional role of education in preserving democracy, as set forth in article IX, section 1. . . ."

California satisfies its obligation to educate its children by means of the compulsory education law. Education Code §48200 provides: "Each person between the ages of 6 and 18 years . . . is subject to compulsory full-time education [and] . . . shall attend the public full-time day school. . . . [E]ach parent . . . shall send the pupil to the public full-time day

7. . . . The dependency court noted that the family was using education packs with copyright dates of 1978 and 1979.

17. [T]here are over 6,200,000 students in California's public schools, . . . over 500,000 students in California's private schools. . . . [I]t is estimated that there are approximately 166,000 students being home schooled in California.

school . . . for the full . . . schoolday. . . ."[18] . . . There are two exemptions relevant to this case: the private school exemption and the private tutor exemption.

(1) Private School Exemption

. . . Education Code §48222 . . . provides, "Children who are being instructed in a *private full-time day school by persons capable of teaching* shall be exempted. Such school shall . . . be taught in the English language and shall offer instruction in the several branches of study required to be taught in the public schools of the state. The attendance of the pupils shall be kept by private school authorities in a register. . . . Exemptions under this section shall be valid only after verification . . . that the private school has complied with the provisions of §33190. . . . The verification . . . shall not be construed as an evaluation, recognition, approval, or endorsement of any private school or course."

Education Code §33190 requires "[e]very person . . . conducting private school instruction on the elementary or high school level" to, between October 1 and 15 of every year, "file with the Superintendent of Public Instruction an affidavit . . . by the owner or other head" setting forth . . . "The . . . place of doing business . . ."; "The names and addresses . . . of the directors, if any, and the principal officers . . ."; and "The school enrollment, by grades, number of teachers, coeducational or enrollment limited to boys or girls and boarding facilities." The affidavit must also contain a statement that "the following records are maintained at the address stated, and are true and accurate: (1) The records required to be kept by §48222. (2) The courses of study offered by the institution. (3) The names and addresses . . . of its faculty, together with a record of the educational qualifications of each." The affidavit must also affirm that "[c]riminal record summary information has been obtained pursuant to §44237."

(2) Private Tutor Exemption

. . . Education Code §48224 . . . provides, "Children not attending a private, full-time, day school and who are being instructed in study and recitation for at least three hours a day for 175 days each calendar year by a private tutor or other person in the several branches of study required to be taught in the public schools of this state and in the English language shall be exempted. The tutor or other person shall hold a valid state credential for the grade taught. The instruction shall be offered between the hours of 8 o'clock A.M. and 4 o'clock P.M."

It cannot reasonably be argued that home schooling conducted by a parent who is *not* a certificated teacher satisfies the private tutor exemption from the compulsory education law. . . . Thus, we turn to principal question in this case: whether a home school can be considered a private school. . . . The term "private full-time day school" could include home schools, or it could refer solely to institutions outside the home, which we term "traditional private schools." . . .

The compulsory education law was initially enacted in 1903. . . . A child was exempt under the statute upon proof "that such child is being taught in a private school, or by a private tutor, or at home by any person capable of teaching, in such branches as are

18. . . . If it appears that the parent has committed a violation, the secretary of the board (or the attendance supervisor) shall refer the parent to a school attendance review board. If the parent still continually and willfully fails to comply, the school attendance review board shall direct the school district to file . . . a criminal complaint charging the violation. . . . The first conviction results in a fine of no more than $100; the penalty for a second conviction is a fine of no more than $250. Subsequent convictions can result in a fine of up to $500. In lieu of fines, the court may order participation in a parent education and counseling program. . . . [T]ruancy of a child who fails to attend school as required . . . could culminate with a declaration that the child is a ward of the juvenile court.

usually taught in the primary and grammar schools of this state." By its express terms, the statute allowed for home schooling by any person capable of teaching. . . .

When the School Code was reenacted [in 1923], the provision regarding the private tutor exemption changed. No longer could a child be tutored by a person "capable of teaching." Now, "Such tutor or other person shall hold a valid state credential for the grade taught." . . . It appears, then, that the Legislature's intent was *not* to permit home schools as part of the private school exemption.

However, in 1991, the Legislature enacted an uncodified law providing, "Notwithstanding §33190 . . . of the Education Code, . . . the State Department of Education shall expend no funds to prepare . . . a compilation of information on private schools with five or fewer students." . . . While it is possible that some private schools with five or fewer students are, in fact, traditional private schools in which the teacher is unrelated to the students, it is much more likely that the private schools referred to by this law are home schools. . . .

Education Code §44237(a) provides that every private school shall require each applicant for employment to submit fingerprints for criminal record checks. The statute, however, exempts "a parent or guardian working exclusively with his or her children." . . . This language was intended to exempt parents and guardians employed in home study programs . . . if they worked exclusively with their own children. From this legislative history, it seems clear that the Legislature both *understood* that some parents home school their children by designating their home schools as private schools, and *sought to benefit* those parents by exempting them from the fingerprint requirement. . . .

The integrity of the apparently contradictory provisions can be maintained if we simply conclude that the compulsory education law is to be interpreted to permit home schools to operate as private schools. . . . If a statute is susceptible of two constructions, one of which renders it constitutional and the other unconstitutional (or raises serious and doubtful constitutional questions), the court will adopt the construction which will render it free from doubt as to its constitutionality. . . . If home schools are not permitted in California unless under the private tutor exemption (requiring the tutor to be credentialed), this raises difficult constitutional questions. . . .

While parents generally have a parental liberty interest, California also has recognized that the "welfare of a child is a compelling state interest that a state has not only a right, but a duty, to protect." . . . *Yoder* recognized that "the power of a parent, even when linked to a free exercise claim, may be subject to limitation . . . if it appears that parental decisions will jeopardize the health or safety of the child." "[A] parent's own constitutionally protected 'liberty' includes the right to 'bring up children', and to 'direct the upbringing and education of children.' As against the state, this parental duty and right is subject to limitation only 'if it appears that parental decisions will jeopardize the health or safety of the child, or have a potential for significant social burdens.'"

We therefore consider the constitutionality of allowing a dependency court to restrict home schooling in order to satisfy the compelling governmental interest of the child's safety. To pose the question is to answer it. We emphasize that we are here concerned with a proceeding in *dependency*. In this case, the restriction on home schooling would arise in a proceeding in which the children *have already been found dependent due to abuse and neglect of a sibling*. We are therefore not concerned with the interference with the rights of a *fit* parent; the parents in dependency have been judicially determined not to be fit. . . . "The juvenile court '"stands *in loco parentis* to the minor in a proceeding whose primary consideration is the minor's welfare."'" . . .

Should a dependency court conclude, in the proper exercise of its discretion, that due to the history of abuse and neglect in the family, requiring a dependent child to have regular contact with mandated reporters is necessary to guarantee the child's safety, that order would satisfy strict scrutiny. There can be no dispute that the child's safety is a compelling governmental interest. Restricting home schooling also appears to be narrowly tailored to achieving that goal. Without contact with mandated reporters, it may well be that the child's safety cannot be guaranteed without removing the child from the parents' *custody*.[33] As such, the restriction on home schooling would be the least restrictive means of achieving the goal of protecting the children; they would be permitted to continue to live at home with their parents, but their educators would change in order to provide them an extra layer of protection. . . .

[W]e will remand for the trial court to consider whether the safety of the children necessitates removing them from home schooling. . . .

We close with an observation that the fact that home schooling is permitted in California as the result of implicit legislative recognition rather than explicit legislative action has resulted in a near absence of objective criteria and oversight for home schooling. In this regard, while we do not attempt a comprehensive review of other states' requirements, we note some of the methods used by other states to guarantee that their home schooled children are receiving an adequate education. In some, discretion to approve home schooling is granted to state, county or district officials.[36] In several, capable teaching is assured by requiring the parent to possess a certain minimum level of education in order to home school, generally a high school diploma or its equivalent.[37] Various states require home schooling parents to regularly submit documents—either reports or samples of the children's work—to authorities. . . .[38] A few states measure home schooling students' progress by means of standardized testing, although alternative means of evaluation are often permitted.[39] In several states, if a child fails to demonstrate sufficient progress, the home schooling of that child is placed on probation, or terminated altogether.[40] A number of states require home visits, although there is some dispute

33. In this regard, we note the following colloquy between the trial court and father:

"The Court: You know where I get about 99 percent of my referrals of sexual abuse?

"The Father: I know what you are going to say. From the public school system.

"The Court: Amazing, isn't it? That is exactly correct.

"The Father: Is that the purpose of the public school system[ ]?

"The Court: One of the purposes of a teacher, one of the obligations is to report abuse, be it physical or sexual, and it is just amazing when little Jenny goes to school and is totally depressed or has got bruises all over them, that a teacher just—what is the matter, Jenny? And Jenny says, I've been struck by Mr. [C.] or he is playing around with me in places that he shouldn't be playing."

"The Father: There is also a lot of time when they say stuff that isn't true.

"The Court: Well, that may be, but because the children are-

"The Father: The panacea for our society is not to have a world of snitches that are going to be there to say things that aren't necessarily true or not."

36. See, e.g., Fla. Stat., §1003.26 [approval by a "home education review committee," which reviews the student's portfolio every 30 days until it deems the program satisfactory]; La.; N.M.; Ohio; Pa.; Vt.; *Care and Protection of Charles* (Mass. 1987) (upholding an advance approval requirement against a constitutional challenge); *State v. Riddle* (W. Va. 1981).

37. See, e.g., Ga.; N.M.; N.C.; Pa.; S.C.; Tenn. Code Ann., §49-6-3050, subd. (b) (high school diploma sufficient to home school through 8th grade; further education required to home school at high school level). Ohio permits a parent without a high school diploma to home school only if supervised. North Dakota requires a baccalaureate degree to home school, and will permit a high school graduate to home school only if monitored.

38. E.g., Iowa; Minn.; Md.; Ohio; Pa.; S.C.; Vt.; Va. Code Ann., §22.1-254.1; *Combs v. Homer Center School Dist.* (W.D. Pa. 2006) (upholding such a requirement against a constitutional challenge).

39. E.g., Ark.; Colo.; Fla.; Ga.; Haw.; Minn.

40. E.g., Colo.; Fla.; Md.

among the courts which have considered the issue whether requiring home visits is a constitutional limitation on parental rights.[41]

A few states have comprehensive regulations imposing several different requirements. For example, New York has promulgated regulations which require: (1) the parent to send an individualized home instruction plan for each student to the school district each year; (2) quarterly reports; (3) an annual assessment including a standardized achievement test (or alternative means of review); (4) a plan of remediation if the student falls below the 33rd percentile on a standardized test; and (5) possible termination of home schooling if the remediation objectives are not met within two years.

In contrast, California impliedly allows parents to home school as a private school, but has provided no enforcement mechanism. As long as the local school district verifies that a private school affidavit has been filed, there is no provision for further oversight of a home school. It appears that the propriety of any parent's home schooling will arise only in dependency (or family law) proceedings, as in this case, or in a prosecution for failing to comply with the compulsory education law. Given the state's compelling interest in educating all of its children, and the absence of an express statutory and regulatory framework for home schooling in California, additional clarity in this area of the law would be helpful.

Does the court's reasoning violate any canons of statutory interpretation that the court did not mention? Arguably the court's interpretation of the statutes is dictum, because unnecessary to its holding, which was essentially that child maltreatment law trumps whatever the statutes say about the permissibility of homeschooling.

Do California statutes, as interpreted by the court in this case, effectively empower parents to deprive their children of what the state regards as an education? How far could private schools and home schools depart from what happens in public schools without violating the law? Are the regulations in any other states that are mentioned adequate to protect children's educational interests?

Suppose the state legislature decided to ban homeschooling because of concerns about ideological rigidity, inadequate socialization, and/or sexist instruction and treatment of pupils. Would those concerns be sufficient to override parental free exercise rights as articulated in *Prince* and *Yoder*?

e. Medical Neglect

Just as a married person has a duty to secure medical care for a seriously ill or injured spouse who is unable to do so independently, parents have a duty to do the same for their children. The basic duty expressed in neglect laws generally does not extend to routine examinations or preventive care, but only to remediation of significant threats to a child's health, though that can include attention to parasitic invasions such as lice and tooth decay. Vaccinations are typically a pre-condition for enrolling a child in a school, so for most parents (but not homeschoolers) there is effectively a duty to obtain them,

41. Compare *Battles v. Anne Arundel County Bd. of Educ.* (4th Cir. 1996) 95 F.3d 41; *Matter of Kilroy* (N.Y. Fam. Ct. 1983) (upholding monitoring requirement); with *Brunelle v. Lynn Public Schools* (1998) 428 Mass. 512 (monitoring is not necessary when standardized testing shows sufficient progress).

embodied in states' education codes. Nearly all states, however, exempt from this duty parents who object to immunization on religious grounds, and some have a broader exemption applying to "philosophical" objections as well. Physical examinations are typically a pre-condition only for a child's participation in school sports programs.

Even as to serious illnesses and injury, there is again special provision in the law for parents who object on ideological grounds to the legal duty. The great majority of states have a religious exemption to the medical care aspect of their neglect laws. See, e.g., Colo. Rev. Stat. §19-3-103 ("No child who in lieu of medical treatment is under treatment solely by spiritual means through prayer in accordance with a recognized method of religious healing shall, for that reason alone, be considered to have been neglected or dependent within the purview of this article."). Cf. Ind. Code §31-34-1-14 ("If a parent . . . fails to provide specific medical treatment for a child because of the legitimate and genuine practice of the religious beliefs of the parent . . . , a rebuttable presumption arises that the child is not a child in need of services because of the failure.").

Many states created these exemptions in the mid-1970s, when Congress made it a condition for receiving federal grants for child protection, and most retained the exemptions even after Congress removed this condition in 1983. A few states limit application to or refer explicitly to Christian Scientists, the group largely responsible for inclusion of the exceptions, even though there are many other groups that also oppose conventional medical care. For example, Connecticut statutes provide that "treatment of any child by a Christian Science practitioner in lieu of treatment by a licensed practitioner of the healing arts shall not of itself constitute maltreatment." Conn. Gen. Stat. §17a-104. But most states confer an exemption to a broader class of parents—all those who choose just to pray or engage in other forms of "spiritual treatment."

These exceptions effectively entitle certain religiously motivated parents to deny their children medical care up to a point. However, such states also authorize courts to order medical care over parental objection, where some standard of need is met (e.g., to avoid preventable death or to prevent "grievous" injury). For example, Colorado statutes state: "[If a] court determines . . . that the child is in a life-threatening situation or that the child's condition will result in serious disability, the court may . . . order that medical treatment be provided for the child. A child whose parent, guardian, or legal custodian inhibits or interferes with the provision of medical treatment in accordance with a court order shall be considered to have been neglected or dependent for the purposes of this article and injured or endangered for the purposes of [criminal child abuse statute]." Colo. Rev. Stat. §19-3-103. See also Ind. Code §31-34-1-14 (stating that the presumption quoted above "does not . . . [p]revent a juvenile court from ordering, when the health of a child requires, medical services from a physician licensed to practice medicine in Indiana" nor apply "to situations in which the life or health of a child is in serious danger").

You might wonder what Colorado means by "a recognized method of religious healing." The Colorado statute goes on to say that a practice is presumptively so if the IRS treats fees for the practice as a deductible medical expense, if most private insurance companies treat such fees as covered medical expenses, or if the practice "provides a rate of success in maintaining health and treating disease or injury that is equivalent to that of medical treatment." It might surprise you to know that the IRS treats payments to Christian Scientist spiritual healers as a deductible medical expense. See Rev. Rul. 55-261, 1955-1 C.B. 307, 307 (1955) (stating allowance of deduction for "authorized Christian Science practitioners"). But cf. 26 U.S.C.A. §213 (disallowing a deduction for a weight loss program). And that the federal Medicaid/Medicare statute requires states to reimburse "religious nonmedical health care institutions" for nonmedical care provided to people who object on religious grounds to medical care. See Children's Healthcare Is a Legal Duty v. De Parle, 212 F.3d 1084 (8th Cir. 2000), *cert. denied*, 121 S. Ct. 1483 (2001) (upholding this provision in 42 U.S.C. §1395x(ss)(1) against Establishment Clause challenge). Do these financial subsidies make the federal and state governments partly responsible for the suffering and deaths of children whose parents forego medical care in favor of "religious healing"?

The expectation reflected in the provision for court-ordered treatment is that children will get the needed medical care without the state having to charge parents with neglect. However, child protection workers typically do not learn about such cases until a child has died or has already incurred permanent damage or suffered much pain. See Wenday Glauser, *United States Still too Lenient on "Faith Healing" Parents, Say Children's Rights Advocates*," Canadian Med. Assoc. J., Aug. 9, 2011. Some states make "spiritual treatment practitioners" mandatory reporters of child neglect, in the hope that these situations will come to the state's attention. See, e.g., Ohio Rev. Code Ann. §2151.421. But religious healers resist reporting, and the spiritual treatment exception in the medical neglect definition could lead them to believe they do not need to make reports at all. For these and other reasons, tragic child deaths continue to occur. In 1998, Rita Swan, a former Christian Scientist and the founder of the leading U.S. organization opposed to religious medical care exemptions, Children's Health Care Is a Legal Duty, Inc., co-authored a study of 172 deaths of children from whom medical care was withheld on religious grounds, in which they found that 140 of the children would have had at least a 90 percent likelihood of survival with medical care. See Seth Asser & Rita Swan, *Child Fatalities from Religion Motivated Medical Neglect*, 101 Pediatrics 625, 625-629 (Apr. 1998). Such deaths continue to occur at a rate of at least ten a year in the United States. See Alicia Galegos, *Miracle vs. Medicine: When Faith Puts Care at Risk*, Am. Med. News, Sept. 19, 2011. Parents might be charged for criminal child neglect, but even if convicted they typically receive a light penalty. See, e.g., id. (reporting 2011 case in which an Alabama mother whose teen son died of untreated pneumonia received only a suspended six-month sentence; a 2010 case in which Pennsylvania parents whose two-year-old died of untreated pneumonia received a sentence of just ten years probation; a 2009 case in which an Oregon father whose 15-month-old died of untreated pneumonia was sentenced to 60 days in jail; and a 2009 case in which Wisconsin parents whose 11-year-old died of untreated diabetes received a prison sentence of 30 days per year for six years).

Parents adhering to a religious faith opposed to medical care naturally assert an entitlement to act on their faith, as an aspect of their First Amendment freedom of religious exercise. Courts always reject that assertion when a child has died. In the small number of reported decisions on child protection agency petitions for a court order of treatment, most courts have adopted a position similar to that reflected in the Colorado statute—that is, that danger of death or serious disability justifies infringement of parents' supposed constitutional right, but that danger of less serious harm or simply suffering does not. See Jessie Hill, *Whose Body? Whose Soul? Medical Decision-making on Behalf of Children and the Free Exercise Clause Before and After* Employment Division v. Smith, 32 Cardozo L. Rev. 1857 (2011). In contrast, the prevailing rule in Europe appears to be that courts should order medical care over parental religious objection whenever physicians recommend it. See Norman Doe, Law and Religion in Europe: A Comparative Introduction (2011), 230-231. Indeed, European officials appear quite willing to prohibit parents from involving children in religious activities that the officials believe to pose a risk to health. See id. at 231 (noting cases relating to the Church of Scientology and the Sahaja Yoga movement).

In criminal prosecutions in the United States of parents whose children die, parents sometimes also assert a procedural due process type of objection, that the state sends mixed messages, by suggesting in civil neglect laws that using only spiritual treatment is not neglectful but then prosecuting under criminal neglect laws. Courts have divided on whether to accept that defense. See, e.g., Commonwealth v. Twitchell, 617 N.E.2d 609 (Mass. 1993) (rejecting the defense); State v. McKown, 475 N.W.2d 63 (Minn. 1991) (accepting the defense).

In cases involving adolescents who share their parents' opposition to medical care, most courts have rejected parents' argument that their adolescent offspring were constitutionally entitled to make the decision themselves or that the state must adopt a "mature minor" rule. See, e.g., Commonwealth v. Nixon, 761 A.2d 1151 (1999) (rejecting mature-minor defense to charges of involuntary manslaughter and endangering the welfare of a child after 16-year-old died from untreated diabetes). But at least one state's highest court has adopted the rule. See In re E.G., a Minor, 549 N.E.2d 322 (Ill. 1989) (in neglect proceeding involving 17-year-old with leukemia who needed blood transfusions, holding that parent who acquiesced in mature minor's decision to reject life-sustaining medical treatment is not guilty of neglect). See also A.C. v. Manitoba (Director of Child and Family Services), 2009 SCC 30; [2009] 2 S.C.R. 181 (Canadian Supreme Court decision upholding court order of blood transfusions for 14-year-old child of Jehovah's Witnesses who had Crohn's disease, but stating that the views of mature minors generally must be respected in religious medical neglect cases, so long as they do not endanger their lives).

In the context of preventive care, courts (in contrast to legislatures) have given very little weight to parents' religious beliefs, even though the danger to children seems much more remote than in medical neglect cases. Part of the explanation is that there is specific U.S. Supreme Court precedent for the constitutionality of the state forcing even adults to receive vaccinations.

Workman v. Mingo County Board of Education

419 F. App'x 348 (4th Cir. 2011)

WYNN, Circuit Judge:

Plaintiff Jennifer Workman . . . is the mother of two school-aged children: M.W. and S.W. S.W. suffers from health problems that appeared around the time she began receiving vaccinations. In light of S.W.'s health problems, Workman chose not to vaccinate M.W. Workman's decision not to allow vaccination of M.W. ran afoul of West Virginia law, which provides that no child shall be admitted to any of the schools of the state until the child has been immunized for diphtheria, polio, rubeola, rubella, tetanus, and whooping cough. W. Va. Code §16-3-4. . . . The statute exempts a person who presents a certificate from a reputable physician showing that immunization for these diseases "is impossible or improper or other sufficient reason why such immunizations have not been done." . . . Workman obtained a Permanent Medical Exemption ("the certificate") from Dr. John MacCallum, a child psychiatrist[, but] . . . Dr. Cathy Slemp, the acting head of the West Virginia Department of Health and Human Resources, . . . recommend[ed] Workman's request for medical exemption be denied. . . .

Workman brought suit individually and as parent and guardian of her minor child, M.W. . . . against the Mingo County Board of Education; . . . State Superintendant of Schools; Dwight Dials, Superintendant of Mingo County Schools; and the West Virginia Department of Health and Human Resources. . . . Workman . . . alleged that Defendants' denial of her application for a medical exemption violated her First Amendment rights . . . [,] constituted a denial of Equal Protection and Due Process[, and] violated West Virginia Code Section 16-3-4. . . .

III.

. . . Workman argues that the laws requiring vaccination substantially burden the free exercise of her religion and therefore merit strict scrutiny. Defendants reply that the Supreme Court in *Employment Div., Dep't of Human Res. of Or. v. Smith* (1990), abandoned the compelling interest test, and that the statute should be upheld under rational basis review. Workman counters that *Smith* preserved an exception for education-related laws that burden religion. We observe that there is a circuit split over the validity of this "hybrid-rights" exception. However, we do not need to decide this issue here because, even assuming for the sake of argument that strict scrutiny applies, prior decisions from the Supreme Court guide us to conclude that West Virginia's vaccination laws withstand such scrutiny.

Over a century ago, in *Jacobson v. Massachusetts* (1905), the Supreme Court considered the constitutionality of a statute that authorized a municipal board of health to require and enforce vaccination. Proceeding under the statute, the board of health of Cambridge, Massachusetts, in response to an epidemic, adopted a regulation requiring its inhabitants to be vaccinated against smallpox. Upon review, the Supreme Court held that the legislation represented a valid exercise of the state's police power, concluding "we do not perceive that this legislation has invaded *any right* secured by the Federal Constitution."

In *Prince v. Massachusetts* (1944), the Supreme Court considered a parent's challenge to a child labor regulation on the basis of the Free Exercise Clause. The Court explained that the state's "authority is not nullified merely because the parent grounds his claim to control the child's course of conduct on religion or conscience. Thus, he cannot claim freedom from compulsory vaccination for the child more than for himself on religious grounds." The Court concluded that "[t]he right to practice religion freely does not include liberty to expose the community or the child to communicable disease or the latter to ill health or death."

. . . Workman also argues that because West Virginia law requires vaccination against diseases that are not very prevalent, no compelling state interest can exist. On the contrary, the state's wish to prevent the spread of communicable diseases clearly constitutes a compelling interest. . . . This conclusion is buttressed by the opinions of numerous federal and state courts that have reached similar conclusions in comparable cases. *See, e.g., McCarthy v. Boozman* (W.D. Ark. 2002) ("The constitutional right to freely practice one's religion does not provide an exemption for parents seeking to avoid compulsory immunization for their school-aged children."); *Sherr v. Northport-East Northport Union Free Sch. Dist.* (E.D. N.Y. 1987) ("[I]t has been settled law for many years that claims of religious freedom must give way in the face of the compelling interest of society in fighting the spread of contagious diseases through mandatory inoculation programs."); *Davis v. State* (Md. 1982) ("Maryland's compulsory immunization program clearly furthers the important governmental objective of eliminating and preventing certain communicable diseases."); *Cude v. State* (Ark. 1964) ("According to the great weight of authority, it is within the police power of the State to require that school children be vaccinated against smallpox, and that such requirement does not violate the constitutional rights of anyone, on religious grounds or otherwise.").

IV.

. . . Workman notes that the statute does not provide an exemption for those with sincere religious beliefs contrary to vaccination. She argues that the statute therefore discriminates on the basis of religion. The district court ruled that, although a state may provide a religious exemption to mandatory vaccination, it need not do so. The Supreme Court held as much in *Zucht v. King* (1922), where it considered an equal protection and due process challenge to ordinances in San Antonio, Texas, that prohibited a child from attending school without a certificate of vaccination. The Court stated that *Jacobson* "settled that it is within the police power of a State to provide for compulsory vaccination." "A long line of decisions by this court . . . also settled that in the exercise of the police power reasonable classification may be freely applied, and that regulation is not violative of the equal protection clause merely because it is not all-embracing." Further, in *Prince*, . . . [t]he Supreme Court explained that . . . "there is no denial of equal protection in excluding [Jehovah's Witnesses'] children from doing [on the streets] what no other children may do."

Here, Workman does not explain how the statute at issue is facially discriminatory; indeed, her complaint is not that it targets a particular religious belief but that it provides no exception from general coverage for hers.[1] . . .

V.

Workman next argues that denying her a religious exemption from the mandatory vaccination statute violates her substantive due process right to do what she reasonably believes is best for her child. Workman asserts that, because the statute infringes upon a fundamental right it must withstand strict scrutiny. . . .

The Due Process Clause "provides heightened protection against government interference with certain fundamental rights and liberty interests." To determine whether an asserted right is a fundamental right subject to strict scrutiny under the Clause, a court must (1) consider whether the asserted right is deeply rooted in the Nation's history and tradition; and (2) require a careful description of the asserted liberty interest. . . .

As in *Boone v. Boozman* (E.D. Ark. 2002), "the question presented by the facts of this case is whether the special protection of the Due Process Clause includes a parent's right to refuse to have her child immunized before attending public or private school where immunization is a precondition to attending school." We agree with other courts that have considered this question in holding that Workman has no such fundamental right. *See Zucht*; *Boone*; *Bd. of Educ. of Mountain Lakes v. Maas* (N.J. Super. Ct. App. Div. 1959). Indeed, the Supreme Court has consistently recognized that a state may constitutionally

1. Several courts have declared unconstitutional religious exemptions from mandatory vaccination statutes. *See, e.g., McCarthy* (invalidating religious exemption from Arkansas compulsory immunization statute); *Brown v. Stone* (Miss. 1979) (invalidating religious exemption from Mississippi compulsory immunization statute).

require school children to be immunized. This is not surprising given "the compelling interest of society in fighting the spread of contagious diseases through mandatory inoculation programs." Accordingly, we conclude that Workman has failed to demonstrate that the statute violates her Due Process rights. . . .

VII.

Finally, . . . "district courts may decline to exercise supplemental jurisdiction over a claim . . . if . . . the district court has dismissed all claims over which it has original jurisdiction." . . . There is no indication that the district court abused its discretion in dismissing Workman's state law claims. . . .

You cannot tell from the opinion how religious belief came into play. Ms. Workman did not object to vaccination per se. Rather, she thought vaccination would be medically bad for her child, and she asserted a religious belief that she should not do anything to harm her child. Could the court have rejected the free exercise claim by taking the position that any asserted religious belief must be opposed specifically to the particular state law or action that is challenged? What is the problem with recognizing the religious belief Ms. Workman asserted as a sufficient basis for a First Amendment challenge?

Despite the consistent doctrine cited by the Fourth Circuit holding that parents have no constitutional right to an exemption from immunization laws, 48 states currently have such an exemption. Only West Virginia and Mississippi extend the protection of the immunization mandate to all children. Do you suppose the interests of the children of religious objectors are well represented in the political process? In the *Brown v. Stone* decision cited by the court in *Workman*, the Mississippi Supreme Court rejected a claim like Workman's that the state must exempt religious objectors, and in doing so noted that allowing an exemption would constitute a denial of equal protection of the law to the children of people religiously opposed to vaccination. Do you suppose many state legislators recognize that they are discriminatorily denying some children an important benefit when they seek to accommodate religious parents? For elaboration of the equal protection argument, see James G. Dwyer, *The Children We Abandon: Religious Exemptions to Child Welfare and Education Laws as Denials of Equal Protection to Children of Religious Objectors,* 74 N.C. L. Rev. 1321 (1996).

States make some effort to protect unvaccinated children, by requiring that during an outbreak of a disease unvaccinated children remain at home. However, unvaccinated children might already be infected by the time school officials identify an outbreak, and in any case the children might have to miss many days of schooling. Some private schools prefer not to take this risk and so refuse to allow any children to enroll without the usual vaccinations, not being bound the way public schools are to take all applicants. Cf. Joshua Rhett Miller, *Parents Sue Catholic School for Denying Admission to Their Unvaccinated Son,* Fox News, Sept. 13, 2010.

Most states also have a religious exemption from laws compelling testing of newborns for genetic conditions dangerous to their health. As with immunization, states that do not let religiously opposed parents deny this benefit to their children risk being sued for violating parents' constitutional rights.

Douglas County v. Anaya

694 N.W.2d 601 (Neb. 2005)

Wright, J.

Rosa Ariel Anaya was born in the Anayas' home, without a physician present, on July 11, 2003. The birth was reported to the Department of Health and Human Services on July 17. In August 2003, a DHHS employee received Rosa Anaya's birth certificate, checked DHHS' database, and determined that the testing for metabolic diseases required by §71-519 had not been performed. A certified letter was sent to the Anayas explaining the statute's requirements. . . . The Anayas declined to submit Rosa Anaya for the screening, stating that it was in direct conflict with their sincerely held religious beliefs that life is taken from the body if blood is removed from it and that a person's lifespan may be shortened if blood is drawn. Douglas County brought an action seeking to compel the Anayas to comply with §71-519 . . . [which] provides:

> (1) All infants born in the State of Nebraska shall be screened for phenylketonuria, primary hypothyroidism, biotinidase deficiency, galactosemia, hemoglobinopathies, medium-chain acyl-CoA dehydrogenase (MCAD) deficiency, and such other metabolic diseases as [DHHS] may from time to time specify. . . .
>
> (2) . . . If a birth is not attended by a physician and the infant does not have a physician, the person registering the birth shall cause such tests to be performed within the period and in the manner prescribed by [DHHS].

The Anayas argue that because they have raised a free exercise of religion claim along with a parental substantive due process claim, they have a hybrid constitutional rights claim, which requires strict scrutiny review. . . . Although *Smith* discussed prior decisions that involved not only the Free Exercise Clause but other constitutional provisions, the Court did not hold that a strict scrutiny review is required simply because more than one constitutional right might be implicated. . . .

The second constitutional rights violation asserted by the Anayas seems to suggest that §71-519 violates their rights as parents to make decisions concerning the upbringing of their children. They rely upon *Pierce v. Society of Sisters* (1925), and *Wisconsin v. Yoder* (1972). In *Pierce*, the Court . . . concluded that the challenged law served no state interest and therefore had no reasonable relation to any state purpose. In *Yoder*, the Court . . . noted that no harm to the physical or mental health of the child was inferred but that when the health and safety of a child was involved, different considerations applied.

> To be sure, the power of the parent, even when linked to a free exercise claim, may be subject to limitation . . . if it appears that parental decisions will jeopardize the health or safety of the child, or have a potential for significant social burdens.

The Court did not conclude that strict scrutiny was required. . . .

This case is analogous to cases in which courts have upheld the State's right to require immunization of children. In *Boone v. Boozman* (E.D. Ark. 2002), the court upheld the constitutionality of an immunization statute. . . . The law applied to all school children except those whose health would be endangered by immunization. Because the law was neutral, heightened scrutiny was not required even though compulsory immunization might burden a plaintiff's right to free exercise. The court stated, "It is well established that the State may enact reasonable regulations to protect the public health and the public safety, and it cannot be questioned that compulsory immunization is a permissible exercise of the State's police power." Society's interest in protecting against the spread of disease takes precedence over parental rights and the right to free exercise of religion. . . .

Section 71-519 is a neutral law . . . generally applicable to all babies born in the state and does not discriminate as to which babies must be tested. Its purpose is not directed at religious practices or beliefs. . . . Section 71-519 does not contain a system of particularized exemptions that allow some children to be excused from testing. . . . Section 71-519 cannot be construed as directly regulating religious-based conduct. There is no evidence that the State had an antireligious purpose in enforcing the law. . . .

We conclude that the effect of §71-519 . . . is properly analyzed under a rational basis review. Evidence was presented concerning the effects of the diseases that are tested for. . . . Early diagnosis allows for prevention of death and disability in children. The State has determined that it is appropriate to test for these diseases soon after a child is born in order to address treatment options. The health and safety of the child are of particular concern, as are the potential social burdens created by children who are not identified and treated. A medical doctor testified concerning the diseases identified in §71-519:

> Phenylketonuria, referred to as "PKU," is an inherited metabolic condition due to a genetic absence of an enzyme. The condition creates an abnormal buildup of amino acid that interferes with the growth of nerve cells in the brain, which is critical in the very first weeks and months of an infant's life. Abnormal chemistry is present and can be diagnosed within hours of birth. Any damage occurs within the first few weeks of life, but clear evidence may not be seen until the second half of the first year. Treatment is a special diet that allows children to develop normally.
>
> Hypothyroidism results in a loss of thyroid function and in newborns causes the brain not to develop, resulting in profound mental retardation and developmental delays. An infant with hypothyroidism would not grow well, and the condition would be obvious within a few weeks of birth.
>
> Galactosemia is a condition due to a missing enzyme. Babies without the enzyme quickly become jaundiced and droopy, and they may have a bloodstream infection that kills them within days.
>
> Biotinidase is an enzyme that helps to conserve a B vitamin. A person who lacks the enzyme can develop acidosis, blindness, mental retardation, seizures, and deafness. Treatment is inexpensive and inoffensive. Signs and symptoms of this disease do not manifest early or at a predictable time. A child who is deficient in biotinidase will probably become symptomatic during the first year, and a child who is partially deficient might become symptomatic during childhood or adolescence.
>
> Hemoglobinopathies can result in diseases including thalassemia and sickle cell disease, which are readily diagnosable and at least partially correctable. Newborns with these diseases are susceptible to bloodstream infections during the first year of life. Symptoms include a low blood count and sometimes an enlarged spleen, which would generally be assessed by a physician.
>
> MCAD, medium chain acyl-CoA dehydrogenase deficiency, is due to the absence of an enzyme that is responsible for burning body fat. MCAD may appear in the first few days or weeks of life or during a childhood illness with fever and vomiting. It can be seen in school-age children. Remedial measures include educating the parents and the child's physician as to the condition and the risks and giving the child a dietary supplement. An episode of severe flu-like symptoms can result in brain damage.

The State has an interest in the health and welfare of all children born in Nebraska, and the purpose of §71-519 is to protect such health and welfare. This is a rational basis for the law, and it is constitutional . . . .

Is the outcome of this case necessarily the best result for children? What effects could compulsory immunization and screening have on families in which parents believe accepting them would pose a grave danger to their and their children's salvation? Even if a state is not *required* to exempt parents who object on religious grounds, should it do so?

There is reference in this opinion to the state's police power role and to its *parens patriae* role. What is the difference between them? Is it possible for the state to occupy both roles in the same situation? Or are the two roles incompatible?

In addition to imposing on parents positive duties of care in relation to children's health, the law empowers parents to force children to undergo certain forms of treatment that the law does not require. We saw one instance of that above, in discussion of circumcision. Another example is commitment to a psychiatric facility or drug rehabilitation program. Courts have generally rejected challenges based on constitutional rights of children to parental commitment decisions. See, e.g., Parham v. J.R., 442 U.S. 584 (1979) (holding that no formal hearing is required for commitment of minor to psychiatric hospital at parents' request when medical professionals at the admitting facility confirm the child's need for treatment); In the Interest of F.C. III, 2 A.3d 1201 (Pa. 2010) (rejecting due process challenge to statute permitting a parent to petition for commitment of a minor to involuntary drug and alcohol treatment services). Parents cannot, however, legally force a daughter to have an abortion.

f. Exposure to Immorality

There are many activities deemed suitable for adults but not for children, and so the state in various ways limits parents' freedom to involve children in or expose children to those activities. There are business regulations that prohibit the presence of minors in, for example, casinos, betting parlors, and bars. In addition, courts generally find some language in child maltreatment laws for deeming such involvement or exposure to be child abuse or neglect. Thus, child protective services might charge with sexual abuse, psychological abuse, or "injurious environment" neglect a parent who has his or her children watch live or filmed sexual activities.

In addition, this is a context, like education, in which the state stands ready to infringe the liberty of a parent upon request of the other parent in ways that it would not otherwise do. Parents make such requests frequently, in part because most parents have standards of decency higher than those reflected in maltreatment laws and in part because many people want to inflict pain on their ex-partners. Public humiliation, state condemnation, and court-imposed restriction of an ex-spouse can be very gratifying. Most states have adopted a rule that a parent's interactions with a new partner, whether of the opposite or the same sex, must be harming a child in verifiable ways in order for a court to condition custody or visitation on forbearance. But the threshold for a finding of harm is much lower in a dispute between parents than it is in a child protective services intervention.

A.O.V. v. J.R.V.

Court of Appeals of Virginia (2007)

BENTON, Judge.

. . . The parties were married in 1987. During the marriage, the mother, a former teacher, remained at home to manage the household and care for the three children, born in 1992, 1998, and 1999. The father's military career required the family to move often throughout the years. Prior to their separation in 2004, the family lived together in a house in Stafford, Virginia. Upon their separation, the mother moved with the children to South Carolina to live with her sister.

The divorce suit stemmed primarily from a separation and the father's homosexuality. The evidence proved the father had affairs before the separation. The father testified that he met his current paramour in May of 2004 and that he and the man are an exclusive couple. They share rent at their house, utilities, and grocery costs. . . .

[T]he trial judge . . . found the father to be a fit father, and further found he has a good relationship with the children. Specifically, he found the children were still young and needed both parents; both parents were physically and mentally fit; and positive relationships existed between each parent and the children. Additionally, the judge considered the children's needs to have relationships with both of their extended families; the propensity and interests of both parents to participate in the children's upbringings; and "the propensity of each parent to actively support the children's contact relationship with the other parent."

The trial judge awarded the parties joint custody of the children, with primary custody to the mother. The trial judge awarded the father visitation one weekend a month, some holidays, and four weeks in the summer. He continued two of the limitations imposed on visitation in the *pendente lite* order. That is, that the father cannot have any companion with whom he has a romantic relationship stay overnight (between midnight and 6:00 A.M.) or demonstrate affection with third parties in the presence of the children. . . .

The mother contends the trial judge erred by not granting her sole custody of the children and by not prohibiting the father from exposing the children to his homosexual lifestyle. She argues she should have received sole custody of the children due to the father's cohabitation with his homosexual lover, his actions which "led directly to the destruction of this family unit," his placement of his own desires over his children's welfare, the negative effects his homosexuality has had on the children, and the parties' inability to communicate. The father responds that . . . no evidence demonstrated his homosexuality had an adverse effect on the children, and that the evidence demonstrated he was a loving father. . . . The father appeals, however, the imposition of visitation restrictions. . . .

Homosexuality by itself does not render a parent unfit. *Doe v. Doe* (Va. 1981) (trial judge cannot assume, without specific proof, that a parent's homosexuality will adversely affect the child). The Supreme Court has held, however, that a parent's "illicit relationship" conducted in the presence of a child is a factor . . . to consider. "In all custody cases . . . , the court must decide by considering all the facts, including what effect a nonmarital relationship by a parent has on the child. . . . An illicit relationship to which minor children are exposed cannot be condoned. Such a relationship must necessarily be given the most careful consideration in a custody proceeding." *Brown v. Brown* (Va. 1977).

In *Brown*, evidence proved the mother's relationship with her lover adversely impacted the children. The mother openly cohabitated with a man in the children's presence for an extended period. Under these facts, the Supreme Court affirmed the trial judge's determination that the adulterous relationship rendered the mother unfit. In *Roe v. Roe,* (1985), the father lived with a man who was his lover. They shared a bed, they kissed and hugged in front of the child, and they permitted "other homosexuals [to visit] the home and engage[ ] in similar behavior in the child's presence." The Supreme Court held that the father's conduct violated the standards discussed in *Brown* but expressly noted that its decision in *Brown* "was not based on the mother's adulterous relationship in the abstract, but rather on the fact that it was conducted in the children's presence." The Court applied *Brown* to hold that "[t]he father's continuous exposure of the child to his immoral and illicit relationship renders him an unfit and improper custodian as a matter of law." This holding was based in part upon the observation that the father engaged in "unlawful" conduct (referencing Code §18.2-361, which criminalized sodomy).

In *Bottoms v. Bottoms* (Va. 1995), the Supreme Court affirmed the circuit court's custody award to the child's grandmother where the mother was engaged in a homosexual affair. Reciting the rule that "a lesbian mother is not *per se* an unfit parent," the Court held that the mother's conduct was still an "important consideration in determining custody," and it specifically referred to the Virginia statute criminalizing sexual "conduct inherent in lesbianism." The *Bottoms* Court noted additional support in the record for the trial judge's custody award, including the mother's habit of disappearing for days, her lack of self-sufficiency, her inability to control her temper, and her neglect of the child when in her care. The Court also noted the record established the child had been harmed by living with his mother, as demonstrated by the child's use of vile language and tantrums. In short, the Court cited a host of factors, other than the mother's lesbian relationship, supporting the trial judge's custody award to the grandmother, including the mother's own neglect of the child and evidence supporting a finding of actual harm to the child.

We note that the holdings in *Roe* and *Bottoms* are weakened to the extent that they relied on Code §18.2-361's criminalization of certain sexual acts. Since then, *Lawrence v. Texas,* 539 U.S. 558 (2003), and *Martin v. Ziherl,* 269 Va. 35 (2005), have cast serious doubts upon the constitutionality of the statute as it applies to private conduct between consenting adults. However, the central holdings of *Roe* and *Bottoms* remain strong: the court's primary concern is the best interest of the child, which requires consideration of actual harm to the child as a factor in determining that best interest.

Ford v. Ford (1992), demonstrated that our concern is with exposing children to actual harm, not with the relationships themselves. There, this Court upheld the joint custody determination where the father and his companion "were sleeping together." The evidence proved the father and the child "spent nights at [the father's companion's] home on a regular basis" and the father later moved into his companion's home, where "the couple maintained separate bedrooms." The evidence showed that the father and his companion "made efforts to establish for [the child] a nonthreatening platonic relationship." Affirming the joint custody ruling, this Court noted that *Brown* had not established a "per se rule prohibiting awarding custody to a parent involved in an adulterous relationship," but rather that the "standard governing . . . review of this issue is 'the extent to which the child is exposed to an illicit relationship.'"

In a more recent case, this Court reviewed the trial judge's award of joint custody of the child after considering both parents' post-separation relationships. *Piatt v. Piatt* (1998). Citing *Brown,* we referenced the general rule that a trial judge "examines the sexual conduct of a parent to determine whether it has had any adverse impact on the child." We noted that "[t]his standard applies to both heterosexual and homosexual conduct." Thus, we held that the parents' post-separation relationships "were facts for the trial court to consider" and affirmed the trial judge's award of primary custody to the father, ruling evidence supported the judge's conclusion that the mother provided a less stable home environment for the daughter.

In sum, Virginia law requires trial judges, when determining custody, to consider the extent to which the child is exposed to a parent's romantic relationship and whether that relationship had an "adverse impact" on the child. The mother primarily cites the father's homosexuality and his "willingness to expose [the] children to the social condemnation resulting from an active homosexual relationship" as rendering him unfit to share custody of the children. The father and his companion testified, however, that they are not open about their relationship to the children. The father calls the man his friend and told the children that they are roommates. When the children visit, the man sleeps at his condominium or at a friend's house instead of the house he shares with the father. At the hearing, the mother admitted the children seemed happy and had not demonstrated any negative effects from their visits with the father.

Ample evidence in the record supports the trial judge's finding that the father is a fit parent. Family friends described him as a good father. The mother described him as an involved parent during their marriage. During visitations, the father either takes leave from his job or works from home in order to be with the children. When the children visit, he takes them hiking, to the park, biking, to museums, and to the movies. In sum, the record provides evidence showing that the father is discreet in the presence of the children about his romantic relationship, that the relationship has not had an adverse impact on the children, and that the father is a good parent. Thus, taking these factors into consideration, the trial judge did not abuse his discretion by granting joint custody.

The mother alternatively argues that, if the trial judge did not err by giving the father joint custody, he erred by not prohibiting the father from exposing the children to his homosexual lifestyle. She asserts his history of self-serving actions demonstrates he should not be allowed discretion in exhibiting his homosexuality around the children. . . .

In . . . imposing visitation restrictions, . . . a trial judge may consider "what effect a nonmarital relationship by a parent has on the child." We have held, however, "[t]he relationship between a child and non-custodial parent should not be subject to the dictates of the custodial parent unless circumstances justify placing restrictions or conditions on the visitation privileges." . . .

During the time between the *pendente lite* order and the custody hearing, the children had visited the father. The record contains no evidence they suffered any harm from being in the presence of the father's companion or from the lack of stricter restraints on visitation. . . . [T]he trial judge attempted to strike a balance between the mother's disapproval of the father's relationship, the Commonwealth's traditional concern over exposing children to extra-marital relationships, and the importance of the father's relationship with his children. In view of the circumstances of this case, we hold that the trial judge did not abuse his discretion in imposing visitation restrictions. The circumstances did not mandate that he bar the father's companion from the children's presence, but neither did he abuse his discretion by prohibiting the father from allowing his companion to occupy the home overnight or engaging in displays of affection while the children visit.

The father argues that restrictions can only be placed on visitation if there has been a showing of harm or a specific danger of harm to the children. This contention is not supported by Virginia case law. . . .

Can it possibly be constitutional to condition a parent's having contact with children on not "engaging in displays of affection" with another adult while the children are present? Is the prohibition on overnights constitutional? The only reasons given for imposing the prohibition were "the mother's disapproval of the father's relationship" and "the Commonwealth's traditional concern over exposing children to extra-marital relationships." Is either of those even a legitimate basis for limiting a person's freedom in child rearing and in personal relationships? If the court allows the children to be in the home during the day, deeming that to have no adverse affect on the children, what is different about night time? What happens to the children at night? Such decisions upholding restrictions on overnight guests are fairly common throughout the Bible Belt. See, e.g., Simmons v. Williams, 660 S.E.2d 435 (Ga. Ct. App. 2008). But see also Mongerson v. Mongerson, 678 S.E.2d 891 (Ga. 2009) (overturning trial court order prohibiting father "from exposing the children to his homosexual partners and friends" in absence of any evidence that this would be contrary to children's welfare). It is also very common throughout the United States for divorcing parties to agree to include such a restriction in a settlement agreement. It is typically only for a limited period, though, such as one year following entry of the divorce decree, because the main concern for most people is not exposure to "illicit" relationships but rather upsetting the children by bringing a new person into their lives too quickly.

g. Other Limitations Imposed at a Co-Parent's Behest

Other types of conduct that frequently trigger petitions to restrict or change custody are alienating the child from the other parent and from extended family; one parent's religiously inspired choices about a child's upbringing that the other believes, on secular grounds, to be harmful to the child; an unhealthy lifestyle; and relocation.

Parental Alienation

Courts are more willing to restrict a parent's speech to children when the other parent objects to it, especially when the speech amounts to maligning the other parent. This situation often arises in a divorce context. Parental Alienation Syndrome is now widely recognized as a common phenomenon in custody battles, especially in cases when a child expresses a preference not to visit a parent. Of course, sometimes there are entirely legitimate reasons why a child does not wish to see a non-custodial parent, such as that the non-custodial parent has abused the child or the custodial parent. But all too commonly the bitterness of the dissolution causes one or both parents to malign the other in front of the children, and even intentionally to alienate the child from the other parent in order to inflict pain on the other parent.

What is the best way for the legal system to react to this? Does telling your child that the other parent is evil, stupid, ugly, etc., amount to psychological abuse, such that child protective services should intervene if it happens even in an intact family? Should it matter in this context whether the maligning arises from moral beliefs or simply from bitterness? Compare Eugene Volokh, *Parent-Child Speech and Child Custody Speech Restrictions*, 81 N.Y.U. L. Rev. 631 (2006) (arguing that ideologically motivated parental speech should receive the same First Amendment protection in a dispute between parents as it receives in a state vs. parent context), with James G. Dwyer, *Parents' Self-Determination and Children's*

Custody: A New Analytical Framework for State Structuring of Children's Family Life, 54 ARIZ. L. REV. 79 (2012) (arguing that courts are not constrained by constitutional rights of parents when adjudicating custody disputes between parents, because the court then acts exclusively as a fiduciary for the child).

Ex parte Snider

929 So. 2d 447 (Ala. 2005)

Laura and William were divorced in May 1997 when their daughter was 5½ months old. By agreement, Laura, who was living in Cullman at the time, was given custody. In November 1999, Laura remarried, and she and the child moved to Birmingham to live with Laura's husband, Brian. . . . Brian and Laura spend a significant portion of their time preparing video documentaries for a missionary named David Cloud. In December 2002, Laura, Brian, and the child moved to a rural area of Indiana in order for Brian and Laura to be located closer to their missionary work. . . .

William petitioned the trial court for a change in custody. . . . In its order granting William's petition for modification, the trial court stated:

> ". . . Brian Snider has engaged in a concerted pattern of behavior intended to control, both physically and emotionally, and isolate the Mother, and as a direct consequence, the parties' minor child, . . . who is presently six years of age. . . . This . . . is extremely detrimental, both physically and emotionally, to the child; and . . . Mother has participated in, condoned, and/or, at the very least, acquiesced to the actions of her husband. The evidence presented to this Court in the trial of this case included:
>
> "(a) The child was encouraged to call Brian Snider 'Papa.'[1]
>
> "(b) Brian Snider hit the child in the head with his hand in an attempt to discipline the child for saying something that he felt was wrong. The child was only five years old at the time. Even though Brian Snider acknowledges that his doing so was totally inappropriate, the testimony of the Mother was that he was 'out of control' at the time, and that she did not do anything about it. When confronted by the Father about his striking the child in the head, Brian Snider refused to assure the Father that it would not happen again.
>
> "(c) Brian Snider whipped the parties' child when she told the Mother and Brian Snider that she had watched a PG-13 movie, 'Miss Congeniality,' with the Father and others while she was visiting with her Father. . . .
>
> "(d) The Mother and Brian Snider relocated their residence, and the residence of the parties' child, to a very rural area in the State of Indiana, even though neither of the parties had any family, nor established business, in the State of Indiana. In doing so, the Mother and Brian Snider isolated and removed this child from the large and loving family support system that she had previously enjoyed in the State of Alabama, which consisted not only of the Mother's family, and the Father, but the family of Brian Snider as well, with whom the child also enjoyed a close and loving relationship. As admitted by the Mother in her testimony, the move to Indiana was of 'no benefit to the child.'
>
> "(e) The Mother and Brian Snider have told this child that her Father and maternal grandfather are 'going to hell'. . . .
>
> "(f) Brian Snider has alienated every member of the Mother's family, with whom the child and the Mother enjoyed a close and loving relationship prior to her marriage to Brian Snider. By doing so, her family support system was eliminated; and Brian Snider succeeded in

1. The divorce judgment prohibited the parties from encouraging the child to address parties other than William and Laura by names such as "mother" and "father" or words of similar import.

becoming the only source of support available to the Mother, making her thereby completely dependent on him and him alone.

"(g) The alienation of the Mother and the child from her family is so complete that the Mother testified that she did not think that it was positive for the parties' child to have contact with her family, except under her direct supervision and only for a short time interval; and that she is not willing to foster a good relationship between the child and the members of her family. The Court notes from the testimony that the family from whom the Mother and child are now alienated provided her not only a place to live, but for the support and care of the parties' child following the separation of these parties; and had at all times prior to her marriage to Brian Snider, enjoyed a close, loving relationship with the child.

"(h) Brian Snider, on one occasion, chastised the child for going with her grandparents to the theater to see the Disney movie 'Finding Nemo.' On another occasion, he and the Mother forcibly removed the child from the physical custody of the Mother's sister during the Father's period of visitation, simply because the Mother's sister had been allowed by the Father to take the child to the birthday party of her maternal grandmother.

"(i) Even though the Mother had only dated Brian Snider for two months prior to their marriage, within six months of their marriage, Brian Snider and the Mother approached the Father and requested that he allow Brian Snider to adopt [the child]. The Father adamantly refused to do so.

"(j) Brian Snider has actively interfered with the communications between the Father and the Mother, and the decisions to be made by them concerning their child, to the point that the exercise of visitation by the Father with the child could only be accomplished with undue and unnecessary pressure and hardship. . . .

"(m) The Mother has indicated that she is submissive to Brian Snider, which is certainly her decision to make; but further asserted that '[the child] is under his (Brian Snider's) control, too.'

"(n) The actions of Brian Snider resulted in a significant and detrimental change in the personality and behavior of the child. . . . [S]ince she has been placed in the pendente lite custody of the Father, the child is now happy and well adjusted. . . .

"(o) Brian Snider and the Mother made demands on the Father for him to conform his household to adhere to their demands, including the child wearing long clothing, no mixed swimming by the child with members of the opposite sex. . . . When the Father refused on one occasion to accede to her demands, the Mother brought law enforcement officers to the Father's home to get the child.

"(p) This Court finds the Father to have a calm and non-aggressive personality; and that he did not exhibit any hostility towards the Mother or Brian Snider in his testimony, but rather exhibited genuine concern for the health and welfare of his child. The Court also found the members of the Mother's family, who testified in support of the Father in this case, to be loving, and without hostility towards the Mother."

We have . . . ample evidence supporting the trial court's findings. Of course, . . . the evidence is not wholly one-sided. We note that Laura testified that she and the child play games together, that they go horseback riding, and that they used to go ice skating.[2]

Laura also testified that she is a competent homeschool teacher, and that the child has progressed under her teaching. She further testified that since she and Brian married, the child has visited Yellowstone National Park, Mount Rushmore, the Statue of Liberty, Washington, D.C., and Nepal. All of this travel was associated with the ministry work in which Laura and Brian are involved. . . . Laura also testified that, after she and William

2. Laura testified that the child's further training in ice skating was discontinued because ice skaters dress in "revealing" outfits and skate to music that is unacceptable to Laura and Brian.

were divorced, William took advantage only of approximately half of his allotted visitation time with the child. She also testified that William is a racist.

Brian testified that William attacked him on one occasion, unprovoked, although William testified that Brian provoked the attack by repeatedly poking him in the chest. There was additional testimony indicating that William drinks regularly, although not to the point of intoxication, and that he has roughly $24,500 in unsecured credit-card debt. Lastly, . . . William's mother, who sometimes cares for the child, has bipolar disorder, although with medication she keeps her symptoms under control. . . .

The existence of conflicts in the evidence at the hearing, standing alone, does not warrant reversal. . . . [T]his Court cannot conclude based on the record before us that the trial court's transfer of custody to William was "plainly and palpably wrong." . . . The record does reveal that the majority, if not all, of the actions taken by Brian and Laura with regard to the child were pursued in adherence to their religious beliefs. . . . *Clift* . . . recognized:

> "[T]hat one's religious beliefs may not serve as the *sole* consideration in a child custody proceeding does not necessarily preclude exploration into those beliefs. . . . [T]he ultimate consideration in determining the proper custody of the child is what is in his best interests. . . . [Q]uestions concerning religious convictions, when reasonably related to the determination of whether the prospective custodian's convictions might result in physical or mental harm to the child, are proper considerations for the trial court in a child custody proceeding."

. . . The trial court found that "[t]he actions of Brian Snider resulted in a significant and detrimental change in the personality and behavior of the child . . . ," and . . . the court expressly states that it did not rely solely on religion in making its decision: ". . . [T]his Court does not find it appropriate, legally or otherwise, to base its decision on whether or not this Court agrees or disagrees with a party's religious beliefs." . . . The trial court was obviously impressed with the solidarity of the child's extended family in its support for the change of custody to William.[5] . . .

. . . Laura . . . [also] contends that the trial court "exceeded its authority by restricting the Mother by only permitting her to train the child in her religious views 'by example.'" . . . [W]e cannot agree with the conclusion in the dissenting opinion that what it describes as the trial court's "sweeping directive" in this proceeding violates Laura's constitutional right to free exercise of religion. The trial court's order states:

> "[T]he religious training of the child while in the home of the Mother for visitation shall be made by example, and not by any religious training which would otherwise be disparaging or critical of in any way the beliefs of the Father, and/or the way in which his household is conducted." . . .

Nothing in the trial court's order prevents Laura from teaching the child every facet of the Christian faith and every principle and lesson contained in the Bible. This can be done by any parent without disparaging or criticizing his or her former spouse. . . .

Laura cites *Ex parte Hilley* (Ala. 1981), a child-custody case. Because the mother in *Hilley*, who had been awarded custody of her children, was an evangelist and church-choir member, she attended church frequently, sometimes until 11:00 P.M. or later, and she

5. Members of Laura's own family supported the change of custody. Indeed, her own parents testified against their daughter, and in favor of their former son-in-law, at the final custody hearing.

would take her children with her. The trial court awarded custody of the children to the mother, but conditioned that custody award as follows:

> "'That during the time that the children are in the care, custody, and control of [the mother], she will curtail all activities that require her to be away from the children, or requires the children to travel from the home during the week except for one church function of reasonable duration and normal school and social functions in which the children may become involved.'"

The trial court stated that, but for the restriction quoted above, it would have awarded custody of the children to their father. This Court held that the trial court's order unduly restricted the mother's right to practice her religion. The Court distinguished orders involved in similar, but not identical, cases:

> "In none of the cited cases did the orders prohibit the parents from themselves following and/or engaging in the beliefs and practices of their chosen religion. The orders merely prohibited the parents from binding the children to their particular beliefs or practices when they threatened the health or welfare of the children. The order in the present case, however, goes beyond that. It effectively restricts [the mother's] free exercise of her chosen religion by providing that 'she will curtail all activities that require her to be away from the children. . . .' Thus, [the mother] is not free to attend church or other church related activities during that time when the children are out of school because *the order does not permit her to leave the children in the care of a babysitter or other suitable attendant.*"

The Court, by noting that a babysitter or other attendant would have been a better means of avoiding keeping the children up and out at all hours of the night, implicitly recognized that it might not be in the best interests of the children to attend all of the church services the mother attended. Put another way, it appears that an order prohibiting the mother from taking her children to all of the church functions would not have run afoul of her right to free exercise of religion. *Hilley*, therefore, does not stand for the proposition that a court may never restrict in any way a custodial parent's exposure of her child to the parent's religion. . . .

The child was only 6½ years of age when this order was entered. . . . The child is now approaching nine years of age. If Laura considers that circumstances with respect to the child's current level of maturity or other circumstances warrant greater freedom on Laura's part during visitation with respect to the child's religious training, including latitude to make comments she might deem appropriate about her father's and grandparents' faith, a motion in the trial court seeking such relief is the appropriate vehicle.[9] . . .

Parker, Justice (dissenting).

The right to worship God according to the dictates of one's conscience is the most cherished star in our constitutional constellation. Thus, civil government can overreach in few ways more egregious than by invoking the law to restrict a mother from teaching her child the worship of God. . . . Laura considered her duties as a parent to include the religious and moral instruction of her child, and she sought to follow Biblical standards in

9. "[M]atters of child custody are never res judicata, and the circuit court retains jurisdiction over the matter for modification upon a showing of changed circumstances."). The same rule applies in matters involving visitation.

child-rearing. Laura tried to protect her daughter from worldly influences, including immoral TV shows and movies, and to have her dress in a feminine and modest way. Laura also followed the Bible by using corporal punishment to discipline the child when she misbehaved. Laura asked William to adhere to these standards during visitation and her father and stepmother to follow them when William left the child in their care.

Although William initially agreed to adhere to Laura's requests, he subsequently reneged on the agreement, drinking beer in front of the child on nearly a daily basis,[12] uttering profanity in her presence, and permitting her to watch TV shows and dress in clothing contrary to the standards he and Laura had agreed upon. William also left the child in day-care arrangements in which those agreed-upon standards were not followed.

Laura's father and stepmother likewise opposed Laura's religious convictions and child-rearing standards and refused to follow them. According to her father, Laura's requirements of long dresses and modest swimwear for her daughter were not "normal," so he and his wife disregarded them. The maternal grandparents also disregarded Laura's instructions regarding the child's TV viewing. Laura's father justified his flouting of her instructions in these and other matters on the theory that grandparents have an independent right to make judgments about what is right for their grandchildren, provided they do not permit anything "objectionable to society as a norm." . . .

Laura implicates the trial court in the infringement of two closely connected, God-given and inalienable rights—the right to free exercise of religion and the right to freedom of expression in the training of one's children. . . .[14]

For innumerable Americans and Alabamians, from the founding of this Nation to the present, the worship of God and faith in His providence have provided hope for a blessed life on earth and salvation in eternity. Recognizing faith in God as the bulwark of our freedom, the Founders deliberately grounded American independence on the "Laws of Nature and of Nature's God." See *Declaration of Independence*. . . . Jefferson asked:

> "Can the liberties of a nation be thought secure when we have removed their only firm basis, a conviction in the minds of the people that these liberties are the gift of God? That they are not to be violated but with His wrath?"

12. In an effort to disguise from the court the quantity of beer he consumed, William altered his check register by whiting out references to the purchase of beer and, in one entry, wrote "root" in a different ink color in front of the word "beer."

14. The majority opinion contends that I read the trial court's order "too broadly" because "[n]othing" in it "prevents Laura from teaching the child *every* facet of the Christian faith and *every* principle and lesson contained in the Bible." . . . Of course, . . . holding firmly and consistently to one interpretation of the Bible (or any book, for that matter) logically precludes other, contradictory interpretations. Where the contradiction is between the understanding of one spouse and the practices of another, to teach the understanding of the one is necessarily to disparage the practices of the other.

For example, if one parent is a Christian and the other is a witch, the Christian parent could not teach that the Bible condemns witchcraft as an "abomination" (see, *e.g.*, *Deuteronomy* 18:10: "There shall not be found among you anyone who burns his son or daughter as an offering, anyone who practices divination or tells fortunes or interprets omens, or a sorcerer or a charmer or a medium or a wizard or a necromancer, for whoever does these things is an abomination to the LORD.") without implicitly disparaging the parent who practices witchcraft.

Furthermore, if the child asked explicitly if the pagan parent was doomed to Hell for practicing witchcraft, the Christian parent would have to choose between teaching what the Bible says (see, *e.g.*, *Galatians* 5:19-21, which teaches that those who practice witchcraft will not go to Heaven) and obeying the court order to refrain from a teaching that would in any way be disparaging of the beliefs of the other parent.

Something very similar occurred in the instant case, in which the child asked her mother if William was going to Hell and, based on her understanding of the Bible and her knowledge of William's beliefs, Laura said "Yes." Such a reply may sound harsh to those who favor a more liberal or universalist view of salvation (certainly the trial court considered it harsh), but it is outside the proper jurisdiction of a state court in Alabama to prohibit such an utterance by favoring the denominational view of one parent over that of the other. . . .

Thomas Jefferson, *Notes on the State of Virginia*, 1782.

. . . In the darkest days of the Constitutional Convention, with delegates strongly divided, Benjamin Franklin brought them together by an appeal to the corporate dimension of worship, reminding those gathered of God's role in the formation and preservation of this Nation: . . .

> "I have lived, Sir, a long time; and the longer I live, the more convincing proofs I see of this truth, that *God governs in the affairs of men*. And if a sparrow cannot fall to the ground without his notice, is it probable that an empire can rise without his aid? We have been assured, Sir, in the sacred writings that 'except the Lord build the house, they labor in vain that build it.' [*Psalm* 127:1]." . . .

George Washington . . . emphasized that "Religion and Morality are the essential pillars of civil society." . . . James Madison . . . recognized and emphasized the individual right and duty to worship God. . . .

> "This duty is precedent both in order of time and degree of obligation, to the claims of Civil Society. Before any man can be considered as a member of Civil Society, he must be considered as a subject of the Governor of the Universe: And if a member of Civil Society, who enters into any subordinate Association, must always do it with a reservation of his duty to the general authority; much more must every man who becomes a member of any particular Civil Society, do it with a saving of his allegiance to the Universal Sovereign."

. . . It therefore stands to reason that they would have regarded any law or court order prohibiting a person from worshipping God as the very epitome of tyranny and would have been shocked by a court order prohibiting a parent from teaching the worship of God to her child. Indeed, no aspect of religious freedom is more treasured than the right of parents to teach their children to worship God. . . . The religious instruction of children is important not only for society generally, but also particularly for parents who believe, as does Laura, that the worship of God through faith in Jesus Christ is the *only* way of salvation and that God Himself has commanded parents to teach His commands to their children. . . . Given the unique importance of fundamental religious rights—particularly where they overlap fundamental rights of free speech—courts should act with the highest caution when considering an order restricting the exercise of these rights. Regrettably, this level of caution appears to have been sorely lacking in . . . the trial court's order. . . .

I can find no precedent in law and no foundation in reason to support the notion that an attempt to ensure the protection of a child from pressure and confusion resulting from differences of opinion between parents falls within the jurisdiction of the state. Even if . . . the state could acquire such jurisdiction, preventing a child's "unnecessary" feelings of pressure or confusion would hardly rise to the level of a "compelling [civil] government interest" as required by the Alabama Constitution to justify state interference with the God-given religious freedom of its citizens.

But even if, arguendo, one could contrive a "compelling state interest" in a child's not feeling unnecessarily pressured or confused . . . the means to that end as chosen by the trial court in the instant case is far from the "least restrictive means" required by the Alabama Religious Freedom Amendment. In fact, . . . paragraph 3(j) of the trial court's order constitutes nothing less than a blanket prohibition on Laura's right to speak to her child about certain core principles of her conservative Christian faith—including absolute standards of right and wrong and absolute beliefs about the afterlife—merely because her former husband does not share these core principles. The trial court's order even prevents Laura from *answering* theological questions posed by her daughter whenever Laura's honest answer would reveal conflicts with the views or practices of the father. . . .

Instead . . . the trial court could have ordered Laura to *qualify* every such comment with a statement to the following effect: "This is what Mommy believes from the Bible, but Daddy believes something different. Sometimes parents disagree." Such an order would acknowledge real differences of opinion between parents without favoring one denominational viewpoint over another. . . . If Laura were to respond to her daughter with, "The judge may punish me if I answer you," or "If I answer you, honey, you may not be able to see Mommy again," or some other, similar answer, the child would be more confused than if her mother could answer sincerely according to her beliefs and merely add the comment that some people, including Daddy, do not believe the same thing. . . .

To view the issue from another perspective: If the Alabama Legislature had passed a bill restricting parental rights in the same manner as does the trial court's order, this Court would not hesitate to strike it down as unconstitutionally vague, overbroad, and violative of fundamental rights. We should be no less vigilant to correct unconstitutional actions in our own branch of civil government.

Is it hopeless to try to protect children of divorce from parental hostility? Would you suppose that religious difference makes hostility between parents and damaging expression of that hostility more likely or less likely?

The dissent treats as part and parcel of the same protected liberty both worshipping according to the dictates of one's conscience and instructing one's child about religion. Are those actually distinct activities, entitlement to which must rest on different grounds?

Unhealthy Lifestyle

Neglect laws prohibit parents from maintaining a grossly unsanitary home and from having dangerous things like guns and drugs lying about the house. And of course the criminal law prohibits all people from engaging in some behaviors that could endanger children, such as taking drugs or driving while drunk. But otherwise the law leaves parents free to adopt a lifestyle that could adversely affect a child's health. Parents can legally feed their children only junk food, get drunk at home every night, smoke cigarettes in the home and while driving their children around, spray chemicals all over their lawns, and leave the television on constantly. But at the request of another parent or custodian, courts will sometimes impose restrictions on particular parents' otherwise lawful activities.

Janice Morse, Court Bans Mom from Smoking Near Child

Cincinnati Enquirer, Nov. 8, 2009

No smoking around your daughter. That was a Warren County court's order to a mother last December—and now an appeals court has sided with that ruling, taking the unusual step of using "judicial notice" to conclude that second-hand smoke is a danger to a child.

In a decision that could apply to many other child-custody and visitation cases, the Ohio . . . [courts forbade] anyone from smoking around Victoria Anderson, 9. Since she was a baby, she has lived with her great-grandmother in suburban Dayton, Ohio; she gets "parenting time" with her divorced mom and dad. In April 2008, Victoria's paternal great-grandmother, Marilyn Anderson, objected to the child's mother, Racheal Hill, smoking around Victoria during visits. The child returned home "smelling of cigarette smoke as a result of Racheal smoking in her home and car," court records say. Eight months later, the court ordered all parties to protect Victoria from second-hand smoke. . . .

Disputes over parental smoking have been cropping up in family-court cases nationwide, legal experts say, and the cases highlight two competing interests: A parent's right to smoke versus a child's right to breathe smoke-free air. Courts appear to be deciding such clashes based on the "best interest of the child," rather than whose "rights" win out. . . . Action on Smoking and Health, a non-smokers' rights group in Washington, D.C., says courts in at least 18 states have ruled that "subjecting a child to tobacco smoke is a factor which should be considered in deciding custody."

In the Warren County case, even with no evidence that Victoria suffers specific reactions or health issues from exposure to smoke, the court ruled that a smoking ban was in the child's best interest. To reach that conclusion, the court . . . "took judicial notice"—without anyone presenting proof in court—of an "avalanche of authoritative scientific studies" that say second-hand smoking poses risks to children. . . .

Often, parties agree they shouldn't smoke in front of kids . . . [But] Hill objects to the court's "intrusion into her home," regulating even a legal activity such as smoking. . . . The court ruling also limits where Hill can take her daughter, such as to the home of a friend who smokes. . . . Hill could be hauled into court on the mere suspicion that she smoked around the child, facing a contempt charge that could bring jail time. . . .

What other lawful activities might a co-parent claim is harmful to a child? Limiting parents' freedom to live as they want and enjoy themselves raises a larger question about how we should view "the deal" that people implicitly agree to when they have children—that is, what trade-off of duties versus rights and benefits. Is there any realistic danger that decisions like that in Racheal Hill's case could make the parental role so burdensome that many people will opt not to have children at all? Or that many people who do become parents will resent their children for the burdens and as a result give the children less nurturing than they otherwise would?

Relocation and Travel

Americans move a lot. They are especially likely to do so after an intimate relationship dissolves, particularly if one party to the relationship previously relocated for the sake of the other or if a desire to relocate partly caused the dissolution. When the parties have co-parented their children, the question arises whether the children will move with the person who is relocating, and often the parties are not able to agree on an answer. There are therefore many reported court decisions deciding the question for parents. The issue occasionally arises in an initial custody determination, but more commonly it arises in a petition by one parent or the other for a later modification of the original order.

Generally, a custodial parent must give advance notice of an intent to relocate, giving the other parent an opportunity to seek a change of custody so that the child will not also move. See, e.g., Ariz. Rev. Stat. §25-408(B) ("If by written agreement or court order both parents are entitled to custody or parenting time and both parents reside in the state, at least sixty days' advance written notice shall be provided to the other parent before a parent may do either of the following: 1. Relocate the child outside the state. 2. Relocate the child more than one hundred miles within the state."). Relocating without notice could subject a custodial parent to loss of custody and/or to tort liability. See, e.g., Stewart v. Walker, 5 So. 3d 746 (Fla. Dist. Ct. App. 4th Dist. 2009) (holding that non-custodial parent can sue custodial parent for IIED based on relocation without notice or court permission). The custodial parent might give notice by initiating a modification action herself, asking for less or different visitation for the other parent.

The prevailing basic rule for modification of custody is that the petitioner must show a material change of circumstances affecting the child's well being and that the proposed change would be in the child's best interests. Such a material change could be a parent's work demands, a parent's losing housing, a parent's starting a new relationship, a child's need to change schools, or any other significant event in the life of parent or child.

Scholars and courts have debated whether relocation should count as a material change of circumstances, and therefore a basis for a non-custodial parent to request transfer of custody to him or her, and whether the basic rule should even apply in relocation situations. Some state statutes prohibit a custodial parent from relocating a child, if the other parent objects, unless the custodial parent can demonstrate that the move would be in the child's best interests. See, e.g., Ariz. Rev. Stat. §25-408(G) ("The court shall determine whether to allow the parent to relocate the child in accordance with the child's best interests."). That rule ostensibly could apply even where the non-custodial parent is not willing or able to assume primary custody, and so could effectively prevent a custodial parent from moving herself, unless she is prepared to leave the child in the custody of a non-parent, if she cannot show that relocating with her would be better for the child. But courts naturally take into account what the living situation would be with a change of custody, and the typical relocation dispute begins with a non-relocating parent asking for primary custody to be transferred to him.

Because restrictions on custodial parent relocation of a child predominantly impact mothers, feminists generally argue for a strong presumption in favor of allowing relocation, as a matter of women's right to move and to pursue careers and new lives. Fathers' rights groups, on the other hand, insist that custodial parents should have to show that a child would be better off as a result of the move despite any loss of time with the non-custodial parents.

Baxendale v. Raich

878 N.E.2d 1252 (Ind. 2008)

Boehm, Justice.

. . . Valerie Baxendale and Sam Raich divorced in 2000. They were granted joint legal custody of their two children, and Valerie was granted physical custody of both. The older child is now a college student, and his custody is not at issue. After the divorce, Valerie, Sam, and the younger child, A.R., continued to live in Valparaiso, Indiana, which is in the greater Chicago metropolitan area. In 2001, Valerie graduated from law school and began employment in Chicago, but her position was eliminated fourteen months later. After a year seeking other legal employment in Illinois, Valerie expanded her search and received a job offer in Minneapolis, Minnesota.

On December 6, 2005, after accepting the position in Minneapolis, Valerie filed a Notice of Intent to Relocate with A.R., and Sam responded with a Petition for Modification of Custody. The parties apparently agreed that pending final resolution of custody, A.R., then eleven years old, would remain in Valparaiso with Sam. Valerie moved for an emergency hearing to resolve the relocation issue before the beginning of the 2006 school year. The trial court . . . interviewed A.R. in camera. The interview was not recorded or attended by counsel, and neither party requested to attend or record the interview.

On September 1, 2006, the trial court entered an order: (1) denying Valerie's request to relocate A.R.; (2) continuing joint legal custody of A.R.; and (3) providing that Sam would be the physical custodial parent if Valerie continued to reside in Minnesota, but if Valerie "returns to Indiana she will be the residential custodial parent." . . .

In general, an initial child custody order is determined "in accordance with the best interests of the child." . . . Modifications are permitted only if the modification is in the best interests of the child and there has been "a substantial change" in one or more of the factors identified in Section 8 as considerations in the initial custody determination. These include the wishes of the child and the interrelationship of the child with parents, siblings, and others "who may significantly affect the child's best interests."

. . . "Relocation" is "a change in the primary residence of an individual for a period of at least sixty (60) days," and no longer requires a move of 100 miles or out of state. A "relocating individual" is someone who "has or is seeking: (1) custody of a child; or (2) parenting time with a child; and intends to move the individual's principal residence." A "nonrelocating parent" is someone "who has, or is seeking: (1) custody of the child; or (2) parenting time with the child; and does not intend to move the individual's principal residence." Upon motion of either parent, the court must hold a hearing to review and modify custody "if appropriate." In determining whether to modify a custody order, the court is directed to consider several additional factors . . . specific to relocation[6] [including] the financial impact of relocation on the affected parties and the motivation for the relocation in addition to the effects on the child, parents, and others identified in Section 8 as relevant to every change of custody.

. . . We agree with the Court of Appeals that relocation does not require modification of a custody order. [W]e do not agree . . . that Section 21 requires that a change in one of the original Section 8 factors be found before a change may be ordered after a relocation[, i.e., that relocation per se is not a basis for modification]. . . . [C]hapter 2.2 is a self-contained chapter and . . . introduces some new factors that are now required to be balanced, but also expressly requires consideration of "other the factors affecting the best interest of the child." . . . Because consideration of the new factors might at least theoretically change this balance, the current statutory framework does not necessarily require a substantial change in one of the original Section 8 factors. . . .

6. These factors are (1) the distance involved in the proposed change of residence; (2) the hardship and expense involved for the nonrelocating individual to exercise parenting time or grandparent visitation; (3) the feasibility of preserving the relationship between the nonrelocating individual and the child through suitable parenting time and grandparent visitation arrangements, including consideration of the financial circumstances of the parties; (4) whether there is an established pattern of conduct by the relocating individual, including actions by the relocating individual to either promote or thwart a nonrelocating individual's contact with the child; (5) the relocating parent's reasons for relocating the child and the nonrelocating parent's reasons for opposing the relocation of the child; and (6) other factors affecting the best interest of the child.

In most cases the need for a change in a Section 8 factor is likely to be academic because a move across the street is unlikely to trigger opposition, and a move of any distance will likely alter one of the Section 8 factors. For example, Section 8 requires evaluation of the effect of relocation on the interaction between the child and other individuals and the community. It is hard to imagine a relocation of any distance where there is no effect on the "interaction" of parents, etc. with the child or the child's adjustment to home, school, and community. The fundamental point recognized in *Lamb* under the 1985 statute is that a relocation may or may not have significant effects on the child's best interests. 600 N.E.2d at 99 ("[W]here a very young child or baby is involved, a move out of state may have little or no effect on the child. For an older child who has formed friendships, attends school, and participates in activities or sports, is involved in church, or enjoys the security of supportive relationships with nearby relatives or others in his community, a move out of state may have a much more significant effect."). . . . Similarly, the effect on the child's relationships with others will vary widely with the individual circumstances of the child and the significant individuals in the child's life. We therefore adhere to the view under the current statute that relocation may or may not warrant a change of custody. . . .

Evidence of the circumstances surrounding this proposed relocation was presented at trial. There are several factors, some more persuasive than others, evidenced in the record that the trial court could have found to support a change in custody to permit A.R. to remain in Valparaiso. These include his improved school performance, proximity to his older brother and grandmother, established athletic and extracurricular relationships, availability of other family members to provide care during temporary parental absences, and the greater cost of proposed education in Minneapolis. Obviously, we can speculate that the court's in camera interview also affected the court's conclusion as to the child's wishes. But there is nothing in the record that gives us any basis to conclude that this factor was significant in the trial court's ruling. Because of the presence of the other factors, however, we cannot say that the trial court abused its discretion in modifying the custody order. Modification is permissible because of substantial changes in A.R.'s interaction with his father, grandmother, and brother, and his adjustment to school and other activities, irrespective of A.R.'s unrecorded wishes. . . .

Finally, Valerie argues that the trial court's order violates her federal constitutional right to travel by forcing her to choose between moving to Minnesota and retaining physical custody of A.R. Only one Indiana case discusses this right in the context of a custody order, . . . reasoning that ". . . the court's order does not impose any necessary burden whatever upon *her* right to travel. She remains free to go wherever she may choose. It is the children who must be returned to Indiana."

We think the *Clark* formulation does not give appropriate recognition to the rights of the relocating parent. The Supreme Court of the United States has held that all citizens have a right to interstate travel "uninhibited by statutes, rules, or regulations which unreasonably burden or restrict this movement," and laws that chill that right with no other purpose are "patently unconstitutional." No Supreme Court case has addressed the interaction between a parent's right to travel and a child custody order, but several state courts have considered how *Shapiro* applies in the child custody context. One state reads *Shapiro* as weighting the scale in favor of the parent's right to travel.[7] Others view the

7. The parent's right to travel with children prevails unless "clear evidence before the court demonstrates another substantial and material change of circumstances and establishes the detrimental effect of the move upon the children." *Watt v. Watt* (Wyo. 1999).

child's best interests as trumping the parent's right to travel.[8] And yet others balance the relocating parent's right to travel with two other important interests—the best interests of the child and the nonrelocating parent's interest in the care and control of the child.

We agree with those courts that take *Shapiro* as recognizing that a chilling effect on travel can violate the federal Constitution, but also acknowledging that other considerations may outweigh an individual's interest in travel. We think it clear that the child's interests are powerful countervailing considerations that cannot be swept aside as irrelevant in the face of a parent's claimed right to relocate. In addition, it is well established that the nonrelocating parent's interest in parenting is itself of constitutional dimension. In short, we agree with the recent well-reasoned opinion of the Colorado Supreme Court that the trial court is to balance these considerations.

In the custody context, Indiana's statutes reflect these concerns by considering whether the relocation is indeed bona fide, and explicitly acknowledging the child's interests and the effect on nonrelocating persons, including a nonrelocating parent. Valerie's reason for relocating certainly appears valid, but this is not a case, as Valerie argues, where she is unable to take employment out of state "for fear that the state will take her child." Under the terms of this final custody order, Valerie retains significant involvement with A.R. A.R.'s interests in continuity of education and contact with other family members and Sam's interest in parenting A.R. are significant and justify the trial court's custody order.

Should a child's best interests be sacrificed at all for the sake of parents' constitutional rights? Comparison with the marital relationship might again be illuminating. If one member of a married couple wishes to relocate and the other thinks that would be, all things considered, not in his or her best interests, the other is absolutely free to remain in place. The moving spouse has no right of any sort against the other staying behind, no entitlement that the other sacrifice what is best for him or her and make the move. If the state were to try to coerce the other spouse to move (e.g., by charging that spouse with desertion in a divorce action and inflicting a financial penalty as a result), that would likely be seen as infringing the other spouse's constitutional right of "travel."

Are all the factors identified for authorizing relocation clearly tied to the child's welfare, or do some reflect a different focus? Many courts also focus on how difficult or costly communication and transportation for visits would be for the non-custodial parent and child following a relocation. There has been little change in transportation in recent decades and no sign that it will become easier or cheaper. Ease of communication, however, has improved dramatically in recent years and likely will continue to do so. Courts are increasingly urging use of new technologies to maintain contact. See Molly McDonald, *Judge Orders Skype Visits as Condition of Mom's Move*, A.B.A. J., Aug. 12, 2010. It might be, however, that cell phones and webcams are more helpful with older children than with infants and toddlers. And both transportation and communication are usually more difficult and/or costly when a parent proposes an international relocation, so courts are especially reluctant to allow it. Safety and reliability of the legal system are additional concerns with some requests for international relocation. See, e.g., J.B. v. A.C., 2009 WL 6303022 (Del. Fam. Ct. 2009) (blocking move to Liberia). But see Goldfarb v. Goldfarb, 861 A.2d 340 (Pa. Super. Ct. 2004) (authorizing move to Israel).

8. *LaChapelle v. Mitten*, 607 N.W.2d 151, 163-64 (Minn. Ct. App. 2000); *Ziegler v. Ziegler*, 107 Idaho 527, 691 P.2d 773, 780 (Idaho Ct. App. 1985).

In addition to sometimes denying custodial parents the power to relocate a child, courts occasionally prohibit a parent even from taking a child on vacation to certain places, if the other parent objects. Usually the proposed destination is another country and the principal reasons for denying permission are that the other country is very unsafe or cannot be counted on to force return of the child to the United States if the traveling parent attempts to remain in the other country with the child. The latter is a great concern for mothers in the United States whose co-parent is a native of a highly patriarchal foreign society. See, e.g., V.U. v. F.U.U., 2008 WL 2898335 (Del. Fam. Ct. 2008) ("Nigeria appears to be a country that cannot provide security for American citizens or its own citizens and . . . is in [a] state of turmoil. Furthermore, although the Court does not necessarily find that a country must be a signatory to the Hague Convention [on the Civil Aspects of International Child Abduction] in order to allow travel to that country, the Court has very little information on whether Nigeria honors its extradition treaties with the United States or what problems Mother might face in trying to have the children returned from Nigeria.").

C. RETHINKING PARENTS' RIGHTS

In several contexts in this chapter, such as education, medical care, and contact with extended family, we have seen that American law treats parents not simply as caretaking guardians of children but also or instead as persons entitled for their own sake to control children's lives. The law does not just impose duties on parents to provide care of particular kinds, but also empowers parents to do things to children that parents are not legally required to do, such as circumcision and committing to a treatment facility, and empowers parents to some extent to prevent other parties, including the state, from providing particular services, such as medical care and education of particular kinds, to children. Such power is characterized as an entitlement of parents.

In fact, that parents have "rights" with respect to the upbringing of "their" children is perhaps the most taken for granted assumption in family law. There is plenty of disagreement about how extensive parents' control rights should be, and some scholars have criticized excessive emphasis on rights generally in connection with family matters. Until recently, however, there was little or no recognition that the very concept of parental entitlement might be problematic, even though we long ago rejected the notion that one adult could properly have a right to control the life of another adult, competent or incompetent. Even when people acknowledged that the "other-determining" parental control right is anomalous, they accepted it based on a belief that parenting is *sui generis,* unlike any other social practice. The following summary critique of parental rights on conceptual and moral grounds rests in large part on a showing that parenting is in fact similar in relevant ways to other relationships and practices, in connection with which our legal and moral cultures reject the notion of "other-determining" rights.

James G. Dwyer, Children's Rights

in A Companion to the Philosophy of Education (Blackwell 2003)

. . . My approach to determining who has moral rights in connection with children's education is in part deconstructive; I critique prevailing views holding that parents or the state possess rights concerning children's education. It is also constructive; I show that a proper understanding of the nature and purpose of rights supports attribution of educational rights to children, including both basic rights and equality rights.

Basic Principles Concerning Rights

I begin with a particular conception of what rights are and what they do. I draw this conception from the history of political and legal theory, and from widely shared moral precepts in our society. Under this conception, rights are claims that impose on others duties of forbearance or assistance, and that override interests and preferences that do not command the protection of rights. Rights carry the moral connotation of entitlement and deservingness; to state that one has a moral right is to make a strong statement about what others owe one as a matter of justice. Because of these characteristics of rights, they are properly ascribed only to protect certain interests. Interests that warrant the protection of rights are defined by their importance and their kind.

First, only interests of great importance command the protection of moral rights. The importance of the interest is determined not by the subjective value an individual places on it, but by reference to objective criteria that select for goods of the greatest intrinsic and instrumental value. Joel Feinberg distinguishes "welfare interests" from "ulterior interests." Welfare interests are those aspects of wellbeing, such as food and education, that one must have in order to carry on in life, that are preconditions for pursuing any higher aims. In Feinberg's terms, they are "the basic requisites of a man's well-being," "generalized means to a great variety of possible goals and whose joint realization, in the absence of very special circumstances, is necessary for the achievement of more ultimate aims." From an objective perspective, these are the most important interests a person has, even if most people take them for granted most of the time. And because of their great importance to an individual's well-being, they "cry out for protection, for without their fulfillment, a person is lost."

Ulterior interests, in contrast, are satisfactions of the higher, individualized aims people form for their lives. Though these aims have great subjective importance for those who hold them, frustration of them does not undermine a person's well-being in the same way or to the same extent as does harm to welfare interests, and frustration of one aim might be compensated for by fulfillment of another. They therefore do not warrant the protection of rights. Feinberg gives as examples of ulterior interests "such aims as producing good novels or works of art, solving a crucial scientific problem, achieving high political office, successfully raising a family, achieving leisure for handicraft or sport, building a dream house, advancing a social cause, ameliorating human suffering, achieving spiritual grace."

Second, some kinds of interests are ruled out as bases for rights. For example, although law and public morality support attribution of rights to ownership of property, they rule out attribution of rights to ownership of persons, even though ownership of a person could be of much greater subjective value and material benefit to a right holder than ownership of any thing. An interest whose satisfaction entails disrespecting the personhood of another cannot give rise to a moral right.

These two limitations on rights—the importance of interests and the kind of interests—generate a general principle that is reflected in all areas of law other than child rearing. That principle is that no individual is morally entitled to control the life of another human being. This principle rests on the empirical assumption that an interest in controlling the life of any other person—however strongly one might wish to do so—is objectively not an aspect of basic welfare, and on the moral premise that deeming one person the object of another's rights fails to accord that person the respect he or she is owed as a person. The principle also rests on a conceptual distinction between a right to self-determination and a right to "other-determination," the former being of fundamental importance and the latter not, the former resting on a sound moral premise of self-ownership and the latter finding no support in general moral principles. Finally, this conceptual distinction presupposes a moral and practical difference between having a right to something—that is, a moral entitlement—and simply being privileged to have or do something. We can recognize that sometimes practical circumstances require that one person direct the life of another person—specifically, when the latter is not sufficiently competent to direct his or her own life—while at the same time denying that having the power to do so is ever a matter of right: that is, is something the power holder is himself or herself entitled to as a matter of justice.

Importantly, our legal system applies this principle to the lives of incompetent adults. Even though those persons must have others exercise control over their lives to some degree, such control is not bestowed or exercised as a matter of the guardian's right. Instead, the state confers on caretakers and surrogate decision-makers a legal privilege to exercise certain powers, subject to regulation and revocation by the state as the welfare of the incompetent adult requires. Guardians for incompetent adults occupy a fiduciary, rather than possessory, role; they are agents rather than owners. They have legitimate power insofar as they act to effectuate the rights of the incompetent adult, and are subject to legal override and removal if they act contrary to the interests—as defined by the state—of the incompetent person. Thus, habilitation decisions on behalf of mentally disabled adults must conduce to the welfare of the incompetent adult. And if there is disagreement between interested parties—for example, a state agency and a ward's parents—courts or administrative agencies resolve that disagreement on the basis of what they find to be best for the ward, and attribute no rights to either the state agency or the parents in the matter.

Against Parents' Rights

Parents' child-rearing rights are of two kinds. Rights to recognition as a parent and to custody of a child are associational rights. They are analogous to rights to enter into other sorts of relationships, such as a marriage. These associational rights of parents are not at issue here. Rights to make decisions concerning specific aspects of a child's life, such as the child's education, are control rights or powers. These are distinct from custodial rights, and denying to parents the power to make certain decisions regarding a child's education does not affect their custodial, associational rights: that is, their right to have a relationship with, live with, and interact with their child.

The general principles relating to control rights identified above *prima facie* rule out parental control rights, while allowing for parents to exercise some authority over their children's lives as a matter of legal privilege and in a fiduciary capacity. Thus, the parental child-rearing rights the United States Supreme Court has fashioned from the First and Fourteenth Amendments to the Constitution (neither of which mentions parents or children) are presumptively morally (and on some views of constitutional interpretation, legally) illegitimate. In the controlling cases, the Court determined that parents have a legal right that trumps state education laws in some instances. The Court has not squarely held that parents have a constitutional right to make educational decisions contrary to their children's interests, because in each case it decided the Court found that the state had not shown its laws necessary to protect children's welfare. Nevertheless, the Court's reasoning in these cases allows for such a result, because the Court did not rest its decisions on the (false) assumption that parents must have rights (rather than simply fiduciary authority) in order to protect the interests of children, but attributed child-rearing rights to parents principally on the basis of parents' own interests. The Court has never addressed the apparent inconsistency between attributing other-determining rights in the parent—child context and refusing to do so in every other context, including contexts involving incompetent adults.

Putting aside what the Supreme Court has done, several moral arguments might appear to support attribution of parental control rights. These arguments can usefully be categorized on the basis of whose interests they champion—children's interests, parents' interests, or societal interests. First, many would argue that parents should have rights concerning their children's education because parents know their children best and are more committed to their children's welfare than anyone else. The alternative of a state right to standardize children for its own purposes is unacceptable in a liberal society that respects the separateness of persons and places moral value on the welfare of the individual. This argument has the virtue of making children—the persons whose lives are directly at stake—the center of moral attention. Nevertheless, it is flawed.

The factual premises underlying this argument are themselves subject to dispute: for example, on the grounds that many parents are not very committed to their children's welfare and that education, like medicine, is a specialized field about which most parents know very little. But even if the factual premises were unassailable, they would not support the conclusion that parents must have rights to control children's education. They would support assignment of some decision-making authority to parents, but only if and to the extent that this is best for children, and as a matter of the children's right, not the parents' right. It is simply nonsensical to attribute rights to one person—that is, to say that moral duties are owed to that person—in order to protect the welfare of another person. If the moral foundation for attributing some rights is the welfare of children, then the rights should be attributed to the children themselves—rights to have decisions about their lives made in a particular way by particular people on the basis of particular standards.

Moreover, in the context of religious objections to state-imposed rules for public or private schools, where parental rights are most hotly contested, the issue is really not who is in the best position to know what is best for a child, but whose values will control. When parents object for religious reasons to some aspect of public school curriculum, such as a course in critical thinking, or to imposition of a particular regulation on private schools, such as one prohibiting sexist teaching and treatment of students, the contest is not between competing positions on empirical facts. It is between competing ideologies.

As such, it is senseless in this context to speak of who knows the child best and cares most about the child. Knowledge of a particular child's characteristics is irrelevant to the question of whether her school should teach her that females have moral worth and social importance equal to that of males and can rightfully pursue all the same careers that males pursue. The answer to such a question turns on whose values will govern the child's schooling—the state's values or the parents' values. And what many people fail to realize is that it is the state that must answer that question, because it is the state that ultimately must determine who will possess legal power over the lives of non-autonomous persons and what the scope and standards for exercise of that power will be. And in making that determination, the state must rely on its own perceptions—from its necessarily secular perspective—of what interests are at stake and which are the most important.

Thus, anyone who accepts that children have the most important interests at stake in connection with their own education, and who believes that education law and policy ought to be driven by the interests of children, must recognize that at this second-order level, in deciding whose values will control a child's upbringing when a conflict arises—parents' religious values or the liberal state's secular values—the state must act on the basis of its own perception of what is, in general, best for children. If the state concludes that it is generally best, in terms of children's temporal well-being, that parents' religious values control their schooling, then it should establish legal rules that give effect to parental religious objections. If, on the other hand, the state concludes that it is generally best for children, in terms of their temporal well-being, that this one aspect of their lives be controlled by liberal secular values, then it should establish legal rules that do not give effect to parental religious objections. In either case, though, the legal rule would be predicated on rights of children, rather than on rights of parents or the state.

A second category of arguments for parental rights rests on interests of parents themselves. Many contend that parents have fundamental interests at stake in connection with their children's upbringing, and that those interests deserve the protection of child-rearing rights. Parents therefore *are* a proper locus of moral entitlement, they argue. The rest of society owes duties *to them* as parents, wholly apart from any duties owed their children. Here the empirical premise is clearly flawed. Parental interests in how their children's lives go are simply not fundamental. They do not constitute a component of basic welfare, satisfaction of which is a prerequisite to pursuing higher aims in life. Instead, they are related to one of the higher aims that many—but not all—adults choose to pursue. They are in the same category as interests in having a particular job (which one might be unable to secure) or in marrying a particular person (who might refuse the proposal)—interests that might be of tremendous subjective importance to a person but are not, from an objective point of view, fundamental in the true sense, such that they warrant the protection of a right. Non-fulfillment of such an interest does not undermine one's capacity for self-determination and pursuit of other ulterior aims.

This is even clearer when it is recognized that formal education is just one facet of a child's life, occupying less than 20 percent of a child's awake hours from birth to adulthood, and that denying parents a right to decide how their child will be educated does not amount to denying them the opportunity to be parents and to teach their children their beliefs. To say that parents have fundamental interests at stake in matters of state regulation of children's schooling is to say that parents have a fundamental interest in having exclusive dominion over their children's minds, and that assertion is utterly implausible as an empirical matter. This conclusion that the parental interest is not fundamental is borne out by the quite common practice in divorce law of completely denying one of a child's parents any authority whatsoever to make decisions concerning the child's education. Significantly, it is not regarded as a tragedy or a grave injustice that a non-custodial parent has no say at all in his child's education, where a court deems that to be in the child's best interests, and non-custodial parents carry on with their lives and maintain rewarding relationships with their children despite denial of that power.

In addition, no matter how important parents' interests in how their children's lives go are, for the state to attribute to them control rights in order to further those interests entails treating children instrumentally, as means to the furtherance of other persons' aims. With respect to any adults, whether competent or not, we regard it as morally inappropriate for the state to treat them instrumentally in this fashion. Thus, the law treats the interests of an incompetent adult's guardian as entirely irrelevant to decisions about the incompetent adult's living situation, training, and medical care. Absent a compelling argument for treating children anomalously in this respect, we should not do so. Children are persons, and the state should not treat them as instruments for furtherance of other persons' aims in life any more so than it should treat any adults in that fashion.

Finally, some defend parental control rights on the grounds that such rights are necessary to promote certain diffuse societal interests, such as interests in pluralism and in avoiding state tyranny. Entitling parents to depart from prevailing norms is said to promote diversity of beliefs and ways of life. Such diversity is valuable because it facilitates societal progress, expands opportunities available to individuals to adopt beliefs and ways of life most conducive to their happiness, and simply makes for a richer, more stimulating and aesthetically pleasing cultural environment (at least for people who value diversity).

One problem with this line of reasoning is that the premise that parental power over children's education is necessary to preserve and promote diversity is false. On a liberal understanding of children's welfare, a state aiming to provide children the best education would provide an autonomy-facilitating education, one that fosters abilities to question received views—including those espoused by current government officials—and to develop one's own views about the world and matters of value (Levinson, 1999; Brighouse, 2000). Such an education would thus tend to produce greater diversity in our society. Parental rights are often asserted as an objection to that type of education, and in that respect actually tend to diminish diversity and to inhibit the progress said to come from the freedom to engage in experiments in living. A diversity of illiberal, authoritarian communities is not the sort of diversity a liberal state values. While a liberal state might properly leave adults free to form illiberal cultural communities for themselves, its interest in pluralism does not support a decision affirmatively to assist such communities in perpetuating themselves, by bestowing on their adult members plenary power over their children's lives, including the power to stifle children's freedom of thought.

Moreover, if and to the extent that the state itself acts illiberally, and itself denies children an education that facilitates their freedom of belief, expression, and self-determination, children's rights—asserted by themselves or by their parents—can serve as an appropriate and sufficient basis for moral condemnation and legal injunction. It is not necessary as a practical matter to attribute rights to parents in order to guard against ideological tyranny by the state. And to say that parents do not possess moral rights to control their education is not to say that they should have no voice in the formation of education policy. To the contrary, it is best for children in general that the process of formulating education policies be open to the public and that all concerned citizens be able to participate in public deliberations about children's welfare.

An additional problem with the argument based on societal interests is that it presupposes the appropriateness of sacrificing children's welfare for the sake of diffuse societal interests. The very point of attributing rights to parents on this basis is that there is a conflict between parents' ideological preferences and what the liberal state deems best for children, and it is supposed that deferring to parents will enable dissident, illiberal subcultures to survive. Those who make this argument never defend the implicit assumption that furthering a societal interest in pluralism by this means is of greater moral importance than protecting the educational interests of children. As an empirical matter, it seems clear that children's interests are weightier than any contrary societal interest at stake. A child's interest in receiving an autonomy-facilitating education is profound, while the interest of any person *qua* citizen in living in a society that contains pockets of illiberal resistance to prevailing norms is insignificant, at least in connection with any single instance of parent—state conflict, if not entirely illusory. Thus, this argument would have to rest on a moral premise that the collectivity is to be favored over the individual regardless of what a balancing of interests would dictate. That is a decidedly illiberal premise, entailing an instrumental view of persons whose basic welfare is at issue, and one to which few if any people would be willing to adhere consistently. . . .

Formal Characteristics of Children's Rights

According children the respect they are owed as persons entails giving proper weight to the interests they have at stake in connection with their education. From an objective standpoint, their educational interests are clearly fundamental, and the most important among all the interests potentially affected by education policy. Schooling is about shaping minds, fostering skills, providing socializing activities, and otherwise preparing young people for adult life. The minds that are being shaped belong to the children, not to any adults. The skills reside in them and largely determine their life prospects, not those of current adults. They are the ones being socialized and they are the ones who will live the adult lives for which schooling is preparation. Ordinarily when we debate policies concerning the fundamental welfare of some group of individuals, those individuals—*their* rights, *their* interests, *their* claim to justice—are the focus of moral inquiry. And so it should be with children's education.

One would be hard-pressed to find any theorist who denies that children possess a moral right to an education of some sort. Disagreement arises principally as to the specific formal and substantive features of children's educational rights. Are children entitled to the best education feasible, or simply to a minimally adequate education, or to something in between? What is the content of a good education? Against whom do children's rights operate or, in other words, who owes duties to children to ensure that they receive an education of the sort to which they are entitled—the federal government, state governments, local communities, or only parents? Are children's rights only entitlements to what others think is best for them, so paternalistic imposition of a curriculum is appropriate, or do children have choice-based rights, such that teachers owe children a duty to secure their assent to particular lessons before administering them? I will not attempt to answer these questions or even to rehearse the many arguments advanced by others, but instead offer just a few observations relevant to these questions.

First, it is generally assumed that any educational rights children have must, as a conceptual matter, be positive rights, rather than negative rights—that is, they are rights to assistance rather than forbearance on the part of others. . . . A strong version of that position would hold that only private parties—specifically, parents—owe any duties to children relating to education. In the legal world, this distinction between positive and negative rights has figured most prominently in United States Supreme Court decisions addressing claims for a federal constitutional right to an education. The Court has largely rejected such claims, in large part because it views the Constitution as an embodiment of negative rights only. On the other hand, most state constitutions in the USA, the national constitutions of many other countries, and several international conventions and declarations contain an explicit affirmation of children's positive right to an education, suggesting that the libertarian view that the state bears only duties of non-interference is not the prevailing view in American society or in other societies.

In any event, the distinction between positive and negative rights is unclear at best, and in some contexts entirely illusory. One could argue, for example, that today's children have a *prima facie* negative right against the state ever imposing legal restrictions on their behavior, a right that is extinguished only insofar as the state ensures them an education adequate to prepare them for responsible self-governance. In the context of disputes between parents and the state over regulation of children's education, it is generally assumed that parents asserting a constitutional right to noninterference with their choices are asserting negative rights, while any claims on behalf of the children to enjoy the benefits of state-imposed standards are presumed to be claims of positive rights. But in fact what parents are demanding is that the state bestow on them a great benefit—namely, plenary legal power over their children's lives. Parents are not demanding that the state dissociate itself entirely from their children's lives, since that would leave them with no legal power at all, but that the state favor them in making the decision—which the state must make—as to who will possess authority over children's education. The parents' claim is therefore very much a positive right claim, a claim for state assistance in advancing their aims. And the claim on behalf of the children whose parents object to state requirements for education can be viewed as a negative right claim; it is a claim against interference with their statutory right to an education that satisfies state standards. The children's claim is essentially that the state—in the form of school officials or a court or a legislative body—must not act to exclude them from benefits they would otherwise receive, simply because their parents do not wish them to have the benefit. It is as much a negative rights claim as is the claim of a property owner against a change in zoning laws that diminishes the value of his or her property.

In addition, children possess equality rights, as a moral and constitutional matter, that significantly constrain state action relating to their education. Regardless of what basic rights children have in connection with their education—that is, what rights they possess because of their developmental needs, children have rights arising from the state's obligation to act impartially and to treat equally persons who are similarly situated. This right is embodied in the Equal Protection Clause of the Fourteenth Amendment to the federal Constitution, and in similar provisions in every state's constitution. This right requires that if the state chooses to bestow particular educational benefits on children generally—for example, by enacting compulsory schooling laws and by providing schooling itself (i.e. public schools), even if it is not morally obligated to provide such benefits to anyone, the state must provide that benefit equally to all children, absent circumstances that make the benefit of no value to some children. Analogously, if the state chooses to provide the benefit of police protection, it must provide it equally to all citizens; it may not create a police force and then limit its operation to protecting only people who are white or male, for example.

Children's equality rights have numerous implications for education. Because all states in the US do confer on children the benefit of a statutory and, in many states, constitutional right to an education, they may not exclude any children from this benefit absent a showing that the children would not benefit from receiving an education. There might be circumstances in which this is the case for some children, but such circumstances would not arise simply from a parental objection on ideological grounds. The Supreme Court's decision in *Wisconsin v. Yoder*, which held, in effect, that the state may not guarantee to children of Amish parents the same education it guarantees for other children, thus violated the Equal Protection Clause and the equality rights of children whose parents are Amish. The Court ought to repudiate the *Yoder* decision on that basis.

The same is true when one looks beyond merely receiving some education to receiving an education of a particular quality or content. If the state determines that children's developmental interests require that they receive an education of a particular sort—for example, one that promotes critical thinking, trains children in the investigative methodologies of many disciplines, instills the knowledge they would need to pursue a higher education in the best universities, and teaches gender equality—and the state acts on this determination by fashioning regulations requiring schools to provide such an education, it bears a moral responsibility to ensure that *all* children receive such an education. To exclude any children from that benefit on the grounds that their parents object to it, or have chosen to place their child in a private school, is to violate the equality rights of those children. The children themselves have not, presumably, chosen to forgo that benefit, and the state cannot justifiably withdraw it from them because of other persons' preferences. Analogously, the state could not justifiably deny police protection to African-Americans on the grounds that some other persons do not want them to have that protection. The state would bear the burden of demonstrating that any children excluded from the protection of state-imposed standards for education would not benefit from that protection, or that providing that protection to them would inevitably entail countervailing costs to them that outweigh the benefits, because of the children's circumstances. Absent such a showing, the state would be precluded from exempting any children from aspects of the public school curriculum that further the objectives identified above, and would be required to extend all its academic standards to all private schools.

Finally, children's equality rights also have implications for state funding of education, which is a very large benefit that the state provides to children. When the state spends large sums of money to operate public schools, or where it funds public schools and some private schools . . . , it has a *prima facie* obligation to fund the education of all children. In other words, every child has a presumptive, equality-based right to a fair (as determined by need) share of state spending on education. This means that children in private schools, including religious schools, have a *prima facie* right to state-provided educational vouchers. With adults, we say that there is no equality-based entitlement to funding of private analogues to public services—for example, museums—because everyone is treated equally by the service being made available to all, and any who freely choose to forgo the state-provided service justifiably bear the consequences of doing so. This understanding of moral responsibility defeats equality-based claims for school vouchers on behalf of parents. But the same cannot be said of children in private schools, who generally do not themselves choose to forgo the state-provided service of public schooling. They should not be made to suffer, by losing out on the important state benefit of funding for education, as the result of other persons' choices, not even the choices of their parents.

This implication of children's equality rights leads to the startling conclusion that children in religious and other private schools are presumptively entitled, as a matter of moral equality rights and constitutional equal protection rights, to state-provided school vouchers. And were it the case that the state regulated private schools sufficiently to ensure that they all strive to provide a good secular education—that is, the kind of education the liberal state determines to be good for children, that right would be controlling. The problem today in the USA is that the state ignores its responsibility to children in private schools to extend to them the benefit of academic standards and rules for treatment of students. Private schools are virtually unregulated with respect to curricular matters and conduct toward students. Beyond requiring that private schools profess to teach certain subjects, states do nothing to ensure that private schools are academically sound. And beyond general criminal prohibitions against serious physical violence, states do nothing to ensure that private schools treat students with respect. As long as this remains the case, children's equality-based rights to state funding of private schooling cannot be effectuated. The state has no reason to believe that in funding any particular private school it will be benefiting the children in it. In fact, in funding some schools, the state would be harming the children in it, because the state would be supporting illiberal schooling practices—for example, stifling of critical and independent thought and teaching of sexist and racist views. Giving effect to the rights of children in private schools would require a major transformation of that sector of the US educational system.

Finally, a distinction can be made between children's welfare rights and their liberty rights or rights of self-determination. It is plausible to regard the value and moral force of rights of self-determination as varying with the capacity of their possessor to make competent decisions, because to the extent that one lacks this capacity one's freedom to make decisions for oneself will not enable one to effectively promote one's interests. Regard for well-being and respect for claims of self-determination converge by-and-large in the case of adults, and this convergence warrants a strong principle of respect for individual liberty rights. But what weight should be given to the claims of children to make decisions, such as educational decisions, on their own behalf? Children have been traditionally regarded as lacking the maturity of judgment necessary to be able to make decisions that will adequately protect their interests, including their developmental interests. Because proper attention to these developmental interests is vital to a child's *future* capacity for effective self-determination, it has been common to regard the promotion of these developmental interests as displaying a kind of prospective or forward-looking respect for the child's interest in self-determination or autonomy.

Against this traditional view, child liberationists have argued that children are rational enough to decide well for themselves, and that they should thus be morally entitled to the same rights of self-determination as adults. On this basis others have derived various conclusions regarding the moral impermissibility of imposing various aspects of schooling on children without their consent. This is not the place to review the evidence which has been brought to bear against this view of children's decisional competence (see Purdy, 1992). I will simply make two points. The first is that a proper respect for children does require that, to the extent education is imposed upon them involuntarily in public or private schools, that education should be one that enhances their autonomy on the whole in the long run (Pritchard, 1996; Brighouse, 2000). Given children's limited maturity of judgment and foresight, their present interest in making choices for themselves cannot be given the weight properly accorded their well-being and the development of their future capacities for competent self-determination. The second point relates specifically to contexts where parents who wish their children to have an authoritarian, illiberal upbringing object to liberal state requirements for education. The point is simply that, as an empirical matter, children of such parents tend to be delayed in their development of the capacity for free and fully informed, independent decisions about their lives. Thus, when children voice agreement with parental objections to liberal educational requirements, their choices are more likely to be heteronomous than autonomous, and heteronomous choices generally command lesser respect than autonomous ones. On the other hand, a child's disagreement with a parent's illiberal objections—for example, if a child says she *wants* to study evolution and other mainstream views in the sciences—might signal an independence that makes all of the child's views worthy of greater respect than if she appeared simply to be obeying parental commands to express a certain position.

Would viewing children's education through a children's rights lens and not a parents' rights lens adequately protect the interests you believe children have? If not, what interests would not be protected and precisely why would they not? What do claims of parental entitlement actually change as a practical matter? Which normative argument in the excerpt above is most persuasive for justifying that change? Which least persuasive?

PROBLEM

Read the following excerpts from an illuminating and engaging book about growing up in a Christian Science family and then analyze a hypothetical custody dispute in a divorce between the parents in the story. Who should receive primary physical and legal custody? Should the other parent have liberal and unsupervised visitation? Should they share joint physical or legal custody?

Lucia Greenhouse, fathermothergod: My Journey Out of Christian Science

(Crown Publishing 2011)

April 1970
Wayzata, Minnesota

One afternoon a couple of weeks before my eighth birthday, my five-year-old brother, Sherman, and I scramble out of the school bus and race each other home up the steep hill. . . . We drop our books in the front hall and dart into the kitchen to find . . . our older sister, Olivia, asleep on the tattered red and white love seat, with a blanket up to her chin. Her long brown hair is pulled back in a ponytail. Her chin, cheeks, nose, forehead, and both hands are covered in little red spots.

"Hi!" Sherman says.

Olivia opens her eyes. "Chicken pox," she says miserably.

"Do they hurt?" I ask.

"They really itch," she says, wincing. . . . .

Mom appears as we help ourselves to the bakery box.

"Olivia has chicken pox?" I ask.

Mom doesn't answer.

"Mom? Chicken po—"

"In Christian Science," she reminds us gently, "we know that there is no illness. No disease. No contagion. Olivia is not sick. She is God's perfect child. We are all going to work very hard to keep our thoughts elevated."

"Does that mean she doesn't have to go to school?" I ask Mom.

"It means I *can't*," Olivia says.

"No fair!" Sherman protests. "How come?"

"Well, even though we know Olivia isn't sick—can't be sick," our mother says, "we need to follow the school's policy on certain . . . matters."

"I can't go back to school until the chicken—I mean, until . . . they . . . crust over," Olivia says.

We know from Sunday school that we're not supposed to name illness, because by naming something, we are giving in to *the lie* about it. Mary Baker Eddy tells us to "stand porter at the door of thought."

For the next several days, life at our house is unbearably dull. My brother and I go to school; our sister doesn't, until her spots crust over. After school, our friends don't come to play kickball or ride bikes in our driveway. We are told it's because of *contagion*, a scary thing other people worry about but we Christian Scientists don't believe in. We know that contagion is about germs spreading; we also know that *prevailing thought* (something we can tell is bad just from the way our parents and other Christian Scientists say it) claims that chicken pox is contagious. But we have learned in Sunday school that there's no such thing as germs.

Before we go to bed, Olivia, Sherman, and I pile into our parents' bed and listen as they read aloud various passages from the Bible and *Science and Health*. "'We weep because others weep, we yawn because they yawn,'" my mother recites. Curiously, I find myself yawning. "'And we have smallpox because others have it; but mortal mind, not matter, contains and carries the infection.'" I think to myself that I'd rather hear the next chapter of *Little House in the Big Woods*, the book Mom was reading to us before Olivia got spots. They read aloud for almost an hour. Snuggled under the soft comforter and between warm bodies, we fall asleep; soon we are carried, half-awake, to our own beds.

"Am I going to get"—I hesitate groggily—"chicken pox?" My father has just brought me a drink of water.

"Let's talk about what you're learning in Sunday school," he says gently. "Is sickness real?"

I shake my head no.

"Are you God's child?"

I nod yes.

"Can you be anything but perfect?"

"Nope."

"Mary Baker Eddy says we must put on *the panoply of Love*. Do you remember what *panoply* means?"

Even though I've heard the word a lot in Sunday school, I can never remember what it means. I make a face that tells my dad I've forgotten.

"A *panoply* is a full suit of armor," he says. "So if we think of God's love as a suit of armor, protecting us, we can never be hurt or sick."

"Well," I ask, "how come Olivia has . . . spots?"

"That's just *erroneous belief—error*," my dad says, "which we all must guard against. She may have the *appearance* of *error*, but we know it's a lie, an illusion."

My Sunday school teacher talks a lot about *error* too, and I remember what that is: sin, disease, and death. She tells us that error is like a mirage in the desert: the vision of a pool of water where there is nothing but sand. So when my dad says Olivia's spots are the *appearance of error*, I understand that he means the spots are not real. But I don't *exactly* understand how that can be; it seems like everything that Christian Science says is *unreal* is *real*, and vice versa. I guess when I'm older it'll make more sense, but for now, it is comforting enough to know that, as Mom and Dad and Sunday school have taught me, Christian Science is a *science that works*.

"Okay, Loosh," Dad says, and I know it is time for bedtime prayers, and he will give me a choice.

"Daily Prayer?"

I shake my head no. "Fathermothergod," I say.

Together, we recite the Children's Prayer, written by Mary Baker Eddy.

Father-Mother God,
Loving me,-
Guard me while I sleep;
Guide my little feet
Up to Thee.

I kick the covers off my bed and levitate my feet toward my canopy.

"Good night, Dad," I say, giggling at our silliness. I pull the covers back up to my chin.

My father gives me a kiss on the forehead, and I wonder if he has just done the same to my sister, who is now asleep in the next room. My sister has gotten to skip four days of school already and hang out in our parents' bedroom watching TV and eating cinnamon buttered toast. As appealing as that sounds, my birthday is only days away. If I get spots, I know I won't be able to have my party.

The next morning, I wake up and my pajamas are damp and cold, and I'm shaking. I crawl out of bed and walk over to the mirror on my wall to see if I have red spots like Olivia. I have only a flushed face (it looks like I'm wearing Grandma's rouge) and bright red ears. My throat stings when I swallow, my head hurts a little bit, and I feel really tired. I return to bed and yell, "*Mo-om*?" Moments later she enters my room. "I don't feel good," I say.

She sits down beside me, tenderly pushes my bangs out of the way, and places her hand on my forehead. I know from TV that this is how you check for fever, but I have never seen my mom do this. Fever, I know, is *error*. Then she presses her lips against my forehead, which should feel like a kiss, but I wonder if she's doing something else. "Hmm, I think we'll give Mrs. Hannah a call," Mom says.

Mrs. Hannah is our Christian Science practitioner. We call her when we are sick—I mean, when we have a problem—and she prays for us. She is also the superintendent of our Sunday school. She leads us each week in singing hymns and reciting the Lord's Prayer with its spiritual interpretation by Mary Baker Eddy. She is not much taller than me, and she is round. She needs to stand on a stool when she's behind the *lectern*, and even then, we can't see her face, only the top of her head and her arms. Sometimes I squint, and her arms look like they're attached to the sides of the tall desk.

I hear my brother, Sherman, calling from down the hall. My mother gets up and goes to his room. I fall back asleep, and when I wake up, my sister has already left for school with Dad (her spots have crusted over), and Mom has brought me a tray with cinnamon toast and orange juice. I don't want to eat it. "How would you and Sherman like to go to Grandma's today?" my mother says, as she sits down beside me again.

Grandma's house could be my favorite place in the whole world. . . . But today, I don't want to go anywhere. "I want to stay home, Mom," I say. "C'mon," she says. And so we go. Mom lets us each bring a blanket and pillow for the twenty-minute car ride. I close my eyes and try to get comfortable, but now I ache all over. I wonder to myself why Mom's making us get out of bed and drive to Grandma's. When we arrive, Grandma greets us at the door with her soft-cheeked hug and the warm squeeze of her hand on my arm. I love the way her charm bracelet jingles.

"Here, let's get you settled. Would you like to watch TV in my bed?" I nod yes. My brother and I climb under the covers and face each other, wondering what to make of today. We should be in school, but instead we'll get to watch *Bewitched* and *Let's Make a Deal*. Grandma brings us a tray, with two tiny glasses of orange juice, two bowls of Lipton instant chicken noodle soup (my favorite), cinnamon toast cut into triangles, and two bowls of applesauce. I frown. I hate applesauce.

"Go on, have some," Grandma says. "It tastes good when you're under the weather." She spoons it into each of our mouths as though we are toddlers. [It] has what looks to me like teeny bits of chalk in it and leaves a taste in my mouth that is yucky and bitter. The cinnamon toast fixes that.

Mom comes into the bedroom, Grandma goes downstairs, and together we—Mom, Sherman, and I—sing "Mother's Evening Prayer," one of the hymns by Mary Baker Eddy that we know by heart. I don't know why, but when I sing it, my eyes tear.

> *O gentle presence, peace and joy and power;*
> *O, Life divine, that owns each waiting hour,*
> *Thou Love that guards the nestling's faltering flight!*

My throat tightens, and when the tune climbs upward on "nestling's faltering flight," I start to cry. I just want to feel better.

> *Keep Thou my child on upward wing to-night. . . .*

Mom rubs my back, my nose gets all runny, and my voice sort of wobbles through the remaining four verses. After we're done with the hymn, we recite the Scientific Statement of Being, just like we do at the end of Sunday school every week:

> There is no life, truth, intelligence, nor substance in matter. All is infinite Mind and its infinite manifestation, for God is All-in-all. Spirit is immortal Truth; matter is mortal error. Spirit is the real and eternal; matter is the unreal and temporal. Spirit is God, and Man is His image and likeness. Therefore man is not material; he is spiritual.

Although the words skip over my tongue as easily as the Pledge of Allegiance, I don't really understand what they all mean, separately or together. But we say the Scientific Statement of Being so often in our house that it just sounds to my ears like the words should make sense.

We stay at Grandma's until two-thirty, when we have to hurry home before Olivia gets back from school. By then, I feel fine.

A few days later, Sherman and I both wake up with red spots. My brother counts eleven on his face, and more on his tummy, back, and arms. I have only two on my face and three on each hand, so I figure I've done a better job of praying than Sherman has. Still, we both stay home from school until the spots crust over. "The school has certain rules we have to obey," my father reminds us. Neither of us asks why.

* * *

SPRING 1975

Several of my friends at school start going to Perkins Cake & Steak for breakfast on Thursday mornings with Bill, a youth leader for Young Life, a Christian organization. I plead with my parents to let me join this group ("All they do is eat breakfast, it's not like they're going to convert me or anything"), and when I point out that our church doesn't have a youth group—no camping trips, not even a choir—Mom and Dad give in.

My first Thursday morning, Bill's old station wagon pulls up to our house. "I see Mimi, Mary, and James among the faces peering through the car windows. . . . I climb into the backseat, say hi to my friends. . . .

Every Thursday at Perkins, I order the same thing: French toast with bacon. . . . "Dear Lord," Bill says, as we are about to dig in. We follow his lead and bow our heads, smiling self-consciously and checking in with one another out of the corners of our eyes. "Bless this meal, and be a comforting presence for these friends who have gathered in Your Name. Teach them what it means to have a deep personal relationship with You. Amen."

Even without a text in front of me, I am sufficiently literate in religious matters to know which of Bill's words should be capitalized. But having a "relationship with Christ"—like He's a person—is something I've never considered. In our church, God has never felt personal. I've been taught to think of God as the Father-Mother, but God has always felt inanimate, more like the three-letter word *air* than the three-letter word *Him.*

Bill's blessing is the only reference to religion at breakfast. After the grace, we dig in. . . . Throughout the meal, there is much laughter and the occasional tossing of food before we pool our dollars to pay the check. We get back into Bill's car for the drive to school. At the first red light, we jump out, chase one another once around the car, and pile back in before the light turns green. Arriving at the school's front entrance just in time for the first bell, I feel like I am—by dint of sheer luck—part of quite possibly the coolest group at school.

One Thursday, as Bill drives us to school after the weekly breakfast, I become aware, very quickly, that I don't feel well. My stomach is uncomfortably full, and a queasy sensation starts making its way from my belly up toward my throat. During the Chinese fire drill I stay put, while my friends climb over me to make their dash around the outside of the car. As everyone piles back into the car, fortunately oblivious to me, I elbow my way to the window seat and pray that, first, I don't barf right then and there; second, I am not forced to ask Bill to stop the car; and, finally, I can make it to school without anybody noticing me. I don't know if this desire for privacy is a function of being a seventh grader and not wanting to stand out at all, in any way, or if everything I've learned from Mom and Dad and Sunday school is kicking in.

> When thou prayest, enter into thy closet, and when thou hast shut thy door, pray to thy Father which is in secret; and thy Father which seeth in secret, shall reward thee openly.

God, please don't let me barf. I crank down the window for some air and pray pray pray.

The car pulls up to the traffic circle at the school's entrance. I run to the bathroom, lock the stall door, and vomit my French toast. I made it. Thank you, God. I try to hold back my hair the way Mom does when I throw up. I wish she were here. Once I've emptied my stomach, I curl up cold and clammy on the tile floor and stay there for a while.

Eventually, I get up and walk down the hall to the nurse's office, a room I've never had to visit. "My goodness, dear, you don't look so good," the nurse says, hands on her hips, before taking my arm and leading me to the cot against one wall.

She asks me my name, and I wonder if she knows I'm a Christian Scientist.

"Can I call your mom? Would you like to go home?"

I nod.

She dials our number, but there is no answer. I remember that Mom plays tennis on Thursday mornings and there is no way to reach her, so the nurse looks up something in my file and tells me she is calling Dad at the office. ". . . she is white as a ghost," the nurse explains when he answers. "Sure, she's right here." The nurse looks over at me and tilts her head sweetly. "Would you like to talk to your dad?"

I get up and move to her desk. "Hi, Dad," I say.

"Hi, kiddo."

"I threw up."

"Would you like me to pray for you?"

I look at the nurse.

"Can I go home?" I ask Dad. I want him to say yes.

"That might not be necessary;" he says. "Lucia, you, as God's perfect creation, cannot be sick. You are the perfect reflection of God."

"Can you come get me?" I whisper.

I stare at the floor, because I know the nurse is looking at me.

He goes on. "Mrs. Eddy says, 'Let unselfishness, goodness, mercy, justice, health, holiness, love—the kingdom of heaven—reign within us, and sin, disease, and death will diminish until they finally disappear.'"

There is silence now, and I am trying to concentrate on what Dad is saying, about disease disappearing if I fill my thoughts with goodness, health, and love, but my eyes are filling with unwelcome tears. My fingers fiddle with the phone cord. I'm embarrassed that the nurse is listening, and Dad is not offering to come get me.

". . . you needn't give in to the erroneous suggestions of mortal mind. You *cannot* be sick, Lucia. Jesus said, 'Be ye therefore perfect, even as your Father which is in heaven is perfect.'"

I wipe my eyes with my sleeve.

"Loosh?" Dad asks. "Do you think you'd like to go back to class?"

"Yes," I say. But what I'd really like is to be in my bed. At home. With Mom.

"That's wonderful," Dad says. "I know you're going to feel fine."

I say good-bye and hand the phone to the nurse.

"My dad's going to call my mom again and she'll come get me," I tell her.

"*Hmm*," the nurse says, an hour later. "Do you want to try her again?"

She dials the number and hands me the phone. I count six rings, seven, eight, and am about to hang up when Mom answers.

"Mom, I'm at the nurse's office. I threw up. Can you come get me?"

"Of course, sweetheart," Mom says. "I'm on my way."

I feel such relief.

D. FINANCES

The final aspect of state regulation of the parent-child relationship we will study concerns distribution and control of wealth. In addition to controlling children's social lives, education, medical care, and daily routines, parents also generally control all wealth within a family. As with dependent spouses, though, there are some ways in which a child has a claim on the dominant party's earnings and property. In fact, there is much more litigation concerning distribution of wealth in intact parent-child relationships than in intact marriages. Property ownership and management is a relatively simple issue, so it appears first below. The larger issue is the duty to support.

1. *Property Ownership and Management*

As with marriage today, both parties to a parent-child relationship can own property. Minor children typically exercise practical control over their own belongings of small value, but this is at the discretion of parents, who are legally empowered to control their children's activities and smaller-value assets. As to assets or financial transactions of larger value—$10,000 is about average among statutory thresholds—state law might require appointment of a guardian of the estate for the minor. Except in the rare case of the child entertainer, such wealth usually comes to minors not through earnings but through gift, inheritance, or lawsuit (e.g., a tort claim). In appointing a guardian to manage an inheritance or to manage and settle a lawsuit for a minor, courts generally give preference to parents, just as they ordinarily give preference to a spouse in appointing a guardian of the estate for a married incompetent adult who has not designated someone else. See, e.g., In re Miller, 2011 WL 4505306 (Pa.) (parent entitled to object to appointment of guardian other than parent); Dengler v. Crisman, 516 A.2d 1231 (Pa. Super. Ct. 1986) (courts to give preference to parents in appointing a guardian of the estate).

What is different in that case relative to parental control over children's minor assets is that the parent is subject to court supervision, to ensure the parent acts as a fiduciary should, acting only to promote the interests of the ward. In part to avoid such supervision, estate planning attorneys encourage clients to give bequests to minors in trust form, and to name a parent as trustee if that is who the testator wants to manage the money. Trustees are also subject to fiduciary duties but typically have greater freedom and are not subject to ongoing court supervision. There are also cases, of course, in which people leave wealth to minors in trust and designate someone other than parents as trustees—some other relative or an institutional trustee. In that case, parents are likely to serve as intermediaries between children and this outside controller of wealth, reporting on the child's needs and possibly handling distributions for the benefit of their children (though trustees generally prefer to make direct payments to providers of goods and services).

The obverse is true with elderly parents who become incompetent. As noted, when courts appoint a guardian of the estate for such incompetent adults, they generally give first preference to someone previously designated by the ward and, if none, then to a capable spouse, but if the spouse declines or is judged incapable, they generally give next preference to adult offspring. The offspring serving as guardian of the estate would owe fiduciary duties to the incompetent parent and be subject to judicial oversight. Parents who wish to minimize the burden on a future caretaker can put their wealth in trust, with themselves as initial trustees and their preferred caretaker as successor trustee, who will take over if and when the parents become incompetent.

2. *The Support Duty*

The greater wealth issue in parent-child relationships is the duty of support, and in particular the duty that parents owe to minor and disabled offspring. Adult offspring also have a duty to support their parents in many jurisdictions, but it is a much more limited duty, ordinarily kicking in only when the parents are destitute and apply for public assistance, and even then entailing relatively small payments. See, e.g., Conn. Gen. Stat. §53-304 (duty to support parent in need who is under age 65); Ind. Code §35-46-1-7-9 (failure to support parent in need is a misdemeanor); Ohio Rev. Code

Ann. §2919.21(A)(3) (failure "to provide adequate support to . . . aged or infirm parent . . . unable to provide adequately for the parent's own support"); Andrea Rickles-Jordan, *Filial Responsibility: A Survey Across Time and Oceans*, 9 Marq. Elder's Advisor 183 (2007). In contrast, the law requires parents to devote a substantial portion of their income to their offspring throughout minority, and often beyond that.

Neglect laws impose a duty even on parents who are cohabiting with a child to use some of the wealth they control to provide basic necessities for children. Neglect laws thus create a duty of support similar to that which spouses have toward each other in an intact marriage; to the extent no one else is providing for a child's most basic needs, parents must do so. How much one must spend to fulfill that particular duty is highly variable based on circumstances; probably one could avoid a neglect charge while spending less than $50 a week on a child, as long as one also kept the child's environment safe and minimally sanitary.

In addition, though, just as when spouses are not cohabiting a court can order one to pay a definite amount to the other each month as support, likewise when a parent is not cohabiting with a child all of the time, a court can order the parent to pay monthly support in behalf of the child. Most commonly, non-custodial parents make support payments to custodial parents, though there can also be situations in some states, as discussed below, in which custodial parents must pay support to a joint custodian or even to a non-custodial parent. In addition, the state attempts to collect support from parents whose children are in foster care or detention. See Daniel L. Hatcher, *Collateral Children: Consequence and Illegality at the Intersection of Foster Care and Child Support*, 74 Brook. L. Rev. 1333 (2009); Wash. Rev. Code §13.32A.175 (support order when court orders out-of-home placement of child).

Before the late nineteenth century, the state generally did not compel non-custodial parents to provide any financial support for their children. This is partly because children were viewed as an asset of the custodian, who would be compensated for investing in the child's upbringing by receiving the child's earnings in the later years of minority and by being able to rely on the offspring's support later in life. If one did not have custody and control of the child and the right to these rewards, it was only fair that one not have any duty to support. Another part of the reason was that fathers had a presumptive right to custody of their children in the event of a break-up of the family, and they were also typically the ex-spouse with the greater financial resources.

As explained in Section I above, in the late nineteenth century, there was a turn-around in the custody presumption to favor mothers. The maternal preference reigned throughout the most of the twentieth century, then was replaced by the ostensibly gender-neutral "primary caretaker" presumption that many observers say amounts in practice to a maternal preference. Along with the change in gender preference from fathers to mothers, it became more common for non-custodial parents, who were now predominantly men, to retain some rights of control and contact with respect to a child. Support duties were then increasingly imposed by legislatures and courts on non-custodial parents, justified as the quid pro quo for these rights. However, enforcement was lax.

Two developments led to stronger enforcement of support duties at the end of the twentieth century. First, moral attitudes changed; we now view a support duty as arising simply from having created a child. Whereas in the past, non-custodial parents' support obligation was tied to their rights—so that, for example, if the court ordered no visitation or if the custodial parent thwarted visitation, a non-custodial parent might be excused from paying support—the modern trend is to reject the "tying" of support and visitation. The second development partly explains the first. The rise of the welfare state has meant that the public treasury is affected when children are not provided for privately. Federal legislation that pushed states to enforce support orders more aggressively was part of the general anti-welfare campaign of the 1990s. Today child support is ordered in the vast majority of divorce and paternity actions, and enforcement has become quite rigorous. Nearly one third of all adult Americans now living are or have been a child support payor or payee.

IRA MARK ELLMAN & TARA O'TOOLE ELLMAN, THE THEORY OF CHILD SUPPORT, 45 HARV. J. ON LEGIS. 107, 129, 145 (2008): "Child support laws reflect the widespread belief that state support of children is appropriate only if parental support is impossible—what might be called the principle of the primacy of the parents' support obligation. . . . While the primacy principle may explain why the law requires support at all, it does not help much in determining support amounts. . . . We suggest that support awards are meant to accomplish three purposes, and that the appropriate amount of the award depends upon the particular blend of these three purposes applicable to any particular case. The three purposes are: (1) to protect the well-being of the child who is the order's intended beneficiary (the "well-being" component); (2) to enforce the social consensus that both parents have a support obligation, even if the child lives primarily with one parent (the "dual-obligation" component); and (3) to limit the size of the gap between the child's living standard and the higher living standard of the support obligor (the "gross-disparity" component). . . . However, claims arising from all three components are also limited by the Earner's Priority Principle . . . [that] everyone may keep what they have earned, in the absence of some very good reason to take it from them."

A separate, but related development in connection with support has been the move to statutory formulae for determining support amounts, and reducing judicial discretion, which was perceived to tend toward under-charging non-custodial parents. Thus, whereas courts act with unguided discretion in fixing the amount of spousal support payments to an estranged spouse, today determination of child support amounts, once parental income has been established, usually entails mechanical application of a percentage or table. It is therefore more predictable, objective, and consistent across cases. Primary sources of litigation today are determining parents' income and adjudicating requests for a deviation from the statutory formulae.

a. The Basic Child Support Rule

Pamela Foohey, Child Support and (In)ability to Pay: The Case for the Cost Shares Model

13 U.C. Davis J. Juv. L. & Pol'y 35, 42-55 (2009)

Prior to the late 1980s, child support obligations were determined by judges on a case-by-case basis. . . . [A]nalysts believed that awards often were deficient as compared to the true cost of raising children; obligations were inconsistent, resulting in unequal treatment of similarly situated individuals; and the adjudication of obligations was inefficient without consistent standards. To remedy these problems, the [federal] Family Support

Act of 1988 ("the Act") required states to implement mandatory numeric child support guidelines. These quantitative guidelines set presumptive child support obligations; if a judge or court wishes to deviate from the presumptive obligation, the judge or court must explain why the obligation is "unjust or inappropriate" in the specific case. . . . In response to the mandate, states have enacted three prevailing types of guidelines: the percentage of income standard, the Income Shares model, and the Delaware Melson Formula. . . .

A. Percentage of Income Standard

The simplest of the guidelines is the percentage of income standard. It currently is enacted in fourteen states. The percentage of income standard calculates child support obligations by applying a set percentage to the income of the obligor parent (some states apply the percentage to gross income, while others use net income). The obligation usually is calculated independent of the income of the custodial parent, who is assumed to meet his or her obligation by living with and caring for the child.

There are two variations of the percentage of income standard. The "flat percentage model" calculates child support based on a fixed percentage across all levels of income of the obligor parent. . . . In contrast, the "varying percentage model" applies different percentages to different levels of income. . . ." In all states that employ the percentage of income standard, the percentage varies based on the number of children supported, and, in some states, based on the children's ages. . . . For example, Wisconsin . . . applies the following percentages to the obligor's gross income: 17 percent for one child, 25 percent for two children, and 29 percent for three children. Similarly, Minnesota's model applies the following percentages to the obligor's net income: 25 percent for one child, 30 percent for two children, and 35 percent for three children. . . .

[The percentage of income model] tends to yield numerically high child support obligations . . . compared to the other guidelines. . . . Also, the flat percentage variation model tends to yield higher obligations than the varying percentage model, particularly at lower levels of obligor income. . . . [T]he percentage of income standard is criticized as being inherently unfair in not taking into account the custodial parent's income. . . . [The flat percentage model] also should be more explicitly criticized for unrealistically expecting lower-income obligors to be financially able to pay such a large percentage of their income in child support. . . . The extra expenses associated with establishing and maintaining a new (and permanent) household, even if that new household is nothing more than a small apartment, combined with other costs of divorce and permanent separation, leaves little for child support. . . . [M]any lower-income fathers (including some middle-class fathers) are not financially able to pay such a high percentage of their income in child support without sacrificing . . . a healthy life. Indeed, the Federal Office of Child Support Enforcement has itself found . . . "a downward adjustment may even be advantageous to the child if it results in an amount of support which can be paid fully, regularly, and timely by the obligor. An unrealistic order . . . may result in only sporadic payments or none. . . ."

B. Income Shares Model

The Income Shares model is the most popular child support guideline, and currently is enacted in thirty-six states. . . . [It] takes into account both the obligor's and obligee's income. . . . It sets child support obligations by first determining what proportion of their combined income the divorcing parents [should devote to] their children. . . . This determination is based on economic data estimating child-rearing expenses; the applicable base child-rearing expense amount is adjusted according to extraordinary expenses unique to the divorcing couple's children such as child care and medical expenses. The final amount, termed the "basic child support obligation," is then pro-rated between the two parents based on their relative incomes.

For example, assume that the custodial parent's yearly income is $50,000, the non-custodial parent's yearly income is $70,000, 25 percent of the parents combined income [would ordinarily be] spent on their two children . . . , and there are no extraordinary expenses. The $30,000 "basic child support obligation" would be apportioned $12,500 to the custodial parent and $17,500 to the non-custodial parent. Accordingly, the non-custodial parent would owe the custodial parent $17,500 per year in child support for their two children. . . . [C]hild-rearing expense estimates vary slightly state-to-state. . . .

[U]nlike the percentage of income standard, the Income Shares model . . . yields higher or lower obligations when the parents' incomes are divergent. . . . However, though the Income Shares model may yield numerically lower child support obligations for lower-income obligors as the other parent's income increases, it still unrealistically expects some lower-income obligors to be financially able to pay a large percentage of their incomes in child support. . . .

C. Delaware Melson Formula

The Delaware Melson Formula . . . currently is used in three states [Delaware, Hawaii, and Montana]. It . . . is a three-step calculation. First, the net income of each parent is calculated; from this net income, a self-support reserve is subtracted. Second, each parent's remaining income is applied to a pre-determined primary support need for the child or children. . . . Third, "[t]o the extent that either parent has income available after covering the self-support reserve and his or her share of the child's [or children's] primary support needs, an additional percentage of the remaining income is applied to the child support obligation." The total child support obligation for each parent is calculated by adding steps two and three. For example, the current Delaware guidelines incorporate a self-support reserve of $970 per month, and provide a minimum child support obligation based on the number of children ($720 per month for two children assuming the parents' combined income is sufficient to pay that amount). This minimum child support obligation is increased by a set percentage to reflect an appropriate standard of living adjustment (24% of remaining net income in the case of two children). . . .

[T]he Melson Formula . . . presumes that "the support of others is impossible until one's own basic support needs are met" and that higher income parents "should share their additional incomes with their children, improving their children's standard of living as their own standard of living improves." . . . [B]ecause of its self-support reserve, the Melson Formula tends to yield obligations that are lower when the parents' income is lower as compared to the other two guidelines, and because of its sharing of additional income, it tends to yield higher obligations when the parents' income is higher as compared to the other two guidelines. . . . [I]t is not the lowest income obligors that are the most likely to not be able to financially pay; rather, it is those obligors whose income falls at the low end of "middle income" that . . . are unable to afford their child support obligations without slipping close to the poverty line on which the allowance for basic needs is built, a line that may not allow them to maintain a life that permits them to sustain their current level of income. . . .

Texas's child support rule embodies a flat percentage-of-income model, at least for middle- and low-income non-custodial parents:

Vernon's Texas Statutes and Codes, Family Code
Title 5, Subtitle B. Suits Affecting the Parent-Child Relationship
Chapter 154, Subchapter C. Child Support Guidelines

§154.125. Application of Guidelines to Net Resources

(a) . . . are specifically designed to apply to situations in which the obligor's monthly net resources are not greater than $7,500. . . .

(b) If the obligor's monthly net resources are not greater than [$7,500], the court shall presumptively apply the following schedule in rendering the child support order:

1 child	20% of Obligor's Net Resources
2 children	25% of Obligor's Net Resources
3 children	30% of Obligor's Net Resources
4 children	35% of Obligor's Net Resources
5 children	40% of Obligor's Net Resources
6+ children	Not less than the amount for 5 children

§154.126. Application of Guidelines to Additional Net Resources

(a) If the obligor's net resources exceed [$7,500], the court shall presumptively apply the percentage guidelines to the portion of the obligor's net resources that does not exceed that amount. Without further reference to the percentage recommended by these guidelines, the court may order additional amounts of child support as appropriate, depending on the income of the parties and the proven needs of the child.

Section 154.126(a) retains for higher-income levels the broad discretion that courts previously exercised at all income levels.

Like the percentage-of-income guidelines, the income-shares approach can apply the same percentages at all income levels or have the percentage vary by income level. New York's child support rule follows the income-shares model using flat percentages:

McKinney's Consolidated Laws of New York
Domestic Relations Law
Chapter 14, Article 13. Provisions Applicable to More Than One Type of Matrimonial Action

§240. Custody and Child Support; Orders of Protection

1-b. . . . (b)

(3) "Child support percentage" shall mean:

(i) seventeen percent of the combined parental income for one child;

(ii) twenty-five percent of the combined parental income for two children;

(iii) twenty-nine percent of the combined parental income for three children;

(iv) thirty-one percent of the combined parental income for four children; and

(v) no less than thirty-five percent of the combined parental income for five or more children.

(4) "Combined parental income" shall mean the sum of the income of both parents.

(c) The amount of the basic child support obligation shall be determined in accordance with the provision of this paragraph:

(1) The court shall determine the combined parental income.

(2) The court shall multiply the combined parental income . . . by the appropriate child support percentage and such amount shall be prorated in the same proportion as each parent's income is to the combined parental income. . . .

(f) . . . Unless the court finds that the non-custodial parents' pro-rata share of the basic child support obligation is unjust or inappropriate, which finding shall be based upon consideration of the following factors:

(1) The financial resources of the custodial and non-custodial parent, and those of the child;

(2) The physical and emotional health of the child and his/her special needs and aptitudes;

(3) The standard of living the child would have enjoyed had the marriage or household not been dissolved;

(4) The tax consequences to the parties;

(5) The non-monetary contributions that the parents will make toward the care and well-being of the child;

(6) The educational needs of either parent;

(7) A determination that the gross income of one parent is substantially less than the other parent's gross income;

(8) The needs of the children of the non-custodial parent for whom the non-custodial parent is providing support who are not subject to the instant action and whose support has not been deducted from income . . . , and the financial resources of any person obligated to support such children, provided, however, that this factor may apply only if the resources available to support such children are less than the resources available to support the children who are subject to the instant action;

(9) Provided that the child is not on public assistance (i) extraordinary expenses incurred by the non-custodial parent in exercising visitation, or (ii) expenses incurred by the non-custodial parent in extended visitation provided that the custodial parent's expenses are substantially reduced as a result thereof; and

(10) Any other factors the court determines are relevant in each case,

the court shall order the non-custodial parent to pay his or her pro rata share of the basic child support obligation . . . .

(g) Where the court finds that the non-custodial parent's pro rata share of the basic child support obligation is unjust or inappropriate, the court shall order the non-custodial parent to pay such amount of child support as the court finds just and appropriate. . . .

Additional provisions dictate additions to the basic support obligation for a child's medical expenses and for child-care expenses if the custodial parent is working or attending school. Another omitted provision authorizes imposition of just a nominal support obligation—$50 or $25 per month—for very low income non-custodial parents.

In Virginia's income-shares model, in contrast, the percentage of combined income designated for support of children varies by income level. The Virginia statute therefore lays out a table that looks like the federal income tax tables, with a combined obligation specified at different combined income levels, in $50 increments, up to a certain level of income. After $10,000 combined monthly income, the statute applies a very small percentage at higher levels. Most of the lines are omitted below.

Code of Virginia
Title 20. Domestic Relations
Chapter 6. Divorce, Affirmation and Annulment

§20-108.2. Guideline for Determination of Child Support

A. There shall be a rebuttable presumption in any judicial or administrative proceeding for child support . . . that the amount of the award which would result from the application of the guidelines set forth in this section is the correct amount of child support to be awarded. In order to rebut the presumption, the court shall make written findings . . . that the application of the guidelines would be unjust or inappropriate in a particular case. . . .

B. . . . [A] basic child support obligation shall be computed using the schedule set out below. . . . "Number of children" means the number of children for whom the parents share joint legal responsibility and for whom support is being sought.

SCHEDULE OF MONTHLY BASIC CHILD SUPPORT OBLIGATIONS

COMBINED MONTHLY GROSS INCOME	ONE CHILD	TWO CHILDREN	THREE	FOUR	FIVE	SIX
0-599	65	65	65	65	65	65
600	110	111	113	114	115	116
. . .						
1000	196	304	344	348	351	355
. . .						
1500	274	426	533	602	656	680
. . .						
3000	445	691	866	975	1064	1138
. . .						
5000	666	1036	1295	1460	1593	1704
5050	671	1043	1305	1471	1605	1716
. . .						
7000	848	1315	1644	1855	2024	2163
. . .						
10000	1014	1577	1977	2222	2427	2596

For gross monthly income between $10,000 and $20,000, add the amount of child support for $10,000 to the following percentages of gross income above $10,000:

ONE CHILD	TWO CHILDREN	THREE	FOUR	FIVE	SIX
3.1%	5.1%	6.8%	7.8%	8.8%	9.5%

For gross monthly income between $20,000 and $50,000, add the amount of child support for $20,000 to the following percentages of gross income above $20,000:

2%	3.5%	5%	6%	6.9%	7.8%

For gross monthly income over $50,000, add the amount of child support for $50,000 to the following percentages of gross income above $50,000:

1%	2%	3%	4%	5%	6.5%

. . .

G. 1. The sole custody total monthly child support obligation shall be established by adding (i) the monthly basic child support obligation, as determined from the schedule contained in subsection B, (ii) costs for health care coverage . . . , and (iii) work-related child-care costs . . . The total monthly child support obligation shall be divided between the parents in the same proportion as their monthly gross incomes bear to their monthly combined gross income. The monthly obligation of each parent shall be computed by multiplying each parent's percentage of the parents' monthly combined gross income by the total monthly child support obligation.

What this statutory provision leaves unstated is that the non-custodial parent should pay the custodial parent each month the amount of the non-custodial parent's monthly obligation. The custodial parent is presumed to fulfill her monthly support obligation by paying directly for child rearing expenses on a daily basis.

Virginia's guidelines are obviously more complicated than those of Texas. Most states have concluded it is worth the complication to achieve fairer results. What makes the Virginia approach fairer? Of course, fairness also depends on what percentages legislatures insert in the guidelines. Calculate the percentages that Virginia uses at different income levels (e.g., at $5,000 combined income, the percentage when there are two children is just over 20%) and compare them with those in the Texas and New York statutes.

The statutory provisions above all assumed a traditional arrangement with a custodial parent and a non-custodial parent, but a significant percentage of non-cohabiting parents share joint custody. Virginia deals with this by adding another, barely comprehensible step in the calculations. Do not puzzle over it too much; practicing attorneys in Virginia do not understand it, but instead just put income figures into a computer program provided by the state that does the calculations for them. The bottom line is that when both parents have the child for more than 90 days of the year, a parent who might otherwise be a non-custodial obligor typically pays substantially less in child support. In fact, as explained below, it is possible under the shared-custody support rule for a parent who has 91 days of visitation per year to be the recipient of child support rather than the payor.

§20-108.2. Guideline for Determination of Child Support

G. . . . 3. Shared custody support.

(a) Where a party has custody or visitation of a child or children for more than 90 days of the year . . . , a shared custody child support amount based on the ratio in which the parents share the custody and visitation of any child or children shall be calculated in accordance with this subdivision. . . .

(ii) Custody share. "Custody share" means the number of days that a parent has physical custody, whether by sole custody, joint legal or joint residential custody, or visitation, of a shared child per year divided by the number of days in the year. . . .

(iii) Shared support need. "Shared support need" means the presumptive guideline amount of needed support for the shared child or children calculated pursuant to . . . [the guideline above] multiplied by 1.4. . . . .

(b) Support to be paid. The shared support need of the shared child or children shall be calculated pursuant to subdivision G3(a)(iii). This amount shall then be multiplied by the other parent's custody share. . . . This total for each parent shall be multiplied by that parent's income share. The support amounts thereby calculated that each parent owes the other shall be subtracted one from the other and the difference shall be the shared custody support one parent owes to the other, with the payor parent being the one whose shared support is the larger. Unreimbursed medical and dental expenses shall be calculated and allocated. . . .

(c) Definition of a day. For the purposes of this section, "day" means a period of 24 hours; however, where the parent who has the fewer number of overnight periods during the year has an overnight period with a child, but has physical custody of the shared child for less than 24 hours during such overnight period, there is a presumption that each parent shall be allocated one-half of a day of custody for that period. . . .

Additional language concerning day care expenses is omitted above; those expenses are usually added on top of the guideline support amount prior to allocating the obligation between parents. A few other things to note about shared custody support:

First, "shared custody" here is independent of how the court or parties characterize the allocation of parenting time in deciding custody. The court order or settlement agreement might say "mother will have primary custody and father visitation," but if father's visitation adds up to over 90 days per year, then they have shared custody for child support purposes. Second, this means that in practice attorneys should be very mindful of the 90-day threshold, and parents are likely to fight about the precise allocation of parenting time when they are close to that threshold, because of this substantial financial implication. An attorney for a parent likely to be a child-support-paying non-custodial parent who unthinkingly accepts a proposal from the other side that his or her client enjoy 87 days of visitation per year is a bad attorney.

Third, it is actually possible that pushing a client's visitation up over 90 days will result in the client *receiving* child support instead of paying it. Whereas the provision for sole custody support says simply that after allocating the children's support need between the parents based on income, the non-custodial pays the amount allocated to him to the custodial parent, paragraph (b) of the shared support provision says that after determining each parent's share of support, whichever parent has the higher amount should pay the other that amount minus the other parent's obligation. It is possible that the parent who has the higher amount is the parent with primary custody, if that parent has a much higher income. For example, suppose a primary breadwinner father assumes primary custody of the children after a divorce, perhaps because the mother is starting professional school, but the mother has visitation with the children for 95 days per year. The father likely will pay child support to the mother (at least absent imputation of income to the mother, a topic addressed below). This is an unusual situation; usually the parent who takes on greater responsibility for physical care of the children has lower income. But it can happen, and as you might imagine, custodial parents in that situation perceive it as quite unjust. Is it?

Utah, which follows the percentage-of-income approach, addresses substantial visitation time in a different way. It reduces the guideline child support amount during any extended period when the children are solely or primarily with the payor. It should be reduced by 50 percent when the child spends "at least 25 of any 30 consecutive days" with the non-custodial parent, or by 25 percent when the child spends "at least 12 of any 30 consecutive days" with the non-custodial parent. Utah Code Ann. §78B-12-216. See also 2008 Mich. Child Support Formula 3.03(A). When parents live far apart, they often divide custody between the school year and the summer, and this provision would allow the non-custodial parent to pay less support during a long summer visit. The basic rationale for reducing or flipping a child support order when a "non-custodial parent" has a lot of visitation is that in such a case the non-custodial parent must set up a household like that of a custodial parent, with bedrooms, toys, etc., and so has greater child-related expenses than the guidelines assume. But cf. William V. Fabricius & Sanford L. Braver, *Non-Child Support Expenditures on Children by Nonresidential Divorced Fathers*, 41 FAM. CT. REV. 321 (2003) (arguing that, because even at levels of visitation time below thresholds like Virginia's 90 days, non-custodial parents typically incur such expenses, there should be a downward adjustment of the child support obligation based on amount of contact also at those lower levels).

POLICY QUESTIONS

It is generally assumed that child support guidelines have produced higher average awards—that is, that guideline formulae are more generous than judges were on average when they exercised unguided discretion. And more aggressive enforcement has certainly resulted in a dramatically higher average of actual payments. Today, therefore, if cohabiting parents take into account the financial consequences of dissolving their relationship when deciding whether to stay together, child support could be a significant consideration. Would you suppose that these child support reforms have increased or decreased the rate of dissolution (including divorce by married parents and separation of never-married parents)? Is it likely to matter whether women or men are more likely to push a relationship toward dissolution? Could the child support rules also affect unmarried couples' decision whether to get married, either before or after they conceive a child? Is it likely to matter whether women or men are more likely to push a relationship toward marriage? Could the rules influence decisions about having children after a couple marries? Cf. Barham, Devlin & Yang, *Public Policies and Private Decisions: The Effect of Child Support Measures on Marriage and Divorce*, 35 J. Legal Stud. 441 (2006) (finding "some evidence to suggest that the probability of marrying has increased as a result of the guidelines" and "a positive and statistically significant (at the 7 percent level) impact on the probability of divorce"). Should any such effects be relevant to child support policy? Imagine yourself in each situation. Could the potential for a child support order influence your decision about whether to have a child with someone or about whether to continue a relationship with someone after having a child with him or her?

Termination of the Support Obligation

Most states mandate payment of child support until offspring reach adulthood, typically defined as age 18, completion of high school, or age 21. In nearly 20 states, though, statutes authorize courts to order parents to continue assisting their children financially while they attend college, at least so long as the children are diligent. Cf. McLeod v. Starnes, 723 S.E.2d 198 (S.C. 2012) (rejecting equal protection objection to compelled payment of college expenses, finding rational basis for treating divorced parents different from parents in intact families). Massachusetts adds a requirement that the offspring be living with the other parent. Mass. Gen. Laws ch. 208, §28 ("The court may make appropriate orders of maintenance, support and education for any child . . . who has not attained age twenty-three, if such child is domiciled in the home of a parent, and is principally dependent upon said parent for maintenance due to the enrollment of such child in an educational program, excluding educational costs beyond an undergraduate degree."). Such court orders are not limited to millionaires; courts are willing to impose this burden even on parents with little net income, potentially forcing them to take out large loans themselves to pay for tuition. See, e.g., In re Marriage of Cianchetti, 815 N.E.2d 17 (Ill. App. Ct. 2004) (upholding order that father pay $15,000 per year toward daughters' college tuition, even though he had zero net income, reasoning that he previously mortgaged his house to pay for prep school and so could do it also for college).

In contrast, the civil codes of many European countries have provisions requiring parents to support their children for as long as they are not financially independent. Young adults in many European countries are much more likely than their American counterparts to live with their parents and to be dependent on them well into their 20s and even beyond 30, and difficult economic times prolong this dependency. Occasionally parents rebel and courts must decide whether chronically lazy offspring (who, surprisingly, are often law school graduates!) still deserve parental beneficence.

Al Goodman, Judge Orders 25-Year-Old Man to Leave Home and Find Job

CNN, Apr. 27, 2011

A 25-year-old Spanish man has been ordered by a judge to leave home and look for a job after he took his parents to court for stopping his allowance money. The man from Andalusia in southern Spain had taken the court action demanding a monthly allowance of $588 after his parents stopped giving him his spending money unless he tried to find a job. However, the judge told the man, who has not been named in court documents, that he must leave his parents' house within 30 days. The judge said the man was studying law, albeit at a slow rate, and would probably not complete the degree for several years, but he thought he was still capable of finding some kind of work.

The family court in Malaga says the situation at the home had seriously deteriorated with the parents claiming their son had physically and verbally assaulted them. The man's mother works in a restaurant while his father works for a garbage collection firm. The judge also ordered that the parents should pay a $292 monthly food stipend for 2 years. The parents have also taken over the monthly repayments on their son's car.

In Spain it is not unusual for offspring to remain living with their parents until well into their 30s, a trend strengthened by a tough labor market where the youth unemployment rate is 40.5%, the highest in the European Union. . . .

Several years before the Spain case, there was a similar one in Italy. See Sarah Delaney, *A Lot of Slack in the Apron Strings*, WASH. POST, Apr. 8, 2002, and Philip Willan, *Italian Court Tells Father to Support Stay at Home Son, 30*, GUARDIAN, Apr. 6, 2002 (describing decision of Italy's highest court that a 70-year-old Naples man must pay his lawyer son $700 per month until the son is able to find a job "adequate to his specific preparation, his attitudes and his interests, stating: 'You cannot blame a young person, particularly from a well off family, who refuses a job that does not fit his aspirations.'"). Such stories inspired the comedy film *Tanguy*.

Note that most European countries also grant offspring a right to inherit from their parents. In contrast, in the United States, apart from Louisiana, states confer no right on offspring to a "forced share" of a parent's estate, even if the parent was at the time of death a non-custodial parent under a child support obligation. See, e.g., Va. Code Ann. §20-124.2 ("The court shall have no authority to decree support of children payable by the estate of a deceased party.") In Australia, the government provides a Common Youth Allowance for full-time students up to age 25, though there is an expectation parents will instead provide support if able. See Bruce Smyth, *Child Support for Young Adult Children in Australia,* 16 INT'L J.L. POL'Y & FAM. 22 (2002). What is the justification for these financial protections of adult offspring? Is there something wrong with the American character that we think parents need to be able to withhold wealth from their adult offspring in order to reward good behavior and punish ungrateful or ne'er-do-well children? Should U.S. states reconsider now given the great difficulty young people are having finding jobs? Do you think your parents should remain legally obligated to support you?

Some scholars argue in this context that the law of child support should mirror ordinary parental choices in an intact marriage, on the theory that children should not suffer loss of an important benefit as a result of their parents' divorcing, and they note that most children whose parents are married to each other when the children attend college receive substantial financial assistance from their parents. See, e.g., Monica Hof Wallace, *A Federal Referendum Extending Child Support for Higher Education*, 58 U. KAN. L. REV. 665 (2010). Why would a parent make different choices about funding an offspring's college education based on his or her relationship with the other parent? Cf. Fabricius & Braver, *Non-Child Support Expenditures on Children by Nonresidential Divorced Fathers*, supra (finding substantial contribution by non-custodial parents to offspring's college education even in states where courts cannot order such contribution, in amounts equivalent to the contributions of custodial parents on an income-adjusted basis, with a strong correlation between amount of contribution and both amount of visitation time the non-custodial parents had enjoyed and having joint legal custody). Is there a downside for college students if a court has ordered their parents to pay for their education against the parents' wishes? Note that in any state, parents can bind themselves in a dissolution agreement to providing post-majority support, and many do so. Courts do enforce contractual promises to provide more support than is legally required.

A widespread exception to the age-based termination of child support is one for offspring who are disabled in a way that delays or precludes independent living. See, e.g., Ind. Code §31-16-6-6 ("The duty to support a child . . . ceases when the child becomes twenty-one years of age unless . . . [t]he child is incapacitated. In this case the child support continues during the incapacity or until further order of the court."). Courts in most states can order support for as long as the offspring remains non-self-sufficient. See Katherine Ellis Reeves, *Post-Majority Child Support Awards for Disabled Children: A Fifty State Survey*, 8 WHITTIER J. CHILD & FAM. ADVOC. 109. Is it fair to parents to impose this obligation, which is greater than that of other parents simply because their child is disabled? Or should the public pick up the full financial burden of disability when an offspring reaches the age of adulthood? Consider that a rule perpetuating such a parent's obligation creates an incentive for people to avoid having a child with a disability or to refrain from extraordinary measures to preserve the life of an offspring with disabilities.

Traditionally, as noted above, child support obligations have also ceased when an obligor parent died, though some states have reversed this rule. See, e.g., 750 Ill. Comp. Stat. 5/510 ("An existing obligation to pay for support or educational expenses, or both, is not terminated by the death of a parent. When a parent obligated to pay support or educational expenses, or both, dies, the amount of support or educational expenses, or both, may be enforced, modified, revoked or commuted to a lump sum payment, as equity may require. . . ."). Moreover, as noted, offspring in nearly all states have no claim on the estate of deceased parents who have wills leaving all their property to other people. However, parents who draft wills ordinarily leave a substantial portion of their estate to any children they had with an ex-partner, and if a parent who had children with an ex-partner leaves no will then all of his or her children are entitled to some share of the estate, even if the parent dies while married to a different partner. In addition, courts routinely order, or parties agree, that an obligor parent will maintain a life insurance policy naming the child as a beneficiary until the child reaches the age at which child support would ordinarily cease.

In addition to monthly payments and life insurance, child support orders and agreements typically also address allocation of expenses for health insurance, medical expenses not covered by health insurance, schooling (if the child will attend private school), extracurricular activities, and vacation camps. These are ordinarily allocated between the parents based on respective income, or if allocated primarily to the child-support-obligor parent they might be a basis for a downward deviation from the support guideline amount.

Under any of the approaches to guidelines, courts are routinely called on to resolve disputes over what constitutes income, when deviation from guideline amounts is appropriate, and whether a parent is voluntarily under-employed and so should have income imputed to him or her.

Income Tax Treatment

Before delving into the most-often litigated details, a note about taxation: In contrast to spousal support payments, child support payments do not affect the income tax obligation of payor or payee. A payor of both kinds of support may deduct alimony payments from income, making the actual loss to the payor less than the nominal amount of the obligation, but cannot deduct child support payments. Conversely, a recipient of both types of payments must declare alimony as taxable income but need not include child support payments in income. We can most readily explain not including child support in the recipient's income, based on the assumption that child support belongs to the child, not the custodial parent. It is less clear why the child support obligor is not permitted to deduct child support payments from income and, conversely, why alimony is not likewise treated as a redistribution of after-tax income. Allowing a deduction for child support would effectively shift some of the cost of raising children in "fractured families" to other taxpayers (assuming no one is taxed for receiving the support, or that a person for whom the support is taxable (the other parent or the child) has a lower marginal tax rate), and it would likely improve rates of compliance with child support orders, so deductibility would seem to be a good thing for children. IRS treatment of spousal support effectively shifts some of the cost of post-divorce recovery for dependent spouses to other taxpayers, insofar as it allows divorcing couples to shift income from the person in a higher tax bracket to the person in a lower tax bracket, so that in the aggregate the ex-spouses pay less tax than they would in the absence of an alimony obligation. Courts and divorce attorneys can take tax effects into account in setting the nominal amount of a support order at an appropriate level, which should result in higher nominal awards than if there were no tax effect.

b. Determining Income

Arriving at figures to which statutory percentages or tables will apply is as complicated as determining taxable income on IRS Form 1040. A great many things count as income for child support purposes, and in addition, many things can be deducted from income.

Vernon's Texas Statutes and Codes, Family Code
Title 5, Subtitle B. Suits Affecting the Parent-Child Relationship
Chap. 154, Subch. B. Computing Net Resources Available for Child Support

§154.062. Net Resources

(b) Resources include:

(1) 100 percent of all wage and salary income and other compensation for personal services (including commissions, overtime pay, tips, and bonuses);

(2) interest, dividends, and royalty income;

(3) self-employment income;

(4) net rental income (defined as rent after deducting operating expenses and mortgage payments, but not including noncash items such as depreciation); and

(5) all other income actually being received, including severance pay, retirement benefits, pensions, trust income, annuities, capital gains, social security benefits other

than supplemental security income, unemployment benefits, disability and workers' compensation benefits, interest income from notes regardless of the source, gifts and prizes, spousal maintenance, and alimony.

(c) Resources do not include:

(1) return of principal or capital;

(2) accounts receivable;

(3) benefits [from] the Temporary Assistance for Needy Families program; or

(4) payments for foster care of a child.

(d) The court shall deduct the following items from resources . . . :

(1) social security taxes;

(2) federal income tax based on the tax rate for a single person claiming one personal exemption and the standard deduction;

(3) state income tax;

(4) union dues; and

(5) expenses for the cost of health insurance or cash medical support for the obligor's child ordered by the court. . . .

Some of the most common issues that arise in calculating income are whether one party is concealing income, whether employer-provided benefits other than pay should be counted as income, whether gifts a party receives from family should be included, and whether income should be imputed to a parent who is accused of being voluntarily underemployed.

Concealing income is easier for those who are self-employed. The following case illustrates this and also how support can be ordered retroactively.

McDonald v. Trihub

173 P.3d 416 (Alaska 2007)

Carpeneti, Justice.

. . . Curtis McDonald and Yvonne Trihub were involved in a relationship but never married. They had one child, Gideon, born in Anchorage in 1992. Six months after Gideon was born, the parties separated. Yvonne and Gideon lived in Oregon during the mid 1990's. During that period and until August or September 1999, Curtis paid Yvonne some level of child support, ranging from $275 to $475 a month. The parties did not seek or obtain a support or custody order. In 1999 Yvonne and Gideon returned to Alaska and resided with Curtis until May 2000. . . .

On May 8, 2006, Judge Tan issued a final order concluding that Yvonne had primary physical custody of Gideon during 2000-2002, 2004, and 2005, calculating Curtis's support obligations from 2000 forward using a wage of twenty dollars per hour, and setting Curtis's support obligation for May 2000 forward. Curtis's monthly support obligation was determined to be approximately $560. . . .

Curtis asserts that the superior court erred in establishing his retrospective support obligation based upon a wage of twenty dollars per hour for a "skilled mechanic." He claims that the court used this figure as imputed income but made no finding that he was underemployed. Contrary to Curtis's contention, the court's decision to approximate income was not based on a finding that Curtis was underemployed, but rather was an effort to estimate Curtis's income accurately in light of the confusing and non-credible nature of the evidence Curtis had presented. We conclude that the decision to do so was reasonable. A trial court must apply the methodology of Rule 90.3 to establish the amount due to a custodial parent for child support during periods not covered by a support order. The court's calculation of income for the purposes of establishing the amount of support owed should be a "reasonable assessment" of the obligor's earning capacity.

Curtis contends that in establishing the retrospective award his actual income should have been used, and that the court's use of the hourly wage was error. Our recent case law provides that actual income is an acceptable basis for establishing past support "accruing over a relatively short duration," but here the superior court was confronted with establishing Curtis's support obligations over a six-year period. Moreover, we have recognized that a trial court may estimate income for the purpose of calculating support where no other accurate or credible information is available.

In this case, the court attempted to approximate Curtis's income amid evidence that was at best contradictory and inchoate, and at worst misleading. . . . Curtis's tax returns were not consistent with his bank records. Judge Tan found that Curtis's cash flow likely underestimated his income, that Curtis "was not careful about keeping business records," and that the various income numbers presented were "guesstimates at best." The court also recognized that while Curtis was doing "favors" for friends by providing labor for excavations in the form of a bartering system, he provided no written record of these transactions. Judge Tan ultimately concluded that the court did not have a "complete picture of Mr. McDonald's actual income."

The court's rejection of Curtis's proffered income evidence is perhaps best justified because . . . it [was] confounding, unreliable, or both. At the April 2006 court hearing, Curtis's counsel contended that Curtis's income from "2000 until present" was in the "$25,000 range." But Curtis's tax returns reflected a much lower figure—his 1999 adjusted gross income was $9,612 and his 2000 income was $8,307. At no time does Curtis explain the discrepancy between these figures. CSSD recognized the discrepancy and rejected Curtis's 2003 tax return, which reflected a business income of $11,186, and instead initially calculated Curtis's 2003 obligation based on the total amount of deposits ($72,897) made to his business checking account. Following the administrative hearing, CSSD . . . instead calculated Curtis's obligations on the total amount of personal checks Curtis withdrew from his business for personal expenses—$25,730.17 in 2003 and $24,101.18 in 2004. The administrative decision subsequently concluded that this latter method was ". . . the best evidence of [Curtis]'s income for child support purposes." . . .

Judge Tan noted that it would be nearly impossible to "go back and recreate" Curtis's income from the information presented. The court chose to approximate Curtis's income using a wage of $20 per hour. . . . Curtis owned and operated a business buying and selling used motor homes, that he worked as an automobile mechanic repairing and upgrading the motor homes for resale, and that as recently as 2004 he held a business license for "auto repair and sales." Evidence established that the mean wage for automotive service technicians and mechanics in Anchorage was $20.51 per hour. Curtis also maintained a commercial driver's license and has performed some excavation work, including putting water lines in for a housing development and laying foundations in the summer of 2004. Evidence established that the mean wage for "machine operators, excavating" was $19.32 per hour. In light of this evidence, Judge Tan's use of a wage of twenty dollars per hour as an estimate of Curtis's income was reasonable. . . .

Curtis's testimony also indicated that he had little memory of or willingness to discuss his prior cash flow, income, and bookkeeping practices. Curtis was asked about the large discrepancies between his business bank statements and his tax returns. . . . He repeatedly responded "I don't know" and added "you'd have to ask the accountant." . . . He also stated that he kept his own books for his business, but that he "didn't really keep any records," he "didn't see any reason why" he needed to maintain accurate bookkeeping, and that the accountant who did his taxes was a friend. . . .

Curtis claims that . . . 2005-2006 . . . a knee injury rendered him incapable of performing anything but sedentary work, that there was no evidence in the record that he worked in 2005, and that his prospective support obligation should therefore have been varied for "good cause." . . . Rule 90.3(c) provides that the court may vary a support award for good cause; however we "will not relieve a noncustodial parent from his child support obligations absent an affirmative showing that the obligor parent cannot meet this obligation." . . . Curtis's evidence of his alleged disability consisted largely of his own testimony. He testified that he "blew . . . out" his ACL ten years before trial and had been receiving injections into his knee to help him get around, that he would need a knee replacement in the future, and that he often wore a knee brace. He testified that he could no longer work on heavy equipment and could only do light-duty work "up until a year ago." He testified that shortly after Christmas 2004 he had a snow machine accident and "blew [his] knee apart," that from late December 2004 on he could perform only limited work, and that his doctor ordered that he be "totally off work" from October 2006 (when Curtis suggested he might undergo knee surgery) until January 1, 2007. However, . . . [h]e admitted to being able to maintain work over the last 14 years despite his knee problems and testified that he continued to go snow machining with his son and stay "pretty active." His wife testified that Curtis was still able to go four-wheeling. And while Curtis testified that he could not work on heavy equipment because his knee was so susceptible to injury, he later explained that when he worked at his shop he would "climb ladders and climb inside and get underneath [the motor homes and vehicles]."

We have previously rejected a trial court's order holding in abeyance a party's support obligation based on its decision that the party could no longer work as a carpenter where there was "no testimony by a physician regarding the nature or extent of the [obligor's] injuries and disability." In this case Curtis presented scant evidence of the nature of his injury. Neither of the one-page forms he produced from the Anchorage Fracture & Orthopedic Clinic contained any formal diagnosis or specific comments on Curtis's injury. Curtis did not call a physician to testify nor did he offer any further medical documentation on the existence or extent of his injury.

Moreover, Curtis's contention that his support obligation should be reduced because there was "no evidence" that he worked in 2005 reverses the burden of proof and is otherwise suspect. Curtis, who had worked continuously for years, never testified that he was unemployed in 2005. . . . And Curtis's counsel contended that Curtis's average income had been about $25,000 "over the years from 2000 *until present.*" Finally, to the extent that Curtis was not working, he made no showing of other job or training opportunities that he had been actively pursuing such that he might have been found to be reasonably underemployed. . . . We therefore conclude that the superior court decision establishing Curtis's prospective support obligation was reasonable.

If you were Curtis's attorney, how would you prepare for trial? What justifications for under-employment does the court suggest are valid? Are there others you think appropriate? Below are two cases addressing non-monetary employment benefits.

Massey v. Evans

886 N.Y.S.2d 280 (App. Div. 2009)

PERADOTTO, J.

. . . Petitioner mother commenced this proceeding seeking a determination that respondent is the father of her then-two-year-old child and seeking an award of child support. After an order of filiation was entered, the parties stipulated that the mother earns $14,226 per year and that the father receives base pay from the military in the amount of $22,186.80 per year. The parties further stipulated that, in addition to his base pay, the father receives BAH [Basic Allowance for Housing] in the amount of $10,776 per year and BAS [Basic Allowance for Subsistence] in the amount of $3,533.16 per year. BAH is a monthly sum paid to members of the military who do not reside in government-supplied housing. The amount of BAH, which is intended to offset the cost of civilian housing, varies according to the member's pay grade, geographic location, and dependency status. BAS is an additional monthly sum paid to active duty members to subsidize the cost of meals purchased for the benefit of the individual member on or off base. The amount of BAS is based upon average food costs as determined by the federal government. . . .

The specific question of whether military allowances may be included in a parent's income for child support purposes has never been addressed by a New York court. The Child Support Standards Act (CSSA), codified in Domestic Relations Law §240 and Family Court Act §413, establishes a formula for calculating a parent's basic child support obligation. One of the primary goals of the legislation is "to establish equitable support awards that provide a 'fair and reasonable sum' for the child's needs within the parents' means," and to enable children to "share in the economic status of both their parents." To that end, the amount of child support required by the statute is based in large part on a determination of parental income. Family Court Act §413(1)(b)(5) provides that a parent's "income" includes, but is not limited to, gross income as reported on the most recent federal income tax return and, to the extent not reflected in that amount, "income received" from eight enumerated sources such as workers' compensation, disability benefits, unemployment insurance benefits, and veterans benefits.

The statute also affords courts considerable discretion to attribute or impute income from "such other resources as may be available to the parent." Such resources include, but are not limited to,

> "meals, lodging, memberships, automobiles or other perquisites that are provided as part of compensation for employment to the extent that such perquisites constitute expenditures for personal use, or which expenditures directly or indirectly confer personal economic benefits [and] . . . fringe benefits provided as part of compensation for employment."

. . . As courts in other states have noted . . . , the purposes underlying the federal tax code and child support statutes are different. The objective of the former is to calculate an individual's taxable income, while the objective of the latter is to determine the amount that a parent can afford to pay for the support of his or her child. . . . Notably, veterans benefits are specifically included in the Family Court Act's definition of income, notwithstanding the fact that such benefits are excluded from taxable income under federal law. . . . In any event, federal law defines "regular compensation" or "regular military compensation" as

> "the total of the following elements that a member of a uniformed service accrues or receives, directly or indirectly, in cash or in kind every payday: basic pay, *basic allowance for housing, basic allowance for subsistence*; and Federal tax advantage accruing to the aforementioned allowances because they are not subject to Federal income tax."

. . . The father also . . . relies on federal tax regulations for the proposition that the value of meals or lodging furnished to an employee for the convenience of his or her employer is excluded from gross income. Even assuming, arguendo, that such regulations are relevant . . . , we note that meals and lodging furnished to an employee or his or her dependents are excluded from income only if "the meals are furnished on the business premises of the employer . . . [and] the employee is required to accept such lodging on the business premises of his [or her] employer as a condition of his [or her] employment." Here, the father receives BAS in the form of additional cash in his paycheck, which can be used to purchase meals or groceries at establishments of his choice, and BAH is applied to the father's choice of dwellings. There is thus no question that the food and housing allowances "directly or indirectly confer personal economic benefits" upon the father. . . . [C]ourts in other states have uniformly held that military allowances are properly included in a parent's income for child support purposes (*see e.g. D.F. v. L.T.* (La. 2006); *Hopkins v. Batt* (Neb. 1998); *Hautala v. Hautala* (S.C. 1988).

The father cannot give any portion of the housing allowance to the child or custodial parent, so why is it considered part of the father's income from which support can be expected? The next case deals with several more common non-monetary employment benefits and also a not uncommon situation in which parents disagree about the necessity for extraordinary expenses.

Murphy v. McDermott

979 A.2d 373 (Pa. Super. Ct. 2009)

Opinion by Lally-Green, J.:

. . . "The parties to this matter have never been married. [Father] is an oncology accounts manager, supplying medications to hospitals, at Glaxo-Smith-Kline. . . . Appellee [Colleen Murphy ("Mother")] is the owner/operator of a nail salon. . . . Two months after the child's birth, [Father] acknowledged paternity, and a month after that, [Mother] commenced a support action. An initial award . . . was entered, and the following June, [Mother] sought modification. . . ." The parties never lived together. . . .

In September 2005, Mother enrolled the child in a private preschool program. Father apparently "disagreed" with that decision. Nevertheless, Father voluntarily paid Mother $1,400.00 of the $1,980.00 cost of the 2005-2006 school year. . . . For the 2006-2007 school year, Mother enrolled the child in the same school's pre-kindergarten program. Father again "did not agree" with the decision. This year, however, Father did not voluntarily contribute. At the time of the hearing, Mother planned to enroll the child in a related school's kindergarten program in September 2007. She testified that it was in the child's best interest to attend "because he has been with these children for two years now, and academically I think they have a great program."

Father testified that he did not agree with the decision to enroll the child in private school. He stated that he began in Catholic school, but graduated from public school. He opined that the public schools "offer[ ] more," and have programs to meet a child's needs, whether they are advanced or in need of special attention. In particular, he testified that he had spoken to some of his friends who teach at the local public school, and concluded that it would be suitable for his son. Father testified that his objection to his son attending private school was "philosophical" rather than financial.

On July 30, 2007, the master entered a recommendation that Appellant pay $1,896.74 per month in child support, including $241.56 per month toward private school tuition. The master reasoned that . . . Father could "easily and adequately" afford to pay for the contribution. . . . In calculating Father's 2007 income, the master included 401(k) and stock contributions by GlaxoSmithKline and perquisite income equivalent to 40% of the total cost for a company-provided car. The master also included two vested stock options which Father exercised. . . .

Father argues that the record is devoid of any evidence that Child would benefit more from attending private school than public school. . . . Under Pa. R.C.P. 1910.16-6(d), the court may direct the obligor to contribute to private school tuition if it is a "reasonable need. . . . In determining whether a need is reasonable, this Court has stated:

> A private school education may be a reasonable need for a child if it is demonstrated that the child will benefit from such and if private schooling is consistent with the family's standard of living and station in life before the separation. . . .

[E]vidence of a family's history of private schooling is not required. . . . Such evidence, however, is relevant to counter an argument that private schooling is not a reasonable need. . . .[5]

The record is limited on these issues.[6] Nevertheless, . . . it is impossible to say that the court acted unreasonably in determining that the child will "benefit." The record reflects that this very young child has been happy in private day care and pre-K classes. . . . He will presumably rejoin some of his classmates from pre-K, and enjoy a similar academic philosophy as the prior school. . . .

Next, the record reflects that attending private school is indeed consistent with the child's and the parents' station in life. The child has known only private school. Father voluntarily paid for a substantial portion of the 2005-2006 school year. Moreover, Father was already under an interim court order directing him to contribute to private school tuition. The new order simply increased that amount (by slightly over $100.00 per month), and directed such payments to continue. Additionally, the record . . . reflects that this contribution poses little, if any, financial burden on Father. . . .

Father contends that in calculating his 2007 income, the court included two stock options he exercised for a total of $23,276.67, and one unexercised stock option valued

5. In the instant case, the parties never married, and thus never separated. Therefore, the qualifier "prior to separation" would not apply. In such cases, it is quite consistent with the established case law that courts are to take into account the parties' financial stations in life regardless of whether they were married prior to the date of the order.

6. . . . We do observe . . . that the issue before the court was the *continued* payment of father of private school expenses. . . . If Father wanted to relieve himself of the burden of continuing to pay for private school, he should have presented additional concrete evidence to support his position.

at $11,100.00.[7] Father argues that because the 2007 stock options were one-time gains, the court should not have included them in determining his 2008 income. . . . We agree.

. . . Stock options are a form of deferred income. A parent who declines to exercise stock options is nonetheless imputed with the monetary gain from exercising those options. The reason for imputing this income is because the support obligation is based on a parent's earning capacity. . . . Father, however, has no potential of earning income in 2008 from the two stock options he exercised in 2007. Because Father's support obligation for 2008 is based on an inflated 2007 income, we are constrained to conclude that there is insufficient evidence to sustain the support order to the extent it applies from January 1, 2008, on forward.

Father also . . . notes that in 2007, it cost his employer $16,798.65 per year for his company-issued vehicle. . . . Father . . . uses the vehicle 40% of the time for personal use. . . . 40% of the gross amount, $16,798.65, is $6,719.46. If Father did not pay his employer for personal use of the vehicle, then that $6,719.46 figure would be attributable to him as personal perquisite income. Father, however, does pay his employer for personal use of the vehicle, specifically $1,820.00 per year. . . . Thus, we subtract $1,820.00 from $6,719.46 and arrive at $4,899.46 as Father's 2007 perquisite income. . . .

Finally, Father claims that the court miscalculated his income by using the gross amount of his employer's contributions to his 401(k) and stock accounts. Father contends that the post-tax and post-penalty amount of his employer's contributions should have been used. . . . Pa. R.C.P. 1910.16-2(c) . . . provides that taxes be deducted from gross income to arrive at net income. . . . We agree that Father is entitled to relief. . . .

> [A]n employer's contribution to an employee's retirement plan could constitute income . . . if the employee could access his employer's contributions (regardless of penalties) at the time of the support calculation. . . . For if an employee/parent is entitled to any portion of these funds at the time of the support calculation, his/her children should presently reap the benefit of the investment.[2]
>
> 2. [I]t is not determinative in the instant case that contributions to a 401(k) are not taxable as income at the time of the contribution. It is well settled that taxable income is not the same as net income for support purposes. . . . [T]ax law contains many preferences that have no relationship to the parties' support obligation.

The *Portugal* Court . . . [stated:] "If the trial court determines that he has such access, employer's contributions, less the penalty incurred for withdrawal, shall constitute additional income for purposes of the child support calculation." Instantly, the trial court erred by not accounting for the withdrawal penalty when it included the employer's gross contributions to Father's 401(k) and stock accounts. . . . We remand for recalculation of Father's net income and support obligation in accordance with this memorandum.

Should it be relevant to a determination of whether a parent must pay for private elementary school that he previously agreed to pay part of the cost of private preschool? What is the thinking behind a "if you paid before then you should pay again" principle?

7. By way of background:

A stock option, typically a "form of compensation," is defined as "an option to buy or sell a specific quantity of stock at a designated price for a specified period regardless of shifts in market value during the period." An option is "vested" when all conditions attached to it have been satisfied and it may be exercised by the employee.

Should employment perquisites figure in at their cost to the employer or something else? What if the employer paid a certain amount for a company car because they get a volume discount and the employee would have to pay much more if purchasing himself? Or what if the employee would buy a different and much cheaper car if the company did not provide a car of its own choice to him? Large disparities between cost to the company and what the employee would pay if purchasing herself could also pertain to other perquisites, such as auto and health insurance, housing, meals, etc.

The next case raises the question whether grandparents should be able to assist financially their divorced offspring who are custodial parents, without that resulting in reduced child support from the non-custodial parent.

State v. Williams

635 S.E.2d 495 (N.C. Ct. App. 2006)

TYSON, Judge.

. . . Cheryl Williams ("plaintiff") and defendant were married on 26 November 1994 and divorced on 1 August 2005. Three children ("the children") were born of the marriage during the years of 1995, 1996, and 1998. Since the date of the parties separation on 10 May 2004, the children have resided primarily with plaintiff. . . . The trial court calculated plaintiff's monthly gross income to be $893.00, defendant's monthly gross income to be $3,200.00, and ordered defendant to pay $728.51 per month in child support. . . .

N.C. Gen. Stat. §50-13.4(c) (2005) determines child support payments and provides:

> Payments ordered for the support of a minor child shall be in such amount as to meet the reasonable needs of the child for health, education, and maintenance having due regard to the estates, earnings, conditions, accustomed standard of living of the child and the parties, . . . and other facts of the particular case.

. . . At the hearing to determine child support, plaintiff testified her father gives Darrel Buck ("Buck"), a friend of plaintiff's, money to pay $1,550.00 per month rent on the home in which plaintiff and the children reside. Plaintiff testified it is her understanding her father will continue to give the rent money to Buck for the remainder of the lease.

Plaintiff also testified the vehicle, of which she has full possession and use, is paid for by her father in the same manner. Buck purchased the car when it was repossessed from plaintiff. The payments of $340.00 a month are paid by plaintiff's father. Over $10,000.00 remained owed on the vehicle. Plaintiff testified her father will continue to make the payments on the vehicle until it is paid in full.

The trial court found as fact plaintiff's father provides money to a friend who in turn makes these payments "in an effort to hide assets and income from the Bankruptcy Court or this Court, or both." The payment of the monthly vehicle obligation and rent payment total $1,890.00.

The North Carolina Child Support Guidelines in effect at the time the child support order at issue was entered defined "'income' [as] income from any source, including but not limited to income from . . . gifts . . . or maintenance received from persons other than the parties to the instant action." In *Spicer v. Spicer*, we stated that income includes "any 'maintenance received from persons other than the parties to the instant action.'"

"'Maintenance' is defined as 'financial support given by one person to another. . . .'" (*Black's Law Dictionary* 973 (8th ed. 2004)). Plaintiff's vehicle and housing payments are to be considered as income to her. The trial court erred by not including these payments in calculating income in the child support order. We reverse and remand . . . to recalculate plaintiff's child support obligation, and take into account plaintiff's gift income. . . .

What arguments can you make for and against reducing child support as a result of the custodial parent receiving financial assistance from family members? Would it be different if a grandparent died and left the mother money in a will? What if grandparents give their daughter money and direct that it be used for a grandchild—should that count as income for the daughter? If the mother is named trustee of a fund for the children?

The final major issue in income determination, imputation of income to a voluntarily under-employed parent, is well illustrated in a case in the next Section that also raises the issue of deviating from guideline amounts in situations of extraordinarily high payor income, the Michael Strahan case.

c. Deviating from the Guidelines

States generally authorize courts to deviate upward or downward from the guideline support amount after considering numerous factors. As to each factor in the Texas list below, try to think of circumstances that would appear to warrant an upward deviation and circumstances that would appear to warrant a downward deviation. Are there reasons to think a particular listed factor should not justify a deviation in either direction?

Vernon's Texas Statutes and Codes, Family Code
Title 5, Subtitle B. Suits Affecting the Parent-Child Relationship
Chap. 154, Subchapter C. Child Support Guidelines

§154.123. Additional Factors for Court to Consider

(a) The court may order periodic child support payments in an amount other than that established by the guidelines if the evidence rebuts the presumption that application of the guidelines is in the best interest of the child and justifies a variance from the guidelines.

(b) In determining whether application of the guidelines would be unjust or inappropriate under the circumstances, the court shall consider evidence of all relevant factors, including:

(1) the age and needs of the child;

(2) the ability of the parents to contribute to the support of the child;

(3) any financial resources available for the support of the child;

(4) the amount of time of possession of and access to a child;

(5) the amount of the obligee's net resources, including the earning potential of the obligee if the actual income of the obligee is significantly less than what the obligee could earn because the obligee is intentionally unemployed or underemployed and including an increase or decrease in the income of the obligee or income that may be attributed to the property and assets of the obligee;

(6) child care expenses incurred by either party in order to maintain gainful employment;

(7) whether either party has the . . . physical custody of another child;

(8) the amount of alimony or spousal maintenance actually and currently being paid or received by a party;

(9) the expenses for a son or daughter for education beyond secondary school;

(10) whether the obligor or obligee has an automobile, housing, or other benefits furnished by his or her employer, another person, or a business entity;

(11) the amount of other deductions from the wage or salary income and from other compensation for personal services of the parties;

(12) provision for health care insurance and payment of uninsured medical expenses;

(13) special or extraordinary educational, health care, or other expenses of the parties or of the child;

(14) the cost of travel in order to exercise possession of and access to a child;

(15) positive or negative cash flow from any real and personal property and assets, including a business and investments;

(16) debts or debt service assumed by either party; and

(17) any other reason consistent with the best interest of the child, taking into consideration the circumstances of the parents.

With respect to the first factor, courts commonly deviate upward because a child has extraordinary needs, often related to medical problems or a disability. A child might also need more than the guideline amount because the custodial parent has moved to a place where the cost of living is much higher—for example, from Kansas to Manhattan. Cf. Ga. Code Ann. §19-6-15(13) (cost of living of community of each parent is a deviation factor); Mont. Admin. R. 46-30-1543 (cost-of-living differential is deviation factor); Wash. Rev. Code Ann. §26.19.075(1)(c)(ii) (significant disparity in the living costs of the parents due to conditions beyond their control is deviation factor). Occasionally a support obligor will argue for a downward deviation on the grounds that the child's needs are less than normal. One reason for that might be an alternative source of support, such as a stepparent or a trust fund established by a grandparent. Another might be that the custodial parent lives in a place with a much lower cost of living than the state whose courts have jurisdiction—for example, in Wyoming rather than Connecticut. Increasingly, courts are seeing cases where custodial parent and child live in another country, as in the case below. This decision also discusses cases in other jurisdictions involving the converse claim, based on the second factor above that the non-custodial parent is not able to contribute as much because he has moved someplace with a much higher cost of living.

Gladis v. Gladisova

856 A.2d 703 (Md. 2004)

Battaglia, J.

Slavomir Gladis and Eva Gladisova, both citizens of the Slovak Republic, married in that country on February 20, 1993. Their daughter, Ivana, was born on November 4, 1993. In 1994, Mr. Gladis moved to the United States, and he last saw Ivana in April of 1994.

On March 11, 1998, Mr. Gladis filed a Complaint for Absolute Divorce in the Circuit Court for Baltimore City. On April 24, 1998, the Circuit Court entered a Judgment of Absolute Divorce, granting Ms. Gladisova custody of Ivana and Mr. Gladis the right to see

Ivana at reasonable times. The decree also charged Mr. Gladis with Ivana's general support and maintenance, but it did not specify the amount.

On June 5, 2002, Ms. Gladisova filed a Petition for the establishment of child support in the Circuit Court of Baltimore City pursuant to the Maryland Uniform Interstate Family Support Act (hereinafter "MUIFSA"). . . . On May 30, 2003, Master Furnari . . . found that Mr. Gladis had a high school education, works as a mechanic at Performance Auto Group, earns $41,773 annually, and has health insurance through his employer. She found that Mr. Gladis lives in Kingsville, Maryland, with his wife, who sells real estate, and their seven-month-old child. . . .

Ms. Gladisova works as a nurse, earns the equivalent of $430 per month, and pays approximately $2.97 per month for health insurance. She lives in the Slovak Republic with Ivana, her brother, and her parents in her parents' home. . . . Ivana attends fifth grade at a public school located 200 yards from her home. She participates in dance and music programs after school, attends summer camp, skis, bicycles, and plays the organ. . . .

Mr. Gladis has provided support for Ivana by sending cash, clothes, and school supplies. . . . [I]n 1998, Mr. Gladis sent $1800 to Ivana through his cousin, who was visiting him and, in 2001, he sent $1500 to Ivana through another cousin. . . . Mr. Gladis gave his father $2000 to give to Ivana in 2002.

Relying on Ms. Gladisova's financial statements, Master Furnari also found that, including monthly and annual expenses, the total average monthly expense for Ivana's care and support was the equivalent of $275.88 in United States dollars. . . .

Section 12-202(a)(1) of the Family Law Article now states unequivocally that "the court shall use the child support guidelines" "in any proceeding to establish or modify child support." The Guidelines apply unless the parents' monthly combined adjusted income exceeds $10,000, in which case "the court may use its discretion in setting the amount. . . ." The Guidelines are based on the Income Shares Model. . . . [I]f the parents' monthly income does not reach $10,000, "the [child support] obligation is calculated by determining each parent's monthly income, using the table at §12-204(e) to determine the parents' combined monthly support obligation, and dividing this obligation between the two parents in proportion to their incomes." "The judge must then add together any work-related child care expenses, extraordinary medical expenses, and school and transportation expenses and allocate this total between the parents in proportion to their adjusted actual incomes." The amount of child support that results from this calculation is presumptively "the correct amount of child support to be awarded."

The presumption of correctness may be rebutted by evidence demonstrating that the result under the Guidelines would "be unjust or inappropriate in a particular case." In determining whether a child support award is unjust or inappropriate, courts may consider a number of factors enumerated by the Guidelines, including:

> 1. the terms of any existing separation or property settlement agreement or court order, including any provisions for payment of mortgages or marital debts, payment of college education expenses, the terms of any use and possession order or right to occupy to the family home under an agreement, any direct payments made for the benefit of the children required by agreement or order, or any other financial considerations set out in an existing separation or property settlement agreement or court order; and
>
> 2. the presence in the household of either parent of other children to whom that parent owes a duty of support and the expenses for whom that parent is directly contributing.

The duty to support other children in the household of either parent, however, cannot form the sole basis for rebutting the presumption that the Guidelines establish the correct amount of child support. . . .

Mr. Gladis contends that the $497 monthly obligation, as derived from the Guidelines, is "unjust and inappropriate" because the monthly cost of raising Ivana in the Slovak Republic is the equivalent of merely $233.[5] . . .

At least two courts in our sister states have determined that differences in the standard of living in different geographic areas do not justify a deviation from statutory child support guidelines. In *In re Marriage of Beecher* (1998), the Supreme Court of Iowa held that the non-custodial father's increased cost of living in California did not justify a departure from the child support award calculated under Iowa's child support guidelines. . . .

> [The father's] move to California was for a higher paying job. His increased income inured to the benefit of his sons and results in the corresponding increase in the amounts due for their support under the guidelines. The more expensive home in California was intended to benefit the boys. Both the income and more expensive home however also inured to [the father's] own benefit. *The California home and the higher living cost there are not grounds for departure from the guidelines.*

In a case that is more on point, *Edwards v. Dominick* (La. App. 2002), the non-custodial father contended that his child support obligation should be less than the amount established by Louisiana's statutory child support guidelines because his daughter's standard of living in South Africa differed from the standard of living in Louisiana. The court . . . observed that the father "failed to cite any Louisiana law to support his argument that the standard of living in the place where the minor child resides is a relevant factor . . ." [and] held that "there is no indication . . . that the application of the guidelines would not be in the best interest of the child or would be inequitable to the parties. . . ."

Other out-of-state courts have held that deviation from the guidelines may be appropriate based on the standards of living in different localities. *Booth v. Booth* (Ohio 1989) . . . concluded that deviation from the guidelines based on the husband's high cost of living in New York was permissible. The court stated, ". . . it *may* have indeed been 'unreasonable' for the court to ignore such economic realities. . . ." S*ee also In re Marriage of Welch* (Mont. 1995) (holding that the non-custodial parent's higher cost of living in Washington, D.C. . . . was an "acceptable reason[ ] for the granting of a variance" from the child support award established by the guidelines); *In re Marriage of Dortch* (Wash. 1990) (noting that the "high cost of living" in the non-custodial parent's domicile "is a consideration which may warrant a deviation from the support schedule. . . ."). *In re Marriage of Andersen* (Col. App. 1995) confirms that a deviation from the Colorado guidelines must be supported by more than just evidence of different standards of living in different localities. There, the court noted "that a finding that one parent has a higher cost of living will not, in and of itself, ordinarily justify deviating from the guidelines." . . .

[W]e believe the better position is to prohibit courts from deviating from the Guidelines based on standards of living in different areas. . . . The Guidelines reflect the Legislature's plan for determining child support, and the courts must follow that plan. The Guidelines were intended to ensure that awards sufficiently met the needs of children,

5. [B]oth parties agree that Mr. Gladis's child support obligation, as determined by the Guidelines, far exceeds the cost of raising Ivana in the Slovak Republic.

improve the consistency and equity of awards, and improve the efficiency of the processes for adjudicating child support. To carry out these goals, the carefully crafted provisions of the Guidelines establish consistent awards notwithstanding what differences may exist in the standards of living in different geographic areas. Simply put, the General Assembly did not make one's geographical standard of living part of the child support formula.

In addition, the General Assembly enacted the Guidelines based on the premise that "a child should receive the same proportion of parental income, and thereby enjoy the standard of living, he or she would have experienced had the child's parents remained together." In *Voishan,* we . . . held that, in an above-guidelines case, the schedule under Section 12-204(e) "could provide a presumptive *minimum* basic award," but the legislature did not intend "to cap the basic child support obligation at the upper limit of the schedule." Rather, the child of parents who earn *more* than $10,000 per month may be entitled to a higher standard of living and more child support than a child of parents who earn *exactly* $10,000 per month.

This rationale applies with equal force in the case at bar. Here, like in *Voishan,* the child support award would allow the child to enjoy an above-minimum standard of living that corresponds to the father's economic position. There is no question . . . [the] support exceeds the *minimum* of what is needed to live normally according to the Slovak Republic's standards. . . . Had Mr. Gladis and Ms. Gladisova remained together (in Maryland), Ivana would have enjoyed certain amenities that are generally not available in her native country. The increased amount of child support will allow Ivana to experience some of those same amenities, allowing her to experience a lifestyle that corresponds more closely to the economic position of Mr. Gladis. The child support calculated under the Guidelines, therefore, only serves Ivana's best interests and is the appropriate measure of Mr. Gladis's obligation.

Further, one of the primary purposes of the Guidelines "was to limit the role of trial courts in deciding the specific amount of child support to be awarded in different cases. . . ." Allowing a deviation from the Guidelines based on the standards of living in different localities would encourage trial courts to examine those circumstances on a case-by-case basis and, no doubt, depart from the guidelines more frequently. How, for instance, could fact finders consistently determine the precise differences in the standards of living in two different countries, given that the value of currency changes constantly and that middle-class living conditions in Maryland may be considered poverty or extravagance elsewhere? If this complex inquiry becomes a factor in determining child support awards, it "would only serve to make the support awards less uniform and predictable and more subject to individual whim and manipulation." This is the very result the General Assembly hoped to avoid in enacting the Guidelines. . . .

Although no Maryland case has addressed the specific issue raised in this case, the Court of Special Appeals, not long ago, faced an analogous question in *Smith v. Freeman* (2002). In *Smith,* Antonio Freeman, a professional football player, sought to prevent an increase to his child support obligation based on an annual salary boost from $1.2 to $3.2 million dollars. . . . The Guidelines did not apply in *Smith* because the parties' income exceeded $10,000 per month, but the Court of Special Appeals discussed . . . : When the child and non-custodial parent have two different standards of living, which standard should determine the amount of the child's support? . . . Judge Hollander . . . observed:

> The . . . concept of "need" is relative, almost metaphysical, and varies with the particular circumstances of the people involved, as well as their culture, values, and wealth. To be sure, many people, adults and children alike, have far more than they truly "need" to survive, or

> even to live comfortably. On the other hand, there is virtually no limit to the luxuries that many extremely wealthy celebrities seem to enjoy regularly. Even among middle class populations, there is a range of tastes with varying costs. While some Marylanders are amply satisfied with a vacation in Ocean City, others prefer to vacation in places like Martha's Vineyard, despite the fact that both beaches front on the Atlantic Ocean. Simply put, given a choice between rhinestones and rubies, many people opt for the latter if they can afford to do so.

The court further noted a "child of a multi-millionaire generally expects a lifestyle of unusual privilege and advantage" and that "children of wealth 'are entitled to every expense reasonable for a child of affluence.'" The court rejected Freeman's suggestion that the child did not deserve increased support because the child was not accustomed to her father's "wealthy economic status." Rather, the court stated, "every child is entitled to a level of support commensurate with the parents' economic position."

In the instant case, like in *Smith*, the . . . child's "needs" . . . depend on the parents' economic position. The advantages of Mr. Gladis's economic strength, accordingly, should flow to his child living in a nation of less wealth, just like the advantages of Freeman's extreme wealth should pass to his child. . . .

Mr. Gladis further asserts that . . . there had been a substantial increase in the cost of caring for the child of his current marriage. . . . Although, according to Section 12-202(a)(2)(iii)(2) of the Family Law Article, the expense of other children in the non-custodial parent's household is relevant to whether an award is "unjust" or "inappropriate," Section 12-202(a)(2)(iv) expressly states that evidence of this support obligation, by itself, cannot rebut the presumption that the award under the Guidelines is correct. . . .

RAKER, J., dissenting, in which HARRELL, J., joins:

. . . In my view, the guidelines are irrelevant under these circumstances . . . The guidelines were enacted to ensure that the custodial parent receive an amount of child support consistent with the *actual monthly costs* of raising the child. . . . The Income Shares Model "establishes child support obligations based on estimates of the percentage of income that parents in an intact household typically spend on their children." . . . It is not plausible that the General Assembly, in developing the schedule, researched or took into account the percentage of income that parents living in different countries spend on their children. . . . Even though there is disparity in the cost of living within jurisdictions in the United States, and the guidelines do apply where the non-custodial parent resides outside Maryland but within the U.S., it is unrealistic to attempt to equalize standards of living throughout the entire world and, in my view, the Legislature did not attempt to do so.

. . . Ivana's monthly expenses . . . are below $280.[1] . . .

Although §12-202(a)(2)(iii) sets forth some factors which the court "may consider" in "determining whether the application of the guidelines would be unjust or inappropriate in a particular case," the use of "may" indicates that the Legislature did not intend this list to be exhaustive. There is nothing in the statutory language that supports Ms. Gladisova's contention that the court is forbidden from considering an international disparity in child-rearing costs as a factor in determining the appropriateness of a Guideline award. . . .

In the case *sub judice*, had Mr. Gladis and Ms. Gladisova remained together, Ivana would not have had a higher standard of living than she does currently. Mr. Gladis earns $42,000

1. The Master found that according to a Slovak Republic government resource, the Slovak Republic the average gross expenses *per household* in 2001 were the equivalent of $168.80 per year.

per year and lives a modest and comfortable life with his new wife and seven-month-old daughter. Had Mr. Gladis and Ms. Gladisova remained together, in either the United States or the Slovak Republic, they would have lived a lifestyle commensurate with the standards of the country in which they resided and not one considered luxurious by the local standard. . . . If Mr. Gladis is required to pay the amount stipulated by the guidelines, Ivana will have the financial ability to live a life of luxury in the Slovak Republic as compared to the ordinary standard of living in that country. Therefore, following the guidelines . . . is contrary to the principle that the child is entitled to the standard of living that she would have enjoyed had the parents remained together.[3]

Even if we ignore the difference between the material expectations held by residents of Maryland and the Slovak Republic, the Circuit Court appears to have ignored the effect of purchasing power differentials. . . . The same bundle of goods and services which would constitute a middle class standard of living in Maryland could be purchased at significantly lower cost in the Slovak Republic. Exporting Mr. Gladis's U.S. dollars to the Slovak Republic and exchanging them for crowns greatly increases their purchasing power. Because she happens to be shopping in the Slovak Republic, Ivana can purchase more skis, bicycles, lessons, and insurance policies with her father's dollars than she could at Maryland prices. It is unjust to provide her (and her mother) this windfall at her father's expense, merely because Mr. Gladis happens to live in a country with a higher cost of living. . . .

Should the court compare Ivana's quality of life in Slovakia with what it would be if she lived in the United States or with what other children in Slovakia have? Could the court have reasoned: "Yes, she will live like a queen in Slovakia, but that is still a worse life than she would have if the parents had remained married in Maryland"? Is that likely true? What effects does it have on a non-custodial parent's freedom to move or change jobs if courts will not take into account the relative cost of living where that parent lives?

It appears that the mother and daughter never came to the United States, so it is odd that a Maryland court handled the divorce and child support. If the father had been able to file for divorce in Slovakia, he would likely have done better on child support. The mother might have realized that and acquiesced to the jurisdiction of the Maryland courts.

Is the court's comparison to high-income cases like the *Strahan* case below apt? The New Jersey court in *Strahan* addressed not only the concept of need in a high-income situation, but also the common concerns that a custodial parent is using child support for her own benefit and not earning as much herself as she could.

Strahan v. Strahan

953 A.2d 1219 (N.J. Super. Ct. App. Div. 2008)

PARKER, J.A.D.

. . . Plaintiff is a football player who has been under contract with the New York Giants since 1993. He began dating defendant in October 1994. At the time they met, defendant

3. Ivana has health insurance through her mother's employer, whereas most people in the Slovak Republic pay for medical services as they are rendered. Ms. Gladisova also has a vehicle, whereas the majority of the population in the Slovak Republic travels by public transportation. Furthermore, Ivana regularly attends dance and music lessons and has skis, a bicycle and an organ.

was employed as a model and manager for a cosmetics company, earning about $70,000 per year. In 1995, the parties moved in together and defendant quit her job, purportedly at plaintiff's request. When plaintiff extended a marriage proposal, defendant agreed to sign a pre-nuptial agreement (agreement) before they married on July 18, 1999. Twin girls were born of the marriage on October 28, 2004.

The complaint for divorce was filed on March 14, 2005. The parties were able to agree on joint legal custody of the children with defendant having primary residential custody. The matter was tried over eleven days in June and July 2006. A dual judgment of divorce was entered on July 20, 2006 dissolving the marriage. . . .

In setting child support, the court shall consider the factors set forth in *N.J.S.A.* 2A:34-23(a):

> (1) Needs of the child;
> (2) Standard of living and economic circumstances of each parent;
> (3) All sources of income and assets of each parent;
> (4) Earning ability of each parent, including educational background, training, employment skills, work experience, custodial responsibility for children including the cost of providing child care and the length of time and cost of each parent to obtain training or experience for appropriate employment;
> (5) Need and capacity of the child for education, including higher education;
> (6) Age and health of the child and each parent;
> (7) Income, assets and earning ability of the child;
> (8) Responsibility of the parents for the court-ordered support of others;
> (9) Reasonable debts and liabilities of each child and parent; and
> (10) Any other factors the court may deem relevant.

"If the combined net income of the parents is more than $187,200 per year, the court shall apply the guidelines up to $187,200 and supplement the guidelines-based award with a discretionary amount based on the remaining family income (i.e., income in excess of $187,200) and the factors specified in N.J.S.A. 2A:34-23. "The key to both the [g]uidelines and the statutory factors is flexibility and the best interest of children."

In the context of high-income parents whose ability to pay is not an issue, "the dominant guideline for consideration is the *reasonable needs of the children,* which must be addressed in the context of the standard of living of the parties. The needs of the children must be the centerpiece of any relevant analysis." The consideration of needs must include the age and health of the children—with the understanding that infants' needs are less than those of teenagers—as well as any assets or income of the children.

Determining a child's "needs" in high-income earning families presents "unique problems." First, a balance must be struck between reasonable needs, which reflect lifestyle opportunities, while at the same time precluding an inappropriate windfall to the child or even in some cases infringing on the legitimate right of either parent to determine the appropriate lifestyle of a child. This latter consideration involves a careful balancing of interests reflecting that a child's entitlement to share in a parent's good fortune does not deprive either parent of the right to participate in the development of an appropriate value system for a child. This is a critical tension that may develop between competing parents. Ultimately, the needs of a child in such circumstances also calls to the fore the best interests of a child.

"Judges must be vigilant in providing for 'needs' consistent with lifestyle without over-indulgence." In *Isaacson,* we referred to the Kansas "Three Pony Rule," which states that "'no child, no matter how wealthy the parents, needs to be provided [with] more than three ponies.'" Even with high income parents, the court still must "determin[e] needs of a child in a sensible manner consistent with the best interests of the child." "[T]he law is not offended if there is some incidental benefit to the custodial parent from increased child support payments." While "some incidental benefit" is not offensive, "overreaching in the name of benefiting a child is." "[A] custodial parent cannot[,] through the guise of the incidental benefits of child support[,] gain a benefit beyond that which is merely incidental to a benefit being conferred on the child." That is especially true where the custodial parent is not entitled to alimony. "The award of nonessential additions to child support requires a careful weighing and determination as to who is the primary and who is the incidental beneficiary of such support."

Here, the parties' experts agreed the marital standard of living was approximately $1 million a year. The court found that the "reasonable current standard of living" of defendant and the two children was $630,000 a year. The court set forth all of the expenses that went into that figure, but did not distinguish defendant's expenses from those of the children's. The court stated that defendant "reported spending approximately $8,000 per month over an approximate twelve month period on the children." The court added: "The historical expenses attributed to the children, to the extent reasonable and recurring, have been reviewed and weighed to their current needs as determined by the court's analysis of the factors under *N.J.S.A.* 2A:34-23(b)." The basic child support amount under the guidelines was $35,984 a year. But, the court found that the children had a supplemental need of $200,000 a year, for a total of $235,984 a year.

The court did not impute income to defendant but considered the funds she would have available at the conclusion of the divorce. The court determined defendant would have $10.5 million in liquid assets to invest, which would return about $525,600 annually in gross income or $341,640 net, or $28,470 net income per month. With monthly expenses of $52,500, however, defendant had a shortfall of $24,030 per month.

Plaintiff's post-divorce income for 2006 was about $5.87 million, with "$292,000 net monthly income available for child support." The parties' combined net monthly income was $330,470, with plaintiff's income being 91% of the total and defendant's 9%. Plaintiff's 91% share of the annual child support amounted to $214,745. This did not include the additional expenses for the children that plaintiff volunteered to pay: medical insurance, uncovered medical expenses, and 80% of the agreed-upon extra-curricular activities and college expenses. . . .

We agree with plaintiff that the court here failed to make the specific findings of fact necessary to sustain its decision regarding the amount of supplemental child support. The court merely repeated defendant's recitation of the children's "needs" as they appeared on her case information statement (CIS) without any determination of what was essential or non-essential or any judgment regarding the accuracy or appropriateness of those needs. Expenses such as the mortgage, taxes, utilities, car expenses, and similar items benefited defendant as well as the children, but the court did not discuss what portion of those expenses was for the benefit of the children and what portion was for the benefit of defendant. . . .

Moreover, the court failed to make any analysis of the reasonableness of the "needs" claimed by defendant on behalf of the twin toddlers. Although in high income families, children are entitled to the benefit of financial advantages available to them, "the custodial parent bears the burden of establishing the reasonableness of those expenses." Some of the expenses claimed by defendant clearly should have been deleted by the court. For example, the "children" sent their nanny and her family to Jamaica for a ten-day vacation, and gave their grandmother diamond jewelry. Defendant claimed that the twin toddlers needed nearly $27,000 a year for clothing because she dressed them in a new outfit every time they saw their father, and one of the three-year-old girls did not like to leave the house without a purse. There was no explanation as to why the children needed $30,000 worth of landscaping per year, or what was included in $3,000 for "audio visual" expenses per year. Defendant listed $36,000 a year for the children's "equipment and furnishings" without explaining what that covered. Other expenses listed in defendant's CIS should have been questioned by the court, as well. . . .

Defendant admitted that many of the expenses she listed for the children were incurred without plaintiff's knowledge or consent. At trial, plaintiff expressed his desire not "to spoil" the children and to teach them the value of money. Nevertheless, the court failed to address plaintiff's "legitimate right . . . to determine the appropriate lifestyle of [his] child[ren]."

Plaintiff further argues that the judge erred in failing to impute any income to defendant for child support purposes. He maintains that defendant has two college degrees, had earned $70,000 per year prior to the marriage, and admitted that she was capable of working but chose not to do so. He contends that her "voluntary decision to be unemployed is not a legitimate basis for failing to impute any income." We agree.

The "fairness of a child support award is dependent on the accurate determination of a parent's net income. If the court finds that either parent is, without just cause, voluntarily underemployed or unemployed, it shall impute income to that parent[.]" . . . [T]he court must first determine whether the parent has "just cause" to be voluntarily unemployed. "In making that decision, the court should consider the employment status and earning capacity of that parent had the family remained intact; the reason for and intent behind the voluntary underemployment or unemployment; the extent other assets are available to pay support; and the ages of the children in the parent's household as well as child-care alternatives." If the court finds that there is no "just cause" for the parent remaining unemployed or underemployed, the guidelines provide that income can be imputed "based on potential employment and earning capacity using the parent's work history, occupational qualifications, educational background and . . . job opportunities." The court also may impute income in accordance with the person's usual or former occupation.

Here, the court concluded that defendant was "neither voluntarily unemployed nor underemployed" and declined to impute income to her. The court explained:

> The defendant was a wife, homemaker, companion, and mother during her relationship with the plaintiff. The plaintiff did not want the defendant to be employed during their cohabitation, both before and after their marriage. The court finds the plaintiff wanted the defendant to be his companion and wife, and ultimately, the full time mother of his children. The parties' relationship was a "shared enterprise" resulting in their living together, becoming engaged and married, and wanting to have children. On the parties' tax returns the plaintiff reported . . . [defendant's occupation] as homemaker. . . . The parties' parenting agreement recognized the defendant's parental responsibilities as the primary caretaker of the parties' children. . . . Under the circumstances of this case, the defendant cannot go back in time and continue her employment or develop her career as if it was 1994, the date of cohabitation, or 1999, the date the parties married, or 2004, the date the parties' twin[s] were born. The defendant testified that she will not seek employment but will raise the parties' children as the parties' intended during her pregnancy and after the birth of the children. Under those circumstances, and based on the assets and income of the parties and quality of life for the children, the court finds it would be unreasonable to impute earned employment income to the defendant.

First, we note that the parties separated when the children were a few months old, so there was virtually no history of their conduct vis-à-vis the children. Second, defendant's employment opportunities were, in all likelihood, enhanced by her celebrity marriage. There is no question that as a healthy, educated, forty-one-year old, defendant is capable of earning her own income. . . . The children . . . have had nannies to care for them since they were born.

Although the court did attribute income to defendant from the interest on her investments, it failed to take into consideration the very substantial assets defendant derived from the marriage and divorce, the opportunities for employment available to her as the former wife of a celebrity and the time available to her as a result of the nannies who care for the children. In short, in the remand hearing, the court should consider all possible sources of income for defendant—earned and unearned—as well as her assets in determining her share of child support.

What is the moral basis for saying a child is entitled to share in a non-custodial parent's good fortune or the fruits of a parent's hard work, as opposed to saying a child is entitled to enough support to live an ordinary, decent life? Is the only limit to that idea a concern that at some point additional wealth just spoils a child? If so, should the court assume that a custodial parent would in fact use huge support payments to spoil the child? What else might a conscientious custodial parent choose to do with the money?

Another moral assumption influencing legislative and court decision making is that children should not be worse off as a result of their parents' decision not to continue their relationship. Everyone acknowledges that there might have to be some economic loss for all family members when a family household breaks up into two households, because of the associated increase in costs. But many believe that, apart from that, children should be no worse off financially—in other words, that parents should spend the same on them and they should have more or less the same standard of living in both households. But does that assumption presuppose the contestable one above, that children are entitled to share in their parents' good fortune? It is a well-established moral principle that one person should not suffer for the actions or choices of another, but by that we usually mean the first person should not lose something to which they are entitled. As to windfalls, it is less clear that this moral principle applies. So to children (or spouses, for that matter) of high-income earners, why do we not instead say: "You were very lucky to have a rich life while the family was intact, and you should be thankful for that, and you have no legitimate basis for complaining that you now have a life more like that of the average person." By way of comparison, suppose when you graduate someone offers you an extraordinary job opportunity, a half million dollars a year for doing very little work, but then after a few years decides to eliminate the job or to reduce the salary to what the average person makes for doing that amount and kind of work (e.g., $50K/year). Would they have done you a moral wrong?

Should the mother in this case be effectively forced to work? Would imputing income to her have the effect of doing so? Why is any agreement or understanding the couple had during the marriage about the mother's working relevant after divorce? When people say while married something like "OK, when we have children, I'd like you to stay home and take care of them," they probably are not also thinking ". . . and I'd want you to continue doing that indefinitely even if we get divorced". Is continuation of the marriage not a crucial assumption of almost anything couples agree to regarding lifestyle and division of responsibilities when they get married?

This divorce proceeding commenced less than five months after twin babies were born, which is quite rare; mothers generally do not look for alternative mates while tending to newborns, and fathers usually have the decency not to seek a divorce right after their wives have done such an extraordinary thing for the family. So the likely explanation in such a case would be that the father did something the wife could not tolerate so she filed for divorce. And that is what Jean Strahan alleged—namely, that after the birth Michael spent all his time with mistresses, especially Nicole "Cupcake" D'Oliveira, or with his buddies at night clubs rather than with her and the babies. But Giants fans would hear none of it. See Jeane MacIntosh, *Strahan Wife Bares Her 'Ex'-tacy,*" N.Y. Post, Jan. 16, 2007.

In most states, a certain percentage applies to an obligor's income no matter how high it is, though the percentage might decline to a very small number. We saw above, though, that the Texas child support statute applies percentages only to income below $7,500 per month and gives courts broad discretion to set a higher amount if parents' income is higher. The Texas statute also contains a provision manifesting hostility to "four pony" awards: "The proper calculation of a child support order that exceeds the presumptive amount established for the portion of the obligor's net resources [up to $7,500] requires that the entire amount of the presumptive award be subtracted from the proven total needs of the child. After the presumptive award is subtracted, the court shall allocate between the parties the responsibility to meet the additional needs of the child according to the circumstances of the parties. However, in no event may the obligor be required to pay more child support than the greater of the presumptive amount or the amount equal to 100 percent of the proven needs of the child." Tex. Fam. Code Ann. §154.126. Thus, a court cannot order a high-income obligor with two children to pay more than $1,875 per month in child support unless the custodial parent proves the children need more than that. How might Michael Strahan have fared under the Texas statute?

Some issues relating to deviation from guideline amounts come up principally in proceedings to modify a prior child support order. The general rule for court-ordered modification is that the party seeking a change to the child support amount must show a change in circumstances relevant to determination of the amount. A change in custody is an obvious basis for modifying a support order. A substantial change in the obligor's income or, in income-shares states, the obligee's income, is also a basis for modification, *provided* that any downward change is involuntary. Whether a parent is voluntarily underemployed is a question courts address frequently, at the time of the initial order or at the time of a modification petition. If they find that a parent is shirking, they can impute income to that parent, based on income received in a prior job or likely obtainable by someone with similar training or experience. Cf. Va. Stat. §20-108.1(H) ("when the earning capacity, voluntary unemployment, or voluntary under-employment of a party is in controversy, the court . . . may order a party to submit to a vocational evaluation by a vocational expert").

An ever more frequent child support issue, as people increasingly marry multiple times, is whether obligations to children from another relationship should reduce one's support amount. An obligor parent might a) seek a downward modification as a result of having subsequent children, or b) seek a downward deviation in an initial award as a result of already being under a support order as to prior children. Are you more sympathetic to this request in situation a) or b)?

Adrienne Jennings Lockie, Multiple Families, Multiple Goals, Multiple Failures: The Need for "Limited Equalization" as a Theory of Child Support

32 Harv. J.L. & Gender 109, 140-155 (2009)

. . . The two primary ways to allocate child support among families are "first family first" and "equalization." The "first family first" policy is premised on the concept of child support as a "nondisclaimable duty that should not be altered by activities chosen by the obligor." The rationale is that permitting retrospective modification gives no incentive to parents to avoid having additional children and in fact may provide an incentive to have additional children, where having additional children leads to a reduction in required child support payments. In . . . calculating support orders for subsequent children under the "first family first" policy, judicial deference is ordinarily given to existing support orders for children born from prior relationships. As of 2004, at least forty state guidelines "provide that a parent's preexisting order is to be subtracted from the parent's income prior to the determination of support." The ALI Principles explain . . . :

> A rule of strict equality among children of different families would require recalculation of existing child-support orders for children not before the court and perhaps not even subject to the court's jurisdiction. A rule of priority is independently justifiable in equitable terms. A parent may be understood to come to a second family already economically diminished by obligations to a prior family, as by obligations to other creditors whose claims are not dischargeable in bankruptcy. Prior obligations should not, as a general matter, be retroactively reduced in light of obligations subsequently undertaken.

"Equalization," the second way to allocate child support among families, calls for "equal treatment of all the children of a particular parent" on the basis that "[h]ad the parents stayed together and produced additional children, there would have been adjustments and a likely reduction in the resources available for the first child." "Equalization" supporters argue that the "first family first" policy limits the freedom to form new families and that denying modifications interferes with a parent's ability to support additional children. . . .

Despite the ostensible simplicity of "first family first," numerous complications may arise. For example, the first family may not have an existing child support order in place prior to the birth of subsequent children. In this situation, . . . preexisting children may be handled as a deviation factor. . . .

Under the guideline models, states handle *subsequent* children in calculating child support orders in a variety of ways: as a mandatory required income deduction, as a discretionary income deduction, as a deviation factor, as a component of a self-serve reserve, or by providing no accommodation. Subsequent children are often considered in a motion to modify a child support order for existing children. As a practical matter, permitting deviations or deductions may eliminate the advantages to the first family, thus rendering the "first family first" policy meaningless. Where parents have multiple subsequent children with different partners, providing accommodation to the subsequent children may result in low awards for all children. . . . To calculate the amount of child support to be reduced, some states use the actual expenses of subsequent children, while others craft a hypothetical child support order for the subsequent children. . . .

Another issue relevant under any model is the extent to which child support orders reflect new families' resources. States rarely consider the income of a new spouse or cohabitant because there is no legal duty of support to the existing children. . . . Connecticut . . . has an expansive definition of income and, while not counting the income of new partners or spouses, allows for a deviation from a presumptive child support award if the new partner or spouse's contributions have led the parent to "experience[ ] an extraordinary reduction of his or her living expenses as a direct result of such contributions or gift." . . .

Limited equalization recognizes the need to provide adequate resources for all children without exacerbating the incentives for a nonresident parent to reduce payments to the first family. . . . First or existing children should receive a preference because nonresident fathers are less likely to pay child support when they have new children; there is empirical support for the idea that fathers "swap" families and may adjust their child support payments informally to account for new biological children. . . . Limited equalization looks at the actual needs and available support for all of the children rather than enforcing a blanket policy of either "equalization" or "first family first." . . .

[O]ne method of allocation is to provide a percentage of income to each child or each family . . . based on the actual need of the children and other available resources, or the number and sequencing of children (where existing children are given a preference). To maintain support for first or existing families, existing children should be entitled to a higher baseline percentage. Alternatively, there could be a baseline percentage of income under which the award for preexisting families could not fall. Once the baseline for the preexisting family is met, the family, or families, with the most need would receive a higher percentage of the obligor's income. . . . One reason to give a preference to existing children is that the hardships caused by a significant child support reduction, and the resulting decrease in standard of living, are more severe than those of having a low initial child support amount ordered. . . . At the same time, in looking to the available resources for children in multiple families, limited equalization allows courts to examine the actual living situation of the children and strive to keep all children out of poverty.

Try to formulate statutory rules that would favor earlier children but allow for lowering their support to some degree based on an obligation to support later-born children. You would need a rule for modification of an existing support order based on later-born children and also a rule for taking into account earlier-born children (with or without orders for them) when initially setting an amount of support for the later-born children (if the obligor is not living with them either). As to the latter, does the Massachusetts rule accomplish this objective? Mass. Gen. Laws ch. 208, §28: "When a court makes an order for maintenance or support, the court shall determine whether the obligor under such order is responsible for the maintenance or support of any other children . . . , even if a court order for such maintenance or support does not exist. . . . If the court determines that such responsibility does, in fact, exist and that such obligor is fulfilling such responsibility such court shall take into consideration such responsibility in setting the amount to be paid under the current order for maintenance or support."

Existing rules in most states invite fairness arguments in every multiple-family case, because obligations to people not before the court can be relevant in one way or another under any guideline, at least until appellate courts establish a definitive rule governing a particular type of situation. If in no other way, it can be "another factor" potentially making the guideline amount "unfair" or "inappropriate" and therefore justifying a deviation. Practicing attorneys should therefore have an arsenal of moral arguments at their disposal and be prepared to deploy them persuasively—for example, "people should not be able to get out of existing obligations by incurring new ones" versus "children should not receive less because of the arbitrary fact of birth order." Does law school prepare lawyers to make effective moral arguments?

Kentucky is a "first family first" state with a clear set-aside of income for support of earlier-born children. Because it is an income-shares state, this protection applies to the potential recipient of child support in an instant action as well as to the potential payor.

Kimbrough v. Commonwealth of Kentucky, Child Support Division ex rel. Belmar

215 S.W.3d 69 (Ky. Ct. App. 2006)

SCHRODER, Judge.

. . . This case began as a paternity action filed in 1995 by the mother, Shantrece Belmar, against Charles Alex Kimbrough regarding two children, Charles, born March 2, 1994, and Charnasia, born March 3, 1995. Paternity was established and a child support order was entered requiring Charles to pay $62.25 a week. On March 15, 2005, Shantrece filed a motion for an increase in child support for child care costs and health care coverage. . . .

The two factors used to determine the amount of child support under the guidelines . . . are "combined monthly adjusted parental gross income" and the number of children. KRS 403.212(2)(g) provides . . . :

> "Combined adjusted parental gross income" means the combined gross incomes of both parents, less any of the following payments made by the parent: . . .
>
> 4. A deduction for the support to the extent payment is made, if a parent is legally responsible for and is actually providing support for other prior-born children who are not the subject of a particular proceeding. If the prior-born children reside with that parent, an "imputed child support obligation" shall be allowed in the amount which would result from application of the guidelines for the support of the prior-born children.

At the time of the motion for increase in support in this case, Shantrece had a 15-year-old child from a prior relationship of whom she had custody, and Charles had an 8-month-old child for whom he was financially responsible who resided with him in a current relationship. According to Charles, there was a child support order in the sum of $50 per week to be paid by the biological father of Shantrece's 15-year-old child. However, the biological father of the child was apparently incarcerated and not paying child support. Thus, in determining Shantrece's monthly adjusted parental gross income for purposes of calculating child support for the two later children, the court allowed Shantrece to deduct $413 as imputed child support for the prior-born child under KRS 403.212(2)(g)(4). This effectively increased the percentage of total child support that Charles was ordered to pay, and resulted in an increase of $50 a week in child support. Whereas, under that same statute, Charles was not entitled to deduct any imputed child support for his later-born 8-month-old child.

Charles argues that because KRS 403.212(2)(g)(4) allows the parent of a prior-born child to deduct imputed child support, but does not allow the same deduction for the parent of a later-born child whom the parent is financially responsible for, the statute denies the parent of the later-born child equal protection under the law. Charles also argues that it denies the later-born child equal protection because there are less financial resources available for the later-born child, effectively giving a benefit to the prior-born child at the detriment of the later-born child. . . .

A statute carries a strong presumption that it is constitutional. . . . In analyzing the equal protection argument, we apply the rational basis standard of review because the claim does not involve a suspect classification or a fundamental right. Under the rational basis standard, this Court must uphold a statute if the statutory classification bears some rational relationship to a legitimate state purpose. . . .

In viewing the language of KRS 403.212(2)(g)(4), it is clear that the purpose of the legislation was to ensure that parents had sufficient financial resources to meet the needs of prior-born children before setting child support for later-born children. We note that this is a question of first impression in Kentucky, and there is little case law on the issue from other jurisdictions.

In *Feltman v. Feltman* (S.D. 1989), the Supreme Court of South Dakota upheld a similar provision in its child support guidelines, adjudging that the provision was rationally related to the state's interest in requiring parents to support all of their children and in protecting the welfare of the children, which includes their standard of living. The Court acknowledged that application of the provision could result in later-born children receiving a lesser amount of economic support than prior-born children. . . . The Court went on to defend the state's justification for enacting the provision:

> The support format set forth in SDCL 25-7-7 provides a fair and logical prioritization of claims against a noncustodial parent's income. Without prioritization, the children from the first family might find their standard of living substantially decreased by the voluntary acts of a noncustodial parent. A noncustodial parent who becomes responsible for supporting the children of a second marriage does so with the knowledge of a continuing responsibility to the children of the first marriage.

Similarly, in Florida, the Court found that a rational basis existed for a statute precluding a decrease in child support for prior-born children because the obligor parent has subsequent children. *Pohlmann v. Pohlmann* (Fla. App. 1997). "The statute assures that noncustodial parents will continue to contribute to the support of their children from their first marriage notwithstanding their obligation to support children born during a subsequent marriage."

And more recently, the Tennessee Supreme Court upheld as constitutional a provision in the child support guidelines allowing the amount of an existing child support order to be deducted in determining that parent's net income, but not taking into consideration children of that parent who are not included in the decree of child support. Gallaher v. Elam, 104 S.W.3d 455 (Tenn. 2003). The Court noted that "the obligor's children who are not receiving support pursuant to a court order and who live with the obligor inherently benefit from the obligor's household expenditures. Children who do not live with the obligor do not enjoy this benefit." The Court also looked to the fact that the deviation from the guidelines is allowed in cases of extreme economic hardship.

We agree with the above courts that the state's interest in seeing that prior-born children are provided for is a rational basis for the provision at issue in KRS 403.212(2)(g)(4). Clearly, the intention of the statute is not to deny financial resources to later-born children, but rather to make sure prior-born children are being supported. While in some cases application of the statute may result in later-born children having access to fewer financial resources than prior-born children, "[e]qual protection does not require there to be a perfect fit between means and ends." And in areas of social welfare and economic legislation, the question is not whether the statute is ideal or could be more just.

We would also note that just because a deduction for imputed child support for prior-born children is allowed, it does not necessarily follow that in every case there will be insufficient financial resources for later-born children. Indeed, in the present case, Charles does not allege that he cannot provide for his 8-month-old child, only that there are less financial resources available for the later-born child. As pointed out by the Tennessee Court, because the 8-month-old child lives with Charles, that child gets the benefit of household expenditures as well. And, in the event there are extraordinary circumstances, KRS 403.211(2) and (3) permit deviation from the guidelines where "application of the guidelines would be unjust or inappropriate."

Charles' next argument is that KRS 403.212(2)(g)(4) as applied in this case violated his due process rights when he was required to pay increased child support because the father of Shantrece's prior-born child was incarcerated and not paying child support. . . . In reviewing the record in this case, there is no evidence regarding . . . the incarcerated father's alleged failure to pay child support . . . or how the failure of this incarcerated parent to pay child support actually affected the child support obligation of Charles . . . although both parties apparently stipulated that the father is required to pay $50 a week. . . . It is the appellant's obligation to see that the record before the appellate court is sufficient for an adequate review. . . . [W]e must affirm the deduction of $413 for imputed child support. . . .

Did the court present any defense of the statutory favoritism for earlier-born over later-born children other than that the legislature was more concerned to protect earlier-born children than it was to protect later-born children? What arguments could you make to an appellate court for or against giving priority to earlier-born children? Is there a realistic concern that child support obligors would, if a state allowed for downward modification based on subsequent children, have more children for the purpose of reducing their obligation? Or unmindful of their existing obligation? Does refusing to reduce an obligation based on subsequent children run counter to the state policy of encouraging marriage? Does it infringe the constitutional right to procreate? Should the father have prevailed on his due process claim if he had presented evidence proving that he was having to pay more because the father of Shantrece's prior-born child was in jail?

Vermont represents a version of the equalization approach. Note the reference to step-children in the statute below; in some states, step-parents have a legal support obligation with respect to their step-children while living with them. Try to figure out the practical effect of paragraph c). Is this a departure from the equalization aim?

West's Vermont Statutes
Title 15, Chapter 11. Annulment and Divorce
Subchapter 3A. Child Custody and Support

§656A. Adjustment for Additional Dependents

(a) As used in this section, "additional dependents" means any natural and adopted children and stepchildren for whom the parent has a duty of support.

(b) In any proceeding to establish or modify child support, the total child support obligation for the children who are the subject of the support order shall be adjusted if a parent is also responsible for the support of additional dependents who are not the subject of the support order. The adjustments shall be made by calculating an amount under the guidelines to represent the support obligation for additional dependents based only upon the responsible parent's available income, without any other adjustments. This amount shall be subtracted from that parent's available income prior to calculating the total child support obligation based on both parents' available income. . . .

(c) The adjustment for additional dependents shall not be made to the extent that it contributes to the calculation of a support order lower than a previously existing support order for the children who are the subject of the modification hearing at which the adjustment is sought. . . .

Lastly, there are a large number of cases in which biological fathers attempt to avoid a child support obligation altogether on the grounds that it is unfair to make them pay, because they were wronged somehow in the process of conception. All such attempts fail; the legal system imposes strict liability on males for any procreation their sperm causes. But hope springs eternal. The following decision addresses constitutional challenges to imposition of a support obligation. It also illustrates how state welfare agencies get involved in child support actions when the mother receives public assistance.

Dubay v. Wells

506 F.3d 422 (6th Cir. 2007)

Clay, Circuit Judge.

. . . In the fall of 2004, Dubay and Wells became involved in a romantic relationship. At that time, Dubay informed Wells that he had no interest in becoming a father. In response, Wells told Dubay that she was infertile and that, as an extra layer of protection, she was using contraception. Dubay, in reliance on these assurances, participated in a consensual sexual relationship with Wells.

The parties' relationship later deteriorated. Shortly thereafter, and much to Dubay's surprise, Wells informed Dubay that she was pregnant, allegedly with Dubay's child. Wells chose to carry the child to term and the child, EGW, was born on an unspecified date in 2005. During the pregnancy and birth of the child, Dubay was consistently clear about his desire not to be a father.

A few weeks after EGW's birth, the County brought a paternity complaint against Dubay in the Saginaw County Circuit Court under the Michigan Paternity Act. Wells and the County sought a judgment of filiation, child support, reimbursement for delivery of the child, and other statutory and equitable relief. . . .

Dubay argues that the Michigan statutes deny him the equal protection of the law by affording mothers a right to disclaim parenthood after engaging in consensual sex *(i.e.,* through abortion) while denying that right to fathers. Second, Dubay contends that Michigan law denies men equal protection by making it easier for a woman to place a child in adoption or drop the newborn off at a hospital or other social service agency. . . .

Dubay cannot prevail under any of these equal protection theories. First, strict scrutiny does not apply because the Michigan Paternity Act does not affect any of Dubay's fundamental rights. In *N.E. v. Hedges,* we found that the right to privacy . . . does not encompass a right to decide not to become a parent after conception and birth. *See also Rivera v. Minnich* (U.S. 1987) (finding that a "putative father has no legitimate right and certainly no liberty interest in avoiding financial obligations to his natural child that are validly imposed by state law"). In doing so, we explicitly rejected the argument . . . that "fairness" dictates that men should receive a right to disclaim fatherhood in exchange for a woman's right to abortion.[3] Our discussion clarified that it is not a fundamental right of any parent, male or female, to sever his or her financial responsibilities to the child after the child is born. Thus, to the extent that Dubay claims Michigan is not affording him equal protection of the law by denying men, but not women, "the right to initiate consensual sexual activity while choosing to not be a parent," his argument must fail.

Second, we do not need to apply intermediate scrutiny because the Michigan Paternity Act does not discriminate on the basis of gender. The statutory provisions that impose the obligation of support upon Dubay, and similarly situated fathers, are gender neutral. *See* Mich. Comp. Laws §722.712(1) ("The *parents* of a child born out of wedlock are liable for the necessary support and education of the child."). Likewise, while the provision allowing for a judgment of filiation is technically based upon gender as it only provides for an order establishing that a man is the legal *father* of the child, this provision must be read in light of Michigan's entire statutory scheme which also requires the identification of a *mother* at the child's birth and establishes a judicial remedy to ensure that this mother is providing adequate support to the child. By requiring the identification of a mother and a father for the child and by demanding that both these parents provide support to the child, the Michigan statutes do not discriminate against either sex in imposing parenting obligations and, thus, do not need to be reviewed under intermediate scrutiny.

Finally, the Michigan Paternity Act withstands rational basis review because it is rationally related to a legitimate government purpose. "The underlying purpose of the Paternity Act is to ensure that the minor children born outside a marriage are provided with support and education." This is undoubtedly a legitimate, and an important, governmental interest. Moreover, the means that the statute uses to achieve this end—requiring support from the legal parents, and determining legal fatherhood based on the biological fatherhood—is substantially, let alone rationally, related to this legitimate, and probably important, government purpose.[5] Accordingly, we find that Dubay has raised no viable equal protection challenge to the Michigan Paternity Act. . . .

Dubay further argues that "[u]nder Michigan's safe haven and abandonment laws, a mother can also unilaterally drop off a newborn at the hospital, police department, or clinic without any legal or financial recourse whatsoever, something not afforded men. It is also easier for a woman to place a child for adoption, and again avoid being forced into

3. . . . The woman's right to abortion is not solely, or even primarily, based upon her right to choose not to be a mother after engaging in consensual sexual intercourse. Rather, the right to abortion, as articulated in *Roe,* derives from the woman's right to bodily integrity and her privacy interest in protecting her own physical and mental health. *See id.* (focusing on the negative mental and physical health effects that would follow from denying a woman's choice to terminate her pregnancy). Moreover, [i]n the case of a father seeking to opt out of fatherhood and thereby avoid child support obligations, the child is already in existence and the state therefore has an important interest in providing for his or her support. When a woman exercises her right to abortion, the pregnancy does not result in a live birth and there remains no child for the state to have an interest in supporting. If the state allowed a mother to unilaterally disclaim the legal rights and obligations incident to motherhood *after the child was born,* then the law would be extending a right to mothers which it does not afford to fathers. . . .

5. As our analysis indicates, while we do not apply intermediate scrutiny to the Michigan Paternity Act because it does not discriminate on the basis of gender, we believe that the law would withstand such review.

unwanted parenthood." As with his challenge to the Paternity Act, this argument lacks legal foundation. . . . [T]he laws that Dubay appears to be challenging are gender neutral and are rationally related to a legitimate government interest. Dubay has produced no evidence that any of these acts were motivated by a discriminatory intent or for a discriminatory purpose. Accordingly, we again find that Dubay cannot demonstrate that the challenged Michigan laws violate the Equal Protection Clause. . . . Therefore, we hold that the district court properly dismissed Dubay's case for "failure to state a claim upon which relief can be granted."

Were you convinced fathers are in no worse position than mothers regarding control over becoming a parent once a child is born? Are there other suspect assumptions, explicit or implicit, in the analysis? For example, does the abortion decision really only affect the well-being of the mother and not also the father? Cf. I. Glenn Cohen, *The Right Not to Be a Genetic Parent?*, 81 S. Cal. L. Rev. 1115 (2008). See also *Phillips v. Irons*, infra. The right not to procreate is also asserted when married couples who have created and frozen embryos disagree about disposition of them at the time of divorce. See Ellen A. Waldman, *The Parent Trap: Uncovering the Myth of "Coerced Parenthood" in Frozen Embryo Disputes*, 53 Am. U. L. Rev. 1021 (2004).

The court noted in a deleted footnote that the father alleged no substantive due process claim. Could he have done so on the grounds that the state may not impose a duty on him, and accordingly take his property away, because of a situation resulting from his being defrauded, if evidence showed the mother intentionally deceived him as to fertility and contraception? Would a due process argument be stronger or weaker when the biological father is a victim of statutory rape? The following decision addresses that more-common-than-you-might-expect situation.

L.M.E. v. A.R.S.

680 N.W.2d 902 (Mich. Ct. App. 2004)

Owens, P.J.

. . . LME was born in 1968 and respondent was born in 1974. In 1989, while married, [LME] gave birth to BME and listed her husband, DLE, as the child's father. In 2000, she and DLE were divorced in New York. In the course of the divorce proceedings, or immediately after the divorce was granted, blood tests established that DLE was not BME's biological father. In 2001, a New York hearing examiner entered a filiation order indicating that respondent had appeared with counsel and admitted being BME's father. . . . Subsequently, the Macomb County prosecutor, on behalf of petitioners, petitioned the trial court for child support. . . .

Respondent argued that he was the victim of an act of criminal sexual conduct committed by LME because he was fourteen years old when she induced him to have sexual intercourse. He reasoned that because he was under the age of consent, his participation was legally involuntary.[7] This argument confuses two distinct legal concepts. Because of

7. Respondent claimed that LME plied him with alcohol and the promise of sex with an older woman to induce him to engage in sexual intercourse with her; there is no support in the record for this allegation so we need not consider it. However, we note that this claim does not assist respondent's argument that the sexual relationship was not consensual.

his age at the time of the sexual conduct, the law refuses to permit the adult in the relationship to claim consent as a defense. Therefore, even if respondent was a willing participant in the sexual intercourse, LME could still have been charged with, at least, third-degree criminal sexual conduct.

However, the issue presented by this case is not LME's criminal culpability for criminal sexual conduct, or whether respondent was—or could have been—a "consensual" participant in that activity. Rather, we are concerned with whether respondent may be liable for child support for the child that resulted from the sexual activity. Child support is not imposed to penalize or victimize either parent. "The purpose of child support is to provide for the needs of the child." "Child support is not imposed for the benefit of the custodial parent, but rather to satisfy the present needs of the child."[8]

Guidance regarding this determination may be derived from the decisions of sister states. . . . The courts that have considered this issue have uniformly concluded that the fact that a child results from the criminal sexual act of an adult female with a minor male does not absolve the minor from the responsibility to pay child support.

For example, in *Schierenbeck v. Minor* (1961), a 20-year old female (who was married to another man) had sexual relations with the plaintiff with the result that a child was born. The Colorado Supreme Court rejected any suggestion that the plaintiff's third-degree rape by the adult female excused his liability to provide for the support of his child and stated:

> Certain it is that his assent to the illicit act does not exclude commission of the statutory crime, but it has nothing to do with assent as relating to progeny. His youth is basic to the crime; it is not a factor in the question of whether he is the father of Sherrie Lynn. . . .

The Wisconsin Court of Appeals in *In re Paternity of JLH* (1989), rejected the claim that a fifteen-year-old boy who had intercourse with an eighteen-and-a-half-year-old female was absolved of responsibility to support the resultant child because he was a victim of a sexual assault and the female should not be permitted to benefit from her crime. The court stated:

> We reject appellant's argument that his paying child support to L.H. would permit her to benefit from her crime. Even assuming that L.H. criminally assaulted appellant, child support is paid to benefit the child, not the custodial parent. The custodial parent receives support payments in trust to be used for the child's welfare.

The Illinois Court of Appeals rejected a similar claim in *In re the Parentage of JS* (1990). The respondent in that case claimed that Illinois public policy protected him, as a minor, from the consequences of his "improvident conduct." The court disagreed and stated:

> We note that contrary to the respondent's position, Illinois public policy has never offered blanket protection to reckless minors. At the same time, Illinois public policy has recognized the blanket right of every child to the physical, mental, emotional, and monetary support of his or her parents. The public has an interest in protecting children from becoming wards of the state. In the instant case, we find that the public policy mandating parental support of children overrides any policy of protecting a minor from improvident acts.

8. This Court has concluded that the securing of support for children is so important that it has held that even where a parent voluntarily releases his parental rights, he is still liable to pay support for the child as long as the child's custody remains with the other biological parent.

In *Mercer Co. Dep't of Social Services v. Alf M* (N.Y. 1992), the county family court rejected the respondent's argument that because he was technically the victim of a crime (he was sixteen when he had sexual relations with the child's mother, who was twenty-one at the time), he should not be held legally responsible to support the child. The court responded:

> [F]ather's recourse under the law as to the mother of the child . . . , was to file criminal charges against her. To penalize this child for the mother's actions would run contrary to the fundamental purpose of this proceeding . . . protecting the best interests of and insuring that adequate provision will be made for, the child's needs.

[T]he Kansas Supreme Court in *State ex rel. Hermesmann v. Seyer* (1993), held that the state could require that the thirteen-year-old juvenile father pay for the support of the child that resulted from his sexual intercourse with his seventeen-year-old babysitter. The Court stated:

> This State's interest in requiring minor parents to support their children overrides the State's competing interest in protecting juveniles from improvident acts, even when such acts may include criminal activity on the part of the other parent. Considering the three persons directly involved, Shane, Colleen, and Melanie, the interests of Melanie are superior, as a matter of public policy, to those of either or both of her parents. This minor child, the only truly innocent party, is entitled to support from both her parents regardless of their ages.

The California Court of Appeals in *San Luis Obispo Co. v. Nathaniel J* (1996), considered a case where the father was fifteen and the mother thirty-four when their consensual sexual relations resulted in the birth of a child. The mother was convicted of unlawful sexual intercourse with a minor and the father then claimed that he was not required to pay child support because he was the victim of a statutory rape. The court rejected this claim. The court observed that the father engaged in consensual sexual intercourse five times over a two-week period, noted that "[o]ne who is injured as a result of criminal conduct in which he willingly participated is not a typical crime victim." . . .

In *Jevning v. Cichos* (Minn. App., 1993), Jevning had a child after having sexual intercourse with Cichos when she was twenty and he was fifteen years old. Cichos argued that he should not be required to pay child support because he was the victim of criminal sexual conduct. The Minnesota Court of Appeals disagreed and reasoned:

> Statutory nonconsent under some definitions of criminal sexual conduct does not translate to a holding that on the civil issue of child support, minors can never be held responsible for their children resulting from sexual conduct. Generally, minors are responsible for their actions; exceptions to that principle are rare. For instances, minors are generally accountable for their economic transactions, allowed to sue and can be sued, are accountable for acts of juvenile delinquency, and may be certified to be tried as adults, depending on the circumstances.

See also *SF v. State ex rel. TM* (Ala. Civ. App. 1996) (the child is an innocent party and the purpose behind the state parentage act is to provide for the welfare of the child; "any wrongful conduct on the part of the mother should not alter the father's duty to provide support for the child"); *Hamm v. Office of Child Support Enforcement* (Ark. 1999) (accepting general rule that "father who had been below the age of consent for sexual intercourse under criminal sexual conduct statutes at the time of conception is liable for supporting the child resulting from that union").

We agree with these authorities. The record indicates that respondent participated in the act of sexual intercourse that resulted in the conception of BME. Respondent is not absolved from the responsibility to support the child because LME was technically committing an act of criminal sexual conduct. The public policy of this state seeks to secure support for children. Contrary to respondent's view, LME does not "profit" from her criminality. "Child support is not imposed for the benefit of the custodial parent, but rather to satisfy the present needs of the child." We recognized in *Pellar* that "[t]he needs of the child are of overriding importance." This important public policy is furthered by requiring respondent to pay child support. . . .

The court quotes from an Illinois decision stating: "Illinois public policy has recognized the blanket right of every child to the physical, mental, emotional, and monetary support of his or her parents. The public has an interest in protecting children from becoming wards of the state." Does this conflate the rights of children with the self-interest of taxpayers? Why do children need protection against having their support come from the state rather than from their biological fathers? Is all the talk of the babies' well-being really disingenuous, an attempt to disguise the fact that the real conflict of interests is not between father and child but between father and taxpayers, and to disguise the courts' undefended choice to elevate the interests of taxpayers above those of boys who are victims of statutory rape?

All of the precedents cited involved an older woman and a boy. Do you suppose the outcomes would be so consistently hostile to the statutory rape objection to a child support obligation if the genders were reversed—that is, if there were a spate of cases involving 13-, 14-, and 15-year-old girls impregnated by boyfriends in their 20s or 30s, in which the men ended up with custody of the children instead of the girls?

The California court in *Nathaniel J* emphasized that the boy was a willing participant in repeated sexual activity—that is, that he enjoyed the experience. Should that matter? Many of the cited decisions in fact suggest that the boy-father is really not innocent in these situations. What if a boy were really not a willing participant—for example, if a babysitter were able to force intercourse? Or would judges likely refuse to believe that that is possible? There have actually been cases in which *adult* men claimed to have been raped—for example, while they were passed out after heavy drinking. Perhaps in part because they simply do not believe the men, courts also uniformly reject those claims.

Even weirder, as reflected in the decision below, there have been several cases in which women took a man's sperm by oral or manual stimulation and, without the man's knowledge, injected themselves with it. Then there was the case of two young couples in Kansas who went on a double date to the drive-in theater, became amorous, discovered they only had one condom between them, and . . . you don't want to know. Across all scenarios, courts effectively apply a rule of strict liability for the behavior of one's sperm.

In some circumstances, a man who is wronged in the process of procreation might have financial recourse other than avoiding the child support obligation—namely, by going after the mother for tort damages.

Phillips v. Irons

2005 WL 4694579 (Ill. App. Ct. 2005)

Plaintiff . . . and defendant began dating in January of 1999, prior to which time defendant informed plaintiff that she was divorced, her prior marriage having occurred one year earlier, and it was a "terrible mistake." In a short period of time, plaintiff and defendant became engaged to be married. During their relationship, the parties discussed the possibility of having children only after they married. Plaintiff informed defendant he did not wish to have children prior to marriage, and intended to use a condom if and when they engaged in sexual intercourse. Defendant understood and agreed.

During the entire course of their relationship, the parties engaged in intimate sexual acts three times, with two of those times occurring on the same date. Vaginal penetration never occurred; the parties engaged only in acts of oral sex. Defendant told plaintiff she did not want to have sexual intercourse due to her menses. On or around February 19, 1999, and March 19, 1999, defendant "intentionally engaged in oral sex with [plaintiff] so that she could harvest [his] semen and artificially inseminate herself," and "did artificially inseminate herself." . . .

[I]n May of 1999, defendant confessed to plaintiff that she still was married to her former husband, Dr. Adebowale Adeleye. She told plaintiff she planned to get a divorce, and showed him a "Petition for Dissolution of Marriage," which was filed on May 20, 1999. In the petition, defendant swore she was not pregnant. The parties' relationship terminated in May of 1999, upon plaintiff learning defendant was not divorced.

On November 21, 2000, defendant filed a "Petition to Establish Paternity and Other Relief" against plaintiff, claiming she and plaintiff had a sexual relationship eight to ten months before the birth of defendant's daughter, Serena, on December 1, 1999. DNA tests have confirmed plaintiff is Serena's biological father. Plaintiff's complaint asserted he had no knowledge of defendant's pregnancy nor the birth of the child until receiving defendant's petition to establish paternity. He also claimed defendant continued to live with Adeleye during her pregnancy, after which defendant led Adeleye and the public to believe Serena is Adeleye's daughter, as evinced by Adeleye's name on Serena's birth certificate. Plaintiff contends Serena still does not know he is her biological father. . . .

I

Plaintiff argues . . . intentional infliction of emotional distress. He claims defendant's conduct was "extreme and outrageous," when she lied about being unable to engage in intercourse or to conceive due to her menses and agreed to prevent conception of children prior to marriage, but then intentionally engaged in oral sex so she could harvest his semen to artificially inseminate herself.[2] Plaintiff asserts defendant falsely claimed not

2. Although the legal issues involved are dissimilar from those presented in the case *sub judice,* there are at least two cases dealing with self-insemination. In *Jhordan C. v. Mary K.* (Cal. Ct. App. 1986), an unmarried woman artificially inseminated herself at home with the semen of a known donor and gave birth to a child she intended to raise jointly with a close woman friend. The donor filed an action to establish paternity and visitation rights. With regard to the mother's ability to inseminate herself, the Court of Appeal of California stated "[i]t is true that nothing inherent in artificial insemination requires the involvement of a physician. Artificial insemination is, as demonstrated here, a simple procedure easily performed by a woman in her own home."

In *State v. Frisard* (La. Ct. App. 1997), the child's mother filed a paternity suit against the father, who denied having sexual intercourse with the mother, to whom he was not married. He alleged that she, a nursing assistant, performed oral sex on him in a hospital, made him wear a condom, and used his sperm to inseminate herself in a

to be pregnant in her petition for dissolution, yet in her response to plaintiff's "Demand for Bill of Particulars" in the pending paternity suit, defendant informed the circuit court she "began to suspect that [she] was pregnant during the week of April 5, 1999."

Plaintiff asserts defendant "intended to inflict emotional distress on plaintiff or knew there was a high probability that her conduct would do so." He claims defendant, as a physician and clinical professor of internal medicine, is well versed in: the functions of the female body; the fact that the mouth is a suitable environment to house live sperm; and the art of artificial insemination. Given defendant's awareness of the circumstances, plaintiff contends defendant knew, or should have known, that filing her petition for paternity would shock him and inflict severe emotional distress.

Plaintiff alleges defendant "actually caused severe emotional distress," as manifested in his nausea; inability to eat; difficulty concentrating and sleeping; feelings of being trapped in a nightmare; diminished ability to trust; and headaches. . . .

Three elements are needed to state a cause of action for IIED: (1) the conduct involved must be truly extreme and outrageous; (2) the actor must either intend that his or her conduct inflict severe emotional distress, or know that there is at least a high probability that it will cause severe emotional distress; and (3) the conduct must, in fact, cause severe emotional distress. . . .

Whether conduct is extreme and outrageous is evaluated on an objective standard based on all of the facts and circumstances. Mere insults, indignities, threats, annoyances, petty oppressions or other trivialities do not qualify as outrageous conduct. Rather, the nature of defendant's conduct must be so extreme as to go beyond all possible bounds of decency, and to be regarded as intolerable in a civilized community. In the case *sub judice*, if proved, defendant's actions would constitute "extreme and outrageous" conduct. Defendant is accused of deliberately misleading plaintiff to believe she did not want to conceive children until after marriage and could not become pregnant due to her menstrual cycle, but deceitfully engaged in sexual acts, which no reasonable person would expect could result in pregnancy, to use plaintiff's sperm in an unorthodox, unanticipated manner yielding extreme consequences. Under these facts, it is cognizable that if an average member of the parties' community were told of these circumstances, a reasonable response could be, "outrageous!"

Next, . . . even if defendant intended to accomplish only conception and procreation, she knew there was at least a high probability that her manner of so doing would inflict severe emotional distress. . . . According to plaintiff, defendant was aware of his desire to have children only after marriage. Further, plaintiff believed defendant could not become pregnant. . . . Months later, however, defendant informed plaintiff he fathered her child. From these facts, if proved, it may be inferred reasonably that defendant knew manipulating plaintiff into unwittingly conceiving a child out of wedlock would inflict severe emotional distress. Further, . . . plaintiff is not claiming the act of filing the paternity suit itself caused him severe emotional distress; it was the result of defendant's actions in their entirety.

Last, . . . plaintiff set forth sufficient facts to allege "severe" emotional distress. Plaintiff claims he "often finds himself nauseated and unable to eat, especially when—as a family practitioner—he treats small children who are the same age as the child he allegedly

---

nearby bathroom with a "red looking bulb with a glass tube." In addition to DNA results and plaintiff's affidavit, in which she stated she had sexual intercourse with defendant and did not have intercourse with any other man 30 days before or after the date of conception, the Court of Appeal explained that defendant's "testimony showed that he had some sort of sexual contact with plaintiff around the time frame of alleged conception, although he denied that they had sexual intercourse."

fathered." He states that his continued thoughts of this child have caused him difficulty sleeping and has interfered with his professional obligations and personal activities. He feels "as if he is trapped in a terrible nightmare," he is "burdened with feelings of betrayal," and "his ability to trust has been greatly diminished," which has "greatly affected his social life." . . . It is the degree of emotional distress actually suffered by plaintiff which separates the actionable from the non-actionable. . . . Here, plaintiff has . . . illustrated with examples the effect of defendant's actions on him. As plaintiff's claim involves a physically and psychologically manipulated non-consensual pregnancy, it is cognizable that the intensity of his emotional distress is great and its duration long-lasting. . . . [I]n "Illinois, unlike some other jurisdictions, physical injury or disability is not required to accompany, or result from, the psychic trauma."

At this stage plaintiff is not required to prove his case. . . . Whether plaintiff will prevail on the elements of his claim for IIED is a quintessential question of fact to be resolved by the trier of fact. Accordingly, the circuit court erred in dismissing count I. . . .

II

Plaintiff contends next the circuit court erred in dismissing count II of his complaint for fraudulent misrepresentation. . . . The elements of a claim for fraudulent misrepresentation are: (1) a false statement of material fact; (2) known or believed to be false by the party making it; (3) intent to induce plaintiff to act; (4) action by plaintiff in justifiable reliance on the truth of the statement; and (5) damage to plaintiff resulting from such reliance. . . . The tort of fraudulent misrepresentation historically has been limited to cases involving business or financial transactions where plaintiff has suffered a pecuniary harm. Fraudulent misrepresentation is a tort distinct from the general milieu of negligent and intentional wrongs; it is an economic tort under which one may recover only monetary damages. Therefore, plaintiff may not recover on allegations of physical and emotional distress. The circuit court did not err in dismissing plaintiff's claim for fraudulent misrepresentation.

III

Plaintiff['s] complaint for conversion . . . asserts that defendant . . . took his "semen, sperm, and genetic material without his permission, for the purpose of conceiving a child. . . ." Defendant responds that where plaintiff did not loan or lease his sperm, where there was no agreement that the original deposit would be returned upon request, or where the transaction did not create a bailment, a claim for conversion cannot be sustained. She asserts that when plaintiff "delivered" his sperm to defendant it was a gift—an absolute and irrevocable transfer of title to property from a donor to donee. Plaintiff's donative intent was clear, she argues, "had he not intended to deliver his sperm to [her], he would have used a condom and kept it and its contents."

Conversion is an unauthorized act that deprives a person of his property permanently or for an indefinite time. . . . The elements of a claim for conversion are: (1) plaintiff's right in the property; (2) plaintiff's right to immediate, absolute, and unconditional possession of the property; (3) defendant's unauthorized and wrongful assumption of control, dominion, or ownership over the property; and (4) plaintiff's demand for possession.

In this case, no set of facts could be proved under the pleadings that would entitle plaintiff to relief for conversion, as he cannot satisfy the requisite elements. Cases from other jurisdictions have recognized the existence of a "property right" in materials derived from the human body; however, plaintiff cannot show he had the "right to immediate, absolute, and unconditional possession" of his sperm. Plaintiff presumably intended, and he does not claim otherwise, that defendant discard his semen, not return it to him. "The essence of conversion is the wrongful deprivation of one who has a right to the immediate possession of the object unlawfully held." Plaintiff is unable to satisfy the second element needed to state a claim for conversion. In light of the foregoing, the third and fourth elements of conversion need not be addressed.

In a case like this, where the custodial parent has ample financial resources for raising the child, the principal rationale of cases like *L.M.E.*—that is, that the child should not become a public charge—does not apply. Should courts excuse defrauded men from a child support obligation when state dependency is not an issue? Would that be preferable to having the men file tort suits against the mothers?

Though this particular form of fraud, secretly inseminating oneself, is rare, another form is quite common—namely, women simply lying about their fertility or their use of contraception prior to having intercourse with men. *Phillips* suggests there is a real harm to men, psychological and even physical, from being deceived into procreation. Imposing an 18-year-or-more financial obligation compounds the trauma. Is it an adequate response to say to such men that they could simply have chosen not to have sex?

d. Enforcement

Non-compliance with child support orders was an especially serious problem before the 1990s, as was the absence of orders as to many non-marital children. Courts had limited ability to compel payments, determine obligors' true income, or locate those who moved. Legislation in the late 1980s and in the 1990s dramatically changed the rates of support orders and of compliance with orders, by pushing states to authorize new mechanisms for courts to track down and pin down non-custodial parents and their assets. See, e.g., Tracy Carbasho, *Allegheny County a National Leader in Child Support Collection and Enforcement*, 12 No. 18 Lawyers J. 7 (2010) (reporting an 81 percent rate of collection of all child support owed in the Pittsburgh area). It is not clear, however, to what extent children rather than state welfare agencies have benefited from these reforms.

Elizabeth G. Patterson, Civil Contempt and the Indigent Child Support Obligor: The Silent Return of Debtor's Prison

18 Cornell J.L. & Pub. Pol'y 95, 99 (2008)

. . . Congressional reform of the welfare program in the 1980's focused on two primary techniques for reducing spiraling welfare costs and welfare recipients' economic dependence on government. The first technique was putting the welfare recipient to work. The second was obtaining support for the recipient's children from absent parents. Between them, earned income and child support were expected to create sufficient household income so that many single parents—the primary welfare population—would no longer require welfare subsidies. Child support payments on behalf of children supported by the welfare program also were seen as a means for repaying the state and federal governments for welfare benefits received by the payor's family. . . . Only when support payments exceeded this debt to the government would the custodial parent/welfare recipient receive any portion of the funds. Almost half the national child support debt is owed not to custodial parents, but to the government.

In fashioning the child support enforcement program, the federal focus was on creating a relentlessly effective system for collecting as much accrued child support debt as possible from absent parents. The federal requirements address every aspect of the process of identifying and locating absent parents, and establishing and enforcing the support obligation. Welfare eligibility is conditioned on identification of the father (in the case of female applicants) and cooperation with efforts to obtain support from the absent parent. Judicial proceedings for determining paternity and ordering payment of child support have been replaced with administrative proceedings. . . .

Once the order is in place, collection of the required support is facilitated through a broad array of mechanisms created or mandated by federal law. A vast network of automated systems provides the child support agency with information on obligors' bank accounts, tax filings, and assets, as well as means for effecting automated seizures of certain assets, including tax refunds. Wage withholding is mandatory in all cases where child support enforcement is being handled by the agency. Employers can be identified through interlinked automated state and national "new hire" directories, to which employers must report information on each newly hired employee. If insufficient funds are obtained through wage withholding and seizure of assets, a variety of coercive mechanisms are available to try to induce payment by the obligor. These include the revocation of occupational, driver's, and other licenses; the denial of passports; and reporting of delinquent obligors to consumer reporting agencies.

The federal statute also provides for interstate cooperation in enforcement efforts and creates state and federal "Parent Locate" systems with access to records of departments of corrections, employment security commissions, utility companies, the postal service, the military, and other entities with extensive records on members of the public. . . .

For various reasons, the court often lacks . . . information with regard to low-income parents. The parent may fail to appear, or the parent's evidence concerning income and employment may be incomplete or confusing, particularly if he does not have a steady job. Commonly, the only evidence of the indigent parent's income and assets comes from the parent's own testimony, which the court may discount as self-serving and lacking credibility. In these cases the amount of child support ordered may represent nothing more than an educated guess. . . . When the noncustodial parent fails to appear at the hearing, the court will impute an income to the parent, which then serves as the basis for the support award. . . . In the absence of . . . evidence, the court may impute to the obligor the ability to earn the minimum wage, or it may simply take a stab in the dark. . . . [T]he court generally assumes a forty-hour work week. Imputation of income frequently overestimates the income of low-income parents, who often work less than a forty-hour week, may receive less than minimum wage, and frequently work sporadically. . . .

A retroactive support award treats the accrual of child support as commencing at some time prior to entry of the order. For divorced or cohabiting parents, this date is generally the date when the parties separated. For other nonmarital parents, the accrual of child support may begin upon the birth of the child. . . . Failure to support the child at any time, whether or not an order is in place, constitutes a legal default subject to later enforcement by the courts. Particularly in the case of nonmarital fathers, whose paternity may not be definitively established until the child support proceeding, the retroactive award may extend over a period of years, resulting in retroactive awards in the thousands of dollars. Some states add costs associated with the birth of the child and possibly a variety of fees as well. . . .

Thus, low-income obligors, who generally lack the assets to pay a large retroactive award, enter a state of permanent arrearage. Courts generally deal with arrearages by adding to the "current" monthly support obligation an additional amount to be applied toward arrearages. Even when the award of current support accurately reflects the amount of support the obligor could afford to pay, the addition of an arrearage component will inherently cause the award to exceed the obligor's ability. . . . [Moreover,] child support guidelines are designed for situations in which it is possible to project an amount that the parent can reasonably be expected to pay each month over an extended period of time. . . . For many low-income persons, however, their job trajectory lacks this kind of consistency. Employment is sporadic, with wages fluctuating from one job to the next and separated by periods of unemployment, thus causing frequent changes in the obligor's ability to pay. . . . [S]tates have limited the availability of the modification remedy by restricting the types of changes that warrant an adjustment in the support amount. . . . Finally, most low-income obligors . . . have limited understanding of their legal rights, do not know how to access the legal system or present their case effectively, and are intimidated by courts and other official fora. They also lack the funds to hire legal counsel to help them navigate the system, and no jurisdiction recognizes a right to appointed counsel in proceedings to establish or modify the child support amount. . . . In any event, it is too late at the point of modification to affect arrearages that have already accumulated as a result of excessive awards, as federal law prohibits retroactive modification of accrued child support. . . .

Other scholars have also taken the view that child support enforcement efforts directed at low-income obligors are often unfair and likely to do more harm than good for children. See, e.g., Ann Cammett, *Deadbeats, Deadbrokes, and Prisoners*, 18 Geo. J. Pov. L. & Pol'y 127 (2011); Solangel Maldonado, *Deadbeat or Deadbroke: Redefining Child Support for Poor Fathers*, 39 U.C. Davis L. Rev. 991 (2006); Jane C. Murphy, *Legal Images of Fatherhood: Welfare Reform, Child Support Enforcement, and Fatherless Children*, 81 Notre Dame L. Rev. 325 (2005).

We saw in Chapter 2 that at least one state, Wisconsin, attempted to encourage payment of child support by denying marriage licenses to delinquents. The U.S. Supreme Court foreclosed that enforcement mechanism with its decision in *Turner v. Safley*. But it has not yet ruled on use of another sort of incursion into intimate life to induce compliance with a support order—namely, ordering delinquent obligors not to have any more children until they are paid up.

State v. Talty

814 N.E.2d 1201 (Ohio 2004)

Moyer, C.J.

. . . On February 27, 2002, the Medina County Grand Jury indicted Talty on two counts of nonsupport . . . , a fifth-degree felony. . . . The trial court . . . found him guilty of both counts . . . [and] sentenced Talty to community control for five years under . . . the Adult Probation Department. As a condition of that community control, the trial court ordered Talty to "make all reasonable efforts to avoid conceiving another child."[1] The court additionally stated, "What those efforts are are up to [Talty], that is not for me to say; I am not mandating what he does, only that he has to make reasonable efforts to do so." . . .

R.C. 2929.15(A)(1) governs the authority of the trial court to impose conditions of community control. That section provides that when sentencing an offender for a felony, the trial court may impose one or more community sanctions, including residential, nonresidential, and financial sanctions, and any other conditions that it considers "appropriate." . . . Nevertheless, a trial court's discretion in imposing probationary conditions is not limitless. . . . The issue in *Jones* was whether a trial court may impose a probation condition that required an offender to "have no association or communication, direct or indirect, with anyone under the age of eighteen (18) years not a member of his immediate family." We . . . concluded that the order "should reasonably be interpreted as meaning an illicit, or potentially unlawful association or communication." Because the Constitution does not confer a right to speech or association for illegal purposes, our opinion in *Jones* thus addressed only a nonconstitutional challenge to the condition.

Having so limited our analysis in *Jones,* we set forth the test for determining whether a condition reasonably relates to the three probationary goals—as reflected in former R.C. 2951.02(C)—of "doing justice, rehabilitating the offender, and insuring good behavior." We stated that courts must "consider whether the condition (1) is reasonably related to rehabilitating the offender, (2) has some relationship to the crime of which the offender was convicted, and (3) relates to conduct which is criminal or reasonably related to future criminality and serves the statutory ends of probation." In addition . . . , we observed that probation conditions "cannot be overly broad so as to unnecessarily impinge upon the probationer's liberty." . . . The United States Supreme Court has explained—albeit in a constitutional context—that the availability of ready alternatives to a regulation is evidence that the regulation is unreasonable. . . .

Talty asserts that his community-control order is overbroad because there was no opportunity to have the antiprocreation condition lifted if he became current on his child-support payments. The government counters that other states have applied a test similar to *Jones* and upheld "virtually identical" conditions. Specifically, the state points to *State v. Oakley* (Wis. 2001), in which the Wisconsin Supreme Court upheld an antiprocreation condition imposed upon a father who had been convicted of intentionally refusing to pay child support. Significantly, however, the antiprocreation condition in *Oakley* included the stipulation that the court would terminate the condition if the defendant could prove to the court that he had supported his children. The Wisconsin Supreme Court considered this portion of the order critical. . . .

Although we do not determine whether a mechanism that allowed the antiprocreation condition to be lifted would have rendered the condition valid under *Jones,* such a mechanism would have been, at the very least, an easy alternative that would have better accommodated Talty's procreation rights at de minimis costs to the legitimate probationary interests of rehabilitation and avoiding future criminality. Nor can the condition be

1. The court further ordered Talty to make regular payments of child support, to pay $150 per week on arrearages, to obtain a GED within five years, and to make reasonable efforts to remain employed on a full-time basis.

considered valid merely because the trial court *could* modify the order if Talty became current on his child-support payments. Our review of a condition of community control is limited, as it must be, to what the sentencing order says and not what a trial court might later modify it to say.

Further, we reject the argument that the antiprocreation order is valid because Talty could have been incarcerated but for the trial judge's "act of grace" and that, if incarcerated, he would have been denied conjugal visits. . . . [T]he United States Supreme Court has rejected the "act of grace" doctrine. Thus, the fact that the state might have incarcerated a defendant does not, in itself, justify a lesser intrusion of his or her rights. . . . [I]nfringements of constitutional rights must be tailored to specific government interests. . . . [A] prisoner who is convicted of a crime wholly unrelated to procreation (say, burglary) may nonetheless be denied conjugal visits . . . because, for example, the regulation is reasonably related to the legitimate government interest of maintaining the security of the prison. For the same crime (burglary), however, a probationer may not be denied the right to procreate on the basis of the same government interest—maintaining the security of a prison—because the probationer is not in prison. It follows, therefore, that a legitimate *penological* interest may be different from a legitimate *probationary* interest, thus rendering unsound the notion that the government may withhold from a probationer any right that it could withhold from a prisoner.

Finally, . . . if a trial judge could deny to a probationer any right that a prison official could deny to an inmate, then a condition of community control need not be related to the rehabilitation of the defendant, the administration of justice, or the prevention of future criminality. Rather, the condition need only infringe the rights of a probationer as much as or less than a prison regulation may infringe those of an inmate. This proposition . . . was expressly rejected in *Gagnon*, 411 U.S. at 782. . . .

[W]e hold that the antiprocreation order is overbroad under *Jones* and vacate that portion of the trial court's sentencing order. Given our disposition, we need not address Talty's constitutional . . . challenges to the antiprocreation condition. . . .

PFEIFER, J., dissenting.

. . . [D]efendant Sean Talty "is a 30-year-old male who has fathered six or seven children. (The evidence was unclear as to the exact number. . . .) Two children were conceived during a marriage: Heather Talty and Shyann Talty. The Defendant owes child support arrears for those children in the amount of $28,044.79. . . . He has one child, Courtney Hunter, for whom he owes child support in the amount of $10,642.51. . . . "The Defendant also has two children by the woman with whom he is currently living and has two children by other women, one of whom lives in Butler County, and he possibly has a child living in Dayton, Ohio." . . . The court found that Talty "never paid" toward his child-support obligations even though he was aware of them. . . .

I am not persuaded that *Jones*, which addressed conditions of probation pursuant to former R.C. 2951.02, applies to this case, which addresses conditions of community control pursuant to R.C. 2929.15. . . . Although community control is in large measure the functional equivalent of probation, the drafting of the two statutes is markedly different. . . . When imposing community-control sanctions for a felony, the trial court "shall be guided by the overriding purposes of felony sentencing," which are "to protect the public from future crime by the offender and others and to punish the offender." To achieve those purposes, the sentencing court "shall consider the need for incapacitating the offender, deterring the offender and others from future crime, [and] rehabilitating the offender." . . . Talty was ordered to "make all reasonable efforts" to avoid fathering another child. . . . [T]he sanction relates directly to the crime of which Talty was convicted and is tailored to prevent even more instances of felony nonsupport. . . .

As the majority clearly states, overbreadth in this context is not constitutional overbreadth, which can be invoked only when the Free Speech Clause of the First Amendment to the United States Constitution is implicated. Rather, overbreadth in this context is more in the nature of a reasonableness argument. . . . R.C. 2929.15(C) provides that "[i]f an offender, for a significant period of time, fulfills the conditions of a sanction . . . imposed in an exemplary manner, the court may reduce the period of time under the sanction or impose a less restrictive sanction." . . . Further, the trial court ordered Talty to make only "reasonable efforts". . . . The language of the antiprocreation condition is reasonable, not excessively rigid or absolute. . . .

Next, I turn to constitutional considerations. As the majority states, "the right to procreate is considered fundamental under the United States Constitution." *Skinner v. Oklahoma* (U.S. 1942). "To a greater or lesser degree, it is always true of probationers (as we have said it to be true of parolees) that they do not enjoy 'the absolute liberty to which every citizen is entitled, but only . . . conditional liberty properly dependent on observance of special [probation] restrictions.'" *Griffin v. Wisconsin* (U.S. 1987). . . . The same is true of community control. Like federal courts that have reviewed similar issues, I do not believe that felons subject to community control are entitled to strict scrutiny even for the deprivation of fundamental rights. . . . "[I]f probation conditions were subject to strict scrutiny, it would necessarily follow that the more severe punitive sanction of incarceration, which deprives an individual of the right to be free from physical restraint and infringes upon various other fundamental rights, likewise would be subject to strict scrutiny analysis . . . [which would be] unworkable . . .

I conclude that "in light of [Talty's] ongoing victimization of his . . . children and extraordinarily troubling record manifesting his disregard for the law, this [antiprocreation] condition—imposed on a convicted felon facing the far more restrictive and punitive sanction of prison—is not overly broad and is reasonably related to [Talty's] rehabilitation. . . . In *Gagnon*, the Supreme Court stated with respect to the "act of grace" concept that a probationer could not be denied his conditional liberty without being afforded due process. In this case, Talty has had due process. . . . Talty is . . . being deprived of a constitutional right . . . because he exercised the constitutional right irresponsibly, and because the deprivation of the constitutional right will make it less likely for him to commit again the offense of which he was convicted. . . .

A simper way to prevent Talty from procreating again would have been to actually send him to prison. Courts do sometimes do that in child support delinquency prosecutions, but often spread out the sentence by ordering many short stays of two or three days, so that the delinquent can continue working to make support payments. If courts did not face this conundrum—that is, that a normal prison sentence would only make payment less likely, would a prison term be justified? Child support arrears are in essence a debt, and the Anglo-American legal system eliminated debtors' prisons long ago. See Patterson, *Civil Contempt and the Indigent Child Support Obligor: The Silent Return of Debtor's Prison*, supra (arguing against use of criminal contempt when obligors are truly unable to pay). But states generally do use the criminal law to enforce child support orders, most commonly with criminal contempt charges. Unlike most other debts, the alternative in the case of child support is state support, and the criminal law is considered an appropriate protection of the public interest, financial and otherwise. Child support obligations also receive special treatment in debtor/creditor law; they are non-dischargeable in bankruptcy and have priority over commercial debts in garnishment proceedings. See Richard M. Hynes, *Bankruptcy and State Collections: The Case of the Missing Garnishments*, 91 CORNELL L. REV. 603, 637-638 (2006).

One common reason non-custodial parents give for not complying fully with support orders is that the custodial parent uses the money for herself instead of for the children. Many ask judges to allow for direct payments to providers of services and goods in lieu of payments to the other parent, or for in-kind payments rather than money. Courts uniformly reject such requests. Professor Wallace proposes that courts order obligors to pay into a bank account and that custodial parents draw on the account using a debit card to purchase things for a child, so that there is a record of where the money goes. See Monica Hof Wallace, *Child Support Savings Accounts: An Innovative Approach to Child Support Enforcement*, 85 N.C. L. REV. 1155 (2007). If you were a custodial parent, would you have any legitimate objection to this way of receiving child support?

Finally, note that international enforcement of child support orders is an increasingly significant issue in practice and has improved with U.S. adoption of the Hague Convention on the International Recovery of Child Support and Other Forms of Family Maintenance. See U.S. Dep't of State Press Release No. 2010/1402 (Oct. 1, 2010).

e. Modification

Parents' financial circumstances relevant to child support change far more frequently than do the circumstances relevant to custody. In particular, at least in good economic times, most people see regular increases in their pay check from year to year. In addition, many parents who have been primary caretakers of young children have little or no income at the time of divorce but within a few years greatly increase their labor force participation, and that could produce a very different outcome in applying an income-shares formula. We saw above that new family relationships are often asserted as a basis for modification, either because new obligations diminish a parent's ability to support a child or because a new spouse represents a new source of wealth for a parent. In addition, children's needs can change dramatically—for example, if a new medical problem develops. How do child support laws deal with such frequent changes?

ELIZABETH G. PATTERSON, CIVIL CONTEMPT AND THE INDIGENT CHILD SUPPORT OBLIGOR: THE SILENT RETURN OF DEBTOR'S PRISON, 18 CORNELL J.L. & PUB. POL'Y 95, 112 (2008): "Federal law requires review and adjustment of support orders every three years at the request of either parent. However, most states will adjust the support amount only if the change exceeds a specified threshold—either a percentage of the existing award or a monetary amount. . . . Both common law and federal statute also provide for modification of child support orders at any time upon a showing of changed circumstances. . . . In all jurisdictions, the change must be "substantial," a requirement that generally translates into a quantitative variance between the existing and adjusted amounts similar to the "threshold amount" requirement discussed above. . . . Some states hold that only changes that were unforeseeable at the time of the original order can serve as grounds for modification. . . . Another common requirement demands that the change be involuntary and in good faith. Quitting a job is likely to be viewed as voluntary, regardless of motivation or rationale, as is termination attributable to the employee's malfeasance. Continued unemployment is considered voluntary if the obligor has failed to make sufficient efforts to find employment. Some courts also view imprisonment as voluntary, based on the voluntariness of the underlying criminal act. . . . [There is] widespread hostility to downward modification of child support obligations. . . . At least one state allows only non-custodial parents without arrears to have their orders adjusted. . . ."

Many attorney-drafted separation agreements build in annual cost-of-living increases, and then the agreement terms can be incorporated into a court decree. But courts generally do not include such automatic adjustment clauses in decrees if not asked to do so. How would you counsel a client about including such a clause in an agreement or asking a court to include one in its decree?

Katzman v. Healy

933 N.E.2d 156 (Mass. 2010)

KAFKER, J.

. . . The parents . . . were married in 1995. They have two children, Hunter, born April 6, 2000, and Kierstin, born September 13, 2001. The parents separated in May, 2003, and in . . . January, 2006, a judgment of divorce nisi issued . . . , which incorporated into the judgment a thirty-nine page separation agreement. Under the terms of the separation agreement, the mother and father were to have joint legal custody of the children and the wife was to have sole physical custody and act as primary child care provider. . . . The children were to be with the father every other weekend and Tuesday and Thursday after school. . . . [T]he father was to pay the mother $2,903.33 per month as child support. . . .

The husband was, at the time of the divorce and trial, . . . chief executive officer of EnerNOC, Inc. . . . earning $150,000 per year and the company had not yet gone public. The mother was employed as a clinical nurse specialist earning $42,000 per year. The parents then had a negative net worth of $34,000. The father did own substantial stock in EnerNOC. Pursuant to the separation agreement, the mother received forty-five percent of the father's stock, which amounted to 605,535 shares.

In March, 2007, the mother filed a complaint for modification . . . seeking an increase in child support. . . . [T]he father's base salary had risen to $325,000. The father filed a cross complaint requesting increased time with the children. By this point the father had married Jaimee Manninen and had his first child in the new marriage.

In May, 2007, EnerNOC's initial public offering occurred with a closing price of $30.16 per share. Also, in May, 2007, the mother met Robert Katzman, a Federal Bureau of Investigation (FBI) agent living in New Jersey and working in New York City. In August, 2007, the mother became engaged to Mr. Katzman. Mr. Katzman did not "wish to transfer from the New York office of the FBI to any other location. . . ." He also believed that he lacked the seniority to transfer to the Boston office. In September, 2007, the mother amended her complaint to seek removal, which the father opposed. . . . In February, 2008, three days before trial, the mother married Mr. Katzman; they were expecting their first child in October, 2009. The father and Ms. Manninen's second child was born in June, 2008.

Trial on the complaint for modification lasted twenty-three days. Both parents were found to have good parenting skills and positive, nurturing relations with the children.

Hunter was found to be strongly attached to his mother, "especially strongly attached to his father," and "strongly attached to Ms. Manninen." He also "gets along well with Mr. Katzman . . . [and] [h]is attachment to Mr. Katzman is newer and not as strong as his attachments to his parents and to Ms. Manninen." . . . Hunter ". . . does not wish to move from the area where his father and step-mother live." . . . Hunter's "fear of having less time with his father in the future is a significant element of his anxiety." The judge found Hunter's anxiety about the family situation to be severe. Kierstin was found to be "clearly emotionally attached" to the mother, Mr. Katzman, the father, and Ms. Manninen. Kierstin was also found to "prefer that the present parenting arrangement stay the same." . . . Also, at the beginning of trial, the mother was earning $85,000 from her employment as a clinical nurse specialist. In June, 2008, the project the mother was working on ended, and the mother became voluntarily unemployed. . . .

1. PARENTING TIME. . . .

As provided by G.L. c. 208, §28 . . . , "the court may make a judgment modifying its earlier judgment as to the care and custody of the minor children of the parties provided that the court finds that a material and substantial change in the circumstances of the parties has occurred and the judgment of modification is necessary in the best interests of the children." . . . The judge, however, without finding a change in circumstances, adopted a "5/2 split" recommended by the guardian ad litem. The children would essentially be with the mother Tuesdays and Wednesdays, and the father would have them Thursdays and Fridays. The parents would alternate having the children on weekends, meaning from Friday until Tuesday morning. . . .

The judge and the guardian considered this significant change to be a continuation of "approximately equal time" because of their focus on time spent with the parent when the children were not at school, camp, or asleep. . . . The judge did not consider it important for his equality analysis that the mother originally had eighty-two percent of the sleep time while the father only had eighteen percent. Under the new schedule, the mother's sleep time percentage would drop to fifty-seven percent while the father's would increase to forty-three percent. The law has not, however, neatly divided custodial parenthood into waking, sleeping, and schooling categories. Nor should it. Disregarding sleep or school time ignores that children get sick, have nightmares, and otherwise require their parent's assistance at unexpected times. See *Kawatra v. Kawatra* (Tenn. 2005) ("The responsibilities of a parent do not end when a child is asleep, at school or day care, or otherwise outside of the parent's presence"). An important part of parenting is being available to children whenever needed, night or day. Under the separation agreement, that role was primarily provided by the mother who had sole physical custody. . . .

To the extent the judge wanted to extend joint physical custody to the father, findings reflecting substantial and material changed circumstances supported by the evidence were required. No such findings were made here, and therefore so much of the amended modification judgment as increases parenting time for the father and decreases parenting time for the mother is reversed.

2. REMOVAL. . . .

Under *Yannas*, the advantages and disadvantages of moving or not moving to the parent who has sole physical custody are a "significant factor in the [best interests of the child] equation." This is true because "the best interests of a child are so interwoven with the well-being of the custodial parent." The judge here . . . finds . . . "[i]t cannot be said that the benefit to the children flowing from their mother's increased happiness in

New York or Connecticut would outweigh the loss to them of the regular and frequent time in their other home." . . .

"[A] remand as to removal is necessary here. As part of that remand, other important factors should be more fully analyzed . . . Most importantly the judge concludes that "[r]emoval would be devastating to Hunter." This conclusion must be grounded in specific subsidiary fact-finding to support it. . . . Assuming Mr. Katzman is unable to relocate, the judge should examine how the mother's unhappiness from raising her children in Massachusetts while living separated from her husband would affect the children. . . . Finally, the judge should give further consideration and make additional fact findings about the practical repercussions of traveling if removal were allowed. . . . [T]he judge should weigh whether plane travel, instead of automobile, would be possible and beneficial, and if so, whether the mother's preferred home is sufficiently close to an airport to facilitate the visits. . . .

3. CHILD SUPPORT.

The mother claims that the judge abused his discretion in calculating the increase in child support by limiting the father's income to his base salary. . . . The judge here based his decisions as to child support on provisions in the parents' separation agreement. The agreement stated that "the amount of child support paid by the Husband to the Wife is based upon his current weekly income . . . exclusive of bonuses. In the event that he receives a *cash* bonus during any year then he shall pay to the wife . . . 20% of the net bonus amount as additional child support." Although the mother argues that "[t]his provision reflected the fact that, at the time of the parties' divorce, stock in the father's closely held company was valued at $0," we agree with the judge's assessment that this issue is something that "the parties should have reasonably foreseen" during the negotiations. . . .

The separation agreement further provided: "Commencing on February 15, 2008 and every three (3) years thereafter, the parties shall exchange with one another financial information . . . to be contained in preparing a child support guidelines worksheet. . . . The purpose of the exchange of such information shall be the calculation of the future weekly child support amount. Said payments shall be retroactive to the first of the year. If the parties are unable to agree upon such a modification, then either party may file a Complaint for Modification. . . ."

Finally, the father contends that the judge erred in calculating the amount of child support, which increased from $2,903.33 to $6,028.33. The judge was justified in ordering a modification as it was contemplated in the parties' separation agreement and supported by the father's substantial increase in income and a material disparity in the parties' respective lifestyles. The judge found that "[t]he income and net worth of each party has increased dramatically since the Judgement of Divorce Nisi, primarily as a result of . . . the increase in the father's compensation as chairman and chief executive officer of [EnerNOC]. . . ." The judge further found that "[e]ven with additional child support, the mother will not be able to match the life style the father has for the children, which is not to suggest that the children will not be very financially comfortable in their mother's care."[8] "Implicit in the judge's consideration of this disparity is consideration of the children's needs, defined in the light of [the father's] higher standard of living."

8. The judge found that the father's new home in Concord "will have six plus bedrooms, multiple baths, a big back yard, a big side yard, an indoor basketball court for the children, an upstairs art studio for the children and a detached carriage house." The mother, for reasons that remain unclear, continued to live in the same two-bedroom apartment she had lived in since the divorce despite her ample stock holdings. As represented in briefing at oral argument, she did, however, eventually buy a large home in Connecticut.

. . . [T]he "guidelines are not meant to apply where the combined annual gross income of the parties exceeds $250,000. In cases where income exceeds this limit, the Court should consider the award of support at the $250,000 level as the minimum presumptive order. Additional amounts of child support may be awarded in the Court's discretion." In the instant case, the judge calculated the presumptive minimum at $2,754.74 per month. . . . The judge then added fifteen percent of the increase of the father's base salary since the judgment of divorce. . . . The fifteen percent marginal rate is assigned to the highest income bracket in the child support guidelines. Given the provision in the separation agreement contemplating adjustment in child support, the substantial increase in the father's income since the divorce and the children's entitlement to share in the lifestyle of the parents, we discern no abuse of discretion in the judge's calculation.

This case illustrates the hazard of including provisions in an agreement about future changes in income; the mother lost out on the benefit of the great increase in value of husband's stock because of the wording of the language about bonuses. In the absence of an agreement, or if the agreement said simply that support would be recalculated every three years, a court might have considered as income the increased value of stock the husband had received as bonuses.

Because Massachusetts is a percentage-of-income state, the mother's earnings were irrelevant to calculation of support by application of the formula, as was any wealth her new husband might have. The father's dramatic rise in salary effectively made it possible for her to continue her voluntary unemployment with almost as much after-tax income as she had while working (taking into account that child support received is not taxed). Does this case illustrate the superiority of the income-shares approach?

f. Rethinking Child Support

How would you respond to the following normative argument:

> A man harms no one by having consensual sex with a woman that results in pregnancy. The woman is not injured, because she is legally free to terminate the pregnancy, and even if she were injured, the injury would not be wrongful, because of her consent to sex. The child that results, if the woman chooses to carry the child to term, is not harmed, because it is better to exist than not to exist. Instead, the child owes the man a debt of gratitude for bringing him or her into existence. The child might not be better off as a result of existing, relative to not existing, if his or her life is horrible, but to say the child will have a life of deprivation unless the man pays child support just begs the question at issue—namely, why should the obligation for a child's support be foisted on the biological father? An obvious alternative is for society as a whole to take up the cost of supporting the child, along with whoever has custody.
>
> Does this mean the man has harmed society if he participates in producing a child and then does not financially support the child? No. That would be true only if a newborn child is a net liability for society. But generally in the United States we assume production of children, who will one day be workers and support current adults in old age, is beneficial to society. If biological parents were to bear the entire cost of raising children, there would be positive externalities, and that is not fair to parents. The rest of us should pay for the future benefit children represent. (The state does now subsidize child rearing, through tax exemptions, deductions, and credits; school funding; and child-directed welfare programs, but could do much more.)

The situation might be different if we had an over-population problem, but currently we do not. Especially with baby boomers now approaching retirement, we need a lot of future workers in the pipeline. Many European countries have a problem with too low a birth rate and have had to import workers. So even if the state takes on full financial responsibility for the children resulting from unintended pregnancies, the creation of those children is a net benefit for society. We should thank the men who do it instead of penalizing them with child support orders.

Scott Altman, A Theory of Child Support

17 Int'l J.L. Pol'y & Fam. 173 (2003)

. . . Three theories favouring coerced payments have traditionally been advanced: . . .

A. CAUSING NEEDS

. . . Parents cause children to need care by procreating, much like drivers cause pedestrians to need care by running them over. Having created a need, . . . parents are obligated to meet the need if they can. . . .

Although causation is relevant to legal and moral duties, it is neither necessary nor sufficient for a duty, and is generally an unappealing principle for distribution. . . . Being peculiarly able to prevent harms can create duties to prevent those harms, especially harm one caused. . . . Similarly, duties are common when someone commits a wrong while causing a need, or profits while causing a need, or agrees to meet needs, or perhaps is in a good position to spread losses associated with needs. When these factors are absent, duties to meet needs one creates lose much of their intuitive appeal.

Consider, for example: Procreating to Cure Cancer—Susan, a gifted cancer researcher, is pregnant. She has discovered a drug that will alter her child's genes so that the child will provide society a cure for cancer. The child will need an expensive treatment to survive. Susan and her child will not profit from the cure. Susan's employer will profit greatly, as of course will millions of people who will not die painful deaths from cancer. Should Susan—who caused the need for expensive treatment—be obligated to pay for it? Or is this duty more properly assigned to her employer, or taxpayers, who benefit from this need? Assuming that Susan did nothing wrong, I see little reason to ask her alone to pay. Similarly, child support seems inappropriate when causation is not accompanied by some other factor. . . .

B. VULNERABILITY

. . . [P]erhaps children's material needs justify imposing financial duties on parents. Welfare benefits or tax relief together with the income of custodial parents often fall short of the amount families believe they should spend to care for children. . . . [H]owever, . . . the argument is circular. . . . [C]hildren are vulnerable to non-support only because government benefits are set so low, or more generally because we conventionally assign primary support duties to parents. The argument from vulnerability cannot justify the conventional arrangements that make children vulnerable to parents unless it can somehow show that parents are especially well situated to provide for their children's financial needs. Given the enforcement problems associated with child support, the opposite conclusion seems more reasonable: vulnerability counsels government, rather than private, support of children, because government funds can more reliably prevent hunger and similar material suffering.

c. CONSENT

The obligation to pay support can be grounded in implied consent. People choose to procreate, or at least to risk procreation, by having sex. As Onora O'Neill explains "[w]herever natural parents are the normal child rearers, decisions to procreate are (and are known to be) decisions to undertake the far longer and more demanding task of bringing up a child or arranging for its upbringing." . . .

We could treat lying about birth control, or refusing to abort when the father asks, or refusing to place a child for adoption as consenting to assume sole financial responsibility for the child. . . . Support orders in these unusual cases . . . might be justified by the need for simple rules. In the usual case, the consent inferred from sex looks a lot like actual consent. Although not everyone knows legal rules, or shares middle-class norms about parental responsibility, most parents act intentionally, knowing that their actions will be treated as consent. Those who do not know arguably should know. . . .

But . . . widespread notice of a custom (such as assignment of support duties to parents) cannot truly justify the custom. Giving people adequate notice of rules does not justify promulgating the rules in the first place. Justifying child support as a truly fair demand on parents requires a good reason for having asked them to make those commitments as a precondition to procreating. . . .

3. JUSTIFYING CHILD SUPPORT AS AN INSTITUTION

. . . The theories below . . . provide guidance on . . . the extent to which taxpayers, rather than parents, should support children; the criteria by which we should identify someone as a parent; and the circumstances under which someone otherwise qualified as a parent should be relieved of support duties.

A. (P)REPAYING A DEBT

. . . Some interpret child-support duties as prepayments for support during old age. Others interpret these duties as repayment for the benefit of having been supported as a child. According to both theories, people receive care and support when they are vulnerable. In exchange those same people provide care and support when they are able. This system is fair in the aggregate because everyone needs care as children, and reasonably expects to need care in old age. . . .

Despite its general appeal, intergenerational bargains offer little justification for coercing parents, rather than taxpayers, to pay child support. The argument makes more sense for direct provision of personal care than for financial support. Most people would gladly provide physical care to a relative or close friend if this act guaranteed that they would be reared by loving parents, or tended at a time of physical need by a trusted companion. The parallel financial bargain is less attractive. The argument turns child support into a form of insurance: I pay child support to get support in old age if I need it; or I pay child support to repay the fund that supported me as a child. Why would a reasonable person seek such a limited and financially random insurance pool? Rather than risk my old-age support on the uncertain income of a small number of children, I would prefer to place risk on the next generation. . . . Similarly, rather than place my financial support as a child at risk by making it depend on the financial success of one or two parents, I would prefer the safety of diversification. The intergenerational transfer theory therefore argues—all else being equal—for a system of public child support.

B. EQUALITY

... Adequate child support funded in large measure by men combats women's subordination materially by making women somewhat less poor. ... This argument ... says little about apportioning support duties between parents and the state. ... Because public funding might provide more money or more reliable money to custodial parents, it could combat female poverty, and therefore promote gender equality, more effectively than traditional child support. ...

C. ENCOURAGING POPULATION CONTROL AND FAMILY PLANNING

... One might expect that child-support duties would lead men—particularly unmarried men—to use contraception. ... The few available empirical studies suggest that couples increase contraceptive use in response to increased child-support enforcement. ... Child support is a way to internalize the costs of procreative decisions. In this respect, child support is like any tax on a socially costly activity. ...

There is evidence, however, that children create net benefits in the US. Public spending on children is a small fraction of spending on public goods and on the elderly. Because additional children reduce the per-capita cost of public goods and support for the growing older population, additional children in the US could create large external benefits. ... One author calculated the present value of the net external benefit per child as more than $100,000 in 1985. A later study put this figure at closer to $200,000. Although these figures include virtually all public spending on children, they omit many external benefits that evade simple measurement, such as any benefit to the child for being alive or to friends and family. The authors calculated net present value of a child by estimating the present value of taxes that the child and all their likely descendants will pay (taking account of the characteristics of the child likely to affect their own and their descendants' earning capacity), and then subtracting the present value of various government expenditures on this child and likely descendants. ...

According to Allen Parkman, private child support is better than government subsidies, because the latter "encourag[e] the wrong people to become parents." By "wrong people" Parkman means those who are not able to provide sufficient financial resources, or who are not willing to rear the child in a two-parent household. Parkman explains:

> [i]n addition to low earning capacities, single parents are less able to instill important social values in their children. Almost two-thirds of rapists, three-quarters of adolescent murderers, and the same percentage of long-term prison inmates are young males who grew up in fatherless homes. ...

Some recent studies find a correlation between welfare and out-of-wedlock births. But they find very small effects on the number or timing of births. To the extent that welfare encourages non-marital teenage births, it does so mostly by deterring marriage. Second, that a large portion of troubled children and young adults were reared in single-parent homes, does not show that a large portion of children reared in such homes end up troubled. In fact, the majority of children reared in single-parent homes become productive, tax-paying, law-abiding, adults. In the aggregate, children born to unwed mothers likely produce net external benefits. Third, the bad outcomes that stem from single-parenting often can be mitigated by more money, suggesting that greater investment might improve rather than worsen effects. ... If teenagers delay procreating, their children ... might contribute slightly more. But ... then the argument ... cannot rely on cost internalization. It would rely instead on value maximization, with perhaps very different policy implications. . . .

D. DISTRIBUTIVE JUSTICE AND THE BENEFIT PRINCIPLE

. . . [J]ustice requires people to pay for goods that benefit them. . . . If parenting is an activity that adults pursue for pleasure or duty, should it not be paid for primarily by those who seek and gain these benefits? . . . Child support is a users' fee.

If receiving the pleasures of parenting is a central justification for child support, should parents who benefit less pay less? . . . Perhaps those who seek children's company (grandparents, step-parents) should pay support, while those who care not at all for children (unwilling parents) should have no duties?

In some settings, linking the duty of support with the benefit a parent gets from the child seems demeaning to children, as if children were toys for adult amusement. . . . Imagine if child support were actually paid on an hourly basis as the price of admission for visitation. Viewing procreation as consumption . . . clashes with how most parents understand their roles. . . . But we do sometimes seem to treat child support as a users' fee. Lawmakers and scholars have debated whether visitation interference should justify reductions of child support, and whether non-payment should justify reduced visitation. Less controversially, most states insulate from child-support duties people who get no access to their children, including sperm and ova donors, people whose parental rights have been terminated, parents who cannot locate their children (such as when the child has been kidnapped), and parents who voluntarily give up children for adoption—even if their children later need funds. Emancipation doctrine might even be understood as linking the benefits and duties of parenting. Children who will not abide by parental direction do not receive parental support. . . .

E. PREVENTING HARM AND BAD BEHAVIOUR

Child support might be used to punish parents who act poorly, to deter others from similar action, to mitigate harms, or to compensate victims. . . .

(i) Insufficient Demonstration of Love

Parents who do not voluntarily pay child support demonstrate little concern for their children's welfare. . . . A duty to demonstrate love for one's biological children (and perhaps also the children in one's home) by providing for them might be grounded in Natural Law. . . . Should we condemn, and demand payment from, those who either do not feel this way, or who overcome these natural feelings? This argument faces at least two problems. First, unless people can control their emotions, a duty to have loving feelings makes little sense. Second, even if the duty is restated as a duty to act like most parents, rather than to feel what most parents feel, the duty might place too much weight on the duty to act lovingly toward biological children or physically near children. . . . We could condemn all reticence toward redistribution as a failure of loving behaviour toward children. Blame on this account would be appropriately on all the adults whose indifference allows millions of children to live in poverty.

A stronger justification for the parental duty to demonstrate love relies on protecting children from psychological harm. . . . It seems intuitively plausible that children view non-payment of support as showing indifference. . . . This indifference violates the expectation of parental love, and the need for being the object of special concern. Non-payment is thus at once betrayal of a social norm, and deprivation of a strong psychological need. Admittedly, feelings of betrayal might be caused by child-support laws themselves. If laws and other social institutions did not demonize non-supporting parents, children might feel less aggrieved by the loss. But at least sometimes non-payment traumatizes children for different reasons. In cases of divorce preceded by a well-established loving relationship, non-payment likely exacerbates the feeling of betrayal and abandonment experienced by the child from the physical departure itself. . . .

Yet if children learn that the payments are coerced, how could such payments represent love? Perhaps children do not always know, and perhaps some parents comply with child-support duties apparently without coercion, but would not do so but for the threat of prosecution.

In addition to its direct effects, voluntarily paid child support might . . . encourage non-custodial parents to establish and maintain loving relationships with their children. . . . Some evidence suggests that even coerced child support would induce visitation. . . . The correlation might reflect a common cause. For example, love might cause some non-custodial parents to visit and to pay support. If so, inducing payments by uncaring parents would do little to induce visitation. Alternatively, . . . "noncustodial parents who pay support [might] visit more frequently to monitor the way custodial parents use the child-support money . . . [or] custodial parents [might] facilitate visits when they receive child-support, and hinder it when they do not." Whether such visitation is valuable remains controversial, particularly since visitation induced by coerced child support might harm some children by increasing family conflict. . . .

Parents are uniquely well situated to demonstrate love and thereby prevent important psychological harm. Because being in a unique position to prevent a harm creates a *prima facie* duty to act, particularly for someone who caused the harm and knew about the likely need, non-payment is a *prima facie* wrong. Coerced child support is an apt punishment and deterrent. And it might prevent the harm from continuing. . . . [T]erminating, rather than failing to establish, a loving parent-child relationship might be a particularly harmful act. . . . Showing indifference toward a child because one no longer loves the other parent is a betrayal. Indeed, we sometimes impose child-support duties on people who act as parents even absent a biological connection for just this reason. . . .

Perhaps in a society that regularly reared children in a communal setting, so that social expectations of family life placed less emphasis on parent-child interactions, the harm of overt parental indifference would be trivial. Similarly, if a state were so generous that children never lived at a lower standard of living than their absent parents, non-payment might have different meanings. In such a society, the argument I advance would not be persuasive. . . .

Child support is obviously not the main way that parents demonstrate love to children. Parents who try to show love though money usually fail. And one can certainly imagine a parent who demonstrates love without paying support. But surely this case is not common enough to justify a special exception to child-support duties. . . .

The duty I posit is not a duty to love children, which is likely not something within one's voluntary control . . . Rather, I ground child support in a duty to show love, even if one does not actually feel love. One might think a duty to feign love hypocritical; how can we have a duty to lie? . . . It is not always wrong to act as if one loves a person one does not love. . . . Unlike a romantic love, children will not necessarily discover later that the parent did not love them. And in any case, the child will not feel that they should have sought another parent. Even if later feelings of betrayal are possible, it seems likely that children benefit more from demonstrations of love during childhood than they are harmed by possible discoveries of insincere loving acts. . . .

(ii) Insufficient Love Between Parents

Perhaps parents owe children a home with two parents who love each other. . . . [P]arents might breach a duty by allowing their relationship to deteriorate, or by procreating without good reason to think they can form a loving, stable relationship. Child support might mitigate harms to children from parental separation, and offer an incentive to make a marriage work. . . .

Th[is] might be thought inappropriate for two reasons. First, . . . the non-custodial parent is not always primarily to blame for failure to provide parents who love each other. Child support seems to reward the custodial parent, who is also guilty of harming the child. Second, liability seems to be imposed without any fault at all: sometimes relationships deteriorate despite all reasonable efforts by both parents.

The first objection misdescribes child-support liability. Non-custodial parents are not alone responsible for child support. Rather, they share this responsibility with custodial parents. Child support is therefore less a reward for custodial parents, than a division of the liability for wrongful behaviour. . . . The second version poses a more serious difficulty. Why should marital dissolution—admitting its harms to children—be treated differently from various unfortunate facts that make people less well off than they might have been, but that were not caused by negligence or intentional wrongdoing? . . . The objection . . . applies to fewer cases than one might think. Those parents who never form long-term relationships should be held accountable for the predictable harms to children. Parents who do marry, or who otherwise reasonably expect an enduring loving relationship, often marry with less caution than they ought, and work less persistently at their relationship than they might. . . . [P]erhaps most children whose parents divorce should be entitled to complain that the parents did not find a way to be happier. . . .

(iii) Implications of a Harm-Based Theory

. . . By treating compelled child support primarily as damages for a wrong, harm-based theories avoid the demeaning account of child support as a users' fee. . . . Harm-based theories also have the advantage of accommodating seeming anomalies. Sperm donors and parents who place children for adoption absent themselves from their children no less than non-resident parents who had casual sex. . . . But they do not leave children so frequently in poverty or demonstrate a preference for their own welfare over the welfare of the child in such a patent way as do parents refusing to pay support. As well, there are strong social reasons to encourage adoption and, to a lesser extent, sperm donation. . . .

[T]he idea that children should live as well as their parents . . . seems hard to justify apart from the harm-based theory. . . . Parents who love their children typically want their children to live as well as they do. By not visibly prospering more than the child, the parent demonstrates love to the child. . . .

Although this theory seems promising, it has problems. . . . If we learn, contrary to initial findings, that voluntary child support benefits children little, that support does not promote visitation or that visitation harms children, and that living with two parents who love each other offers no advantage, then harm-based arguments for child support might fail. . . . The two wrongs I discuss also raise controversial moral issues. In particular, the second theory—a duty to form and sustain a loving relationship with the other parent—diverges from many people's understanding of a right to intimate association. . . . The specific harms I identify might be thought insufficient to justify tort-like duties. Inaction, even in the face of patent need and the ability to meet it, usually creates no liability. Isn't failure to demonstrate love, or failure to create and sustain a marriage or long-term relationship, much like failure to rescue someone in need? I do not think the comparison is apt. Parents are not mere bystanders who happen to find themselves well-positioned to provide aid. Parents act intentionally and for their own benefit when they have sex, and do so knowing that this act causes (or risks causing) someone to need their aid, and that they will be in an especially good position to provide the assistance. . . .

This argument undoubtedly sounds like I have now accepted the very claims I started the article by rejecting—justifications of child support based on causation, vulnerability, and consent. . . . However, causation can be relevant. It distinguishes parents' failure to meet psychological needs from a wider duty to act whenever one is well positioned to help someone. Vulnerability, I argued, does not justify private child support because parents are not especially well situated to support children. However, . . . parents are especially well situated to provide children with love and a loving home. . . . Consent, I explained, does not fully justify child support absent an independent reason for demanding that parents accept this duty as a precondition to procreating. Children's psychological needs provide such a reason. We should often treat sex as consent to support children because children are less well protected from psychological harm when governments relieve parents of all support duties. . . .

[A]lthough my arguments might support a *prima facie* moral duty to visit children, they do not necessarily justify making such a moral duty into a legal duty through damage awards. There are many practical problems—such as proving whether non-visitation was wrongful rather than excused because it was caused by interference of the custodial parent. It is not clear whether coerced visitation would benefit children. . . . Those coerced to visit might certainly behave badly in a way that harmed children. Forced visitation constrains life choices by some non-custodial parents (such as by limiting relocation) more dramatically than forced payments. . . .

Professor Altman's view might be summarized thus: There is no justification for imposing a child support obligation on a non-custodial parent (rather than on taxpayers) except that doing so prevents children from feeling unloved by that parent and compensates children for the harm of having parents who do not live together. Is his refutation of other theories or the case he makes for his own theory persuasive? In refuting other theories, he supposes an alternative of robust taxpayer support for child rearing. If we assume the same alternative when assessing his positive theory, is it less persuasive? Does his theory then ultimately rest on the empirical supposition that imposing a support obligation induces parents to visit who otherwise would not do so, and that such induced visitation would make the child feel loved? Any studies showing that parents who pay are more likely to seek and show up for visitation have been done in a society where shame and recrimination attach to non-payment. The same causal relation might not exist in a society where payment is not expected. In addition, we might ask whether there is another way to induce visitation that is neither forcing to pay regardless of visits nor forcing to pay for not visiting. One possibility is a system of rewards for visiting, perhaps through income tax rules. Another is sending a message to non-custodial parents opposite to what current law arguably does—that is, communicating to them that it is really their attention and love that is needed, not just their money. Lastly, we might ask to what extent the current child support system generates resentment in non-custodial parents toward children, and whether that might be even more damaging to children than parental indifference.

Is there a third alternative source of support for children, someone other than parents or the state? Consider the principle of "solidarity of the generations" embodied in the German civil code, under which grandparents can be ordered to pay support for children whose parents lack sufficient resources. Such a rule was also part of the Elizabethan Poor Laws, which were generally adopted in the American colonies but later abandoned. Today in the United States only a small number of states authorize imposition of a support obligation on grandparents per se, and then only if and while the parents are minors, and in some states only if the parent with custody has applied for welfare benefits. See, e.g., Ariz. Rev. Stat. §25-810(A) ("parents having custody or control of the putative mother or father . . . may be held jointly and severally liable with the minor until the minor reaches the age of majority"); Md. Code Ann., Family Law §5-203(c) ("If one or both parents of a minor child is an unemancipated minor, the parents of that minor parent are jointly and severally responsible for any child support for a grandchild that is a recipient of temporary cash assistance to the extent that the minor parent has insufficient financial resources to fulfill the child support responsibility of the minor parent."). (Note: Standing in *loco parentis* can give rise to a support obligation for any adult, including grandparents.) What would be the policy pros and cons of enacting throughout the United States a broad rule like that in Germany that grandparents are liable for the support of children whose parents have insufficient income, regardless of the parents' age and regardless of whether the parents are in the grandparents' custody or home? Note that the rule in Germany is actually reciprocal; adult grandchildren can be ordered to support grandparents in need.

Further readings: ANNE L. ALSTOTT, NO EXIT: WHAT PARENTS OWE THEIR CHILDREN AND WHAT SOCIETY OWES PARENTS (2005) (arguing on justice grounds for greater public financial support of child rearing); Jennifer M. Collins, Ethan J. Leib & Dan Markel, *Punishing Family Status*, 88 B.U. L. REV. 1327 (2008) (questioning policy of predicating financial and other burdens on being in family relationships); Sally Sheldon, *Unwilling Fathers and Abortion: Terminating Men's Child Support Obligations?*, 66 MOD. L. REV. 175 (2003) (examining the basis of paternal obligation where women retain sole control over the abortion decision).

Part III

DISSOLUTION OF FAMILY LEGAL RELATIONSHIPS

Just as with formation of family relationships, dissolution of the *social* aspect of a relationship might occur without state involvement, but state action is required for termination of the *legal* relationship and of the rights and duties that accompany the legal relationship. And as with formation, we will ask with respect to dissolution whether and to what extent the choice of private parties is necessary or sufficient for the state to take action. Insofar as private party choice is not determinative, what other considerations drive state decision making? Do the same policy considerations underlie the legal rules for termination as for creation?

This unit begins with the parent-child relationship, in part for the sake of continuity with the prior chapter and in part because you are probably already somewhat familiar with the basic rules for divorce, so comparison of the rules for the two relationships will be easier this way. Divorce, as you know, can and often does result from the unilateral choice of one party to the relationship, and that choice need not be based on any particular showing of fault by the other party nor, in actual practice, of any unusual problems in the relationship. If one spouse thinks she would be better off terminating the relationship, that is enough for the state to release her from the legal bond. With the parent-child relationship, we will see, it is often legally sufficient for termination that *the parent* decides she would be better off terminating the relationship, but it is generally not sufficient that anyone decides the child would be better off.

Children are thus the only people unable ever to escape legal family relationships based simply on a showing that they would be better off if that happened. Children's welfare is not irrelevant to the termination decision in the way it was with creation of parent-child relationships; a best-interests showing is a *necessary* condition for termination of parental rights. It is simply not a *sufficient* condition. With adults, the state says (with some exceptions), in effect: "Even though you chose (in some sense) to enter this (marital or parent-child) relationship, we will not force you to sacrifice at all what you think is best for yourself for the sake of preserving the relationship." With children, the state says, in effect: "Even though you did not choose to enter this relationship, we will force you to sacrifice your welfare to some extent for the sake of preserving the relationship, because the other party to the relationship wants it to continue." In this Part, we will be searching for justifications for this seemingly disparate treatment of children and adults.

5

DISSOLUTION OF THE PARENT-CHILD RELATIONSHIP

The social relationship between parent and child might end even though the legal relationship continues, if a parent declines to have any contact or communication with a child or if a court in a maltreatment, divorce, or parentage action orders a parent not to have contact or communication because of past misconduct. The social parent-child relationship might also end as a result of offspring running away from custodial parents or refusing contact and communication with a non-custodial parent, but in either case the state generally will step in at the parent's request to force renewed contact, so long as the offspring remain unemancipated minors. And while the legal relationship continues, the parent still has at least the financial support duty and at least some of the rights you studied in Chapter 4. In this chapter, you will study the means by which the state dissolves parent-child relationships and any lingering post-dissolution consequences of the relationship.

A. LEGAL ROUTES TO DISSOLUTION OF THE PARENT-CHILD RELATIONSHIP

Termination of the legal relationship between parent and child can occur in a few different ways. With babies, the most common ways are parental relinquishment of rights and adoption of a child by other adults, and those two ways often go hand-in-hand. With older children, the more common way is through child protection proceedings, based on serious parental misconduct.

1. Voluntary Relinquishment

People can give up their legal parent status by executing a consent to adoption by others or by executing a relinquishment of rights to a social services or adoption agency.

California Family Code
Division 13, Part 2. Adoption of Unmarried Minors
Chapter 2. Agency Adoptions

§8700. Relinquishment of Child to Department or a Licensed Adoption Agency

(a) Either birth parent may relinquish a child to the department or a licensed adoption agency for adoption by a written statement signed before two subscribing witnesses and acknowledged before an authorized official of the department or agency. The relinquishment, when reciting that the person making it is entitled to the sole custody of the child and acknowledged before the officer, is prima facie evidence of the right of the person making it to the sole custody of the child and the person's sole right to relinquish.

(b) A relinquishing parent who is a minor has the right to relinquish his or her child . . . , and the relinquishment is not subject to revocation by reason of the minority. . . .

(e) (1) . . . The relinquishment shall be final 10 business days after receipt of the filing by the department . . . :

(2) After the relinquishment is final, it may be rescinded only by the mutual consent of the department or licensed adoption agency to which the child was relinquished and the birth parent or parents relinquishing the child.

(f) The relinquishing parent may name in the relinquishment the person or persons with whom he or she intends that placement of the child for adoption be made. . . .

(g) and (h) [If the agency ends up not placing with the persons whom the birth parents named, then the birth parents can rescind the relinquishment.]

(j) The filing of the relinquishment with the department terminates all parental rights and responsibilities with regard to the child, except as provided in subdivisions (g) and (h).

After seeing such an authorization voluntarily to exit a parent-child relationship, you might wonder what all the fuss was about involuntary declarations of paternity and imposition of support orders. Can a biological father ordered to pay child support simply file a paper saying "I don't want to be a parent"? States avoid that result by several means: 1) requiring court approval of any relinquishment before it is effective and permitting approval only after a finding that ending the relationship would be in the child's best interests, which usually will only be true when there is a pending petition to adopt the child; 2) making a relinquishment effective only upon approval of an adoption or acceptance of the child by an adoption agency; or 3) continuing the child support obligation despite termination of parental status unless and until the child is adopted. See, e.g., In re Brue R, 662 A.2d 107 (Conn. 1995) (holding that in applying a best-interests test for acceptance of a voluntary termination of parental status, trial court must consider the financial condition of the relinquishing parent and of the parent who retains parental status and custody, given that termination eliminates the support obligation); Tex. Fam. Code Ann. §§ 161.103 (affidavit of relinquishment must identify an agency or adoptive parents who will take custody of the child); In re Carr, 938 A.2d 89 (N.H. 2007) (imposing support duties notwithstanding agreement to relinquish all parental rights).

Thus, relinquishments are usually only effective as a complete severance of the legal tie between parent and a minor child when there is an accompanying adoption. This is not unlike dissolution of a "traditional" marriage in which one spouse was financially dependent on the other; courts commonly impose a post-divorce support obligation on the primary breadwinner spouse until the dependent spouse becomes self-supporting or becomes dependent on a different spouse by remarrying.

2. *Involuntary Termination by Adoption*

State laws create a presumption that adoption will occur only with the consent of existing legal parents. However, they authorize adoption, and the attendant termination of existing parents' status, despite an existing parent's objection, in some circumstances. The most common such circumstance is some form of abandonment. See, e.g., 750 Ill. Comp. Stat. 50/8(a) (requiring "consents . . . in all cases, unless the person . . . shall be found by the court: (1) to be an unfit person . . . , by clear and convincing evidence") and 50/1(D) (defining "unfit person" to include: "(a-1) Abandonment of a newborn infant in a hospital. (a-2) Abandonment of a newborn infant in any setting where the evidence suggests that the parent intended to relinquish his or her parental rights. (b) Failure to maintain a reasonable degree of interest, concern or responsibility as to the child's welfare. (c) Desertion of the child for more than 3 months next preceding the commencement of the Adoption proceeding."); N.J. Stat. Ann. §9:3-46 (failure to communicate or provide financial support for the six months preceding placement of the child for adoption).

Many states also waive the consent requirement as to a parent who has demonstrated unfitness in other ways. Illinois's adoption code, for example, also lists among the bases for finding parental unfitness, warranting court approval of an adoption despite a legal parent's objection, more than one past finding of child abuse, multiple criminal convictions, a mother's drug use during pregnancy, and chronic substance abuse by either parent. See 750 Ill. Comp. Stat. 50/1(D)((f) ("There is a rebuttable presumption . . . that a parent is unfit if: (1) Two or more findings of physical abuse have been entered regarding any children . . ."), (i) ("Depraved. . . . There is a rebuttable presumption that a parent is depraved if the parent has been criminally convicted of at least 3 felonies . . . and at least one of these convictions took place within 5 years of the filing of the petition"), (k) "Habitual drunkenness or addiction to drugs, other than those prescribed by a physician, for at least one year immediately prior to the commencement of the unfitness proceeding. There is a rebuttable presumption that a parent is unfit under this subsection with respect to any child to which that parent gives birth where there is a confirmed test result that at birth the child's blood, urine, or meconium contained any amount of a controlled substance . . . and the biological mother of this child is the biological mother of at least one other child who was adjudicated a neglected minor . . .").

A much less common basis for dispensing with consent, one of uncertain constitutionality, is simply a finding that the biological parent is withholding consent "contrary to the best interests of the child." See, e.g., D.C. Code §16-304(e); Va. Code Ann. §63.2-1203. This ostensibly permits courts to terminate parent-child relationships simply because the child would be better off in a relationship with other persons who want them. This puts children in a position similar to that of spouses, who are able to exit if they find they would be better off in a relationship with someone else. The U.S. Supreme Court has not yet decided whether such rule is consistent with the substantive due process rights it created in the *Stanley v. Illinois* to *Lehr v. Robertson* line of cases discussed in Chapter 1. Lower courts have mostly avoided the constitutional question by interpreting such statutes as requiring that the child would be harmed by continuing in a legal relationship with the existing parent or that the parent refusing consent is unfit. See, e.g., Copeland v. Todd, 715 S.E.2d 11 (Va. 2011). If there is a practical difference between "adoption without consent if it would be better for the child" and "adoption without consent only if not doing so would be harmful to the child" or "adoption without consent only if the parent is unfit," then this reinterpretation creates a category of cases in which children must remain in relationships contrary to their best interests in order to serve the interests of the other party to the relationship. Is the following potentially such a case? Does the court resort to double-talk to avoid acknowledging that?

In re S.M.

985 A.2d 413 (D.C. 2009)

Steadman, Senior Judge:

. . . This case first came to court on a neglect complaint filed by the District of Columbia on December 22, 2003, against K.D. (mother)[2] and H.O. (father, appellant) with respect to their two biological children, Ka.D. and J.D., twin boys born in April of 2001. The complaint asserted both unsanitary conditions in the home and an allegation of sexual abuse by K.D.'s biological daughter, T.D., age 12, against H.O.[3] At the time, K.D. and H.O. were living with the boys and with S.D., age 7, another daughter of K.D.'s, in H.O.'s apartment. S.D. and T.D. are not related to H.O., and T.D. was not living with H.O., K.D., and the other children at the time of the alleged abuse.

On January 12, 2004, K.D. stipulated that the boys were neglected. Because K.D. had been admitted to the Family Treatment Court Program (FTCP) for drug abuse, the boys were placed there in order to remain with their mother, a decision to which H.O. understandably did not object. No ruling with respect to neglect chargeable to H.O. was ever made. The treatment provided to K.D. at the FTCP was unsuccessful, and later in 2004 she violated the terms of the FTCP. In November, the court revoked K.D.'s protective supervision and placed the boys into the custody of the Child Family Services Agency. At that time, custody with H.O. was not an option for the boys because H.O. was temporarily in prison following his arrest for sexual abuse. Upon removal from their mother at the end of September, the boys were placed with a foster parent, Ms. Wright, with whom they would reside for the next two years.

At a January 6, 2005, hearing, the court changed the boys' permanency goal from reunification with K.D. to reunification with H.O., saying it would wait to make further changes to the permanency goal pending the outcome of H.O.'s criminal case. In August, 2005, H.O. was convicted of two counts of misdemeanor sexual abuse and one count of simple assault, stemming from the charges leveled against him by T.D. At a September 13, 2005, permanency hearing, the permanency goal was changed to adoption. H.O. objected, through counsel, requesting custody for himself. . . .

S.M. and R.S., the petitioners in the adoption case, . . . [began] meeting with the boys pending receipt of a necessary license, but the boys remained in foster care. . . . H.O. faithfully and regularly visited with the boys during this period. The boys moved into S.M.

2. K.D., the boys' mother, is not a party to this case, having consented to the boys' adoption on August 1, 2007.

3. At the initial hearing on probable cause, the magistrate judge relied on a third factor: lack of parental control. This stemmed from the drug activity of K.D. and her mother, I.D., and from H.O.'s decision to leave the children with K.D. and I.D., despite knowing them to be drug abusers. No evidence of drug use by H.O. himself was ever presented. At the time of the initial hearing, H.O. had already been employed by the same company for over 25 years.

and R.S.'s home on December 22, 2006. The adoption petition was formally filed on March 22, 2007. H.O. was served with notice of the adoption petition. . . . On November 9, 2007, the court issued its order waiving parental consent on the ground that the father was withholding consent against the best interests of the boys. . . . A final decree of adoption was issued on July 15, 2008. H.O. timely appealed. H.O.'s brief asserts that he last saw the boys on August 16, 2008, little more than a year ago. . . . The [criminal] charges against H.O. remain pending. . . .

The parental rights of the appellant, H.O., were terminated as a result of the adoption. District of Columbia law provides two methods by which this may lawfully be accomplished. One method is through a termination proceeding brought by the District or the child's legal representative under D.C. Code §16-2353 (2001). The other is through an adoption proceeding commenced by a private party, as part of which a court may grant the adoption over the objection of a natural parent "when the court finds, after a hearing, that the consent or consents are withheld contrary to the best interests of the child" under D.C. Code §16-304(e) (2001). . . . [T]he second method is the functional equivalent of the first. . . . [T]he consequence for the parent is the same: termination of his or her parental rights. . . . Under either method, the paramount consideration is the best interest of the child. Under either method, the court making the decision on what is in the child's best interest must be guided by the factors set forth in §16-2353(b). Those factors are:

> (1) the child's need for continuity of care and caretakers and for timely integration into a stable and permanent home . . . ;
>
> (2) the physical, mental and emotional health of all individuals involved . . . ;
>
> (3) the quality of the interaction and interrelationship of the child with his or her parent . . . ;
>
> (4) to the extent feasible, the child's opinion of his or her own best interests . . . ; and
>
> (5) evidence that drug-related activity continues to exist in a child's home. . . .

These factors are applied, however, against a broader background. We have followed the Supreme Court in recognizing the gravity of a decision whether to terminate parental rights. "Repeatedly, we have stated that biological parents have a 'fundamental liberty interest . . . in the care, custody, and management of their child. . . .'" *In re J.T.B.* (D.C. 2009) (quoting Santosky v. Kramer, 455 U.S. 745 (1982)). *See also Troxel v. Granville* (2000) (recognizing precedent protecting fundamental right to parent).

In this jurisdiction, we have held "that the [termination] statute incorporates into the best interest standard a preference for a fit unwed father who has grasped his opportunity interest and that this preference can be overridden only by a showing by clear and convincing evidence that it is in the best interest of the child to be placed with unrelated persons."[6] Otherwise put, application of the statute must take into account the presumption that the child's best interest will be served by placing the child with his natural parent, provided the parent has not been proven unfit. It follows that the question of a natural parent's fitness must be a relevant consideration. The presumptive right of a fit parent over an adoptive parent is not absolute. The presumption must necessarily give way in the face of clear and convincing evidence that requires the court, in the best interest of the child, to deny custody to the natural parent in favor of an adoptive parent. Thus, in *In re*

6. The District of Columbia does not require, as some jurisdictions do, a "discrete and preemptory unfitness finding [before the court can move to a best interest analysis]."

Baby Boy C. (D.C. 1993), we affirmed the adoption decree where, despite the preference for the fit father, the trial court found by clear and convincing evidence that the child would suffer significant psychological harm from being removed from the home in which the child had lived for nine years.

In *Appeal of H.R.*, we reversed and remanded the trial court's granting of an adoption petition because the court merely conducted a traditional "best interest" balancing test without including a custodial preference for a fit parent.[7] We conclude we must do so again here. . . .

[I]n a pretrial hearing . . . , the court stated to H.O.'s counsel:

> I understand, but you're asking them to assess the suitability of your client as a parent. They don't have any obligation to do that. . . . [I]t's up to you to defend your client's interest and to negate what they say as well as to build your own case to say that your client is a fit and proper parent. . . .

[On another occasion, the court stated:] "[T]he Government's burden in this is not to prove the unfitness of the parents. . . . It is, rather, the child's need for continuity of care and caretakers."

It is noteworthy that H.O. had not been explicitly adjudicated unfit or even neglectful at any point prior to the show cause hearing.[9] Nor did the court after the hearing find that H.O. was unfit. . . . While the trial court did find that H.O. was withholding consent contrary to the best interests of the children, it made no express finding that clear and convincing evidence showed that it was in the best interests of the children to be placed with the adoptive parents as opposed to the presumptive preference for H.O.[10] . . .

To be sure, at the end of the day, the paramount consideration must of course be the best interest of the child. The rights of even fit parents "are not absolute, and must give way before the child's best interests." But here, the trial court approached the issue without according H.O. the presumption and preference to which our case law entitles him. "[W]e cannot properly assume that the court's application of [its findings], while looking through the prism of an erroneous legal test, would be the same when looking through another prism intended to grant presumptive custody to a fit natural father as against strangers." In the circumstances here, we must agree with the District that neither the adoption decree nor the termination of parental rights can stand. . . . The boys as well

7. We have held that noncustodial fathers are entitled to the presumption in favor of a fit parent only after they have "grasped" their "opportunity interest," *i.e.*, after they have "early on, and continually, done all that [they] could reasonably have been expected to do under the circumstances to pursue [their] interest in the child." Appellees do not claim that H.O., who had been involved with the boys since birth, failed to grasp his opportunity interest.

9. . . . [W]e cannot say that the [sexual abuse] conviction necessarily implies a finding of unfitness. . . . [I]f it attempted to establish neglect on the part of H.O. based on abuse of another child, the District would have to show the abused child lived in the same household or was "under the care of the same parent, guardian or custodian" as J.D. and Ka.D. T.D. was not a biological child of H.O.'s and was not living in the same household as the boys at any relevant time. Even if she were, the District acknowledges that "a finding of imminent danger 'because another child in the same household has been abused cannot be automatic.'" Rather, we have held that an individualized finding must be made for each child.

10. The court did express the view that removal of the boys from the custody of S.M. and R.S., with whom they had lived for barely six months at the commencement of the hearing, would be "very harmful" to the boys. However, this conclusion came largely from the testimony of an art and play therapist who had never seen H.O. interact with the boys, or met with H.O. in any capacity. H.O. was hardly a stranger to these boys: unlike so many cases that come before us, the father had been involved in the boys' lives since birth and shown a faithful commitment to visitation during the pendency of these proceedings. . . . In any event, . . . with the . . . relatively short time of residence with petitioners, . . . the typical consideration of "bonding" may not apply with its usual force.

as H.O. are entitled to a fresh assessment of the present situation in which the presumption and preference in favor of H.O. is fully taken into account. . . . [T]he trial court should fashion appropriate visitation for H.O. with the boys pending further determinations on remand.

The court of appeals did not find the trial court erred in concluding it would be best for the boys to be adopted despite the biological father's refusal of consent. So if it were really true that "at the end of the day, the paramount consideration must of course be the best interest of the child," what would be the point of a remand? Is the ruling here just about burdens of proof? Or is the appellate court dictating a different substantive test, some sort of balancing of interests, and potential sacrifice of what is best for the boys?

Did H.O. in fact do "all that [he] could reasonably have been expected to do under the circumstances to pursue [his] interest in the child[ren]"? Or does committing a crime that makes you unable to care for children because you are in jail preclude such a finding? As we will see in Section I.C. below, courts are divided on whether to treat incarceration as a form of abandonment or as an excuse for not caring for and supporting a child.

3. *Involuntary Termination by Child Protection Proceeding*

We saw in Chapter 1 that states create legal parent-child relationships with no regard for adults' parenting qualifications, almost exclusively on the basis of biological parentage, even though legislators know a significant percentage of biological parents are unfit to raise children. We saw in Chapter 4 that states have chosen to deal with unfitness instead by reacting after children incur maltreatment, authorizing child protection agencies to investigate reports of abuse or neglect, remove children from unsafe home environments, and condition return of the child on parental rehabilitation. Only if parents prove unable or unwilling to reform after being offered extensive rehabilitation services do child protection agencies petition a court to terminate parental rights.

How bad must parents be for the state to sever their relationships with children? In reviewing the statutory provision below setting forth four substantive bases for termination of parental rights (TPR) in Virginia, think about how they are similar to or divergent from the reasons why adults typically seek to break off relationships with each other. In addition, try to anticipate which terms in each paragraph present the greatest interpretive problems or are most often contested.

Code of Virginia
Title 16.1. Courts Not of Record
Chapter 11. Juvenile and Domestic Relations District Courts
Article 9. Disposition

§16.1-283. Termination of Residual Parental Rights

A. . . . The local board of social services or a licensed child-placing agency need not have identified an available and eligible family to adopt a child for whom termination of parental rights is being sought prior to the entry of an order terminating parental rights. . . .

B. The residual parental rights of a parent or parents of a child found by the court to be neglected or abused and placed in foster care . . . may be terminated if the court finds, based upon clear and convincing evidence, that it is in the best interests of the child and:

1. The neglect or abuse suffered by such child presented a serious and substantial threat to his life, health or development; and

2. It is not reasonably likely that the conditions which resulted in such neglect or abuse can be substantially corrected or eliminated so as to allow the child's safe return to his parent or parents within a reasonable period of time. . . .

Proof of any of the following shall constitute prima facie evidence of the conditions set forth in subdivision B 2 hereof:

a. The parent or parents are suffering from a mental or emotional illness or mental deficiency of such severity that there is no reasonable expectation that such parent will be able to undertake responsibility for the care needed by the child . . . ;

b. The parent or parents have habitually abused or are addicted to intoxicating liquors, narcotics or other dangerous drugs to the extent that proper parental ability has been seriously impaired and the parent, without good cause, has not responded to or followed through with recommended and available treatment . . . ; or

c. The parent or parents, without good cause, have not responded to or followed through with appropriate, available and reasonable rehabilitative efforts on the part of social, medical, mental health or other rehabilitative agencies. . . .

C. The residual parental rights of a parent or parents of a child placed in foster care . . . may be terminated if the court finds, based upon clear and convincing evidence, that it is in the best interests of the child and that:

1. The parent or parents have, without good cause, failed to maintain continuing contact with and to provide or substantially plan for the future of the child for a period of six months after the child's placement in foster care notwithstanding the reasonable and appropriate efforts of . . . agencies to communicate with the parent or parents and to strengthen the parent-child relationship. . . . ; or

2. The parent or parents, without good cause, have been unwilling or unable within a reasonable period of time not to exceed twelve months from the date the child was placed in foster care to remedy substantially the conditions which led to or required continuation of the child's foster care placement, notwithstanding the reasonable and appropriate efforts of social, medical, mental health or other rehabilitative agencies. . . .

D. The residual parental rights of a parent or parents of a child found by the court to be neglected or abused upon the ground of abandonment may be terminated if the court finds, based upon clear and convincing evidence, that it is in the best interests of the child and that:

1. The child was abandoned under such circumstances that either the identity or the whereabouts of the parent or parents cannot be determined; and

2. The child's parent or parents, guardian or relatives have not come forward to identify such child and claim a relationship to the child within three months following the issuance of an order by the court placing the child in foster care; and

3. Diligent efforts have been made to locate the child's parent without avail.

E. The residual parental rights of a parent or parents of a child who is in the custody of a local board or licensed child-placing agency may be terminated if the court finds, based upon clear and convincing evidence, that it is in the best interests of the child and that

(i) the residual parental rights of the parent regarding a sibling of the child have previously been involuntarily terminated;

(ii) the parent has been convicted of an offense . . . that constitutes murder or voluntary manslaughter, or a felony attempt, conspiracy or solicitation to commit any such offense, if the victim of the offense was a child of the parent, a child with whom the parent resided at the time such offense occurred or the other parent of the child;

(iii) the parent has been convicted of an offense . . . that constitutes felony assault resulting in serious bodily injury or felony bodily wounding resulting in serious bodily injury or felony sexual assault, if the victim of the offense was a child of the parent or a child with whom the parent resided at the time of such offense; or

(iv) the parent has subjected any child to aggravated circumstances.

As used in this section:

"Aggravated circumstances" means torture, chronic or severe abuse, or chronic or severe sexual abuse, if the victim of such conduct was a child of the parent or a child with whom the parent resided at the time such conduct occurred, including the failure to protect such a child from such conduct, which conduct or failure to protect: (i) evinces a wanton or depraved indifference to human life, or (ii) has resulted in the death of such a child or in serious bodily injury to such a child.

"Chronic abuse" or "chronic sexual abuse" means recurring acts of physical abuse which place the child's health, safety and well-being at risk.

"Serious bodily injury" means bodily injury that involves substantial risk of death, extreme physical pain, protracted and obvious disfigurement, or protracted loss or impairment of the function of a bodily member, organ or mental faculty.

"Severe abuse" or "severe sexual abuse" may include an act or omission that occurred only once, but otherwise meets the definition of "aggravated circumstances."

The local board or other child welfare agency having custody of the child shall not be required by the court to make reasonable efforts to reunite the child with a parent who has been convicted of one of the felonies specified in this subsection or who has been found by the court to have subjected any child to aggravated circumstances.

Notice that every basis for TPR contains a "clear and convincing" evidentiary standard. As Section III below reveals, the Supreme Court has held that parents' procedural due process rights require that the state meet at least this standard of proof.

More importantly, note that being in the child's best interests is in all cases a necessary but not sufficient condition for termination. A court must also find one of the specified "fault" predicates, such as serious abuse, abandonment, or failure to respond to rehabilitative efforts. In contrast, states no longer require spousal fault as a precondition for divorce.

INTERPRETIVE QUESTIONS

1. Describe some circumstances in which it might it be in a child's best interests to terminate the parent-child relationship yet termination is not possible under the Virginia

statute. In any such circumstances, would it be accurate to say that the state has chosen to sacrifice children's welfare in order to serve parents' interests?

2. Is it possible under this statute in any circumstance to terminate the rights of one parent if the child is in the custody and care of the other parent?

Paragraph E was added in the late 1990s under pressure from the federal government, exerted through the Adoption and Safe Families Act (ASFA) of 1996. ASFA effected three major changes in child protection practice. First, it required states, as a condition for receipt of certain federal funds, to direct local CPS agencies to petition for TPR as to any child who has been in foster care for 15 of the past 22 months, unless an agency can show that continuation of foster care would be in the child's best interests, or unless the agency has failed to provide needed services to the parents, or unless the foster parents are biological relatives of the child. This was a reaction to a widespread perception that children lingered too long in foster care because social workers were giving unfit parents too many chances to reform. This provision has been effective in shortening the average stay of children in foster care who are not in a placement with relatives.

Second, ASFA required states to authorize TPR without first undertaking to rehabilitate parents when the parents have committed especially egregious abuse against the child at issue. As with the 15/22 rule, this "no reasonable efforts" or "reunification bypass" aspect of ASFA aimed to spare children from pointless waiting in foster care for permanency.

Third, and most dramatically, ASFA required states to authorize termination of a parent's relationship with one child based on that parent's conduct toward another child, again without first attempting rehabilitation, in cases where that conduct resulted in termination of the parent's relationship with the other child or a felony conviction. By means of this "reunification bypass" provision, Congress aimed to eliminate the problem that each child of an unfit parent had to suffer maltreatment before receiving state protection. However, child protection agencies rarely use this "bypass" authorization. When they do, it is usually in a situation like that in the next case below, where CPS removes a group of children from an unsuitable home environment, petitions for TPR as to one of the children based on severe maltreatment, and then petitions for TPR as to another child based on the abuse finding and TPR as to the first, because proving the prior TPR occurred is easier than proving maltreatment as to the second child. In such cases, the child who is the subject of the second TPR really has already incurred maltreatment.

In re Jenks

760 N.W.2d 297 (Mich. Ct. App. 2008)

PER CURIAM.

. . . The minor children came to the attention of petitioner, the Department of Human Services, on September 1, 2006, when it was discovered that the children's home was in deplorable condition and without running water. Thereafter, on October 23, 2007, respondent pleaded guilty to one count of first-degree criminal sexual conduct with a person under 17 years of age for his conduct in sexually abusing his stepdaughter, who is the minor children's half-sister. As part of his plea, respondent admitted his sexual penetration of the stepdaughter. On November 27, 2007, respondent was sentenced to serve a prison term of 5 to 15 years for that offense. Petitioner sought to terminate respondent's parental rights on the basis of his admitted sexual abuse of the other child. . . .

MCL 712A.19b(3)(b) provides for termination if the

> child or a sibling of the child has suffered physical injury or physical or sexual abuse . . . [and] there is a reasonable likelihood that the child will suffer from injury or abuse in the foreseeable future if placed in the parent's home.

The record clearly established that respondent sexually abused the minor children's half-sister; respondent does not dispute this. And the statute clearly encompasses such conduct.[2]

Further, considering the nature of respondent's criminal sexual conduct with the other child, which included penetration, the trial court did not clearly err in determining that there is a reasonable likelihood that the minor children would suffer injury or abuse in the foreseeable future if placed in respondent's home. Therefore, the trial court did not clearly err in finding that this ground for termination was established by clear and convincing legally admissible evidence. . . .

Having found that at least one statutory ground for termination was established by clear and convincing evidence . . . , the trial court was required to terminate respondent's parental rights unless there was clear evidence, on the whole record, that termination was not in the children's best interests. . . . [W]e find no clear error in the trial court's conclusion that, considering the nature of respondent's criminal sexual conduct with the minor children's half-sister and the length of his incarceration for that offense, termination was not clearly contrary to the minor children's best interests.

2. This Court previously interpreted the prior version of MCL 712A.19b(3)(b)(i) as applicable only to conduct perpetrated by the parent of the injured or abused child. Therefore, this Court reluctantly determined that the prior version of this section did not apply if the injured or abused child was not also the child of the parent whose parental rights the petitioner sought to terminate. *In re Powers* (1995). However, the Legislature amended MCL 712A.19b(3)(b)(i) in 1997 to clarify that grounds for termination are established when the parent against whom termination is sought is responsible for the physical injury or physical or sexual abuse of a sibling of the minor child, regardless of whether that parent is also a parent of the injured or abused sibling. . . .

Is it clear that Mr. Jenks's biological offspring were in danger of sexual abuse? Suppose the sexual abuse with his step-daughter was mutually voluntary intercourse and she was 16. That is illegal and arguably immoral, but does it necessarily mean that Mr. Jenks is an indiscriminate pedophile? Was the statutory amendment described in footnote 2 wise?

The following is an extraordinary case in which the state did take custody of a child who had not yet incurred maltreatment and petitioned immediately for TPR. The petitioning agency found the trial court judge receptive but met with repeated resistance at the appellate court level.

In re D.L.D.

771 N.W.2d 538 (Minn. Ct. App. 2009)

LARKIN, Judge.

. . . Appellant-mother's parental rights to the children D.D. and C.D. were involuntarily terminated by the district court in 1995. Appellant-parents' parental rights to the child D.L.R.D. were involuntarily terminated in 2002. . . . Finally, appellant-parents' parental rights to the child S.L.H. were involuntarily terminated in September 2007. . . . The prior terminations were based on appellant-mother's drug use and mental-health issues and appellant-father's abuse of appellant-mother and the parties' child.

This case concerns the child S.M.H., who was born to appellant-parents on August 29, 2008. On September 2, respondent St. Louis County Public Health and Human Services (county) filed a termination-of-parental-rights (TPR) petition under Minn. Stat. §260C.301, subd. 1(b), alleging that the parents are presumed to be palpably unfit based on their previous involuntary terminations. On October 7, the district court ordered that the county was not required to make reasonable efforts to rehabilitate and reunify appellant-parents with S.M.H. given the prior involuntary termination of their parental rights. . . .

The evidence indicates that appellant-parents contacted the Intensive Family Based Services (IFBS) program in October to request admission into the program. IFBS offers counseling and parenting education to families. Appellant-mother had participated in the IFBS program prior to termination of her parental rights to S.L.H. IFBS was unwilling to provide services to appellant-parents because S.M.H. was not in appellant-parents' custody, there was no plan for reunification, and IFBS's resources were limited. Unable to obtain services from IFBS, appellant-parents began attending parenting classes at the Family Investment Center (FIC) on October 29. The parents attended classes at FIC on November 5 and 26, and on December 10. They attempted to attend a class on October 12, but no instructor was available. The parenting classes were client-based and included a parenting discussion group. . . . Topics included appropriate discipline, Christmas safety, and HIV awareness.

The evidence also shows that appellant-mother continued to engage in therapy to address her documented mental-health issues. Appellant-mother had engaged in counseling with John Seldon at Range Mental Health Center until October 2007. Seldon testified at the TPR trials concerning D.L.R.D. and S.L.H. Appellant-mother testified that she changed therapists because she felt that Seldon did not appear to be listening to her. Appellant-mother also alleged that Seldon fell asleep during a therapy session. Appellant-mother began counseling with psychologist Robert Stehlin in October 2007. Stehlin diagnosed appellant-mother with anxiety, depression, and post-traumatic stress disorder. Around this time, appellant-mother applied for and was deemed eligible for permanent social-security-disability benefits. Appellant-mother attends cognitive behavioral therapy with Stehlin at least two times per month and has never cancelled an appointment. Stehlin does not believe that appellant-mother poses a risk of harm to herself or others and that her condition does not impair her ability to care for a child. Stehlin observed no reason to believe that appellant-mother has ever been under the influence of illegal substances during the time he has treated her.

With regard to chemical use, the evidence indicates that appellant-mother received an updated chemical-dependency evaluation on December 24, 2008, which recommended outpatient treatment. Appellant-mother testified that she is willing to participate in outpatient treatment, but had not started treatment by the time of trial. Appellant-mother had participated in urinalysis testing. Her last positive test was in April 2007, and it indicated the presence of methamphetamine and cocaine. Appellant-mother provided samples that tested negative in May, June, July, August and September 2007, and in March, April, June, August, October and December 2008. And appellant-mother documented her attendance at 22 Narcotics Anonymous (N.A.) meetings between October 11 and November 26, 2008. Appellant-mother testified that she began attending N.A. regularly during her pregnancy with S.M.H. but did not begin documenting her attendance until

October. Appellant-mother's supervising probation officer, Kelli Horvath, testified that at the time of trial, appellant-mother was current on all conditions of probation.[1] . . .

The evidence shows that appellant-mother has stable housing. Appellant-father lives separately from appellant-mother, but occasionally stays at appellant-mother's apartment. Appellant-mother acknowledges that appellant-father has subjected her to domestic abuse in the past and states that she will immediately end the relationship if there is another incident of domestic violence. Appellant-parents sought couples counseling with therapist Stehlin but had not started counseling by the time of trial due to insurance issues.

Appellant-father presented evidence that he began . . . a program to address domestic violence issues, the Range Intervention Project. . . . Appellant-father did not complete the program because he was incarcerated as a result of a new conviction of fleeing a police officer in a motor vehicle, which stemmed from conduct that occurred on March 29, 2008. Appellant-father reportedly was under the influence of alcohol when he committed the offense. . . . Appellant-father was incarcerated at the time of S.M.H.'s birth. While incarcerated, appellant-father attended Alcoholic Anonymous (A.A.) groups and participated in cognitive-thinking groups three times a week. Appellant-father also attended A.A. meetings prior to his incarceration in an effort to reinstate his driving privileges. Appellant-father testified that he has maintained sobriety since March 29, 2008. . . .

The undisputed evidence indicates that appellant-parents consistently attended weekly visits with S.M.H. during the termination proceeding. There were no reports of inappropriate behavior by the parents during visits. And appellant-parents presented the testimony of relatives who reported seeing no signs of recent domestic violence between the parents and expressed no concerns regarding appellant-parents' past parenting abilities.

Social worker Nancy Melin testified that she has worked with appellant-parents since June 2005. Melin testified that appellant-parents had not presented evidence of their participation in any service that they had not already received in the past. Melin acknowledged that appellant-parents could parent adequately under close supervision but believes that if supervision ended, the parents would return to old habits that would create unsafe situations for a child, as they had done in the past. Melin opined that there are no services that would allow S.M.H. to safely return to her parents' custody. But if a case plan had to be developed, Melin would recommend that the parents reside separately, participate in IFBS, participate in counseling, and follow the recommendations of their chemical-dependency assessments. . . .

Analysis

It is presumed that a parent is palpably unfit to be a party to the parent-child relationship upon a showing that the parent's parental rights to one or more other children were involuntarily terminated. . . . When the presumption of unfitness applies, a parent must affirmatively and actively demonstrate her or his ability to successfully parent a child. We recognize this is a particularly onerous task when, because of the prior termination of parental rights, the statute has relieved the county of the obligation to develop a case plan and make reasonable efforts to reunite the parent and child. To shoulder this burden, the parent, with the assistance of counsel, is inevitably required to marshal any available community resources to develop a plan and accomplish results that demonstrate the parent's fitness.

1. Appellant-mother was on probation following her guilty plea to third-degree burglary for an offense that occurred on August 1, 2004.

Despite the parents' participation in services, the record does not demonstrate that they are able to successfully parent S.M.H. or that they have accomplished results that demonstrate parental fitness. Despite the recent order terminating their parental rights to S.L.H., appellant-parents did not seek services from the county during appellant-mother's pregnancy with S.M.H. Instead, appellant-parents waited until after the county petitioned for termination of their parental rights to seek services specific to their parenting abilities. Despite recent recommendations for outpatient chemical-dependency treatment, neither parent had started treatment by the time of trial. Despite a history of domestic violence and a court-order for appellant-father to complete domestic-abuse counseling, appellant-father had not completed domestic-abuse counseling and the parties had not engaged in couples counseling by the time of trial. These delays support the district court's finding that the parents' apparent willingness to cooperate with services and the county is superficial.

Appellant-parents offer several explanations for their failure to complete services. Appellant-father was unable to complete domestic-abuse counseling because he was incarcerated for a new felony-level offense. Appellant-parents sought admission to IFBS but were not accepted into the program because their child was not in their care and reunification was not in progress. They sought couples counseling but were unable to begin due to insurance issues. But regardless of the reasons, appellant-parents did not "accomplish results that demonstrate [parental] fitness." Despite appellant-parents' efforts and their cooperation with some services, there is insufficient evidence of change.

Moreover, the services that appellant-parents utilized in this case are the same or similar to the services that they engaged in during their previous TPR proceedings. And their parental rights were previously terminated despite their participation in these services. It is unlikely that the current services are adequate to bring about results that demonstrate parental fitness given appellant-parents' previous inability to maintain their parental rights despite participation in similar services. Thus, the district court did not err by concluding that "nothing has changed" since appellant-parents' last TPR trial. . . . In order to rebut a presumption of palpable unfitness, a parent must do more than engage in services; a parent must demonstrate that his or her parenting abilities have improved. . . . By the time of S.M.H.'s birth, appellant-father had engaged in felony-level criminal activity during appellant-mother's pregnancy, had been convicted of fleeing a police officer in a motor vehicle, and was incarcerated as a result. Appellant-mother had also been charged with a criminal offense as a result of her attempt to help appellant-father avoid arrest. These behaviors are inconsistent with a finding of parental fitness. . . .

If a statutory ground for termination of parental rights is proved, the paramount consideration in determining whether parental rights will be terminated is the best interests of the child. . . . The county acknowledges that the district court's order does not contain findings or conclusions regarding S.M.H.'s best interests. But the county argues that a best-interests determination can be "implied" from the current record, which includes judicial notice of appellant-parents' prior involuntary terminations and the best-interests findings made in those proceedings. . . . Section 260C.301, subdivision 7, clearly states: "In any proceeding under this section, the best interests of the child must be the paramount consideration." The word "any" is broadly applied in statutes. Thus, a district court's findings in support of any TPR order must address the best-interests criterion. . . . See Minn. R. Juv. Prot. P. 39.05, subd. 3(b)(3) (2009) ("Before ordering termination of parental rights, the court shall make a specific finding that termination is in the best interests of the child and shall analyze: (i) the child's interests in preserving the parent-child relationship; (ii) the parent's interests in preserving the parent-child relationship; and (iii) any competing interests of the child."),

42.08 (requiring that an order granting involuntary termination of parental rights contain "findings regarding how the order is in the best interests of the child"). . . .

Under the best-interests doctrine, every child who is the subject of a TPR proceeding deserves the court's full consideration. . . . An exception to the requirement that a child's best interests be the paramount consideration in any TPR proceeding would constitute a significant departure from the policy embodied in section 260C.301, subdivision 7. . . . [T]he absence of district court findings on the child's best interests in a TPR proceeding precludes effective appellate review because it prevents us from determining whether the district court adequately considered the child's best interests as the paramount consideration. . . . [W]e remand for best-interests findings.

Does the state go too far when it terminates a parent's legal relationship with a child whom the parent has not harmed? Should the mother have received another chance with her fifth child? What more could she do to demonstrate preparedness to care for a child if the child protection agency swoops in every time she has another baby and takes the baby away? Do her clean drug tests for over a year not show that her efforts are more than superficial?

Reread the last paragraph of the opinion. The court's statement that TPR statutes make a child's best interests "paramount" is implausible, given that no state's statutes make the best interests of the child a sufficient basis for termination; rather, courts get to the best-interests inquiry only after the parental fault prong of the TPR tests is met. And in a follow-up decision after remand (below), the same court interprets "best interests of the child" in a bizarre way that further diminishes the power of juvenile courts to do what is best for children. How much confidence in the ability of the court system to achieve permanence and the best outcome for children does this decision give you?

In re Welfare of Child of D.L.D.

2010 WL 1192310 (Minn. Ct. App. 2010)

HUDSON, Judge.

. . . On remand, the district court ruled that termination is in the child's best interests. . . . The order . . . lacks findings addressing the child's best interests, but its conclusions of law state that "[t]he consideration of 'best interests' in this case is identical to the consideration of 'palpable unfitness'; it is precisely and logically the same issue, involving the exact same relevant evidence." The district court concluded that it "is unable to envision any sort of factual scenario wherein it would possibly be in a child's 'best interests' to deny a termination petition, notwithstanding evidence that leads to factual findings as well as a legal conclusion of 'palpable unfitness.'" . . .

Because a parent's palpable unfitness means that the district court "may" terminate parental rights, the existence of that condition does not *require* termination. . . . Because a child's best interests . . . can preclude termination of parental rights despite the existence of a statutory condition allowing termination, evaluating a child's best interests involves an inquiry distinct from that used to determine the existence of a statutory condition allowing termination. Thus, . . . a ruling that it is in a child's best interests to terminate parental rights *because* of the existence of a statutory basis to terminate is a misapplication of the law. . . . [It] preclude[s] the possibility of non-termination permanency dispositions in cases where such a disposition is possible. *See* Minn. Stat. §260C.201, subd. 11(c), (d) (noting multiple permanency options including, but not limited to, termination of parental rights). . . . Therefore, we remand for the district court to readdress the child's best interests, and to do so in a way that is unambiguously distinct from its determination that the appellants are palpably unfit to be parties to the parent-child relationship.

After trial in this matter, Minn. R. Juv. Prot. P. 39.05, subd. 3(b)(3), was amended to require the district court, in its best-interests analysis, to consider the child's interest in preserving the parent-child relationship, the parent's interest in preserving that relationship, and any competing interest of the child. This amendment of the rule was an incorporation of pre-existing caselaw reciting the same analysis. . . . Therefore, on remand, the district court's best-interest analysis shall include . . . considering the child's interest in preserving the parent-child relationship, the parent's interest in preserving that relationship, and any competing interest of the child. . . . [T]he district court shall make findings adequate to facilitate effective appellate review, to provide insight into which facts or opinions were most persuasive of the ultimate decision, and to show its consideration of the factors relevant to its best-interests analysis.

How, as a conceptual matter, could "the parent's interest in preserving that relationship" be part of an analysis of what is best for the child, and how could it be consistent with making the child's welfare "paramount"? Do you suppose S.M.H. has yet achieved permanency? What do you think are the effects on a child of protracted TPR litigation like this, with repeated appeals and remands?

Are there other bases you would add for TPR without rehabilitative efforts? Given that in every situation the test is something plus best interests of the child, one could view the fault basis for TPR as simply a trigger for a best-interests hearing. So we could ask instead, what should trigger court consideration of whether it would be best for a particular child to end a parent-child relationship immediately? Should drug use during pregnancy be such a trigger? As noted above, it is a basis in Illinois for waiving the requirement of maternal consent in an adoption proceeding, as is habitual drunkenness or drug abuse. Birthing facilities are now required to report any positive toxicology finding in newborns to the local CPS office. The usual CPS response, however, is to place the baby in foster care for a year or more and try to get the mother to stop using drugs. See, e.g., Idaho Dep't of Health & Welfare v. Doe, 219 P.3d 448 (Idaho 2009) (TPR trial only after child spent first three years of life in foster care).

In the following case, a Virginia appellate court interpreted paragraph B of the statutory section above as also authorizing TPR without rehabilitative efforts. Is this in fact an appropriate case for immediate termination upon discovery of the maltreatment, or should a court have ordered rehabilitative efforts?

Toms v. Hanover Department of Social Services

616 S.E.2d 765 (Va. Ct. App. 2005)

KELSEY, Judge.

. . . Frazier and Laura Toms are the biological parents of eight children—seven boys and one girl. On January 28, 2003, Laura Toms left the family home and walked to a neighbor's house. Her husband was holding her against her will, she told the neighbor, and had abused her. The children were home alone.

When the sheriff's office responded to the Toms house, two deputies met one of the boys standing at the gate to the property. The boy told the deputies to leave and that his father was not at home. Concerned about the safety of the children, the deputies entered the property several minutes later. The boy ran into the woods. When the deputies walked into the house, they noticed a two-year-old boy standing on a bed. The rest of the children could not be found. They too had fled into the woods.

What appeared to be the Toms residence was a 16′ by 16′ unfinished structure. The structure had three stories, but no access between the floors. The family lived together on the first floor. The house had no electricity or indoor plumbing. There were no rooms, no indoor sinks or bathtubs, and no kitchen. The structure was "full of trash." The family used an outdoor tub for bathing and a primitive outdoor latrine. The yard around the structure was littered with alcohol bottles and cans.

About thirty minutes after the deputies arrived, Fraizer Toms appeared at the house. He was visibly intoxicated and agitated. The deputies sought his assistance in finding the children, but he refused to cooperate and was eventually arrested. A K-9 unit and multiple aircraft assisted in the search for the children. It was near freezing temperatures, and the children had no coats, hats, or gloves to protect them against the cold. About eight hours later, at around 3:30 A.M., the children emerged from the woods. The rescue unit took the children to the hospital for examination for potential hypothermia.

Laura Toms was hospitalized that same evening due to a psychiatric condition. The children were placed in a foster home by Hanover Department of Social Services (HDSS) the next day. . . . The Hanover Juvenile and Domestic Relations District Court approved the removal, holding that the children were abused or neglected by their parents. The JDR district court also approved foster care plans for the children presented by HDSS and allowed HDSS to perform additional evaluations and assessments. . . .

In October 2003, the JDR district court approved HDSS's goal of adoption for the children and, in February 2004, ordered that Frazier and Laura Toms's residual parental rights be terminated.[1] Both appealed these decisions to the circuit court.

At the circuit court hearing, the children's psychologists testified to the profound neglect evidenced by the children's underdeveloped speech, intelligence, motor skills, and social and emotional functioning. The children scored below the first percentile on standardized child developmental tests. The children had "received no health care, no education, no social skills, no speech skills." The Toms residence "was so pathetically substandard that it itself demonstrates abuse and neglect." The guardian *ad litem* for the children reported . . . their "speech was almost wholly unintelligible, consisting of 'grunts' and various forms of body language."

Psychological testing revealed that Frazier Toms suffered from episodes of delusional thinking, social phobias, paranoia, obsessive-compulsive disorder, depression, severe anxiety, and avoidant personality features. The extent of his mental illness led one psychologist to conclude that his prognosis for rehabilitation was poor. . . . Frazier's mother reported that her son had been diagnosed as a teenager with paranoid schizophrenia and was hospitalized for that condition. . . . [A] psychologist who prepared a parenting assessment of Toms noted: "Signs of his paranoia were clearly evident during this

1. HDSS sought the termination of the Toms's parental rights with respect to six of their eight children—the oldest son reached the age of majority, and both Frazier and Laura Toms voluntarily terminated their parental rights to their infant son.

assessment process." The parenting assessment concluded that the "children would be at serious risk if returned to Mr. Toms at this time or in the near future."

The evidence also showed that Toms started drinking alcohol at age six. In 1995, Toms had his driving privileges suspended after a DUI conviction. By 1998, he was consuming up to six beers and a pint of alcohol on a daily basis. He typically passed out at least twice a week from intoxication. Toms's counsel . . . acknowledged that "this family lived in nothing short of absolute crisis conditions for three years. . . ."

. . . [T]he circuit court approved the goal of adoption and ordered that Toms's parental rights be terminated under Code §16.1-283(B). . . .[2]

In a related criminal proceeding, the circuit court convicted Toms of seven misdemeanors and two felonies for the abuse and neglect of his children. He remains incarcerated at this time on those convictions.

II.

. . . Because "the rights of parents may not be lightly severed," clear and convincing evidence must establish the statutory grounds for termination. In the end, the "child's best interests" remain the "paramount consideration" of the court. . . .

In this case, the factual record supports the circuit court's decision to terminate Toms's parental rights under Code §16.1-283(B). After the lengthy hearing, the trial court found the evidence was "overwhelming that the Toms children have experienced abuse or neglect that has demonstrably had a serious and substantial detrimental effect on their lives, health and development." Especially in regards to the older children, the court was "utterly convinced" that their "health and development has been harmed to such an extent that it may well be permanent." "Given the abuse and neglect heaped upon them that has so profoundly affected them, it is without a doubt that it is in their best interests." . . .

We also hold that the record supports the circuit court's finding that Toms could not, within a reasonable period of time, substantially remedy the conditions that resulted in the children going into foster care. Toms's life has been badly scarred by destructive patterns of alcohol abuse and debilitating bouts of mental illness. These longstanding conditions go back to his childhood and cannot be explained away as recent, readily correctable, maladies. And they were severe enough to cause Toms to cloister his children in inhumane living conditions, to deprive them of routine medical care, and to do nothing to stop the steep regression in their developmental skills.

Toms complains that the circuit court did not give him a "fair chance" because it appeared to gauge the probability of his future reformation by examining the severity of his past actions. . . . "No one can divine with any assurance the future course of human events. Nevertheless, past actions and relationships over a meaningful period serve as good indicators of what the future may be expected to hold." Toms had the opportunity to explain his past actions and to offer promises of future self-reformation. . . . "Suffice it to say," the trial judge found, he "was not convinced of either Mr. Toms's sincerity or dedication to remedying what are obvious functional disabilities." "His testimony was vague and nonspecific," the judge added, "and particularly revealed that he had taken virtually no steps since January 2003 to remedy anything (recognizing that he was in jail for some period of time)." . . .

2. The circuit court also terminated the residual parental rights of Laura Toms, a decision she did not appeal. . . .

Whatever permissible inferences flow from his past actions, Toms argues, the circuit court still erred as a matter of law in granting the petition for termination because HDSS failed to provide him with rehabilitation services required by Code §16.1-283(B). Toms concedes the text of subsection B does not literally impose such a requirement. But the "larger statutory scheme" does, he contends. . . . Code §16.1-283(B) requires only that the circuit court consider whether rehabilitation services, if any, have been provided to a parent. Nothing in Code §16.1-283 or the larger statutory scheme requires that such services be provided in all cases as a prerequisite to termination under subsection B.

(i) The Difference Between Code §16.1-283(B) & (C)

Code §§ 16.1-283(B) and 16.1-283(C)(2) both "set forth individual bases upon which a petitioner may seek to terminate residual parental rights." Though we have sometimes blurred the distinctions between the discrete subsections of Code §16.1-283, on this one issue a significant dissimilarity exists. Subsection C(2) specifically requires a showing that DSS has provided "reasonable and appropriate" services to a delinquent parent prior to terminating his rights. In this way, the statute establishes a time frame after the child has entered foster care for the parents "to receive rehabilitative services to enable them to correct the conditions that led to foster care placement." Subsection B(2), on the other hand, merely requires the court to "*take into consideration* the efforts made to rehabilitate the parent or parents by any public or *private* social, medical, mental health or other rehabilitative agencies *prior to* the child's initial placement in foster care." . . . Subsection B does not create specific time frames, "nor does it mandate that a public or private agency provide any services to a parent after the child enters foster care."

That is not to say that a trial court considering a subsection B termination case should ignore a parent's inexcusable failure to respond to rehabilitative services offered by DSS or other assisting agencies after the child's removal. Subsection B(2)(c) specifically recognizes this circumstance as a *prima facie* ground justifying termination. But it is to say that the provision of such services, while a relevant circumstance, cannot be viewed as a prerequisite to a subsection B termination—one, which if not met, would render termination legally invalid no matter the unique circumstances of the case. The *prima facie* examples listed in Code §16.1-283(B)(2)(a) to (B)(2)(c) do not purport to be the only conceivable methods of proof. The list is illustrative, not exhaustive. . . .[4]

This dissimilarity stems from the differing precipitating events leading to the need to remove the child from the home in the first place. The precipitating event of subsection B is a judicial finding of neglect or abuse. Subsection C termination cases, however, start off with no such finding of parental culpability. Subsection B, unlike C, often addresses situations farther along the continuum toward termination—thus making the continued provision of rehabilitative services a relevant concern, but not an absolute prerequisite to termination.

(ii) The Larger Statutory Scheme

. . . Toms points us to Code §16.1-281, the statute requiring DSS to prepare a foster care plan and submit it to the court for approval. . . . Prior to . . . amendment, the statute required that the initial foster care plan "shall be designed to lead to the return of the child to his parents or other prior custodian within the shortest practicable time which shall be specified in the plan." The 1998 amendment rewrote that sentence: "*If consistent*

4. Subsection B, after all, also lists another example of *prima facie* evidence (severe "mental or emotional illness") that makes no mention of a parent's failure to respond to any rehabilitative services. . . .

with the child's health and safety, the plan shall be designed to *support reasonable efforts which* lead to the return of the child to his parents. . . ." The amendment, therefore, gave DSS the initial discretion to abstain from reunification efforts if it deems them inconsistent with the "health and safety" of the child. . . .[8]

. . . Code §16.1-281(B) now renders DSS's duty to provide rehabilitation services contingent upon its belief that the reunification goal would be "consistent with the child's health and safety." . . . In this case, HDSS in fact included in the initial foster care plan a summary of anticipated rehabilitative services in aid of reunification.[9] As various psychological reports and parenting assessments came in, however, HDSS concluded that reunification was inconsistent with the children's "health and safety." . . . [T]he circuit court concurred. . . . [T]he evidence supports the circuit court's decision. . . .

No judicial precedent has imposed a *constitutional* duty to provide rehabilitative services prior to termination when the statutory grounds for termination do not otherwise require them. And we know of no principled basis for asserting there to be one. . . . "All that the Constitution requires under the majority opinion in *Santosky* is for the state to establish by clear and convincing evidence that the parent is currently unfit to provide proper care and custody for the child as defined by state [parental termination] statutes." . . .

Should the outcome in this case have been different if the father expressed a commitment to rehabilitation and took some initial steps toward turning his life around? Do you think his current imprisonment influenced the court's decision? Presumably in prison he was forced to stop drinking. Should the state have waited to see if that change positively affected him?

How could the older children have spent years in this environment without state intervention? At what point in the family's history should the child protection agency have first become involved? Note that such horror stories occur not only in rural environments; every year children are discovered after spending years locked up and starving in urban homes. See, e.g., *6 Kids Found in Horror House Case*, myfoxphilly.com, Oct. 18, 2011; Kimberly Dick, *6 Children Found Living in Deplorable Conditions*, heraldonline.com (Rock Hill, SC), Sept. 29, 2011. Should the state be supervising all family situations more than it does at present, in order to ensure that no children are living in environments like the Toms's home, rather than waiting for maltreatment reports to come in? How could it do that? Could a situation like this exist within a mile of your law school?

Toms was in prison at the time of the appellate court decision. Does any provision in the Virginia TPR statute authorize termination on the basis of imprisonment per se? Should

8. The General Assembly enacted the 1998 amendments to accommodate changes in federal grant requirements imposed by the Adoption and Safe Families Act (ASFA) passed by Congress in 1997. . . . ASFA superseded the much criticized Adoption Assistance and Child Welfare Act of 1980, which had the unintended effect of encouraging the use of state termination statutes to "trap children in temporary foster care placements." To remedy this problem, ASFA recognizes the "health and safety of the child" as the paramount public policy concern and allows states flexibility in determining whether reunification efforts serve that goal.

9. . . . HDSS committed to "diligently work to thoroughly assess" all treatment recommendations to determine whether "Return Home to Parents" was a viable goal. Subsequently, Toms was compelled by a JDR district court order to complete a mental health assessment (to which he objected) and a substance abuse evaluation (which he refused to complete until a motion to show cause on his failure to do so had been filed). The social worker referred Toms to the Hanover Community Services Board to obtain substance abuse treatment (which he refused to do), gave him information about parenting classes (which he never attended), and arranged with Central Virginia Counseling Group for his parenting assessment. . . .

long-term incarceration, along with a best-interests finding, be a basis in and of itself for TPR? In several states it is.

West's Tennessee Code
Title 36. Domestic Relations

§36-1-113. Termination of Parental Rights

. . . (g) Initiation of termination of parental rights may be based upon . . .

(6) The parent has been confined in a correctional or detention facility . . . under a sentence of ten or more years, and the child is under eight years of age at the time the sentence is entered by the court. . . .

Is this provision too limited? Suppose a mother is sentenced to eight years in prison just before the child is born, with parole possible after five. Should she retain parental status? Colorado has a shorter time line, but incarceration is a basis for TPR only if the child has been declared dependent, which will only be true when the child has no other private caregiver and the state has to assume custody, which rarely happens when a parent enters prison. See Colo. Rev. Stat. §19-3-604(1)(b)(III) ("The court may order a termination of the parent-child legal relationship upon the finding . . . [t]hat the child is adjudicated dependent . . . [and] no appropriate treatment plan can be devised to address the unfitness of the parent. . . . [T]he court shall find one of the following as the basis for unfitness: . . . (III) Long-term confinement of the parent of such duration that he is not eligible for parole for at least six years from the date the child was adjudicated dependent or neglected. . . ."). Arizona and Rhode Island do not specify a particular time. See Ariz. Rev. Stat. §8-533(B)(4) (parent-child relationship may be terminated on the grounds that "the parent is deprived of civil liberties due to the conviction of a felony . . . if the sentence of that parent is of such length that the child will be deprived of a normal home for a period of years."); R.I. Gen. Laws §15-7-7(a) ("The court shall . . . terminate any and all legal rights of the parent to the child . . . , if the court finds as a fact by clear and convincing evidence that: . . . (2) The parent is unfit by reason of . . . (i) . . . imprisonment, for a duration as to render it improbable for the parent to care for the child for an extended period of time"). Cf. 750 Ill. Comp. Stat. 50/1 (establishing "depravity" as a basis for finding parental unfitness, and including in the definition of depravity that "the parent has been criminally convicted of at least 3 felonies . . . and at least one of these convictions took place within 5 years of the filing of the petition . . ." or that the "parent has been criminally convicted of either first or second degree murder of any person . . . within 10 years of the filing date of the petition . . .").

In states where TPR statutes do not address incarceration explicitly, a child protection agency will sometimes assert that a parent's incarceration constitutes abandonment or failure to provide for a child in need if the child is in foster care. Courts in those instances have generally held that incarceration per se is not a basis for termination. See, e.g., Hatch v. Anderson, 4 A.3d 904 (Me. 2010); In re Parental Rights to Q.L.R., 54 P.3d 56 (Nev. 2002). They require other evidence of parental unfitness or indifference, such as child maltreatment prior to incarceration or not communicating with the child while in prison.

A significant percentage of women sentenced to prison are pregnant at the time they enter prison, and most spend at least a few years in prison. Yet there is virtually no reported court decision concerning petitions to terminate the parental rights of such women. This is in part because of a general CPS reluctance to terminate parental rights without giving parents a chance at some time to parent their child. It is also in part because those babies typically do not even come to CPS attention. Most states' prison regulations do not require prison officials to notify CPS of an inmate's giving birth, but rather instruct them to notify family and hand the baby over to a family member who comes forward to claim custody. Usually, the birth mother will contact a family member (most often, her own mother) and ask that she take custody. The law then, in effect, treats the situation like one in which a birth mother leaves her baby in the care of someone else and then voluntarily goes off to live elsewhere.

Best-Interests Prong

In all cases, courts must deny a petition to terminate a parent-child relationship if they find termination would not be in the child's best interests, even if they find the fault predicate exists. As noted above, that TPR would be best for the child is not a sufficient condition, but it is a necessary condition. When might it *not* be in the child's best interests to terminate if a court has determined that the fault predicate has been established—that is, that the parent has abandoned, neglected, and/or abused a child, or has determined that the parent is unable and/or unwilling in the future to provide minimally adequate care? Well, try to imagine situations in which an intimate partner has abused or neglected you and yet you decide it is not in your best interests to end the relationship, so you stay in it.

One possibility is that you are so emotionally attached to your partner that the cost of ending the relationship exceeds the gain for you from doing so. Likewise, children can attach even to parents who abuse them, and where there is an attachment courts should balance the emotional and psychological costs to the child of severing the relationship against the gains of avoiding further maltreatment and of potentially having a better relationship with another set of parents. An additional consideration in the parent-child relationship is the biological connection, which is psychologically of some importance to most people. It is precisely because of these interests of children in favor of staying with a parent despite maltreatment that a best-interests-only test for termination would not produce the willy-nilly reallocation of children that some fear.

A second situation in which one might decide to stay with an abusive or neglectful partner is when you have good reason to think he or she will change. Perhaps a mental illness or drinking problem was the source of the problem, and your partner has found and accepted the right medication or rehabilitation program. Likewise, with a fault predicate for TPR that does not itself include exhaustion of rehabilitative efforts, the possibility of reform should be an aspect of the best-interests analysis. As you saw with the Virginia statute above, there are bases for TPR based on conduct toward another child, such as a severe assault, but a parent might not pose a danger to a later child despite that past conduct, either because the nature of the relationship is different or because the parent has changed. See, e.g., State *ex rel.* Dep't of Hum. Servs. v. A.C., 213 P.3d 844 (Or. Ct. App. 2009) (denying termination petition because abuse of other children stemmed from methamphetamine use that mother had since discontinued).

A third situation in which you might stay with a partner who mistreats you is one in which you do not see any prospect for a better relationship with someone else and you think it better to be with a lousy partner than to be alone. Cf. Florence & The Machine, *Kiss with a Fist, on* Lungs (Island Records 2009). Likewise, a common consideration in the best-interests prong of a TPR proceeding is the likelihood of adoption. When there is little chance of adoption, it might be better for the child to remain in the legal parent-child relationship even if there can be little or no contact with the parent. See Ellis, Malm & Bishop, The Timing of Termination of Parental Rights: A Balancing Act for Children's Best Interests, a Child Trends Research Brief, http://www.childtrends.org (reporting on survey of judges as to their attitude toward TPR when no adoptive placement is yet available for a child, in which some judges expressed concern about creating "legal orphans").

B. CONSEQUENCES OF TERMINATION

The effect of a TPR is to make an adult no longer a legal parent of a child and vice versa, just as a divorce makes one no longer a spouse to the other person. And as with termination of the marital relationship, termination of the parent-child relationship generally removes most of the rights and responsibilities that attend the relationship.

1. Post-TPR Contact

After TPR, a parent generally cannot seek court-ordered custody of or visitation with a child, cannot demand information concerning the child, and has no say in how a child is raised. The termination order might direct that the adult is to have no contact with the child, but if it does not, the adult will ordinarily have contact, if at all, only at the discretion of the child's custodian or, when the child is older, of the child. Some state legislatures or courts have modified traditional practice to allow courts to order some post-TPR visitation with a biological parent, but courts are reluctant to do this, because it might frighten a child, hamper bonding with adoptive parents, or deter people from adopting.

2. Child Support

One significant exception with respect to both divorce and TPR is the possibility of post-termination support of a dependent person until such time as that person has another source of support. In some states, TPR ends the child support obligation. See, e.g., Tenn. Code Ann. §36-1-113(l)(1) ("An order terminating parental rights shall have the effect of severing forever all legal rights and obligations of the parent or guardian of the child against whom the order of termination is entered and of the child who is the subject of the petition to that parent or guardian. . . . It shall terminate the responsibilities of that parent . . . for future child support or other future financial responsibilities even if the child is not ultimately adopted."). Courts in those states are therefore more reluctant to order TPR unless they anticipate an adoption by another adult who can support the child.

In other states, the support obligation continues after TPR unless and until an adoption occurs. See, e.g., Ill. Dep't of Healthcare & Fam. Servs. v. Warner, 882 N.E.2d 557

(Ill. 2008). Similarly, remarriage typically ends an alimony obligation, unless the ex-spouses executed an agreement to the contrary.

3. *Inheritance*

In all states but Louisiana, children have no right to demand an inheritance when a parent dies leaving a will that disposes of all property to others. That does not change after termination of the parent-child relationship. On the other hand, state laws do give offspring a share of a legal parent's intestate estate—that is, any portion of the parent's estate not disposed of by will—if the parent was not married to the offspring's other parent at the time of death. In many states, this claim of children to a share of the intestate estate survives a TPR so long as the child remains unadopted. See, e.g., Tenn. Code Ann. §36-1-113(l)(2) ("a child who is the subject of the order for termination shall be entitled to inherit from a parent whose rights are terminated until the final order of adoption is entered"); Va. Code Ann. §64.1-5.1 ("an order terminating residual parental rights under §16.1-283 shall terminate the rights of the parent to take from or through the child in question but shall not otherwise affect the rights of the child, the child's kindred, or the parent's kindred to take from or through the parent or the rights of the parent's kindred to take from or through the child").

Such statutory provisions maintaining a child's inheritance prospect post-TPR and pre-adoption find no parallel in divorce law, and they seem an extension of the support obligation rather than based on the usual rationale for intestacy rules, which is that they aim to match what most decedents would have wanted. Probably most terminated parents would not have wanted to leave part of their estate to biological offspring who are no longer their legal offspring.

4. *Property Distribution*

In contrast to spouses in a divorce, children receive no share of family property upon dissolution of a family relationship. Can you construct an argument for distributing property between parent and child in a TPR proceeding? The primary rationale for equitable distribution of marital property in divorce, as you have already seen, rests on an assumption that a spouse contributes to acquisition in wealth, in part by taking care of household tasks and in part by providing emotional support and comfort. Do children contribute in a similar way to a parent's ability to earn? Is there another rationale apart from contribution that might justify a court's imposing on a terminated parent a debt to the child or an order to transfer some property to the child?

C. DUE PROCESS RIGHTS OF PARENTS IN TERMINATION PROCEEDINGS

As noted in the *Toms* case above, there is no precedent establishing a constitutional right of parents to a particular *substantive* showing by the state before a court can terminate parental rights. In other words, there are currently no established constitutional constraints on what any state may make a basis for finding a parent unfit and taking his or her child away for good. We did see in the Supreme Court's *Lehr v. Robertson* decision dictum to the effect that it would violate a *fit* biological parent's substantive due process rights to deny or sever legal parenthood solely on the basis that this would be in the child's best interests. But the Court has never actually held that that is the case, nor has it presumed to define what "fit" means.

On the other hand, there is a substantial body of federal constitutional law on the *procedural* rights of parents in connection with termination proceedings, including their rights to counsel and to a relatively high evidentiary standard. The Supreme Court's decisions regarding these rights are of interest to us not so much because of their holdings, which are unremarkable, but principally because they contain deep theoretical assumptions that are typically unstated in the reasoning of lower courts and in public discussion of family issues. Ask yourself whether the Justices would convince anyone who does not share their assumptions that their position is correct. And ask yourself whether the reasoning from assumptions to conclusions is sound.

1. *Right to Counsel*

Lassiter v. Department of Social Services of Durham County

452 U.S. 18 (1981)

Justice Stewart.

In the late spring of 1975, after hearing evidence that the petitioner, Abby Gail Lassiter, had not provided her infant son William with proper medical care, the District Court of Durham County, N.C., adjudicated him a neglected child and transferred him to the custody of the Durham County Department of Social Services, the respondent here. A year later, Ms. Lassiter was charged with first-degree murder, was convicted of second-degree murder, and began a sentence of 25 to 40 years of imprisonment. In 1978 the Department petitioned the court to terminate Ms. Lassiter's parental rights because, the Department alleged, she "has not had any contact with the child since December of 1975" and "has willfully left the child in foster care for more than two consecutive years without showing that substantial progress has been made in correcting the conditions which led to the removal of the child, or without showing a positive response to the diligent efforts of the Department of Social Services to strengthen her relationship to the child, or to make and follow through with constructive planning for the future of the child."

Ms. Lassiter was served with the petition and with notice that a hearing on it would be held. Although her mother had retained counsel for her in connection with an effort to invalidate the murder conviction, Ms. Lassiter never mentioned the forthcoming hearing to him (or, for that matter, to any other person except, she said, to "someone" in the prison). At the behest of the Department of Social Services' attorney, she was brought from prison to the hearing. . . . The hearing opened, apparently at the judge's instance, with a discussion of whether Ms. Lassiter should have more time in which to find legal assistance. Since the court concluded that she "has had ample opportunity to seek and obtain counsel prior to the hearing of this matter, and [that] her failure to do so is without just cause," the court did not postpone the proceedings. Ms. Lassiter did not aver that she was indigent, and the court did not appoint counsel for her.

A social worker from the respondent Department was the first witness. She testified that in 1975 the Department "received a complaint from Duke Pediatrics that William had not been followed in the pediatric clinic for medical problems and that they were having difficulty in locating Ms. Lassiter. . . ." She said that in May 1975 a social worker had taken William to the hospital, where doctors asked that he stay "because of breathing difficulties [and] malnutrition and [because] there was a great deal of scarring that indicated that he had a severe infection that had gone untreated." The witness further testified that, except for one "prearranged" visit and a chance meeting on the street, Ms. Lassiter had not seen William after he had come into the State's custody, and that neither Ms. Lassiter nor her mother had "made any contact with the Department of Social Services regarding that child." When asked whether William should be placed in his grandmother's custody, the social worker said he should not, since the grandmother "has indicated to me on a number of occasions that she was not able to take responsibility for the child" and since "I have checked with people in the community and from Ms. Lassiter's church who also feel that this additional responsibility would be more than she can handle." The social worker added that William "has not seen his grandmother since the chance meeting in July of '76 and that was the only time."

After the direct examination of the social worker, the judge said:

> "I notice we made extensive findings in June of '75 that you were served with papers and called the social services and told them you weren't coming; and the serious lack of medical treatment. And . . . the grandmother . . . filed a complaint on the 8th day of May, 1975, alleging that the daughter often left the children, Candina, Felicia and William L. with her for days without providing money or food while she was gone."

Ms. Lassiter conducted a cross-examination of the social worker, who firmly reiterated her earlier testimony. The judge explained several times, with varying degrees of clarity, that Ms. Lassiter should only ask questions at this stage; many of her questions were disallowed because they were not really questions, but arguments.

Ms. Lassiter herself then testified, under the judge's questioning, that she had properly cared for William. Under cross-examination, she said that she had seen William more than five or six times after he had been taken from her custody and that, if William could not be with her, she wanted him to be with her mother since "He knows us. Children know they family. . . . They know they people, they know they family and that child knows us anywhere. . . . I got four more other children. Three girls and a boy and they know they little brother when they see him." Ms. Lassiter's mother was then called as a witness. She denied, under the questioning of the judge, that she had filed the complaint against Ms. Lassiter, and on cross-examination she denied both having failed to visit William when he was in the State's custody and having said that she could not care for him.

The court found that Ms. Lassiter "has not contacted the Department of Social Services about her child since December, 1975, has not expressed any concern for his care and welfare, and has made no efforts to plan for his future." Because Ms. Lassiter thus had "wilfully failed to maintain concern or responsibility for the welfare of the minor," and because it was "in the best interests of the minor," the court terminated Ms. Lassiter's status as William's parent. On appeal, Ms. Lassiter argued only that, because she was indigent, the Due Process Clause of the Fourteenth Amendment entitled her to the assistance of counsel, and that the trial court . . . erred in not requiring the State to provide counsel for her. . . .

A

[A]n indigent's right to appointed counsel . . . has been recognized . . . only where the litigant may lose his physical liberty if he loses the litigation. . . . [T]hus *Argersinger v. Hamlin* established that counsel must be provided before any indigent may be sentenced to prison, even where the crime is petty and the prison term brief. . . . [And] *In re Gault* [held] that "the Due Process Clause of the Fourteenth Amendment requires that in [juvenile delinquency proceedings that] may result in commitment to an institution . . . ," the juvenile has a right to appointed counsel even though proceedings may be styled "civil" and not "criminal." . . .

Significantly, as a litigant's interest in personal liberty diminishes, so does his right to appointed counsel. . . . In *Morrissey v. Brewer*, . . . the Court had said: "[Probation] revocation deprives an individual, not of the absolute liberty to which every citizen is entitled, but only of the conditional liberty properly dependent on observance of special parole restrictions." Relying on that discussion, the Court in *Scarpelli* declined to hold that indigent probationers have, per se, a right to counsel at revocation hearings, and instead left the decision whether counsel should be appointed to be made on a case-by-case basis. Finally, the Court has refused to extend the right to appointed counsel to include prosecutions which, though criminal, do not result in the defendant's loss of personal liberty . . . [stating] "that actual imprisonment is a penalty different in kind from fines or the mere threat of imprisonment." . . .

B

The case of *Mathews v. Eldridge* propounds three elements to be evaluated in deciding what due process requires, viz., the private interests at stake, the government's interest, and the risk that the procedures used will lead to erroneous decisions. We must balance these elements against each other, and then set their net weight in the scales against the presumption that there is a right to appointed counsel only where the indigent, if he is unsuccessful, may lose his personal freedom.

This Court's decisions have by now made plain beyond the need for multiple citation that a parent's desire for and right to "the companionship, care, custody and management of his or her children" is an important interest that "undeniably warrants deference and, absent a powerful countervailing interest, protection." *Stanley v. Illinois.* Here the State has sought not simply to infringe upon that interest but to end it. If the State prevails, it will have worked a unique kind of deprivation. A parent's interest in the accuracy and injustice of the decision to terminate his or her parental status is, therefore, a commanding one.

Since the State has an urgent interest in the welfare of the child, it shares the parent's interest in an accurate and just decision. For this reason, the State may share the indigent parent's interest in the availability of appointed counsel. If, as our adversary system presupposes, accurate and just results are most likely to be obtained through the equal contest of opposed interests, the State's interest in the child's welfare may perhaps best be served by a hearing in which both the parent and the State acting for the child are represented by counsel, without whom the contest of interests may become unwholesomely unequal. . . .

The State's interests, however, clearly diverge from the parent's insofar as the State wishes the termination decision to be made as economically as possible and thus wants to avoid both the expense of appointed counsel and the cost of the lengthened proceedings his presence may cause. But though the State's pecuniary interest is legitimate, it is hardly significant enough to overcome private interests as important as those here, particularly in light of the concession in the respondent's brief that the "potential costs of appointed counsel in termination proceedings . . . is [sic] admittedly de minimis compared to the costs in all criminal actions."

Finally, consideration must be given to the risk that a parent will be erroneously deprived of his or her child because the parent is not represented by counsel. . . . The respondent argues that the subject of a termination hearing—the parent's relationship with her child—far from being abstruse, technical, or unfamiliar, is one as to which the parent must be uniquely well informed and to which the parent must have given prolonged thought. The respondent also contends that a termination hearing is not likely to produce difficult points of evidentiary law, or even of substantive law, since the evidentiary problems peculiar to criminal trials are not present and since the standards for termination are not complicated. In fact, the respondent reports, the North Carolina Departments of Social Services are themselves sometimes represented at termination hearings by social workers instead of by lawyers.[5]

Yet the ultimate issues with which a termination hearing deals are not always simple, however commonplace they may be. Expert medical and psychiatric testimony, which few parents are equipped to understand and fewer still to confute, is sometimes presented. The parents are likely to be people with little education, who have had uncommon difficulty in dealing with life, and who are, at the hearing, thrust into a distressing and disorienting situation. . . . Thus, courts have generally held that the State must appoint counsel for indigent parents at termination proceedings. . . .[6]

C

. . . To summarize the above discussion of the *Eldridge* factors: the parent's interest is an extremely important one (and may be supplemented by the dangers of criminal liability inherent in some termination proceedings); the State shares with the parent an interest in a correct decision, has a relatively weak pecuniary interest, and, in some but not all cases, has a possibly stronger interest in informal procedures; and the complexity of the proceeding and the incapacity of the uncounseled parent could be, but would not always be, great enough to make the risk of an erroneous deprivation of the parent's rights insupportably high.

If, in a given case, the parent's interests were at their strongest, the State's interests were at their weakest, and the risks of error were at their peak, it could not be said that the *Eldridge* factors did not overcome the presumption against the right to appointed counsel, and that due process did not therefore require the appointment of counsel. But since the *Eldridge* factors will not always be so distributed, and since "due process is not so rigid as to require that the significant interests in informality, flexibility and economy must always be sacrificed," neither can we say that the Constitution requires the appointment of counsel in every parental termination proceeding. We therefore adopt the standard found appropriate in *Gagnon v. Scarpelli*, and leave the decision whether due process calls for the appointment of counsel for indigent parents in termination proceedings to be answered in the first instance by the trial court, subject, of course, to appellate review.

5. [T]he Columbia Journal of Law and Social Problems (1968), . . . questioned the New York Family Court judges who preside over parental termination hearings and found that 72.2% of them agreed that when a parent is unrepresented, it becomes more difficult to conduct a fair hearing (11.1% of the judges disagreed); 66.7% thought it became difficult to develop the facts (22.2% disagreed).

6. A number of courts have held that indigent parents have a right to appointed counsel in child dependency or neglect hearings as well. E.g., [decisions from Fifth Circuit, Ninth Circuit, and Western District of Tennessee].

III

Here, as in *Scarpelli*, "[i]t is neither possible nor prudent to attempt to formulate a precise and detailed set of guidelines to be followed in determining when the providing of counsel is necessary to meet the applicable due process requirements," since . . . "[t]he facts and circumstances . . . are susceptible of almost infinite variation. . . ." Nevertheless, because child custody litigation must be concluded as rapidly as is consistent with fairness,[7] we decide today whether the trial judge denied Ms. Lassiter due process of law when he did not appoint counsel for her.

The respondent represents that the petition to terminate Ms. Lassiter's parental rights contained no allegations of neglect or abuse upon which criminal charges could be based, and hence Ms. Lassiter could not well have argued that she required counsel for that reason. The Department of Social Services was represented at the hearing by counsel, but no expert witnesses testified and the case presented no specially troublesome points of law, either procedural or substantive. While hearsay evidence was no doubt admitted, and while Ms. Lassiter no doubt left incomplete her defense that the Department had not adequately assisted her in rekindling her interest in her son, the weight of the evidence that she had few sparks of such interest was sufficiently great that the presence of counsel for Ms. Lassiter could not have made a determinative difference. True, a lawyer might have done more with the argument that William should live with Ms. Lassiter's mother—but that argument was quite explicitly made by both Lassiters, and the evidence that the elder Ms. Lassiter had said she could not handle another child, that the social worker's investigation had led to a similar conclusion, and that the grandmother had displayed scant interest in the child once he had been removed from her daughter's custody was, though controverted, sufficiently substantial that the absence of counsel's guidance on this point did not render the proceedings fundamentally unfair.

Finally, a court deciding whether due process requires the appointment of counsel need not ignore a parent's plain demonstration that she is not interested in attending a hearing. Here, the trial court had previously found that Ms. Lassiter had expressly declined to appear at the 1975 child custody hearing, Ms. Lassiter had not even bothered to speak to her retained lawyer after being notified of the termination hearing, and the court specifically found that Ms. Lassiter's failure to make an effort to contest the termination proceeding was without cause. In view of all these circumstances, we hold that the trial court did not err in failing to appoint counsel for Ms. Lassiter.

IV

In its Fourteenth Amendment, our Constitution imposes on States the standards necessary to ensure that judicial proceedings are fundamentally fair. A wise public policy, however, may require that higher standards be adopted than those minimally tolerable under the Constitution. Informed opinion has clearly come to hold that an indigent parent is entitled to the assistance of appointed counsel not only in parental termination proceedings, but also in dependency and neglect proceedings as well. . . . The Court's opinion today in no way implies that the standards increasingly urged by informed public opinion and now widely followed by the States are other than enlightened and wise.

7. According to the respondent's brief, William Lassiter is now living "in a pre-adoptive home with foster parents committed to formal adoption to become his legal parents." He cannot be legally adopted, nor can his status otherwise be finally clarified, until this litigation ends.

Justice BLACKMUN, with whom JJ. BRENNAN and MARSHALL join, dissenting.

The Court . . . revives an ad hoc approach thoroughly discredited nearly 20 years ago in Gideon v. Wainwright. . . . At stake here is "the interest of a parent in the companionship, care, custody, and management of his or her children." This interest occupies a unique place in our legal culture, given the centrality of family life as the focus for personal meaning and responsibility. "[F]ar more precious . . . than property rights," parental rights have been deemed to be among those "essential to the orderly pursuit of happiness by free men," and to be more significant and priceless than "'liberties which derive merely from shifting economic arrangements.'" Accordingly, although the Constitution is verbally silent on the specific subject of families, freedom of personal choice in matters of family life long has been viewed as a fundamental liberty interest worthy of protection under the Fourteenth Amendment. Within the general ambit of family integrity, the Court has accorded a high degree of constitutional respect to a natural parent's interest both in controlling the details of the child's upbringing, and in retaining the custody and companionship of the child.

In this case, the State's aim is not simply to influence the parent-child relationship but to extinguish it. A termination of parental rights is both total and irrevocable. Unlike other custody proceedings, it leaves the parent with no right to visit or communicate with the child, to participate in, or even to know about, any important decision affecting the child's religious, educational, emotional, or physical development. It is hardly surprising that this forced dissolution of the parent-child relationship has been recognized as a punitive sanction by courts,[4] Congress,[5] and commentators. The Court candidly notes . . . that termination of parental rights by the State is a "unique kind of deprivation." . . .

Surely there can be few losses more grievous than the abrogation of parental rights. . . .

The method chosen by North Carolina to extinguish parental rights resembles in many respects a criminal prosecution. Unlike the probation revocation procedure reviewed in *Gagnon v. Scarpelli,* on which the Court so heavily relies, the termination procedure is distinctly formal and adversarial. The State initiates the proceeding by filing a petition in district court,[9] and serving a summons on the parent. A state judge presides over the adjudicatory hearing that follows, and the hearing is conducted pursuant to the formal rules of evidence and procedure. In general, hearsay is inadmissible and records must be authenticated.

In addition, the proceeding has an obvious accusatory and punitive focus. In moving to terminate a parent's rights, the State has concluded that it no longer will try to preserve the family unit, but instead will marshal an array of public resources to establish that the parent-child separation must be made permanent.[10] The State has legal representation through the county attorney. This lawyer has access to public records concerning the family and to professional social workers who are empowered to investigate the family situation and to testify against the parent. The State's legal representative may also call

4. E.g., [decisions of federal courts in the Fifth Circuit and Nevada and state courts in West Virginia, Maryland, and Louisiana].

5. See H.R. Rep. No. 95-1386, p. 22 (1978) ("removal of a child from the parents is a penalty as great, if not greater, than a criminal penalty. . ."). . . .

9. A petition for termination may also be filed by a private party, such as a judicially appointed guardian, a foster parent, or the other natural parent. Because the State in those circumstances may not be performing the same adversarial and accusatory role, an application of the three *Eldridge* factors might yield a different result with respect to the right to counsel.

10. . . . The possibility of providing counsel for the child at the termination proceeding has not been raised by the parties. That prospect requires consideration of interests different from those presented here, and again might yield a different result with respect to the right to counsel.

upon experts in family relations, psychology, and medicine to bolster the State's case. And, of course, the State's counsel himself is an expert in the legal standards and techniques employed at the termination proceeding, including the methods of cross-examination.

. . . The provision of counsel for the parent would not alter the character of the proceeding, which is already adversarial, formal, and quintessentially legal. It, however, would diminish the prospect of an erroneous termination, a prospect that is inherently substantial, given the gross disparity in power and resources between the State and the uncounseled indigent parent. The prospect of error is enhanced in light of the legal standard against which the defendant parent is judged. As demonstrated here, that standard commonly adds another dimension to the complexity of the termination proceeding. Rather than focusing on the facts of isolated acts or omissions, the State's charges typically address the nature and quality of complicated ongoing relationships among parent, child, other relatives, and even unrelated parties.

In the case at bar, the State's petition accused petitioner of two of the several grounds authorizing termination of parental rights under North Carolina law:

> "That [petitioner] has without cause, failed to establish or maintain concern or responsibility as to the child's welfare. . . .
>
> "That [petitioner] has willfully left the child in foster care for more than two consecutive years without showing that substantial progress has been made in correcting the conditions which led to the removal of the child [for neglect], or without showing a positive response to the diligent efforts of the Department of Social Services to strengthen her relationship to the child, or to make and follow through with constructive planning for the future of the child."

The legal issues posed by the State's petition are neither simple nor easily defined. The standard is imprecise and open to the subjective values of the judge.[13]

A parent seeking to prevail against the State must be prepared to adduce evidence about his or her personal abilities and lack of fault, as well as proof of progress and foresight as a parent that the State would deem adequate and improved over the situation underlying a previous adverse judgment of child neglect. The parent cannot possibly succeed without being able to identify material issues, develop defenses, gather and present sufficient supporting nonhearsay evidence, and conduct cross-examination of adverse witnesses. . . .

Faced with a formal accusatory adjudication, with an adversary—the State—that commands great investigative and prosecutorial resources, with standards that involve ill-defined notions of fault and adequate parenting, and with the inevitable tendency of a court to apply subjective values or to defer to the State's "expertise," the defendant parent plainly is outstripped if he or she is without the assistance of "'the guiding hand of counsel.'" When the parent is indigent, lacking in education, and easily intimidated by figures of authority,[14] the imbalance may well become insuperable.

13. Under North Carolina law, there is a further stage to the termination inquiry. Should the trial court determine that one or more of the conditions authorizing termination has been established, it then must consider whether the best interests of the child require maintenance of the parent-child relationship. This Court more than once has adverted to the fact that the "best interests of the child" standard offers little guidance to judges, and may effectively encourage them to rely on their own personal values. Several courts, perceiving similar risks, have gone so far as to invalidate parental termination statutes on vagueness grounds.

14. See . . . *Davis v. Page* (S.D. Fla. 1977) (uncounseled parent, ignorant of governing substantive law, "was little more than a spectator in the adjudicatory [dependency] proceeding," and "sat silently through most of the hearing . . . fearful of antagonizing the social workers").

The risk of error thus is severalfold. The parent who actually has achieved the improvement or quality of parenting the State would require may be unable to establish this fact. The parent who has failed in these regards may be unable to demonstrate cause, absence of willfulness, or lack of agency diligence as justification. And errors of fact or law in the State's case may go unchallenged and uncorrected.[15] . . . By intimidation, inarticulateness, or confusion, a parent can lose forever all contact and involvement with his or her offspring. . . .

[T]he case-by-case approach advanced by the Court itself entails serious dangers for the interests at stake and the general administration of justice. The Court assumes that a review of the record will establish whether a defendant, proceeding without counsel, has suffered an unfair disadvantage. But in the ordinary case, this simply is not so. The pleadings and transcript of an uncounseled termination proceeding at most will show the obvious blunders and omissions of the defendant parent. Determining the difference legal representation would have made becomes possible only through imagination, investigation, and legal research focused on the particular case. Even if the reviewing court can embark on such an enterprise in each case, it might be hard pressed to discern the significance of failures to challenge the State's evidence or to develop a satisfactory defense. Such failures, however, often cut to the essence of the fairness of the trial, and a court's inability to compensate for them effectively eviscerates the presumption of innocence. Because a parent acting pro se is even more likely to be unaware of controlling legal standards and practices, and unskilled in garnering relevant facts, it is difficult, if not impossible, to conclude that the typical case has been adequately presented.[19]

. . . The problem of inadequate representation is painfully apparent in the present case. . . . In December 1977, she was visited in prison by a Durham County social worker who advised her that the Department planned to terminate her parental rights with respect to William. Petitioner immediately expressed strong opposition to that plan and indicated a desire to place the child with his grandmother. After receiving a summons, a copy of the State's termination petition, and notice that a termination hearing would be held in August 1978, petitioner informed her prison guards about the legal proceeding. They took no steps to assist her in obtaining legal representation, nor was she informed that she had a right to counsel. Under these circumstances, it scarcely would be appropriate, or fair, to find that petitioner had knowingly and intelligently waived a right to counsel.

At the termination hearing, the State's sole witness was the county worker who had met petitioner on the one occasion at the prison. This worker had been assigned to William's case in August 1977, yet much of her testimony concerned events prior to that date; she represented these events as contained in the agency record. Petitioner failed to uncover this weakness in the worker's testimony. That is hardly surprising, for there is no indication that an agency record was introduced into evidence or was present in court, or that petitioner or the grandmother ever had an opportunity to review any such record. The social worker also testified about her conversations with members of the community.

15. See Parent Representation Study (parents appearing in Kings County, N.Y., Family Court, charged with neglect and represented by counsel, had higher rate of dismissed petitions, 25% to 7.9%, and lower rate of neglect adjudications, 62.5% to 79.5%, than similarly charged parents appearing without counsel); Brief for Respondent (study of state-initiated termination actions in 73 North Carolina counties; parent prevailed in 5.5% of proceedings where represented by counsel, and in 0.15% of proceedings where unrepresented).

19. Of course, the case-by-case approach . . . places an even heavier burden on the trial court, which will be required to determine in advance what difference legal representation might make. A trial judge will be obligated to examine the State's documentary and testimonial evidence well before the hearing so as to reach an informed decision about the need for counsel in time to allow adequate preparation of the parent's case.

In this hearsay testimony, the witness reported the opinion of others that the grandmother could not handle the additional responsibility of caring for the fifth child. There is no indication that these community members were unavailable to testify, and the County Attorney did not justify the admission of the hearsay. Petitioner made no objection to its admission.

The court gave petitioner an opportunity to cross-examine the social worker, but she apparently did not understand that cross-examination required questioning rather than declarative statements. . . . [T]he judge became noticeably impatient with petitioner

"*THE COURT:* All right. Do you want to ask her any questions?

"*[PETITIONER]:* About what? About what she—

"*THE COURT:* About this child.

"*[PETITIONER]:* Oh, yes.

"*THE COURT:* All right. Go ahead.

"*[PETITIONER]:* The only thing I know is that when you say—

"*THE COURT:* I don't want you to testify.

"*[PETITIONER]:* Okay.

"*THE COURT:* I want to know whether you want to cross-examine her or ask any questions.

"*[PETITIONER]:* Yes, I want to. Well, you know, the only thing I know about is my part that I know about it. I know—

"*THE COURT:* I am not talking about what you know. I want to know if you want to ask her any questions or not.

"*[PETITIONER]:* About that?

"*THE COURT:* Yes. Do you understand the nature of this proceeding?

"*[PETITIONER]:* Yes.

"*THE COURT:* And that is to terminate any rights you have to the child and place it for adoption, if necessary.

"*[PETITIONER]:* Yes, I know.

"*THE COURT:* Are there any questions you want to ask her about what she has testified to?

"*[PETITIONER]:* Yes.

"*THE COURT:* All right. Go ahead.

"*[PETITIONER]:* I want to know why you think you are going to turn my child over to a foster home? He knows my mother and he knows all of us. He knows her and he knows all of us.

"*THE COURT:* Who is he?

"*[PETITIONER]:* My son, William.

"*[SOCIAL WORKER]:* Ms. Lassiter, your son has been in foster care since May of 1975 and since that time—

"*[PETITIONER]:* Yeah, yeah and I didn't know anything about it either."

Petitioner then took the stand, and testified that she wanted William to live with his grandmother and his siblings. The judge questioned her for a brief period, and expressed open disbelief at one of her answers:

"*[THE COURT]:* Did you know that your mother filed a complaint on the 8th day of May, 1975 . . . ?

"*A:* No,'cause she said she didn't file no complaint.
"*[THE COURT]:* That was some ghost who came up here and filed it I suppose."

The judge concluded his questioning by saying to the County Attorney: "All right, Mr. Odom, see what you can do."

The final witness was the grandmother. Both the judge and the County Attorney questioned her. She denied having expressed unwillingness to take William into her home, and vehemently contradicted the social worker's statement that she had complained to the Department about her daughter's neglect of the child. Petitioner was not told that she could question her mother, and did not do so. The County Attorney made a closing argument, and the judge then asked petitioner if she had any final remarks. She responded: "Yes. I don't think it's right." . . .

An experienced attorney might have translated petitioner's reaction and emotion into several substantive legal arguments. The State charged petitioner with failing to arrange a "constructive plan" for her child's future or to demonstrate a "positive response" to the Department's intervention. A defense would have been that petitioner had arranged for the child to be cared for properly by his grandmother, and evidence might have been adduced to demonstrate the adequacy of the grandmother's care of the other children. The Department's own "diligence" in promoting the family's integrity was never put in issue during the hearing, yet it is surely significant in light of petitioner's incarceration and lack of access to her child. . . .

Petitioner plainly has not led the life of the exemplary citizen or model parent. It may well be that if she were accorded competent legal representation, the ultimate result in this particular case would be the same. But the issue before the Court is not petitioner's character; it is whether she was given a meaningful opportunity to be heard when the State moved to terminate absolutely her parental rights. . . . I find virtually incredible the Court's conclusion today that her termination proceeding was fundamentally fair. . . .

Finally, I deem it not a little ironic that the Court on this very day grants, on due process grounds, an indigent putative father's claim for state-paid blood grouping tests in the interest of according him a meaningful opportunity to disprove his paternity, *Little v. Streater*, but in the present case rejects, on due process grounds, an indigent mother's claim for state-paid legal assistance when the State seeks to take her own child away from her in a termination proceeding. . . . If the Court in *Boddie v. Connecticut* (1971), was able to perceive as constitutionally necessary the access to judicial resources required to dissolve a marriage at the behest of private parties, surely it should perceive as similarly necessary the requested access to legal resources when the State itself seeks to dissolve the intimate and personal family bonds between parent and child. . . .

Notice that in this decision, a majority of the Court views the greatest constitutional evil (and perhaps only substantial due process concern) to be state deprivation of physical liberty. If you were given a choice between losing your children forever or spending a certain amount of time in jail, how long would that time have to be before you would agree to give up your children?

Many states have opted since *Lassiter* to make appointment of counsel for indigent parents automatic once a petition for termination has been filed. They likely concluded that it would cost more to litigate the right to counsel than to pay for one to handle the case, especially given that compensation for the appointed counsel is in most states quite low. In states where appointment is discretionary, how should courts go about deciding whether to exercise their discretion to appoint counsel for the parents? Imagine drafting a form for parents to fill out, an application for appointed counsel, based on the Court's analysis in *Lassiter*. What questions would you include?

The majority contends that everyone involved in termination proceedings—parents, children, and the state—share an interest in the parents' case being adequately presented. Yet when it weighs the interests in favor of appointing counsel against the "presumption" against a right to appointed counsel established by precedent, the majority considers only the parents' interests. Might this be a case where giving greater consideration to children's interests would have produced a better result *for the parents*? Or would children's interests be wholly protected by appointment of counsel for the child? Does Justice Burger disagree with the premise that children's interests are aligned with parents' interests in connection with appointing counsel for parents?

The dissenters note other Supreme Court decisions creating constitutional rights for indigent persons to waiver of normal litigation-related expenses, such as fees for blood tests to disprove fatherhood in a paternity action (*Little v. Streater*) and court fees for divorce actions (*Boddie v. Connecticut*). Are those rights distinguishable from the right claimed here other than on the basis of the degree of cost the right would entail for the state?

2. *Right to Minimum Standard of Proof*

Santosky v. Kramer

455 U.S. 745 (1982)

Justice BLACKMUN.

Under New York law, the State may terminate, over parental objection, the rights of parents in their natural child upon a finding that the child is "permanently neglected." The New York Family Court Act requires that only a "fair preponderance of the evidence" support that finding. Thus, in New York, the factual certainty required to extinguish the parent-child relationship is no greater than that necessary to award money damages in an ordinary civil action. Today we hold that the Due Process Clause of the Fourteenth Amendment demands more than this. Before a State may sever completely and irrevocably the rights of parents in their natural child, due process requires that the State support its allegations by at least clear and convincing evidence.

I

. . . The State bifurcates its permanent neglect proceeding into "fact-finding" and "dispositional" hearings. At the factfinding stage, the State must prove that the child has been "permanently neglected". . . . The Family Court judge then determines at a subsequent dispositional hearing what placement would serve the child's best interests.

At the factfinding hearing, the State must establish, among other things, that for more than a year after the child entered state custody, the agency "made diligent efforts to encourage and strengthen the parental relationship." The State must further prove that during that same period, the child's natural parents failed "substantially and continuously or repeatedly to maintain contact with or plan for the future of the child although physically and financially able to do so." Should the State support its allegations by "a fair preponderance of the evidence," the child may be declared permanently neglected. That declaration empowers the Family Court judge to terminate permanently the natural parents' rights in the child. Termination denies the natural parents physical custody, as well as the rights ever to visit, communicate with, or regain custody of the child. . . .

Petitioners John Santosky II and Annie Santosky are the natural parents of Tina and John III. In November 1973, after incidents reflecting parental neglect, respondent Kramer, Commissioner of the Ulster County Department of Social Services, initiated a neglect proceeding . . . and removed Tina from her natural home. About 10 months later, he removed John III and placed him with foster parents. On the day John was taken, Annie Santosky gave birth to a third child, Jed. When Jed was only three days old, respondent transferred him to a foster home on the ground that immediate removal was necessary to avoid imminent danger to his life or health. In October 1978, respondent petitioned the Ulster County Family Court to terminate petitioners' parental rights in the three children.[5]

II

. . . The fundamental liberty interest of natural parents in the care, custody, and management of their child does not evaporate simply because they have not been model parents or have lost temporary custody of their child to the State. Even when blood relationships are strained, parents retain a vital interest in preventing the irretrievable destruction of their family life. If anything, persons faced with forced dissolution of their parental rights have a more critical need for procedural protections than do those resisting state intervention into ongoing family affairs. When the State moves to destroy weakened familial bonds, it must provide the parents with fundamentally fair procedures.[7]

In *Lassiter*, the Court and three dissenters agreed that the nature of the process due in parental rights termination proceedings turns on a balancing of the "three distinct factors": the private interests affected by the proceeding; the risk of error created by the State's chosen procedure; and the countervailing governmental interest supporting use of the challenged procedure. . . . In *Addington v. Texas* (1979), the Court, by a unanimous vote of the participating Justices, declared: "The function of a standard of proof, . . . is to 'instruct the factfinder concerning the degree of confidence our society thinks he should have in the correctness of factual conclusions for a particular type of adjudication.'" [I]n any given proceeding, the minimum standard of proof tolerated by the due process requirement reflects not only the weight of the private and public interests affected, but also a societal judgment about how the risk of error should be distributed between the litigants.

Thus, while private parties may be interested intensely in a civil dispute over money damages, application of a "fair preponderance of the evidence" standard indicates both

5. Since respondent Kramer took custody of Tina, John III, and Jed, the Santoskys have had two other children, James and Jeremy. The State has taken no action to remove these younger children. At oral argument, counsel for respondents replied affirmatively when asked whether he was asserting that petitioners were "unfit to handle the three older ones but not unfit to handle the two younger ones."

7. We therefore reject respondent Kramer's claim that a parental rights termination proceeding does not interfere with a fundamental liberty interest. The fact that important liberty interests of the child and its foster parents may also be affected by a permanent neglect proceeding does not justify denying the natural parents constitutionally adequate procedures. . . .

society's "minimal concern with the outcome," and a conclusion that the litigants should "share the risk of error in roughly equal fashion." When the State brings a criminal action to deny a defendant liberty or life, however, "the interests of the defendant are of such magnitude that historically and without any explicit constitutional requirement they have been protected by standards of proof designed to exclude as nearly as possible the likelihood of an erroneous judgment." The stringency of the "beyond a reasonable doubt" standard bespeaks the "weight and gravity" of the private interest affected, society's interest in avoiding erroneous convictions, and a judgment that those interests together require that "society impos[e] almost the entire risk of error upon itself."

This Court has mandated an intermediate standard of proof—"clear and convincing evidence"—when the individual interests at stake in a state proceeding are both "particularly important" and "more substantial than mere loss of money." Notwithstanding "the state's 'civil labels and good intentions,'" the Court has deemed this level of certainty necessary to preserve fundamental fairness in a variety of government-initiated proceedings that threaten the individual involved with "a significant deprivation of liberty" or "stigma." See, e.g., *Addington v. Texas* (civil commitment); *Woodby v. INS* (deportation); *Chaunt v. United States* (1960) (denaturalization). . . . Yet juvenile delinquency adjudications, civil commitment, deportation, and denaturalization, at least to a degree, are all reversible official actions. Once affirmed on appeal, a New York decision terminating parental rights is final and irrevocable. Few forms of state action are both so severe and so irreversible.

Thus, the first *Eldridge* factor—the private interest affected—weighs heavily against use of the preponderance standard at a state-initiated permanent neglect proceeding. We do not deny that the child and his foster parents are also deeply interested in the outcome of that contest. But at the factfinding stage of the New York proceeding, the focus emphatically is not on them. The factfinding does not purport—and is not intended—to balance the child's interest in a normal family home against the parents' interest in raising the child. Nor does it purport to determine whether the natural parents or the foster parents would provide the better home. Rather, the factfinding hearing pits the State directly against the parents. The State alleges that the natural parents are at fault. The questions disputed and decided are what the State did—"made diligent efforts,"—and what the natural parents did not do—"maintain contact with or plan for the future of the child." . . . Victory by the State not only makes termination of parental rights possible; it entails a judicial determination that the parents are unfit to raise their own children.[10]

At the factfinding, the State cannot presume that a child and his parents are adversaries. After the State has established parental unfitness at that initial proceeding, the court may assume at the dispositional stage that the interests of the child and the natural parents do diverge. See Fam. Ct. Act §631 (judge shall make his order "solely on the basis of the best interests of the child," and thus has no obligation to consider the natural parents' rights in selecting dispositional alternatives). But until the State proves parental unfitness, the child and his parents share a vital interest in preventing erroneous termination of their natural relationship.[11]

10. . . . Nor is it clear that the State constitutionally could terminate a parent's rights without showing parental unfitness. See *Quilloin v. Walcott* (1978) ("We have little doubt that the Due Process Clause would be offended '[i]f a State were to attempt to force the breakup of a natural family, over the objections of the parents and their children, without some showing of unfitness and for the sole reason that to do so was thought to be in the children's best interest.'")

11. For a child, the consequences of termination of his natural parents' rights may well be far-reaching. . . . In this case, for example, Jed Santosky was removed from his natural parents' custody when he was only three days

Thus, at the factfinding, the interests of the child and his natural parents coincide to favor use of error-reducing procedures.

However substantial the foster parents' interests may be, they are not implicated directly in the factfinding stage of a state-initiated permanent neglect proceeding against the natural parents. If authorized, the foster parents may pit their interests directly against those of the natural parents by initiating their own permanent neglect proceeding. Alternatively, the foster parents can make their case for custody at the dispositional stage of a state-initiated proceeding, where the judge already has decided the issue of permanent neglect and is focusing on the placement that would serve the child's best interests. For the foster parents, the State's failure to prove permanent neglect may prolong the delay and uncertainty until their foster child is freed for adoption. But for the natural parents, a finding of permanent neglect can cut off forever their rights in their child. Given this disparity of consequence, we have no difficulty finding that the balance of private interests strongly favors heightened procedural protections.

[W]e next must consider both the risk of erroneous deprivation of private interests resulting from use of a "fair preponderance" standard and the likelihood that a higher evidentiary standard would reduce that risk. . . . Permanent neglect proceedings employ imprecise substantive standards that leave determinations unusually open to the subjective values of the judge. In appraising the nature and quality of a complex series of encounters among the agency, the parents, and the child, the court possesses unusual discretion to underweigh probative facts that might favor the parent.[12]

Because parents subject to termination proceedings are often poor, uneducated, or members of minority groups, such proceedings are often vulnerable to judgments based on cultural or class bias.

The State's ability to assemble its case almost inevitably dwarfs the parents' ability to mount a defense. No predetermined limits restrict the sums an agency may spend in prosecuting a given termination proceeding. The State's attorney usually will be expert on the issues contested and the procedures employed at the factfinding hearing, and enjoys full access to all public records concerning the family. The State may call on experts in family relations, psychology, and medicine to bolster its case. Furthermore, the primary witnesses at the hearing will be the agency's own professional caseworkers whom the State has empowered both to investigate the family situation and to testify against the parents. Indeed, because the child is already in agency custody, the State even has the power to shape the historical events that form the basis for termination.[13]

. . . Coupled with a "fair preponderance of the evidence" standard, these factors create a significant prospect of erroneous termination. A standard of proof that by its very terms

---

old; the judge's finding of permanent neglect effectively foreclosed the possibility that Jed would ever know his natural parents.

12. For example, a New York court appraising an agency's "diligent efforts" to provide the parents with social services can excuse efforts not made on the grounds that they would have been "detrimental to the best interests of the child." In determining whether the parent "substantially and continuously or repeatedly" failed to "maintain contact with . . . the child," the judge can discount actual visits or communications on the grounds that they were insubstantial or "overtly demonstrat[ed] a lack of affectionate and concerned parenthood." When determining whether the parent planned for the child's future, the judge can reject as unrealistic plans based on overly optimistic estimates of physical or financial ability.

13. In this case, for example, the parents claim that the State sought court orders denying them the right to visit their children, which would have prevented them from maintaining the contact required by the Family Court Act. The parents further claim that the State cited their rejection of social services they found offensive or superfluous as proof of the agency's "diligent efforts" and their own "failure to plan" for the children's future. . . . Of course, the disparity between the litigants' resources will be vastly greater in States where there is no statutory right to court-appointed counsel.

demands consideration of the quantity, rather than the quality, of the evidence may misdirect the factfinder in the marginal case. . . . Raising the standard of proof would have both practical and symbolic consequences. The Court has long considered the heightened standard of proof used in criminal prosecutions to be "a prime instrument for reducing the risk of convictions resting on factual error." An elevated standard of proof in a parental rights termination proceeding would alleviate "the possible risk that a factfinder might decide to [deprive] an individual based solely on a few isolated instances of unusual conduct [or] . . . idiosyncratic behavior." "Increasing the burden of proof is one way to impress the factfinder with the importance of the decision and thereby perhaps to reduce the chances that inappropriate" terminations will be ordered.

The Appellate Division approved New York's preponderance standard on the ground that it properly "balanced rights possessed by the child . . . with those of the natural parents. . . ." The court's theory assumes that termination of the natural parents' rights invariably will benefit the child.[15] . . . Even accepting the court's assumption, we cannot agree with its conclusion that a preponderance standard fairly distributes the risk of error between parent and child. Use of that standard reflects the judgment that society is nearly neutral between erroneous termination of parental rights and erroneous failure to terminate those rights. For the child, the likely consequence of an erroneous failure to terminate is preservation of an uneasy status quo.[16] For the natural parents, however, the consequence of an erroneous termination is the unnecessary destruction of their natural family. A standard that allocates the risk of error nearly equally between those two outcomes does not reflect properly their relative severity.

Two state interests are at stake in parental rights termination proceedings—a parens patriae interest in preserving and promoting the welfare of the child and a fiscal and administrative interest in reducing the cost and burden of such proceedings. A standard of proof more strict than preponderance of the evidence is consistent with both interests. Since the State has an urgent interest in the welfare of the child, it shares the parent's interest in an accurate and just decision" at the factfinding proceeding. As parens patriae, the State's goal is to provide the child with a permanent home. Yet while there is still reason to believe that positive, nurturing parent-child relationships exist, the parens patriae interest favors preservation, not severance, of natural familial bonds. . . .[17]

The State's interest in finding the child an alternative permanent home arises only "when it is clear that the natural parent cannot or will not provide a normal family home for the child." At the factfinding, that goal is served by procedures that promote an accurate determination of whether the natural parents can and will provide a normal home. . . .

New York also demands at least clear and convincing evidence in proceedings of far less moment than parental rights termination proceedings. See, e.g., N.Y. Veh. & Traf. Law §227.1 (requiring the State to prove traffic infractions by "clear and convincing

15. This is a hazardous assumption at best. Even when a child's natural home is imperfect, permanent removal from that home will not necessarily improve his welfare. Nor does termination of parental rights necessarily ensure adoption. Even when a child eventually finds an adoptive family, he may spend years moving between state institutions and "temporary" foster placements after his ties to his natural parents have been severed.

16. When the termination proceeding occurs, the child is not living at his natural home. A child cannot be adjudicated "permanently neglected" until, "for a period of more than one year," he has been in "the care of an authorized agency." Under New York law, a judge has ample discretion to ensure that, once removed from his natural parents on grounds of neglect, a child will not return to a hostile environment. In this case, when the State's initial termination effort failed for lack of proof, the court simply issued orders . . . extending the period of the child's foster home placement.

17. Any parens patriae interest in terminating the natural parents' rights arises only at the dispositional phase, after the parents have been found unfit.

evidence") and . . . *Ross v. Food Specialties, Inc.* (N.Y. 1959) (requiring "clear, positive and convincing evidence" for contract reformation). We cannot believe that it would burden the State unduly to require that its factfinders have the same factual certainty when terminating the parent-child relationship as they must have to suspend a driver's license. . . .

Thus, at a parental rights termination proceeding, a near-equal allocation of risk between the parents and the State is constitutionally intolerable. The next question, then, is whether a "beyond a reasonable doubt" or a "clear and convincing" standard is constitutionally mandated. In *Addington,* the Court concluded that application of a reasonable-doubt standard is inappropriate in civil commitment proceedings for two reasons—because of our hesitation to apply that unique standard "too broadly or casually in noncriminal cases," and because the psychiatric evidence ordinarily adduced at commitment proceedings is rarely susceptible to proof beyond a reasonable doubt. . . . Like civil commitment hearings, termination proceedings often require the factfinder to evaluate medical and psychiatric testimony, and to decide issues difficult to prove to a level of absolute certainty, such as lack of parental motive, absence of affection between parent and child, and failure of parental foresight and progress.

The substantive standards [now] applied vary from State to State. . . . A majority of the States have concluded that a "clear and convincing evidence" standard of proof strikes a fair balance between the rights of the natural parents and the State's legitimate concerns. We hold that such a standard adequately conveys to the factfinder the level of subjective certainty about his factual conclusions necessary to satisfy due process. We further hold that determination of the precise burden equal to or greater than that standard is a matter of state law properly left to state legislatures and state courts.

J. Rehnquist, with whom Chief Justice Burger, and Justices White and O'Connor join, dissenting.

. . . By parsing the New York scheme and holding one narrow provision unconstitutional, the majority invites further federal-court intrusion into every facet of state family law. If ever there were an area in which federal courts should heed the admonition of Justice Holmes that "a page of history is worth a volume of logic," it is in the area of domestic relations. This area has been left to the States from time immemorial, and not without good reason. . . .

Adoption of the preponderance-of-the-evidence standard represents New York's good-faith effort to balance the interest of parents against the legitimate interests of the child and the State. . . . Having in this case abandoned evaluation of the overall effect of a scheme, and with it the possibility of finding that strict substantive standards or special procedures compensate for a lower burden of proof, the majority's approach will inevitably lead to the federalization of family law. Such a trend will only thwart state searches for better solutions in an area where this Court should encourage state experimentation. "It is one of the happy incidents of the federal system that a single courageous State may, if its citizens choose, serve as a laboratory; and try novel social and economic experiments without risk to the rest of the country. This Court has the power to prevent an experiment." It should not do so in the absence of a clear constitutional violation. [N]o clear constitutional violation has occurred in this case. . . .

[By its] termination procedures . . . , the State seeks not only to protect the interests of parents in rearing their own children, but also to assist and encourage parents who have lost custody of their children to reassume their rightful role. Fully understood, the New York system is a comprehensive program to aid parents such as petitioners. Only as a last resort, when "diligent efforts" to reunite the family have failed, does New York authorize the termination of parental rights. The procedures for termination of those relationships which cannot be aided and which threaten permanent injury to the child, administered by a judge who has supervised the case from the first temporary removal through the final termination, cannot be viewed as fundamentally unfair. . . .

In determining the propriety of a particular standard of proof in a given case . . . , it is not enough simply to say that we are trying to minimize the risk of error. Because errors in factfinding affect more than one interest, we try to minimize error as to those interests which we consider to be most important. . . . Because proof by a preponderance of the evidence requires that "[t]he litigants . . . share the risk of error in a roughly equal fashion," it rationally should be applied only when the interests at stake are of roughly equal societal importance. . . . On one side is the interest of parents in a continuation of the family unit and the raising of their own children. The importance of this interest cannot easily be overstated. . . .

On the other side of the termination proceeding are the often countervailing interests of the child.[13] A stable, loving homelife is essential to a child's physical, emotional, and spiritual well-being. It requires no citation of authority to assert that children who are abused in their youth generally face extraordinary problems developing into responsible, productive citizens. The same can be said of children who, though not physically or emotionally abused, are passed from one foster home to another with no constancy of love, trust, or discipline. If the Family Court makes an incorrect factual determination resulting in a failure to terminate a parent-child relationship which rightfully should be ended, the child involved must return either to an abusive home or to the often unstable world of foster care.[15] The reality of these risks is magnified by the fact that the only families faced with termination actions are those which have voluntarily surrendered custody of their child to the State, or, as in this case, those from which the child has been removed by judicial action because of threatened irreparable injury through abuse or neglect. Permanent neglect findings also occur only in families where the child has been in foster care for at least one year.

13. The majority dismisses the child's interest in the accuracy of determinations made at the factfinding hearing because . . . [o]nly "[a]fter the State has established parental unfitness," the majority reasons, may the court "assume . . . that the interests of the child and the natural parents do diverge." This reasoning misses the mark. The child has an interest in the outcome of the factfinding hearing independent of that of the parent. To be sure, "the child and his parents share a vital interest in preventing erroneous termination of their natural relationship." But the child's interest in a continuation of the family unit exists only to the extent that such a continuation would not be harmful to him. An error in the factfinding hearing that results in a failure to terminate a parent-child relationship which rightfully should be terminated may well detrimentally affect the child. . . .

New York's adoption of the preponderance-of-the-evidence standard reflects its conclusion that the undesirable consequence of an erroneous finding of parental unfitness—the unwarranted termination of the family relationship—is roughly equal to the undesirable consequence of an erroneous finding of parental fitness—the risk of permanent injury to the child either by return of the child to an abusive home or by the child's continued lack of a permanent home. Such a conclusion is well within the province of state legislatures. . . .

15. The New York Legislature recognized the potential harm to children of extended, non-permanent foster care. It found "that many children who have been placed in foster care experience unnecessarily protracted stays in such care without being adopted or returned to their parents or other custodians. Such unnecessary stays may deprive these children of positive, nurturing family relationships and have deleterious effects on their development into responsible, productive citizens." . . . One commentator recently wrote . . . : "Over fifty percent of the children in foster care have been in this 'temporary' status for more than two years; over thirty percent for more than five years. During this time, many children are placed in a sequence of ill-suited foster homes, denying them the consistent support and nurturing that they so desperately need." In this case, petitioners' three children have been in foster care for more than four years, one child since he was only three days old. Failure to terminate petitioners' parental rights will only mean a continuation of this unsatisfactory situation.

In addition to the child's interest in a normal home life, "the State has an urgent interest in the welfare of the child." Few could doubt that the most valuable resource of a self-governing society is its population of children who will one day become adults and themselves assume the responsibility of self-governance. "A democratic society rests, for its continuance, upon the healthy, well-rounded growth of young people into full maturity as citizens, with all that implies." Thus, "the whole community" has an interest "that children be both safeguarded from abuses and given opportunities for growth into free and independent well-developed . . . citizens."

When, in the context of a permanent neglect termination proceeding, the interests of the child and the State in a stable, nurturing home life are balanced against the interests of the parents in the rearing of their child, it cannot be said that either set of interests is so clearly paramount as to require that the risk of error be allocated to one side or the other. Accordingly, a State constitutionally may conclude that the risk of error should be borne in roughly equal fashion by use of the preponderance-of-the-evidence standard of proof. . . .

The decision in *Santosky* requires that states apply *at least* a clear and convincing standard regarding unfitness in termination proceedings. It left states free to apply the higher "beyond a reasonable doubt" standard if they wish. However, nearly all states today use the clear and convincing standard. The *Santosky* decision does not speak to abuse and neglect proceedings that are not termination proceedings, and most states use a lower "preponderance of the evidence" standard in adjudicatory hearings, which determine whether there has been sufficient abuse or neglect to justify removal of a child and/or state-mandated parental rehabilitation.

The (liberal) majority in *Santosky* postulates, as did the (conservative) majority in *Lassiter*, that parents and children (and the state) share an interest in accurate decision making in termination proceedings. Is that true even though, as the majority here notes, the best interests of the child is not the sole standard for termination? Are the *Santosky* dissenters (who were in the conservative majority in *Lassiter*) now suggesting in their footnote 13 that parents' interests and children's interests actually diverge in the unfitness determination? Is it because a parent's interest is not necessarily in having an accurate determination?

The *Santosky* majority also states that, even if there were a conflict of interests between parent and child with respect to whether there should be a termination, the balancing of their respective interests would tip in favor of the parent, because termination harms a parent more than mistaken non-termination harms a child. Does the majority underestimate the consequences for a child of remaining in the limbo of foster care, as the dissenters suggest? What if the interests of children in "a stable, nurturing homelife" are in conflict with, and are more important than, the "interests of the parents in the rearing of their child"? What evidentiary rule could a legislature then create to allocate properly the risk of error?

Near the end of their opinion, the dissenters voice the "statist" position that children are societal "resources" on whose proper nurturance democratic society depends. This is ironic, given that in cases assessing the constitutionality of state efforts to restrict religiously motivated parenting choices, particularly those relating to children's education, the conservative justices tend to denounce the idea that children are "creatures of the state." Should the diffuse social interest in producing self-supporting, productive citizens be given much weight in abuse and neglect proceedings, or any other legal decisions concerning children's lives?

A third Supreme Court decision, M.L.B. v. S.L.J., 519 U.S. 102 (1996), held that states must waive court fees for indigent parents who wish to appeal termination orders. The *M.L.B.* decision, unlike *Lassiter* and *Santosky*, rested heavily on an equal protection rationale; the Court noted that there is no general constitutional right to an appeal of a TPR decision. The Court cited for support its prior holdings in Boddie v. Connecticut, 401 U.S. 371 (1971), that court costs should not prevent indigent persons from filing for divorce, and Little v. Streater, 452 U.S. 1 (1981), that the state must pay for blood tests sought by an indigent man wanting to contest a paternity allegation. Those two prior cases both involved poor people who did not want to be in a legal relationship. Is the case for state financial assistance stronger or weaker for a poor person fighting to *remain in* a legal relationship? Consider that the *M.L.B.* decision also cited the Court's prior decision in Rivera v. Minnich, 483 U.S. 574 (1987), which declined to extend *Santosky* to paternity proceedings, holding that a preponderance standard of proof is constitutionally adequate for attributing biological parenthood and on that basis forcing a man to be in a legal parent-child relationship. In assessing the strength of due process claims in TPR cases relative to divorce and paternity cases, should we consider not only the interests of the person asserting the constitutional claim but also any competing interests? The *M.L.B.* Court assumed the only competing interest was the state's interest in saving money. Should it also have considered children's interest in finality?

Thinking ahead to the next chapter, on divorce, is there a good argument to be made that the constitutional guarantees the Court read into the Due Process Clause in *Lassiter* and *Santosky* should also extend to spouses who oppose a divorce, who want to remain married? Is the loss to them of the state's ordering the divorce potentially even greater than that experienced by an abusive or neglectful parent as a result of TPR? Is it not also the case for divorce that granting the petition is more drastic for the person who opposes it than denying the petition would be for the person who filed it? Is it the case with marriage that until the statutory grounds for divorce are proven, the interests of both spouses are presumptively aligned against granting the divorce petition, so that courts should demand clear and convincing evidence of extreme marital fault or of irretrievable breakdown of the marriage? Is the best policy, on utilitarian grounds or in order to respect the rights of persons who want to remain married, to err on the side of denying divorce petitions? If you think instead that one spouse's petitioning should give rise to a presumption that divorce is best, despite the ease with which a divorce can be initiated, why not think the same of a CPS decision to petition for TPR after prolonged efforts to rehabilitate the parents?

D. NO-FAULT TERMINATION?

As a final point of comparison between TPR and divorce, revisit the comparison of substantive bases for ending the two relationships. Why is the legal standard for terminating parents' rights not simply that it would be in a child's best interests all things considered? Modern no-fault divorce essentially makes the substantive rule for divorce that one spouse thinks a divorce would be in his or her best interests all things considered. The things to be considered in a TPR analysis based solely on the child's best interests would include the importance to a child's happiness and well-being of being in a family with biological parents, of maintaining existing psychological ties, of avoiding a radical change in living environment, and anything else you might think would count against termination despite any abuse or neglect. If after considering every reason not to terminate it is still the case that, on balance, it would be better for the child to remove them permanently from a parent-child relationship, are there any plausible moral arguments against doing so? One possibility is that maltreated children owe a debt of gratitude to their parents, because their parents created (or adopted) them. Can you construct a plausible argument along those lines? Another possibility is that parents have a natural right to possess their offspring that, to some degree, overrides the children's well-being. Can you present an argument for that position? On the other side, can you construct an argument that children have a right as strong as that of adults, if not stronger, to exit relationships that are not good for them? Does it help in making that argument to note that parents legally can refuse to have contact with a child and, with some limitations, can voluntarily exit the legal parent-child relationship at any time, possibly subject only to a continuing duty of support?

6

DISSOLUTION OF MARITAL RELATIONSHIPS

Divorce is the largest component of family law practice and involves many highly contested legal issues. You already studied, in Chapter 4, two major components of divorce practice, those that relate to the parent-child relationship—namely, allocation of custody/visitation and imposition of a child support obligation. Those issues also arise when parents who were never married are not living with each other. This chapter covers issues more or less unique to the ending of a legal marriage—namely, the substantive bases for dissolution and the financial claims spouses have against each other during the course of and after dissolution.

The focus here is on just the marriage relationship, though initially we looked more broadly at adult intimate relationships. Chapter 2 indirectly addressed what little law exists on dissolution of non-formalized, non-marital intimate relationships, in assessing what protections marriage uniquely affords that provide a motivation for getting married. Rules for dissolution of marriage-equivalent relationships that received state recognition, such as civil unions, are essentially the same as those for marriage. But cf. Cal. Fam. Code §299 (providing a somewhat simpler way to end registered domestic partnerships in some circumstances). Localities that offer their own registered partnerships might have their own rules for dissolving those relationships, but that is beyond the scope of this course.

The chapter title uses "dissolution" rather than "divorce" because there are steps other than divorce that couples can take to end a marriage or purported marriage. Recall from Chapter 2 that some purported marriages are absolutely void. No court decree is necessary to make the parties unmarried in that situation. See, e.g., Va. Code Ann. §20-43 ("All marriages which are prohibited by law on account of either of the parties having a former wife or husband then living shall be absolutely void, without any decree of divorce, or other legal process."). However, clients might wish to have formal recognition of their unmarried condition—for example, in order to reassure a new partner, and state laws authorize courts to issue a declaration. Clients might also or instead wish for a legal remedy in tort or contract, if they believe they have been wronged.

In other situations, a marriage is voidable, which means the parties are legally married unless and until one of them secures a court order voiding the marriage. See, e.g., 23 Pa. Cons. Stat. §3305(b) ("In all cases of marriages which are voidable, either party to the marriage may seek and obtain an annulment of the marriage but, until a decree of annulment is obtained from a court of competent jurisdiction, the marriage shall be valid."). The concept of annulment is closely related to, and in some states statutorily conflated with, voiding a marriage, so the two are combined for analysis purposes below.

Divorce is the most common way by which couples dissolve marriages, so the bulk of the chapter relates to divorce. As an interim step toward divorce, couples commonly live separately for a period of time, and some legal rules address this situation, so there is also a section below covering separation.

A. VOIDING A MARRIAGE/ANNULMENT

A declaration of void marriage or annulment has the consequence of deeming the parties never to have been married. Some people prefer this to a divorce, because the process is very quick (there is no required waiting period, even in the absence of fault); because they might avoid some common consequences of ending a marriage, such as post-divorce spousal support; and because they might have better prospects for a subsequent marriage if they do not have this divorce in their personal history. The Catholic Church has long embraced annulment as a way for people to avoid the strictures of its rule prohibiting divorce and remarriage.

The grounds for a legal annulment are, in theory, very narrow. In reading the Nevada statute below, think about which basis for annulment is probably easiest to satisfy and about how demanding courts should be in reviewing petitions.

Nevada Revised Statutes
Title 11. Domestic Relations
Chapter 125. Dissolution of Marriage

125.320. Cause for Annulment: Lack of Consent of Parent or Guardian

. . . If the consent [of a parent or court] required [for under-age marriage] is not first obtained, the marriage . . . may be annulled upon application by or on behalf of the person who fails to obtain such consent, unless such person after reaching the age of 18 years freely cohabits for any time with the other party to the marriage as husband and wife. . . .

125.330. Cause for Annulment: Want of Understanding

When either of the parties to a marriage for want of understanding shall be incapable of assenting thereto, the marriage shall be void from the time its nullity shall be declared by a court of competent authority. . . .

125.340. Cause for Annulment: Fraud

1. If the consent of either party was obtained by fraud . . . , the marriage shall be void from the time its nullity shall be declared by a court of competent authority.

2. No marriage may be annulled for fraud if the parties to the marriage voluntarily cohabit as husband and wife having received knowledge of such fraud.

125.350. Cause for Annulment: Grounds for Declaring Contract Void in Equity

A marriage may be annulled for any cause which is a ground for annulling or declaring void a contract in a court of equity.

One of the more prominent annulment actions in Nevada was that of Britney Spears in 2004, filed just two days after an impulsive middle-of-the-night Las Vegas wedding with her hometown buddy Jason Allen Alexander. Spears was reported to have worn to the wedding a baseball cap, "tummy" shirt, torn jeans (with garter belt on top), and sneakers, and to have handed a bottle of Jack Daniels to a homeless person upon exiting the Little White Wedding Chapel. See Paula Froelich & Dan Kadison, *Judge Nixes Nuptials After Brit Says She Was Too Dumb,* N.Y. Post, Jan. 6, 2004. Spears's annulment petition alleged that she "lacked the understanding of her actions to the extent that she was incapable of agreeing to the marriage because, before entering into the marriage, [she] and defendant did not know each other's likes and dislikes, each other's desires to have or not have children, and each other's desires as to state of residency." Alexander consented to the annulment, even though an entitlement to a share of Spears's earnings, even for just a brief marriage, could have been quite lucrative. His take on it then was: "'That wasn't a very cool thing we did,'" Id. Eight years later, he claimed it was a real wedding for him and that he regretted not demanding his financial due. See John Berman, *Britney Spears' Ex, Jason Alexander, Reflects on 55-hour Marriage: "I Was in Love,"* ABCnews.com, Feb. 4, 2012.

This was not an instance of aberrant celebrity behavior; "hangover annulment" petitions are quite common in early January in Las Vegas, and courts there readily grant them, typically within a couple of days. See Alfred Lubrano, *Luckily for Britney, the Knot Untied,* Phila. Inquirer, Jan. 6, 2004. Is there any reason to be strict in applying the annulment rules? The Catholic Church is much more so; though it grants roughly 85 percent of petitions, it does deny a significant portion of them, and even successful requests take a year to be processed. Id. What does the church gain by denying some and requiring real proof of a legitimate reason for annulment? If it gains something important, would the state not also do so by making annulment more difficult? Or is it pointless to resist when people quickly realize they should not have married?

As a result of the annulment, Britney's marriage to dancer Kevin Federline later that same year was legally her first. Illustrating again her sophisticated understanding of family law, she separated the legal formalization of that marriage—which occurred on October 6, 2004—from the private ceremony on September 18, to allow sufficient time for working out a pre-nuptial agreement. That marriage lasted two years. Is there anything in the Nevada statute that precludes seeking an annulment two years after the wedding? Spears did not attempt that route, but instead filed for a no-fault divorce. A few years later she began a very long engagement with manager Jason Trawick. Other celebrities that have had marriages annulled include Jennifer Lopez, Frank Sinatra, Julio Iglesias, Jack Kerouac, Tupac Shakur, Rudy Giuliani, and King Henry VIII.

The fraud basis in the Nevada statute is typical for annulment statutes. How might someone be defrauded into marrying another person? Virginia spells out some specific post-nuptial surprises that can justify erasing the wedding:

VA. CODE §20-89.1. SUIT TO ANNUL MARRIAGE

. . . (b) In the case of natural or incurable impotency of body existing at the time of entering into the marriage contract, or when, prior to the marriage, either party, without the knowledge of the other, had been convicted of a felony, or when, at the time of the marriage, the wife, without the knowledge of the husband, was with child by some person other than the husband, or where the husband, without knowledge of the wife, had fathered a child born to a woman other than the wife within ten months after the date of the solemnization of the marriage, or where, prior to the marriage, either party had been, without the knowledge of the other, a prostitute, a decree of annulment may be entered upon proof, on complaint of the party aggrieved. . . .

Virginia courts have been more stringent in applying this rule than Nevada courts appear to be with the "want of understanding" rule. For example, in Sanderson v. Sanderson, 186 S.E. 2d 84 (Va. 1972), the Virginia Supreme Court held that an annulment could not be granted on the basis of a wife's having represented to her husband before marriage that she was previously married and divorced only once when in fact she had been five times. Professor Abrams explains that the doctrine aims to limit successful fraud claims to those that go to the "essentials" of marriage. See Kerry Abrams, *Marriage Fraud*, 100 CAL. L. REV. 1 (2012). Does the number of times one's spouse has been divorced previously go to the essentials of marriage? More or less so than finding out that your wife was once convicted of a felony or once worked as a prostitute? A defrauded spouse might also, or instead, be able to sue in tort and recover damages, as the former first lady of New Jersey initially attempted to do in her 2008 divorce from Jim McGreevey, who resigned as governor when news surfaced that he had been having a homosexual affair. Dina Matos McGreevey alleged in the divorce that Jim had defrauded her by concealing his homosexuality when they married. See Associated Press, *Wife of Former New Jersey Gov. Jim McGreevey Drops Fraud Claim*, N.Y. DAILY NEWS, Sept. 10, 2008.

POLICY QUESTION

Should the law enable couples, for a certain period of time after the wedding—for example, one year—to erase their marriages simply on the grounds that they think they made a mistake? What reasons could there be for forcing such couples instead to go through a divorce? Pennsylvania effectively allows couples two months to rescind a marriage, by authorizing annulment within that period based solely on an assertion that either party had a drink or took a Prozac before the wedding. See 23 Pa. Cons. Stat. §3305(3) ("Where either party to the marriage was under the influence of alcohol or drugs and an action for annulment is commenced within 60 days after the marriage ceremony.") Lawmakers in Mexico City have proposed transforming legal marriage there into a limited-term contract, with a minimum term of two years, subject to renewal by mutual consent but otherwise automatically expiring. See Douglas Stanglin, Mexico City Lawmakers Propose "Renewable" Marriage Contracts, USA Today (Sept. 30, 2011). Diametrically opposed is the law of Northern Ireland, which prohibits married people from petitioning to dissolve a marriage until they have been married for at least two years, having as its aim preventing overly hasty decisions during the supposedly more difficult early years.

B. SEPARATION

Married couples can cease cohabiting without needing to do anything legally. Even if they do this in contemplation of divorce, perhaps to satisfy a no-fault divorce ground of having lived separate and apart for a period of time, they do not need any court authorization or recognition of this decision; they can simply split their households. (Until 2010, couples in New York could not satisfy that state's no-fault ground of living separately for one year unless they had a separation decree or agreement, but a statutory amendment in 2010 added an irretrievable breakdown basis for divorce, making formal separation unnecessary to a no-fault divorce.) In an extreme case, a primary breadwinner who moves out and leaves behind a spouse and children with no means of support might be charged with desertion. And a spouse who moves out and leaves children behind might be at a disadvantage in a custody dispute. But otherwise there are no legal consequences simply from separating.

However, states have long had a legal mechanism, short of becoming "divorced," for couples to effect a formal termination of their cohabitation. First, in the days when divorce was difficult or impossible to obtain—there was great social stigma attached to divorce, and many people felt bound by religious proscriptions against divorce—states created a legal action called divorce *a menso et thoro*, or "divorce from bed and board." Through this legal action, a court could authorize spouses to live separately without risking a charge of desertion, allocate marital assets between the spouses, determine the residence of any children of the couple, and order ongoing support of spouse and/or children, but without permanently ending their legal tie and without freeing the parties to remarry. It was thus similar in some ways to placing a child in foster care. And as with temporary suspension of the parent-child relationship, a party seeking a divorce *a menso et thoro* generally had to show marital fault by the other person. Some states retain statutory provision for this form of court-sanctioned separation.

Baldwin's Kentucky Revised Statutes
Title XXXV. Domestic Relations
Chapter 403. Dissolution of Marriage

403.050 DIVORCE FROM BED AND BOARD; GROUNDS AND LEGAL EFFECT

Divorce from bed and board may be rendered for any cause that allows divorce, or for any other cause that the court in its discretion considers sufficient. A divorce from bed and board shall operate as to property thereafter acquired, and upon the personal rights and legal capacities of the parties, as a divorce from the bond of matrimony, except that neither shall marry again during the life of the other. . . .

Divorce from bed and board is also like temporary removal of a child from parental custody insofar as a court can later make the suspension of the relationship permanent and complete. A person in a status of divorce *a menso et thoro* can petition for a divorce *a vinculo matrimonii,* or "absolute divorce," whenever grounds for it exist (which might require that a certain amount of time in the intermediate status has elapsed).

Petitions for divorce *a menso et thoro* are rare today. Most state codes now contain provisions simply authorizing married persons to seek temporary protection of their interests when they physically separate from a spouse, without seeking to change their marital status even in an intermediate way and without needing to establish any grounds for the separation. See, e.g., Minn. Stat. §518.06 ("A decree of legal separation shall be granted when the court finds that one or both parties need a legal separation."). Courts addressing petitions for separation routinely issue temporary orders as to child custody, financial support, and occupation of the marital residence.

Illinois Compiled Statutes
Chapter 750, Act 5. Illinois Marriage and Dissolution of Marriage Act
Part IV. Dissolution and Legal Separation

5/402. Legal Separation

(a) Any person living separate and apart from his or her spouse without fault may have a remedy for reasonable support and maintenance while they so live apart. . . .

Part VI. Custody

5/601. Jurisdiction; Commencement of Proceeding

. . . (b) A child custody proceeding is commenced in the court: (1) by a parent, by filing a petition: (i) for . . . legal separation. . . .

In some states, a court-decreed separation halts the creation of "marital property"—that is, the property subject to division at divorce; each spouse's income from then on will be treated as separate property. See, e.g., Mo. Rev. Stat. §452.330.2(3). It might also make clear that a new romantic relationship will not constitute adultery. Cf. Romulus v. Romulus, 715 S.E.2d 308 (N.C. Ct. App. 2011), infra (finding based on detailed examination of facts that separation had not occurred before wife's sexual encounters with another man). These are additional reasons for making separation more formal.

Most couples who separate, though, do not go to court for protection of their interests. Some simply do not worry about finances or child custody enough to take any self-protective steps. Many negotiate and sign a separation agreement, which can cover all of the matters that a court would decide in a separation or divorce action. The agreement might ultimately be incorporated into or merged with a divorce decree, but the spouses do not need to file the agreement with a court at the time they sign it. A very common service family law attorneys provide, then, is negotiation and drafting of separation agreements. In fact, in most divorces, that is the main thing lawyers do. Some legal rules pertaining to separation agreements are discussed below.

PRACTICE CONSIDERATION

A client wishing to separate might worry that whatever arrangement exists as to child custody during the separation, as a result of agreement or court order, will become permanent following divorce. They will therefore be anxious to get the best possible result at the time of separation. There is justification for this worry; judges, like other human beings, manifest a status quo bias and so feel most comfortable ordering continuation of an existing arrangement. Judges might also view any agreement that co-parenting spouses made during marriage or at the time of separation as indicative of the parents' own assessment of the children's best interests or of the parents' genuine interest in caring for the children. However, so that terms of separation do not become as contested as terms of divorce, state laws create no formal presumption that arrangements adopted during a period of separation will continue after divorce, and some states' statutes explicitly reject such a presumption. The Virginia provision below does so, and it also sets forth additional remedies a spouse might seek in separating—importantly, including a mechanism for protection from partner abuse other than initiating a civil or criminal domestic violence proceeding.

Code of Virginia
Title 20. Domestic Relations
Chapter 6. Divorce, Affirmation and Annulment

§20-103. Court May Make Orders Pending Suit for Divorce

A. In suits for . . . separate maintenance, . . . the court having jurisdiction of the matter may . . . make any order that may be proper (i) to compel a spouse to pay any sums necessary for the maintenance and support of the petitioning spouse . . . , (ii) to enable such spouse to carry on the suit, (iii) to prevent either spouse from imposing any restraint on the personal liberty of the other spouse, (iv) to provide for the custody and maintenance of the minor children of the parties . . . , (v) to provide support . . . for any child of the parties to whom a duty of support is owed . . . , (vi) for the exclusive use and possession of the family residence during the pendency of the suit, (vii) to preserve the estate of either spouse, so that it be forthcoming to meet any decree which may be made in the suit . . .

E. An order entered pursuant to this section shall have no presumptive effect and shall not be determinative when adjudicating the underlying cause.

Subsection A.ii. above is significant and quite irksome to primary breadwinner spouses. A homemaker wife might move out of the family home, over the strenuous objections of the husband, and seek a court order that she receive custody of the children and spousal and child support during the separation, and that on top of that the husband pay for her divorce attorney! Why would states give their courts the power to force one spouse to pay for the other to sue him for divorce? Should they? Should the cause of the separation matter? Note the limitation on spousal support in the Illinois statute above, precluding a spouse who is at fault from petitioning for temporary support.

Also irksome to many is subsection A.vi. In a not uncommon situation, the husband is the sole owner of the family home, but a court orders him to move out of and stay away from the home, so that his wife and children can live there peacefully until the divorce is finalized. Outside the marriage context, this would seem bizarre—that is, to order the owner of a house to move out and pay for someone else to live in it. So again we might ask whether the state can justify such a dramatic infringement of rights just by pointing out that the person voluntarily chose to get married once upon a time.

Separation Agreements

The great majority of divorces today are uncontested. Even spouses who do not wish to divorce ultimately recognize that they cannot prevent it if the other spouse is determined to end the marriage. And most come to the conclusion that, even if they might secure a better outcome by litigating financial and child custody issues, the flame is not worth the candle. They therefore reach an agreement on such issues, and that agreement is controlling, at least for some period of time and at least insofar as no terms are contrary to a state's laws or public policies (e.g., as to child custody and support). Typically, the court's divorce decree incorporates the agreement in some way. The agreement should specify whether it is to be "incorporated but not merged," and so retain its character as an independently enforceable contract, or is instead to be "merged" into the divorce decree, so that the only remedy for violation of its terms is an action to enforce the court order. Different procedures and remedies might pertain to the two types of legal action. In some states, there is a presumption of merger, so if the agreement is silent on the issue, it will be deemed merged and thereafter of no independent effect. See, e.g., LaPrade v. LaPrade, 941 P.2d 1268, 1274 (Ariz. 1997).

Once the parties execute an agreement, if neither spouse asks for a trial as to the granting of the divorce, the specific grounds for the divorce, or any ancillary aspects of the divorce, then the parties need not ever appear in court. The petitioning party might need to supply evidence that the alleged basis for divorce exists, but that is commonly done by deposition in the office of that party's attorney. For example, if the basis for divorce is having lived separate and apart, the petitioner and a friend or relative might go to the lawyer's office and on the record answer a series of questions aimed at proving that fact. The lawyer for the petitioning spouse can then submit this evidence and any other pertinent documents to the court, and some time later the parties will receive a divorce decree in the mail.

Thus, your client's entire experience of the legal process of getting divorced might consist only of visits to your office. Does this make divorce too easy? Should the decision to divorce instead be as public as the decision to marry, perhaps in recognition of the community's interest in the marriage or as a way to ensure the decision is well thought through? Is it wrong to make people experience public shame at having failed at marriage? Perhaps local newspapers should publish a list of recent divorces and the grounds therefor, similar to the "police blotter" that some papers regularly print. Might that not be a good way to motivate people to strive harder for marital success?

It is possible in most jurisdictions to execute an agreement to govern only the period of separation, and then to litigate or execute a separate agreement as to what will happen at and after divorce. This might be desirable if there is an urgent need for some things to be put in place for the separation period but negotiation of a permanent settlement is likely to be protracted. But usually the assumption is that the separation agreement will operate at and after divorce, if divorce occurs. The drafting and negotiation of the agreement is therefore of great importance; it largely determines central aspects of the future life of divorcing clients—namely, their financial well being and their relationship with their children.

States today encourage use of separation agreements, because agreements save the state and the parties from the substantial expense of litigation and usually lessen the parental stress and conflict to which children are exposed. Many states have enacted a Uniform Dissolution of Marriage Act (UDMA) provision pertaining to separation agreements.

Arizona Revised Statutes
Title 25. Marital and Domestic Relations
Chapter 3, Article 2. Dissolution of Marriage

§25-317. Separation Agreement; Effect

A. To promote amicable settlement of disputes between parties to a marriage attendant on their separation or the dissolution of their marriage, the parties may enter into a written separation agreement containing provisions for disposition of any property owned by either of them, maintenance of either of them, and support, custody and parenting time of their children. . . .

B. In a proceeding for dissolution of marriage or for legal separation, the terms of the separation agreement, except those providing for the support, custody and parenting time of children, are binding on the court unless it finds, after considering the economic circumstances of the parties and any other relevant evidence produced by the parties, on their own motion or on request of the court, that the separation agreement is unfair.

C. If the court finds the separation agreement unfair as to disposition of property or maintenance, it may request the parties to submit a revised separation agreement or may make orders for the disposition of property or maintenance.

D. If the court finds that the separation agreement is not unfair as to disposition of property or maintenance and that it is reasonable as to support, custody and parenting time of children, the separation agreement shall be set forth or incorporated by reference in the decree of dissolution or legal separation and the parties shall be ordered to perform them. . . .

E. Terms of the agreement set forth or incorporated by reference in the decree are enforceable by all remedies available for enforcement of a judgment, including contempt.

Why is there a need for a statutory provision authorizing two private individuals to enter into an agreement? Notice that the basis for court rejection of agreement terms is broader in this provision than in the typical statutory provision governing pre-nuptial agreements. Arizona has an "unfair" standard. Other UDMA states have an "unconscionable" standard. Colo. Rev. Stat. §14-10-112; Ky. Rev. Stat. Ann. §403.180; Mo. Rev. Stat. §452.325. As seen in Chapter 2, states have moved toward recognizing only standard contract defenses with respect to pre-nups. Why the different treatment of separation agreements? Recall the rationales courts offered for rejecting fairness-based efforts to set aside pre-nups. Which of those are weaker or inapplicable in the case of a separation agreement?

Separated couples often retain strong feelings for each other and many make sincere efforts at reconciling before petitioning for divorce. Indeed, the very purpose of one common no-fault basis for divorce, that requiring that spouses live "separate and apart" for a specified period, is to force petitioners to take time to make sure they truly do want to divorce. Even when spouses retain no hope of fixing their problems, separating permanently from each other can be somewhat like overcoming a drug habit; ambivalence, sadness, and loneliness can cause "relapses." What effect might any temporary reunions have on a separation agreement? How would you counsel a client who is thinking about moving back in with a spouse after executing an agreement, or who tells you he or she is still occasionally having sex with the estranged spouse?

Cameron v. Cameron

265 S.W.3d 797 (Ky. 2008)

Opinion of the Court by Justice CUNNINGHAM.

. . . The parties in this case were married twice, first in 1988. There was one child born of this marriage on April 21, 1989. The parties lived on a large farm of approximately 1,200 acres which was managed by Donald, but owned by his father. It appears that all of the parties' expenses were paid for by Donald's father as part compensation for Donald managing the farm.

In 1998, Donald filed for divorce. . . . The parties were divorced, but there was never a property settlement following the divorce. Donald remarried and was subsequently divorced from that wife, with whom he had a son. On January 4, 2002, the parties reconciled and remarried and lived together until October 10, 2002. In between their divorce and remarriage, Donald's father gifted him several farms located in Nicholas County, Kentucky, totaling approximately 1,400 acres. After the January 2002 remarriage, the parties resided together on the real estate gifted to Donald by his father. Unfortunately, the parties only lived together for less than a year when, in October of 2002, Donald filed for a second divorce. . . .

Shortly after Donald filed for dissolution, Lynea moved in with her mother in Mason County, Kentucky. In late November, Donald, who was represented by an attorney, contacted Lynea, who was not represented by an attorney, about the prospects of once again reconciling. It appears from the record that both parties were serious about the reconciliation attempt, but that Lynea insisted upon the parties attending marriage counseling. It also appears that Donald wanted to reassure his wife that if their reconciliation attempt failed, she would be taken care of with a sufficient amount of property. Therefore, on December 20, 2002, both parties signed a document entitled, "Separation Agreement," which is the subject of this action.

The agreement drawn by Donald's lawyer is a short and concise contract, but contains the significant provision which is at the center of this controversy. . . . Paragraph three, which deals with property issues, states specifically that the parties would equally divide all property, to include "whether said property be classified as marital or nonmarital property." It has not been refuted that this clause was included specifically for the purpose of including the property that had been gifted to Donald by his father.

Significantly missing from the agreement are any provisions for either maintenance or child support.

The steps taken toward reconciliation are particularly germane to the issue before us. Lynea did not move back into the Nicholas County property with her husband. None of her personal possessions were moved back into that home. She and Donald did spend quite a bit of time together visiting on weekends. They even took two separate trips to Mexico, the latter being in February or March of 2003 when their daughter and another person went with them. During this latter visit, at least, the parties slept in separate rooms. The evidence reveals that during this attempted reconciliation the parties spent frequent weekends together. Their activities during this period of time are consistent with a genuine attempt to reconcile, as well as constructive, joint parenting of their fourteen-year-old daughter. Finally, in August of 2003, after giving up on attempts at reconciliation, Lynea filed her own divorce action. . . . Donald then moved that the separation agreement be set aside because they had reconciled subsequent to the making of it, as well as claiming that it was unconscionable. . . .

The trial court in this case found that there was no reconciliation between the parties. . . . [R]econciliation of the spouses and a resumption of cohabitation of the parties nullifies the agreement. . . . With a societal interest in the preservation of marriage, we are careful to . . . not put a chilling effect upon reconciliation attempts. Absent an outright rescission of the agreement, whether reconciliation has actually occurred can be a most difficult call to make. Of course, the intentions of the parties are certainly an important factor for the trial court to consider. Obviously, if either party does not intend to reconcile, then reconciliation cannot occur. We could not possibly enumerate all of the factors which might come into play for a trial court to consider in determining whether reconciliation has occurred. We mention only a few: (1) whether the parties have resumed residing with each other; (2) the nature in which they hold their personal property, including bank accounts; (3) their failure to carry out other executory provisions of the contract; (4) activities of the parties in which normally only married couples participate; (5) whether the parties attended marriage counseling (here, both parties attended, but Lynea stopped going); and (6) other factors of which this Court is not now mindful. A guiding light might be that reconciliation occurs where, from all appearances and for a substantial period of time, it seems purely an oversight that the agreement has not been rescinded or the divorce action dismissed. . . .

Here, the trial court was confronted with the fact that the parties had already been divorced once. Lynea continued to reside with her mother in Mason County and kept her personal property separate from that of Donald. And while the parties had spent some time together, including two short vacation trips to Mexico and several weekends, . . . they had never resumed cohabitation after signing the separation agreement.[2]

Finally, Donald testified that the marriage had been reconciled and Lynea testified that it had not. Considering all of the circumstances of this case, we do not believe that the trial court was clearly erroneous in accepting the testimony of Lynea.

2. We note that in *Peterson*, even cohabitation for a short time [did] not constitute reconciliation. In that case, the couple moved back in with each other some four months after the agreement was signed and lived together for almost a month.

The second question raised in this appeal seems much easier to deal with. That is, the allegation by Donald that the agreement entered into was unconscionable. KRS 403.180(2) states in relevant part, "[T]he terms of the separation agreement . . . are binding upon the court unless it finds, after considering the economic circumstances of the parties and any other relevant evidence . . . that the separation agreement is unconscionable." . . .

[T]he burden of proof in challenging the agreement was upon Donald. The separation agreement was prepared by Donald's lawyer and signed by both parties. Lynea signed the agreement without benefit of counsel. Also, the trial court found that Donald was a college graduate and that the agreement was not the result of fraud, undue influence, or overreaching. All of this was supported by substantial evidence. Neither does this Court find that the trial court was erroneous in finding that the separation agreement was not manifestly unfair or inequitable.

It is true that Donald divested himself of half the property which was non-marital. While the second marriage between the parties was of short duration, neither divorce provided for maintenance or child support. This was a cumulative ten year marriage. In light of this, it can hardly be said that the agreement was lopsided. We do not think that the trial court was clearly erroneous in its finding that Donald had failed to meet his burden of proof necessary to show that the separation agreement was unconscionable.

Was the agreement in this case more like a pre-nup than a separation agreement? If so, should that matter to enforceability? What would motivate someone in either situation—that is, prior to marriage or when moving toward divorce—unilaterally to "give up the farm" to the other? Ordinarily, assets a spouse receives by gift or prior to marriage would be separate property and off limits in property distribution at divorce, and the 1,400 acres in this case was both a gift and received when the parties were not married to each other. Did Lynea give any consideration in exchange for Donald's promise to give her 700 acres of land if their reconciliation failed? Recall that a marital agreement in which the promise on one side is just to care for the other is generally unenforceable, for lack of mutual consideration, because spouses have a duty to care for each other anyway. Does it matter that the agreement said nothing about alimony, as opposed to saying that there would be no alimony?

Did Donald's attorney commit malpractice? He or she drafted for Donald what was effectively a contractual obligation to give Lynea a 700-acre reward for *not* reconciling with him. Is it any wonder that she never moved back in with him? What would you do if your client was determined to offer an estranged spouse such a deal?

It is odd that the court rested its conclusion as to the agreement's fairness in part on the fact that the agreement said nothing about child support. A divorcing spouse who would otherwise likely receive child support payments cannot legally bargain away child support in a separation or divorce settlement agreement. Thus, Lynea could still go to court at any time and get a child support order, even though the agreement is still effective. The law treats child support as a right of the child, not of the custodial parent. In addition, states worry about a) children ending up on welfare even though the non-custodial parent is capable of supporting them, and b) primary caretaker parents being frightened into forgoing child support in exchange for assurance that they will have primary custody after divorce. Some states authorize a court to ignore even provisions of a separation agreement relating to alimony, if a former spouse would end up on welfare, so determined is the state to privatize support of persons who are not self-sufficient.

New York Family Court Act
Article 4. Support Proceedings
Part 6. Effect of Action for Separation, Divorce or Annulment

§461. Duty to Support Child . . .

(a) A separation agreement, a decree of separation, and a final decree or judgment terminating a marriage relationship does not eliminate or diminish either parent's duty to support a child of the marriage. . . .

§463. Effect of Separation Agreement on Duty to Support a Spouse

A separation agreement does not preclude the filing of a petition and the making of an order . . . for support of a spouse who is likely to become in need of public assistance or care. . . .

Is there much chance of divorcing couples cooperating to game the welfare system through terms of a separation agreement? Or of a dependent spouse waiving alimony in order to secure some other benefit (e.g., custody), all the while thinking that she will just apply for welfare to obtain the money she needs to live?

Negotiation of a separation agreement takes place "in the shadow of the law" of divorce, which is the subject matter of the remainder of this chapter. The parties and any attorneys involved argue for particular terms not only or even principally on the basis of what they think is fair or utility-maximizing, but also or exclusively on the basis of what a court would likely decide if the matter were litigated. Rational actors will agree to a compromise outcome somewhere in between the best plausible litigation outcome for one party and the best plausible litigation outcome for the other. Of course, many people are at their least rational when going through a divorce.

PROFESSIONAL ETHICS QUESTION

To what extent should an attorney try to convince a highly emotional client to accept a deal when the attorney believes it is in the client's best interests to do so? The client might want to make unreasonable demands out of spite or with the hope of having a public battle in court. What ethical obligations, if any, come into play for the attorney? An unfortunate reality in practice is that some attorneys do the opposite, in order to drive up their fees; they encourage clients to insist on unreasonable demands, knowing full well that opposing counsel will have to discourage the other spouse from acceding to the demands. Is there any way the state can prevent this, or must it depend on competition in the legal market to do this?

C. DIVORCE

"Divorce" today means a final severance of the legal relationship between spouses. The law in Western society has evolved from a regime in which absolute divorce was nearly impossible, through a period in which it was widely available but only on limited fault grounds and without much protection for dependent spouses, to the current regime of what some characterize as "unilateral divorce on demand," with substantial financial protection for dependent spouses. We take legally easy divorce for granted today, but this is really a modern phenomenon. In the mid-nineteenth century, 5 percent of first marriages ended in divorce; today nearly 50 percent do. Some Western countries authorized divorce only very recently—for example, Malta in 2011, Ireland in 1996. Two states—the Philippines and Vatican City—still do not allow it. The following U.S. Supreme Court decision provides a window onto the early history of divorce in America.

Maynard v. Hill

125 U.S. 190 (1888)

. . . In 1828, David S. Maynard and Lydia A. Maynard intermarried . . . In 1850 the husband left his family in Ohio and started overland for California, under a promise to his wife that he would either return or send for her and the children within two years, and that the mean time he would send her the means of support. He left her without such means, and never afterwards contributed anything for her support or that of the children. On the 16th of September following he took up his residence in the territory of Oregon . . . , and continued ever afterwards to reside there. . . . On the 22d day of December, 1852, an act was passed by the legislative assembly of the territory, purporting to dissolve the bonds of matrimony between him and his wife. . . . On or about the 15th of January, 1853, the husband, thus divorced, intermarried with one Catherine T. Brashears, and thereafter they lived together as husband and wife until his death. . . . [Upon David's death, title to certain property he had held depended on his marital status vis-à-vis Lydia and Catherine. Lydia argued that the legislative divorce was improper.]

Mr. Justice Field delivered the opinion of the court.

. . . Marriage, as creating the most important relation in life, as having more to do with the morals and civilization of a people than any other institution, has always been subject to the control of the legislature. That body prescribes the age at which parties may contract to marry, the procedure or form essential to constitute marriage, the duties and obligations it creates, its effects upon the property rights of both, present and prospective, and the acts which may constitute grounds for its dissolution. . . .

Many causes may arise, physical, moral, and intellectual, such as the contracting by one of the parties of an incurable disease like leprosy, or confirmed insanity, or hopeless idiocy, or a conviction of a felony, which would render the continuance of the marriage relation intolerable to the other party, and productive of no possible benefit to society. When the object of the relation has been thus defeated, and no jurisdiction is vested in the judicial tribunals to grant a divorce, it is not perceived that any principle should prevent the legislature itself from interfering, and putting an end to the relation in the interest of the parties as well as of society. If the act declaring the divorce should attempt to interfere with the rights of property vested in either party, a different question would be presented.

When this country was settled, the power to grant a divorce from the bonds of matrimony was exercised by the parliament of England. The ecclesiastical courts of that country were limited to the granting of divorces from bed and board. Naturally, the legislative assemblies of the colonies followed the example of parliament and treated the subject as one within their province. And, until a recent period, legislative divorces have been granted, with few exceptions, in all the states. . . . Says Kent, in his Commentaries: "During the period of our colonial government, for more than a hundred years preceding the revolution, no divorce took place in the colony of New York, and for many years after New York became an independent state there was not any lawful mode of dissolving a marriage in the life-time of the parties but by a special act of the legislature." . . .

The power is not prohibited either by the constitution of the United States or by that of the state. . . . The adoption of late years, in many constitutions, of provisions prohibiting legislative divorces would also indicate a general conviction that, without this prohibition, such divorces might be granted, notwithstanding the separation of the powers of government into departments, by which judicial functions are excluded from the legislative department. We are therefore . . . compelled to hold, that the granting of divorces was a rightful subject of legislation . . . when either of the parties divorced was at the time a resident within the territorial jurisdiction of the legislature. . . . One of the parties, the husband, was a resident within the territory. . . .

The facts alleged in the bill of complaint, that no cause existed for the divorce, and that it was obtained without the knowledge of the wife, cannot affect the validity of the act. Knowledge or ignorance of parties of intended legislation does not affect its validity, if within the competency of the legislature. The . . . loose morals and shameless conduct of the husband can have no bearing upon the question of the existence or absence of power in the assembly to pass the act. . . .

It is also to be observed that, while marriage is often termed by text writers and in decisions of courts as a civil contract, generally to indicate that it must be founded upon the agreement of the parties, and does not require any religious ceremony for its solemnization, it is something more than a mere contract. The consent of the parties is of course essential to its existence, but when the contract to marry is executed by the marriage, a relation between the parties is created which they cannot change. Other contracts may be modified, restricted, or enlarged, or entirely released upon the consent of the parties. Not so with marriage. The relation once formed, the law steps in and holds the parties to various obligations and liabilities. It is an institution, in the maintenance of which in its purity the public is deeply interested, for it is the foundation of the family and of society, without which there would be neither civilization nor progress.

This view is well expressed by the supreme court of Maine in *Adams v. Palmer* . . .: "When the contracting parties have entered into the married state, they have not so much entered into a contract as into a new relation, the rights, duties, and obligations of which rest not upon their agreement, but upon the general law of the state, statutory or common, which defines and prescribes those rights, duties, and obligations. They are of law, not of contract. It was a contract that the relation should be established, but, being established, the power of the parties as to its extent or duration is at an end. Their rights under it are determined by the will of the sovereign, as evidenced by law. They can neither be modified nor changed by any agreement of parties. It is a relation for life, and the parties cannot terminate it at any shorter period by virtue of any contract they may make. . . ."

And again: "It is not then a contract within the meaning of the clause of the consitution which prohibits the impairing the obligation of contracts. It is rather a social relation like that of parent and child, the obligations of which arise not from the consent of concurring minds, but are the creation of the law itself, a relation the most important, as affecting the happiness of individuals, the first step from barbarism to incipient civilization, the purest tie of social life, and the true basis of human progress." In Noel v. Ewing, 9 Ind. 37, the . . . supreme court of Indiana . . . said: "Some confusion has arisen from confounding the contract to marry with the marriage relation itself. . . . At common law, marriage as a *status* had few elements of contract about it. [I]t is not so much the result of private agreement as of public ordination. In every enlightened government it is pre-eminently the basis of civil institutions, and thus . . . a great public institution. . . ."

When . . . the act was passed divorcing the husband and wife, he had no vested interest in the land, and she could have no interest greater than his. . . . After the divorce she had no such relation to him as to confer upon her any interest in the title subsequently acquired by him. A divorce ends all rights not previously vested. . . . It follows that the wife was not entitled to the east half of the donation claim. . . . The judgment of the supreme court of the territory must therefore affirmed. . . .

Today we take for granted that courts issue divorce decrees and that the decrees typically order a division of marital assets even if title to all significant assets (house, cars, financial accounts) was in the name of just one spouse. The *Maynard* opinion reveals that in the late nineteenth century, there was generally no legislative authorization of such judicial acts and indeed no explicit conferral of the power to grant a divorce on any government branch. Legislatures assumed this power to be within their general power to regulate social life for the public good.

But note that the Supreme Court expressed doubt that the legislature could legitimately go beyond dissolving the legal tie between spouses to ordering a reassignment of property from one spouse to another. Bear this in mind when you study property distribution below. The Court's explanation for the legislature's interest in exerting control over divorce, invoking the idea that marriage is not merely a contract but also a state-conferred status that the parties voluntarily assumed, might also justify the state's forcing a transfer of property at divorce. Indeed, it would seem a justification for boundless state power over married people; the state could always point out that couples have chosen to enter the state-created status, and were free not to if they did not like the rules the state had created for the relationship and its dissolution. Can you present an argument that, despite the voluntariness of becoming legally married, there are some constitutional limits on the power of the state to define the substantive bases for divorce, to determine ownerhsip of divorcing parties' assets, or to order one party to keep supporting the other? Or is the state really constitutionally free to do anything it wishes to married people in the name of legitimate public policies?

In addition to the change in how divorces are granted—that is, from legislative act to judicial decree—there has been a dramatic transformation of public attitudes toward divorce since the time of *Maynard.* The idea that individual happiness must give way to the societal interest in stability absent extraordinary circumstances has largely given way to the idea that individuals have a right to be happy and need not sacrifice their happiness for the sake of any collective good, so that divorce is now an accepted common fact of life. In recent years, American society appears to have accepted even multiple divorces in a person's life, and a corresponding view of marriage as a short-term contract, renewable if both parties wish but not presumptively life-long. "Three is the new two" when it comes to remarriage, and some refer to the first as a "starter marriage." See Mimi Avins, *Marriage in the Third Degree*, L.A. TIMES, Feb. 9, 2003 (noting that societal reactions to multiple divorces depends in part on a person's age and whether a marriage produced children).

Is a cavalier attitude toward divorce and remarriage anomalous or pervasive? What do you suppose your classmates' attitudes toward divorce are? Does the multiple-marriage phenomenon suggest the state should take a new approach to marriage and divorce, either to accept it and adjust or to try new ways of stopping it? If state actors were to assume that marriage is a temporary arrangement rather than a permanent one, they might treat marriage the way they have traditionally treated dating—that is, by ignoring it. Or is there a way to maintain legal recognition of marriage but revise the rules and expectations that go with it in a way that reflects the normalcy of repeated transitions from single to married to unmarried to remarried?

Alternatively, states might try new strategies for getting people to stay married. Past efforts such as shaming and making divorce difficult largely failed, but perhaps the state could try something else. Might it make people more content to be married if the state found ways to reduce the expectations, pressures, and restrictions of marriage? Perhaps the state should encourage a return to the unromantic view of marriage as predominantly an economic, functional arrangement, and discourage the view that a spouse should satisfy one's emotional and social needs. Alternatively, the state might try to frighten people into working harder on their marriages, by limiting the number of marriages any one person can have in a lifetime—say, to two or three. There are still two jurisdictions in the world, the Philippines and Vatican City, where the limit is one, because, as noted above, divorce in the full sense is not allowed. Would you support any of these approaches? Can you suggest any other?

1. The Lived Experience of Divorce

It is often said that divorce has become too easy. Usually what people mean by that is the legal process, which as the next part shows has changed dramatically in the past half century. But probably the great majority of people who have gone through a divorce would say that it was quite traumatic, no matter how easy the legal proceedings were, and one of the worst experiences of their lives. Chapter 4 presented empirical research on divorce's effects on children, a subject of extensive study in recent decades. Much less scientific study has been devoted to the emotional and psychological consequences for the adults. The effects typically begin long before legal proceedings commence.

PAUL R. AMATO, THE CONSEQUENCES OF DIVORCE FOR ADULTS AND CHILDREN, J. MARRIAGE & FAM. 1269, 1271-1272, 1275 (2000): "Uncoupling begins with feelings of estrangement—feelings that typically emerge after a period of growing dissatisfaction with the relationship. Because virtually all people enter marriage with the expectation (or the hope) that it will be a mutually supportive, rewarding, lifelong relationship, estrangement from one's spouse is typically a painful experience. Estranged spouses might spend considerable time attempting to renegotiate the relationship, seeking advice from others, or simply avoiding (denying) the problem. Consequently, the first negative effects of divorce on adults can occur years prior to final separation and legal dissolution. . . . [T]he spouse who is considering divorce might mourn the end of the marriage even though it is still legally and physically intact. . . . In fact, Kitson's (1992) respondents reported (retrospectively) that they had experienced the greatest level of stress prior to making the decision to divorce. . . . [R]eports of unhappiness and psychological distress begin to rise a few years prior to marital separation. . . . Mastekaasa (1997) observed personal problems (such as greater alcohol consumption among wives) as early as 4 years prior to divorce."

A therapist who specializes in divorce summarizes her experience with divorcing clients, describing the stages they typically go through:

Darlene Lancer, Growing Through Divorce

Whole Life Times, Feb. 1992

In any case, divorce is painful. It ranks just above death in severity of stress, and is often combined with other stressors, such as marital discord, serious financial problems, a move, single parenting, multiple losses and litigation, all at once. Divorce is a life cycle crisis that is unpredictable, and unlike other transitions, there still is no social protocol for the divorcees and their friends. . . . Divorce presents a crucial period of increased vulnerability. . . .

Divorce is a process of several stages: The cognitive, emotional, physical, legal and spiritual. . . . Prior to the cognitive stage, the family has lived with marital problems for some time, and often in denial. Marital discord may have increased, or it may have gone underground. . . . Gradually one or both spouses become willing to risk going into the unknown and pain of divorce—it appears preferable to the pain they are already in. . . . Some will protest that they never wanted a divorce, blaming it on their spouse, all the while precipitating or allowing the marital break-up, and provoking or permitting their spouse to carry it out. . . . Naturally, it is optimal if the family can and has been talking openly. . . . More often, there is high dysfunction and . . . fear and anger are intensified and reactivity escalates. . . . Both still have ambivalent, though often unconscious, feelings of love and hate which intensify their reactivity. At this point, confusion sets in, old roles and rules and parenting begin to deteriorate. . . . Often neither spouse wants to leave, and the question of who will vacate the family residence is frequently the first heated legal dispute. . . . Especially if one spouse still wants to be married and is angry or feels like the victim of his or her mate, s/he will resist any change in lifestyle. . . .

Confusion, mood swings, and strong emotions, such as fear, guilt, lust, rage, jealousy, resentment and grief are "normal" during this period. . . . Upon separation, feelings generally are still ambivalent; many couples attempt to reconcile from one to three times, and sixteen percent continue to have sex. . . . This creates a constant state of disequilibrium. . . . [T]he family cannot reorganize to establish new roles and boundaries in regard to money, living space, household responsibilities, dating, and parenting. . . .

Parents often reverse roles. One who was over-functioning becomes irresponsible; the under-functioning spouse tries to be the perfect mom or dad. After a few months, the legal and economic realities of legal fees, maintaining two households, dividing property and determining child custody and visitation arrangements increase the stress and emotional reactivity. In the first six months of separation, women are more prone to symptoms of depression, such as poor health, loneliness, work inefficiency, insomnia, memory difficulties and increased substance abuse. Studies show that men feel empty, guilty, anxious, depressed, deep loss, and strong dependency needs of which they were theretofore unaware. Although initially the person left feels worse, over time the impact is the same on both spouses.

During the first year both parents continue to feel anxious, angry, depressed, rejected, and incompetent. Women feel more helpless, vulnerable and low self-esteem, while men tend to work harder, sleep less, and function ineffectively. These feelings are more intense in older spouses and longer marriages. Both spouses have almost twice as many car accidents and three times as many traffic citations as before the separation. . . . The custodial parent may take on dual parenting roles, and the children, particularly boys, challenge the new regime, especially single mothers. . . . [U]nresolved emotional conflicts fuel adversarial posturing. The legal divorce can be a long, drawn out battle, in which couples stay connected through their anger by breaking agreements and violating court orders, or by taking either intransigent or ever-changing positions. . . .

Divorce represents loneliness, change of lifestyle, imagined losses of what might have been, and of memories of what once was, as well as real losses on every front, such as a home, family, children, financial, and often friends and in-laws. It may entail a move to a different city or school, a job change, or a homemaker going back to school or entering the work force for the first time. These changes are also stressful, because the transition to the unfamiliar provokes anxiety and fears. Divorce can also shatter a spouse's self-esteem and identity, as a wife, a husband, and possibly as a father or mother. In order to bolster their self-esteem, some difficult spouses continue to argue, resisting compromise and escalating disputes. They are really fighting for validation because they feel disrespected or devalued. . . . Unfortunately, too often attorneys become pawns and act out their clients' rage. Divorce also rekindles the pain associated with past losses, such as an abortion, a death, immigration, or their own parents' divorce. . . . With such spouses the threat of loss is overwhelming. They may create disputes and obstacles to settlement in order to postpone the divorce, thereby avoiding their grief, feelings of helplessness, emptiness and abandonment. . . . This endless struggle for control over every last detail represents the spouses' last-ditch effort to avoid finality of the marriage and the pain of separation and abandonment. . . .

Social scientists' summary of research findings is consistent with this narrative:

MEGAN M. SWEENEY & ALLAN V. HORWITZ, INFIDELITY, INITIATION, AND THE EMOTIONAL CLIMATE OF DIVORCE: ARE THERE IMPLICATIONS FOR MENTAL HEALTH?, 42 J. HEALTH & SOC. BEHAV. 295, 296, 300 (2001): "Divorce is associated with numerous psychopathological conditions, and indeed may be among the most stressful events that many individuals experience over the course of their lvies. Compared to married people, those who divorce display higher rates of depression, suicide, alcohol abuse, and out and inpatient mental health treatment. . . . [D]ivorce. . . . lead[s] to a chain of 'secondary stressors' that further reduce well-being. For example, estimates suggest that women's standard of living falls by 27 percent after divorce, although men's post-divorce standard of living increases slightly. Divorce may also cause former sources of interaction—including networks based on couples, in-laws, and married friends—to attenuate or dissolve. . . . [T]wo-thirds report seeing less of friends previously shared with their spouse than they did before the separation. Indeed 40 percent of respondents report no contact at all with previously shared friends. . . . [This] is associated with a 62 percent increase in the odds of depression."

AMATO, supra, J. MARRIAGE & FAM. at 1274-1275: "Compared with married individuals, divorced individuals also have more health problems and a greater risk of mortality. . . . [D]ivorced individuals report more social isolation, less satisfying sex lives, and more negative life events. . . . [S]everal studies show that divorced individuals report higher levels of autonomy and personal growth than do married individuals. . . . Riessmann (1990) found that women reported more self-confidence and a stronger sense of control . . . and men reported more interpersonal skills and a greater willingness to self-disclose. . . . But . . . longitudinal studies show that people who make the transition from marriage to divorce report an increase in symptoms of depression, an increase in alcohol use, and decreases in happiness, mastery, and self-acceptance."

Amato's metaanalysis supported a conclusion that there is some selection effect—that is, that many people who divorce had characteristics prior to marriage that played a role in causing the divorce and in creating the post-divorce negative emotional states, but that even after controlling for that, divorce itself had a demonstrable adverse effect along many dimensions. Id. at 1275.

Research has also revealed how particular aspects of divorce can have an emotional impact. In particular, "qualitative studies of the divorce experience highlight the enormous psychological consequences of adultery, including outrage, betrayal, resentment, embarrassment, anger, grief, shame, guilt, fear and anxiety." Sweeney & Horwitz, supra, at 297. If one's spouse has been unfaithful, it appears far better to be the petitioner than the respondent in the divorce; being the initiator of the divorce in that situation reduces the odds of depression by 20 percent, whereas those whose spouses cheat on them and then petition for a divorce from them are among those hardest hit by divorce, feeling doubly victimized. Id. at 304, 305. When one's spouse has not committed adultery, on the other hand, being the initiator appears to cause greater post-divorce depression, probably because of guilt. Id. After the divorce, lower income is associated with greater depression, but some studies find that even after controlling for income, women experience higher levels of depression than men. Id. at 302. Having children raises the odds of being depressed by 73 percent, but the effect is more pronounced for fathers than for mothers, likely because fathers typically experience a substantial reduction in contact with their children. Id. at 302, 304.

The worst period emotionally for the spouses after separation is typically the first two years, but intense feelings of hurt and anger can last much longer for spouses who feel wronged. "Wallerstein found that even after ten years 40% of the women and 30% of the men experienced continuing anger and bitterness. . . . In women, continuing anger was related to loneliness and economic issues (especially for the former wives of high income husbands). Even remarriage did not seem to reduce the anger. . . ." Ferreiro, Warran & Konanc, *ADAP: A Divorce Assessment Proposal*, 35 FAM. REL. 439, 442 (1986). "Leavers," on the other hand, are often surprised to find they suffer from guilt for many years, worried about having hurt the former spouse and any children. Id. Either party is likely to feel guilt if they have strong religious beliefs as to the wrongfulness of divorce. Id. at 443. Negative post-divorce emotions are more intense when the divorce was sudden than when it was the culmination of a long deterioration in the relationship. Id.

Separated couples typically experience great awkwardness or discomfort in many of their social relationships. First, they do not know how to act toward each other, and the emotional bond between them usually persists despite any negative feelings they have toward each other. Id. at 440. "Five years may be the norm for diminution of strong attachment bonds. . . . Former spouses often experience 'flashbacks' to stronger levels of feeling during times of change i.e., the remarriage or divorce of either spouse or a major illness. . . . [M]oderate levels of attachment are associated with consistent child support payments and ease of agreement in settling practical matters. Either high or low levels of attachment were related to increased difficulty in negotiating agreement." Id. at 444-445. In addition, former spouses who are not custodial parents usually become completely estranged from in-laws, and any contact (e.g., running into each other if they live in the same community, or at children's major life events) can be stressful. Id. at 442.

Age is relevant to post-divorce recovery, especially for women. Those who are over 40 at the time of divorce fare the worst. They are more likely to suffer financially from the divorce, and they are much less likely to remarry compared to men or to younger women. Id. at 445-446. "Loneliness and depression were major problems for these women and the feelings were not ameliorated by the benefits of increased autonomy and competence . . . which was a source of self-esteem for many of the younger women." Id. at 446. At the same time, men who were very dependent on their wives typically have substantial difficulty adjusting to divorce, id., and rates of alcohol abuse are especially elevated for them. Education level is positively associated with post-divorce adjustment, as are formation of a new romantic relationship and remarriage. See Amato, supra, J. MARRIAGE & FAM. at 1276. Having social support can, of course, help in some ways, but receiving help from others can also generate distress tied to feelings of inadequacy, indebtedness, and having to accept possibly unwelcome advice. Id. Amato found mixed results on the relative psychological impact of divorce on men and women, at least when there is control for economic situation. Because they tend to suffer a substantial decline in standard of living, women generally experience more stress and anger. Id. at 1277. Studies also produce mixed results as to the relative effect on different racial groups. Id. Finally, cross-national studies show that the consequences of divorce are fairly uniform across cultures and nationalities. Id.

Paul Amato's overall assessment of the policy debate, based on his review of the empirical literature is this: "On one side are those who see divorce as an important contributor to many social problems. On the other side are those who see divorce as a largely benign force that provides adults with a second chance for happiness and rescues children from dysfunctional and aversive home environments. Based on the accumulated research . . . it is reasonable to conclude that both of these views represent one-sided accentuations of reality. The increase in marital instability has not brought society to the brink of chaos, but neither has it led to a golden age of freedom and self-actualization. Divorce benefits some individuals, leads others to experience temporary decrements in well-being that improve over time, and forces others on a downward cycle from which they might never fully recover." Id. at 1282.

2. *Legal Grounds for Divorce*

Before the mid-twentieth century, divorce in the United States could be had only by showing serious marital fault, such as adultery or physical abuse. In most U.S. states today, a spouse can still petition for a divorce based on fault, but a substantial minority of states has eliminated fault grounds. In all states today, a spouse can petition for a divorce on "no-fault" grounds, which typically means a claim either that there has been an irretrievable breakdown of the marriage or that the spouses have lived separately for a certain period of time. After studying modern statutes and developing an understanding of the substantive standards courts apply today in granting divorces, you will examine the causes of the "divorce revolution," in which states dramatically liberalized divorce rules and moved away from public airing of marital fault.

The Pennsylvania statutory provisions below represent the most common form of divorce law today, offering both fault and no-fault bases for petitioning. They also refer to some traditional defenses to the fault grounds.

Purdon's Pennsylvania Statutes
Title 23 Pa. C.S.A. Domestic Relations
Part IV. Divorce, Chapter 33. Dissolution of Marital Status

§3301. Grounds for Divorce

(a) Fault.—The court may grant a divorce to the innocent and injured spouse whenever it is judged that the other spouse has:

(1) Committed willful and malicious desertion, and absence from the habitation of the injured and innocent spouse, without a reasonable cause, for one or more years.

(2) Committed adultery.

(3) By cruel and barbarous treatment, endangered the life or health of the injured and innocent spouse.

(4) Knowingly entered into a bigamous marriage. . . .

(5) Been sentenced to imprisonment for a term of two or more years upon conviction of having committed a crime.

(6) Offered such indignities to the innocent and injured spouse as to render that spouse's condition intolerable and life burdensome.

(b) Institutionalization.—The court may grant a divorce from a spouse upon the ground that insanity or serious mental disorder has resulted in confinement in a mental institution for at least 18 months immediately before the commencement of an action under this part and where there is no reasonable prospect that the spouse will be discharged from inpatient care during the 18 months subsequent to the commencement of the action. . . .

(c) Mutual consent.—The court may grant a divorce where it is alleged that the marriage is irretrievably broken and 90 days have elapsed from the date of commencement of an action . . . [and] each of the parties consents to the divorce.

(d) Irretrievable breakdown.—

(1) The court may grant a divorce where a complaint has been filed alleging that the marriage is irretrievably broken and an affidavit has been filed alleging that the parties have lived separate and apart for a period of at least two years and that the marriage is irretrievably broken and the defendant either:

(i) Does not deny the allegations set forth in the affidavit.

(ii) Denies one or more of the allegations set forth in the affidavit but, after notice and hearing, the court determines that the parties have lived separate and apart for a period of at least two years and that the marriage is irretrievably broken.

(2) If a hearing has been held pursuant to (1)(ii) and the court determines that there is a reasonable prospect of reconciliation, then the court shall continue the matter for [90 to] 120 days unless the parties agree to a period in excess of 120 days. . . . If the parties have not reconciled at the expiration of the time period and one party states under oath that the marriage is irretrievably broken, the court shall determine whether the marriage is irretrievably broken. If the court determines that the marriage is irretrievably broken, the court shall grant the divorce. Otherwise, the court shall deny the divorce.

§3302. Counseling

(a) Indignities.—Whenever indignities . . . is the ground for divorce, the court shall require up to . . . three counseling sessions where either of the parties requests it.

(b) Mutual consent.—Whenever mutual consent under section 3301(c) is the ground for divorce, the court shall require up to a maximum of three counseling sessions within the 90 days following the commencement of the action where either of the parties requests it.

(c) Irretrievable breakdown.—Whenever the court orders a continuation period as provided for irretrievable breakdown in section 3301(d)(2), the court shall require up to three counseling sessions within the time period where either of the parties requests it or may require such counseling where the parties have at least one child under 16. . . .

§3307. Defenses

(a) General rule.—Existing common-law defenses are retained as to the grounds enumerated in section 3301(a) and (b). The defenses of condonation, connivance, collusion, recrimination and provocation are abolished as to the grounds enumerated in section 3301(c) and (d).

(b) Adultery.—In an action for divorce on the ground of adultery, it is a good defense and a perpetual bar against the action if the defendant alleges and proves, or if it appears in the evidence, that the plaintiff:

(1) has been guilty of like conduct;

(2) has admitted the defendant into conjugal society or embraces after the plaintiff knew of the fact;

(3) allowed the defendant's prostitution or received hire from it; or

(4) exposed the defendant to lewd company whereby the defendant became involved in the adultery.

§3309. General appearance and collusion

. . . Collusion shall be found to exist only where the parties conspired to fabricate grounds for divorce . . . , agreed to and did commit perjury or perpetrated fraud on the court. . . .

PRACTICE CONSIDERATIONS

Many clients ask whether it will help them to be the first to file for a divorce. State laws do not explicitly confer any formal advantages on the spouse who files first. Why is that a good thing from a policy perspective? There might, however, be practical advantages and disadvantages to filing first. The first to file usually has more control over the pace at which a case proceeds. In addition, if dispute over child custody or financial matters is anticipated, the first to file can create the first impression in the judge's mind as to the equities of the case. The other spouse can file a counter-petition, alleging his or her own bases for divorce, and in doing so respond to any accusations in the initial complaint, but they will be on the defensive.

One downside to being the petitioner can be higher legal fees, as the attorney for the petitioner is likely to do somewhat more work simply by virtue of having to draft a petition and take responsibility for moving the case along, keeping the court informed, etc. In addition, clients who want to exit a marriage quickly could suffer if they file first and allege fault grounds, because they might trigger a responsive pleading alleging fault against them, which can produce litigation that might otherwise have been avoided and which can result in a judge denying the petition because there is no "innocent" party, forcing the couple to refile on no-fault grounds. Many clients would be well-served by instead negotiating an agreement with their spouse as to who will file and on what grounds, as part of a larger separation agreement covering custody and financial issues as well. Courts are increasingly ordering couples to attempt mediation before litigation anyway, and that along with other causes of delay usually precludes a quick divorce absent an early agreement. This leads to an important ethical question: When an unhappy married person comes to you looking for a "barracuda" lawyer, as many people contemplating divorce do, what obligations do you have in counseling them, if you know that in the great majority of cases your being barracuda-like is unlikely to accomplish anything except higher fees for you?

How you represent your clients can have a great impact not only on their resources but also on the long-term well being of their fractured families; an ugly divorce is likely to deepen wounds and damage children, whereas lawyers who calm their clients, mute hostile communications between the spouses, and avoid litigation can facilitate healing and positive post-divorce interactions. The dilemma for practicing divorce lawyers, though, is that the market is not likely to reward a positive, therapeutic approach, because people typically do not realize the benefits of that approach until after the divorce is over, and often not until long after. When people first look for a lawyer to represent them in a divorce, they usually want someone who promises to be tough and aggressive, regardless of what divorced friends and family tell them, because they are angry or afraid or both.

Mandatory Counseling

The counseling requirement in the Pennsylvania statute is unusual; in most U.S. states, courts lack authority to order marital counseling per se. More commonly, they have and exercise authority to order mediation and classes on post-divorce parenting, either of which can cause parties to rethink the decision to divorce. See, e.g., Mo. Rev. Stat. §452.605 (providing that in any divorce or post-divorce custody dispute, courts must "order the parties to attend educational sessions concerning the effects of custody and the dissolution of marriage on children," unless they agree on custody or "the safety of a party or child may be endangered"). See also Ariz. Rev. Stat. §§ 25-312, 25-381.23 (authorizing transfer of divorce petitions to "conciliation courts"). Even in Pennsylvania, the authority to order counseling is limited to particular situations, ones that do not include abuse, desertion, or adultery. Contrast this with the legal rules for dissolving parent-child relationships, which require in most cases that abusive or neglectful parents have received rehabilitation services for a year or more. Why are abused or abandoned spouses not similarly required to give "maltreating" spouses time to rehabilitate themselves? Why not a blanket rule that anyone who files for divorce must have attended or be willing to attend several marriage counseling sessions?

Only if the sole basis for divorcing in a state were living separate and apart for a certain time would there be an approach to divorce similar to that for termination of parental rights in this respect, insofar as it would compel a waiting period even where there has been serious misconduct, during which time the offending spouse might have a chance for redemption. In the United States, however, this appears to be true only in the District of Columbia, where a unilateral divorce is possible only after living apart for a year and a consensual divorce only after living apart for six months. See D.C. Code §16-904(a). In other states, mandated mediation is likely to cause some delay in finalizing the divorce, but it could be very brief. And in no U.S. jurisdiction is the government required to provide rehabilitation services to a philandering or cruel spouse. Should not the widespread belief in the possibility of redemption apply to people in marital relationships as well in parent-child relationships? If parents are entitled to second, third, etc., chances, should not an abusive, neglectful, or adulterous spouse be entitled to multiple chances as well? Do we effectively hold people to a higher standard in marriage than in parent-child relationships? If so, does that make sense? Is an unhappy spouse's judgment about whether divorce is best for him or her inherently superior to the judgment of a child protection agency and court that termination of parental rights would be best for a child?

In an earlier age, extended family, clergy, and social organizations would exert pressure on couples to resolve any marital difficulties. Today, given that community and extended family ties are generally weaker, one might think it all the more important that the state step in to exert such pressure, which it might do by requiring couples contemplating divorce to bring in some sort of third-party mediator to attempt a reconciliation. Until a recent and rapid turn toward individualism in Chinese society, Chinese law required divorcing couples to undergo mediation under the direction of the local governing unit. See Maureen Fan, *Chinese Slough Off Old Barriers to Divorce*, WASH. POST, Apr. 7, 2007. Under the influence of the Catholic Church, Italian law has required court hearings to attempt a reconciliation when a spouse files for divorce or separation. Compulsory mediation in Japan often entails pressure on a petitioning spouse to accept the marital situation and withdraw the petition. See Jeremy Morley, *Non-Recognition of Japanese Consent Divorces in the U.K.*, 2005 INT'L FAM. L. 161, 183. The state is even more invasive in India; there, when someone files for divorce, a court might assign a social worker not only to counsel the couple and attempt a reconciliation but also to investigate the couple's situation by, for example, questioning neighbors or co-workers. See GOPIKA SOLANKI, ADJUDICATION IN RELIGIOUS FAMILY LAW: CULTURAL ACCOMMODATION, LEGAL PLURALISM, AND GENDER EQUALITY IN INDIA (2011), 121, 164. This is very much like the practice in the United States for determining whether a parent-child relationship should be terminated. Why do we not do the same in the United States with divorce petitions? Can you explain the comparative unwillingness of private parties and public officials in the United States to exert pressure on couples to stay married in a way that does not ultimately rest on a supposition that American society has embraced selfishness as a defining characteristic of persons, to a degree that some collectivist or more traditional societies (including pre-Enlightenment Western society) have not?

a. Fault Grounds

The Pennsylvania divorce statute is chock-full of terms whose meaning is ambiguous and/or likely to generate factual disputes—for example, "malicious desertion" (is moving out always malicious or must there be more to it?), "absence from the habitation" (must it be uninterrupted?), "innocent spouse" (does that mean one who has not committed a form of fault listed in the statute or one who bears no responsibility whatsoever for the marital difficulties?), "endangered the health" (physical only, or also mental?), "been sentenced" (recently, during the marriage, at any time in life?), "reasonable cause," "cruel and barbarous," "indignities," "intolerable," "burdensome," and "irretrievably broken." As we saw in earlier chapters, even the meaning of the terms "adultery" and "bigamy" is not entirely definite.

In practice, however, evidentiary hearings and arguments on divorce grounds are unusual. There is usually little point for defendants in fighting fault accusations or for petitioners in pushing for a fault finding if the defendant denies the allegation. In most jurisdictions that retain fault grounds, the singular consequence of petitioning on the basis of fault rather than proceeding on no-fault grounds is a quicker divorce, and that benefit is likely to be lost if the parties choose to litigate whether fault exists. If a defendant manifests an inclination to litigate, the petitioner can simply withdraw the petition and file a new one based on no-fault grounds.

Moreover, in most jurisdictions, fault is either irrelevant to other aspects of the divorce such as property distribution or, if it is relevant, the blameworthy conduct can be alleged and proven even if it is not the asserted basis for petitioning for or opposing the granting of a divorce. For example, Pennsylvania's equitable distribution rule states that "the court shall equitably divide . . . the marital property between the parties without regard to marital misconduct. . . ." 23 Pa. Cons. Stat. §3502. See also Kinsella v. Kinsella, 696 A.2d 556 (N.J. 1997) (holding, in absence of statutory reference to fault as a factor in property distribution, that courts shall not consider it). Connecticut's equitable distribution law directs courts to consider "the causes for the . . . dissolution of the marriage," without requiring that the divorce be predicated on one of the statutory fault grounds. Even in some states where only no-fault grounds exist for divorce, spouses can allege bad conduct as a basis for receiving more property. For example, the equitable distribution statute in Missouri, which grants divorces only on the basis that a marriage is "irretrievably broken," states broadly that courts may consider the "conduct of the parties during the marriage." Mo. Ann. Stat. §452.330.1(4). In Virginia, adultery can be a bar to receiving alimony, but the statute does not require that a potential alimony payor have filed for divorce based on adultery in order to resist imposition of the obligation on that basis. Va. Code Ann. §20-107.1(B). But see *Kinsella v. Kinsella* (N.J. 1997), below, for a contrary rule.

Nevertheless, fault-based petitions for divorce are common, and sometimes there is litigation over whether the fault actually exists. Reported decisions give attorneys and the public some idea of what conduct constitutes particular types of fault.

(1) Adultery

Adultery is relatively straightforward. Having intercourse with someone who is not your spouse is clearly adultery, and though we can debate whether online romances constitute infidelity, divorce petitions generally allege adultery only when there has been actual rather than virtual sexual conduct. We do not yet have a jurisprudence of virtual adultery.

Why was adultery the first basis for divorce recognized in America? Note that originally it was only available to husbands. Is adultery so prominent because of the implications for the quality of the marriage? Many people have been content to remain in their marriages while they or their spouses carry on an intimate relationship on the side. Is it because of the insult or threat to well being that it represents? If so, is the insult or threat on average greater for men than for women, or vice versa?

(2) Cruelty

The other most common fault ground for divorce is cruelty. Most states that include it in their divorce law ostensibly require "extreme cruelty." Certainly a pattern of serious domestic violence would satisfy that standard. But where is the line between ordinary marital tensions and cruelty, or between extreme and non-extreme cruelty? Do you suppose courts require a strong showing of severe conduct? Should they?

Wuebker v. Wuebker

3d Dist. No. 2-03-04, 2003-Ohio-2954

Bryant, P.J.

. . . On June 16, 1973, Myrle and Peggy were married. On July 16, 2002, Peggy filed a complaint for divorce alleging that Myrle was guilty of gross neglect of duty and extreme cruelty, and that the parties were incompatible. . . . Myrle denied that he was guilty of gross neglect of duty and extreme cruelty, and denied that the parties were incompatible. . . . A claim of incompatibility cannot be grounds for divorce if it is denied by the other party. . . . [T]he trial court had no option but to find fault with one of the parties if, in its discretion, the trial court determined that a divorce was appropriate. . . .

The definition of extreme cruelty is sufficiently broad to encompass acts and conduct which destroy the peace of mind and happiness of one of the parties to the marriage and make the marital relationship intolerable to that party. In this case, the evidence demonstrated that although Myrle did not engage in any one act that could be defined as cruel, there was a pattern of conduct that resulted in Peggy being very unhappy in the marriage. . . . Peggy received very little help with the household chores even though she worked a full time job outside of the home. . . . Myrle would make major decisions, such as the purchase of a new car, without consulting Peggy. The couple rarely socialized with others. Additionally, the couple frequently went for weeks without speaking to each other. Although Peggy may have some responsibility for the situation, the result was that she was miserable and wanted out of the marriage. Myrle, on the other hand, sees nothing wrong with the situation and wants the situation to continue as it has. Based upon this evidence, the trial court . . . finding of extreme cruelty . . . was justified. . . .

Did Myrle's conduct fit within the ordinary language meaning of "extreme cruelty"? We do not ordinarily think of slugs as cruel, however unattractive they might be as companions. Would you have reached a conclusion different from that of the trial court judge, if the result of doing so would be to deny Peggy a divorce from Myrle? Is there something wrong with a statute that forces courts to reach implausible fault findings in order to reach what the appellate court seems to think is the right result—that is, to enable an unhappy spouse to exit a marriage?

The following case discusses cruelty indirectly, in the context of a dispute over the admissibility of evidence, but presents an historical and policy perspective on fault-based divorce. Would you like to be a judge who has to hear this kind of case?

Kinsella v. Kinsella

150 N.J. 276 (N.J. 1997), 696 A.2d 556

STEIN, J.

. . . Plaintiff John Kinsella and defendant Mary Kinsella married in May 1977 in New York City. The couple subsequently moved to Glen Ridge, New Jersey. Two children were born of the marriage: John, Jr. on April 6, 1982, and Anastasia on September 14, 1985.

In January 1992, plaintiff filed for divorce on the ground of his wife's extreme cruelty, dating from approximately 1986. Specifically, plaintiff alleged that defendant had been verbally abusive, that she would "fly into a rage for no reason," and that she had intentionally involved the children in the couple's arguments. Plaintiff also alleged that defendant had spent excessive time with a male friend and that she had devoted too much time to her interior design business. Further, plaintiff alleged that defendant had alienated family and friends by her "bizarre behavior." Plaintiff sought dissolution of the marriage, custody of the children, and equitable distribution of the marital property.

In March 1992, defendant filed an answer and counterclaim, denying extreme cruelty on her part and alleging extreme cruelty on the part of the plaintiff, commencing with the birth of the couple's son in 1982. Defendant alleged that plaintiff had undergone a change of character due to heavy use of alcohol and illegal drugs. She alleged a pattern of belittling and humiliating behavior by plaintiff towards her, both at home and in public. Defendant further alleged that plaintiff had verbally and physically abused her and the children on a number of occasions. One such episode allegedly had resulted in a miscarriage. On another occasion, allegedly resulting in defendant's hospitalization, she asserted that the couple's six-year-old son had intervened by hitting plaintiff with a chair, allowing defendant to flee and call the police.

Defendant sought dissolution of the marriage, custody of the children, equitable distribution of the marital property, alimony and child support, as well as court costs and counsel fees. Defendant also sought compensatory and punitive damages for injuries set forth in the counterclaim. . . .

In the fall of 1992, the designated motion judge appointed a psychologist, Sharon Ryan Montgomery, Psy.D., to assist in determining whether plaintiff should have overnight visitation with the children. . . . Before rendering her fourteen-page report, Dr. Montgomery had met four times with each parent individually, once with each child individually, and once with each parent together with the children. Her report included summaries of these interviews. Dr. Montgomery had also consulted with Madelyn S. Milchman, Ph.D., from whom the Kinsellas briefly had received therapy as a couple beginning in 1988 and from whom plaintiff continued to receive therapy on an individual basis. . . . In addition, Dr. Montgomery apparently had reviewed a court-ordered addiction evaluation of plaintiff. Dr. Montgomery had not consulted with defendant's therapist, with John Jr.'s therapist, or with the family therapist treating the children and defendant.

According to Dr. Montgomery's report, defendant reported to Dr. Montgomery that plaintiff had had a drinking problem and had been physically abusive to both her and the children. She stated that the children were very fearful of their father and did not want to visit with him overnight. Defendant wanted plaintiff to have only very limited visitation. She also stated that she did not want plaintiff to have input into decisions regarding the children's welfare because she did not think that he and she could agree.

Plaintiff, on the other hand, admitted to Dr. Montgomery that he had been volatile and abusive with his wife at times, but claimed that she exaggerated the behavior. Plaintiff also admitted use of cocaine until November 1991 and excessive use of alcohol, but stated that his alcohol use diminished after he had decided to leave the marriage and that he currently did not suffer from an alcohol problem. That conclusion was confirmed . . . by the addiction evaluation. . . .

On January 15, 1995, defendant, who had obtained new counsel, filed an amended answer and counterclaim. The first count of the counterclaim again sought divorce on the ground of extreme cruelty, but contained more detailed factual allegations than the original counterclaim. Defendant alleged that plaintiff's physical and sexual abuse of her had dated from the beginning of the marriage in 1977, and that plaintiff had had a severe drinking problem from that time. Defendant also alleged that plaintiff had begun using cocaine in 1985.

Defendant alleged many specific instances of physical abuse against her and her children. She alleged that plaintiff had once severely injured her arm by twisting it in an attempt to make her drop her baby. . . . Other instances of alleged abuse against defendant included striking, dragging, choking, kicking and cutting her, throwing objects at her, and attempting to run her over with a car. Defendant also alleged that plaintiff had tortured her with razor blades and a leather whip and that he had threatened both her and her son with knives and baseball bats. She alleged that plaintiff had refused to help her obtain critical medical assistance when she was suffering from a dangerous kidney infection related to her diabetic condition, and that he had attempted to force her to ingest overdoses of her medications. Defendant stated that she had lived in an attitude of constant fear and had contemplated suicide. Defendant alleged that plaintiff had threatened to kill her and had tried to convince her to kill herself.

Defendant claimed that she had been hospitalized in connection with some of those incidents, had required several surgeries, and continued to suffer medical consequences. She also claimed to have fled on one occasion to a Rhode Island hotel with her children. Defendant further alleged that plaintiff had been arrested in connection with incidents of abuse and had been the subject of a restraining order.

Defendant alleged that plaintiff's threats and abuse had continued after the separation. She alleged that . . . plaintiff had entered the marital home and broken the third floor windows. Additionally, defendant alleged that plaintiff had hired men to stalk and terrorize her. . . .

In her letter brief, defendant stated that she believed that plaintiff had revealed to his therapist a course of abusive conduct towards defendant. . . . We do not find it necessary to decide whether . . . an exception to the psychologist-patient privilege exists, however, because we find that, to the extent that the communications at issue in this appeal would come under such an exception, they are protected by the marriage and family therapist privilege rule. . . . [I]n contrast to the attorney-client privilege rule, the marriage and family therapist privilege rule makes it clear that one party may not force disclosure of communications made by another party at a time when both parties were engaged in common therapy. . . .

On appeal, defendant argued for the first time that release of plaintiff's psychotherapy records was required because plaintiff had put communications in those records "in issue," and thus waived the psychologist-patient privilege, by pleading extreme cruelty as a ground for divorce. . . . The facts put "in issue" by a claim of extreme cruelty are a function of the requisite elements of proof of that cause of action. The statutory provision for divorce on the ground of extreme cruelty reads:

Divorce from the bond of matrimony may be adjudged for the following causes heretofore or hereafter arising: . . .

> c. Extreme cruelty, which is defined as including any physical or mental cruelty which endangers the safety or health of the plaintiff or makes it improper or unreasonable to expect the plaintiff to continue to cohabit with the defendant; provided that no complaint for divorce shall be filed until after 3 months from the date of the last act of cruelty complained of in the complaint, but this provision shall not be held to apply to any counterclaim; [*N.J.S.A.* 2A:34-2.]

That provision as it currently exists is the result of a general overhaul and liberalization of the divorce laws accomplished in 1971. In drafting the new laws, the Legislature relied heavily on the report of the Divorce Law Study Commission (Commission). The Commission announced that a primary policy objective was "to make it legally possible to terminate dead marriages." The Commission therefore recommended the establishment of a "no-fault" ground for divorce based on a period of separation. Similarly, the Commission recommended abolition of all defenses to divorce based on mutual fault. The Commission declined to advocate at that time the complete elimination of fault as a consideration in the law of divorce; rather, it recommended retaining some fault-based grounds, including extreme cruelty, and also stated that fault could continue to be considered in making alimony and child support determinations. However, the report demonstrates that an effort had been made "to move away from the concept of fault on the part of one spouse as having been solely responsible for the marital breakdown, toward a recognition that in all probability each party has in some way and to some extent been to blame."

Revisions to the provision for divorce on the ground of "extreme cruelty" were an important part of the Commission's recommendations. That cause of action was first adopted in 1923. The term came to be judicially defined as "that degree of cruelty, either actually inflicted or reasonably inferred, which endangered the life or health of the aggrieved party, or rendered his or her life one of such extreme discomfort and wretchedness as to incapacitate him or her physically or mentally from discharging the marital duties." The Commission blamed the "current rigidity of New Jersey divorce law" in large part on that narrow definition. Therefore, the Commission recommended the current statutory definition, which includes behavior that "makes it improper or unreasonable to expect the plaintiff to continue to cohabit with the defendant." The Commission explained that definition as follows:

> The above definition constitutes an effort to modernize the concept of cruelty in a moderate fashion. It is broad enough to cover serious marital misconduct which endangers health or safety, *or* makes it improper or unreasonable to expect continued cohabitation. The terms are flexible but do not include trivial misconduct or ordinary contretemps. Minor frictions or frustrations, such as nagging or bullying, would not suffice unless in the aggregate when combined with other misconduct the cumulative effect endangers health or makes the relationship so intolerable that further cohabitation cannot reasonably be expected.
>
> An attempt is made to focus upon the effect of extreme cruelty upon the plaintiff, rather than upon the defendant's *mens rea* or intent to inflict pain. The result, insofar as the plaintiff is concerned, is the same whether the "cruelty" is calculated and designed or a by-product of the defendant's self-centeredness. Moreover, the result to the marriage relationship may be the same regardless of the defendant's motives. The focus should be upon what the misconduct has done to the marriage, not on punishing the defendant.

The Commission also stated that the phrase "improper or unreasonable" was purposely vague and intended to be adapted to community standards of marital misconduct as they evolve. . . . Even prior to the 1971 revisions, the standard for proving extreme cruelty had an important subjective element. The test has been stated to focus on three factors: (1) the acts of the defendant; (2) the intent of the defendant; and (3) the effect on the plaintiff. The third factor was accorded special significance. After the 1971 revision, it became even clearer that the subjective experience of the plaintiff, rather than the objective quality of the acts complained of, was determinative. A 1977 case illustrates this trend. In *Gazzillo v. Gazzillo,* the court applied the subjective standard as follows:

> Two basic findings are apparent. First, that the marriage is "dead." The acts did, in fact, affect plaintiff so that it cannot reasonably be expected that she "continue to cohabit with the defendant." To quote the statute is to make the finding. The parties have not, in fact, "cohabited" for at least 14 months (according to defendant) and probably over two years. The future offers no relief. Second, defendant knew, or should have known, the effect upon plaintiff of his stiff-necked attitude, his lack of sympathy and his acts which did, in fact, affect plaintiff to the point where the marriage is now beyond rehabilitation. Yet, I find no "fault." It is, in large part, the peculiar sensibilities of plaintiff which permit the invocation of 2A:34-2(c).

Because the standard for establishing extreme cruelty is a largely subjective one, the primary evidence required is the plaintiff's testimony that, due to the defendant's behavior, he or she in fact finds it improper or unreasonable to continue to cohabit with the defendant. Because the definition of "extreme cruelty" no longer requires a threat to the plaintiff's health, expert medical testimony is not required to prove the effect of the defendant's behavior on the plaintiff. Therefore, the Chancery Court has held that merely alleging "extreme cruelty" in a divorce complaint does not put the plaintiff's mental condition in sufficient issue to constitute "good cause" for the purpose of justifying a court-ordered psychological examination under *Rule* 4:19.

Neither is it always necessary to corroborate the plaintiff's testimony regarding the defendant's behavior. The traditional rule requiring that proof of each element of an action for divorce be corroborated was eliminated by court rule in 1975. Although corroboration may still be required at the discretion of the trial judge, it was generally recognized, even before the new rule was enacted, that "[w]here . . . the testimony of plaintiff ma[kes] out a case of extreme cruelty, . . . 'the rule of corroboration only requires that belief in its truthfulness must find support in the testimony of others, or of surrounding established circumstances.'" Today, courts frequently do not require corroboration for extreme cruelty claims.

Whether pleading extreme cruelty as a ground for divorce puts the plaintiff's psychotherapy records "in issue" also depends on the functional importance to the parties of the award of divorce on that ground. In practice, claims of extreme cruelty are frequently uncontested. The court is empowered to enter dual divorce decrees, regardless of the grounds for divorce. Moreover, parties who institute actions for divorce by alleging extreme cruelty may, by consent of the other party or leave of court, amend their complaints to include the eighteen month separation ground for divorce when that cause of action accrues. Presumably influenced by convenience and the chance to minimize acrimony, parties frequently choose to do so.

The ground of extreme cruelty remains functionally important in obtaining a divorce decree in limited circumstances. . . .

> There will be some instances where the separation ground will be inapplicable such as the situation where a party seeks a divorce immediately after the defendant's misconduct and does not want to wait a year or more before separation ripens into a cause for divorce. A victim of extreme cruelty should not be required to wait.

In addition, because the parties do not have to live apart to obtain a divorce based on extreme cruelty, this cause of action may serve an important role where the parties are unable to afford separate lodging immediately, or where a party seeking a divorce from a recalcitrant spouse does not have the means herself to move out of the marital home or is unable to do so because of children. *Cf. Gazzillo* (dismissing defendant's assertion that law affords no relief to plaintiff in face of defendant's lack of objective bad behavior unless plaintiff leaves marital home for eighteen months).

In most cases, the practical consequences of succeeding in a divorce action on fault-based grounds, as opposed to separation, are minimal. The provision for equitable distribution of property under *N.J.S.A.* 2A:34-23 does not refer to concepts of fault, and this Court has concluded that "the concept of 'equitable distribution' requires that fault be excluded as a consideration." Similarly, "marital fault" is not a relevant consideration in determining the extent of child support obligations under the statute. Moreover, a determination of "marital fault" does not disqualify a parent from obtaining custody, except as far as such fault is independently determined to be proof of parental unfitness.

According to the statute, except where the judgment is granted solely on the ground of separation, proofs made in establishing the grounds for divorce may be considered "in determining an amount of alimony or maintenance that is fit, reasonable and just." However, the focus of the decision regarding alimony is generally on the financial circumstances of the parties. . . . Our perception is that, in today's practice, marital fault rarely enters into the calculus of an alimony award. . . .

Based on the elements of proof required by the cause of action for extreme cruelty, and the function of that cause of action in New Jersey divorce law, piercing the psychologist-patient privilege should be permitted only very rarely in order to enable a party to defend that cause of action. Because of the subjective and liberal standard for proving extreme cruelty, the plaintiff in the vast majority of cases is not required to allege facts that would need to be tested by reference to any information likely to be contained in a psychologist's treatment records. Moreover, where both parties seek divorce, there invariably will not be a genuine need for this type of evidence to defend the claims of the other party. . . .

Plaintiff is not seeking to introduce any evidence related to his treatment by Dr. Milchman and he has not alleged any specific psychological damage to himself. He apparently intends to rely for his proof of extreme cruelty on proof of the alleged acts of defendant, consisting primarily of argumentativeness, neglect and aberrational behavior, and his own testimony concerning their emotional effects on him, focusing on why defendant's conduct makes it improper or unreasonable for him to continue in the marriage. We conclude that defendant has failed to show any likelihood that information contained in Dr. Milchman's records would have unique bearing on plaintiff's case. To the extent that defendant has an interest in defending the extreme cruelty claim, and specifically the charges regarding "misconduct" on her part, other evidence, such as the testimony of lay witnesses, is available. . . . We hold that defendant has not made a *prima facie* showing that the psychologist-patient privilege should be pierced for the purpose of defending the divorce action. . . .

The court refers to evolving standards of marital cruelty. In which direction are our collective standards headed? Should spouses be expected to endure some quantum of boorishness, inconsiderateness, and meanness? Or would that require people to lower their expectations for marriage? Should we have high expectations, or should we excuse unattractive behavior as an inevitable consequence of human imperfection?

(3) Abandonment

The third most common statutory ground for divorce is abandonment or "willful desertion," being listed in the divorce statutes of nearly 30 states. It generally entails leaving the marital home a) without the other spouse's consent, b) without justification arising from the other spouse's conduct, such as domestic violence, and c) for a substantial period (some statutes specify one year). In Hanley v. Hanley, 493 S.E.2d 337 (N.C. Ct. App. 1997), a wife took off to Hawaii for a couple of months to hang out with some new friends she made while on vacation, leaving husband and children back in North Carolina, and the court found abandonment even though the husband had not objected to her doing so, after finding that he had not done anything to drive her away. As a result of this finding, the court denied alimony to the wife, even though she had been a financially dependent spouse during the marriage.

CLIENT COUNSELING SITUATION

A typical marital dissolution situation is one in which the spouses become emotionally estranged, making cohabitation unpleasant, and then begin to think about establishing separate residences, as a prelude to filing for divorce. In some states, as you will see below, the simplest way to get divorced is to file based on having lived separately for the statutorily prescribed period of time, such as a year. Suppose you live in a state where abandonment is a fault ground for divorce and fault can influence property distribution and/or alimony. And you know that in any state a judge might be influenced in a custody determination by the status quo during separation or by perception of who caused the breakup of the family. How would you counsel a client who comes to you and says she is contemplating moving out of the marital home? Or a client who says that her husband has proposed his moving out and who wants to know whether she should encourage him to do so? Lastly, suppose a couple has young children, the mother has been the primary caretaker, and she has met another person with whom she would like to pursue a relationship. How would you advise either her or the husband with respect to the possibility of her moving out and getting her own apartment, with or without the children?

b. No-Fault Grounds

Even when a petition asserts no-fault grounds, defendants sometimes wish to contest it, perhaps with the (unrealistic) hope that the court will order the parties to remain married or perhaps hoping the court will order them to first get counseling. We saw above that Pennsylvania courts can order counseling in a contested no-fault case. Do courts in any state actually put petitioners to the proof before they will grant a no-fault divorce?

If the no-fault ground is living separate and apart, there is usually little room for dispute about the relevant facts, and so a petitioner might prefer for the sake of simplicity to allege this ground instead of irreconcilable differences or irretrievable breakdown. One situation in which proof might be more involved is where the parties have effected an "in-house separation," living under the same roof but in separate quarters, perhaps because one spouse has insufficient resources for living alone and the other refuses to move out. Courts in some states treat this as satisfying the rule, but require real proof of estrangement. Beyond the obvious requirement of separate bedrooms, courts will inquire as to such things as whether the spouses, during the period of alleged separation, had any sexual contact with each other or ate their meals, watched TV, or went to social engagements together. On rare occasion, courts will deny a petition based on separation even when the parties did sleep in separate houses and did not have sexual relations, if they otherwise continued to act as a couple. See, e.g., Garner v. Garner, 659 S.E.2d 98 (N.C. Ct. App. 2008) ("Although the Garners did not sleep in the same bed for that time period, or even stay under the same roof, they ate together, shopped together, spent significant time together at home and at social and family gatherings, attended church together, and in all respects appeared to have the same relationship and affection for each other as they had prior to beginning their separate sleeping arrangements.").

Another exception might be if the couple reunited and cohabited very briefly and courts are receptive to pleas to ignore that episode. U.S. courts generally require uninterrupted separation for the required period. In contrast, Ireland's divorce statute itself contemplates and accommodates unsuccessful attempts at resumed cohabitation; it authorizes divorce when "the spouses have lived apart from one another for a period of at least four out of the previous five years," although it also requires the petitioner to show that there is no reasonable prospect of a reconciliation. Analogously, one now-universal basis for terminating parental rights in the United States, the "15/22 rule" discussed in Chapter 5, contemplates overlooking unsuccessful episodes of reunification. What are the pros and cons of overlooking temporary reunions versus restarting the clock after one overnight?

States vary substantially in the period of time they require a couple to be separated before granting a divorce on this ground. In Montana it is six months, whereas in neighboring Idaho it is five years. Mont. Code Ann. §40-4-104(1)(b)(i); Idaho Code §32-610.

Some states have a shorter period when the couple has no children and/or have entered into an agreement as to the incidents of divorce. See, e.g., Va. Code Ann. §20-91(A)(9) (six months if there is an agreement and no children, otherwise one year).

The other type of no-fault rule, allowing for divorce based on "irretrievable breakdown," as in Pennsylvania, or "irreconcilable differences," as in the California statute below, would seem to invite factual dispute. In a significant number of states, this is the only basis for seeking a divorce. Is the statutory definition of the standard here helpful?

West's California Family Code
Division 6, Part 3. Dissolution of Marriage and Legal Separation

§2310. Grounds for Dissolution or Legal Separation

Dissolution of the marriage or legal separation of the parties may be based on either of the following grounds, which shall be pleaded generally:

(a) Irreconcilable differences, which have caused the irremediable breakdown of the marriage.

(b) Incurable insanity.

§2311. Irreconcilable Differences Defined

Irreconcilable differences are those grounds which are determined by the court to be substantial reasons for not continuing the marriage and which make it appear that the marriage should be dissolved.

§2335. Misconduct; Admissibility of Specific Acts of Misconduct

Except as otherwise provided by statute, in a pleading or proceeding for dissolution of marriage or legal separation of the parties, . . . evidence of specific acts of misconduct is improper and inadmissible.

§2336. Default; Proof Required

(a) No judgment of dissolution or of legal separation of the parties may be granted upon the default of one of the parties . . . but the court shall . . . require proof of the grounds alleged, and the proof, if not taken before the court, shall be by affidavit. . . .

(b) If the proof is by affidavit, the personal appearance of the affiant is required only when it appears to the court that any of the following circumstances exist:

(1) Reconciliation of the parties is reasonably possible.

(2) A proposed child custody order is not in the best interest of the child.

(3) A proposed child support order is less than a noncustodial parent is capable of paying.

(4) A personal appearance . . . would be in the best interests of justice.

What would you expect to find in an affidavit supporting a claim of irreconcilable differences? If the central problem in a marriage is one spouse's infidelity or violence toward the other, does Sec. 2335 make it impossible to satisfy Sec. 2336? Should the parties not be required even to appear in court to get a divorce? Notably, there are no reported California court decisions since 1972 addressing an opposition to a divorce petition, even though in a substantial percentage of cases one spouse wishes to remain married. Have no-fault states effectively created unilateral divorce on demand, enabling people to exit marriage on an impulse, without having to try first to save the marriage or even to give the decision much thought? Is there much danger of people doing that?

The policy debate relating to no-fault divorce is typically framed as pitting interests of individuals against interests of the state. But the fact that often one member of the couple wishes to remain married means that there is really a conflict of interests, or at least a conflict of desires, between two private individuals. Do people who want to save their marriages not have a right to greater protection of that desire and of the profound interests they have tied up in the relationship?

Richter v. Richter

625 N.W.2d 490 (Minn. Ct. App. 2001)

SHUMAKER, Judge.

The parties married in 1983 and wife petitioned to dissolve the marriage in September 1999. . . . [H]usband, pro se, moved to dismiss the proceeding, alleging, among other things, that (a) there was no irretrievable breakdown of the marriage; (b) marriage is a contract; and (c) the statutes allowing dissolution of a marriage infringed on the constitutional right to contract. . . .

Minnesota allows marriages to be dissolved if there has been an "irretrievable breakdown of the marriage relationship." Minn. Stat. §518.06, subd. 1. While husband denies challenging the constitutionality of the Minnesota's dissolution statute, he argues that to be constitutional, the statute cannot be construed to allow "divorce on demand" because that would interfere with his right to contract. See U.S. Const. art. I, §10 (prohibiting laws "impairing the obligation of contracts"). . . . Such an argument assumes that the Minnesota dissolution statutes allow "divorce on demand" and that marriage is a contract. Both assumptions are incorrect.

I.

In Minnesota, if there is a dispute about whether a marriage is irretrievably broken, "the court shall consider all relevant factors" and find whether the marriage is irretrievably broken. Minn. Stat. §518.13, subd. 2 (2000). "Irretrievable breakdown" occurs when "there is no reasonable prospect of reconciliation." To find irretrievable breakdown of a marriage in a case where the existence of such a breakdown is contested,

> [t]he finding [of irretrievable breakdown] must be supported by evidence that (i) the parties have lived separate and apart for a period of not less than 180 days immediately preceding the commencement of the proceeding, or (ii) there is serious marital discord adversely affecting the attitude of one or both of the parties. Id.

Here, the parties had been separated, but not for 180 days, before wife petitioned to dissolve the marriage. The district court, however, believed wife's testimony about the state of the parties' marriage and found an irretrievable breakdown of the marriage. . . . See *Hagerty v. Hagerty* (Minn. 1979) (stating irretrievable breakdown "can also be shown by evidence of only one party's belief that it is the existing state, particularly where the parties have been living apart"). A statute that requires proof of "no reasonable prospect of reconciliation" and "serious marital discord adversely affecting the attitude of one or both of the parties" before a marriage can be dissolved does not allow "divorce on demand." Moreover, husband's withdrawal from the courtroom means he neither entered evidence contrary to wife's assertions on this point nor cross-examined her regarding the state of the marriage. Thus, the only evidence regarding the state of the parties' marriage was wife's uncontradicted testimony.

II.

Marriage, "so far as its validity in law is concerned," is a contract. Minn. Stat. §517.01 (2000). That marriage is a contract for determining its validity does not mean marriage is a contract in the usual sense of that term. . . . [I]n *Maynard v. Hill* (1888) . . . [t]he Supreme Court stated . . . that the prohibition of the federal constitution against the impairment of contracts by state legislation [is not implicated, because] . . . marriage is not a contract within the meaning of the prohibition. As was said by Chief Justice Marshall in the *Dartmouth College* Case . . . "The provision of the constitution never has been understood to embrace other contracts than those which respect property or some object of value, and confer rights which may be asserted in a court of justice. It never has been understood to restrict the general right of the legislature to legislate on the subject of divorces." . . .[3]

The *Richter* court implied that the husband might have had better luck if he had presented evidence to refute the wife's assertion. What sort of evidence would you muster for a client who wanted to prove that his marriage is not irretrievably broken?

Is there any practical difference between "divorce on demand" and divorce based solely on one party's assertion that the marriage is irretrievably broken? Rarely do courts require much by way of proof from petitioners who seek divorce based on breakdown or irreconcilable differences. In effect, courts grant divorce based simply on a declaration by one spouse that he or she wishes to divorce, making the process of getting out of marriage about as easy, in terms of legalities, as getting in. Under Sharia law, a Muslim husband is similarly able to exit a marriage simply by declaration; he need only utter the word "talaq" three times to his wife and then they are divorced. The ease of divorce for men under Islamic law is illustrated by this bizarre story:

Associated Press, Man Accidentally Divorces His Wife in His Sleep

Mar. 28, 2006

NEW DELHI—Village elders ordered a Muslim man in eastern India to leave his wife after he accidentally divorced her in his sleep . . . Aftab Ansari uttered the Urdu word for

3. Even if marriage is a contract, appellant failed to introduce any evidence of the terms of his "contract." Therefore, the terms of his "contract" would be those provided by statute. And, the statute provides that a marriage can be dissolved if it is irretrievably broken. Thus, to prevail in this appeal, husband would have to show that the district court's finding of an irretrievable breakdown of the marriage is clearly erroneous. . . . Viewing that evidence in the light most favorable to the district court's finding . . . , the finding is not clearly erroneous.

divorce, "talaq," three times in his sleep, prompting his worried wife to discuss the matter with her friends. . . . Muslim leaders in the couple's village in West Bengal state found out and decreed that Ansari's unconscious utterances constituted a divorce. . . . But 30-year-old Ansari said he had no intention of leaving his wife of 11 years. "I have not given talaq. When I uttered talaq three times I had taken medicines to help me sleep," he was quoted as saying in the report.The religious leaders said that before remarrying, the couple would have to be apart for at least 100 days and that the wife, Sohela, would also have to spend a night with another man and then be divorced by him.

American law technically does not authorize divorce by declaration, and it is unlikely that someone would download, fill out, and mail and serve a divorce petition while sleeping. But might someone do so while drunk or high? Of course, they could withdraw the petition upon returning to a normal state of mind, if they recall what they did. . . .

POLICY QUESTIONS

1. Which type of no-fault approach is preferable from a public policy standpoint—requiring a period of separation before filing or allowing immediate divorce based on a showing (or mere allegation) of irremediable breakdown? Which policies are relevant to answering that question? If a waiting period is desirable, how long should it be?

2. Hindu divorce law combines fault-based unilateral divorce with bilateral no-fault divorce. In other words, someone who wants to get divorced must get the other spouse's consent or show that the other spouse has engaged in misconduct. Thus, a spouse who does not wish to divorce and who has not engaged in any marital misbehavior has a right to remain married. Correspondingly, someone who simply becomes disenchanted with his spouse and finds another intimate partner he wants to be with cannot legally free himself from his spouse without her consent. But if both spouses wish to divorce, they can do so quickly without having to show that either was at fault (though they might have to convince a court that reconciliation is impossible). See SOLANKI, supra, at 120-128. Is that a reasonable compromise between the old fault-only regime and the current U.S. unilateral divorce-on-demand regime? Which problems of each regime does it avoid? Which problems does it still present? An approach intermediate between the Hindu and the prevailing U.S. approaches today is that of England, whose Matrimonial Causes Act authorizes immediate fault-based divorce, no-fault divorce by consent after a two-year separation, and no-fault divorce without consent (i.e., "unilateral no-fault") after a five-year separation. How would you assess that regime relative to the others?

c. Disability

The Pennsylvania divorce statute makes mental illness a ground for divorce, but only when it has resulted in institutionalization. Most other states in which mental illness is a basis for divorce also require a substantial period of hospitalization for it. See, e.g., Ala. Code §30-2-1(a)(8) (five years); Conn. Gen. Stat. §46b-40 (five years); Md. Code Ann.,

Fam. Law §7-103 (three years); N.J. Stat. Ann. §2A:34-2 (two years); Wyo. Stat. Ann. §20-2-105 (two years). Some other states make mental illness per se a ground for divorce. See, e.g., Cal. Fam. Code §2310 ("incurable insanity"); Ga. Code Ann. §19-5-3; Ind. Code Ann. §31-15-2-3(4) ("Incurable insanity of either party for a period of at least two years."); Nev. Rev. Stat. §125.010(1) (same); Utah Code Ann. §30-3-1(3)(i). In either case, the petitioning spouse might have to remain responsible for the mentally ill person's financial support. See, e.g., Iowa Code §598.17; Nev. Rev. Stat. §125.010(1). Paradoxically, insanity was once a common defense to marital fault in a divorce action. See, e.g., Minn. Stat. §518.06 ("Defenses to divorce, dissolution and legal separation, including . . . insanity, . . . are abolished.").

Other grounds for divorce in some states might also be characterized as illness or disability, such as drug addiction and impotence. See, e.g., Ala. Code §30-2-1(a)(6) ("becoming addicted after marriage to habitual drunkenness or to habitual use of opium, morphine, cocaine or other like drug"); Ga. Code §19-5-3 (12) ("Habitual drug addiction"); W. Va. Code §48-5-207(b) ("addiction of either party, subsequent to the marriage, to the habitual use of any narcotic or dangerous drug"); Me. Rev. Stat. Ann. tit. 19-A, §902 ("A divorce may be granted for . . . Impotence"); Mass. Gen. Laws ch. 208, §1 ("impotency"); Miss. Code Ann. §93-5-1("natural impotency"); N.H. Rev. Stat. Ann. §458:7(I) ("impotency"); R.I. Gen. Laws §15-5-2 (same). Most states that make sexual dysfunction a basis for divorcing require that the condition have existed at the time of the marriage. See, e.g., Ala. Code §30-2-1(a)(1) (court may award divorce "In favor of either party, when the other was, at the time of the marriage physically and incurably incapacitated from entering into the marriage state"); Ark. Code Ann. §9-12-301(b) ("either party, at the time of the contract, was and still is impotent"); Ga. Code §19-5-3(3); 750 Ill. Comp. Stat. 5/401 ("was at the time of such marriage, and continues to be naturally impotent"); Ind. Code Ann. §31-15-2-3(3) ("Impotence, existing at the time of the marriage."); Tenn. Code Ann. §36-4-101(a)(1) ("at the time of the contract, was and still is naturally impotent and incapable of procreation"). What is the reason for requiring that the condition pre-existed the marriage? Is that requirement backward from a modern perspective?

MORAL THEORY QUESTION

Does the commitment most people make at their wedding to be devoted to each other "in sickness and in health" embody a genuine moral obligation not to leave because one's spouse gets sick? Consider the question from utilitarian (i.e., maximizing aggregate welfare), deontological (i.e., whether a mentally ill person has a moral right not to be abandoned), and virtue ethics (i.e., what kind of person one should strive to be) perspectives. To which of these different forms of moral reasoning might the degree of mental incapacity be relevant? Which, if any, should be the basis for the legal rule?

d. Defenses

Divorce rules historically contained several defenses—that is, bases for a court to refuse to grant a divorce petition and thereby to force someone to remain married. In today's no-fault era, we find it difficult to understand the point of these defenses, and many states have eliminated some or all of them. Try to articulate the thinking that lay behind each.

- **Connivance** means encouraging and facilitating the conduct alleged as fault—for example, asking someone to seduce your spouse so you can charge him with adultery.
- **Collusion** means cooperating with one's spouse in fabricating grounds for divorce before a court—that is, agreeing simply to lie to the court and perhaps concocting false evidence to support the lie.
- **Recrimination** means reciprocal fault—for example, one spouse is charged with adultery and defends by saying she was driven to it by the other's cruelty.
- **Provocation** means provoking one's spouse to engage in illicit conduct—for example, nagging a spouse until it triggers a violent response.
- **Condonation** means forgiving the fault and resuming cohabitation.

The last of these retains some popularity. A common divorce scenario involves one spouse having done something destructive of the relationship, the other spouse having agreed for a time to work on forgiving and forgetting, and that effort failing. The "injured spouse" files for divorce alleging fault and the other points to the reconciliation effort as a defense to the fault allegation. Courts do still apply the defense, with the effect that the petitioning party must proceed on no-fault grounds.

Hoffman v. Hoffman

762 A.2d 766 (Pa. Super. Ct. 2000)

JOYCE, J.:

. . . The parties met in Hawaii in 1986, when Appellee [husband] was employed as an admiral in the United States Navy. Appellee was thereafter transferred to Washington, D.C. Appellant [wife] accompanied Appellee and the parties resided together. Upon Appellee's retirement from the service in 1988, the parties moved to Washington, Pennsylvania. They married in 1990. One child, a daughter, was born in 1991.

In April of 1998, Appellee discovered that Appellant had engaged in an adulterous affair with one of his relatives. Appellant thereafter went to Florida for a vacation. During Appellant's absence, Appellee filed a complaint for custody of the parties' minor child.

The parties tried to reconcile upon Appellant's return to Pennsylvania. However, Appellee curtailed Appellant's access to monies during this time period and refused to withdraw his custody complaint. Consequently, Appellant filed a support complaint on May 27, 1998. The reconciliation proved unsuccessful. Appellant left the marital residence in August of 1998. . . .

With regard to the issue of spousal support, the rule is that "[a] dependent spouse is entitled to support until it is proven that the conduct of the dependent spouse constitutes grounds for a fault divorce. . . . Adultery is among the enumerated grounds for a divorce on fault grounds. In this case, it was undisputed that Appellant had engaged in adulterous behavior. However, Appellant asserts that the parties' reconciliation attempt constituted a condonation of the conduct. Condonation is a defense to adultery.

The defense of condonation has been defined as "complete renewal of the marital relationship, or a single act of sexual intercourse, after knowledge or belief that adultery had been committed." "Condonation means the blotting out of the offense imputed, so as to restore the offending party to the same position he or she occupied before the offense was committed. . . . Condonation restores equality before the law."

The parties admittedly attempted a reconciliation, although Appellee explained that he doubted Appellant's sincerity. The parties also conceded that they resumed their marital relations during this time period. . . . We recognize there was not a complete renewal of the marital relationship. . . . However, . . . Appellee accepted Appellant back into the marital residence and resumed relations with her. He further began courting her in an attempt to restore the parties' relationship. Appellee's conduct thus evinced an intent to forgive or condone Appellant's prior adulterous behavior. It is only logical to conclude that had the parties' attempted reconciliation been successful, this matter would not now be before this Court.

It is the policy of the courts to promote reconciliation and keep families together whenever possible. It may seem a harsh result that a single act of intercourse would equate to condonation of the adulterous conduct. However, this Court must have an objective and conclusive test to utilize in determining whether condonation has occurred. Once one party to the marriage has knowledge of the other party's adultery . . . , then that party must decide whether he or she thinks the marriage can be saved. Once that party decides to attempt to reconcile with the adulterous spouse, he or she may decide to resume sexual relations. The resumption of sexual intercourse in this situation is an objective standard by which to judge the condonation of that behavior by the other spouse. The surrounding circumstances, such as the state of mind of that spouse, are subjective and cannot be accurately gauged. To find otherwise would require this Court to engage in a subjective review of the parties' marital relationship.

Under these circumstances, we are compelled to conclude that the trial court abused its discretion in denying Appellant's request for spousal support. . . . Condonation "means the blotting out of the offense imputed, so as to restore the offending party to the same position he or she occupied before the offense was committed." . . . We therefore reverse that portion of the trial court's order dealing with the denial of spousal support and remand for a calculation of Appellee's spousal support obligation.

We saw that reconciliation can nullify a separation agreement, which might in effect penalize a spouse for trying to save a marriage. Here we see that resuming intimate relations in an effort to reconcile can prejudice an injured spouse who tries to forgive and forget the other's adultery. What rationale does the court offer for wiping the slate clean, and is it weightier than the deterrent the holding creates to attempting reconciliation? Does the condonation defense on the whole really serve the state's interest in preserving marriages? What are the incentive effects of the defense on the two parties?

Religious Defense?

The world's major religions have largely been opposed to divorce, and those that allow it have required that couples married within the faith receive a dissolution from religious authorities in order to remarry within the faith. Such religiously imposed constraints have at times conflicted with civil divorce law and procedure.

Ann Laquer Estin, Unofficial Family Law

94 Iowa L. Rev. 449, 463-472 (2009)

. . . For Catholics and Hindus, whose religions prohibit divorce, secular laws that narrowly limited access to divorce were a better fit with unofficial religious norms. For this reason, the Roman Catholic Church worked strenuously for many years against the easing of official divorce laws in the United States. Once lawmakers enacted no-fault divorce laws, some individuals attempted without success to resist civil divorce actions on religious grounds, arguing that entry of a no-fault divorce decree would violate their rights under the First Amendment. Citing free-exercise and establishment barriers, courts identified the central problem with this defense as a conflict between religious views: to deny a divorce based on one partner's religious convictions would impose those religious values on the other partner. . . . Implicit in this response is the court's conclusion that civil divorce belongs to the state, as a purely secular matter, and that questions of religious belief and practice are entirely beyond its ken.

Religious communities have maintained the norms that discourage or prohibit divorce; yet as divorce rates have risen across societies, they have also increased for the membership of these groups. For members of groups that prohibit divorce, a civil dissolution of marriage creates the possibility of a limping marriage, terminated in official law but still binding in religious law. This is a concern for Roman Catholics, divorced in the civil courts, who cannot participate fully in the religious life of their community if they remarry without first obtaining an annulment of their marriage under canon law. To accommodate this concern, the numbers of annulments granted by the Church have increased dramatically over the past thirty years. . . .

For Muslims and Jews, whose religious law has permitted divorce for many centuries, civil divorce laws create a different limping marriage problem. Both systems of law permit divorce, but just as the state does not recognize a religious divorce, the religious community does not recognize a civil divorce as ending a religious marriage. The intersection of civil and religious law is made more complicated by the fact that in these systems the legal rights of husbands are different than the legal rights of wives. These differences create opportunities for strategic behavior in civil divorce proceedings.

To conclude a divorce, Jewish law requires that a husband deliver a document known as a get to his wife in a process carried out before a rabbinic tribunal. As this requirement has been implemented in rabbinic tradition, both husband and wife must participate willingly in the process, and neither party is free to remarry until the get has been given and accepted. A married woman who no longer lives with her husband but has not received a get is known as an agunah, a woman "chained" or "anchored" to her husband. The consequences for a married woman who remarries without a get are much more serious than the consequences for a married man. Many writers have described the dilemma created when a spouse refuses to cooperate in a get proceeding unless his or her demands for custody or a financial settlement are met. Traditional Jewish communities take the agunah problem quite seriously, and may attempt to pressure a spouse to participate in a get procedure through the use of sanctions such as shaming or ostracism.

. . . In these cases, state courts have considered whether the written agreement signed by a Jewish couple prior to their marriage, known as a ketubah, can be construed as a promise to cooperate in a get proceeding before a rabbinic tribunal should the marriage come to an end, and whether such a promise can be enforced by a secular court. Courts have reached different conclusions in these cases, and the problem is made more complex by the fact that a get given or accepted under pressure from a civil court may be invalid as a matter of Jewish law. One innovative approach, approved by the New York Court of Appeals in *Avitzur v. Avitzur*, was the inclusion of explicit language in a ketubah that recognized the jurisdiction of a specific rabbinic tribunal or bet din over marital disputes. The court viewed this provision as analogous to an arbitration clause and held that it provided the civil court with authority to order the parties to appear before the bet din. . . .

Jewish communities in New York and elsewhere have attempted to address the agunah problem by seeking civil statutes that prevent a Jewish spouse from securing a secular divorce until the get process has been concluded. Under New York's get law, enacted in 1979, a court cannot grant a divorce or annulment to any petitioner whose marriage was solemnized in the state by a religious official until the petitioner provides a sworn statement that he or she has "taken all steps solely within his or her power" to remove any religious barriers to the other party's remarriage. A second law, enacted in 1992, permits the civil courts to take religious barriers to remarriage into account in determining the financial incidents of a divorce decree. . . .

From this process, a new model has emerged in which religious courts or clergy function as arbitrators to resolve marriage and divorce disputes. After arbitration, one member of the couple may bring the settlement or judgment to a secular court for enforcement as an arbitration award. A number of these cases that have reached the courts raise a concern that the applicable religious or customary law or procedures put women at a disadvantage. Courts have set aside arbitration awards when there is evidence of undue pressure or overreaching, and courts generally refuse to enforce agreements to arbitrate custody or child-support matters. In practice, in order to ensure that their orders will be upheld and enforced by secular courts, religious arbitrators have learned to address these concerns. . . .

Under Islamic law, a husband has the power to divorce his wife unilaterally by pronouncing talaq, but a wife's options for obtaining a divorce are more limited. Typically, she must obtain her husband's consent to a khula divorce, which usually requires that she relinquish her right to the marriage payment (or mahr) promised by the husband in their marital agreement. Informal conciliation or arbitration within the Muslim community may achieve a settlement, but some disputes over mahr reach the official courts, where the question is whether the courts can enforce a Muslim marital agreement as a civil contract. In countries with Islamic courts, judges have developed a judicial khula divorce that may be available to a wife whose husband refuses to consent to divorce. Where there are no recognized Islamic courts, a wife may have no means to overcome her husband's refusal to agree to a divorce, and no leverage to negotiate over keeping her mahr or obtaining a financial settlement. In London, . . . [i]n both the Muslim and Jewish communities, religious tribunals are now conducting arbitrations under religious law as a form of alternative dispute resolution within the larger framework of English law. . . . [A]n agreement to submit to the jurisdiction of religious authorities poses particular problems not found in other arbitration agreements or marital contracts. . . . [O]ne member of a couple or family might have conscientious or religious objections to appearing before a religious tribunal. . . .

In nations with civil marriage and divorce laws, individual members of religious communities may turn to the secular legal system even when these laws are at odds with religious or other group norms. These choices are protected by the official family-law system as well as constitutional principles of freedom of religion. Some group members make this choice even as they intend to maintain their membership in the religious community. Religious groups, which cannot use the power of the state to enforce their internal norms, are then challenged to find other means of influencing or responding to the choices of group members. The requirement to obtain a religious annulment or divorce as a condition of remarriage within the community is one response that is often, but not always, successful in maintaining the group norm. Sanctions such as shunning or excommunication are a stronger response. . . .

Over time, groups may come to accommodate the choices made by their members with new institutions and practices. . . . These include the development of new types of premarital agreements in different Muslim and Jewish communities, designed to be enforceable in secular courts, which address some of the gender inequalities of traditional practices. . . . Pluralism within a broad tradition provides individuals with important alternatives to a complete exit from the group. . . . [T]he fluidity of belief, practice, and membership in religious communities in these circumstances may contribute to their flourishing.

Recall the rules for enforcement of pre-nuptial agreements. Suppose that in some religious community a standard marriage contract included a waiver by the bride-to-be of all claim to property or support in the event of dissolution. Women cannot marry within this community without signing this contract. Should a civil court enforce this agreement if a married woman from this community petitioned for a civil divorce? See also Nathan B. Oman, *How to Judge Shari'a Contracts: A Guide to Islamic Marriage Agreements in American Courts,* 2011 UTAH L. REV. 287, 313-318 (describing refusal of some U.S. state courts to enforce such agreements, based on failure to comply with the formalities of execution required under local law, but willingness of other courts to do so, particularly when it is the wife seeking to enforce the contract).

Apparently courts in France "may refuse a divorce which one party opposes on religious grounds if this would cause that party 'exceptional hardship' given that party's commitment to religious teaching on the indissolubility of marriage." See NORMAN DOE, LAW AND RELIGION IN EUROPE: A COMPARATIVE INTRODUCTION (2011), 223. In seeming tension with that position, however, French courts also may order a Jewish husband who refuses to issue a *get* to pay compensation to the wife. Id. And U.K. courts can refuse to grant a Jewish husband a civil divorce if he refuses to give his wife a *get.* Could any U.S. court do any of those things without running into constitutional problems?

As the article above suggests, the divorce laws of several cultures have at times given husbands greater control over the divorce decision than wives. In fact, at one time the Anglo-American legal tradition granted the power to seek divorce solely to husbands. This was consistent with the coverture law regime's eviscerating wives' legal personhood, rendering them incapable of bringing suit in court, which in turn reflected a view of women as property and/or as incapable of rational decision making. Today there remains some asymmetry in Muslim law; husbands can divorce by declaration, but wives must show fault and/or return their dowry.

THOUGHT EXPERIMENT

Imagine that some state's legislature concluded (rightly or wrongly) that men on average are not especially rational about relationship decisions, being driven more by sexual impulse than by reason and caring, and so instantiated an opposite sort of gender-asymmetrical divorce rule, one granting wives alone the power to divorce. What consequences, good or bad, might such a rule have? And which of those consequences might the patriarchal rule putting control entirely in the husband's hands also have had? Does it influence your conclusions to take into account that today in the United States wives file roughly 70 percent of all divorce petitions?

e. A Counter-Revolution?

You now have some sense of the substantive bases for divorce and how use of one or another can impact other aspects of a marital dissolution. The following article presents some of the social history underlying the move from fault-based to no-fault divorce in the Western world. It also serves as a segue to the financial aspects of divorce, by identifying some policy debates that have motivated or resulted from developments in the law governing property distribution and alimony.

Laura Bradford, The Counterrevolution: A Critique of Recent Proposals to Reform No-Fault Divorce Laws

49 Stan. L. Rev. 607 (1997)

On Valentine's Day 1996, Michigan State Representative Jessie Dalman launched "the divorce counter-revolution." In an announcement made on the steps of the Michigan Capitol Building, Ms. Dalman unveiled a series of bills designed to strengthen the institution of marriage by ending easy "no-fault" divorces. . . . On Michigan's heels, at least nine other states have introduced similar bills. As David Blakenhorn, the founder of . . . the Institute for American Values, stated, "[w]e as a society are becoming sick and tired of a culture of divorce and non-marriage. . . . For the past twenty years, the image of divorce was of rebirth and renewal, a pathway to greater happiness. . . . The divorce revolution has not delivered the goods, and now we're beginning to view divorce as the problem."

The Michigan proposal is the latest attempt to define the "problem" with the American family, which is widely viewed as being in a crisis. Evidence of this crisis includes soaring divorce rates and an increasing number of children being raised in nontraditional, often one parent, families. Female headed households make up the "new poor" in America with median incomes of one-third those of married couples. Fathers are behind in child support payments to the tune of several billion dollars. Children raised in single parent households are more likely to have emotional or behavioral problems, become sexually active, use drugs, and fare poorly in school. Politicians have been quoted as saying that, "[a]lmost every problem we have in this society can be attributed to the breakdown of the marriage-based, two-parent family."

The breakdown in the American family has prompted nostalgia for the old fault-based divorce system. Under this system, marriage was an unbreakable union, dissoluble only in the face of certain well-defined moral transgressions by one party. Courts used fault to determine property and support allocations after divorce. If the wealthier party, usually the husband, was at fault, courts would require him to support the "innocent" spouse, while a transgression by the wife forfeited her right to any support from the injured husband. Those who advocate a return to this system argue that the current divorce regime does not encourage spouses to remain responsible and committed throughout the marriage. Academics and legislators alike have proposed reforms that would impose a cost for immoral or irresponsible behavior by one partner. . . .

I. The Move to No-Fault Divorce Laws

A. The Fault Regime

Before the 1960s, legal rules regulating marriage reflected the belief that the state had a profound interest in the institution, and therefore could closely regulate its formation, organization, and dissolution. A couple could only obtain a divorce where one member had clearly engaged in one of a few acts defined by the state to constitute a fault. . . . Only the "innocent" spouse could apply for divorce. . . .

B. Changes in Social Views

As attitudes about the individual and the family began to change and divorce became more prevalent in the early 1960s, distaste for public intrusion into the marital relationship led to the decline of the fault system. The secularization of divorce led to less restrictive attitudes about breaking the marriage contract. Gradually, society began to accept a view of marriage as a partnership between individuals, terminable at will when it failed to meet the needs or desires of either party. The restrictive fault regime had imposed intolerable obstacles in front of a procedure desired by more and more couples.

The spectacle of couples parading their marital problems in front of judges fed the impetus for reform. The movement toward no-fault was supported by the fact that divorce-seeking couples often subverted or ignored the restrictive fault rules. The most common evasions were migration and collusion; couples would either go to a jurisdiction with more lenient divorce laws, or would perjure themselves before the court to manufacture instances of marital "fault." In the 1960s, ninety percent of divorces on fault grounds were granted without contest. The judicial system participated in this evasion; divorce hearings became "brief and perfunctory" as judges sought to avoid ugly airings of marital grievances. This new view of marriage questioned the idea that divorce could be fully explained by simplistic notions such as "fault." More complex conceptions of human psychology led people to understand divorce as stemming not from one factor but from a variety of complicated circumstances affecting both parties. . . .

At the same time, attitudes regarding the law's proper role in moral discourse about the family were undergoing revolutionary change. . . . Changing moral values, as evidenced by the sexual revolution and the decline of religion in American life, have reduced popular consensus about marital norms. In particular, the decline of religious homogeneity has weakened the moral base of family law. Another factor . . . is . . . the rise of "Psychologic Man." According to this theory, modern individuals crave self-realization and personal well-being more than they seek to fulfill religious and moral duties. For members of this new generation, marriage is a relationship that should continue only as long as it "works" for the partners. Thus, the traditional view of the wife as a family caretaker unselfishly devoted to the home and the husband as the provider and protector have given way to demands for self-fulfillment and self-development. Concomitantly, changing gender roles contributed to the modern conception of marriage as an equal partnership. As women seek equality with men, the patriarchal family unit has given way to relationships where men and women enter as equal, autonomous partners who agree that the marriage should dissolve if and when it fails to provide both partners with opportunities for self-fulfillment.

Finally, . . . the Supreme Court increasingly redefined family privacy in terms of individual autonomy and respect for individual choice in areas such as marriage, procreation, and child-rearing. . . . By coming to the defense of a practice that states had identified as hostile to the purity and sanctity of the marriage relationship, the Court in *Eisenstadt* indicated that it was bestowing protection not on the family as the foundation of society, but on the individual as a personal decisionmaker. This move both mirrored and perhaps drove the popular conception that marriage and the decision to divorce are personal ones which should remain outside the purview of the law. . . .

C. NO-FAULT REFORM: ITS HISTORY AND PROBLEMS

The central goal of the movement toward no-fault was preservation of judicial integrity; it was originally conceived neither as a way of encouraging easy divorces and revolving door marriages nor as a method for reforming the basis upon which courts should determine spousal support and child custody awards. However, these unintended effects have become its legacy. The academics, lawyers, and clerics who were the original proponents of no-fault reform sought to shore up the integrity of the law and to preserve the dignity of the couple. The reformers realized that the fault requirement was out of step with American society, and they sought through reform to eliminate the widespread, elaborate, and embarrassing ruses staged by divorcing couples. Therefore, although the no-fault "revolution" simply mirrored what was already occurring in practice, reformers believed that bringing the law in conformity with practice would yield benefits both to the legal system as well as individuals who sought divorce.

Between 1969 and 1985, all 50 states incorporated no-fault provisions into their laws governing divorce. . . . Although the primary objective of the no-fault movement was to change the grounds for divorce, reformers also proposed to eliminate fault as a basis for property division and alimony awards. Reformist legislators sought to replace the punitive element of these determinations with a focus on the economic circumstances of the parties. Indeed, many states . . . eliminated fault as a factor in the allocation of property and the setting of spousal support. Other states have retained fault as one of many factors that a court may consider. . . . However, even when fault is considered, it no longer guarantees permanent support from a guilty spouse. Emphasis instead falls on letting the partners make a "clean break," by providing for lump sum settlements to avoid prolonged financial relationships between the parties. Under this system, the court designs "equal" or "equitable" property awards and, where appropriate, minimal alimony allocations, which are gradually phased out as the supported spouse retrains for a new career.

Critics of this trend toward equal property awards point out its catastrophic effects on women and children. For example, they note that the new rules penalize a spouse who sacrificed her own career potential to care for her family. Most couples who apply for divorce have been married for only a short time, have accumulated only minimal assets, such as a mortgage-encumbered home, and have young children in need of full-time supervision. Yet, following the divorce, the husband frequently has an established career and a sufficient job, while the wife typically has no marketable skills to show for her years of marriage. Under these highly disadvantageous circumstances, she is then expected to assume joint financial responsibility for her children and sole responsibility for herself. Therefore, "clean break" dissolutions effectively burden the wife with more responsibility and less support, while awarding the husband sole enjoyment of all future increases in earning capacity.

One example of the burden "equal" divorce places on women and children is the award of the family home. Under the old fault system, courts generally awarded the marital home to the wife; however, courts now are more likely to sell the home and divide the proceeds equally between the spouses. The sale compounds the disorienting effect of the divorce on the wife and children by separating them from their community at a time when they most need its support. . . .

Compounding the problem is a reluctance of many courts to characterize intangible property such as professional degrees or enhanced earning capacity as marital property subject to division. The argument for characterizing such intangibles as marital property is that one spouse sacrificed her own career potential, so that the other spouse could concentrate fully on his career. Thus, courts should award at least some of the property value to the spouse who either worked at home or worked in a dead end job to provide money that enabled the wealthier spouse to obtain his degree or increase his earning capacity. Courts and academics have two standard responses to this argument. First, these assets are simply too speculative and remote to appraise. Second, such compensation would be unfair because the wealthier spouse would probably have completed the degree or achieved at work regardless of his spouse's help.

The move to no-fault divorce also undermined the traditional justifications for alimony, and therefore caused additional problems for women. Under the fault system, the notion of marriage as a lifelong commitment justified a guilty husband's obligation to support his wife after the divorce. Under no-fault, no such justification exists. With the new emphasis on dividing family assets equally, alimony has become a temporary entitlement for the wife until she can obtain "retraining" to support herself. This arrangement only makes sense if one believes that women can find easy access to new jobs and achieve economic parity with men in the labor market. Unfortunately, the real story is not so rosy. . . . Evidence shows that "[a] homemaker displaced through divorce often suffers an immediate and dramatic decline in economic status." Approximately 57% of women who were formerly homemakers earn incomes at or below the poverty level and the percentage is higher for women of color. Women's efforts to get ahead in the work world are frustrated by continuing wage discrimination and insufficient experience, education, and training. Moreover, if the woman is younger, she often still has full-time child care responsibilities. . . .

The effect of divorce on children has also been devastating both emotionally and economically. For any child, the separation of their parents causes stress and uncertainty. After the divorce, the children will usually see less of one parent and may see less of both parents if the primary caretaker has to return to work. Ninety percent of all children remain in their mother's custody after divorce. In addition to experiencing the same financial hardships as their mother, these children must often deal with the stress of changing schools or attending day care. Social science research suggests that these children are also more at risk for depression, emotional, and behavioral problems, and poor performance in school . . . [as well as] juvenile crime and teenage suicide. . . .

II. The Fault-Based Proposals

In a 1986 . . . survey, 79.6 percent of those questioned agreed with the statement, "Divorce is so easy to get today that people don't really work as hard as they should to stay married." A 1995 survey . . . found that 31 to 55% of Americans surveyed favored "divorce reform to strengthen the rights of spouses who want to save the marriage." . . . In step with the rising dissatisfaction, [Michigan, Idaho, Georgia, Iowa, Virginia,

Washington, Minnesota, Illinois, Pennsylvania, Indiana, and Hawaii] have considered . . . proposals to repeal or modify their no-fault divorce laws. . . . [T]he "Michigan Proposal" . . . would make it harder both to get married and to obtain a divorce. To obtain a marriage license . . . , couples would either complete a program in premarital counseling or wait thirty days and pay an extra eighty dollars for the license. Spouses seeking a divorce would face even greater hurdles. Couples who mutually consented to the split would still be eligible for a no-fault divorce. However, if one spouse does not want to end the marriage, the old fault requirements would apply. In addition, all divorcing couples with children have to fill out parenting plans and complete a "parenting educational program" before filing for divorce. The course would teach them about the effects of divorce on children of different ages. . . .

Elizabeth Scott . . . suggests . . . the problem with modern marriage is that adults have been trained to leave the relationship if it fails to meet their current needs or expectations. The fault system, although inadequate in many ways, had the overlooked benefit of imposing considerable costs on the decision to terminate the marriage. Scott proposes a number of "precommitment" remedies, such as economic penalties, mandatory waiting periods, and prenuptial agreements to fulfill fault's old role of inducing couples to stay together. She also argues that the state should apply a separate set of more restrictive laws to couples with children to further hinder their ability to obtain a divorce. . . .

[E]ach of the proposals explicitly seeks to restore the lost bargaining power of the innocent spouse. . . . [T]he fault requirement had provided an important bargaining advantage for the spouse who was reluctant to leave the marriage. Where the guilty spouse was eager for release, the other spouse could agree to sue for divorce in return for significant concessions under the settlement agreement. Weitzman . . . argued that the loss of this bargaining power was largely responsible for many of the meager settlements women were receiving under the no fault scheme. . . .

Finally, fault proposals satisfy the popular expectation that the family organization is predicated on moral as well as economic and social terms. When a spouse who commits adultery walks away with half or more of the family's assets . . . , most people believe an injustice has been done. Injecting fault back into divorce and into the division of assets and maintenance after divorce satisfies the popular expectation that society will reward those who observe their marital vows and commitments. This sentiment probably accounts for the wide political appeal of the fault proposals.

Are the arguments for resurrecting barriers to divorce persuasive? Do they adequately address the problems with the fault regime that led to the no-fault revolution? Would they be more persuasive if the new barriers avoided some of the problems with fault-only divorce law—for example, if the reform involved eliminating fault grounds while putting teeth into no-fault grounds and/or imposing serious pre-filing counseling requirements? Might the ideal role for the state be one that is highly paternalistic but not judgmental? Cf. Clare Huntington, *Repairing Family Law*, 57 Duke L.J. 1245 (2008) (urging that the state focus on repairing emotional relationships within families even while it is severing legal family relationships).

Ultimately, the Michigan legislation failed. Instead Louisiana led the anti-divorce movement with its "Covenant Marriage" law, discussed in Chapter 2. Arizona and Oklahoma later enacted similar laws. Surprisingly few people opted into Covenant Marriage in these states, even though the terms are not radically different from those in a typical state that combines fault grounds with a no-fault divorce based on having lived separate and apart, and despite the unrealistic optimism people have at the time of marrying about the permanence of their union.

3. *Financial Aspects of Divorce*

The financial aspects of a divorce decree include property division, alimony, and child support. You studied child support in Chapter 4, because it is an aspect of the ongoing legal relationship between parents and younger offspring. Courts generally look at property division and alimony in combination and try to arrive at an appropriate package of financial provisions. The modern trend is to restrict or avoid alimony and to account for the needs of ex-spouses as much as possible through property division. We saw that child support is usually determined by mechanical application of a formula. In contrast, courts in most states must allocate property and award alimony based on quite subjective, factor-based judgments. Thus, the primary sites of lawyering in connection with the financial aspects of divorce are property division and spousal support. Be aware that, in addition to the rules we will study, tax, bankruptcy, and other laws may affect how you structure a settlement or proposed decree as to property division.

a. Property Division

The judge in a divorce action must answer four questions regarding property division. Ordered conceptually, they are:

What is property?
Which property is subject to division by the court?
What is the value of property that is subject to division?
How should that property be divided?

You might suppose the answer to the first question is straightforward. We all know what property is—a house, a car, furniture, bank accounts, stocks. But the past few decades have brought recognition in divorce actions of "new property"—intangible interests that may be the product of joint spousal effort. Is a pension property? What about goodwill in a family business? Is your law degree property? Although this question of what is property is conceptually first, we will address it after studying the rules dictating which property is subject to division, because an understanding of the basic principles underlying the latter will better enable you to comprehend courts' analysis of the former.

The second question essentially asks which property the courts treat as separate and which as community or "marital property" at the time of divorce. In the great majority of states, courts may only divide marital property; any separate assets remain entirely the property of the nominal owner. This "characterization" issue generates much litigation.

Answering the third question often requires, as several of the cases below reveal, application of fairly complex accounting principles. For example, how a divorce court should value a contingency fee that a spouse who is a lawyer might receive after divorce depends partly on how one calculates the present value of future income and partly on an estimate of the probability of success in the litigation and the size of the fee if ever received. Divorce attorneys must sometimes retain accounting or valuation experts to handle valuation disputes effectively.

The fourth question is often the most difficult at the trial level, because in most states it cannot be answered simply by reference to general rules, such as that each spouse shall receive 50 percent of marital assets, but rather requires case-specific application of subjective factors such as contribution, need, and fault. We will discuss the virtues and vices of this factor-based inquiry and of specific factors courts apply.

(1) Which Property Is Subject to Division?

As explained in Chapter 3, the distinction between community property regimes and common-law property regimes largely disappears in the context of divorce, because states in both categories have largely converged on a single approach to property division—the "marital property system." This approach treats some property of spouses as "marital property" subject to division and some as separate property. The legal basis for characterizing property as marital at the time of divorce is the same as that for characterizing property as community during marriage in community property states—namely, that it was acquired by labor of a spouse during marriage. Insofar as common-law property states today overlook title to property and treat any property acquired by labor during the marriage as marital and subject to division between the spouses, they have essentially adopted the idea of community property and its underlying view of marriage as an economic partnership. As the Bradford article above indicated, 50 years ago courts in common-law property states had no jurisdiction over individually owned assets, even if the owner acquired the assets by labor during marriage; they could allocate between the spouses only jointly owned assets.

Most states still ostensibly exclude separate property—that is, property acquired before the marriage or received by gift or inheritance, from the total pie to be divided at divorce, leaving it entirely to the owning spouse. A significant minority of states, though, are "hotchpot" states that make separate property also potentially subject to forced transfer from the owner to the other spouse. For example, Connecticut law confers on divorce courts sweeping power over married persons' property: "At the time of entering a decree . . . dissolving a marriage . . . , the court may assign to either the husband or wife all or any part of the estate of the other." Conn. Gen. Stat. §46b-81(a). Other hotchpot states include Indiana, Massachusetts, Oregon, and Vermont. How can such states justify taking away from someone property that they earned before getting married or property that a family member gifted to them? Professor Motro suggests a justification by criticizing the prevailing rule's tying of entitlement to marital labor.

Shari Motro, Labor, Luck, and Love: Reconsidering the Sanctity of Separate Property

102 Nw. U. L. Rev. 1623 (2008)

. . . First, the labor-centered rule naively assumes that spouses with unequal separate holdings will be equally invested in the marriage as a joint venture. In many cases, spouses with widely divergent wealth have a disproportionate exposure to risk. As a result, they may not expend the same efforts toward income production—both before and during marriage. . . .

Also, the line between acquisitions attributable to marital labor and those attributable to other factors—like premarital labor and sheer luck—is impossible to draw accurately. Many gifts and inheritances are not the result of pure altruism, but rather reflect, at least in part, a quid pro quo, an unarticulated exchange. On the flip side, earnings are rarely attributable solely to contemporaneous effort. Most often, earnings reflect a combination of past and current labor, as well as circumstances over which the individual worker has little control—circumstances that can often be traced to gifts, favors, or inherited privilege. An individual's education, cultural fluency, and professional contacts accessed through social and familial networks are just some of the lucky breaks that impact financial success.

Finally, the labor-centered partnership theory conflicts with widely held intuitions and typical practices in ongoing marriages. Property that would be considered separate as a legal matter is hardly ever kept wholly separate from the marriage. Rather, propertied spouses tend to share more and more of their individual assets as marriage progresses, mixing labor- and luck-generated property as their relationship grows and deepens.

Professor Motro proposes a rule by which a non-owning spouse would become entitled to a share of the owning spouse's separate property at divorce at a percentage that increases with the length of the marriage. It is fairly clear how one of her points supports this proposal—namely, the one about "unarticulated exchange"; if husband's inheritance from his mother is secured by taking care of her in her declining years, it is reasonable to suppose wife contributes to that effort. Some people do have to work for their inheritance. But do any of Professor Motro's other points support an argument for forced transfer of separate property at divorce? If a trust-fund-beneficiary wife feels free not to work, how does that make her husband entitled to a share of her trust fund? Why should her husband do better financially in the divorce than he would if she had had no income from any source and chose not to work outside the home? And what is the implication for separate property from the fact that a spouse's high-paying job might have been secured through nepotism? It is still a job requiring expenditure of effort, is it not? And does not the assertion that earnings in marriage partly reflect premarital effort, or privilege, count against sharing even marital income? Lastly, if one spouse chooses to share pre-marital or inherited wealth with the other, how does that make the other spouse entitled to even more of that wealth at time of divorce? Is Professor Motro suggesting that the choice to share some during marriage logically entails a commitment to share all even after the marriage ends?

In the vast majority of states, courts allocate whichever property is in the divisible pie "equitably," which could be anything from 50/50 to 100/0. Most states' statutes set forth a list of factors deemed relevant to equity, an example of which you will study shortly. Three community property states—California, New Mexico, and Louisiana—divide property at divorce based strictly on equitable ownership during marriage. Thus, what was community property during marriage (property acquired by effort during marriage) is divided *equally*, and what was separate property during marriage (property owned before marriage or acquired during marriage by gift or inheritance) remains the separate property of the title holder. Some states' statutes establish a presumption in favor of equal distribution of marital assets, or direct that courts use 50/50 as a starting point, putting the burden of persuasion on a spouse who demands more than 50 percent.

In every state, the "characterization question"—that is, what is marital and what is separate, is important. Even in hotchpot states, courts generally treat as a relevant equitable consideration what contribution each spouse made to acquisition of any property, and with separate property the assumption should be that they made none. See, e.g., Vt. Stat. Ann. tit. 15, §751(b)(10) (listing as an equitable distribution factor "the party through whom the property was acquired"). Situations that give rise to litigation over characterization include deferred compensation (i.e., income received during marriage for pre-marital labor or income expected after divorce for labor expended during the marriage); sale of separate assets and use of the proceeds to purchase new assets; increases in value of, or income from, separate property; and commingling of marital and separate assets. Reading the Virginia equitable distribution statute below should give you some idea of why property distribution is usually the most complex aspect of divorce litigation and practice. To make it somewhat more readable, key terms are highlighted.

Code of Virginia
Title 20. Domestic Relations
Chapter 6. Divorce, Affirmation and Annulment

§20-107.3. Court May Decree as to Property of the Parties

A. Upon decreeing . . . a divorce from the bond of matrimony, . . . the court, upon request of either party, shall determine the legal title as between the parties, and the ownership and value of all property, real or personal, tangible or intangible, of the parties and shall consider which of such property is separate property, which is marital property, and which is part separate and part marital property in accordance with subdivision A 3. The court shall determine the value of any such property as of the date of the evidentiary hearing on the evaluation issue. . . .

1. **Separate property** is (i) all property, real and personal, acquired by either party before the marriage; (ii) all property acquired during the marriage by bequest, devise, descent, survivorship or gift from a source other than the other party; (iii) all property acquired during the marriage in exchange for or from the proceeds of sale of separate property, provided that such property acquired during the marriage is maintained as separate property; and (iv) that part of any property classified as separate pursuant to subdivision A 3. . . .

2. **Marital property** is (i) all property titled in the names of both parties, whether as joint tenants, tenants by the entirety or otherwise, except as provided by subdivision A 3, (ii) that part of any property classified as marital pursuant to subdivision A 3, or (iii) all other property acquired by each party during the marriage which is not separate property as defined above. All property . . . acquired by either spouse during the marriage, and before the last separation of the parties, . . . is presumed to be marital property in the absence of satisfactory evidence that it is separate property. For purposes of this section marital property is presumed to be jointly owned unless there is a deed, title or other clear indicia that it is not jointly owned.

3. The court shall classify property as part marital property and part separate property as follows:

a. In the case of **income received from separate property** during the marriage, such income shall be marital property only to the extent it is attributable to the personal efforts of either party. In the case of the **increase in value of separate property** during the marriage, such increase in value shall be marital property only to the extent that marital property or the personal efforts of either party have contributed to such increases, provided that any such personal efforts must be significant and result in substantial appreciation of the separate property. . . .

d. When marital property and separate property are **commingled by contributing one category of property to another**, resulting in the loss of identity of the contributed property, the classification of the contributed property shall be transmuted to the category of property receiving the contribution. However, to the extent the contributed property is retraceable by a preponderance of the evidence and was not a gift, such contributed property shall retain its original classification.

e. When marital property and separate property are **commingled into newly acquired property** resulting in the loss of identity of the contributing properties, the commingled property shall be deemed transmuted to marital property. However, to the extent the contributed property is retraceable by a preponderance of the evidence and was not a gift, the contributed property shall retain its original classification.

f. When **separate property is retitled** in the joint names of the parties, the retitled property shall be deemed transmuted to marital property. However, to the extent the property is retraceable by a preponderance of the evidence and was not a gift, the retitled property shall retain its original classification.

g. When the **separate property** of one party is **commingled** into the separate property of the other party, or the separate property of each party is commingled into newly acquired property, to the extent the contributed property is retraceable by a preponderance of the evidence and was not a gift, each party shall be reimbursed the value of the contributed property in any award made pursuant to this section.

h. Subdivisions A 3 d, e and f of this section shall apply to jointly owned property. No presumption of gift shall arise under this section where (i) separate property is commingled with jointly owned property; (ii) newly acquired property is conveyed into joint ownership; or (iii) existing property is conveyed or retitled into joint ownership. For purposes of this subdivision A 3, property is jointly owned when it is titled in the name of both parties, whether as joint tenants, tenants by the entireties, or otherwise.

B. For the purposes of this section only, both parties shall be deemed to have rights and interests in the marital property. However, such interests and rights shall not attach to the legal title of such property and are only to be used as a consideration in determining a monetary award, if any, as provided in this section.

C. Except as provided in subsection G, the court shall have no authority to order the division or transfer of separate property or marital property which is not jointly owned. The court may, based upon the factors listed in subsection E, divide or transfer or order the division or transfer, or both, of jointly owned marital property, or any part thereof. The court shall also have the authority to apportion and order the payment of the debts of the parties, or either of them, that are incurred prior to the dissolution of the marriage, based upon the factors listed in subsection E.

As a means of dividing or transferring the jointly owned marital property, the court may transfer or order the transfer of real or personal property or any interest therein to one of the parties, permit either party to purchase the interest of the other and direct the allocation of the proceeds, provided the party purchasing the interest of the other agrees to assume any indebtedness secured by the property, or order its sale by private sale by the parties, through such agent as the court shall direct, or by public sale as the court shall direct without the necessity for partition. . . .

D. In addition, based upon (i) the equities and the rights and interests of each party in the marital property, and (ii) the factors listed in subsection E, the court has the power to grant a **monetary award**, payable either in a lump sum or over a period of time in fixed amounts, to either party. . . .

E. The amount of any division or transfer of jointly owned marital property, and the amount of any monetary award, the apportionment of marital debts, and the method of payment shall be determined by the court after consideration of the following **factors**:

1. The contributions, monetary and nonmonetary, of each party to the well-being of the family;
2. The contributions, monetary and nonmonetary, of each party in the acquisition and care and maintenance of such marital property of the parties;
3. The duration of the marriage;
4. The ages and physical and mental condition of the parties;
5. The circumstances and factors which contributed to the dissolution of the marriage, specifically including any ground for divorce under the provisions of subdivisions (1), (3) or (6) of §20-91 or §20-95;
6. How and when specific items of such marital property were acquired;
7. The debts and liabilities of each spouse, the basis for such debts and liabilities, and the property which may serve as security for such debts and liabilities;
8. The liquid or nonliquid character of all marital property;
9. The tax consequences to each party;
10. The use or expenditure of marital property by either of the parties for a non-marital separate purpose or the dissipation of such funds, when such was done in anticipation of divorce or separation or after the last separation of the parties; and
11. Such other factors as the court deems necessary or appropriate to consider in order to arrive at a fair and equitable monetary award.

F. The court shall determine the amount of any such monetary award without regard to maintenance and support awarded for either party or support for the minor children of both parties and shall, after or at the time of such determination and upon motion of either party, consider whether an order for support and maintenance of a spouse or children shall be entered or, if previously entered, whether such order shall be modified or vacated.

G. In addition to the monetary award made pursuant to subsection D, and upon consideration of the factors set forth in subsection E:

1. The court may direct payment of a percentage of the marital share of any pension, profit-sharing or deferred compensation plan or **retirement benefits**, whether vested or nonvested, which constitutes marital property . . . as such benefits are payable. . . .
2. To the extent permitted by federal or other applicable law, the court may order a party to designate a spouse or former spouse as irrevocable beneficiary during the lifetime of the beneficiary of all or a portion of any **survivor benefit** or annuity plan of whatsoever nature, but not to include a life insurance policy. . . .

I. Nothing in this section shall be construed to prevent the affirmation, ratification and incorporation in a decree of an agreement between the parties pursuant to §§ 20-109 and 20-109.1. Agreements, otherwise valid as contracts, entered into between spouses prior to the marriage shall be recognized and enforceable.

Note the stark contrast between Virginia law and Connecticut law as to the power of courts to order a transfer of title. The Connecticut statute quoted above empowers courts to transfer any assets, even individually owned non-marital assets, from one spouse to another. See also Vt. Stat. Ann. tit. 15, §751(a) ("All property owned by either or both of the parties, however and whenever acquired, shall be subject to the jurisdiction of the court. Title to the property, whether in the names of the husband, the wife, both parties, or a nominee, shall be immaterial, except where equitable distribution can be made without disturbing separate property.") The Virginia statute, in paragraphs B and C, prohibits courts from retitling any property that the couple did not jointly title; instead, courts must effect a distribution of the value of individually titled marital property by giving the non-owner a monetary award, which the title holder may satisfy however he or she chooses. The practical difference is that property owners going through a divorce in Virginia retain more control over which particular assets they keep and which they transfer to the other spouse. Though most married couples own the marital home jointly, in many couples only one spouse holds title to the home, and that spouse will get to keep the house after the divorce, forcing the other to move out.

The following case addresses the issue of how to characterize income from an increase in value to separate property, under a Minnesota statute similar to that of Virginia.

Baker v. Baker

753 N.W.2d 644 (Minn. June 26, 2008)

MEYER, Justice.

. . . Appellant Dr. Daniel Remember Baker married respondent Carol Bernice Baker on May 12, 1990. On May 6, 2003, Ms. Baker filed a petition for dissolution of the marriage. . . . Ms. Baker was 57 and Dr. Baker 69½ years of age. They had no children together, although both have children from previous relationships. . . .

Dr. Baker's former employer, Specialists in General Surgery, Ltd. (SIGS), provided a qualified retirement plan. At the time of the marriage, Dr. Baker's SIGS accounts were worth $957,473. During the marriage, SIGS made contributions to the plan totaling $396,455. Although both parties agree that the balance at the date of the marriage remains nonmarital and that the contributions made during the marriage and the investment return attributable to those contributions ($243,122) are marital, they dispute the characterization of the $1,491,022 investment return attributable to the nonmarital portion. Ms. Baker contends that it is entirely marital. Dr. Baker contends that it is nonmarital.

These disputed amounts reflect a total of 11 separate accounts holding SIGS funds. In late 1991 or early 1992, Dr. Baker moved some of the SIGS accounts to Merrill Lynch under management of Randy Trask. According to Thomas William Harjes, Dr. Baker's valuation expert,

> Dr. Baker pays a management fee to Merrill Lynch based on a percentage of the assets under management. . . . [T]here are different money managers that Merrill Lynch has hired to manage different accounts. . . . Mr. Trask manages and reviews the annual . . . information from those money managers to determine whether different money managers would be hired.

. . . Trask testified that he and the money managers he retained had discretion to invest the money in the accounts. According to Trask, Dr. Baker also had the power to direct investments and to transfer funds at will from one investment to another at either the same or different institutions. At least since Dr. Baker turned 59½, the funds were available without a penalty as liquid assets. Before that, he could have accessed them if he paid a penalty.

Trask characterized Dr. Baker's involvement in the Merrill Lynch accounts as "[v]ery passive" and recalled only one stock purchase during the course of their 13-year relationship that was made at Dr. Baker's behest: a purchase for "a few thousand dollars" of stock in a company with which Dr. Baker's son was associated. Trask recalled that in 1998 or 1999, Dr. Baker "transferred his accounts to another firm for a while, but—and then he came back."

The Bakers made no withdrawals and received no distributions from the accounts during the marriage. All investment return was added to the principal. For purposes of Harjes's calculations "any elements of increase in value be it interest, dividends, capital gains distributions or stock appreciation was considered a return on the account." Harjes did not trace individual investments or distinguish between specific premarital and post-marital investments. Because SIGS contributed to the accounts during the marriage, marital and nonmarital funds were commingled in the accounts.

Dr. Baker moved SIGS funds, both within and among investment institutions, at various times during the marriage. In each of the years from 1999 to 2003, he closed at least one account and transferred the funds into new accounts. Of the two present accounts that are not with Merrill Lynch, one is with Charles Schwab and one is with U.S. Bank. There is very little in the record about these accounts or Dr. Baker's role in those investments. . . .

The issue in this case is whether the total investment return on the nonmarital portion of Dr. Baker's SIGS accounts is marital property. . . . As we noted above, there were no withdrawals from Dr. Baker's SIGS accounts during the marriage, and all income earned on the accounts during the marriage-interest, dividends, and capital gains-was reinvested in the accounts. We consider whether the appreciation on the accounts-the increase in the value of the investments as opposed to the income earned on the accounts-during the marriage is marital or nonmarital property. . . .

Minnesota Statutes §518.003, subd. 3b (2006), defines marital property as "property, real or personal, . . . acquired by the parties, or either of them, to a dissolution . . . at any time during the existence of the marriage relation between them, . . . but prior to the date of valuation." Nonmarital property is "property real or personal, acquired by either spouse . . . , which . . . (b) is acquired before the marriage; [or] (c) is acquired in exchange for or is the increase in value of" nonmarital property. All property acquired by either spouse during the marriage is presumptively marital, but a spouse may defeat the presumption by showing by a preponderance of the evidence that the property acquired is nonmarital.

In determining whether the appreciation in the value of a nonmarital investment is marital or nonmarital, we look to whether or not the appreciation is the result of active management of the investment, classifying active appreciation as marital property and passive appreciation as nonmarital property. We have explained the difference between active and passive appreciation as follows:

> [I]ncrease in the value of nonmarital property attributable to the efforts of one or both spouses during their marriage, like the increase resulting from the application of marital funds, is marital property. Conversely, an increase in the value of nonmarital property attributable to inflation or to market forces or conditions[] retains its nonmarital character.

Dr. Baker argues that appreciation is active only if caused by the application of marital effort. He argues that by focusing on control rather than effort, the court of appeals eliminated the possibility of passive appreciation of nearly any asset and, by extension, the possibility that any asset can remain nonmarital. Ms. Baker counters that the investment in this case was actively managed. Dr. Baker disputes this and argues that he expended "virtually no time, effort, or funds from the marriage to appoint an investment advisor to manage the accounts."

The classification of property as marital or nonmarital is grounded in the principle that marriage is a partnership and that each partner should get out of the marriage a fair share of what was put into it. Our discussion in *Nardini* is illustrative:

> [M]arriage is a joint enterprise whose vitality, success and endurance is dependent upon the conjunction of multiple components, only one of which is financial. . . . [T]he extent to which each of the parties contributes to the marriage is not measurable only by the amount of money contributed to it during the period of its endurance but, rather, by the whole complex of financial and nonfinancial components contributed. The function of equitable distribution is to recognize that when a marriage ends, each of the spouses, based on the totality of the contributions made to it, has a stake in and right to a share of the marital assets accumulated while it endured. . . .

We have never addressed how §518.003, subd. 3b, and its underlying rationale should affect the classification of investment portfolios such as those at issue here. We have, however, decided a number of cases involving the classification of other kinds of property. *See Gottsacker* (holding that an Accumulated Adjustment Account (AAA) in a subchapter S corporation was nonmarital property on the dual bases that the wife had no control over distributions from the AAA and that no marital effort increased the value of the wife's interest in the AAA); *Antone* (holding that there was "marital equity" in rental properties to the extent that the rental income during the marriage reduced the properties' mortgage balances; that there was a marital component to the homestead, even though the husband had bought it before the marriage and its mortgage balances had actually increased during the marriage; and that the husband's interest in a business was marital because it was purchased with marital funds, even though it was a successor to a similar failed nonmarital business); *Nardini* (holding that increase in value of couple's closely held corporation, in which the husband had acquired 50% ownership before the marriage, was marital because it was attributable to the efforts of the spouses during the marriage); *Faus v. Faus* (Minn. 1982) (affirming trial court's conclusion that a homestead purchased with nonmarital assets was marital because much of its value came from improvements made by the couple during the marriage); *Schmitz v. Schmitz* (Minn. 1981) (holding that a duplex purchased with nonmarital assets was marital property to the extent that the mortgage had been paid with rental income during the marriage).

In *Schmitz*, we endorsed the use of a formula to apportion the marital and nonmarital components of a single asset. We later summarized the formula as follows:

> The present value of a nonmarital asset used in the acquisition of marital property is the proportion the net equity or contribution at the time of acquisition bore to the value of the property at the time of purchase multiplied by the value of the property at the time of separation. The remainder of equity increase is characterized as marital property. . . .

In light of the foregoing, we conclude that central to the classification of appreciation of nonmarital property as marital or nonmarital is the principle that effort expended to generate property during the marriage—that is, "marital effort"—should benefit both parties rather than one of the parties to the exclusion of the other. In all of the cases where we have held appreciation of nonmarital property to be marital, significant effort that otherwise could have been devoted to the generation of marital property was diverted and applied toward nonmarital property instead.

In contrast, in this case the court of appeals based its decision in significant part upon the fact that Dr. Baker had control over the SIGS accounts. ("[T]he ability to control investments or withdraw funds can defeat a claim that the increases in value of premarital funds were the result of passive appreciation."). We agree with Dr. Baker that whether appreciation is generated through marital effort has been central to our decisions and that the court of appeals erred in adopting a different test. As Dr. Baker argues, the court of appeals' control test all but eviscerates the statutory intent to protect the nonmarital character of increases in the value of nonmarital property. Many traditionally nonmarital assets are within a spouse's control. For example, a gift or inheritance to only one spouse may be hers to do with as she pleases, and yet it is expressly nonmarital under Minn. Stat. §518.003, subd. 3b(a). We have held that property over which a party has control may be nonmarital in whole or in part. *Gottsacker* (degree of control shareholder spouse can exercise over corporation determines whether retained earnings are marital or nonmarital asset). Therefore, we reaffirm *Nardini* and hold that the single test for whether appreciation in the value of nonmarital property is marital or nonmarital is the extent to which marital effort—the financial or nonfinancial efforts of one or both spouses during the marriage—generated the increase.

We turn next to the question of whether Dr. Baker's actions in this case constitute "marital effort." This case differs materially from our earlier "marital effort" cases, which have dealt primarily with small businesses or real estate. Here instead we consider a portfolio of stocks and bonds of publicly traded companies and government securities. We conclude that in evaluating a portfolio of investments, we look to the character of the underlying investments themselves. . . . We further conclude that absent evidence that the efforts of one or both spouses directly affected the value of an investment, the appreciation in the value of the investment is properly characterized as passive. . . .

Other jurisdictions have reached the same conclusion. *Warner* (Maine) ("As publicly traded securities, any increase in the market value of the shares of Exxon, General Electric, Procter & Gamble, and Union Pacific during the marriage was the product of market forces, not . . . marital effort."); *Lane v. Lane* (La. Ct. App. 1978); *O'Brien v. O'Brien* (N.C. 1998) (holding "that if either or both of the spouses perform substantial services during the marriage which result in an increase in the value of an investment account, that increase is to be characterized as an active increase and classified as a marital asset"). . . .

Dr. Baker's activity with respect to the accounts consisted of selecting and occasionally changing investment advisors; authorizing money managers to make discretionary decisions about the investments; retaining discretion to direct investments but exercising that discretion on only one occasion (to invest in a business with which his son was involved); and declining to withdraw from the funds although they were available as liquid assets.

We note that by utilizing professional investment institutions, Dr. Baker avoided the need to devote significant personal effort to managing his retirement funds. Dr. Baker worked full time and contributed his earnings to the marriage. The court of appeals' decision compels us to ask, if Dr. Baker expended too much marital effort to avail himself of the statutory definition of nonmarital property, what less could he have done? How else could he have invested his premarital retirement funds so as to ensure that their appreciation during marriage would remain nonmarital? We conclude that on this record,

Dr. Baker's role in the investments was insufficient to render active the appreciation in the value of the overall portfolio.

The court of appeals also reasoned that the money managers' actions with respect to the SIGS funds are attributable to Dr. Baker under agency principles. We disagree. Although we acknowledge that had Dr. Baker done what Merrill Lynch did any appreciation would have been active, we find no authority for the proposition that a third party's activities constitute marital effort for purposes of determining whether property is marital or nonmarital. . . . [O]nly the financial and nonfinancial efforts of the spouses themselves are relevant to the assessment of marital effort.

Alternatively, Ms. Baker argues that even if the appreciation in the nonmarital portion of the SIGS accounts would otherwise be nonmarital, the entire increase in the value of the SIGS accounts attributable to the value of the account at the date of the marriage should be considered marital property for two reasons. First, Ms. Baker points out, Dr. Baker failed to meet his burden to distinguish between the increase due to income earned by the nonmarital portion of the SIGS accounts, which is marital property, and the increase due to appreciation. Second, nonmarital and marital funds were admittedly commingled in the SIGS accounts, and the court of appeals has held that commingling of marital and nonmarital funds can render the nonmarital funds marital property. *See, e.g., Wiegers v. Wiegers* (Minn. App. 1991) ("When nonmarital and marital property are commingled, the nonmarital investment may lose that character unless it can be readily traced."). The court of appeals did not address these arguments, and they are not before us on review. Accordingly, we remand to the court of appeals for consideration of these alternative arguments.

Is it right to look only at affirmative actions a spouse took in determining whether they expended "marital effort"? Or should the court also consider any effort expended studying and evaluating a portfolio that ultimately results in a decision not to make any changes? Deciding not to make a transaction could entail as much research and deliberation as deciding to make a transaction.

Stock ownership and trading is, of course, very common among married people. The increase-in-value question often arises as well with real property holdings, which can increase in value as a result of improvements or of market forces. If improvements result from either spouse's efforts, the value they add is marital. In addition, if improvements result in part from infusion of marital assets—for example, money the couple has saved from earnings during the marriage, then the portion of the added value reflecting that infusion might be characterized as marital (depending on how well documented is the amount of the contribution). On the other hand, a market-driven rise in the value of real estate that is separate property should also be separate property.

The following case illustrates the characterization rules relating to both increases in value and income from real property. Most real property that is not the marital home generates income—for example, rental property, farmland, commercial space. With income from separate property, the crucial fact is again whether either spouse expended significant effort to generate the additional value. The case below also exemplifies the phenomenon of welfare-type payments that substitute for income. In this case, it is government farm subsidies. Other examples are disability insurance and workers compensation payments and personal injury compensation. In each context, general characterization principles suggest one should ask whether the payments substitute for income that would have been earned by effort during marriage, and treat payments as subject to equitable distribution only to the extent that they do. Many states treat these wage substitutes that way, but a number focus on when the right to payment accrued and treat the entire value as divisible property if it accrued during the marriage, even if some is intended to substitute for post-dissolution wages. See Lopiano v. Lopiano, 752 A.2d 1000 (Conn. 1998) (holding that entire personal injury award was property subject to division and citing court rulings in other states). The following case further illustrates how a valid agreement between the parties can override the state's characterization rules.

Jones v. Jones

245 S.W.3d 815 (Ky. Ct. App. 2008)

TAYLOR, Judge.

. . . Ricky and Lynn M. Jones were married on June 21, 1986. Two children were born of the marriage. Prior to marriage, Ricky inherited from his grandfather a life estate in a farm consisting of 215 acres. . . . During the marriage, the parties resided in a residence located on the farm, and Ricky conducted farming operations thereupon. By decree entered May 18, 2005, the family court dissolved the parties' marriage. Ricky and Lynn entered into an agreement disposing of issues relating to child custody, visitation, and support. [T]he family court disposed of all outstanding issues related to property division and maintenance. This appeal follows. . . .

To correctly allocate and divide property owned by parties in a dissolution of marriage proceeding, the court must: (1) classify the property as marital or nonmarital, (2) assign to each party nonmarital property owned by that party, and (3) divide in just proportions marital property. Kentucky Revised Statutes (KRS) 403.190. KRS 403.190(1) directs that "the court shall assign each spouse's property to him." While the court possesses discretion in the division of marital property, the classification of property as nonmarital and assignment of such nonmarital property to its owner is not open to the court's discretion. . . .

Throughout the parties' marriage, tobacco was routinely raised on the 215-acre farm. The farm contained a basic tobacco quota. Through the Fair and Equitable Tobacco Reform Act of 2004, the federal tobacco quota and price support programs were repealed. In exchange for termination of such programs, the United States Department of Agriculture distributes payments to quota owners (quota owner TTPP payments) and growers of tobacco (grower TTPP payments) equally over a ten-year period, beginning in 2005 through 2014. These payments are designed, in part, to compensate quota owners and growers of tobacco for loss of the tobacco quota and price support programs. Generally, a quota owner is one who owned a farm with a tobacco market quota or allotment, and a grower is a producer of tobacco in the years of 2002, 2003, or 2004.

In the case *sub judice*, it is uncontroverted that Ricky inherited the life estate in the farm from his grandfather before the marriage and simultaneously inherited the tobacco quota pertaining to the farm. As such, the life estate in the farm and the tobacco quota are clearly classified as Ricky's nonmarital property. Pursuant to his nonmarital tobacco quota, Ricky routinely grew tobacco on the farm. . . . As Ricky owned a tobacco quota and also grew tobacco, both quota owner TTPP payments and grower TTPP payments are at issue. . . .

For purposes of a dissolution proceeding, we view the quota owner TTPP payments as essentially "compensation" by the government for taking of the property interest in the tobacco market quota. It is tantamount to Ricky selling his nonmarital tobacco quota and receiving compensation over a ten-year period. [I]t follows that the quota owner TTPP payments are necessarily classified as Ricky's nonmarital property and must be assigned to him.

Conversely, the grower TTPP payments . . . do not compensate for the taking of a property interest but, rather, compensate for the loss of income incurred by a grower of tobacco. Thus, for purposes of a dissolution proceeding, we conclude that grower TTPP payments are income. . . . Ricky routinely grew tobacco on the farm, and the income derived from the sale of such tobacco was income produced by the farm . . . The grower TTPP payments essentially supplanted this tobacco income and, likewise, constitute income produced by the farm . . .

[However, u]nder the terms of the prenuptial agreement, Ricky and Lynn agreed that Ricky's life estate in the farm "together with the income produced thereby, shall continue and remain the separate property" of Ricky. As such, the grower TTPP payments are properly classified as Ricky's nonmarital property and must be assigned to him.

Ricky further contends the family court erred by finding a marital interest in the increased value of his life estate in the farm and in valuing such marital interest. . . . The . . . parties made substantial improvements to the farm with marital assets. These improvements included renovation of the main house and construction of a garage and lake. The family court found that the actual cost of improvements to the farm totaled $67,000. The family court then adjusted this amount ($67,000) by Ricky's "life estate valuation formula" and concluded the marital property interest was $44,648.

KRS 403.190(2)(e) provides that marital property includes all property acquired by either spouse after marriage except:

> The increase in value of property acquired before the marriage to the extent that such increase did not result from the efforts of the parties during marriage.

. . . To the extent that marital assets increased the value of the life estate in the farm, such increase in value must be classified as marital under KRS 403.190(2)(e).

The more troublesome question presented is the proper valuation of such marital increase in value of the life estate in the farm. The family court essentially equated actual cost of improvements to the life estate in the farm with increase in value to the life estate in the farm. We view this as clear error. . . . To properly calculate the increase in value attributed to marital improvements upon property acquired before marriage, the court must subtract the fair market value (FMV) of the property at the time of dissolution without marital improvements from the FMV of the property at the time of dissolution with marital improvements.[3] The difference between such FMVs yields the increase in value attributed to marital improvements upon the property. As to a life estate acquired before marriage, a party may be compensated for the increased value attributed to marital improvements thereon, "not to exceed the value of the improvements."

When determining the FMV of real property with improvements and without improvements, expert opinion is ordinarily necessary. . . . Simply stated, the mere ownership of property does not qualify a lay person to give an opinion upon market value. In any event,

3. In this Commonwealth, the proper date to value marital assets is the date the decree of dissolution is entered. Thus, any appreciation in value of an asset occurring after the decree of dissolution is entered is generally nonmarital.

the actual cost of improvements may be considered as evidence bearing upon FMV but should not be the sole factor. Where the parties fail to offer sufficient proof as to FMV of real property, we remind the family court of our Court's decision in *Robinson*:

> . . . If the parties come to the end of their proof with grossly insufficient evidence on the value of the property involved, the trial court should either order this proof to be obtained, appoint his own experts to furnish this value, at the cost of the parties, or direct that the property be sold.

Upon remand, the family court shall calculate the marital increase in value of the life estate in the farm by subtracting the FMV of the farm at the time of dissolution without marital improvements from the FMV of the farm at the time of dissolution with marital improvements; then, the court shall adjust this amount by a life estate valuation formula. However, in no event, shall the compensation for the marital increase in value to a life estate exceed the "value of the improvements" thereon. Considering the complexity of such FMVs, expert testimony will most likely be required. . . .

Ricky finally contends the family court abused its discretion by awarding attorney fees to Lynn. Specifically, Ricky contends that Lynn possesses the financial resources to pay her attorney fees and that the award of $5,000.00 was an abuse of discretion. We disagree. The trial court has broad discretion in awarding attorney fees to either party in a dissolution proceeding. It is well-established that the court must consider the financial resources of both parties and may award attorney fees only where an imbalance of such resources exists. . . . Ricky continued to live "rent free" on the farm and retained his nonmarital interest in the livestock and farm gate inventory. The court further noted that Lynn was leaving the marriage with only "a small home which is fully encumbered," a vehicle, a one-half interest of the couples' retirement account. . . . Based upon the apparent imbalance of financial resources between the parties, we are unable to conclude that the family court abused its discretion in awarding Lynn a portion of her attorney fees. . . .

Did you find plausible the court's approach to determining the value contributed by marital effort? Is it possible to determine what a property's value would have been in the absence of a marital investment? Does it depend on the type of investment?

Some timing issues: States vary as to when a spouse's labor ceases to be marital. It can be the date when a petition for legal separation or divorce is filed, the date when the parties execute a separation agreement, the date when a court orders a separation decree, the date of any trial on property distribution, the date of final physical separation without intention to reunite, or the date of the divorce decree. Some clients might have reason to slow down or speed up the steps toward divorce, in order to maximize what they take away in property distribution. For example, someone expecting his spouse soon to do some especially highly remunerative work might want to hold off on filing or separating until that work is done. Someone expecting to do such work herself might want the determinative date to be before she does it. Another pertinent date is that on which valuations will be set. The *Jones* court noted that Kentucky law establishes the date on which the decree of dissolution is entered, which suggests that Kentucky courts commonly enter divorce decrees prior to resolving disputed financial issues. The Virginia statute specified "the date of the evidentiary hearing on the evaluation issue" as the proper date for determining value.

A final characterization question is whether property has been transmuted from separate to marital or vice versa, as a result of gift or commingling. Property might change from marital to separate by gift if, for example, a wife uses her income during marriage to purchase an expensive birthday present for her husband. Property might change from marital to separate by commingling if, for example, a spouse who inherited a vacation home routinely pays for small upkeep expenses at the home with cash he gets for doing odd jobs (given that such payments likely cannot be traced at the time of divorce to the marital font). The following case presents also the opposite possibility of separate property being transmuted into marital.

Pratt v. Pratt

2011 WL 6412226 (Va. Ct. App.)

ALSTON, Judge.

J. David Pratt (husband) . . . and Morgan Patricia Pratt (wife) were married in December 1996. During the parties' marriage, husband worked as an ordained minister until he retired in 2000, at which point he continued to work as a handyman and wedding officiant. Wife was also employed until she retired in 2001, then becoming a homemaker. Wife left the marital residence in June 2006, and husband filed a complaint for divorce in August 2009. . . .

Prior to the parties' marriage, in 1986, husband and his previous wife Agatha bought a house located in Springfield, Virginia, for $165,182.66. . . . When husband and Agatha divorced in 1996, Agatha's name was removed from the title of the house, leaving the house titled solely in husband's name. . . . [T]he house remained solely titled in husband's name. . . . Bank statements from an account at the Eastern Ohio United Methodist Conference Credit Union (the Eastern Ohio account) show that mortgage payments on the residence were made from this account.[2] In 2009, the Fairfax County Department of Tax Administration assessed the value of the house at $431,560. . . .

[W]ife . . . performed many of the household chores and errands, such as picking up dry-cleaning, washing, shopping, cleaning the house, doing the laundry, cooking, and gardening. According to wife, she decorated and furnished the house, including purchasing fabric and making drapes for the master bedroom. Wife also claimed that she paid to have the master bedroom repainted and the ceiling altered. Wife also testified that during the marriage, she and husband undertook several home improvement projects such as painting, removing wallpaper, and putting up drywall. According to wife, she and husband used "household money" to purchase various appliances for the house, and wife used her salary for household expenses. Wife also testified that she had written checks to husband totaling $10,000 for household and other expenses in 2000 and 2001. Wife testified that husband deposited his earnings from his handyman work and wedding officiating into the Eastern Ohio account . . .

In 2005, husband received an inheritance of $70,525.59. Husband deposited the inheritance into the Eastern Ohio account, which, at the time of deposit, was solely in husband's name. Husband used approximately $16,000 of the inheritance money to purchase a 2006 Toyota Matrix, which was jointly titled in husband's and wife's names. At trial, the parties stipulated that the car's value was $10,000. Wife testified that she test

2. For most of the parties' marriage, the Eastern Ohio account was in husband's name only. In 2006, husband added wife's name to the Eastern Ohio account. . . .

drove and chose the Toyota prior to its purchase. According to wife, she typically drove the Toyota, and when husband wanted to drive it he would ask her if he could borrow it.

An account statement introduced at trial showed that the value of the Oppenheimer Value Fund was $9,962.29 and was registered in both parties' names as of June 30, 2010. Husband testified . . . that he did not contribute to or remove money from the Oppenheimer Value Fund during the course of the parties' marriage. . . .

THE SPRINGFIELD, VIRGINIA RESIDENCE

The trial court held that the Springfield, Virginia residence was marital property based on wife's non-monetary, personal efforts as a homemaker and wife's monetary contributions to the mortgage. . . . Although the house was husband's separate property at the beginning of the parties' marriage, "depending on how property is utilized during the marriage, property that was at one time 'separate' can be converted into either 'marital' property or 'part marital property and part separate property.'" . . . [T]he increase in value of separate property may be classified as marital property . . . if "marital property or the personal efforts of either party have contributed to such increases," provided that any personal efforts are "significant and result in substantial appreciation of the separate property." . . . [W]ife's personal efforts amounted to no more than customary care, maintenance, and upkeep of the house. Wife testified that she performed household chores and errands, gardened, decorated and furnished the house, and undertook home improvement projects such as painting and installing drywall and appliances. Similar to the wife in *Martin*, who had "personally painted, wallpapered, and carpeted parts of the house," these activities do not . . . prove a significant personal effort. Moreover, wife offered no evidence that her personal efforts, or any marital property contributed to household maintenance or renovations, caused an increase in the value of the residence. . . .

[T]he trial court also relied upon wife's monetary contributions to the mortgage payment. . . . However, . . . when marital property is contributed to enhance or maintain separate property, the *marital property* contribution is transmuted to *separate property*, unless the marital property is retraceable and was not a gift. Here, . . . the parties used marital property to pay the mortgage on the residence. . . . Wife testified that she had written checks to husband totaling $10,000 for household and other expenses. . . . Because this money was earned during the parties' marriage, it is marital property. . . . "[T]he trial court did not consider marital funds losing [their] classification as marital property when commingled with the receiving property. It did not consider whether wife traced the marital funds. . . ." Thus, we remand to the trial court for a determination of what property, if any, used to pay the mortgage can be retraced to marital property and thus retains its classification as marital property. . . .

THE 2006 TOYOTA

The trial court found that the Toyota was wife's separate property, concluding it was a gift from husband to wife. Code §20-107.3(A)(1) defines separate property, in pertinent part, as "all property acquired during the marriage by bequest, devise, descent, survivorship or gift *from a source other than the other party*." Thus, . . . the trial court erred in determining that because the Toyota was a gift *from husband,* it was wife's separate property. . . . [T]he Toyota is properly classified as husband's separate property. . . . The Toyota was purchased using husband's separate property, i.e., money from his inheritance. As a result, the Toyota was originally husband's separate property. However, the Toyota was then titled jointly in the parties' names. Thus, the Toyota was transmuted to marital property unless it is retraceable by a preponderance of the evidence and was not a gift. *See* Code §20-107.3(A)(3)(f).

We find that the Toyota is retraceable to husband's separate property, his inheritance. . . . [I]f a party successfully retraces assets obtained during the marriage to his separate property, the burden is on the opposing party to prove that those assets were a gift in order to prove that the property is marital. . . . To establish the existence of a gift, the non-owning party must prove, by clear and convincing evidence "'(1) the intention on the part of the donor to make the gift; (2) delivery or transfer of the gift; and (3) acceptance of the gift by the donee.'" . . . Although the Toyota was jointly titled in the parties' names, no presumption of a gift arises simply from a party's decision to jointly title separate property. Code §20-107.3(A)(3)(g). Moreover, even though wife typically drove the Toyota and husband asked to "borrow" the car when he wished to drive it, that does not prove by clear and convincing evidence that husband intended the Toyota to be a gift to wife. We find that this evidence could do nothing more than suggest that husband intended merely to provide wife with the *use* of a car. Thus, . . . the Toyota . . . retains its original classification as husband's separate property. . . .

THE OPPENHEIMER VALUE FUND

. . . Code §20-107.3(A)(1) defines separate property, in pertinent part, as "all property, real and personal, acquired by either party before the marriage." Because the evidence shows that husband established the Oppenheimer Value Fund before marriage, with property that was therefore his separate property, we find that the Oppenheimer Value Fund is retraceable to husband's separate property. . . . Although the Oppenheimer Value Fund was jointly registered in the parties' names, as noted above, no presumption of a gift arises from a party's decision to jointly title separate property. There was no other evidence regarding any donative intent on husband's part. Therefore, we find that, as a matter of law, the Oppenheimer Value Fund was not a gift from husband to wife. Consequently, under Code §20-107.3(A)(3)(f), the Oppenheimer Value Fund is husband's separate property, and the trial court erred in classifying it as marital property.

ATTORNEYS' FEES

Both parties have requested appellate attorneys' fees. Because this litigation "addressed appropriate and substantial issues," and "neither party generated unnecessary delay or expense in pursuit of its interests," we deny both parties' requests. . . .

What policy considerations counsel for or against a liberal versus stringent approach to reclassification of separate property as marital? Might people's decision making about getting married or getting divorced be influenced by the approach a state adopts?

Were you convinced as to the lack of donative intent with respect to the car? The court might have been more convincing if it said there was intent to gift, but only conditionally, with the condition being continuation of the marriage. Instead the court implicitly assumes that any gift would have to be absolute. There are occasions when a spouse gives a gift to the other with the idea that it will be hers forever regardless of what happens with their marriage. But that seems more likely with personal items like a dress or jewelry than it is with an automobile, so one might expect more evidence than the wife presented. Should courts require an explicit statement of donative intent, perhaps in writing?

The court's treatment of "increase in value" in this and other cases raises at least two questions. One is, how someone could prove that home improvement efforts increased the value of a house? The most common way to do this is to subtract from market value at the time of dissolution the value of the property at the time of marriage or, if it was purchased after the marriage began, the value when purchased, and then further subtract any increase attributable to market forces. For example, if husband brings a house into the marriage, worth $200,000 on the day of the wedding, its appraised value is $400,000 at the time of divorce after wife has devoted substantial efforts to improving it, and the average increase in house value in that market during that time was 50 percent. $100,000 of the increase in value would be passive and not marital, and $100,000 of the increase would be active—that is, attributable to the wife's labor—and therefore marital. But this method is not possible if a property brought into the marriage was not appraised at or near the time of the wedding, as was likely true in this case.

Another, related question the case raises, though, is whether the comparison of market values at two points in time is always the right one to make. Suppose the market was flat and the husband's house would have *declined* in value without the wife's efforts, rather than remaining static. The court characterized the wife's work in the house, including "painting and installing drywall and appliances" as "no more than customary care, maintenance, and upkeep," but a house not kept in good repair can lose value as a result. Should the wife not get the benefit of maintaining the house's value? Or suppose the market had been declining, as was likely true in this case, and the wife's efforts kept it from declining as much as it would have without her efforts. Again, why should she lose out on the value she created because of the fortuity of market trends? Indeed, even if the market was rising and her efforts merely permitted their house's value to rise by the average rate, along with other houses that were properly maintained, why is no portion of the value at the time of dissolution marital, if the value would have been less without her efforts? Calculating a value in that situation would be difficult, but you will see below that in other contexts courts are quite willing to speculate in order to avoid the unjust result of giving nothing where clearly something is due. An earlier decision by the same court more clearly presented this question of what baseline value a court should adopt:

Robinson v. Robinson

621 S.E.2d 147 (Va. Ct. App. 2005)

ROBERT J. HUMPHREYS, Judge.

. . . Husband and wife married on November 22, 1999, and they separated on September 5, 2002. . . . During their relatively short marriage, neither party was employed in any capacity. Rather, the parties' only source of income was a trust fund husband inherited from his mother. Husband receives a net monthly income of approximately $50,000 from the trust. . . . Shortly after the marriage, the parties established a joint checking account and a joint savings account. The parties arranged for husband's trust income to be electronically deposited directly into the joint checking account, and the majority of the parties' expenses, including their car loans and mortgage payments, were paid from that account. During the course of the marriage, husband deposited a total of $2,156,351.14 into the joint checking account, and wife deposited $3,703.80 into the checking account during that same time frame.

Wife's primary contribution to the marriage involved handling the parties' finances. In addition to paying the bills, wife encouraged husband to set aside additional money in the savings account and to curb his spendthrift habits. . . . As of the date of separation, the joint savings account contained $244,137, and the joint checking account had a balance of $68,887. . . . Wife contends that . . . , as a result of her "personal efforts" to control the parties' finances, husband saved a portion of his trust income in the joint bank accounts. . . . However, . . . with the exception of any passive interest that may have been generated, placing the trust income into a savings account did not increase the "value" of the income. The decision to save a portion of husband's trust income merely prevented that income from being spent on another asset. "Preserving" and "maintaining" an asset is not necessarily equivalent to enhancing the value of that asset. Because there is no evidence that wife's "personal efforts" actually caused the separate asset to "increase in value," Code §20-107.3(A)(3)(a) and (A)(1) are inapplicable.[15]

Moreover, . . . because "the record contains no evidence of the value of wife's contributions" in managing and administering husband's trust income, "her contributions were transmuted into husband's separate property when they were commingled with husband's separate property." *Rowe*, 24 Va. App. at 136 (holding that, where wife failed to produce any evidence relating to the "value" of the "time and energy" she spent refurbishing a home that was husband's separate property, those efforts also became husband's separate property). . . . For these reasons, . . . the trial court clearly erred in classifying the joint bank accounts containing husband's trust income as marital property. . . .

15. It is also questionable whether wife's conduct actually constitutes a "personal effort." . . . [T]he statute "contemplates a significant personal effort that substantially affects the value of property, *not merely a joint decision that may have been influenced by one spouse.*"

Here again the court appears to assume that the proper baseline is the value an asset (in this case, cash) had when first received, rather than what its value would be in the absence of the spouse's efforts. Presumably if the wife had caused the couple's wealth to increase in value by investing it, any increase in value above the amount originally received would be deemed an increase in value subject to distribution. But why should any management efforts that prevent it from being depleted (e.g., in gambling) not generate a similar result?

(2) What Is Property?

Difficulty in answering this question arises principally from the intangible nature of some modern property interests. The most common intangible sources of wealth that a spouse may have at the time of divorce are an interest in a pension or other retirement fund, goodwill in a family business, and a professional license or educational degree. Traditionally, these were not treated as property subject to division, but rather as potential sources of future income that could be used to pay alimony. With the modern movement away from alimony and adoption of the economic partnership view of marriage, courts have increasingly treated these interests as property, insofar as they appear to have value or generate wealth. Doing so allows a court to order a one-time payment to a spouse to compensate him for his contribution to acquisition of the interest. A major problem this creates is that courts sometimes are making awards based upon a *potential* for future income that may never be realized, and property awards (unlike alimony awards) are not modifiable on the basis of an unforeseen change in circumstances. Another source of conceptual uncertainty is dispute at divorce over living things, such as pets and embryos.

(a) Pensions

Along with the family home, pension interests constitute one of the largest assets divorcing couples possess, so it is important for a practitioner to understand at least some basics concerning them. Pensions also illustrate some economic concepts that are important to property distribution more broadly.

Pensions are an employer-facilitated financial provision for retirement. Some large employers manage a pension fund internally, but increasingly pensions have come to be managed by separate corporations. Employers contribute at least part of the money to the fund used to provide post-retirement payments to employees. Importantly, the employer's payment is part of the employee's compensation package, an alternative form of salary; it is not a gift. Under many plans, employees can also contribute to the pension fund, by having some amount deducted from each paycheck.

The two basic types of pension plans are "defined contribution" and "defined benefit." The former is like a savings account or brokerage account. The employer—and possibly also employee—periodically contributes a definite amount to an account established for the employee. Its value at any given time is easily determined, which makes this type of plan easy to deal with in a divorce. Employees usually receive a statement quarterly or annually stating the current value of their account, so the value added during marriage is presumptively simply the value at time of divorce or separation minus the value at the time of the wedding or when employment began (if that was during marriage). Employees might even be able to control how the money in their account is invested—for example, by selecting from among mutual funds that the pension fund operates.

A defined benefit plan, in contrast, is like an annuity. It is a promise by the employer to pay to the employee after retirement an income whose amount typically depends on total years of service and/or final salary at time of retirement. The precise value of an employee's retirement benefits under that kind of plan thus ordinarily cannot be determined until the employee actually retires, and that presents a problem when the divorce occurs long before the employee is of retirement age. In fact, a defined benefit pension can, at the time of divorce, be unvested, meaning that if the employee terminated employment immediately, he or she would never receive any pension from that employer, making its value zero. A defined benefit pension typically vests only after an employee has been with a company for some time (e.g., five or ten years). While a pension remains unvested, the employee forfeits any claim to a pension if she leaves the company.

Another variable is whether a vested pension benefit has "matured"—that is, whether the employee is presently entitled to receive it or instead must wait until a certain date or age. An employer might impose a longer period for maturing of a defined benefit pension than it does for its vesting. That pension rights are unmatured in and of itself usually does not create a problem for valuation. It principally just delays the time at which the employee could remove funds in order to give an ex-spouse his share. If an employee dies before maturation of a defined benefit plan, his or her pension benefit might vanish, but today the law generally preserves an ex-spouse's interest in a defined benefit plan even when the employee dies before maturation. What creates problems for valuation at the time of divorce are a) when the pension value depends on years of service and final salary, as in a defined benefit plan, and b) when rights have not yet vested and might never vest.

All states treat vested pension rights earned during marriage as marital property, even if there will be no payments to the employee from the pension until long after the divorce and even if the ultimate value is uncertain at the time of divorce. Any employee contribution to a defined contribution plan is always vested, and typically the employer contribution is vested from day one as well. Unvested defined benefit pensions, because of their contingent nature, are more problematic, raising questions about the fairness of attributing their value to a spouse and about how to determine their value, but many states nevertheless treat them as divisible property. See, e.g., Bender v. Bender, 785 A.2d 197 (Conn. 2001) (unvested pension benefits were sufficiently certain to constitute divisible property because "susceptible to reasonably accurate quantification"). Many courts will retain jurisdiction to wait and see whether the rights ever vest, and with defined benefit plans they might suspend judgment even after vesting and until the employee spouse retires, when the value of the pension right becomes definite.

In re Marriage of Richardson

884 N.E.2d 1246 (Ill. App. Ct. 2008)

Justice Karnezis delivered the opinion of the court:

. . . Petitioner started participating in the pension plan when he was hired by the Village of Hoffman Estates police department on October 12, 1973. He married respondent on June 14, 1984. The court entered the dissolution of marriage order on March 27, 1995. Pursuant to the terms of the parties' oral settlement agreement, the judgment of dissolution of marriage provided:

> "Wife is hereby awarded one-half (1/2) of Husband's pension as it has accrued form [*sic*] the date of the marriage to the date of the entry of this Judgment of Dissolution of Marriage. This court shall retain jurisdiction of this cause for the purpose of entering a Qualified Domestic Relations Order."

In December 2002, petitioner retired and started collecting his benefits.

Pursuant to the Illinois Pension Code, for service in excess of 20 years, a pension is calculated at 50% of the employee's final salary, plus an additional 2.5% of salary for each full year of service up to 30 years. Petitioner worked 29 full years. His yearly benefit was, therefore, calculated at 72.5% of his final salary, for a monthly benefit of $6,012.83 gross. This amount is uncontested.

In September 2003, petitioner started paying respondent what he considered her share of the benefits, admittedly guessing at the amount. He contacted the pension fund requesting a calculation of how much he should be paying respondent. The fund informed him he should be paying respondent $625.40 per month. . . .

In July 2003, respondent moved for compliance with the judgment for dissolution and requested the court order petitioner to consent to having respondent's share of the pension remitted directly to her by the pension fund through a qualified domestic relations order. . . . Respondent asserted her half share of the marital portion of petitioner's pension should be either $1,118.44 or $1,112.67 per month, depending on which of the two allocation formulas suggested by her expert applied, plus her share of the 3% cost of living increases petitioner would receive annually starting in January 2005. . . .

There are two approaches to valuing an unmatured pension upon dissolution of a marriage: the "immediate offset" approach and the reserved jurisdiction approach. Using the immediate offset approach, the court determines the present value of a pension benefit, awards the value of the benefit to the employee spouse and offsets that award with an award of marital property to the nonemployee spouse. This approach is usually used "when there is sufficient actuarial evidence to determine the present value of a pension, when the employee spouse is close to retirement age, and when there is sufficient marital property to allow an offset." Neither party asserts that the immediate offset approach should have been used here.

The reserved jurisdiction approach is used in cases where it is difficult to place a present value on a pension due to uncertainties regarding vesting or maturation or when the present value can be ascertained but lack of marital property makes an offset impractical or impossible. Under the reserved jurisdiction approach, the court does not immediately compensate the nonemployee spouse at the time of dissolution. Instead, it awards the nonemployee spouse a percentage of the marital interest in the pension and retains jurisdiction over the case in order that the employee spouse pays the nonemployee spouse his or her portion of that marital interest "'if, as and when'" the pension becomes payable. The reserved jurisdiction approach is particularly appropriate where an interest has not vested at the time of dissolution, because it divides the risk that a pension will fail to vest.

The parties agree the pension plan is a defined benefit pension plan, pursuant to which the value of an employee's pension benefit is dependent on the total number of years the employee participated in the plan and the final salary the employee was collecting at the time of retirement. The value of the benefit cannot be determined until retirement. Further, petitioner's interest in the pension had neither matured nor vested at the time of dissolution because he was not yet eligible to collect his pension. . . . Because the plan itself is of a type which makes valuation virtually impossible until retirement and petitioner's interest had neither vested nor matured at time of dissolution, use of the reserved jurisdiction approach was appropriate in this case.

Under the reserved jurisdiction approach, the court can either (1) devise a formula at the time of dissolution that will determine both the marital interest on the pension benefits and the nonemployee spouse's share of that marital interest or (2) wait to determine the marital interest until the benefits are to be paid, *i.e.*, until the employee spouse starts to collect his pension. . . . But, whether determined at the time of dissolution or at the time of benefit payment, the calculation of the value of the marital interest under the reserved jurisdiction approach is the same: pension benefits actually received multiplied by marital interest percentage (length of time pension benefits accrued during the marriage divided by total length of time benefits accrued prior to retirement/payment).

The value of the marital interest is calculated as a percentage of each benefit payment, rather than of the value of the pension benefit at the time of dissolution and, therefore, takes into account the entire time the employee spouse accrued benefits. Petitioner argues, however, that by taking into account the entire term of petitioner's participation in the pension plan, including the time the pension accrued after the divorce, and the benefit earned on the date of retirement rather than that applicable on the date of the dissolution, the reserved jurisdiction approach violates the literal terms of the judgment for dissolution. He asserts the judgment is clear and unambiguous and means respondent should receive one-half of only that portion of petitioner's pension accrued from June 14, 1984, the date of the marriage, to March 27, 1985, the date of the dissolution judgment, *i.e.*, that the 10-year marital portion of the pension must be calculated in isolation from the years petitioner accrued benefits before and after the marital period.

Petitioner argues that the correct calculation for the marital portion of his pension . . . is that suggested by his expert: take only the 10 full years of pension benefit accrual from the date of marriage to the date of dissolution; multiply each year by 2.5% as provided by the Code for service of less than 20 years, for a total of 25%; and multiply this 25% by petitioner's salary on the date of dissolution to determine the marital portion of the pension benefit accrued between the date of marriage and the date of dissolution per year. Respondent's share of this marital portion would be 50%, or $625.40 per month.

Marital assets generally must be valued as of the date of the judgment of dissolution. However, valuing pension rights as of the date of dissolution as petitioner suggests, rights which may not be actualized until years in the future, only determines the present value *at the time of dissolution* of the benefits expected to be received upon retirement and necessarily assumes the employee spouse will no longer accrue additional benefits after the date of dissolution, such as if he stopped working on that date. Valuing pension rights at the time of dissolution freezes those pension benefits as of that date. It does not take into account the years worked after the dissolution, the cumulative effect of all the years on the pension benefit or the higher salary the employee spouse will be receiving upon his retirement, even though the plan calculates the final benefit based on these cumulative totals. . . .

Because petitioner is collecting his pension based on the full 29 years of his participation therein, the value to him of his 50% of the marital portion of his pension is $1,112.67 per month (50% x [37.01% x 72.5% of December 2002 salary]). However, he is arguing that the value to respondent *of that identical share* should be $625.40 per month (50% x [25% of March 1995 salary]). The marital shares in the pension are the same. The parties' agreement to award 50% of the marital portion of the pension to respondent necessarily means they agreed petitioner should receive the remaining 50%, *i.e.*, they agreed to evenly split the marital portion between them and each share is the same. If each share is the same, they should be valued the same. The parties did not agree that respondent's marital share would be valued differently than petitioner's marital share, yet that is what petitioner essentially argues.

Pension benefits are property interests. At dissolution, respondent obtained an actual co-ownership interest in the benefits as marital property; she became a co-owner of the pension benefits accrued during the marriage. Freezing respondent's interest in the pension as of the date of dissolution denies her the growth in the value of the marital share occurring during the period between dissolution and petitioner's retirement, a growth in value that petitioner, the co-owner holding an identical share, will collect. The identical percentage of a single pension benefit cannot be worth more to one person than another. . . .

Petitioner argues respondent should not share in any increase in his pension benefits accrued between the time of the dissolution and his retirement because such increase is solely due to his postmarital efforts, that any spousal efforts respondent contributed to the accrual of his pension occurred only during the marital period and she should not get the benefit of any pension accrual thereafter. Respondent's efforts were indeed limited to the period of the marriage. However, the pension plan provides petitioner's pension benefit is calculated based on the cumulative total of his full years in the plan, here 29 years. That 29-year cumulative total is only possible because of all the years of benefit accrual, the cumulative result of his solo efforts before the marriage, his and respondent's efforts as equal partners during the marriage[3] and his efforts after the marriage. Respondent's efforts during the marriage contributed to that cumulative total, not only to the benefits accrued during the marriage years.

The parties agreed respondent should receive a 50% share in the benefits to which she contributed. Petitioner, as the holder of any remaining share in those marital benefits, necessarily, therefore, holds the remaining 50% share, a share equal to respondent's. Petitioner's 50% share is worth $1,112.67 per month. If spouses agree to equally divide a marital asset, each spouse's share of that asset must obviously be valued the same, or the division would not be equal. Equal shares must be valued the same, and the judgment for dissolution does not provide otherwise. The court did not abuse its discretion in applying the widely accepted reserved jurisdiction approach and awarding respondent $1,112.67 per month as her 50% share of the marital portion of petitioner's pension benefit. . . .

What is it about a pension that justifies awarding some of it to someone who will no longer be the spouse of the employee at the time the latter retires? Many clients are perplexed by this, because they view a pension as retirement income, providing for them and for the family they have at that time because they are no longer able to work.

What are the equities on each side in deciding whether to give a non-employee spouse an award at the time of divorce for his or her share of an unvested pension fund, rather than taking the "if, as, and when" approach that reserving jurisdiction entails? Imagine yourself in a job where your pension will vest only if you remain with that company for another three or five years, and where you are perhaps not very happy. Then imagine yourself someone whose spouse has an unvested pension from several years of work during marriage, which you supported in various ways, but who at the time of divorce is so spiteful that he would shoot himself in the foot if that could somehow cause you pain.

Does the *Richardson* court implicitly treat all years of employment as contributing equally to the value of the pension? Does it make sense to do that, or might later years generate more value than earlier ones (as higher salaries for more senior employees might suggest)? How does the court justify giving the ex-wife any share of "the growth in the value of the marital share occurring during the period between dissolution and petitioner's retirement"? It makes sense that if one spouse for a long time after the divorce holds onto a marital asset whose value has not yet been allocated (e.g., imagine that a couple divorced without an agreement or court order as to division of marital property, and one spouse held onto the marital home), and that asset appreciates in value because of market forces, then the increase in value should be shared. But should an increase be shared if it is entirely the result of post-divorce effort by one spouse (e.g., if the spouse holding onto the marital home made improvements after divorce)? Ordinarily, a person's labor ceases to be marital at the time of divorce or separation.

3. Courts consider a marriage to be a partnership of coequals, the partners working together to enhance the wealth and security of the marital unit. Any accumulation of assets during the marriage, including pensions and other less tangible assets, is considered to be due to both partner's efforts, no matter that one spouse may have been employed while the other stayed at home, and such assets are considered marital property, subject to division between the spouses upon dissolution.

QUALIFIED DOMESTIC RELATIONS ORDERS

Although the preference is for an immediate resolution of property issues, to effect a "clean break" between the spouses, and although a pension is treated as property subject to distribution at divorce, it may be impossible for an employee spouse at the time of divorce to pay over all the other spouse's share of a pension. It might be the employee spouse's only significant asset. In such cases, courts may order that the other spouse receive a share of the pension only after the employee spouse retires, when the pension is actually paid out.

This often generates some insecurity on the part of the other spouse, because of the contingencies inherent in pensions. The employee typically has complete control over the timing of retirement, so the other spouse cannot know when, if ever, she will begin to receive benefits. Partly to solve this problem, the federal government enacted legislation, the Employee Retirement Income Security Act of 1974, that directed state courts to enter Qualified Domestic Relations Orders (QDROs) at the time of divorce. A QDRO ordinarily instructs an employer to begin paying out to an employee's ex-spouse her share of a pension as soon as the pension is vested and matured, regardless of whether the employee has retired. Thus, if at the time of divorce an employee spouse's pension is already vested and matured, the other spouse can immediately begin receiving monthly payments from the employer. Not all pension plans fall under the federal legislation, so you would need to check whether a particular client's plan is eligible for a QDRO. In particular, state employees' pensions are generally outside the purview of ERISA.

There are other complexities to pension plans, pension rights, and divorce court assignment of pension rights, which a divorce lawyer must learn, but for now you should just grasp the difference between defined contribution and defined benefit, why ex-spouses are entitled to a share of pension rights acquired during marriage, and how vesting and maturing can create difficulties in property distribution. If you want more information, you might consult the federal Department of Labor website for QDROs: http://www.dol.gov/ebsa/publications/qdros.html. And now for something more entertaining. . . .

(b) Academic Degrees and Professional Licenses

A "new property" question of great interest to lawyers in the last few decades is whether educational degrees and professional licenses, such as a law degree and license to practice law, are property of which the professional's spouse can claim a share upon divorce if the spouse has contributed to attainment of the degree and license. Are you surprised to learn that the legal community has largely answered "no" to this question?

Simmons v. Simmons

708 A.2d 949 (Conn. 1998)

CALLAHAN, Chief Justice.

. . . The plaintiff and the defendant were married on September 23, 1983, in Fayetteville, North Carolina. At the time of their marriage, the plaintiff was 23 years of age and was a sergeant in the United States Army. The defendant was 43 years of age and was working as a bartender. There are no children of the marriage. The defendant, however, had six children of her own prior to her marriage to the plaintiff.

During the course of the marriage, both the plaintiff and the defendant pursued their individual educational goals. The defendant obtained two associates degrees, one as a surgical technician and one in nursing, culminating in her becoming a registered nurse in 1991. The plaintiff received his undergraduate degree in 1990 and entered medical school. He completed medical school in 1994 and entered a surgical residency program at St. Raphael's Hospital in New Haven, causing the family to relocate to Connecticut from North Carolina. The defendant and the plaintiff both paid their own educational expenses and both were employed and jointly supporting the family unit until the plaintiff entered medical school, when he was prohibited from maintaining outside employment. The plaintiff received loans and grants to pay for medical school and to defray some of the household expenses. The defendant worked and supported the family while the plaintiff attended medical school. She provided financial and emotional support as well as her services as a homemaker. She did not, however, make any direct financial contribution toward the cost of the plaintiff's medical school education.

In the third year of his five-year surgical residency, the plaintiff filed an action for dissolution of marriage. At trial, the defendant . . . presented an expert witness, Steven Shapiro, an economist, who testified . . . that the plaintiff's future earning potential, reduced to present value, was approximately \$3.4 million as a plastic surgeon and \$2.8 million as a general surgeon. He concluded that the average of the two, \$3.1 million, represents the appropriate value to be assigned to the plaintiff's medical degree. The defendant claimed that the degree's present value should be equitably distributed between the parties and demanded in excess of \$1.5 million as a property settlement. . . .

I

The first issue raised by the defendant is whether the plaintiff's medical degree is property subject to equitable distribution pursuant to §46b-81 upon dissolution of the marriage. This is a question of first impression for Connecticut. It is not, however, a new question nationwide. At least thirty-five states have addressed the issue. . . . It has been labeled with a number of appellations, the most common of which is the "working spouse/student spouse syndrome," apparently so called because it represents an unfortunate circumstance that too often arises in family courts. In its most basic form, it is typified by one spouse who works to provide primary support for the family unit while the other spouse obtains an education, meanwhile earning either nothing or substantially less than he or she otherwise might have earned. Typically, it is also characterized by a relatively short marriage and a working spouse who has made significant sacrifices, for example, forgoing or delaying educational or childrearing opportunities and the current enjoyment of income that could have been produced by the student spouse. The expectation that the future benefit of increased earning capacity would be the reward shared by both is dashed when the marriage disintegrates and one of the parties files an action for dissolution before the anticipated benefits are realized.

The critical problem in these situations is that the couple usually has few, if any, assets to be distributed at the time of the dissolution of the marriage. The degree, with its potential for increased earning power, is, therefore, the only thing of real economic value to the parties. . . .[4]

In *Krafick*, we were called upon to determine whether the term property in §46b-81, which is not defined by the statute or clarified by its legislative history, was broad enough to include vested, though unmatured, pension rights. To that end, we concluded that the legislature intended to adopt the commonly accepted legal definition of property as set forth in Black's Law Dictionary, which "defines 'property' as the term 'commonly used to denote everything which is the subject of ownership, corporeal or incorporeal, tangible or intangible, visible or invisible, real or personal; everything that has an exchangeable value or which goes to make up wealth or estate. It extends to every species of valuable right and interest, and includes real and personal property, easements, franchises, and incorporeal hereditament.'" By adopting that definition, we acknowledged that the legislature intended the term to be broad in scope. While we do not retreat from the definition of property espoused in *Krafick*, we also recognize that it is not without limits. We conclude that the plaintiff's medical degree falls outside those limits.

Whether the interest of a party to a dissolution is subject to distribution pursuant to §46b-81, depends on whether that interest is: (1) a "presently existing property [interest]" or (2) a "mere expectanc[y]." "[Section] 46b-81 applies only to presently existing property interests, not 'mere expectancies.'" Therefore, the former interest is subject to equitable distribution upon dissolution, while the latter is not. The prototypical nonproperty interest is an anticipated inheritance, which we consistently have deemed to be a mere expectancy that is precluded from equitable distribution under §46b-81. . . . "The term expectancy describes the interest of a person who merely foresees that he might receive a future beneficence. . . . *[T]he defining characteristic of an expectancy is that its holder has no enforceable right to his beneficence.*"

By contrast, . . . "vested pension benefits represent an employee's *right* to receive payment in the future, subject ordinarily to his or her living until the age of retirement. The fact that a *contractual right* is contingent upon future events does not degrade that right to an expectancy." Consequently, the defining characteristic of property for purposes of §46b-81 is the present existence of the right and the ability to enforce that right.

The defendant first argues, by analogy, that a medical degree is substantially similar to pension benefits because both are a means to obtain deferred compensation. In both circumstances, she argues, the marital unit forgoes current income and invests those resources to acquire the benefit of future income. . . . *Krafick* . . . acknowledged in dicta that a vested pension represents deferred compensation and is often the only substantial asset of the marital unit. Relying on the law of contracts, however, we went on to conclude that "*[a]s contractual rights,* pension benefits are 'a type of *intangible* property,' and, as such, are encompassed in Black's definition of 'property.'" We repeatedly emphasized the fact that the owner of the pension has a presently existing, enforceable contract right attendant to a vested pension. In conclusion, we stated "that 'property' as used in §46b-81, includes the right, *contractual in nature,* to receive vested pension benefits in the future." Thus, it is not the pension's character as deferred compensation

4. Although the present facts are not an exact fit with the more typical model, the relationship here generally falls within the basic framework of the paradigm. Unlike the typical working spouse who has forgone educational opportunities, the defendant here did attain a postsecondary education during the marriage and is currently working in her chosen field. Moreover, there is no allegation that the defendant has forgone childrearing opportunities as is often the case. The parties do, however, lack substantial assets, and the marriage was of only moderate duration.

that makes it property subject to equitable distribution pursuant to §46b-81, but the presently existing, enforceable contract right to receive the benefits that does so.

The defendant's argument is, therefore, unpersuasive because an advanced degree entails no presently existing, enforceable right to receive any particular income in the future. It represents nothing more than an *opportunity* for the degree holder, through his or her own efforts, in the absence of any contingency that might limit or frustrate those efforts, to earn income in the future.

The defendant next relies on our statement in *Krafick* that "[t]he fact that a contractual right is contingent upon future events does not degrade that right to an expectancy." She argues, again by analogy, that the fact that an advanced degree is also subject to contingencies in the future should not prevent its classification as property. This argument misses the crucial prerequisite that the interest must first qualify as an *existing* right before it qualifies as property subject to distribution pursuant to §46b-81. The enforceable rights inherent in a vested pension make it distinctly different from the expectation of possible benefits afforded by an advanced degree. Additionally, the right to a vested pension benefit has already accrued prior to the action for dissolution. It is presently existing and enforceable, notwithstanding that it is contingent on certain factors such as survival of the pensioner until maturity.

By contrast, the benefits attendant on a newly acquired professional degree have not vested at the time of dissolution, and any benefits derived will accrue only after the dissolution of the marriage. These benefits may never accrue for any number of reasons because the holder has no enforceable right to earn any particular income in his or her chosen profession. Consequently, we conclude that an advanced degree is properly classified as an expectancy rather than a presently existing property interest. It is not, therefore, subject to equitable distribution upon dissolution pursuant to §46b-81.

The great weight of authority supports this conclusion.[7] The oft-cited rationale for concluding that a degree is not property subject to distribution is found in *Graham v. Graham* (1978). There, the Colorado Supreme Court concluded that "[a]n educational degree . . . is simply not encompassed even by the broad views of the concept of 'property.' It does not have an exchange value or any objective transferable value on an open market. It is personal to the holder. It terminates on death of the holder and is not inheritable. It cannot be assigned, sold, transferred, conveyed or pledged. An advanced degree is a cumulative product of many years of previous education, combined with diligence and hard work. It may not be acquired by mere expenditure of money. It is simply an intellectual achievement that may potentially assist in future acquisition of property. In our view, it has none of the attributes of property in the usual sense of the term."

We agree that an advanced degree has no inherent value extrinsic to the recipient. Its only value rests in the possibility of the enhanced earning capacity that it might afford sometime in the future. The possibility of future earnings, however, represents a mere expectancy, not a present right. We previously have concluded that "[t]he terms 'estate' and 'property,' as used in the statute [§46b-81] *connote presently existing interests.* 'Property' entails '*interests that a person has already acquired* in specific benefits.'" In *Rubin,* we declined to allow a property division in contemplation of an anticipated inheritance. We concluded that "the relevance of probable future income in determining the fair and equitable division of *existing* property . . . does not establish jurisdiction to make allowances

7. 35 states have addressed this issue. Of them, 34 have declined to consider an educational degree marital property subject to equitable distribution.

from . . . property *other than that held at the time.*" "Until our legislature amends §46b-81 to authorize contingent transfers of expected property, we shall not read such an intent into the statute."

In this regard, we find the rationale of the Supreme Court of Pennsylvania persuasive. In *Hodge v. Hodge* (1986), the court denied a professional degree the status of property, concluding that "[i]n instances such as the one now before the Court, the real value being sought is not the diploma but the *future* earned income of the former spouse which will be attained as a result of the advanced degree. The property being sought is actually acquired subsequent to the parties' separation. Thus, the future income sought cannot be 'marital property' because it has not been earned. If it has not been earned, it has not been acquired during the marriage."

The court in *Hodge* went on to note that "the contribution made by one spouse to another spouse's advanced degree plays only a small part in the overall achievement." In the same vein, the Supreme Court of Appeals of West Virginia, concluded that "[o]n the whole, a degree of any kind results primarily from the efforts of the student who earns it. Financial and emotional support are important, as are homemaker services, but they bear no logical relation to the value of the resulting degree." The defendant maintains in her reply brief that this assertion "reflects a paleolithic view of marriage" that is inconsistent with the partnership theory of marriage embraced in Connecticut. We disagree.

The defendant reminds us that "the primary aim of property distribution is to recognize that marriage is, among other things, 'a shared enterprise or joint undertaking in the nature of a partnership to which both spouses contribute—directly and indirectly, financially and nonfinancially—*the fruits of which* are distributable at divorce.'" She argues that the only way to effectuate this purpose in these circumstances is to conclude that the plaintiff's medical degree is marital property. We disagree.

There are other ways to compensate the defendant for her contribution to the plaintiff's degree without subjecting it to classification as property subject to equitable distribution. Furthermore, while we have acknowledged that the marital union is *akin* to a partnership, we have never held that it is an actual economic partnership. The parties to a marriage do not enter into the relationship with a set of ledgers and make yearly adjustments to their capital accounts. "Marriage is not a business arrangement, and this Court would be loathe to promote any more tallying of respective debits and credits than already occurs in the average household." Reducing the relationship, even when it has broken down, to such base terms serves only to degrade and undermine that relationship and the parties.

Of the numerous states that have passed on this question, only one has concluded that an advanced degree is distributable as marital property. The New York Court of Appeals, in *O'Brien v. O'Brien* (1985), . . . concluded that New York's unique statutory scheme was broader than those of other states that had declined to consider degrees and licenses marital property, and that, unlike other states, "*our statute* recognizes that spouses have an equitable claim to *things of value* arising out of the marital relationship and classifies them as subject to distribution by focusing on the marital status of the parties at the time of acquisition. . . . [T]hey hardly fall within the traditional property concepts because there is no common-law property interest remotely resembling marital property." The court [said] that "the New York Legislature deliberately went beyond traditional concepts when it formulated the Equitable Distribution Law. . . ."

By contrast, we have interpreted our equitable distribution scheme under §46b-81 as embracing the traditional, albeit broad, legal concept of property as defined in Black's Law Dictionary. In *Krafick*, we concluded that this definition represents the "common understanding" of the term. Furthermore, the New York statute *specifically states* that the court must consider the contribution and expenditures of each spouse *to the career of the other spouse* when making a property distribution. There is no concomitant directive in §46b-81(c), which requires only that courts consider various factors including "occupation, amount and sources of income, vocational skills, employability, estate, liabilities and needs of each of the parties and the opportunity of each for future acquisition of capital assets and income . . . [and] the contribution of each of the parties in the acquisition, preservation or appreciation in value of their respective estates." Accordingly, we are not persuaded that we should follow New York's minority approach, which is based exclusively on its unique statute and the statute's illustrative legislative history. We conclude that the plaintiff's medical degree is not property subject to equitable distribution pursuant to §46b-81 upon dissolution of the parties' marriage.

II

The second issue raised by the defendant is whether, if it is assumed that the plaintiff's degree is not property subject to distribution pursuant to §46b-81, the trial court abused its discretion by failing to take proper account of the plaintiff's degree in structuring a property settlement and in denying her alimony. The following additional facts are relevant to this issue. When this case was decided by the trial court, the plaintiff was 36 years of age with an annual gross income of $45,660 from his residency position. The defendant was 56 years of age and employed part time as a registered nurse earning approximately $36,000 annually. She had earned approximately $67,000 in the previous year. The parties owned minimal assets, including their older automobiles, approximately $5800 in cash, some collectibles, including rare books and stamps, and other miscellaneous personalty.[9] . . .

"The well settled standard of review in domestic relations cases is that this court will not disturb trial court orders unless the trial court has abused its legal discretion or its findings have no reasonable basis in the facts. . . . As has often been explained, the foundation for this standard is that the trial court is in a clearly advantageous position to assess the personal factors significant to a domestic relations case, such as demeanor and attitude of the parties at the hearing." . . . Accordingly, "it is only in rare instances that the trial court's decision will be disturbed." . . .

The . . . trial court did take account of the plaintiff's degree and the potential for enhanced earning capacity when it distributed property pursuant to §46b-81. . . . On the liabilities side of the ledger were two significant debts—the plaintiff's $40,000 in education loans and a debt to the Internal Revenue Service. The plaintiff was ordered to assume both of those debts. The plaintiff also was ordered to pay over the full amount of the parties' cash assets [$5,800] to the defendant. Each was allowed to keep his or her own automobile and any other miscellaneous personalty already within his or her possession. . . . The purpose of a distribution of property upon dissolution of the marriage is to "giv[e] each spouse what is *equitably* his [or hers]." Of the assets that did exist at the time of trial, all that were liquid went to the defendant and all the debt went to the plaintiff. We cannot say that this distribution is inequitable. . . .

9. The defendant alleges that the plaintiff owns $70,000 to $80,000 worth of collectibles including rare books and a stamp collection. . . . The plaintiff admits that he owned these items, but alleged that the defendant retained these items for a time after their separation. The defendant returned some of the stamp collection during the trial, but a significant number of stamps were missing. The plaintiff maintained that he is no longer in possession of the rare books and believes that the defendant destroyed them. The defendant admits that she left the books outside the house when she left the house permanently. . . .

We do, however, find merit in the defendant's second claim, that the trial court abused its discretion in failing to award her alimony. . . . The defendant was fifty-six years of age at the time of trial, while the plaintiff was thirty-six years of age. Although the defendant may be able to continue to pursue her chosen career, she is significantly limited in the duration of that career because of her age. Moreover, she currently has no significant assets and she is not likely to accumulate any prior to her retirement. Any savings she might have garnered in anticipation of her retirement were necessarily consumed during the years of the plaintiff's medical education because she was the sole support of the family unit. It is not unlikely or unreasonable to believe that the plaintiff's medical degree was the defendant's retirement plan.

We also take exception to the trial court's emphasis of the fact that the defendant did not contribute direct financial aid to the cost of the plaintiff's schooling. The absence of direct financial contribution is of little consequence in an award of alimony in these circumstances. The defendant provided emotional support and homemaker services during the years of the plaintiff's medical education. Moreover, she was the primary financial support of the family unit and forsook earnings by her spouse during his years in medical school in anticipation of the future enhanced earning capacity of the family. Just prior to the time when she reasonably might have anticipated a return on her sacrifice, the breakdown of the marriage effectively prevented her from realizing anything for her efforts.

Finally, we are concerned by the trial court's reference to the defendant's ability to sustain herself at a level to which she had become accustomed during the marriage. . . . The only reason the defendant was accustomed to a standard of living commensurate with her salary alone is that she had become the sole support of the family unit in order to allow the plaintiff an opportunity to attain his medical degree. . . . The conclusions of both the Massachusetts and Rhode Island courts that the unmodifiable nature of a property settlement sometimes makes it an inappropriate method for sharing the wealth generated by the student spouse's increased earning capacity is persuasive. . . .

We previously have concluded that "property distributions, unlike alimony awards, *cannot* be modified to alleviate hardships that may result from enforcement of the original dissolution decree in the face of changes in the situation of either party." An alimony award, on the other hand, is an appropriate method to take into account future earning capacity because it can be modified whenever there is a change in the circumstances of the parties that justifies the modification. . . . To conclude that the plaintiff's medical degree is property and to distribute it to the defendant as such would, in effect, sentence the plaintiff to a life of involuntary servitude in order to achieve the financial value that has been attributed to his degree. The plaintiff may become disabled, die or fail his medical boards and be precluded from the practice of medicine. He may chose an alternative career either within medicine or in an unrelated field or a career as a medical missionary, earning only a subsistence income. An award of alimony will allow the court to consider these changes if and when they occur. . . .

Additionally, we are mindful that in ordering alimony or a property distribution in cases where there is an advanced degree obtained with the aid of a working spouse, the trial court also must take into account . . . the fact that the student spouse has worked and studied hard to obtain the degree and will have to continue to work hard in the future to realize the earning potential attributable to the degree. . . .

Finally, we recognize that a nominal alimony award may often be appropriate when the present circumstances will not support a substantial award. Nominal awards . . . are all that are necessary to afford the court continuing jurisdiction to make appropriate modifications. We have stated that "because some alimony was awarded, [$1.00 per year] with no preclusion of modification, if the circumstances warrant, a change in the award can be obtained at some future date." Concededly, in this case, no significant alimony appears to have been warranted at the time of trial . . . because, at the time of dissolution, the defendant's salary was roughly equal to that of the plaintiff and, with further effort, could have been increased significantly. The failure to award any alimony at the time of trial, however, permanently precluded the defendant from seeking alimony at a future date should those circumstances change.[18]

III

The final issue presented for our consideration is the existence of an implied in fact contract between the parties with respect to the plaintiff's medical degree. There are two subparts to this issue articulated by the defendant. First, she asks *this* court to find that a contract did exist between the parties, and, second, she asks us to conclude that the trial court improperly failed to enforce that contract. Because these issues were not properly raised in the trial court, we decline to address them.

There are many questionable steps in the court's reasoning. One is the supposition that "the contribution made by one spouse to another spouse's advanced degree plays only a small part in the overall achievement." In many cases, the supporting spouse's contribution will be a but-for cause of the degree acquisition; absent that spouse's payment for daily living expenses and/or tuition, the student-spouse might have been entirely unable to pursue the degree. And if the supposition were true that one spouse makes only a small contribution to career efforts of the other, even when the first "provided financial and emotional support as well as her services as a homemaker" durying the other's years in professional school, that would seem to undermine altogether the economic partnership idea that underlies equitable distribution. If it is true in that situation, would it not be even more so when a spouse supports the other only by providing emotional support and housework, and still more so if a spouse provides only emotional support and neither income nor housework as might be true in some high-income families?

Also questionable is the court's assertions that "[f]inancial and emotional support are important, as are homemaker services, but they bear no logical relation to the value of the resulting degree" and that "[t]here are other ways to compensate the defendant for her contribution to the plaintiff's degree." The same things could be said with respect to income earned by a primary breadwinner in a traditional family—that is, that there is no logical reason to assume that the other spouse's homemaking services and emotional support are worth half the value of the income, and that there are other ways to compensate the homemaker (e.g., calculating what the breadwinner would have had to pay for a maid, a counselor, etc.).

18. We are also mindful of our prior holdings recognizing that "'[t]he rendering of a judgment in a complicated dissolution case is a carefully crafted mosaic, each element of which may be dependent on the other.'" In light of that truism, we concluded in *Sunbury* that "[t]o limit the remand in this case to the issue of periodic alimony would impede the trial court's ability to weigh the statutory criteria for financial orders to achieve an equitable result [because t]he issues involving financial orders are entirely interwoven." Accordingly, notwithstanding our conclusion that the property distribution pursuant to §46b-81 was fair and within the discretion of the trial court, it is necessary on remand for the trial court to reevaluate its prior order distributing the marital property in light of our conclusion that an award of alimony should be granted. . . .

The court also wants to avoid degrading marriage by "tallying of respective debits and credits." But does a reimbursement approach better avoid this than does just assuming both spouses are entitled to an equal share of the value of the degree?

The court assumes the degree has no exchange value and cannot be bought. Is it possible to square that supposition with the common practice of the military to pay someone's tuition in exchange for a post-graduation work commitment—for example, in the JAG Corps? Or with the reality that it is close to impossible to flunk out of most law schools?

What is primarily driving courts' hostility to the idea of a license or degree as property? Is the outcome here consistent with the expectations of husband and wife when they married? What weight did the court give to their expectations in analyzing property distribution? Do they factor into the alimony analysis? Does the discussion of alimony suggest the court viewed the ex-wife as entitled to a share of the value produced by the degree in the future, or just to reimbursement for her financial sacrifices in helping the ex-husband acquire the degree? If the latter, and if the ex-husband had the ability to give the ex-wife full reimbursement right away, what would be gained by ordering periodic payments instead of awarding property? What is lost?

Why does the court focus so much on entitlement rather than likelihood of receipt? Does a contractual right to a pension make receipt of the benefit a 100 percent certainty? When a pension is unvested, nothing will ever be received by means of it unless the employer continues to employ the spouse and unless the employee-spouse continues to show up for work. Thus, it is entirely dependent on exactly the same things as is the value of a degree—namely, having a job and performing it. Even when a defined benefit plan is vested, an employee might be entitled to nothing unless and until he lives to retirement age. Comparison might be made also to other types of licenses, such as a liquor license or taxi medallion, which can be of great value even though they do not entitle holders to an income but rather just authorize them to try to earn income in a certain way. Cf. Corey Kilgannon, *"Want a Cab? He Owns the Keys,"* N.Y. TIMES, March 23, 2012 (stating that in New York City "Fleet medallions are said to be worth $1 million apiece these days.").

A trial court subsequently ordered Duncan to pay Aura $125/week in alimony, based on assumed gross annual income of $100,000 for Duncan and $67,000 for Aura. The Simmonses were back in court five years later, because Duncan's income had increased to around $150,000, and a trial court then increased the alimony for 63-year-old Aura to $175/week. Simmons v. Simmons, 2003 WL 21152874 (Conn. Super. Ct.).

Were you persuaded by the court's attempts to distinguish *O'Brien* on the grounds that New York had a special sort of equitable distribution statute? Did the *O'Brien* court actually misuse the statute, conflating legislative direction as to what considerations are relevant to *distributing* property with legislative direction as to what *constitutes* property? That decision was and remains an anomaly, but is still good law in New York State.

O'Brien v. O'Brien

489 N.E.2d 712 (N.Y. 1985)

SIMONS, Judge.

. . . Plaintiff [husband] and defendant [wife] married on April 3, 1971. At the time both were employed as teachers at the same private school. Defendant had a bachelor's degree and a temporary teaching certificate but required 18 months of postgraduate classes at an approximate cost of $3,000, excluding living expenses, to obtain permanent certification in New York. She . . . had relinquished the opportunity to obtain permanent certification while plaintiff pursued his education. At the time of the marriage, plaintiff had completed only 3.5 years of college but shortly afterward he returned to school at night to earn his bachelor's degree and to complete sufficient premedical courses to enter medical school.

In September 1973 the parties moved to Guadalajara, Mexico, where plaintiff became a full-time medical student. While he pursued his studies defendant held several teaching and tutorial positions and contributed her earnings to their joint expenses. The parties returned to New York in December 1976 so that plaintiff could complete the last two semesters of medical school and internship training here. After they returned, defendant resumed her former teaching position and she remained in it at the time this action was commenced. Plaintiff was licensed to practice medicine in October 1980. He commenced this action for divorce two months later. At the time of trial, he was a resident in general surgery.

During the marriage both parties contributed to paying the living and educational expenses and they received additional help from both of their families. [I]n addition to performing household work and managing the family finances, defendant was gainfully employed throughout the marriage [and] contributed all of her earnings to their living and educational expenses, and her financial contributions exceeded those of plaintiff. The trial court found that she had contributed 76% of the parties' income exclusive of a $10,000 student loan obtained by defendant. . . .

Defendant presented expert testimony that the present value of plaintiff's medical license was $472,000. [The expert] arrived at this figure by comparing the average income of a college graduate and that of a general surgeon between 1985, when plaintiff's residency would end, and 2012, when he would reach age 65. After considering Federal income taxes, an inflation rate of 10% and a real interest rate of 3% he capitalized the difference in average earnings and reduced the amount to present value. He also gave his opinion that the present value of defendant's contribution to plaintiff's medical education was $103,390. Plaintiff offered no expert testimony. . . . The court, after considering the life-style that plaintiff would enjoy from the enhanced earning potential his medical license would bring and defendant's contributions and efforts toward attainment of it, made a distributive award to her of $188,800, representing 40% of the value of the license, and ordered it paid in 11 annual installments. . . . The court also directed plaintiff to maintain a life insurance policy on his life for defendant's benefit for the unpaid balance of the award. . . . It did not award defendant maintenance. . . .

Plaintiff does not contend that his license is excluded from distribution because it is separate property; rather, he claims that it is not property at all but represents a personal attainment in acquiring knowledge. . . . [T]he New York Legislature deliberately went beyond traditional property concepts when it formulated the Equitable Distribution Law. Instead, our statute recognizes that spouses have an equitable claim to things of value arising out of the marital relationship and classifies them as subject to distribution by focusing on the marital status of the parties at the time of acquisition. Those things acquired during marriage and subject to distribution have been classified as "marital property" although . . . they hardly fall within the traditional property concepts because there is no common-law property interest remotely resembling marital property. "It is a statutory creature, is of no meaning whatsoever during the normal course of a marriage and arises full-grown, like Athena, upon the signing of a separation agreement or the commencement of a matrimonial action. . . .'" Having classified the "property" subject to distribution, the Legislature did not attempt to go further and define it but left it to the courts to determine what interests come within the terms. . . .

Section 236 provides that in making an equitable distribution of marital property, "the court shall consider: . . . (6) any equitable claim to, interest in, or direct or indirect contribution made to the acquisition of such marital property by the party not having title, including joint efforts or expenditures and contributions and services as a spouse, parent, wage earner and homemaker, and to the career or career potential of the other party [and] . . . (9) the impossibility or difficulty of evaluating any component asset or any interest in a business, corporation or profession" Where equitable distribution of marital property is appropriate but "the distribution of an interest in a business, corporation or profession would be contrary to law" the court shall make a distributive award in lieu of an actual distribution of the property. The words mean exactly what they say: that an interest in a profession or professional career potential is marital property which may be represented by direct or indirect contributions of the non-title-holding spouse, including financial contributions and nonfinancial contributions made by caring for the home and family. . . .

The determination that a professional license is marital property is also consistent with the conceptual base upon which the statute rests. . . . [F]ew undertakings during a marriage better qualify as the type of joint effort that the statute's economic partnership theory is intended to address than contributions toward one spouse's acquisition of a professional license. Working spouses are often required to contribute substantial income as wage earners, sacrifice their own educational or career goals and opportunities for child rearing, perform the bulk of household duties and responsibilities and forego the acquisition of marital assets that could have been accumulated if the professional spouse had been employed rather than occupied with the study and training necessary to acquire a professional license. . . . The Legislature has decided, by its explicit reference in the statute to the contributions of one spouse to the other's profession or career, that these contributions represent investments in the economic partnership of the marriage and that the product of the parties' joint efforts, the professional license, should be considered marital property. . . .

There is no reason in law or logic to restrict the plain language of the statute to existing practices. . . . An established practice merely represents the exercise of the privileges conferred upon the professional spouse by the license and the income flowing from that practice represents the receipt of the enhanced earning capacity that licensure allows. . . . A professional license is a valuable property right, reflected in the money, effort and lost opportunity for employment expended in its acquisition, and also in the enhanced earning capacity it affords its holder, which may not be revoked without due process of law. That a professional license has no market value is irrelevant. Obviously, a license may not be alienated as may other property and for that reason the working spouse's interest in it is limited. The Legislature has recognized that limitation, however, and has provided for an award in lieu of its actual distribution.

Plaintiff also contends that alternative remedies should be employed, such as an award of rehabilitative maintenance or reimbursement for direct financial contributions. . . . Limiting a working spouse to a maintenance award, either general or rehabilitative, not only is contrary to the economic partnership concept underlying the statute but also retains the uncertain and inequitable economic ties of dependence that the Legislature sought to extinguish by equitable distribution. Maintenance is subject to termination upon the recipient's remarriage and a working spouse may never receive adequate consideration for his or her contribution and may even be penalized for the decision to remarry if that is the only method of compensating the contribution. . . .

Turning to the question of valuation, it has been suggested that even if a professional license is considered marital property, the working spouse is entitled only to reimbursement of his or her direct financial contributions. By parity of reasoning, a spouse's down payment on real estate or contribution to the purchase of securities would be limited to the money contributed, without any remuneration for any incremental value in the asset because of price appreciation. . . . If the license is marital property, then the working spouse is entitled to an equitable portion of it, not a return of funds advanced. Its value is the enhanced earning capacity it affords the holder and although fixing the present value of that enhanced earning capacity may present problems, the problems are not insurmountable. Certainly they are no more difficult than computing tort damages for wrongful death or diminished earning capacity resulting from injury and they differ only in degree from the problems presented when valuing a professional practice for purposes of a distributive award, something the courts have not hesitated to do. . . .

MEYER, Judge (concurring).

I concur in Judge Simons' opinion but write separately to point up for consideration by the Legislature the potential for unfairness involved in distributive awards based upon a license of a professional still in training. An equity court normally has power to "'change its decrees where there has been a change of circumstances.'" . . . [But] a distributive award pursuant to section 236(B)(5)(e), once made, is not subject to change. Yet a professional in training who is not finally committed to a career choice when the distributive award is made may be locked into a particular kind of practice simply because the monetary obligations imposed by the distributive award made on the basis of the trial judge's conclusion (prophecy may be a better word) as to what the career choice will be leaves him or her no alternative. The present case points up the problem.

A medical license is but a step toward the practice ultimately engaged in by its holder, which follows after internship, residency and, for particular specialties, board certification. Here it is undisputed that plaintiff was in a residency for general surgery at the time of the trial, but had the previous year done a residency in internal medicine. Defendant's expert based his opinion on the difference between the average income of a general surgeon and that of a college graduate of plaintiff's age and life expectancy, which the trial judge utilized, impliedly finding that plaintiff would engage in a surgical practice despite plaintiff's testimony that he was dissatisfied with the general surgery program he was in and was attempting to return to the internal medicine training he had been in the previous year.

The trial judge had the right, of course, to discredit that testimony, but the point is that equitable distribution was not intended to permit a judge to make a career decision for a licensed spouse still in training. Yet the degree of speculation involved in the award made is emphasized by the testimony of the expert on which it was based. Asked whether his assumptions and calculations were in any way speculative, he replied: "Yes. They're speculative to the extent of, will Dr. O'Brien practice medicine? Will Dr. O'Brien earn more or less than the average surgeon earns? Will Dr. O'Brien live to age 65? Will Dr. O'Brien have a heart attack or will he be injured in an automobile accident? Will he be disabled? . . ."

[If] the assumption as to career choice on which a distributive award payable over a number of years is based turns out not to be the fact (for example, if a general surgery trainee accidentally loses use of his hand), it should be possible for the court to revise the distributive award to conform to the fact. And there will be no unfairness in so doing if either spouse can seek reconsideration, for the licensed spouse is more likely to seek reconsideration based on real, rather than imagined, cause if he or she knows that the nonlicensed spouse can seek not only reinstatement of the original award, but counsel fees in addition, should the purported circumstance on which a change is made turn out to have been feigned or to be illusory.

The decisions of the Connecticut and New York courts were unanimous. Is the New York statute really so different from the Connecticut statute as to explain such diametrically opposed results? Are the two courts in complete disagreement, or are there just one or two points of minor disagreement that lead to different outcomes? Does the New York court respond to all the policy concerns raised by the Connecticut court, and vice versa?

Whereas the *Simmons* court denied that a medical degree or license amounted to any kind of right, the *O'Brien* court states that "a professional license is a valuable property right." Which court is correct? A right entails duties others owe to the right-holder. Are there duties others will owe you when you get your J.D. or when you become licensed to practice law?

The New York court asserts that a degree or license has value even though it cannot be sold. The value must therefore exist only for the holder. In that sense, it is like a skill. So suppose the wife had taught the husband to play the guitar, sufficiently well that the husband can now earn substantial money playing in a band. Should that skill be deemed property whose value—namely, ability to generate income—should be shared with the wife at the time of divorce? As with a degree, there might be the option of awarding alimony instead, and by that means directing some of the future earnings obtained through use of the skill to the ex-spouse. Make sure you understand why alimony might not be a satisfactory alternative.

(c) *Goodwill*

In what ways relevant to the claims of a spouse at time of divorce does the goodwill component of a private professional practice—for example, your reputation as an excellent lawyer and the contacts you have developed over the years—differ from a pension fund and from a license or degree? Only in the relative difficulty of valuing it? While states uniformly treat goodwill in a non-professional family business, such as a retail store, as property for divorce purposes, the states are divided today in how they treat goodwill in a professional practice, such as a medical or legal practice.

Gaskill v. Robbins

282 S.W.3d 306 (Ky. 2009)

Opinion of the Court by Justice Noble.

. . . Gaskill had a very successful [oral surgery] practice, and Robbins worked as a salaried employee with several businesses throughout the marriage, so that at the time of trial, the parties had amassed a marital estate of over four million dollars, including a value of $669,075 for the practice. . . . There was no dispute that Gaskill was highly skilled and earned roughly 90% of the income received during the marriage. The testimony also indicated that she was extremely hard working, and managed her practice with frugality. The practice consisted of her as the sole oral surgeon, with office staff. She was also primarily responsible for management of the office, though Robbins did take care of some paper work such as paying bills, and he often brought supplies to the office. Gaskill alone was responsible for patient acquisition. Robbins testified that he helped her set up the office initially, and was generally supportive. Since the practice in Bowling Green was established after the marriage, there is no question as to its marital character.

At trial, . . . Gaskill's accountant, Steve Wheeler, who collected data from the business records and actually talked with personnel at the practice location, did a detailed report laying out all of the financial information, . . . various accounting methods, and definitions of frequently used accounting terms. . . . [H]e settled on an asset-based analysis . . . because the business was not actually to be liquidated, no similar sales of a reasonably similar business were available, and there was no previous transaction in this business with which to compare. He testified at trial that the practice had a value of $221,610. . . . Wheeler assigned a value of zero to goodwill because Gaskill's role in the business amounted to a "non-marketable controlling interest." To illustrate, he asked, "Why would a purchaser pay more than fair market value of the tangibles if Dr. Gaskill can take her patients, go down the hall, and set up a practice?"

Robbins's expert, Richard Callahan, did not independently collect data and did not visit the practice to interview staff or view the physical aspects and working procedures of the office, but instead used Wheeler's detailed data. He used four different methodologies to evaluate the business: capitalized earnings, excess earnings, adjusted balance sheet, and the market approach. He calculated a value for the business under each method, then averaged the four numbers to arrive at a value of $669,075, which included an assumed non-compete agreement and goodwill. He specifically objected to one of Wheeler's calculations doubling the wages of the employees to allow for the cost of acquiring similarly trained personnel, arguing that a willing buyer could utilize the same employees that Gaskill currently had. He testified that using Wheeler's calculations on this item would reduce the practice's value by $315,890.

The trial court accepted Callahan's view "to be more credible," particularly referencing the employee salary calculations, and fixed the value of the practice at $669,075. However, the trial court primarily relied on the premise that there is no legal authority for a distinction between personal and enterprise goodwill in Kentucky law.

The total value of the marital property was determined, and the trial court . . . found that the parties contributed equally in obtaining the marital estate, to duties at home, and to the raising of their son. The trial court also considered that at the time of the dissolution, Gaskill remained able to earn approximately 7.5 times the amount Robbins could, giving her a far greater ability to rebuild her estate. The trial court then found that "just proportions" required that the marital estate be divided equally, and ordered a 50-50 division of the marital property. The practice was assigned to Gaskill, as were a number of other non-liquid assets, and most of the cash was assigned to Robbins in order to equalize the distribution. Gaskill appealed.

A. VALUATION OF GOODWILL

The valuation of a business is complicated, often speculative . . . , and at best subjective. This is particularly true . . . where the business is a professional practice with only one practitioner, clients or patients come to the business to receive that particular person's direct services, the business is not actually being sold, and the success of the business depends upon the personal skill, work ethic, reputation, and habits of the practitioner.

Nonetheless, when a business is established during a marriage and is thus marital property, the trial court is required to fix a value and divide it between the spouses. To do this, . . . the court must . . . answer at least the following questions . . . :

1. What can be earned from the business over a reasonable period of time? This value . . . includes the concept of transferable goodwill.
2. What is the value of the hard assets? This includes real estate, equipment, client lists, cash accounts or anything else the business may own or control.
3. What is the value of the accounts receivable? This has a potential discount because all the accounts may not be collectible.
4. What is the value of the training of the personnel who will remain with the practice, or what is the cost to train new personnel?
5. What are the liabilities that will remain after the purchase? This includes personnel salaries, taxes, debt service, and other costs of doing business.

While some of these questions are comparatively easy to answer, some of them are complex and require application of accounting and business valuation methods. The concept of goodwill and how it may affect continuing profitability is one of the complex questions. The question of how to value goodwill of a business has been a source of contention for many years, with trial courts left to decipher competing and frequently inconsistent theories and accounting practices into something meaningful. It is generally accepted in existing Kentucky law that goodwill is a factor to be considered in arriving at the value of a business, but whether goodwill can be divided between the business *and* the individual is a question of first impression for this Court.

Heller is the first in a line of Court of Appeals cases recognizing that at times a business can be sold for more than just the value of its assets. The idea is premised on the notion that the reputation of the business will draw customers, get them to return, and thus contribute to future profitability. Obviously, future business is of primary importance to a potential buyer. *Heller*'s concept of goodwill has been applied in a line of cases. . . . This line of cases focuses on professional practices, and assumes that there is a buyer for the practice (in *Heller*, an accounting practice; . . . in *Drake,* an interest in a medical practice . . . ; and in *Gomez*, a hospital-based radiology practice). In order to evaluate the fair market value of the practice, everything of value, including transferable goodwill, must be counted. None of these published cases recognize a distinction between personal and enterprise goodwill; however, they do not prohibit such an analysis. They merely establish that goodwill is a factor to be considered in valuation. This Court agrees with that conclusion.

In this case, Gaskill is the sole proprietor, or only practitioner, in the oral and maxillofacial surgery practice. Every patient of the practice is treated by her. Only she exercises the professional judgment and skill required to perform surgery on her patients. The evidence indicates that she has been a prudent and frugal office manager as well, a fact that Wheeler claimed was responsible for the large cash account of the business. Gaskill alone has performed the treatment in this practice for over thirteen years. Clearly, the practice is, in general, marital property, and therefore subject to division, but how are we to divide a person's reputation, skill and relationships? To what extent can a buyer of a business assume that his performance will equal that of the present owner? To what extent can he take on the seller's reputation in the community?

This Court has held that an advanced professional degree is not to be treated as marital property because it is personal to the holder and cannot be transferred to another. *Lovett v. Lovett* (Ky. 1985). This is because the degree

> does not have an exchange value or any objective transferable value on an open market. . . . It terminates on the death of the holder and is not inheritable. It cannot be assigned, sold, transferred, conveyed or pledged. An advanced degree is a cumulative product of many years of previous education, combined with diligence and hard work. It may not be acquired by the mere expenditure of money. It is simply an intellectual achievement that may potentially assist in the future acquisition of property . . . [.]

In *Heller*, the Court of Appeals held that there was at least "limited marketability" of goodwill where practices "*can be* sold for more than the value of their fixtures and accounts receivable. . . ." Based on this, that court held that it could distinguish professional degrees and professional goodwill. This is correct to the extent that, unlike for a professional degree, some businesses may be able to establish value beyond fixtures and accounts receivable. Examples of this include when a practitioner is part of a group practice, or is selling the name of a practice such as "Smith Pharmacy," or any other reputational thing a buyer could reasonably be expected to pay for. The analysis falls short in that it fails to consider that part of goodwill that is personal and nontransferable, much like the professional degree. It is obvious that in some cases, depending on the facts, goodwill can belong primarily or only to the person, precisely as a professional degree belongs only to the person. If value is to be decided on a fair and reasonable basis, and property divided equitably, this must be considered.

Since the mid-eighties, when *Heller* was decided, trial courts have had increasing opportunities to look at this issue, not only in Kentucky but throughout the nation. This led to development of the concepts of "personal" and "enterprise" goodwill, recognizing that there could be some goodwill associated with a business, and some that was solely due to the personal qualities of the practitioner. In states adopting this view, valuations take into consideration, based on the factual proof, whether any goodwill could reasonably be marketable as continuing with the business absent the presence of a particular person. . . .

In *May*, the Supreme Court of West Virginia found from its survey that 13 courts made no distinction between personal and enterprise goodwill, 5 courts held that goodwill is not a part of marital property, and 24 states differentiated between personal and enterprise goodwill. . . . The *May* court joined the 24 jurisdictions that distinguish between enterprise and personal goodwill. In reaching its decision, the court relied substantially on an opinion of the Supreme Court of Indiana in *Yoon*, which explained . . . :

> Goodwill has been described as the value of a business or practice that exceeds the combined value of the net assets used in the business. . . . Enterprise goodwill is based on the intangible, but generally marketable, existence in a business of established relations with employees, customers and suppliers. Factors affecting this goodwill may include a business's location, its name recognition, its business reputation, or a variety of other factors depending on the business. Ultimately these factors must, in one way or another, contribute to the anticipated future profitability of the business. Enterprise goodwill is an asset of the business and accordingly is property that is divisible in a dissolution to the extent that it inheres in the business, independent of any single individual's personal efforts and will outlast any person's involvement in the business. It is not necessarily marketable in the sense that there is a ready and easily priced market for it, but it is in general transferrable to others and has a value to others. . . .

> In contrast, the goodwill that depends on the continued presence of a particular individual is a personal asset, and any value that attaches to a business as a result of this "personal goodwill" represents nothing more than the future earning capacity of the individual and is not divisible. . . .
>
> [W]e join the states that exclude goodwill based on the personal attributes of the individual from the marital estate. . . . [B]efore including the goodwill of a self-employed business or professional practice in a marital estate, a court must determine that the goodwill is attributable to the business as opposed to the owner as an individual. If attributable to the individual, it is not a divisible asset and is properly considered only as future earning capacity that may affect the relative property division. In this respect, the future earning capacity of a self-employed person (or an owner of a business primarily dependent on the owner's services) is to be treated the same as the future earning capability and reputation of an employee. . . .

In this first look at the subject, this Court finds the reasoning of *Yoon* and *May* to be compelling. . . . In a case such as this one, there can be little argument that the skill, personality, work ethic, reputation, and relationships developed by Gaskill are hers alone and cannot be sold to a subsequent practitioner. In this manner, these attributes constitute nonmarital property that will continue with her regardless of the presence of any spouse. To consider this highly personal value as marital would effectively attach her future earnings, to which Robbins has no claim. Further, if he . . . were then awarded maintenance, this would amount to "double dipping," and cause a dual inequity to Gaskill. On the other hand, if she were willing to leave her name on the practice, such as "Gaskill's Oral and Maxillofacial Surgery," even though she herself did not continue to practice, there arguably could be some reputational reliance that she would stand behind the quality of the practice which could have some pecuniary value. Such scenarios do occur, but this is not the case here. Additionally, this type of distinction is as susceptible to expert valuation as goodwill on the whole is. . . .

B. VALUATION METHODS

In this case, both experts testified to multiple accounting methods of measuring value. Wheeler chose a specific method, gave his reasons for choosing that method, and explained where his data came from. Callahan, in contrast, did not directly obtain data, and calculated the value of the practice using four different methods, with a different value derived from each. He found all the methods to be reliable, and unable to choose, averaged the numbers to get a value.

While the trial court is free to determine the credibility of any witness, it cannot make a determination that is clearly erroneous or an abuse of discretion. Using an average to obtain a value, without some basis other than an inability to choose between conflicting and competing valuation methods, is nothing more than making up a number, for there is no evidentiary basis to support that *specific* number. Employing all four methods, then averaging them, is tantamount to no method at all. If an expert believes four methods are valid, yet each produces a different number, this provides little or no help to the trial court. The trial court must fix a value, and there should be an evidence-based articulation for why that is the value used. While an average may present the easiest route, it lacks the proper indicia of reliability. Thus, the trial court abused its discretion in relying on Callahan's estimate of $669,075 as the value of the practice. . . .

Further complicating the matter, the practice is not actually being sold and was assigned in its entirety to Gaskill. Part of the value the trial court relied on that could impact a goodwill valuation was the assumption by Callahan that a non-compete agreement should be a part of the valuation. While fair market value of Gaskill's practice anticipates what a willing buyer would give a willing seller, the fictional sale must be viewed as a "fire sale," meaning that it must be valued in its existing state. This precludes factoring in a non-existent non-compete clause, as there is no requirement that she enter into one other than as a possible negotiated term of a real sale. It was improper to include such a speculative item to enhance the value of the practice.

C. EQUITABLE DIVISION OF MARITAL PROPERTY

KRS 403.190 requires a trial court to divide marital property in "just proportions," considering "all relevant factors," and specifically includes four factors that must be considered: contribution of each spouse to the acquisition of marital property, value of nonmarital property to each, duration of the marriage, and the economic circumstances of each spouse when the division of property is to become effective. . . . [T]he trial court divided the marital estate 50-50 between the parties.

Gaskill argues that the most significant factor in division of the marital property is the great disparity between the respective financial contributions of the two parties . . . She and the Court of Appeals inferred that the trial court acted under a mistaken belief that it must presume a 50-50 division, or that there is at least a "disturbing trend" for trial courts to do so. The law is clear that there is no presumption of a 50-50 division without regard to the evidence. . . . [However], . . . starting the parties off in an even position in order to determine how to apportion is not unreasonable. . . . In fact, given that each party is an equal owner in the marital estate until the trial court divides it, the parties are in exactly the same position when the court begins dividing marital property. How the trial court ends up splitting the property must be based on record evidence, with an eye toward equity.

The property division statute looks at each spouse's contribution to acquiring the marital estate, and there is no question that on that factor the weight of the evidence lies in favor of Gaskill if numbers alone are considered. However, while the amount of the marital estate may be easily allocated between earners, the ability to work with the support of a spouse and co-parent is an intangible that goes beyond dollars. All of the work done by either spouse during the marriage is done for the marital purpose: having someone, within the bounds of law, with whom one shares a union that allows for joint homemaking, co-parenting if children are born, and experiencing life in general with another. Within the marital arrangement, abilities are often unequal, the use of one's time varies according to present need, and each spouse does things to accommodate the other. How the parties earn money and build wealth is affected by these variables, but is done for common purpose. The term "contribution" thus has tangible and intangible components that must be weighed by the trial court.

Another important statutory factor is what the economic circumstances of the parties will be at the time the property division becomes effective. . . . Just as the actual earnings disproportionately come from Gaskill, her ability to earn after the divorce is disproportionate. . . . Because of the disposition the trial court made of the marital property, it did not award maintenance to Robbins even though the great disparity in income earning ability would otherwise have supported it.

This Court will not infer that the trial court believed it *must* divide the marital estate 50-50 in light of the express statement in its opinion that "Just proportions does not require equal division," and that "a presumption of equal division absent evidence to the contrary is improper." There was evidence to support the trial court's determination that the marital estate should be divided 50-50, which is clearly reflected on the video record of the testimony of both parties about the participation each had during the marriage. While other reasonable courts may have weighed the evidence differently, this Court cannot find that the trial court abused its discretion in dividing the marital estate as it did. . . .

Why do the courts focus on whether goodwill can be sold? How does salability relate to the equitable claim of the spouse? Recall the example above of a non-transferrable license to operate a certain kind if business, such as a taxi or a bar. Some people pay a lot of money for them, even if they cannot resell them. Similarly, even if one cannot sell one's personal reputation, it can have income-producing value and some people expend a lot of marital funds developing it—for example, through advertising.

In addition, are there not in fact ways by which a professional can effectively sell her personal reputation, by associating herself with and vouching for someone else, as celebrities do when they endorse products? Suppose Gaskill did want to sell her practice. Could she not get a higher price by offering to continue working at the practice after the sale, to gradually transition her patients over to the buyer, using her customers' confidence in her personally to preserve the client base by introducing them to and recommending the buyer? Or by agreeing to appear in a local television or newspaper advertisement or story with the buyer?

Do decisions relating to professional licenses and reputations reflect simply a squeamishness about commodifying human capital? Would treating personal goodwill as property look too much like treating a person as property?

Courts in a majority of states take the same approach as in *Gaskill*, calling on experts to distinguish between enterprise and personal goodwill and treating only the former as property subject to distribution. See, e.g., Wilson v. Wilson, 706 S.E.2d 354 (W. Va. 2010) (value of real estate development management firm entirely personal); In re Marriage of Slater, 245 P.3d 676 (Or. Ct. App. 2010) (value of chiropractic business a mix of enterprise and personal); Held v. Held, 912 So. 2d 637 (Fla. Dist. Ct. App. 4th Dist. 2005) (insurance agency).

(d) Living Things

Those who are not pet owners might be surprised to learn that some divorcing couples argue as bitterly over custody of a pet as many couples do over custody of children. The traditional and still prevailing rule treats pets as personal property and awards them to one spouse or the other in the same way as any prized piece of furniture. Courts are happy to enforce agreements that married or non-married couples execute for custody of a pet. See, e.g., Houseman v. Dare, 966 A.2d 24 (N.J. Super. Ct. App. Div. 2009) (upholding order of specific performance of oral agreement boyfriend made to let girlfriend have dog upon ceasing cohabitation); DeSanctis v. Pritchard, 803 A.2d 230 (Pa. Super. Ct. 2002) (dismissing former husband's petition for shared custody of dog acquired during marriage, because under clear and unambiguous terms of agreement parties entered into pursuant to their divorce, dog and his social schedule belonged exclusively to wife). In the absence of agreement, judges decide pet disputes in divorces based on title, if any, and otherwise as they see fit. And they will not award visitation to the loser in the battle. See John DeWitt Gregory, *Pet Custody: Distorting Language and the Law*, 44 FAM. L.Q. 35 (2010) (describing case law and arguing that the prevailing treatment is preferable to treating pets like children and awarding custody based on the animal's best interests). Cf. Ann H. Britton, *Bones of Contention: Custody of Family Pets*, 20 J. AM. ACAD. MATRIMONIAL

L. 1, 15-23 (2006) (contending that public opinion is contrary to treatment of pets as property, and suggesting that judges decide who should have the pet after divorce based both on property-like considerations such as who paid to purchase the pet and custody-like considerations such as who assumed primary responsibility for care of the pet).

A significant number of couples undertake in vitro fertilization in order to have a child, and in the process they often create and freeze a surplus of embryos, rather than go through the extraction procedure more than once. If the couple divorces before using all the embryos, there might be a dispute about what is to be done with them. In the typical dispute, the ex-wife wants to use some to have more children, and the ex-husband wants them destroyed.

In the first decision by a state's highest court to address such a dispute, *Davis v. Davis,* 842 S.W.2d 588 (Tenn. 1992), the Tennessee Supreme Court attributed to the husband a constitutional right not to procreate and held that the embryos should be destroyed. Professor Strasser describes the court's reasoning.

Mark P. Strasser, You Take the Embryos But I Get the House (and the Business): Recent Trends in Awards Involving Embryos Upon Divorce

57 Buff. L. Rev. 1159, 1162-1179 (2009)

While recognizing that embryos "are accorded more respect than mere human cells because of their burgeoning potential for life," the *Davis* court rejected that embryos should be classified as persons. After all, the court noted, "even after viability, they are not given legal status equivalent to that of a person already born." . . . Yet, abortion jurisprudence may be much less helpful than first appears. . . . While the Fourteenth Amendment to the United States Constitution does not accord personhood to the fetus or embryo, an entirely separate question is whether a state law (or state constitution) accords such a status to an embryo or fetus, especially if the conferral of that status would not impinge on existing abortion rights. . . .

The *Davis* court not only rejected that embryos are persons, but also rejected that they are property. Instead, they "occupy an interim category that entitles them to special respect because of their potential for human life." The Davises' interest in the embryos was "not a true property interest". . . . Ultimately, the court suggested that Junior could not be forced to become a father against his will . . . The *Davis* court . . . recognized that an individual can have an interest in avoiding genetic parenthood, even if he would not acquire any legal responsibilities toward any child produced as a result of implantation. The court took seriously that an individual might suffer emotionally were he to know that a child biologically related to him was being raised by strangers, referring to "the relative anguish of a lifetime of unwanted parenthood." . . . [S]omeone who donates semen knowing that it will be used by someone else is not in the same position as someone who produces semen so that he can father a child with his partner. . . .

However, the *Davis* court did not analogously consider whether the right to be a genetic parent might also suffice to trigger constitutional guarantees. . . . Perhaps that is because Mary Sue wanted to donate the embryos purely out of altruism. . . . On the other hand, it may be that Mary Sue valued being a genetic parent, and wanted to donate the embryos to another couple because Junior would then not then face potential financial responsibility as the legal father. Indeed, she might have preferred to raise the child or children herself, but might also have believed that Junior would only consent to implantation were he assured that he would be a legal stranger to any children resulting from the implantation. In any event, regardless of why Mary Sue wanted to donate the embryos, someone else might want to donate them precisely because she would receive psychic benefit just from knowing that she had become a genetic parent. . . . For example, while many egg donors feel good about having given their eggs to others, some say that they would like to know whether the eggs resulted in live births. Presumably, at least some of those . . . would take pleasure in knowing that children had indeed been born from those eggs. That pleasure might result from knowing that one had helped others in need but also might result from knowing that one has a genetic connection to other living beings in the next generation. . . .

After noting that the decision about whether to grant Mary Sue custody of the embryos would have been more difficult had she wanted to use them herself, the *Davis* court cautioned that it would not have been willing to override Junior's wishes unless Mary Sue had had no other reasonable options. . . . [T]he *Davis* court understood that her having to undergo another egg retrieval would be painful, but did not believe that the painfulness of the procedure would render the option unreasonable. . . . [A]fter noting that there might be reasons precluding Mary Sue from going through the entire process again, the court offered the consolation that "she could still achieve the child-rearing aspects of parenthood through adoption." Yet the whole focus of discussion had been on the genetic parenting interests of the parties, so . . . [this] seems to undercut the claim that the Davises were being treated equally as gamete providers. . . . [E]ven were it true that Junior or someone like him might feel badly about being genetically connected to a child raised by others, the court seemed unwilling to consider that an analogous argument might be made about the feelings of the parent who wants the embryos donated, i.e., that he or she might feel terribly were the embryos discarded rather than given the opportunity to flourish. . . .

The *Davis* court explained that a much different result would have been reached had the Davises initially agreed about the disposition of the embryos in the event of divorce. Had there been such an agreement, it would have been enforceable. . . .

Professor Forman describes the current, inconsistent state of the law:

Deborah L. Forman, Embryo Disposition and Divorce: Why Clinic Consent Forms Are Not the Answer

4 J. Am. Acad. Matrimonial L. 57, 58-59, 89-93 (2011)

It has become increasingly common for clinics to require couples undergoing IVF to sign a cryopreservation consent or agreement . . . prior to initiating treatment. These . . . typically ask patients to choose from a number of options for disposition under a variety of contingencies, such as death, divorce or abandonment of the embryos. A few states now require by statute that physicians provide their fertility patients with a form covering dispositional choices. While these documents might appear to settle the matter, . . . [c]ase law to date evinces the uncertainty plaguing the validity of these forms and how to resolve disputes over embryo disposition at divorce more generally. Courts in most states have yet to consider the issue. In those that have, the judicial decisions range from those that purport to view such agreements as binding and enforceable to those that explicitly refuse to enforce certain dispositions chosen at the time of treatment, in the absence of contemporaneous consent.

Moreover statutory proscriptions related to embryo disposition . . . bring[] confusion rather than clarity to the question of embryo disposition in cases of divorce. The statutes fall into roughly two groups: those specifically dealing with embryo disposition and those that address parental status related to embryos used after divorce. California Health & Safety Code §125315 typifies the first category. It provides that physicians offering fertility treatment must obtain written, informed consent regarding embryo disposition. It then instructs that the informed consent form shall include "advanced written directives" offering statutorily delineated options to the patients in the event of a variety of contingencies. . . . Yet the statute says nothing about whether these dispositions will constitute a binding legal agreement between the progenitors in the event the relationship ends. . . . Massachusetts has a statute that . . . provides that the physician present the patient with the options of storing, donating to another person or to research or destroying any unused embryos "as appropriate." It does not address any specific contingencies, such as divorce, and Massachusetts will not compel procreation in the absence of contemporaneous consent. [See A.Z. v. B.Z., 725 N.E.2d 1051 (Mass. 2000).] New Jersey and Connecticut also have statutes dealing with stem cell research that require physicians treating fertility patients to present patients with the options of storing or donating excess embryos to another or to research, but they do not address contingencies such as divorce. New Jersey, too, has adopted the rule of contemporaneous consent by case law. . . .

The second category of statutes . . . resides in code sections related to family law and parentage. These statutes seek to clarify that if a marriage dissolves or, in some cases, a dissolution action is filed, prior to placement of gametes or embryos, the former spouse will not be considered the legal parent of any subsequently resulting child, unless the former spouse consented in writing to be a parent of a child if the assisted reproduction occurred after marital dissolution. This provision addresses one of the significant uncertainties surrounding the use of embryos after divorce: whether a progenitor should shoulder legal responsibilities as a parent if the other progenitor is allowed to use the embryos. These statutes also allow a former spouse to revoke consent to the assisted reproduction "anytime before placement of eggs, sperm, or embryos," which seems to undercut the reliability of the contract considerably, as either party can apparently withdraw consent, at least prior to filing for divorce. . . .

POLICY/THEORY ANALYSIS

Is it possible to reason to a conclusion about the best legal rule for such conflicts without resort to contested moral beliefs—e.g., about the moral status of embryos? Try to think of all the more empirically verifiable pros and cons of routinely favoring one preference or the other (i.e., to use the embryos or to destroy them). Do they show one private party's interests to be weightier than the other's? Are the costs or benefits for the state sufficiently great as to warrant the state overriding any constitutional rights the parties might have, or to control the decision in the face of opposing rights? Consider that a woman who wishes to impregnate herself post-divorce will effectively be intentionally creating a single-parenthood situation. Is any compromise position tenable, such as assigning the right to one side but requiring that party to compensate the other for their psychic costs, perhaps by granting more property in equitable distribution to the latter? If the court bestows the embyos on the wife, should the state relieve the husband of any child support obligation?

(3) Equitable Division

In a small number of states, principally some of the community property states, courts divide the value of marital or community property equally between the spouses. This could involve some further exercise of discretion insofar as a couple might dispute which ex-spouse should receive a particular marital asset or which valuation method is appropriate, but courts are spared from making a judgment about what allocation of value is fair. In most states, however, including some community property states, courts are charged, in the absence of agreement by the parties, with determining what allocation of value is "equitable." For explanation of the various community property states' approaches to property distribution, see James R. Ratner, *Distribution of Marital Assets in Community Property Jurisdictions: Equitable Doesn't Equal Equal*, 72 La. L. Rev. 21 (2011).

As you have already seen, determining what distribution is equitable is not a simple matter of applying a formula or clearly defined factors. Rather, it entails subjective judgments of deservingness and need. As you read the cases in this section, ask whether the appellate court gives you or trial courts much guidance as to how to apply the relevant factors and whether judges recognize all the accounting problems their approach to financial issues entails.

Many states have adopted, more or less, the Uniform Marriage and Divorce Act provision regarding equitable distribution. Note that the example from Colorado below explicitly prohibits consideration of fault. Approximately 20 states now exclude consideration of marital misconduct in dividing property, by virtue either of statutory command or judicially created rule. A majority of states continue to consider it as one factor among many, as in the Virginia statute at the beginning of this section.

Colorado Revised Statutes
Title 14. Domestic Matters
Article 10. Uniform Dissolution of Marriage Act

§14-10-113. Disposition of Property

(1) In a proceeding for dissolution of marriage . . . the court . . . shall divide the marital property, without regard to marital misconduct, in such proportions as the court deems just after considering all relevant factors including:

(a) The contribution of each spouse to the acquisition of the marital property, including the contribution of a spouse as homemaker;

(b) The value of the property set apart to each spouse;

(c) The economic circumstances of each spouse at the time the division of property is to become effective, including the desirability of awarding the family home or the right to live therein for reasonable periods to the spouse with whom any children reside the majority of the time; and

(d) Any increases or decreases in the value of . . . separate property . . . during the marriage or the depletion of the separate property for marital purposes.

Note that the first factor in this non-exclusive list is contribution and the other three all have to do mostly with need. The contribution factor is odd, given the assumption basic to equitable distribution that just having a spouse helps one acquire property, for reasons set out above in *Gaskill v. Robbins*—namely, that a spouse provides emotional security and typically takes on a number of tasks to help the household function. Courts resist calculating the value of that assistance by any means other than an assumption of equal partnership. This factor would seem logically to operate, if at all, only in a negative way, as a justification for punishing a spouse who actually made the income earner unhappy or who did little or no work for the household. Yet courts are also unwilling to pass negative judgments of that sort on any spouse, which can make it difficult to explain the underlying rationale of equitable distribution to some clients. See if you can make any sense of how courts use the contribution factor in the cases you read in this chapter.

Consideration of separate property is also odd, yet many states include among equitable distribution factors whether either spouse has substantial separate property. See, e.g., 750 Ill. Comp. Stat. 5/503; 23 Pa. Const. Stat. §3502; Tenn. Code. Ann. §36-4-121; Wash. Rev. Code §26.09.080. Some states' courts will even reduce a divorcing spouse's share of marital property if he or she is likely to receive a sizeable inheritance or trust benefit *after* the divorce. See Billings v. Billings, 35 A.3d 1030 (Vt. 2011) (holding as such and citing decisions of other states). Considering separate property is odd because, practically speaking, if a court gives a spouse less marital property because that spouse has more separate property than the other spouse, the result can be the same as if "separate" property were in the divisible pie—that is, were not really separate, as in hotchpot states. For example, imagine that a couple has $125,000 in marital assets, the wife has $75,000 in separate property (a recent inheritance, let's say), and the husband has no separate property. If the court finds that all the other factors support a 50/50 split, but then decides to give the husband $100,000 of the marital property because the wife has the separate property, this result is the same as if the court treated all of the wife's inheritance as divisible property and applied the 50/50 equitable proportion. To whatever extent a judge reduces a spouse's share of marital property based on her having separate property, it is the same as if the court treated twice as much of her separate property as divisible property.

Given this effect of factor (b) in the Colorado statute, the main difference between the rules in Colorado and in a hotchpot state would be that in Colorado the absolute value of the marital estate creates a cap on how much a spouse can be forced to sacrifice because of having separate property. For example, if the marital property were only $25,000 and the wife's separate property $75,000, the most a judge in Colorado could do is give all $25,000 to the husband, thus reducing the wife's share of marital property by $12,500, which is equivalent to treating $25,000 of her separate property as divisible. But if the marital estate is larger than a spouse's separate property, that spouse might end up the same financially as if the court included all of that separate property in the divisible pie, if the court reduces that spouse's share of the marital estate based on his having the separate property and therefore less need.

With respect to "marital misconduct," do the same reasons for allowing a divorce without a showing of fault support exclusion of fault from the property distribution decision? Would you guess that women or men have benefited more from the trend toward disregarding or minimizing, fault? Should states limit consideration of fault to the most egregious forms of misconduct? Or to those that cause demonstrable harm other than simply the fact of getting divorced? You might conclude that the Florida court in the case below takes the no-fault idea too far. Or that the Alabama decision that follows it goes too far in the other direction, finding fault too easily.

Mosbarger v. Mosbarger

547 So. 2d 188 (Fla. Dist. Ct. App. 2d Dist. 1989)

Altenbernd, Judge.

. . . The parties were married in Spokane, Washington, in 1959. At that time, Mr. Mosbarger was in the air force. Mrs. Mosbarger dropped out of high school to marry her husband. During the next fourteen years, the parties lived in various states as the husband was transferred from one air force base to another. The couple raised two children, who were adults by the time of the divorce. After completing twenty years of service, the husband was discharged from the air force in 1973. The family moved to the Tampa Bay area, and the husband went to work for Honeywell, Inc., as a program manager. At the time of the divorce proceeding, Mr. Mosbarger was earning in excess of $47,000 a year at Honeywell and was also receiving a military pension of $819 a month. During the marriage, Mrs. Mosbarger worked outside the home at various jobs. In the later years of the marriage, she did clerical work and basic accounting. In 1986, she earned approximately $8,500.

Mrs. Mosbarger suffered from numerous health problems during the marriage. In the summer of 1986, she injured her back in a boating accident. In addition to physical problems, she also suffered from psychological problems during the marriage. Her husband encouraged her to receive psychological treatment, but she was unwilling to undergo testing or hospitalization. In January 1987, Mr. Mosbarger moved out of the marital residence and into his own apartment. When he advised his wife that he wanted a divorce, she attempted suicide. She received emergency medical treatment at a local hospital and then spent a month in a psychiatric hospital. While in that hospital, she was served with the divorce papers and again attempted suicide.

Following her release from the hospital, Mrs. Mosbarger continued psychiatric treatment as an outpatient and returned to work in April 1987. In early June 1987, she went to her husband's place of employment to have him sign some papers. She observed him getting into his car with another woman and assumed they were romantically involved. Mrs. Mosbarger became irate and committed numerous acts over the next several days which can best be described as irrational. She repeatedly threatened to kill her husband. On June 7, she fired two shots from a revolver at her husband. Fortunately, she wounded a small oak tree rather than her husband. She was arrested at the scene and charged with attempted murder.

Mrs. Mosbarger spent the next twenty days in the Hillsborough County Jail. With the assistance of a psychiatrist . . . , she was transferred to a psychiatric hospital. She remained hospitalized for the next five months. In September 1987, Mrs. Mosbarger was found competent to stand trial in her criminal proceeding. She pled guilty to attempted second degree murder in exchange for a sentence including out-of-state counseling and probation for one year, followed by one year of Florida community control and two years of Florida probation. The final hearing in the divorce proceeding occurred . . . while [she] was still hospitalized. By that time, she had made plans to accompany her sister to the state of Washington where she planned to live for the first year of her criminal sentence.

At the time of the final hearing, the trial court was required to equitably distribute assets and liabilities. Each party received an automobile and a portion of the furniture. The husband received his boat and motorcycle along with the liabilities encumbering those vehicles. He received all rights to his Honeywell pension which had a pre-tax valuation of approximately $31,000. The couple had sold their home and the proceeds had been placed in a money market account. Of that account, Mrs. Mosbarger received approximately $28,000 and her husband received the remaining $11,000. Up to this point, the distribution of assets was approximately equal. The trial court, however, then awarded the entire military pension to the husband.

The wife had incurred uninsured medical bills between the time of the parties' separation and the time of the final hearing which totaled more than $20,000. At least a portion of those bills were incurred prior to the filing of the divorce. Although the trial court could have made the husband responsible for these expenses and for future, reasonable medical expenses, the trial court made Mrs. Mosbarger primarily responsible for all of her medical bills.

Finally, the trial court awarded Mrs. Mosbarger permanent periodic alimony in the amount of $500 a month beginning in February 1988. The trial court appears to have considered the military pension in determining this amount. The wife's financial needs, however, clearly exceeded $1,000 a month. While the husband may need to curtail his expenditures for boats, motorcycles, vacations, and gifts to afford the payment of periodic alimony without utilizing the military pension, it is clear that Mrs. Mosbarger has the need for greater support and Mr. Mosbarger has the ability to pay greater support. . . .

[I]t appears that the trial court based the size of the alimony award, in part, upon a decision to impute income to Mrs. Mosbarger during the year of her probation in Washington. The trial court reasoned that Mrs. Mosbarger's unemployment was caused by her criminal activity and should not result in an increased payment by the husband. The record, however, contains expert psychiatric testimony which suggests that Mrs. Mosbarger could not have worked during the year of probation and counseling in Washington due to her major depressive disorder. . . . Mrs. Mosbarger may have employment difficulties due to her mental illness for an extended time.

Concerning the wife's request for attorney's fees, her counsel testified that he had expended approximately 122 hours in her representation. . . . . The trial court, however, without the aid of expert testimony, found that forty hours would have been reasonable and the additional expenditure of time would not have been necessary but for the criminal complications. The trial court required the husband to pay only two-thirds of this reasonable fee, i.e., $2,400. Thus, the wife was left with an obligation to her attorney in excess of $8,000.

In summary, the trial court awarded Mr. Mosbarger a significant distribution of marital assets. His liabilities are modest. Including the military pension and excluding alimony payments, his gross income exceeds $50,000. Mrs. Mosbarger received an equitable distribution which appears insufficient to pay her existing obligations for medical and legal services, and an award of alimony which is no more than 50% of the amount necessary to modestly support this fifty-year-old woman who is suffering from a psychiatric disorder that will undoubtedly limit her employment opportunities.

While the trial court has broad discretion to fashion the overall distribution scheme in a divorce proceeding, we find that the trial court abused its discretion by awarding an overall scheme which shortchanged the wife. The trial court was clearly bothered by the wife's attempt to kill her husband. We do not condone her actions, and she should not benefit in this proceeding because of her criminal conduct. Nevertheless, Florida's divorce system generally attempts to apply no-fault principles. Since adultery, as a statutorily recognized act of marital misconduct, is only considered when it translates into a greater financial need for the spouse or a depletion of the family resources, we are not inclined to believe that Mrs. Mosbarger's criminal conduct, which is not a statutorily recognized act of marital misconduct, should be treated more severely in this domestic proceeding. . . .

This case requires a careful delineation between Mrs. Mosbarger's isolated criminal activity and her more pervasive psychiatric illness. Before the trial court imputes income to Mrs. Mosbarger during her period of probation, that court should first expressly determine that she would have been employable, even in light of her mental illness, except for the criminal sentence. If Mrs. Mosbarger had been suffering from a severe, but curable, physical disease, one suspects that the trial court would have responded more generously to her predicament. When the mental disorder is clearly manifested and professionally diagnosed, we are not inclined to believe it should be treated with less compassion. Among the factors which the trial court must consider in awarding alimony are both the physical and emotional condition of each party. §61.08(2)(c), Fla. Stat. . . . We vacate the final judgment and remand to the trial court to conduct a new evidentiary hearing for purposes of revising . . . the equitable distribution, the alimony, and the award of attorney's fees.

Daugherty v. Daugherty

606 So. 2d 157 (Ala. Civ. App. 1992)

THIGPEN, Judge.

The parties divorced in May 1990. At the time of trial, the wife and the husband were 51 and 47 years old respectively, and both parties were in good health. They had one son who was eighteen years old . . . , and he had expressed a desire to go to college. . . . [H]usband was receiving a net income of $2,000 per month from his occupation installing outdoor sprinkler systems. Prior to the divorce, the parties had separated and the husband was maintaining responsibility for some of the marital debts, and he was contributing to the ongoing expenses of the marriage, which included two monthly mortgage payments totalling $700. . . . The wife was self-employed as an art teacher and earned supplemental income by selling art supplies. The wife's testimony was that she realized only small profits. . . . The record contained testimony from the husband that he had conveyed his interest in one lot owned by the parties, to his brother for $100 just prior to the divorce.

The trial court awarded the wife all of the marital assets (which included the home, its furnishings and two lots), . . . alimony of $1,000 per month for 36 months, and $750 a month thereafter. . . . We found that the award of periodic alimony, coupled with the award of virtually all of the marital assets to the wife, exceeded the husband's ability to pay, and we reversed and remanded the cause to the trial court for consideration. . . . [T]he trial court reduced the periodic alimony award to $400 per month and did not disturb its earlier ruling that the marital assets, including the marital home, should remain with the wife. The husband appeals, contending that this award equals almost half of his monthly income because he is now earning only $927 per month, as opposed to the original $2,000. . . .

A trial court may properly consider the following factors in determining the division of property and the award of alimony . . . : 1) the earning ability of the parties; 2) their probable future prospects; 3) their age, sex, health and station in life; 4) the duration of their marriage; and 5) the conduct of the parties as related to the cause of divorce. . . .

The testimony revealed that the husband, immediately upon leaving the wife, moved to Virginia and began living with another woman and her son. The . . . woman's son previously worked for him, and . . . he had not met the woman prior to his move, because her son had made the living arrangements for the husband prior to his departure for Virginia. The . . . son [had] told him that his mother, who lives in a trailer, took in "boarders" for rental income. The husband . . . is still living in that arrangement, although the son has moved out, and . . . the woman is now his girlfriend. The husband . . . pays the rent on her trailer, the utility bills, the telephone bills, her car payment, and her insurance. The husband also pays a monthly life insurance premium which names his son and his girlfriend's son as the beneficiaries. The husband testified that his ex-wife was a hard worker during the marriage, but that she also expected him to work all of the time and would get upset if he relaxed. He . . . "couldn't take it anymore," so he left for Virginia. . . .

Fault during the term of the marriage is an appropriate factor for the trial court to consider in fashioning its awards. . . . In view of the above, we find the property division and alimony award to be . . . equitable under the circumstances. . . .

Would you view the husband in *Daugherty* as having committed any marital misconduct? Is he being punished financially because he did not petition for divorce sooner, before moving to Virginia?

As noted earlier in this section, in some states with only no-fault grounds for divorce, a party might still be able to allege fault in connection with property distribution and receive a larger share of property as a kind of compensation. Others, however, are "pure no-fault states," meaning that statutes render fault irrelevant to every aspect of the divorce. In a pure no-fault state, a spouse injured by the other's fault might feel cheated by the law's failure to join in condemning and punishing it. Should couples be able to create their own penalties for fault, in a pre-nuptial or marital agreement?

In re Marriage of Mehren & Dargan

118 Cal. App. 4th 1167 (Cal. Ct. App. 2004)

RYLAARSDAM, J.

. . . Husband has suffered an off-and-on addiction to cocaine for many years. . . . [S]everal years after their marriage, the parties separated after another episode resulting from husband's use of cocaine. Months later, the parties agreed that husband would return to the family home. Subsequently, the parties entered into an "Agreement re Transfer of Property." The agreement recited that wife "consented to the resumption of marital relations on the condition that [husband] abstain from the deliberate, intentional use or ingestion of any mind altering chemical or substance excluding such use that may be prescribed or approved by a medical doctor. In the event of such deliberate, intentional use or ingestion of mind altering chemicals or substances by [husband], [husband] agrees that he will forfeit all of his right, title and interest in [described property]." Husband and wife signed the document before a notary public. Unfortunately, husband did not keep his promise. Thereafter wife filed for divorce, asking that the property described in the agreement be confirmed to her as her separate property. . . .

THE CONTRACT VIOLATES PUBLIC POLICY

. . . Although reported cases have dealt with contracts between spouses, many of these deal with premarital agreements. But we can look to these cases for guidance. In *In Re Marriage of Bonds* (2000), our Supreme Court noted the difference between commercial contracts and contracts regulating the marital relationship (in that case, a premarital agreement). Commercial contracts have a specific object, and parties to such contracts generally enter into them intending that the objects be achieved. Marital contracts, on the other hand, are generally entered into in the expectation that they will never be invoked. "Furthermore, marriage itself is a highly regulated institution of undisputed social value, and there are many limitations on the ability of persons to contract with respect to it, or to vary its statutory terms, that have nothing to do with maximizing the satisfaction of the parties or carrying out their intent."

The *Bonds* opinion rejects a freedom-of-contract analysis of marital contracts and recites a number of examples of marital contracts that will not be enforced as violating public policy. *Bonds* also draws a distinction between premarital and postmarital contracts when it notes a difference in the fiduciary relationship between the parties; no such relationship exists preceding the marriage. It does following marriage and therefore affects spouses' ability to enter into contracts between themselves. . . . [W]e must decide whether the statutory regulations pertaining to marriage would be frustrated were we to enforce the agreement. We answer this query in the affirmative. Because the conduct of one spouse would affect the division of community property, the agreement frustrates the statutory policy favoring no-fault divorce.

[In] *Diosdado v. Diosdado* (2002) . . . husband and wife entered into a written agreement wherein each promised to remain faithful to the other; the agreement also provided for $50,000 liquidated damages, to be paid upon dissolution of the marriage, should either spouse breach the agreement. The court adopted the reasoning of the trial court that the agreement was not enforceable "because it was contrary to the public policy underlying California's no-fault divorce laws." The court noted that since the 1969 enactment of . . . Fam. Code, §2310, "[f]ault is simply not a relevant consideration in the legal process by which a marriage is dissolved. Recovery in no-fault dissolution proceedings 'is basically limited to half the community property and appropriate support and attorney fee orders-no hefty premiums for emotional angst.'" The *Diosdado* court concluded the liquidated damage clause "attempt[ed] to impose just such a premium for the 'emotional angst' caused by [husband's] breach of his promise of sexual fidelity." As such, the contract had an unlawful object and was invalid under Civil Code section 1667.

We see little analytical difference between the angst experienced by the wife in *Diosdado* and the angst undoubtedly suffered by wife here. In this case too, the agreement purports to award a community property premium because of the behavior of husband. Thus, as in *Diosdado*, the agreement attempts to avoid the no-fault provisions of Family Code section 2310. As such, its objective is illegal under Civil Code section 1667, which renders a contract unlawful if it is "[¶]1. [c]ontrary to an express provision of law; [¶]2. [c]ontrary to the policy of express law, . . . or, [¶]3. [o]therwise contrary to good morals."

Wife seeks to distinguish *Diosdado* by arguing that the present "agreement was a contract independent of the court, and required no court action," while the agreement in *Diosdado* "could only be implemented in the context of a divorce suit." True, the *Diosdado* agreement would only be effective upon a dissolution. Thus the policy considerations are slightly different. It is also correct that in theory, and assuming the agreement were valid, once husband started again using illicit drugs, wife could have invoked her rights under the agreement and acquired the community property assets without obtaining a divorce. But such a scenario would not affect the relationship of the parties in the same manner as a transfer of these property interests following a divorce. And, significantly, wife did not seek to obtain the transfer of husband's share of the community property when he again relapsed into his addiction; she sought it as part of the dissolution proceedings. Further, the very issue determining whether she was entitled to the property would necessarily involve a judicial determination concerning husband's drug use, a factual adjudication of fault that the no-fault statute seeks to avoid. . . .

THE CONTRACT FAILS FOR LACK OF LEGAL CONSIDERATION

The Restatement of Contracts provides: "A bargain, the sole consideration of which is refraining or promising to refrain from committing a crime or tort, or from deceiving or wrongfully injuring the promisee or a third person, is illegal." Here the sole consideration offered by husband was his promise to refrain from using illegal drugs, a crime. Hence the contract fails.

Would such a contract fare better in a state that has retained fault grounds? Are there reasons to enforce such contracts that the court does not consider? For example, might a rule that such contracts will be enforced save some marriages? Imagine yourself a wronged spouse debating whether to give your spouse another chance.

Professor Laufer-Ukeles argues that although a victim of marital misconduct should have some avenue of redress, that avenue should be entirely apart from the divorce proceeding, in a separate tort suit: "Keeping the process of punishing culpable behavior and providing monetary recourse in tort will best allow judges to focus on what I argue should be the goal of divorce: ensuring adequate support of dependents of the marriage and optimizing post-divorce relations between parents and children." See Pamela Laufer-Ukeles, *Reconstructing Fault: The Case for Spousal Torts,* 79 U. CIN. L. REV. 207, 247 (2010). She would have the legal system recognize tort causes of action against a former spouse for battery and for intentional infliction of emotional distress. She maintains, however, that a cause of action ordinarily ought not to lie for adultery. See if you find her reasoning persuasive and adequate to distinguish adultery from physical abuse: "Historically, the purpose of marriage was community building and the complete, life-long 'channeling of sexual expression' into a monogamous relationship. Accordingly, children born out of wedlock were treated particularly harshly by the law as 'bastards.' Yet, now, we do not treat children born out of wedlock as illegitimate and any such treatment has largely been deemed unconstitutional. Moreover, while adultery clearly is still frowned upon, and can have significant effects on people's careers if they are in the public spotlight, it is also relatively common. It is not deemed a huge impingement on societal interests and is not punished with direct legal ramifications as it once was, particularly in the age of no-fault. . . . In fact, spouses themselves are often willing to overlook adultery and remain in their marriages. . . . [M]odern marriage—in accordance with the ideal of joining with one's soul mate—is more complex than just the context for monogamous sexual relations. Marriage, in other words, is built on more than its sexual 'essentials.' While infidelity is a common reason for divorce, surveys indicate that the majority of people who know or have reason to know their spouse is cheating remain married for years afterward.'" Id. at 249-250.

Economic Misconduct

Whereas the states are split on whether marital misconduct (i.e., conduct manifesting a betrayal of the marriage bond) should factor into financial dispositions, nearly all treat "economic misconduct" or "dissipation" (i.e., wasting of marital assets in contemplation of divorce) as relevant. Why the different treatment?

The prevailing test for a finding of economic misconduct has two elements: the spouse alleging it must show that the other 1) used marital assets for a non-marital purpose "in derogation of the marital relationship" 2) at a time when divorce was anticipated. The remedy is to treat the dissipated assets as part of the distribution of the marital estate to the guilty spouse, as if he already received that much of his share. Thus, suppose $20,000 was wasted, the remaining marital assets are worth $100,000, and the court orders an equal division. The court will ascribe an artificial value of $120,000 to the marital estate (as if the $20,000 had never been wasted), and then award $60,000 of the actual marital estate to the innocent spouse, $40,000 to the guilty spouse. Charges of economic misconduct are fairly common in divorce actions.

Kittredge v. Kittredge

803 N.E.2d 306 (Mass. 2004)

SOSMAN, J.

. . . Elizabeth A. Kittredge (wife), and the defendant, Sidney Kittredge (husband), were married in 1967. . . . The wife acknowledges that, throughout the marriage, the husband was "an excellent economic provider," enabling the family to live "an upper class lifestyle," including "a fine home, clothing, vacations, travel, and recreational activities." Over the many years that the husband was the sole financial provider for the family, the wife and children did not "want[ ] for anything."

The husband was, however, a heavy gambler, regularly placing large bets through bookies, plus occasionally gambling at casinos. Most of his bets were placed on professional and college sporting events, and his sole form of entertainment was to gamble and watch television games on which he had placed bets. This gambling activity—which the wife characterized as "compulsive"—occurred throughout the course of their twenty-seven year marriage.

The wife's father died in 1987, and in 1990 she received an inheritance valued at approximately $1.3 million. With the income from that inheritance, the wife began to pay some of the daily household expenses, while the husband paid the taxes on that additional income and paid for the children's education. As of the time of the master's hearing, the wife estimated that the husband had spent over $350,000 on the children's educational expenses,[1] and it was anticipated that the husband would be paying $50,000 for the upcoming weddings of two of their daughters.

1. At the time of the hearing, one of the daughters was in her third year of medical school, and the youngest child was in her sophomore year in college. The eldest daughter had completed law school and was a practicing attorney.

The wife filed for divorce in February, 1991, alleging an irretrievable breakdown of the marriage. . . . An attempt at marriage counselling, undertaken over a period of months after the wife filed for divorce, was unsuccessful, and the husband moved out of the marital home in January, 1992. . . . The marital estate, including the wife's inheritance from her father,[2] was valued at $4,442,284, of which $2,442,065 was held by the husband and $2,000,219 was held by the wife. . . .

Expert accountants for both sides agreed, at least in concept, as to how the net gambling losses (which had never been documented or recorded in any fashion) could be reconstructed from existing records of that ten-year period. . . . By identifying and quantifying deposits and expenditures that were not related to gambling, the parties' experts proceeded on the assumption that everything else was attributable to gambling—any deposit that could not be attributed to some other source was treated as gambling winnings, and every expenditure from the account that could not be identified for some other purpose was treated as a gambling loss. . . . Based on differing treatment of those items, the experts reached vastly disparate calculations of the husband's net gambling losses over that ten-year period, with the wife's expert opining that the losses amounted to $707,543, while the husband's expert arrived at a figure of $296,690.

The judge ultimately found that the net gambling losses over that time period were $400,000, but he concluded . . . that only $40,000 of that amount should be characterized as "waste" of marital assets. He ordered the husband to make an additional $40,000 transfer to the wife in order to account for that "waste." . . . As a result of these adjustments, the over-all division of marital property awarded sixty-four per cent of the estate to the wife and thirty-six per cent to the husband. . . . Although the judge did not articulate his reasons for selecting the figure of $400,000 (a figure $100,000 less than the average of the two opinions), he did articulate general grounds for placing somewhat greater, although not total, credence in the husband's expert, thus making it rational to select a figure closer to the husband's expert's opinion. . . .

The wife contends that the entirety of the husband's [net] gambling losses must, as a matter of law, be treated as dissipation of marital assets, and that the judge therefore erred when he determined that only $40,000 (or ten per cent of the total [net] gambling losses) constituted dissipation. In large measure, her argument rests on the theory that any "illegal" expenditure is, by definition, a form of financial misconduct that qualifies as dissipation, and that her husband's involvement with an unlawful form of gambling requires the court to treat all his gambling losses as dissipation. . . .

While there is no definition of "dissipation" in our own case law, other jurisdictions define dissipation as a spouse's expenditures for his or her own personal enjoyment at a time when the marriage is apparently coming to an end, from which it can be inferred that the spouse's expenditures were made in order to deprive the other spouse of his or her fair share of the marital estate. See *Herron v. Johnson* (D.C. 1998) (dissipation is "disposition of marital property by a spouse in a manner intended to 'circumvent the equitable distribution of the marital estate,'" which may be shown by evidence that "spouse used marital property for his or her own benefit and for a purpose unrelated to the marriage at a time when the marriage was undergoing an irreconcilable breakdown"); *McCleary v. McCleary* (Md. App. 2002) (dissipation consists of spending marital assets "for the principal purpose of reducing the funds available for equitable distribution"). The concept thus incorporates an element of timing (referring to the time period after it becomes evident that the marriage will not last), and an element of intent (that the expenditure is

2. By the time of hearing, the value of the wife's inheritance had appreciated to $1.8 million.

made for the purpose of thwarting the other spouse's rights to a share of the estate in the impending divorce). Conspicuously absent from these attempts to define or describe the concept of dissipation is any requirement that the allegedly wasteful expenditure be unlawful or any pronouncement that unlawful conduct will automatically constitute dissipation.

Cases in Massachusetts have similarly invoked the concept of dissipation when dealing with expenditures by a spouse made solely for that spouse's pleasures, incurred at a time when the marriage is ending, and done in a manner that evinces a disregard for the obligations to the other spouse. See, e.g., *Ross v. Ross* (Mass. 1982) (awarding wife one-half of stock owned at time of judgment nisi, where husband had thereafter failed to make payments on loans secured by that stock, lost significant portion of that stock as a result, and spent money on another woman); *Johnston v. Johnston* (Mass. 1995) (following separation from wife, husband "embarked on a binge of high living" with other women, including frequent vacation trips and purchase of lavish homes, while transferring and encumbering other real estate in violation of court order).

However defined, the concept of dissipation must be viewed within the context of the statutory factors governing the equitable division of marital property under G.L. c. 208, §34. . . . [D]issipation can be considered as part of the "conduct of the parties during the marriage" (which the judge must consider under §34), and it can also be considered in the assessment of a spouse's "contribution" to "the acquisition, preservation or appreciation in value" of assets (which the judge may consider under §34). . . . [I]t is conduct having an adverse impact on the marriage or the marital estate, not simply conduct that is in some other sense considered "good" or "bad," that is to be weighed. An equitable division of marital property is intended to effect fairness between the parties in light of all of the circumstances, not to punish "bad" behavior or enforce the criminal laws. . . .[12]

Courts have also identified dissipation as a factor that affects a spouse's "contribution" to the marital assets, in the sense that it offsets or diminishes the value of whatever positive contributions that spouse has made. See *E.E.C. v. E.J.C.* (Del. 1983); *Anstutz v. Anstutz* (Wis. Ct. App. 1983). Thus, determination whether a spouse's expenditures constitute dissipation considers them in the light of that spouse's over-all contribution, including whether the expenditures have rendered the spouse unable to support the other spouse from the much-diminished estate at the time of divorce. See *Wilner v. Wilner* (N.Y. A.D. 1993) (marital assets almost entirely depleted by husband's gambling); *Marriage of Rodriguez* (Kan. 1998) (where wife contributed majority of assets to marriage, and husband's arrest for drug dealing resulted in substantial forfeitures and legal fees, court equitably distributed most of remaining $90,000 in assets to wife). . . .

[V]arious courts have found dissipation in a spouse's gambling. However, that finding of dissipation has not been predicated on some inherent feature of gambling (either lawful or unlawful) but rather on the circumstances of the gambling activity in question—its timing, the gambler's intent to deprive the other spouse, and the resulting inability to meet financial obligations to the other spouse—that make it equitable for the gambling

12. For example, a spouse who is a scofflaw with respect to parking and traffic restrictions may, over the course of a long marriage, incur a large total of fines and expenses—the "unlawful" nature of that spouse's driving habits does not compel the judge to tally up those fines and expenses and treat them as dissipation. A spouse's failure to make timely payment of taxes, improper disposal of hazardous waste, running a red light and striking another vehicle, or failure to carry workers' compensation insurance for his or her employees would all be examples of "unlawful" conduct that could result in significant fines, civil judgments, and legal fees. If all wrongful or unlawful conduct by a spouse that resulted in additional expenditures had to be treated as dissipation of marital assets, determinations of the equitable division of marital property would routinely be bogged down in uncovering and quantifying the financial ramifications of prior misconduct committed by either spouse.

spouse to bear the brunt of the losses that he or she has incurred. See *Marriage of Bell* (Iowa Ct. App. 1998) (increase in amount of distribution to wife justified where husband spent significant amounts on gambling after commencement of divorce proceedings); *Barriger v. Barriger* (Ky. Ct. App. 1974) (on being told that wife was filing for divorce, husband liquidated stocks and spent proceeds on gambling, cruises, and women; dissipation justified adjustment to property division); *Carrick v. Carrick* (Minn. Ct. App. 1997) (wife dissipated marital assets when she spent significant sums gambling at casinos during pendency of divorce proceedings).

However, gambling losses are not always treated as dissipation of assets, again dependent on the attendant circumstances surrounding that gambling, including the impact it has had on the other spouse and the other spouse's acquiescence in the activity. See *Jones v. Jones* (Alaska 1997) (losses occurred prior to separation and did not interfere with husband's support of family); *Beck v. Beck* (Md. App. 1996) (husband converted $127,000 of assets to cash, spending . . . an unknown amount on gambling trips; in light of finding that both parties enjoyed "high" standard of living, no error in determination that husband had not dissipated assets); *Marriage of Williams* (Wash. App. 1996) (although wife spent "large sums" on gambling over period of years, no dissipation found where she also brought in "substantial amount of income" from three jobs and husband was aware of her gambling); *Askinazi v. Askinazi* (1994) (wife's claim that husband dissipated assets through gambling rejected where she accompanied husband to jai alai games, voiced no disapproval of his betting on games, and shared in winnings). . . .

The husband's gambling occurred throughout the parties' marriage—it was not something that started in response to the breakdown of the marriage or in anticipation of divorce. There is no suggestion that the husband intended to deprive the wife of her share of the marital estate, or that he gambled away the money rather than see it go to her. At no time was the husband derelict in his support of the wife and children—to the contrary, the wife and children were more than comfortably provided for at all times, leading "an upper class lifestyle," with college and graduate education for the children. And, notwithstanding the magnitude of the husband's gambling losses, the marital estate to be divided now supplies the wife with ample means to maintain that same "upper class lifestyle" following divorce. See *Denninger v. Denninger* (Mass. App. 1993) (one objective of §34 award is to "provid[e] means, to the extent the marital assets allow, which enable the parties to approximate the standard of living enjoyed during marriage"). . . . Finally, while the wife did not herself participate in her husband's gambling, she was aware of it for many years and, whatever concerns she may have harbored about it, there is no evidence that she did anything to protest it. On these facts, the husband's gambling was not a form of "conduct" that harmed the marriage, nor did it prevent him from making a very substantial financial "contribution" to the marital estate. As such, the judge did not err in refusing to treat the entirety of the gambling losses as dissipation. . . .

The basis for the judge's decision to charge the husband with $40,000 in dissipation of marital assets . . . is not identified in his decision. The absence of any explanation . . . does not compel us to vacate the order of property division. . . . Here, although heavy gambling had been a regular feature of the husband's conduct throughout the parties' marriage . . . , the judge could view with particular concern the fact that the husband's gambling—and all of the risks that such heavy gambling entails—continued unabated even after the wife filed for divorce, counselling proved unsuccessful, and the husband vacated the marital home. . . . [D]uring the final year . . . , it was clear that the divorce would proceed and that the marital estate would need to be divided. . . . [H]usband knew that the wife was entitled to her share of that estate. Charging the husband with dissipation for the gambling losses he incurred in that final year . . . is thus not arbitrary.[14]

Though the *Kittredge* trial court limited the dissipation finding to the post-separation period, most courts in the United States will include pre-separation waste if a spouse frittered away assets in anticipation of divorce. See Finan v. Finan, 949 A.2d 468 (Conn. 2008) (holding as such and citing decisions in other states). Why impose any temporal limit or intent requirement? Why not hold a spouse accountable for wasteful behavior at any point in the marriage, just as statutes generally direct courts to consider to what extent each spouse has made a positive contribution to acquisitions of wealth at any time during the marriage? Doing the former makes determination of what is equitable more difficult, but so does the latter. The *Finan* court suggested that actions done in anticipation of divorce are more condemnable because they appear intended to "deprive the other spouse of assets that would otherwise be available for equitable division." Id. at 477. But when spouses gamble or spend extravagantly while the marriage is intact, too, they are at least knowingly, even if not intentionally, risking loss to or depriving the other spouse. A minority of states authorize courts to find dissipation at any time. Indiana, for example, makes it a relevant factor but not a requirement that the wasteful transaction have occurred during the breakdown of the marriage. See Kondamuri v. Kondamuri, 852 N.W.2d 939, 952 (Ind. Ct. App. 2006).

Note that the trial court's order that the husband "make an additional $40,000 transfer to the wife in order to account for that 'waste'" of $40,000 in gambling losses reflected a misunderstanding on the judge's part. The $40,000 found to be wasted was marital money, which means that it was partly Mr. Kittredge's money, which he was free to spend however he wanted. He should not have to pay Mrs. Kittredge for the portion of the $40,000 that was his. Thus, if the equitable division of marital assets was ⅔ for Mrs. and ⅓ for Mr., then any payment from Mr. to Mrs. to compensate her for his wasting of her share of the $40,000 should have been roughly $27,000.

What if Mr. Kittredge always won when he gambled? Presumably his winnings would be marital property, just like any other income received during marriage as a result of either spouse's efforts using marital property, and Mrs. Kittredge would be entitled to a share of them. (And note that Massachusetts law treats income as marital right up to the time of the divorce, absent an agreement otherwise, regardless of when the parties establish separate households.) If she would share in winnings, then why should she not share in losses also? Conversely, if courts are to adopt an asymmetric rule in the special case of highly risky financial behavior, a rule that allows the other spouse to share in any gains but immunizes her from losses, then should not the Massachusetts courts have calculated the amount of waste only by adding up all losses, and ignoring gains, rather than by looking at net losses? In other words, if the *net* loss figure of $400,000 represented $600,000 in gambling winnings and $1,000,000 in gambling losses, should not the courts have concluded either that there was $1,000,000 in waste (applying an asymmetric rule) or that there was none (applying a symmetric rule)?

14. . . . This extremely contentious divorce proceeding has been ongoing for over twelve years, with the $40,000 charge for dissipation the sole remaining issue affecting the division of an estate worth over $4 million. . . . [W]e see no purpose in remanding . . . for further clarification of the justification for that figure. . . .

Is there something special about gambling, or would you expect the court to rule the same way if the husband had instead lost the money on stock and/or real estate investments? Would it depend on how risky the investments were? Are the odds at Blackjack worse than the odds on an initial public offering for a high-tech startup? Should the line between misconduct and non-misconduct be drawn based on a degree of risk, or should it be between activities that might yield a profit and those which cannot yield a profit (e.g., spending on a mistress, giving money away to friends and family, destroying personal property)? In the latter case, gambling would not constitute economic misconduct.

Why did the courts not view Mr. Kittredge's gambling simply as entertainment, as his hobby, and consider whether it is reasonable for people to continue their hobbies even when their marriage is dissolving? If he had spent an average of $40,000 of his income per year throughout the marriage on vacation trips (safari in Africa, climbing Mount Everest, etc.), could his wife charge him with waste if he continued doing that even after she initiated divorce proceedings? Note that the court made no finding of illicit intent in this case, and it seems Mr. Kittredge was simply continuing a form of entertainment he had enjoyed for decades, so how could any of his gambling losses have satisfied the waste test? The cited precedents in which gambling was treated as waste involved behavior that was new for the offending spouse at the time the marriage fell apart.

The *Kittredge* court cited a few other decisions treating expenditures on a mistress as economic misconduct, and most people would think that straightforwardly true in all cases. But some courts have held to the contrary if the timing element of the dissipation test was not satisfied—that is, if the spending occurred before either spouse became inclined toward divorce.

Malin v. Loynachan

736 N.W.2d 390 (Neb. Ct. App. 2007)

. . . [T]he parties began dating in August 1988 and were married on February 6, 1999, after living together for 3 years. Paula attended medical school from 1996 through 1999 and subsequently completed a 4-year residency. . . . Brian was employed with Auburn Consolidated Industries, Inc. (ACI), from 1997 through 2004. . . .

Paula testified that she had reviewed Brian's credit card statements and that there were a number of charges for things such as trips, jewelry, and lingerie purchases that were not incurred for her benefit. . . . Those credit card statements show that Brian owed $12,526.67 for charges he made from July 2002 to January 2005. Brian testified that he incurred some expenses for someone other than his wife during the marriage, but that he spent only $9,000, not $12,000, for himself and a third party. Brian testified that he paid these credit card charges with his own income. . . . The trial court declined to order Brian to reimburse the marital estate for the $9,000 he admitted spending for the benefit of himself and a third party. The trial court divided the marital estate equally, with each party receiving assets of $197,319.53. . . .

Marital assets dissipated by a spouse for purposes unrelated to the marriage after the marriage is irretrievably broken should be included in the marital estate in dissolution actions. "Dissipation of marital assets" is one spouse's use of marital property for a selfish purpose unrelated to the marriage at the time when the marriage is undergoing an irretrievable breakdown. In *Brunges v. Brunges* (2000), . . . the Nebraska Supreme Court held that the trial court erred in not including in the marital estate certain assets (a retirement fund and proceeds from a sale of real estate) "liquidated" by the husband after the parties had separated and for which he had not properly accounted. Although the husband testified that these assets were "'put towards . . . bills,'" he did not offer any testimony or documentation as to the specific bills that were paid.

In *Harris v. Harris* (Neb. 2001), the wife "'asked'" the husband for a divorce in April 1995, but did not file to dissolve the parties' marriage until May 1998. However, the testimony established that the parties were estranged in 1995. Beginning in May 1995, the husband began making large withdrawals from the parties' savings fund. The husband was able to account, through testimonial and documentary evidence, for a portion of the withdrawals as having been used for marital expenses. The balance of the unaccounted-for funds accumulated during the marriage was treated as marital property that the husband had dissipated, and the balance was assigned to the husband in the division.

In *Harris v. Harris,* the parties were estranged at the time of the dissipation of the marital assets, while in *Brunges v. Brunges,* the parties were separated. In the instant case, the parties were not separated or estranged during the time that Brian allegedly dissipated marital assets. We do not conclude that an irretrievable breakdown can be found only when the parties are estranged or have separated. However, in the present case, there is no evidence to support a finding that the parties' marriage was undergoing an irretrievable breakdown during the time period that Brian allegedly dissipated assets. It is true that Brian was spending money on a third party at that time, but that fact, in and of itself, is insufficient to allow us to conclude that an irretrievable breakdown of the parties' marriage was occurring. Therefore, the trial court did not err in failing to require Brian to reimburse the marital estate for approximately $9,000 in funds alleged by Paula to have been dissipated while the marriage was undergoing irretrievable breakdown.

The Virginia Court of Appeals reached the same conclusion by similar reasoning in Smith v. Smith, 444 S.E.2d 269 (Va. Ct. App. 1994). Might having a mistress actually keep some husbands in a marriage they would otherwise leave? If you had a client who claimed that was true of him, could you argue with a straight face that his gifts to the mistress were for a marital purpose?

Alternative Factors?

Whereas fault can be a consideration in property distribution in many U.S. states, who filed for the divorce generally cannot be. Suppose one spouse wants to end the marriage despite the lack of clear fault by the other, and so petitions on no-fault grounds, but the other spouse wants to stay married and is willing to undertake counseling and other efforts at fixing the couple's problems. Should courts reward greater commitment to the marriage by one spouse through property distribution or, looked at another way, penalize a spouse who heads for the exit without making substantial effort to save the marriage? Could the state not serve its interest in preserving marriages well by imposing a financial penalty on the petitioner, at least in some circumstances? Are there other factors you think should influence equitable distribution?

Practicalities of Distribution

Having determined what division of property is equitable, the trial court often must orchestrate the sale and transfer of assets to accomplish the distribution, because usually not all of the marital estate is in liquid form. Often the family home is the largest asset, and often most of the couple's wealth is tied up in a family-run business. Sometimes a court will order sale of properties, but courts try to avoid forcing sale of assets that one of the parties continues to use or rely on for a livelihood. When a major asset cannot be sold, the court may order the party who retains ownership to pay the other party the value of the other party's share of that asset. The payment can be made in a single lump sum or, in the common case when the owning spouse does not have enough cash on hand to do that, spread out over many payments during a long period of time. When payments are spread out, property distribution comes to resemble alimony.

One feature that distinguishes property distribution from alimony in the United States is that the former is final whereas the latter is modifiable subsequent to the divorce. In some other countries, property distribution is also subject to later modification in light of changed circumstances—for example, if one former spouse unexpectedly lost his or her job. See, e.g, Civil Code of Spain, Chapter IX, Art. 90. The concurring judge in *O'Brien* (medical degree case) urged the New York legislature to consider making property awards modifiable. Which approach to property distribution is preferable? What arguments are there for making alimony modifiable that do not also apply to property distribution?

(4) Critique of Equitable Division

Laura A. Rosenbury, Two Ways to End a Marriage: Divorce or Death

2005 Utah L. Rev. 1227, 1282-1289

. . . [M]any feminists . . . seek to ensure that legal reforms benefit a wide range of women, and that such reforms provide women with meaningful choices about how to live their lives. The partnership theory of marriage falls short of meeting each of these goals.

. . . [T]he underlying premise of the partnership theory is that intangible contributions to a marriage, such as child care, housework and other care work, should be valued on par with tangible financial contributions, thus leading to an equal or equitable division of tangible assets. This premise most advances the material well-being of those wives who forego market work in order to do care work. . . . [H]istorically only certain women—namely white middle- to upper-middle-class women—could afford to forego market work, and, increasingly, many of those women have found that they must work to make ends meet. Thus, today, the partnership theory of marriage most benefits only those women who can afford to stay at home and choose to do so. In addition, the amount of material benefit received by these women is directly tied to the amount of money earned by their husbands. Under the partnership theory, the value of care work is not independently set. Rather, wives who forego market work receive half of every dollar earned by their husbands. Therefore, the more money earned by the husband, the more the wife benefits from the partnership theory of marriage. . . .

Of course wives who do not forego market work can also benefit from the partnership theory of marriage, but their care work is valued less than the care work of the wives who forego market work. Every dollar earned by a wife in the market translates into a dollar by which her care work is undervalued, at least when compared to the wife who foregoes market work. Thus, women who both work outside of the home and do the bulk of the care work within the home may not benefit from the partnership theory of marriage and may even be harmed by it. For example, the intangible contributions of a wife who earns as much as her husband yet also does most of the housework and child-care coordination—a situation that is increasingly common—will be completely unvalued pursuant to the partnership theory of marriage. . . . And a wife who earns more than her husband yet also does most of the housework and child-care coordination will be hurt by the partnership theory because she must share her wages with her husband even though he did not make significant intangible contributions to the marriage. . . .

[M]ost women of color do not forego market work and those who do tend not to be married to wealthy men. Moreover, . . . it is doubtful that married lesbians would benefit from the partnership theory in the same way that straight women married to wealthy men do because women tend to earn less than men, particularly at the highest levels of the professions, and lesbians tend not to adopt the traditional division of care work and market work that maximizes the material benefits of the partnership theory. The partnership theory of marriage thus seems to be a vestige from the time when feminist reforms primarily benefited privileged women. . . .

[E]ven if most women receive some material benefit from the partnership theory, this may come at the cost of women's ability to make choices free of gender-role expectations. By providing the greatest material benefits to women who forego market work, the partnership theory of marriage reinforces the traditional division of labor allocating wage work to men and care work to women. . . . Some scholars praise this role division as economically efficient. Most feminists, however, have long criticized the separate spheres ideology underlying such gender-role divisions. . . . The partnership theory is also at odds with attempts by some men to escape from the expectation that they fill the breadwinner role, to the exclusion of care work. . . .

[B]acking away from the partnership theory of marriage would not harm many women because most do not greatly benefit from it. Moreover, even those women who do materially benefit from the partnership theory are also constrained by it. Their benefits increase based on the length of their marriages and their continued abstention from wage work. These women may therefore be constrained to stay in their marriages and forego wage work even when they may desire otherwise.

In addition, the assumption that women benefit from the partnership theory of marriage seems to rest in large part on the assumption that most wives will also be mothers raising children. . . . This . . . ignores the fact that the partnership theory of marriage applies to all marriages, including childless marriages or second or other subsequent marriages in which child care is not required because the children are grown. The assumption thus contributes to repronormativity by defining all women as mothers. . . .

[S]ome feminists may object that a focus on freeing women (and men) from traditional gender-role expectations simply perpetuates the liberal feminist fiction that women are the same as men. . . . However, . . . biology determines childbearing, not childrearing. Thus, the primary gender difference to be taken into account would be a psychological one: many cultural feminists argue that women are more relational than men, and hence value autonomy less than men do. As such, according to those feminists, increasing women's individual agency would not take into account women's actual desires and needs. However, women may very well value connection and care work over wage work because they have been constructed, or even pressured, to do so. Laws that reinforce the gendered division of care work and wage work play a role in this construction. Moving away from the partnership theory of marriage . . . would be a step toward uncovering what individual women might desire in the absence of traditional gender-role expectations. Some women might choose to prioritize care work over wage work, whereas other women might negotiate to share responsibility for care work with their spouses, or to shift care work entirely to their spouses in order to devote more time to wage work or other self-satisfying pursuits. At the moment, however, although many women believe they have the ability to make free choices about work and family—a recent *New York Times* headline read: "Why Don't More Women Get to the Top? They Choose Not To"—many women's choices are likely constrained by social expectations and laws like those motivated by the partnership theory of marriage that put a thumb, or worse, on the care work side of the scale.

As such, although the partnership theory of marriage may have been a useful interim tool for ensuring that women were not left destitute after the introduction of no-fault divorce, it is not a long-term strategy for eliminating gender-role oppression. . . .

Can you explain how "[e]very dollar earned by a wife in the market translates into a dollar by which her care work is undervalued"? Is Professor Rosenbury justified in assuming that all wives who make less than their husbands make a great intangible contribution to the marriage but that any husband who makes less than his wife and does less than half of the "housework and child-care coordination" does "not make significant intangible contributions to the marriage"? Is doing forty percent of housework and childcare an insignificant contribution? And are housework and child care the only efforts upon which partnership theory's assumption of equal contribution and reciprocity rests? Does that matter to any aspects of her argument? Professor Rosenbury's coercion point appears to presuppose that many married people are cognizant of the equitable distribution rule for divorce when they make career choices. Is it plausible to suppose that?

In addition to the possibility that equitable division principally benefits women of privilege, "reinforces the traditional division of labor" and so encourages dependency in women, and "contributes to repronormativity," modern equitable division of "marital property" is vulnerable to challenge on other grounds. First, even if one concedes that there is something to the "economic partnership" idea that a homemaker spouse contributes to the earning of a breadwinner spouse, it is exceedingly difficult to justify an assumption that the value of that contribution is definitely or presumptively equal to half of the latter's income. As Professor Rosenbury suggested, this has the perplexing consequence of making the value of a homemaker spouse's contribution depend not on what she actually does but rather on how much her spouse earns. And there are obvious alternative approaches to valuing the contribution. For example, it could be based on the market price of services similar to what the homemaker spouse provides (e.g., those of a maid, cook, nanny, counselor, etc.)—that is, what the breadwinner spouse might have had to pay for those things if unmarried. Another interesting possibility is to speculate as to what percentage of his income the breadwinner would have had to offer prior to the marriage to get the future homemaker to sign a pre-nuptial agreement, perhaps taking into account the alternatives available to each. Might that percentage tend to be lower the higher the income? Can you think of other plausible approaches to valuing a spouse's contribution to the other's earnings? Or can you develop an argument for a moral entitlement to a 50% share of a spouse's earnings?

Apart from the question of what a dependent spouse deserves, there is the question of what effect the change to equitable distribution law has had on incentives to enter into and remain in a marriage. For higher-income persons, the change has meant a transition from a time when marriage was a relatively low-risk proposition financially (they would share what wealth they chose during marriage and, in the unlikely event of a divorce (the divorce rates were dramatically lower then), would keep all their property and possibly have just a modest support obligation) to a time when marriage—or at least a traditional marriage to a homemaker—is a high-risk proposition financially (in the now-much-more-likely event that the marriage ends, they will likely lose half or more of all the property they accumulated from working during the marriage). So there is now a large deterrent to marriage for high-income people that did not previously exist. On the other hand, there is now for them also a large deterrent to getting divorced after they have entered into marriage. For poorer persons who expect to be financially dependent on a spouse, the change has meant a transition from a time when marriage was a medium-risk proposition financially (they would benefit from a spouse's wealth during marriage and divorce was much less likely, but if there were a divorce they could be left fairly impoverished and without great prospects for remarriage) to a time when marriage is almost a no-risk proposition financially (they benefit from the spouse's wealth during marriage and, though divorce is more likely now, they can count on a substantial property award, possibly indefinite alimony, and relative ease of remarrying). So today persons who expect to be dependent in a marriage have much less reason to fear getting in or getting out of marriage with a high-income earner, and in fact they have a strong incentive to get in and little deterrent to exiting. This hypothesis is consistent with the reality that roughly seventy percent of divorce petitions today are filed by wives. And with the reality that husbands today are much more supportive of their wives' working outside the home. Would you judge the changes in incentives described above to be good, bad, or neutral from a social policy standpoint?

b. Alimony

"Alimony," "spousal support," and "spousal maintenance" are synonyms. A lower-income spouse can request in a separation or divorce that the other make ongoing support payments. What justification could there be for ordering one adult to support another adult when they no longer have any social relationship with each other? Should the state have stronger justification for seizing a single person's income and giving it to another person simply because the two were once in a marriage together than for ordering at the time of divorce that spouses share the assets acquired during the marriage regardless of how they are titled?

Historically, in common-law property states, alimony was the only financial benefit a dependent spouse could hope to receive from a dissolved marriage, because whoever held title to property walked away with it. Nevertheless, it was typically not especially generous. Today a couple's wealth is likely to be divided more or less equally, without regard to title, at the time of divorce, and in addition courts are still authorized to award ongoing spousal support payments to an ex-spouse with much lower earning potential. As noted above, courts generally view property distribution and alimony as two components of a single financial package, and will make tradeoffs between the two to achieve what feels like a fair balance between the parties in the overall disposition. We have already seen one reason why a court or party might prefer alimony to property distribution or vice versa—namely, that alimony is modifiable based on later changes in circumstances. In this section, you will discover additional reasons to prefer one or the other in particular circumstances. A connection between the two financial decisions is suggested by factor (10) in the list of alimony factors in the New Jersey statute below.

New Jersey Statutes
Title 2A. Administration of Civil and Criminal Justice
Subtitle 6., Chapter 34. Divorce and Nullity of Marriage

2A:34-23 ALIMONY, MAINTENANCE

Pending any matrimonial action or action for dissolution of a civil union brought in this State or elsewhere, or after judgment of divorce or dissolution or maintenance, whether obtained in this State or elsewhere, the court may make such order as to the alimony or maintenance of the parties . . . as the circumstances of the parties and the nature of the case shall render fit, reasonable and just. . . .

b. In all actions brought for divorce, dissolution of a civil union, divorce from bed and board, legal separation from a partner in a civil union couple or nullity the court may award one or more of the following types of alimony: permanent alimony; rehabilitative alimony; limited duration alimony or reimbursement alimony to either party. In so doing the court shall consider, but not be limited to, the following factors:

(1) The actual need and ability of the parties to pay;

(2) The duration of the marriage or civil union;

(3) The age, physical and emotional health of the parties;

(4) The standard of living established in the marriage or civil union and the likelihood that each party can maintain a reasonably comparable standard of living;

(5) The earning capacities, educational levels, vocational skills, and employability of the parties;

(6) The length of absence from the job market of the party seeking maintenance;

(7) The parental responsibilities for the children;

(8) The time and expense necessary to acquire sufficient education or training to enable the party seeking maintenance to find appropriate employment, the availability of the training and employment, and the opportunity for future acquisitions of capital assets and income;

(9) The history of the financial or non-financial contributions to the marriage or civil union by each party including contributions to the care and education of the children and interruption of personal careers or educational opportunities;

(10) The equitable distribution of property ordered and any payouts on equitable distribution, directly or indirectly, out of current income, to the extent this consideration is reasonable, just and fair;

(11) The income available to either party through investment of any assets . . . ;

(12) The tax treatment and consequences to both parties of any alimony award, including the designation . . . of the payment as a non-taxable payment; and

(13) Any other factors which the court may deem relevant. . . .

c. In any case in which there is a request for an award of permanent alimony, the court shall consider and make specific findings on the evidence about the above factors. If the court determines that an award of permanent alimony is not warranted, the court shall make specific findings on the evidence setting out the reasons therefore. The court shall then consider whether alimony is appropriate for any or all of the following: (1) limited duration; (2) rehabilitative; (3) reimbursement. In so doing, the court shall consider and make specific findings on the evidence about factors set forth above. . . .

An award of alimony for a limited duration may be modified based either upon changed circumstances, or upon the nonoccurrence of circumstances that the court found would occur at the time of the award. The court may modify the amount of such an award, but shall not modify the length of the term except in unusual circumstances. In determining the length of the term, the court shall consider the length of time it would reasonably take for the recipient to improve his or her earning capacity to a level where limited duration alimony is no longer appropriate.

d. Rehabilitative alimony shall be awarded based upon a plan in which the payee shows the scope of rehabilitation, the steps to be taken, and the time frame, including a period of employment during which rehabilitation will occur. An award of rehabilitative alimony may be modified based either upon changed circumstances, or upon the nonoccurrence of circumstances that the court found would occur at the time of the rehabilitative award.

This section is not intended to preclude a court from modifying permanent alimony awards based upon the law.

e. Reimbursement alimony may be awarded under circumstances in which one party supported the other through an advanced education, anticipating participation in the fruits of the earning capacity generated by that education. . . .

g. In all actions for divorce or dissolution other than those where judgment is granted solely on the ground of separation the court may consider also the proofs made in establishing such ground in determining an amount of alimony or maintenance that is fit, reasonable and just. . . .

2A:34-25. Remarriage of Former Spouse or Partner; Termination of Alimony

If after the judgment of divorce or dissolution a former spouse shall remarry or a former partner shall enter into a new civil union, permanent and limited duration alimony shall terminate as of the date of remarriage or new civil union. . . . The remarriage or establishment of a new civil union of a former spouse or partner receiving rehabilitative or reimbursement alimony shall not be cause for termination of such alimony by the court unless the court finds that the circumstances upon which the award was based have not occurred or unless the payer spouse or partner demonstrates an agreement or good cause to the contrary. Alimony shall terminate upon the death of the payer spouse or partner, except that any arrearages that have accrued prior to the date of the payer spouse's or partner's death shall not be vacated or annulled.

Note first that there are several types of alimony, or several rationales for awarding it. Traditionally, any alimony award was indefinite in time, what the New Jersey statute calls "permanent." Really no award is made permanent at the time of divorce, because it is always subject to later modification or, if the recipient remarries or if either party dies, to termination. Permanent alimony is simply support without a court-specified termination date. The other forms of alimony listed—limited duration, rehabilitative, and reimbursement—usually have an inherent temporal limit. Their purpose is explained in the New Jersey court decision below. As with child support, alimony can in many states be paid through the court or a government agency established for that purpose, and it might even be possible to have the payments withheld from the payor's wages. See, e.g., Mo. Rev. Stat. §§ 452.345, 452.350.

The factors for determining the type, duration, and amount of alimony boil down to a) the requesting party's need for support, b) the other party's financial ability to provide support, c) the justness of making the other party support the requesting party (which depends in particular on whether the need is the result of sacrifices made for the family or of harmful conduct by the other party), and d) the inadequacy of property distribution to generate a fair overall financial result.

Regarding a), courts generally do not interpret "need" as "avoiding poverty" but rather something more like maintaining the standard of living the parties had during the marriage, while recognizing that it is usually not possible for both parties to maintain the marital standard of living when the efficiency of a joint household is lost. As to b), courts generally look to all potential sources of financial resources, just as they do with child support. See, e.g., Urbaniak v. Urbaniak, 2011 WL 6276005 (S.D.) (holding that husband's veteran disability pay and social security disability payments constituted income for alimony purposes). With respect to c), this might include conduct during the marriage and also the post-divorce situation, such as the New Jersey statute's reference to relative parental responsibility. But why should the custody arrangement affect alimony when a primary custodial parent is likely to receive child support payments?

Ultimately, the decision whether to award spousal support and how much is a very subjective one. Child support provisions used to invite similarly subjective determinations of support amounts, but all states have moved to formula-based calculations that make awards more uniform and predictable. Should states do that with spousal support as well? A number of local courts have adopted their own guidelines for spousal support, and at least one state has codified a formula, though only for support during the pendency of the divorce action:

New York Domestic Relations Law §236(B)(5-a)(c)(1):

The court shall determine the guideline amount of temporary maintenance in accordance with the provisions of this paragraph after determining the income of the parties: . . .

(a) the court shall subtract twenty percent of the income of the payee from thirty percent of the income . . . of the payor.

(b) the court shall then multiply the sum of the payor's income . . . and all of the payee's income by forty percent.

(c) the court shall subtract the income of the payee from the amount derived from clause (b) of this subparagraph.

(d) the guideline amount of temporary maintenance shall be the lower of the amounts determined by clauses (a) and (c). . . .

Is that formula likely to produce a generous support award? Calculate what the award would be using different hypothetical incomes for the two spouses.

In making their subjective decisions in the absence of a formula, judges are guided by their sense of what the goal is. It could be to allow the recipient spouse to maintain the same standard of living the couple enjoyed during the marriage, or it could be just to keep an ex-spouse off of welfare or out of homeless shelters. The New Jersey statute above suggests the former, insofar as it lists among the relevant factors: "The standard of living established in the marriage or civil union and the likelihood that each party can maintain a reasonably comparable standard of living." In contrast, Texas's alimony rule suggests the latter goal:

Vernon's Texas Family Code
Title 1, Subtitle C. Dissolution of Marriage
Chapter 8, Subchapter B. Court-Ordered Maintenance

§8.051. Eligibility for

In a suit for dissolution of a marriage . . . , the court may order maintenance . . . only if the spouse seeking maintenance will lack sufficient property . . . on dissolution of the marriage to provide for the spouse's minimum reasonable needs and:

(1) the spouse from whom maintenance is requested . . . [committed] family violence . . . against the other spouse or the other spouse's child . . . or

(2) the spouse seeking maintenance:

(A) is unable to earn sufficient income . . . because of an incapacitating physical or mental disability;

(B) has been married to the other spouse for 10 years or longer and lacks the ability to earn sufficient income . . . ; or

(C) is the custodian of a child of the marriage of any age who requires substantial care and personal supervision because of a physical or mental disability that prevents the spouse from earning sufficient income to provide for the spouse's minimum reasonable needs.

What could the justification be for making a person obligated to ensure that an ex-spouse continues to live at the same standard of living? That goal seems to reflect an assumption about an entitlement of the ex-spouse, rather than any state interests. But what argument could there be for saying that, if a person is able to enjoy a much higher standard as a result of being married to someone with a much better income than their own, then they become entitled to live at that standard forever after? Or looked at another way, what basis is there for imposing on a wealthy person who marries a poor person a legal duty to give that poor person a wealthy lifestyle for the rest of his or her life? Is there even adequate justification for obligating a person to keep an ex-spouse off welfare? As with child support, the question arises why financial assistance to people who are not self-sufficient must be privatized, rather than being the duty of society collectively.

Role of Marital Misconduct

Note that under the Texas statute just above, one kind of fault is relevant to alimony—namely, physical abuse by the potential payor. It is one partial basis for awarding alimony.

A few other states' alimony rules speak more broadly of the conduct of the parties during the marriage as a factor, and this could mean awarding more alimony because of any misconduct by the potential payor. See, e.g., Mo. Ann. Stat. §452.335.2(9). No state, however, makes misconduct by the potential payor a *necessary condition* for alimony. In contrast, Hindu Law in India does make fault by a spouse a necessary condition for imposing an alimony obligation on him or her. See SOLANKI, supra, at 141-143. Thus, a primary breadwinner whose spouse decides to divorce him simply because she concludes she does not love him or enjoy being with him anymore cannot demand support payments from him, even if she is unable to support herself. Is that a fairer rule? Is there any social cost to such a rule?

Look again at New Jersey's alimony statute. Does it make the cause of marital breakdown relevant? Does fault influence the court's decision in the following case?

Cetin v. Cetin

Superior Court of New Jersey, Appellate Division (2006)

PER CURIAM.

The parties are natives of Turkey and speak minimal English. Defendant moved to the United States in 1989, and has owned and operated a produce/convenience grocery in Absecon, New Jersey since 1993. Plaintiff completed two years of study at the University of Istanbul, where she studied accounting. She moved to the United States in 1996. The parties met in Florida and were married there on May 16, 1997. They have one child, John, born on May 3, 2000.

Throughout the marriage, the parties rented their residence, and maintained a lower middle-class lifestyle. Defendant operated his store between the hours of 8:00 A.M. and 8:00 P.M., seven days per week. Plaintiff worked at defendant's store without compensation for the first four years of the marriage, under defendant's threat that she would have to return to Turkey if she stopped working at the store. The parties' monthly housing expenses were $850 in rent, and $150 to $200 in utilities. Defendant controlled the parties' assets, and plaintiff had limited access to funds for personal use.

Defendant gambled heavily and regularly consumed large quantities of alcohol. When defendant drank, he became abusive, and struck plaintiff on numerous occasions throughout the marriage. A temporary restraining order (TRO) was entered on January 26, 1998, based on alleged physical and sexual abuse, but was dismissed at the hearing on February 19, 1998, for insufficient evidence. Thereafter, during an altercation, defendant banged plaintiff's head against a bathroom sink in his store, resulting in injuries to plaintiff's head and face. The police responded, and plaintiff was taken to the hospital. A TRO was entered on April 29, 1998, and a final restraining order (FRO) was entered on May 14, 1998. On August 27, 1998, the FRO was dismissed at plaintiff's request. On occasion, plaintiff stayed at the Northfield Women's Center due to fears of abuse, and she received psychiatric and psychological counseling in 1997 and 1998.

In June 2001, plaintiff obtained employment as a cashier at an Atlantic City casino, and desired to send the parties' son, John, to preschool so that he could learn English. Although defendant objected to John attending preschool, plaintiff sent John to All God's Children preschool in Absecon in early 2002, at a cost of $150 per week. Plaintiff began taking "English as a Second Language" (ESL) courses at Atlantic Cape Community College (ACCC), while she worked at the casino.

In summer 2003, plaintiff found approximately $100,000 cash in a closet in their residence, and an altercation ensued. Defendant told plaintiff that she was not going to receive any of the money, and demanded that she leave the residence. Plaintiff moved to Atlantic City, and took a job at a different casino as a room service attendant. She was unable to continue attending classes at ACCC, arresting her studies at the fifth of nine levels in ESL. John also stopped attending preschool due to lack of funds. His English speaking skills are minimal. Defendant continued to reside in the marital home, and operate the store. His monthly expenses remained the same, but he was later able to obtain a roommate to share housing costs.

Plaintiff filed for custody and child support on July 29, 2003, and the parties reached an agreement providing for joint legal custody of John, with plaintiff as the parent of primary residence. . . . On November 24, 2003, plaintiff filed for divorce based on grounds of extreme cruelty. . . .

At the time of trial, defendant's monthly expenses totaled $1,100, including $163 for parenting expenses; $58 for food and household supplies; $20 for clothing; $20 for dining expenses; and $15 for gifts. Defendant refused to provide the court with reliable figures for his income, and only supplied tax returns from his business. Defendant was also approximately $3,500 behind in child support payments.

Plaintiff's wages were $4.30 per hour, plus tips that averaged $100 to $150 per week. Her average gross income was $1,300 monthly, and her average net income was $1,000 monthly. Plaintiff's monthly expenses totaled $2,867, including $837 for shelter expenses; $426 for transportation expenses; and $1,604 for personal expenses, inclusive of $387 for child care, John's preschool costs, and plaintiff's estimated tuition and fees at ACCC. Plaintiff had three credit cards totaling $950 in debt, and one additional credit card with an unknown balance. In order to supplement her monthly earnings, plaintiff's siblings and friends sent her money, and at the time of trial, plaintiff owed $6,000 to family, and $2,500 to friends.

Plaintiff presented an accounting expert . . . [Morowitz, who] testified that although defendant stated that his net income for 2002 was $9,466, as reflected on defendant's business tax returns defendant's net income for 2002 was approximately $62,800 and the store was valued at $84,000. These estimates were based on . . . various underreported and overstated expenses in the 2002 tax return, industry comparisons, and Morowitz's experience.

On December 21, 2004, . . . Judge Middlesworth concluded that defendant's conduct constituted "extreme cruelty, making it improper and unreasonable to expect the plaintiff to continue to cohabit with the defendant, and entitling the plaintiff to a divorce." . . . [H]e ordered defendant to undergo substance abuse evaluation and treatment as a condition of continued parenting time.

As to equitable distribution, Judge Middlesworth found that there was no evidence as to the present value of plaintiff's checking account; that defendant's business was pre-marital and had not increased in value during the marriage due to plaintiff's efforts; and that the net value of plaintiff's car was $1,250. The judge also found that defendant had at least $100,000 cash on hand. . . . Considering the factors under *N.J.S.A.* 2A:34-23.1, Judge Middlesworth allocated defendant the entire sum of $100,000, subject to plaintiff's claim for one-half; his pre-marital business free from any claim by plaintiff; and his personal and business debts. Plaintiff was allocated her checking account, her automobile, and her debts. As an equalization payment, the judge ordered that defendant pay plaintiff the sum of $44,465, with interest (5% per annum), in payments of $1,000 per month. . . .

Judge Middlesworth . . . ordered defendant to pay $302 per week in child support, along with $148 per week toward arrears. . . . He also awarded plaintiff $10,000 in compensatory and punitive damages on her tort claims of assault. . . . Based on his finding that plaintiff's counsel fees were reasonable . . . and that defendant engaged in bad faith in an attempt to conceal his actual income and prevent plaintiff from obtaining support, Judge Middlesworth ordered defendant to pay plaintiff's counsel fees and costs of $10,708.78 . . . [and] to reimburse plaintiff's attorney for Morowitz's fee of $1,500, and to reimburse the court for the "expense of the Turkish Interpreter requested by the parties, $1,122.40." . . .

I.

In awarding alimony pursuant to a divorce decree, the trial court must "'consider and make specific findings' under *N.J.S.A.* 2A:34-23[b]." The thirteen factors in *N.J.S.A.* 2A:34-23b apply to all alimony awards. Subsection "c," which directs the court to consider limited duration, reimbursement, and rehabilitative alimony when the court finds permanent alimony inappropriate, mandates that the same factors as relevant to an award of permanent alimony be considered. *N.J.S.A.* 2A:34-23c. . . .

Our courts have awarded rehabilitative alimony when a party may be placed in a self-support economic position, after a period of educational advancement. It is "payable for a specific time period, ceasing when the dependent spouse is in a position of self-support," and it permits a spouse "'to complete the preparation necessary for economic self-sufficiency.'" "The focus of rehabilitative alimony is upon the ability of the depend[e]nt spouse to engage in gainful employment, combined with the length of the marriage, the age of the parties, and the spouse's ability to regain a place in the workplace." Typically, the award is appropriate when the marriage is "relatively short and the recipient spouse is capable of full employment based on experience, additional training or further education."

This court has found insufficient evidence for a rehabilitative alimony award where there was only "casual reference" to the intention to resume studies. While rehabilitative alimony is warranted where the payee demonstrates the necessary steps, time frame, and scope to rehabilitate the dependent spouse, *N.J.S.A.* 2A:34-23d, contrary to defendant's assertion, a rigid "plan" is not always necessary; the plan need only be reasonable. Wass v. Wass, 311 N.J. Super. 624, 635-36, 710 A.2d 1053 (Ch. Div. 1998) (granting four years of rehabilitative alimony where there was testimony as to anticipated time (three years) and cost to complete a certification program, but no testimony as to time or cost to complete GED and basic skills training). Plaintiff testified that she needed to complete at least four additional levels of ESL studies, and that it would take about nine months or two semesters to complete the ESL program. She testified that she had been attending ACCC, had studied accounting in Turkey, and that accounting was her desired field of employment. The judge determined that in today's market, plaintiff would need at least an Associate's degree in accounting to be able to realistically compete for employment in the accounting field. We conclude that the determination was reasonable.

While ESL studies may generally prepare plaintiff for engaging in day-to-day conversation, her studies in accounting may require an advanced level of language ability. Accounting is a technical field, involving many complex theories and terms, which may not be taught in a regular ESL program. It was reasonable for the judge to determine that ESL studies alone would be insufficient. Further, ACCC's cost of attendance is public knowledge, and any individual may inquire as to the cost per credit hour, and the number of credits and length of time for completion of an Associate's degree in accounting. That plaintiff did not explicitly testify to these facts should not thwart her recovery, especially considering her limited ability to comprehend English. . . . Plaintiff provided sufficient testimony for the judge to determine that an Associate degree in accounting at ACCC costs approximately $7,000.

The intention of rehabilitative alimony is to make the dependent spouse self-supporting, and an award would be useless if it did not set out to achieve that goal. As such, that the judge determined that at minimum plaintiff would require an Associate's degree in order to be self-supporting, and that the cost of the degree was $7,000, was consistent with the substantial credible evidence adduced at trial.

Reimbursement alimony is meant to "recognize past forbearances," and a trial court's authority to award it is permissive. The statutory language in *N.J.S.A.* 2A:34-23e, indicates that where a specific forbearance exists, the court "may" award reimbursement alimony, whereas other kinds of alimony "shall" be awarded where appropriate. Even where the facts of a case satisfy subsection "e," the court is not obligated to order reimbursement alimony. In addition, although the statute indicates that one party's educational support of the other during the marriage may warrant reimbursement alimony, the court's authority to so order is not limited to only situations which satisfy subsection "e." *See N.J.S.A.* 2A:34-23f (indicating the court has broad discretion to award any kind of alimony that is warranted and just, in light of the circumstances and facts . . .).

Generally, courts have ordered reimbursement alimony in situations where one party supported the other throughout his or her pursuit of an advanced educational goal. Here, Judge Middlesworth found plaintiff's "forbearance" to be the years she spent working in defendant's store without compensation, and awarded reimbursement alimony at $200 per week for two years. Although there was no pursuit of advanced education by defendant, the payment of alimony in addition to rehabilitative alimony for a short transitional period, was not unwarranted by the facts of the case.

Judge Middlesworth's comprehensive memorandum of decision provides adequate reasons for an award of limited duration alimony, although he did not consider such an award. Since the marriage of six and one-half years was one of intermediate duration, and the judge found permanent alimony unwarranted, he should have considered limited duration alimony, as suggested by *N.J.S.A.* 2A:34-23c. "[I]n recognition of a dependent spouse's contributions to a relatively short-term marriage," limited duration alimony is to be awarded. Such alimony is intended for situations where "an economic need for alimony is established, but the marriage was of short-term duration such that permanent alimony is not appropriate." . . . Judge Middlesworth recognized the shortfall between plaintiff's expenses and her income. Based on the intended scope of limited duration alimony when compared with that of reimbursement alimony, it appears that plaintiff's award of for $200 per week for two years should have been "labeled" as limited duration alimony rather than reimbursement alimony. . . .

A trial court's alimony findings may only be vacated if this court concludes that the trial court "clearly abused its discretion. . . ." Judge Middlesworth engaged in a thorough analysis of the factors in *N.J.S.A.* 2A:34-23b. . . . As to defendant's income, because defendant failed to supply the court with proper documentation as to his income, the court relied on plaintiff's expert's analysis of defendant's tax returns and valuation of his business. . . . "[D]efendant provided no expert testimony to refute the . . . expert's conclusions." . . . [T]he judge's findings as to defendant's income and the necessity for the awards of alimony were sufficiently based on substantial, credible evidence.

We affirm the awards of rehabilitative and reimbursement alimony . . . [and] direct that the order be amended to label plaintiff's award of reimbursement alimony as limited duration. . . .

Does the amount of alimony awarded seem adequate, in light of the couple's history and the ex-wife's current situation? Would you want to know more about the ex-wife's prospects for forming a new intimate relationship, or should that be legally irrelevant?

What about fault by the potential payee? At one time, most states made adultery a bar to receiving alimony, and some made other forms of fault also a bar. See Gross v. Gross, 318 N.E.2d 659, 663 (Ill. App. Ct. 1974) (noting the "almost universal rule that permanent alimony will be denied to a wife who is guilty of adultery"). Today two states, Louisiana and North Carolina, make adultery an absolute bar to receiving alimony, and Louisiana extends the bar to any form of fault. See La. Civ. Code Ann. art. 111 ("the court . . . may award final periodic support to a party who is in need of support and who is free from fault"). Louisiana courts often deny alimony to a dependent spouse even in cases where the dependent spouse's fault was not as extreme as adultery or physical abuse and where the other spouse was also at fault. See, e.g., Wolff v. Wolff, 966 So. 2d 1202 (La. Ct. App. 2007) (upholding denial of alimony to wife based on finding that she, because of jealousy, had "subjected Mr. Wolff to a pattern of mental harassment, nagging and griping which rendered the marriage insupportable," where husband was also found at fault, and stating "for a claimant spouse to prove entitlement to final support, that spouse must affirmatively prove freedom from fault."); Gilley v. Gilley, 976 So. 2d 727, 07-568 (La. Ct. App. 2007) (upholding denial of alimony based on finding "both parties committed numerous and consistent acts which constituted cruel treatment and behavior, defamatory acts, and habitual intemperance").

The North Carolina statute limits the absolute bar to sexual misconduct and is more even-handed, insofar as it makes adultery by the potential payor a basis for awarding alimony. See N.C. Gen. Stat. Ann. §50-16.3A ("If the court finds that the dependent spouse participated in an act of illicit sexual behavior during the marriage and prior to or on the date of separation, the court shall not award alimony. If the court finds that the supporting spouse participated in an act of illicit sexual behavior during the marriage and prior to or on the date of separation, then the court shall order that alimony be paid to a dependent spouse. If the court finds that the dependent and the supporting spouse each participated in an act of illicit sexual behavior during the marriage and prior to or on the date of separation, then alimony shall be denied or awarded in the discretion of the court after consideration of all of the circumstances. Any act of illicit sexual behavior by either party that has been condoned by the other party shall not be considered by the court."). The North Carolina statute additionally makes any other form of marital misconduct by either spouse a relevant consideration. But only adultery by the supporting spouse can remove the bar created by a dependent spouse's adultery.

Romulus v. Romulus

715 S.E.2d 308 (N.C. Ct. App. 2011)

STROUD, Judge.

The parties were married on 27 August 1988 and separated on 1 July 2006. On 12 April 2007, Rebecca Romulus ("plaintiff") filed a complaint alleging claims for post-separation support, alimony, child custody, child support, and equitable distribution. . . . The trial court made the following findings of fact . . .:

> 11. During the marriage in the summer and fall of 1999, the Plaintiff was involved in an act or acts of illicit sexual behavior with a man by the name of Steve Cline by allowing Mr. Cline to penetrate her vagina either with his finger or his penis on at least one or more occasions.

12. . . . Plaintiff admitted under oath to having "sexual relations" or "sexual encounters" with Steve Cline in 1999.

13. . . . At the subsequent hearing, the Plaintiff testified that she considered kissing to be "sexual relations." This testimony is not believable to this Court. Steve Cline . . . testified that he remembered having sexual relations with the Plaintiff on two occasions, once on Bald Head Island and once in a pool. . . . Mr. Cline testified that . . . even though sexual intercourse may have failed due to his failure to obtain or maintain an erection, he rubbed the Plaintiff's vaginal area and she touched his penis. . . .

14. . . . Defendant was not ever made aware of these encounters until the trial of this matter and as such, did not condone such actions. . . . .

17. . . . Defendant committed marital misconduct by the following:

a. His excessive viewing of pornography, in spite of Plaintiff's request to the contrary and to the extent that one of the parties' children "caught" him viewing same. He was in . . . therapy for this problem.

b. His multiple incidents of violence against the Plaintiff, the most violent one being the incident intentionally breaking her right arm.

c. His violence against the parties' minor children pushing them, hitting them and in one instance choking one of the minor children until he lost consciousness.

d. His repeated verbal abuse of Plaintiff and the minor children. . . .

"Illicit sexual behavior" is treated differently from all other forms of "marital misconduct,"[3] as the trial court has the discretion to weigh all of the other forms of "marital misconduct" and to determine what effect, if any, the misconduct should have upon the alimony award. *See* N.C. Gen. Stat. §50-16.3A(b) (". . . In determining the amount, duration, and manner of payment of alimony, the court shall consider all relevant factors, including: (1) The marital misconduct of either of the spouses. . . ."). As to "illicit sexual behavior" only, N.C. Gen. Stat. §50-16.3A(a) eliminates the trial court's discretion to weigh the marital misconduct of the parties unless both parties have committed "illicit sexual behavior." If only the dependent spouse has engaged in uncondoned "illicit sexual behavior" during the marriage and prior to the date of separation, the trial court cannot award alimony, even if the supporting spouse has committed egregious "marital misconduct" of another sort.

N.C. Gen. Stat. §50-16.1A(3)a defines "illicit sexual behavior" as "acts of sexual or deviate sexual intercourse, deviate sexual acts, or sexual acts defined in G.S.

3. N.C. Gen. Stat. §50-16.1A(3) lists the others:

"b. Involuntary separation of the spouses in consequence of a criminal act committed prior to the proceeding in which alimony is sought;

c. Abandonment of the other spouse;

d. Malicious turning out-of-doors of the other spouse;

e. Cruel or barbarous treatment endangering the life of the other spouse;

f. Indignities rendering the condition of the other spouse intolerable and life burdensome;

g. Reckless spending of the income of either party, or the destruction, waste, diversion, or concealment of assets;

h. Excessive use of alcohol or drugs so as to render the condition of the other spouse intolerable and life burdensome;

i. Willful failure to provide necessary subsistence according to one's means and condition so as to render the condition of the other spouse intolerable and life burdensome."

14-27.1(4), voluntarily engaged in by a spouse with someone other than the other spouse[.]" . . .

Plaintiff is correct that there was no direct evidence of "sexual intercourse" between herself and Mr. Cline. Defendant responds that under the doctrine of "inclination and opportunity," the evidence was sufficient to support the trial court's finding of "sexual intercourse." Our Supreme Court has declared that:

> Adultery is nearly always proved by circumstantial evidence. Circumstantial evidence "is often the only kind of evidence available, as misconduct of this sort is usually clandestine and secret." . . . [Under] the opportunity and inclination doctrine . . . , adultery is presumed if the following can be shown: (1) the adulterous disposition, or inclination, of the parties; and (2) the opportunity created to satisfy their mutual adulterous inclinations. . . .

[T]he testimony of both plaintiff and Mr. Cline demonstrates their mutual "adulterous inclination" and their opportunity to "satisfy their mutual adulterous inclinations." Since the trial court phrased its finding of fact in the alternative, it is unclear if it actually did find that plaintiff and Mr. Cline had "sexual intercourse." We must therefore also address the finding as to penetration of plaintiff's vagina by Mr. Cline's finger, which arguably falls under . . . "sexual acts. . . ."

N.C. Gen. Stat. §14-27.1(4) (2009) defines "sexual act" as follows:

> (4) "Sexual act" means cunnilingus, fellatio, analingus, or anal intercourse, but does not include vaginal intercourse. Sexual act also means the penetration, however slight, by any object into the genital or anal opening of another person's body. . . .

"Sexual acts" are distinguished from other forms of "sexual contact" . . . as "(i) touching the sexual organ, anus, breast, groin, or buttocks of any person, (ii) a person touching another person with their own sexual organ, anus, breast, groin, or buttocks, or (iii) a person ejaculating, emitting, or placing semen, urine, or feces upon any part of another person." Thus, a "sexual act" requires "penetration, however slight . . . ," while touching without penetration would be "sexual contact." The trial court's finding of fact that Mr. Cline's finger penetrated plaintiff's vagina is a finding of a "sexual act." . . .

Just as for "sexual intercourse," the testimony of plaintiff and Mr. Cline provides sufficient evidence to support the trial court's finding of fact. . . . [T]he doctrine of inclination and opportunity . . . would . . . also apply to other forms of "illicit sexual behavior." . . .

Pursuant to N.C. Gen. Stat. §50-16.1A(3)a, the dependent spouse's "illicit sexual behavior" must occur "during the marriage and prior to or on the date of separation" in order to be a bar to alimony. The trial court's findings of fact as to the date of separation are as follows:

> 15. . . . Although there was some physical separation of the parties after a choking incident involving the parties' youngest son in the summer of 1999, neither party had expressed to the other party they wanted to separate nor in fact intended to permanently separate during the summer of 1999 through Christmas of 1999. Defendant continued to maintain all of his belongings at the marital residence and continued to have his mail delivered there. He did household chores and only occasionally slept at his dental office during this period of time.
>
> 16. Neither party sought the advice of attorneys, executed any type of separation or property settlement agreement nor expressed a contention to permanently end their marriage.

. . . The phrase "the date of separation[,]" . . . is not defined by the statutory provisions regarding alimony, but has been addressed by our courts in the context of N.C. Gen. Stat. §50-6, which addresses absolute divorce. [It] provides that "[m]arriages may be dissolved and the parties thereto divorced from the bonds of matrimony on the application of either party, if and when the husband and wife have lived separate and apart for one year. . . ." . . . "The words 'separate and apart' . . . mean that there must be both a physical separation and an intention on the part of at least one of the parties to cease the matrimonial cohabitation." . . .

> [S]eparation implies . . . the living apart for such period in such a manner that those in the neighborhood may see that the husband and wife are not living together. . . . Marriage is not a private affair, involving the contracting parties alone. Society has an interest in the marital status of its members, and when a husband and wife live in the same house and hold themselves out to the world as man and wife, a divorce will not be granted on the ground of separation, when the only evidence of such separation must . . . "be sought behind the closed doors of the matrimonial domicile." Our statute contemplates . . . the complete cessation of cohabitation.

Here, there was evidence that at times, the parties would have an argument and defendant "would go to the office for a couple of days and cool down or whatever . . . and then [he] would basically come back." However, even during these times when he went to stay in his office, defendant still would return to the marital home to take care of household chores, pay bills, and take the children to activities. Some of the parties' family members and acquaintances testified that they were unaware of any separation of the parties prior to their final separation in 2006; others testified that the parties had separated for a period of time in 1999. . . . The trial court's findings of fact and conclusions of law do not indicate any error of law as to the definition of "separation."

Why is the interest of society in its members' marital status relevant to the empirical question of whether the parties lived apart and intended to cease cohabiting?

Should the adultery be excused if the husband had ceased cohabitation a few months prior, or should spouses be expected to refrain from intimacy with others until a divorce is final? Many other states treat as adultery sex with a non-spouse during separation from one's'spouse. If it is an aim of the state to avoid unnecessary divorce, does authorizing new intimate relationships during the separation period, as North Carolina implicitly does, undermine that aim? Or might it even advance it, by helping people figure out whether they really do want a divorce?

Why is sexual behavior singled out for special treatment in some states' alimony provisions? In Louisiana there is an asymmetrical adultery penalty; dependent spouses can expect a financial penalty for cheating but supporting spouses need not fear that. Is that justifiable? Does the more symmetrical nature of the North Carolina statute make it fair? Or should it go farther and provide that any misconduct by the supporting spouse, such as Mr. Romulus's violence, nullifies the dependent spouse's "sexual acts"? Recall the scenario posited in Chapter 3 of a battered spouse who manages to escape from her husband but who is terrified of initiating a divorce action. On the other side of the equation, should violence by a dependent spouse be a bar to receiving alimony?

In a couple of states, adultery or other misconduct by a dependent spouse presumptively precludes alimony, but courts may nevertheless award it if denying support would be unjust, given the spouse's circumstances and the behavior of the supporting spouse. For example, Virginia's alimony statutes provides that "no permanent maintenance and support shall be awarded from a spouse if there exists in such spouse's favor a ground of divorce under the provisions of [code section relating to adultery]," unless "denial of support and maintenance would constitute a manifest injustice, based upon the respective degrees of fault during the marriage and the relative economic circumstances of the parties") Va. Code Ann. §20-107.1(B). See also Retzer v. Retzer, 578 So. 2d 580, 592-593 (Miss. 1990) (stating "a general rule that alimony will not be allowed a wife when the husband is granted a divorce because of her fault" but an "exception to this rule has been made in cases where the marriage has been of long duration, the husband is able to pay alimony in some amount, and the wife has no means of livelihood").

Congdon v. Congdon

578 S.E.2d 833 (Va. Ct. App. 2003)

Kelsey, Judge.

. . . Mary Evelyn Davis (known as Lynn) and John Rhodes Congdon married in 1977. During their twenty-two year marriage, the couple had three children. . . . Lynn conceded that she was guilty of adultery. . . . The evidence showed that she engaged in an extramarital affair for at least five years during the marriage. Viewed in the light most favorable to Lynn, however, the evidence also portrayed John as a profane and verbally abusive man. John frequented "strip joints and topless bars" and told Lynn about, among other things, the "oil wrestlers" that performed at these places. He would indiscriminately engage in these conversations in the presence of his children and Lynn's family, at times even "boasting or bragging about those places." . . . John "frequently talked crudely about sexual type things." . . .

John also directed his profanity toward his children. In one instance, John's son Michael had accidentally kicked his father's head while both were lying on a bed watching television. Though realizing it was simply an accident, John "started yelling . . . God damn you, Michael. Why in the f— did you kick me in the face. . . . Why did you f—ing have to kick me in the face?" In response, Michael ran out of the house. On another occasion, John was having a "food fight" with his twelve-year-old daughter when John accidentally got hit in the eye. He "started screaming . . . God damn you. God damn, you hit me in the eye." His daughter "just sat there and started crying," not at all understanding her father's outburst. Other times John would come home from work angry and declare, in ear-shot of his children, that "one of the girls at the office" was a "bitch or a c—." His use of vulgarity, in the presence of his family and others, "was quite frequent."

Several witnesses who knew John and Lynn over the years testified that they had never once seen John show any affection or any kindness toward Lynn. Over the course of the marriage, John chronically complained (both to Lynn and others) about Lynn's weight, appearance, housekeeping, and spending habits. John referred to Lynn as "Witch." He was a "heavy drinker," sometimes starting as early as "10:00 in the morning." . . . John particularly disliked Lynn's family and threatened on one occasion to move her out of town if she did not "stop speaking with her parents."

Despite these problems, John and Lynn enjoyed considerable financial security. John has a college degree, a stable and long-term career in a family trucking business, an annual salary exceeding $250,000, and additional income from corporate dividends and family related gifts. John's interests in stocks, real estate, and tangible assets exceeded $6 million. In contrast, Lynn has not held a full time job since the early years of her marriage, choosing instead to stay at home to raise their three children. She has no college degree, giving her a future earning capacity far below her husband's. At the time of trial, Lynn was earning $10.00 an hour as a receptionist. . . .

[T]he court invoked the "manifest injustice" exception . . . [and] awarded support of $2,300 per month to Lynn to continue until her death or remarriage. . . . On the "respective degrees of fault" factor, the trial court correctly observed that in this context fault "encompasses all behavior that affected the marital relationship, including any acts or conditions which contributed to the marriage's failure, success, or well-being." . . . We believe a reasonable jurist could put John's "fault" in a league apart from the type of mere incivility or petulance of manners ordinarily alleged, and often proved, in nearly every contested divorce case. . . . Nor do we believe, as John contends, that the trial court's finding essentially declares that John's behavior "amounted to a justification for adultery." The law does not excuse, condone, or justify Lynn's infidelity. . . .

On the second factor, . . . the trial court found "extreme disparities in their relative economic situations, both in terms of earning capacity, current incomes and other economic assets and resources." Ample evidence supports this finding.

For these reasons, the trial court was not plainly wrong in finding, by clear and convincing evidence, that denying spousal support under Code §20-107.1(B) would constitute a "manifest injustice" . . . , [and] we affirm the trial court on this issue.

Why is John's treatment of and speech in front of their children relevant to alimony? Does the court's decision really not amount to condoning Lynn's five-year adulterous affair?

A handful of other states simply identify marital misconduct as a relevant factor in deciding whether and how much alimony to award. See, e.g., Fla. Stat. §61.08(1) ("The court may consider the adultery of either spouse and the circumstances thereof in determining the amount of alimony, if any, to be awarded."); Mass. Gen. Laws ch. 208, §34 ("the court . . . shall consider . . . the conduct of the parties during the marriage"); Mo. Rev. Stat. §452.335.2(9); 23 Pa. Const. Stat. §3701. This could mean increasing the amount where the potential payor's abusive conduct makes the potential payee less able to support herself, or it could mean lowering the amount in light of abuse or other misconduct by the potential payee. Consideration of fault could also enter the equation in the many states whose alimony statutes have a catch-all "any other factor the court deems relevant" sort of clause. See, e.g., Ga. Code Ann. §19-6-5(a) ("The following shall be considered in determining the amount of alimony, if any, to be awarded . . . (8) Such other relevant factors as the court deems equitable and proper.").

On the other hand, some states forbid courts from considering fault in alimony decision making. See, e.g., 750 Ill. Comp. Stat. 5/504 ("the court may grant a temporary or permanent maintenance award for either spouse in amounts and for periods of time as the court deems just, without regard to marital misconduct"); Ariz. Rev. Stat. §25-319B; Colo. Rev. Stat. §14-10-114 (similar); Wash. Rev. Code §26.09.090 (similar).

POLICY QUESTION

Which forms of marital fault provide the strongest basis for denying alimony? Is there any justification for an asymmetrical approach, in which fault is a basis either for awarding or for denying alimony but not both? If not, what explanation could there be for the asymmetry in states such as Texas and Louisiana?

Modification and Termination of Alimony

Some agreements and court decrees on alimony provide for automatic adjustments to alimony amounts, based on inflation or on periodic disclosure of income. In addition, either payor or payee can petition for a modification before the original order expires based on a change of circumstances subsequent to the original order. The change could be anything that would be relevant to an original order, but state laws typically require that the change be a substantial one not anticipated at the time of the original order or agreement. As with child support, the change is usually a substantial increase or decrease in the income or resources of one or both parties, as a result of a promotion, a layoff, a career change, an inheritance, a new source of support, or some other cause. And as with child support, courts will scrutinize any decline in income to ensure that the petitioning party is not voluntarily unemployed or under-employed, and will impute income to a party who is so. Another common basis for requesting modification is that the payor has new family financial obligations, as a result of remarriage and/or birth of a child with another partner.

Alimony can terminate by its own terms, if it is any form other than "permanent." Death of either payor or payee terminates the obligation in most states. See, e.g., Fla. Stat. §61.08(5), (7), (8). In most states, unless the parties have agreed otherwise, a recipient's remarriage terminates the obligation to pay any form of alimony other than reimbursement. Section 2A:34-25 of the New Jersey code above embodies such a rule. See also Ga. Code Ann. §19-6-5(b); 23 Pa. Const. Stat. §3701(e) ("Remarriage of the party receiving alimony shall terminate the award of alimony.").

Cynthia Lee Starnes, One More Time: Alimony, Intuition, and the Remarriage-Termination Rule

81 Ind. L.J. 971, 972-976, 994, 999 (2006)

Roughly 75% of divorcing women remarry within ten years; 54% remarry within five years. Unfortunately, these second marriages are at least as likely to fail as first ones. For some who marry a second time, marriage demands a hefty admission price not imposed on first-timers: any alimony claim against a former spouse will likely terminate, often automatically and without regard to financial impact. The intuition of most observers is that this is the right result: an ex-husband should not pay alimony to a former wife who has married someone else. . . . Notwithstanding the near-universality of this remarriage-termination rule, . . . the underlying rationale for the remarriage-termination rule is "remarkably unclear."

Intuition is not enough to sustain a rule with such a brutal impact. Consider, for example, the case of Helen and Anthony, who divorce after a twenty-six year marriage.

During marriage, Helen worked as a full-time homemaker and caretaker of the couple's children while Anthony pursued a career. At divorce, Anthony earned $158,000 annually as a bank executive while Helen "qualified for only unskilled, entry level positions at minimum wage." A divorce decree divided the couple's marital property; ordered Anthony to pay $500 per week in alimony and $300 per week in child support . . . Helen soon found work as a part-time medical assistant earning $90 per week. One and one-half years later, Helen married again, and upon Anthony's petition, a court terminated her alimony.* . . .

Suppose that her second marriage, sadly, also ends in divorce, as very many remarriages do. Unable to qualify for alimony based on a short second marriage, Helen is left to fend for herself, armed with two years of undergraduate education, $90 per week in earnings, and a twenty-six-year history as a caretaker for the family she and Anthony once shared. Helen's brief remarriage has freed Anthony to enjoy all the career rewards of his role as family breadwinner and left Helen alone to bear all the career costs of her role as family caretaker. . . . [I]f Anthony's payments had been part of the division of property—perhaps installments on a buyout of Helen's interest in the marital home—rather than alimony, her remarriage would have had no effect on Anthony's obligation. Why is Helen's right to a buyout of her interest in a house, a Mercedes, or a yacht more deserving of protection than her right to a buyout of her interest in the marital partnership, or at least to compensation for her lost career opportunities? . . .

[T]he ALI [American Law Institute] suggests a rationale for termination based on recovery of psychic loss. "The most important loss on divorce," observes the ALI, "may be the failed expectation of having a close and caring lifetime companion." Because such loss ordinarily cannot be measured, it is necessarily disregarded at divorce. "Remarriage presumptively solves this measurement problem," claims the ALI, "for the inference naturally arises that the obligee derives great nonfinancial rewards from the new relationship overall, whatever its financial component." The ALI then reaches the dubious conclusion that "[c]ontinuing compensatory payments after the obligee's remarriage would make overcompensation likely because the obligee could combine the first spouse's earnings with both the personal and financial qualities of the second spouse." The message is that an alimony recipient's presumed joy on remarriage should trigger financial loss in order to avoid her overcompensation. What? In the end, the ALI's rhetoric is an embarrassing effort to explain intuition rather than an uncompromising attempt to provide a compelling rationale for the remarriage-termination rule. . . .

[J]udicial efforts to explain the rule only confirm the suspicion that the roots of the remarriage-termination rule lie in archaic principles of coverture, which cast a wife not as a marital partner, but rather as a man's burden, dependent on her husband for protection and survival until the next man comes along to relieve him of the task. . . .

Is there nothing to the ALI's "overcompensation theory"? Can you think of any better rationale? Put yourself in the place of an alimony payor whose ex-wife remarries. How would you feel about continuing to pay alimony to her while she is married to and living with another man? Is it plausible that the termination rule, even if not fair, serves the societal interest in minimizing violence? On the other hand, should legislators be concerned that the termination rule might deter alimony payees from remarrying?

* The facts in this paragraph are taken from Keller v. O'Brien, 652 N.E.2d 589 (Mass. 1995)—Ed.

We saw above that there are several types of alimony, reflecting different purposes. And as noted above, reimbursement alimony generally is not terminated by remarriage, because that is akin to a debt. Florida also excludes from the remarriage automatic-termination rule rehabilitative alimony, leaving to a court's discretion whether a new "supportive relationship" constitutes a change of circumstances warranting reduction or termination of alimony. See Fla. Stat. §§ 61.08(6), 61.14(1)(b). How would you explain the special protection for this form of alimony? In light of it, would you advise a divorcing client to request rehabilitative alimony instead of permanent alimony?

Should alimony also cease if the *payor* remarries? Or should remarriage by either party simply be a factor in an original or modification petition if it affects need or ability to pay? That is the approach in a minority of states. See, e.g., In re Frost, 260 P.3d 570 (Or. Ct. App. 2011) (terminating ex-husband's alimony obligation before expiration of the eight-year term the parties had negotiated at divorce, because wife had remarried to a man whose income gave her a higher standard of living that she had had with her ex-husband). If you are representing a client likely to receive alimony, you might aim to include in a settlement agreement a provision that remarriage will not terminate the obligation, though the other side is likely to resist this.

Alimony Reconsidered

Pamela Laufer-Ukeles, Selective Recognition of Gender Difference in the Law: Revaluing the Caretaker Role

31 Harv. J.L. & Gender 1, 56-64 (2008)

The Uniform Marriage and Divorce Act ("UMDA") provides for alimony based upon need. . . . Need has alternately been interpreted as social need, dependent on the pre-divorce standard of living, and basic need, dependent on the spouse's ability to support himself at a basic standard of living. . . . Leaving a court with the discretion to determine the meaning of financial need with regard to people's lives seems hardly justifiable. . . . Moreover, the existence of need alone does not explain why such need should be fulfilled by a divorcing spouse. Furthermore, focusing on absolute need allows ghastly discrepancies between the financial circumstances of spouses post-divorce and entirely fails to acknowledge the plight of the primary caretaker post-divorce.

Alternately, the obligation to pay maintenance can be understood to belong to the spouse because of something implicit to the marital agreement—a contract-based expectation rationale for alimony. As Mark Ellman has persuasively argued, this rationale for alimony works far better in conjunction with fault-based divorce in which fault is considered in determining whether to grant alimony:

> The wife expects that the marriage itself will compensate her economic sacrifice, by providing not only personal satisfaction but also a share in her husband's financial success. This expectation presumably lies at the heart of any contract claim she may have, and is frustrated only because the marriage has ended. A formal contract claim would therefore require, as its basis, an allegation that the marriage's termination is due the husband's breach.

A contractual entitlement to a spouse's wage and living standard is much less convincing in the context of a person whose own actions cause the divorce. . . . [In any event,] such a contract theory does not provide a justification for alimony in modern marriages in which both spouses engage in some form of market work and in which the expectation for lifetime commitment is much less embedded. . . .

A compensatory theory of alimony is also insufficient. The most recent formulation of the compensatory theory is promulgated by the ALI Principles of Family Dissolution. . . . Section 5.05 provides . . . : "A spouse should be entitled at dissolution to compensation for the earning-capacity loss arising from his or her disproportionate share during marriage of the care of the marital children, or of the children of either spouse." Section 5.05 further provides compensation for loss of marital standard of living. . . . It is not clear why only the caretaker spouse is entitled to compensation upon termination of a marriage. What about the other spouse's contribution? Why is it less worthy of some form of restitution/compensation, perhaps for all those late nights at the office spent to support the family as opposed to being with the children? Compensation theory focuses only on the financial aspects of marriage and does not consider the benefits of caretaking. . . . Caretakers are neither "suckers" nor "victims" deserving of compensation for their sacrifices; they are important contributors to society. . . .

According to the partnership justification for alimony, the primary caretaker spouse would be entitled to receive a portion of her husband's salary as determined by some factor corresponding to the length of the marriage and/or the existence of dependent children. The theory is that both spouses . . . are entitled to their fair share of the total product created by the marriage, including the primary earner's wage, which has been facilitated by the spouse's caretaking efforts. . . . Arguing that a caretaking spouse is entitled to half her ex-spouse's future income is to pretend that spouses have not made different choices. . . . The spouse who chooses caretaking does more than just facilitate her spouse's earning potential; she lives her own life, obtains her own benefits and drawbacks. The view of women as tied up with their husband's job and social status post-divorce is outdated, inconsistent with basic notions of equality, and should not be encouraged. Joint income theorists are clearly worried that caretaking parents should not end up "worse off" than the income-earning spouse post-divorce with regard to earning capacity. But the concept of "worse off" is not only based on finances. . . . The primary caretaker retains custody of her children and receives child support. . . .

Professor Laufer-Ukeles's last point in this excerpt provides an answer to the "expectation of gain" theory of alimony that some find the most compelling. See, e.g., Cynthia Lee Starnes, *Alimony Theory*, 45 FAM. L.Q. 271, 291 (2011) ("gain theory offers the most satisfactory theoretical basis for alimony . . . [because of] the status it assigns alimony claimants, who are cast as equal partners in marriage, rather than victims of marriage"). Both parties might expect and deserve to gain something from marriage, but it is not clear why the gain for both must be financial. A primary caretaker enjoyed the spouse-subsidized opportunity to spend a lot of time with the couple's children during the marriage, and she leaves the marriage with the profound benefit of a closer bond with the children and a much greater prospect than the primary wage earner has of enjoying a complete life with the children after the divorce.

In addition to the difficulty of justifying alimony, and the concern that alimony might reinforce the perception and reality of female dependency, Twila Perry suggests there is a troubling racial implication of alimony law or of scholarly preoccupation with alimony.

Twila L. Perry, Alimony: Race, Privilege, and Dependency in the Search for Theory

82 Geo. L.J. 2481, 2488-2514 (1994)

. . . The whole notion of separate spheres and the "cult of domesticity" that defined women as naturally suited for motherhood rather than public life has not been a part of Black women's experience in this country. . . . During slavery, Black women engaged in physical labor while white women's roles were more that of companion or mother. After slavery, Black women continued to be workers, entering the labor force in numbers that far exceeded those of white women. . . . And although today the majority of married women have jobs, Black women continue to hold jobs outside of the home in greater numbers than white women.

Nor does the present structure of most marriages of Black couples fit the paradigm generally assumed in discussions of the theory of alimony. Whereas historically many white women have been able to enhance their standards of living by "marrying well," this has seldom been the case for Black women. Because Black men typically earn less than white men, for most Black families, having the mother in the workforce has always been a necessity. Black women are less likely than white women to have the option of choosing part-time work in order to spend more time with their children, and, obviously, Black women are less likely than white women to be confronted with the "dilemma" of having to decide whether to leave a promising job to follow a husband whose company has transferred him or who has found a job opportunity elsewhere. . . .

Black women were taught by their mothers that, rather than aspiring to be financially cared for by a man, they should expect their lives to include working and mothering simultaneously. Thus, Gloria Joseph explains that "Black females are socialized by adult figures in early life to become strong, independent women who, because of precarious circumstances growing out of poverty and racism, might eventually have to become heads of their own households." . . .

As a result of these sometimes different experiences of marriage and motherhood, Black women and middle or upper-middle class white women may have somewhat different perspectives on the relationship between caring for home and children and expecting economic rewards at a later point in their marriages. . . . Black women's views of their roles as mothers may be more independent from how they view their roles as wives. . . . Even those relatively few Black women able to spend some years exclusively as homemakers may see themselves differently than white women in the same position. Thus, some scholarship suggests that Black women may see their unpaid domestic work more as a form of resistance to oppression than as a form of exploitation by men. . . . A Black mother performing domestic work outside of the home for whites may particularly cherish performing those services at home for people she loves, instead of for the people who employ her. In addition, a Black woman in the position of being a full-time homemaker may enjoy the opportunity to occupy a role so often denied Black women. A Black mother's caring for her home and children . . . may not be accompanied by a view that she is investing in her husband's career with the expectation of future return. . . .

For a Black woman, however intense her emotional devastation may be at the end of a marriage, she probably has less of an expectation of economic compensation than a middle class or upper-middle class white woman might have. Black families have much less tangible economic wealth than white families have, and Black men, on the average, earn substantially less than white men earn. Indeed, in some cases, . . . a wife who has been the primary economic provider for her family may find her economic situation unchanged or even improved upon divorce because there is one less person who is dependent on her for financial support. . . . Because the paradigm marriage does not fit most Black marriages, the theories of alimony based on it are, for the most part, inapplicable to most Black marriages. . . .

[T]o the extent that theories of alimony depend on the premise that women have "sacrificed" their careers, this analysis has relevance primarily to upper middle-class, well-educated women. For women who do not have the option of attractive, well-paying professional jobs, staying home may not be considered a sacrifice; it may be seen as a luxury. Working at a full-time, low-paying, dead-end job may seem quite unattractive in comparison to staying home and taking care of the home and children. Moreover, contract-based arguments premised on the idea of an "expectation" by the partners that the wife would continue to be financially supported by her husband seem particularly limited to this privileged class of woman. The justification for such an expectation is questionable in a marriage where the wife has always been employed, has always been a major contributor to family finances, and has always been expected to be self-supporting. . . .

Consequently, although it is important to recognize that middle and upper-middle class women may be exploited during marriage, it is equally important to recognize that this exploitation is often accompanied by an element of privilege that may operate both during marriage and after divorce. It is also important to recognize that privileging more advantaged women by awarding alimony can easily reinforce hierarchies that view women as being deserving or undeserving of economic support based solely on their attachment to men. In this hierarchy, . . . Black women . . . will always occupy the bottom rung of the ladder.

The privileges and images of privilege that alimony reinforces can confirm to Black women, and especially to poor, Black women, the difference between the ways white and Black women are treated and valued in this society. These women are already likely to see white women as pampered individuals with whom they have little in common. The perception . . . is reflected in the following comment on the women's movement by an anonymous, low-income Black woman born and raised in Mississippi: "They just a bunch a women that don't know what they want. . . . If they so tired of staying at home, let them change places with me for a while and see how tired they get."

Another danger of focusing on theories of alimony relevant primarily to privileged women is that it reinforces society's unfortunate tendency to divide women into categories of those who are deserving of economic support and those who are not. . . . Professor Fineman describes a hierarchy of mothers based on their relationships to men. . . . Let us take the example of two women, neither of whom has ever held a job in her adult life. The first woman was married right out of college to a young man with a promising career. The other woman never married but had three children and ended up receiving public assistance. Both women have been out of the workforce caring for their children at home for the last several years. In one case, the husband has now decided that he wants to end the marriage. In the other case, the government has decided to take more severe measures against mothers receiving public assistance and to force them into workfare programs. It is likely that many people would be sympathetic to the privileged woman, believing that she is deserving of continued economic support. If circumstances required that she work after divorce, the feeling would probably be that she should be trained for a job that has long-term potential for financial and personal growth. There would be concern about the decline in her economic status as a result of the divorce. There would also probably be concern about her loss of status and about possible resulting psychological harm. On the other hand, many people would feel that the welfare mother should take any job, however low-paying and dead-end, even if it causes her to lose important benefits, such as medical care for her and her children. . . . For many people, a woman's economic dependency is acceptable as long as that dependency is on a man. . . . Both women may have been superb homemakers and wonderful, attentive mothers, yet only one is viewed as deserving. . . .

Reinforcing a system in which the value of women is determined primarily by the status of the men to whom they are attached can also have profound implications for the relationships between white and Black women. As Patricia Hill Collins has noted, "[r]elationships among Black and white women are framed by the web of sexual politics that seduces white women with an artificial sense of specialness and vests them with the power to sustain that illusion." She also has noted that Black women often feel that far too many white women are unwilling to acknowledge—let alone challenge—the actions of white men because, in part, they have benefitted from them. Indeed, it is that attachment to powerful white men that has enabled white women to participate in the subordination of Black women ever since slavery, and it is those white women with higher family income levels—where alimony would most likely be received in the event of a divorce—who are in the best position to subordinate. These are the women most likely to have the opportunity to employ Black women to do domestic work in their homes, where a complex relationship of racial domination and subordination is often played out. It is, in part, this relationship, as well as Black women's awareness of a past rooted in slavery, that stands as one of the barriers to the formation of effective coalitions between white and Black women. . . .

What would it mean for privileged women to envision a world that does not embody a Cinderella story, in which they marry a powerful man who provides them with lots of "choices." What if they said to themselves: "I alone am responsible for my economic status and my economic well-being whether or not I choose to be with a man?" The prospect may be frightening as well as liberating. Eliminating the idea of a man as the assumed economic backdrop would result in all women having an increased incentive to address those problems in the workplace that impact most severely upon poor women, but also limit the opportunites of all women to succeed. The struggle could intensify and focus on a number of goals: to eliminate sex discrimination, to ensure that child-care facilities are made available for all, to establish appropriate leave policies to care for children or other relatives, and to initiate innovations such as job-sharing and more flexible work hours. Well-educated professional women could bring significant political and economic strength to efforts aimed at making changes in the workplace that would benefit all working women. . . .

See also Laura T. Kessler, *Transgressive Caregiving*, 33 FLA. ST. U. L. REV. 1, 4 (2005) ("A woman who does significantly more housework and child care than her husband is likely to view caregiving work differently than an unmarried welfare recipient who wishes to gain an exception to her state's workfare program in order to spend more time with her infant child or a lesbian choosing to bring a child into her family through alternative insemination."). Is advocacy for more generous alimony misplaced? Should efforts instead be directed toward increasing state support for poor single parents, regardless of whether they were previously in a state-sanctioned heterosexual union?

Most of the women in your law school class will marry and have children. How many of them do you think will give up their careers, or at least substantially reduce their commitment to it, in order to devote themselves to caring for home, partner, and children? If any, which ones and why? Do any feel family or societal pressure to be domestic rather than professional? Or the opposite? To the extent society does still impose a gendered expectation of domesticity, should society collectively bear responsibility for any resulting dependency? Most of the men in your class also will marry and have children. How many of them do you think will make substantial career sacrifices in order to do more homemaking or child care?

The greatest pressure on women to adopt traditional, gendered family roles and not pursue a career might be in some conservative religious communities. Many of those communities, however, also exert great pressure on married couples to stay married and not divorce. They might also offer greater collective support for dependent people who lose their family source of support as a result of death or divorce. There might therefore be little need for court-ordered alimony for women in these communities.

Primary breadwinners sometimes also express the view that being a homemaker is a privilege and luxury, rather than a sacrifice. They could be correct even if they would not want to change places, just as one could say that spending a day golfing is a luxury even if one has no interest in golf and would rather spend a day at home cutting the grass and cleaning the gutters. Working husbands at time of divorce might also say that while they benefitted from the homemaking and childcare efforts of their wives, they have also had to live without the income their wives could have earned if employed outside the home—and so have sacrificed something themselves—and that their wives were fully compensated for their efforts by being supported during the marriage. What weaknesses, if any, are there in this view? If it is persuasive, what implications, if any, does it have for the law and theory of alimony?

c. Additional Financial Consequences of Divorce

Decedents' Estates: We saw in Chapter 3 that marriage entitles a spouse to a share of a decedent's estate, regardless of any will provisions. That entitlement vanishes at divorce. The prevailing rules of trusts and estates relating to divorce are that divorce eliminates any right to intestate succession for a spouse and revokes any provision in a will for a spouse. Traditionally, divorce had no effect on non-probate transfers, but increasingly states have adopted rules that cause divorce to remove spouses from trust instruments, beneficiary designation in life insurance policies, and payable-on-death (POD) designations in accounts with financial institutions. In counseling a divorcing client, it is important to know what the law in your state is regarding such non-probate transfers, because many divorcing persons do not think to change these beneficiary designations. If the law in your state does not provide for automatic revocation of beneficiary and POD designations, you should advise your client to contact the trustees or financial institutions in order to make any desired changes to those designations.

Tax: Tax filing status depends on one's family situation on the last day of the tax year. Thus, anyone divorced earlier in the year than December 31 must, absent remarriage, file as single (or possibly "head of household" if the primary custodian of a child"). With respect to exemptions for children, the IRS assumes that the spouse who has custody of the children is entitled to the exemptions, but the spouses are allowed to trade exemptions back and forth freely, using IRS Form 8332. Often the exemptions are assigned to one spouse or the other in a separation agreement. The person who has the exemptions typically also gets the child credit, if eligible. Rational divorcing couples will calculate what assignment of exemptions and credits generates the lowest collective tax burden and agree on that assignment, and have the person getting the tax benefits compensate the other in some way to effect a fair splitting of the benefit. But divorcing couples are not typically paragons of rationality. Usually it is better for the higher-income parent to use the exemptions, because he is likely to be in a higher tax bracket, but that is usually the parent who does not have custody, and some primary custodians might be resistant to the idea of signing over the exemptions to the non-custodial parent. Use of the child credit usually goes hand in hand with the exemption for children. This can complicate calculations, because a high-income non-custodial parent might be able to save more with the exemptions than the custodial parent can, but be unable to claim the child credit because his income is too high. You might urge clients in this situation to work with an accountant or professional tax preparer.

Clients should also know the income tax treatment of support payments. Alimony is deductible for the payor, and it is income that the payee must report. As noted in Chapter 4, this is different from IRS treatment of child support, which is not deductible by the payor and is not reportable income for the receiving parent or for the child. Some clients might also need to be concerned about capital gains taxes arising from sale of the marital residence.

Government Benefits: Ex-spouses who were married for at least ten years enjoy a permanent, but to some extent conditional, entitlement to social security payments based upon their former spouses' employment, regardless of whether the former spouses remarry. They are entitled to survivor benefits from Social Security if the former spouse predeceases them. In addition, upon reaching age 62, they can collect retirement benefits on their former spouse's Social Security record if the former spouse is entitled to or receiving benefits, *and if* they are unmarried at that time (regardless of whether there has been an intervening subsequent marriage). These retirement benefits are in lieu of benefits based upon one's own employment, so it is significant for divorced persons who have lower lifetime earnings than their ex-spouses. One might suggest to a client contemplating divorce from a higher-income spouse in the eighth or ninth year of marriage that he or she hold on for another year or two to lock in these social security benefits.

The military has a number of special rules for distribution of financial benefits to ex-spouses at the time of divorce and at the time of the service member's retirement. Some domestic relations attorneys develop a specialty in military divorces.

Part IV

This final Part contains three client-situation exercises. Their purpose is partly to help you review and apply the substantive law you learned in the prior units. In addition, they raise some special ethical and practical issues that commonly arise in family law practice, and after each exercise there are some additional short readings that will enable you to address those issues.

CLIENT EXERCISE 1

Patrick comes to your office for a consultation. He is a 19-year-old man who has not had steady employment since dropping out of school at age 15. He appears to you to be of below-average intelligence. He has been convicted of a few misdemeanors, most recently driving while intoxicated. It is now late November, and he tells you that until this past summer he was dating a girl named Molly, who was 16 and a junior in high school. Their relationship had included sex, sometimes with condoms and sometimes without. Their relationship ended during the summer, when Molly worked as a waitress at a Denny's restaurant and started a relationship with the 24-year-old manager, Henry. Patrick remains in love with Molly and has continuously tried to communicate with her since she broke up with him in July, but Molly has been unresponsive. Patrick has just heard from a mutual friend that Molly is "very pregnant" and is planning to marry Henry on New Year's Eve. Patrick believes he could be the one who got Molly pregnant, and he tells you that if he is the biological father, then he will want to act as a parent to the child. He wants to know what legal steps he can take, and he wants to act as quickly as possible.

A. SUBSTANTIVE QUESTIONS

1) If Patrick is the biological father, can he ensure that he becomes the legal father even if Molly does marry Henry and they want to raise the child without Patrick's interference?
2) How would Patrick go about determining whether he is the biological father?
3) If Patrick is the biological father but fails to secure legal parent status for himself, is there still a way for him to demand a role in the child's life?
4) Is there anything legally Patrick can do now, before the wedding occurs, to help his cause?
5) Can anyone legally stop Molly and Henry from marrying?

B. ETHICAL QUESTIONS

1) Patrick has little money to pay you. What should you do about that? Family law is one of those areas of practice in which attorneys frequently receive pleas for help from low-income persons. There might or might not be a local legal aid office that does family law cases and that can take on new clients. There probably is not a system in your area for court appointment of lawyers for adults involved in paternity disputes. If there is, the lawyers likely receive little compensation, and they might get paid by the case rather than by the hour, giving them no financial incentive to do more than a bare minimum. Do you have any obligation, as a matter of professional ethics or of morality, to help Patrick in any way? Does it depend on how good his alternatives for legal assistance are? Or on how helpful local judges and court clerks are with pro se litigants?
2) You have a strong conviction that the child would be better off if Patrick would just disappear and leave Molly and Henry undisturbed to create a family together. You also suspect that if Patrick succeeded in a paternity claim, his present enthusiasm for parenthood would evaporate after a few months of awkward visits with the baby and an accruing child support obligation. Is it ethically permissible to try to convince Patrick to give up his quest for paternity? Or to refuse to represent him because you disapprove of his aims? Family law is also an area of practice in which lawyers often find their clients' wishes to be morally objectionable.

Here are provisions of the Model Rules of Professional Conduct that might be relevant:

Rule 1.2 Scope of Representation and Allocation of Authority Between Client and Lawyer

(a) . . . [A] lawyer shall abide by a client's decisions concerning the objectives of representation. . . . A lawyer shall abide by a client's decision whether to settle a matter. . . .

(b) A lawyer's representation of a client, including representation by appointment, does not constitute an endorsement of the client's political, economic, social or moral views or activities.

Rule 1.14 Client with Diminished Capacity

(a) When a client's capacity to make adequately considered decisions in connection with a representation is diminished, whether because of minority, mental impairment or for some other reason, the lawyer shall, as far as reasonably possible, maintain a normal client-lawyer relationship with the client.

Rule 1.16 Declining or Terminating Representation

(b) . . . [A] lawyer may withdraw from representing a client if:

(1) withdrawal can be accomplished without material adverse effect on the interests of the client; . . .

(4) the client insists upon taking action that the lawyer considers repugnant or with which the lawyer has a fundamental disagreement; . . .

(6) the representation will result in an unreasonable financial burden on the lawyer or has been rendered unreasonably difficult by the client; or

(7) other good cause for withdrawal exists.

RULE 2.1 ADVISOR

In representing a client, a lawyer shall exercise independent professional judgment and render candid advice. In rendering advice, a lawyer may refer not only to law but to other considerations such as moral, economic, social and political factors, that may be relevant to the client's situation.

RULE 6.1 VOLUNTARY PRO BONO PUBLICO SERVICE

Every lawyer has a professional responsibility to provide legal services to those unable to pay. A lawyer should aspire to render at least (50) hours of pro bono publico legal services per year. In fulfilling this responsibility, the lawyer should:

(a) provide a substantial majority of the (50) hours of legal services without fee or expectation of fee to:

(1) persons of limited means or

(2) charitable . . . organizations. . . .

American Academy of Matrimonial Lawyers, Bounds of Advocacy

The primary purpose of the Bounds of Advocacy: Goals for Family Lawyers is to guide matrimonial lawyers confronting moral and ethical problems. . . . The ABA's Model Rules of Professional Conduct ("RPC") are addressed to all lawyers, regardless of the nature of their practices. . . . Many Fellows of the American Academy of Matrimonial Lawyers have encountered instances where the RPC provided insufficient, or even undesirable, guidance. . . . These Goals are . . . directed primarily to the "gray" zone where even experienced, knowledgeable matrimonial lawyers might have concerns. . . . Conduct permitted by the RPC cannot form the basis for state bar or court discipline. Hence, the Goals here established for matrimonial lawyers use the terms "should" and "should not," rather than "must," "shall," "must not" and "shall not." . . . [I]t is inappropriate to use the Goals to define the level of conduct required of lawyers for purposes of malpractice liability or state bar discipline. . . .

[E]mphasis on zealous representation of individual clients . . . is not always appropriate in family law matters. . . . A counseling, problem-solving approach for people in need of help in resolving difficult issues and conflicts . . . is sometimes referred to as "constructive advocacy." . . . Effective advocacy for a client means considering with the client what is in the client's best interests and determining the most effective means to achieve that result. The client's best interests include the well being of children, family peace, and economic stability. Clients look to attorneys' words and deeds for how they should behave while involved with the legal system.

1.3 An attorney should refuse to assist in vindictive conduct and should strive to lower the emotional level of a family dispute by treating all other participants with respect.

Comment

Although the client has the right to determine the "objectives of representation," after consulting with the client the attorney may limit the objectives and the means by which the objectives are to be pursued. . . . If the client is unwilling to accept the attorney's limitations on objectives or means, the attorney should decline the representation. . . .

2.4 An attorney should share decision-making responsibility with the client, but should not abdicate responsibility for the propriety of the objectives sought or the means employed to achieve those objectives.

Comment

. . . It is appropriate as part of the lawyer's counseling function to assist the client in reframing the client's objectives when to do so would be in the client's best interests. A lawyer may counsel a client not only as to the law, but also as to "other considerations such as moral, economic, social and political factors that may be relevant to the client's situation." . . . "In questions of means, the lawyer should assume responsibility for technical and legal tactical issues" (e.g., choosing forum, type of pleadings, or judicial remedy), "but should defer to the client regarding expenses to be incurred and concern for third persons who might be adversely affected." . . .

2.5 When the client's decision-making ability appears to be impaired, the attorney should try to protect the client from the harmful effects of the impairment.

Comment

. . . The lawyer is not compelled to follow irrational or potentially harmful directives of a client, particularly one who is distraught or impaired, even if the client is legally competent. . . . The attorney should attempt to dissuade the client before accepting any clearly detrimental decision. The attorney should consider consulting others who might have a stabilizing influence on the client such as the client's therapist, doctor or clergy. . . .

2.7 An attorney should not allow personal, moral or religious beliefs to diminish loyalty to the client or usurp the client's right to make decisions concerning the objectives of representation.

Comment

. . . [T]he lawyer should withdraw from representation if personal, moral or religious beliefs are likely to cause the attorney to take actions that are not in the client's best interest. If there is any question as to the possible effect of those beliefs on the representation, the client should be consulted and consent obtained. . . .

CLIENT EXERCISE 2

You work in a small, general-practice firm whose work includes real estate, employment, criminal, domestic relations, and other matters. Several times someone you encountered in a business dealing has come to you later with a family law issue. One day a woman, Angela, comes to your office and you remember her from a home refinancing you handled for her partner, Bianca, a few years ago. Angela and Bianca have lived together for nine years, and they had a wedding ceremony six years ago. Twice they arranged together for Angela to have a baby by artificial insemination at an assisted reproduction facility using sperm from an anonymous donor. Angela quit her job as a high school math teacher to devote herself full-time to taking care of the children, who are now three and five years old, and to maintaining the home. The children view both women as their parents, though Bianca has never attempted to adopt them. Bianca has provided all the income to the family from her service in the army, where she has achieved the rank of Staff Sergeant. Bianca owns and controls all the family's wealth; the bank and investment accounts are solely in her name, as are the house and two cars. So that Angela can pay for daily expenses, Bianca has given Angela a credit card and cash as needed.

Angela tells you Bianca has been physically abusive toward her since the first pregnancy. The abuse escalated recently as a result of Bianca's unhappiness at work. On two occasions, Bianca even attacked Angela while the children were present. Angela has decided to move out for the sake of her safety and her children's well being. She wants you to counsel her and to help her to make this transition. She has no money to live independently, and no family or friends who can take her in.

A. SUBSTANTIVE QUESTIONS

1) Can Angela initiate a civil or criminal domestic violence action against Bianca?
2) Could either woman be charged with child maltreatment if CPS learned about the domestic violence?

3) Does Angela need permission from Bianca or a court to take the children out of the home to live elsewhere?
4) Would a court order Bianca to provide support to Angela and/or the children, temporarily or long-term? Would Angela do anything wrong by continuing to use the credit card, if Bianca does not immediately cancel it?
5) Will Angela have any claim on the wealth Bianca accumulated during the time they lived together? Will she need to leave behind the car she has been using?
6) Could a court award Bianca visitation with or even custody of the children?
7) Could Bianca adopt the children now, to secure her relationship with them?

B. ETHICAL QUESTIONS

1) Can you represent Angela, given that you previously handled the house refinance for Bianca?
2) You know that the army might discipline, demote, or even discharge Bianca if a court determines that she committed domestic abuse, and that Bianca might suffer a substantial drop in income as a result. How should you deal with that fact in counseling Angela about whether she should initiate a domestic violence action? Is it ethical to try to extract concessions from Bianca on financial or child-rearing issues by threatening to initiate a civil or criminal action?

These provisions of the Model Rules of Professional Conduct might be relevant:

RULE 1.9 DUTIES TO FORMER CLIENTS

(a) A lawyer who has formerly represented a client in a matter shall not thereafter represent another person in the same or a substantially related matter in which that person's interests are materially adverse to the interests of the former client unless the former client gives informed consent, confirmed in writing. . . .

(c) A lawyer who has formerly represented a client in a matter . . . shall not thereafter:

(1) use information relating to the representation to the disadvantage of the former client . . . ; or

(2) reveal information relating to the representation. . . .

RULE 3.1 MERITORIOUS CLAIMS AND CONTENTIONS

A lawyer shall not bring or defend a proceeding, or assert or controvert an issue therein, unless there is a basis in law and fact for doing so that is not frivolous. . . .

RULE 4.1 TRUTHFULNESS IN STATEMENTS TO OTHERS

In the course of representing a client a lawyer shall not knowingly:

(a) make a false statement of material fact or law to a third person;

RULE 4.4 RESPECT FOR RIGHTS OF THIRD PERSONS

(a) In representing a client, a lawyer shall not use means that have no substantial purpose other than to embarrass, delay, or burden a third person. . . .

RULE 8.4 MISCONDUCT

It is professional misconduct for a lawyer to: . . .
(c) engage in conduct involving dishonesty, fraud, deceit or misrepresentation;
(d) engage in conduct that is prejudicial to the administration of justice;
(e) state or imply an ability to influence improperly a government agency or official or to achieve results by means that violate the Rules of Professional Conduct or other law. . . .

American Academy of Matrimonial Lawyers, Bounds of Advocacy

7.3 . . . The attorney believes that the opposing party has engaged in activity that the party would not want made public. It is improper to bluff the other side into settlement by hinting that the matrimonial lawyer will use damaging evidence of the conduct if that evidence does not exist. It is also improper to threaten public disclosure if the evidence exists, but would likely be inadmissible or irrelevant at trial.

6.6 An attorney should not make or assist a client in making an allegation of child abuse unless there is a reasonable basis and evidence to believe it is true.

Comment

An attorney who is made aware of abuse . . . is permitted, if not obligated, to provide that information during divorce or custody proceedings. While reporting the existence of child abuse is crucial, however, a claim that a parent has abused a child is ugly and leads to the most unpleasant and harmful litigation in the field of family law. Such claims draw the child into testing or some other form of examination, which itself may be traumatic. The harm to both the accusing and accused parent will almost always be very great. . . . Use of such charges to obtain an unfair advantage in the dispute is inexcusable. . . . The lawyer should use all available information and resources—including evaluation by a doctor, therapist, or other health professional—to be sure there is a reasonable basis and substantial supporting evidence for such a charge. Even when the allegation is believed to be justified, it should be made in a manner least harmful to any children and least likely to inflame the dispute.

C. JURISDICTIONAL QUESTIONS

1) Could Bianca insist that proceedings relating to any of the substantive questions above occur in a military court? If so, would it be to her advantage to do so?
2) If the army relocated Bianca to a base in another state, could Bianca initiate legal proceedings relating to any of the substantive issues in a court in that state, forcing

Angela to hire another lawyer there, or would Bianca have to file in the state where the family has lived?

Below are some materials that might help you answer those jurisdictional questions.

1. Military Jurisdiction

The military question is a significant one; there are roughly 1.5 million Americans on active military duty at any given time, a high percentage of them are in intimate relationships, and they disproportionately have family law problems. Unfortunately, there are no clear and comprehensive authorities on when military or civilian courts have jurisdiction over a particular type of matter involving military personnel. The following documents provide some pieces of the puzzle.

Solorio v. United States

483 U.S. 435 (1987)

Chief Justice REHNQUIST delivered the opinion of the Court.

. . . While petitioner Richard Solorio was on active duty in the Seventeenth Coast Guard District in Juneau, Alaska, he sexually abused two young daughters of fellow coastguardsmen. . . . [A] commander convened a general court-martial to try petitioner for crimes. . . . Petitioner's . . . offenses were committed in his privately owned home. . . . [P]etitioner moved to dismiss the charges for crimes committed in Alaska on the ground that the court lacked jurisdiction.

The Constitution grants to Congress the power "[t]o make Rules for the Government and Regulation of the land and naval Forces." U.S. Const., Art. I, §8, cl. 14. Exercising this authority, Congress has empowered courts-martial to try servicemen for the crimes proscribed by the U.C.M.J., Arts. 2, 17, 10 U.S.C. §§802, 817. The Alaska offenses with which petitioner was charged are each described in the U.C.M.J. . . .

In an unbroken line of decisions from 1866 to 1960, this Court interpreted the Constitution as conditioning the proper exercise of court-martial jurisdiction over an offense on one factor: the military status of the accused. . . . Implicit in the military status test was the principle that determinations concerning the scope of court-martial jurisdiction over offenses committed by servicemen was a matter reserved for Congress:

> "[T]he rights of men in the armed forces must perforce be conditioned to meet certain overriding demands of discipline and duty, and the civil courts are not the agencies which must determine the precise balance to be struck in this adjustment. . . ."

In 1969, the Court in *O'Callahan v. Parker* departed from the military status test and announced the "new constitutional principle" that a military tribunal may not try a serviceman charged with a crime that has no service connection. Applying this principle, the *O'Callahan* Court held that a serviceman's off-base sexual assault on a civilian with no connection with the military could not be tried by court-martial. On reexamination of *O'Callahan*, we have decided that the service connection test announced in that decision should be abandoned. . . . Whatever doubts there might be about the extent of Congress' power under Clause 14 to make rules for the "Government and Regulation of the land and naval Forces," that power surely embraces the authority to regulate the conduct of persons who are actually members of the Armed Services. . . . Alexander Hamilton described these powers of Congress "essential to the common defense" as follows:

> "These powers ought to exist without limitation, because it is impossible to foresee or define the extent and variety of national exigencies, or the correspondent extent and variety of the means which may be necessary to satisfy them. . . ."

The *O'Callahan* Court's historical foundation for its holding . . . , however, is less than accurate. . . . We think the history of court-martial jurisdiction in England and in this country during the 17th and 18th centuries is far too ambiguous to justify the restriction on the plain language of Clause 14 which *O'Callahan* imported into it. . . . The only other basis for saying that the Framers intended the words of Art. I, §8, cl. 14, to be narrowly construed is the suggestion that the Framers "could hardly have been unaware of Blackstone's strong condemnation of criminal justice administered under military procedures." In his Commentaries, Blackstone wrote:

> ". . . [M]artial law, which is built on no settled principles, but is entirely arbitrary in it's [sic] decisions, is . . . something indulged in rather than allowed as a law. The necessity of order and discipline in an army is the only thing which can give it countenance; and therefore it ought not to be permitted in time of peace. . . ."

Although we do not doubt that Blackstone's views on military law were known to the Framers, we are not persuaded that their relevance is sufficiently compelling to overcome the unqualified language of Art. I, §8, cl. 14. . . . [T]he plain language of the Constitution, as interpreted by numerous decisions of this Court preceding *O'Callahan,* should be controlling on the subject of court-martial jurisdiction. . . . Congress has primary responsibility for the delicate task of balancing the rights of servicemen against the needs of the military. . . . The notion that civil courts are "ill equipped" to establish policies regarding matters of military concern is substantiated by experience under the service connection approach. . . . [In addition,] the service connection approach . . . has proved confusing and difficult for military courts to apply. . . .

We therefore hold that the requirements of the Constitution are not violated where, as here, a court-martial is convened to try a serviceman who was a member of the Armed Services at the time of the offense charged. . . .

Justice MARSHALL, with whom Justice BRENNAN joins, and with whom Justice BLACKMUN joins in all but the last paragraph, dissenting.

. . . The rights to grand jury process and to trial by jury are . . . of restricted application in military cases. . . . These protections should not be lightly abrogated. . . . One of the grievances stated in the Declaration of Independence was King George III's assent to "pretended Legislation: For quartering large bodies of armed troops among us: For protecting them, by a mock Trial, from punishment for any Murders which they should commit on the Inhabitants of these States." The Framers thus were concerned both with protecting the rights of those subjected to courts-martial, and with preventing courts-martial from permitting soldiers to get away with murder—literally—in the civilian community. . . .

Application of the service connection requirement of *O'Callahan* . . . demonstrates that petitioner's Alaska crimes do not have an adequate service connection to support the exercise of court-martial jurisdiction. Petitioner's offenses did not detract from the performance of his military duties. He committed these crimes while properly absent from his unit, and there was no connection between his assigned duties and his crimes. Nor did petitioner's crimes threaten people or areas under military control. The crimes were committed in petitioner's private home in the civilian community. . . . Petitioner's acts were not likely to go unpunished; the court-martial judge determined that the offenses were of a type traditionally prosecuted by civilian courts, that such courts were available, and that, while the Alaska courts had deferred prosecution in light of the court-martial proceeding, the State had not declined to prosecute the offenses. . . . Moreover, the crimes caused no measurable interference with military relationships. . . . Because the crimes did not take place in an area within military control or have any effect on petitioner's military duties, their commission posed no challenge to the maintenance of order in the local command. . . . It is true that the test requires a careful, case-specific factual inquiry. But this is not beyond the capacity of the military courts. . . . Unless Congress acts to avoid the consequences of this case, every member of our Armed Forces, whose active duty members number in the millions, can now be subjected to court-martial jurisdiction—without grand jury indictment or trial by jury—for any offense, from tax fraud to passing a bad check, regardless of its lack of relation to "military discipline, morale and fitness." . . .

United States Code Title 10. Armed Forces
Subtitle A. General Military Law, Part II.
Personnel Chapter 47. Uniform Code of Military Justice
Subchapter X. Punitive Articles

§928. Art. 128. Assault

(a) Any person subject to this chapter who attempts or offers with unlawful force or violence to do bodily harm to another person, whether or not the attempt or offer is consummated, is guilty of assault and shall be punished as a court-martial may direct.

(b) Any person subject to this chapter who . . . commits an assault and intentionally inflicts grievous bodily harm with or without a weapon is guilty of aggravated assault and shall be punished as a court-martial may direct.

§933. Art. 133. Conduct Unbecoming an Officer and a Gentleman

Any commissioned officer, cadet, or midshipman who is convicted of conduct unbecoming an officer and a gentleman shall be punished as a court-martial may direct.

§934. Art. 134. General Article

. . . [A]ll disorders and neglects to the prejudice of good order and discipline in the armed forces, all conduct of a nature to bring discredit upon the armed forces, and crimes and offenses not capital, of which persons subject to this chapter may be guilty, shall be taken cognizance of by a general, special, or summary court-martial, according to the nature and degree of the offense, and shall be punished at the discretion of that court.

Department of Defense, Instruction Number 6400.06

(August 21, 2007)

. . . 6. Procedures . . .

6.1.1. Commanders shall:

6.1.1.1. Ensure that the alleged military [domestic] abusers are held accountable for their conduct through appropriate disposition under the UCMJ and/or administrative regulations, as appropriate.

6.1.1.2. Respond to reports of domestic abuse as they would to credible reports of any other crime and ensure that victims are informed of services available. . . .

6.1.1.5. Refer any incident of domestic abuse reported or discovered independent of law enforcement to military law enforcement or the appropriate [military] criminal investigative organization for possible investigation. . . .

6.1.1.9. Ensure safe housing has been secured for the victim as needed.

6.1.1.9.1. The preference is to remove the alleged abuser from the home when the parties must be separated to safeguard the victim.

6.1.1.9.2. If necessary, the alleged abuser will be directed to find alternative housing. . . .

6.1.1.17. Document . . . that a Service member engaged in conduct that is a dependent-abuse offense when referring such action for court martial and when initiating action to administratively separate, voluntarily or involuntarily, the Service member from active duty so that the family members may apply for transitional compensation benefits. . . .

E2. Enclosure 2: Definitions

E2.8. . . . "crime of domestic violence" means an offense that has as its factual basis, the use or attempted use of physical force, or threatened use of a deadly weapon; committed by a current or former spouse, parent, or guardian of the victim, by a person with whom the victim shares a child in common, by a person who is cohabitating with or has cohabitated with the victim as a spouse, parent, or guardian, or by a person similarly situated to a spouse, parent or guardian of the victims.

E2.13. Domestic Abuse. Domestic violence or a pattern of behavior resulting in emotional/psychological abuse, economic control, and/or interference with personal liberty that is directed toward a person of the opposite sex who is:

E2.13.1. A current or former spouse.

E2.13.2. A person with whom the abuser shares a child in common; or

E2.13.3. A current or former intimate partner with whom the abuser shares or has shared a common domicile.

E2.14. Domestic Violence. An offense under the United States Code, the Uniform Code of Military Justice, or State law involving the use, attempted use, or threatened use of force or violence against a person of the opposite sex, or a violation of a lawful order issued for the protection of a person of the opposite sex, who is:

E2.14.1. A current or former spouse.

E2.14.2. A person with whom the abuser shares a child in common; or

E2.14.3. A current or former intimate partner with whom the abuser shares or has shared a common domicile.

E5. Enclosure 5: Sample Memorandum of Understanding Between the Installation Staff Judge Advocate and the Local District Attorney's Office

. . . 3. responsibilities:

A. The (COUNTY/CITY) DA agrees to perform the following actions: . . .

(2) When investigating or prosecuting domestic abuse cases, the (COUNTY/CITY) District Attorney (DA) shall determine whether the alleged offender is an active duty Service member assigned to (INSTALLATION). If the alleged offender is an active duty member assigned to (INSTALLATION), the DA shall contact the (INSTALLATION) SJA to inform the SJA of the pending investigation or prosecution.

(3) . . . [T]he DA shall consult with the SJA with respect to prosecution of the individual under the appropriate state law or under the Uniform Code of Military Justice (UCMJ).

(5) When, after consultation, the SJA and the DA have determined that the alleged offender will be subject to procedures under the UCMJ, the DA shall cooperate during the investigation and disciplinary action to the greatest extent possible.

B. The (INSTALLATION) SJA agrees to perform the following actions: . . .

(2) When investigating a domestic abuse case involving an active duty member assigned to (INSTALLATION) who is alleged to be the offender, the SJA shall, in cases where the state has jurisdiction, consult with the local DA to determine whether the individual will be prosecuted under the appropriate state law or whether the command will pursue disciplinary action under the UCMJ. . . .

(4) When, after consultation, the DA and the SJA have decided that the alleged offender will be prosecuted under state law, the SJA shall cooperate during the investigation and prosecution . . . by sharing information and facilitating the interviewing of witnesses.

Domestic Violence Amendment to the Gun Control Act of 1968

Army Regulation 600-20, Army Command Policy, para. 4-23

a. The Domestic Violence Amendment to the Gun Control Act of 1968, the Lautenberg Amendment, makes it unlawful for any person to transfer . . . firearms or ammunition to any person . . . convicted of a misdemeanor crime of domestic violence. It is also unlawful for any person who has been convicted of a misdemeanor crime of domestic violence to receive any firearm or ammunition that has been shipped or transported in interstate or foreign commerce. This chapter applies to all Soldiers throughout the world. . . .

b. Definitions. For the purpose of this paragraph only, the following definitions apply:

(1) *Crime of domestic violence.* An offense that involves the use or attempted use of physical force, or threatened use of a deadly weapon committed by a current or former spouse, parent, or guardian of the victim; by a person with whom the victim shares a child

in common; by a person who is cohabiting with or has cohabited with the victim as a spouse, parent, or guardian; or by a person who was similarly situated to a spouse, parent, or guardian of the victim. Persons who are similarly situated to a spouse include two persons who are residing at the same location in an intimate relationship with the intent to make that place their home.

(2) *Qualifying conviction.* A state or Federal conviction for a misdemeanor crime of domestic violence and any general or special court-martial for an offense that otherwise meets the elements of a crime of domestic violence, even though not classified as a misdemeanor or felony. A qualifying conviction does not include a summary court-martial conviction or the imposition of nonjudicial punishment under UCMJ, Art. 15. . . .

c. Commander's responsibilities.

(1) The commander will ensure that all Soldiers who have a qualifying conviction are notified that it is unlawful to possess . . . firearms and ammunition. . . .

(5) The commander will ensure that procedures are implemented to track domestic violence arrests and convictions in the civilian community. . . .

(6) . . . Soldiers with qualifying convictions must be identified and reported to HQDA. . . .

(8) Domestic violence is incompatible with Army values and will not be tolerated or condoned. However, Soldiers will be given a reasonable time to seek expungement of or to obtain a pardon for a qualifying conviction. . . . The following factors will be considered in the commander's determination: . . .

(b) Whether firearms or deadly weapons were used in the offense that formed the basis for the Soldier's domestic violence conviction. . . .

(e) Whether serious injury was caused during the crime of domestic violence. . . .

(9) Commanders must detail Soldiers whom they have reason to believe have a qualifying conviction to meaningful duties that do not require bearing weapons or ammunition. . . . Commanders will not appoint or assign Soldiers with qualifying convictions to leadership, supervisory, or property accountability positions that would require access to firearms or ammunition.

d. Personnel policies.

(1) . . . Soldiers with a qualifying conviction will be barred from reenlistment and are not eligible for the indefinite reenlistment program. Soldiers in the indefinite reenlistment program will be given an expiration of term of service (ETS) not to exceed 12 months from the date HQDA is notified of the qualifying conviction. . . .

(2) Applicants with a qualifying conviction will not be approved for commissioning . . . and are ineligible for voluntary indefinite status. Officers with a qualifying conviction will be separated not later than 12 months from the date HQDA is notified of the qualifying conviction.

(6) Officers with a qualifying conviction may not be promoted to the next higher grade. . . .

(8) All Soldiers . . . [with] a qualifying conviction are not mobilization assets and are nondeployable for missions that require possession of firearms or ammunition. . . .

(10) . . . Soldiers with a qualifying conviction are not eligible for overseas service. . . .

Spouses of military members often complain that military officials ignore or underreact to reports of abuse, after informing civilian authorities that the military will address the situation. See, e.g., Lizette Alvarez, *Despite Assurances from Army, an Assault Case Founders,* N.Y. TIMES, Nov. 23, 2008; Miles Moffeit & Amy Herdy, *While Civilian Prosecutors Crack Down on Domestic Abuse, the Military Emphasizes Counseling and Tells Commanders to Consider the Accused's Career,* DENV. POST, Nov. 17, 2003.

2. *Interstate Jurisdiction*

Interstate movement is so common in the United States that the question of which state has jurisdiction over a domestic relations matter arises routinely. Fortunately, there is a fairly universal set of rules for resolving the forum question, because the uniform act below has been adopted throughout the United States, with some minor variations from one state to another.

Uniform Child-Custody Jurisdiction and Enforcement Act

[ARTICLE] 1. . . .

SECTION 102. DEFINITIONS

In this [Act]:

. . . (4) "Child-custody proceeding" means a proceeding in which legal custody, physical custody, or visitation with respect to a child is an issue. The term includes a proceeding for divorce, separation, neglect, abuse, dependency, guardianship, paternity, termination of parental rights, and protection from domestic violence, in which the issue may appear. . . .

(5) "Commencement" means the filing of the first pleading in a proceeding. . . .

(7) "Home State" means the State in which a child lived with a parent or a person acting as a parent for at least six consecutive months immediately before the commencement of a child-custody proceeding. . . .

(8) "Initial determination" means the first child-custody determination concerning a particular child. . . .

(13) "Person acting as a parent" means a person, other than a parent, who:

(A) has physical custody of the child or has had physical custody for a period of six consecutive months, including any temporary absence, within one year immediately before the commencement of a child-custody proceeding; and

(B) has been awarded legal custody by a court or claims a right to legal custody under the law of this State.

SECTION 103. PROCEEDINGS GOVERNED BY OTHER LAW

This [Act] does not govern an adoption proceeding. . . .

Comment

. . . Adoption . . . is thoroughly covered by the Uniform Adoption Act (UAA) (1994). . . . However, . . . if a State adopts the UAA then Section 3-101 of the Act specifically refers in places to the Uniform Child Custody Jurisdiction Act which will become a reference to this Act. Second, the UAA requires that if an adoption is denied or set aside, the court is to determine the child's custody. UAA §3-704. Those custody proceedings would be subject to this Act. . . . Children that are the subject of interstate placements for adoption or foster care are governed by the Interstate Compact on the Placement of Children. . . .

SECTION 106. EFFECT OF CHILD-CUSTODY DETERMINATION

A child-custody determination made by a court of this State that had jurisdiction under this [Act] binds all persons who have been served in accordance with the laws of this State or notified in accordance with Section 108 or who have submitted to the jurisdiction of the court, and who have been given an opportunity to be heard. As to those persons, the determination is conclusive as to all decided issues of law and fact. . . .

SECTION 110. COMMUNICATION BETWEEN COURTS

(a) A court of this State may communicate with a court in another State concerning a proceeding arising under this [Act]. . . .

(d) . . . [A] record must be made of a communication under this section. The parties must be informed promptly of the communication and granted access to the record.

[ARTICLE] 2. JURISDICTION

SECTION 201. INITIAL CHILD-CUSTODY JURISDICTION

(a) . . . [A] court of this State has jurisdiction to make an initial child-custody determination only if:

(1) this State is the home State of the child on the date of the commencement of the proceeding, or was the home State of the child within six months before the commencement of the proceeding and the child is absent from this State but a parent or person acting as a parent continues to live in this State;

(2) a court of another State does not have jurisdiction under paragraph (1), or a court of the home State of the child has declined to exercise jurisdiction on the ground that this State is the more appropriate forum under Section 207 or 208, and:

(A) the child and the child's parents, or the child and at least one parent or a person acting as a parent, have a significant connection with this State other than mere physical presence; and

(B) substantial evidence is available in this State concerning the child's care, protection, training, and personal relationships;

(3) all courts having jurisdiction under paragraph (1) or (2) have declined to exercise jurisdiction on the ground that a court of this State is the more appropriate forum to determine the custody of the child under Section 207 or 208. . . .

(c) Physical presence of, or personal jurisdiction over, a party or a child is not necessary or sufficient to make a child-custody determination.

SECTION 202. EXCLUSIVE, CONTINUING JURISDICTION

(a) . . . [A] court of this State which has made a child-custody determination consistent with Section 201 or 203 has exclusive, continuing jurisdiction over the determination until:

(1) a court of this State determines that neither the child, nor the child and one parent, nor the child and a person acting as a parent have a significant connection with this State and that substantial evidence is no longer available in this State concerning the child's care, protection, training, and personal relationships; or

(2) a court of this State or a court of another State determines that the child, the child's parents, and any person acting as a parent do not presently reside in this State.

(b) A court of this State which has made a child-custody determination and does not have exclusive, continuing jurisdiction under this section may modify that determination only if it has jurisdiction to make an initial determination under Section 201.

SECTION 203. JURISDICTION TO MODIFY DETERMINATION

. . . [A] court of this State may not modify a child-custody determination made by a court of another State unless a court of this State has jurisdiction to make an initial determination under Section 201(a)(1) or (2) and:

(1) the court of the other State determines it no longer has exclusive, continuing jurisdiction under Section 202 or that a court of this State would be a more convenient forum under Section 207; or

(2) a court of this State or a court of the other State determines that the child, the child's parents, and any person acting as a parent do not presently reside in the other State.

SECTION 206. SIMULTANEOUS PROCEEDINGS

(a) . . . [A] court of this State may not exercise its jurisdiction under this [article] if, at the time of the commencement of the proceeding, a proceeding concerning the custody of the child has been commenced in a court of another State having jurisdiction substantially in conformity with this [Act], unless the proceeding has been terminated or is stayed by the court of the other State because a court of this State is a more convenient forum under Section 207. . . .

SECTION 207. INCONVENIENT FORUM

(a) A court of this State which has jurisdiction under this [Act] to make a child-custody determination may decline to exercise its jurisdiction at any time if it determines that it is an inconvenient forum under the circumstances and that a court of another State is a more appropriate forum. The issue of inconvenient forum may be raised upon motion of a party, the court's own motion, or request of another court.

(b) Before determining whether it is an inconvenient forum, a court of this State shall consider whether it is appropriate for a court of another State to exercise jurisdiction. For this purpose, the court shall . . . consider all relevant factors, including:

(1) whether domestic violence has occurred and is likely to continue in the future and which State could best protect the parties and the child;

(2) the length of time the child has resided outside this State;

(3) the distance between the court in this State and the court in the State that would assume jurisdiction;

(4) the relative financial circumstances of the parties;

(5) any agreement of the parties as to which State should assume jurisdiction;

(6) the nature and location of the evidence required to resolve the pending litigation, including testimony of the child;

(7) the ability of the court of each State to decide the issue expeditiously and the procedures necessary to present the evidence; and

(8) the familiarity of the court of each State with the facts and issues in the pending litigation. . . .

SECTION 208. JURISDICTION DECLINED BY REASON OF CONDUCT

(a) [I]f a court of this State has jurisdiction under this [Act] because a person seeking to invoke its jurisdiction has engaged in unjustifiable conduct, the court shall decline to exercise its jurisdiction unless:

(1) the parents and all persons acting as parents have acquiesced in the exercise of jurisdiction;

(2) a court of the State otherwise having jurisdiction under Sections 201 through 203 determines that this State is a more appropriate forum under Section 207; or

(3) no court of any other State would have jurisdiction under the criteria specified in Sections 201 through 203.

Comment

. . . Most of the jurisdictional problems generated by abducting parents should be solved by the prioritization of home State in Section 201; the exclusive, continuing jurisdiction provisions of Section 202; and the ban on modification in Section 203. For example, if a parent takes the child from the home State and seeks an original custody determination elsewhere, the stay-at-home parent has six months to file a custody petition under the extended home state jurisdictional provision of Section 201, which will ensure that the case is retained in the home State. . . .

[ARTICLE] 3. ENFORCEMENT. . . .

SECTION 303. DUTY TO ENFORCE

(a) A court of this State shall recognize and enforce a child-custody determination of a court of another State if the latter court exercised jurisdiction in substantial conformity with this [Act]. . . .

SECTION 312. COSTS, FEES, AND EXPENSES

(a) The court shall award the prevailing party . . . necessary and reasonable expenses incurred by or on behalf of the party, including costs, communication expenses, attorney's fees, investigative fees, expenses for witnesses, travel expenses, and child care during the course of the proceedings, unless the party from whom fees or expenses are sought establishes that the award would be clearly inappropriate.

CLIENT EXERCISE 3

You work in a medium-sized law firm, and you are one of the two attorneys in the firm that handles divorce cases. Sandra comes to your office one day and says she wants to hire you to represent her in a divorce, because she heard good things about your work.

Sandra is 30 years old. She married a man named Preston nine years ago. She worked as a nurse until six years ago, when she and Preston decided to have a child. He was in medical school at the time. Their child, Lamar, recently turned five. Sandra is pursuing the divorce, against the wishes of Preston, because she feels entirely estranged from him. During the past four years, Preston has been doing his medical residency and has rarely been at home, because of the extraordinary demands of the program. When he has been at home, he has given nearly all his attention when not sleeping to Lamar and has shown little interest in her. Whenever she has expressed unhappiness about this, he has accused her of being selfish and unsupportive, insisting that he was working so hard for the good of the family and for the good of his future patients, and that it was important for his son to bond with him. Sandra does not believe Preston has been unfaithful, but rather that Preston is simply so completely absorbed by his career that he has no interest in or energy for intimacy. As a result, they have drifted apart emotionally, and Sandra says she is lonely and not sure she still loves Preston. She and Lamar have been spending a lot of time with Lamar's gymnastics teacher, Grant, and his six-year-old son, Danny. Sandra says she feels closer to Grant than to Preston and thinks she might like to pursue a romantic relationship with Grant. Grant is 35 and widowed, and the two boys have become great friends.

You run a conflicts check in your firm's client database and discover that a week earlier Preston met with the other divorce attorney in your firm for a 30-minute free consultation. You ask your colleague if she discussed the marital situation with Preston. She says that she did, but that Preston did not reveal anything that his wife would not already know and mostly asked general questions about divorce law. You call several other local divorce attorneys to see if they might be able to represent Sandra, but they all say that Preston has also been in for a consultation with them. You stop making calls when you run out of people whom you respect enough to recommend.

You ask Sandra to find out if Preston has retained a lawyer. She reports back that a "barracuda" lawyer named Shirley Strike is representing him. You give Ms. Strike a call, and she tells you that Preston a) does not want a divorce and will seek court orders aimed at forcing reconciliation efforts; b) will not agree to waive any conflict of interest problem; c) when his residency ends in six months, will open his own medical practice serving the indigent, with hours limited to the time (9-4, Monday-Friday) that Lamar will be in school, so that he can assume primary responsibility for care of his son; d) believes that because he is African American and Lamar's skin color is closer to his than to that of his Korean-American mother, it is better for Lamar to be primarily in his father's custody; and e) is willing to support Sandra financially for one year while she gets retraining so she can resume her nursing career.

You estimate that the couple has only about $50,000 in accumulated assets, including a BMW that Preston bought ten years ago (now worth $6,000) and a Toyota 4Runner that Preston got for Sandra just before Lamar was born (now worth $16,000) and just finished paying for. The other $28,000 comprises household belongings (furniture, electronics, jewelry Preston has given to Sandra) and $10,000 in bank accounts, all accumulated during the marriage except for Sandra's $8,000 engagement ring. They have been renting a two-bedroom apartment. Preston's residency salary is $50,000/year. Doctors with his training on average have a salary of $200,000/year in their first position after residency, if they work in a hospital or other large, for-profit medical facility. With a year of retraining, Sandra could return to nursing. If she stays where the family now lives, she could expect to earn around $60,000/year as a nurse. But if they divorce, Sandra would have to choose whether to stay where she is; move to wherever Preston gets his first post-residency position, if that is in a different city; or move back to the small town 300 miles away where she grew up, to be near her family. Back home she likely would make only $40,000 per year as a nurse.

A. SUBSTANTIVE QUESTIONS

1) On what grounds could Sandra petition for divorce? What defenses, if any, could Preston assert in an effort to have the court deny the petition?
2) When would it be "safe" for Sandra to become intimate with Grant?
3) What could Sandra expect to receive in property and/or alimony if she petitions for divorce now?
4) If custody of Lamar is contested, what should the court order if the parents will remain where they have been living? If Preston wants to take a post-residency position a thousand miles away? If Preston stays in that town but Sandra wants to return to her home town?
5) If Sandra were awarded primary custody of Lamar, will she still be expected to work? If she does return to nursing, will the size of her salary influence how much child support she receives from Preston? If she refuses to work and claims that Lamar needs her full attention, what reaction would a court likely have to that?
6) If Preston were awarded primary custody of Lamar, would Sandra have to pay him child support? Does it matter to child support whether they have joint legal custody? What if they share joint physical custody?

B. ETHICAL QUESTIONS

1) It is not uncommon nor inappropriate for someone contemplating divorce to meet with two or three attorneys for a consultation before choosing one to represent him. An especially devious person, however, might try to prevent his spouse from hiring a decent attorney by arranging such a consultation with every well-regarded attorney in town, in the expectation that they will all be "conflicted out." It appears that is what Preston has done. Is that stratagem likely to succeed? Are you precluded from representing Sandra in this matter? Should Ms. Strike be urging Preston to waive any conflict of interest problem?
2) Given that Sandra does not now have access to much money for your retainer, can you agree to represent her on a contingency fee basis—for example, that one third of any property and/or alimony award she receives will go to you?
3) If you do counsel Sandra, should you urge her to attempt a reconciliation?

As to the conflicts problem, in addition to the ethical rules set out in Client Exercise 1 above, consider the following materials:

RULE 1.18 DUTIES TO PROSPECTIVE CLIENT

(a) A person who discusses with a lawyer the possibility of forming a client-lawyer relationship with respect to a matter is a prospective client.

(b) Even when no client-lawyer relationship ensues, a lawyer who has had discussions with a prospective client shall not use or reveal information learned in the consultation, except as Rule 1.9 would permit with respect to information of a former client.

(c) A lawyer subject to paragraph (b) shall not represent a client with interests materially adverse to those of a prospective client in the same or a substantially related matter if the lawyer received information from the prospective client that could be significantly harmful to that person in the matter, except as provided in paragraph (d). If a lawyer is disqualified from representation under this paragraph, no lawyer in a firm with which that lawyer is associated may knowingly undertake or continue representation in such a matter, except as provided in paragraph (d).

(d) When the lawyer has received disqualifying information as defined in paragraph (c), representation is permissible if:

(1) both the affected client and the prospective client have given informed consent, confirmed in writing, or

(2) the lawyer who received the information took reasonable measures to avoid exposure to more disqualifying information than was reasonably necessary to determine whether to represent the prospective client; and

(i) the disqualified lawyer is timely screened from any participation in the matter and is apportioned no part of the fee therefrom; and

(ii) written notice is promptly given to the prospective client.

RULE 1.9 DUTIES TO FORMER CLIENTS

. . . c) A lawyer who has formerly represented a client in a matter or whose present or former firm has formerly represented a client in a matter shall not thereafter:

(1) use information relating to the representation to the disadvantage of the former client except . . . when the information has become generally known; or

(2) reveal information relating to the representation. . . .

In re Marriage of Newton

955 N.E.2d 572 (Ill. App. Ct. 2011)

Justice PUCINSKI delivered the judgment of the court, with opinion.

. . . David . . . and . . . Hadley Newton were divorced . . . March 8, 2010. In the underlying divorce proceedings, David filed an emergency motion to disqualify Hadley's attorney, Grund, and the law firm of Grund & Leavitt . . . , due to Grund's former representation of David in the same proceeding. . . . David testified that he met alone with Grund in Grund's office for between 1½ and 2 hours. They discussed information and issues related to his marriage and impending divorce from Hadley, including issues regarding the children and his financial situation, and Grund took notes.

Hadley . . . learned that there was a conflict with Grund representing her because Grund himself told her there was a conflict when she came in to see him. However, he entered into a retainer agreement with her and represented her. . . . Grund and Leavitt filed a petition for attorney fees on behalf of Hadley . . . , seeking prospective and interim fees and costs from David in the amount of $250,000. . . .

Grund testified that he told David that representation would not begin until David actually signed a contract, that no attorney-client privilege would attach during their meeting, and that David should not disclose anything to Grund that could not appear in answers to interrogatories or in the public record. Grund testified that David "volunteered some information," but Grund did not recall anything specifically. Grund denied taking any notes. Grund believed David never intended to actually hire him. Grund also denied giving David a business card with his private cellular telephone number, but was impeached by the production by David of Grund's business card with his cellular telephone number written on the back of the card. In rebuttal, David testified that Grund assured him everything they discussed was confidential.

On March 3, 2009, the circuit court entered its memorandum opinion and order finding that there was an attorney-client relationship between David and Grund and disqualifying Grund and Leavitt from representing Hadley. . . . [T]he court concluded that it could not award attorney fees . . . because of counsel's disqualification. Grund and Leavitt argued strenuously for fees . . . , and the court offered to find them in contempt so that they could immediately appeal. The court asked counsel to step away from the bench, but counsel did not do so, and the court found them in contempt. . . .

Rule 1.9(a) of the Illinois Rules of Professional Conduct provides: . . .

(a) A lawyer who has formerly represented a client in a matter shall not thereafter:

(1) represent another person in the same or a substantially related matter in which that person's interests are materially adverse to the interests of the former client, unless the former client consents after disclosure; or

(2) use information relating to the representation to the disadvantage of the former client, unless:

(A) such use is permitted by Rule 1.6; or

(B) the information has become generally known.

We find the circuit court's determination correct. . . . "An attorney/client relationship can be created at the initial interview between the prospective client and the attorney, and it is possible that confidential information passed during the interview sufficient to disqualify the attorney from representing the opposing party in related litigation." "[T]he relationship can come into being during the initial contact between the layperson and the professional and appears to hinge on ' "the client's belief that he is consulting a lawyer in that capacity and his manifested intention to seek professional legal advice."' " . . . David's consultation with Grund gave rise to an attorney-client relationship.

Furthermore, since David and Hadley were parties in the identical case, there was clearly a substantial relationship between Grund's representation of David and Grund's representation of Hadley regarding their divorce. " 'Once a substantial relationship is found between the prior and present representations, it is irrebuttably presumed that confidential information was disclosed in the earlier representation.' " Thus, . . . Grund was prohibited by Rule 1.9 from representing Hadley. . . .

Section 508(a) of the Act provides: "The court . . . may order any party to pay a reasonable amount for his own or the other party's costs and attorney's fees. . . . Section 508(c)(3) specifically conditions the enforceability of a fee agreement on meeting applicable court rules: "(3) The determination of reasonable attorney's fees and costs either under . . . subsection (a), is within the sound discretion of the trial court. . . . [I]f the court finds that the former client and the filing counsel, pursuant to their written engagement agreement, *entered into a contract which meets applicable requirements of court rules* and addresses all material terms, then the contract shall be enforceable. . . ." Here, Grund and Leavitt's contract with Hadley did not meet the applicable requirements of our court rules, as it violated Rule 1.9, and therefore the contract was unenforceable under section 508 of the Act. . . . [In] fact . . . Grund and Leavitt's fee agreement with Hadley is void for violation of Rule of Professional Conduct 1.9. . . . While Illinois courts strongly favor the freedom of contract, a court will declare a contract void if it contravenes the public policy of the state. . . . Where attorney conduct is at issue, we look to the Supreme Court Rules for expressions of public policy. . . . Rule 1.9 is a clear prohibition on representing a party with a conflicting interest. Thus, the contract was void *ab initio.*

Furthermore, . . . the judicial decisions of our state are clear and long standing that attorney fees will not be allowed if counsel is disqualified due to a conflict of interest. . . . Precedent holds that, "[g]enerally, an attorney may not receive fees after representing adverse, conflicting, and antagonistic interests in the same litigation." King v. King, 52 Ill. App. 3d 749 (1977) . . . involved a divorce case where an attorney represented one spouse after he initially consulted with the other spouse, just as in this case. . . . In *King*, the husband visited the law office of the attorney to discuss his marital problems and the possibility of divorce. He consulted with the attorney for less than one-half hour and did not retain him. The wife filed a complaint for separate maintenance and retained the attorney who previously consulted with her husband. The husband filed a motion to exclude the attorney, but the trial court denied it. The court entered a decree of separate maintenance and ordered the husband to pay the wife's attorney fees in the amount of $6,000, and the husband appealed. The appellate court found that an attorney-client relationship existed between the attorney and the husband and that it was improper for the attorney to then undertake the representation of the wife. The court reversed the award of attorney fees. The court held that "[t]he rule [against representing conflicting interests] applies even though the attorney acquired no knowledge which could operate to the client's disadvantage," and "[i]t makes no difference that the client offered no compensation and the attorney neither made nor expected to make any charge for his services." Further, the motives or intentions of the attorney are irrelevant. . . . Where the ethical rules have been violated . . . , counsel's purported good faith is irrelevant. . . .

Finally, Grund and Leavitt argue . . . to "level the playing field" for economically disadvantaged spouses to obtain counsel of their choosing despite intimidation tactics of wealthier spouses. However, counsel cannot simply flout the ethical rules. . . . [A]mended Supreme Court Rules of Professional Conduct, though not in effect at the time of Grund's attorney-client relationship with David, now help resolve the problem suggested by Grund and Leavitt. . . . Under Rule 1.18, a lawyer who has had discussions with a prospective client shall not represent a client with interests materially adverse to those of a prospective client in the same or a substantially related matter if the lawyer received information from the prospective client that could be significantly harmful to that person in the matter, except if:

> (1) both the affected client and the prospective client have given informed consent, or
>
> (2) the lawyer who received the information took reasonable measures to avoid exposure to more disqualifying information than was reasonably necessary to determine whether to represent the prospective client; and that lawyer is timely screened from any participation in the matter and is apportioned no part of the fee therefrom.

Committee comment 5 to Rule 1.18 provides how this result can be achieved:

> (5) A lawyer may condition conversations with a prospective client on the person's informed consent that no information disclosed during the consultation will prohibit the lawyer from representing a different client in the matter.

This blueprint for representing a spouse after having an initial consultation with the other spouse should discourage the tactical "conflicting out" of divorce attorneys by wealthier spouses that Grund and Leavitt suggest is a pervasive practice in the area of divorce law.

We emphasize that the Rules of Professional Conduct recognize that the practice of law is a public trust and lawyers are the trustees of the judicial system. . . . "[A]nything which might tend to debase the learned professions is at war with the public interest and is therefore contrary to public policy." . . . [I]t is inexplicable that Hadley made it past screening and that Grund agreed to represent her. . . .

We note the well-established rule that where a " 'refusal to comply with a trial court's order constitutes a good-faith effort to secure an interpretation of [an issue without direct precedent], it is appropriate to vacate a contempt citation on appeal.' " However, under the facts of this case, we find that Grund and Leavitt's refusal to comply with the circuit court's order denying them fees did not constitute a good-faith effort to secure an interpretation without direct precedent. Rule 1.9 . . . is clear that representing clients with conflicts of interest is prohibited. Precedent is clear that fees for such prohibited representation are barred. . . . We find that the purging provision which would allow Grund and Leavitt an opportunity to purge the contempt by paying the $100 fine was well within the court's discretion . . . and was remarkably restrained, given the entire record of this case.

American Academy of Matrimonial Lawyers, Bounds of Advocacy

2.8 An attorney should discourage the client from interfering in the spouse's effort to obtain effective representation.

Comment

Clients who file or anticipate the filing of a divorce proceeding occasionally telephone or interview numerous attorneys as a means of denying their spouse access to effective representation. The attorney should discourage such practices, and should not assist the client, for example, by responding to the client's request for a list of matrimonial lawyers, if improper motives are suspected. When the client has already contacted other lawyers for the purpose of disqualifying them, the client's attorney should attempt to persuade the client to waive any conflict so created.

7. Professional Cooperation and the Administration of Justice
. . . Allowing the adverse emotional climate to infect the relations between the attorneys and parties inevitably harms everyone, including the clients, their children and other family members. . . . Combative, discourteous, abrasive, "hard ball" conduct by matrimonial lawyers is inconsistent with both their obligation to effectively represent their clients and their role as problem-solvers. . . . In fact, candor, courtesy and cooperation: (1) facilitate faster, less costly and mutually-accepted resolution of disputes; (2) reduce stress for lawyers, staff and clients; (3) reduce waste of judicial time; and (4) generate respect for the court system, the individual attorney and the profession as a whole.

7.1 An attorney should strive to lower the emotional level of marital disputes by treating counsel and the parties with respect.

Comment

Some clients expect and want the matrimonial lawyer to reflect the highly emotional, vengeful relationship between the spouses. The attorney should explain to the client that discourteous or uncivil conduct is inappropriate and counterproductive, that measures of respect are consistent with competent and ethical representation of the client, and that it is unprofessional for the attorney to act otherwise.

With respect to fees, there is this guidance:

Model Rule of Professional Conduct 1.5

(a) A lawyer shall not make an agreement for, charge, or collect an unreasonable fee or an unreasonable amount for expenses. The factors to be considered in determining the reasonableness of a fee include the following:

(1) the time and labor required, the novelty and difficulty of the questions involved, and the skill requisite to perform the legal service properly;

(2) the likelihood, if apparent to the client, that the acceptance of the particular employment will preclude other employment by the lawyer;

(3) the fee customarily charged in the locality for similar legal services;

(4) the amount involved and the results obtained;

(5) the time limitations imposed by the client or by the circumstances;

(6) the nature and length of the professional relationship with the client;

(7) the experience, reputation, and ability of the lawyer or lawyers performing the services; and

(8) whether the fee is fixed or contingent. . . .

(c) A fee may be contingent on the outcome of the matter for which the service is rendered, except in a matter in which a contingent fee is prohibited by paragraph (d) or other law. A contingent fee agreement shall be in a writing signed by the client and shall state the method by which the fee is to be determined, including the percentage or percentages that shall accrue to the lawyer in the event of settlement, trial or appeal. . . .

(d) A lawyer shall not enter into an arrangement for, charge, or collect:

(1) any fee in a domestic relations matter, the payment or amount of which is contingent upon the securing of a divorce or upon the amount of alimony or support, or property settlement in lieu thereof. . . .

American Academy of Matrimonial Lawyers, Bounds of Advocacy

4.4 An attorney's fee should be reasonable, based on appropriate factors, including those listed in RPC 1.5(a).

Comment

. . . Although the starting point in determining a reasonable fee is often the lawyer's hourly rate multiplied by the hours spent on the case, a number of other factors may be relevant in determining an appropriate fee in a particular representation. . . . Clients, as consumers, should be able to negotiate fee agreements that best suit their needs and circumstances. In addition to fees based solely on hourly rate, a fee agreement may provide for a contingent fee, or one based on "value," a specified result, or some combination of factors. No single factor is appropriate in all family law cases. . . .

Some jurisdictions have prohibited fees in domestic relations cases that were in any way based on the results obtained in the case, holding that such fees constituted contingent fees. Courts in other jurisdictions have held that the fact that an hourly fee is enhanced on the basis of results obtained does not necessarily make it a contingent fee [citing decisions in Maryland and Illinois]. . . .

A fee based on the attorney's usual hourly rate, but enhanced by achieving a specified result, may be justified in a given case by any combination of the following circumstances: the complexity of the case; the shortness of the time between the attorney's retention and impending proceedings; the difficult, aggressive nature of the opposing party and counsel; a particular attorney's unique ability to settle a case quickly and avoid lengthy and acrimonious trial proceedings; and a substantial risk that the representation will be unsuccessful due to unfavorable factual or legal context. A fee based in part on results obtained is permissible under this Goal so long as the specified "result" does not include obtaining a divorce, custody or visitation provisions, or the amount of alimony or child support awarded, and if the fee is: (1) reasonable under the circumstances; (2) in addition to the attorney's usual hourly rate; (3) based on factors clearly stated in writing and provided to the client at the outset of the agreement; and (4) agreed to in writing by the client at the outset of the representation after full consultation and an opportunity to seek independent legal advice.

4.5 An attorney should not charge a fee the payment or amount of which is contingent upon: (i) obtaining a divorce; (ii) custody or visitation provisions; or (iii) the amount of alimony or child support awarded. An attorney may charge a contingent fee for all other matters. . . .

Comment

. . . Although attorneys and informed clients are generally able to determine that a contingent fee arrangement is more beneficial to the client than one based, for example, on an hourly rate, there has long been a total ban on contingent fees in domestic relations cases. The primary basis for the prohibition in divorce cases is that the arrangement would "put strong economic pressure on the lawyer to assure that reconciliation did not occur." In addition, the rationale that contingent fee arrangements are necessary in other civil cases to enable indigent litigants to obtain counsel is believed not to be applicable in divorce cases. The spouse in possession of marital assets will usually have little difficulty in obtaining representation, while the other spouse is assumed to be protected by the court's authority to compel the spouse with the greater assets to pay attorney's fees.

A third basis for the ban on contingent fees is that it may "disrupt the pattern of wealth distribution that the court intended in making the award," unless the existence of the contingent fee is made known to the court in advance. And, to the extent that the contingent fee applies to the amount of a property settlement and not to support or alimony, the attorney may be tempted to advocate more for the former, even if not in the best interests of the client and any children.

At the same time, however, the complete ban on contingent fees at all stages of domestic relations cases, . . . is unsupported by the above policies. Such a ban also undermines the freedom of attorneys and informed clients to enter into fee arrangements that best suit the nature of particular cases and the interests of both. . . . For example, although courts may have the power to compel the spouse with the greatest assets to pay attorney's fees, they often do not do so. Therefore, if the client is unlikely to pay the attorney's fee unless the client receives a substantial award, the client's ability to obtain quality legal representation may be dependent upon the availability of a contingent fee agreement.

In addition, the amount of effort involved in a difficult case might result in an hourly fee that the client could only afford if he or she won. And yet, it is in just such a case that the client would need an experienced attorney, who would be unlikely to undertake a risky case, solely on the basis of the attorney's hourly rate. At the same time, the client might be reluctant to commit to the attorney's hourly rate in a complex and costly case, without a way of assuring there will be adequate funds from which to pay the fee. . . . For these reasons, this Goal limits the prohibition of contingent fees to those aspects of divorce cases supported by the historic policy bases. . . . Jurisdictions that completely ban all contingent fees should be urged to adopt a rule similar to this Goal.

Finally, regarding non-legal personal advice or encouragement:

Model Rule of Professional Conduct 2.1 ("In rendering advice, a lawyer may refer not only to law but to other considerations such as moral, economic, social and political factors, that may be relevant to the client's situation.").

American Academy of Matrimonial Lawyers, Bounds of Advocacy

1.2 An attorney should advise the client of the emotional and economic impact of divorce and explore the feasibility of reconciliation.

Comment

The divorce process can exact a heavy economic and emotional toll. . . . An attorney should discuss reconciliation and whether the client has considered marriage counseling or therapy. If the client exhibits uncertainty or ambivalence, the lawyer should assist in obtaining help. A lawyer's role in family matters is to act as a counselor and advisor as well as an advocate. . . . Although few attorneys are qualified to do psychological counseling, a discussion of the emotional and monetary repercussions of divorce is appropriate. . . . It is important, however, for the attorney to be mindful that a "breathing spell" afforded by counseling could harm the client's interests. The other spouse may take advantage of the delay for financial or other advantage. The lawyer should warn the client of these risks and recommend precautions to protect the client in the interim.

6.1 An attorney representing a parent should consider the welfare of, and seek to minimize the adverse impact of the divorce on, the minor children.

Comment

. . . Matrimonial lawyers should counsel parties to examine their wishes in light of the needs and interests of the children and the relationship to other family members. . . . Parents owe a continuing fiduciary duty toward each other, as well as toward their children, to serve their children's best interests. In many instances, parents should subordinate their own interests to those of their children. . . .

C. PRACTICAL QUESTIONS

1) Assuming any attempts at reconciliation fail, what are the options for getting this couple through the divorce without a court battle? What role would you play in any form of alternative dispute resolution (ADR)?
2) What other professionals are likely to get involved in the divorce, if litigation occurs or if the parties attempt some form of ADR ?
3) To what extent can Sandra insulate Lamar from the legal proceedings? Would you have any obligation as Sandra's lawyer to protect Lamar's well being as well?

Alternative Dispute Resolution and Other Professionals

Jana B. Singer, Dispute Resolution and the Postdivorce Family: Implications of a Paradigm Shift

47 Fam. Ct. Rev. 363 (2009)

Over the past two decades, there has been a paradigm shift in the way the legal system handles most family disputes—particularly disputes involving children. This paradigm shift has replaced the law-oriented and judge-focused adversary model with a more collaborative, interdisciplinary, and forward-looking family dispute resolution regime. It . . . [reflects] a profound skepticism about the value of traditional adversary procedures . . . for resolving disputes involving children. . . . [C]hildren's adjustment to divorce and separation depends significantly on their parents' behavior during and after the separation process: the higher the levels of parental conflict to which children are exposed, the more negative the effects of family dissolution. . . . Family courts across the country . . . have adopted an array of nonadversary dispute resolution mechanisms designed to avoid adjudication of family cases. . . .

A second element of the paradigm shift in family dispute resolution is the belief that most family disputes are not discrete legal events, but ongoing social and emotional processes. . . . Thus recharacterized, family disputes call *not* for zealous legal approaches, but for . . . nonlegal professionals. . . . [J]udges no longer function primarily as fault finders or rights adjudicators, but rather as ongoing conflict managers . . . by attempting to understand and address underlying family dynamics and by using judicial authority "to motivate individuals to accept needed services and to monitor their compliance and progress." . . . [F]amily courts have adopted systems that deemphasize third-party dispute resolution in favor of capacity-building processes that seek to empower families to resolve their own conflicts. Consistent with this philosophy, jurisdictions across the country have instituted mandatory divorce-related parenting education and other programs designed to enhance litigants' communication and problem-solving skills. . . . More recently, a number of family courts have added parenting coordinators to their staffs; these quasi-judicial officials assist high-conflict families to develop concrete parenting plans and to resolve ongoing parenting disputes that arise under these plans. . . .

American Academy of Matrimonial Lawyers, Bounds of Advocacy

1.5 An attorney should attempt to resolve matrimonial disputes by agreement and should consider alternative means of achieving resolution.

Comment

. . . Matrimonial law is not a matter of winning or losing. At its best, matrimonial law should result in disputes being resolved fairly for all parties, including children. Major tasks of the matrimonial lawyer include helping the client develop realistic objectives and attempting to attain them with the least injury to the family. The vast majority of cases should be resolved by lawyers negotiating settlements on behalf of their clients.

Parties are more likely to abide by their own promises than by an outcome imposed on them by a court. When resolution requires complex trade-offs, the parties may be better able than the court to forge a resolution that addresses their individual values and needs. An agreement that meets the reasonable objectives of the parties maximizes their autonomy and their own priorities. A court-imposed resolution may, instead, maximize legal principles that may seem arbitrary or unfair within the context of the parties' family. An agreement may establish a positive tone for continuing post-divorce family relations by avoiding the animosity and pain of court battles. It may also be less costly financially than a litigated outcome. . . . These issues should be discussed with the client. . . . The matrimonial lawyer's task includes informing the client about the availability and nature of mediation or other alternatives to traditional negotiation or litigation.

5.2 An attorney should advise the client of the potential effect of the client's conduct on a child custody dispute.

Comment

. . . Predivorce planning is an ideal opportunity to advise the client on ways to make the divorce transition easier for the children. For example, the lawyer might describe ways for the parents in concert to inform the children of the divorce and to reassure the children that both parents will always be there for them. The lawyer might describe programs available in the client's community to aid both parents and children in adjusting to divorce. Most important, predivorce planning is an opportunity to orient the client toward consideration of the children's needs first and toward the desirability of working out a cooperative parenting plan. The lawyer should describe how mediation of child custody disputes might assist in effecting a cooperative parenting plan. It is appropriate to tell the client that children suffer from parental conflict and that a child custody dispute involving the searching inquiry of a custody evaluation and rigors of a trial is likely to be harmful to every member of the family.

6.1 An attorney representing a parent should consider the welfare of, and seek to minimize the adverse impact of the divorce on, the minor children.

Comment

Matrimonial lawyers and parents alike should collaboratively seek parenting arrangements that eliminate fractious contact between parents, minimize transition or transportation difficulties and preserve stability for the children. . . . If the parents are in conflict and disagree about custody and other parenting issues, the attorney should consider, with the cooperation of the other parent's attorney, sending the parties to a neutral mental health professional who is a family therapist. The goal of this referral is to resolve their disputes through counseling with the help of that mental health professional. The referring agreement should include confidentiality for all contacts with the therapist and exclusion of that therapist as a witness in the divorce case. . . . The attorney should discourage the client and refuse to participate in multiple psychological evaluations of children for the purpose of finding an expert who will testify in their favor. Repeated psychological evaluations of children are contrary to the children's best interest. . . .

The attorney should warn the client against leaving papers from the attorney out where children can read them and to avoid talking about the case when children can overhear.

7.1 An attorney should strive to lower the emotional level of marital disputes by treating counsel and the parties with respect.

Comment

. . . Ideally, the relationship between counsel is that of colleagues using constructive problem-solving techniques to settle their respective clients' disputes consistent with the realistic objectives of each client. Examples of appropriate measures of respect include: cooperating with voluntary or court-mandated mediation; meeting with opposing counsel to reduce issues and facilitate settlement. . . .

John Lande & Gregg Herman, Fitting the Forum to the Family Fuss

42 Fam. Ct. Rev. 280 (2004)

Not long ago, divorce lawyers and clients had few alternatives available to negotiate a settlement. Some divorcing parties would negotiate an agreement and complete the legal process of divorce without hiring any professionals. Others would negotiate an agreement themselves, and one of them would hire a lawyer to write the agreement and process the divorce papers in court. . . . When both spouses hired lawyers, they typically used a process that Marc Galanter called "litigotiation," referring to the strategic pursuit of settlement by using the court process. . . . In typical litigotiation, lawyers try to build strong cases for trial and often engage in a ritual charade of being reluctant to negotiate out of fear of losing advantage by appearing weak. Most cases eventually do settle, but this process often adds unnecessary costs and harms family members. . . .

In recent decades, many parties, lawyers, and courts have used mediation to focus explicitly on negotiation. In mediation, a neutral third-party helps parties negotiate without representing either party or the authority to impose a decision. States have enacted statutes authorizing or requiring courts to order parties to mediate as a condition to get a court hearing, particularly in cases involving child custody or visitation disputes. In many places, mediation has become the most common procedure for resolving family disputes in litigation.

Starting in the 1990s, family lawyers and other professionals . . . developed collaborative law as an alternative to traditional litigotiation and mediation. . . . In collaborative law, both parties hire lawyers who focus exclusively on negotiation from the outset of the case. Under a written agreement, the lawyers and parties explicitly commit to avoid litigation by providing that the lawyers are disqualified from representing parties in litigation and must withdraw if either party chooses to litigate or even threatens to litigate. . . . A much smaller movement has developed a "cooperative law" procedure, which is . . . similar to collaborative law except that it does not use a disqualification agreement. . . . [C]ooperative law assumes that in some cases, parties may need to threaten litigation to motivate the other side to negotiate appropriately. . . .

The modern mediation movement dates back several decades and has benefited from intensive work . . . to develop mediation theory and practice. . . . Numerous organizations have developed . . . standards of conduct for mediation. . . . Moreover, many states and mediation programs have developed credentialing systems. . . . The collaborative and cooperative law fields are much newer, and there has been much less development. . . . Research on collaborative law is just beginning. In just the past few years, local collaborative law groups have been developing membership criteria and procedures. . . . The cooperative law field has been developed the least because it is much smaller, with practitioners in only a handful of communities. . . .

MEDIATION

In mediation, neutral professionals, whose sole goal is to impartially promote negotiation benefiting both parties, manage the negotiation process. . . . [T]he parties are responsible for making substantive decisions in their case rather than the professionals that they hire or the courts. Mediation often uses an interest-based . . . approach to negotiation in which the parties explicitly identify their interests and select options maximizing the interests of both parties. Whether the parties have lawyers and whether lawyers attend mediation varies widely based on local culture. Similarly, mediation processes vary in how much, if at all, the negotiation focuses on legal issues and rules and possible court outcomes. This may vary based on the disciplinary background of the mediator (e.g., if the mediator is trained as a lawyer or mental health professional), whether lawyers participate in the mediation, the preferences of the parties, and local norms. The discussion may focus on emotional and therapeutic issues, especially if the mediator is a mental health professional. Mediators often refer clients to get professional help from others such as lawyers, mental health professionals, appraisers, and financial experts; these professionals can attend mediation if desired. . . .

COLLABORATIVE LAW

Collaborative law provides each side with a lawyer who can provide legal advice and advocacy that mediators cannot offer. As advocates, collaborative lawyers are not required to be neutral and thus can strongly present clients' interests and positions . . . [but] the disqualification agreement and collaborative law culture create incentives to satisfy their clients' interests through negotiation. . . . Although some believe that zealous advocacy requires lawyers to seek every possible partisan advantage for their clients, lawyers often best serve their clients' interests by negotiating agreements that satisfy important interests of the other parties. This is especially true in divorce cases involving minor children because both parties have strong interests in future cooperation. If either party seeks to maximize its gain at the expense of the other party, such action can stimulate a spiral of retaliatory actions and undermine the potential for cooperation. . . . Lawyers are committed to "keep the process honest, respectful, and productive on both sides." The parties are expected to be respectful, provide full disclosure of all relevant information, and address each other's legitimate needs. . . . Collaborative law theory provides that each lawyer is responsible for moving parties from artificial bargaining positions to focus on their real needs and interests to seek "win-win" solutions. . . . The collaborative law process may include other professionals such as coaches, who are mental health professionals hired by each client to help identify and change unproductive communication patterns and to educate clients about the divorce process and coparenting. . . . Collaborative law clients may also hire joint experts such as accountants, appraisers, and child development specialists. . . .

Proponents say that lawyers are so used to litigating that at the first sign of disagreement, many lawyers would quickly threaten legal action if not precluded from doing so by an enforceable mechanism like the disqualification agreement. If clients feel angry and want to litigate, the disqualification agreement gives the lawyers an absolute excuse why they cannot do so. . . . [T]he disqualification agreement focuses the lawyers on settling in collaborative law because termination of the process would end their income from the case. The agreement focuses the clients on settling in collaborative law because termination of the process would raise the cost, end the representation by lawyers who they have educated and may trust, and require hiring new lawyers who are likely to be more adversarial. . . . Many collaborative law clients appreciate feeling protected from adversarial pressures. . . . On the other hand, the disqualification agreement can harm clients if they feel trapped. . . . [S]ome may feel heavy pressure to accept agreements that they believe are not in their interests. Some of the pressure may come from their own lawyers because of the lawyers' incentives to press for settlement. . . .

COOPERATIVE LAW

Cooperative law . . . includes a written agreement to make full, voluntary disclosure of all financial information, avoid formal discovery procedures, utilize joint rather than unilateral appraisals, and use interest-based negotiation. The choice not to use a disqualification agreement offers advantages and disadvantages. In some cases, parties and lawyers may act reasonably only if they face a credible threat of litigation. . . . Some clients may especially appreciate the security of knowing that they can retain their lawyers if the parties engage in contested litigation. . . . [A]lthough parties who use a cooperative law procedure may eventually settle, the implicit or explicit threat of litigation may taint the negotiation by undermining a problem-solving atmosphere.

CONCLUSION

. . . Professionals working with divorcing families . . . should effectively convey the benefits and especially the risks of the procedures. . . . When describing these procedures, professionals may convey this information more effectively by describing the implications concretely, such as any requirements to disclose new romantic relationships and to correct each other's mistakes, as well as potential difficulties of terminating collaborative law after investing substantial time and money in the process. . . .

[M]ediation is appropriate if parties are capable of negotiating for themselves with or without lawyers present. Collaborative law and cooperative law are appropriate if the parties need or want lawyers to participate directly in the negotiations. Conversely, mediation is appropriate if parties want neutral professionals to manage the process, especially if they cannot afford or do not want to engage lawyers at all or to take the lead in managing the negotiation process. In some cases, parties might benefit from having collaborative or cooperative lawyers as well as mediators. In a case starting as a mediation, parties who need legal advice and support during a mediation session may benefit from having lawyers oriented to problem-solving attend. Conversely, if parties and lawyers in a collaborative or cooperative law negotiation have substantial difficulties, they may engage a mediator to help manage the process and resolve disputes. . . . If parties place a high value on reaching an agreement and avoiding the adversarial pressures of contested litigation, collaborative law would be especially appropriate. . . . On the other hand, if the parties want to avoid potentially increased pressure to settle in collaborative law and to preserve ready access to litigation without changing lawyers, they would do better to choose one of the other procedures.

Roughly a dozen states now require mediation as to some aspects of a divorce dispute (principally, those relating to children) in some circumstances. In addition to the California statutes below, mediation mandates can be found in the codes of Delaware, Florida, Hawaii, Maine, Maryland, New Jersey, North Carolina, South Dakota, Tennessee, Utah, Virginia, and Wisconsin.

California Family Code
Division 8. Custody of Children, Part 2. Right to Custody of Minor Child
Chapter 11. Mediation of Custody and Visitation Issues

§3160. MEDIATORS; AVAILABILITY; DUTIES OF COURT

Each superior court shall make a mediator available. . . .

§3161. PURPOSE OF MEDIATION PROCEEDINGS

The purposes of a mediation proceeding are as follows:
(a) To reduce acrimony that may exist between the parties.
(b) To develop an agreement assuring the child close and continuing contact with both parents that is in the best interest of the child. . . .
(c) To effect a settlement of the issue of visitation rights of all parties that is in the best interest of the child.

§3162. UNIFORM STANDARDS OF PRACTICE; CONTENTS; ADOPTION BY JUDICIAL COUNCIL

(a) Mediation of cases involving custody and visitation concerning children shall be governed by uniform standards of practice adopted by the Judicial Council.
(b) The standards of practice shall include, but not be limited to, all of the following:
(1) Provision for the best interest of the child and the safeguarding of the rights of the child to frequent and continuing contact with both parents. . . .
(3) The conducting of negotiations in such a way as to equalize power relationships between the parties. . . .

§3164. QUALIFICATIONS OF MEDIATORS

(a) The mediator may be a member of the professional staff of a family conciliation court, probation department, or mental health services agency, or may be any other person or agency designated by the court.
(b) The mediator shall meet the minimum qualifications required of a counselor of conciliation. . . .

Article 2. Availability of Mediation

§3170. Setting Matters for Mediation

(a) If it appears on the face of a petition, application, or other pleading to obtain or modify a temporary or permanent custody or visitation order that custody, visitation, or both are contested, the court shall set the contested issues for mediation. . . .

Article 3. Mediation Proceedings

§3177. Confidentiality of Proceedings

Mediation proceedings pursuant to this chapter shall be held in private and shall be confidential. All communications, verbal or written, from the parties to the mediator made in the proceeding are . . . [confidential, inadmissible in court, and not subject to discovery].

§3178. Restrictions on Mediation Agreements

An agreement reached by the parties as a result of mediation shall be limited as follows:
(a) Where mediation is required to settle a contested issue of custody or visitation, the agreement shall be limited to the resolution of issues relating to parenting plans, custody, visitation. . . .

§3180. Duties of Mediators

(a) . . . [T]he mediator has the duty to assess the needs and interests of the child involved in the controversy, and is entitled to interview the child where the mediator considers the interview appropriate or necessary.
(b) The mediator shall use his or her best efforts to effect a settlement of the custody or visitation dispute that is in the best interest of the child. . . .

§3181. Domestic Violence History Between the Parties; Separate Meetings

(a) In a proceeding in which mediation is required pursuant to this chapter, where there has been a history of domestic violence between the parties or where a protective order . . . is in effect, at the request of the party alleging domestic violence in a written declaration under penalty of perjury or protected by the order, the mediator appointed pursuant to this chapter shall meet with the parties separately and at separate times. . . .

§3182. Authority of Mediators; Exclusion of Counsel

(a) The mediator has authority to exclude counsel from participation in the mediation proceedings pursuant to this chapter if, in the mediator's discretion, exclusion of counsel is appropriate or necessary. . . .

§3183. Child Custody Recommending; Investigation When Agreement Not Reached

(a) . . . [T]he mediator may . . . submit a recommendation to the court as to the custody of or visitation with the child. . . .

(b) If the parties have not reached agreement as a result of the mediation proceedings, the mediator may recommend to the court that an investigation be conducted . . . or that other services be offered to assist the parties to effect a resolution of the controversy. . . .

§3184. Appointment of Counsel to Represent Minor Child; Recommendations

. . . [N]othing in this chapter prohibits the mediator from recommending to the court that counsel be appointed . . . to represent the minor child. . . .

§3185. Failure to Reach Mediation Agreement; Visitation Rights Hearing

(a) If issues . . . are not resolved by an agreement . . . , the mediator shall inform the court in writing and the court shall set the matter for hearing on the unresolved issues. . . .

D. LEGISLATIVE INTENT QUESTIONS

1) What do you suppose is the reason for the limitation on the content of a mediated agreement in §3178?
2) What circumstances might warrant a mediator's recommending appointment of counsel for the child at issue under §3184?

American Academy of Matrimonial Lawyers, Bounds of Advocacy

8.1 An attorney should act as a mediator only if competent to do so.

Comment

No lawyer should act as the mediator of marital disputes without adequate education, training or experience. There are many ways to acquire the necessary knowledge and skill, including law school training programs, AAML mediation training certification, continuing legal education, formal training programs, and informal training by peers. . . . A matrimonial lawyer may be a better mediator because the lawyer may be in the best position to understand the likely outcome of litigation and is best able to ensure the understanding and validity of a mediated agreement. . . .

8.2 An attorney acting as a mediator in a marital dispute should remain impartial.

Comment

The primary responsibility for resolution of a marital dispute rests with the participants. A neutral person trying to help people resolve disputes in an amicable way should help the parties reach an informed and voluntary settlement. At no time should a mediator coerce a participant into agreement or make a substantive decision for a participant. The mediator should remain completely impartial in assisting the participants in reaching agreement, permitting neither manipulative nor intimidating practices. . . . Although the mediator should not have a vested interest in any particular terms of a settlement, the mediator should "be satisfied that agreements in which he or she has participated will not impugn the integrity of the process" and are fundamentally fair. If the mediator is "concerned about the possible consequences of a proposed agreement, and the needs of the parties dictate, the [mediator] must inform the parties of that concern. In adhering to this Standard, the [mediator] may find it advisable to educate the parties, to refer one or more of the parties for specialized advice, or to withdraw from the case." The mediator should assist the clients . . . also in considering the interests of unrepresented parties, and in particular the interests of their children. . . .

8.3 An attorney acting as a mediator in a marital dispute should urge each party to obtain independent legal advice.

Comment

. . . Review of a proposed mediated settlement agreement with a party's consulting attorney affords that party the opportunity to reflect on the fairness of the agreement before signing it and helps ensure that the party understands the agreement and enters into it voluntarily.

8.4 An attorney acting as a mediator in a marital dispute should only give advice that will enable the parties to make reasonably informed decisions.

Comment

. . . Some information, such as the tax consequences of certain transactions, legal principles about the characterization of assets, and the need for formal parenting plans, is neutral and beneficial to both parties. . . . The extent to which a mediator should provide advice (as opposed to information) is a controversial issue. On the one hand, it is difficult for the mediator to maintain impartiality while providing advice to one of the participants. Also, in some circumstances providing advice might be seen as constituting legal representation, which is inappropriate for a mediator and might bring into play the conflict of interest rules. There is the danger that the participants will perceive advice from the mediator as a directive that they must follow. On the other hand, the participants may be unable to make informed decisions without some guidance. They may seek that guidance from a lawyer-mediator rather than obtain outside expert advice on every issue that arises. . . .

A mediator choosing to provide advice or evaluation should tell the participants they are free to reject it. "Evaluations, particularly of a predictive nature, generally should be resorted to only after other more facilitative measures have failed to break an impasse." The mediator should, if possible, offer suggestions in the guise of questions, rather than definitive statements, because doing so is less coercive. . . . The mediator should provide in writing to all participants a statement such as the following:

> 1. Although I am a lawyer, I am not acting as a lawyer for either of you. You are not my clients. I do not represent either of you. I will help you reach a fair, informed agreement. I will

give you advice about how the law might affect your decisions and aspects of your agreement, but I will not favor either of your interests, or provide advice that is beneficial to one of you but detrimental to other participants.

2. You should obtain independent advice from someone who is looking out only for your interests. You should consult your own attorney before signing any agreement reached during this mediation. . . .

Many family law scholars and practitioners harbor some skepticism about alternative dispute resolution procedures in divorce cases. The most prevalent concern is that wives who were victims of domestic violence will be intimidated and coerced in any informal proceedings, especially if they do not have counsel present. Do you think the California statute addresses that concern adequately? In addition, Martha Fineman has argued that giving non-legal professionals such as social workers and psychologists an influential role in resolution of custody disputes creates too much pressure for shared physical custody, even when the wife has clearly been the primary caretaker, because compromise, cooperation, and sharing are the default preferences in therapeutic work. See Martha Fineman, *Dominant Discourse, Professional Language, and Legal Change in Child Custody Decisionmaking,* 101 HARV. L. REV. 727 (1988).

Child's Involvement

The prevailing rule in the United States for divorces involving children (and for child custody disputes between unmarried parents) is that the court may, but need not, appoint a legal representative for the child. Many states do mandate appointment when there is a well-founded allegation of child maltreatment by one of the parents. See, e.g., Fla. Stat. §61.401; Mo. Rev. Stat. §452.423(2); Minn. Stat. §518.165(2).

In most states, the representative would be a "guardian ad litem," who is usually a lawyer but whose role is more paternalistic than the usual attorney role, having a duty to advocate for or assist the court in determining the child's best interests, rather than advocating strictly for satisfaction of the child's wishes per se. In some states, the representative is "counsel" or "attorney for the child," and is expected to operate as much like an attorney for an autonomous client as possible. There is great debate among scholars and practitioners about which of these is the best model for representation of a child, and this is reflected in the variation among states and from one judge to the next in preference for a traditional advocate model, a surrogate parent model, or a court investigator model. See Barbara A. Atwood, *Representing Children Who Can't or Won't Direct Counsel: Best Interests Lawyering or No Lawyer At All?,* 53 ARIZ. L. REV. 381 (2011). Increasingly, states are relying on Court Appointed Special Advocates (CASA) to gather information and guide the best-interests determination. CASA volunteers are lay persons trained to assist an attorney representative for a child, by doing much of the interviewing and investigating. In many states, the court may also or instead order an investigation of and report on the child's situation by a neutral, specially trained custody evaluator or a mental health professional or social worker.

When divorcing parents submit a custody agreement to the court, the court will almost never appoint a representative for the child nor order a custody evaluation, even though the court is supposed to make an independent assessment of whether the agreement is in the child's best interests. See, e.g., N.J. Stat. Ann. §9:2-4(d) ("The court shall order any custody arrangement which is agreed to by both parents unless it is contrary to the best interests of the child."). In an exceptional case, allegations in a pleading that a parent has committed child abuse might cause the court to order some investigation of the situation even if the parties reach an agreement on custody.

When parents litigate custody, the prevailing rule directs courts to appoint a representative for the child when they have reason to believe the child's interests will not otherwise be adequately protected in the proceeding. In practice in most jurisdictions, guardian ad litem appointment is automatic in litigated custody disputes. Some courts will wait until after mediation has been attempted, others not. Texas's rule is typical (except for the unusual term "amicus attorney," which appears to apply to the court investigator model):

Vernon's Texas Family Code
Title 5. . . . Suit Affecting the Parent-Child Relationship
Subtitle A, Chapter 107. Special Appointments and Social Studies
Subchapter A. Court-Ordered Representation . . .

§107.021. Discretionary Appointments

(a) In a suit in which the best interests of a child are at issue, other than a suit filed by a governmental entity . . . , the court may appoint one of the following:

(1) an amicus attorney;

(2) an attorney ad litem; or

(3) a guardian ad litem. . . .

(b) In determining whether to make an appointment . . . , the court:

(1) shall:

(A) give due consideration to the ability of the parties to pay reasonable fees to the appointee; and

(B) balance the child's interests against the cost to the parties that would result from an appointment by taking into consideration the cost of available alternatives for resolving issues without making an appointment;

(2) may make an appointment only if the court finds that the appointment is necessary to ensure the determination of the best interests of the child. . . .

§107.001. Definitions

(1) "Amicus attorney" means an attorney . . . whose role is to provide legal services necessary to assist the court in protecting a child's best interests rather than to provide legal services to the child.

(2) "Attorney ad litem" means an attorney who provides legal services to a person, including a child, and who owes to the person the duties of undivided loyalty, confidentiality, and competent representation. . . .

(5) "Guardian ad litem" means a person appointed to represent the best interests of a child. The term includes:

(A) a volunteer advocate . . .

(B) a professional, other than an attorney, who holds a relevant professional license and whose training relates to the determination of a child's best interests;

(C) an adult having the competence, training, and expertise determined by the court to be sufficient to represent the best interests of the child; or

(D) an attorney ad litem appointed to serve in the dual role.

§107.008. SUBSTITUTED JUDGMENT OF ATTORNEY FOR CHILD

(a) An attorney ad litem appointed to represent a child . . . may determine that the child cannot meaningfully formulate the child's objectives of representation in a case because the child:

(1) lacks sufficient maturity to understand and form an attorney-client relationship with the attorney;

(2) despite appropriate legal counseling, continues to express objectives of representation that would be seriously injurious to the child; or

(3) for any other reason is incapable of making reasonable judgments and engaging in meaningful communication.

(b) An attorney ad litem . . . who determines that the child cannot meaningfully formulate the child's expressed objectives of representation may present to the court a position that the attorney determines will serve the best interests of the child. . . .

§107.002. POWERS AND DUTIES OF GUARDIAN AD LITEM FOR CHILD

(a) A guardian ad litem appointed for a child under this chapter is not a party to the suit but may:

(1) conduct an investigation to the extent that the guardian ad litem considers necessary to determine the best interests of the child; and

(2) obtain and review copies of the child's relevant medical, psychological, and school records. . . .

(b) A guardian ad litem appointed for the child under this chapter shall:

(1) within a reasonable time after the appointment, interview:

(A) the child in a developmentally appropriate manner, if the child is four years of age or older;

(B) each person who has significant knowledge of the child's history and condition, including any foster parent of the child; and

(C) the parties to the suit;

(2) seek to elicit in a developmentally appropriate manner the child's expressed objectives;

(3) consider the child's expressed objectives without being bound by those objectives;

(4) encourage settlement and the use of alternative forms of dispute resolution; and

(5) perform any specific task directed by the court.

(c) A guardian ad litem appointed for the child under this chapter is entitled to:

(1) receive a copy of each pleading or other paper filed with the court . . . ;

(4) attend all legal proceedings in the case but may not call or question a witness or otherwise provide legal services unless the guardian ad litem is a licensed attorney who has been appointed in the dual role;

(5) review and sign, or decline to sign, an agreed order affecting the child; and

(6) explain the basis for the guardian ad litem's opposition to the agreed order if the guardian ad litem does not agree to the terms of a proposed order.

(d) The court may compel the guardian ad litem to attend a trial or hearing and to testify as necessary for the proper disposition of the suit.

(e) Unless the guardian ad litem is an attorney who has been appointed in the dual role . . . , the court shall ensure in a hearing or in a trial on the merits that a guardian ad litem has an opportunity to testify regarding, and is permitted to submit a report regarding, the guardian ad litem's recommendations relating to:

(1) the best interests of the child; and

(2) the bases for the guardian ad litem's recommendations.

(f) In a nonjury trial, a party may call the guardian ad litem as a witness for the purpose of cross-examination regarding the guardian's report without the guardian ad litem being listed as a witness by a party. . . .

§107.003. Powers and Duties of Attorney ad Litem for Child and Amicus Attorney

An attorney ad litem appointed to represent a child or an amicus attorney appointed to assist the court:

(1) shall . . .

(A) . . . interview:

(i) the child in a developmentally appropriate manner, if the child is four years of age or older;

(ii) each person who has significant knowledge of the child's history and condition . . .

(iii) the parties to the suit;

(B) seek to elicit in a developmentally appropriate manner the child's expressed objectives of representation;

(C) consider the impact on the child in formulating the attorney's presentation of the child's expressed objectives of representation to the court;

(D) investigate the facts of the case to the extent the attorney considers appropriate;

(E) obtain and review copies of relevant records relating to the child . . . ;

(F) participate in the conduct of the litigation to the same extent as an attorney for a party;

(G) take any action consistent with the child's interests that the attorney considers necessary to expedite the proceedings;

(H) encourage settlement and the use of alternative forms of dispute resolution; and

(I) review and sign, or decline to sign, a proposed or agreed order affecting the child;

(2) must be trained in child advocacy or have experience determined by the court to be equivalent to that training; and

(3) is entitled to: . . .

(B) request a hearing or trial on the merits;

(C) consent or refuse to consent to an interview of the child by another attorney;

(D) receive a copy of each pleading or other paper filed with the court; . . .

(G) attend all legal proceedings in the suit.

§107.004. Additional Duties of Attorney ad Litem for Child

(a) Except as otherwise provided by this chapter, the attorney ad litem appointed for a child shall, in a developmentally appropriate manner:

(1) advise the child;

(2) represent and . . . follow the child's expressed objectives of representation during the course of litigation if the attorney ad litem determines that the child is competent to understand the nature of an attorney-client relationship and has formed that relationship with the attorney ad litem. . . .

§107.006. Access to Child and Information Relating to Child

(a) In conjunction with an appointment under this chapter, . . . the court shall issue an order authorizing the attorney ad litem, guardian ad litem for the child, or amicus attorney to have immediate access to the child and any information relating to the child. . . .

(b) . . . including records regarding social services, law enforcement records, school records, records of a probate or court proceeding. . . .

(c) . . . medical, mental health, or drug or alcohol treatment record of a child. . . .

(d) The disclosure of a confidential record under this section does not affect the confidentiality of the record, and the person provided access to the record may not disclose the record further except as provided by court order or other law. . . .

(f) Records obtained under this section shall be destroyed on termination of the appointment.

§107.007. Attorney Work Product and Testimony

(a) An attorney ad litem, an attorney serving in the dual role, or an amicus attorney may not . . . be required to disclose the source of any information. . . .

§107.031. Volunteer Advocates

. . . (b) . . . [T]he court may appoint a charitable organization composed of volunteer advocates whose training provides for the provision of services in private custody disputes or a person who has received the court's approved training regarding the subject matter of the suit and who has been certified by the court to appear at court hearings as a guardian ad litem for the child or as a volunteer advocate for the child. A person appointed under this subsection is not entitled to fees. . . .

§107.051. Order for Social Study

(a) The court may order the preparation of a social study into the circumstances and condition of:

(1) a child who is the subject of a suit or a party to a suit; and

(2) the home of any person requesting . . . possession of, or access to a child. . . .

§107.0514. Elements of Social Study

(a) The basic elements of a social study under this subchapter consist of:

(1) a personal interview of each party to the suit;

(2) an interview, conducted in a developmentally appropriate manner, of each child at issue in the suit who is at least four years of age;

(3) observation of each child at issue in the suit, regardless of the age of the child;

(4) the obtaining of information from relevant collateral sources;

(5) evaluation of the home environment of each party seeking . . . possession of or access to the child, unless the condition of the home environment is identified as not being in dispute in the court order requiring the social study;

(6) for each individual residing in a residence subject to the social study, consideration of any criminal history information and any contact with the Department of Family and Protective Services or a law enforcement agency regarding abuse or neglect; and

(7) assessment of the relationship between each child at issue in the suit and each party seeking possession of or access to the child. . . .

Regardless of which of the three types of roles a court-appointed representative adopted, she or he would have to meet with Lamar, explain the court proceedings to him, and attempt to elicit Lamar's thoughts and feelings about his post-divorce living arrangement. In theory, there would also be follow-up meetings after any major developments in the case, so that the representative could attempt to explain the developments to Lamar. Ideally such meetings would occur in Lamar's home or some other place that is a normal and comfortable part of Lamar's life, but the reality is that many lawyers who represent children insist that parents bring the children to the lawyer's office for the conversation.

In addition to the potential intrusion into the child's life of a lawyer representative, CASA volunteer, and/or custody evaluator, a judge might ask to meet with the child in chambers, typically without parents present but often with all of the lawyers in the case present, to interview the child about his or her wishes and interests. See, e.g., Ohio Rev. Code Ann. §3109.04(B)(1) ("In determining the child's best interest . . . , the court, in its discretion, may and, upon the request of either party, shall interview in chambers any or all of the involved children regarding their wishes and concerns. . . ."). Judges who conduct such interviews might strive to make the child feel comfortable, and some are fairly skilled at doing so, but it is still likely to be a stressful event for the child, especially if what they say to the judge could become known to their parents. Cf. Va. Code Ann. §20-124.2:1 ("In any proceeding in a court of record to determine custody or visitation, when the court conducts an in camera interview of a minor child whose custody or visitation is at issue without the presence of the parties or their counsel, a record of the interview shall be prepared, unless the parties otherwise agree. The record of the interview shall be made a part of the record in the case unless a decision is made by the court that doing so would endanger the safety of the child.").

As for your responsibility toward a child when you represent a parent, the ethics rules have little to say, but the domestic relations bar has offered some guidance:

Model Rules of Professional Conduct

Rule 4.3 Dealing with Unrepresented Person

In dealing on behalf of a client with a person who is not represented by counsel, a lawyer shall not state or imply that the lawyer is disinterested. When the lawyer knows or reasonably should know that the unrepresented person misunderstands the lawyer's role in the matter, the lawyer shall make reasonable efforts to correct the misunderstanding. The lawyer shall not give legal advice to an unrepresented person, other than the advice to secure counsel, if the lawyer knows or reasonably should know that the interests of such a person are or have a reasonable possibility of being in conflict with the interests of the client.

Rule 4.4 Respect for Rights of Third Persons

(a) In representing a client, a lawyer shall not use means that have no substantial purpose other than to embarrass, delay, or burden a third person, or use methods of obtaining evidence that violate the legal rights of such a person.

American Academy of Matrimonial Lawyers, Bounds of Advocacy

6. Children

. . . The lawyer must competently represent the interests of the client, but not at the expense of the children. The parents' fiduciary obligations for the well being of a child provide a basis for the attorney's consideration of the child's best interests consistent with traditional advocacy and client loyalty principles. It is accepted doctrine that the attorney for a trustee or other fiduciary has an ethical obligation to the beneficiaries to whom the fiduciary's obligations run. Statutory and decisional law in most jurisdictions imposes a fiduciary duty on parents to act in their child's best interests. . . .

6.2 An attorney should not permit a client to contest child custody, contact or access for either financial leverage or vindictiveness.

Comment

. . . Proper consideration for the welfare of the children requires that they not be used as pawns in the divorce process. Thus, for example, in states where child support is determined partly on the basis of the amount of time a parent spends with the child, the lawyers should negotiate parenting issues based solely on considerations related to the child, then negotiate child support based on financial considerations. If despite the attorney's advice the client persists, the attorney should seek to withdraw.

6.3 When issues in a representation affect the welfare of a minor child, an attorney should not initiate communication with the child, except in the presence of the child's lawyer or guardian ad litem, with court permission, or as necessary to verify facts in motions and pleadings.

Comment

. . . There is a risk of harm to the child from an attorney's contacts and attempts to involve the child in the proceedings. Advice to or manipulation of the child by a parent's lawyer has no place in the lawyer's efforts on behalf of the parent. . . .

6.4 An attorney should not bring a child to court or call a child as a witness without full discussion with the client and a reasonable belief that it is in the best interests of the child.

Comment

Taking sides against either parent in a legal proceeding imposes a large emotional burden on a child. Some children do not want to express a preference in child custody disputes; they want their parents to resolve the issue without calling them. Other children want their views expressed, and their views may be highly relevant. . . . All participants in a family law proceeding . . . should strive to permit a child's views and information to be expressed in a manner that least exposes the child to the rigors of the courtroom. The attorney should weigh carefully the risks and benefits to the child of testifying, including consulting with appropriate experts as to the potential for harm.

TABLE OF CASES

Principal cases are in italics.

INDEX